Sicut lilium inter spinas sic amica mea inter filias

On The Cover: We use the symbol of the "lily among the thorns" from Song of Solomon 2:2 to represent the Baptist History Series. The Latin, ***Sicut lilium inter spinas sic amica mea inter filias***, translates, "As the lily among thorns, so is my love among the daughters."

THE
HISTORY
OF THE
English Baptists

Vol. II

WILLIAM KIFFIN
1616-1701

THE
HISTORY
OF THE
English Baptists,

FROM THE

REFORMATION
To the Beginning of the
Reign of King GEORGE I.

VOL. II.

CONTAINING
Their HISTORY from the RESTORATION of King
CHARLES II. to the End of his Reign.

By THO. CROSBY.

LONDON:

Printed for the AUTHOR, and sold by him at his House on
Horse-ly-down, Southwark; and AARON WARD,
Bookseller, at the *King's Arms* in *Little Britain*.
MDCCXXXIX.

he Baptist Standard Bearer, Inc.
NUMBER ONE IRON OAKS DRIVE • PARIS, ARKANSAS 72855

Thou hast given a *standard* to them that fear thee;
that it may be displayed because of the truth.
-- *Psalm 60:4*

*Reprinted
by*

THE BAPTIST STANDARD BEARER, INC.
No. 1 Iron Oaks Drive
Paris, Arkansas 72855
(501) 963-3831

THE WALDENSIAN EMBLEM
lux lucet in tenebris
"The Light Shineth in the Darkness"

ISBN #1-57978-902-1

TO THE
READER.

IT *may be expected, and I did intend, that this Volume should have contained all I at first proposed to the publick. But since my publication of the former Volume, I have had such materials communicated to me, that I could not in justice to the communicators omit them, without incurring the just censure of a partial historian. Besides, it having been objected to me, that a more early account of the* English Baptists *might be obtained; it gave a new turn to my thoughts, and put me upon considering the state and condition of the* Christian Religion, *from the first plantation of the Gospel in* England. *Now in this enquiry, so much has occurred to me, as carries in it more than a probability, that the first* English *Christians were* Baptists. *I could not therefore pass by so material a fact in their favour: And because it cannot now be placed where it properly belongs, I have fixed it by way of preface to this second Volume. Moreover, in my first Volume, I did exhibit part of a* Confession of Faith, *published by the* Baptists *about the year* 1611, *taken from Mr.* Robinson, *pastor of the* English *Church at* Leyden; *who in the year* 1614, *printed some remarks upon it, and said, it was published by the remainder of Mr.* Smith's *company. Whether Mr.* Smith *had left this people, or whether upon some disagreement, they departed from him, I cannot say. It is not very material, nor at this distance of time very easy to determine. But as I have lately obtained a* Declaration of Faith *published by them; and as the same may give us some light, respecting the opinions of the* English Baptists, *in those early days of the Reformation; so I have placed it, tho' out of due time, in the* Appendix *of this Volume,* N°. I.

And

To the READER.

And the rather, because they declare, ' *they are forced a-*
' *gainst their whole minds to publish it, for the clearing of*
' *their innocency in such things, as men do commonly keep up*
' *in their account ; and all to further their reckoning in con-*
' *tempt with men of all estates.*' I may justly add ; the
same practice is continued among some of the Pædobaptists,
even to the present time: as appears by the late histories of
the Reverend Mr. Neal, and Mr. Lewis; both which I
have already replied to.

Also in my first Volume I took notice, that the Baptists
presented an Humble Supplication to King James I. the
Parliament then sitting ; and gave only a short account thereof. This has been questioned by some: and the Reverend Mr.
Lewis seems to doubt it, because he says, The Anabaptists are said to have presented unto King James I. in
Parliament time, their Humble Supplication. —— But this
I have not seen. Therefore I have now placed it also in
the Appendix of this Volume, N°. II.

I take this opportuntity to acknowledge and amend a mistake, pointed out to me by a worthy learned gentleman, (whose
modesty deemed his information of so little importance, as to
chuse not to be mentioned) in the preface to the first Volume,
p. 28. where I denominate Monsieur Bayle a Papist. I
did not then know he had again embraced the reformed religion: and desire my Readers to correct that paragraph, by
erasing being, and over-writing who had been.

THE PREFACE.

HE gospel of *Christ Jesus*, the Son of God, was begun by the ministry of *John*; who, as the herald of the Lord *Messias*, went before him to proclaim his first approaches, and prepare men, by *Repentance* and *Baptism*, for this new dispensation, which was the accomplishment of ancient prophecies.

This was the first person that we read of in the Holy Scriptures, that used *Baptism* as a sacrament, and initiated his disciples by it. From hence he derived the title of *Baptist*, or *Baptizer*; as being therein the author of some new and strange practice among them. For although there were *divers washings* used among the *Jews*, by God's appointment, yet that it was their custom to baptize those that were made proselytes, and initiate them, and their children, into the mystery of the *Jews* religion by *baptism*, as some pretend, is a groundless opinion. There is no such thing mention'd in the law of *Moses*;

^{John the first baptizer.}

The *PREFACE.*

Moses; and therefore, if there was such a practice, it must be a *tradition of the elders*, and fell among their other superstitions, under the censure of our blessed Saviour. And is it reasonable to suppose, an Institution of the gospel was founded upon a sinful custom of the *Jews?* But the scriptures give no account of any such practice. Those *Rabbies* that do make mention of any such thing, lived many years since the death of our blessed Saviour. Their writings are full of lies and blasphemy, and therefore no credit can be given to them; nay, they contradict one another even in this very point; and those who deny it, are as ancient and as learned as the affirmers of it.

Received his commission from heaven. Luke iii. 2.

This great prophet *John*, had an immediate commission from heaven, before he enter'd upon the actual administration of his office. And as the *English Baptists* adhere closely to this principle, that *John* the *Baptist* was by divine command, the first commissioned to preach the gospel, and *baptize* by *immersion*, those that received it; and that this practice has been ever since maintained and continued in the world to this present day; so it may not be improper to consider the state of religion in this kingdom; it being agreed on all hands, that the plantation of the gospel here was very early, even in the *Apostles* days. I shall therefore enquire, when, and by whom (as far as history can inform us) the gospel was first preach'd in *Great Britain*. And here it must be granted, that historians give a very different account; yet they agree in this, that the early reception of the gospel was either from an

Apostle

Apostle or apostolical men; and that Christianity was maintained at first in its purity, and preserved it self for some years, from the errors and superstitions of the church of *Rome*.

I shall begin with the account of that honest historian, the reverend Mr. *Fuller*; 'Who it was, *says he*, that first brought over the gospel into *Britain*, is very uncertain. The conversioner (understand *Parsons* the Jesuit) mainly stickleth for the Apostle *Peter* to have first preach'd the gospel here.' *Ch. History, Book I. p. 3.* And having confuted *Parsons*'s five arguments, which he had brought to prove it, says; 'We have staid the longer in confuting these arguments, because, from *Peter*'s preaching here, *Parsons* would infer an obligation of this *Island* to the see of *Rome*.' He further observes; That some would have *James*, the son of *Zebedee*; others St. *Paul*; others *Simon* the *Canaanite*; and others *Aristobulus*, though not an *Apostle*, yet an Apostle's mate, to be the first planters of religion in this *Island*. 'The result of all is this, says he, *Churches* are generally ambitious to entitle themselves to *Apostles* for their founders; conceiving they should otherwise be esteemed but as of the *second form*, and *younger house*, if they received the faith from any inferior preacher.—— Whereas, indeed, it matters not if the *doctrine* be the *same*, whether the *Apostles* preached it by themselves, or by their successors. We see little certainty can be extracted, who first brought the gospel hither. 'Tis so long since, the *British church* hath forgotten her own *infancy*, who were her first *Godfathers*. *Anno 41.* *Ibid. p. 4.*

a 2 'We

'We see the *light* of the *Word shined* here;
'but see not who *kindled it.*'

Anno 63. Now amongst the converts of the natives of this Island, in this first age to Christianity, *Claudia*, surnamed *Ruffina*, is reputed a principal; she was wife to *Pudens*, a *Roman* senator; and that this is the *Claudia*, a *Briton*
2 Tim. iv. 21. born, mentioned by St. *Paul*, then living at *Rome*. Mr. *Fuller* endeavours to prove against the exceptions of *Parsons* the Jesuit, by answering his objections to the contrary; and then says, 'The issue of all is this: *Clau-*
'*dia*'s story, as a *British* Christian, stands
'unremov'd, for any force of these objecti-
'ons; tho' one need not be much engaged here-
'in.—— But now to return again to the prime
'planters of religion in *Britain*. As for all
'those formerly reckon'd up, there is in au-
'thors but a tinkling mention of them; and
'the sound of their preaching low and little,
'in comparison of those loud peals which are
'rung of *Joseph* of *Arimathea* his coming
Ibid. p. 6, 7. 'hither.—— Whilst *Philip* (whether the
'Apostle or Deacon, is uncertain) continued
'preaching the gospel in *France*, he sent *Jo-*
'*seph* of *Arimathea* over into *Britain*, with
'*Joseph* his son, and ten other associates, to
'convert the natives of that Island to Chri-
'stianity. These coming into *Britain*, found
'such entertainment from *Aviragus* the king,
'that though he would not be dissuaded from
'his idolatry by their preaching, yet he al-
'low'd them twelve hides of ground (an hide
'is as much as, being well manur'd, will
'maintain a family; or, as others say, as
'much as one plow can handsomely manage)
'in a desolate Island, full of fens and bram-
               'bles,

The PREFACE.

'bles, called the *Ynis Wittrin*; since, by
'translation, *Glassenbury*. Here they built
'a small church; and, by direction from
'*Gabriel* the Archangel, dedicated it to the
'Virgin *Mary*, encompassing it about with a
'church-yard; in which church, afterwards,
'*Joseph* was buried: And here these twelve
'lived many years, devoutly serving God,
'and converting many to the Christian re-
'ligion.'

Mr. *Fuller* says, he '' dares not wholly
'deny the substance of this story, though
'the leaven of monkery hath much swollen,
'and puffed up the circumstance thereof; —
'and that as this relation is presented unto
'us, it hath a young man's brow with an old
'man's beard. I mean, says he, novel su-
'perstitions disguised with pretended an-
'tiquity. In all this story of *Joseph's* living
'at *Glassenbury*, there is no one passage re-
'ported therein beareth better proportion to
'time and place than the church which he is
'said to erect; whose dimensions, materials,
'and making, are thus presented unto us.
'It had in length sixty foot, and twenty six
'in breadth, made of rods watled or interwo-
'ven:— In this small oratory, *Joseph* with
'his companions, watched, prayed, fasted,
'and preached, having high meditations un-
'der a low roof, and large hearts betwixt nar-
'row walls. Let not then stately modern
'churches disdain to stoop with their highest
'steeples, reverently doing homage to this
'poor structure, as their first platform and
'precedent. And let their chequer'd pave-
'ments no more disdain this Oratory's plain

'floor,

'floor, than her thatched covering doth envy
'their leaden roofs.

Ibid. p. 8. 'By all this it does not appear, says *Fuller*, That the first preachers of the gospel
'in *Britain* did so much as touch at *Rome*;
'much less that they received any command
'or commission thence to convert *Britain*.

Vol. I. p. 69. Mr. *John Fox*, when treating of the first planters of the gospel in *Britain*, cites *Nicephorus*; who saith, 'That *Simon Zelotes*
'came into *Britain*. Some others alledge,
'out of *Gildas*, de *Victoria Aurel. Ambrosii*,
'That *Joseph* of *Arimathy*, after the disper-
'sion of the *Jews*, was sent by *Philip* the
'*Apostle*, from *France* to *Britain*, about the
'year of our Lord, threescore and three;
'and here remained in this land all his time;
'and so, with his fellows, laid the first
'foundation of Christian faith among the
'*Britain* people. Whereupon other preach-
'ers and teachers coming afterward, con-
'firmed the same, and increased it more."
And, for confirmation hereof, he alledges the testimonies of *Gildas*, *Tertullian*, *Origen*, and the words also of the letter of *Eleutherius*; which import no less, but that the faith of Christ was here in *England*, among the *British* people, long before *Eleutherius*'s time, and before *king Lucius* was converted.

'*Gildas*, our countryman, *says he*, in his
Vol. I. p. 137. 'history affirmeth plainly, That *Britain* re-
'ceived the gospel in the reign of *Tiberius*
'the emperor, under whom Christ suffered.

'The second reason is out of *Tertullian*;
'who living near about, or rather somewhat
'before

' before the time of this *Eleutherius*, in his
' book *Contra Judæos*, manifeſtly importeth
' the ſame. Where the ſaid *Tertullian*, te-
' ſtifying how the goſpel was diſperſed abroad
' by the found of the *Apoſtles*, and there rec-
' koning up the *Medes, Perſians*, &c. reciteth
' alſo the parts of *Britain* which the *Romans*
' could never attain to ; and reporteth the
' ſame now to be ſubject to Chriſt.—— Note
' here, how, among other, divers believing
' nations, he mentioneth alſo the wildeſt
' places of *Britain*, to be of the ſame num-
' ber, and theſe, in his time were *chriſtned*,
' who was in the ſame *Eleutherius*'s time,
' as is aboveſaid. Then was not Pope *Eleu-
' therius* the firſt which ſent the Chriſtian
' faith into this realm ; but the goſpel was
' here received before his time, either by
' *Joſeph* of *Arimathea*, as ſome chronicles
' record, or by ſome of the *Apoſtles*, or of
' their ſcholars, which had been here preach-
' ing Chriſt before *Eleutherius* wrote to
' *Lucius*.

' My third probation I deduct out of *Ori-
' gen. Hom.* IV. *in Ezchielem*, whoſe words
' be theſe: *Britanniam in chriſtianam conſen-
' tire religionem.* Whereby it appeareth,
' that the faith of Chriſt was ſparſed here
' in *England*, before the days of *Eleuthe-
' rius.*

' For my fourth probation, I take the
' teſtimony of *Beda*; where he affirmeth,
' That, in his time, and almoſt a thouſand
' years after Chriſt here in *Britain, Eaſter*
' was kept after the manner of the Eaſt-
' church, in the full of the moon, what day
' in the week ſoever it fell on ; and not on

' the

The PREFACE.

'the *Sunday*, as we do now: Whereby it is
'to be collected, that the first preachers in
'this land, have come out from the East part
'of the world, where it was so used, rather
'than from *Rome*.

'*Fifthly*, I may alledge the words of *Nice-
'phorus*, lib. ii. cap. 40. where he faith,
'That *Simon Zelotes* did spread the gospel of
'Christ to the West ocean, and brought the
'same unto the Isles of *Britain*.

'*Sixthly*, May be here added also the
'words of *Petrus Cluniacensis*; who writing
'to *Bernard*, affirmeth, That the *Scots*, in
'his time, did celebrate their *Easter*, not after
'the *Roman* manner, but after the *Greeks*, &c.
'And as the said *Britains* were not under
'the *Roman* order, in the time of this ab-
'bot of *Cluniake*; so neither were they, nor
'would be under the *Roman* legate, in the
'time of *Gregory*; nor would admit any pri-
'macy of the *bishop* of *Rome* to be above
'them.

'For the *seventh* argument, moreover, I
'may make my probation by the plain
'words of *Eleutherius*; by whose epistle [a],
'written to *king Lucius*, we may understand
'that *Lucius* had received the faith of Christ
'in this land, before the king sent to *Eleu-
'therius* for the *Roman* laws; for so the ex-
'press words of the letter do manifestly pur-
'port. By all which conjectures, it may
'stand, probably, to be thought, that the
'*Britons* were taught first by the *Grecians*
'of the East church, rather than by the
'*Romans*.'

[a] Which may be seen both in *Fuller* and *Fox*.

Mon-

The PREFACE.

Monsieur *Rapin*, a late author, gives this account of the first plantation of the gospel in *Britain*. He says; 'Before the birth of our *Hist. of* Engl. Vol. I. p. 27.
'Saviour, the *Britons*, like the rest of the
' world, the *Jews* only excepted, were *gross*
' idolaters; they not only worshipped *false*
' gods, but, if their own historians are to be
' credited, had as *many*, and as *extravagant*
' ones, as the *Egyptians* themselves.——

' Though it be difficult to know the pre-
' cise time, yet all agree the gospel was
' preached in *Great Britain* soon after our
' Saviour's death. But those who place this
' event in the reign of *Tiberius*, do not con-
' sider, the first Gentile *Cornelius*, was not
' converted till the year of our Lord 40;
' that is, three years after the death of that
' emperor.

' *Baronius*, upon the questionable autho-
' rity of *Simeon Metaphrastes* [b], which he
' himself justly rejects on several other occa-
' sions, says; St. *Peter* first preach'd to the
' *Britons*. This opinion is the more impro-
' bable, because it is certain St. *Peter* per-
' form'd the office of an Apostle chiefly in
' the *Eastern* countries. Others affirm, That
' *Simon Zelotes*, one of the twelve Apostles,
' undertook the conversion of the *Britons*.
' *Nicephorus Callistus*, *Dorotheus*, in his *Sy-*
' *nopsis*, and the *Greek Kalendar*, say; This
' Apostle was crucified and buried in *Britain*.
' At the same time, we find in the *Roman*
' *Martyrology*, and in those of *Bede*, *Adon*,

[b] A writer of the tenth century, says Mr. *Tindal*; so called from writing the lives of the saints. He was a lay-man. *Notes upon* Rapin, *p.* 28.

' and

The PREFACE.

'and *Usuard*, that St. *Simon* suffer'd martyr-
'dom in *Persia*.

  'The most current opinion, for some time,
'was, That *Joseph* of *Arimathea* first preach-
'ed to the *Britons*. Though this tradition,
'supported by the sole testimony of *William*
'of *Malmsbury* [c], in proof of the antiquity
'of the church of *Glaston*, or *Glassenbury*,
'says, after *Frecu'phus*, that upon the mar-
'tyrdom of saint *Stephen*, the Apostles were
'dispersed throughout the whole world. St.
'*Philip* (continues the historian) at his com-
'ing among the *Francs*, sent twelve of his
'disciples, with *Joseph* of *Arimathea*, as
'their head, to propagate the gospel in
'*Great Britain*; where they arrived in the
'year of our Lord 61. After some oppo-
'sition from the inhabitants, a certain king
'gave them a little spot of ground, surround-
'ed with fens and bushes to dwell in. Not
'long after, two other neighbouring kings,
'having allow'd them twelve *hides* of land
'for their subsistance, the Angel *Gabriel*
'commanded them, from God, to build a
'church in the place now called *Glaston*, but,
'at that time, *Inswitrin*. This chuch was
'finished in the year 63; and, as the histo-
'rian adds, was dedicated by our Saviour
'himself, as a mark of distinction to the *Vir-
'gin Mary*.'

  Rapin, after a refutation of the proofs
brought in vindication of this tradition of
Joseph of *Arimathea*, observes, That 'though

---

[c] A writer of the twelfth century stands upon no better foundation than those above mention'd; it has however been deem'd incontestable. *Malmsbury*,

'the

‘ the exact time of the conversion of the
‘ *Britons* be uncertain, it is very probable
‘ the gospel was preached in the Island not
‘ long after the death of Christ. *Theodoret*
‘ assures us, the *Britons* were converted by
‘ the Apostles. *Eusebius*, speaking of the
‘ dangers the Apostles were exposed to in
‘ propagating the gospel in the most remote
‘ countries, mentions, among the rest, the
‘ *British* Isles. Now, says he, the likeliest
‘ time to be assigned for the conversion of the
‘ *Britons*, if it was in the apostles days, is
‘ that between the victory of *Claudius* and
‘ the defeat of *Boadicea*. For, at the time of
‘ the general revolt, there were in the Island
‘ above eighty thousand *Romans*, among
‘ whom, very probably, were some *Chri-*
‘ *stians*, the gospel having now got footing
‘ in many places, particularly at *Rome*: Up-
‘ on this supposition there is no absurdity in
‘ asserting, with several modern authors,
‘ that St. *Paul* first preach'd the gospel in
‘ *Britain*. It is certain this Apostle, in the
‘ eight years between his first imprisonment
‘ at *Rome*, and his return to *Jerusalem*, pro-
‘ pagated the *Christian* religion in several
‘ places, especially in the *Western* countries.
‘ He informs us of his design of going to
‘ *Spain*; and it is not unlikely but his desire
‘ of converting the *Britains* might carry him
‘ into their Island. This opinion may be
‘ supported by the testimony of *Venutius For-*
‘ *tunatus*, in his poem upon the life of saint
‘ *Martin*; where he speaks of the travels of
‘ St. *Paul*. But after all, these are only con-
‘ jectures, and of no other use but to make it
‘ more credible, that the gospel was planted
‘ in

'in *Britain* soon after the death of our
'Lord.'

The true *Christian* doctrine, and form of worship, as delivered by the *Apostles*, was mantained in *England*, and the *Romish* government and ceremonies zealously withstood, till the *Saxons* enter'd into *Britain*, about the year 448. during which time there is no mention of any baptizings in *England*, but of adult persons only. And from this silence in history, touching the baptizing of any *Infants* in *England*; from the *Britons* being said to keep so strictly to the holy Scriptures, in doctrine and ceremonies; in which there is no mention of baptizing *infants*; and from the accounts of those who were baptized, which expresly mention their faith and conversion, the *English Baptists* have concluded, that there was no such practice as baptizing of *Infants* in *England*, for the first three hundred years after it received the gospel; and certainly he would have a very hard task that should undertake to prove there was.

b. History,
ib. i. p. 10.

Mr. *Fuller* informs us, That *Lucius*, king of *Britain*, in the year 167, 'being much
' taken with the miracles which he beheld
' truly done by pious Christians, fell in ad-
' miration of, and love with their religion;
' and sent *Elvanus* and *Meduinus*, men of
' known piety and learning in the scriptures,
' to *Eleutherius*, bishop of *Rome*, with a
' letter; requesting several things of him,
' but principally that he might be instructed
' in the Christian faith. The reason why he
' wrote to *Rome* was, says *Fuller*, because,
' at this time, the church therein was the
' most

'most eminent church in the world, shining
'the brighter, because set on the highest *can-*
'*dlestick*, the *imperial city*. We are so far
'from grudging *Rome* the happiness she
'once had, that we rather bemoan she lost
'it so soon, degenerating from her primi-
'tive purity.

'*Eleutherius*, says he, at the request of — Ibid. p. 12.
'king *Lucius*, sent unto him *Faganus* and
'*Derwianus*, or *Dunianus*, two holy men,
'and grave divines, to instruct him in the
'Christian religion; by whom the said king
'*Lucius*, called by the *Britains*, *Lever-Maur*,
'or the *Great light*, was baptized, with ma-
'ny of his subjects.

Mr. *John Fox* thus relates the story of — *Martyrology,*
king *Lucius*. 'About the time and year of Vol. I. p. 138.
'the Lord 180, says he, king *Lucius*, son
'of *Toilus*, which builded *Colchester*, king
'of the *Britains*, who then were the inha-
'biters and possessors of this land, which
'now we *Englishmen* call *England*, hearing
'of the miracles and wonders done by the
'Christians at that time, in divers places, as
'*Monumetensis* writeth, directed his letters to
'*Eleutherius*, bishop of *Rome*, to receive of
'him the Christian faith.—— The good bi-
'shop, hearing the request of this king, and
'glad to see the godly towardness of his well
'disposed mind, sendeth him certain teachers
'and preachers, called *Fugatius*, or, by some,
'*Faganus*, and *Damianus*, or *Dunianus*;
'which converted first the king and people
'of *Britain*, and baptized them with the
'baptism and sacrament of Christ's faith.'

In the year 178, says Mr. *Fuller*, 'Some — *Church Hist.*
'report, That, at this time, three thousand p. 13.

'philo-

xiv The *PREFACE*.

'philosophers of the university of *Cambridge*,
'were converted and baptized; that king
'*Lucius* came thither, and bestowed many
'privileges and immunities on the place, with
'much more improbable matter.'

Hist. of Engl. Vol. I. p. 28.   *Rapin* observes, That 'from the conver-
'sion of *Lucius*, to the *Dioclesian* persecution,
'the *ecclesiastical* history of *Britain* is intirely
'unknown. It is very probable, however,
'says he, that, during that interval of eighty
'years, the *Christian* religion made great
'progress in the Island; as appears from
'*Tertullian, Origen, Bede,* and *Gildas*: But
'what puts the thing out of all dispute, is,
'the multitude of *British* martyrs [whom I
must (till the Pædobaptists convince me to
the contrary) believe were all *English* Bap-
tists] 'that suffer'd during the dreadful per-
'secution under *Dioclesian* and *Maximian* his
'collegue.'

It was in the year 469, that the *Saxons* in-
vaded *England*. They made a compleat
conquest; overthrew *Christianity*, and set up
the Heathen *idolatry*. But those *Christians*
which escaped, fled into *Cornwall* and *Wales*;
where they secur'd themselves, and maintained the true Christian faith and worship.
Jeffery of *Monmouth*, in his book, *De Bri-
tannorum Gestis*, Lib. iv. cap. 4. as cited
Treat. of Bap- by Mr. *Danvers*, tells us, 'That in the
tism, p. 333.   'country of the *Britains*, Christianity flou-
'rished, which never decayed, even from
'the *Apostles* times. Amongst whom, says
'he, was the preaching of the gospel, sincere
'doctrine, and living faith, and such form of
'worship, as was delivered to the churches
'by the *Apostles* themselves; and that they,
'even

'even to death it self, withstood the *Romish*
'rites and ceremonies; and that about the
'year 448, the *English Saxons* began to pos-
'sess *Britany*; and that about 593, they
'having made a compleat conquest of the
'*Britains*, and began to settle their *Heptar-*
'*chy*.'—— That, 'as long as the *British* chur-
'ches possessed the country, they kept them-
'selves sound in the faith, and pure in the
'worship, order, and discipline of Christ, as
'it was deliver'd to them from the *Apostles*,
'or their *Evangelists*.' But to strengthen this
testimony, I will cite others.

Mr. *John Fox* thus introduces the entering *Martyrology,* and reigning of the *Saxons* in the realm of Vol. I. p. 141. *England.* 'This, says he, was the coming
'in first of the *Angles* or *Saxons* into this
'realm, being yet *unchristen'd* and *Infidels*;
'which was about the year of our Lord, as
'*William Malmsbury* testifieth, four hundred
'sixty and nine; the captains of whom were
'*Hengistus* and *Horsus*—— and at length
'possess'd all, driving the *Britains*, such as
'remained, into *Cambria*, which we call
'now *Wales*.' This, as Mr. *Fox* observes, Ibid. p. 149.
'was by *Gurmundus*, a *Pagan*, king of the
'*Africans*; who, joining in league with the
'*Saxons*, wrought much grievance to the
'*Christians* of the land: Insomuch that *Theo-*
'*nus*, bishop of *London*, and *Thadioccus*, bi-
'shop of *York*, with the rest of the people,
'so many as were left, having no place
'wherein to remain with safety, did fly some
'to *Cornwall*, and some to the mountains of
'*Wales*, about the year of our Lord 550.

'Most miserable, says Mr. *Fuller*, at this *Church Hist.*
'time, was the *British* commonwealth, croud- Lib. i. p. 39.
'ed

'ed up into barren corners, whilst their ene-
'mies, the *Pagan Saxons*, possessed the East
'and South, if not the greatest, the best part
'of the *Island*——— needs then must reli-
'gion, now in *Britain*, be in a doleful con-
'dition; for he who expects a flourishing
'church in a fading common-wealth, let him
'try whether one side of his face can smile,

Ibid. p. 40. 'when the other is pinch'd.——— The intire
'body of the *British* church, at this time,
'was in *Wales*; where *Banchor* on the
'*North*, and *Caer-lion* on the *South*, were
'the two *Eyes* thereof, for learning and
'religion.'

Hist. of Engl. *Rapin*, upon the state of the *British* church,
Vol. I. Lib. ii. from the arrival of the *Saxons*, to the retreat of
p. 43. the *Britons* into *Wales*, begins thus: 'After,
'says he, having seen what calamities *Britain*
'was exposed to by the *Saxon* wars of a hun-
'dred and thirty years, a regular account of
'the *British* church is not to be expected

Ibid. p. 44. 'during that space.——— It is very likely,
'says he, all the monuments of the *British*
'churches were destroy'd, where-ever the
'*Saxons* became masters; and that it was
'not possible to preserve any but those of the
'churches of *Wales*, where the *Saxons* could
'never penetrate. It is easy to imagine,
'that the church was in a very mournful state,
'while the *Saxons* were exercising their fu-
'ry. These merciless idolaters, as well out
'of duty as wantonness, not only trampled
'upon every thing relating to the Christian
'religion, but let loose their rage against the
'Christians themselves. *Gildas* and *Bede*
'have painted out their inhuman proceedings,
'in such a manner as shows their barbarities
'were

'were carried to the highest Degree imagi-
'nable. *From the east to the west,* says Gil-
'das, *nothing was to be seen but churches
'burnt, and destroy'd to their very founda-
'tions. The inhabitants were extirpated by
'the sword, and buried under the ruins of
'their own houses. The altars were daily
'profaned by the blood of those slain thereon.*
'Bede, who was a *Saxon,* and therefore not
'to be supposed to aggravate the cruelty of
'his country-men, expresses himself thus:
'*By the hands of the* Saxons, *a fire was light-
'ed up in* Britain, *that served to execute the
'just vengeance of God upon the wicked* Bri-
'tons, *as he had formerly burnt* Jerusalem *by
'the* Chaldeans. *The Island was so ravaged
'by the conquerors, or rather by the hand of
'God, making use of them as instruments;
'that there seemed to be a continued flame
'from sea to sea, which burnt up the cities,
'and covered the surface of the whole Isle.
'Publick and private buildings fell in one com-
'mon ruin. The priests were murdered on the
'altars; the bishop, with his flock, perished
'by fire and sword, without any distinction,
'no one daring to give their scattered bodies
'an honourable burial.*

'To these mournful descriptions, says *Ra-
'pin,* may be added, That the *Britons,* who
'escaped the fury of their enemies, not find-
'ing wherewithal to subsist in the woods and
'mountains, were forced, at length, to sur-
'render to the conquerors, deeming them-
'selves happy in being able to purchase their
'lives, with the loss of their liberty. Some
'fled into foreign parts, and those whom the
'love of their native country kept at home,

b
'and

xviii   The *PREFACE*.

'and the dread of slavery prevented from sub-
'mitting to the *Saxons*, dragged on a wretch-
'ed life, in miserable want and perpetual
'fear. It is therefore no wonder that the
'accounts of the *British* church are so imper-
'fect; since the *Saxons* used their utmost en-
'deavours to destroy all the monuments that
'might have been preserved.'

The Christian *Britons* being thus pent up in *Wales*, kept their ground a good while there; till at length they were intirely subdued by a massacre, procured, as some think, by St. *Austin*, for their refusing to comply with him in embracing the erroneous principles of the church of *Rome*.

The Accounts of this *Austin* are as follow:

Fox's *Martyr*. p. 149.
About the year 596. saint *Austin*, with about forty more, were sent into *England* by *Gregory* bishop of *Rome*, to preach the gospel, and endeavour to plant Christian churches among the *Saxons*. He met with great success, the king, and great numbers of the people, being converted and bap-

Ibid. p. 154.
tized. Yea, they came in so fast, that he is said to have baptized ten thousand on a *Christmas* day, in the river *Swale* by *York*. Mr. *Fuller* gives an account of the manner how this was performed; though he is in doubt whether saint *Austin* or *Paulinus* were the doer thereof; and says, it would argue too much morosity in us to demur in our

Church *Hist*. Lib. ii. p. 66.
faith to the whole fact. 'And if so many, '*says he*, were baptized in one day, it ap-
'pears plainly, that in that age, the admini-
'stration of that sacrament, was not loaded
'with those superstitious ceremonies, as essen-
'tial thereunto, of crossing, spittle, oil, cream,
                                    'salt,

'salt, and such like trinkets; which *Prote-*
'*stants* generally as little know what they
'are, as *Papists* why they use them. I say,
'in that age, nothing was used with baptism,
'but baptism; the *Word* and the *Water*
'made the sacrament. Yea, the archbishop
'is said to have *commanded, by the voice of*
'*cryers, that the people should enter the river*
'*confidently, two by two, and in the name of*
'*the Trinity baptize one another by turns:*
'This, indeed, says Mr. *Fuller*, was the
'most compendious way; otherwise *Joshua*'s
'day, wherein the sun stood still, had been
'too short for one man's personal perform-
'ance of such an employment.'

Rapin, after having given an account of St. *Austin*'s mission by *Gregory*, and the kind reception he met with from *Ethelbert* the king, says; 'The queen got leave for the *missionaries* to settle at *Canterbury*, the ca- [Hist. of Engl. Vol. I. p. 66.]
'pital of *Kent*; where she took care to pro-
'vide them with convenient lodgings, and
'procure them the liberty of preaching to as
'many as had the curiosity to hear them.
'They made so good use of this favourable
'juncture, that in a short time, several of
'the principal *Saxons* embraced the Christian
'faith. The swift progress of the gospel at
'*Canterbury*, raised the king's curiosity to
'be more particularly instructed in the nature
'of the religion these strangers preached. At
'length, by the persuasions of the queen,
'and frequent conferences with *Austin*, he re-
'ceived baptism, about a Year after the ar-
'rival of the *missionaries*. The conversion
'of the king being followed by that of mul-
'titudes of his subjects, the queen's chapel,
                    'which

'which stood without the city, soon became
'too little to hold them.—— Thus began
'the conversion of the *Saxons* in *England*.
'*Austin* and his fellow labourers were the In-
'struments made use of, by divine Provi-
'dence, to turn them from their idolatrous
'superstitions, to the light of the gospel; a
'blessing their brethren in *Germany* enjoyed
'not till two hundred years after, in the
'reign of *Charles* the Great. *Ethelbert* pro-
'moted to his utmost, the conversion of his
'subjects, but without using the least vio-
'lence or compulsion; having learn'd of his
'instructors, as *Bede* expresly observes, that
'God requires none to serve him, but those
'who do it with a willing mind. It were to
'be wished, says *Rapin* [with whom all
Baptists, and sincere Christians, will unite]
'that all Christian princes would follow his
'example! The *Saxons* were so eager to em-
'brace the gospel, that, if historians may be
'credited, *Austin*, in one day, baptized ten
'thousand in the river *Swale*, which runs in-
'to the *Thames*.'

 Baptism was not, in those times, administer'd in a font in the church (much less in
houses) but in rivers; nor attended with so
many ceremonies as practised now by those of
the *Roman* faith, as Mr. *Fox* observes, speaking of St. *Austin*; 'After he had baptized
'and christen'd, *says he*, ten thousand *Saxons*,
'or *Angles*, in the *West* river, that is called
'*Swale*, beside *York*, on a *Christmas* day;
'perceiving his end to draw near, he or-
'dained a successor, named *Laurentius*, to
'rule after him the archbishop's sea of *Doro-*
'*bernia*. Where note, by the way (Chri-
            'stian

Martyrology,
Vol. I. p. 154.

The PREFACE.

'ſtian reader) that whereas *Auſtin* baptized
'then in rivers, it followeth, there was then
'no uſe of fonts. Again, if it be true that
'*Fabian* ſaith, he baptized ten thouſand in
'one day, the rite then of baptizing at *Rome*
'was not ſo ceremonial; neither had ſo many
'trinkets at that time, as it hath had ſince;
'or elſe it could not be, that he could baptize
'ſo many in one day.'

 Auſtin meeting with ſuch ſucceſs, in that Anno 604.
part of *Britain* called *England*, held a ſynod
near the borders of *Wales*, and ſent to the Fox's *Martyr.*
biſhops of the ancient *Britons*, who had fled Vol. I. p. 153.
into thoſe parts, and were now encreaſed to a
very great number, to perſuade them to ſub- Fuller's *Ch.*
mit to the authority of the ſee of *Rome*, as *Hiſt.* p. 61.
many *Saxons* had done, and to embrace the
ceremonies of that church, particularly in the
time of keeping *Eaſter, and in baptizing
their children.* 'To theſe, ſays Mr. *Fox*,
'the *Scots* and *Britains* would not agree,
'refuſing to leave the cuſtom which they ſo
'long time had continued.'

 Thus far it appears, that the doctrine and
worſhip which the *Britains* received from the
Apoſtles, they cloſely adhered to, cleaving to
the ſcriptures, utterly renouncing all *Romiſh*
Traditions and Superſtitions: But inaſmuch
as they refuſed to be ſeduced by *Auſtin*, he
not only threaten'd their ruin, but accompliſhed the ſame in a ſhort time after. For,

 When *Auſtin* found the *Britons* refuſed to
comply with his extravagant propoſals, he
abated in his demands, and only deſired their
compliance with him in three things. His
words, according to *Fabian*, were theſe: Part v. p. 119.
'Sins ye wol not aſſent to my heſts general-
'ly,

'ly, affent ye to me fpecially in iii things. The *firſt* is, that ye keep *Eſter* day in due fourme and tyme as it is ordayned. The *ſecond*, that ye geve Chriſtendome to chil- dren: And the *thyrde* is, that ye preach unto the anglis the word of God as afore- times I have exhorted you. And all the other deale, I ſhall ſuffer you to amende and refourme within your ſelves. But, *ſaith he*, they would not thereof. Then *Auſtayne* ſaid unto them, and warned them by man- ner of infpyracion, that ſins they wolde not receave peace of their brethren, they ſhould of other receive warre and wretche.'

Hiſt. of Engl. Vol. I. p. 68.
Bede, an author much more ancient than *Fabian*, as cited by *Rapin*, expreſſes this threat of St. *Auſtin* thus: 'Since you refuſe peace from your brethren, you ſhall have war from your enemies; and ſince you will not join with us in preaching the word of eternal life to your neighbours, you ſhall receive death at their hands: Which, ſaith Mr. *Danvers*, *Auſtin* accompliſhed accor- dingly, by bringing the *Saxons* upon them to their utter ruin.'

How far St. *Auſtin* might be concerned in bringing upon the *Britons* their ruin, does not appear. *Fabian* commends him as a great faint and a prophet: indeed, immediately af- ter his words above quoted, and at the end of the paragraph, he adds, 'the which was put in experience by *Ethelfridus* king of *Northumberland*.' Some authors do look upon it as the accompliſhment of his predi- ction: But be that as it will, the *Britains* ſtill held their integrity; neither promiſes nor threats could prevail with them to admit

mit of the least change in their ancient customs.

Rapin, upon this head, observes; 'That 'Austin had not only pressed the *Britons* to a 'conformity with the *church of Rome*, and 'obedience to the *Papal* authority, but also 'had reproached them for their negligence 'and want of zeal, in not promoting the conversion of the *Saxons*. Perhaps, *says he*, 'he designed to intimate to them, that the 'conversion of all *England* stuck only at the 'union he proposed to them. However this 'be, these words of *Austin* were looked upon 'as a prediction of the *massacre* of the monks 'of *Bangor*:' Which, says Mr. *Fox*, ' not 'long after, so came to pass, by the means 'of *Ethelfride*, king of *Northumberland*; 'who being yet a *Pagan*, and stirred with 'a fierce fury against the *Britains*, came, 'with a great army, against the city of *Chester*, where *Brockmaile*, the consul of that 'city, a friend and helper of the *Britains* 'side, was ready with his force to receive 'him. There was at the same time at '*Bangor* in *Wales*, an exceeding great Monastery, wherein was such a number of monks, 'as *Galfridus* with other authors do testify, that if the whole company were divided 'into seven parts, in every of the seven parts 'were contained not so few as three hundred monks, which all did live with the 'sweat of their brows, and labour of their 'own hands, having one for their ruler named *Dino*. Out of this *Monastery* came 'the monks of *Chester*, to pray for the good 'success of *Brockmile*, fighting for them against the *Saxons*. Three days they conti-

Ibid. p. 68.

not *Martyrology*, Vol. I. p. 154.

'nued

'nued in fasting and prayer. When *Ethel-
'fride*, the aforesaid king, seeing them so
'intentive to their prayers, demanded the
'cause of their coming thither in such a com-
'pany; and when he perceived it was to
'pray for their consul; then saith he, al-
'though they bear no weapon, yet they fight
'against us; and, with their prayers and
'preachings they persecute us. Where-
'upon, after that *Brockmaile* being over-
'come did flee away, the king commanded
'his men to turn their weapons against the
'silly unarm'd monks, of whom he slew, at
'the same time, or rather martyr'd, eleven
'hundred [*Fuller* says twelve] only fifty
'persons of that number did flie and escape
'away with *Brockmaile*; the rest were all
'slain.'

The late reverend Dr. *Calamy*, who seems to have taken not a little pains on this head: He quotes *Gildas*, who wrote about the year of Christ 564. and said; 'That *Christ* '*shewing his bright light to all the world,* '*afforded his rays, that is, his precepts, in* '*the latter end of the reign, as we know, of* 'Tiberius Cæsar, *when his religion was pro-* '*pagated without any hindrance.* And if he 'meant this, says the doctor, of the publica- 'tion of the gospel in *Britain*, which has 'been the most prevailing opinion, we must 'allow him to have had better advantages 'for the *knowing* this with certainty then, 'than we can have at this distance. Accord- 'ing to this account, this Island had Christi- 'anity preach'd in it, within five years of 'our Saviour's crucifixion, which was very 'early; perhaps too early, says he, all cir-
'cum-

God's Concern for his glory in the British Isles, p. 6.

'cumstances consider'd, for a place that lay
'so remote. A late learned writer therefore Stillingfleet's
'asserts, That those words of *Gildas* have Orig. Brit.
'been misunderstood, and applied to the Lib. I. Ch. i.
'particular preaching of the gospel in *Bri-*
'*tain*; whereas they were meant of the ge-
'neral liberty of preaching it throughout the
'world. But be it as it will, as to that, all
'ancient writers agree, that Christianity was
'planted in this land very soon, considering
'its distance from *Judea*.

'Tis evident, that after Christianity ob-
'tained here, a great part of the inhabitants
'still continued *Pagans*, and yet our holy
'religion made a progress. As it got ground,
'the temples of their ancient idols were some
'of them destroy'd, and others of them de-
'dicated to the true and living God. We
'have no account of such severities here in
'the primitive times against the followers of
'a crucified Jesus as in other countries. That
'which was the last of the ten persecutions
'under the *Roman* emperors seems to have
'been the first that affected this Island. But
'in that general calamity, in the reign of
'*Dioclesian* and *Maximian*, about the year 303,
'the Christians here were very great sufferers.

''Tis said, That Maximian *almost rooted out* Usser Brit.
'*the Christian religion from* Britain; *and* Eccl. Antiq.
'*that they who suffered martyrdom were almost* Cap. 7.
'*beyond number.* Gildas tells us, That *their*
'*churches were thrown down, and all the*
'*books of holy scriptures that could be found,*
'*were burnt in the streets; and the chosen*
'*priests of the flock of our Lord, together*
'*with the innocent sheep, murdered.* St. *Al-*
'*ban* of *Verulam,* and *Aaron,* and *Julius* of
'Carlisle

'*Carlisle* upon *Usk* in *Monmouthshire*, and many others, sealed the truth of Christianity with their blood.

'But when the storm was over, which did not last much above a year, the Christians here, as well as in other parts, fled out of the woods and dens and caves, where they had hid themselves, and rebuilt their demolished churches, and flourished to a great degree, both in peace and unity. They were much favour'd by *Constantius*, the father of *Constantine*, who continued for the latter part of his life here in *Britain*; and would suffer no man to die for his religion in his dominions. It was here also that *Constantine* himself, who was a native of this Island, first declared himself a Christian, or inclined that way; which it is not likely he would have publickly done, had not a good part of his army been of that religion: And upon his advancement to the imperial throne, 'tis not to be wonder'd at, if more splendor attended Christianity as it was here professed, than had been known before. But I have not, says the doctor, upon the strictest enquiry I have been able to make, hitherto been able to discern sufficient ground to apprehend, that from the beginning, churches, or places of worship, were so nobly adorn'd, or church government so modelled in this Island, as some time after; or that the prelatical form of government was any part of that *glory* that was at first *declared* in this Island.' And he spends some pages in vindication of his own opinion thereupon, in opposition to what had been written in favour of the prelatical par-

Euseb. de vit. Const. M.I.1. c. 13. Soz. Hist. Eccles. I. 1. c. 6.

'ty;

The PREFACE.

'ty; which I pass, as foreign to my design.

'*Britain*, says the doctor, was also sadly
'infested with the *Picts* and *Scots*; which,
'after various struggles, when no more help
'could be had from the *Romans*, was the
'occasion of calling the *Saxons* to their assi-
'stance. These *Saxons*, whom *Gildas* calls,
'*A nation, odious both to God and Man*,
'came hither to be a scourge to the *Britons*,
'about the year of Christ 450. They were
'at first received as guests, and treated as
'stipendiaries, in opposition to the barbari-
'ans; but at length found themselves strong
'enough to set up for masters; laid the
'whole country waste, and drove the old
'*British* Christians into the barren mountains
'of *Wales*; and occasion'd such confusion
'and desolation, as *Gildas*, who wrote a few
'years after, thought could never be enough
'lamented. That writer describes their cruel-
'ties, and the judgment of heaven upon a sin-
'ful people, which they were the instruments
'of inflicting, in such a manner, as must
'needs affect all that read his account. He
'says, That *all the towns, with the beating
'of the rams, and all the townsmen, pastors
'priests and people, with naked swords, that
'glittered on all sides, and crackling flames,
'were together whirled to the ground.* And
'our historians say, that they scarce left the
'face of Christianity where they prevailed.
'And yet pure religion was not even then
'extirpated out of the Island.' Ranulph. *Nig. in Chronic.* and Mat. Westmonast. A. D. 586, 596.

The doctor goes on, and says; '*Bede*,
'who wrote his history about the year 731,
'gives us a great deal of light; though al-
'lowance must be made for his being himself

'a

'a *Saxon*, and not very friendly to the *Bri-*
'*tish* churches, and for his having a mona-
'ſtick tincture. Chriſtianity, in a new edi-
'tion of it, with great improvements, as to
'outward pomp, was, during this period,
'received from *Rome*, through the hands of
'*Auſtin* the monk, about the year 598. But
'there was a purer Chriſtianity in the Iſland
'before, that was much freer from adultera-
'tions and corruptions, than that which was
'now introduced under the ſame name. There
'were great conteſts between thoſe of the old
'ſtamp, and thoſe of the new. The former
'lived in *Wales* and *Scotland*, and the latter
'in the heart of the country. So that there
'were conſiderable debates on foot in this
'Iſland, between *Conformiſts* and *Nonconfor-*
'*miſts*, in ancient as well as in modern times:
'And the one ſort was apt to carry it with
'an high hand, and the other was forced to
'be ſatisfied with the conſcience of their own
'integrity then, as well as now. The *Con-*
'*formiſts* then were, in all things, for the me-
'thods of the church of *Rome*; and the *Non-*
'*conformiſts* were for the ways and methods
'of the ancient Chriſtians, and diſowning

Hiſtorical Ac- 'impoſitions. And *they were called too, The*
count, p. 69. '*Schiſmaticks of* Britain *and* Ireland; *becauſe*
'*they would not receive the Romiſh altera-*
'*tions, nor ſubmit to the authority by which*

Eccleſ. Hiſt. '*they were impoſed.* In the year 601, *ſays*
Lib. ii. Cap. ii.'*the doctor,* there was a ſynod, called by
'*Auſtin*, to which, *Bede* tells us, the biſhops,
'or doctors of the next province of the *Bri-*
'*tons*, were ſummon'd; in which the abbot
'of *Bangor* gave him a free anſwer to his de-
'mand of conformity to *Rome*. He told
'him,

' him, That *they, the ancient Christians of*
' *this Island, were obedient, and subjects to*
' *the church of God, and to the pope of*
' *Rome, and to every godly Christian*; *to*
' *love every one in his degree, in perfect cha-*
' *rity*; *and to help every one of them by word*
' *and deed, to be the children of God: And*
' *other obedience than this he knew not to be*
' *due to him whom he called the pope,* &c.
' And many of the poor monks, not long
' after, lost their lives, in return for this free-
' dom and resolution.'

The doctor, having shewn the great contest in the church about *Easter*, says, ' It ought
' not to be forgotten, that the difference be-
' tween these old *Conformists* and *Nonconfor-*
' *mists*, did not lie only in the time of keep-
' ing *Easter*; they differed also about *Bap-*
' *tism*: For that was one of the three things
' *Austin* insisted on in his conversation with
' the *British* doctors; that they should, for
' the future, administer baptism after the man-
' ner of the church of *Rome*; which is an
' argument they did not use to do so before.'

The doctor here seems to be at a stand, lest his ancient *Nonconformists*, which may very well be supposed to be *English Baptists*, should, by his readers, be taken as such: And therefore, in a comment upon the account he has given, tells us thus: ' Where-
' in the difference, *says he*, between the old
' *Britons* and the *Romans*, properly lay about
' *Baptism*, is not so evident. *Pits* frankly
' owns, he did not know what it was. *Relat.*
' *Hist. de rebus anglicis*, p. 19. Nor does
' *Bede* explain it, nor any of our ancient
' writers that I have conversed with. Some
' have

The *PREFACE*.

'have thought they differ'd about the *subjects*
'of *baptism*; and that whereas the *Romans*
'baptized infants, the *Britons* were againſt
'infant baptiſm; and an argument has been
'drawn from thence by the *Antipædobap-*
'*tiſts*: But an anſwer is returned to it by
'Mr. *Wall*, in his *Hiſtory of infant baptiſm*,
'p. 327. where he obſerves, that *Pelagius*
'being a native of *Britain*, his declaring
'that he never heard of any Chriſtian, Ca-
'tholick or Sectary, that deny'd infant bap-
'tiſm, is a good evidence that his country-
'men did not do it. It ſeems more likely,
'that this difference ſhould have been about
'the *mode of Baptiſm*, and the very words
'of *Auſtin*, as *Bede* relates the matter, ſeem
'to look that way. For he would have them
'adminiſter baptiſm, for the future, *after*
'*the manner of the church of Rome*. Now I
'know of nothing ſo remarkable in the man-
'ner of baptizing in the church of *Rome* at
'that time, as the *trine immerſion*. That
'this was cuſtomary in that church, is aſſert-
'ed by *Walafridus Strabo, de rebus Eccleſiæ*,
'Cap. 26. And though we have no poſitive
'evidence, as I know of, that a ſingle im-
'merſion, or aſperſion, or pouring of water,
'was uſed among the ancient *Britons* in their
'baptiſm; yet, till ſomething elſe is menti-
'on'd, with a ſurer appearance of probability,
'I am inclined to believe, this was the mat-
'ter of that part of the difference.'

I muſt beg leave to obſerve here, That this worthy gentleman, upon the ſtricteſt enquiry, as he ſays, could not diſcern ſufficient ground to apprehend, that churches, or places of worſhip, were ſo nobly adorned;

or

or church-government so modelled in this Island, as sometime after; or that the prelatical form of government was any part of that glory, that was at first declared in this Island; and takes some considerable pains to prove it, in opposition to a venerable prelate of the church of *England*, who, in an historical account of church government, as it was in *Great Britain* and *Ireland*, when they first received the Christian religion, undertook to prove, that it was much the same from the first, that it is at present. But the doctor did not tell us he could not discern sufficient ground for *infant* baptism; which, I think, is as undiscernable as the other: Neither has he taken notice of any of those many instances we have of the churches practice respecting baptism. It may be, his eyes were so fixed on the *prelatical* point, he could not see those trifling points of *adult* baptism, and by *immersion*; which were apparently the practice of the church in those days: For we have no mention of the practice of christening or baptizing children in *England* before the coming of St. *Austin*: And it is evident, he being the pope's legate, brought it from *Rome*: And the doctor himself owns, the *British* church was not yet corrupted with the superstitions of the *Romish* church. But the doctor seems to be under a necessity to own (because he says it ought not to be forgotten) That one of the points in difference between St. *Austin* and the *British* Christians, was that of baptism; and should we allow the doctor his way of reasoning on the *trine* immersion (which we cannot) what will become of his *sprinkling?*

But,

But, to me, the evidence of *Fabian*, for ought that appears to the contrary, is as good, if not much better, than that of *Pelagius*: Because, if *Pelagius* did say so, it is rather a proof of his great ignorance. For it is undeniable, that many, before his time, denied infant baptism. Besides, that he did say so, only depends upon the veracity of a pope; and but few Protestants will believe what the pope says, merely upon his own word, in opposition to any of their doctrines. However, the arguments for and against this point, you may see in *Wall*, *Wills* and *Danvers*. But this is evident, *Austin* did not use many ceremonies in baptism; as appears by his performing it in rivers, and baptizing ten thousand in one day, as aforesaid; and therefore could not insist upon their baptizing after the manner of *Rome*, as one of the three fundamental points, to be comply'd with by the *Britains*; unless the *Romish* manner of baptizing was quite different then from what it has been since: Because *Bede*, an author vastly more ancient than *Fabian*, does affirm, that one of the three things insisted on by *Austin* was, That the *Britons* should ' compleat the ministration of baptism (by which ' we are born again unto God) according to ' the custom of the holy *Roman* and apostolic ' church.' *Lib.* ii. *Cap.* ii.

That the controversy about the baptizing of infants, was agitated in *England*, at this time, appears from hence; because one of those difficulties that *Austin* met with was this. For when he sent over certain difficult cases to the bishop of *Rome*, for his advice and direction, after he had desired to know, what

The PREFACE.

what he should do with the bishops of Britain, who had rejected his proposals, he made this enquiry; *How long a child may be left unbaptized, if there was no present danger of death.* Fox's *Martyr.* Vol. I. p. 151.

The *subject* of baptism being now changed in *England*, and by a *Romish* emisary, so ignorant in the rite, as appears by his question to the pope, and introduced by such a *bloody massacre* of those glorious witnesses of Christ, which did arise from their Christian courage and zeal against those antichristian impositions of the *Romish* church: One would think the *pædobaptist* Protestants could not be so tenacious about a rite sprung from so foul a beginning, as to martyr such a multitude as has been martyr'd in this kingdom for opposing it. Yet the *mode* of baptism (which has been, and is still too much ridicul'd by the rigid part of the *pædobaptists*) continued about one thousand Years longer; and baptism was performed by *dipping* those who were baptized, into the water.

Baptizing in churches did not begin in *England* till about the year 627; when king *Edwin* built one on purpose to be baptized in himself. He was one of the *Saxon* kings in *England*; and having a Christian queen, was persuaded to have his daughter, and twelve more, baptized by *Paulinus*; and afterwards was baptized himself at *York*, by the same person. From the conversion of this king, to the end of his reign, which was about six years, *Paulinus*, bishop of *York*, continued christening in the rivers *Gwenie* and *Swala*, using the said rivers for his *fonts*. He was forced to fly from his bishoprick in a time of persecution; but one *James*, his deacon, a good and holy man, continued there baptizing and preaching in the north parts of *England*.

Ch. History, Mr. *Fuller*'s Account is this: He says,
Lib. ii. p. 73. ' King *Edwine*, almost three years a *candi-*
' *date at large* of Christianity, cordially em-
' braceth the same; and, with many of his
' nobles, and multitudes of his subjects, is
' solemnly baptized by *Paulinus*, in the little
' church of St. *Peter*'s in *York*, hastily set up
' by the king for that purpose, and after-
' ward by him changed into a firmer and fairer
' fabrick.'

Martyrology, Mr. *Fox* tells us, That ' after this [an in-
Vol. I. p. 156. ' tended assassination which king *Edwin* esca-
' ped] about *Whitsontide*, the king being
' scantly whole of his wound, assembled his
' host, intending to make war against the
' king of *West Saxons* [who sent the assassin
' privily to slay him] promising to Christ to
' be christened, if he would give him the
' victory over his enemies; and in token
' thereof caused his daughter, born of *Edel-*
' *burge*, the same *Easter* day when he was
' wounded, named *Eufled*, to be baptized,
' with twelve others of his family, of *Pauli-*
' *nus*'—— who addressed himself to the king,
after his conquest, in these words; ' Behold,
' O king, you have vanquished your ene-
' mies; you have obtained your kingdom;
' now perform the third thing, which you pro-
' mised, that is, to receive the faith of Christ,
' and to be obedient to him. Whereupon,
' says Mr. *Fox*, the king conferring with his
' counsel, and his nobles, was baptized of the
' said *Paulinus* at *York*, with many of his

' other

The PREFACE.

other subjects with him.' And in the margin says, he was baptized in St. *Peter's* church at *York*; which he first caused to be made of wood, which after, by St. *Oswald*, was builded of stone—— 'From that time
' forth, during the life of *Edwin*, which was
' the term of six years more, *Paulinus* chri-
' sten'd continually in the rivers of *Gwenie*
' and *Swala*, in both provinces of *Deira* and
' *Bernicia*, using the said rivers for his *fonts*,
' and preached in the shire of *Lincescie*,
' where he builded also a church of stone at
' *Lincolne*.' And in the margin, says, Note, *Paulinus* christen'd in rivers.

Rapin agrees in his testimony as to this; *Hist. of Engl.* and gives a full account from *Bede*, of the Vol. I. p. 69, several facts before related. He says, ' *Que-* 70.
' *celin*, one of the kings of *Wessex*, bore the
' yoke of *Edwin* with that impatience, that
' he resolved to free himself from it, by
' means of an assassin, whom he sent to him
' on some pretence, privately armed with
' a poisoned dagger. The Ruffin being in-
' troduced into the presence chamber, took
' his opportunity, and made so furious a *pass*
' at the king, that he was wounded through
' the body of *Lilla* his favourite, who inter-
' posed himself, and received the blow. *Pau-*
' *linus* being informed of this accident, ha-
' stily ran into the room; and finding *Edwin*
' in a great rage with the king of *Wessex*, told
' him, God, to whom such wretches were an
' abomination, would not fail to punish so
' horrid a villany. It is said, that *Edwin*,
' whom the queen had hitherto solicited in
' vain, promised, at the same time, to re-
' nounce idolatry, if the God of the Christi-

' ans

'ans would revenge him of his enemy. At
'the fame inftant news was brought him,
'That the queen, after a hard labour, was
'brought to bed of a princefs; for which he
'returned thanks to his gods. *Paulinus*, for
'his part, having been in great fears for the
'queen, fell upon his knees, and thanked
'God for her deliverance. The prelate's zeal
'was fo pleafing to the king, that immedi-
'ately conceiving a favourable opinion of
'the Chriftian religion, he confented, *Pauli-*
'*nus* fhould baptize the new born infant.——
'*Edwin* however, not forgetting the perfidi-
'oufnefs of the king of *Weffex*, marched with
'an army into his dominions; and, after
'defeating him feveral times, compelled him
'humbly to fue for peace, and make him
'ample fatisfaction. But though he returned
'with victory, according to his wifh, he de-
'ferred the performance of his promifes.
'When the queen and *Paulinus* preffed him
'upon that head, he told them, the quitting
'his religion feemed to him to be of that im-
'portance, that he could not refolve upon it
'without a thorough examination of mat-
'ters. —— The queen and *Paulinus* continued
'to folicit the king to perform his promife;
'and to give the greater weight to what they
'faid to him, they got the *pope* to write
'him a letter. But all would not do; *Ed-*
'*win* ftill demurred, and could not come to
'a refolution: at laft, the circumftances of the
'*vifion* he had formerly feen in the garden of
'*Redowald*, being, as it is pretended, re-
'vealed to *Paulinus*, the work was accom-
'plifhed in an extraordinary way. *Bede* re-
'lates, How that one day, as the king was

'fur-

'furrounded with a cowd of courtiers, *Paulinus*
'came in fuddenly, and laying his hand on
'*Edwin*'s head, afk'd him, Whether he un-
'derftood the meaning of that *token*. At
'thefe words, *Edwin* recollecting what had
'paffed between him and the *ftranger* in *Re-*
'*dowald*'s garden, threw himfelf at *Pauli-*
'*nus*'s feet; who, with an air of authority,
'faid to him thus: *My Lord, You have efca-*
'*ped the hands of your enemies, and are be-*
'*come a great king. All that was foretold*
'*you is come to pafs; it is your duty now to*
'*make good your promife.* Upon hearing this,
'*Edwin* is faid to reply, he was fully fatis-
'fied, and ready to receive the *Chriftian*
'*faith*. From that moment he ftrove not
'only to be better informed himfelf, but alfo
'to prevail with his fubjects to follow his ex-
'ample and embrace the gofpel.—— *Edwin*
'being fure of the concurrence of the high
'prieft, and fome of his principal courtiers,
'called a *Wittena gemot*, or parliament, to
'debate whether the Chriftian religion fhould
'be received or not.—— It paffed without
'any oppofition.—— The fame day *Ed-*
'*win* was baptized, with his neice *Hilda*, af-
'terwards *Abbefs* of *Whitby*.

'The *Northumbrians* following the exam-
'ple of their king; *Paulinus*, who till then
'had lain idle, on a fudden found himfelf
'fully employ'd by the prodigious crowds
'that daily came to be taught and baptized.'
[*Bede* fays, that *Paulinus* coming one time Tindal's *note*
with the king and queen, to a place called *on* Rapin,
Adregrin, fpent there thirty fix days from P. 70.
morning till night, in inftructing and baptizing (in the river *Gleni*) the people that
flocked

flocked to him from all quarters] 'But if it
'be true, as some affirm, That he baptized
'in one day ten thousand, his instructions
Ibidem. 'must needs have been very concise.' [The
same is said of St. *Austin*, and both the rivers
are called *Swale*. It may seem incredible,
that *Paulinus* should baptize so many in one
day. But this difficulty is removed in an ancient fragment quoted by Mr. *Cambden*:
The archbishop, after he had consecrated the
river *Swale*, commanded by the cryers and
principal men, that they should, with faith,
go in two by two, and in the name of the
holy Trinity baptize each other.] 'A church
'of timber was hastily run up at *York* for
'the new converts, who were very numerous.
'Shortly after, *Edwin* laid the foundation
'of a church of freestone round the former,
'which stood till the other of stone was
'built. He had not the satisfaction to finish
Anno 640. 'it; which was done by *Oswald* his suc-
'cessor.'

The custom of having godfathers for adult
persons as well as children, I find was used so
early as the year 640.

Martyrology, Mr. *Fox*, after having related a fable of
Vol. I. p.158. *Berinus*'s walking upon the sea, says; 'This
'*Berinus* being received in the ship again,
'with a great admiration of the mariners,
'who were therewith converted and bap-
'tized, was driven, at last, by the weather,
'to the coast of the *West Saxons*; where *Ki-*
'*nigilsus*, and his brother *Quicilinus*, did
'reign. Which two kings, the same time,
'by the preaching of *Berinus*, were convert-
'ed and made Christian men, with the people
'of the country, being before rude and bar-
'barous.

'barous. It happen'd the same time, when
'the foresaid kings should be christen'd,
'that *Oswaldus*, king of *Northumberland*,
'was then present, and the same day marri-
'ed *Kinigilsus* his daughter, and also was
'godfather to the king.'

Mr. *Fuller* agrees as to the fact; but places *Church Hist.* it in the year 636. His words are these: Lib. ii. p. 79.
'*Birinus* here [in the South-west part of
'*England*] sets up his staff episcopal; fixeth
'himself; falls a preaching; converts many,
'and amongst the rest, *Kyngils*, the *West*
'*Saxon* king, whom he baptized. *Oswald*,
'king of *Northumberland*, chanced to be
'present at that time, and was first *godfather*,
'then father in law to king *Kyngills*, to
'whom he gave his daughter to wife.'

St. *Chad* 'was, says Sir *John Floyer*, one *History of cold*
'of the first converters of our nation, and *bathing*, p. 17.
'used *immersion*, in the baptism of the *Saxons*.
'And the well near *Stow*, which may bear
'his name, was, probably, his *baptistry*, it
'being deep enough for *immersion*, and con-
'veniently seated near the church, and that
'has the reputation of curing sore eyes, scabs,
'*&c.* as most holy wells in *England* do;
'which got that name from the baptizing the
'first Christians in them, and to the memory
'of the holy bishops who baptized in them,
'they were commonly dedicated, and called
'by their names.'

This saint *Chad* lived about the year 656; Anno 656.
and, says Mr. *Fuller*, was 'born in *Nor-* *Church Hist.*
'*thumberland*, bred likewise in *Holy island*, Lib. ii. p. 84.
'and scholar to *Aidanus*. He was bishop of
'*Litchfield*, a mild and modest man—who
'made

The PREFACE.

'made many Christians, and amongst the
'rest *Wulfade* and *Rufine*.'

Anno 689.   Among the ecclesiastical laws of *Inas*, or
Iva, one of the *West Saxon* kings, who be‐
gan his reign in the year 689, and reigned
Fox. Vol I.   thirty seven years, this was one; 'That in‐
p. 1016.   'fants should be baptized within thirty days:'
Which supposes that some, in those times,
were for delaying their baptism.

History of cold   '*Wilfrid*, says Sir *John Floyer*, converted
bathing, Pt. I. ' the *South Saxons* to the faith, *et lavacrum*
p. 57.   '*salutis ministrabat*. *Edilmalch*, their king,
'was baptized in *Mercia*, whose king, *Wulf‐*
'*here* being present, *Bede*, in his fourth book,
'makes him his godfather: *A quo etiam de*
'*fonte egressus loco filii susceptus est*. *Bede*, in
'his first book, relates how *Ceadwella*, the
'king of the *West Saxons*, left his kingdom
'and went to *Rome*; *ut ad limina beatorum*
'*apostolorum fonte baptismatis ablueretur*;
'and that he was baptized, *die sancti sabbati*
'*paschalis*, Anno 689.' And in another
Ibid. p. 11.   place, says Sir *John*, 'The Christian bap‐
'tism succeeded the *Gentile* purifications;
'and that was performed by *immersion* in
'*England*, and all parts, at the first planting
'of Christianity. In the life of *Ælfredus*
Anno 872.   '[who began his reign over *England* in the
'year 872.] we find that *Guthrumnus the*
'*Dane*, with thirty of his companions, were
'baptized in a fountain; and *Alfredus de*
'*baptisterio susceptum nominat Athelston*;
'and they used a second rite of ablution, *cum*
'*vestes candidæ deponerentur*, such practices
'of ablution of children, which is both reli‐
'gious and physical, is practised in the *East‐*
'*Indies*,

' *Indies*, as *Albert de Mandeshoes* informs us
' in his travels among them.—— And be-
' cause it is usually objected, says Sir *John*,
' that these religious practices of immersion
' are suitable to hot regions, and not to cold,
' I will give some quotations from the wri-
' ters of travels into those cold countries; to
' shew that the northern people use such
' practices.

' The *Muscovites*, says Sir *John*, from   Ibid. p. 13.
' *Olearius*, believe themselves the only Chri-
' stians, because they are immersed into the
' water, and not sprinkled; and they will
' receive no proselytes till they are rebaptized
' by immersion. They therefore dip their
' children in the fonts; and all persons of
' riper years are plunged into rivers at their
' baptisms. And *Olearius* farther affirms,
' *page 96*. That they often break the ice to
' get them into the water.

' *Olearius* also delivers the manner of the   Ibid. p. 14.
' baptism of the *Arminians*, who set their
' children naked in the font, and pour water
' on their heads and bodies three times.

' In *Tavernier*'s travels 'tis observed, that
' the Christians of *Balsara* in *Asia*, who anci-
' ently lived near *Jordan*, never baptize but in
' rivers; and that the godfathers plunge the
' child all over into the water. And every
' year these disciples of St. *John* celebrate a
' feast for five days; during which time
' they are baptized, according to the bap-
' tism of St. *John*. *Tavernier* also farther
' observes, That the *Arminians* plunge their
' children into rivers at *Christmas*; and he
' wonders that the extremity of the weather
' does not kill the children. The king of
'   ' *Persia*

The PREFACE.

'*Persia* is oft present at this ceremony, performed at *Christmas*, near *Ispahan*.'

I have been informed, says Sir *John*, that our *Highlanders* oft dip their children in cold water.

Anno 976. King *Ethelred*, who came to the crown in the year 976, appears to have been baptized by a total *immersion*, from an accident that happen'd at his *baptism*.

Acts and Monuments, Mr. *Fox*, who calls him *Egelred*, says:
Vol. I. p.206. 'Of this *Egelred*, it is read, That when *Dunstan* the archbishop should christen him, as he did hold him over the font, something there happen'd that pleased not *Dunstan*; whereupon he sware, *per sanctam Mariam, iste ignavus homo erit,* by the mother of Christ, he will be a prince untoward and cowardly.'

Ch. History, Mr. *Fuller* is more plain; and says,
Lib. ii. p.135. '*Ethelred*—— with whom *Dunstan* had a quarrel from his cradle; because, when an infant, *he left more water in the font then he found there* at his baptizing—— from such his *addition*, *Dunstan* prognosticated an inundation of *Danes* would ensue in this *Island*.'

Sir *John Floyer*, plainer yet, in answer to the objection, That it never was the custom
Dedication. to immerse children in *England*, says, 'I will give this remarkable instance of the *baptism* of king *Edgar*'s son *Ethelred*, in *Polydore Virgil*'s own words: *Is dum baptizabatur, cum subito in sacrum fontem confecti cibi reliquias ex alvo emisisset, traditur Dunstanus predixisse ita futurum, ut ille quandoque ingens patriæ incommodum dedecusque afferret.'*

Mr.

The *PREFACE.*

Mr. *Fox*, to shew that the government of Christ's church in *England*, did not depend upon the pope, but hath been directed by such princes as God had placed under him to govern the people of this realm, has given us a table of the ecclesiastical laws made by several of the kings of *England*, for the government of the *British* church. I shall only take notice of that of *Canutus* the *Dane*, who began to reign in this land *Anno* 1016. Among many other ecclesiastical laws, he made this: 'That every Christian man under‑ 'stand the points of his faith; and that, at 'the least, he learn perfectly the Lord's 'prayer and the creed; and that whosoever 'cannot, the same shall be excluded from 'the eucharist, and shall not be received, to 'undertake for others in baptism.' *Anno* 1016. *Acts and Mon.* Vol. I. p. 1017.

Though the *baptism* of infants seems now to be pretty well established in this realm; yet the practice of *immersion* in *baptism* continued many years longer; and there were not persons wanting to oppose *infant baptism*. For in the time of *William* the conqueror, and his son *William Rufus*, it appears; that the *Waldenses* and their disciples, out of *France*, *Germany* and *Holland*, had their frequent recourse and residence, and did abound in *England*. Mr. *Danvers* cites bishop *Usher*, who, he says, tells us, 'That the *Beringa‑* 'rian, or *Waldensian* heresy, as the chrono‑ 'loger calls it, had, about that time, *viz.* '*Anno* 1080. generally corrupted all *France*, '*Italy* and *England*. And further, the said 'bishop tells us, out of *Guitmond*, a popish 'writer of that time, That not only the '*meaner sort* in the *country villages*, but the *Treat. of Bapt.* p. 275.

'nobi‑

xliv				The PREFACE.

'*nobility* and *gentry* in the chiefest towns and
' cities, were *infected* therewith; and there-
' fore doth *Lanfrank*, who was *archbishop*
' of *Canterbury*, in the time of both these
' kings, about the year 1087, write a book
' against them.

'In the time of *Henry* I. and king *Ste-*
'*phen*, the said bishop *Usher* tells us, out of
'*Popliner*'s history of *France*, That the *Wal-*
Anno 1100. '*denses* of *Aquitain* did, about the year 1100.
' spread *themselves* and their *doctrines* all
' *Europe over*, whereof he mentions *England*
' in particular.'

Anno 1158.   About the year 1158, there came about
thirty persons of the *Waldensian* sect over into
England, and endeavour'd to seminate their
doctrines here: These are supposed to reject
infant baptism; the two chief of them were
Gerberdus and *Dulcinus*.

Acts and Mon.   Thus, says Mr. *Fox*, ' *Gerbardus* and *Dul-*
Vol. I. p.262. ' *cinus Nauarensis*, who, in their time, ac-
' cording to their gift, did earnestly labour and
' preach against the church of *Rome*, defend-
' ing and maintaining, that prayer was not
' more holy in one place than in another;
' that the pope was antichrist; that the clergy
' and prelates of *Rome* were reject, and the
' very whore of *Babylon* prefigured in the
' apocalypse, &c. Peradventure, says Mr.
' *Fox*, these had received some light of know-
' ledge of the *Waldenses*, who, at length,
' with a great number of their followers,
' were oppressed and slain by the pope.

' *Illyricus*, in his book *De testibus*, refer-
' reth the time of these two to the year of our
' Lord 1280. But, as I find in the story of
' *Robert Guisbarne*, these two, about the
'				year

'year of our Lord 1158, brought thirty
'with them into *England*; who, by the king
'and the prelates, were all burnt in the fore-
'head, and so driven out of the realm; and
'after, were slain by the pope.'

Mr. *Danvers* cites *Roger Hoveden*; who *Treat. of Bapt.*
in his annals upon the year 1182, saith, p. 277.
'That *Henry* II. was then very favourable to
'the *Waldensian* sect in *England*; for where-
'as they burnt them in some places of
'*France*, *Italy* and *Flanders*, by great num-
'bers, he would not in the least suffer any
'such thing here, he being in his own wives
'right, possest of *Aquitain*, *Poictou*, *Guien*,
'*Gascoyn*, *Normandy*, &c. the principal pla-
'ces where the *Waldenses* and *Albigenses* in-
'habited, and who being his subjects in
'*France*, had the freer egress into his *terri-*
'*tories* here.

'In the time of *Richard* I. and king *John*,
'we read of no opposition made against
'them, being times of great trouble, what
'by *Richard*'s absence in the *holy wars*, and
'his imprisonment by the *emperor* at his re-
'turn; and the grievous wars, both foreign
'and domestic, that attended king *John*,
'and the great contests he had with the
'*pope*, who interdicted his kingdom, forbad
'all publick *worship* in the nation, for the
'space of *six years*, only admitting of pri-
'vate baptism to infants, procured the greater
'freedom to the Christians, as well as the
'greater opportunity in those disturbances to
'propagate the truth.——

'In the time of *Henry* III, about the year
'1235, as saith bishop *Usher* out of *Matth.*
'*Paris*, The orders of the *Friers Minorites*
'came

' came into *England*, to suppress this *Wal-*
' *densian* heresy.'

Anno 1315.   In the time of king *Edward* the second, about the year 1315. *Walter Lollard,* a *German* preacher, a man of great renown among the *Waldenses,* came into *England*; he spread their doctrines very much in these parts; so that afterwards they went by the name of *Lollards.*

Ch. History,   Says Mr. *Fuller :* ' By *Lollards,* all know
Lib.iv p.163. ' the *Wicklivites* are meant; so called from
' *Walter Lollardus,* one of their *teachers*
' in *Germany,* flourishing many years before
' *Wickliffe,* and much consenting with him in
' judgment.'

Of *Wickliff,* his opinions, and his followers, who were called *Lollards,* I have given an account in *Chap.* i. of the first volume. I shall only now further observe, That the practice of *immersion* or dipping in *baptism,* continued in the church until the reign of king *James* I. or about the year 1600. which I shall transcribe from that ingenious and worthy gentleman, Sir *John Floyer* of *Litchfield,* Knt. who begins his third letter concerning the ancient *immersion* of infants in baptism, thus :

History of cold ' *To the Reverend the Dean and Canons, Re-*
bathing. Ed.3. ' *sidentiaries of the Cathedral Church of*
p. 50. ' *Litchfield.*

' *My Reverend friends,*

' MY design being to recommend the
' use of cold bathing to this country,
' I thought it necessary for the assuring all
' people of the innocency of that practice, to
' represent

'represent to them the ancient custom of our
' church in the immersion of infants, as well
' as all other people at their baptism. And I
' do here appeal to you, as persons well versed
' in the ancient history, and canons, and ce-
' remonies of the church of *England*; and
' therefore are sufficient witnesses of the mat-
' ter of fact which I design to prove, *viz.*
' That *immersion* continued in the church of
' *England* till about the year 1600. And from
' thence I shall infer, that if God and the
' church thought that practice innocent for
' 1600 years, it must be accounted an unrea-
' sonable nicety in this present age, to scruple
' either *immersion* or cold bathing as danger-
' ous practices.'

To prove that it was the general practice of the primitive church to baptize their converts in fountains, ponds, or rivers; ' After
' that manner, says he, all nations, whether
' *Northern* or *Southern*, received the baptis-
' mal ablution.
 ' The holy scriptures inform us, that St.
' *John* baptized in *Jordan*; and this was part
' of our *English* liturgy, *That by the baptism*
' *of thy well beloved son, Jesus Christ, did*
' *sanctify the flood* Jordan, *and all other waters.*
' *Paul* baptized *Lydia* in a river. And *Phi-*
' *lip* baptized the eunuch in a water; of
' whom 'tis writ, *That they went both down*
' *into the water.* *Tertullian* affirms, That
' *Peter* baptized many in the *Tyber*.
 ' 'Tis certain, says he, that there were no
' baptisteries built till after the second century;
' and then they were not built in the church,
' but out of it, and near to some cathedral;

' where

The *PREFACE*.

' where the bishop used to baptize at the *Eves*
' of *Easter* and *Whitsontide*.'

He cites St. *Chrysostom*, St. *Ambrose* and St. *Cyprian*, to prove that *baptism* was perform'd by *immersion*: And then tells us, That
' in the time of *Cludoveus*, the *French* king's
' baptisteries were built in the *Western* church,
' and placed near the door on the left hand;
' they were parted in the middle by a travers
' of wood; one part was allotted to the wo-
' men, and the other to the men; and Dea-
' conesses were appointed to assist in the bap-
' tizing of the women ———

' In all these baptisteries, says he, they
' used *immersion*; and they descended by
' steps into them as into a sepulchre; be-
' cause we are said to be *buried with him*
' *in baptism*; and it was the custom of the
' godfathers to receive the men, and the God-
' mothers the women, as they came out of
' the water.'

To answer the objection, That this practice may be fitter for hot climates than the cold. He cites the baptism of king *Lucius* and his people by *Phaganus* and *Deruvianus*; and how *Paulinus* baptized king *Edwin* at *York*, and great numbers in the rivers *Glen*, *Swalva*, and *Trakenta*, with other instances to the same purpose. And in conclusion says; ' By
' all the preceding quotations from *Bede*, 'tis
' clearly prov'd, that *immersion* was the gene-
' ral practice in the first planting of Christi-
' anity in *England*, and by the following in-
' stances it will appear, that it was continued
' in the *English* church till the time of king
' *James* I.

' In

The PREFACE.

'In *Spelman*'s *Concilia*, part the first, in
'the synod of *Cheluchyth*, under *Wulfred*
'archbishop of *Canterbury*, *An.* 821. *cap.* 22.
'I find these words; *Sciant etiam presbyteri,*
'*quando sacrum baptisma ministrant, ut non*
'*effundant aquam sanctam super capita in-*
'*fantum, sed semper mergantur in lavacro,*
'*sicut exemplum præbuit per semet ipsum Dei*
'*filius omni credenti, quando esset ter mersus*
'*in undis Jordanis.*

'That the same custom continued after-
'wards, appears by the *Cassillian* council in
'*Ireland*, *Anno* 1172. in part second of *Spel-*
'*man*'s *Concilia*; where it was order'd, *Ut*
'*pueri deferrentur ad ecclesiam, et ibi bapti-*
'*zentur in aqua munda, trina mersione.* And
'in the year 1195, in the council at *York*, it
'was order'd, *Ne in baptismate plures quam*
'*tres suscipiant puerum de sacro fonte.* And
'*Spelman* shews the continuance of *immer-*
'*sion*, by a statute made in the council at
'*London*, held 1200; *Si vero puer in necessi-*
'*tate baptizetur a laico; sequentia immersio-*
'*nem, non præcedentia per sacerdotem exple-*
'*antur.* Many more testimonies of the *im-*
'*mersion* may be observed in *Spelman*.

'In the constitutions of *Ric. Episc. Sa-*
'*rum*, 1217, 'tis order'd, That in baptizing
'of a boy, there shall be but three, *ad*
'*levandum puerum de fonte.* And in the con-
'stitutions of *Ric. Episc. Dunelm.* 1220, 'tis
'order'd, That the water where the child is
'baptized, shall not be kept above seven
'days: And in the *Synodus Wigornensis,*
'*Trina semper fiat immersio baptizandi*, An-
'no 1240. And in the *Synodus Exoniensis,*
'1287. *Si puer rite baptizatus, non ipsa sub-*
'*mersio,*

'*mersio, nec præcedentia, sed subsequentia per
'*sacerdotem suppleantur.* And the *Synodus
'Wintoniensis*, Anno 1306, mentions the
'*immersion.* I have quoted all the preceding
'passages, says Sir *John*, from *Spelman*,
'whose credit cannot be questioned: and I
'desire also thence to observe, That the *im-
'mersion* was always used to children as well
'as adult persons.

'I will next, says he, produce *Linwood*,
'who began to write his *Constitutiones An-
'gliæ*, about the year 1422. And he gives
'the provincial constitutions of *Edmund Episc.
'Cant. Anno Dom.* 1234. *Baptisterium habe-
'atur in qualibet ecclesia baptismali lapideum,
'vel aliud competens.* And a competent bap-
'tistery *Linwood* interprets big enough for the
'immersion of the person to be baptized.
'And *Linwood*, p. 242. gives these remarks
'on the different ways of baptizing; al-
'though *baptism* may be performed by *asper-
'sion*, or *effusion* of water, where there is
'such a custom, yet the more laudable cu-
'stom is, that it should be done by *immersion*;
'and though the *immersion* may be one, yet
'the custom of the trine *immersion* is more to
'be approved, because it signifies our faith in
'the Trinity, and the three days sepulture of
'Christ. Though this was the opinion of the
'*Canonists* in his days, yet, 'tis plain, that the
'trine *immersion* continued longer in *England*;
'for *Erasmus* noted it as a piece of singularity
'in the *English* church; because, in his time,
'they used immersion. And it is evident, by
'the rubrick in king *Edward* VIth's days,
'that the *English* church used that practice.

'Then

The PREFACE.

'Then shall the priest take the child in his
' hands, and ask the name, and naming the
' child, shall dip it in the water thrice; *first*,
' dipping the right side, *secondly*, the left side,
' and the *third* time, dipping the face towards
' the font, so it be discreetly and warily done.
' In the Common-prayer-book, in queen *Eli-*
' *zabeth*'s days, the *rubrick* says, naming the
' child, you shall *dip* it in the water, so it
' be discreetly and warily done; but if the
' child be weak, or be baptized privately,
' in case of necessity, it was sufficient to pour
' water upon it.

'King *Edward*'s injunctions were pub-
' lish'd, 1547. by which all people were for-
' bid the breaking obstinately the laudable
' ceremonies of the church. And in *Sparrow*'s
' *collection of articles*, &c. in the articles of
' queen *Elizabeth*, 1564, 'tis order'd, That
' the font be not remov'd, nor that the curate
' do baptize in any parish churches in any ba-
' son, nor in any other form than is already
' prescribed. And 1571, *Liber canonum,*
' *postremo curabunt ut in singulis ecclesiis sit*
' *sacer fons, non pelvis, in quo baptismus mi-*
' *nistretur, riteque, decenter et mundè con-*
' *servetur.*

'I have now given, says Sir *John*, what
' testimony I could find in our *English* authors,
' to prove the constant practice of *immersion*,
' from the time the *Britons* and *Saxons* were
' baptized, till king *James*'s days, when the
' people grew peevish with all ancient cere-
' monies; and through the love of novelty,
' and the niceness of parents, and the pretence
' of modesty, they laid aside *immersion*;
' which never was abrogated by any canon;

d 2 'but

The *PREFACE.*

'but is still recommended by the present
'*rubrick* of our church; which orders the
'child to be *dip'd* discreetly and warily.'

Hist. of cold bathing, p.63.
He observes, That 'when Christianity was
'first planted, the bath structures were turn-
'ed into temples, and the *Piscina*'s or cold
'baths, were called *Baptisteria* by *Pliny*, ju-
'nior, and in them they baptized frequently.

Ibid. p. 164.
'And that the *Saxons* who succeeded the *Ro-*
'*mans*, brought in the *German* custom of
'washing in rivers for the preserving of their
'healths; and that made them receive the
'baptismal *immersion* in rivers and fountains,
'without any scruple; and, 'tis probable,
'that on these the first Christians imposed the
'names of their saints, and religion taught the
'Heathens to change the names of their
'springs, and dedicate them to their Christian
'saints; which, for their great cures, were
'formerly dedicated to their demons. So
'*Virgo*, the famous spring at *Rome*, which
'was dedicated to *Diana*, was afterwards
'consecrated *Divæ Mariæ Virgini*, as the
'learned *Baccius* affirms.'

Though the practice of *immersion* was now
generally disused in *England*, yet there were
some who were unwilling to part with this
laudable and ancient practice.

Ibid. p. 61.
'I have been credibly informed, says Sir
'*John Floyer*, by a person of quality, who
'had the relation from Mrs. *Shaw*, an anci-
'ent midwife; that Sir *Robert Shirly*, in
'king *Charles* I's days, caused three of his
'sons to be *dipped* in the font without any
'prejudice to them: and that one of that ho-
'nourable family, who was thus baptized is
'now living. I mention this, says he, to
'shew

'shew the opinion of some in those days,
'who thought that *immersion* innocent; and
''tis probable, that many others were very
'unwilling to part with this laudable and
'ancient practice of *immersion*.'

And in another place he says, 'That I may Ibid. p. 182.
'farther convince all my countrymen, that
'*immersion* in *baptism* was very lately left off in
'*England*; I will assure them, that there are
'yet persons living who were so *immersed*;
'for I was informed by Mr. *Berisford*, mini-
'ster of *Stretton* in *Derbyshire*, that his pa-
'rents *immersed* not only him, but the rest
'of his family at his *baptism*. He is now
'about sixty six years old;' which, by the
date of the letter must be about the year 1640.

In another place, says Sir *John*, 'A per- Ibid. p. 14.
'son of eighty years old, who was then ve-
'ry sensible, told me, that in his time he
'could not remember the dipping of infants
'in *England* at their baptism, but that his
'father oft spoke of it; and farther told him,
'That the parents used always at the bap-
'tism of their children, to desire the priest to
'dip that part very well, in which any dis-
'ease used to afflict themselves, to prevent its
'being hereditary.'

And he asserts, That 'it has been a pro- Ibid. p. 65.
'verbial saying amongst the old people, *That
'if any one complained of any pain in their
'limbs, surely that limb had never been dip-
'ped in the font.*

'The *Welsh*, says he, have more lately left Ibid. p. 14.
'*immersion*; for some middle aged persons
'have told me, That they could remember
'their *dipping* in *baptism*.' And he endeavours to prove that custom useful to the

health

Ibid. p. 15. health of infants and others; and says, 'That it is only a vain fear in the parents, which has occasioned the disuse of it; to which the Canon 1603, in king *James*'s days, might a little contribute, through the mistake of its sense; for there all baptism, whether by *immersion* or *aspersion*, is declared valid.'

Thus have I traced the practice of the *British* churches in the point of baptism till sprinkling took place. And to me it seems evident beyond contradiction, that about three hundred years after the first plantation of the gospel in *Britain*, no other baptism was used but that of *adult persons*, by immersion, or dipping the body of the person, upon the profession of his faith; and that after the subject was changed, and infant baptism introduced by a massacre of almost all that refused to comply with the change; yet the *mode of baptism* by immersion continued about twelve hundred years; and though the *mode* be now changed, and sprinkling has gained the ascendant, yet I must beg of the pædobaptist gentlemen (and I doubt not but all the *English baptists* will join with me) to shew us, where Christ has given to any men or church, a dispensation to change his laws and ordinances, or make them void by their traditions, seeing they are all, except the *Papists*, ready to join with us, in declaring God's word to be our rule in all points of faith and practice, to the end of the world; as I shall shew in my preface to the next volume.

How doth God complain, by the prophet, of his people of old, for presuming to change his laws? He gave a particular command, that his altars should be made of earth or

rough

rough stone; and reprov'd their horrid transgression and disobedience in acting contrary to his express institution; *A people, saith God,* Isa. lxv. 3. *that provoke me to anger continually to my face, that sacrificeth in gardens, and burneth incense upon altars of brick.*

I shall leave the reader to judge, whether *changing baptism,* which God has expresly commanded to be administred by dipping believers, on profession of repentance and faith, into that of sprinkling infants, be not a transgression of his precept, in as bad or worse a manner, than that of building altars of brick, which God himself declares was a provoking him continually to his face.

But the *English Baptists* dare not do thus, though the Pædobaptists have said much, and they think to little purpose, to prove that the word *baptism* may be taken in a larger sense than strictly to signify immersion in water; because, unless it can be shewed from the holy scriptures, that the word *baptism* was, or may be taken for *sprinkling* or *pouring* water upon a person, as well in the administration of this ordinance, as in any common use, they conceive, there cannot be from thence drawn any solid argument for the change of this sacred rite.

It is true, some attempts have been made by gentlemen of great learning towards it; and they have been replied to by the *Baptists.* And as far as I can find, in pursuing their history, they have always had an open ear to conviction, and been a people who love and honour all men fearing God, whether they agree with, or disagree from them, in their opinion concerning baptism. But instead of a fair and candid conviction in a Christian way, it has too much been their lot to be render'd by their opponents, *as odious as they could, and as if they had nothing to say for their practice.* Thus the reverend Mr *Neal*, in his *History of the Puritans*, a work that is a sufficient evidence of his great industry and good judgment, yet labours under this prejudice against the *Baptists*; not for want of being better informed, for then something might be said in his excuse. He says, 'The advocates of 'this doctrine were, for the most part, of 'the meanest of the people; their preachers 'were generally illiterate.'

This Gentleman's candour and justice will appear, if we do but compare this with the account Captain *Richard Deane* gave to that worthy prelate Dr. *Barlow*, bishop of *Lincoln*, of the *English Baptists*, in this very time Mr. *Neal* mentions. He says, he hopes they will, in his lordship's charity (so far as their conversation suits with their doctrine) be admitted among the number of sincere Christians: and further, thus expresses himself.

Letter, p. 7.
'That your lordship may make the better 'judgment of the disciples and state of this 'Sect, concerning whom I write this; I 'crave leave to bring to your remembrance 'some of their leaders, and the occasions 'which prepared the way for the increase of 'their numbers.

'About thirty eight years since, in the heat 'of our late troubles, *Episcopacy being laid* '*aside, and Presbytery* only, as it were by 'way of experiment, for a season attempted, 'but never, in a national way prosecuted with 'effect, every man was at liberty to pursue
'the

'the persuasions of his own mind, as to en-
'tering into church fellowship in distinct con-
'gregations, and therein to join with such as
'he conceived came nearest to the primitive
'pattern in worship and discipline.

'About that time, says he, and a little af-
'ter, there were many ministers, some who
'had been before ordained, and others who
'were admitted to parochial and other pub-
'lick charges. Among whom, of my ac-
'quaintance, were Mr. *Tombes*, sometime
'preacher at the *Temple*, Mr. *Christopher*
'*Blackwood* in *Kent*, Mr. *Benjamin Cox* at
'*Bedford*, Mr. *Edward Harrisson*, Mr. *Da-*
'*niel Dyke*, and some others in or near *Hert-*
'*fordshire*, Mr. *Hanserd Knollys*, and many
'others, who did openly profess, and several
'of them write, and publish their opinions
'concerning the proper subject and manner
'of baptism. Some of them voluntarily left
'their parochial charges and benefices, as not
'approving the baptizing of infants, and col-
'lected distinct congregations of such as a-
'greed with them in this doctrine of baptism;
'which, by a succession of ordained mini-
'sters, in the place of such as are dead, re-
'main to this day.'

I shall add to this, the names of other worthy Gentlemen who left the practice of *Infant baptism*, were themselves baptized by immersion, and joined themselves with the baptized churches, viz. *John Harding*, D. D. ——— *Duveil*, D. D. Mr. *Vavasor Powel*, Mr. *James Brown*, Mr. *Robert Brown*, Mr. *Henry Jessey*, Mr. *Thomas Hardcastle*, Mr. *Francis Cornwell*, Mr. *John Gosnold*, Mr. *Henry Denne*, Mr. *Samuel Fisher*, Mr. *Henry*

Mor-

The *PREFACE*

Morriss, Mr. *Richard Claridge,* Mr. *John Keith,* Mr. *Francis Bampfield,* Mr. ———— *Abbot,* Mr. ———— *Seykmore,* Mr. *William Kaye,* Mr. *William Britten,* Mr. *Henry Forty,* Mr. *Joseph Maisters,* Mr. *Robert Steed,* Mr. ———— *Williams,* Mr. ———— *London,* Mr. *Richard Adams,* Mr. *John Canne.*

These were *Advocates,* who the reverend Mr. *Neal* would have us to esteem, *illiterate, and of the meanest of the people.* And if so, I hope he will not look upon it as an hard task to make a reply to the account which the Captain has given of their judgment and practice (the which I have placed in the *Appendix,* N°. 3.) and the rather, because, in my opinion, all the *Baptists* ever since have, by their doctrine and conversation attested what is asserted by this author.

THE

THE

CONTENTS.

CHAP. I.

From the reſtoration of king *Charles* II. to the baniſhment of the earl of *Clarendon*, in 1667.

CAPTAIN Dean's *account of the Baptiſts in the parliament army*, page 2. *King* Charles II. *reſtor'd*, p. 5. *The regicides tried*, p. 8. *Some account of Major General* Harriſon, p. 9. *Of Sir* Robert Tichborne, p. 11. *The Baptiſts of the county of* Lincoln *petition the king*, p. 19. *A petition of the Baptiſts in* Maidſtone *goal*, p. 23. Vavaſor Powel, Jenkin Jones, *and others, impriſon'd*, p. 26. *The ſufferings of the Baptiſts in* Glouceſterſhire, p. 27. *Some remarkable rebukes on their perſecutors*, p. 30. Venner's *rebellion*, p. 35. *The Baptiſts apology and*
pro-

The CONTENTS.

protestation against it, p. 35. *The tragedy of* Munster *unjustly cast on the Anabaptists*, p. 66. *Antipædobaptism no more repugnant to magistracy than Pædobaptism*, p. 68. *Baptist principles as consistent with human society*, &c. *as any other*, p. 69. *Pædobaptists as much or more Fifth Monarchists than Baptists*, p. 70. *Oppression of the magistrates, the cause of the rebellion in* Germany, p. 72. *The* German *sedition also charged upon* Luther, p. 76. *Enthusiasm*, &c. *unjustly charged on the Baptists*, p. 78. *Errors called anabaptistical, as much or more held by the Pædobaptists*, p. 79. *The* German *historians account very doubtful*, p. 80. *if true, make not against the* English *Baptists*, p. 82. *A declaration concerning ecclesiastical affairs*, p. 83. *A commission granted*, p. 84. *No Baptists in this commission*, ibid. Hanserd Knollys, Vavasor Powel, *and others, imprisoned*, p. 91. John Bunyan *imprisoned*, p. 92. *Baptists imprisoned at* Reading, p. 94. *The Baptists address to the king, parliament and people for a toleration*, p. 100. *Dr.* John Griffith's *complaint of the oppressed against oppressors*, p. 145. John Sturgion's *plea for toleration*, p. 146. Thomas Grantham, *and others, seized by soldiers*, p. 149. *A letter to the mayor of* Dover, *by* James Atkins, p. 151. *The imprisonment of the Baptists at* Dover, p. 154. *Their petition to the king*, p. 155, *and another to the duke of* York, p. 159. *The persecution of the Baptists about* London, p. 160. John James's *meeting disturbed*, p. 165. *He is committed to* Newgate, p. 169, *and executed at* Tyburn,

The CONTENTS.

burn, p. 171. *Other meetings disturbed, and many persons sent to prison by* John Robinson, *&c.* p. 172. *The Baptists prisoners assaulted in* Newgate *and* White-lyon *prison,* Southwark, p. 179. *Twelve Baptists condemned at* Ailsbury, p. 181. *The king pardons them,* p. 184. *Mr.* Benjamin Keach, *his life attempted,* p. 185. *He publishes a primmer, is taken up for it, and bound over to the assizes,* p. 186. *His trial,* p. 187. *His sentence,* p. 202. *His behaviour in the pillory,* p. 204. *An account of the pestilence at* London, p. 209. *And the fire,* p. 213.

CHAP. II.

From the banishment of the earl of *Clarendon,* to the end of the reign of king *Charles* II.

*A*Ttempts *for a comprehension,* p. 217. *The House of Commons revive the conventicle act,* p. 220. *The Dissenters prosecuted thereupon,* p. 224. Vavasor Powel *imprisoned,* p. 227. *A disputation between the Baptists and Quakers,* p. 231. Robert Shalder *taken out of his grave,* p. 240. Robert Wright *conforms to the establish'd church,* p. 241. *Persecutions in* Suffex, p. 244. *An account of some persecutors in* Oxfordshire, p. 259. *The king designs to govern absolutely,* p. 264. *Forms the Cabal, who resolve upon a war with* Holland, p. 265, *and an indulgence to Dissenters,* p. 267. *A declaration for liberty of conscience,* p. 269. *The* Commons

The CONTENTS.

Commons address the king against his declaration, p. 272. *The king's answer*, p. 273. *He calls in his declaration*, p. 275. *The laying on of hands controverted among the Baptists*, p. 277. *A wicked slander against the Baptists confuted*, p. 279. *The Baptists contend with the Quakers*, p. 294. *The Baptists publish confessions of their faith*, p. 312. Francis Bampfield *imprison'd*, p. 355. *Dies in* Newgate, p. 361. Dr. John Griffith's *case*, ib. Mr. Thomas Delaune *imprison'd*, p. 366. *Remarks on his sufferings*, p. 376. John Child's *apostacy*, p. 379.

ERRATA.

PREFACE.
PAGE 37. line 1. for *cowd* read *croud*.

HISTORY.
Page 17. line 10. for *they* read *have*.
—— 98. —— 1. for *diftuburbance* r. *difturbance*.
—— 103. —— 2. read *in* all.
—— 125. —— 22. read *to* them.
—— 132. —— 13. read *of* them.
—— 206. —— 11. for *he which* r. *which he*.
—— 294. —— 15. for *from* r. *of*.
—— 299. —— 21. for *abfured* r. *abfurd*.
—— 363. —— 29. for *any* r. *an*.

APPENDIX.
Page 24. line 33. for *Trinty* read *Trinity*.

THE
HISTORY
OF THE
English Baptists

Vol. II

THE HISTORY
OF THE
Engliſh Baptiſts.

CHAP. I.

From the reſtoration of King Charles II. to the baniſhment of the Earl of Clarendon in 1667.

SAD and melancholy was the ſtate of theſe kingdoms, during the late uſurpation. Whether they were *Papiſts, Epiſcopalians, Presbyterians, Independants,* or *Baptiſts,* who were the inſtruments made uſe of by Providence to bring about that ſad revolution, is not much material

Anno 1660.

to the present generation. Tho' great pains have been taken by historians, to clear the party on whose side they wrote, from the *odium* thereof, and to fix it upon the rest; the truth is, in my judgment, they were all in some measure concern'd in it. This is certain, and beyond contradiction, that the *Presbyterians* assumed the government; and had not Providence in so wonderful a manner appeared, and defeated their designs, the whole kingdom must have speedily conformed, or have felt the smart of their government.

BUT because some have charged the *Baptists*, upon a presumption, from the favour of *Cromwell* towards them, till his assuming the supreme power; I shall cite the evidence of Capt. *Richard Dean*, who in his letter to Dr. *Barlow*, bishop of *Lincoln*, having spoken of the great increase of the *Baptists* in the year 1649, says: That ' in that time, did this opinion spread itself also into some of the regiments of horse and foot in the army; and that in 1650, and afterwards, some professing this opinion were called from their private employments, and preferr'd to commands at sea. Among others, Capt. *Mildmay*, to command the Admiral Flagship, under the late Duke of *Albemarle*, when he was one of the generals at sea. Capt. *Pack* to command the Flagship under
' Sir

Edit. 1693, p. 10, &c.

'Sir *George Afcue*, Rear-Admiral; Sir *John Harman*, to command the Admiral Flagſhip, under his Royal Highneſs the Duke of *York*.

'But notwithſtanding ſome of this ſect had that countenance given them, as I have mentioned, by ſuch as had the principal management of affairs; yet this ſect in general, as they have publiſh'd in their *Apologies*, were the leaſt of any ſort of people concern'd in any viciſſitudes of government that happen'd among us: My ſtation within the afore mention'd ten years, gave me opportunity to know moſt perſons and actions of note, in reference as well to civil, as martial affairs, and particularly thoſe of this ſect. And although in and after the year 1649, their numbers did encreaſe, inſomuch that the principal officers in divers regiments of horſe and foot became *Anabaptiſts*; particularly in *Oliver Cromwell*'s own regiment of horſe, when he was Captain-General of all the Parliament's forces; and in the Duke of *Albemarle*'s own regiment of foot when he was General of all the *Engliſh* forces in *Scotland*: Yet by the beſt information I could have, there were not at any time, before the year 1649, twenty *Anabaptiſts* in any ſort of command in the whole army; and until after the year 1648, there were no more 'than

'than two; *viz.* Mr. *Laurence,* and Mr.
'*John Fiennes,* one of the Lord *Say*'s
'sons, who made profession of this opi-
'nion, chosen into the Common's House
'of Parliament; and both these did in that
'year, and in the life-time of K. *Charles* I.
'as I have been credibly inform'd, vo-
'luntarily depart from that Parliament,
'as not approving their proceedings
'against the person of the King, and
'sat no more in it, but liv'd privately
'until about six years aferwards, a new
'form of government being then formed,
'and in appearance settled, Mr. *Laurence*
'was called again into publick employ-
'ment.

'I confess to your Lordship, I ne-
'ver heard of any *Anabaptist* in the King's
'army, during the contest between his
'Majesty and the Parliament. And per-
'haps, because there were some in the
'Parliament's army, and none in the
'King's army, some persons have from
'thence taken occasion to affirm, that
'the opinion of Anabaptism in the church
'is opposite to monarchy in the state.
'It is true, says he, as before is men-
'tion'd, that this opinion was no gene-
'ral bar to the continuance of such as
'did embrace it, in publick employment,
'tho' I have cause to believe, one special
'reason of disbanding one entire regiment
'in the Earl of *Essex*'s army, was, for
'that

‘ that the Colonel entertained and gave *Colonel*
‘ countenance to *Separatists* and some A- Holm-
‘ nabaptists. And that which occasion'd stead's.
‘ *Oliver Cromwell*, after he usurped the
‘ government of Lord Protector, to dis-
‘ charge at once all the principal officers
‘ of his own regiment upon other pre-
‘ tences, was, for that they were all *A-*
‘ *nabaptists.*'

HENCE I think it evidently appears, that the *Baptists* were not in power, at the time of the King's death; and that afterwards they were not so much in favour with the Protector, who was the chief author of the King's death, as to give any grounds to charge that action upon them.

KING *Charles* II. was receiv'd with the *King* general acclamation of the people. ‘ At Char. II.
‘ his arrival, says *Rapin* [a], the face of *restor'd.*
‘ *England* was entirely changed; and
‘ joy, pleasures, publick and private re-
‘ joicings, succeeded to trouble, fear and
‘ consternation. The people were so ti-
‘ red of the life they had led for twenty
‘ years past, that they did not believe it
‘ possible to be in a worse state. Every
‘ one rejoiced to see at last a calm, af-
‘ ter so long a storm; and expected to
‘ enjoy a tranquillity, sought in vain for
‘ so many years. The *Royalists* and *E-*
‘ *piscopalians* were at once raised to the

[a] Vol. II. p. 618.

‘ height

'height of their wishes, in beholding
'*Charles* II. on the throne of his ances-
'tors, and the church of *England* about
'to resume her former lustre. The
'*Presbyterians* flatter'd themselves, that
'their late services for the King, would
'at least procure them an entire liberty
'of conscience, and the free exercise of
'their religion. The *Republicans, Inde-
'pendants, Anabaptists*, could not indeed
'hope to be restor'd to the state, they
'had enjoy'd so many years; but expec-
'ted at least an intire impunity, agreea-
'bly to the *Breda* declaration.' In which
was this clause [b]: ' And because the pas-
'sion and uncharitableness of the times
'have produc'd several opinions in reli-
'gion, by which men are engaged in
'parties, and animosities against each o-
'ther, which, when they shall hereafter
'unite in a freedom of conversation, will
'be composed or better understood: We
'do declare, *a liberty to tender consci-
'ences; and that no man shall be disquiet-
'ed, or called in question, for differences of
'opinion in matters of religion, which do
'not disturb the peace of the kingdom*;
'and that we shall be ready, to consent
'to such an Act of Parliament, as upon
'mature deliberation shall be offered un-
'to us for the full granting that indul-
'gence.'

[b] Rapin, Vol. II. p. 616.

'The *Regicides*, says *Rapin*[c], that is, the late King's judges, were the only persons, that could not but expect the punishment they justly deserved. And yet, even they despaired not of the King's clemency, as indeed, such as cast themselves upon it were not wholly disappointed. It is not therefore strange, that the whole kingdom should resound with joyful transports, and unite in receiving with loud acclamations, a King, who, according to the general expectation, was to restore the publick tranquillity and happiness, and put all things in their natural order.

'As soon as the King was arriv'd in England[d], the Assembly which from the 25th of *April*, had been honoured with the name of *Parliament*, was only called the *Convention*, the King being unwilling to own for Parliament an assembly which had not been summoned by his writs. But this change of name was of no long continuance. Two days after his arrival, the King went to the House of Lords; where he sent for the Commons, and gave the royal assent to three acts; the first was to change the *Convention* into a *Parliament*.' And to prevent all doubts and scruples concerning this Parliament, it was enacted;

Declares the Convention a free Parliament.

Stat. 12. Car. II. *c*. 1.

[c] Rapin, Vol. II. p. 618.
[d] Ib. Vol. II. p. 619.

That the Lords and Commons, then sitting at *Westminster*, were the two Houses of Parliament, and so should be declar'd and adjudg'd to be, notwithstanding any want of the King's writs of summons.

This Parliament began with the act of *indemnity*: And the Commons in an address presented to the King, declar'd, they accepted the gracious pardon offer'd by his Majesty in his declaration from *Breda*, with reference to the excepting of such as should be excepted in an act of pardon. The Lords likewise, says *Rapin* [e], presented a petition of the like import.

Publishes a proclamation.

IMMEDIATELY after, the King publish'd a proclamation; declaring, that all such of the late King's judges, as did not surrender themselves within fourteen days, should be absolutely excluded from the general pardon. In consequence of this proclamation, twenty of them voluntarily surrendred themselves; others withdrew out of the kingdom, and some were taken in attempting to escape. During the adjournment of the Parliament [f], the King appointed commissioners for trial of the *Regicides*. The number of those concern'd in the late King's death, as judges, officers of the court of justice and others, amounted to fourscore and one; of whom

The Regicides tried.

[e] Rapin, Vol. II. p. 619.
[f] Ib. Vol. II. p. 621.

twenty

twentyfive were dead, *nineteen* had made their escape; *seven* others, for having been less engaged in the crime, were thought worthy of the King's clemency; and *twentynine* were condemn'd to die, *ten* only were executed; the rest were pardoned as to life; but reserv'd for other penalties, as imprisonment, banishment, and forfeiture of estate. Of those that were executed, says *Rapin*, they were almost all *Anabaptists*, *Enthusiasts*, *Fifth Monarchy-men*, &c. *And some executed.*

I do not find that any of the King's judges were *Baptists*, except Major-General *Harrison*; and if there were more of them such, it reflects no more *odium* on the profession of the *English Baptists*, than on the other denominations to which the rest belonged. But it is easy to see the partiality of *Rapin* towards the Dissenters, who were not of his own profession. And I believe none will deny the difficulties that must consequently attend those, be their profession of religion what it will, when they are under the power of them, who have the sword of government in their hands. *Major Gen. Harrison.*

Mr. *Baxter* records the Major as an *Anabaptist*; and yet acknowledges, that he was a man of excellent natural parts for affection and oratory: And further tells us, that *Cromwell*, when he thought himself well settled in his Protectorship, began *Life*, Part I. p. 57. *Ib.* p. 74.

began to undermine the *Sectarians*, of whom Mr. *Harrison* he fays, was become the head and tho' *Cromwell*; had often fpoken for the *Anabaptifts*, he defign'd now to fettle himfelf in the people's favour by fuppreffing them. Hereupon Mr. *Harrison* was by him made contemptible, who, but yefterday, fays Mr. *Baxter*, thought himfelf not much below him.

THE controverfy between him and the ftate is a point too tender to be touch'd upon. But his behaviour under his fufferings, publifh'd in the year 1660, fhews him to be a man of great piety, and one who believ'd in his confcience he was not culpable: Nor did he upon his trial attempt to evade any thing he was charg'd with, but own'd his hand to the warrant for convening the *High Court* of *Juftice*, and alfo to that for execution of the fentence againft the King. ' I do not come, ' fays he, to be denying any thing, that ' in my own judgment and confcience I ' have done or committed, but rather to ' be bringing it forth to the light.' And in his defence he faid, he had two things to offer to the court in matter of law. One is fays he, ' That this, that hath been ' done, was done by a *Parliament* of ' *England*, by the Commons of *England* ' affembled in *Parliament*; and that be-' ing fo, whatever was done by their ' commands, or their authority, is not ' quef-

Trial of the Regicides, p. 54.

Ib. p. 59.

'questionable by your Lordship's, as be-
'ing, as I humbly conceive, a power in-
'ferior to that of an High Court of Par-
'liament.' That's one. A second is this;
'That what therefore any did in obedi-
'ence to that power and authority, they
'are not to be question'd for it; other-
'wise we are in a most miserable condi-
'tion, bound to obey them that are in
'authority, and yet to be punish'd if obey'd.
'We are not to judge what is lawful or
'what is unlawful. My Lords, upon
'these two points I do desire, that those
'that are learned in the laws may speak
'to on my behalf. It concerns all my
'countrymen. There are cases alike to
'this, you know in King Richard IId's
'time; wherein some question had been,
'of what had been done by a Parlia-
'ment; and what follow'd upon it, I
'need not urge in it. I hope it will
'seem good to you, that Councel may be
'assign'd; for it concerns all my country-
'men.'

THERE are some circumstances attend- *Sir Rob.*
ing the conduct of Sir *Robert Tichborne*'s Tich-
family, respecting the baptism of his grand- borne.
children, which may give some ground to
suspect that Sir *Robert* was a Baptist, tho'
I do not find it recorded in any books I
have perus'd. However it appears, that
he was a man of strict piety, an excellent

lent magiftrate, and one that aim'd at the publick good.

In his book intitled, a *Clufter of Canaan's Grapes*, licenfed by Mr. *Jofeph Caryll*, and printed in the year 1649, when he is proving, that love to all faints fhews union with Chrift; it plainly appears that he was againft the *Prefbyterian* eftablifhment. For he thus expreffes himfelf: 'If the world, like itfelf, be froward to us, we can foon be fenfible and complain of it; when at the fame time we, *altogether unlike faints*, are froward, and become thorns in the fides of our brethren; and can fooner fay, 'tis impoffible to be otherwife, than complain of our bafe hearts. And, fays he, with an index in the margin, *I may juftly fear, that many a foul, which but few years fince would creep into corners with other faints, to complain to God of the injuftice and unkindnefs of the world to them; yet now their feet have been out of the ftocks, are become the firft that lift up their hands againft their brethren.*' And further adds, 'Perfecution is fuch a foreigner to heaven, that I may fafely fay, whatever brings it into a perfon or a nation never came from God; and it will beget a pale countenance at the day of death, when confcience fhall witnefs, that faints have done

'done that to faints, which they judg'd 'unjuft from the world to them.'

WHETHER Sir *Robert* was a *Baptift* or not, my long and intimate acquaintance with the family, and the refpect I bear to them, having been both an eye and ear witnefs of fome infults on them upon his account, will not permit me to pafs him, without fome further notice.

WHEN he was before his judges, he declared, it was his unhappinefs to be called to fo fad a work, and that he could fay with a clear confcience, he had no more enmity in his heart to his Majefty, than he had to his wife that lay in his bofom; and fo pleaded *guilty* to his indictment. The council replied thus; 'We fhall give no evidence againft the 'prifoner; he fays he did it ignorantly: 'and I hope and do believe he is peni- 'tent; and as far as the Parliament thinks 'fit to fhew mercy, I fhall be very glad.' *Trial of the regicides, p. 293.*

IT is recorded of him by the author of *his cafe*, that he was of an honeft and genteel parentage in the city of *London*; a linnendraper, anciently defcended from a worfhipful family, well efteem'd and honoured, no picque, blemifh, or ftain upon them, his growth and education advancing him alike, to be foon a man, which put him very early into action. He foon became *Captain* over a foot company in the trained-bands. This he difcharged abroad *His parentage.*

abroad with valour and discretion; and at home with courtesy, his enemies bearing him witness. During the war he ascended the several steps of military honours in order; made *Colonel* of a regiment, and for a time *Lieutenant* of the tower; not taxed by them whom he served with any baseness or deficiency.

Made Sheriff of London. p. 7.

He was made *Sheriff* of *London* in the year 1650. And, says the author *of his case,* 'During his session and continu-
' ance in the court of *Aldermen,* betwixt
' his *shreivalty* and *maioralty,* he perform-
' ed the office of a good citizen, to com-
' mon justice. Many can bear him wit-
' ness of much uprightness and integrity
' manifested by him in private businesses,
' the decision whereof being referred to
' committees of *aldermen* (of which very
' seldom, but he was one, thro' the sense
' that court had of his abilities) he al-
' ways justly and impartially accommo-
' dated; and envy her self cannot speak
' less, but gratitude —— would speak
' more.

Lord Mayor.

' We will take a full view of him in
' this his next dignity, the supreme ma-
' gistracy of the *city,* as *Lord-maior* of
' *London.* And we use to say, *magis-*
' *tratus indicat virum*; but here, *vir in-*
' *dicat magistratum*; very few persons that
' arrived at this honour, after a full ripe-
' ness of years, and digestion of a long
' obser-

'observation of custom and manners, go-
'verned the *city* better, nor revived
'more wholesome laws, and reduced
'things methodically to their first state;
'the severest punisher of fraud and in-
'justice, a most rigid exactor of all dues
'and rights belonging to the *city*; keep-
'ing a constant inquisition of all the
'abuses and trespasses committed or suf-
'fered on its privileges; neither favour
'nor affection, as we use to say, making
'him to connive at such unlawful prac-
'tices.

He was not against the restoration of the King; but stood still, and engaged in no new designs, counsels, or practices, to withstand that blessed work, but with all submission and patience expected the results of providence. There were few of that temper and moderation in that critical juncture of time, who yet were in less danger than himself; which afterwards amounted to a confidence of surrendering himself, according to the proclamation, and putting himself within the danger of the law.

Surrenders himself.

What he did as a member of the *committee of safety*, was rather of necessity than choice. And doubtless had he had that state insight, he might have taken hold on occasion's foretop, and redeemed himself by some signal seasonable
demon-

demonstration of *loyalty*, as well as others in the same predicament.

p. 11.
 ' H o w he behaved himself, saith the
' author *of his case*, as to his imprison-
' ment in that place where he once com-
' manded, with all humility and fair car-
' riage, the noble Sir *John Robinson*, and
' his *warders* and *officers*, will give him
' a sufficient and good character. At that
' late strange, and rebellious insurrection
' in the *city* by the *Fifth Monarchists*, he
' professed an utter detestation thereof,
' and not so much for the butchery and
' murder committed, as that the peace
' of the kingdom was thereby endan-
' gered, by such a riotous wicked attempt.
' The danger and scandal brought by it
' on him and his fellow-sufferers, to the
' acceleration of their ends, he weighed
' not so much; being resolved either liv-
' ing or dying to pray for the prosperity
' of the King's government.

 ' H E hath continued ever since his first
' restraint a most strict, austere, and mor-
' tified life, without any grudgings or re-
' pinings at these his sad dispensations;
' bearing with an even mind the loss of
' a considerable estate, besides sundry dis-
' comforts in his near relations grieving
' excessively at his condition. And a
' deeper wound can hardly be given to a
' man in misery: so falls it out in the
' extreams of sorrow, that even our friends
          ' invo-

' involuntarily shall contribute to the load
' of it.'

In the many volumes I have perused, I do not find many *English Baptists* acting in high *magistratical stations*. But when it has so happened, they have appeared to be men of strict justice, great humility, and such as aimed at the publick good, not enriching themselves by the benefits of their *high stations*. It is observed of this great and good gentleman, that notwithstanding the several rich *places* and *offices* he went through during the *usurpation*, his wealth did not answer the sum requir'd to a *Lord-Mayor*'s estate; and that his constant affability, and humility, was sufficient to convince all men that he was not arrogant.

The King publish'd a proclamation concerning Religion, containing eight articles; most of which prescribed certain rules to the Bishops, in the exercise of their spiritual jurisdiction. The two last deserve a particular notice, because they discover, that the Dissenters were not like to continue long undisturb'd.

A proclamation concerning religion.

' The seventh ran, says *Rapin* *, that
' a certain number of Divines should be
' appointed to revise the Liturgy, and
' make such alterations in it, as should
' be judg'd necessary; and that *scrupu-*

* Vol. II. p. 261.

' lous *perfons* fhould not be punifh'd or
' troubled for not ufing it, at prefent.'

' THE eighth was, concerning *cere-*
' *monies*; to which for the prefent, no
' perfon fhould be oblig'd to conform.'

ABOUT this time was publifh'd by the *General Baptifts*, a brief confeffion or declaration of faith, fubfcrib'd by certain Elders, Deacons, and Brethren met at *London*, in behalf of themfelves and many others unto whom they belong, in *London* and in feveral counties of this nation, who were of the fame faith with them.

IT was prefented to, and approv'd of by his Majefty: And the fame was reprinted at *London*, in the year 1691, with the addition of fome names thereunto. I have plac'd it in the *Appendix*, N° IV.

THE great encreafe of the *Baptifts*, ftirr'd up their enemies to reproach and villify them, and to render them odious to the government. They are generally charg'd, as a people whofe principles tended to the deftruction of the civil power: But I do not find, that their enemies were ever able to produce any thing upon which they could juftly found fuch a charge. Indeed, I have receiv'd from the Rev^d. Mr. *Calamy*, a declaration fign'd but by three perfons, who apologize for their paucity, and are very zealous againft *bearing of arms*, and *taking an oath*, and feem to be not pleas'd with
their

their brethren, for not being of their judgments in these points. They are so far from opposing magistracy, that if the greatest zealots for *passive obedience* and *non-resistance*, had been of their judgment, King *James* II. might quietly have kept his throne, and impos'd what religion and laws he had pleas'd upon these kingdoms. I have plac'd their declaration in the *Appendix*, N° V.

On the 26th of *July* 1660, was presented to the King a petition, with a narrative and complaint, and the confession of faith of sundry honest and well-dispos'd *Baptists*; the messengers whereof, by the assistance of an honourable Member of Parliament, were procur'd to deliver the same into his Majesty's own hand; to which he was pleas'd to return a most gracious answer. Part of this narration and complaint, which may suffice to shew the innocency of the complainants, and the cruelty of their persecutors, is recorded by Mr. *Jessey*, and is as followeth:

The Lord's loud Call to England, *p.* 15.

May it please you, &c.

'BEING commanded thereto by
' the Lord, we have met often to-
' gether, to acquaint each other, what
' God hath done, doth daily, and will do
' for our souls, and what therefore, we
ought

'ought to do towards him, each other,
'and all men.

'From which assemblings, O King!
'we have been discharg'd by some in
'magistratical capacity in these parts; al-
'though therein, we bless God, none
'hath ever found us with multitude or
'with tumult. But being taught of God
'to obey him in the things by him com-
'manded, rather than man, though in
'the place of magistracy, when com-
'manding things contrary; we therefore
'durst not receive that discharge. Where-
'fore some of us have been silenc'd from
'making mention of the name of the
'Lord, as formerly, by being intangled
'in bonds, pretendedly impos'd upon us
'for this good behaviour. To which in
'our innocency we readily yielded; be-
'ing bound to the good behaviour in
'conscience, we fear'd not to be bound
'thereto by law. But such is the sad
'estate of this generation, that *they call*
'*good evil, and evil good*; with sorrow
'we speak it; taking their advantage a-
'gainst us, in our serving the Lord. Up-
'on account of the condition of these obli-
'gations, accounting us, O King! peace-
'breakers, when in the sincerity of our
'hearts, and innocency of our souls, we
'peaceably meet to worship our God in his
'fear, we affirm it. Since thus entangl'd,
'O King! we have been much abus'd as
'we

' we pass in the streets, and as we sit in
' our houses; being threatned to be
' hang'd, if but heard praying to the
' Lord in our families, and disturb'd in
' our so waiting upon God, by uncivil
' beating at our doors, and sounding of
' horns; yea, we have been ston'd, when
' going to our meetings, the windows of
' the place where we have been met,
' struck down with stones, yea, taken
' as evil-doers, and imprison'd, when
' peaceably met together to worship the
' Most High, in the use of his most pre-
' cious ordinances. We have, O King!
' spread these things before them in au-
' thority in these parts, but can have no
' redress from them; but the rage of our
' adversaries hath been augmented, by
' hearing us abus'd by some of them in
' open court, who sat on the bench of
' justice, under the odious terms of *kna-*
' *vish, juggling, impudent, and phanatick*
' *fellows*, &c. And as if all this were too
' little, they have, to fill up their mea-
' sure, very lately indicted many of us at
' the *Sessions*; and intend, as we are in-
' form'd, to impose on us the penalty of
' *twenty pounds per month*, for not com-
' ing to hear such men, as they provide
' us, of whose principles and practices,
' we could give a most sad and doleful, yet,
' O King! a most true relation, *&c.*'

Lincoln-
shire.

This was sign'd by thirty five men, in the behalf of many others.

The substance of the King's answer to the messengers, that were sent with this narration and petition was this: 'That it was not his mind, that any of his good subjects who liv'd peaceably, should suffer any trouble upon the account of their judgments, or opinions in point of religion; and that he had declar'd the same in several declarations. He promised us also, say they, upon our declaring our grievances, that he would have particular care over us, that none should trouble us upon the account of our consciences in things pertaining to religion. And while we were present before him, he order'd an honourable Member of Parliament to go to the Lord *Chancellor* and *Secretary*, and get something done to that purpose. The Member of Parliament promis'd he would do as the King had order'd him.'

The petition and representation of the Baptists in Maidstone goal.

In this year also was publish'd, *The humble petition and representation of the sufferings of several peaceable and innocent subjects, call'd by the name of* Anabaptists, *inhabitants of the county of* Kent, *and prisoners in the goal of* Maidstone, *for the testimony of a good conscience*; and was as followeth:

To

'To his Majesty Charles II. King of England, Scotland, France and Ireland, and the Dominions thereunto belonging.

'May it please your Majesty,

'FORASMUCH as by authority deriv'd from yourself, several of us your subjects, inhabitants in the county of Kent, are now imprison'd; it therefore much concerns thee, O King! to hear what account we give of our present distress'd condition. Thou hast already seen our Confession of Faith, wherein our peaceable resolutions were declar'd. We have not violated any part thereof, that should cause that liberty promis'd from Breda to be withdrawn. And now for our principles, that most particularly relate to magistrates and government, we have with all clearness laid them before thee; humbly beseeching they may be read patiently, and what we say weighed in the ballance of the sanctuary; and then judge how worthy we are either of bonds or imprisonment. And this we the more earnestly desire, because not only our own lives are in danger, but also an irresistable destruction cometh on our wives and little ones, by that vio- 'lence

' lence which is now exercis'd on us. Dif-
' dain not our plainness of speaking, see-
' ing the great God accepts of the like.
' And now, O King! that all thy pro-
' ceedings, both towards us and all men,
' may be such as may be pleasing unto
' the Eternal God, in whose hands your,
' and our breath is, who e'er long will
' judge both quick and dead, according
' to their works, is the prayers of thy
' faithful subjects and servants,

> ' The prisoners in the goal of
> ' *Maidstone*, for the testimo-
> ' ny of a good conscience.'

P. 5. THEN follows, their free and faithful acknowledgment of the King's authority and dignity in civil things, over all manner of persons ecclesiastical and civil, within his Majesty's dominions. Wherein they thus complain: ' We, thy impri-
' son'd subjects, have some of us, had our
' houses broken open in the dead of the
' night, without producing any authori-
' ty from thee, or any inferior minister
' under thee; our goods and cattle taken
' away from some others, and yet detain-
' ed from us; our bodies, some taken
' from our own dwellings, and others from
' our peaceable meetings, and made pri-
' soners; and this done unto many of us,
' some

English Baptists.

' some days before thy proclamation was
' publish'd: which proceedings doth bring
' great distress and ruin to ourselves and
' families.'

Then follows their reasons for meriting the King's protection, in their spiritual and civil rights, equal with other his Majesty's obedient subjects. After which they say: ' From all that we have P. 13.
' said, Thou, O King! mayst see, that
' not without grounds do we deny the
' taking the oath of thy supremacy, which
' calls for obedience, as well in spiritual
' and ecclesiastical things and causes, as
' temporal; not but that we can freely
' acknowledge thee to be supreme go-
' vernor of all persons, as well ecclesias-
' tical as temporal, but still in temporal
' causes and things.'

They conclude thus: ' And now hav- P. 15.
' ing faithfully laid our condition and prin-
' ciples, so far as they relate to *magistrates*
' or *government*, before thee. We there-
' fore beseech thee, O King! that liberty
' may be given us to worship our God;
' and such bowels of compassion be in
' thee, as to give us such speedy relief,
' as may be agreeable to the mind of
' God, *Which made heaven and earth*, Psa. cxlvi.
' *which executed judgment for the oppres-* 7.
' *sed, which giveth food to the hungry: the*
' *Lord looseth the prisoners.*'

Signed

SIGNED by us in the name of the *Baptists*, now *prisoners* in the goal at *Maidstone*.

William Jeffery.
George Hammon.
John Reve.
James Blackmore.

<small>Vavasor Powel imprison'd.</small>

IN this year Mr. *Vavasor Powel*, a famous *Baptist* Minister, well known to be an able and painful Preacher of the Gospel, in a great part of *North* and *South-Wales*, <small>Lord's loud Call, p. 13.</small> 'Was, says Mr. *Jessey*, seiz'd 'upon, and imprison'd in *Shrewsbury*, 'and many of his friends in several Nor- 'thern counties in *Wales*; and not for 'any crime committed by him or them; 'yea, and divers of their houses plun- 'der'd by soldiers, shewing no warrant 'for their proceedings therein.'

<small>Jenkin Jones and others imprison'd.</small>

ALSO in *South-Wales*, Mr. *Jenkin Jones*, another *Baptist* Minister, with some of the congregation, were imprison'd; as appears by a letter wrote to Mr. *Jessey*, *June* 29, 1660, from Mr. *Tho. Guin*, who had been a Gentleman Cavalier in *Wales*, but was converted under the ministry of the said Mr. *Jones*, and became a member of his Church, and a sufferer with him for the truth of the Gospel. Part of this letter Mr. *Jessey* <small>Lord's loud Call, p. 14.</small> publish'd, And is as followeth:

'SOME

'Some of our brethren were for a month's space imprison'd in *Caermarthen*, merely because they would not forego their meetings, and join with them again in their traditional worship, from whom the Lord had separated them. They bore their testimony so full, and their sufferings so patiently and chearfully, that we have much cause to bless the Lord for his gracious and tender dealings towards them. Their conversation was such, that made those that threw stones at them, and shouted when they were brought thither, part with them with tears, confessing they suffer'd for *well-doing*, and judg'd them happy therein. I suppose the Lord was more glorified by them, in those sufferings, than by any one thing, which happen'd since I came to understand any thing of his particular dealings with his people. They had his promises in an ample manner fulfill'd unto them, and his presence very frequent, glorious and powerful. This tended much to the strengthning of others, to endure the like trials, if call'd unto it by the wife Disposer of all things.'

GREAT were the sufferings of the Baptists in *Glocestershire*. The most eminent Cavaliers, imbitter'd persecutors, rode about arm'd with swords and pistols; ran-

The sufferings of the Baptists in Glocestershire.

ranfack'd their houfes, and abus'd their families in a violent manner. Mr. *Jeffey* has publifh'd part of many letters fent to him, fetting forth the hard ufage, and great perfecutions that befel the people of God in that county; more particularly thofe of the *Baptift* perfuafion; as will appear by a letter from the houfe of a godly ftrict *Presbyterian*: Which fays;

<small>Lord's loud Call, p. 21.</small> ' That they of that family, as others
' fearing the Lord, were as a beacon on
' a hill, and under great reproach, ac-
' counted not worthy to live, and count-
' ed as *Elias* was by *Ahab*, *troublers of*
' *Israel*, troublers of the place they liv'd
' in, with other fuch like afperfions,
' counting them *Anabaptifts* and *Quakers*,
' and were in fear of being plunder'd
' therefore.'

<small>The houfes of feveral perfons ranfack'd.</small> IN a letter wrote to Mr. *Jeffey*, April 3, 1660. it is faid, that the houfes of Captain *Crofts*, Mr. *Palmer* of *Borton*, Mr. *Helme* of *Winchcombe*, and many o-
<small>Ib. p. 17.</small> thers, were ranfack'd for arms. ' It fo
' fell out, fays the writer of the letter,
' that Mr. *Helme* not being at home, on
' the 6th day of the laft week, they came
' to his houfe, ranfacked his trunks, ftudy,
' and all his goods, for arms, not fpar-
' ing the bed whereon his children lay,
' to their great affrightment, being in bed.
' One of them held up his piftol to ftrike
' Mrs. *Helme*, having given her moft uncivil

English Baptists.

'civil language; so that the terrour hath
'brought upon her a very sore distem-
'per, and brought her nigh unto death.
'They drink the King's health stoutly,
'and rage against any that have the face
'of godliness; and not only soldiers, but
'the people who had long obscured their
'malice to the people of God, are now
'confident, and act barbarously. Take
'two late examples. One was of Mr. *Mr.* War-
'*Warren*, a minister in the county, who ren *perse-*
'upon the ejection of a malignant (as *death.*
'then that denomination was given men)
'was put into the parsonage of *Rencome*;
'upon this new encouragement, the said
'ejected minister (one Mr. *Broade)* brake
'in with a company of rude companions
'into the parsonage house, penned up
'Mr. *Warren*, and his wife and family
'into an upper room; so distressing and
'afflicting the poor man, night and day,
'making a noise with hautboys, so that
'he died in the place. His blood will
'cry. Another was one Mr. *Fletcher*, a *Mr.* Flet-
'godly man, who lately came out of *New-* cher *and*
'*England*, being put into a vacant place *ly forced*
'by authority, a rude cavalier in the pa- *to fly for*
'rish came in upon him in his house, *their lives.*
'beat him and used him very inhumanly,
'threatned to cut off his head with a bill,
'which one of them carried; at last, af-
'ter much vile carriage, one took his
'coat and carpet off his table, and marched
                                        'with

'with them in the streets on the top of
'a bill, so that the poor man and his
'family are fled for their lives.

Lord's loud Call, p. 19.

IN another letter of *April* 19. it is said, 'Since my last letter, the perse-
'cution in these parts breaks out more
'and more. Last week there was a godly

Mr. Finch abused and imprison- ed.

'minister sorely injured, as he was en-
'tring the pulpit to preach; and the
'same week, another was violently pulled
'out of his house, his wife, and children
'and goods, thrown into the street by
'the rude multitude; none of the parish
'daring to give them entertainment; the
'former ejected notorious person, getting
'again into possession, where he trium-
'phantly abides without controul, and
'some rudely haling the poor minister
'thus abused to the *goal*, as they said
'they would.'

THERE are part of several other letters published in the same treatise, confirming the aforesaid account of the sufferings of these people in *Glocestershire*.
To which I refer the reader for his fuller

Some re- markable rebukes on persecu- tors.

satisfaction: and shall take notice, of some
notable rebukes to the enemies of these
poor persecuted people, recorded by the
said Mr. *Jessey*.

Lord's loud Call, p. 29.

ON the day of the King's proclamation at *Waltham* near *Theobalds*, in the
evening there was a bonefire made to express

press the people's joy. A cooper who was *On a*
present ' swore and tore, and struck the *cooper.*
' ground, and said, now have at the *Ana-*
' *baptists.* Now as the fire burned he
' took a faggot, and said, here is a round
' head, and cast it into the fire which
' burn'd; and then took another faggot,
' and said, here is an *Anabaptist,* and
' that burn'd, &c. But the Lord struck
' him that night, so that he never saw
' the morning. Attested by several of the
' same town.

' Mr. O—— a minister, in his ser- *On Mr.*
' mon using many hard speeches against *O---a mi-*
' those peaceable people there, that he *nister.*
' call'd *Anabaptists,* there being many
' such there at that time: Even whilst *Lord's loud*
' he was preaching in that manner, fell *Call,* p. 8.
' into a swoon, and was speechless, as
' one dead for about two hours, and it
' was fear'd he would never have reco-
' ver'd out of it. At a meeting (at Bro- *Ib.* p. 3.
' kington in *Glocestershire, June* 3, 1660,)
' were many met; B. *Collet* and B. *Col-*
' *lings,* gifted brethren, from *Burton* on
' the water, and divers others thence, and
' from *Stow,* and other places. It was
' rumour'd about that some of the coun-
' ty troop would then come and seize up-
' on them, and imprison some and rout
' them all. The *Clerk*'s daughter came *On the*
' with her mother, who had oppos'd and *Clerk's*
' *daughter*
' revil'd them, uttering hard speeches a- *at* Bro-
' gainst *kington.*

' gainſt them, and their meetings, and
' ways; and theſe two ſtood by in a
' corner. When they came, *B. Collet*
' was ſpeaking upon *Jude* 14 and 15
' verſes, with much affection, upon theſe
' words, *Behold the Lord cometh, with ten
' thouſand of his ſaints to execute judgment
' upon all, and to convince all that are un-
' godly amongſt them, of all their ungod-
' ly deeds, which they have ungodly com-
' mitted, and of all their hard ſpeeches,
' which ungodly ſinners have ſpoken againſt
' him*. Whilſt he was preaching upon
' theſe words, the hand of the Lord of
' Hoſts went out againſt that *daughter*,
' as it appear'd; for ſhe gave a ſudden
' great ſhriek, and fell down dead before
' them all. Thoſe that were about her
' rubb'd and chaf'd her for her reſtoring;
' but there was no appearance of life at
' all. *B. Collet* was much affected with
' this hand of the Lord, and look'd pale,
' being of a very tender ſpirit. *B. Col-
' lings* ſeeing it, was about to ſeek the
' Lord for raiſing her up again; but her
' *mother*, being much out of patience, hin-
' der'd their prayers for her; and ſhe ne-
' ver recover'd. As ſome were carrying
' her corps out, Mr. *H*—— met them,
' who led that party of the troop; and he
' came in, and would have them away
' *priſoners*; and he charg'd them with
' the death of the *maid*, that they had
                                    ' kill'd

'kill'd her. *B. Collings* anfwer'd to this
'effect, *Nay, we have not kill'd her; but
'the Moft High hath done it, in whofe
'hand is both your breath and ours.* Af-
'ter he had pull'd the fpeakers towards
'the door, and fpoke more to them, he
'and the foldiers left them. Since this
'time the *Clerk* hath fpoke well of that
'people; faying, *thefe are the people of
'God*.'

I shall add but one inftance more from this author, of this kind; and that is a flagrant one; for the fufferings and hardfhips of the Diffenters in general, were made a *jeft* upon the ftage at *Oxford*, and became the fubject of their fport and laughter.

'There was a play acted by *fcho-*
'*lars*, wherein *one* acted the *Old Puri-*
'*tan*. He that acted that part, came in
'with a narrow band, fhort hair, and a
'broad hat; a boifterous fellow comes
'after him, and trips up his heels, call-
'ing him *Puritan Rogue*; at which
'words, the *Old Puritan* fhook off the
'dirt of his feet againft him. Two of
'thefe actors were alfo cut off, and he
'that acted the *Old Puritan* broke a vein,
'and vomited fo much blood in the
'place, that they thought he would have
'died in the room; but he now lieth def-
'parately fick. This is all very true. Al-

Lord's loud Call, p. 1, 2.

On the players at Oxford.

' fo

'so a woman, that join'd with them in
'their play, is dead.

'THE year 1661, says *Rapin* *, was
'usher'd in by an extraordinary event.
'The 6th of *January*, while the King
'was attending the Queen-mother, and
'the Princess his sister to *Dover*, in their
'return to *France*; about fifty of these
'men (fifth-monarchy-men) under the
Venner's 'conduct of one *Thomas Venner*, assembled
rebellion. 'in the evening in St. *Paul*'s church-yard,
'and kill'd a man, who upon demand,
'had answer'd, *for God and the King*.
'This giving an alarm to the *city*, some
'train'd-bands were sent against them,
'whom these men quickly routed; and
'then march'd through several streets, and
'at last retir'd to *Cane-wood*, betwixt
'*Highgate* and *Hampstead*; from whence
'a party of horse and foot, sent by Gene-
'ral *Monk*, dislodg'd them, and took some
'prisoners. But this did not prevent the
'rest from returning to the *city*, where
'they fought furiously, till they were
'oblig'd to take sanctuary in an house.
'They there defended themselves like
'men fearless of death, or rather, as se-
'cure from all danger, under the protec-
'tion of *Jesus Christ*. Here it was that
'*Venner* being wounded, and twenty of
'his men kill'd, with as many of the af-
'failants, was taken with the rest of his

* Vol. II. *p.* 623.

'fel-

'fellows. A few days after they were
'all tried, condemn'd and executed, with-
'out any confeffion of guilt, and perfift-
'ing in their extravagancies to the laft;
'two young men only fhew'd fome figns
'of repentance.'

THE King took occafion from this in- *A procla-*
furrection to publifh a proclamation, for- *mation a-*
bidding all *meetings* and *conventicles* under *meetings.*
pretence of religion, and commanding the
oath of *allegiance* and *fupremacy* to be tendred to all perfons difaffected to the government, and in cafe of refufal, they
were to be profecuted on the ftatute of
the 7th of *James* I.

THE *Englifh Baptifts* prefently after
this infurrection, publifh'd two *Apologies*,
wherein they protefted both againft the
principles and practices of that rebellious
party, and are as followeth:

The humble Apology of fome commonly Apology of
call'd Anabaptifts, *in behalf of them-* *the* Eng-
felves, and others of the fame judgment tifts.
with them; with their proteftation a-
gainft the late wicked, and moft horrid
treafonable infurrection and rebellion,
acted in the city of London; *together*
with an Apology, formerly prefented to
the King's moft Excellent Majefty. *Printed at*
London *in*
the year
'WE fhould be ftupid and fenfe- 1660.
'   lefs, if we did not deeply re-
D 2 , fent

' sent those black obloquies and re-
' proaches cast upon those of our profes-
' sion and practice in the point of Bap-
' tism, by occasion of the late most hor-
' rid treason and rebellion in this *city* of
' *London.*

' WE most sadly see, and feel, that
' among many it is become enough to
' render any man criminal to be call'd
' an *Anabaptist*; or at least a ground suf-
' ficient, to question his loyalty and fide-
' lity to the King's Majesty.

' WE may not therefore be so negli-
' gent of our duty unto God, in respect
' of our profession, or unto ourselves and
' families, as silently to suffer our names
' and profession, to be buried under such
' causeless infamy; neither may we be
' so much wanting of our duty to our
' King, as by such sullen silence, to of-
' fer his Majesty just occasion of being
' jealous, and suspicious of our loyalty
' and obedience, or to leave him with-
' out all possible, rational security, of
' our humble subjection and fidelity to
' him.

' WE acknowledge, that the histories
' of *Germany* relate most dreadful things,
' of the impious opinions and practices of
' some reputed *Anabaptists*, destructive to
' all government and human society. Al-
' tho' it is to be observ'd, what *Cassander*,

'a learn'd and moderate *Papiſt*, relates in
'his epiſtle to the Duke of *Gulick* and
'*Cleve*, to this purpoſe, That there were
'certain people in *Germany* bearing the
'denomination of *Anabaptiſts*, who reſiſt-
'ed and oppos'd the opinions and prac-
'tices of thoſe at *Munſter*, and taught
'the contrary doctrine, whereby in his
'opinion they appear'd to be incited by a
'godly mind, and render'd themſelves ra-
'ther worthy of pity, than perſecution
'and perdition; and that in *Holland*,
'thoſe who have ſucceeded them, do in
'doctrine and practice, adhere to the
'ſame peaceable principles, is publickly
'known. But the miſguided zeal of
'ſome, otherwiſe minded in the point of
'*Baptiſm*, hath frequently, tho' undu-
'ly imputed the like impious opinions,
'deſigns and intentions, unto all that are
'call'd by that name; altho' their ſouls
'abhor the very memory of ſuch impi-
'ous doctrines, and their bloody conſe-
'quences. That ſuch evil opinions and
'practices, are no natural or neceſſary
'concomitants or conſequences of the
'doctrine about *Baptiſm*, nor of any poſ-
'ſible connexion with it, is eaſy to be
'diſcern'd; yet by the like miſtake we
'now ſuffer under jealouſies, thro' the
'wicked treaſon, rebellion, and murder,
'of a few heady and diſtemper'd perſons,

'pretending to introduce a civil and tem-
'poral reign and government of *Jesus*
'*Christ* by their swords, and to subvert
'all civil government and authority.

'YET we cannot imagine a reason
'why, their bloody tenets, and tragical
'actings, should reflect upon those of our
'persuasion, the persons not being of our
'belief or practice about *Baptism*; but to
'the best of our information, they were
'all, except one, assertors of *Infant-Bap-*
'*tism*, and never had communion with
'us in our assemblies, nor hath there
'been any correspondence or converse be-
'tween us; but contrariwise, in their
'meetings, they have inveigh'd bitterly
'against us, as worshippers of the beast,
'because of our constant declaring against
'their conceited, wild interpretations of
'dark prophecies, and enthusiastical im-
'pulses; and profess'd and practis'd our
'duty of subjection to the civil magis-
'tracy.

'AND it is notoriously known, the very
'same *persons*, or at least the *leaders*, and
'the most of them, formerly advanc'd
'their pretended standard of *Jesus Christ*,
'as much against us, as against any o-
'thers.

'AND it is as publickly known, that e-
'ven in this their rebellion, such of us
'as were call'd thereunto, which were
'many,

'many, were ready to hazard our lives
'to suppress them.

'And if such a constant continu'd op-
'position unto the impious tenets and
'practices of these *persons*, both in our
'doctrines and lives, will not be esteem'd
'a pregnant and cogent evidence of our
'unspotted innocence, from their treason
'and rebellion, and satisfy every man,
'that our souls never enter'd into their
'secrets; we can only appeal to the All-
'seeing God, the judge of all the earth,
'to vindicate us in his righteous judg-
'ment, who we are assur'd will judge Gen.
'and do right. xviii. 25.

'In whose presence we protest, that
'we neither had the least foreknowledge
'of the said late treasonable *insurrection*,
'nor did any of us, in any kind or degree
'whatsoever, directly or indirectly con-
'trive, promote, assist, abet, or approve
'the same; but do esteem it our duty to
'God, to his Majesty, and to our neigh-
'bour, not only to be obedient; but al-
'so to use our utmost industry, to pre-
'vent all such treasons, murders, and re-
'bellions; and to use in all our assemblies,
'constant prayers and supplications for
'his Majesty.

'Wherefore we humbly beseech
'his Majesty, and desire all our fellow
'subjects, that our actions, doctrines and
'lives, may be the only glasses, thro'
'which

'which they will look into our hearts,
'and pass judgment upon us; and that
'the tenets or opinions of others, either
'in this or foreign kingdoms, may not be
'imputed to us, when our doctrines and
'lives, do declare our abhorrency of them:
'We believing, that *Jesus Christ* himself,
'his *Apostles*, and Christian Religion, did
'consist with, and obey the imperial go-
'vernment, that then was in the world,
'and that we ought to obey his Majesty
'not only for wrath, but for conscience
'sake.

'WE desire, therefore, that it may be
'considered without prejudice, whether
'our perswasion in the matter of *Baptism*,
'hath any connexion with these doctrines
'against government; or whether these
'can be the probable consequences or in-
'ferences from our doctrine concerning
'*Baptism*? And we pray that it may be
'seriously considered, whether it be ra-
'tional, just, or christian, to impute all
'the errors, and wickedness of any *sect*
'of Christians in one age or country, to
'the persons of another age or country,
'called by the name of the former? es-
'pecially when these errors, or impieties,
'gave not the name to the *sect*, as in our
'case, nor can be reasonably supposed to
'be the consequences of that opinion,
'from whence the *sect* had its denomi-
'nation.

'IT

'IT would not be holden juft to aver,
'every *Proteftant* to believe *Confubftan-*
'*tiation*, or abfolute *Predeftination*, and
'*Reprobation*, becaufe *Luther* was zea-
'lous in the one, and *Calvin* in the other;
'why therefore fhou'd the errors and im-
'pieties of others, be imputed to us,
'whilft we earneftly contend againft
'them? And as to our doctrine of *Bap-*
'*tifm*, we hope every Chriftian, that hath
'fearch'd the fcriptures, knoweth, that
'there wants not fo much evidence, at
'leaft for our opinion and practice, as
'Chriftian charity may well allow, tho'
'in fome mens judgments we fhould be
'efteemed miftaken; and it will be eafily
'granted by the learned, that there is no
'impiety in our doctrine of *Baptifm*, nor
'oppofition to civil government, or his
'Majefty's authority; neither can the in-
'jury of our neighbour, be the natural
'confequence of it.

'AND therefore we humbly hope,
'that the omnipotent Power of heaven
'and earth, will fo difpofe his Majefty
'and his people's hearts, that we may
'worfhip God in peace and freedom, ac-
'cording to the faith we have receiv'd,
'living a peaceable and quiet life, in all
'godlinefs and honefty.

POST-

42 *The* History *of the*

POSTSCRIPT.

'That it may yet more fully appear,
'That our principles suggested in this
'apology, about subjection to magistracy
'and government, against the contrary
'opinions and practices are not new, much
'less proceeding from us upon the suc-
'cessfulness of this tragical enterprise; we
'have thought fit herewith, to publish
'an apology of our ancient and constant
'principles, presented with our humble
'petition, to the King's most excellent
'Majesty, some months since, in the
'year 1660.'

This was subscribed by thirty ministers and principal members of the *Baptist* congregations.

Another apology of the English *Baptists.*

'*An Apology of some call'd* Anabaptists,
'*in and about the city of* London, *in*
'*behalf of themselves and others of the*
'*same judgment with them.*

'FORASMUCH * as it hath been
' our portion all along to suffer not
'only some hard things in many of our

* Let the Rev^d. Mr. *Neale* seriously consider this paragraph, and if his own conscience do not smite him, for that unfair representation of his, I think he is rather an object of pity than resentment.

' persons

'persons, but also very much in our re-
'putations, thro' the unjust aspersions
'and calumnies of our adversaries, and
'such, who, tho' they daily behold our
'inoffensive conversation, and do or may
'know our faith and doctrine, will not
'yet be deliver'd from those groundless
'and injurious reports, which they have
'without proof, concerning things or
'persons taken up; but contrariwise con-
'tinue in press, pulpit, and common
'discourse, industriously to divulge things
'tending to our defamation; and more
'especially for that purpose, watching
'the opportunity of all revolutions and
'changes of persons exercis'd in govern-
'ment, which hath often happen'd in
'these nations of late years. And inas-
'much as the design of our adversaries
'therein, hath appear'd to be the rendring
'of us obnoxious to those, that have had
'most power in their hand to offend and
'harm us, and have for that purpose,
'invented such calumnies, as might best
'accomplish that design; which altho'
'they have been various, and sometimes
'manifestly cross and contradictory one
'to another, yet having no other ground,
'that we know of, than the fore-men-
'tion'd evil purpose; they have there-
'fore, both one and the other, even all
'of them, been generally accompany'd
'with

'with the charge of disobedience to ma-
'giſtracy and civil government.

'WE have therefore been neceſſitated,
'as alterations in government have hap-
'pen'd, to renew our vindications in this
'publick manner, having very ſeldom
'opportunity, otherwiſe to inform ei-
'ther magiſtrates or people of the injuries
'done unto us, and which is much more,
'to the truth we do profeſs. And that
'in this preſent conjuncture of affairs,
'the miſrepreſentation of us either for-
'merly or now, may not take impreſſion
'upon any, to the damage of us and our
'profeſſion, we have thought it requiſite
'not to bring to light any new matter;
'but only to extract out of our former
'confeſſions of faith and declarations,
'our conſtant principles, to which we
'have been, and ſhall always endeavour,
'the Lord aſſiſting us, that our practice
'may ſtill be conformable in this great
'point, concerning magiſtracy and civil
'government, as by theſe extracts fol-
'lowing may appear.

'THAT civil * *magiſtracy* is an ordi-
'nance of God, ſet up by him for the pu-
'niſhment of evil-doers, and for the praiſe
'of them that do well; and that in all

---

* Confeſſion of faith of thoſe churches in *London*, which are commonly, tho' unjuſtly, call'd *Anabaptiſts*, Art. 47. Printed in the ſeveral years 1651, 1646, 1644, &c.

'law-

' lawful things commanded by them, fub-
' jection ought to be given by us in the
' Lord, not only for wrath but for con-
' fcience fake, and that we are to make
' fupplications and prayers for *Kings*, and
' all that are in *authority*, that under
' them we may live a peaceable, a quiet
' life, in all godlinefs and honefty.

' W E who are falfely call'd *Anabap-*
' *tifts* *, being as ready to obey our civil
' *magiftrates*, as to profefs our fubjection
' to them in all lawful commands ; what-
' ever is preach'd or printed of us, by any
' to the contrary, and whofoever have
' or fhall accufe us, either to the *magif-*
' *trates*, or to the common people, that we
' will not obey *authority* do falfely ac-
' cufe us.

' AND however † it be a thing very
' defireable to godly men, to have fuch
' to be their *governors* as fear the Lord,
' inafmuch, as together with their moral
' principles, they are under more folemn
' bands of engagement as chriftians, to
' execute judgment and juftice, and faith-
' fully to difcharge their truft, and in-
' afmuch alfo, as they will be more rea-
' dy to protect godly men, which gene-

---

* Declaration concerning a publick difpute. Printed in the year 1645, *p*. 4.

† Declaration by the feveral congregational focieties in and about the city of *London*, in way of vindication of themfelves, touching liberty, magiftracy, &c. Printed 1647, p. 7. Sect. 3, & 4.

' rally

'rally are the hated of the world, and to
'propagate the Gospel in their territories,
'than other men will be; yet whatever
'the magistrate is in point of religion,
'he is to be reverenc'd and obey'd in all
'those commands of his, which do not
'intrench upon, or rise up in opposition
'to the commands of God. And we do
'freely acknowledge, that kingly govern-
'ment establish'd, guided and bounded
'by just and wholesome laws, is both
'allow'd by God, and a good accommo-
'dation to men.

'THAT all people in every nation,
'as well members of * churches as o-
'thers, ought for conscience sake to ho-
'nour such, as by the wise disposing
'providence of God are their rulers, and
'are to submit to the civil commands
'not only of such rulers as are faithful,
'but even to infidels.

'ALTHO' we cannot answer in justi-
'cation † of every individual person,
'that is of our profession in matters of
'religion, no more than our christian
'friends of other persuasions can do in
'behalf of all of their persuasions; yet
'we can say this, and prove it to all the

* Declaration of divers elders and brethren of congregational societies in and about the city of *London, Nov.*
10. 1651.
† Declaration of several of the people call'd *Anabaptists* in and about the city of *London, Dec.* 12. 1659.
The answer to the first crimination.

'world,

' world, that it hath been our profession,
' and is our real practice, to be obedient to
' *magistracy* in all things civil, and will-
' ing to live peaceably under the go-
' vernment establish'd in this nation: For
' we do believe and declare, *magistracy*
' to be an *ordinance* of God, and ought
' to be obey'd in all lawful things.

' These things we have herein recit-
' ed, the rather, because that such judg-
' ment as shall be made by any concern-
' ing us, may be fairly and duely taken,
' and calculated from our own writings,
' and not from the aspersions unjustly
' cast upon us by such, who have not
' only render'd many guilty for the of-
' fence-sake of some one person; but also
' call'd others, after the same name given
' to us, with whom we have had or held
' no correspondency or agreement, en-
' deavouring to blemish our profession, by
' charging the whole party, not only
' with the guilt of many strange unsound
' opinions, such as were never receiv'd or
' allow'd by them; but also with many
' actions wherein they have been least of
' all, if at all concern'd. And as for
' those things wherein any of us, or o-
' thers of our judgment have been actually
' concern'd, we hope it has proceeded
' from a due regard to those invariable
' rules given in the Holy Scripture for
' the ordering of our conversation, with
' respect

'respect unto *magiſtracy*, according to
'the beſt judgment could be made of
'them, and purſuant thereunto, done in
'obſervance of thoſe publick edicts and
'declarations, whereunto the moſt uni-
'verſal obedience and conſtant adherence
'hath been requir'd by thoſe that have
'had the power over us, and who have
'admitted us the leaſt of any people, to
'diſpute the reaſon of governments and
'laws.

'And for that the ſubjection yielded
'by us, to the powers that have been
'over us, hath proceeded from a conſci-
'ence not daring to diſobey, unleſs in
'ſuch things which we could not un-
'derſtand to be lawful, and the affections
'that have been manifeſted therein, have
'ariſen from the enjoyment of that due
'liberty and protection, which we have
'had in matters of religion; we do hope
'and deſire, that none of us upon the
're-eſtabliſhment of the preſent govern-
'ment, ſhall now be adjudg'd criminal
'by our preſent governours; but that we
'may notwithſtanding reap the benefit of
'that favour, that hath been declar'd and
'tender'd by the King's Majeſty, and be
'protected from all injury and violence
'whatſoever, equally with others his Ma-
'jeſty's ſubjects, in the quiet and peace-
'able enjoyment of our religious and civil
'rights and liberties, we deſiring and en-
                                    'deavouring

ENGLISH BAPTISTS.

' deavouring to behave ourselves in all
' good conscience towards God and man,
' remembring that rule of our Lord, that
' we are to render unto *Cæsar* the things
' which are *Cæsar*'s, and to God the
' things which are God's; and that we,
' as well as rulers, must certainly at the
' great day be accountable, to the just
' and righteous judge of all the earth, for
' all our doings.'

I FIND in short-hand, added to the end of these printed Apologies, these words, *viz.*

MR. *Jessey* preaching soon after, declar'd to his congregation, that *Venner* should say, that he believ'd there was not one *Baptist* amongst them, and that if they succeeded, the *Baptists* should know that Infants Baptism was an ordinance of *Jesus Christ*. Mr. *Gravener* was present at his meeting-house in *Coleman-street*, and heard him say this; from whose mouth, says the writer, I had this account.

As this mad insurrection in *England*, so also that at *Munster* in *Germany*, is improv'd by the generality of the *Pædobaptist* authors, to reflect an *odium* on all those who are stil'd *Anabaptists*; I shall in this place transcribe what I find in a certain *Author*, who about this time wrote a small Treatise, which he intitled *Moderation, or Arguments and Motives tending thereto; humbly tendred to the honourable Members of Parliament*.

IN this Treatise, he says[*], 'Now forasmuch, as *among others* bearing the name of *Sectaries*, the name of *Anabaptists* is mainly singled out for *publick reproach*, if not for *ruin*, and that their grand impeachment is their opposing *magistracy, government*, &c. Upon which account the *Munster Tragedy* is so *much* and *often* in all places (by prints and otherwise) laid to *their* charge, as indeed it could not *rightly* be *more*, if those bearing that name in *England* had been the very *individual* actors thereof at *Munster*; will not the *stones speak*, if all *men* should be wholly *mute* under such *clamours?* Wherefore in answer hereunto, I hope it will not be a crime very briefly to *apologize* so far as to do *them truth*, and *justice* itself a *little right*, without doing *others* any *wrong*, further than to undeceive them, and exonerate *all* as much as may be from *misprisions*, which in this and other things, are the *bane* and *poison* of publick peace and amity.

The tragedy of Munster unjustly cast on the Anabaptists.

[*] Sect. 19. p. 13.

' FIRST,

'First, Let it be noted, that *other* *sorts* of men * in *England* do impeach one the other with the *same crime*; some charge the *whole Parliament*, both *Lords* and *Commons*, and *all* their adherents, with *resisting the authority of the King*; saying, such of them were only *loyal obedient subjects*, who went to *Oxford* upon the *King's summons*, to sit in *Parliament* there, or to aid and assist him in his war. *Others* charge all those *members* who have *espous'd the seclusion* of so many of their *own house*, and turn'd out the *house of Lords*. Others have been adjudg'd and proceeded against as *delinquents*, both formerly and lately, for *resisting the Parliament* upon the King's account. I modestly mention *only* matters of *fact*, and that but *hints*, without judging the *merit* of them, only to the end, it may be observ'd, that (setting *these* aside) others do and will mutually charge with *illegalities* and *exorbitances* relating to *civil power* and *government*: And indeed *things are not judg'd illegal* (now in our days) *so much for what they are simply*

Others in England charg'd as opposers of magistracy.

---

* Vide Vindiciæ Regum, or the grand rebellion. Gr. *Williams*, Bishop of *Ossory*. Dr. *Fern, Salmasius,* Mr. *Edw. Symons*. The loyal subjects belief, with the several answers unto these by other ministers.

68   *The* HISTORY *of the*

'in *themselves*; but either as they may not
'*prosperously succeed*, or as being done by
'other hands, and not in prosecution of
'their own *interest* and *opinion*, who so
'judge of them: Which favours more of
'*faction*, *passion* and *interest*, than of *rea-*
'*son* and *justice*, in the eyes of *wise* ob-
'servers.

Antipædo-baptism *no more repugnant to magistracy than Pædobaptism.*

'SECONDLY, Their opinion, wherein
'other *Christians* differ from them about
'the *subject* and *form* of that instituted or-
'dinance of *Baptism*, is as far *off* the
'point of *magistracy* and opposition to
'it, as *Pædobaptism* itself, or any *other*
'thing in the world. What though,
'therefore, some holding that opinion,
'either in this or other nations, should
'be in any wise *enormous?* yet their o-
'pinion and practice of *Baptism* would
'be no *more* impair'd, nor *untrue*, than
'our Saviour *Christ's* and his *Apostles*
'doctrine was, by the treachery of *Ju-*
'*das*, and the apostacy of *multitudes* in
'the *primitive times*. And why the
'denomination of *Anabaptists* (which
'they disown) should be fasten'd upon
'them, they are yet to seek of suffici-
'ent reason ; not only seeing they ac-
'knowledge *but once baptizing*; but also
'they laying *no more* weight upon that
'instituted ordinance, than upon that o-
'ther of like institution, *the Lord's-Sup-*
'*per*,

'*per*, and than *others* do, who hold the
' *other* way of *baptizing*; yet this *name* is
' *abusively* put upon them, as if all their *re-*
' *ligion* lay in *baptism*; whereas the course
' of their doctrine touching principles of
' faith, and piety, and morality in *chris-*
' *tian* practice, is such as is generally re-
' ceiv'd for *orthodox*; even by the most
' accounted *such*, who have read the con-
' fessions of their faith, and heard their
' common doctrine.

' THIRDLY, The generality of per- Baptist
' sons who hold this opinion, have gi- *principles*
' ven *sufficient* proof for divers years, that *stent with*
' their principles and practices are as *con-* *human so-*
' *sistent* with human *society*, peaceable *as any o-*
' *co-habitation*, and *due subjection* to civil *ther.*
' *establish'd* government, as any other in
' the land. Not only do their manifold
' *declarations*, if examin'd, give satisfacti-
' on in this point; but withal, neither
' the *time*, nor *place*, nor *persons of them*,
' can be mention'd, touching any *insur-*
' *rection* they ever made against the *ma-*
' *gistracy* in *England*. But if any per-
' sons of them had done it, would it be
' *justice* to impute that to the *whole*?
' Would those of *other ways* be so judg'd?
' Of whom there have been *many*, who
' have both plotted and actually perpetra-
' ted publick insurrections, which yet
' was never call'd the *Munster Tragedy*

E 3 ' *of*

'of *Pædobaptists*; becaufe, though the
'*fame* reafon, yet *moderation* would not
'allow it. For *perfonal faults* ought to
'have only *perfonal imputations*; and *they*
'defire to do therein, as they would o-
'*thers* fhould *deal* with them.

'As what has been faid will much
'*obviate* an objection, touching thofe *few*
'of *this way* in the *army*; fo let me add,
'that what they they done in that *pub-*
'*lick capacity*, under an opinion of *pub-*
'*lick obligation*, hath been fo far *perfonal*,
'and as members of the *nation*, that
'fuch do wrongfully who impute it unto
'their *profeſſion*. But if it muſt needs
'be fo, then let it be try'd and prov'd,
'whether there have not been *many* call'd
'*Pædobaptiſts*, join'd in all thofe very
'actions, for *one of thoſe* call'd *Anabap-*
'*tiſts*, even in the *higheſt acts* done,
'whatever unfairly and difingenuouſly hath
'been by any repreſented *otherwiſe* to the
'world. Neither have thefe things been
'done in *corners*, to be hid from the eyes
'of *indifferent* fpectators, who are well
'able to judge of partiality.

Pædobap-
tiſts as
much or
more
Fifth-mo-
narchiſts
than Bap-
tiſts.

'FOURTHLY, As touching *thofe now*,
'who hold fome opinions about Chriſt's
'kingdom on earth in a reputed offen-
'five way; is it not notorious, that they
'are many of them *Pædobaptiſts* them-
'*felves*, and as much againſt thofe call'd
'*Ana-*

' *Anabaptists* as others, even as well as in
' the subject of *baptism?* And on the
' *other hand,* the generality of those call'd
' *Anabaptists,* are as much against all
' their offensive opinions in those points
' (tho' some few of *one,* as well as the
' *other* sort may own them) as any o-
' thers in the world, pitying those who
' *err* therein; and *publickly* in their
' congregations and doctrines detecting
' such *errors,* disclaiming and refuting
' them. Yet albeit there are many such
' call'd *Pædobaptists* of them, the *others*
' have more of *reason* and *moderation,*
' than to lay the *Munster Tragedy* upon
' that *name,* though there may be the
' *same* ground. If, therefore, there should
' be any *exorbitant irruption* in *words* or
' *actions* of that sort of people, *thus mix'd;*
' either let such fault be reputed merely
' *personal,* and no further; or else *indif-*
' *ferently, justly* and *impartially* be imput-
' ed to *one sort* as well as *another,* more
' than hitherto it hath been; which in-
' deed, among other things, may *justly*
' call in question the *justice* of *historians*
' touching the *Munster people,* which was
' about 130 years past; forasmuch as
' *truth* and *justice* is so much *wrong'd* be-
' fore our *eyes,* and at our own *doors,* as
' it is by *publick prints* and *otherwise*
' daily.

E 4 ' FIFTH-

Oppressions of the magistrates the cause of the rebellions in Germany.

'FIFTHLY, All historians about the seditions in *Germany* confess *thus far ingenuously*; that the *intolerable oppressions* of the *magistrates* then, gave one *great* occasion of their *rise* and *progress* to that heighth. Wherefore at the same time (about the year of our Lord 1525,) in *Suevia* and *Franconia*, there arose in arms about forty thousand men, (who pretended nothing at all to that call'd *Anabaptism*) to exonerate and acquit themselves by force from their heavy burthens. Which was more a rebellion than the other; for they kill'd the greatest part of the *Nobility*; pillag'd, sack'd and burn'd their houses, castles and fortresses; and violently overflow'd, and destroy'd the country like an inundation. Yet concerning *these*, we have *only* the *gentle tender hints* of our *Historiographers*, giving us in few lines *merely narrative of fact*, without any *odium* on their *fault*, or any *black characters* at all upon their *names, persons* or *religion*; when as the same *history* of the same fact, imputed to some call'd *Anabaptists* there, is wrote in most dreadful letters of *blood*, concerning their persons, names and religion; which (by the way) may guide the impartial reader in his observation and credit of *histories* wrote by *adversaries.*

ENGLISH BAPTISTS.

'*faries.* Now somewhat contemporary
' with this great insurrection (according
' to the same stories) *Caroloftadius, Stock,*
' *Muntzer,* and other publick ministers of
' the Gospel (as *Luther* then was) fell
' from good principles to dangerous opi-
' nions, dreams, enthusiasms, pretences of
' extraordinary visions and revelations (all
' which, those call'd *Anabaptists* that I
' defend, do, and ever did as much dis-
' claim and abhor, as any others in the
' world, holding firmly to the sacred word
' of God, the holy Scriptures) of whom,
' *Muntzer* chiefly manageth these opinions
' with the oppressions unto disturbous
' practices, to his and others ruin and re-
' proach. About six or seven years af-
' ter, which was about the years 1531,
' 1532, and forward, broke out like the
' unhappy bustle at the city of *Munster*
' in *Westphalia,* by *John Becold Knipper-*
' *doling,* and one *Bernard Rotman,* a
' publick preacher in that city; and this
' was accompany'd with the like foolish,
' mad, vain opinions; being as far *remote*
' from, and as *foreign* unto *these* people
' in *England,* in their *opinions,* as they
' were in their *persons, place* and *time;*
' who therefore are unduly and unwor-
' thily call'd their *spawn,* their *offspring*
' and *generation,* &c. and what not?
' Howbeit, let it be obferv'd, how *mon-*
   ' *strous*

' ſtrous and *prodigious* this is made; and
' how the world is made to *ring* of the noiſe
' of this *one* diſaſter, that happen'd in *one*
' little compaſs of time; and how unchri-
' ſtianly and unreaſonably it is now *rak'd*
' up, and *reckon'd* to a company of people,
' who in ſuch things are as innocent now
' of the like, as they were of that very fact
' there, being then unborn. Whereas I
' have mention'd *like fact* at the *ſame*
' *time in others*, and may add the like
' hints in thoſe hiſtories of the *Switzers*,
' who about 200 years before, aroſe and
' violently deſtroy'd their *Lords*, and as
' violently chang'd (without blame) both
' their *governours* and *government*, not re-
' verting to this day; which if thoſe of
' *Germany* had ſucceeded as proſperouſly,
' they might have been no more blam'd.
' I might infinitely multiply examples, if
' I ſhould rake in the duſt and aſhes of
' other ſorts throughout all ages in *Chriſ-*
' *tendom*. But what need I go farther
' then our divers and manifold inſurrec-
' tions in *England*, againſt all kinds and
' degrees of *authority*? Neither need I
' mention *by whom* they have been per-
' petrated. Yet all this without the
' leaſt remembrance or reckoning of *Mun-*
' *ſter* unto them, or any of them; ſuch
' is the power of partiality and prejudice.
' Moreover I muſt not omit to return

' the

'the reader's *eye* again to *Munster*, of
'which *same* city we have had certain
'account year by year to this very day,
'for some considerable time; *that they
'rise in arms, resist and oppose their law-
'ful magistrate, refuse obedience to his e-
'dicts, and maintain the same city against
'him by publick force*, and all without
'the least *brand* of *infamy on them*. On
'the other hand, such are very great
'strangers in the world, who know not
'that in *Holland* are *very many*, and have
'been *very long*, that bear the same name
'of *Anabaptists*, that are as *famous* for
'peaceable living and subjection, as any
'others have been *infamous* for the con-
'trary.

 'ALL which strongly results and con-
'cludes in this; that there is no *end* nor
'*bounds* of impeaching, if there be not
'*strict restraint* of publick faults unto
'their *proper authors*, acquitting *other o-
'pinions* they hold, except only such o-
'pinions as do naturally and directly tend
'to such faults. Wherein, indeed, Mr.
'*Joshua Scotton* (tho' a *Pædobaptist*) deals
'the most ingenuously of all other, who
'in his translation of *Guy de Brez*'s
'*German* story, calls it *The German En-
'thusiast*, in the title page, and not the
'*German Anabaptist:* and in the latter
'end of his epistle to the reader, hath
'these

'these words; *those*, saith he, *which he
'stileth* Anabaptists, *between whom and
'other mere Dissenters in the point of
'Pædobaptism, being otherwise orthodox
'and peaceable, the reader ought always
'conscientiously to distinguish.*

<small>German sedition also charg'd upon Luther.</small>

'SIXTHLY, Let me a little further
'enforce this by observing, that all this
'*German* sedition that is now (about 130
'years after) put to the account of the
'*innocent* reputed *Anabaptists* in *Eng-
'land*; was in *like* manner *as much* charg'd
'upon *innocent Luther* at that very day, as
'the *same historians* do jointly and gene-
'rally report; and is confess'd by Mr.
'*Samuel Clark* in his *lives of the fathers*.
'Yet had they *as much* reason for that
'(though none at all) seeing the *princi-
'pal* fomenters of the sedition had been
'*publick preachers* of the Gospel, as *Lu-
'ther* was, who then and thereupon could
'but purge himself by publick *mani-
'festo*, (which is yet extant) as *these* in
'*England* have done, time after time, *not
'only* by their *confession of faith* oft im-
'printed, shewing their constancy, be-
'sides their manifold declarations, *more
'particularly* upon this point in hand, but
'confirm'd by *constant practice*, in their
'*peaceable co-habitation* with their seve-
'ral neighbourhoods both in *city* and
'*country*.

'SEVENTH-

English Baptists.

' Seventhly, Is not this *same* impu-
' tation tofs'd like a *ball*, or rather a
' *stone*, between the *Protestants* in gene-
' ral, and the *Papists* in all their paper
' contests? And *which*, and *who* can ac-
' quit every *individual* of their party? If,
' therefore, any *particular persons* of this
' *name* should (among others) prove ex-
' travagant; it will no more make this
' *their glorying void*, than that of *others*,
' who may rather (for want of modera-
' tion) watch for haltings in these more
' than in *all other* sorts besides. Its evi-
' dent then, that the prevalency of *inte-*
' *rest* and *faction* above *commutative jus-*
' *tice, right and reason*, in too many of
' this age, doth influence them to this
' great unfairness. Which whether the
' design be (in this way) to *stifle* their
' *opinion* about *baptism*, or to bring *swift*
' *destruction* upon those who hold it,
' though they hold it with never so much
' *piety* towards God, *righteousness and*
' *peace* towards men, *moderation and re-*
' *spect* towards those *christians* who con-
' scientiously differ from them, yet (leav-
' ing that to God, that knows their
' purposes, and is above them) they desire
' the Lord to forgive those who thus *tra-*
' *duce* them, and *detract* them, and that
' (through the assistance of God's grace)
' they may be enabled to walk inoffen-
' sively

The HISTORY *of the*

Enthu-
fiafm, &c.
unjuftly
charg'd on
the Bap-
tifts.

'sively towards *Jew* or *Gentile*, or church
' of God, so as to put to silence the ig-
' rance of all foolish men, who delight
' to speak evil of *what* and of *whom* they
' know not, at least many of them.

' EIGHTHLY, As touching extraordi-
' nary *impulses, enthusiasms, dreams, visions,*
' &c. Such who lay all this upon those
' call'd *Anabaptists* promiscuously in *Eng-*
' *land*, they shew themselves to be *very*
' *great strangers, not understanding where-*
' *of they do affirm.* The contrary where-
' of shineth so bright, *as* in their ordi-
' nary teachings and church-government,
' *so* in the manifold treatises, commenta-
' ries, *&c.* printed and publish'd by many
' learned of them, upon all points in the
' christian religion. Wherein let it be
' *duly* noted, that one grand occasion of
' this and such like imputations, is plain-
' ly this: That one writing author meet-
' ing with *heterodox* and gross opinions
' in his readings of others, laid upon that
' *name*, he transmits it to another that
' follows; and so the *second* to the *third*, and
' none of all (for the most part) receiv-
' ing any such assertions from the persons
' themselves, much less from any confes-
' sion of faith, comprehending the judg-
' ment of the *generality* of that name.
' By which both writers and readers both
' do, and suffer wrong in creating to
' them-

'themselves and others groundless pre-
'judices conveying them over from age
'to age, and rendring them a hideous,
'monstrous people. And though I could
'multiply instances hereof in my own
'small readings, yet I shall mention but
'*one*, which was call'd a catalogue of the
'damnable errors of the *Anabaptists*, e-
'numerating *thirty and one*; yet of *all*
'these, there was but that *one* reputed
'error of *Antipædobaptism*, which they
'will espouse, disavowing the rest as
'much as he that accus'd them, who
'was a minister of no inferior note. Yet
'I shall forbear to mention any names,
'because I want not due regard to such
'persons, who may be otherwise godly
'and serviceable in both teaching and wri-
'ing, setting aside such misprisions. And
'withal few observing readers are unac-
'quainted herewith, to need instances.

'NINTHLY, Neither is it less mani- *Errors*
'fest, that most of those very errors are *call'd A-*
'held and maintain'd by *Pædobaptists* one *cal as*
'against the other. The manifold contests *much or*
'among them about the *principal* points of *by the Pæ-*
'*doctrine*, and also most things apper- dobaptists.
'taining to *church-government* and *admi-*
'*nistration of all ordinances*, have been
'upon the house-top, to be publickly
'known and read of *all* men. More
'particulary those call'd of the *Episcopal*,
'Pres-

'Presbyterian and Erastian ways, not to
' mention more; nor yet these with the
' least immoderate spirit towards them,
' but *rather* desiring it may be us'd by
' them to a *moderation* of mind towards
' each other; and also to enquire whether
' the *reputed errors* chargeable upon those
' call'd *Anabaptists*, are any way compa-
' rable in *number* or *weight* to those in
' controversy among themselves; and
' whether the cause of such estrangedness
' and enmity on their part, be not mis-
' understanding or interest of some kind
' or other, which in like manner hath
' led themselves to such *heat* of opposi-
' tion, as hath ended in *removing* and *re-*
' *volving* of *church-government*.

The German historians account very doubtful.

' TENTHLY, To conclude these par-
' ticulars upon this general section, we
' find the stories of a company of people
' in *Germany*, who are long since dead
' and buried, under the greatest reproach
' and infamy that can be. Of whom
' none can be left to answer for them-
' selves; their reported *extirpation* and *ex-*
' *tinction* being about 130 years past;
' their rise and fall, *lives* and *deaths*,
' wrote by their *adversaries*; no *aggrava-*
' *ting* circumstances, either for *opinion* or
' *practice*, seems to be omitted; no *exte-*
' *nuating* passages *confessedly* inserted. Now
' that upon the *whole*, there might be such

' a

'a *people*, and such *persons* bearing that
'appellation of *Anabaptists*, who mix'd
'with others, may be faulty in opinions
'and practices, is a matter much un-
'doubted. But that every *aggravating*
'*passage* is true; or that any *one historian*,
'admitting him otherwise just, was an
'*ear witness* of all their *opinions*, and an
'*ocular witness* of all their *tragical ac-*
'*tions*, is reasonably to be *doubted*. And
'consequently their testimony in every
'*puncto* not so much to be *regarded*; be-
'cause false reports of contrary minded
'men, touching both such and other per-
'sons and things, are so *abounding* and
'*notorious* in *our own* nation and age, like
'that of *Jer.* xx. 10. *Report, say they,*
'*and we will report*; *they watched for my*
'*halting*, &c. Insomuch that, indeed,
'we have little ground of credit to com-
'mon fame, at least, touching *particu-*
'*lars* of *words* or *acts* spoken or done at
'the very next town; and least of all
'from *adversaries* to the persons and things
'reported of. Yet all such things, thus
'brought upon the *wings* of *fame*, is not-
'withstanding as commonly and credibly
'*receiv'd*, and thereupon again *reported*,
'yea *printed* and *publish'd*, even in all the
'aggravating circumstances, as if nothing
'in the world were more authentick and
'indubitable; such is the blind and rash
'*credulity* of men (though some other-
'wise

If true, make not against the English Baptists.

'wife honeft) where they are *pre-difpof-*
'*ed* and *prefix'd* in their affections or
'difaffections.

'BUT fuppofe, and admit it granted
'to be *wholly true*; yet obferve what
'*proximity* and *nearnefs* of relation is there
'between *thofe* perfons and enormities in
'*Germany*, to *thefe* now in *England*; that
'*their eating of four grapes fhould fet the*
'*teeth of thefe on edge?* For there is not
'any *one* thing of *agreement* is or can be
'pretended, but in that of *Baptifm*. And
'if the ftories themfelves be true, they
'do not *fo much* agree in that neither (all
'things confider'd and obferv'd) as thofe
'call'd *Anabaptifts* and *Pædobaptifts* do
'here agree; for they relate, that they
'grounded their practice of *Baptifm*, up-
'on pretences of *immediate revelations*;
'that they baptized *all* who came unto
'them; that they threaten'd *damnation* to
'*all* who neglected it; that they forc'd
'*all* perfons to be baptized, by proclaim-
'ing that all who refus'd it fhould be
'kill'd. All which fignify fo much of
'frenzy and madnefs, that to thofe of
'*that name* in *England*, nothing is more
'abfurd and abominable: And that there
'were ever any fuch rude and heady per-
'fons, anfwerable to this their portrai-
'ture and picture, fcarce any thing to
'*them* is more *incredible*. Befides their
'practices of *polygamy*, and deftroying
'pro-

' propriety, is unto thefe in *England* de-
' teftable; and *both* among other things
' detected in their *declaration* 1647.
' Wherefore, I do humbly and fairly
' propofe, on their behalf in *England*;
' that if the *denomination* of *Anabaptift* be
' deriv'd *from*, or at leaft imputed re-
' proachfully *upon*, that abominable abufe
' of *Baptifm*, by thefe men in *Germany*
' (waving the proper fignification of the
' word as unduly applied) that then, and
' from henceforth, thefe who bear the
' *name* of *Anabaptifts* in *England*, may be
' for ever acquitted and difcharg'd there-
' of, never more to be call'd by that
' *name*; which difcharge is a *due debt*
' from *juftice itfelf*, feeing they can as
' clearly and truly plead *not guilty*, as
' any other people in the world.'

ON the 25th of *Octob.* 1660. The King put forth a declaration concerning ecclefiaftical affairs, wherein he eftablifh'd again the book of *Common-prayer*. Yet to quiet the minds of the people, he therein affur'd them, that he would appoint an equal number of Divines of both perfuafions, to review the fame, and confider the feveral objections rais'd againft it; and if there was occafion, to make fuch reafonable and neceffary alterations and amendments therein, as fhould be agreed upon, for the fatisfaction of *tender confciences*,

A declaration concerning ecclefiaftical affairs.

and

84   *The* HISTORY *of the*

A commiſ-
ſion grant-
ed.

and preſerving peace and unity in the churches. Accordingly a commiſſion was granted *March* 25. following, with full power and authority to the perſons therein mention'd, to make ſuch amendments and alterations, as they ſhould agree upon, ſubjecting the ſame to his Majeſty's approbation. The perſons appointed on the ſide of the eſtabliſh'd Church were, the Biſhops of *York, London, Durham, Rocheſter, Sarum, Worceſter, Lincoln, Peterborough, Cheſter, Carliſle, Exeter* and *Norwich.* And of the *Preſbyterian* perſuaſion were, the Reverend *Anthony Tuckney, John Conant, William Spurſtow, John Wallis, Thomas Manton, Edmund Calamy,* Doctors of Divinity: *Richard Baxter, Arthur Jackſon, Thomas Caſe, Samuel Clark,* and *Matthew Newcomen,* Clerks. To whom were added, Dr. *Earles,* Dean of *Weſtminſter,* Peter *Heylin, John Hackett, John Berwick, Peter Gunning, John Pearſon, Thomas Peirce, Anthony Sparrow, Herbert Thorndike, Thomas Horton, Thomas Jacomb,* Doctors of Divinity; *William Bates, John Rawlinſon, William Cooper,* Clerks; Dr. *John Lightfoot,* Dr. *John Collins,* Dr. *Benjamin Woodbridge,* and *William Drake,* Clerk.

No Bap-
tiſts *in this*
commiſſi-
on.

THOUGH the *Baptiſts* in *England* were at this time very numerous, and as famous men amongſt them for learning and piety, as moſt in this commiſſion; yet

no

no regard was had to their cafe, nor any one of that perfuafion appointed to have any fhare in it. They did not defign to reform fo far; for if they could but bring the *Prefbyterian* party in, which was the moft numerous of the Diffenters, that might be fufficient to fecure their power; though by the confequence of this proceeding it feems probable, there was no defign of reformation; but only to quiet the minds of the people, till they could gain time.

This controverfy was manag'd by writing, and publifh'd the fame year. Among many other things, the doctrine and manner of Baptifm was debated. Both perfuafions charg'd each other, with advancing fuch principles therein, as gave encouragement to *Anabaptifm* *. For the *Epifcopal* Divines afferted, that it is uncharitable to punifh the children for their parents faults: That the children of *heathens* or excommunicate perfons, have as much right to *Baptifm* as thofe of believers; that the efficacy of children's *Baptifm*, depends neither upon their own faith and repentance, nor that of their parents: That to fay, that every child that is baptized, is not regenerated by God's Holy Spirit, tends to

---

* By the account of the proceedings, publifh'd in 1661, it feems to me very evident, that the controverfy on the doctrine of *Baptifm*, did much tend to promote what they call *Anabaptifm*.

bring the *baptism* of *Infants* into contempt, and makes it not material whether the sacrament be administred to children or not. These were reasons sufficient to fasten that charge upon them. On the other hand, the *Presbyterian* Divines asserted: That the making a cross in *Baptism* was an human invention; that *Godfathers* and *Godmothers* have no power to covenant and vow in the *child*'s name: That those who do not consent themselves, or do it by some other, who have a right to act for them, are not taken into covenant: That it cannot be said in faith, every *child* baptized is regenerated by God's Holy Spirit: That those who receive the benefit of *Baptism* must be qualified *subjects*, having the conditions requir'd of such: That if *Baptism* justify and save those that receive it, Christianity is another kind of thing than the *Apostles* understood it to be; who taught, that it was not the washing of *water*, but the answer of a good conscience, that saves in baptism: That if *baptism* had such a virtue in it, then it were a charitable practice to catch the *children* of *Heathens*, and dip them, and so save them against their wills. Let the reader judge whether these could be excus'd from the like charge.

I HAVE been inform'd, that when the *Presbyterians* were pleading hard for such
con-

conceffions from his Majefty, as they thought would bring about an union; the Lord-Chancellor told them, his Majefty had receiv'd petitions from the *Anabaptifts*, who defir'd nothing more but to have liberty to worfhip God according to their confciences. At which they were all ftruck dumb, and remain'd in a long filence.

Mr. *Baxter* has given us this in another light; therefore I fhall make ufe of his own words. He fays.

'The moft of the time being fpent *Life*, Part
' thus in fpeaking to particulars of the II. *p.* 277.
' declaration as it was read; when we
' came to the end, the Lord-Chancellor
' drew out another paper, and told us,
' that the King had been petition'd alfo
' by the *Independants* and *Anabaptifts*:
' And tho' he knew not what to think of
' it himfelf, and did not very well like
' it; yet fomething he had drawn up,
' which he would read to us, and defire
' us alfo to give our advice about it.
' Thereupon he read, as an addition to the
' declaration; *That others alfo be permitted*
' *to meet for religious worfhip, fo be it*
' *they do it not to the difturbance of the*
' *peace, and that no Juftice of peace or offi-*
' *cer difturb them.* When he had read
' it, he again defir'd them all to think
' on it, and give their advice; but all
' were filent. The *Prefbyterians*, fays he,
' all

'all perceiv'd as soon as they heard it,
'that it would secure the liberty of the
'*Papists*. And one of them [Dr. *Wallis*]
'whisper'd me in the ear, and intreated
'me to say nothing, for it was an *odious*
'*business*; but let the Bishops speak to it.
'But the Bishops would not speak a
'word, nor any one of the *Presbyterians*
'neither; and so we were like to have
'ended in that silence. I knew if we
'consented to it, it would be charg'd on
'us, that we spake for a toleration of
'*Papists* and *Sectaries*, (but yet it might
'have lengthen'd out our own.) And if
'we spake against it, all sects and parties
'would be set against us, as the causers
'of their sufferings, and as a partial peo-
'ple, that would have liberty ourselves, but
'would have no others have it with us.
'At last seeing the silence continue, I
'thought our very silence would be
'charg'd on us a consent if it went on;
'and, therefore, I only said this: *That
'this reverend brother, Dr*. Gunning, *even
'now speaking against sects, had nam'd
'the* Papists *and the* Socinians. *For our
'parts we desir'd not favour to ourselves a-
'lone, and rigorous severity we desir'd a-
'gainst none. As we humbly thank'd his
'Majesty for his indulgence to ourselves, so
'we distinguish the tolerable parties from
'the intolerable. For the former, we hum-
'bly crave just lenity and favour; but for
'the latter, such as the two sorts nam'd be-
                                         ' fore,*

'fore, by that reverend brother, for our
'parts we cannot make their toleration our
'request. To which his Majesty said,
'That there were laws enough against the
'Papists. And I reply'd, That we under-
'stood the question to be, whether those laws
'should be executed on them or not. And
'so his Majesty brake up the meeting of
'that day.'

HAD these two great bodies united in their opinions, what could the *Baptists* have expected, unless Divine Providence had interpos'd, but an entire extirpation by banishment or death? But I think it would be but just, that the *Pædobaptists* should first agree in the principles on which they found their practice of *Infant-baptism*, rather then persecute the *Baptists* for dissenting in that point from them. For in my judgment, if *Infant-baptism* was an institution of Christ, the *Pædobaptists* could not be at such a loss about the grounds of the right *Infants* have to *Baptism*. Some affirm, it is to take away original sin. Others say, it is their right by the *covenant*, they being the seed of *believers*. Others again say, *Infants* have *faith*, and therefore have a right. Others, that they have a right by the *faith* of their *sureties*. Some ground their right from an *apostolical tradition*. Others upon the *authority* of the *scriptures*. Some say all *children* of *professing christians* ought to
be

be baptized. Others say, *none* but the *children* of *true believers* have a right to it. Sure if it was an *ordinance of Christ*, his word would soon end this *controversy*.

IT is very remarkable, and worthy the reader's observation, how much the *assertors* of *Infant-baptism* differ among themselves, about that *faith* they suppose to be in infants. For some of them assert, they have the *faith* of the *church*, that being entail'd upon all that are within the pale thereof. Thus the *Roman Catholicks*. Others say, they have the *faith* of the *gossips* or *sureties*. Thus the *Church* of *England*. *Musculus* seems to assert they have an *imputed faith*. Mr. *Baxter* intimates they have a *dogmatical faith* only; but does not tell us how it agrees with, or differs from the *faith* of the *adult*. Some say it is a *physical faith*; some a *metaphysical*; and some a *hyperphysical faith*: Hard words and unscriptural I must confess; no wonder they are so little understood. Some say they are born *believers*, which proceeds from their parents being in *covenant*, and being *believers*; but this is to entail *grace* to *nature*, and *regeneration* to *generation*; nay, and to assert, all are not children of wrath by *nature*, or as they are born and come into the world. Others say they are made *believers* by *baptism*, that ordinance conveying *grace*. But to which of all these shall we give credit?

dit? The truth is, they all speak without book, having no ground from *God's word* to say as they do

NOTWITHSTANDING the *Baptists* were some of the first of the Dissenters from the establish'd Church, who shew'd their abhorrence of *Oliver*'s usurpation, and made overtures to the King for his restoration; and although they fully clear'd themselves from being any ways concern'd in the *insurrection* made by *Venner* and his accomplices: Yet they were so far from being allow'd the liberty of their religion, that the first and most violent persecution was chiefly levell'd against them; as the following relations will make appear.

IMMEDIATELY after the rising of *Venner* and his accomplices, Mr. *Hanserd Knollys*, and divers other godly and peaceable persons, were hal'd out of their houses, and committed, some to *Woodstreet-counter*, some to *Newgate*, and many to other prisons. Hanserd Knollys and others imprison'd.

MR. *Vavasor Powel* was taken from his house by a company of soldiers, and carried to prison, from thence he was conducted to *Salop*, and committed with several others, to the custody of a marshal; where they continu'd prisoners about nine weeks; and then by order of the King and Council, he was releas'd with the rest of his brethren. Vavasor Powel and others imprison'd.

IT

The HISTORY *of the*

John Bun-yan impri-son'd.

IT was about this time, that the famous Mr. *John Bunyan* was apprehended at a meeting, and carried before a Justice of the peace; who committed him to prison, though he offer'd security for his appearing at the next sessions. At the sessions he was indicted for an upholder and maintainer of unlawful assemblies and conventicles, and for not conforming to the Church of *England*. He was a man of a free and open spirit, and would not dissemble to save himself, especially in his Master's cause; and therefore frankly own'd his being at a meeting and preaching to the people, and that he was a dissenter from the establish'd church. The Justices took his open and plain dealing with them, for a confession of the indictment; and sentenc'd him to perpetual banishment, because he refus'd to conform, in pursuance of an Act made by the then Parliament. Upon which he was again committed to prison; where, though his sentence of banishment was never executed upon him; yet he was kept in prison 12 years, and suffer'd much under cruel and oppressing goalers. There were in the prison with him, two eminent dissenting ministers, *viz.* Mr. *Wheeler* and Mr. *Dun*, both very well known in *Bedfordshire*; and above threescore dissenters besides. After he had suffer'd twelve years imprisonment for the testimony of a good conscience, he was releas'd releas'd on the importunity of Dr. *Barlow*, Bishop of *Lincoln*.

THEY were neither abbettors of this treasonable insurrection, nor privy to it, nor could their enemies fix any thing of that nature upon them; but they had the oaths of *supremacy* and *allegiance* tender'd to them, which it was impossible for any dissenter to take; because by this, they must acknowledge the King *supreme head* of the Church, and swear allegiance to him in all ecclesiastical matters, as well as civil: And their refusing to take this, was made the pretence for keeping them in custody. So that from the time of this *mad insurrection*, to the coronation of the King, which was about 18 weeks, many upon this account were kept close prisoners. Above 400 were crouded into *Newgate*, besides what were in the other prisons belonging to the *city* and places adjacent: But then an act of pardon being granted to all offenders, except murderers, they were all set at liberty.

ANOTHER instance of their severity towards the *Baptists* above all others, appear'd in this. 'The parliament assembled upon the restoration, says Dr. *Wall*, express'd the dislike the nation had conceiv'd against the tenets and behaviour of these men [meaning *Anabaptists*] when making an act, for the confirming all ministers in the possession of
'their

Hist. of Bapt. Vol. II. *p.* 215.

' their benefices, how *heterodox* foever they
' had been, provided they would con-
' form for the future, they excepted fuch
' as had been of this way.'

As they would give this people the leaft encouragement to conform, fo they treated them the moft cruelly and barbaroufly for their diffenting; as will appear by the following relations.

Baptifts imprifon'd at Reading.

MR. *Jeffey*, an eminent and learned minifter of the *Baptifts*, gives us an account from *Reading-prifon*, where divers peaceable *Baptifts* were put, having oaths put upon them, which they were not fatisfied to take; who wrote to him of the Lord's inftructing and comforting them under thefe their fufferings for his fake. Their words are thefe:

The Lord's loud Call, p. 24.

' OUR Lord and King, whom we
' ferve, hath brought us under his own
' pavilion; and *his banner over* us hath
' been ,and ftill *is love*; and hath been
' teaching of us thefe leffons following.

' FIRST, In the lofs of all outward
' things, having Chrift, we enjoy all
' things, and are fatisfied in the Lord;
' we fhall take the fpoiling of our goods
' with far more comfort, than the enemy
' will do in the fpending of them, for
' that word is very much upon our hearts
' concerning him.

Job xx. 22, 23.

' SECONDLY, We hope we have learn-
' ed, in whatfoever condition we are in,
' to

'be therewith contented; and are perſuad-
'ed in our hearts, this is given us in as an
'anſwer of many prayers breath'd forth
'unto the Lord on our behalfs.

'THIRDLY, That whereas formerly
'we could hardly part with any thing for
'the Lord, we are now made willing by
'him, to part with all things for him, and
'to ſay with good old *Ely, It is the Lord,*   1 Sam. iii.
'*let him do what he pleaſeth*; and that   18.
'in *Job*, is ſet before us for our exam-
'ple, upon whom the ends of the world
'are come; *The Lord giveth, and the Lord*   Job i. 22,
'*taketh away; bleſſed be the name of the*   23.
'*Lord. In all this* Job *ſinned not,* &c.

'FOURTHLY, We have ſince our
'confinement taſted a greater ſweetneſs
'in the promiſes of the Lord than for-
'merly; and particularly theſe places   Phil. iv.
'following, we have ſweet experience of,   19.
'and we can truly ſay by experience, *That*   1 Pet. v. 7.
'*faithful is he, that hath thus promiſed, for*   Deuteron.
'*he hath alſo done it; it is the Lord's doing*   xxxiii. 25.
'*and is marvellous in our eyes.* We are
'alſo brought by the power of his grace,
'to a more watchful frame over our
'hearts, thoughts, and actions, by theſe
'trials than formerly. One thing had
'almoſt ſlip'd our memory, the know-
'ledge of which will we hope rejoice our
'hearts; that our relations that are pre-
'cious to the Lord, and to us, bear this
'our ſuffering with incomparable pati-
                            'ence;

'ence, rather singing for joy, than weeping for grief: Also our *societies* from whence we were taken, are exceeding chearful, and a very lively spirit of faith and prayer is amongst them; and their meetings rather encreaseth than otherwise. Sure, *That the Lord is near, his wondrous works declare; for the singing of birds is come, and the turtle is heard in our land.*

'AND now, brethren, forasmuch as the mercies expected and pray'd for by us, are to be enjoy'd in the way of righteousness, it greatly concerns us, we cry mightly to the Lord, as did his servant of old. Then shall we have that new name which God will give us, which is express'd in the last verse of that chapter.

Isa. lxii. 1.

'Now the God of all peace fill you with peace and joy in believing; so pray your brethren through grace,

John Jones,
Robert Keate,
John Peck,
Richard Steed,
Thomas Jones,
John Coombes.

BY a letter from *Newport* in *Wales,* about this time, came to Mr. *Jessey* the following account.

'To

' To give you a full account of the hard
' dealings we now meet with from fome.
' Laſt Lord's-day with naked fwords and
' ſtaves, they attempted to fet upon Mr.
' *H. W.* and Mr. *W. J.* but theſe by
' their peaceable carriage ſtay'd their hands
' from blows; it being an aſſembly of
' rude foldiers, and moſt or many *Papiſts*,
' that came together againſt fermon was
' ended in *Lauvihaugel Laularnum*, which
' they had defign'd fince the night before,
' efpecially as we underſtand to cut off
' Mr. *W.* Mr. *J.* and another friend that
' lives in that town; though 'tis like, if
' they had but the leaſt juſt occafion or
' any pretence to fall upon them, they
' would have fpared none of the reſt.
' Since the Lord was pleas'd to bring us
' fafe from under their hands, they con-
' tinu'd, it feems; their carouſing all that
' day till midnight, and fought, and dan-
' gerouſly wounded one another. And
' as we underſtand, made uſe of that to
' accufe us at *London*; though we have
' neither fpoken, nor acted any thing
' contrary to the publick peace, though
' for our own defence, we were fuffici-
' ently provok'd thereunto. This is writ,
' that as occafion is, a true relation here-
' of may be given.'

THE kingdom being in a great fer- Anno
ment, fo that the *Baptiſts* could promife 1661.
them-

themselves no security from distuburbance. They therefore publish'd an address to the King, Parliament and People, entitled, *Sion's groans for her distress'd*; or, *sober endeavours to prevent innocent blood*, &c. The occasion of the publication of it, they deliver in this short epistle to the reader, thus:

'*Courteous Reader*,

'WITH burthen'd hearts, as once
' the two disciples travelling un-
' to *Emaus* spoke to Christ, a suppos'd
' stranger, so speak we unto thee. Art
' thou a stranger in our *island*, and hast
' not known the things that have come
' to pass in these our days; while the
' father hath been divided against the
' son, and the son against the father,
' three against two, and two against
' three. Even a man's foes, they of his
' own houshold; so great have been our
' divisions like *Reuben*, that no sooner
' light hath been by God's grace mani-
' fested to the begetting children of the
' free-woman, but presently they are per-
' secuted by the children of the bond-
' woman. And how unpleasing this is
' to *Jesus Christ*, and how unlike his
' golden rule that saith; *And all things*
' *whatsoever ye would that men should do*
' *to*

English Baptists.

' *to you, do ye even so to them; for this is
' the law and the prophets:* We say,
' how unpleasing this is to him; judge
' upon thy serious perusal of this fol-
' lowing treatise, which we commend
' to thy perusal in thy most retir'd con-
' sideration, when thou canst read with
' thy thoughts least cumbred with other
' business. Our design in what we beg
' may be perused, is general good, in
' setting at liberty that which God
' made free, even the conscience. Thou
' canst not be ignorant of the great
' controversy that now is on foot, as
' to *uniformity in worship,* to impose
' by violence, where they cannot per-
' suade, under seeming pretence of scrip-
' ture-warrant and antiquity; the con-
' trary to which is asserted in the words
' of truth and soberness, by scripture,
' reason, and practice of the primitive
' times.

' And least violence and oppressing
' of conscience should run up to that
' heighth, till it terminate in the blood
' of some who are dear, and their blood
' precious in the eyes of the God of all
' the earth; therefore have we commit-
' ted this unto the view of all men, as
' part of the work of our generation, in
' singleness of heart: And remain lovers
' and prayers for all men, *that we might*
' live

'live a peaceable and a quiet life in all
'godliness and honesty.

The 8th day of the 3d month, 1661.   '*Farewel*,

Thomas Monck,   *Francis Stanley,*
Joseph Wright,   *William Reynolds,*
George Hammon,   *Francis Smith.*
William Jeffery,

HAVING in my former volume shewn the opposition made to a *toleration*, by the city magistracy, the Assembly of Divines, the ministers of *London*, *Lancashire* and *Warwickshire*, &c. I should not do justice to the *English Baptists*, if I should pass by, or abridge this their address to the King, Parliament and People, for a *toleration*. Which seems to me so full and strong, and containing such cogent arguments, urg'd with so much life and spirit; that he would have an hard task, that should undertake to confute them. I shall, therefore, deliver the whole in their own words.

' As *all the holy scriptures*, say they,
' *have been written aforetime for our learn-*
' *ing and admonition, upon whom the ends*
' *of the world are come*; so that particu-
' lar book of the *Revelation*, is of such
' excellent worth, *That blessed is he that*
' *readeth, and they that hear the words of*
' *this prophecy, and keep those things that*
' *are written therein; for the time is at*
                                        ' *hand.*

' hand. In which book, in no less than ^(Rev. xiv. 8.)
' three several texts it is testified; that ^(Rev. xvii. 2.)
' the nations of the world, and inhabiters
' of the earth with their kings, would ^(Rev. xviii. 3.)
' drink the wine of the fornication of
' that *abominable harlot*, that sitteth upon
' people, and multitudes, and nations, and
' tongues; and by her sorceries deceiveth
' all nations, until they become drunk,
' and altogether uncapable, in that condi-
' tion, to receive the pure waters of life,
' tender'd to them in the plain way of the
' Gospel of our Lord *Jesus*.

' THIS, with grief of heart, we see
' too visible. For the doctrine and tra-
' ditions of *Rome*, who is mystery *Ba-*
' *bylon*; and since her apostacy the mo-
' ther of harlots; (*For the woman which* ^(Rev. xvii. 18.)
' *thou sawest, is that great city which*
' *reigneth over the kings of the earth*;)
' have so corrupted the earth, and cloud-
' ed the understandings of the sons of
' men, that the great and most impor-
' tant truths of God cannot be receiv'd
' or believ'd. The reason why the na-
' tions are so generally beguil'd in the
' concernments of their souls is, because
' the greatest part being carnal and un-
' regenerate persons, they are naturally
' inclin'd to such ways of worship, as
' are accompany'd with external pomp
' and glory. And therefore the Spirit
' of the Lord testifies, that the *great har-* ^(Rev xvii.)
' *lot* ^(4.)

'*lot* filleth her abominations, and filthy
' fornications in a golden cup; like the
' phyfician that gilds his bitter pill, that
' his patient may the better fwallow it.

' Thus doth the *Romifh* church, and
' her followers; who to make their *car-*
' *nal ordinances* find the better reception,
' deliver them to the inhabitants of the
' earth, by fuch as are honourable a-
' mongft men; in worldly fanctuaries,
' moft magnificently built and adorn'd,
' endow'd with lordly revenues, accom-
' pany'd with mufick and voices, and
' pontifical veftments; yea, many fuper-
' ftitions and cuftoms merely earthly and
' fenfual, if not worfe. Which, we fay,
' fo pleafeth the earthly and unregenerate
' man, that he is ready to fay, this is the
' beft religion, which is of moft efteem
' in the nations, and accompany'd with
' all earthly glory and delights: Altoge-
Matt. vii. ' ther forgetting, *That ftrait is the gate,*
14. ' *and narrow is the way that leads to life,*
Luke xvi. ' *and few there be that find it.* And
15. ' that which is highly efteem'd among
' men, is abomination in the fight of
' God.

' And if it had been the mind of the
' Lord *Jefus*, that the Gofpel fhould have
' been recommended unto the world, and
' accompany'd with thefe ceremonies and
' formalities that are practis'd in the wor-
' fhip of the nations, or were us'd amongft
' the

' the *Jews*; it is very strange we should
' not have one word for it all the scrip-
' tures of the New Testament; when Heb. iii.
' Christ was as faithful over his house, 2, 5, 6.
' as *Moses* was over his, and is to be Deut.
' heard in all things, as *Moses* himself xviii. 18,
' commanded. And there will be little 19.
' encouragement to touch with the *Gen-*
' *tile* nations in their superstitious ceremo-
' nies, when it shall be consider'd, that
' the rites and ceremonies of the *Mosaical*
' law, being once the appointment of
' God, did far exceed in glory what the
' shallow inventions of the *Romish* or any
' of the national churches are able to pro-
' duce; yet wholly taken away. Which
' the author to the *Hebrews* notably
' proves: saying, *Then verily the first co-*
' *venant had also ordinances of divine ser-*
' *vice, and a worldly sanctuary; for there*
' *was a tabernacle made, the first wherein*
' *was the candlestick, and the table, and*
' *the shew-bread, which is call'd the sanc-*
' *tuary; and after the second vail the ta-*
' *bernacle, which is call'd the holiest of all.*
' They had also their High-Priest and of-
' ferings, and linen ornaments belonging
' to this covenant. But, saith our au-
' thor, *If that first covenant had been* Heb. viii.
' *faultless, then no place had been sought* 7.
' *for the second; and, he taketh away the* Heb. x. 9.
' *first, that he might establish the second.*
' And now under the second covenant,
                G 4   ' which

'which is the Gospel, the *Romish* Bishop,
'or any man on earth, cannot be our
'High-Preist. *For we have such an High-*
'*Priest, who is set on the right-hand of*
'*the throne of the Majesty in the heavens;*
'*a minister of the sanctuary, and of the*
'*tabernacle which the Lord pitcheth, and*
'*not man.*

'And under this second covenant,
'God hath not promised his presence to
'any temple built with wood and stone,
'as of old; *For now the Most High* [Acts vii. 48.]
'*dwelleth not in temples made with hands,*
'as the superstitious clergy would per-
'suade us; but *where two or three are*
'*gather'd together in the name of Christ,*
'*there is he in the midst of them;* altho'
'it be in a house, by a river's side, on
'a mountain, or in a wilderness; such
'little respect hath he to *place*.

'As little respect hath God to *persons*,
'because of any honour or esteem they
'may have in the world, either for birth or
'natural endowments; but such as usu-
'ally are *foolish, weak, and base in the eyes*
'*of the world*, doth he make use of in
'the work of the Gospel; that so the
'learned *Doctors*, and *Masters of Art* [1 Cor. i. 26, &c.]
'may not have wherewithal to boast.

'Which despis'd way of the Gospel,
'we well know, becomes a *stumbling*
'*block* to the *Gentile Nations*, as in the
'first delivery of it, it did unto the
'*Jews,*

'*Jews*, who *would not receive the Lord*
'*of life*, nor his doctrine, becaufe not
' accompany'd with that earthly glory
' which their corrupt hearts affected:
' And rather would retain that exploded
' difpenfation of the law, which God had
' departed from, than they would receive
' the glorious Gofpel by thofe hands the
' wifdom of God thought fit to tender
' it. For which obftinacy, as the Apo-
' ftle *Paul* faith, *The wrath of God is*
' *come upon them to the uttermoft*, even
' to the laying wafte their temple and ci-
' ties, the great flaughter of their perfons,
' and captivating their pofterity, as at
' this day. Let therefore the *Gentile Na-* 1 Thef.
' *tions* fear; but more efpecially this na- ii. 16.
' tion. For fome fuch fpirit feems to ap-
' pear amongft thofe that would retain
' their empty and dead forms of wor-
' fhip, which God hath fhewed his dif-
' pleafure againft, and have no footing in
' the whole book of God, rather than
' they will receive the pure way of God,
' without the mixture of human inven-
' tions and traditions.

' BUT the bare rejection of truth, and
' embracing of error, is not all the evil,
' that the nations generally are engag'd
' in by the Church of *Rome*, and her
' followers; but for to compleat and fill
' up the meafure of their iniquities, like
' *Nebuchadnezzar*, nothing lefs muft be

'inflicted on the servants of the Most High
'God, that cannot bow down to the
'*Golden Image* of their inventions, than
'the *fiery furnace* of *persecution*; many
'times unto death itself.

'And this the people of the Lord must
'endure; it being as certain their portion
'to be persecuted, as it is the practice of
'the false Church to persecute; who
'build their superstructures of will-wor-
'ship on no other foundations but violence
'and cruelty. Else what mean these im-
'prisonments, banishments, wars, and
'massacres, which have been made in
'*Europe* for religion? What troubles and
'desolations in *Germany*; civil commo-
'tions in *France*; cruelties exercis'd in
'the *Netherlands*, by that darling of
'the *Romish* Church, the Duke of *Al-*
'*va*, and others? What massacres in
'*France*, *Piedmont* and *Ireland*, to car-
'ry on the business of religion, for the
'satisfaction of a blood-thirsty and insa-
'tiable Clergy; when the disciples of the
'Lord *Jesus* were to use no other vio-
'lence against those that rejected them,
'than to *shake the dust from their feet*,
'which would be a witness against them
'at the tribunal of *Jesus*, not *Cæsar*'s?
'Yea, this *Popish* principle of propagat-
'ing religion by the sword, hath reach'd
'the poor *Americans*; many hundred
'thousands of them having been destroy'd,
'because

Acts xiii. 51.
Matt. x. 14, 15.

English Baptists.

'because they would not be *proselytes*,
'no other cause being to be given. For
'it cannot be suppos'd, those remote and
'simple people had so much as known
'the *Spaniard*, much less done any in-
'jury unto him. Our own nation hath
'also felt the rage of this fury, both be-
'fore, and in the reign of Queen *Mary*.
'And the wise may judge, whether the
'Bishops endeavours to impose their li-
'turgy in *Scotland*, with their cruelties in
'*England*, did not contribute much to
'our late unhappy troubles. But cer-
'tainly if the *Romish* and national clergy
'were guided by the Spirit of God, the
'authority of Scripture, or force of argu-
'ment to support their forms of worship;
'they would not then impose them by
'external force; when by such proceed-
'ings they render themselves altogether
'unlike the Lord *Jesus*, the prince of
'peace; *who came not to destroy men's*
'*lives, but to save them.*

'But on the contrary, it will evince
'to all that have their eyes open, how
'like they are to that woman, which is
'*drunken with the blood of saints, and* Rev. xvii. 6.
'*with the blood of the martyrs of* Jesus;
'*in whom will be found the blood of pro-* Rev. xviii. 24.
'*phets, and of saints, and of all that were*
'*slain on the earth.* Altho' as our Lord
'and master hath foretold, in killing o- John xvi. 2.
'thers,

'thers, she may think she doth God ser-
'vice.

'LEST, therefore, those unchristian
'principles of persecution for conscience,
'which troubleth the world, should take
'root in this nation, to the stirring up
'men's minds to shed the blood of the
'innocent, the guilt whereof is able to
'sink the most flourishing kingdoms into
'an ocean of misery and calamity; we
'have here following written some argu-
'ments, which we humbly offer to all
'men, to prove how contrary to the
'Gospel of our Lord *Jesus*, and to good
'reason, it is for any magistrate, by out-
'ward force, to impose any thing in the
'worship of God, on the consciences of
'those whom they govern; but that li-
'berty ought to be given to all such, as
'disturb not the civil peace, though of
'different persuasions in religious matters.
'In which discourse we neither desire
'nor design to diminish any of that pow-
'er which God hath given to the King's
'Majesty that now reigneth: Whom we
'own to be chief magistrate and gover-
'nour of these nations, over all persons, as
'well ecclesiastical as temporal. And to
'all his commands that do not oppose the
'scriptures of truth, shall we yield active
'obedience, not only for wrath, but al-
'so for conscience sake. And if any
'thing otherwise shall be requir'd, we
'shall

'shall be paffive, and fuffer what may
'be inflicted on us for our confciences.
'For whatever hath been fuggefted by
'evil men; yet that magiftracy and go-
'vernment is an ordinance of God, hath
'been frequently afferted in our difcourfes
'and writings, and is by us believ'd, as
'fully as the Apoftle *Paul* in the 13th
'of the *Romans* hath taught. And all
'that we defire, which is dearer to us
'than our lives, is, that our fpirits and
'confciences may be left free to ferve
'the Eternal God: Which ought to be
'granted us, feeing, as the fame Apoftle
'faith in thefe cafes, *We fhall every one*
'*of us give an account of himfelf to God.*
'But to our arguments. The firft of
'which fhall be that, which fome of us
'made ufe of to the King's Majefty from
'*Maidftone*; which we have not yet feen
'weaken'd.

See the confeffion of faith, printed in March 1659; and fince re-printed, and pre-fented to his Majefty.

Rom. xiv. 12.

'LET it, therefore, be confider'd, If
'any magiftrate under heaven, in the
'days of the Gofpel, hath power by out-
'ward force to impofe any thing in the
'worfhip and fervice of God on the con-
'fcience; it is given him as he is a ma-
'giftrate only, or as a chriftian fo con-
'fider'd. But that no fuch power is
'given by God to any magiftrate, ap-
'pears,

'1. BECAUSE if magiftrates as fuch,
'have fuch an authority; then all magi-
'ftrates

' ſtrates in all nations have the fame pow-
' er. Then, if we liv'd in *Turkey*, muſt
' we receive the *Alcoran*, and be wor-
' ſhippers of *Mahomet*; if in *Spain*, be
' *Papiſts*; in *England*, ſometimes *Papiſts*,
' as in *Henry* VIII's days, *Proteſtants* in
' *Edward* VI's, *Papiſts* again in Queen
' *Mary's*; and *Proteſtants* again in Queen
' *Elizabeth's*. And ſo for ever, as the
' authority changes religion, we muſt do
' the ſame; but God forbid, for nothing
' is more abſurd.

' 2. SEEING in the days of the Goſ-
' pel, the Lord *Jeſus* is that great *Pro-*
' *phet, which as Moſes* ſaid, *is to be heard*
' *in all things*; and as himſelf teſtifieth,
Matt. ' *Hath all power in heaven and earth gi-*
xxviii. 18. ' *ven unto him:* Then if magiſtrates have
' power to impoſe any thing by outward
' force on the conſcience, it muſt be com-
' mitted unto them from the Lord *Jeſus*,
' and written in the ſcriptures of the New
' Teſtament; or elſe how doth it appear?
1 Cor. iv. ' *Let no man think of men above that*
6. ' *which is written*. But the whole ſtream
' of the New Teſtament ſcriptures run
' clear in another channel. And there is
' no colour for any ſuch impoſition, as
' farther appears,

' 3. BECAUSE the Apoſtles themſelves,
' that gave forth thoſe commands which
' are written in ſcripture, to be obedient
' to magiſtrates, refus'd to be obedient to
' their

'their rulers, when they were command-
'ed to forbear, that which they judg'd
'part of the worship of God: And said,
'*Whether it be right in the sight of God,* Acts iv.
'*to hearken unto you more than unto God,* 19, 20.
'*judge ye.*

'4. ALL the scriptures of the New
'Testament, that enjoin obedience unto
'magistrates, were written when the *Ro-*
'*mans* had the empire of the world;
'whose Emperors were for the most part,
'if not all, *heathenish* idolators, for the
'first three hundred years, until *Constan-*
'*tine's* time. It, therefore, cannot be
'suppos'd, that any of those texts of scrip-
'ture, that call for obedience to magis-
'trates, intend an obedience in matters of
'faith: For then the Christians that liv'd
'under those Emperors must needs have
'denied Christ, and worshipped the *Ro-*
'*man* Gods, as some of the Emperors *As Dio-*
'commanded. *clesian,*
Euseb.
'5. IF magistrates, as such, have *Book*
'power from God in the days of the Gos- *VIII.*
'pel to command in spiritual matters, *chap. 3.*
'and to punish those that obey not: Then
'must Christians surely be actually obe-
'dient, *not only for wrath, but also for*
'*conscience sake*: because else they should
'*resist the ordinance of God.* But if this
'were true, the way to heaven would be
'so far from being *strait and narrow*, that
'any might be a *disciple of Christ*, with- Luke xiv.
 'out 17.

'out *taking up the cross and following*
'*him*; yea all sufferings and persecutions
'should wholly be at an end, and they
'that undergo them should utterly be
'condemn'd. For it is not to be sup-
'pos'd there could be persecutions, if all
'the commands of the magistrate in spi-
'ritual causes were actually to be obey'd.
'It, therefore, reasonably follows; that
'no magistrate, as such, hath power from
'God to compel in spiritual causes. But
Rev. vii. 'on the contrary, for saints to endure
14, 15. 'persecutions and sufferings rather than
Jam. i. 12.
Acts xiv. 'actually obey, is abundantly by the Lord
22. 'foretold, rewarded and justified; as by
2 Tim. ii. 'the scriptures of the New Testament
11, 12. 'appears.

'BUT if it be objected, that neither
'the magistrate is to command, nor the
'subjects actually to obey, any thing but
'what is according to the mind of God; it
'is answer'd, that all magistrates suppose
'whatever they impose to be so; but the
'question is, who is to determine. For
'if the magistrate, or any other man, or
'men, have power from God to judge
'and determine what is lawful for men
'to obey; then no room is left for them
'to dispute the lawfulness of any of his
'commands, it being their duty to obey
'whatever is commanded; and so as it hath
'been said before, *the cross of Christ ceases.*
Rom. xiv. '*But if every one shall give account for*
12. '*himself*

'*himself to God*; then it reasonably fol- Josh. xxiv.
'lows, that every man must judge for 15.
'himself in matters spiritual: And there-
'fore, for the magistrate to compel, can-
'not be warrantable by scripture or rea-
'son.

'AGAIN: That the power to judge
'and determine in spiritual matters, is
'not in a magistrate as such, *Gallio* the
'*Roman* deputy of *Achaia* well under-
'stood, when the *Jews* made insurrec-
'tion with one accord against *Paul*, and
'brought him to the judgment-seat, say-
'ing, *This fellow persuadeth men to wor-*
'*ship God contrary to the law*. Which
'almost ever since hath been the great
'cry by all sorts of the *national clergy*,
'whose turns it hath been to have the
'magistrate on their sides, against all o-
'thers that have differ'd from them. But
'*Gallio* said; *If it were a matter of* Acts xviii.
'*wrong, or wicked lewdness, O ye Jews,* 12, &c.
'*reason would that I should bear with*
'*you: But if it be a question of words,*
'*and names, and of your law, look ye to*
'*it, for I will be no judge of such matters.*
'*And he drave them from the judgment-*
'*seat*. Which worthy example, if ma- *But in tha.*
'gistrates would be persuaded to follow, *he suffer'd*
'by judging and punishing only civil *to be beaten*
'injuries and wrongs, and leaving spiri- *he did not*
'tual differences to be decided and judg'd, *being a*
'and punish'd by *Jesus Christ* according *civil in-*
VOL. II. H 'to *jury.*

'to the Gospel; they then would find
'themselves and governments quickly
'free from many inconveniences that
'now they are involv'd in, about decid-
'ing religious controversies, with exter-
'nal force and power.

'AND now that no magistrate, altho'
'a christian, hath power to be a lord over
'another's faith, or by outward force to
'impose any thing in the worship of
'God, is also very clear.

'1. BECAUSE the Lord *Jesus* him-
'himself would never by any outward force
'compel men to receive him or his doc-
'trine. For when his disciples, supposing
'they might use violence, as under the
'law, would have commanded fire to
'come down from heaven, as *Elias* did, to
'consume them that would not receive
'him, Christ turn'd and rebuk'd them;
'saying, *Ye know not what spirit ye are* Luke ix. 54, &c.
'*of; for the son of man is not come to de-*
'*stroy mens lives, but to save them.* And
'most remarkable doth it appear, that it
'is not the intent of the Lord *Jesus*, that
'judgment should be executed on those
'that reject his words, to the punishing
'them in their bodies and estates in this
'life, as under the law, from his own
'sayings, which speak thus: *If any man* John xii. 47, 48.
'*hear my words, and believe not, I judge*
'*him not: for I came not to judge the*
'*world, but to save the world.* He that
're-

' rejecteth me, and receiveth not my words,
' hath one that judgeth him: the word
' that I have spoken, the same shall judge
' him at the last day. And the Apostles
' also, were so far from propagating the
' Gospel by outward violence and force, Matt. x.
' that all their proceedings were by in- 14.
' treaty and persuasion; and in case of re- 52.
' sistance, to shake the dust from their
' feet as a witness against their opposers.
' Nor will it avail to say, because the
' magistrate exercises authority on civil
' and temporal things, which the Lord *As the*
' Christ would not, that therefore in spi- *dividing*
' ritual things they may do the same; *tances,&c.*
' unless it may be suppos'd the magistrates
' right to have supremacy over the world
' to come, in all heavenly and eternal
' things; because God hath given him
' power over the world that now is, in
' earthly and temporal things. Which
' may be conjectur'd upon as good ground
' from what is written, as that a magis-
' trate under the Gospel dispensation hath
' more power in spiritual causes, than the
' Lord Christ or his Apostles would ex-
' ercise; especially, seeing there is not
' the least warrant for any such power
' from Christ or the Apostles, from any
' thing that is written in the scriptures
' of the New Testament. *And to the
' law, and to the testimony; if they speak*
                                    ' *not*

' not according to this word, it is because
' there is no light in them.

' 2. IF any men, as Christians under
' heaven, have had any such power in
' the days of the Gospel, the Apostles and
' Elders in the primitive times must needs
' have had it. But this they utterly dis-
2 Cor. i. ' claim'd: As *Paul, Not for that we
24. ' have dominion over your faith, but are
' helpers of your joy: for by faith ye stand.*
' Yea, the Lord *Jesus*, when they strove
Matt. xx. ' for domination, forbids it, saying: *Ye
25. ' know that the princes of the Gentiles ex-
' ercise dominion over them, and they that
' are great, do exercise authority upon
' them; but it shall not be so amongst
' you.* Even so saith *Peter*, speaking to
1 Pet. v. ' the Elders; *Feed the flock of God which
2, 3. ' is amongst you, taking the oversight
' thereof, not by constraint, but willingly;
' not for filthy lucre, but of a ready mind.
' Neither as being lords over God's heri-
' tage, but being examples to the flock.*
' Why therefore the Christian Religion
' should be built and supported by vio-
' lence and cruelty, when the foundation
' was laid, and the work carried on all
' the Apostles days, and some hundred of
' years after, by a quite contrary means;
' is a question would be resolved by those,
' whose strongest argument for the sup-
' port of their religion is, TAKE HIM,
' JAYLOR. For such is the difference
' between

'between the way which the Apostles and
'primitive saints took, in carrying on the
'work of the Gospel, and approving
'themselves to be the Ministers of God,
'and the way now used by the *national*
'*Clergy*, than which nothing is more un-
'like. They being ambassadors for the 2 Cor. v.
'prince of peace, did in his stead beseech 20.
'and pray the disobedient to be reconcil'd
'to God; never stirring up the nations
'to ruin, and destroy by external violence
'those that oppos'd them in their mini-
'stry; but as the Apostle *Paul* saith, *Be-* 1 Cor. iv.
'*ing reviled, we bless; being persecuted, we* 12, 13.
'*suffer it: Being defamed, we entreat.*
'*Giving no offence in any thing, that the* 2 Cor. vi.
'*ministry be not blamed: But in all things* 3, &c.
'*approving ourselves as the ministers of*
'*God, in much patience, in afflictions, in*
'*necessities, in distresses, in stripes, in impri-*
'*sonments, in tumults, in labours, in watch-*
'*ings, in fastings, by pureness, by knowledge,*
'*by long-suffering, by kindness, by the Holy*
'*Ghost, by love unfeigned*, &c. O ye ru-
'lers of the world, and inhabitants of the
'earth, this was the way, the Lord of all
'things, with his disciples and followers,
'took to plant and establish the doctrine
'of the Gospel in the hearts and affec-
'tions of the sons of men. Be ye not
'therefore unlike those whom you say you
'follow, by imposing your doctrines and
'traditions by the violence of penal laws and
'edicts,

'edicts, to the *imprisoning, banishing*, and
'*spoiling* the goods of the conscientious;
' causing them, as the saints of old, to
Heb. xi. ' be *destitute, afflicted, and tormented*, al-
36, &c. ' though for their innocency and upright-
' ness, *the world is not worthy of them.*

' 3. It is very plain, that the Lord *Je-*
Matt. xiii. ' *sus* himself, in his parable of the *tares*
' and *wheat*, forbids any outward force
' or violence to be exercised upon false
' worshippers and hereticks as such. For
' by the *tares*, which he forbids the pul-
' ling up, cannot be intended the tranf-
' gressors of the second table, such as
' *thieves, murderers*, or any that should
' do that civil injury or wrong unto ano-
' ther, which he would not have done
' unto himself. For all confess with one
' consent, that the magistrates authority
' reaches such. Neither can it be in-
' tended that *the children of the wicked*
' *one*, in any sense, that visibly appear to
' be so, should be tolerated in the church;
' for that destroys the power of excom-
' munication. That which unavoidably
' then follows is, that although men are
' *tares*, or *the children of the wicked one*,
' by erring in the worship of God, yet
' should they not be *plucked up*, but *to-*
' *lerated in the field of the world*, until
' the *harvest* shall come, *at the end of*
' *this world*; when the *angels*, who are to
' be the reapers, and infallibly can diftin-
' guish

' guish between the *tares* and the *wheat*,
' which no magistrate now can, shall
' gather the *tares* in bundles, and *cast*
' *them into a furnace of fire*; *there shall*
' *be wailing and gnashing of teeth*. Which
' scripture so eminently concludes for a
' toleration; that the greatest enemies to
' true liberty have been at a great loss,
' when they have endeavour'd to make it
' speak some other thing. As that ex- J. T. *Sup-*
' positor is, who says; *It seems to him,* plement,
' *not to note the duty of the civil magis-* p. 29.
' *trate, but the event of God's providence,*
' *that God would permit the co-habitation*
' *of the wicked in the world with the just*;
' *not that magistrates or ministers should*
' *permit them, and not by civil punishment*
' *or ecclesiastical, remove them out of the*
' *church or the world.* But if men did
' not fight against truth, they would not
' so evidently contradict their own sayings.
' For who can believe that it should be the
' mind of God, to permit the co-habita-
' tion of the wicked in the world with
' the just, as aforesaid, and yet the ma-
' gistrate should not permit them; but
' remove them by civil punishment out of
' the world? Hath the magistrate power
' to remove those out of the world, that
' God would have permitted to live?
' How soon may a magistrate, if guided
' by such doctrine, bring the blood of
' the innocent upon himself and nation?

' *And*

' *And innocent blood the Lord will not*
' *pardon.* It therefore highly concerns
' all magistrates, before they persecute
' any for matters of faith or wor-
' ship, to see they have a better warrant
' for so doing, than the word of men;
' which will not secure them at that day,
' *when God shall judge the secrets of men,*
' *by Jesus Christ, according to the Gospel.*
' Which will be found to be *the book*
' *that shall be opened,* when *the dead,*
' *both small and great, shall stand before*
' *God, to be judged by what is written*
' *therein, according to their works.* As
' the Lord *Jesus* saith: *The word that I*
' *have spoken, the same shall judge you at*
' *the last day.* And this is his word, to
' let both tares and wheat grow together
' in the field of the world, until the har-
' vest.

' 4. It can in no wise be safe for ma-
' gistrates, in the days of the Gospel, to
' persecute and destroy those that are
' contrary minded in religious matters,
' because of their fallibility. And that is
' the very reason why the Lord *Jesus,*
' in the fore-mention'd parable, forbids
' gathering up the *tares; least the wheat*
' *be rooted up* along *with them.* That
' magistrates may err in spiritual and re-
' ligious matters, woful experience hath
' taught the world in all ages. The Lord
' of Life himself was put to death, for
' sup-

Margin notes:
2 Kings xxiv 4.
Rom. ii. 16.
Rev. xx. 12.
So many as have lived where the word of the Gospel comes.
Matt. xiii. 3.

'suppos'd blasphemy and wickedness, and
'accus'd for being *an enemy unto Cæsar*.
'Which great mistake was committed
'through ignorance; as *Peter* saith, *And* Acts iii.
'*now, brethren, I wot that through igno-* 17.
'*rance ye did it, as also did your rulers.*
'And at this day, what mistakes are con-
'tinu'd in magistrates about religion?
'Some being *Calvinists*, as in *Holland* and In Europe.
'*Geneva*, more *Lutherans*, but the great-
'est part *Papists*: And each of these
'condemneth, and many times persecut-
'eth the other for heresy, or superstition.
'Unavoidably therefore it follows, that
'some of these must err: But we need not
'go far for the proof of this in one and the
'same person, who receives that at one
'time for truth, which at another time
'must be persecuted for error. This ap-
'pear'd notably in King *Henry* VIII. who
'persecuted the *Protestants* to death; and
'writes against *Luther*, for which the
'*Pope* gives him the title of *defender of*
'*the faith*: And yet a while after re-
'ceives some of *Luther*'s doctrines, and
'rejects the supremacy and authority of
'the *Pope*; and serves the *Papists* as he
'did the *Protestants*. Nor will magis-
'trates be the more free from mistakes,
'by relying on the authority of Synods,
'Popes, or general Councils, because
'such eminent contradictions and opposi-
'tions have appear'd amongst each of them,
'that

'that nothing is more uncertain than their
'conclusions. As for general Councils,
'whose authority is in the greatest esti-
'mation of the three, it is plain, they
'are so far from being infallible, that
'their decrees have been not only directly
'opposite to plain texts of scripture, and
'the practice of the primitive church,
'but also against each other. Which
'appear'd first in the Council of Con-
'*stance*, in the thirteenth session; where
'it was decreed, that the Lord's-Supper
'should be given but in one kind;
'when nothing is more plain, than that
'the Lord *Jesus* instituted it; the A-
'postle *Paul* afterwards deliver'd it to
'the *Corinthians*; and the primitive
'church receiv'd it, with both the bread
'and the cup.

'So for the Council of *Trent*, to de-
'cree that the service in the church
'should be perform'd in *Latin*; how
'contrary is it to the doctrine of *Paul*;
'who said, *In the church he had rather
'speak five words with understanding, that
'he might teach others, than ten thousand
'words in an unknown tongue.* So also
'have they clash'd one with another: The
'Council of *Trent* allowing picturing of
'God the father; the Council of *Nice*
'altogether disallowing it. And in the
'great *Arian* controversy, which was
'no circumstantial business, how many
'Coun-

As Jer. Taylor *now Bishop of Down, in his liberty of Proph.* Sect. VI. *at large proves.*

Mat. xxvi. 26, 27.

1 Cor. xi. 24, 25.

1 Cor. xiv. 19.

' Councils and Conventions, were both
' for and against it?
    ' As little reliance can be put on any
' suppos'd infallibility the *Pope* may have;
' there having been two or three at one   Benedict.
' time, each raging against the other, with Silvester
'   III. Gre-
' their censures and decrees. And noto- gory VI.
' rious it is, what dissention there was
' amongst the Popes and Cardinals about
' Pope *Formosus*; who being first Bishop
' of *Pontiniack*, was degraded by Pope Fox's *acts*
' *John* VIII. and made to take an oath *and mon.*
'   p. 188.
' to lead a secular life all his days. Yet
' by Pope *Martin* that succeeded *John*,
' was *Formosus* releas'd from his oath, re-
' stor'd to his Bishoprick, and afterwards
' came to be *Pope*, and so continu'd 5 years,
' making several decrees. But *Stephen* VI.
' coming to the Popedom, abrogates the
' decrees of *Formosus*, takes up his body,
' cut off two of his fingers, throws them
' into the river *Tyber*, and then buries
' him in a *Layman*'s sepulchre. Next to
' *Stephen* succeeds *Romanus*; who on the
' the other hand repeals the acts and de-
' crees of his predecessor *Stephen* against
' *Formosus*. And Pope *John* X. in a sy-
' nod at *Ravenna*, ratifies all the decrees
' and doings of *Formosus*. Yet after all
' this, comes Pope *Sergius*, digs up again
' *Formosus*, cuts of his head and three
' more off his fingers, and throws his
' body into the *Tyber*, and likewise de-
                                    ' pos'd

' pos'd all such as had been consecrated by
' him. All which schisms and dissen-
' tions make it plain to the world, that
' there is nothing of infallibility in the
' *Popes*.

' AND for national conventions and
' synods; they are so far from any shew
' of infallibility, that the same complec-
' tion and temper the nation is of, where-
' in they are call'd, and have their pro-
' motions, you shall be sure to find them
' of; because they have their dependency
' on the authority that calls them toge-
' ther. So that although the last nation-
' al synod in this nation, would have e-
' stablish'd *Presbytery*, because that then
' was most like to take; yet it is very
' questionable, if now a convention be
' call'd, whether it will be much talk'd
' of amongst them.

' THEN this must be concluded from
' all, that seeing magistrates themselves,
' general Councils, Popes, or national Sy-
' nods may err, in judging and determi-
' ning the most weighty controversies in
' religion; there can therefore be no se-
' curity for a magistrate that he doth well
' in persecuting or putting to death the
' contrary minded in religious matters;
' seeing through mistake, he may as soon
' persecute or put to death the true fol-
' lowers of the Lord *Jesus*, as any other.
' Yea, in likelihood much sooner; be-
' cause

'cause they in conscience towards God,
'cannot receive the inventions and tradi-
'tions of men, in the worship of God;
'but must be a witness for the eternal
'God against them, for which they are
'accounted as the saints of old, *pestilent* Acts xiv.
'*fellows, movers of sedition, turners of the* 5.
'*world upside down,* enemies to Cæsar, and Acts xvii. 6, 7.
'upon this account persecuted; when the
'greatest part of men being unregenerate,
'and having no other spirit in them but
'what is of this world, there is therefore
'no reason why the world should per-
'secute and hate his own.

'5. For magistrates to inflict tempo-
'ral punishments upon any of their sub-
'jects, for not conforming to their de-
'crees, that enjoin any spiritual worship
'or service, is undoubtedly a breach of that
'royal law, which says, *Whatsoever ye* Matt. vii.
'*would that men should do to you, do you* 12.
'*even so them, for this is the law and the*
'*prophets*; and is a sure and standing rule,
'by which all men, if they would deal in-
'genuously by themselves, might measure
'the justice of their proceedings towards
'others. For who, that was not a despe-
'rate enemy to himself, would put out
'another man's eye, if he was sure his
'own should be put out as soon as he
'had done; as he was to be serv'd by
'the judicial law. Neither would those
'that are forward to persecute, be very

'zealous

'zealous in their proceedings, if they
' were sure, that those whom they perse-
' cute should have power on their sides,
' to *mete the same measure unto them.* And
' this is worthy of observation; that this
' rule of doing as we would be done un-
' to, can be receiv'd and pleaded by all
' sorts of men, whilst they are under af-
' fliction and persecution; but who re-
' members it, when they have power to
' afflict and persecute others? The *Pa-*
'*pists* themselves, when out of power,
' in this and other nations, can plead a-
' gainst persecution for their conscience;

Cambden's *Annals of Eliz. p.* 20.
' as they did in the reign of Queen *Eli-*
'*zabeth*, procuring the letters of the Em-
' peror, and other Princes, to intercede
' for some places to be allow'd, where
' they may worship by themselves. But
' in this they desir'd more than themselves
' would allow to others when in power.

As in France.
' So, many of the *Protestants*, where the
' magistrate is different from them in re-
' ligion, can be well pleas'd with a *tole-*
'*ration*: And *Martin Luther* in his ser-
' mon of the good shepherd; english'd
' by *W. G.* in the year 1581, speaking
' of the kingdom of Christ, saith, it is
' not govern'd at all by any force or pow-
' er, but by outward preaching alone,
' that is, by the Gospel. Why, there-
' fore, cannot the *Protestants*, who would
' seem to have an honourable esteem of

' this

'this man, be of the same spirit; and
'the *Papists* be as much for liberty in
'prosperity, as in adversity; seeing the
'Lord *Jesus* hath not directed at one
'time, to the use of force and violence,
'in the work of the Gospel; and at ano-
'ther time, if the civil sword be not to be
'procur'd, then to use arguments and
'persuasions? No, at all times the rule
'which his disciples must take notice of,
'says, *Whatsoever ye would that men should* Matt. vii.
'*do to you, do you even so to them; for* 1, 2.
'*with what measure ye mete, it shall be*
'*measured to you again.*

'And because mystery *Babylon* hath
'not regarded these sayings, but exercis-
'eth all manner of cruelties, and deaths
'upon such as cannot believe as she be-
'lieves and practises; therefore God will
'find out a way to retaliate upon her all
'the blood of his servants; *And in the* As at this
'*cup which she hath filled, shall it be filled to* day.
'*her double. How much she hath glorified* Rev. xviii.
'*herself, and lived deliciously, so much tor-* 6, &c.
'*ment and sorrow give her: for she saith*
'*in her heart, I sit a queen, and am no wi-*
'*dow, and shall see no sorrow. Therefore*
'*shall her plagues come in one day, death,*
'*and mourning and famine, and she shall*
'*be utterly burnt with fire, for strong is*
'*the Lord God who judgeth her. And the*
'*kings of the earth who have committed*
'*fornication, and lived deliciously with*
                                      'her,

'her, shall bewail and lament for her. And
'her merchants, which are the great men
'of the earth, who traffick with her in
'things costly, delicate, and of esteem in the
'world, and in slaves, and souls of men,
'or as by the margin it may be read,
'bodies and souls of men, these also shall
'mourn over her; for no man buyeth their
'merchandize any more. And thus the
'fierceness of God's wrath will overtake
'her, to the sinking of her like a mill-
'stone, into the bottom of the sea; be-
'cause the great weight of innocent blood
'lieth upon her. For in her will be
'found the blood of prophets, and of saints,
'and of all that were slain upon the earth.
'He that therefore would not partake
'with her in any of her plagues, let
'him flee from her, and partake not
'with her in any of her sins; one of the
'greatest being the persecution of men
'for keeping a good conscience. For
'except the great God should cease to be
'what he is, if men repent not of their
'deeds, there will be as certainly punish-
'ment, as there is sin; and it shall not
'be the arm of flesh that will be able to
'support this strumpet, although many
'kingdoms should engage in her quar-
'rel; neither shall the wisdom and pru-
'dence of great statesmen be able to keep
'off her judgments. For if men should
'cease to do any thing against her, yet
'God

'God will make the very elements to
' fight againſt her; and will contend
' with her by famine and peſtilence, yea,
' and fword too, altho' fhe fears it not.
' For God will ſtir up the ten Kings to do
' his will upon her; and by his great
' works, and judgments that he will ma-
' nifeſt in the earth, will he gain him-
' felf a name, and great honour and glory.
' Even ſo, *Amen.*

'As it is no ways lawful from the
' word of God, for chriſtian magiſtrates,
' in the days of the Goſpel, to deſtroy
' and root out the contrary-minded in re-
' ligious matters, tho' idolaters; ſo ſuch
' proceedings may ſometimes prove in-
' conſiſtent, with the very being of nations.
' For ſuppoſe any nation were wholly
' heatheniſh idolaters, and the word of
' God coming in amongſt them, ſhould
' convert the chief magiſtrate, and one
' twentieth part of the nation more; muſt
' he then, with that twentieth part, de-
' ſtroy all the other nineteen, if they will
' not be converted, but continue in their
' heatheniſh idolatry? It cannot poſſibly
' be ſuppos'd to be warrantable. And
' this reaſon holds good, likewiſe, againſt
' the rooting up and deſtroying hereticks
' out of the world; becauſe if the church
' proceeds againſt any of her members to
' excommunication, the church's deport-
' ment towards him ſo caſt out, is to be

Vol. II. I ' the

'the same, as towards a *heathen*. So
'saith Christ himself; *If he neglect to hear
'the church, let him be unto thee as an
'heathen man, and a publican*; who, for
'the aforesaid reason, is not to be de-
'stroy'd because he is so. And moreover,
'seeing the Lord, who is abundantly
'merciful, many times gives repentance
'not only to the unbelieving idolater, but
'also to the excommunicated person; he
'therefore that destroys the body of such a
'one, doth as much as in him lieth destroy
'his soul also. For the Lord, you see, brings
'into his vineyard *some at the third hour,
'some at the sixth, some at the ninth, and
'others at the eleventh*. He, therefore,
'that shall destroy any at the third, or
'sixth hour of the life, hinders his con-
'version, that possibly may be call'd at
'the ninth or eleventh hour; and so may
'be charg'd with bringing eternal loss
'and damage to him whom he destroys.

'OBJECTION. But whereas the example
'of the Kings of *Israel* and *Juda*, is
'made the greatest pillar to support the
'magistrates proceedings under the Gos-
'pel, in persecuting and punishing the
'contrary-minded in religious matters, or
'such as shall be adjudg'd guilty of blas-
'phemy or idolatry; therefore the second
'*canon* of the *English* Church tells us,
'*Whosoever shall affirm, that the King's
'Majesty hath not the same authority in
'causes*

Matt.
xviii. 17.

' caufes ecclefiaftical, that the godly Kings
' had amongft the Jews, fhall be excom-
' municated. But if magiftrates would
' defer perfecuting any man for religion,
' until the clergy had prov'd this unto
' them, it would be happy for the moft
' confcientious under them, and them-
' felves too.

' ANSWER. But in anfwer, we deny
' not, but the Kings of the *Jews* had
' power to punifh idolaters, and blafphe-
' mers, and fome other trangreffors of
' the then law of God: Which power was
' given them of God, and written in plain
' precepts, in the *Mofaical* law. But
' who tells them, that magiftrates under
' the Gofpel difpenfation, hath fuch
' power? Hath the Lord *Jefus* faid any
' fuch thing? Or if he have, where is it
' written? Nay, where is it written from
' the beginning of *Genefis*, to the end of
' the *Revelations*, that magiftrates under
' the Gofpel fhould have the fame power
' in religious caufes, as thofe under the
' law? If the judicial law be a rule for
' magiftrates under the Gofpel to walk
' by; then why 'muft it be mangled in
' pieces, and juft fo much taken of it as
' fuits their intereft, and all the reft re-
' jected? Is it left to magiftrates now, or
' was it ever left to the *Jewifh* Kings, to
' take what part of it they pleafe to be a
' rule to them, and reject all the reft? And

I 2 ' it

'it is eminently remarkable, how this
'plea is by the Clergy themselves, that
'most contend for it, made altogether
'invalid. For by it they will stir up
'the civil magistrate, to punish those that
'dissent from them about the doctrine
'and worship, under the notion of a blas-
'phemer or heretick; and against such
'this law must be held authentick: But
'he that *smiteth, or curseth his father or
'mother*, or *stealeth a man*, or him that
'*committeth adultery*, or *breaketh the sab-
'bath*, who were all them sure to be put
'to death, by the same judicial law;
'yet in these cases they will not tell the
'magistrate it is any rule; but it is to
'be rejected, because here they cannot
'much make it reach their suppos'd here-
'ticks, who they are more jealous of,
'than any of the afore-mention'd offen-
'ders.

'BUT besides; it is observable, that
'the Kings of the *Jews*, all the time
'they kept to the Law of God, had ad-
'vantages to give righteous judgment in
'spiritual causes, which magistrates un-
'der the Gospel have not. For they had
'that standing oracle of God amongst
'them, the *Urim* and *Thummim*, together
'with extraordinary prophets, which in
'all difficult cases they had recourse unto,
'and would infallibly direct them to
'judge according to the mind of God.

'But

' But when thefe Kings became wicked,
' and loft the benefit of the abovefaid ora-
' cle, and extraordinary prophets; then, al-
' though they had the written law a-
' mongft them, did they run headlong into
' fuch grofs miftakes, that the true pro-
' phets of the Lord were fure to be per-
' fecuted; and thofe prophets which
' would prophefy fmooth things unto
' them, were cherifh'd, although many
' times, by heark'ning unto them, they
' loft their kingdoms, lives, and it is to
' be fear'd, fouls and all. How grofly
' did *Ahab* miftake, when he accounted
' *Elijah* the *troubler of Ifrael*; and caus'd
' poor *Micajah* to be imprifon'd, and *fed*
' *with bread and water of affliction*, be-
' caufe he would not help to deceive him,
' as his 400 * time-ferving prophets had
' done? So *Jeremiah* was accus'd for
' feeking the hurt of his nation, and not
' the welfare, and muft be put in a miry
' dungeon; becaufe he in plainnefs deli-
' ver'd the mind of the Lord to the
' King, his princes and people. How,
' therefore, can the *Gentile* rulers affure
' themfelves they do any better than thefe
' rulers did, if they fhall perfecute the
' contrary-minded in religious matters;

* 400 Falfe Prophets muft eat bread at *Jezabel's* table, when *Micajah* muft have bread and water of affliction, *Jer.* xxxviii. 4, 5, 6. as it hath been in our day.

'seeing they have neither an infallible ora-
'cle to enquire at, nor extraordinary pro-
'phet, nor yet such written precepts, as
'the *Jews* under the *Mosaical* law had;
'that did not only direct them what of-
'fenders should be punish'd, but also
'what the particular punishment to every
'several offence should be?

'FURTHERMORE, it is very plain,
'that the Gospel which we live under, is
'clear another dispensation, far different
'in all its ordinances and administrations
'from the law; under which the Lord
'*Jesus* is the only law-giver. Who doth
'not, as *Moses*, proceed against the trans-
'gressors of his precepts by external force
'and power, to the destroying them in
'their bodies and estates in this life;
'but in long-suffering waits on men,
'*not willing they should perish, but rather* 1 Thess. i. 9.
'*that they should repent and be saved.* And 2 Pet. i. 9.
'when any continues in disobedience to Acts xvii. 31.
'the Gospel, his punishment is eternal in
'the world to come. Therefore, as the
'Apostle *Paul* saith, *Judge nothing be-*
'*fore the time, until the Lord come; who*
'*will bring to light hidden things of darkness,*
'*and will make manifest the councels of the*
'*hearts; and then shall every man have*
'*praise of God.* The same Apostle testi-
'fieth of himself, *that he was a blasphemer* 1 Tim. i. 13.
'*and persecutor*; and if the mind of God
'had been, that he should have suffer'd
'death

' death in that condition, how should he
' have had repentance given him, and
' been such a glorious instrument in the
' church, as afterwards he was?

' AND it is too well known, that the
' *Jews* are the great blasphemers against
' our Lord *Jesus Christ*, that are on earth.
' Yet it is not the mind of the Lord,
' they should be destroy'd from the face
' of the earth. For how then should
' the scripture be fulfilled, wherein God
' hath promis'd to call them, and make
' them the most glorious nation on the
' earth? Or how can they be converted,
' if they be not permitted, where the
' Gospel is preach'd? We speak not this
' in favour of any blasphemy, for our
' souls abhor it; but because all men that
' have power in their hands, might be as
' tender of the lives of men, as the most
' righteous and holy God is: Who would
' have men be imitators of himself, in
' mercy and goodness towards others;
' *and maketh his sun to rise on the evil,*
' *and on the good, and sendeth rain on the*
' *just and unjust.*

' IF it shall still be objected, that it is
' inconsistent with the safety and well-
' being of any nation, to allow or tole-
' rate any more ways of worship than
' one: We answer, experience hath
' taught the contrary to several countries
' of *Europe*; as *France*, and the *United*

' Pro-

'Provinces, and several countries of Ger-
'many. Besides, those that say they are
'the servants of God, should conclude
'that to be most for the safety and
'well-being of their countries, which is
'most agreeable to his heavenly will, de-
'clar'd in his word. It was the ruin of
'*Jeroboam*, and almost all the Kings of
'*Israel*, that succeeded him, that they
'would rather act by corrupt principles
'of state policy, than by the word which
'God had spoken. And although God
'had rent ten tribes from *Rehoboam*, and
'given them to him, yet he wanted faith
'to believe his new kingdom could any
'ways be secur'd to him, or kept from
'going back to the lineage of *David*, un-
'less he devis'd some new way of wor-
'ship, to keep the people in their own
'land. And for his so doing, he thought
'he had much reason of state: For what
'*Prince* now will conclude it good po-
'licy, to permit his people to go up
'yearly, into his enemies chief *city* to
'worship; but will conclude it to be a
'notable way to alienate the affections
'of his subjects from him, to his great
'prejudice and detriment? Thus *Jero-*
'*boam* reasons, as by his words appear.

1 Kings
xii. 26,
27, 28.

'Take them at length. *And* Jeroboam
'*said in his heart, Now shall the kingdom*
'*return to the house of* David: *If this*
'*people go up to do sacrifice in the house*
'*of*

' of the Lord at Jerusalem, then shall the
' heart of this people turn again unto their
' lord, even unto Rehoboam king of Ju-
' dah; and they shall kill me. Whereup-
' on the king took counsel, and made two
' calves of gold; and said to them, it is too
' much for you to go up to Jerusalem; be-
' hold thy Gods, O Israel, which brought thee
' out of the land of Egypt. Which policy
' of his procur'd this event, which God
' denounc'd against him; saying, *I will* 1 Kings
' *bring evil upon the house of* Jeroboam, xiv. 10,
' *and will cut off from* Jeroboam *him that* 11.
' *pisseth against the wall, and him that is*
' *shut up, and left in* Israel; *and will take*
' *away the remnant of the house of* Jero-
' boam, *as a man taketh away dung, till*
' *it be all gone*. And for the sin where-
' in he made *Israel* to sin, is he branded
' to all posterity. But on the other hand,
' had he permitted the people to go up to
' *Jerusalem* to worship, and kept the ap-
' pointments of God, tho' seemingly a-
' gainst his present interest; then had the
' promise of God been made good unto
' him, which the prophet *Abijah* declar'd
' long before he came to the kingdom;
' saying, *And it shall be, if thou wilt* Chap. xi.
' *hearken unto all that I command thee, and* 38.
' *wilt walk in my ways, and do that is*
' *right in my sight, to keep my statutes*
' *and commandments, as* David *my servant*
' *did; that I will be with thee, and build*
' thee

'thee a sure house, as I built for David, and will give Israel unto thee. Which things were written for the example of such, as should come after. *Be wise now therefore, O ye kings; be instructed, ye judges of the earth. Serve the Lord with fear, and rejoice with trembling. Kiss the son, lest he be angry, and ye perish from the way, when his wrath is kindled but a little; blessed are all they that put their trust in him.*

Psa. ii. 10, 11, 12.

'WE shall take leave to mind and keep in memory the *liberty of tender consciences*, which the King's Majesty declar'd from *Breda*; and shall yet live in hope and expectation to be partakers of the benefit thereof; being reasonably persuaded, that the same principle that led his Majesty to assert such *Christian Liberty*, still remains with him, to the allowing and protecting his peaceable subjects, in their religious concernments: Humbly praying, that God may order his heart, and the hearts of his great council, to proclaim *liberty* by a law, and *the opening of the prisons to them that are bound*. That these desires may not seem novel, or suggested by us in the day of our distress, we have herewith inserted the testimony of the ancients; which we have collected out of Dr. *Jer. Taylor's liberty of prophesying*, which we pray may be impartially consider'd.

'IT

'IT is obfervable, that reftraining of liberty, impofing upon other mens un-derftanding, being mafters of their con-fciences, and lording it over their faith, came in with the retinue and train of Antichrift: That is, they came as other abufes and corruptions of the church did, by reafon of the iniquity of the times, and the cooling of the firft heats of chriftianity, and the increafe of in-tereft, and the abatement of chriftian fimplicity; when the church's fortune grew better, and her fons grew worfe, and fome of her fathers worft of all. For in the firft 300 years, there was no fign of perfecuting any man for his o-pinion, though at that time there were very horrid opinions commenc'd: For they then were affaulted by new fects, which deftroy'd the common principles of nature, of chriftianity, of innocence, and publick fociety. And they who us'd all the means, chriftian and fpiri-tual, for their difprovement and con-viction, thought not of ufing corporal force, otherwife than by blaming fuch proceedings. To which I add; that all wife princes, till they were overborn with faction, or folicited by peevifh perfons, gave *toleration to differing fects*, &c.

Epift. *p.* 18.

'AND the experience which *Chrift-endom* hath had in this laft age, is ar-
'gument

'gument enough, that *toleration of differing opinions* is so far from disturbing the publick peace, or destroying the interest of princes and commonwealths, that it does advantage to the publick. It secures peace, because there is not so much as the pretence of religion left to persons to contend for it, being already indulg'd to them.

'When the *French* fought against the *Hugonots*, the spilling of her own blood was argument enough, of the imprudence of that way of promoting religion. But since she hath given permission to them, the world is witness, how prosperous she hath been ever since. Indeed, there is great reason for princes to give *toleration to disagreeing persons*, whose opinions by fair means cannot be alter'd. For if the persons be confident, they will serve God according to their persuasions: And if they be publickly prohibited, they will privately convene.

'And it is also a part of Christian Religion, that the liberty of mens consciences should be preserv'd in all things, where God hath not made a limit, or set a restraint; that the soul of man should be free, and acknowledge no master but *Jesus Christ*; that matters spiritual should not be restrain'd by punishments corporal; and that the same meekness

' meekness and charity should be preserv'd
' in the promotion of christianity, that
' gave it foundation, and increment, and
' firmness in the first publication; that
' conclusions should not be more dogma-
' tical than the virtual resolution and effi-
' cacy of the premise; and that the per-
' sons should not more certainly be con-
' demn'd, than their opinions confuted;
' and lastly, that the infirmity of man
' and difficulty of things should be both
' put in ballance, to make abatement in
' the definitive sentences against mens
' persons.

' AND therefore the best of men, and
' most glorious of princes, were always
' ready to give *toleration*, but never to make
' executions for matters disputable: As
' *Eusebius*, in his second book of the life
' of *Constantine*, reports.

' ALSO King *James*, writing to the
' state of the *United Provinces*, dated the
' 6th of *March* 1613, among other
' things, saith; that you charge them to
' maintain peace, by bearing one with
' another, in such differences of opinions
' and judgments. The like counsel in
' the divisions of *Germany*, at the first
' reformation, was thought reasonable by
' the Emperor *Ferdinando*, and his ex-
' cellent son *Maximilian*. For they had
' observ'd that violence did exasperate,
' was unblessed, unsuccessful, and unrea-
                          ' sonable;

'sonable; and therefore they made de-
'crees of *toleration*, and appointed tem-
'pers and expedients to be drawn up by
'discreet persons. And *Emanuel Philibert*,
'Duke of *Savoy*, repenting of his war
'undertaken for religion against the *Pe-
'demontani*, promised them *toleration*,
'and was as good as his word. As much
'is done by the nobility of *Polonia*. So
'that the best princes and best bishops
'gave *toleration* and impunities. Also in
'*Rome* itself, till the time of *Justinian*
'the Emperor, the *Catholicks* and *Nova-
'tians* had churches indifferently permit-
'ted: And the *Popes* were the first
'preachers of force and violence in mat-
'ters of religion; and yet it came not so
'far as death. But the first that preach'd
'that doctrine was *Dominick*, the founder
'of the begging order of *Fryers*; the
'*Fryer's* preachers; in memory of which
'the inquisition is intrusted only to the
'*Fryers* of his order.

'In *England*, altho' the *Pope* had as
'great power here as any where, yet
'there were no executions for matter of
'opinion, until *Henry* IV. who, because
'he usurp'd the crown, was willing by
'all means to endear the clergy, by de-
'stroying their enemies, that so he might
'be sure of them to all his purposes.
'And, indeed, it may become them well
'enough, *who are wiser in their genera-
'tion*

A.D. 525.

' *tion than the children of light:* It may
' possibly serve the policies of evil per-
' sons, but never the pure and chaste de-
' signs of christianity.

' By this time I hope it will not be
' thought reasonable to say; he that teach-
' eth mercy to erring persons, teaches in-
' differency in religion; unless so many
' fathers, and so many churches, and the
' best of Emperors, and all the world,
' till they were abused by tyranny, po-
' pery, and faction, did teach indifferen-
' cy. For I have shew'd, that christiani-
' ty does not punish corporally, persons
' erring spiritually; but, indeed, *popery*
' does; and hath done ever since they
' were taught it by their St. *Dominick*.

' And yet after all this, I have some-
' thing to exempt myself from the cla-
' mour of this objection. For let all er-
' rors be as much and as zealously sup-
' press'd as may be; but let it be done
' by such means, as are proper instru-
' ments of their suppression, by preach-
' ing and disputation (so that neither of
' them breed disturbance) by charity and
' sweetness, by holiness of life, and as-
' siduity of exhortation, by the word of
' God and prayer; For these ways are
' most natural, most prudent, most peace-
' able and effectual. Only let not men
' be hasty in calling every dislik'd opi-
' nion by the name of heresy; and when
'   ' they

'they have resolv'd that they will call it
'it so, let them use the erring person
'*like a brother*; not beat him like a dog,
'or convince him with a gibbet, or vex
'him out of his understanding and per-
'suasion.

'Why are we so zealous against those
'we call *Hereticks*, and yet great friends
'with drunkards, and fornicators, and
'swearers, and intemperate and idle per-
'sons? I am certain that a drunkard is as
'contrary to God, and lives as contrary to
'the laws of christianity, as a *Heretick*:
'And I am also sure, that I know what
'drunkenness is; but I am not sure, that
'such an opinion is heresy, *&c.* Thus
'far Dr. *Taylor*, now Bishop of *Down*.

'Now whereas we have given pub-
'lickly an account of the former ages, in
'their carriages and behaviours towards
'persons differing in judgment in religi-
'ous things; we take the leave humbly
'to desire, and beg the same privilege,
'as was granted unto the *Waderdopers*,
'by the Prince and State of the *Nether-
'lands*: Which was to admit a publick
'dispute, between the ministers and the
'persons aforesaid, in the presence of the
'Prince, which we humbly conceive is
'but a reasonable request.'

In this year was publish'd a small piece, written by Dr. *John Griffith*, a *Baptist* mini-

minister, who afterwards suffer'd a long imprisonment in *Newgate* for the cause of Christ; entitled, *A complaint of the oppress'd against oppressors: or, The unjust and arbitrary proceedings of some Soldiers and Justices, against some sober godly persons in and near* London, *who now lie in stinking goals for the testimony of a good conscience; with some reasons why they cannot swear allegiance to obtain their liberty.* It is introduc'd thus:

John Griffith's complaint of the oppress'd against oppressors.

‘THE unjust proceedings of some
‘ in present power, against many
‘ in this nation fearing God, cannot but
‘ be manifest to such sober men, that
‘ do or will take a view of the same. I
‘ having knowledge of the sufferings of
‘ many godly persons, especially in and
‘ about *London*, whom their very adver-
‘ saries cannot blemish justly with the
‘ least spot of infamy, dare not but
‘ let the world know the innocency of
‘ the men, and the tyranny of their op-
‘ pressors. And in what I shall say, I
‘ dare appeal to the consciences of all so-
‘ ber and judicious persons, of what per-
‘ suasion soever, except the proud *prelate*;
‘ whether it be not *tyranny* to the height,
‘ for men to be seiz'd and taken out of
‘ their beds, at midnight by soldiers, in
‘ a hostile manner, with their swords
‘ drawn; by means of which their wives

‘ and

'wives and children have been much af-
'frighted to their great detriment in point
'of health; and this done in a time of
'peace, and without warrant from any,
'no not so much as a warrant from a Ju-
'stice of Peace. Others taken from their
'peaceable meetings, when they have
'been in the Lord's service in a publick
'manner, the doors being open for all
'that would come in to see what they
'did, and hear what they said. Others at-
'tack'd as they have pass'd along the streets,
'about their lawful employments. And
'all this done by soldiers, without war-
'rant from any, and by them carried be-
'fore some men call'd *Justices*, but such
'only in name and title, nothing so in
'truth.'

John Sturgion's plea for toleration.

In this year also, Mr. *John Sturgion*, a *Baptist*, wrote a Tract, which he entitled, *A plea for toleration of opinions and persuasions in matters of religion differing from the Church of* England*: Humbly presented to the King's most excellent Majesty.* Which he introduces in this manner:

' *May it please your Majesty,*

' I HAVE had strong impulses upon
' my mind, for some days, to present
' this paper to your Majesty. And I
' humbly hope it will not be made to
' suffer

'suffer much under an evil resentment,
'upon its presentation to your hand,
'because it bears a testimony of the
'*Author*'s good affection to your roy-
'al self. For my witness is on high;
'that I did not write this paper because I
'love you not, because I honour you
'not, because I own you not, in your
'royal capacity of magistracy and civil
'power. God knoweth, that you have
'not any subject more christianly real or
'cordial unto you. I humbly beg, that
'your Majesty would be pleas'd so far to
'deny yourself, as to read it with pati-
'ence, and to judge of it as you shall
'see cause.'

AFTER some reasonings with his Majesty, respecting the prohibition of all *meetings* whatsoever, he thus expresseth himself:

'AND may it further please your Ma- P. 7.
'jesty, to consider your afflicted and in-
'nocent subjects, how they have been
'hall'd from their peaceable habitations,
'and thrust into *prisons*, almost in all
'*counties* in *England*; and many are still
'detain'd, to the utter undoing of them-
'selves and families: And most of them
'are poor men, whose livelihood, under
'God, depends upon the labour of their
'own hands. So that they lie under
'more than an ordinary calamity; there
'being

'being so many thrust into little rooms
'together, that they are an annoyance each
'to other; especially in the *City* of *Lon-*
'*don*, where the *Lord-Mayor* crouds
'them very close together; that it hath
'been observ'd, the keepers have com-
'plain'd they have had too many guests;
'and whilst they suffer there, some of
'their wives and tender babes want bread
'at home.'

THEN he lays before his Majesty six reasons against restraining, or using force in matters of religion: And says,

P. 17.
'Now if your Majesty will but con-
'sider, what it is which the *baptized peo-*
'*ple*, and divers others, have made such
'earnest suit to your Majesty for: It is
'not for *titles of honour*, nor for *places*
'*of great profit*, either in a *civil* or *eccle-*
'*siastical capacity*: But only this is their
'request and humble desire, that we may
'serve the Lord without molestation, in
'that faith and order, which we have
'learn'd in the Holy Scripture; giving
'honour to our King, to whom honour
'belongs, fear to whom fear, tribute to
'whom tribute belong; in every thing,
'as far as we have abilities, to render to
Rom. xiii. 'God the things that are God's, and to
7. 'the magistrate the things that are
'his.'

A

A SUDDEN ſtorm ariſing now, from I know not what ſurmiſe of a plot, and thereby danger ariſing to the government; the meetings of the Diſſenters were broken up throughout the city, and ſuch as were there found, were put into priſon. Among whom Dr. *John Griffith*, author of the afore-mention'd complaint of the oppreſs'd, was apprehended and committed to *Newgate*, where he lay ſeventeen months for no other crime but preaching to a congregation of *Proteſtants*.

THIS ſtorm was not confin'd to the city, but alſo reach'd the country. For the worthy Mr. *Thomas Grantham*, and ſome others, were taken from their meeting at *Boſton* in *Lincolnſhire*, by ſome ſoldiers, who lodg'd them all night in a publick inn: Where they continu'd ſwearing and curſing inceſſantly, to the no ſmall grief of Mr. *Grantham* and his companions, he and two more only being detain'd, and the reſt being diſmiſs'd. In the morning he with his companions were convey'd to the common goal at *Lincoln*, and there confin'd; where they met with one Mr. *Cox*, who had been committed there before them. In this place were they detain'd till the aſſizes, without ſo much as the leaſt pretence of any crime laid to their charge. It was rumour'd about by ſome, that Mr. *Grantham* was a *Pa-piſt*;

Ellwood's *life.*

pift; and several of the clergy, who came to see him during his confinement, affirm'd to his face that he was a *Jesuit*. In order to remove this slander, he publish'd a controversy he had with a *Roman Catholick*; and entitled it, *The Baptist against the Papist*. By which prudent conduct he happily put an end to that scandalous report; tho' it was the ordinary aspersion cast on those of the *Baptist persuasion*, and then design'd not so much to bring reproach on their persons as their profession. However at the assizes no one appearing, and no crime being alledg'd against them, they were dismiss'd: And they return'd to the churches to which they belong'd, who express'd no little joy for their deliverance, after fifteen months imprisonment. During this confinement, Mr. *Grantham* wrote his book, entitled, *The prisoner against the prelate: or, a dialogue between the common Goal of* Lincoln, *and the Cathedral*. From several passages, in which it appears, that the sufferings of the *Baptists* were numerous, the persecutions against them, were carried on with great vehemence by the clergy, who thought it not sufficient to imprison their persons, and take away their liberty, unless they could also take away their good names. They therefore spread several scandalous reports about them, as if the persons they

they injur'd were *Papists, Jesuits,* and immoral persons. However their demeanour was so peaceable, and their behaviour in prison so edifying, they being very much employ'd in praying to, and praising God; and in holy conversation with one another, or private meditations; that they gain'd the reputation of being godly men, who suffer'd for conscience sake: while the clergy were look'd on as persecutors of those, who were better than themselves; and as having an eye in what they did more to their own interest than the honour of Christ.

The Mayor of *Dover,* Mr. *John Home,* and the Justices there, began very early to shew themselves, and their zeal against their dissenting neighbours, more particularly the *Baptists.* Upon which, one who stil'd himself *a poor subject,* wrote the following letter to them.

' *To the honour'd the Mayor, and Justices*
  ' *of this town.*

' WE desire to let you know, yet *Manuscipt*
' once more, that we do acknow- *penes me.*
' ledge your power, and do desire to
' submit unto it, so far as we are engag'd
' by the rule of truth. But we do hum-
' bly conceive, that your power doth not
    ' reach

'reach so far as to tie our consciences, to
'worship our God according to your man-
'ner. We must not see with your eyes,
'but we must worship God according to
'that light, that he hath been pleas'd to
'give unto us from the scriptures of truth.
'But haply you may say, that you have
'the scriptures as well as we, and more
'learning than we have to understand
'them. And so far we may agree, that
'you have the scriptures, and more human
'learning than we: But we must intreat
'you to excuse us in this, that we dare
'not worship the true God in a false
'manner, according to the traditions of
'men, according to the revolutions of
'ages; as we humbly conceive you do,
'with the rest of the nations, tho' not
'in such a gross manner of idolatry as
'some other nations do. But we do not
'know how soon you may be as vile as
'the worst of them. We have great cause
'to fear such a thing, because in one
'thing you are more vile already; in
'that there is liberty given by some o-
'ther nations, and also in this nation,
'more than in this place. We intreat
'you in the bowels of love to consider
'of it. We know you have knowledge,
'but we intreat you to take heed you be
'not puff'd up in your knowledge;
'which if you be, it will cause you to
'be

'be so blind, that you will act quite
'contrary to truth, and to your own
'knowledge. We hope you will not be
'offended, because you know it is the
'exhortation of the Apostle *Paul*, and
'it is his testimony, that *knowledge* will
'*puff up*, if there be not good care taken.
'So we shall leave at present, these
'things to your judgment and considera-
'tion.

'If any friend, says he, seem to be offend-
'ed with my beginning, and judge me to
'offend in giving such titles unto men,
'judging it to be flattering titles; I de-
'sire to be excus'd, inasmuch as I have
'no intent to flatter. But as at present, I
'judge it my duty to give that honour
'unto men in their places, as they are
'set; so I judge not without the provi-
'dence of God, or at least, God doth
'suffer it so to be, that they have the
'power; and I am bound to honour
'them, however they may be persuaded
'to persecute me, and think it their duty
'so to do, and judge me to be an here-
'tick. But that I must leave to God,
'that will judge all in righteousness, with-
'out respect of persons, powers and sub-
'jects, rich and poor; there will be no
'respect with God in judgment. There-
'fore whatsoever the judgment of some
'may be, as touching the civil honour
'and titles belonging to men in power;

'I

'I defire to be excus'd, in giving to man,
'that belongs to him in his place, altho'
'I may fuffer never fo much evil at
'their hands.

'By me *James Atkins*, in the
'behalf of us all, that are like
'to be prohibited of our liber-
'ties, by the envy of fome in-
'ftruments, that are foliciting
'the magiftrate to that pur-
'pofe.'

THE magiftrates of *Dover* were very fevere upon thefe people. They took them from their meeting-houfe in the year 1660, and committed them to prifon. After keeping them there four and twenty days, they were admitted to bail, paying their charges; and appearing at the next *feffions*, were forbid to meet any more at their meeting-houfe, and allow'd to meet together in one of the churches. The which they did every Lord's-day for about the fpace of five months, meeting together about eleven in the morning, and continuing till about three in the afternoon. This privilege being denied them by the fucceeding *Mayor*, they affembled again at their own meeting-place. The *Mayor* difturb'd them, took their names, and warn'd them to appear at the *hall*. They appear'd, and four of them, viz.
Thomas

Thomas Williams, Chriſtopher Streetind, John Hales and *James Houſon*, were committed to priſon. The next Lord's-day the *Mayor* diſturb'd them again, took their names, and ſent ſix who were country-men to priſon; viz. *Thomas Partridge, John Finis, Edmund Finis, Simon Loveleſs, John Barrows,* and *John Hobbs*: And the next Lord's-day after ſent four more. The *Mayor* diſturb'd them a fourth time, and then committed them all, being ten in number. At the *Quarter-ſeſſions*, a bill of indictment was found againſt them, ſome travers'd it, others ſubmitted to the court, and the reſt were remitted to priſon again.

These hardſhips under which they groan'd, at length ſtirr'd them up to ſeek for mercy from the higher powers: And thereupon they drew up a petition to the King, and ſoon after another to the Duke of *York*. I have plac'd them together; and they are in their own words, as followeth:

' *To the ſupreme magiſtrate of theſe Na-*
' *tions,* Charles II. *King of* England,
' Scotland *and* Ireland, *and the Domi-*
' *nions thereto belonging, together with*
' *his honourable Privy-Council.*

' THE humble petition of many *Manu-*
' of thoſe poor ſuffering diſtreſs'd *ſcript pe-*
' people, falſely call'd *Anabaptiſts*, in the *nes me.*
             ' behalf

'behalf of themselves and many others,
'differing from those called *Church of
'England*, in matter of faith, and also
'form of worship; who, notwithstanding,
'do walk in all good conscience to-
'wards God, and in sincerity of heart,
'do also acknowledge the King to be
'chief in all temporal things, and there-
'fore do and shall yield, in all temporal
'things, due obedience unto him, *not only
'for wrath but for conscience sake*; and so
'in all things shall give unto the King that
'which is his, and unto God that which
'only belongs unto himself.

'Now therefore, may it please your
'Highness to lay to heart what hath
'been formerly in humility presented
'unto you, by way of petition and ad-
'vice relating to liberty of conscience,
'the innocent desires of your peaceable
'subjects; and let our lives, and the lives
'of our wives and children be precious
'in your eyes, for we are free-born
'*Englishmen*, and one flesh as the flesh
'of others. O be pleased to consider,
'that those that have had the greatest
'means of light, and have been as zea-
'lous as any, yet they have pluckt up
'the wheat instead of tares, and have kil-
'led the most precious children of God
'instead of the children of the wicked
'one. O let our words be acceptable
'unto you, *for the wisdom that comes
'from*

'*from above is first pure*, and teacheth all
' men to do as they would be done
' unto ; *it is peaceable, gentle, and easy to
' be intreated, full of mercy*; yea, the
' great things of God's law, *are judgment,
' mercy and faith.* Moreover, the Gospel
' is *the Gospel of peace* ; and so the Apo-
' stles made it their work, not to force,
' but to persuade men. And as our *Savi-*
' *our* saith, that five should be in one house,
' three against two, and two against three,
' and so commonly the poor sheep and
' lambs of Christ have much tribula-
' tion, but in him having peace they
' bear it patiently. O be pleased there-
' fore to consider, how disagreeable it
' is with christianity, to bring tribula-
' tion upon any for conscience sake, see-
' ing all things in worship must be done
' in faith and love. But nevertheless,
' your peaceable subjects are liable to
' the penalty of such laws and statutes,
' as enjoin such service and conformity,
' as in conscience to God we cannot do
' in faith and love ; the penalty of which
' statutes are such, as in a little time,
' if prosecuted, will work out ruin to
' ourselves and families.

' Now here, we humbly beseech
' your Highness, to take into serious
' consideration the deplorable condition of
' your peaceable Subjects, and to grant unto
' us what you were pleased to promise,

' upon

'upon the word of a King, at *Breda*,
'and also since your arrival; not only
'by your declaration for ecclesiastical
'affairs, but also at several other times
'to several of us, when we made our
'addresses unto you; and therefore we
'do crave these things with the more
'boldness and confidence, forasmuch as
'innocency is found in us, and against
'the King and his Government we
'have done no harm, whatever may be
'reported to the contrary, to our re-
'proach. These premises considered,
'we pray, we may not be interrupted
'in our worshipping the God of Hea-
'ven, as we are taught in his holy
'word, which indeed we do prize
'above all the world. The which, if
'we shall enjoy, will greatly encourage
'us to pray and praise the Lord on
'your behalf, which *rules the hearts*
'*of Kings, as the rivers of water.*

'BUT if notwithstanding what hath
'been and is desired, we shall be denied,
'that which we humbly conceive, the
'law of God and Nature doth allow
'us; yet we shall, in the strength of
'the Lord, patiently suffer what shall
'be inflicted upon us. *For the weapons*
'*of our warfare are not carnal, but spi-*
'*ritual and mighty, to the pulling down of*
'*strong-holds.*

To his Highness the Duke of York.

'FORASMUCH as the all-disposing hand of God's providence hath brought your Highness into this place; we hope it is, that by you, as a fit instrument to so good a work, to deliver us, his harmless people, and peaceable subjects to the King. And inasmuch as what is done unto us, is done in your name; we humbly lay before you, that many of us inhabitants of this town, [*Dover*] for the space of six weeks, have been imprisoned, for no other cause, but for our peaceable meeting to worship our God, and thereby are brought into great straits; some of our families, being numerous, whose daily supply dependeth on our daily labour; so that our wants and straits are like to be very great, by reason of our present sufferings. And forasmuch as the like is not done to our friends in other places, but the King is pleased to protect them as his peaceable subjects, we think it hard measure to be thus dealt withal, our offence being no more criminal than theirs.

' THE premises considered, we humbly intreat your Highness to shew mercy to us, your peaceable yet oppressed subjects, in setting us at liberty, that
' the

'the cries of our little ones and fami-
'lies, by reason of our sufferings, do
'not provoke the great God of mercy
'and truth against this land of our na-
'tivity. And if you please to answer
'our desires, we are sure God will re-
'ward you an hundred fold; since he
'hath promised, that he that giveth
'but a cup of cold water to any of his
'suffering people, shall not lose his
'reward; and you will engage us so
'much the more, both to speak well
'of, and pray for you. In this reso-
'lution we subscribe ourselves, in the
'innocency of our souls, in the sight
'of God,

James Houson   *John Finis*
Simon Loveless *Tho. Partridge*
John Hales   *Tho. Williams.*

From the Prison in Dover, *the
17th day of the 9th month,* 1661.

The perse-   IN the year 1662, was published a
cution of small pamphlet, intitled, *Behold a Cry;*
the Bap-
tists about or, a true relation of the inhuman and violent
London. outrages *of divers Soldiers, Constables and
others, practised upon many of the Lord's
people, commonly, tho' falsely called* Anabaptists, *at their several meetings in and about*
London, and is thus introduced:

THE

English Baptists.

'THE sundry and divers abuses that hath been offered time after time to the free-born people of *England*, contrary to *Magna Charta*, and the *Petition of right* and all the known laws of the land, the declaration and proclamation of the King that now is, we cannot suppose the nation wholly ignorant of. But how inhumanly they have been used, and with what violence soldiers and others have proceeded in several places where they have, in the fear of the Lord, been assembled: Their usual manner being to come with soldiers, which commonly were most of them rude youths or mercenary men, of the ruder and viler sort; and they with their muskets, and some with their swords drawn, to the affrighting of women and children, breaking and spoiling their goods, doing violence to their persons, by pulling, halling, and beating some of them, the which they may not understand. Now that all, both *Magistrates* and People, may be rightly informed, the mouth of falsehood and scandal stopped, and such abuses redressed; we shall, in particular, give a brief hint of some of them as followeth:

'IN *June* 1661, there came divers rude soldiers, wicked, swearing, and

Brick-lane Meeting-house disturb'd and more than 20 seiz'd.

'debauched persons, to the meeting-
' house in *Brick-lane* near *White-Chapel*,
' and laid hands on several men, to the
' number of more than *twenty*; who,
' in a peaceable manner, demanded of
' them their warrant for so doing, but
' they would not shew them any, which

Wm. Caswell sorely abused.

' one *William Caswell* seeing, he said to
' this purpose, that if they had a warrant
' he would obey it; but if they had
' none they should carry him for he
' would not go: With that they beat
' him with their hangers about the head,
' and pulled him along by force; and
' sometimes taking him up between
' three or four of them, and then let-
' ting him fall with violence into the
' dirt; pulling by great force his sto-
' mach and breast against the rails; inso-
' much that with blows and falls he is
' deprived of health to this day. And
' when there were several of the actors
' of this tragedy arrested, * and sute be-
' ing, according to law, commenced a-
' gainst them, and the persons abused
' intending to go on, they were sudden-
' ly surprized and prevented by *John*
' *Robinson*, who granted a warrant to
'   seize

---

* The King in his proclamation, *Jan.* 10, 1660, declared that if any should be so hardy as to seize the persons of any without warrant, &c. that then they should be left open to the law to be proceeded against, and receive according to their demerit.

'seize the body of *Thomas Hull* and
'the abovesaid *William Caswel*. The
'said *Thomas Hull* being taken in the
'street, by virtue of the aforesaid war-
'rant, and carried before *John Robin-*
'*son*, who in a fury demanded how he
'durst arrest his soldiers, and would
'not take bail, but sent him to *New-*
'*gate,* and one with him, who only
'came along with his friend, the said
'*Thomas Hull,* and desired to bail him;
'where they both lay about ten or twelve
'days before they could be bailed, and
'were held bound from sessions to ses-
'sions, for a long time after, before they
'could be discharged. So little was the
'King's proclamation regarded by *John*
'*Robinson.*

Tho. Hull and his friends who came to bail him, both imprisoned by John Robinson, a great prosecutor.

'Secondly, ON the 20th of *October*
'1661, there came a parcel of the afore-
'said rude soldiers to the meeting at
'*Brick-lane,* and took away one that
'was then preaching. Some there de-
'sired them to shew their warrant for
'their so doing: One lieutenant *Wilton*
'shewed his commission as he was an
'officer; which being read, he said,
'that was sufficient. One answering,
'said, that was not sufficient, he ought
'to have a particular warrant, with the
'name of the person seiz'd expressed in
'it, and under the hand and seal of
'some one justice or more. One en-
'sign

'sign *Spike* answered, if that were not
'sufficient, it was sufficient, Sir *John
'Robinson*, as he called him, bid them
'by word of mouth to do what they
'did. To which was answered, that
'a verbal order from him, or any other
'justice else, was not according to law
'in such a case, neither did the law in-
'title them to be executioners of it;
'but if they had a warrant, as they
'had none, it ought to be directed to
'some peace officer, and not to them.

A Baptist Minister seiz'd without warrant, and sent to Newgate.

'Yet notwithstanding they carried him
'away to the *Tower*, before *John Robin-
'son*, who sent him to *Newgate*, pre-
'tending and inserting great matters in
'his *mittimus*; where he lay *thirty weeks*,
'without any thing laid to his charge,
'and then they released him.

'Thirdly, On the 3d day of *Novem.*
'1661, they came again in the like
'manner to the aforesaid place, in as rude
'a manner as before, and with as little
'a shew or face of law: They seized
'him that was preaching, as one was
'at that time; and when they had ta-
'ken him down, they took away three
'more; two of which were sitting at
'the table. Whom they carried before

Another Minister and three more sent to New-Prison.

'*John Robinson*, who committed them
'all to *New-Prison*; inserting in their
'*Mittimus*, things of an high nature;
'as their speaking of treasonable words,
'and

' and the like. When some questioned
' the legality of their seizure, he, *John*
' *Robinson,* reply'd, with some indigna-
' tion, that he sent them to do what
' they did; as if his verbal command
' were sufficient to justify their illegal
' proceedings. And at *Sessions* following,
' there was one of them remov'd in time
' of *Sessions*, only by *John Robinson's*
' warrant from *New-Prison* to *Newgate*;
' in order, as he said, to his trial, which
' he could never attain to have, nor
' any thing laid to his charge, tho' he
' often called for it in the face of the
' *Court*, but had no notice taken of him,
' nor never returned in the calendar;
' yet was he kept in *Newgate* twelve weeks
' unjustly, 'till he was fetched out by a
' person in authority. He suffered in all
' near *eighteen weeks* imprisonment; and the
' rest of his fellows suffered *twenty-eight*
' *weeks* imprisonment, and then were re-
' leased, nothing being laid to their charge.'

IT was about this time, that a con-gregation of *Baptists* holding the *seventh-day* as a *sabbath*, being assembled at their meeting-house in *Bulstake Alley*, the doors being open, about three of the clock in the afternoon, whilst Mr. *John James* was preaching, one Justice *Chard*, with Mr. *Wood*, an *Headborough*, came into the meeting-place. *Wood* commanded him in the King's name to be silent, and come down,

J. James's meeting disturbed.

down, having spoken treason against the King: But Mr. *James* taking little or no notice thereof, proceeded in his work. The *Headborough* came nearer to him in the middle of the meeting-place, and commanded him again in the King's name to come down, or else he would pull him down; whereupon the disturbance grew so great, he could not proceed, but told the *Headborough* he would not come down, except he was pulled down: Whereupon he pulled him down, and halled him away, being charged with treasonable words uttered in his sermon, by one *Tipler*, a pipe-maker's journey-man. Who being a scandalous idle-fellow, the Justice took not much notice of what he said; but bringing a neighbour with him, he was provok'd by him to regard his testimony.

His hearers sent to prison.

John Robinson with three more Justices of the Peace, sitting at the *Half-moon* tavern, both *men* and *women* who were at the meeting, were brought before them by *sevens*. To whom they tender'd the oath of allegiance, and committed those that refus'd, some to *Newgate*, both *men* and *women* being guarded thither by the *Hamlets*.

Narrative p. 8

‘ AFTERWARDS the same *Justices*,
‘ entring the meeting-place, sat down a-
‘ bout the table with their clerk; and
‘ Major *Stanley* standing by, did send for
‘ *John*

'*John James.* And in the mean time
' the Lieutenant of the Tower read a pa-
' per which he pull'd out of his pocket;
' saying, he would read to them what
' doctrine was preach'd there that day;
' being of the nature of a charge, which
' they drew up from *Tipler*'s mouth a-
' gainst *John James*; demanding of cer-
' tain *women*, relating to the meeting,
' yet detain'd, and whose names they
' were then taking, how they could hear
' such things as those? To which they
' unanimously reply'd in the fear of the
' Lord, *That they never heard such words,
' as they shall answer it before the Lord,
' and they durst not lie.*

John James being brought before them into the meeting-place, *John Robinson* examin'd him. Among other questions put to him, were these following, *viz.* *Himself examined.*

' WHETHER he had not been before
' him before this? Who answer'd, he had:
· And whether he had not been civilly
' us'd? He reply'd, yea; and for his ci
' vility he thank'd him. Then the *Lieu
' tenant* ask'd him, if he was not coun
' sell'd for to take heed for the future?
' He answer'd, yea; and he had taken it
' so far as he could with a good consci
' ence. Upon which the *Lieutenant* told
' him, he should *stretch* for it; and if he
' were not *hang'd*, he would be *hang'd*
for him. *John James* told him, he was
' not

'not careful in that matter; and that they
'could do no more, then they should be
'suffer'd by the Lord to do. The *Lieu-
'tenant* told him, he thought he was not
'careful; for he had a mind to be *hang'd*,
'as some of his *holy brethren* that went
'before him? *John James* desir'd he
'would not speak so lightly. The *Lieu-
'tenant* spake something to him about
'the *fifth kingdom*; and ask'd him, whe-
'ther that was his principle? Who told
'him, he did own the *fifth-kingdom*,
'which was to come. Whereupon they
'laugh'd one upon another, and said, now
'they had it from his own mouth. Some-
'thing also was charg'd upon him about his
'learning to sound a trumpet, in order
'to a rising with *Venner*'s party. To
'which he said, there was a friend of
'his who lay in his house, minding to
'go to sea, being to learn to sound, de-
'sir'd he might have liberty to be
'taught in his house; but he never
'learn'd himself, neither was he one of
'those in that *rising*, judging it to be a
'*rash act*.

'Then the *Lieutenant* of the *Tower*,
'call'd in Captain *Hodgskin*, who com-
'manded the party of soldiers that stood
'at the door: And said, take this *man*,
'be careful of him, and commit him
'close prisoner to *Newgate*. So they
'carried him away with his *Mittimus*,
'hereafter express'd.   'To

'To the keeper of the goal of Newgate,
' or his deputy; Middlesex.

'THESE are in the King's Majesty's
' name, to require you to receive into
' your custody, the body of *John*
' *James*, whom we send you here-
' with; being taken this present day
' at a *Conventicle* or private meeting,
' in the parish of *White-chapel*; and
' there speaking in the audience of the
' people present, *treasonable words* a-
' gainst his Majesty's royal person.
' You shall therefore keep him close
' prisoner until further order; and this
' shall be your warrant. Given under
' our hands, this 19th day of *October*
' 1661.

And committed to prison.

        ' *John Robinson*, Lieut. of
' the Tower; *Thomas Bide*,
' *Edw. Chard*, *Tho. Swallow*.

I SHALL refer the reader to the narrative, publish'd in 1662, where he may see the crimes charg'd against him; how prov'd, by whom, and in what manner; with his defence and avow'd innocency, from first to last; and his solemn appeals to the Lord thereupon, that by some signal testimony, he would manifest the same. Of which no judgment is there
pass'd,

pass'd, but submitted to the discerning and impartial reader.

His wife petitions the King for him.

IN the interval between his casting and condemnation, upon *Wednesday* evening, his wife, by the advice of some friends, endeavour'd to make address to the King, to acquaint him with her husband's innocency, and the condition of those loose persons, who had falsely accus'd him. Which she put in writing, lest she might either want an opportunity, or not have courage enough to speak to him. With some difficulty at last she met the King, and presented him with the paper, acquainting him who she was. To whom he held up his finger and said,

Narrative, p. 24.

'Oh! Mr. James, *he is a sweet gentle-* '*man;*' but following him for some further answer, the door was shut against her.

Is rejected.

THE next morning she attended again; and an opportunity soon presenting, she implor'd his Majesty's answer to her request. Who then reply'd, '*That* '*he was a rogue, and should be hang'd.*' One of the Lord's attending him, ask'd her of whom she spake. The King answer'd, '*Of* John James, *that rogue; he* '*shall be hang'd; yea, he shall be hang'd.*'

WHEN he was brought to the bar to receive sentence; he was ask'd what he had to say for himself, why sentence of death should not be pass'd upon him.

He

He anſwer'd, 'That he had not much to ſay, only two or three ſcriptures he would leave with them.

'THE firſt ſcripture was, *Jer.* xxvi. *v.* 14, 15. *As for me, do as ſeemeth good unto you. But know ye for certain, that if you put me to death, you ſhall ſurely bring innocent blood upon yourſelves, and upon this city, and upon the inhabitants thereof.*

'THE ſecond ſcripture was, *Pſalms* cxvi. 15. *Precious in the ſight of the Lord is the death of his ſaints.* He alſo minded that good word of the Lord: *He that toucheth the Lord's people, toucheth the apple of his eye.*

'HE told them, he had no more to ſay for himſelf; only one word for the Lord, and ſo he had done:

'THAT *Jeſus Chriſt*, the ſon of God, was King of *England*, *Scotland*, and *Ireland*, and of all the kingdoms of this world.'

WHICH being ſpoken, they ſilenc'd him, and the court proceeded to ſentence; and the Judge pronounc'd ſentence of death againſt him; and he was executed, according to his ſentence, at *Tyburn, Nov.* 26. 1661. *He is executed at Tyburn.*

Now if there was any undue combination againſt this poor man; if it was for ſome reaſon of ſtate, rather than for any real guilt on his part; if his judgment

ment and confcience, rather than any juft crime, were the caufe of his thus fuffering; his blood muft be innocent blood.

SOME remarkable things are taken notice of in the Narrative, publifh'd after his death, as befalling thofe, who had been inftruments in his fufferings, or had exprefs'd a delight in them. But I chufe to pafs them over in filence.

THE blood of this poor man, did not fatiate that devouring wolf *John Robinfon*: For many (who fuffer'd much from the brutifh hands of his foldiers, to whom he gave money to encourage them in their barbarity) were by him committed to prifon.

Anno 1662.
Behold a cry, p. 5.

' ON the 25th of *May* 1662: At a
' meeting in *Shakefpear's-walk*, near *Wapping-wall*, where fome people were
' peaceably met, there came foldiers in a
' hoftile manner, with fwords and muskets,
' pulling and halling fome of them; and
' the man that was preaching, they pull'd
' violently down from the place where
' he ftood, though it was his own hired
' houfe. And fuch was their rage, notwithftanding he was their prifoner, because he continu'd fpeaking, they cry'd,
' fhoot him, before he had any *trial*, or
' was found worthy or not worthy of
' death. And fuch was their violence,
' that a child belonging unto the family,
' about

' about a year and a quarter old, was so
' affrighted and awak'd out of its sleep,
' as it lay in the cradle; with which
' fright it fell sick, and never recover'd
' its sickness, but died three days after.
' And whether they were the cause of
' its death or no, is left to the Lord to
' determine at the last day. They car- *Two more*
' ried *two* of the said meeting before *imprison'd*
' *John Robinson*; who committed them *by John Robinson:*
' to *Newgate*, where they still remain,
' nothing being laid to their charge.

' On the same 25th of *May*, the sol- *Ibidem,* p.
' diers came to *Beech-lane*, to a meeting 6.
' there, with their swords drawn, pul-
' ling and halling of them violently: And *Two car-*
' *two* of them they carried in the morn- *ried to*
' ing to *Newgate*; where they were kept, *Newgate without a*
' and never had before any *magistrate* to *mittimus.*
' be heard, nor accus'd by any till the
' *quarter-sessions*, which was a month or
' five weeks after.

' On the first day of *June* 1662, they
' came to the aforesaid *Beech-lane*, with
' their swords drawn as before. The *En-*
' *sign* came in with his sword drawn,
' holding it over the head of him that
' was preaching; pulling them violently
' down the stairs, carrying them to
' *Paul's-yard*, and from thence to *Ri-* *Some sent*
' *chard Brown*, who committed them to *to New-*
' *Newgate.* *gate by Richard*
' On *Brown.*

'On the first day of *June* 1662, the
'soldiers came to *Brick-lane* in like vio-
'lent manner, with swords and muskets;
'and forced him that was speaking down,
'with great outrage; and carried *ten* of
'the men before *John Robinson*, who
'after his wonted manner committed
'them to *New-prison*. This was in the
'morning. And in the afternoon they
'came again with far greater violence;
'broke the pulpit all to pieces, they left
'not a whole piece of wood; and car-
'ried *eight* more to the *Tower*, before
'*John Robinson*, who committed them to
'*New-prison* also. But not to omit an
'act worthy the observing; *John Robin-*
'*son* as he came at night by the watch-
'house, at *Brick-lane* end, where the
'valiant soldiers were keeping guard;
'they told him what they had done, how
'they had broken the pulpit? He, *John*
'*Robinson*, answer'd, it was well done;
'and gave the soldiers a piece of gold, as
'a reward for their good service.

Ten sent to New-Prison by Robinson.

Eight more committed by him.

'On the eighth of *June* 1662, the
'soldiers came again to *Brick-lane*, exer-
'cising their wonted violence and tu-
'multuous behaviour. They carried a-
'way *seven* men before *John Robinson*,
'who committed them to *New-prison*,
'where they yet remain. On the same
'eighth of *June*, the soldiers came to the
'meeting in *Beech-lane*, manifesting their
'fury

Ibid. p. 7.

Seven more committed by Robinson.

'fury and rage: They took away only
'him that was preaching, and carried *A minister*
'him before *Richard Brown*; when the *committed by Brown.*
'man was before him, amongst the rest
'of his learned discourse, he told him,
'*He should teach him a new trade* (mean-
'ing, as we suppose, that he would send
'him to *Bridewell*) *and have the skin
'from his back:* He committed him to
'*Newgate.*

'ON the fifteenth of *June* 1662, the
'soldiers came again to *Brick-lane,* in
'such manner as they were wont. They
'took *six* men and carried them to *John* *Six com-*
'*Robinson,* who committed them to *New-* *mitted by*
'*gate.* And on the same day they came *Robinson.*
'to the meeting at *Beech-lane,* and vio-
'lently set upon them with drawn swords,
'pulling of them out of their meeting-
'place with great rage. The place they
'stood to preach in they broke it down
'with such fury, that they broke their
'muskets: They struck several persons
'to their detriment in point of health.
'After which they took *two* men more,
'carried them to *Paul's-yard,* and from
'thence to *Newgate,* where they were
'kept while *Sessions,* not being at all com- *Two com-*
'mitted, or had before any *magistrate;* *mitted without*
'and at Sessions returned to *Newgate,* *Mittimus.*
'nothing being laid to their charge,
'where they still remain.

'ON

'ON the same fifteenth of *June*, 1662,
'the soldiers came with great fury and
'rage, with their swords drawn, to the
'meeting at *Petty-France*; where they
'very inhumanly wounded a boy almost
'to death; it was doubtful whether he
'would recover. They took away him
'that preached, and carried him to *New-*
'*gate*, and never had him before any
A minister '*magistrate*, where he remained till Ses-
committed 'sions, and from thence was returned
without a 'to *Newgate* again, where he yet re-
mittimus. 'mains.

'ON the twenty-ninth of *June*, sol-
'diers came to *Petty-France*, full of rage
'and violence, with their swords drawn.
'They wounded some, and struck others,
'broke down the gallery, and made
'much spoil: This was in the morning.
'In the afternoon the soldiers came to
'*Brick-lane*, practising their wonted cruel-
'ty, by pulling, halling, and beating them;
Several 'and took several, had them before *J.*
committed '*Robinson*, who committed them to *New-*
by Robin- '*Prison.*
son.

Ibidem, p. 'ON the sixth of the month called
8. '*July*, the soldiers came like beasts of
'prey, to *Brick-lane*, where they shut
'the door, and kept in all that were
'there, and with great violence they
'broke the forms before their faces;
'they left not one form whole, taking
'the legs and hurling them against the
'win-

'dows, pulling and hauling many; not
'regarding *sex*, *childhood*, nor *old age*.
'They took *six* men, and had them be-
'fore *John Robinson*, who committed them *Six com-*
'to *New Bridewell*. In the morning fol- *mitted by*
'lowing, they were by the keepers of *Robinson.*
'*Bridewell*, call'd *to beat hemp*: Which
'they refusing to do, were put into *New-*
'*prison*, to the rest of their fellow-suffer-
'ers, where they still are.

'On the 27th of the same month,
'the soldiers came to *Brick-lane* afore-
'said, with a multitude of rude people,
'as butchers out of *White-chapel*, bailiff's-
'followers, boys and such like unruly
'and debauch'd fellows, with a consta-
'ble like themselves: Who, as we heard,
'told *John Robinson*, that he could not
'overcome them, nor break the meet-
'ing at *Brick-lane*. *John Robinson* an-
'swer'd, as was said, *That then he should
'let in the multitude upon them, and let
'them tear the cloaths from their backs*;
'or words to that purpose: Which may
'very well be judg'd to be true, for the
'abovesaid ungodly wretches, soldiers and
'constables, after they had beat, pull'd,
'and hall'd them in a very inhuman
'manner themselves, set the great gates
'wide open: The constable, namely
'*Bartlet* a cook, and *Brown* the mar-
'shal, a wicked lewd fellow, calling the
'rude multitude in, march'd down be-

'fore

'fore them, saying to them, *Do your
'work, boys:* Which they did, for they
'beat the women and maids, broke the
'forms, the glass windows, and the door,
'making such spoil and havock as was
'seldom heard of; sparing none, no not
'women big with child. This *Brown*
'the marshal being ask'd, why he beat
'the women? he said, Who saw me?
'Who will swear it? And with those
'words, fell more violently upon the wo-
'men, some whereof were with child;
'striking of them with his fists, such
'blows that made them reel. Again, a
'maid had her bible snatch'd away; she
'labouring to get it again, was struck
'over the eye, that it was black a long

Seven committed by Robin-son.

'time after. Then the soldiers took *six*
'men and a woman, and carried them to
'*John Robinson;* who notwithstanding
'committed them all to *New-prison.*

Ibidem, p. 9.

The Baptists prisoners assaulted in Newgate.

Heb. x.

'On the third day of the month
'call'd *August* 1662, when the prison-
'ers in *Newgate*, call'd *Baptists*, were in
'their chamber, seeking the Lord, and
'speaking to one another, that they might
'as their duty is, provoke one another
'to love and good works: About four
'of the clock in the afternoon, the thieves,
'as house-breakers, pick-pockets, high-
'waymen, came with violence into our
'room, one took up a bible from the
'table, and threw it down to the ground,
'asking

'	asking what we did there? Struck one in the face with his fist, and he with the rest fell upon us, drew their knives, and endeavour'd to stab some of us. But the Lord was pleas'd to deliver us from their cruelty; for we took courage to defend ourselves, and escaped their bloody hands. And on the same day, the like violence, as we were in-form'd, was offer'd to those brethren in the *White-Lyon, Southwark*, by the felons there. And on the first of *June* so called, 1662; which was upon the first day of the week, after we were brought to *prison*, some of the keepers did come up to us, and charge us that we should not pray nor preach; for if we did, they had order to put us into the hole, and that they must do it. And though that was not executed; yet the felons did come violently upon us in our room, and did beat some of us, and threaten us all, saying, they would now order us well enough, for they had commission so to do.

And in White-Lyon prison in Southwark.

POSTCRIPT.

'WE would not be understood by any, that we send out this *cry*, be-cause we are wearied with what we have suffer'd, or afraid of what we may further suffer; but that we might

Ibidem, p. 15.

'shew

'shew to the world that our sufferings
'are altogether contrary to law and hu-
'manity itself.

'For did they no more than were
'law, we should be silent, and willing,
'with much rejoycing, to endure and
'suffer it, in that blessed cause of the
'Gospel, which we are not asham'd of,
'nor of the testimony of the Lord *Je-*
'*sus*; for whom we are willing to suf-
'fer the loss of all things, esteeming it a
'very choice mercy, that the Lord should
'accept of such poor nothing and un-
'worthy creatures as we are, to bear a
'testimony for him, against idolatry and
'prophaness.'

Anno 1664. The persecution against the *Baptists* still increas'd; and many more instances might be produc'd of the severities us'd against them, both in *London*, and in almost all the counties in *England*; and in the country was usually the greatest cruelty and injustice practis'd.

Manuscript penes me. Near *Ailsbury* in *Buckinghamshire*, there were several Gentlemen, if they deserve that name, in the commission of the peace, who endeavour'd to distinguish themselves, by their zeal in prosecuting the *Non-conformists*. They not only fill'd the county goal, with prisoners of this character; but also took two large houses in *Ailsbury*, and turn'd them into *prisons*, to make room

English Baptists.

room for their great numbers. Nor were they contented with the ordinary severities in this case, such as imprisonment and confiscation of goods, which were their daily exercise; but they endeavour'd to revive the old practice of punishing *Hereticks* with *banishment and death*.

There was a clause, in an Act made the 35th of *Elizabeth* against *Protestant Dissenters*, to this purpose, that if any person had been legally convicted of being at a *Conventicle*, and should after three months imprisonment for the same, refuse to conform to the Church of *England*, they should be oblig'd to abjure the land, that is, be banished, and swear never to come back again without leave; and if they should refuse, *either to conform or abjure the realm*, they should then be guilty of *felony*, without benefit of the *clergy*. This clause seem'd not to have been taken notice of since the *Restoration*, or at least none would so mind it, as to put it into execution.

[margin: Draconica, p. 2. Pulton's Stat. p. 1030.]

There were twelve persons, ten men and two women, all *Baptists*, who had been taken at their meeting, in or near *Ailsbury*; and having been legally convicted of the same, three months before, were now brought before the bench of justices at their *Quarter-sessions*; and there required, either to conform themselves to the *Church of England*, and

[margin: Ten men and two women condemned at Ailsbury.]

and take the oaths of *allegiance* and *supremacy*, or to abjure the realm, as this law directed; and were assured, that if they refused to do either of these, *sentence of death* should be passed against them. However, that there might be some shew of clemency, they gave them 'till the afternoon to consider of it. Mr. *Farrow*, one of the justices of that county, who liv'd at *Ailsbury*, was the principal agent in this prosecution: And the better to carry on his malicious design, he was this day made their *Chairman*. Several of the *Justices* left the bench, either being ashamed of these rigorous proceedings, or afraid of the consequences of such severity. But *Farrow* and three or four more continued, and were resolved to push on this matter.

WHEN the *prisoners* were again brought forth, they all declared, that *they could neither conform to the Church of England, nor abjure their native country and relations,* and therefore must throw themselves on the mercy of the *court*. Upon this they were by virtue of the aforecited law, declared guilty of *felony*, and sentence of *death* accordingly passed on them, and they were remitted back to *goal*, 'till their *execution*. The men were, *Stephen Dagnal*, minister; ——— *Ellit*, a teacher; *William Whitchurch*, a glover and deacon of their congregation; *Thomas Hill*, a linnen-draper; *William Welch*, a tallow-chandler; *Thomas Monk*, a farmer; —— *Brandon*, a shoemaker; and three more, whose names I cannot obtain: The women were, *Mary Jackman*, a widow, who had six children; *Ann Turner*, spinster.

The sentence was no sooner passed against them, but the officers were sent to their several houses, to seize on their goods, and whatever effects of theirs could be found: Which order was executed immediately, and great havock made of what little possessions they had. The rest of the *Dissenters* who lived in that town were not a little alarmed at this proceeding, and expected it would quickly come to their turns, to be treated after the same manner. These therefore shut up their shops also; who being the greatest part of the inhabitants, it put a great stop to commerce, and struck the whole *town* with great horrour and surprize. *Brandon*, one of the condemned persons, was prevailed upon, by the tears and earnest entreaties of his wife, to make a recantation, and take the oaths; but he presently found such horrour and distress in his mind, for what he had done, as exceeded all his former fears of death, or grief for his family. He voluntarily returned to the *Prison* again, declared, with the greatest signs

The Town much alarmed thereat.

signs of grief and trouble, his repentance of what he had done, and there continued with his companions, refolving to die with them, in defence of that caufe he had fo fhamefully renounced.

Thomas Monk, fon to him of that name, among the condemned, upon the paffing of the fentence, immediately took horfe for *London*, where he applied himfelf to Mr. *William Kiffin*, a man of great note among the *Baptifts*. and one that had as great an intereft at court, as any of that profeffion, and particularly with chancellor *Hide:* When he had revealed the whole matter to him, they go with great expedition to *Hide*, and intreat him to lay their cafe before his Majefty, which he readily did. The King feemed very much furprized, that any of his fubjects fhould be put to death for their religion only, and enquired whether there was any law in force that juftified fuch proceedings. When he was fatisfied about this, he promifed his pardon, and gave orders to the Lord Chancellor accordingly: But when they confidered, that the form of paffing a pardon would require fome time, and that thofe who had fo haftily paffed *a fentence of death*, might be as rafh alfo in the execution of it; they renewed their fuit to his Majefty, that an immediate reprieve might be granted, which his Majefty as gracioufly

The King pardons them.

ously comply'd with; and it was immediately given to the said *Thomas Monk*, who thereupon made all possible haste down again to *Ailsbury*.

WHEN he reported the success he had met with at court, and produced his Majesty's reprieve, it was not more joyful to his friends, than surprizing to their persecutors; and this put some stop to the violence of their proceedings in those parts.

HOWEVER, the condemned persons were continued close prisoners 'till the next assizes, and then the judge brought down his Majesty's pardon with him, and they were all set at liberty again.

THE reverend and famous Mr. *Benjamin Keach* had no small share in the sufferings of these times: He was often seized, when preaching, and committed to prison, sometimes bound, sometimes released upon bail, and sometimes his life was threatened. The troopers, who were sent down into *Buckinghamshire*, where he was, to suppress such meetings of the *Dissenters* as they could find; having discovered a meeting where Mr. *Keach* was preaching, they came with great rage and violence upon the assembly, and swore they would kill the *preacher*. Accordingly he was seiz'd, and four of the troopers declared their resolution to trample him to death with
their

Mr. Ben. Keach.

His Life attempted.

their horses; and laying him bound on the ground, prepared themselves for the fact. But the officer seeing their design, rode up towards them, and just as they were going to spur all their horses at once upon him, interposed and prevented them. Then he was taken up and tied behind one of the troopers cross his horse, and so carried to *goal*; from whence after some time of suffering great hardships and trouble, he was released.

He publish-es a Primmer. In this year he wrote a little book, intitled, *The Child's Instructor; or, a new and easie Primmer*. Several of his friends desired him to print it for the use of their children; and accordingly he sent it to *London* to be printed, without fixing his name thereunto, and had a recommendatory preface fixed to it by another hand. In this book were several things asserted, contrary to the doctrines and ceremonies of the *Church of England*: As that *infants* ought not to be baptized. That *Laymen* having abilities may preach the Gospel. That *Christ* should reign personally upon the earth in the latter day. &c.

Is taken up for it, and bound over to the Assizes. THIS book was no sooner printed, and some few of them sent down to him, but one Mr. *Strafford*, a Justice of the Peace for that county, was inform'd thereof; who taking a Constable with him, went presently to the house of

Mr.

Mr. *Keach*, seized all the books he found there, and bound him over to the *Assizes*, in a recognizance of *one hundred pounds*, and two sureties with him, *fifty pounds* each.

THE *Assizes* began at *Ailsbury*, *Octo.* 8. *His Trial.* 1664, and Lord Chief Justice *Hide* was Judge. On the first day of the *Assize*, in the afternoon, Mr. *Keach* was called, who answering to his name, was brought to the bar. After the Judge had made some unjust reflections upon his person and profession, to render him odious to the court, he held up one of the *Primmers* in his hand, and said unto him, did not you write this book? Mr. *Keach* readily acknowledged, that he writ the greatest part of it. Upon this the Judge answered, with a great shew of indignation, what have you to do to take other mens trades out of their hands? *I believe you can preach as well as write books.* Thus *A brave* it is, to let you, and such as you are, *protestant* *to have the scriptures, to wrest to your own* *Judge.* *destruction.* In your book you have made a new *creed*; I have seen three *creeds* before, but never saw a fourth till you made one.

Keach. I have not made a *creed*, but a confession of the *christian faith*?

Judge. WHAT is a *creed* then?

Keach. YOUR Lordship said, that you had never seen but three *creeds*; but
thou-

thousands of christians have made a confession of their faith.

THEN the judge said several things concerning *baptism* and the *ministers* of the Gospel; and when Mr. *Keach* began to make answer, the Judge stopt him, saying, you shall not preach here, nor give the reasons of your *damnable doctrine*, to seduce and infect the King's subjects; these are not things for such as you to meddle with, nor to write books of divinity, I will try you for it before I sleep, and then gave directions to the *Clerk* to draw up the indictment. But he was not so good as his word; for tho' he was very dilligent, and spent much of his own time to assist the *Clerk*, in preparing the bill, yet they could not get all things ready for the tryal till the next day.

WHILE the *Indictment* was drawing up, the witnesses were sworn, and bid to stand by the *Clerk*, 'till it was finish'd, and then to go with it to the *Grand Inquest*. During this interval, the Judge endeavoured to incense the *Jury* against the *prisoner*, representing him as a base and dangerons fellow. I shall send you presently, said he, a bill against one, that has taken upon him to write a new *Primmer*, for the instruction of your children; and if this be suffered, children by learning of it will become such as he is, and

and therefore I hope you will do your duty; and then the court broke up for that day. The next day, the court being set, the *Grand Jury* found the bill against him, and brought it in, endorsed, *billa vera*; and Mr. *Keach* being called to the bar, the *Clerk* said,

Benja. Keach, hear your charge, and then read his *indictment*, which was to this effect:

THOU art here indicted by the name of *Benjamin Keach*, of *Winslow* in the county of *Bucks*, for that thou being a seditious, heretical, and schismatical person, evilly and maliciously disposed, and disaffected to his Majesty's government, and the government of the *Church of England*; didst maliciously and wickedly, on the first day of *May*, in the sixteenth year of the reign of our sovereign Lord the King, write, print, and publish, or cause to be written, printed, and published, one seditious and venemous book, entitled, *The Child's Instructor; or, a new and easy Primmer*; wherein are contain'd by way of question and answer, these *damnable positions*, contrary to the book of Common Prayer, and the Liturgy of the *Church of England*; that is to say, in one place you have thus written.

Q. WHO are the right subjects of *baptism*?

A.

A. Believers, or godly men and women only, who can make confession of their faith and repentance. And in another place, you have maliciously and wickedly written these words.

Q. How shall it go with the saints?

A. O very well, it is the day that they have longed for; then shall they hear that sentence, *Come ye blessed of my Father, inherit the kingdom prepared for you*; and so shall they reign with Christ on the earth a thousand years, even on mount *Sion*, in the new *Jerusalem*, for there will Christ's throne be, on which they must sit down with him.

Then follows this question with the answer thereunto in plain English words:

Q. WHEN shall the rest of the wicked and the fallen angels, which be the devils, be judged?

A WHEN the thousand years shall be expired, then shall all the rest of the devils be raised and then shall be the general and last judgment; then shall all the rest of the dead, and devils be judg'd by Christ, and his glorified Saints, and they being arraigned and judged, the wicked shall be condemned, and cast by the angels into the lake of fire, there to be burned for ever and ever.

IN another place, you have wickedly and maliciously written, these plain English words: *Q.*

Q. WHY may not *Infants* be received into the church now, as they were under the law?

A. BECAUSE the fleshly seed is cast out, tho' God under that dispensation did receive *Infants* in a lineal way by generation; yet he that hath the key of *David, that openeth and no man shutteth, that shutteth, and no man openeth,* hath shut up that way into the church, and hath opened the door of regeneration, receiving in none now but *believers.*

Q. WHAT then is the case of *Infants?*

A. Infants that die are members of the kingdom of glory, tho' they be not members of the visible church.

Q. Do they then that bring in *Infants* in a lineal way by generation, err from the way of truth?

A. YEA, they do; for they make not God's holy word their rule, but do presume to open a door, that Christ hath shut, and none ought to open.

AND also, in another place, thou hast wickedly and maliciously composed *A short confession of the Christian Faith*; in which thou hast affirmed this concerning the second person in the Blessed Trinity, in these plain English words:

I ALso believe, that he rose again from the dead, and ascended into Heaven above, and there now sitteth at the right hand of God the Father, and from thence

thence he shall come again, at the appointed time, to reign personally upon the earth, and to be judge of the quick and dead.

AND in another place, thou hast wickedly and maliciously affirmed these things concerning true Gospel Ministers, in these plain English words following:

CHRIST hath not chosen the wise and prudent men after the flesh, not great *Doctors* and *Rabbies*, not many mighty and noble faith, St. *Paul*, are called, but rather the poor and despised, even tradesmen, and such like, as was *Matthew*, *Peter*, *Andrew*, *Paul* and others. And Christ's true Ministers have not their learning and wisdom from men, or from universities, or human schools; for human learning, arts and sciences, are not essential, in order to the making of a true minister; but only the gift of God, which cannot be bought with silver or gold. And also, as they have freely received the gift of God, so they do freely administer; they do not preach for hire, for gain or filthy lucre, they are not like false teachers, who look for gain from their quarters; who eat the fat, and cloath themselves with the wool, and kill them that are fed. Those that put not into their mouths they prepare war against. Also, they are not Lords over God's heritage, they rule them not by force and cruelty ty, neither have they power to force and compel men to believe, and obey their doctrine, but are only to perfuade and intreat; this is the way of the Gofpel as Chrift taught them. And many other things haft thou feditioufly, wickedly, and malicioufly written in the faid book, to the great difpleafure of Almighty God, the fcandal of the Liturgy of the *Church of England*, the difaffection of the King's people to his Majefty's government, the danger of the peace of this Kingdom, to the evil example of others, and contrary to the ftatute in that cafe made and provided.

THE *Indictment* being read, the *Clerk* faid,

How fay you, *Benjamin Keach*, are you guilty or not guilty?

Keach. THE *Indictment* is very long, I cannot remember half of it, nor have I been accuftomed to plead to *Indictments*; I defire to have a Copy of it, and liberty to confer with council about it, in order to put in my exceptions; and then I fhall plead to it.

Judge. IT is your intention to delay your trial 'till the next *Affizes*.

Keach. No, my Lord, I have no defign by this to delay my trial.

Judge. I will not deny you what is your right, but you muft firft plead to the

Indictment, and afterwards you shall have a copy of it.

Keach. I desire I may have a copy of it, before I plead, in order to put in my exceptions against it.

Judge. You shall not have it before you plead, *guilty or not guilty*.

Keach. It is what has been granted to others.

Judge. You shall not have a copy of it first, and if you refuse to plead *guilty or not guilty*, I shall take it *pro Confesso*, and give *judgment* against you accordingly.

When Mr. *Keach* saw he was thus over-ruled by the Judge, and that he was denied his right as an Englishman, he pleaded *not guilty*.

Judge. Now you may have a copy of your *Indictment*; and I will give you *an hour's time* to consider of it.

Keach. If I may have no longer time, I don't desire one.

Judge. I have something else to do than to wait upon you, you are not a person fit to go abroad 'till the next *Assizes*, and you would think it hard if I should commit you to *Goal* till then; but because you shall not say, but that you were offered fair, if you will find sufficient sureties for your appearance at the next *Assize*, and for your good behaviour till then, you shall not be tried till then.

But

But Mr. *Keach* knowing, that his appearing at any diffenting-meeting, would be deemed in thofe evil times a breach of his good behaviour, dared not to accept of this propofal, and faid, I am willing to be tried now.

Judge. Go on then, a God's name.

Then the *Jury* were called by their names, and fworn well and truly to try the *Traverfe* between the King and the Prifoner.

Upon this the *Clerk* read the *Indictment*, and told them that he had pleaded *not guilty*, and that their charge was to enquire whether he was *guilty* or not; and fo the witneffes were called, whofe names were *Neal* and *Whitehall*.

Neal fwore, that Juftice *Strafford* fending for him to wait upon him, he coming to his worfhip, was commanded to fetch his *ftaff of authority*, and come to him again, and then they went to one *Moody*'s ftall, and asked for fome *Primmers* which he had; but he anfwered he had none; from thence they went to *Benjamin Keach*'s houfe, where firft they faw his wife, he himfelf being in an inward room; they asked her if there were not fome *Primmers* in the houfe; fhe faid there were, and there were about thiry brought forth, and delivered to him.

Justice *Strafford* alfo depofed, That going to the houfe of the *Prifoner*, he found

found and seized the said *Primmers*; and that the *Prisoner* at the bar confessed before him, that he writ and composed the said book; and then a copy of the *Prisoner*'s examination before the said deponent, signed with his own hand, was produced and read. Wherein was contained, that the *Prisoner* being asked whether he was the *Author* or writer of the said book, answered, yes he was, and further declared, that he delivered part of the *Copy* to one *Oviat*, a printer, since dead, and that the rest of the said *Copy* he sent up by another hand, but that he knew not who printed it; that about forty of them were sent down to him, of which he had disposed about twelve, and that the price was five pence each book.

THEN the Judge called for a *Common Prayer Book*, and ordered one of the *Primmers* to be given to the *Jury*, and commanded the *Clerk* to read those sentences in the *Indictment*, that were taken out of the said book, that the *Jury* might turn to them, to see that the said positions were contained therein.

THE first position, which affirms that *Believers only are the right subjects of Baptism*, being read. This, says the Judge, is contrary to the book of *Common Prayer*, for that appoints *Infants* to be baptized, as well as men and women; and then read

read several places, wherein the baptizing of such is enjoined and vindicated.

THE next position is that, which affirms, that *the Saints shall reign with Christ a thousand years.*

THIS, says the Judge, is contrary to the *Creed*, in the book of *Common Prayer*, and is an old *Heresy*, which was cast out of the Church a thousand years ago, and was likewise condemned by the council of *Constance*, about five hundred years after, and hath lain dead ever since, 'till now this *Rascal* hath revived it.

UPON reading that position in the *Indictment*, which denies that *Infants are to be received into the Church now, as they were under the Law*: The Judge said, this also is contrary to the book of *Common Prayer*; which appoints *Infants* to be received into the Church, and directs the Priest to say, when he hath sprinkled the Child, *We receive this Child into the Congregation of Christ's Flock*, &c.

AND to the next position in the *Indictment*, wherein it is affirmed, that *Infants that die, are Members of the Kingdom of Glory, tho' not of the visible Church.* The Judge said, this he speaks of *Infants* in general; so that the Child of a *Turk*, is made equal to the Child of a *Christian*; but our Church hath determined otherwise, *viz.* That if an *Infant* die after *Baptism*, and before it hath actually sinned,

ned, it is faved; becaufe *original Sin* is wafhed away in *Baptifm*.

AFTER this was read, that pofition in the *Indictment* which was taken out of the *confeffion of Faith*, made by *Benja. Keach*. This, faith the Judge, is contrary to our *Creed*; for whereas this faith of Chrift, *that he afcended into Heaven above, and there now fitteth at the right hand of God the Father, and from thence he fhall come again, at the appointed time of the Father, to reign perfonally upon the Earth, and to be the judge both of the quick and dead.* Our Creed faith only, *from thence he fhall come to judge both the quick and dead.* And as to that concerning *Gofpel Minifters*, he faid, this is alfo contrary to the book of *Common Prayer*: For whereas the pofition in the *Indictment* faith, *that Chrift hath not chofen great Rabbies and Doctors, but rather the Poor and Defpifed, and Tradefmen*: The book of *Common Prayer*, does admit of fuch *viz. Doctors and Rabbies*, and then read fome paffages, concerning the qualifications of *Minifters*, and their manner of confecration in proof of it. And afterwards faid, becaufe Chrift when he was upon earth made choice of tradefmen to be his Difciples, this *Fellow* would have *Minifters* to be fuch now; *Taylors, Pedlars*, and *Tinkers*, fuch *Fellows* as he is; but it is otherwife now, as appears from the manner in which
the

the Church has appointed them to be chofen, ordained, and confecrated.

THE Judge having done, the *Prifoner* thought now he might have liberty to fpeak for himfelf, and accordingly began.

Keach. As to the *Doctrines* ———

Judge. YOU fhall not fpeak any thing here, except to the matter of *Fact*, that is to fay, whether you wrote this book or not.

Keach. I DESIRE liberty to fpeak to the particulars of my *Indictment*, and anfwer thofe things that have———

Judge. YOU fhall not be fuffered to give the reafons of your *Doctrine* here, to feduce the King's fubjects.

Keach. Is my *Religion* fo bad, that I may not be allow'd to fpeak?

Judge. I KNOW your *Religion*, you are a *fifth monarchy man*, and you can preach as well as write books, and you would preach here if I would let you; but I fhall take fuch order, as you fhall do no more mifchief.

THIS threatning, made Mr. *Keach* and fome of his friends, who were unacquainted in the law in this cafe, fear, that he intended to have him hanged.

Keach. I DID not write all the book, for there is an *Epiftle* wrote to it by another hand, neither can it be proved, that I writ all that is put into the *Indictment*.

Judge. IT is all one, whether you

writ it yourself, or dictated to another, that wrote it; but it appears, by your examination, under your own hand, that you wrote it all.

Keach. BECAUSE I writ the greater part of it, I was contented to let it go with the word *all* in my examination before Justice *Strafford*; but I cannot in conscience say that I writ it all, nor is it proved, that I published it.

Judge. YES, for *Moody* had six books of you.

Keach. I DID neither sell them nor deliver them unto him.

Judge. HE had them at your house, and tis not likely he should take them without your consent.

Keach. I Do not say he had them without my consent.

Judge. IT is all one then.

SOME few more words passed; but Mr. *Keach* being not permitted to answer to the particulars charged upon him, was content not to insist upon more proof of his being the *Author* of the book.

THEN the Judge summed up the evidence, and gave his charge to the *Jury*, wherein he cast many reflections on the *Prisoner,* to incense them against him, like as he had done before to the *Grand Inquest*.

THE *Jury* having received their charge, withdrew, and staid for some hours. At length one of the Bailiffs who attended them, came and told the Judge, that the Jury about the

the *Primmer* could not agree. But, said the Judge, they muft agree; the *Bailiff* replied, they defire to know whether one of them may not fpeak to your Worfhip, about fomethimg whereof they are in doubt. Yes, *privately*, faid the Judge; and ordered that one fhould come to him on the bench. And when the *Officer* had fetched one, he was fet upon the *Clerk*'s table, and the Judge and he whifpered together a great while. And it was obferved, that the Judge having his hands upon his fhoulders, would frequently fhake him, as he fpake to him.

Upon the Perfon's returning, the whole *Jury* quickly came in, and being according to cuftom, called over by their names, the *Clerk* proceeded.

Clerk. How fay you, is *Benja. Keach* guilty of the matter contained in the *Indictment* againft him, or not *guilty*?

Foreman. Guilty in part.

Clerk. Of what part?

Foreman. There is fomething in the *Indictment* which is not in the book.

Clerk. What is that?

Foreman. In the *Indictment*, he is charged with thefe words; when the thoufand years fhall be expired, then fhall all the reft of the *Devils* be raifed; but in the book it is, then fhall the reft of the *Dead* be raifed.

Clerk. Is he guilty of the *Indictment*, that fentence excepted?

One

One *of the Jurymen.* I cannot in conscience find him *guilty,* because the words in the *indictment,* and the book do not agree.

Judge. That is only thro' a mistake of the *Clerk,* and in that one sentence only: And you may find him guilty of all, that sentence excepted. But why did you come in before you were agreed?

Foreman. We thought we had been agreed.

Judge. You must go out again and agree. And as for you that say, you cannot in *conscience* find him *guilty,* if you say so again, without giving reasons for it, I shall take an order with you.

Then the *Jury* withdrew, and in a little time return'd again, and brought in this verdict, that he was guilty of the indictment; that sentence, wherein *devils* is inserted instead of *dead,* only excepted.

His sentence. Upon this *Benjamin Keach* was call'd to the bar; and the Judge proceeded, and pass'd *sentence* as follows:

Judge. Benjamin Keach, you are here convicted, for writing, printing and publishing, a seditious and schismatical book, for which the court's judgment is this, and the court doth award: That you shall go to *goal* for a fortnight without bail or mainprize; and the next *Saturday,* to stand upon the *pillory* at *Ailsbury*

bury, in the open market, for the space of two hours, from eleven of the clock to one, with a paper upon your head with this inscription: ' For writing, printing ' and publishing, a schismatical book, ' intitled, *The Child's Instructor, or, a* ' *new and easy Primmer*.' And the next *Thursday*, to stand in the same manner, and for the same time, in the market of *Winslow*; and there your book shall be openly burnt, before your face, by the common hangman, in disgrace of you and your doctrine: And you shall forfeit to the King's Majesty the sum of *twenty pounds*; and shall remain in *goal*, until you find *sureties* for your good behaviour, and appearance at the next *Assizes*, there to *renounce your doctrines*, and make such publick submission as shall be enjoined you: Take him away, keeper.

Keach. I hope I shall never *renounce those truths*, which I have written in that book.

Clerk. My Lord, he says, he hopes he shall *never repent*; but the Judge making no answer to this, the *Jaylor* took him away.

It is easy to discover, that this trial was carried on in a very arbitrary manner, and a *verdict* extorted against him from the *Jury*. Not could any pardon be obtain'd, or the least relaxation of the

severe

severe sentence, and the *Sheriff* took care that every thing should be punctually performed, and that other things should be expected: For according to the rigour of the law, he was kept close prisoner till the *Saturday*; when according to the sentence, he was brought to the *pillory* at *Ailsbury*; several of his religious friends and acquaintance accompanying him: And when they expressed his hard case, and the injustice of his sufferings, he said with a chearful countenance, *the cross is the way to the crown*. His head and hands were no sooner fixed in the pillory; but he began to address himself to the spectators to this effect. Good people, I am not ashamed to stand here this day, with this paper on my head; my Lord *Jesus* was not ashamed to suffer on the cross for me; and it is for his cause that I am made a gazing-stock. Take notice, it is not for any wickedness that I stand here; but for writing and publishing his truths, which the Spirit of the Lord hath revealed in the Holy Scriptures.

A CLERGYMAN that stood by could not forbear interrupting him: And said, it is for writing and publishing *errors*; and you may now see, what your *errors* have brought you to.

MR. *Keach* reply'd, Sir, can you prove them errors; but before the *Clergyman* could

Is put into the pillory at Ailsbury.

His behaviour there.

could return an answer, he was attacked by some from among the people. One told him, of his being pulled *drunk out of a ditch:* Another upbraided him with being lately found *drunk under a haycock.* At this all the people fell to laughing; and turn'd their diversion from the sufferer in the pillory to the *drunken priest*; insomuch that he hasten'd away with the utmost disgrace and shame.

After the noise of this was over, the *prisoner* began to speak again; saying, It is no new thing for the servants of the Lord to suffer, and be made a gazing-stock; and you that are acquainted with the scriptures know, that the way to the crown is by the cross. The Apostle saith, *That thro' many tribulations we must enter into the kingdom of heaven;* and Christ saith, *He that is ashamed of me and my words, in an adulterous and sinful generation, of him shall the son of man be ashamed, before the father, and before his holy angels.* But he was frequently interrupted by the *Jaylor*, who told him that he must not speak, and that if he would not be silent, he must force him to it. After he had stood some time silent, getting one of his hands at liberty, he pull'd his *Bible* out of his pocket, and held it up to the people; saying, take notice, that the things which I have written and pub-

publifhed, and for which I ftand here this day, a fpectacle to men and angels, are all contain'd in this *book*, as I could prove out of the fame, if I had an opportunity.

AT this the *Jaylor* interrupted him again; and with great anger enquired, who gave him the *book*; fome faid, his wife, who was near unto him, and frequently fpoke in vindication of her hufband, and the principles for he which fuffered. But Mr. *Keach* reply'd, and faid, that he took it out of his own pocket. Upon this the *Jaylor* took it from him, and faftened up his hand again. But it was almoft impoffible to keep him from fpeaking; for he foon began again, faying to this effect: It feems I cannot be fuffered to fpeak to the caufe for which I ftand here; neither could I be fuffered the other day (on his trial I fuppofe he meant) but it will plead its own innocency, when the ftrongeft of its oppofers fhall be afhamed.

I DO not fpeak this out of prejudice to any perfon, but do fincerely defire, that the Lord would convert them, and convince them of their errors, that their fouls may be faved in the day of the Lord *Jefus*. *Good people*, the concernment of fouls is very great; fo great, that Chrift died for them: And truly a concernment

cernment for fouls was that which moved me to write and publish those things, for which I now suffer, and for which I could suffer far greater things than these. It concerns you therefore to be very careful, otherwise it will be very sad with you, at the revelation of the Lord *Jesus* from heaven, for we must all appear before his tribunal. Here he was interrupted again, and forced to be silent for some time. But at length he ventur'd to speak again; saying, I hope the Lord's people will not be discouraged at my suffering. Oh! did you but experience, says he, the great love of God, and the excellencies that are in him, it would make you willing to go through any sufferings for his sake. And I do account this the greatest honour, that ever the Lord was pleas'd to confer upon me. After this, he was not suffered to speak much more: For the *Sheriff* came in a great rage; and said, if he would not be silent, he should be *gagged*; and the *officers* were ordered to keep the people at a greater distance from him, though they declar'd they could not do it. At the end of a long silence he ventur'd again: This, says he, is one *yoke of Christ*, which I can experience *is easy* to me, and a *burthen* which he doth make *light*. But finding he could not be suffer'd to speak, he kept silence till the

whole

whole two hours were expired; only uttering this sentence, *Blessed are they that are persecuted for righteousness sake, for theirs is the kingdom of heaven.* When the full time according to his sentence was expired, the *Under-keeper* lifted up the board, and as soon as his head and hands were at liberty, he blessed God with a loud voice for his great goodness unto him.

He is put into the pillory again, and his book burnt.

ON the *Saturday* following, he stood in the same manner, and for the like time, at *Winslow*, the town where he liv'd; and had his book *burnt before him*, according to the sentence. But I cannot obtain any particulars of his behaviour there; and therefore therein must be silent, not doubting but that it was with the same christian spirit and courage, as before.

THE person who preserved this relalation, being present, wrote down all he heard and saw, at the very instant; and makes this observation of his suffering, *viz.* That he stood in the pillory full two hours to a minute, which was a more strict execution than ever he saw in town or country; that others always had their hands at liberty; but this *sufferer* had his carefully kept in the holes, almost all the time which must render his suffering so much the more painful, yet, says he, *Thus judg-*

judgment is turned away backward, and justice standeth afar off: for truth is fallen in the streets, and equity cannot enter. He that departeth from evil, maketh himself a prey, and the Lord saw it, and it displeased him, that there was no judgment. Isa. lxix. 14, 15.

THE persecution against the professing people of God, was carried on with great violence, and much innocent blood shed. But two dreadful judgments, one upon the back of the other, befel the great city of *London*; the *Pestilence*, and the *Fire:* Which by many in that day, were look'd upon as tokens of God's anger against that persecuting spirit gone forth amongst the people.

THE account of the plague is taken notice of by Dr. *Calamy*, in his *continuation* of the account of the ministers, &c. silenced after the Restoration, by or before the Act for Uniformity, taken from the treatise of Mr. *Thomas Vincent*, intitled, *God's terrible voice in the city*; which is very affecting. Anno 1665.

' HE there tells us, says the Doctor,
' that it was in *Holland* in 1664; and
' the same year began in some remote
' parts of this land; though the weekly
' bills of the city took notice but of three
' that then died there of that disease. In
' the beginning of *May* 1665, nine died of
Continuation, p. 33.

' it

'it in the heart of the city, and eight in
'the suburbs; the next week the bill
'fell from nine to three; in the next
'week it mounted from three to four-
'teen; in the next to seventeen; in the
'next to forty-three. In *June* the num-
'ber encreased from forty-three to one
'hundred and twelve; the next week to
'one hundred sixty-eight; the next to
'two hundred sixty-seven; the next to
'four hundred and seventy. In the first
'week of *July*, the number arose to se-
'ven hundred twenty-five; the next week
'to one thousand and eighty-nine; the
'next to one thousand eight hundred and
'forty-three; the next to two thousand
'and ten. In the first week in *August*,
'the number amounted to two thousand
'eight hundred and seventeen; the next
'to three thousand eight hundred and
'eighty; the next to four thousand
'two hundred thirty-seven; the next to
'six thousand one hundred and two. In
'*September* a decrease of the distemper
'was hop'd for; but it was not yet come
'to its height: In the first week, there
'died of it six thousand nine hundred
'eighty-eight: And though in the second
'week the number abated, to six thou-
'sand five hundred forty-four; yet in the
'third week it arose to seven thousand
'one hundred sixty-five, which was the
                                       'highest.

' higheft. And then of the one hundred
' and thirty parifhes, in and about the
' city, there were but four which were
' not infected: And in thofe there were
' but few people remaining, that were
' not gone into the country. In the
' houfe where he lived [Mr. *Thomas Vin-*
' *cent*] there were eight in family, three
' men, three youths, an old woman and
' a maid. It was the latter end of *Sep-*
' *tember* before any of them were touch-
' ed. The maid was firft feized with the
' diftemper, which began with a fhiver-
' ing and trembling in her flefh, and
' quickly feized on her fpirits. This was
' on the *Monday*, and fhe died on *Thurf-*
' *day* full of tokens. On *Friday* one of
' the youths had a fwelling in his groin,
' and on the *Lord's-day* died, with the
' marks of the diftemper upon him. On
' the fame day, another of the youths
' fickened, and on the *Wednefday* follow-
' ing he died. On the *Thurfday* night
' the mafter of the houfe fell fick, and
' within a day or two was full of fpots,
' but was ftrangely recover'd, beyond his
' own or others expectation. In the fourth
' week of *September* there was a decreafe,
' to five thoufand five hundred thirty-
' eight. In the firft week of *October*, there
' was a farther decreafe to four thoufand
' nine hundred twenty-nine; in the next

'to four thousand three hundred twenty-
'seven; the next to two thousand six
'hundred sixty-five; the next to one
'thousand four hundred twenty-one; and
'the next to one thousand and thirty-one.
'The first week in *November* there was
'an increase to one thousand four hun-
'dred and fourteen; but it fell the week
'after to one thousand and fifty; and
'the week after to six hundred fifty-two;
'and so lessened more and more to the
'end of the year. And the whole number
'of those that were reckoned to die of the
'plague in *London*, this year, was sixty-
'eight thousand five hundred ninety-six.

'THE main body, says Dr. *Calamy*,
'of the publick ministers retired from
'the danger, and left their pulpits va-
'cant. In this case, the ministers that
'had been silenced three years before,
'and had preached only privately, and
'to small numbers, thought it their duty
'to give the best help they could to the
'many thousands that remained in the
'city. They staid and preached to vast
'congregations; and the immediate views
'of death before them, made both
'preachers and hearers, serious at an un-
'common rate.

Anno 1666.

'THE vices and immoralities of the
'nation, says Mr. *Neal* *, not being suf-

* Hist. of the Puritans, Vol. IV. p. 404.

'ficiently

' ficiently punished by the *Plague*, it
' pleased Almighty God this year to suf-
' fer the City of *London* to be laid in
' ashes, by a dreadful *conflagration*, which
' began behind the *Monument* in *Pud-*
' *ding-lane*, Sept. 2. and within three or
' four days consumed thirteen thousand
' two hundred dwelling houses, and eigh-
' ty-nine churches; among which was
' the Cathedral of St. *Paul's*; many pub-
' lick structures, schools, libraries, and
' stately edifices. Multitudes of people
' lost their estates, their goods and mer-
' chandize, and some few their lives;
' the King, the Duke of *York*, and many
' of the Nobility, were spectators of the
' desolation, but had not power to stop
' it; till at length it ceas'd almost as
' wonderfully as it began. *Moorfields* was
' filled with houshold-goods, and the
' people were forced to lie in huts and
' tents. Many families, who the last
' week were in large circumstances, were
' now reduc'd to beggary, and oblig'd to
' begin the world again. The authors of
' this *fire* were said to be the *Papists*, as
' appears by the inscription upon the *Mo-*
' *nument*. The Parliament being of this
' persuasion, petitioned the King to issue
' out a proclamation, requiring all *Popish*
' *Priests* and *Jesuits* to depart the king-
' dom within a month; and appointed a
' com-

'committee who received evidence of
'some *Papists*, that were seen to throw
'fire-balls into houses, and of others who
'had materials for it in their pockets;
'but the men were gone, and none suf-
'fer'd but one *Hubert*, a *Frenchman*,
'by his own confession.'

In this general confusion, the churches being burnt, and many of the parish ministers gone, for want of places of worship, the *Nonconformists* resolved again to supply the necessities of the people. Some churches were rais'd of boards, which they called *Tabernacles*: And the *Dissenters* fitted up large rooms with pulpits, seats and galleries; and many citizens frequented their meetings. But these calamities had no further influence upon the court prelates, than that they durst not at present prosecute the preachers so severely as before.

Anno 1667.

This year put a stop to the power of the great Earl of *Clarendon*, Lord High Chancellor of *England*, who had made himself obnoxious to the court, by his magisterial air towards the King. He was impeached at the bar of the House of Lords, in the name of all the Commons of *England*, of High-Treason, for sundry arbitrary and tyrannical proceedings, contrary to law, by which he had acquir'd a

greater

English Baptists.

greater eftate, than could be honeftly gotten in that time. The Earl did not think fit to abide the ftorm, but withdrew to *France*; leaving a paper behind him, in which he denied almoft every article of his charge; but the Parliament voted it fcandalous, and order'd it to be burnt by the hands of the common hangman. He was banifhed the King's dominions for life, by Act of Parliament: ' And fpent, ' fays Mr. *Neal*, the remaining feven years ' of his life at *Roan* in *Normandy*, among ' *Papifts* and *Prefbyterians*, whom he ' would hardly fuffer to live in his own ' country; and employ'd the chief of his ' time, in writing the hiftory of the Grand ' Rebellion.' He gloried, fays *Rapin* *, in his hatred of the *Prefbyterians*: And, perhaps, contributed more than any other, to that excefs of animofity, which ftill fubfifts among the followers of his maxims and principles. But what gives a luftre to his glory, is, that from the marriage of his daughter with the Duke of *York*, fprung two *Princeffes*, fucceffively Queens of *England*. ' His Lordfhip, ' fays Mr. *Neal*, was a perfon of very ' confiderable abilities, which have been ' fufficiently difplay'd by his admirers; ' but I have not been able to difcover

* Hiftory of *England*, Vol. II. p. 650.

' any

'any of his great or generous actions
'for the service of the publick; and how
'far his conduct with regard to the *Non-*
'*conformists* was consistent with honesty,
'religion or honour, must be left with
'the reader.'

CHAP. II.

From the banishment of the Earl of Clarendon, *to the end of the reign of King* Charles II.

Anno 1668.

LORD *Clarendon*, the great patron of persecuting power, having lost the King's favour; and Archbishop *Sheldon* and Bishop *Morley* being likewise under his displeasure, affairs began to take another turn. For Bishop *Burnet* observes *,
'That when complaints were made of
'some disorders, and of some Conventi-
'cles, the King said, the Clergy were
'chiefly to blame for these disorders, for
'if they had liv'd well, and gone about
'their parishes, and taken pains to con-
'vince the *Nonconformists*, the nation

* Hist. of his own Time, Vol. I. p. 258.

'might

ENGLISH BAPTISTS. 217

' might have been well settled; but they
' thought of nothing, but to get good
' benefices, and to keep a good table.'
He adds, that the King once said the
following things to him in his closet; ' If
' the Clergy had done their parts, it had
' been an easy thing to run down the
' *Nonconformists*; but they will do no-
' thing, and will have me do every thing;
' and most of them do worse, than if they
' did nothing. That he had a Chaplain
' a very honest man, but a very great
' blockhead, to whom he had given a li-
' ving in *Suffolk*, that was full of that
' sort of people [*Nonconformists*.] That this
' Chaplain had gone about among them
' from house to house, tho' he could not
' imagine what he could say to them;
' but that he believ'd, his nonsense suited
' their nonsense, for he had brought
' them all to church; and that in re-
' ward of his diligence, he had given him
' a Bishoprick in *Ireland*.'

SOME attempts began now to be made by Anno 1669.
Lord-Keeper *Bridgman*, Lord Chief Justice *Hale*, Bishop *Wilkins*, *Reynolds*, Dr.
Burton, *Tillotson*, *Stillingfleet*, and others,
for a comprehension of such as could be
brought into the church, by some abate-
ments, and a *toleration* for the rest. But
this project was blasted by the Court Bishops, and Lord *Clarendon*'s friends; who
took

took the alarm, and rais'd a mighty outcry of the *danger of the church*. So when the Parliament met, notice was taken, that there were rumours without doors, of a bill to be offer'd for *comprehension* and *indulgence*. Upon which a vote was passed, that *no man should bring such a bill into the house*. ' And to crush the *Noncon-*
' *formists* more effectually, says Mr.
' *Neal* *, Archbishop *Sheldon* writ a cir-
' cular letter to the Bishops of his pro-
' vince, dated *June* 8. to send him a
' particular account of the Conventicles
' in their several Dioceses, and of the
' numbers that frequented them, and
' whether they thought *they might be*
' *easily suppressed by the civil magistrate*.
' When he was provided with this in-
' formation, he went to the King, and
' obtain'd a proclamation to put the laws
' in execution against the *Nonconformists*,
' and particularly against the *preachers*;
' according to the Statute of the 17th of
' King *Charles* II. which forbids their
' inhabiting in corporations.

' Thus, says he, the persecution was
' revived: And the Parliament still bent
' on severities, appointed a committee to
' enquire into the behaviour of the *Non-*
' *conformists*. Who reported to the house,
' that divers Conventicles, and other se-

---

* History of the Puritans, Vol. IV. p. 418.

' ditious

'ditious meetings, were held in their very neighbourhood, in defiance of the laws, and to the danger of the peace of the kingdom. General *Monk*, who was near his end, and funk almoft into contempt, was employ'd to difperfe them; and received the thanks of the houfe for his zeal in that important fervice, wherein he was fure to meet with no oppofition. They alfo returned his Majefty thanks, for his proclamation for fuppreffing Conventicles, defiring him to take the fame care for the future. By this means, the private meetings of the *Diffenters*, which had been held by connivance, were broken up again,' and many of them imprifoned.

But this was contrary to the King's inclination *: Who was only for playing the *Diffenters* againft the Parliament for a fum of money. When the houfe therefore was up, his Majefty ordered fome of the *Nonconformifts* to be told, that he was defirous to make them eafy; and that if they would petition for relief they fhould be favourably heard: Upon which an addrefs was drawn up and prefented to him. The King receiv'd them gracioufly, and promis'd to do his utmoft to get them comprehended within the eftablifhment. He wifh'd there had been no bars

---

* *Neale*, Vol. IV. p. 420.

at all; signified that he was forced to comply for peace sake, but that he would endeavour to remove them, tho' it was a work of difficulty. When he dismissed them, he told them, *That he was against persecution, and hoped e're long to be able to stand upon his own legs.* But, says Mr. *Neale*, his Majesty's promises were always to be bought off by a sum of money to support his pleasures.

<small>Anno 1670.</small>

THE House of Commons were violently set upon persecution; and the Court sided therewith, to reduce the *Dissenters* to the necessity of petitioning for a *general toleration.* They revived the *Conventicle* Act, and added two extraordinary clauses thereto. The Court Bishops were for the bill, but the moderate Clergy were against it. Bishop *Wilkins* spoke against it in the house: And when the King desired him in private to be quiet, he reply'd, that he thought it an ill thing, both in conscience and policy; therefore as he was an *Englishman* and a Bishop, he was bound to oppose it: And since by the laws and constitution of *England*, and by his Majesty's favour, he had a right to debate and vote, he was neither afraid nor ashamed to own his opinion in that matter.

<small>Burnet, p. 272.</small>

HOWEVER the bill passed both houses; and received the Royal Assent, *Ap.* 11. 1670.

1670. 'It was, says Mr. *Neal* *, to the
' following effect: That if any person
' upwards of sixteen years, shall be pre-
' sent at any Assembly, Conventicle or
' Meeting, under colour or pretence of
' any exercise of religion, in any other
' manner than according to the Liturgy
' and practice of the Church of *England*;
' where there are five persons or more
' present, besides those of the said house-
' hold; in such cases the offender shall
' pay five shillings for the first offence,
' and ten shillings for the second. And
' the preachers or teachers in any such
' meetings, shall forfeit twenty pounds
' for the first, and forty for the second
' offence. And lastly, those who know-
' ingly suffer any such Conventicles in
' their houses, barns, yards, &c. shall
' forfeit twenty pounds. Any Justice of
' Peace on the oath of two witnesses, or any
' other sufficient proof, may record the of-
' fence under his hand and seal, which
' record shall be taken in law for a full
' and perfect conviction, and shall be cer-
' tified at the next Quarter-Sessions. The
' fines above-mention'd may be levied, by
' distress and sale of the offender's goods
' and chattels; and in case of the pover-
' ty of such offender, upon the goods
' and chattels of any other person or per-

---

* History of the Puritans, Vol. IV. p. 426.

' sons

'sons that shall be convicted of having
'been present at the said Conventicle, at
'the discretion of the Justice of Peace,
'so as the sum to be levied on any one
'person, in case of the poverty of
'others, do not amount to above ten
'pounds for any one meeting: The Con-
'stables, Headboroughs, &c. are to levy
'the same by warrant from the Justice,
'and to be divided, *one third for the use
'of the King, another third for the poor,
'and the other third to the informer or his
'assistants; regard being had to their di-
'ligence and industry in discovering, dis-
'persing, and punishing the said Conven-
'ticles.* The fines upon ministers for
'preaching, are to be levied also by di-
'stress; and in case of poverty, upon
'the goods and chattels of any other pre-
'sent; and the like upon the house where
'the Conventicle is held; and the money
'to be divided as above.

'And it is further enacted; That the
'Justice or Justices of Peace, Constable,
'Headboroughs, &c. may by warrant,
'with what aid, force, and assistance
'they shall think necessary, break open, and
'enter into any house or place, where
'they shall be informed of the Conven-
'ticle, and take the persons so assembled
'into custody.—— And the Lieutenants,
'or other commissioned officers of the
'militia, may get together such force
                                    'and

' and affiftance as they think neceffary
' to diffolve, diffipate, and difperfe fuch
' unlawful meetings, and take the per-
' fons into cuftody.—— That if any Juf-
' tice of Peace refufe to do his duty in
' the execution of this Act, he fhall for-
' feit five pounds.

' AND be it farther enacted; That all
' claufes in this Act *fhall be conftrued
' moft largely, and beneficially for the fup-
' preffing Conventicles, and for the juftifi-
' cation and encouragement of all perfons
' to be employed in the execution thereof.* No
' *warrant* or *mittimus* fhall be made void,
' or reverfed, for any default in the form:
' And if a perfon fly from one county
' or corporation to another, his goods
' and chattels fhall be feizable wherever
' they are found. If the party offend-
' ing be a wife co-habiting with her huf-
' band, the fine fhall be levied on the
' goods and chattels of the hufband, pro-
' vided the profecution be within three
' months.

' THE wit of man, fays Mr. *Neal*,
' could hardly invent any thing fhort of
' capital punifhment, more cruel and in-
' human. One would have thought fuch
' a merciful Prince as King *Charles* II.
' who had often declared againft perfecu-
' tion, fhould not have confented to it;
' and that no Chriftian Bifhop fhould
' have voted for it. Mens houfes are to

' be

'be plundered, their persons imprisoned,
'their goods and chattels carried away,
'and sold to those who would bid for
'them. Encouragement is given to a
'vile set of *Informers*, and others, to
'live upon the labour and industry of
'their conscientious neighbours. Multi-
'tudes of these sordid creatures spent their
'profits in ill houses, and upon leud
'women, and then went about streets
'again to hunt for further prey. The
'law is to be construed in the favour of
'these wretches, and the power to be
'lodged in the hand of every single Jus-
'tice of Peace; who is to be fined five
'pounds if he refuses his warrant. Upon
'this many honest men, who would not
'be the instruments of such severities,
'left the bench, and would sit there no
'longer.

'GREAT numbers were prosecuted
'on this Act *, and many industrious
'families reduced to poverty. Many
'ministers were confined in goals and
'close prisons; and warrants were issued
'out against them, and their hearers, to
'the amount of great sums of money. In
'the diocese of *Salisbury* the persecution
'was hottest, by the instigation of Bishop
'*Ward*; many hundreds being prosecuted
'with great industry, and driven from

* *Neal*, Vol. IV. p. 429.

'their

'their families and trades. The Act was
'executed with such severity in *Starling*'s
'mayoralty, that many of the trading
'men in the city were removing with
'their effects to *Holland*, 'till the King
'put a stop to it. *Informers* were every
'where at work; and having crept into
'religious assemblies in disguise, levied
'great sums of money upon ministers
'and people. Soldiers broke into the
'houses of honest Farmers, under pre-
'tence of searching for conventicles; and
'where ready money was wanting, they
'plundered their goods, drove away their
'cattle, and sold them for half price:
'These vile creatures were not only en-
'couraged, but pushed on vehemently
'by their *spiritual guides*. For this pur-
'pose Archbishop *Sheldon* sent another
'circular letter to all the Bishops of his
'province; and copies of this letter were
'sent by the Archdeacons to the of-
'ficers of the several parishes within
'their jurisdictions, earnestly desiring
'them to take a special care to perform
'whatsoever is therein required, and to
'give an account at the next visitation.
'Many of the Bishops chose to lie be-
'hind the curtain, and throw off the
'*odium* from themselves to the *Civil*
'*Magistrate:* But some of the more zea-
'lous could not forbear appearing in
'perfon

'person; as Bishop *Ward*, already men-
'tioned, and Bishop *Gunning*, who of-
'ten disturbed the *Meetings* in person.
'Once finding the doors shut, he or-
'dered the Constable to break them o-
'pen with a sledge. Another time he
'sat upon the bench at the Quarter-Ses-
'sions: Upon which the Chairman de-
'sired his Lordship to give the *Charge*,
'which he refusing, received a very
'handsome rebuke; it being hardly con-
'sistent with one that is an Ambassador of
'the prince of peace, to set in judg-
'ment upon the consciences of his poor
'countrymen and neighbours, in order
'to plunder and tear them to pieces.
'The Bishop was so zealous in the cause,
'that he sunk his character by giving
'a publick challenge to the *Presbyterians*,
'*Independants*, *Anabaptists* and *Quakers*;
'and appointed three days for the dis-
'putation. On the first of which his
'Lordship went into the pulpit in the
'Church, where was a considerable con-
'gregation, and charged the former with
'sedition and rebellion out of their books,
'but would hear no reply. When the
'day came to dispute with the *Quakers*,
'they summoned their friends; and when
'the Bishop railed, they paid him in his
'own coin, and followed him to his
'very

'very house, with repeated cries, the 'Hireling fleeth.

Mr. *Vavasor Powell*, was in these times greatly harrassed by his persecutors. The *High Sheriff* of the county of *Montgomery*, for his refusing to give over preaching, according to his prohibition, had wrote to Secretary *Morrice*, and accused him of *Sedition*, *Rebellion* and *Treason*. And before he received a return, so willing was he to be doing, that he directed a warrant to apprehend him, and so he became a *Prisoner*, and continued such several months; all ordinary ways of relief by law allowed in such cases, being wholly obstructed.

Vavasor Powell imprisoned in Wales.

When the Sessions came on, after much importunity, Mr. *Powell* was called, but instead of being released, or having just cause rendered why he should be continued in prison, the oaths of *Allegiance* and *Supremacy* were tendered to him; and upon his refusal of taking those oaths, so arbitrarily imposed, he was again committed to *Prison*, the Judge refusing to take any bail for him till the next Sessions.

But he had not long continued there, when upon a false information, Mr. *Wickham*, a messenger of the Council, was sent down with a *warrant* to bring him before the King and Council. From whence

Is brought before the King and Council, and sent to the Fleet-Prison.

whence he was sent to the *Fleet-Prison*; where he was detained almost two years; and for twelve months in so close a confinement, that he was not suffered to go out of his chamber. Which, together with the offensive smell of a dunghill under his window, did so much impair his health, that he never after perfectly recovered it.

Is remov'd to South-Sea Castle. FROM the *Fleet* in 1662, he was suddenly removed to *South-Sea Castle* near *Portsmouth*, where he continued about five years; and upon the removal of Chancellor *Hide*, he and many others sued for an *Habeas Corpus*, and so at length he obtained his liberty.

THIS scarcely lasted ten months. For one *George Jones*, the Parson of *Merthur* in *Glamorganshire*, a man noted for whoredom, drunkenness, cheating, and putting away his wife, made complaint, and false information against him, before two deputy *Lieutenants*; and swore, that Mr. *Powell*, and the congregation to which he preached, were met near two miles from *Cardiff*, and many of them armed; both which were false. Yet upon this information, or deposition, a *warrant* was granted against him; and he *Is imprison'd again in Wales.* was thereupon apprehended and imprisoned again at *Cardiff*; and at a general meeting of the deputy *Lieutenants* at *Cowbridge*, on the 17th of *October*, he was

exa-

examined before them, by an *Officer* of the *Bishop*'s *Court*; the contents of which you may find in his *Life*, too long to be inserted here.

Upon the eighth of *November*, 1668, and the thirteenth of *January* following, he was convened before the *Justices*, and the Oaths of *Allegiance* and *Supremacy* tendered to him. Much *pro* and *con*, as may be seen in his *Life*, was spent upon this subject. In conclusion, Mr. *Powell* asked, whether they would be pleased to take sufficient bail till the next Sessions? ' * The *Justices* were silent. But the *Jay-*
' *lor* made answer publickly, No. Says
' Mr. *Powell*, Sir, are you one of the
' *Judges* of the Court, that your No
' should stand? But the Justices did not
' give him the least check for his saw-
' ciness. Then *P.* said further; Gen-
' tlemen, I have been near eight years a
' *Prisoner*, and in thirteen *Prisons*, and
' yet in all these, I have not received
' so much incivility as from this man;
' Mr. *Jaylor*; and therefore I desire li-
' berty to take a private chamber in the
' town, giving security for my true im-
' prisonment. But to this the *Justices*
' returned no answer; but commanded
' the *Jaylor* to take the *Prisoner* away,
' which was done accordingly, and re-

* Powell's Life, *p.* 187, &c.

P 3 ' turned

'turned to Prison again. About three
'months after this, a friend in *London* got
'a *Habeas Corpus*, to remove him to the
'*Common Pleas* bar; which the *Sheriff*
'refused to obey. Then came an *Alias*,
'under penalty of 100 *l.* upon which
'they sent him up; but would not let
'him know of his journey before hand.
'But about eight o'clock one night, the
'*Under-Sheriff* came to give him notice
'to be gone in half an hour, and so
'took him with a guard, eight miles
'that night, being the sixteenth of the

Is remov'd to the Common Pleas bar Westminster.

'eighth month 1669; and brought him
'to *Westminster* to the *Common Pleas* bar
'the twenty second of the same; where,
'upon the examination of the return, it
'was found illegal. But *S. M.* their
'Council, pleaded he had not time to
'view it, and desired time till next day,
'which the Judges granted.

'THEREUPON Mr. *P.* moved the
'Court to take bail then, and discharge
'his guard; which had been granted,
'but that *S. M.* said, No, my Lord, then
'he will go preach. To which the *Prisoner* replied, that it was as lawful for
'him to preach, as for him to talk
'there at the bar.

'THE next day he was brought in-
'to the Court again; and the return
'was again argued, the *Prisoner* having
'the liberty to open his case himself.
                                   ' And

' And tho' the return was by all the
' Judges judged falſe and and illegal;
' yet was Mr. *Powell* committed to the
' *Fleet Priſon* by the Court; where he
' remained a Priſoner from the twenty-
' fourth of the third month, 1669, 'till
' he was diſcharged by death, the twenty-
' ſeventh of the eight month, 1670.

IT was about this time, that ſome bickerings happened between ſome of the *Baptiſts*, and ſome of the people called *Quakers*, in or about *High Wicomb* in *Buckinghamſhire*; occaſioned by ſomething a *Baptiſt* preacher had ſaid from the pulpit, againſt the *Quakers* doctrines, but eſpecially ſomething that *William Penn* had written. It came at length to this iſſue, that a publick diſpute was to be holden at *Wicomb*, between *Jer. Ives*, who eſpouſed his brother's Cauſe, and *William Penn*.

A diſputation between the Baptiſts and Quakers.

Ives argued againſt *the light within*, and *univerſal grace conferred by God on all men.* At laſt, after a long diſputation, when neither ſide could agree with the other, *Ives* ſtept down and departed, with a purpoſe to have broken up the Aſſembly: But the *Quakers* ſtaid and harangued the people. Which Mr. *Ives* underſtanding, came in again, and expreſſed his diſlike at the proceedure; as well he might be diſpleaſed at the detaining

taining of the people in order to prejudice them to their side.

HOWEVER the *Quakers* remaining thus masters of the field of battle, triumphed; and *Thomas Ellwood* sent a brief account of their victory to his friend *Isaac Pennington* (by his Son and Servant who returned home, tho' it was late that evening) in the following distich:*

' *Prævaluit veritas* ; *inimici terga dedêre* :
' *Nos sumus in tuto* ; *laus tribuenda Deo.*

  Which he thus *englishes* :
' Truth hath prevail'd, the enemies did
  ' fly;   (high.
' We are in safety; praise to God on

BUT he had no such occasion to triumph at *Jeremy Ives*'s quitting the disputation, since it was time by what I can find, to give it over; for it was very late in the evening before Esq; *Pennington*'s son and servant set out homewards.

' BUT both they [*Baptists*] and we
' (*Quakers*) saith *Ellwood*, had quickly
' other work found us: It soon became
' a stormy time; the clouds had been
' long gathering, and threatened a tem-
' pest; the parliament had sat some-
' time before, and hatched that unaccoun-

* Ellwood's Life, *p.* 273.

         ' table

' table law, which was called the *con-*
' *venticle Act*: If that may be allowed
' to be called a law, by whomsoever
' made, which was so directly contrary
' to the fundamental laws of *England*,
' to common justice, equity and right
' reason, as this manifestly was. For,

' 1. It brake down, and overrun the
' bounds and banks, antiently set for the
' defence and security of *Englishmen*'s
' lives, liberties and properties, *viz. Trial
' by Juries*: Instead thereof, directing
' and authorizing Justices of the Peace,
' and that too, privately, out of *Sessions*,
' to convict, fine, and by their warrants
' distrein upon offenders against it, di-
' rectly contrary to the *great charter*.

' 2. By that Act, the *Informers*, who
' swear for their own advantage, as be-
' ing thereby entitled to a third part
' of the fines, were many times conceal-
' ed, driving on an underhand private
' trade; so that men might be, and
' often were, convicted and fined without
' having any notice or knowledge of it,
' 'till the Officers came and took away
' their goods; nor even then could they
' tell by whose evidence they were con-
' victed: Than which, what could be
' more opposite to common justice?
' which requires, that every man should
' be openly charged, and have his ac-
' cuser face to face; that he might both
' answer

'answer for himself, before he be con-
'victed, and object to the validity of the
'evidence given against him.

' 3. By that Act, the innocent were
'punished for the offences of the guilty.
'If the wife or child was convicted of
'having been at one of those assemblies,
'which by that Act was adjudged un-
'lawful, the fine was levied on the
'goods of the husband or father of such
'wife or child; though he was neither
'present at such an assembly, nor was
'of the same religious persuasion that
'they were of; but perhaps an enemy
'to it.

' 4. It was left to the arbitrary plea-
'sure of the Justices, to lay half the fine for
'the house or ground where such assembly
'was holden, and half the fine for a
'pretended unknown preacher; and the
'whole fines of such, and so many of
'the meeters as they should account
'poor, upon any other or others of the
'people who were present at the same
'meeting, not exceeding a certain limi-
'ted sum, without any regard to equity
'or reason; and, yet this, such blind-
'ness doth the spirit of persecution bring
'on men, otherwise sharp-sighted enough,
'that this unlawful, unjust, unequal, un-
'reasonable, and unrighteous law took
'place in almost all places, and was vi-
                                    ' gorously

'goroufly profecuted againft the meet-
' ings of *Diffenters* in general.'

WHEN the Bifhops had obtained this law, they and fome others of the Clergy of all ranks, and fome others too over-officious perfons, encouraged all they could *Informers*, and preferred to ecclefiaftical offices fuch as they thought would be moft obfequious and active this way. Yet it took not alike every where; but fome were forwarder in the work than others, according as the *Agents* employ'd therein had been predifpofed thereto.

FOR in fome parts of the nation, fays P. 276. Ellwood, care had been timely taken by fome, not of the loweft rank, to chufe out fome particular perfons, men of fharp wit, clofe countenances, pliant tempers, and deep diffimulation, and fend them forth among the *Sectaries*, fo called, with inftructions to thruft themfelves into all focieties, conform to all, or any fort of religious profeffions —In a word, to be all things to all, not that they might win fome, but that they might, if poffible, ruin all, at leaft many. The drift of this defign was, that by this means, they who employ'd them, might get a full account of the number of diffenting meetings in each county, when they were kept, what number of perfons frequented them, and of what ranks, who

were

were persons of estates, and where they lived, that they might know where afterwards to cast their nets with advantage. He who was sent on this errand in the county of *Bucks*, adventured to thrust himself on a *Quaker*, as one of their number. But being suspected by him, and thereon dismissed unentertained, he betook himself to an inn, and there getting a little disordered in liquor, he discovered what he was, and that he was sent forth by Dr. *Mew*, then Vice-chancellor of *Oxford*, on the design before related, and under the protection of Justice *Morton*; a warrant under whose hand and seal he there produced.

Sensible of his error too late, when sleep had restored him to some degree of sense, and vexed at the successlessness of his attempt on the *Quakers*, he left that place, and crossing the country, cast himself among the *Baptists*, at a meeting they held in a private place, of which the over easy credulity of some who went among them (when he had craftily insinuated himself into their favour) gave him notice. The entertainment he met amongst them deserved a better return than he made them; for having smoothly wrought himself into their good opinion, and cunningly drawn some of them into an unwary freedom, and openness of conversation with him,
upon

upon the unpleasing subject of the severity of the times, he most villanously impeached one of them whose name was —— *Headach*, a man well reputed amongst his neighbours, of having spoken *treasonable words*, and thereby brought the man in danger of losing both his estate and life, had not a seasonable discovery of his abominable practices elsewhere (imprinting terrour, the effect of guilt, upon his mind) caused him to fly both out of the *Court* and *Country*, at the very instant of time, when the honest man stood at the bar, to be arraigned upon his false accusation: For he on the laying this false charge on the *Baptists*, was forced to lay off his *vizor*. And now the better to act, he resolved to get a partner, which he soon after did, one who was not long before releafed out of *Ailsbury* goal, where he had been put for cow-stealing.

The country-people not knowing their names, called the one, the *Trepan*, the other the *Informer*; tho' afterwards they came to know, that the one was named *John Poulter*, a butcher of *Salisbury*'s son, an egregiously wicked fellow; and that the *Informer* was called *Lacy* of *Risborough*.

These two resolved to make the first onset on a *Quakers* meeting, in the parish of *St. Giles Chalfont*, in the county ty of *Bucks:* But wanting a place to lurk in, they were obliged to apply to Parson *Philips*. Very ready, able, and willing to assist them, he recommended them to one *Anne Dell*, once his parishioner, but since removed to a farm called *Whites*, in the parish of *Beaconsfield*; who readily received them, and what she had was at their command. She had two sons; the youngest of them *John Dell*, hoping to enrich himself with the spoil of their honest neighbours, listed himself with his mother's new guests, as their guide, who were too much strangers to know the names of any persons they were to inform against.

ON *July* twenty fourth they came to the *Quakers* meeting; but *Poulter* did not stay in the country long after; for he was discovered to have *christened a Cat*, as the term is, by the name of *Catherine Catherina*, in derision of the *Queen*, and of feloniously taking certain goods from one of *Brainford*, whom also he had cheated of money. These things forced him to leave the country. And thus *Headach* was preserved, and the *Quakers* delivered at that time.

THO' it pleased God to put a stop, in a great measure, to the persecution in this county, yet it was carried on with very great severity and rigour in other parts both of the city and country: The worst
of

of men, for the moſt part, being ſet up for *Informers*, the worſt of Magiſtrates encouraging and abetting them; and the worſt of Prieſts, who firſt began to blow the fire, now ſeeing how it ſpread, clapping their hands and hallooing them on to this evil work.

The people thus ſet on by the encouragement of Magiſtrates and wicked Prieſts, their enmity roſe to ſuch a pitch againſt the *Baptiſts*, that they denied the benefit of the common burying places. Yea, ſo inhuman, ſays Mr. *Grantham*, hath been the uſage of ſome, that they have been taken out of their graves, drawn upon a ſledge to their own gates, and there left unburied. ' Thus, ſays he, did the
' inhabitants of *Croft* in the county of
' *Lincoln*, deal by one *Robert Shalder*, a
' baptized believer, in the year 1666, to
' the infamy of the vile doers of that cruel
' act; whilſt this epitaph lives, to keep
' in memory their cruel action:

<small>Chriſtianiſmus Primitivus, Lib. 3. c: 10.</small>

' Sleep, pious *Shalder*, ſleep in thy
  ' ſequeſtred grave,
' Chriſt's faith thou well didſt keep,
  ' maugre the fierceſt wave
' Which Satan's ſtorms could raiſe againſt
  ' thy faith, and now
' In vain he findeth ways, his malice
  ' ſtill to ſhew.

' Thy

'Thy Saviour had no grave, but what
  'a friend did lend;
'Enough, if the servant have like fa-
  'vour at the end.
'And now thy faith divine, I'll pin
  'upon thy herse,
'It bright, tho' brief doth shine; *Heb.*
  'vi. 1, 2, verse.

<small>Robert Shalder ta-ken out of the grave.</small> This Mr. *Shalder* had suffered much by imprisonment for his zeal towards God, and dying soon after his release from prison, was interred in the common burying-ground amongst his ancestors. The same day that he was buried, certain of the inhabitants of *Croft* in the county of *Lincoln*, opened his grave, took him from thence, and dragged him upon a sledge to his own gates, and left him there; upon which some verses were written, and placed upon the grave, entitled, *The Dead Man's Complaint*, designed to check the envy of the Spiritual Court, who thus disgraced the dead. Part of which ran as follows:

Your sad presenting men alive and dead,
What text will warrant, where can it be
  read?
That *Christ* his *Church*, did ever thus proceed
'Gainst any man. Oh! then behold your
  dead.
                                    Whilst

ENGLISH BAPTISTS.

Whilſt you pretend to chriſtianity,
Shew that you have no true humanity:
Let *Croft* beware, if ſhe behave her thus,
Her actions prove not ſadly ominous;
Of ſome impending evils (at the leaſt
Such as my corps being us'd worſe than
    a beaſt:)
On them or theirs; for as the Lord is juſt,
He'll plead his ſervants cauſe, tho' in the
    duſt.
They lie without regard from men, yet he
Accounts they touch the apple of his eye;
That toucheth his, nor ſhall it long time be;
E're I your face before his face ſhall ſee,
And there implead you at his awful bar,
For that which you have done. Oh! then
    prepare,
For death tends on you, as he did on me,
And you muſt to the ſame mortality.

    THE chief actors in this inhumanity, ſo prodigiouſly rude and unnatural, did not long ſurvive it. For one of them died ſuddenly, and the other languiſhed for ſome time; being greatly terrified with the remembrance of what he had done to the dead.

    IT was about this time that Mr. *Robert Wright* conformed to the Church of *England*. He had been a *Baptiſt* preacher, but was excluded for his irregular life and converſation. He continued in his evil courſe of life ſome years, and hav-

R. Wright conforms to the eſtabliſhed Church.

ing spent his estate, in the end made application to the then Bishop of *Lincoln* for some benefice, promising to renounce his principles of baptism, and preach against the *Baptists*. The Bishop accepted his offer, and he was accordingly admitted into their ministry, and preached up the Baptism of infants in opposition to that of believers. This did not a little affect the generality of the Church people, who from the impetuous discourses and daring pretences of this suppos'd champion, expected that most, if not all the ministers of the baptized churches would be easily overcome. The *Baptists* in order to vindicate themselves, did in the open Assize time, draw, and post up four papers, containing a challenge or protestation against the said Mr. *Wright*, as follows:

<small>Manuscript *penes me*.</small>

> 'To the citizens and inhabitants of the
>   'city and county of Lincoln, *salu-*
>   '*tation.*

> 'FORASMUCH as you have heard,
> 'that one *Robert Wright*, once a
> 'member of the churches reproachfully
> 'call'd *Anabaptists*, hath lately recanted
> 'his principles; in token whereof he
> 'hath preached publickly in the city of
> '*Lincoln*, by allowance of the Bishop or
> 'Clergy of the same, to the great re-
>   'proach

' proach of the truth, touching the bap-
' tifm of repentance for the remiffion of
' fins: Know therefore, that if the faid
' *Robert Wright* will accept of a friendly
' conference in the place where he preach-
' ed, and fhall give convenient and pub-
' lick notice of the fame, he fhall find
' fome, if God permit, to maintain the
' doctrine and baptifm of repentance to
' be from heaven, and the fprinkling
' and crofling of Infants to be man's tra-
' dition.

' *The 11th day of the 1st month (Vulg.)*
' March, 1670.

' Written by *Tho. Grantham*.
' Pofted by *Wm. Pann*.

Two of thefe papers which were fet above the hill were taken down in the morning, and, as was fuppofed, carried to the Bifhop and the Judge; the other two below the hill, were read by many, and in the afternoon taken down by the Clergy, who threatened that they who wrote them fhould anfwer for it before the council-table. However, nothing more was done, but the drawing up an angry ill-natured paper, which was fent to the *Baptifts* by Mr. *William Silverton*, the Bifhop's Chaplain, dated from *Scroaby*, *Aug.* 6. 1669: By which it appeared, how much he was chafed at the *Baptifts* proceedings; nor was the Bishop himself a little moved upon the same account, as was then well known. Mr. *Grantham*, to check the confidence of Mr. *Silverton*, drew up some counter positions and concluded his answer thus:

'Finally, Whereas Mr. *Silverton*
'saith, he will defend his propositions; it is
'hereby certified, that if he will either
'publish any thing upon the last two
'proposals, or dispute of them peacea-
'bly in a free audience, some of those
'whom he in the height of his wit
'stiles, *erroneous antick Baptists*, are re-
'solved in the strength of Christ, to
'hear and try that which he shall de-
'clare, time and place being conveni-
'ent.
  '*Thomas Grantham.*

This paper was delivered to Mr. *Silverton* by *William Pann*; but Mr. *Silverton* neither thought fit to enter into the controversy by disputation, nor to make any reply by writing, and so his great boasting ended in a shameful silence.

Persecutions in Sussex.

This year was published a *Narrative of the late proceedings of some Justices and others, pretending to put in execution the late act against Conventicles*; *against several peaceable people in and about the town of of* Lewes *in* Suffex, *only for their being quietly met to worſhip God: Together with a brief account of the like proceedings againſt ſome at* Brighthelmſtone, *and others at* Chillington *in the ſame county.*

THE Author of this Narrative begins with a ſhort epiſtle thus:

READER,

'THOU art here preſented with an
' account of ſome proceedings,
' pretended to be grounded upon the late
' Act againſt *Conventicles.* Of the Act
' itſelf I ſay nothing at all; nor do I
' call theſe proceedings pretended to be
' grounded thereon, either arbitrary or
' illegal. Read, and be judge thyſelf:
' Only be ſure of this; that thou haſt
' a *faithful narrative.* What you find
' therein, relating to the conviction of
' theſe perſons, was reported by ſome
' *Officers* then preſent, or dropt from the
' *Imformers* themſelves: And the witneſs
' of an enemy (we uſe to ſay) is a dou-
' ble teſtimony.

' THAT, of the unreaſonableneſs of the
' diſtreſs, &c. will (if occaſion require)
' be atteſted by many, who were both
' eye and ear witneſſes; *for theſe things*
' *were not done in a corner.* Many ma-
' terial circumſtances are herein, for bre-
' vity ſake, omitted; none but what are
' upon

'upon due examination found true in-
'ferted. The defign of this *Narrative*
'is not to imbitter the fpirits of any a-
'gainft *lawful fuperiors*. And I dare be
'fo charitable as to judge, that fuch a
'defign would be as contrary to thefe
'*fufferers* themfelves, being men that are
'peaceable, and faithful in the land. In
'matters of the kingdom, malice itfelf
'can find nothing wherewith to accufe
'them; only in this matter of their God.
'And when they fuffered thus the fpoil-
'ing of their goods, they endured it with
'patience and joyfulnefs. But my end
'in this relation, is for the general in-
'formation of all; that thofe who are
'fellow fufferers with them in this caufe,
'may not think ftrange of thefe fiery
'trials; knowing that the fame are
'accomplifhed in their brethren that are
'in the world; who are with them
'filling up that which is behind of the
'fufferings of *Chrift*. Befides, hereby
'thefe harfh proceedings againft a *peacea-
'ble people*, may come to the ear of fome
'in authority, who may, out of pity
'to the diftreffed, and juftice to their
'righteous caufe, redrefs thefe grievances.
'And who knows, but that, (as *Morde-
'cai* faid of *Efther*) fome of them are
'come to thefe places of truft for fuch a
'time as this? Wifhing (whoever thou art
'that readeft thefe lines) that thou mayeft
'never

'never meet with the like severity from
'any, that thefe have done from fome;
'I refer thee to the *Narrative* itfelf,
'which immediately enfueth:

'On the twenty-ninth of *May*, 1670.
'being the Lord's-day, fays the *Author*,
'[whom I take to be Mr. *Jerem. Ives*]
'fome chriftians in and about *Lewes*,
'in the county of *Suffex*, (to the num-
'ber of 500, fay their adverfaries) were
'met together to hear the word of God,
'and that they might, if poffible, avoid
'exafperating their enemies on one hand,
'and provide for their own fecurity on
'the other, the meeting was appointed at
'three a-clock afternoon (by reafon of the
'peoples being at the publick) an hour
'of the greateft privacy. People were
'appointed to go to a houfe, where ufu-
'ally they met, within a mile of *Lewes*;
'but from thence were directed to a pri-
'vate by-lane, within a quarter of a mile
'of the houfe. This may be enough to
'take of that imputation of contempt
'of authority, fo frequently caft upon
'them by fome; and that of rafhnefs
'as frequently objected by others.

THERE were two perfons, who feeing Relf *and*
fome people go that way, followed them Goring.
to the place of meeting, and became *In-*
formers. Upon which Sir *Thomas Nutt*, Sir. Tho.
Nutt, *a*
a violent perfecutor, and three other *violent*
Juftices, whom he had drawn into a com- *perfecutor:*
pliance

pliance with him, convicts the *Minister* and above forty of the hearers, without hearing what they had to plead in their own defence.

Many fin'd for being at a meeting.

THE hearers were fined 5 *s.* a piece, and the minister 20 *l.* The minister's fine was laid upon five of the hearers; so that *Walter Brett* and *Thomas Barnard* were fined each 6 *l.* 5 *s.* *Richard White* 3 *l.* 15 *s.* *Thomas Ridge* 1 *l.* 10 *s.* and the rest in smaller fines; the lowest 5 *s.* Warrants were issued out under the hands of the Justices for recovery of the said fines by distress and sale of goods; and directed to the Constable of the hundred, the Church-wardens and Overseers of the parish. And, says the Author of the Narrative, ' after one of the warrants,

p. 3.

' and beneath the hands and seals of the
' Justices, was written as a postcript some-
' what to this purpose, *That all other*
' *officers whatever were required, within*
' *their liberties, to assist the said officers in*
' *making the distress.*

Warrant granted to make distress.

' SIR *Thomas Nutt* sends out these
' warrants by his Clerk; who carrying
' them to the Headborough of *Ring-*
' *mire*, told him, that Sir *Thomas* had
' sent him those warrants, and that if
' he knew any others that had been at
' the meeting, he must put in their names,
' and levy 5 *s.* a piece of them. The
' Headborough telling him he was at
' church,

' church, and so knew not who was at
' the meeting; the other reply'd, that if he
' heard of any that were there he should
' put them in.

' THE constable declared to one of
' the Justices, that he would rather for-
' feit his 5 *l*. than act. The Justice
' told him he was only to go with
' them, and see the peace kept; it was
' the others that were to distrain : Which
' he did accordingly, but would not med-
' dle in the distress.

ON the first of *June* they began to make their distresses, and took from *John Prior* (who was fined 10 *s*. for himself and his wife) four cheeses : He only told them, *he never sold any thing for so great advantage, for this would bring him in an hundred fold.* Within a few days after, he was by warrant brought before Sir *Thomas*, for bidding *Goring* the informer, repent of being such a *Judas*, and warning him of the judgment to come. But Sir *Thomas* only obliged him to pay 2 *s*. for the warrant. On the same day they made distress upon *Thomas Ridge*, being fined 30 *s*. and took as many goods from his shop as amounted to 50 *s*. He peaceably submitted, only assuring them, *he parted as willingly with them as with any goods he ever sold.* They would have deposited their spoil at the sign of the *Cats* in the Cliff,

P. 4.

Distress made on J Prior.

And on T. Ridge.

Cliff, but the master of the house, tho' a churchman, said he would let no such goods come within his doors; which made them take up quarters in another place.

On Rich. White *and* Richard Thomas, Edward Henly, Samuel Cruttenden,

ON the seventeenth of *June*, at the town of *Lewes*, they distrained from *Rich. White* as many brass kettles, with a still, which were worth 10 *l*. 13 *s*. tho' his fine was but 3 *l*. 15 *s*. From *Richard Thomas*, a butcher, they took his weights for 5 *s*. From *Edward Henly*, a shoemaker, they took five pair of shoes; his fine was 5 *s*. From *Samuel Cruttenden*, a haberdasher, they took three hats, worth 15 *s*. for 5 *s*. From *Thomas Elphick*, a shoemaker, three pair of shoes, worth 9 *s*. for 5 *s*. From *Richard Bennet*, a taylor, fined 10 *s*. they plunder'd his kitchen; taking goods of several sorts. From *Edward Whiskets*, a victualler, fined 5 *s*. they took goods to a considerable value. From *Nicholas Grisbrooks*, a blacksmith, they took, amongst other things, part of a flitch of bacon.

Thomas Elphick, Richard Bennet,

Edward Whiskets,

N. Grisbrooks,

J. Tabret,

June the twentieth, *John Tabret* of the *Cliff*, fined 55 *s*. they took from him a cow. She not liking her new masters, at night returned home, but they soon fetch'd her back again.

William Humphry,

June the twenty first, they visit *Lewes* again, and took from *William Humphry*, a barber, a looking-glass of a considerable value, with other things belonging to his

English Baptists.

his employment. Entering the houſe of Benjamin *Wood*, a maſon, they took the ſheets from the bed, and four of the good woman's new ſhifts, but ſhe being unwilling to part with them, redeemed them by paying the 5 *s.* for which they diſtrained. They plundered the ſhop of *John Knapp*, a barber, fined 5 *s.* He deſired them, amongſt the reſt, to take Mr. *Dodd*'s ſayings hanging by; but, ſays the *Author*, them they refuſe, knowing, belike, that they propheſied no good to them. From *Henry Owden*'s, a carpenter, fined 5 *s.* they took a good muſket and a jack, worth 10 *s.* From *Thomas Tourle*, a butcher, fined 5 *s.* they took his horſe. And from *Richard Mantle* they took another, for the like fine. They took from *Walter Brett*, a grocer, fined 6 *l.* 5 *s.* two barrels of ſugar, which coſt him above 15 *l.*

Benjamin Wood,
J. Knapp,
Henry Owden,
T. Tourle,
R. Mantle,
Walter Brett.

' Two days after this, ſays the *Author*, ' being the twenty third of *June*, theſe ' *mauling* officers rally their forces, con- ' ſiſting of *Relph* the *informer*, a brother ' of *Goring*'s the *informer*, and another, ' who encouraged by Sir *Thomas Nutt*, ' newly entered on that employment. ' To which the Conſtable and Head- ' borough of that hundred, within which ' *Northeaſe* farm in the pariſh of *Rad-* ' *mill* lies, being added, they intend ' to make a diſtreſs there for 11 *l.* 10 *s.*

P. 7, 8, &c.

' being

'being the fines impofed on *Thomas* and
'*Richard Barnard* of *Lewes*. The dif-
'treffors pretended, that thefe brothers
'were with their mother partners in the
'ftock, and the goods by partnerfhip
'diftrainable. It was offered to be made
'appear, that *Thomas*, upon whom 6 *l*. 5 *s*.
'of the fine was laid, had no propriety
'in the ftock for above three years paft.
'But it feems they think it a good rea-
'fon, that his mother (though not at
'the meeting) fhould pay for him, as
'that he fhould pay for others. Befides,
'when thefe things were queftioned to
'Sir *Thomas Nutt*, he bid them diftrain
'however: For, faid he, come the
'worft, they can but appeal to us. The
'diftreffors comfort themfelves alfo with
'this, that how illegally foever they act,
'perfons can but appeal to the feffions,
'and they have four of the Juftices
'hands to their warrant already. Sir
'*Thomas* told one whilft this diftrefs was
'levying, that if he pleafed he would
'levy their fines upon him, and how
'would he help himfelf, though the par-
'ty were not at the meeting.

'Before thefe blades could make up
'their full company, the oxen, which
'*Buckland* had efpecially threatned, were
'by the fervants belonging to the farm
'locked up. When the Conftable came,
'*Buckland* commands him to break the
'door.

' door. The Constable demanded of him
' a warrant to empower him to do it.
' Many sore strains *Buckland* himself gave
' the door, but finding himself prevented
' here, in a fume he steers his course ano-
' ther way, threatning that he would take
' the whole herd of about twenty cows;
' upon which the dairy-maid is said to tell
' him, *that then she believed they would
' have store of sillibubs, having gotten so
' much sugar from Mr.* Brett. The bars
' where the cows were, being lockt, the
' Constable durst not break them open,
' at least not without a warrant. *Buck-
' land* took his old warrant out of his
' pocket, and purposely misreading it,
' would have made the Constable believe,
' that he was included in the warrant;
' and producing the act (at the rate he
' read it) made as if that clause, empow-
' ering the breaking open of a house
' in order to the taking of a meeting,
' had empowered him to break open
' upon a distress. Moreover *Buckland* of-
' fered him his word, if not his bond,
' to bear him harmless; but his word and
' bond were both of like value in the Con-
' stable's account; who willing to have
' better security for what he did, imme-
' diately went to the Justices concerned
' in the conviction, desiring a special war-
' rant to break open if he must do it.
' Two of them civilly told him they

' should

'should give out no other warrant.
'Sir *Thomas Nutt* could say more than
'both the others; he tells him, that the
'Constables at *Lewes* had broke open
'doors, and so might he as well: A
'further warrant he denied him, but
'threatned immediately to fine him if he
'did not assist them in the distress.

'THEY were from eight in the morn-
'ing till nigh two in the afternoon, be-
'fore they made their distress.

'*Buckland* sent to *Lewes*, being about
'two miles, to inform Sir *Thomas Nutt*,
'that there was such a company there,
'that he dare hardly to do his office.
'Upon which Sir *Thomas* was heard to say,
'that he would make a riot of it, and
'that it should cost the two *Barnards* an
'100 *l.* a man. It seems there were pre-
'sent most of the servants, few else; and
'these only to be witnesses of what was
'done; the best armed amongst them
'had only an ox-goad, which was he
'that drove the oxen. It seems *Buck-
'land* esteemed him a second *Shamgar*, &c.

Distress on Tho. and Richard Barnard.

'THE Constable returns in great per-
'plexity; if he breaks the door he lays
'himself open to an action from the own-
'ers; if he do not, Sir *Thomas* threatens
'that he shall be fined; who in such cases
'useth not to be worse then his word.
'The Constable chose rather, though im-
'portunately desired by *Buckland* to break
'open

'open the bars for cows, than the barn
'for oxen. They took fix cows, three
'of which, indifferently fold, would more
'than countervail their fines. One of
'the parties diſtrained told them, he won-
'dred that men skilled in the worth of
'cattle, ſhould make ſuch an unreaſon-
'able diſtreſs. *Buckland* replied, but we
'take one for your peremptorineſs, and
'another for our pains. Some of their
'own gang report, that the diſtrainers
'will get above 10 *l.* apeice by the bar-
'gain —— There was ſeverally by both
'the perſons diſtrained demands made of
'a copy of the warrant, which the other
'refuſed to give them. They then de-
'manded the ſight of it, which was
'likewiſe denied.

'THE fix kine aforeſaid, ſays the
'*Author*, were driven to *Buckland*'s, who
'had ſome land he hired, that wanted
'ſtock. The next Saturday ſevennight,
'being the ſecond of *July*, theſe with
'the cow taken from *John Tabret*, were
'brought to *Lewes* market, and placed
'juſt before Sir *Thomas Nutt*'s door. It
'being quickly known upon what account
'they were taken, they had many ſpecta-
'tors, but few chapmen; probably they
'had lain in their hands, but that there
'being at Sir *Thomas Nutt*'s, an own bro-
'ther of his, he becomes the purchaſer,
'buyeth the ſeven cows, for what is not cer-
'tainly

' tainly known, for 14 *l.* 5 *s.* fay they
' that report the higheft, though they
' were not ill worth 27 *l.* Having no
' ground of his own, he firft fends them,
' and then felleth them to one that is
' tenant to Sir *Thomas.*

' IT was ftranged by fome, why Sir
' *Thomas* fhould, beyond others, beftir
' himfelf to procure them diftrained. But
' now that riddle may be eafily read ;
' his brother is to have the firft purchafe
' of them, and his tenant the fecond.
' The fame day, fale was cry'd in the
' market, to be held at the *Star* in *Lewes,*
' the *Monday, Tuefday* and *Wednefday* fol-
' lowing, for the reft of the goods, where
' they fold cheap, I cannot fay good pen-
' nyworths.

' THE fame day with that at *Lewes,*
' there was a meeting at the town of
' *Brighthelmftone,* fome fix miles off. To
' take away all occafion of offence, they
' did leffen their number, and alter their
' place of meeting ; but were befet by
' Captain *Tetterfol,* Conftable of the place,
' and his gang : Finding the door fhut,
' that they could not enter, they furroun-
' ded the houfe, that none of the meeters
' might come out. Thus they kept them
' prifoners till they fent to *Lewes,* to Sir
' *Thomas Nutt* for a warrant to break open
' the door. When the warrant came, en-
' trance was given ; they find no minifter,
' nor

' nor were the people, when they came
' in, about any religious exercise. They
' pretended they had heard the sound of
' a voice, which they please to say is
' preaching. These men going to Sir *Tho-*
' *mas Nutt*, and making some deposition
' upon oath, a warrant is issued out to
' bring the meeters before him and some
' other Justices.

' WHEN they came, the business was
' to pump something by way of confes-
' sion out of them; in which, if they
' would be ingenuous, a promise is made
' that they should set their own fines;
' but these, keeping their own counsel,
' the Justices not being able to convict
' them by the parties confession, are
' forced to do it, by that notorious evi-
' dence before specified. They fine *Wil-* W. Beard
' *liam Beard*, master of the house, where *fined 20 l.*
' the meeting was, 20 *l.* *Tetterfol* breaks *stress made*
' open locks to come at malt: Being *for it.*
' gotten to the heap, filleth, without all
' measure, sixty of five bushel sacks,
' which he hath sold to one of his gang
' for 12 *s. per* quarter. One that went
' out of the house where the meeting was,
' just as the disturbers were coming to it,
' is notwithstanding convicted.

' AT *Chillington*, three miles from Nicholas
' *Lewes*, one *Nicholas Martin* was upon Martin
' slight evidence convicted by Sir *Thomas* *fined 20 l.*
' *Nutt*, for having a meeting at his house; *stress made*
' and *for it.*

' fined 20 *l.* for which they drain his
' land, and took from him six cows, two
' young bullocks and a horse, being all
' the stock he had. These were return-
' ed to him again upon his entring an
' appeal; but being strangely cast at the
' Sessions, he was by the court fined 60 *l.*
' which was at last remitted to 23 *l.*
' For non-payment whereof, he was com-
' mitted to the Jaylor's hands; nor could
' he be released, though one *Salisbury,*
' Vicar of the place, his grand persecu-
' tor, being convinced he had dealt inju-
' riously with him, offered to give bond
' to pay the whole fine within a quar-
' ter of a year.'

Appeals, was cast, and fin'd 60 l

Such was the great rage and malice, with which in those days, the persecutions were carried on against the *Nonconformists*, by the *Justices* and *Clergy* throughout the kingdom, that more mercy was extended to *criminals*, than to those whom they could charge with no *crimes*, either against the church or state.

Manuscript penes me.

It is observed by one Mr. *Josiah Diston*, who had been often committed to prison, and bound over to several *Assizes* and *Sessions*, for having private meetings in his house; that he found the spirit and temper of the *Judges* and *Justices* in those times to be such, that when any person or accusation came before them concerning *Dissenters*, they were zealous in aggravating

vating their crimes; and many who were usually silent in other cases, were very forward speakers in these: Whereas, in other *criminal matters* they were cool, and very willing to shew all the favour they could.

BUT to pass by such melancholly relations of barbarity, used upon people for no other crime but because they feared God, and could not in conscience conform to the rites and ceremonies, which they would have imposed upon them, of which I have many instances now before me; I shall produce some testimonies of God's dislike of such proceedings, by his hand of providence stretched out against some of the *chief persecutors* and *informers* against the *Protestant Dissenters* in *Oxfordshire*; collected by the aforesaid Mr. *Diston*, and several others, who had a personal knowledge of what I am about to relate.

An account of some persecutors in Oxfordshire.

ONE *Anne Clemens*, wife of *Matthew Clemens*, a baker, a man that had an house and land of his own freehold, in good business, and lived plentifully: This woman was noted, at *Chipping-Norton*, for her rage and malice against the *Dissenters*. She in a violent manner attacked a *Minister* in the pulpit, tore his cloak, and with some others assisting her, forced him from the pulpit, and set up an *episcopal one* in his room; for which action she gained the

Anne Clemens.

Mr. Ford.

title

title of Captain *Clemens*. Soon after this, her family funk in their eftate; and though fhe had feveral children, not one that lived thereabout was in a condition of living comfortably in the world. One of her daughters went beyond fea; the family grew poor, the land was fold, the houfe mortgaged for near its worth, the hufband died, and fhe was left fo poor, that fhe was in a little time forced to beg alms of thofe fhe had hated and perfecuted; and under a grievous judgment, of having an appetite to eat as much as would fatisfy two or three people, and fo fubject to breed vermin, that her daughter-in-law faid, that though fhe had wafhed and oven'd her cloaths, yet fhe could not keep her clean. In this deplorable condition fhe lived fome years, and then died miferably as to this world, and it is to be feared, fays the Relator, as to the life to come.

R. Allein. Mr. *Richard Allein* was another who appeared very foon in difquieting his religious neighbours; and though he had formerly been a member of a diffenting congregation, yet all the time of the Diffenters troubles, till near his death, he was a very active *informer* againft them, and took all opportunities of afflicting them, till fome very afflicting providences befel himfelf, and fuch as were thought to be the means of fhortning his life. His eldeft eldest *Son* was killed at *London*; and near the same time, his second *Son* was accused and arraigned at *Oxford* Assizes, for robbing on the highway, and it was by great friends and fees, that he escaped with his life, but was never after heard of in these parts. The father never enjoyed himself after this, nor acted any more against the *Dissenters*; but shortly after died a sudden death.

Mr. *Thomas Lodge*, having in this county T. Lodge. a free estate of about fifty pounds *per Ann.* and twenty pounds a year left him by his father, and besides was an officer in the county troops. This man set himself violently to persecute the Dissenters, and resolved to suppress them intirely; but before he could accomplish his design, and ruin them in their persons and estates, he sunk very much in his own estate, sold part of it, and died greatly in debt: The remainder of his estate being much incumbred, was soon after sold by his son, whose children are now so poor, that they are common beggars.

Robert Werg, when he was Constable, Robert was a very forward and busy man, at Werg. informing against Dissenters, watching to discover their meetings, and in making distress on their goods: He lived not long after he came out of office. In his sickness he was heard to say, that he caught his death by watching one cold night, to take the Dissenters at their meeting.

Thomas Samuel, Thomas Pannier, Thomas Houlton, William Knowlis, Richard Adcock.

Thomas Samuel, Thomas Pannier, Thomas Houlton, William Knowlis and *Richard Adcock,* were all persons whom those in power employ'd to watch the Dissenters meetings, and inform against them, and received pensions for what they did in this wicked service: But it was observed, that they did not prosper in their worldly affairs afterwards, and that shortly after every one of them died.

Lord Falkland, *Sir* Tho. Pennystone, *Sir* Wm. Moreton, *Sir* Tho. Roe.

THE Lord *Falkland* an *Irish* Peer, Lord Lieutenant of the County, Sir *Thomas Pennystone,* deputy Lieutenant, Sir *William Moreton,* and Sir *Thomas Roe,* were Justices of the Peace, and bitter persecutors of the Dissenters, employing their whole power to ruin them; and it is observed concerning them, that by some blast of Providence they came to be utterly ruin'd themselves, their estates sold, and most of their families became extinct, and that some of them were cut off by death, before they could accomplish their threatnings of the further mischief they designed.

Sir Littleton Obaldiston.

Sir *Littleton Obaldiston,* another Justice of the peace, has been sometimes heard to rail against Dissenters, it being accounted a mark of loyalty, to reproach and villify them. He did also join with other Justices in committing Dissenters to prison;

but,

but, says the Relator, there is ground to hope, that he saw his evil afterwards; because he was inftrumental in releafing feveral, and carried himfelf friendly towards them the refidue of his life. He is dead, and his eftate is continued to his pofterity.

—— *Howard*, Efq; being a Juftice of the peace, and an Officer in the county troops, at the beginning of the Diffenters troubles, was, like *Saul*, a zealous perfecutor of them; he broke up a meeting, and committed feveral to prifon, out of zeal, as he then faid, for the church: But fhortly after, being apprehenfive that there was a defign to bring in Popery, he releafed thofe whom he had committed to prifon, and never acted againft Diffenters any more; but, on the contrary, expreffed great friendfhip towards them, and was not backward to own to them, and others, that he was miftaken in the perfons and their principles; and for his moderation to them, was by others reproached, and accounted as one of them, tho' ftill a conftant adherer to the eftablifhed worfhip. This gentleman, fays the Relator, is the only perfon in this part of the county, that was a difturber of the Diffenters that is now living, this 30th of *Dec.* 1707. being now an old man, full of days, wealth and honour.

Howard.

Anno.
1671.
The King designs to govern absolutely.

THE large supplies of money which the parliament had given to support his Majesty's pleasures, kept up a pretty good agreement between him and them: But now the King having assurance of large remittances from *France*, he resolved to govern by the *prerogative*, and stand upon his own legs. And,

*Hist.*Engl. vol. 2. p. 655.

HAVING taken up a resolution to become absolute, he easily saw, says *Rapin*,
' that the execution of it required an art-
' ful and cautious conduct, and such se-
' cret and imperceptible methods, as would
' not too plainly discover his intentions.
' For he could not suppose, that because
' he desired to be absolute, the people of
' *England* would immediately give up
' their liberties and privileges: It was
' therefore necessary to lead them to it
' insensibly and by degrees; and to that
' end he wanted a secret council com-
' posed of few persons, in whom he might
' entirely confide, and whose interest it
' was to accomplish this design. The
' ordinary council consisting of twenty
' one persons, was not proper to con-
' duct this affair. For, besides that some
' Counsellors had a right to their places,
' as for instance, the Archbishop of *Can-
' terbury*, it was very difficult to ingage
' so many persons of the first rank in such
' a plot. To effect therefore this under-
' taking

' taking with the more caution, the King
' eſtabliſhed a cabinet council of five per- *Forms the*
' ſons only; namely, *Cabal.*

  ' *Clifford,*
  ' *Arlington,*
  ' *Buckingham,*
  ' *Aſhley,*
  ' *Lauderdale.*

' As the initial letters of theſe five
' names compoſe the word C A B A L,
' this ſecret council was from thence
' called the *Cabal.*

' IF to theſe five members of the Ca- *Ib. p.* 656.
' bal, ſays *Rapin,* are joined, as in rea-
' ſon they ought, the King and the Duke
' of *York,* it will be found, that all the
' ſeven were for an abſolute and arbitrary
' government; and that, with regard to
' religion, four were Papiſts, namely, the
' King, the Duke, *Arlington* and *Clif-*
' *ford*; and three without any religion,
' or at leaſt they conſidered it only as an
' engine of ſtate. Theſe were *Bucking-*
' *ham, Aſhley,* and *Lauderdale.*

' IT would be difficult to know the *Who re-*
' tranſactions of the *Cabal,* if Father *Orleans,* *ſolve upon*
'   *a war*
' inſtructed by King *James* II. had not *with Hol-*
' told us, that a war with *Holland* was land.
' there reſolved, in order to furniſh the
' King with a pretence to keep on foot
' both land and ſea-forces. For it is ma-
           ' nifeſt,

'nifeft, that such a design could be ac-
'complished, but by force or fear. The
'pretence for this war was to be taken
'from the dispute about the flag, which
'might easily be renewed; and from
'the general complaints of the *English*
'merchants concerning their commerce,
'of which so great use had been made
'for undertaking the former war: *But*,
'adds Father *Orleans, the true reason of
'making this war upon* Holland, *was the
'secret correspondence between the repub-
'licans of* England *and the* Dutch; *who
'were incessantly exciting them to rebel-
'lion, and to shake off the yoke of monarchy,
'being ever ready to support those that should
'attack it.* This seems, says *Rapin*, to
'contradict what the same author ad-
'vances a few lines before; namely, that
'the true ground of this war was to fur-
'nish the King with a pretence for rais-
'ing an army. There is, however, no
'contradiction, for it must be considered,
'that the design of the King and the
'Cabal concerned two points, which went
'hand in hand, and formed properly but
'one design; namely, to introduce an ar-
'bitrary government, and to extirpate the
'protestant religion. As it could not be
'expected, that the *English* would tamely
'give up their religion and liberty with-
'out any resistance, it was natural to be-
'gin with depriving them of the only as-
' sistance

' fiftance they could hope for, by at-
' tacking the *Dutch*, and difabling them
' to fuccour *England*. Thofe therefore
' who are called by Father *Orleans* the
' Republicans of *England*, were the per-
' fons, who it was fuppofed, would op-
' pofe the King's defigns, as well Epif-
' copalians as Prefbyterians, and the Re-
' publicans properly fo called. It is there-
' fore clear, that the true reafon of mak-
' ing war upon the *States*, was as much
' to put it out of their power to affift
' the *Englifh*, as to have a pretence for
' raifing forces, and that this was but one
' and the fame reafon.'

To fhew, that one of the branches of the project formed by the Cabal, was to make the King abfolute, and that under that branch was comprized the extirpation of the Proteftant, or at leaft the intro- duction of the Popifh Religion; *Rapin* quotes an extract from the hiftory of Fa- ther *Orleans*, who after fpeaking of what had paffed concerning the *Papifts* and other *Nonconformifts*, adds, ' The King who
' was no good chriftian in his actions,
' tho' a Catholick in his heart, did all
' that could be expected from his indolent
' temper, to preferve the common liberty,
' that the Catholicks might partake of it.
' But the church of *England* prevailed,
' and Chancellor *Hide* was fo warm up-
' on this occafion, that the King was ob-
         ' liged

And an indulgence to Diffen- ters.

Ib. p. 662.

'liged to yield rather to his importuni-
'ties than his reasons. It was therefore
'the re-establishment of this liberty
'of conscience, that the Lord *Ashley*
'believed necessary to the execution
'of the projected design: He commu-
'nicated his thoughts to his colleagues
'of the Cabal, who were of the same
'opinion, not only on account of the
'reason he alleged, which was, the gain-
'ing of the *Nonconformists*, who were
'justly feared; but also upon another,
'which he readily approved, namely, the
'favouring of the *Catholicks*, whom most
'of them loved, and the rest esteemed.
'*Arlington* and *Clifford* were secretly
'*Catholicks*, and both died in the com-
'munion of the Church. *Buckingham*
'had no occasion to be converted, could
'he only have prevailed with himself as to
'libertinism. *Ashley* was not averse to the
'catholick religion, till interest and ma-
'lice threw him into the contrary party.
'It will easily be conceived, that the
'King readily consented to it, since he
'was a *Catholick*, and continued so to
'his death, though policy caused him to
'pretend the contrary. As for the Duke
'of *York*, he supported the design with
'all his power. All the difficulty lay in
'the extent of this liberty; and the two
'Kings, of *France* and *England*, acting
'in concert, debated this affair in the ne-
                                'gotiation

' gotiation of their treaty. Several propo-
' fals were made, fome more, fome lefs
' advantagious to the Catholicks. *France*
' was for the moſt moderate, fafeſt, and
' moſt feafonable methods. At laſt it was
' agreed, that *Charles* ſhould grant liberty
' of confcience to all his fubjects in gene-
' ral.

' It appears from hence, fays *Rapin*, *Anno*
' that religion was concerned in the pro- 1672.
' jects of the Cabal. But probably fome
' were for having the progrefs of the
' popiſh religion fubfervient to render the
' King abfolute; and others were for
' rendering the King abfolute, to favour
' the progrefs of Popery: Wherefore,
' thefe two articles were never feparated,
' nor indeed could be, fince they entirely
' depended on each other. The King plain- *A decla-*
' ly ſhewed it, when he publiſhed his de- *ration for*
' claration for liberty of confcience; fince *confcience.*
' he could not grant this liberty, without
' affuming a power to abrogate acts of
' parliament, or at leaſt fufpend the exe-
' cution thereof fo long as he pleafed.
' This declaration, dated the 15th of
' *March*, 1672. confiſted of various ar-
' ticles,' of which *Rapin* has given the
fubſtance.

' 1. His Majeſty publiſhes it, *in vir-*
' *tue of his ſupreme power in ecclefiaſtical*
' *matters*, which is a right inherent in his
' perfon,

'person, and declared to be so by several
'acts of parliament.

' 2. He declares his express resolution
' to be, that the church of *England* be
' preserved and remain intire in her doc-
' trine, discipline and government, as
' now it stands established by law.

' 3. That no person shall be capable
' of holding any ecclesiastical benefice or
' preferment of any kind, who is not ex-
' actly conformable.

' 4. That the execution of all penal
' laws in matters ecclesiastical, against
' whatsoever sorts of Nonconformists or
' recusants, be immediately suspended.

' 5. He declares, that he will from
' time to time allow a sufficient number
' of places, as shall be desired, in all parts
' of his kingdom, for the use of such as
' do not conform to the church of *Eng-
' land*, to meet and assemble in, in order
' to their publick worship and devotion.

' 6. That none of his subjects do pre-
' sume to meet in any place, until such
' place be allowed, and the teacher of that
' congregation be approved by him.

' 7. He declares, that this indulgence,
' as to the allowance of publick places of
' worship, and approbation of teachers,
' shall extend to all sorts of Nonconfor-
' mists and recusants, except the recusants
' of the *Roman* Catholick religion, to
' whom he will no ways allow publick
' places

' places of worship, but only indulge
' them their share in the common exemp-
' tion from the executing the penal laws,
' and the exercise of their worship in their
' private houses only.'

This indulgence did not please the *Presbyterians* in general; for many of them had far rather have had any tolerable state of unity with the publick ministry, than such a *toleration*. However, they went in a body, and were introduced by the Lord *Arlington*; and Dr. *Manton*, in their name, thanked the King for his declaration. Most of them, says Dr. *Burnet*, had yearly pensions of fifty pounds; and the chief of them of one hundred pounds.

Vol. 2. *p.* 308.

This deep laid design, under the plausible pretence of *toleration*, to introduce *popery*, plainly appeared: For the Protestant Dissenters, till they could get meeting-houses built, were more terribly restrained from meeting together than before; and it is not to be imagined they would be very forward to erect meeting-houses, when they had by this *indulgence* no security to enjoy them, even for a week; when the *Papists* were immediately put into possession of a securer and fuller liberty, being permitted in their houses, any where under their own government, without limitation or restriction to any number of places or persons, or any necessity of getting approbation.

bation. Thus, tho' this *indulgence* was said to be for avoiding the danger of conventicles in private; yet the *Papists* were allow'd such conventicles, in as many houses as they pleased.

Vol. 2. p. 662.

Mr. *Tindal* observes, in his notes on *Rapin*, from *Kennet*'s History, ' That
' the Lord *Clifford* told a Person of Qua-
' lity in private discourse, that the King,
' if he would be firm to himself, might
' settle what religion he pleased, and carry
' the government to what height he would;
' for if men were assured, in the liberty
' of their consciences, and undisturbed in
' their properties, able and upright Judges
' made in *Westminster-Hall*; and if, on
' the other hand, the fort of *Tilbury* was
' finished to bridle the *City*, the fort of
' *Plymouth* to secure the *West*, and arms
' for twenty thousand men in each of
' these, and in *Hull* for the northern parts,
' with some addition (which might be
' easily and undiscernedly made to the
' forces on foot) there were none who
' would have either will, opportunity or
' power to resist.'

The Commons address the King against his declaration.
Vol. 2. p. 667.

The House of Commons, alarmed with the proceedings of the King and his Cabal, presented an address to him against his *declaration for liberty of conscience*. In which they told him, says *Rapin*, ' That
' having taken into consideration his de-
' claration for *indulgence* to *Dissenters*, they
' found

'found themselves bound in duty to in-
'form his Majesty, *That penal laws in*
'*matters ecclesiastical cannot be suspended*
'*but by act of parliament.* They therefore
'most humbly besought his Majesty to
'give such directions, *that no apprehensions*
'*or jealousies might remain in the hearts*
'*of his faithful subjects.* To this address,
'says he, the King sent the following *The King's*
'answer: That he is very much troubled, *answer.*
'that the declaration which he put out for
'ends so necessary to the quiet of this king-
'dom, especially in that conjuncture,
'should prove the cause of disquiet, and
'give occasion to the questioning of his
'power in ecclesiasticks, which he finds
'not done in the reigns of any of his an-
'cestors. That he never had thoughts
'of using it otherwise than as it had been
'intrusted in him to the peace and esta-
'blishment of the church of *England*, and
'the ease of all his subjects in general.
'Neither doth he pretend to suspend any
'laws wherein the properties, rights or
'liberties of any of his subjects are con-
'cerned; nor to alter any thing in the
'established doctrine or discipline of the
'church of *England*. But his only de-
'sign in this was, to take off the penal-
'ties inflicted by statutes upon the Dis-
'senters, and which he believed, when
'well considered of, they themselves would
'not wish executed according to the ri-
'gour

'gour of the law. Neither hath he done
'this with any thought of avoiding, or
'precluding the advice of his parliament;
'and if any bill shall be offered to him,
'which shall appear more proper to at-
'tain the aforesaid ends, and secure the
'peace of the church and kingdom, when
'tendered in due manner to him, *He will
'shew how readily he will concur in all
'ways that shall appear for the good of the
'kingdom.*'

THE King and the *Cabal* found, that this declaration was far from engaging the Dissenters on their side. For tho' liberty of conscience was so greatly desirable, they did not desire it to the ruin of the church and kingdom. Alderman *Love*, a *city* member, and an eminent Dissenter, spoke in the house with the greatest warmth against the declaration; and said, *he had much rather still go without their desired liberty, than have it in a way that would prove so detrimental to the Nation* *.

THE Commons seeing the Dissenters so ready to sacrifice their own, to the interest of religion and the kingdom, order'd a bill to be brought in for their ease, by which all the penalties against them in the act of *uniformity* were removed, and nothing required but the taking the oaths of *supremacy* and *allegiance*. This bill in a

* Kennet, *p.* 318.

few

few days was compleated; but the Lords having made some amendments, the King prorogued the parliament before these amendments could be agreed to by the Commons.

THE difficulties into which the King by his *Cabal* had involved himself were so great, that to prevent a rupture between him and his parliament, after some hesitation, at the solicitation of his Ladies, called for the declaration, and with his own hands broke the seal; and in his speech to his parliament, tells them *, ' If ' there be any scruple yet remaining with ' you, touching the suspension of the pe-
' nal laws, I here faithfully promise you, ' that what hath been done in that par-
' ticular, shall not for the future be drawn ' into example and consequence; and as ' I daily expect from you a bill for my ' supply, so I assure you, I shall as wil-
' lingly receive and pass any other you ' shall offer me, that may tend to the ' giving you satisfaction in all your just ' grievances.' *He calls in his declaration.*

THE King having not courage and resolution enough to withstand the complaints of the parliament, gave a check to the hopes of the *Cabal*, which were founded on the King's steadiness, and threw them into a great consternation; *The Cabal in confusion.*

* Rapin, *Vol.* 2. *p.* 669.

for they looked upon themselves in danger of being abandoned by the King, and left to the resentment of the parliament : some of them therefore deserted the King, and hereby the grand designs of this *Cabal* were frustrated.

THE bill in favour of the Protestant Dissenters met with another disappointment; for the King adjourned the parliament before the Lords had given their assent to it; which shews, his Majesty had no concern for the interest of the Dissenters; for if he had, he might have deferred the adjournment a few days, till the bill passed in their favour had been ready, or at least might have pressed the two houses to have finished it. Thus the poor Dissenters, being deprived of the shelter of his Majesty's declaration, were left by the parliament to the storm of the severe laws which were in force against them, and by some Justices were rigourously put in execution; but the greater part were then more moderate; and so the Dissenters had in many places a liberty of performing their worship in their own way. But this hardly lasted three years, and the persecution of them revived, and continued to the end of this reign; and, says Dr. *Welwood* *, ' was one continued in-

---
* Memoirs, *p.* 119.

' vasion

' vafion upon the rights of the people,
' and the nation feemed unwilling now
' to contend for them any more.'

Our worthy Patriots now began to have a fcent of a plot to bring in popery, and ftood upon their watch. Something they difcerned to be in hand, and that the project was deeply laid, but on what perfons to charge it they knew not, and were wholly in the dark, as to the methods and particulars of it, till in the year 1678. Dr. *Oates* entered upon that never-to-be-forgotten fervice to his country, at once faving the life of his fovereign, the government of the nation, and the proteftant religion, from a total extirpation, and all good proteftants from a maffacre.

This confpiracy, or as it is more generally called the *Popifh plot*, gave occafion to many Politicians to exercife their talents, fome in fupporting the reality, others in expofing the falfity of it. A full account of the confpiracy, and of the reafons and proofs alledged in maintenance of the reality or falfhood, you may fee in *Rapin*; which is both foreign to my purpofe, and too large to be inferted here.

It was about this time, that the controverfy among the *Baptifts* about *laying on of hands*, called by the Clergy *confirmation*, created not a little trouble to thofe who were for the practice of that apofto-lical

The laying on of hands controverted among the Baptifts.

lical ordinance, occasioned by the publication of a treatise, entitled, *A Search after Schism*, by a nameless company, in opposition to it.

This was answered by Dr. *John Griffith*, in a piece, entitled, *The Searchers after Schism searched*; and drew from Mr. *Grantham*, his *Sigh for Peace, or, the Cause of Division discovered*. The publication of this book occasioned a meeting between Mr. *Grantham* and Mr. *Ives*, where a dispute upon that head was had with much temperance and good humour. Mr. *Ives* finding himself much gravelled, broke up the meeting, as I am informed, very peaceably and friendly.

About three years after Mr. *Danvers* wrote a treatise against *laying on of hands*, which was answered by Mr. *Benjamin Keach*; and also by Mr. *Grantham*, who annexed to his answer, *A treatise of the successors of the Apostles*. In which he pleaded for the *Jus Divinum* of the *Messenger's* office; which is continued among some of the *Baptists* to the present day.

Anno 1673.

That the persons and principles of of those termed *Anabaptists* might be held in disgrace, and rendered odious to the people: In the year 1673, was published a Pamphlet, entitled, *Mr. Baxter baptized in Blood*, which, says * Mr. *Hooke*,

* *Apology*, p. 6-7.

the author of the *Apology for the baptized churches,* 'gave an account of a
' barbarous murder, committed by four
' *Anabaptists,* at *Boston* in *New-England,*
' upon the body of a godly Minister,
' called Mr. *Josiah Baxter,* for no other
' reason, but because he had worsted
' them in disputation; which was set
' forth, with all the circumstances and
' formalities of names, speeches, actions,
' time and place, to make it look the
' more authentick; orderly and most
' pathetically describing the most execra-
' ble murder, that ever was known, *viz.*
' of first stripping, and cruelly whip-
' ping, then unbowelling, and fleeing a-
' live, a reverend godly Minister in his
' own house, in the midst of the howl-
' ing groans and schreechings of his dear
' relations, lying bound before him. And
' the better to create belief, this sad story
' is pretended to be published by the
' mournful brother of the said murdered
' Minister, named *Benjamin Baxter,* liv-
' ing in *Fenchurch*-street, *London.* More-
' over, the *Authors* had dealt so cunning-
' ly, that they had prevailed with Dr.
' *Samuel Parker* to licenfe it.'

A wicked slander against the Baptists confuted.

It hath been always the malicious practice of that grand slanderer *Satan* and his *Instruments,* since the first times of christianity, when they could not resist the power of religion, to defame the persons and assemblies of all Christians, with foul and hateful crimes laid to their charge; as appears by the apologies of *Justine Martyr*, *Tertullian*, and others. But the *Authors* of this slander have hatched a *forgery* beyond all story; not only under the specious pretence of piety, intitling God himself, his holy Word, and all that is sacred therein, but with the formalities of names, speeches, actions, time and place, orderly and most pathetically describing the most execrable murder that ever was known, exceeding the cruelties of the most savage Heathens.

I THINK it may be truly said, that the bounds of christian profession are not wide enough to afford us an example parallel to the prodigious malice of these lying *defamers*; pretending this horrid fact as done by *Anabaptists*, that they might the better expose the whole profession of them in all parts, tho' never so innocent, to the hatred and rage of the people in all places against them.

FOR it concludes in these words, *viz.*

' I HAVE penn'd and published this
' narrative, *in perpetuam rei memoriam*;
' that the world may see the spirit and
' temper of these men, and that it may
' stand as an eternal memorial of their
' cruelty and hatred to all Orthodox Mi-
' nisters.'

Now

Now this was enough to perfuade any body, that the report was true, especially being publifhed with allowance; and might make men, not only afham'd to be *Anabaptifts*, but to abhor the name and *Sect* for ever. Neverthelefs, by divine providence, this was foon difcovered to be all falfe and forged, not a tittle of truth in it; for a fhip coming from *Bofton* in *New-England*, about twenty days after this murder was faid to be committed, two of the men, the *Mafter* of the veffel, and a *Merchant* that was with him, attefted upon oath, before the Lord Mayor of *London*, that they never knew fuch a man as Mr. *Jofiah Baxter*; that they had heard of no fuch report, nor knew any occafion of fuch a thing; but did believe it was a very great falfhood.

The *Officers* of the two wards of *Aldgate* and *Langburn*, in which *Fenchurch*-ftreet is fituate, gave a certificate under their hands, that within their memories, no fuch man as *Benjamin Baxter*, the pretended brother that publifhed the ftory, had lived in *Fenchurch*-ftreet. The King's Privy Council examined the cafe, and detected the *forgery*, and accordingly ordered the publifhing the fame in the *Gazette*; and Dr. *Parker*, that had been too credulous, and hafty in licenfing this tragical ftory, confeffed his error,

error, and gave a teftimonial under his hand, acknowledging the fame.

The affidavit of the two *New-England men*.

By two Men's affidavit.

'*Rich. Martin*, mafter of the good fhip,
' the *Bloſſom* of *Boſton*, of *New-England*,
' Merchant, and *Henry Mountfort* of *Boſ-*
' *ton*, aforefaid, Merchant, make oath,
' that on the 26th day of *February* laſt
' paſt, they thefe deponents fet fail from
' *Boſton* aforefaid, for the port of *London*;
' and thefe deponents alfo fay, and affirm,
' that they, the faid deponents, for di-
' vers years laſt paſt, have had their con-
' ſtant refidence and abode in or near *Boſ-*
' *ton* aforefaid; but thefe deponents, and
' either of them, for himfelf faith, that
' they never heard of, or knew any Mi-
' nifter, called or known by the name of
' *Joſiah Baxter*; nor was there to thefe
' deponents knowledge or belief, any dif-
' pute or controverfy whatfoever, between
' the faid *Baxter* and the *Anabaptiſts* in
' *New-England*, of or concerning any
' points of religion; neither was there
' any report at *Boſton* aforefaid, or any
' other place in *New-England*, of or con-
' cerning any murder, pretended to have
' been committed upon the faid *Baxter*,
' or any other perfon or perfons what-
' foever, by any *Anabaptiſts* in *New-Eng-*
' *land*. And thefe deponents do verily
' believe

'believe that the late book, intitled, Mr.
'*Baxter baptized in blood*, is an abfolute
' pamphlet, and a very great falfhood;
' for that thefe deponents were refiding
' at *Bofton* aforefaid, two and twenty days
' after the faid murder, in the faid pamph-
' let mention'd, is pretended to have been
' committed.'

May 21, 1673. Ambo *Richard Martin.*
jurat. fuer. coram me,
Rob. Hanfon, Mayor. *Henry Mountfort.*

Hereupon the Lord-Mayor was pleafed by his officers, not only to interdict the vending the faid fcandalous pamphlet, but to feize it in the hands of the hawkers and mercuries that fold the fame; and to fupprefs a fecond impreffion thereof in the prefs; committing alfo to *prifon* feveral of the publifhers.

The certificate of the officers of the Ward. *By the officers of the parifh.*

' Whereas we have lately feen a
' pamphlet, entitled, Mr. *Baxter bap-*
' *tized in blood*, faid to be publifhed by
' his mournful brother, *Benjamin Baxter*,
' living in *Fenchurch-ftreet, London:* We
' the Church-wardens, Overfeers and
' Beadles, do certify, that there is no
' fuch man, doth or hath, within our
' memory, lived in the two wards of
' *Aldgate* and *Langbourne*, in which *Fen-*
' *church-ftreet* is fituate. To the truth of
' which

' which attestation, we whose names are
' under written, have set our hands, this
' 27th day of *May,* 1673.'

Thomas Baylie,
William Wickins,   } Church-wardens.
Gordard Fletch,
Thomas Fisher,

Samuel Loveday, } Overseers.
Ralph Almond,

Will. Tiplington, } Beadles.
Thomas Smith,

An address being made to the *Council-board,* they upon examination of the business, find it false and fictitious, and accordingly ordered the publishing the same in the Gazette, *viz.*

The order of Council.

By the order of Council.
' WHEREAS there is a pamph-
' let lately published, entitled,
' Mr. *Baxter baptized in blood,* contain-
' ing a horrible murder, committed by
' four *Anabaptists,* upon the person of
' Mr. *Josiah Baxter,* near *Boston* in *New-*
' *England:* The whole matter having
' been enquired into, and examined at
' the Council-board, is found altogether
' false and fictitious.
' *Edw. Walker.'*

The licenser, Dr. *Samuel Parker*, being also made acquainted with the whole matter, confesseth his mistake and too sudden credulity in the licensing so strange a pamphlet, as appears by the testimonial under his hand, *viz.*

Dr. *Parker*'s Testimonal.

'WHEREAS there was a certain pamphlet, lately published under the title of, Mr. *Baxter baptized in blood*, containing a Narrative, of a murder committed on the person of one *Josiah Baxter*, a Minister, near *Boston* in *New-England*; which *Narrative* was allowed of, licensed, and publickly exposed to sale: These are to certify, that the allowance and licence thereof, was obtained at the desire and suggestion of one *Laurence Savil*: Who in order to procure the same, did really produce to the licenser, letters and testimonals, under the hands, as he pretended, of several persons in *New-England*, containing the particular circumstances of the said relation, and asserting the truth of the same, as in the printed copy is expressed. All which, upon further enquiry and examination, the said licenser hath since evidently 'found

By Dr. Parker.

'found to be fictitious and untrue, con-
'trived and invented here in *England*,
'without any warrant or atteftation from
'beyond the feas. And fo much he hath
'thought fit to publifh, to the end that
'no perfon may be abufed or impofed
'upon by a report, which, as he is now
'fufficiently convinced, is both falfe and
'groundlefs.

Read in Council, 30th of *May*, 1673.   *Samuel Parker.*

<small>The fuppofed publifher of this notorious forgery was one Seymer, a pretended Doctor of Phyfick, who upon diligent fearch was difcovered and met with.

* Seymer.

By a letter from Laurence Savil.</small>

Laurence Savil, who obtained the licenfing of this infamous pamphlet, thro' guilt hiding his head, could not be met with; but wrote a letter to one of them who were in fearch after him, and confeffeth himfelf drawn in and cheated, by this imaginary and fuppofitious *Benjamin Baxter.* The letter was thus:

'SIR,

'THE Doctor * has urged and preffed me by feveral letters, to give
'the world a full and fatisfactory ac-
'count of this bufinefs, of Mr. *Baxter's*
'pamphlet. Mr. *Benjamin Baxter*, the
'Author of the late pamphlet, about nine
'weeks fince, infinuated into my acquain-
'tance: firft in *Gray's-inn-walks*, and
'afterwards at a Coffee-houfe in *Holbourn.*
'I met him often in the walks, from
'thence

' thence we went to the Coffee-houses:
' I was well-pleased with his company,
' because he seemed an ingenious person,
' a good scholar, and an *orthodox member*
' *of the Church of England*. He used
' always to dispute against the *Anabap-*
' *tists*; and in Coffee-houses, to be so
' fierce in his invectives against that *party*,
' that sometimes he became ridiculous
' to the company. He would often much
' comment on the increase of that party.
' Afterwards he told me, he was compo-
' sing a general *History* of the first ori-
' ginal and progress of the *Anabaptists*,
' with a full confutation of their tenets,
' which he was confident would be a
' work very acceptable to the sober part
' of the nation.

' THEN he told me, he had a parti-
' cular kindness for me, and that I should
' have the publishing of it; by which he
' was sure I might gain no less than
' 100 *l*. I returned him thanks for his
' kindness, and told him, I was not ac-
' quainted in things of that nature; but
' that it was more fit for some Bookfel-
' ler to deal in, and that it would re-
' quire a disbursement of a considerable
' sum of money, which I was loath to
' venture. He instantly replied, that tho'
' I was ignorant in the business of print-
' ing, yet he understood it well, and had
' printed several things, but now his bu-
' siness

' finefs coming on fo faft, he had no time
' to follow it himfelf; but if I pleafed,
' would wholly employ me in it, and
' would difburfe the money for printing
' and paper, but leave the profit entirely
' to me. I muft confefs thefe offers
' feemed very fair; I could not hand-
' fomely refufe fuch kindnefs. So the
' bufinefs was concluded, and I every
' day expected this elaborate work for the
' prefs. I faw him no more for eight
' days together, at which I much won-
' dered: but one evening at *Gray's-inn*, I
' met him in a moft heavy and difcon-
' folate condition. After I had preft
' him to difcourfe the caufes of his grief,
' he told me his forrows were unexpref-
' fible; that his dear brother, that was
' formerly gone to *Virginia*, he heard
' was killed by the *Anabaptifts*. And
' then in a great paffion, he flung me
' three letters, and bad me read them.
' He faid he was refolved to *immortalize*
' *the fact*, and let it ftand for ever as an
' *eternal memorial againft that party*. I
' was much troubled at the fad fate of his
' brother, and fo we parted. Some three
' days after we met again; and then he
' fhewed me the copy of this *pamphlet*,
' and told me he came juft then from *Lam-*
' *beth*, and that Dr. *Parker* had licenfed
' it; for, faid he, I fhewed Dr. *Parker*
' the three letters, and could not forbear
                                                    weeping.

'weeping. Could you yourſelf have
'doubted of the reality of the buſineſs,
'if you had ſeen the licenſe to it, his
'tears and paſſionate expreſſions, and al-
'ſo the three letters? So at laſt I conde-
'ſcended to do it. The next day I went
'to Mr. *Darby*, and deſired him to print
'it. He took a view of the copy, and
'ſaid he was not ſatisfied of the truth of
'it; but he would recommend me to a
'*Cavalier* printer, as he expreſſed it, in
'*Jewin-ſtreet*, who would readily per-
'form the buſineſs. I deferred the pub-
'liſhing for ſeven or eight days, expect-
'ing to hear ſome objection againſt it,
'but meeting not with any, I publiſhed
'it. Mr. *Baxter* conſtantly met me eve-
'ry day, and always urged the expedite,
'and ſudden publication of the *Narra-*
'*tive*. I told him it was coming forth.
'He told me, I ſhould command what
'money I deſired, for this and ſeveral
'other books he had to come forth. I
'replied, that none was wanting yet;
'but when it was printed, the printer
'was to be paid. Upon *May* 15, I
'ſhewed him a proof ſheet; he ſaid, he
'was glad the buſineſs was ſo forward,
'he would go to the goldſmith to-mor-
'row; for, ſaid he, that will ſoon be enough
'for the printer. But in the mean time,
'ſays he, pray let me have four or five
'Guineas till to-morrow. I told him I
'had

'had not so much about me, but what I
'had he should have: so I let him have
'forty shillings, and we parted. The
'next day I expected him, but he came
'no more, neither have I ever seen or
'heard from him since.

'FORMERLY, when I asked him con-
'cerning his lodging, he said he lived in
'*Fenchurch-street*, but he was seldom at
'home, and it was impossible for me to
'meet with him. He said he was an
'Attorney, and had good employment
'that way. Thus has this fellow put
'upon me a business, and now unwor-
'thily deserted me. And now I begin
'too late, to perceive him either to be a
'cheat, or to be grosly cheated, and
'gulled with false letters; for he several
'times said, he had not heard of his
'brother, since his departure out of *Eng-
'land* till now. If I can do any further
'service in the matter, I shall be very
'ready and willing; for unless *Baxter*
'appears in his own defence, and pay
'me the money I lent him, I shall cer-
'tainly conclude him a cheat.

'As for my friend the *Doctor*, he
'was altogether unconcerned in the mat-
'ter, and did only recommend me to a
'printer, at my request. All this that
'I have writ, I will avouch to be most
'true, and if you please to print it, I
'will

' will stand to it, and justify it to be the
' naked truth of the business.'

Your real friend,

May 20, 1673.

Laurence Savill.

THUS this dark cloud was dissipated, that threatened a perillous storm to the *Anabaptists*, so called, in *Old England*; the sun shone bright in our horizon again; and the *Anabaptists* looked as fair as their neighbours. And altho' to be falsely accused, directly or indirectly, is a great exercise; yet to be cleared, and timely acquitted, is God's good providence, and an encouragement patiently to bear such slanderous reports; especially remembering, it was the common case of all christians, even from the beginning, to be defamed and evil spoken of without cause. We may from hence see, how injuriously and cruelly the malice of some men hath vented itself against the *Baptists* and their profession; and how speedily and opportunely the goodness and favour of God, have appeared in their timely and successful vindication.

DR. *Parker* was suspected to be the Author of this *scandalous libel*. And no wonder, since from a *Nonconformist*, when the times changed, he changed too, and became

became not only a *Conformist*, but wrote bitterly against the *Nonconformists*, calumniating all the foreign *Protestants*, and stirring up of persecution against those at home, creating a misunderstanding betwixt the King and his people; so that the whole design of his books tended to the disturbance of all government. Mr. *Andrew Marvel*, a zealous *Conformist*, in his *Rehearsal transprosed*, takes notice of this *Libel*, and says, ' It was indeed a
' piece of *Ecclesiastical History*, which he
' [Dr. *Parker*] thought, it seems, very fit,
' to reconcile to the present juncture of
' affairs, and recommend to the present
' *genius* of the age. And yet from be-
' ginning to end, there never was a com-
' pleater falshood invented —— and in
' good earnest, says he, I dare not swear
' but it was the Author of the *Ecclesias-*
' *tical Polities* own handy-work. — And,
' indeed, what reason could there be,
' what likelihood, that any other man
' should go so far out of the way with
' such a book to him, who was the most
' improper licenser of such things of that
' nature? Unless he may have therefore
' been the most proper licenser, because he
' had given so many testimonies, as books,
' of his good inclination to such matters;
' and that (not only in *History*, but even
' in *Doctrine* too) he did not so nearly
' consider the *truth*, as the *interest*. And
' there-

Part II.
p. 100.

'therefore, if, perhaps, he was not the
'Author, yet I dare undertake, that
'when he came to the licenfing of that
'*pamphlet*, he felt fuch an expanfion of
'heart, fuch an adlubefence of mind,
'and fuch an exaltation of fpirit, that
'betwixt joy and love, he could fcarce
'refrain from kiffing it. And this,
'fays he, no man living can deny,
'that either, if he thought there were
'any fault in it, he took care to correct
'and fit it for the prefs, with that ad-
'vantage, that it came out; or elfe,
'he found it fo fatisfactory, that it paf-
'fed his approbation without any amend-
'ment and fo tranfporting, that he forgot
'to keep a copy for his own juftification.
'And truly, had it not chanced that
'there was prefent and immediate proof
'upon the place to convict the *forgery*,
'as foon as publifhed, it might probably
'have had the effect for which it was de-
'figned; however, adds Mr. *Marvel*, no
'thanks to the licenfer, who either was
'alfo the Author, or the more criminal
'of the two; by how much the licenfer
'is always prefumed to have the ftricter
'infpection, the better judgment, and
'more honefty; and is therefore intruft-
'ed by my Lord Archbifhop to give
'the ftamp of publick authority ―― I
'know he will, fays he, take it un-
'kindly, that this fhould be revived, after,

'he

'he will say, he hath given so ample sa-
'tisfaction since for it, in his *testimonial*
'to the contrary; but he may please to
'consider, that this was since the late act
'of general pardon, that it all happened
'since the writing of the *reproof*; that he
'hath only given a masterly certificate,
'as it were, from a justice of peace,
'instead of making an humble recanta-
'tion as an offender. Had he but, as
'they say indeed, he complimented the
'*Anabaptists* on this occasion, so printed
'it too, *that he esteemed them to be the near-*
'*est to truth of all the Dissenters from the*
'*Church from England*, it had been some
'sign of penitence and integrity, and a-
'mounted to some degree of restitution.'

Anno 1674. The Baptists contend with the Quakers.

IN this year were several books published by the *Baptists* against the *Quakers*, and by the *Quakers* in their own defence. Much more noise was made thereupon than was designed; and the matter having been carried to a great height, requires more notice to be taken thereof than otherwise it would have merited.

Thomas Hicks, a Baptist preacher, published several pamphlets in succession, under the title of *A Dialogue between a Christain and a Quaker*; at which the *Quakers* were much offended, stiling them malicious forgeries and fictions, stuft with manifest slanders against their persons and princi-

G. Whitehead, Dippers *plea*, *p. 1.*

principles. To the firſt and ſecond Dialogues *William Penn* replied, in a book entitled, *Reaſons againſt railing, and Truth againſt fiction.* Unto which Mr. *Hicks* made a reply in a third dialogue, intitled, *The Quaker condemned out of his own mouth.* To this Mr. *Penn* replied, in a book, entitled, *The counterfeit Chriſtian detected;* wherein he charges Mr. *Hicks,* with manifold perverſions, downright lies and ſlanders, &c. In this book he appealed to the *Baptiſts* in and about *London,* for juſtice againſt *Thomas Hicks;* threatning in caſe of a refuſal, to purſue him, not only as *Thomas Hicks,* but as the *Baptiſts* great Champion, peculiar agent or repreſentative: and that it might be the more taken notice of, they employ'd perſons to give the book away at the doors of ſeveral meeting-houſes.

Upon this, the *Baptiſts* appointed a day; and to prevent the *Quakers* from pleading any ſurprize, they ſent a letter to *Will. Penn,* and another to *George Whitehead,* to be preſent at the appointed day, for the examination of *Thomas Hicks;* but receiving notice that they were out of the way, they ſent to *John Oſgoods,* to tell him, that he, or any of their friends, might be preſent at the time appointed; for the matter, ſay they, being only matter of fact, and not of diſpute, we conceive we may proceed to hear *Thomas Hick's*

Hicks's defence. So that the *Quakers* had no need to complain of the *Baptists* taking the advantage of the absence of *William Penn* and *George Whitehead*, who were most concerned, and who should make good the charge, since they having the charge before them, had nothing more to do but to hear the defence of *Thomas Hicks*.

ON the day appointed, neither *William Penn, George Whitehead*, nor any other *Quaker* appeared. Several did affirm, says my Author, that *William Penn* was not far from *London*, several days before the day of meeting, after the Letter (of advice) was sent to him: And others reported that he was at his own house, at no great distance from town, the very day preceding. If these things be true, *William Penn* could not be absent for want of information.

Manuscript penes me.

ON the twenty-eighth of *August*, the appointed day, Mr. *William Kiffin* opened the assembly, and gave an account of the occasion of it; then read the *Quakers* appeal, and told them, that the business of the day was not to dispute, but to hear, examine and judge, whether *Thomas Hicks* was guilty of charging the *Quakers* falsely.

THEN *Thomas Hicks*, endeavoured to prove that he had not accused the *Quakers* falsely, either in doctrine or practice.

First,

First, as to doctrine; he proved, that they held all the corrupt opinions he charged them with.

1. *That the light in every man is God.*

THIS *William Penn* owns, when he says, where we never charged him with forgery, he, *viz. Thomas Hicks*, hath taken opportunity, and that with confidence of innocence to cry out, Is that candid to call me forger, when you own the thing ? Examine, says he, *Dial.* 3. *p.* 4, 5, 6, 9. your pages referred to, relate to the point in hand. Counterfeit Christian, *p.* 9.

HE (meaning *GeorgeWhitehead*) owns it, the life which is the light of men, is God himself. Again, we assert the true light, with which every man is enlightened, to be in itself the Christ of God. This light is divine, because it is the life of the world, which is God. *Ib. p.* 56. Reasons against railing. Quakerism a nick name.

HE quotes other passages, where they call the light divine and uncreated.

THAT light which was before conscience or creature, before sun, moon, and stars, and that by which all things were made that were made. Christ by whom the world was made, which was before any thing was made, or conscience named, the eternal ever-living God, the King of Saints, which he gave to me his Servant, to declare to the inhabitants of the Earth, the Lord whose name is the G. Fox's Great mystery,*p.*18, 23, 185, 331. Whitehead, Dippers plea, *p.* 13. G. Fox, junr. *p.* 47, 49, &c.

light

light. That light is also represented as thus speaking of himself; I the light created all things, I the light gave unto every one of you life and breath, you scorn me, the light in you, &c.

<small>Dial. 1. p. 16.</small>

2. *That the Soul is part of God, of God's being, without beginning, and also infinite.*

<small>Reason against railing, p. 65. G. Fox. Gr. Myst. p. 90, 29, 100, 68.</small>

THIS charge, *William Penn* says, is false. To prove it, Mr. *Hicks* quotes this passage out of the Quakers writings. Is not the soul without beginning? And produces plain places where they say expresly, 'tis without beginning or ending, infinite, not a creature, but part of God, of God's being.

<small>Dial. 3. p. 2.</small>

3. I DO accuse the *Quakers, that they deny Jesus Christ to be a distinct person without us.*

William Penn says, this is an unsound inference, from their asserting the true light with which every man is enlightened to be the Christ of God and Saviour of the world.

IN answer to this, Mr. *Hicks* cites some passages, which shew he was not mistaken, from their own books.

<small>G. Fox. Dip. plea, p. 13. App. to Reasons against railing, p. 21, 27.</small>

Jesus Christ, a person without us, is not scripture language; but to suppose him to be so, is anthropomorphism, mugletonianism and socinianism; and the thoughts of a human and personal Christ, are carnal imaginations and dark thoughts.

GIVE

GIVE me one place that mentions Chrift to be a diftinct perfon without us. God's Chrift, and Chrift is not diftinct from his Saints. If there be any other Chrift but he that is crucified within us, he is the falfe Chrift. *Counter-feit Chriftian. G. Fox's GreatMyftery, p. 207, 16, 206.*

4. *That Chrift redeems himfelf.* *Dial. 4. p. 47.*

William Penn fays, that this is a grofs perverfion. *Reafons againft railing.*

FOR the proof of this, Mr. *Hicks* refers to feveral paffages, fuch as thefe:

FEW are come to know what it is wants redemption, and that the promife is to; for there is a feed to which the promife is. Chrift is the election and the feed. *James Naylor's Love to the loft, p. 47, 32.*

THE promife of God is to the feed, that hath been laden as a cart with fheaves by the finner, which feed is the hope Chrift. We affert the redemption of the feed. 'Tis not abfured to affirm, that the end of God's manifefting himfelf in the flefh, was for the redemption and deliverance of his holy life, that was in man, as a fmall feed, that had been long vex'd, grieved and preffed down by fin and iniquity. This feed was and is pure forever, &c. *G. Fox GreatMyftery, p. 324. Reafon againft railing, p. 62, 63, 64, &c.*

5. THAT the *Quakers* deny *the Scriptures to be the rule of life and practice to Chriftians.*

WE deny the fcripture to be the rule
of

of faith and practice, in honour of the Divine light their author. He that persuades people the scriptures are so, is darkness; 'tis a setting the scriptures in the place of Christ.

<small>Reas. against railing.
Ed. Burroughs, p. 62.
G. Whitehead.
Christ ascend.
Dial. 1. p. 28.</small>

6. *That the speaking of the spirit in any one is of greater authority than the Scriptures.*

This is proved expresly by the answer of a *Quaker* to one who put the question to him.

<small>G. Whitehead, Serious Apol. p. 49.</small>

7. *That is no command of God to me, which God hath given to another; neither did any of the saints act by that command which was given to another; every one obeyed their own command.*

<small>Ed. Burroughs, p. 47, 105.</small>

8. *That justification by that righteousness which Christ fulfilled for us, wholly without us, is a doctrine of devils.*

<small>W. Penn's Serious apol. p. 146.</small>

9. *That the Quakers hold justification by works, in the strictest notion.*

God accepts not any when there is any failing, or who do not fulfil the whole law, and answer all the demands of justice. We must not conceive *Abraham*'s personal offering was not a justifying righteousness, but that God was pleased to count it so; nor was there any imputation of another righteousness to *Abraham*; but on the contrary, his personal righteousness

<small>Ed. Burroughs. p. 33.
W. Penn Reas. against railing, p. 80.</small>

oufnefs was the ground of that juft imputation: Therefore that any fhould be juftified by another righteoufnefs imputed, and not inherent in him, is both ridiculous and dangerous.

10. *That Chrift fulfilled the law only as our pattern.* Dial. 2. p. 52.

William Penn fays, the word *only* is not there, nor is the fulfilling of the law, the fubject there treated of. Sandy Found. p. 26.

The citation at large, *Rom.* ii. 13. from whence I obferve, unlefs we become doers of that law, which Chrift came not to deftroy, but as our example to fulfil, we can never be juftified before God; wherefore obedience is fo abfolutely neceffary, that fhort of it there can be no acceptance; nor let any fancy, that Chrift hath fo fulfilled it for them, as to exclude their obedience from being requifite to their acceptance, but *only* as their pattern.

11. *That the doctrine of Chrift's fatisfaction is irreligious and irrational.*

O the infamous portraicture, this doctrine draws of the infinite goodnefs! Is this your retribution, O injurious fatisfactionifts? Sandy Found. p. 22.

12. *That this body which dies fhall not rife again.*

George Whitehead faid thefe words before feveral witneffes.

William

William Penn says, This doctrine is inconsistent with scripture and reason; it out-does transubstantiation in absurdity.

<small>Reas. against railing, p. 133, 134.</small>

As to the *second* head or matter of practice.

1. *That it concerns them to render their adversaries as ridiculous as they can, and to make their friends believe, they do nothing but contradict themselves; and if this fail, to insinuate something by way of question, that may slander them.*

That that is their practise, Mr. *Hicks* proves from *William Penn*'s complaint, that he had not an opportunity to do thus by the Author of *the spirit of the Quakers tried*, because he had not set down his name.

<small>Spirit of truth vindicated, p. 6.</small>

George Whitehead, in answer to Mr. *Dunson*, who stiles himself minister of the Gospel at *Sandwich*, asks, But is not rather that report true, that he was given to gaming, &c?

<small>Divinity of Christ, p. 49.</small>

To excuse him *William Penn* says, who knows not, that priests don't scruple these things? and if *George Whitehead*, to detect the priest, did make this query, must it be presumed, he took him for such? It is not just therefore for *William Penn* to charge me with forgery in that particular.

<small>Spirit of truth vindicated, p. 137.</small>

2. *I charged the Quakers, that they called such as asked them questions, reprobates; and saying, they are in the sorcery and the witchcraft.*

William

William Penn says, it is a great lie. See *Edward Burrough's Works*, p. 29, 34.

3. That William Penn, *by the sense of the eternal spirit doth declare, that these cursing, railing, and lying answers of* Edward Burroughs, *were the only fit answers to the Priest's trepanning questions.* William Penn calls that an ungodly slander; but see the very words.

4. *They prefer their own pamphlets to the bible; for they call the one the voice of wisdom, breathings of true love, shield of faith, a spiritual glass, light risen out of darkness: But the scriptures are called letter, dead letter, paper, ink, and writing, carnal letter, &c.* Reas. against railing, p. 164.

5. *They bid people follow the light within, and if they don't, they revile them.*

William Penn calls it a great lie; but it is plain from their railings at such as oppose them and their error.

6. *They say God himself is the immediate teacher of his people, and yet they appoint their ministers to speak in such a place.* Dial. 2. p. 66.

See this urged against them by the Author of *the Spirit of the hat*, one no stranger to their practices.

7. *They entitle God to sleeveless errands.* Dial. 1. p. 27.

8. *They refuse publick meetings to debate the chief things in difference between them*

and

and others, under pretence of their being cautious of running theirs into jeopardy.

William Penn says, this is a notorious falsehood. Mr. *Hicks* answers, I can prove it by several witnesses. Mr. *Prior's* letters to Mr. *Haworth*, has those very words in it.

9. *That they own the Scripture as far as it agrees with the light within.*

William Penn says, this is a forgery. Mr. *Hicks* says, this is proved before, in that they assert the scripture to be given forth from the light within.

10. *That the light within created heaven and earth, and is the immediate object of divine worship.* This is proved under the first doctrinal charge, tho' *William Penn* says, it is a forgery.

<small>Reas. against railing.</small>

11. *That if these things objected in the two first dialogues be true*, William Penn *hath confessed* a Quaker *is no Christian*.

William Penn charges this also as a forgery, tho' he has writ these words. He, Mr. *Hicks*, to vindicate himself from injustice, has given us a second part, wherein he hopes to make good what he has charged on us by quotations out of our own books; which if faithfully done, I shall freely acknowledge, that a *Quaker* is quite another thing from a *Christian*.

<small>Reas. against railing, *p.* 4.</small>

12. *William Penn* accuses me of *forgery*, in saying he has these words, viz. *That were*

were we what he represents us, the worst plagues, and judgments of God would be our portion. Which are his own words, with this little alteration, that he says, *we might justly expect them to be our portion for ever.*

13. *William Penn* charges me with a downright lie, in giving this answer to *George Whitehead*'s name, viz. *That the plagues and judgments of God will follow thee;* tho' it is attested too under Mr. *John Gladman*'s own hand. Reaf. against railing, p. 163. Dial. 3. p. 85.

14. *That their owning Christ is no other than a meer mystical romance; and that the light within them sees no necessity of a mediator*: And tho' *William Penn* calls these lies and slanders, yet they are true, *since they deny Christ to be a distinct person, and maintain, that God accepts not of any who do not fulfil the law, and every demand of justice.* Reaf. against railing, p. 154.

15. ANOTHER lie, *William Penn* charges me with, is this; *That the* Quakers *deny Christ's visible coming, and appearance in the World*: Whereas *Edward Burroughs* having returned answer to a certain gentleman, that Christ never was visible to him or his generation; I only noted, that the *Quaker* denied Christ was ever visible to such wicked men as he esteemed the Querist. Ibid.

16. *That they account the blood of Christ but as the blood of a common thief*; which

306　*The* History *of the*

Ibid.　tho' *William Penn* says is an ungodly
Dial. 2 p.　aspersion, is fully made out.
3-4.
Dial. 2. p.　　17. *That one of their friends bid her hus-*
63.　*band take another woman.*

Dial. 1. p.　　18. *That a revelation hath been pretended*
26.　*to excuse the payment of a just debt.*

　　19. *That some of their friends have excus-*
Dial. 3.　*ed some of their villanies, by pretence to an in-*
Epist.　*nocent life.*

CONCERNING these three last I propose this unto the *Quakers*, That if they will chuse six sober and disinterested persons, I also will do the like, and if I cannot give sufficient reasons for what I have objected against them, I will contentedly submit unto what these men will determine.

WE whose names are under-written do certify, that the aforesaid quotations are truly recited out of the books to which they refer.

Witness our hands,

Dan. Dyke	*Tho. Plant*
Thomas Paul	*John Hunter*
Tho. Wilcocks	*John Vernon*
Jona. Jennings	*John Gosnold*
Owen Davis	*John Norcott*
Wm. Dix	*Maur. King*
Robert Maton	*Joseph Morton*
Hanserd Knollys	*John Snelling*
Hen. Forty	*Edw. Noble.*
Rob. Snelling	THERE

English Baptists.

There were many more Ministers and others, who were ready to attest the same.

N.B. We have abbreviated the account by much. There was an advertisement giving notice, that Mr. *William Kiffin* was not present by reason of business; but that he had since examined and found the quotations just.

William Kiffin.

Thomas Hicks having thus met at the time and place appointed, made it appear out of the *Quakers* own books, that he had not wronged them in the least. The Church therefore to which he belonged, in publick print cleared him from the *Quakers* charge; and declared to the world, that they as yet see no just cause of blame to be laid unto *Thomas Hicks*; but that if any one shall object any new matter against him, if they signify the particulars in writing, they will return such answers thereunto, as to them may seem just, and that may also be to the satisfaction of all indifferent and unprejudiced minds, hoping that nothing shall lie upon them in point of duty towards him, but that by the grace of God, they shall be ready to do it.

Epistle to the Quakers appeal answered.

William Kiffin	*Daniel Dyke*
Thomas Paul	*Hanserd Knollys.*
Henry Forty	

Mr. *Wills*, in his appeal to the *Baptists* against Esqr; *Danvers*, observes, that tho' the *Quakers* were disappointed as to the issue of their Appeal, ' yet it doth ap-
' pear, says he, to all impartial and unpre-
' judiced persons, that the *Baptists* have
' carried the whole business with a great
' deal of fairness and impartiality to both
' sides, as became just judges and good
' Christians, and vindicated the honesty
' of their brother from the unjust asper-
' sions of his adversaries.'

The *Quakers* exhibited a new complaint, in which they desired a rehearing of the whole matter, which at last was granted them. Wherein they behaved themselves so disorderly, as displeased the whole auditory; and finding themselves not able to get the better of the *Baptists*, being disappointed of the success they hoped for, appointed a meeting at their own house in *Wheeler-street*: Thither Mr. *Hicks* would not go, because they who had appealed were no fit judges to condemn in that case, upon which they had appealed; but sent Mr. *Ives* thither with some others, who so managed the *Quakers*, that they were obliged to break up, without any further proceedings in the matter.

Life, p. 310.

Thomas Ellwood tells us, that he let fly a broad-side at the *Baptists*, in a single sheet of paper, under the title of *A fresh Pursuit*. ' In which, says he, having re-
stated

' stated the controversy between them and
' us, and reinforced our charge of forge-
' ry, &c. against *Thomas Hicks* and his
' *abettors*; I offered a fair challenge to
' them, not only to *Thomas Hicks* him-
' self, but to all those his *compurgators*,
' who had before undertaken to acquit
' him from our charge, together with
' their companion *Jer. Ives*, to give me
' a fair and publick meeting, in which
' I would make good our charge against
' him as *principal*, and all the rest of
' them as *accessaries*; but nothing could
' provoke them to come fairly forth.'

Though Mr. *Ives* lived some years after this, yet Mr. *Ellwood* would never forgive him, for so smartly handling them in the controversy then between them. For he tells us himself, that when he heard of his death, the impression made upon his mind as well at this time, as before, drew from him something like an *Epitaph*, which is published in the *history of his Life*, page 313, &c. But it is such a barefaced piece of *defamation*, and a confirmation of one of the articles respecting their practice, which Mr. *Hicks* charged them with, that I believe the *Quakers* of the present day, who are a more sober and inoffensive people, would rather have it buried in oblivion; and therefore I omit it.

THE *Baptists* did publish an account of the two last meetings between them and the *Quakers*, together with the occasion of these meetings, as also what letters passed in order thereunto; it was entitled, *A contest for Christianity*, with some reflections upon several passages that were published in the account which the *Quakers* gave of the said meetings. The same is submitted to the judgment of all judicious and impartial men, and too long to be inserted in this history, I must therefore refer the reader thereunto; and shall only observe in this place, that the *Quakers* being so chaf'd in their disputes with the *Baptists*, that they did not only brand them with infamy, but denounced curses and judgments upon them, because they so strongly withstood that spirit of delusion which they seemed to them to be under at this time; as appears in the following instance.

Mr. *Ralph James*, Pastor of the *Baptist* church at *North-Willingham* in the county of *Lincoln*, having either disputed or otherwise declared his testimony, and bore witness against the errors of the *Quakers*, one *Richard Anderson*, a *Quaker*, who lived at *Panton* in the same county, impiously assumed to himself the character of a prophet sent of God, and in the name of God denounced this heavy judgment upon Mr. *James* in his presence, *viz*. That he he should become a leper from head to foot for his opposing the spirit of the *Quakers*, or their light within; adding at the same time, that if he was deceived, the self-same plague should befal both him and his family: which accordingly came to pass, for in a little time they were all leprous, and then the *Quaker* in extremity of pain, came sorrowing and making his complaint to Mr. *James*, begging and intreating his prayers to God on his behalf, that he might be released from that severe judgment; and accordingly Mr. *James* and his congregation kept days of fasting and prayer for him, and God was graciously pleased to give them ease and to heal them, which Mr. *Anderson* freely confessed, and then addressed himself to their meetings.

This surprising instance with two others of the like nature, were soon after printed under the title of *A true and impartial Narrative of the eminent hand of God, that befel a* Quaker *and his family*. This starting piece soon alarmed the *Quakers*, and left it should farther expose their delusion, and injure their cause, *Thomas Rudyard*, a lawyer, published in answer to it, a book entitled, *The Anabaptists lying Wonder*, to which a reply soon followed, intitled, *The Quakers subterfuge or evasion overturned*, wherein the truth of the foregoing Narrative was farther confirmed and established, and the *Quakers* thereupon became silenced upon this head, tho' they fell to disputation in several parts of the kingdom; in which Mr. *Thomas Grantham*, and others of the *Baptists* were very much engaged.

Anno 1677.

IN the year 1677, was published by the *Baptists, a Confession of their Faith, put forth by the elders and brethren of many congregations of Christians, baptized upon profession of their faith, in* London *and the country.* It is introduced with an Advertisement *to the judicious and impartial Reader.* Wherein they observe, that it was many years since divers of them, with others, did conceive themselves under a necessity of publishing a confession of their faith; and that many others have since embraced the same truth which was owned therein. They judged it necessary to join together in giving a testimony to the world of their firm adhering to those wholesome principles, by the publication of this. And as their method and manner of expressing their sentiments, doth vary from the former, altho' the matter of the substance is the same; so they give the reasons thereof in the following words.

'ONE thing, say they, that greatly
' prevailed with us to undertake this
' work, was (not only to give a full ac-
' count

'count of ourselves, to those Christians
'that differ from us about the subject of
'baptism, but also) the profit that might
'from thence arise, unto those that have
'any account of our labours, in their in-
'struction, and establishment in the great
'truths of the Gospel; in the clear un-
'derstanding and steady belief of which,
'our comfortable walking with God,
'and fruitfulness before him, in all our
'ways, is most nearly concerned. And,
'therefore, we did conclude it necessary
'to express ourselves the more fully, and
'distinctly; and also to fix on such a me-
'thod as might be most comprehensive
'of those things which we designed to
'explain our sense and belief of. And
'finding no defect, in this regard, in that
'fixed on by the Assembly, and after
'them by those of the congregational
'way, we did readily conclude it best to
'retain the same *order* in our present con-
'fession. And also, when we observed
'that those last mentioned did in their
'confession, (for reasons which seemed
'of weight both to themselves and o-
'thers) chuse not only to express their
'minds in words concurrent with the for-
'mer in sense, concerning all those arti-
'cles wherein they were agreed, but al-
'so for the most part without any varia-
'tion of the terms; we did in like man-
'ner conclude it best to follow their ex-
'ample,

'ample, in making use of the very same
'words with them both, in these arti-
'cles, (which are very many) wherein
'our faith and doctrine is the same with
'theirs. And this we did, the more a-
'bundantly to manifest our consent with
'both, in all the fundamental articles of
'the Christian Religion; as also with
'many others, whose orthodox confes-
'sions have been published to the world,
'on the behalf of the Protestants in di-
'vers nations and cities: And also to
'convince all, that we have no itch to
'clog religion with new words, but do
'readily acquiesce in that form of sound
'words, which hath been, in consent
'with the Holy Scriptures, used by o-
'thers before us; hereby declaring before
'God, angels, and men, our hearty a-
'greement with them, in that wholesome
'Protestant Doctrine, which with so
'clear evidence of scriptures they have
'asserted. Some things indeed, are in
'some places added, some terms omitted,
'and some few changed; but these alte-
'rations are of that nature, as that we
'need not doubt any charge or suspicion
'of unsoundness in the faith, from any
'of our brethren upon the account of
'them.
 'IN those things wherein we differ
'from others, we have expressed our-
'selves with all candour and plainness,
                                'that

'that none might entertain jealoufy of
' ought fecretly lodged in our breafts, that
' we would not the world fhould be ac-
' quainted with; yet we hope we have
' alfo obferved thofe rules of modefty,
' and humility, as will render our free-
' dom in this refpect inoffenfive, even to
' thofe whofe fentiments are different
' from ours. We have alfo taken care to
' affix texts of fcripture in the margin,
' for the confirmation of each article in
' our confeffion. In which work we
' have ftudioufly endeavoured to felect
' fuch as are moft clear and pertinent,
' for the proof of what is afferted by us.
' And our earneft defire is, that all, into
' whofe hands this may come, would
' follow that never enough commended
' example of the noble *Bereans*, who
' fearched the fcriptures daily, that they
' might find out whether the things
' preached to them, were fo or not.

' THERE is one thing more which
' we fincerely profefs, and earneftly de-
' fire credence in, *viz.* that contention is
' moft remote from our defign in all that
' we have done in this matter. And we
' hope the liberty of an ingenuous un-
' folding our principles, and opening our
' hearts unto our brethren, with the
' fcripture grounds on which our faith
' and practice leans, will by none of
' them be either denied to us, or taken ill

' from

'from us. Our whole defign is accom-
'plifhed, if we may obtain that juftice,
'as to be meafured in our principles and
'practice, and the judgment of both by
'others, according to what we have now
'publifhed; which the Lord, whofe eyes
'are as a flame of fire, knoweth to be
'the doctrine, which with our hearts we
'moft firmly believe, and fincerely en-
'deavour to conform our lives to. And
'oh! that other contentions being laid a-
'fleep, the only care and contention of
'all upon whom the name of our Bleffed
'Redeemer is called, might for the fu-
'ture be, *to walk humbly with their God,*
'and in the exercife of all love and meek-
'nefs towards each other; *to perfect holi-*
'*nefs in the fear of the Lord*; each one
'endeavouring *to have his converfation*
'*fuch as becometh the Gofpel*; and alfo
'fuitable to his place and capacity, vi-
'goroufly to promote in others the prac-
'tice of true religion, and undefiled in the
'fight of God and our Father: And that
'in this backfliding day, we might not
'fpend our breath in fruitlefs complaints
'of the evils of others, but may every
'one begin at home, to reform in the
'firft place our own hearts and ways,
'and then to quicken all that we may
'have influence upon, to the fame work;
'that if the will of God were fo, none
'might deceive themfelves, by refting in,
'and

'and trusting to a form of godliness, 'without the power of it, and inward 'experience of the efficacy of those truths 'that are professed by them.'

This Confession of Faith was reprinted in the year 1689, and was approved of, and recommended by the ministers and messengers of above an hundred congregations met in *London*; and is still generally received by all those congregations, that hold the doctrine of personal election, and the certainty of the saints final perseverance: And therefore, I shall reserve the exhibition thereof till I come to treat of that time; and only add the Appendix they annexed to the Confession, published at this time.

They say, 'Whosoever reads, and 'impartially considers, what we have in 'our foregoing Confession declared, may 'readily perceive, that we do not only 'concenter with all other true Christians 'on the word of God, revealed in the 'scriptures of truth, as the foundation and 'rule of our faith and worship; but that 'we have also industriously endeavoured 'to manifest, that in the fundamental 'articles of Christianity we *mind the same* '*things*, and have therefore expressed our 'belief in the same words, that have on 'the like occasion been spoken by other 'societies of Christians before us.

'This

'This we have done, that those who are desirous to know the principles of religion which we hold and practise, may take an estimate from ourselves, who jointly concur in this work; and may not be misguided, either by undue reports, or by the ignorance or errors of particular persons; who going under the same name with ourselves, may give an occasion of scandalizing the truth we profess.

'And altho' we do differ from our brethren who are *Pædobaptists*, in the subject and administration of baptism, and such other circumstances as have a necessary dependance on our observance of that ordinance, and do frequent our own Assemblies for our mutual edification, and discharge of those duties and services which we owe unto God, and in his fear to each other: Yet we would not be from hence misconstrued, as if the discharge of our own consciences herein, did any ways disoblige or alienate our affections or conversation from any others that fear the Lord; but that we may and do, as we have opportunity, participate of the labours of those, whom God hath indued with abilities above ourselves, and qualified, and called to the ministry of the *word*; earnestly desiring to approve ourselves to be such, as follow after peace with holiness. And
'therefore

' therefore we always keep that bleſſed
' *Irenicum*, or healing *word* of the Apo-
' ſtle before our eyes: *If in any thing* Phil. iii.
' *ye be otherwiſe minded, God ſhall reveal* 15.
' *even this unto you: Nevertheleſs whereto*
' *we have already attained, let us walk*
' *by the ſame rule, let us mind the ſame*
' *thing*.

' Let it not therefore be judged of
' us (becauſe much hath been written on
' this ſubject, and yet we continue this
' our practice different from others) that
' it is out of obſtinacy; but rather, as the
' truth is, that we do herein according to
' the beſt of our underſtandings, worſhip
' God out of a pure mind, yielding obe-
' dience to his precept, in that method
' which we take to be moſt agreeable to
' the ſcriptures of truth, and primitive
' practice.

' It would not become us to give any
' ſuch intimation, as ſhould carry a ſem-
' blance that what we do in the ſervice
' of God is with a doubting conſcience;
' or with any ſuch temper of mind that
' we do thus for the preſent, with a re-
' ſervation that we will do otherwiſe here-
' after upon more mature deliberation.
' Nor have we any cauſe ſo to do; be-
' ing fully perſuaded, that what we do
' is agreeable to the will of God. Yet
' we do heartily propoſe this; that if any
' of the ſervants of our Lord *Jeſus* ſhall

'in the spirit of meekness, attempt to
'convince us of any mistake either in
'judgment or practice, we shall diligent-
'ly ponder his arguments; and account
'him our chiefest friend that shall be an
'instrument to convert us from any error
'that is in our ways: For we cannot wit-
'tingly do any thing against the truth,
'but all things for the truth.

'AND therefore we have endeavoured
'seriously to consider what hath been
'already offered for our satisfaction in
'this point: And are loth to say any
'more, lest we should be esteemed defi-
'rous of renewed contests thereabout.
'Yet forasmuch as it may justly be ex-
'pected, that we shew some reason, why
'we cannot acquiesce in what hath been
'urged against us, we shall with as much
'brevity, as may consist with plainness,
'endeavour to satisfy the expectation of
'those, that shall peruse what we now
'publish in this matter also.

'1. As to those Christians who con-
'sent with us, *That repentance from dead
'works, and faith towards God, and our
'Lord* Jesus Christ, *is required in per-
'sons to be baptized*; and do therefore
'supply the defect, of the infant being
'uncapable of making confession of either,
'by others, who do undertake these things
'for it: Altho' we do find by Church-
'History, that this hath been a very an-
'cient

'cient practice; yet considering, that the
'same scripture which does caution us
'against censuring our brother, with
'whom we shall all stand before the
'judgment-seat of Christ, does also in-
'struct us, *That every one of us shall give* Rom. xiv.
'*an account of himself to God*, and *what-* 4, 10, 12,
'*soever is not of faith is sin*; therefore 23.
'we cannot for our parts be persuaded
'in our minds, to build such a practice
'as this, upon an unwritten tradition: But
'do rather choose in all points of faith
'and worship, to have recourse to the
'holy Scriptures, for the information of
'our judgment, and regulation of our
'practice; being well assured that a con-
'scientious attending thereto, is the best
'way to prevent and rectify our defects
'and errors. And if any such case happen 2 Tim.
'to be debated between Christians, which iii. 16.
'is not plainly determinable by the Scrip-
'tures, we think it safest to leave such
'things undecided until the second com-
'ing of our Lord *Jesus*; as they did in
'the church of old, until there should
'arise a priest with *Urim* and *Thummim*, Ezra ii.
'that might certainly inform them of 62.
'the mind of God thereabout.

'2. As for those our christian bre-
'thren, who do ground their arguments
'for infants baptism, upon a presumed
'foederal holiness, or church-member-
'ship; we conceive they are deficient in

Vol. II.   X   'this,

'this, that albeit this covenant-holiness
'and memberſhip ſhould be as is ſuppoſ-
'ed, in reference unto the infants of be-
'lievers; yet no command for infant-
'baptiſm does immediately and directly
'reſult from ſuch a quality, or relation.
'All inſtituted worſhip receives its ſanc-
'tion from the precept, and is thereby
'governed in all the neceſſary circum-
'ſtances thereof. So it was in the cove-
'nant that God made with *Abraham*
'and his ſeed. The ſign whereof was
'appropriated only to the male, notwith-
'ſtanding that the female ſeed, as well as
'the male, were comprehended in the co-
'venant, and part of the Church of God.
'Neither was this ſign to be affixed to
'any male-infant till he was eight days
'old, albeit he was within the covenant
'from the firſt moment of his life. Nor
'could the danger of death, or any o-
'ther ſuppoſed neceſſity, warrant the
'circumciſing of him before the ſet time.
'Nor was there any cauſe for it; the
'commination of *being cut off from his
'people* being only upon the neglect, or
'contempt of the precept.

'RIGHTEOUS *Lot* was nearly related
'to *Abraham* in the fleſh, and contem-
'porary with him, when this covenant
'was made: Yet inaſmuch as he did not
'deſcend from his loins, nor was of his
'houſhold-family, altho' he was of the
'ſame

' same houshold of faith with *Abraham*;
' yet neither *Lot* himself, nor any of his
' posterity, because of their descent from
' him, were signed with the signature
' of this covenant, that was made with
' *Abraham* and his seed.

'This may suffice to shew, that
' where there was both an express cove-
' nant, and a sign thereof, such a cove-
' nant as did separate the persons with
' whom it was made, and all their off-
' spring, from all the rest of the world,
' as a people holy unto the Lord, and
' did constitute them the visible Church
' of God, tho' not comprehensive of all
' the faithful in the world; yet the sign
' of this covenant was not affixed to all
' the persons that were within this cove-
' nant, nor to any of them till the pre-
' fixed season; nor to other faithful ser-
' vants of God, that were not of de-
' scent from *Abraham*. And consequent-
' ly that it depends purely upon the will
' of the Law-giver, to determine what
' shall be the sign of his covenant; unto
' whom, at what season, and upon what
' terms, it shall be affixed.

' If our brethren do suppose baptism to
' be the seal of the covenant, which God
' makes with every believer, of which the
' Scriptures are altogether silent; it is not
' our concern to contend with them here-
' in. Yet we conceive, the seal of that co-
' venant

'venant is the indwelling of the Spirit of
' Chrift, in the particular and individual
' perfons in whom he refides, and no-
' thing elfe. Neither do they or we fup-
' pofe, that baptifm is in any fuch manner
' fubftituted in the place of circumcifion,
' as to have the fame, and no other la-
' titude, extent, or terms, than circum-
' cifion had. For that was fuited only
' for the male-children; baptifm is an or-
' dinance fuited for every believer, whe-
' ther male or female: That extended to
' all the males that were born in *Abra-*
' *ham*'s houfe, or bought with his money,
' equally with the males that proceeded
' from his own loins; but baptifm is not
' fo far extended in any true Chriftian
' Church that we know of, as to be ad-
' miniftred to all the poor infidel fer-
' vants, that the members thereof pur-
' chafe for their fervice, and introduce in-
' to their families; nor to the children
' born of them in their houfe.

' BUT we conceive the fame parity of
' reafoning may hold for the ordinance
' of baptifm, as for that of circumcifion:
Exod. xii. ' *viz. One law for the ftranger, as for the*
49. ' *home-born.* If any defire to be admit-
' ted to all the ordinances and privileges
' of God's houfe, the door is open, up-
' on the very fame terms that any one
' perfon was ever admitted to all, or
' any of thofe privileges, that belong to
          ' the

' the Christian Church, may all persons
' of right challenge the like admission.
' As for that text of Scripture, *He re-* Rom. vi.
' *ceived circumcision, a seal of the righte-* 11.
' *ousness of the faith which he had, yet be-*
' *ing uncircumcised*; we conceive if the
' Apostle's scope in that place be duely
' attended to, it will appear that no ar-
' gument can be taken from thence to
' inforce Infant-baptism. And foras-
' much as we find a full and fair ac-
' count of those words given by the
' learned Dr. *Lightfoot*, a man not to be
' suspected of partiality in this contro-
' versy, in his *Hor. Hebraic.* on the
' 1 *Cor.* vii. 19. p. 42, 43. we shall
' transcribe his words at large, without
' any comment of our own upon them.

Circumcisio nihil est, ratione habita temporis, jam enim evanuerat, ad impleto præcipue ejus fine ob quem fuerat instituta: Istum finem exhibet apostolus in verbis istis, Rom. iv. 11. σφραγιδα της δικαιοσυνης της πιστεως της ἐν ἀκροβυστια. *At vereor ne a plerisque versionibus non satis aptentur*

' Circumcisi-
' on is nothing, if
' we respect the
' time, for now it
' was without use;
' that end of it be-
' ing especially ful-
' filled, for which
' it had been insti-
' tuted; this end the
' Apostle declares
' in these words,
' *Rom.* iv. 11. σφρα-
' γιδα, &c. But I
' fear

aptentur ad finem circumcisionis & scopum Apostoli, dum ab iis interseritur aliquid de suo.

'fear that by most
'translations they
'are not sufficient-
'ly suited to the
'end of circumci-
'sion, and the scope
'of the Apostle,
'whilst something
'of their own is
'by them inserted.

'AND after the Doctor hath repre-
'sented diverse versions of the words, a-
'greeing for the most part in sense with
'that which we have in our Bibles, he
'thus proceeds.

Aliæ in eundem sensum, ac si circumcisio daretur Abrahamo in sigillum justitiæ istius, quam ille habuit, dum adhuc foret præputiatus; quod non negabimus aliqualiter verum esse; at credimus circumcisionem longe alio præcipue respexisse.

'OTHER versi-
'ons are to the
'same purpose, as
'if circumcision
'was given to *A-*
'*braham* for a seal
'of that righteous-
'ness which he had,
'being yet uncir-
'cumcised; which
'we will not deny
'to be in some sense
'true; but we
'believe that cir-
'cumcision had
'chiefly

Liccat.

Liccat mihi verba sic reddere. Et signum accepit circumcisionis, sigillum justitiæ fidei, quæ futura in præputio; quæ futura dico; non quæ fuerat Abrahamo *adhuc præputiato, sed quæ futura semini ejus præputiato, id est, gentilibus, fidem olim* Abrahami *imitaturis.*

Nunc adverte bene, qua occasione instituta Abrahamo *circumcisio, ponens tibi ante oculos historiam ejus,* Gen. xvii.

Fit

' chiefly a far dif-
' ferent respect.

' GIVE me leave
' thus to render the
' words. *And he*
' *received the sign*
' *of circumcision, a*
' *seal of the righteous*
' *ness of faith, which*
' *was to be in the un-*
' *circumcision:* which
' was to be, I say;
' not *which had*
' *been*, nor that
' which *Abraham*
' had whilst he was
' yet uncircumcised;
' but that which
' his uncircumcised
' seed should have,
' that is, the *Gen-*
' *tiles*, who in time
' to come should
' imitate the faith
' of *Abraham.*

' Now consider
' well, on what oc-
' casion circumcisi-
' on was instituted
' unto *Abraham,* set-
' ting before thine
' eyes the history
' thereof, *Gen.* xvii.

X 4 ' THIS

Fit primo ei hæc promissio, multarum gentium eris tu pater (quonam sensu explicat Apostolus, isto capite.) Et subinde subjungitur duplex sigillum rei corroborandæ: immutatio scilicet nominis Abrami *in* Abrahamum, *& institutio circumcisionis,* v. 4. *Ecce mihi tecum est fœdus, eris tu pater multarum gentium. Quare vocatum est nomen ejus* Abrahamus? *In sigillationem hujus promissionis: Tu pater eris multarum gentium. Et quare instituta ei circumcisio? In sigillationem ejusdem promissionis; Tu pater eris multarum gentium. Ita ut hic sit sensus Apostoli, institutioni circumcisionis congruentissimus: accepit signum circumcisionis,*	' This promise is first made unto him, *Thou shalt be the father of many nations* (in what sense the Apostle explaineth in that Chapter.) And then there is subjoined a double seal for the confirmation of the thing: to wit, the change of the name *Abram* into *Abraham*, and the institution of circumcision, v. 4. *Behold as for me, my covenant is with thee, and thou shalt be the father of many nations.* Wherefore was his name called *Abraham?* For the sealing of this promise; *Thou shalt be the father of many nations.* And wherefore was circumcision instituted to him? ' For

nis, figillum justitiæ fidei, quam olim erat in circumcisio (vel Gentiles) habitura & adeptura.

Duplex semen erat Abrahamo: *naturale, Judæorum; & fidele, gentilium credentium. Signatur naturale signo circumcisionis: primo quidem in sui distinctionem ab omnibus aliis gentibus, dum eæ non adhuc forent semen* Abrahami: *at præcipue in memoriam justificationis gentium*

' For the sealing of
' the same promise,
' *Thou shalt be the*
' *father of many*
' *nations*. So that
' this is the sense
' of the Apostle,
' most agreeable to
' the institution of
' circumcision: He
' received the sign
' of circumcision, a
' seal of the righte-
' ousness of faith,
' which in time to
' come the uncir-
' cumcision, or the
' *Gentiles* should
' have and obtain.

' *Abraham* had
' a twofold seed:
' *natural*, of the
' *Jews*; and *faith-*
' *ful*, of the believ-
' ing *Gentiles*. His
' natural seed was
' signed with the
' sign of circumcisi-
' on: First, indeed,
' for the distin-
' guishing of them
' from all other na-
' tions, whilst they
    ' as

um per fidem, cum tandem forent ejus semen. Cessatura ergo merito erat circumcisio, cum introducerentur Gentiles ad fidem; quippe quod tunc finem suum ultimum ac præcipuum obtinuerat; & perinde ἡ περιτομὴ οὐδέν.

' as yet were not
' the seed of *Abra-*
' *ham*; but especi-
' ally, for the me-
' morial of the
' justification of the
' *Gentiles* by faith,
' when at length
' they should be-
' come his seed.
' Therefore circum-
' cision was of right
' to cease when the
' *Gentiles* were
' brought into the
' faith; forasmuch
' as then it had ob-
' tained its last and
' chief end; and
' thenceforth *cir-*
' *cumcision is no-*
' *thing.*

' Thus far he: Which we earnestly
' desire may be seriously weighed; for
' we plead not his authority, but the e-
' vidence of truth in his words.

' 3. Of whatsoever nature the *holi-*
' *ness* of the children, mentioned 1 *Cor.*
' vii. 12. be; yet they who do conclude,
' that all such children (whether infants
' or of riper years) have from hence an
' immediate right to baptism, do as we

' conceive put more into the conclusion,
' than will be found in the premises.

' For altho' we do not determine po-
' sitively concerning the Apostle's scope in
' the *holiness* here mentioned, so as to
' say, it is this or that, and no other
' thing; yet it is evident, that the Apo-
' stle does by it determine not only the
' lawfulness, but the expedience also of a
' believer's co-habitation with an unbeliev-
' er, in the state of marriage.

' And we do think that although the
' Apostle's asserting of the unbelieving
' yoke-fellow to be *sanctified by the be-
' liever*, should carry in it somewhat more
' than is in the bare marriage of two in-
' fidels, because altho' the marriage-cove-
' nant have a divine sanction, so as to
' make the wedlock of two unbelievers a
' lawful action, and their conjunction and
' co-habitation in that respect undefiled;
' yet there might be no ground to sup-
' pose from thence, that both or either of
' their persons are thereby *sanctified*; and
' the Apostle urges the co-habitation of
' a believer with an infidel in the state of
' wedlock from this ground, that the un-
' believing husband is *sanctified* by the be-
' lieving wife. Nevertheless here you
' have the influence of a believer's faith,
' *ascending from an inferior to a superior
' relation*; from the wife to the husband
' who is her head, *before it can descend to*
' their

' *their offspring.* And therefore we say,
' whatever be the nature or extent of the
' *holiness* here intended, we conceive it
' cannot convey to the children an im-
' mediate right to baptism; because it
' would then be of another nature, and
' of a larger extent, than the root and
' original from whence it is derived. For
' it is clear, by the Apostle's argument,
' that *holiness* cannot be derived to the
' child from the sanctity of one parent
' only, if either father or mother be (in
' the sense intended by the Apostle) *un-
' holy* or unclean. So will the child be
' also; therefore, for the production of an
' holy seed, it is necessary that both the pa-
' rents be sanctified. And this the Apostle
' positively asserts in the first place to be
' done by the believing parent, although
' the other be an unbeliever: And then
' consequentially from thence argues the
' holiness of their children. Hence it
' follows, that as the children have no
' other *holiness* than what they derive from
' both their parents; so neither can they
' have any right by this *holiness* to any
' spiritual privileges but such as both their
' parents did also partake of. And there-
' fore, if the unbelieving parent, tho'
' *sanctified* by the believing parent, have
' not thereby a right to baptism; nei-
' ther can we conceive, that there is any
' ' such

'such privilege derived to their children
'by their *birth-holiness*.

'Besides, if it had been the usual
'practice in the Apostle's days, for the
'father or mother that did believe to
'bring all their children with them to be
'baptized: Then the holiness of the be-
'lieving *Corinthians* children would not
'at all have been in question, when this
'epistle was written; but might have
'been argued from their passing under
'that ordinance, which represented their
'new birth, altho' they had derived no
'holiness from their parents, by their
'first birth; and would have lain as an
'exception against the Apostle's infe-
'rence, *else were your children unclean*,
'&c. But of the *sanctification* of all the
'children of every believer by this or-
'dinance, or any other way, than what
'is before-mentioned, the Scripture is al-
'together silent.

'This may be also added, that if
'this *birth-holiness* do qualify all the
'children of every believer, for the ordi-
'nance of baptism; why not for all o-
'ther ordinances? For the Lord's-sup-
'per, as was practised for a long time
'together? For if recourse be had to
'what the Scriptures speak generally of
'this subject, it will be found that the
'same qualities, which do intitle any
'person to baptism, do so also for the
'partici-

'participation of all the ordinances and
' privileges of the house of God, that are
' common to all believers.

' Whosoever can and does interro-
' gate his good conscience towards God,
' when he is baptized (as every one must
' do that makes it to himself a sign of
' salvation) is capable of doing the same
' thing, in every other act of worship
' that he performs.

' 4. The arguments and inferences
' that are usually brought for, or against
' infant-baptism, from those few instances
' which the Scriptures afford us, of whole
' families being baptized, are only con-
' jectural; and therefore cannot of them-
' selves be conclusive on either hand: Yet
' in regard most that treat on this sub-
' ject for infant-baptism, do, as they con-
' ceive, improve these instances to the
' advantage of their argument, we think
' it meet (in like manner as in the cases
' before-mentioned, so in this) to shew
' the invalidity of such inferences.

' *Cornelius worshipped God with all his
' house.* The *Jaylor*, and *Crispus*, the
' chief ruler of the synagogue, *believed
' God with each of their houses. The hous-
' hold of* Stephanas *addicted themselves to
' the ministry of the saints.* So that thus
' far *worshipping* and *believing* runs paral-
' lel with *baptism.* And if *Lydia* had
' been a married person when she be-
' lieved,

'lieved, it is probable her hufband would
'alfo have been named by the Apoftle,
'as in like cafes, inafmuch as he would
'have been not only a part, but the head
'of that baptized houfhold.

'Who can affign any probable rea-
'fon, why the Apoftle fhould make men-
'tion of four or five houfholds being
'baptized, and no more? Or why he
'does fo often vary in the method of his
'falutations: Sometimes only mentioning Rom. i. 6.
'particular perfons of great note; other
'times fuch, *and the church in their*
'*houfe; the faints that were with them;*
'and *them belonging to* Narciffus, *who*
'*were in the Lord:* Thus faluting either
'whole families, or parts of families, or only
'particular perfons in families, confidered
'*as they were in the Lord?* For if it had
'been an ufual practice to baptize all
'children, with their parents; there were
'then many thoufands of the *Jews* which
'believed, and a great number of the
'*Gentiles*, in moft of the principal cities
'in the world; and among fo many thou-
'fands, it is more than probable there
'would have been fome thoufands of
'houfholds baptized: Why then fhould
'the Apoftle in this refpect fignalize one
'family of the *Jews*, and three or four
'of the *Gentiles*, as particular inftances
'in a cafe that was common? Whoever
'fuppofes that we do wilfully debar our
'children

'children from the benefit of any pro-
'mise, or privilege, that of right be-
'longs to the children of believing pa-
'rents; they do entertain over severe
'thoughts of us. To be *without natural
'affections* is one of the characters of the
'worst of persons in the worst of times.
'We do freely confess ourselves guilty
'before the Lord, in that we have not
'with more circumspection and diligence
'trained up those that relate to us in the
'fear of the Lord; and do humbly and
'earnestly pray, that our omissions here-
'in may be remitted, and that they may
'not redound to the prejudice of our-
'selves, or any of ours. But with re-
'spect to that duty that is incumbent on
'us, we acknowledge ourselves obliged by
'the precepts of God, *to bring up our
'children in the nurture and admonition
'of the Lord*, to teach them his fear,
'both by instruction and example; and
'should we set light by this precept, it
'would demonstrate, that we are more
'vile than the unnatural *Heathen*, that
'*like not to retain God in their knowledge*;
'our baptism might then be justly ac-
'counted as no baptism to us. There
'are many special promises that do en-
'courage us, as well as precepts that do
'oblige us, to the close pursuit of our
'duty herein. That God, whom we
'serve, being jealous of his worship,
'threatens

' threatens the *visiting of the fathers
' transgressions upon the children, to the
' third and fourth generation of them that
' hate him:* Yet does he more abundant-
' ly extend his *mercy, even to thousands,*
' respecting the offspring and succeeding
' generations, of them *that love him, and
' keep his commands.*

' WHEN our Lord rebuked his disci-
' ples, for prohibiting the access of little
' children that were brought to him, that
' he might pray over them, lay his hands
' upon them, and bless them, does de-
' clare, *that of such is the kingdom of
' God:* And the Apostle *Peter*, in an-
' swer to their enquiry, that desired to
' know *what they must do to be saved,* does
' not only instruct them in the necessary
' duty of repentance and baptism; but
' does also thereto encourage them, by
' that *promise* which had reference both
' *to them and their children.* If our Lord
' *Jesus* in the fore-mentioned place, do
' not respect the qualities of children, as
' elsewhere, as to their meekness, humi-
' lity and sincerity, and the like, but in-
' tend also that those very persons and
' such like, appertain to the kingdom of
' God: And if the Apostle *Peter*, in
' mentioning the aforesaid *promise*, do re-
' spect not only the present and succeed-
' ing generations of those *Jews,* that
' heard him, in which sense the same

' phrase

'phrafe doth occur in fcripture, but alfo
'the immediate offspring of his audi-
'tors; whether the promife relate to the
'gift of the Holy Spirit, or of eternal life,
'or any grace or privilege tending to the
'obtaining thereof: It is neither our con-
'cern, nor our intereft to confine the
'mercies, and promifes of God, to a
'more narrow or lefs compafs than he
'is pleafed gracioufly to offer and intend
'them; nor to have a light efteem of
'them; but are obliged in duty to God,
'and affection to our children, to plead
'earneftly with God, and ufe our utmoft
'endeavours, that both ourfelves and our
'offspring may be partakers of his mer-
'cies and gracious promifes. Yet we
'cannot from either of thefe texts, col-
'lect a fufficient warrant for us to bap-
'tize our children, before they are in-
'ftructed in the principles of the Chrif-
'tian Religion.

'For as to the inftance in *little chil-
'dren*; it feems by the difciples *forbid-
'ding* them, that they were brought up-
'on fome other account, not fo frequent
'as baptifm muft be fuppofed to have
'been, if from the beginning believers
'children had been admitted thereto:
'and no account is given, whether their
'parents were baptized believers or not.
'And as to the inftance of the Apoftle; if
'the following words and practice may
  'be

' be taken as an interpretation of the
' fcope of that *promife*, we cannot con-
' ceive it does refer to infant-baptifm;
' becaufe the text does prefently fubjoin;
' *then they that gladly received the word*
' *were baptized*.

' That there were fome believing
' children of believing parents in the A-
' poftle's days, is evident from the Scrip-
' tures, even fuch as were then in their
' father's family, and under their parents
' tuition, and education; to whom the
' Apoftle in feveral of his epiftles to the
' churches, giveth commands *to obey their*
' *parents in the Lord*; and does allure
' their tender years to hearken to this
' precept, by reminding them, that it is
' *the firft command with promife*.

' And it is recorded by him for the
' praife of *Timothy*, and encouragement
' of parents betimes to inftruct, and chil-
' dren early to attend godly inftruction,
' that ἀπὸ βρέφους, *from a child, he had*
' *known the Holy Scriptures*. The Apoftle
' *John* rejoyced greatly, when he found
' of *the children of the elect lady* walking
' in the truth; and *the children of her e-*
' *lect fifter* join with the Apoftle in his
' falutation.

' But that this was not generally fo,
' that all the children of believers were
' accounted for believers, as they would
' have been, if they had been all bap-
' tized,

'tized, may be collected from the cha-
'racter which the Apostle gives of per-
'sons fit to be chosen to eldership in the
'church, which was not common to all
'believers. Among others, this is ex-
'pressly one; *viz. if there be any having
'believing, or faithful children*, not ac-
'cused of riot or unruly. And we may
'from the Apostle's writings on the same
'subject, collect the reason of this quali-
'fication; *viz.* that in case the person
'designed for this office to teach and
'rule in the house of God, had children
'capable of it, there might be first a
'proof of his ability, industry and suc-
'cess in this work in his own family, and
'private capacity, before he was ordain-
'ed to the exercise of this authority in
'the church, in a publick capacity; as a
'bishop in the house of God.

'THESE things we have mentioned
'as having a direct reference unto the
'controversy between our brethren and us.
'Other things, that are more abstruse and
'prolix, which are frequently introduced
'into this controversy, but do not neces-
'sarily concern it, we have purposely a-
'voided; that the distance between us
'and our brethren may not be by us
'made more wide: For it is our duty,
'and concern, so far as is possible for
'us, retaining a good conscience towards
                                    'God,

'God, to seek a more entire agreement
'and reconciliation with them.

'WE are not insensible, that as to
'the order of God's house, and entire
'communion therein, there are some
'things wherein we, as well as others,
'are not at a full accord among our-
'selves. As for instance, the known
'principle and state of the consciences
'of divers of us, that have agreed in
'this confession is such, that we cannot
'hold church-communion with any other
'than baptized believers, and churches
'constituted of such. Yet some others
'of us have a greater liberty and freedom
'in our spirits that way; and therefore
'we have purposely omitted the mention
'of things of that nature, that we might
'concur in giving this evidence of our
'agreement, both among ourselves, and
'with other good Christians, in those im-
'portant articles of the Christian Reli-
'gion mainly insisted on by us. And
'this notwithstanding we all esteem it
'our chief concern, both among ourselves
'and all others, that in every place call
'upon the name of the Lord *Jesus Christ*
'our Lord, both theirs and ours, and
'love him in sincerity, *to endeavour to*
'*keep the unity of the Spirit, in the bond*
'*of peace*; and in order thereto, to exer-
'cise *all lowliness and meekness, with long-*
'*suffering, forbearing one another in love.*

' And

'And we are persuaded, if the same me-
'thod were introduced into frequent prac-
'tice between us and our christian friends,
'who agree with us in all the fundamen-
'tal articles of the Christian Faith, tho'
'they do not so in the subject and adminis-
'tration of baptism; it would soon beget
'a better understanding, and brotherly
'affection between us.

'IN the beginning of the Christian
'Church, when the doctrine of the bap-
'tism of *Christ* was not universally un-
'derstood, yet those that knew only the
'baptism of *John*, were *the disciples of*
'*the Lord Jesus*; and *Apollos* an emin-
'ent minister of the gospel of *Jesus*.

'IN the beginning of the reformation
'of the Christian Church, and recovery
'from that *Egyptian* darkness, wherein
'our forefathers for many generations
'were held in bondage; upon recourse
'had to the Scriptures of truth, different
'apprehensions were conceived, which
'are to this time continued, concerning
'the practice of this ordinance.

'LET not our zeal herein be misin-
'terpreted. That God whom we serve is
'jealous of his worship. By his gracious
'providence the law thereof is continued
'amongst us; and we are forwarned by
'what happened in the church of the
'*Jews*, that it is necessary for every ge-
'ration, and that frequently in every ge-
'neration,

'neration, to confult the divine oracle, compare our worfhip with the rule, and take heed to what doctrines we receive and practife.

'If the ten commands, exhibited in the *popifh* idolatrous fervice-book, had been received as the entire law of God, becaufe they agree in number with his ten commands, and alfo in the fubftance of nine of them; the fecond commandment, forbidding idolatry, had been utterly loft. If *Ezra* and *Nehemiah* had not made a diligent fearch into the particular parts of God's law, and his worfhip; the feaft of tabernacles, which for many centuries of years had not been duely obferved, according to the inftitution, though it was retained in the general notion, would not have been kept in due order.

'So may it be now, as to many things relating to the fervice of God, which do retain the names proper to them in their firft inftitution; but yet through inadvertency, where there is no finifter defign, may vary in their circumftances from their firft inftitution. And if by means of any ancient defection, or of that general corruption of the fervice of God, and interruption of his true worfhip, and perfecution of his fervants by the antichriftian bifhop of *Rome*, for many generations; thofe
'who

'who do consult the word of God, can-
'not yet arrive at a full and mutual sa-
'tisfaction among themselves, what was
'the practice of the primitive Christian
'Church, in some points relating to the
'*worship* of God: Yet inasmuch as these
'things are not of the essence of christi-
'anity, but that we agree in the funda-
'mental doctrines thereof; we do appre-
'hend, there is sufficient ground to lay
'aside all bitterness and prejudice, and in
'the spirit of love and meekness, to em-
'brace and own each other therein; leav-
'ing each other at liberty to perform
'such other services, wherein we cannot
'concur, apart unto God, according to
'the best of our understanding.'

THE great increase of the *Baptists*, and the many converts gained by the force of their arguments and the exemplariness of their lives, brought upon them many clamours and defamations; the chiefs were represented as Jesuits, Hereticks, and what not; many books were published, misrepresenting them.

THIS necessitated them to publish many Confessions of Faith; some in vindication of particular churches, others of particular persons, too numerous to be taken notice of in this history. I shall confine myself only to such as were put forth by congregated bodies. And as I have before
ob-

observed, the *Baptists* in general consist of two parties, distinguished by the title of *general* and *particular* ; so I find when the one have published a general Confession of their Faith, the other have soon after likewise done the same; both which I shall place in order of time, that so a just estimation of their principles, and their near coherence with the other Protestant parties in this kingdom may appear. This seems to me the best and only method to answer the many misrepresentations which have been published by their ill-natured opponents, both of their principles and practices.

In the year 1678, a Confession of Faith was agreed to, and signed, by fifty-four ministers and messengers of the churches, in the several counties of *Bucks*, *Hertford*, *Bedford* and *Oxford*, in behalf of themselves and many others; containing fifty articles, which they did most heartily and unfeignedly own, believe and profess, and desired through the grace of God to persevere in. It was soon after published under the title of, *An Orthodox Creed; or, a Protestant Confession of Faith ; being an Essay to unite and confirm all true Protestants in the fundamental articles of the Christian Religion, against the Errors and Heresies of the Church of* Rome. But the same being too long to be contained in the Appendix of of this Volume, I shall place it in the Appendix of Vol. III. Nº. I.

THE *Popish* plot * having fixed a brand of infamy and ingratitude on the whole body of the *Roman Catholicks*; the courtiers attempted to relieve them, by setting on foot a *Sham Protestant Plot*, and fathering it upon the *Presbyterians*. For this purpose mercenary spies were employed to bring news from all parts of the town, which was then full of cabals. At length a plot was formed by one *Dangerfield*, a subtle and dangerous *Papist*, but a very villain. Who when he had informed the King and Duke of *York*, *That he had been invited to accept of a commission; that a new form of government was to be set up; and that the King and Royal Family were to be banished*; the story was received with such pleasure, that he had a present, and a pension of three pounds a week, to carry on his correspondence. But in the end finding himself undone, if he persisted in what he could not support, made an ample confession of the whole matter: And published a Narrative, wherein he testified; *That he was employed by the* Popish *party, and chiefly by the* Popish *Lords in the* Tower, *with the Countess of* Powis, *to invent the* Meal-tub-plot, *which was to have*

---

* *Neal*, Vol. IV. p. 488.

thrown the Popish Plot *wholly upon the* Presbyterians.

THE last Parliament being dissolved abruptly, a new one was called this year: In which the elections went pretty much as before; the cry of the people, being, *no popery, no pensioners, no arbitrary government.* But the King prorogued them from time to time, for above a year, without permitting them to do business. The confusion of the times brought the Parliament to an inclination to relieve the *Nonconformists:* And they appointed a committee, who agreed upon a *comprehension* with the *Dissenters*; and those that could not be comprehended within their terms, were to have a *toleration* and freedom from the penal Statutes, upon condition of subscribing a declaration of allegiance, &c. and of assembling with open doors. Bishop *Burnet* says *, there was a bill of comprehension offered by the Episcopal Party in the House of Commons, by which the *Presbyterians* would have been taken into the church; but that to the amazement of all people, their party in the house did not seem concerned to promote it, but on the contrary neglected it. Mr. *Neal* says †, the reason was, because they found the bill would not

Anno 1680.

* Vol. I. *p.* 495.
† Vol. IV. *p.* 496.

go;

go; or that if it had paffed the Commons, it would have been thrown out by the Bifhops in the Houfe of Lords; the Clergy, as *Kennet* fays, *being no farther in earneſt, than as they apprehended, the knife of the* Papifts *at their throats.*

BUT while the Parliament, fays Mr. *Neal* *, was endeavouring to relieve the *Diſſenters*, and charging the miferies of the kingdom upon the *Papiſts*; many of the Biſhops and Clergy of the Church of *England*, were pleafed to fee the *Court* enclined to profecute the *Nonconformiſts*.

Rapin † reprefents the clergy in general, at this time, as attached to the Court and the intereft of the Duke of *York*; and confiders this as the occafion of the *Diſſenters* charging the Church of *England* with being *popiſhly* inclined. He adds, that in the difpofition of the Court in favour of the *Papiſts*, ever fince the beginning of this reign, or at leaſt ever fince the Earl of *Clarendon*'s difgrace, it may eafily be imagined, that care had been taken, to introduce among the clergy, men of a doubtful religion, and from whom the Court had nothing to fear. And it is certain that even fome of the better fort who wrote againſt *Popery*, went fo far into the court meafures, as to charge the calamities of the times upon

* Vol. IV. *p.* 499.
† Vol. II. *p.* 718.

the *Nonconformifts*, and to raife the cry of the populace againft them. Dr. *Edward Stillingfleet*, who had wrote an *Irenicum* in favour of liberty, and againft *impofitions*, now turned about; and in his fermon before the Lord-Mayor, *May* 2. intitled, *The Mifchief of Separation*, condemned all the *Diffenters* as *Schifmaticks*, and very gravely advifed them not to complain of perfecution. When the fermon was publifhed, it brought upon the Doctor, fays Mr. *Neal*, feveral learned adverfaries; as Mr. *Baxter*, Mr. *Alfop*, Mr. *Howe*, Mr. *Barrett*, and Dr. *Owen*. From which laft Divine, who wrote with great temper and ferioufnefs, I will venture, fays he, to tranfcribe the following paffage, without entering into the argument *.
‘ After fo many of the *Nonconformifts*
‘ have died in common goals; fo many
‘ have endured long imprifonments, not a
‘ few being at this day in the fame du-
‘ rance; fo many driven from their ha-
‘ bitations into a wandering condition,
‘ to preferve for a while the liberty
‘ of their perfons; fo many have been
‘ reduced to want and penury by the
‘ taking away their goods, and from fome
‘ the very inftruments of their livelihood;
‘ after the profecution that has been a-
‘ gainft them in all Courts of Juftice in

* Vol. IV. *p.* 500.

'this nation, on informations, indict-
'ments and suits, to the great charge of
'all who have been so persecuted, and
'the ruin of some; after so many mini-
'sters and their families have been brought
'into the utmost outward straits, which
'nature can subsist under; after all their
'perpetual fears and dangers, wherewith
'they have been exercised and disquiet-
'ed: They think it hard to be censured
'for *complaining*, by them who are at
'ease.'

Anno 1681.

THE King having parted with his last Parliament in displeasure *, without being able to obtain any money, resolved once more to try a new one: And apprehending that the malcontents were encouraged by the neighbourhood of the city of *London*, he summoned them to meet at *Oxford*. The members for *London* being the same as before, had a paper put into their hands, by four merchants, in the name of all the citizens then assembled in common-hall; containing a return of their most hearty thanks, for their faithful and unwearied endeavours in the two last Parliaments, to search into the depth of the *Popish* Plot, to preserve the *Protestant* Religion, to promote an Union among his Majesty's *Protestant* subjects, to repeal

* *Neal*, Vol. IV. *p.* 501.

the 35th of *Elizabeth*, and the *Corporation Act*, and to promote the *Bill of Exclusion*; and requesting their continuance of the same. The members being afraid of violence, were attended to *Oxford* with a numerous body of horse, having ribbons in their hats, with these words, *No popery, no slavery*; the citizens having promised to stand by them with their lives and fortunes. The Parliament revived the *Bill of Exclusion*. Upon which the King went suddenly, and not very decently, says *Burnet* *, to the House of Lords in a *sedan*, with the crown between his feet; and having put on his robes in haste, called up the Commons, and dissolved his fifth and last Parliament, after they had sat but seven days. As soon as his Majesty got out of the house, he rid away in all haste to *Windsor*, as one that was glad he had got rid of his Parliament, which was the last he called, tho' he lived three or four years after. And here was an end of the constitution and liberties of *England* for the present; all that followed, to the King's death, was no more than the convulsions and struggles of a dying man.

The abject and servile flattery of the University of *Cambridge*, and others, in their addresses to the King, being not

* Vol. II. *p.* 499.

joined by the *Nonconformists*, did necessarily bring down vengeance upon them, who were now doomed to suffer under a double character, as *Whigs* and as *Dissenters*. Witnesses were brought over from *Ireland* *, and employed to swear away men's lives. Spies were planted in all Coffee-houses to furnish out evidence for the witnesses. Mercenary Justices were put into commission all over the kingdom; juries were packed. And with regard to the *Nonconformists*, informers of the vilest of the people, were countenanced to a shameful degree; insomuch that the goals were quickly filled with prisoners; and large sums of money extorted from the industry and labour of honest men, and put into the hands of the most profligate wretches in the nation.

THE Justices of *Middlesex* shewed great forwardess, and represented to his Majesty, that an intimation of his pleasure was necessary at this time, to the putting the laws in execution against *Conventicles* †; because when a charge was lately given at the Council-board, to put the laws in execution against *Popish Recusants*, no mention was made of suppressing *Conventicles*. Upon this, his Majesty commanded the Lord-Mayor, Aldermen and Justices, to use their utmost en-

* *Burnet*, p. 501, 505, 506.
† *Neal*, Vol. IV. *p.* 507.

deavour

deavour to suppress all *Conventicles* and unlawful meetings, upon pretence of religious worship; for it was his express pleasure, that the laws be effectually put in execution against them, both in city and country.

It was not in the power of the moderate Churchmen to relieve the *Nonconformists*, nor deliver them from the edge of the penal laws, which were in the hands of their enemies. All that could be done, says Mr. *Neal* [*], was to encourage their constancy, and to write some compassionate treatises, to move the people in their favour, by shewing them, that while they were plundering and destroying their Protestant dissenting neighbours, they were cutting the throat of the whole reformed religion, and making way for the triumphs of *Popery* upon its ruins. Among other writings of this sort, the most famous was, *The Conformists Plea for the Nonconformists*, in four parts; *by a beneficed Minister, and a regular son of the Church of* England. In which the Author undertakes to shew. 1. The greatness of their sufferings. 2. The hardness of their case. 3. The reasonableness and equity of their proposals for union. 4. The qualification and worth of their ministers. 5. Their peaceable behaviour. 6. Their

---
[*] Vol. IV. *p.* 508.

354   *The* HISTORY *of the*

agreement with the Church of *England* in the articles of her faith. 7. The prejudice to the Church by their exclusion. And then concludes, with an account of the infamous lives and lamentable deaths, of several of the *informers*. It was, says Mr. *Neal* * [and, indeed, really so it is] a rational and moving performance, but had no influence on the *Tory Justices* and tribe of *informers*.

MOST of the Clergy were with the Court, and distinguished themselves on the side of persecution. The pulpits every where resounded with the doctrines of *Passive-obedience* and *Non-resistance*: A *Mahometan* principle, says Dr. *Welwood* †, which since the times of that *Impostor*, who first broached it, has been the means to enslave a great part of the world. No *Eastern* monarch, according to them, was more absolute than the King of *England*. They expressed such a zeal, says *Burnet* ‡, for the Duke's succession, as if a *Popish* King over a *Protestant* Country, had been a special blessing from heaven.

THERE was a great change made in the *Commissions* all over *England*. None were left, either on the bench, or in the militia, that did not go with zeal into the humour of the court. And such of the

* Vol. IV. *p.* 509.
† Memoirs, *p.* 112.
‡ Vol. II. *p.* 501.

clergy

English Baptists. 355

clergy as would not engage in that fury, were declaimed againſt as *betrayers of the Church*, and ſecret favourers of the *Diſſenters*. But the truth is, ſays the Biſhop, *the number of ſober honeſt clergymen was not great*; for where the carcaſe is, the eagles will be gathered together: The ſcent of preferment, will draw aſpiring men after it.

Upon the whole, the times were very black at preſent, and the proſpect under a *Popiſh* ſucceſſor more threatning.

It would fill ſome volumes to go into all the particulars of the unchriſtian proceedings that did attend the *Nonconformiſts*; and even too much, to attend thoſe that have particularly concerned the *Baptiſts*. But I muſt not paſs by the ſufferings of ſome of them, who at this time bore a teſtimony for liberty, and ſealed the ſame with their blood. And to do juſtice to the Reverend Mr. *Neal*, I muſt obſerve here, that he has treated the *Baptiſts*, where he has had occaſion to mention them in this volume, much more like a friend, than in his former volumes.

Mr. *Francis Bampfield*, was a famous *Baptiſt*. He was in this reign firſt committed to *Dorcheſter* goal; and a conſiderable fine laid upon him, for preaching, praying, and refuſing to conform to the Church of *England*; in which place he was kept a *priſoner* above eight years.

Mr. Francis Bampfield impriſoned at Dorcheſter, and fined.

Z 2 He

He bore his long imprisonment with great courage and patience, being filled with the joys and comforts of the Holy Spirit. Nor did he cease to preach Christ, and promote his interest, by prayers and exhortations. And so successful was he in his labours, that he gathered a *Church* even in this place of confinement.

After eight years imprisonment is discharged Anno 1675.
Upon his being discharged from hence, in the year 1675. he went up and down in several *counties*, preaching the word as he had opportunity. But it was not long before he was taken up again, for preaching to a congregation in *Wiltshire*. He

Is imprisoned again at Salisbury, and fined.
was apprehended and imprisoned at *Salisbury*. A certain fine or mulct being laid upon him, he continued in *prison* about eighteen weeks. From hence he writ *a Letter to the Saints*, which was quickly printed; wherein he gave a brief account of the occasion of his imprisonment, and declared what satisfaction and joy he had in his present sufferings for the sake of

Is released and comes to London.
Christ. After his release from hence, he came to *London*: And the heat of persecution being somewhat abated, he here enjoyed liberty for several years to preach the Gospel, tho' privately; but with such success, that in a little time he gathered a people unto Christ, who submitted to *Believers Baptism*, and soon after entered

Hires Pinners hall.
into a *Church-State*, and hired *Pinnershall* in *Broad-street*, for the meeting-place.
Which

Which being fo publick, foon expofed them to the rage of their perfecutors.

On the 17th of *Feb.* 1682. when they were met together in the forenoon at their ufual hour, Mr. *Bampfield* being in the pulpit, a Conftable with his ftaff, and feveral men with halberts, rufhed into the affembly. The Conftable commanded him in the King's name to give over and to come down: To which he anfwered, that he was in the difcharge of his office, in the name of the King of Kings. I have, faid the Conftable, a warrant from the *Lord-Mayor* to difturb your meeting. I have, fays Mr. *Bampfield*, a warrant from Chrift, who is *Lord Maximus*, to go on; and fo did proceed in his difcourfe. Then the Conftable commanded one of the officers to pull him down. Upon which Mr. *Bampfield* repeated his text; the latter part of which was, *The day of vengeance is in his heart, and the year of the redeemed ones is come, and he would pull down his enemies.* After they had feized Mr. *Bampfield*, they carried him and fix more before the *Lord-Mayor*. When the Conftable had given an account to his Lordfhip, of the occafion of his bringing thefe men before him; the *Lord-Mayor* examined him firft, and afterwards the other fix; after feveral of them were fined ten pounds a man, were bid to de-

Anno 1682.

Ifa. lxi 1.

Is taken from thence with fix more, and had before the Lord-Mayor.

Some fined 10 l.

part.

part. And Mr. *Bampfield*, who was detained laft, was foon after told he might be gone alfo.

IN the afternoon of the fame day, they went to their meeting-place again, at the ufual time of affembling. As foon as Mr. *Bampfield*, and a few with him were gotten into the place, the officer immediately came, fhut the door againft thofe that were without, and required thofe within to depart. But they kept their places for fome time; and took this opportunity to tell the officers, of the fin and bafenefs of perfecuting men thus for religion. This feemed to touch their confciences; for they all declared their unwillingnefs to meddle in fuch a work, but that they were by their places obliged to it.

HEREUPON *one* demanded of the Conftable to produce his warrant for what he did, but it feems he had none; only he told them, he would fend to the *Lord-Mayor* for one. At length no frefh warrant being produced, the Conftable commanded one of the officers to pull Mr. *Bampfield* down from his pulpit: Who, after fome time tremblingly, and with a pale face, took hold of him, and fo led him out into the ftreet, where there was a great number of people got together. The Conftable not caring to proceed any farther, Mr. *Bampfield* with a great

great company went to his own houfe, and there performed thofe duties of worfhip, which they defigned to have done in their meeting-place.

ON the 24th of the fame month, they met together again at *Pinners-hall*; but they had not long been affembled, and Mr. *Bampfield* in prayer, before another Conftable with feveral officers rufhed in upon them. Mr. *Bampfield* continued his prayer, till one of the officers came and pulled him away. Then they carried him under a guard of officers to the Lord-Mayor: As he went along the ftreet, he carried his bible in his hand, expofing it to the view of the people, who flocked after him in great numbers. He endeavoured briefly to declare, practically as well as verbally, that it was for the fake of Chrift and his word, that his liberty was taken away. When they came to the Lord-Mayor, he was gone to the Seffions; and thither now they were refolv'd to drag him The fpectators as he paffed along, paffed different verdicts upon him; fome condemning him, others fpeaking in his favour. One called him a *Chriftian Jew*; another faid, fee how he walks with his bible in his hand, like one of the old Martyrs.

BEING brought to the Seffions, after examination, he and three more were fent to prifon. Next day in the afternoon, he was

He is taken again, and had before the Lord-Mayor.

He with three more imprifoned.

was brought to the bar with three or four more, who were examined on the like case, and remitted to *Newgate*.

Anno 1683.

ON the 17th of *March* 1683. he with some more who were committed for not taking the oaths of *allegiance* and *supremacy*, were brought before the Sessions-Court in the *Old-Bailey*; indicted, tryed, and by the Jury, directed by the Judge so to do, brought in guilty.

March 28. they were again brought to the Sessions to receive their sentence: And when at the bar, the *Recorder*, without asking whether they would take the oaths, or whether they had any thing to offer, why sentence should not be given against them; after odiously aggravating their not taking of the oaths, and casting reflections on scrupulous consciences, read the sentence; which was: *That they were out of the protection of the King's Majesty; that all their goods and chattels were forfeited during life; that they were to remain in goal during their lives, or during the King's pleasure.*

UPON this Mr. *Bampfield* would have spoken something. But there was a great uproar, crying, *Away with them, put them away from the bar, we will not hear them.* While they were thrusting them away, Mr. *Bampfield* said, *The righteous Lord loveth righteousness, the Lord be judge in this*

this cafe. And then they were returned to *Newgate*, from whence they came.

Mr. *Bampfield* being of a tender conftitution, could not long bear the hardfhip to which they expofed him. He was kept at his laft trial, ten hours in the *Bail-dock*, a cold and loathfome place, where he received great hurt: And foon after died in *Newgate*, very much la- *Dies in* mented by his fellow-prifoners, as well as *Newgate.* friends and acquaintance.

ONE of whom was Dr. *John Griffith*; who publifhed his cafe under his own hand: Which is as followeth, *viz.*
' The cafe of Mr. *John Griffith*, mini- *Dr. John*
' fter of the Gofpel, and now prifoner in *Griffith's*
' *Newgate.* Being a true and impartial *cafe.*
' account of what he fpake at the *Seffions-*
' *houfe* in the *Old-Bailey*, on the 18th
' day of this inftant *April* 1683. before
' the Lord Chief-Juftice *Saunders*, and
' three Judges more, the Lord-Mayor,
' Recorder, and feveral Aldermen of the
' City of *London.*

' ON the day and year abovefaid, a-
' bout four in the afternoon, Mr. *Bamp-*
' *field* and myfelf were fent for by the
' Court; and foon after we came were
' both brought to the inward bar. Mr.
' *Bampfield* was firft required to take the
' *oath of allegiance*; it being again ten-
' dered him, according to the ftatute in
' the third of King *James.* After fome
' difcourfe

'discourse between the Judges and the
'Recorder, had with Mr. *Bampfield*, he
'refusing to swear, they made an end for
'that time with him.

'THE Clerk of the Peace, I took
'him to be, said unto me, Take off your
'glove. I asked him *what to do?* He an-
'swered, *to lay your hand on the book*;
'which book he had in his hand, and
'held it out unto me. I then spake with
'a loud voice, *and said*, My Lord, I
'hope you will give me the liberty to speak
'for myself in my own defence. One
'of the Judges replied, that, my friend,
'meaning Mr. *Bampfield*, had spoke for
'me, or to that effect. I said again;
'that I desired to speak for myself, for I
'had other things to offer, as my reasons
'why I could not take that oath. Hav-
'ing liberty granted, as I took it from
'their silence, I with an audible voice
'said unto them; I am in the Scripture
'commanded, when I take an oath, *to
'swear in truth and judgment, and in
'righteousness*; unto which the Church
'of *England* doth agree. It is one Article
'of their Faith, that he that taketh an
'oath, being required of the magistrate,
'ought to swear, so he do it *in truth, in
'righteousness, and in judgment.* Now
'for me to swear, as my duty is accord-
'ing to the Scripture, and as the Church
'of *England* directs, I cannot, should I
                                    'take

Art. 39, of the Church of England.

' take this oath; becaufe I cannot know,
' but muft be ignorant of, what I bind
' my foul to perform; and then it is im-
' poffible I fhould fwear *in truth, in judg-*
' *ment, and in righteoufnefs.*

' I CANNOT know, but muft be ig-
' norant, both of what hereafter by law
' I may be required to do, and alfo to
' whom I fwear to be obedient; for it is
' not poffible I fhould forefee what laws
' may hereafter be made: And I do not
' only bind my foul to obey the King,
' that now is, but his heirs and fuccef-
' fors alfo: And I know not what his fuc-
' ceffor may be; for ought I know he
' may be a *Popifh* fucceffor, a *Papift*;
' and I cannot fwear to obey laws not
' yet in being, nor to be obedient to a *Po-*
' *pifh* fucceffor. Therefore I cannot take
' the oath of allegiance,

' UPON thefe words there was a hum
' in the court. Which being ceafed, af-
' ter a little paufe, one of the Judges
' made this fhort reply. I, faith he,
' *doth he ftick in there?* I then went on,
' and faid, I cannot conform to the
' Church of *England.* Should I take this
' oath, I fwear to conform; for I am
' bound by any oath to obey all the
' King's laws, as much thofe laws which
' refpect the worfhip of God, as thofe
' relating to civil government: And then I
' am fworn to hear Common-prayer once

' a

'a month. Here one of the Judges said,
'*so you are*; and to receive the Sacra-
'ment with the Church of *England*, as oft
'as the law requires; yea, and to conform
'to all the rites and ceremonies of the
'said Church. To this it was answered,
'*so you are*; and not to frequent private
'meetings any more, for there are laws
'that forbid it. It was again answered,
'*so you are*.

'THEREFORE I cannot take this
'oath.

'I THEN prayed the Judges to give
'me all their opinions, whether it were
'as I had said or not. They answered
'with one consent, as one man, that it
'was as I had said, *viz.* that I did, in
'taking the oath, swear to obey all the
'King's laws without exception. Then
'I returned them thanks, that they were
'pleased to give me their opinion and judg-
'ment in the case. And withal added
'these words: I am well satisfied and
'settled in my religion; and the more
'confirmed by what you said: And if it be
'so, do with me what you please: Come
'life, come death, the Lord assisting me,
'I will never take the oath of allegiance.

'THEN I desired to speak a few
'words more. Which being not denied,
'I said; Be it known unto you, that I
'do not refuse to take the oath of alle-
'giance in any dislike I have of any thing
'con-

'contained therein against the authority
'of the Pope, or the see of *Rome*; but
'do in all points therein with you agree.
'And further I do declare, that I do be-
'lieve the Pope hath no power, nor au-
'thority over the King's person, nor his
'government; no, nor over the meanest
'subject in his kingdom. And do yet
'further declare; that I believe in my
'conscience, popery to be idolatrous,
'damnable and devilish. I was then had
'back again to the *Press-yard*, where
'I remain the Lord's prisoner; and am
'ready further to bear my testimony for
'him, against Antichrist, the Pope, and
'See of *Rome*; and for his Holy Word,
'the purity of the Gospel, and the or-
'dinances thereof, against *Popish* darkness,
'filthy idolatries, fornications, blasphe-
'mies, and abominations, and all tradi-
'tions of men; as one made willing,
'through the free mercy and rich grace
'of God, my heavenly father, to forsake
'all for Christ, who hath loved me, and
'given himself for me; not counting
'my life dear to myself, so I may finish
'my course with joy, and the ministry
'I have received of the Lord *Jesus*, to
'testify the Gospel of the grace of God.
'Thus have I given an account of what
'I spake, and was said to me, to the
'very best of my memory, though it
'may be not word for word. Yet for
'the

'the substance of what was spoke, it is
'true.'
John Griffith.

Mr. Thomas Delaune. Not long after this, the famous and learned Mr. *Thomas Delaune*, fell a sacrifice to the rage and malice of the persecuting clergy of those times; and by imprisonment lost his life.

He was born at *Brini* in *Ireland*, about three miles from *Riggsdale*. His parents were *Papists* and very poor; they rented a part of the estate of ——*Riggs*, Esq; who observing the early and forward parts of young *Delaune*, placed him in a Friary at *Kilcrash*, about seven miles distant from *Cork*, where he received his education. When Mr. *Delaune* was about fifteen or sixteen years of age, he left the Friary and went to *Kingsale*, where he met with Mr. *Bampfield*, who then had a pilchard fishery in that place. He finding Mr. *Delaune* to be a young man of good parts and learning, took him into his service, and made him clerk of the fishery, and became the happy instrument of his conversion. He continued some years in great esteem and intimacy with Major *Riggs* and Mr. *Bampfield*; till thro' persecution and troubles he left *Ireland*, and went over to *England*. Meeting there with Mr. *Edward Hutchinson*, who was pastor of a congregation at *Ormond*,
but

but removed from thence on account of the troubles of the times, at length married his daughter *Hannah*, and went with her to *London*, where he fell into an intimacy and ſtrict friendſhip with Mr. *Benjamin Keach*, and tranſlated the *Philologia Sacra*, prefixed to his elaborate book in Folio, intitled, τροπολογια, *A Key to open Scripture Metaphors*, much eſteemed by the learned.

The occaſion of Mr. *Delaune*'s laſt ſufferings was this; Dr. *Benjamin Calamy*, one of the King's Chaplains, having publiſhed the *London Caſes*, Mr. *Delaune* wrote an anſwer to one of them. For which he was apprehended, and committed to *priſon*; where the ſtraitneſs of his confinement caſt him into a diſtemper of which he ſoon died. And tho' the *Doctor* in his caſes pretended himſelf very deſirous of an anſwer, he never made the leaſt attempt to get him releaſed; but ſuffered him to be perſecuted with all imaginable violence, tho' he anſwered him ſo modeſtly, ſo like a Gentleman, and ſo like a ſcholar!

Thus, ſays Mr. *Pierce*, ' the cham- ' pions of the church ſecured themſelves ' from being attacked by the *Nonconfor-* ' *miſts*; and wrote, when they could not ' be anſwered, with either conveniency or ' ſafety. For the perſecuted condition of ' the *Nonconformiſts* deprived them of lei- ' ſure

Vindication of the Diſſenters, p. 259.

'sure for writing; and if they wrote, 'they brought upon themselves fresh 'troubles and persecutions.' I would not be thought by any means, to reflect upon the Church of *England*, nor its *professors* in the present day, for actions committed by their *predecessors*. Facts are like the laws of the *Medes* and *Persians*, not to be obliterated; but according as they are good or bad, to stand upon *record*, for our imitation, or avoiding. I ever had a great value for the Church of *England*, tho' in conscience I could not conform to all her requirements; and have always esteemed it as the best constituted reformed national church in the world.

'Tis known and professed, says the *Author* of the preface to the *Plea* of the learned Gentleman now before me; 'That 'persecution merely for conscience is con- 'trary to the principles of the Christian 'Religion, and the doctrine of the Church 'of *England*. Who they were that per- 'secuted in those days, we all know, 'and with what real design: To destroy 'the church of *England* itself, is plain. 'How they acted all against the very 'principles of the church is plain. But 'that they acted under the church's au- 'thority, in her name, debauched her 'Clergy, to fall in with the hellish pro- 'ject; made use of her ecclesiastical 'Courts to put their wicked designs in 'execu-

P. 5.

'execution, till the world could hardly
'discover whether it was the Church's
'act and deed, or no, to the indelible
'scandal of the Clergy of those times;
'is a truth too plain to be debated.'

MR. *Delaune* was apprehended *Nov.* 29. 1683. and by Sir *Thomas Jenner*, Recorder of *London*, committed to *Wood-street-Compter*, and put in amongst the common-side prisoners, where he had a hard bench for his bed, and two bricks for his pillows. He was removed from thence by the *Recorder's* warrant, committed to *Newgate*, and lodged amongst *felons*. Whose horrid company, says he, in his letter to Dr. *Calamy*, made a perfect representation of that horrible place, which you describe when you mention hell. *Sent to Wood-street-Compter, and removed to Newgate.*

IN another letter to Dr. *Calamy*, he expresses himself thus:

'I HAVE no malignity against any
'person whatsoever; much less a-
'gainst your church, or any of its mem-
'bers. All I desire is, that scrupulous
'consciences, who trouble not the peace
'of the nation, should be dealt withal,
'at least, as weak brethren, according to
'*Rom.* xiv. 1. and not ruined by penal-
'ties, for not swallowing what is impos-
'ed, under the notion of *decency* and *or-
'der*, tho' excentrick to the scheme, we
'have of it, in our only rule of faith.
Narrative of Mr. Delaune's sufferings, p. 119. His letter to Dr. Calamy.

VOL. II.   A a   'Sir,

'Sir, I entreat you to excuse this
trouble from a stranger, who would
fain be convinced by something more
like *Divinity* than *Newgate*; where any
message from you, shall be welcome to

'Your Humble Servant,

'Thomas Delaune.

To this letter, in which are many things worthy of notice, but too long to be transcribed here, he received an answer to this effect: That if he had been imprison'd upon the account of answering his book, he would do him any kindness that became him.

But how well the *Doctor* performed his promise, will appear in the sequel.

Some days passing, and Mr. *Delaune* hearing nothing from the *Doctor*, sent him the following letter, written in *Latin*, but translated thus:

Ibidem, p. 121.

Jan. 9. 1683.

'*Reverend Sir,*

Another letter to Dr. Calamy.

'WHAT you once and again preached, and then printed, respecting a doubtful conscience, has loudly enough called all such as were dissatisfied about some rites and ceremonies, to examine the reasons on both sides.

'Others

'OTHERS being silent, I obeyed you
'in that particular; not merely to wrangle,
'for the encounter is unequal, betwixt a
'man so eminent as you are, and so mean
'a person as I am; but that an occasion
'may be given, in compliance to what
'you desired, to conclude controversies of
'this nature.

'IF merely for such obedience I must
'be punished, I know not how, nor in
'what manner; is there not a new way
'of conquering [scrupulous consciences]
'unheard of in the Holy Scriptures, start-
'ed by some certain ring-leaders?

'I PURPOSED, from Holy Writ and
'approved writers, to examine what we
'ought to judge of these things. From
'that *light of our paths*, and from that
'*lanthorn*, Psal. cxix. 105. I gathered
'some reasons against those various and
'multiplied errors, which have crept into
'the church. For that only thing am I
'brought to a *prison*, where there is no-
'thing amiable.

'WHETHER arguments of that kind
'will prevail to prove the suppositions in
'your sermon, let the Supreme Judge
'determine.

'OR whether any of the doubting per-
'sons can that way be compelled into the
'spiritual sheepfold, judge you: There is
'nothing against the King's Majesty, no-
'thing about the Civil Government, no-
'thing

'thing against the peace of this monar-
'chy there asserted.

'THE only dispute is about the ori-
'ginal of rites and ceremonies, and some
'things, which under a shew of truths,
'though not righteously, are charged on
'doubting persons. What the court will do
'with me, I know not: The will of the
'Supreme Father be done. Inward and
'outward peace in this, and everlasting
'peace in the world [to come] to all
'such as worship the Saviour of mankind,
'according to his word, is prayed for by

'*Thomas Delaune.*

'I DESIRE you to return me some
'answer, becoming a Divine, by
'my beloved wife, as you have
'promised.'

To this letter he answered by word of mouth to his wife, for he gave none in writing: That he looked on himself unconcerned, as not being mentioned in the sheet he saw with the *Recorder*. To satisfy which doubt, Mr. *Delaune* sent him another letter, with the first sheet of the book he was imprisoned for. Which was a plain demonstration, that it was an answer to his call. The letter was thus:

Jan.

Jan. 14. 1683.

'SIR,

'WHEREAS in anſwer to my *Another letter to Dr. Calamy.*
' two letters, you ſaid to my wife,
' that my papers no way concerned you,
' *viz.* ſuch as I am indicted for: To ſa-
' tisfy you with reſpect to that matter, I
' here ſend you the firſt ſheet; and leave
' you to conſider, whether in pure gene-
' roſity, you are not obliged to procure
' a *priſoner* (whoſe obedience to you made
' him ſo) his liberty.

'I am, Sir,

'Your Humble Servant,

'Thomas Delaune.

'I APPEAL to your conſcience, ſays
' Mr. *Delaune*, whether I had not
' ſome reaſon to expect ſome return to
' theſe applications?
' BUT I had none to any purpoſe: And
' that too but in few words by my wife.
' I had ſome thoughts, that you would
' have performed the office of a *Di-*
' *vine*, in *viſiting* me in my place of
' confinement; either to argue me out
' of my doubts, which your promiſed
' *Scripture* and *Reaſon*, not a *Mitti-*
' *mus* or *Newgate*, could eaſily do. To
' the *former* I can yield.——— To the
' *latter*

' *latter* it seems I muſt. ⸺ This is a
' ſevere kind of *logick*; and will pro-
' bably diſpute me out of this world,
' as it did Mr. *Bampfield* and Mr.
' *Ralphſon* lately; who were my dear
' and excellent companions in trouble.'

On the 10th of *Dec.* a Bill was found againſt him by the *Grand Jury* of *London*: And on the 13th day, he was called to the *Seſſions-Houſe* in the *Old-Bailey*; and his indictment was read, to which he pleaded, not guilty.

In *January*, he was with Mr. *Bampfield*, and Mr. *Ralphſon*, called again to the *Seſſions-Houſe*. But there being ſome trials that proved very tedious, theirs were not brought on at that time; but on the next day they were called to the outer bar;
' after the attendance, ſays Mr. *Delaune*,
' of divers hours, in a place not very
' lovely, and in the ſharpeſt winter that
' you have known; which it is likely
' proved the original of that indiſpoſition,
' which carried my two friends beyond
' the juriſdiction of *Seſſions*, *Bail-docks*, or
' *Preſs-yards*, to a glorious manſion of
' reſt.'

Mr. *Ralphſon* was tried firſt, Mr. *Delaune* next. He deſired his indictment might be read in *Latin*; which was done. The Gentlemen of the Law aggravated things in their uſual rhetorick. One of them

them was pleased to say, that the prisoner that stood there before, did labour to undermine the *State*; and this man would undermine the *Church*. So that, to incense the Jury, he said, here's *Church* and *State* struck at. A thing very improbable. For as Mr. *Delaune* himself observed, ' 'Tis
' wonderful, that any *Church* and *State* so
' potent as this, should fear two such un-
' derminers, as that extravagant harangue
' termed us.' In the end, he was found *guilty:* And the next day received his sentence. Which he has recorded as follows:
' *Thomas Delaune* fined 100 marks,
' and to be kept prisoner, *&c.* [which,
' *&c.* they interpret till he pay his fine]
' and to find good security for his good
' behaviour for one whole year afterwards;
' and that the said books and seditious li-
' bels, by him published, shall be burnt
' with * fire, before the *Royal-Exchange*
' in *London*; and if he be discharged, to
' pay † six shillings.
                   ' Signed, *Wagstaff*.'

Whom Mr. Delaune thought to be the Attorney-General.

His sentence.

THE book which this learned Gentleman wrote, and for which he so severely suffered, is entitled, *A Plea for the Nonconformists.* The Gentleman who prefixed a preface thereto; says,

* ' Not with water you must note.
† ' To the Hangman, for the faggots, I suppose.

' THIS

Remarks on Mr. Delaune's sufferings.

'This book has been printed at least seventeen times. And without doubt, if the adversaries of the *Dissenters* were for coming to the test, either of Scripture, reason or antiquity, it would before now have received some answer.

''Tis one of there own challenges accepted. The reasons for our dissenting are fairly, modestly, and closely applied. If saying nothing be taken *pro Confessa*, the Gentlemen of the Church of *England* would do well to consider of some *mediums*, to defend Dr. *Calamy*, or ingenuously own he was fairly confuted.

'There remains nothing to be added to the argument, till some attempts to confute them shall make a rejoinder necessary: Nor, indeed, can the *Dissenters* desire to have their case more fairly stated, or the conduct of their adversaries be more concurring to their justification.

'When arguments drive the opponents into passions and excesses, like strong purges; 'tis a proof of their operation, that they cause griping pains, in the very bowels of the patient.

'To answer sober arguments, with four coercives, to dispute by the *goal* and the *hangman*, to debate by the prison and not by the pen; these have been the peculiar of the party: And the
'power

'power of persecution, not of persuasion,
'has been the way of their usage to the
'Dissenters.

'THE treatment the reverend and
'learned *Author* of this book met with,
'will for ever stand as a monument of
'the cruelty of those times. And they
'that affirm the *Dissenters* were never
'persecuted in *England* for their religi-
'on, will do well to tell us, what name
'we shall give to the usage of this man
'of merit; than whom few greater scho-
'lars, clearer heads, or greater masters
'of arguments, ever graced the *English*
'nation.

'I AM sorry to say, he is *one* of near
'*eight thousand Protestant Dissenters*, that
'perished in prison, in the days of that
'merciful Prince, King *Charles* II. and
'that merely for dissenting from the
'church, in points, which they could
'give such reasons for, as this Plea af-
'signs; and for no other cause were
'stifled, I had almost said murdered, in
'goals, for their Religion, in the days of
'these Gentlemen's power, who pretend
'to abhor persecution.'

THE same Author declares, that he cannot conclude his preface, without giving the world the rest of the history of this Gentleman, which it was impossible for him to give of himself.

'His

P. 11. 'His sentence, says he, as the Reader
'will find in his book, was a hundred
'marks; the expensive prosecution, depriv-
'ing him of his livelihood, which was a
'Grammar-School, and long imprison-
'ment, had made him not only unable
'to pay his fine, but unable to subsist
'himself and his family.

'He continued in close confinement,
'in the *prison* of *Newgate*, about *fifteen*
'months; and suffered there great hard-
'ships by extreme poverty; being so en-
'tirely reduced by this disaster, that he
'had no subsistence, but what was con-
'tributed by such friends as came to visit
'him.

'His behaviour in this distress was
'like the greatness of mind, he discover-
'ed at his trial. And the same spirit
'which appears in his writings, appeared
'in his conversation, and supported him
'with invincible patience under the great-
'est extremities. But long confinement
'and distresses of various kinds, at last
'conquered him. He had a wife and
'two small children, all with him in the
'prison; for they had no subsistence else-
'where. The closeness and inconvenien-
'cies of the place first affected them; and
'all *three* by lingring sorrows and sick-
'ness, *dyed* in the *prison*. At last worn
'out with trouble, and hopeless of relief,
'and too much abandoned by those,
'who

'who should have taken some other care
'of him, this excellent person, sunk un-
'der the burden, and died there also.
'I cannot refrain saying, such a Cham-
'pion of such a *cause*, deserved better u-
'sage. And it was very hard, such a
'Man, such a Christian, such a Scholar,
'and on such an occasion, should starve in
'a *dungeon*; and the whole body of *Dis-*
'*senters* in *England*, whose cause he died
'for defending, should not raise him 66 *l.*
'13 *s.* 4 *d.* to save his life.'

THE opinion this *Author* had of this book, is summed up in a few words. 'The book, says he, is perfect of itself. 'Never *Author* left behind him a more 'finished piece; and I believe the dis- 'pute is entirely ended. If any man ask 'what we can say, why the *Dissenters* 'differ from the Church of *England*, 'and what they can plead for it? I can 'recommend no better reply than this. 'Let them answer, in short, *Thomas* '*Delaune*; and desire the Querist to read 'the book.'

IT was about this time, it pleased God to shew his displeasure against Apostacy, by pouring forth the vials of his wrath upon one Mr. *John Child*, a preacher of long standing among the *Baptists*. The Authors of the Narrative, intitled, *The Mis-* *chief of Persecution exemplified, by a true Narrative of the life and deplorable end of*

John Child's Apostacy.

Mr.

Mr. John Child, *who miserably destroyed himself*, Oct. 13. 1684. which was published in the year 1688. in the Postscript annexed thereunto, declare: 'That
' it is a true and dreadful instance of a
' man scared into conformity, by the se-
' verity he saw on others, and in part felt
' himself; that the temptation met with
' his corruptions, which if his own
' charge on himself be not too severe,
' you see verified by his own papers.
' Yet this, say they, excuseth not the
' doctrine and practice of persecution: If
' so, Satan might wash his hands also of
' the sins of men. And tho' some men
' may know the beginnings of sin, yet
' none knows the bounds of it. So af-
' ter his conformity, he drew his pen,
' and dipt it in gall against his brethren;
' going on to do violence to his consci-
' ence, till God in a dreadful manner a-
' wakened it against himself, so as prov-
' ed terrible to all the beholders, as well
' as to himself.——We account it a loud
' voice against persecution; and durst not
' silence it, lest we should betray this
' witness of God against it. We know
' authorities of scripture and reason are
' best to work upon the judgment, to
' convince the world of the error of do-
' ing that to others, that would not they
' should do to them. But a fact of this
' nature may move the affections, and
' cor-

‘ corroborate that light, that men receive
‘ from thence: And for this end it was
‘ at firſt intended to be publiſhed. It's
‘ a dreadful thing, not only to break in
‘ upon the civil rights of men, on account
‘ of religion; but far more to be inſtru-
‘ ments, to put any upon ſuch ways,
‘ which not only endanger their peace of
‘ conſcience here, but their eternal wel-
‘ fare hereafter. And this evil we are
‘ bold to charge perſecution with, and
‘ have evidence enough for it in this
‘ very inſtance.

‘ WE hope, ſay they, we may with-
‘ out vanity ſay, that it's written with a
‘ temper ſuitable to the profeſſion we
‘ have always made, of love and charity
‘ to thoſe that differ from us. And tho'
‘ the face of affairs in this nation be ſince
‘ changed, thro' the goodneſs of God, and
‘ the gracious favour of his Majeſty towards
‘ us; we purpoſe in all our actings to ſhew
‘ the ſame ſpirit and temper towards all
‘ Chriſtians, of what perſuaſion ſoever.
‘ And we would by no means have this
‘ conſtruction paſs upon the publication
‘ of this *Narrative* at this time, as if we
‘ deſigned to make the Church of *Eng-*
‘ *land* odious, by refreſhing the memory
‘ of ſo dreadful an accident, which was
‘ the natural effect of ſome of their per-
‘ ſecutions. God is our witneſs, ſay they,
‘ our naked deſign being only to arraign
                                             ‘ the

'the practice of perfecution itfelf, with-
'out reflecting on any, who have been
'the inftruments; hoping time, and this
'glorious defign of his Majefty, will
'have fuch an happy iffue, as to put all
'that profefs to be the followers of
'Chrift, into fuch a condition, as to fee
'it is their intereft, as well as their du-
'ty, not to contend for perfecution.'

This Mr. *John Child* was a man of fome confiderable fubftance, good natural parts and ability; being much followed wherever he preached, both in the city and country; and fo conceited of his abilities, that he feared not to difpute with any man. 'In his judgment, fays Mr.

Golden Mine, p. 48.

'Benjamin Keach, he was a *Baptift*, be-
'ing againft infant's baptifm, and for the
'baptifm of believers. For many years
'he lived in *Buckinghamfhire*, near me, I
'being intimately acquainted with him
'for near thirty years. But a little before
'the laft perfecution of *Diffenters*, he re-
'moved his dwelling and came to *Lon-
'don*, and lived near to my habitation in
'*Paul's, Shadwell*. Now the firft time
'I came to fear him, was thro' fome
'words he uttered to me, which was to
'this effect. *I have*, faid he, *ferioufly
'confidered, whether there be any thing in
'religion worth fuffering for.* Which
'words I wondred at from fuch-a-one as
'he. But foon after he conformed,
'(trou-

'(troubles rifing high) and then wrote a
' curfed book, rendring the *Diffenters*, e-
' fpecially the *Baptifts*, very odious; caft-
' ing reproaches upon their faithful mini-
' fters, becaufe fome of them were not
' learned men, I mean with the knowledge
' of the tongues. And quickly after this,
' he fell under fearful defperation. I
' was one of the firft men that he fent
' for; and I found him in a difmal ftate
' and condition; being filled with horror,
' faying, *he was damned*; and crying out
' againft himfelf, for writing that book;
' faying, *he had touched the apple of God's
' eye*. I faid all I was well capable to
' fpeak, to comfort him; but all in vain.
' ------ His poor wife, as I remember,
' intimated to me, that the very ends of
' the hair of his head, in the night-fea-
' fon, did ftand in drops, thro' the an-
' guifh of his foul.

' Thus he continued, fays Mr. *Keach*,
' for feveral months, under moft dreadful
' horror and fearful defparation, until
' *October* 13. 1684. when to put an end
' to his miferable life, he hanged himfelf,
' in his own hired houfe in *Brick-lane*,
' near *Spittlefields*, *London*, leaving a for-
' rowful widow and feveral children.'
And farther adds: ' I am of opinion, that
' if any *Atheift* in the world, who had
' formerly known this man, had conver-
' fed with him in his bitter agonies, he
' would

'would have seen sufficient demonstra-
' tions to have convinced him, that there
' is a dreadful God, or a power besides
' and above nature, who can touch,
' shake and disorder, and turn into con-
' fusion, the strongest constitution of bo-
' dy, by ministring and fastning terrible
' things upon the soul. And, as he saith,
' let this *Pillar of Salt*, tend to warn and
' season the people of this present and
' future ages, of the danger of sinning
' against the light of their understanding.'

THE book Mr. *Child* published after his conformity to the Church of *England;* which did afterwards fill him with so great horror of soul, bore the title of as charitable an argument, as could be undertaken by the best of Christians: *viz. A second Argument, for a more full and firm union amongst all good Protestants.*

'BUT though in this title, says Mr. *Plant* and Mr. *Dennis,* the Authors of the *Narrative,* ' his words were as the
Psal. lv. ' *Psalmist* speaks, *Softer than oil; yet*
21. ' *were they drawn swords.* He put forth
' his hand against such as were at peace
' with him, his equals, his acquaintance,
' who had walked with him to the house
' of God in company. The sense where-
' of, when he was awakened to see, and
' feel in his own conscience the heinouf-
' ness of his crime, in slandering his bre-
' thren, did so terrify him, that it could

' not

English Baptists. 385

' not be difcerned, (either by his relations
' or any of thofe many of his brethren
' whom he had offended, who came to
' vifit him, and endeavoured to pour
' balm into, bind up, and heal his deep
' wounds) that at any time afterwards he
' enjoyed any peace in his foul.'

THE many conferences that were had with this man, and the papers on this fubject that were left behind him, are publifhed at large in the faid *Narrative*: To which I muft refer the reader, being too much to be inferted in this place.

THIS is not the only inftance of the hand of God on *Apoftates*: Some *Pædobaptifts* have alfo been made publick examples. *Francis Spira*, having received the light of the Gofpel, became a teacher of the bleffed truths thereof, amongft his friends and familiar acquaintance. And (fays the *Narrative*) in comparifon feemed to neglect all other affairs, much preffing this main point of doctrine, *viz. That we muft wholly and only depend on the free and unchangeable love of God in the death of Chrift, as the only way of falvation.*

THE Pope's Legate, refident at *Venice*, was ftirred by the malice of the *Papifts* to accufe *Spira*. And by the craft and policy of the Legate, and thro' flavifh fear, *Spira* firft fled, and afterwards renounced his teftimony to the truth. The Legate commanded him to return to his own town, and there to confess and acknowledge the whole doctrine of the Church of *Rome*, to be holy and true, and to abjure the opinions of *Luther*, &c.

AFTER this, he signed an *Instrument of Abjuration*, and then fell under horrid desparation.

MELANCTHON that famous divine, makes mention of a certain man that was a servant, one that he knew, who for a while was a zealous professor of the Protestant Religion, but by the temptation of Satan fell from it; and some time after, having received the sacrament in the *Popish* manner, he fell under fearful despair, roaring out most horribly. *I have*, said he, *denied the Gospel, and am become the Devil's perpetual vassal.* And whilst the words were yet in his mouth, he suddenly flung himself headlong out of the window, and with the force of the fall, all his bowels gushed out.

MR. *John Fox*, in his acts and monuments, relates a sad story of one Judge *Hale*, who in Queen *Mary*'s time was a Protestant, but by the subtilty of the enemy, it was supposed he was overcome; and thereby fell under such horror of mind, that once or twice he did attempt to destroy himself with a knife, yet was prevented; but afterwards, which was in the year 1555, he cast himself into the river, and was drowned.

To conclude this reign, I shall only observe from the character given of the King by Dr. *Welwood* *: 'That his re- *The cha-* 'ligion was Deism, or rather that which *racter of* 'is called so. And if in his exile, or at *King Char. II.* 'his death, he went into that of *Rome:* 'the first was to be imputed to a com- 'plaisance for the company he was then 'obliged to keep; and the last to a lazy 'diffidence in all other religions, upon 'the review of his past life, and the near 'approach of an uncertain state.

'He was for the most part, says the 'Doctor †, not very nice in the choice 'of his mistresses, and seldom possess'd 'of their first favours: yet would sacri- 'fice all to please them, and upon every 'caprice of theirs, denied himself the 'use of his reason, and acted contrary 'to his interest.

'No age, says he ‡, produced a great- 'er master in the art of dissimulation; 'and yet no man was less upon his guard, 'or sooner deceived in the sincerity of o- 'thers. If he had any one fixed maxim 'of government, it was to play one par- 'ty against another, to be thereby the 'more master of both: and no Prince un- 'derstood better, how to shift hands up- 'on every change of the scene.

---

* Memoirs, *p.* 128.
† Ib. *p.* 129.
‡ Ib. *p.* 131.

' To sum up his character: he was
' dextrous in all the arts of insinuation,
' and had acquired so great an ascendant
' over the affections of his people, in spite
' of all the unhappy measures he had tak-
' en, that it may in some sense be said,
' that he died opportunely for *England*;
' since if he had lived, its probable, we
' might in compliance with him, have
' complimented ourselves out of all the
' remains of liberty, if he had but a
' mind to be master of them; which its
' but charity to believe he had not, at
' least immediately before his death.'

The End of the Second VOLUME.

APPENDIX.

NUMB. I.

A Declaration of FAITH *of* English *People, remaining at* Amsterdam *in* Holland: *Printed* 1611.

Wee BELIEVE *and* CONFESSE,

I.

THAT there are THREE which bear record in heaven, the FATHER, the WORD, and the SPIRIT; and these THREE are ONE GOD, in all equality: By whom all things are created and preserved, in heaven and in earth.

1 John v. 7.

Phil. ii. 5, 6.
Gen. i.

II.

THAT this GOD in the beginning created all things of nothing, and made man of the dust of the earth, in his own image, in righteousness and true holiness; yet being tempted, fell by disobedience. Through whose disobedience all men sinned: His sin being imputed unto all, and so death went over all men.

Gen. i. 1.
—— ii. 7.
—— i. 27.
Eph. iv. 24.
—— iii. 1, 7.
Rom. v. 12, 19.

A   III. THAT

III.

Rom. v. 19.
1 Cor. xv. 22.

THAT by the promised seed of the woman, JESUS CHRIST his obedience, all are made righteous, all are made alive: His righteousness being imputed unto all.

IV.

Eph. ii. 3.
Psal. li. 5.
Jer. iv. 22.
1 Cor. ii. 14.

THAT notwithstanding this, men are by nature the children of wrath, born in iniquitie, and in sin conceived: Wise to all evil, but to good they have no knowledge. *The natural man receiveth not the things of the Spirit of God.* And therefore man is not restored unto his former estate: But that as man, in his estate of innocency, having in himself all disposition unto good, and no disposition unto evil, yet being tempted might yield, or might resist; even so now being fallen, and having all disposition unto evil, and no disposition or will unto any good, yet GOD giving grace, *man* may receive grace, or may reject grace,

Deut. xxx. 19.

according to that saying, *I call heaven and earth to record this day against you, that I have set before you life and death, blessing and cursing: Therefore choose life, that both thou and thy seed may live.*

V.

Eph. i. 4, 12.
Mark xvi. 16.
Rom. viii. 29.

THAT GOD before the foundation of the world hath predestinated that all that believe in him shall be saved, and all that believe not shall be damned; all which he knew before. And this is the *election* and *reprobation* spoken of in the scriptures, concerning salvation, and condemnation; and not that GOD hath predestinated men to be wicked, and so to be damned,

damned, but that men being wicked, shall
be damned; for God would have all men — 1 Tim. ii. 4.
saved, and come to the knowledge of the
truth, and would have no man to perish, but — 2 Pet. iii. 9.
would have all men come to repentance, and
willeth not the death of him that dieth. And — Ezek. xviii.
therefore God is the author of no mens con- 32.
demnation, according to the saying of the
prophet, Thy destruction, O *Israel*, is of thy — Hos. xiii. 9.
self, but thy help is of me.

VI.

That man is justified only by the righ- Rom. iii. 28.
teousness of Christ, apprehended by faith; Gal. ii. 16.
yet *faith without works is dead*. — James ii. 17.

VII.

That men may fall away from the grace — Heb. xii. 15.
of God, and from the truth, which they have —— x. 26.
received and acknowledged, after they have
tasted of the heavenly gift, and were made
partakers of the Holy Ghost, and have —— vi. 4, 5.
tasted of the good word of God, and of the
powers of the world to come; and after they
have escaped from the filthiness of the world, 2 Pet. ii. 20.
may be entangled again therein, and over-
come. That a righteous man may forsake Ezek. xviii.
his righteousness, and perish. And therefore 24, 26.
let no man presume to think, that because he
hath, or had once grace, therefore he shall
always have grace. But let all men have assurance, that if they continue unto the end,
they shall be saved. Let no man then presume; but let all work out their salvation
with fear and trembling.

A 2   VIII.

AP.PENDIX.

VIII.

Rom. i. 3.
—— ix. 5.
Gal. iv. 4.

Luke i. 35.
Heb. iv. 15.

That JESUS CHRIST, the Son of GOD, the second person or subsistance in the Trinity, in the fulness of time was manifested in the flesh, being the seed of *David*, and of the *Israelites*, according to the flesh, the son of *Mary* the Virgin, made of her substance, by the power of the HOLY GHOST overshadowing her; and being thus *true man*, was like unto us in all things, sin only excepted, being *one person* in two distinct natures, TRUE GOD, and TRUE MAN.

IX.

1 Tim. ii. 5.
Matt. xxviii. 18.
Luke i. 33.
Heb. vii. 24.
Acts iii. 22.

Rev. xxii. 18, 19.

That JESUS CHRIST is mediator of the New Testament between GOD and man, having all power in heaven and in earth given unto him, being the only KING, PRIEST, and PROPHET of his Church: He also being the only Law-giver, hath in his testament set down an absolute and perfect rule of direction, for all persons, at all times, to be observed; which no prince, nor any whosoever, may add to, or diminish from, as they will avoid the fearful judgments denounced against them that shall so do.

X.

1 Cor. i. 2.
Eph. i. 1.
2 Cor. vi. 17.
1 Cor. xii. 13.
Acts viii. 37.
Matt. iii. 6.

That the *Church* of CHRIST is a company of faithful people, separated from the world by the word and Spirit of GOD, being knit unto the LORD, and one unto another, by *baptism*, upon their own confession of the faith, and sins.

XI.

XI.

That though in respect of Christ the Church be one, yet it consisteth of divers particular congregations, even so many as there shall be in the world; every of which congregation, though they be but two or three, have Christ given them, with all the means of their salvation; are the body of Christ, and a *whole church*; and therefore may, and ought, when they are come together, to pray, prophesy, break bread, and administer in all the holy ordinances, although as yet they have no *officers*, or that their *officers* should be in prison, sick, or by any other means hindred from the church.

Eph. iv. 4.
Matt. xviii. 20.
Rom. viii. 32.
1 Cor. iii. 22.
―― xii. 27.
―― xiv. 23.
1 Pet. iv. 10.
―――― ii. 5.

XII.

That as one congregation hath Christ, so hath all. And that the word of God cometh not out from any one, neither to any one congregation in particular, but unto every particular *church*, as it doth unto all the world: And therefore no *church* ought to challenge any prerogative over any other.

2 Cor. x. 7.
1 Cor. xiv. 36.
Col. i. 5, 6.

XIII.

That every *church* is to receive in all their members by *Baptism*, upon the confession of their faith and sins, wrought by the preaching of the gospel, according to the primitive institution and practice: And therefore *churches* constituted after any other manner, or of any other persons, are not according to Christ's testament.

Matt. xxviii. 19.
Acts ii. 41.

XIV.

Rom. vi. 2, 3, 4.
THAT *baptism*, or washing with water, is the outward manifestation of dying unto sin, and walking in newness of life; and therefore in no wise appertaineth to *infants*.

XV.

1 Cor. x. 16, 17.
—— xi. 26.
THAT the LORD's Supper is the outward manifestation of the spiritual communion between CHRIST and the faithful, mutually to declare his death until he come.

XVI.

Matt. xviii. 15.
1 Theff. v. 14.
1 Cor. xii. 25.
Acts xx. 28.
1 Pet. v. 2, 3.
THAT the members of every *church* or congregation ought to know one another, that so they may perform all the duties of love one towards another, both to soul and body. And especially the *elders* ought to know the whole flock, whereof the HOLY GHOST hath made them overseers. And therefore a *church* ought not to consist of such a multitude, as cannot have particular knowledge one of another.

XVII.

Matt. xviii. 17.
1 Cor. v. 4, 13.
THAT brethren impenitent in any one sin, after the admonition of the *church*, are to be excluded the communion of the saints. And therefore not the committing of sin doth cut off any from the church, but refusing to hear the church to reformation.

XVIII.

2 Theff. iii. 15.
Matt. xviii. 17.
THAT excommunicants, in respect of civil society, are not to be avoided.

XIX.

APPENDIX. 7

XIX.

THAT every *church* ought, according to the example of CHRIST's disciples and primitive churches, upon every first day of the week, being the LORD's Day, to assemble together, to pray, prophesy, praise. GOD, and break bread, and perform all other parts of spiritual communion for the worship of GOD, their own mutual edification, and the preservation of true religion and piety in the *church:* And they ought not to labour in their callings, according to the equity of the moral law; which CHRIST came not to abolish, but to fulfil. <small>John xx. 19, Acts ii. 42. — xx. 7. 1 Cor. xvi. 2. Exod. xx. 8, &c.</small>

XX.

THAT the *officers* of every *church* or congregation are either *elders,* who by their office do especially feed the flock concerning their souls; or *deacons,* men and women, who by their office relieve the necessities of the poor and impotent brethren, concerning their bodies. <small>Acts xx. 28. 1 Pet. v. 2, 3. Acts vi. 1, 4.</small>

XXI.

THAT these *officers* are to be chosen when there are persons qualified according to the rules in CHRIST's testament, by election and approbation of that *church* or congregation whereof they are members, with fasting, prayer, and laying on of hands: And there being but one rule for *elders,* therefore but one sort of *elders.* <small>1 Tim. iii. 2, 7. Tit. i. 6, 9. Acts vi. 3, 4. — xiv. 23. — xiii. 3. — xiv. 23.</small>

XXII.

THAT the *officers* of every *church* or congregation are tied by office only to that particular

A 4

ticular congregation whereof they are chosen; and therefore they cannot challenge by office any *authority* in any other congregation whatsoever, except they would have an *apostleship*.

Acts xiv. 23.
—— xx. 17.
Tit. i. 5.

XXIII.

THAT the scriptures of the Old and New Testament are written for our instruction; and that we ought to search them, for they testify of CHRIST; and therefore to be used with all reverence, as containing the holy word of GOD, which only is our direction in all things whatsoever.

2 Tim. iii.16.
John v. 39.

XXIV.

THAT *magistracy* is a holy ordinance of GOD; that every soul ought to be subject to it, not for fear only, but for conscience sake. *Magistrates* are the ministers of GOD for our wealth, they bear not the sword for nought. They are the ministers of GOD, to take vengeance on them that do evil. That it is a fearful sin to speak evil of them that are in dignity, and to despise government. We ought to pay tribute, custom, and all other duties. That we are to pray for them; for GOD would have them saved, and come to the knowledge of his truth. And therefore they may be members of the *church* of CHRIST, retaining their magistracy; for no ordinance of GOD debarreth any from being a member of CHRIST's church. They bear the sword of GOD; which sword, in all lawful administrations, is to be defended and supported by the servants of GOD that are under their government, with their lives, and all that they have, according as in the first institution of

Rom. xiii.

2 Pet. ii. 10.

1 Tim. ii. 1, 4.

APPENDIX.

of that holy ordinance. And whosoever holds otherwise, must hold, if they understand themselves, that they are the ministers of the devil, and therefore not to be prayed for, nor approved, in any of their administrations; seeing all things they do, as punishing offenders, and defending their countries, state, and persons by the sword, is unlawful. That it is lawful in a just cause, for the deciding of strife, to take an *oath* by the Name of the LORD. Heb. vi. 16, 2. 2 Cor. i. 23. Phil. i. 8.

XXVI.

THAT the dead shall rise again, and the living be changed in a moment; having the same bodies in substance, though diverse in qualities. 1 Cor. xv. 52. Job xxxviii. 19. —— xv. 28. Luke xxiv. 30.

XXVII.

THAT after the resurrection, all men shall appear before the judgment-seat of CHRIST, to be judged according to their works. That the godly shall enjoy life eternal: The wicked, being condemned, shall be tormented everlastingly in hell. Matt. xxv. 46.

NUMB.

APPENDIX.

NUMB. II.

A most Humble SUPPLICATION *of many of the King's Majesty's Loyal Subjects, ready to testify all Civil Obedience, by the Oath of Allegiance, or otherwise, and that of Conscience; who are persecuted (only for differing in Religion) contrary to Divine and Human Testimonies: As followeth.* Printed 1620.

To the High and Mighty KING JAMES, *by the Grace of God, King of* Great Britain, France *and* Ireland, *Our Sovereign Lord on Earth.*

To the Right Excellent and Noble PRINCE CHARLES, *Prince of* Wales, *&c.*

To all the Right Honourable NOBILITY, *Grave and Honourable* JUDGES, *and to all other the Right Worshipful* GENTRY, *of all Estates and Degrees, assembled in this present* Parliament.

Right High and Mighty, Right Excellent and Noble, } { *Right Honourable,* AND *Right Worshipful.*

AS the consideration of that divine commandment of the King of kings (*Let supplications, prayers, intercessions, and giving of thanks, be made for kings, and for all that are in authority, that we may lead a quiet and peaceable life, in all godliness and honesty*) doth cause in us a daily practice thereof in our

secret

APPENDIX.

secret chambers for you all, as in duty we are bound, of which the searcher of all hearts beareth us witness; so let it be pleasing unto your Majesty, and the rest in authority, that we make humble supplications and prayers to you, for such our bodily miseries and wants as are upon us, in that it is in your power to redress them; and especially at this present, in this high meeting, assembled for the publick weal of all your loyal subjects. Our miseries are long and lingring imprisonments for many years, in divers counties of *England*, in which many have died and left behind them widows, and many small children; taking away our goods, and others the like, of which we can make good probation; not for any disloyalty to your Majesty, nor hurt to any mortal man, (our adversaries themselves being judges) but only because we dare not assent unto, and practise in the worship of God such things as we have not *faith* in, Heb. xi. 6. because *it is sin against the Most High*, Rom. xiv. 23. as your Majesty well observeth in these words: *It is a good and safe rule in theology,* Med. on Lord's *that in matters of the worship of God,* Quod Prayer. *dubitas, ne feceris,* according to *Paul*'s rule: *Let every man be fully persuaded in his own* Rom. xiv. 5. *mind.* If we were in error herein, these courses of afflicting our bodies for conscience-cause, are not of *Christ*, but of *Antichrist*, as hereafter is most plainly shewed; and if no *church* be the rule of faith, *but only the Holy Scriptures*, as the learned *Protestants* do truly confess, and that therefore the doctrine of the church of *Rome* (that all must believe as the church believes, and so practise, or else be cruelly persecuted) be most ungodly, as it is;

then

then how can they avoid the like censure, that practise the same thing, contrary to their own judgment? For the learned *Protestants* do say, it is high cruelty for the *Papists* to constrain them to practise those things in God's worship, which we have not *faith* in, nay, which they know to be evil, with imprisonment, fire, and faggot. And therefore why may not we say, it is great cruelty for the learned *Protestants* to constrain us to practise those things in God's worship, which we have not faith in? Nay, which we certainly know to be evil, with lingring imprisonment, loss of goods, and what other cruelties they can procure against us, of your Majesty, and the civil state. If your learned say, they have the truth, and we are in error; that resteth to be tried by the true touchstone, the holy scriptures. *If they* [the learned] *be our judges, the verdict must needs go against us.* If their sayings be a safe rule for us to be saved by, we will rest upon them: And then, why may not the sayings of the *Papists* be sure also, and they be the *Protestants* judges, and so bring us all to believe as the church believes? The iniquity of which we have discover'd as briefly as we could; beseeching your Majesty, and all that are in authority, to hear us. *It concerneth our eternal salvation, or condemnation, and is therefore of great importance: For what can a man give for the ransom of his soul?* Oh be pleased to remember the saying of that great and good man *Job: I delivered the poor that cried, and the fatherless, and him that had none to help him. The blessing of him that was ready to perish came upon me: And I caused the widows heart to rejoice.*

Job xxix. 12, 13.

APPENDIX.

I was a father to the poor, and when I knew Job xxix. *not the cause, I sought it out diligently. I 16, 17. brake also the jaws of the unrighteous man, and plucked the prey out of his teeth.*

OUR prayers are, and shall be for you day and night, to that *God of glory*, by whom you reign and are advanced, that *he* will put it into your heart, to let these things enter into your thoughts; and then we doubt not (the evidence of them being such) that you will be moved to repeal and make void all those cruel laws (which we most humbly beseech) that persecute poor men, only for matters of conscience: Not that we any way desire for our selves, or others, any the least liberty from the strict observation of any civil, temporal or human law, made or to be made, for the preservation of your Majesty's person, crown, state, or dignity; for, *all that give not to* Cæsar *that which is his*, let them bear their burthen; but we only desire, *that God might have that which is his*, which is the *heart* and *soul*, in that worship that he requireth, over which *there is but one Lord*, and *one Law-* Eph. iv. 5. *giver, who is able to save it, or to destroy it,* James iv. 12. which no mortal man can do. It is not in your power to compel the heart; you may compel men to be hypocrites, as a great many are, who are false-hearted both towards God and the state; which is sin both in you and them. The vileness of persecuting the body of any man, only for cause of conscience, is against *the word of God*, and *law of Christ*. It is against the profession of *your Majesty*; against the profession and practice of *famous princes*; the *ancient and later approved writers witness against it*; so do the *Puritans*,

yea,

APPENDIX.

yea, the establishers of it, the *Papists themselves*, inveigh against it: So that God and all men do detest it, as is herein shewed. And therefore, in most humble manner, we do beseech your Majesty, your Highness, your Honours, your Worships, to consider of it, and do as God directeth you in his word, that cannot lye: *Let the wheat and tares grow together in the world, until the harvest.*

Matt. xiii. 30.

And so in humble manner we proceed.

CHAP. I.

The rule of faith is the doctrine of the Holy Ghost, contained in the sacred scriptures, and not any church, council, prince, or potentate, nor any mortal man whatsoever.

PROVED by the scriptures themselves, which are the writings of *Moses*, and the *Prophets*, the *Evangelists*, and *Apostles*: These are a sufficient rule alone, to try all faith and religion by. Our reasons are, 1. *They are inspired of God, and are able to make us wise unto salvation, and perfect to every good work.* 2. Because these writings are written, *that we might have certainty of the things whereof we are instructed. That our joy might be full. And that we might believe, and in believing might have life.* 3. We are commanded *not to presume* (or be wise) *above what is written.* For with this weapon *Christ put to flight the devil*; and *taught his disciples*; and *Paul taught Christ Jesus.* The godly are commended

2 Tim. iii. 15, &c.

Luke i. 4.

1 John i. 4.
John xx. 31.
1 Cor. iv. 6.

Matt. iv. 4.
Luke xxiv. 27.
Acts xvii. 2.

for

APPENDIX.

for searching the scriptures. All are com- Acts xvii. 11.
manded *to search them.* And *they that will* John v. 39.
not believe these writings, will not believe —— v. 47.
Christ's words; nor one that should come from Luke xvi. 31.
the dead. If any ask, how we know all, or
any of these scriptures to be inspired of God?
We answer, *The ear discerneth words, and* Job xii. 11.
the mouth tasteth meat for it self. And as
the eye discerneth the light of the sun, so
doth our spirit discern these scriptures to be
inspired of God, and that for these reasons.
1. In regard of the majesty, wisdom, and
grace of them, above all other writings: For
there is as great glory in these scriptures, as
in the making of this *wonderful world*, which Heb. xi. 1.
is most evidently discerned. 2. By their
teachings; which excelleth all human teachings, leading us from Satan, from this world,
and our selves, to God, in holiness, faith,
love, fear, obedience, humility. 3. The true
events of them, or fulfilling of the prophecies
contained in them. 4. The consent and agreement of all the parts of them; the like whereof
cannot be shewed, of so many several writers,
since the world began. 5. The admirable
preservation thereof, against time and tyrants;
all which could not extinguish them. 6. The
devil and his instruments rage against those
that practise the doctrines contained in them.
7. The conversion of thousands to God, by
the power of their doctrine. 8. The vengeance that hath come upon such as have not
obeyed them. 9. The acknowledgment of
them, by the very professed adversaries thereof.
10. The miracles confirming them from
heaven. 11. The sight of a Saviour to man,
is only by and from them. And lastly, The
sim-

simplicity of the writers, and plainness of the writings; for God hath chosen the mean, contemptible, and despised, to manifest unto the world his mysteries. These are sufficient to persuade, that these holy writings are inspired of God; and so able to make wise unto salvation, and perfect to every good work. These scriptures contain the law and testimony; and if any church, council, prince, or potentate, *speak not according to this word, it is because there is no light in them.* And we are *commanded to hold them accursed.* For *whosoever shall add unto these things,* God shall add the plagues written herein: And, *Whosoever shall take away from these things, God shall take his name out of the book of life, and out of the holy city, and from those things that are written.*

<small>1 Cor. i.</small>

<small>Isa. viii. 20.</small>

<small>Gal. i. 8, 9.</small>

<small>Rev. xxii.</small>

Much by us shall not need to be written on this subject, the thing is so evident, and so generally acknowledged; at least in words (excepting the *Papists*, with whom we have not here to do) Only we will add some human testimonies.

<small>White's *Way to the Church*, dedicated to two bishops, Page 12.</small>

THE learned Protestants affirm and prove, that it is the doctrine of the church of *England*, Art. 6. *That the scripture comprehended in the Old and New Testament, is the rule of faith so far, that whatsoever is not read therein, nor cannot be proved thereby, is not to be accepted as any point of faith, or needful to be followed;* but *by it, all doctrines taught, and the churches practice, must be examined; and that rejected, which is contrary to it, under what title or pretence soever it come unto us.* And further, they say, *That the Pope, or any mortal man, should be the rule,*

<small>Page 1.</small>

that

that must resolve in questions and controversies of faith, is an unreasonable position, void of all indifferency; when common sense teacheth, that he that is a party cannot be judge. And again; *Which is the church is controversal; which is the scriptures is not; therefore let that be the rule which is out of doubt.* And again; *The scriptures contain the principles of our faith, and shall we not believe them? or cannot we know them infallibly of themselves, without we let in the authority of the church?* This, and much more, the learned *Protestants* have written, and sufficiently confirmeth, that no church, nor man whatsoever, may be the judge, rule or umpire in matters of faith, but only the holy scriptures; and whosoever teacheth, and practiseth otherwise, they must hold and maintain the *Papists* creed, or *Collier's* faith, which the *Protestants* so much in words detest, and mention out of *Staphilus* his *apology*, thus, *The Collier being at the point of death, and tempted of the Devil, what his faith was? answered, I believe and die in the faith of Christ's church.* Being again demanded, what the faith of Christ's church was? *That faith*, said he, *that I believe in. Thus the Devil getting no other answer, was overcome and put to flight. By this faith of the Collier, every unlearned man may try the spirits of men, whether they be of God or no; by this faith he may resist the Devil, and judge the true interpretation from the false, and discern the Catholic from the heretical minister, the true doctrine from the forged.*

If the answer of the *Collier* and the *Papists* conclusion upon it be not found, but detestable,

White, p. 17

Page 6.

B

ble, as the *Protestants* confess, and cry *wo unto* the *Papists* for the same, and that justly; then is it no less detestable in the *Protestants*, or any other to require, or any to yield so far in religion and faith, that upon such a temptation he hath no better answer to make than as the *Collier*, to say, *I believe and die in the faith of the church*, or *of the prince*, or *of the learned*; for being demanded what that faith is? If he be not able to prove it by God's word, contained in the scriptures, it is no better nor no other than the answer of the *Collier*, *The faith that I believe in.* Oh how many millions of souls in this nation, not *Papists* but *Protestants*, live and die, and have never other faith than this, whereunto they are constrained and compelled by persecution, without either faith or knowledge.

CHAP. II.

The interpreter of this rule is the scriptures, and Spirit of God in whomsoever.

THE next thing, as the immediate question from this former, is, Who must interpret this rule? because, as is objected, *There are many dark places in it, hard to be understood.* Unto which we answer, The two witnesses of God shall be the only interpreters thereof; which are, the Word of God contained in the same scriptures, and the Spirit of God; so are they called. *First*, For the scriptures themselves; though some doctrines, in some places, be dark and obscure, as *Peter* speak-

2 Pet. iii.
John xv. 26, 27.
Acts v. 32.

APPENDIX.

speaketh, yet the self same doctrines, in other places, are plain and manifest. For, *all the words of the Lord are plain to him that will understand, and straight to them that would find knowledge.* And *knowledge is easy to him* Prov. viii. 9. *that will understand.* Secondly, The Spirit —— xiv. 6. of God, so saith the Apostle, *It is the Spirit* 1 John ii. 6. *that beareth witness: for the Spirit is truth.* But *the Comforter, which is the Holy Ghost, whom* John xiv. 26. *the father will send in my name, he shall teach you all things, and bring all things to your re-* —— xvi. 3. *membrance which I have told you. Howbeit, when he is come, which is the Spirit of truth, he will lead you into all truth: for he shall not speak of himself, but whatsoever he shall hear, shall he speak, and he will shew you of the things to come. For the Spirit searcheth all things, even* 1 Cor. ii. 10, *the deep things of God. For the things of God* 11. *knoweth no man, but the Spirit of God. But the anointing that ye have received of him,* 1 John ii. 27. *dwelleth in you; and ye need not that any man teach you, but as the same anointing teacheth you of all things, and it is true, and is not lying, and as it hath taught you; you shall abide in him. Hereby we know that he abideth in* —— iii. 24. *us, even by the Spirit that he hath given us. For to one is given by the Spirit, the word of* 1 Cor. xii. 8. *wisdom; and to another the word of knowledge, by the same Spirit.*

The scriptures be so plain in this, that the greatest adversaries thereof do acknowledge the truth of it; only herein lieth the difficulty; who it is that hath this Spirit of God to interpret the scriptures; which is this sure rule? which in the next place is to be handled.

B 2 CHAP.

CHAP. III.

That the Spirit of God, to underſtand and interpret the ſcriptures, is given to all and every particular perſon that fear and obey God, of what degree ſoever they be; and not to the wicked.

Pſal. xxv. 12, 14.
—— cvii. 43.
Dan. xii. 10.
Amos iii. 7.
Pſal. cxix. 99.

Prov. xxviii. 7.
John xiv. 15, 23.

—— vii. 17.

Acts v. 32.
Luke xxi. 15.

—— xii. 12.

Matt. x. 20.
Mark iv. 11.

PRov'd, *What man is he that feareth the Lord, him will he teach the way that he ſhall chooſe. The ſecret of the Lord is revealed to them that fear him, and his covenant to give them underſtanding. Who is wiſe that he may obſerve theſe things, he ſhall underſtand the loving kindneſs of the Lord. None of the wicked ſhall have underſtanding; but the wiſe ſhall underſtand. For God will do nothing; but he revealeth his ſecrets to his ſervants. I have had more underſtanding than all my teachers, and than all the ancients; becauſe I kept thy precepts: For he that keepeth the law is a child of underſtanding. If ye love me, keep my commandments; and I will pray the Father, and he ſhall give you the ſpirit of truth. If any man love me he will keep my word; and my Father and I will come unto him, and will dwell with him. If any man will do his will, he ſhall know of the doctrine whether it be of God or no. Yea, and the Holy Ghoſt, whom God hath given to all that obey him. I will give you* (my diſciples that obey me, and ſuffer for my ſake) *a mouth and wiſdom,* &c. *The Holy Ghoſt ſhall teach you what ye ſhall ſay. For, It is not you that ſpeak, but the Spirit of my Father that ſpeaketh in you. And, to you* (my followers) *is given to know the myſteries*

of

APPENDIX.

of the kingdom of God ; but not to them that are without: For the myftery of the gofpel is made Col. ii. 2. *manifeft to the faints.*

The church and faints of God have revealed unto them *by the Spirit*, the things *that eye hath not feen*, &c. And *they have* 1 Cor. ii. 9, *received the Spirit of God, that they might know* 10, 14. *the things that are given them of God.* But *the natural man perceiveth not the things of the Spirit of God ; for they are foolifhnefs to him : neither can he know them, becaufe they are fpiritually difcerned. But he that is fpiritual difcerneth all things*, &c.

Hence it is moft plain to whom the Spirit of God is given ; even to every particular faint of God. And *it is no private fpirit* ; but even *the publick Spirit of God*, which is in him, which enableth him to underftand, and fo to declare the things gi- 2 Pet. i. 20. ven him of God. That is, a *private fpirit*, that is not of God, though it be in multitudes ; but the Spirit of God, though but in one faint, is not private. God's Spirit is not private; for it is not comprehended only within one place, perfon, or time, as man's is ; but it is univerfal and eternal ; fo is not man's : Therefore man's is private, though they be many ; God's is publick, though but in one Perfon.

CHAP. IV.

Those that fear and obey God, and so have the Spirit of God to search out and know the mind of God in the scriptures, are commonly, and for the most part, the simple, poor, despised, &c.

Matt. xi. 5, 25.

PRov'd. Our Saviour faith, *The poor receive the gospel;* and *I thank thee, Father, because thou hast opened these things unto babes; it is so, O Father, because thy good pleasure was such.*

James ii. 5.

Hearken my beloved brethren, Hath not God chosen the poor of this world that they should be rich in faith, and heirs of the kingdom which he hath promised?

1 Cor. i. 26, &c.

&c. *Brethren, you see your calling, that God hath chosen the foolish of this world, the weak of this world, the vile of this world and despised, and which are not.*

Prov. i. 4.

God's dealing is, *to give unto the simple sharpness of wit, and to the child knowledge and discretion.*

John iii. 8.

The spirit bloweth where it listeth, and is not ty'd to the learned.

1 Kings xxii.

Poor persecuted *Micaiah* had the truth against four hundred of king *Ahab's* prophets. So had *Jeremiah* against all the priests and prophets of *Israel*. The Lord of life himself, in his fleshly being, What was he, but a man full of sorrows? in his birth,

Luke ii. 7.

laid in a cratch, because *there was no room for him in the inn.*

Mark vi. 3.

A carpenter by trade:

Matt. viii. 20.

Having not a hole to rest his head in. And in his death, contemned and despised. His Apostles, in like manner, what were they, but mean men, *fishermen, tentmakers,* and

1 Cor. iv. 11.

such like, *having no certain dwelling place,*
which

which the worldly-wife, Scribes and Pharisees took notice of, and reproachfully said; *Doth any of the rulers, or of the Pharisees believe in him? But this people that know not the law are accursed.* John vii. 48, 49.

THE truth of this is as plain as may be; that the scriptures being the rule of faith, perfect and absolute, and that the plainness of them is such, as by the Spirit of God they may be easily understood of those that fear and obey God, but of none else, and that such are most commonly the poor and despised; for, *if any man want wisdom* (be he never so simple) *let him ask of God, and he will give him.* Which is also confirmed by human testimonies. James i. 5.

THE *Protestants* confess, That *in the primitive church, the doctrines, and several points of religion, were known and discovered by the most mean of the people, and the bishops exhorted them thereunto,* &c. Also that *this rule is of that nature, that it is able to direct any man, be he never so simple; yea, the most unlearned alive may conceive and understand it sufficiently for his salvation.* White, p. 7. Page 9.

AND they relate the sayings of the ancients in this thing. First, *Clemens Alexandrinus. The word is not hid from any; it is a common light that shineth unto all men; there is no obscurity in it: Hear you it, you that be far off, and you that be nigh.* Next him *Austin. God hath bowed down the scriptures to the capacity of babes and sucklings; that where proud men will not speak to their capacity, yet himself might.* After him *Chrysostom. The scriptures are easy to understand, and exposed to the capacity of every servant, and plowman, and widow,* Page 12.

dow, and boy, and him that is *moſt unwiſe*. Therefore God penned the *ſcriptures* by the hands of *publicans, fiſhermen, tentmakers, ſhepherds, neatherds,* and unlearned men; that none of the *ſimple* people might have any excuſe to keep them from reading, and that ſo they might be eaſy to be underſtood of all men; the *artificer,* the *houſe-holder* and *widow woman,* and *him* that is *moſt unlearned.* Yea, the *Apoſtles* and *Prophets,* as ſchoolmaſters to all the world, made their *writings* plain and evident to all men; ſo that every man of himſelf, only by *reading* them, might learn the things ſpoken therein. Next *Juſtin Martyr* ſaith, *Hear the words of the ſcripture;* which be ſo eaſy, that it needs no *expoſition,* but only to be *rehearſed.* And this the *Proteſtants* ſay was the perpetual and conſtant judgment of the ancient *church,* &c.

White, p. 21. And further, he alledgeth, *Theodoret* who writ of his times, *You ſhall every where ſee theſe points of our faith to be known and underſtood,* not only by ſuch as are *teachers* in the *church,* but even of *coblers* and *ſmiths,* and *webſters,* and all kind of *artificers;* yea, all our *women,* not they only which are book learned, but they alſo that get their living with their needle; yea, *maid ſervants* and *waiting women;* and not *citizens* only, but *huſbandmen* of the country are very ſkilful in theſe things; you may hear among us *ditchers,* and *neatheards,* and *woodſetters,* diſcourſing of the *Trinty* and the *Creation,* &c. The like is reported by others. And ſay the *Proteſtants,* his *doctrine* that was preſident in the *Trent conſpiracy, That a diſtaff was fitter for women than a Bible,* was not yet hatched, *&c.* Oh!

APPENDIX.

Oh! it were well if the contempt of these pious practices were paled only within the *Romish* profession, and were not practised in and among those that profess themselves to be separated therefrom; and what is more frequent in the mouths of many *Protestants*, yea, the bishops themselves, than these and such like words: Must every base fellow, *cobler, taylor, weaver,* &c. meddle with the exposition, or discoursing of the scriptures, which appertain to none but to the learned? Yea, do they not forbid their own ministers to expound or discourse of the scriptures? Read their 49th *Canon*, which is; *No person whatsoever, not examined and approved by the bishop of the diocese, or not licensed, as is aforesaid, for a sufficient and convenient preacher, shall take upon him to expound in his own cure, or elsewhere, any scripture, or matter or doctrine; but shall only study to read plainly and aptly (without glozing or adding) the homilies already set forth, or hereafter to be published by lawful authority,* &c. So that not only Jesus Christ and his Apostles (who are alive in their doctrine, though not in their persons) are forbidden all exposition of the holy scriptures, or matter, or doctrine, not being licensed by the bishops; but also their own ministers, who have sworn canonical obedience to them. Yet when they are put to answer the *Papists,* who practise the same thing, they take up both scriptures and ancient writers to confute it.

CHAP.

CHAP. V.

The learned in human learning, do commonly, and for the most part, err, and know not the truth, but persecute it, and the professors of it; and therefore are no further to be followed than we see them agree with truth.

THE next thing in order is, seeing the Lord revealeth his secrets to the humble, though wanting human learning, that we now prove on the contrary. That God usually, and for the most part, hideth his secrets from the learned, and suffereth them to err and resist the truth; yea, so far as to persecute it, and the professors of it.

AND *First*, Let us begin with the learned Heathen, who were behind none in human learning. The wise men of *Egypt*, how did they resist the glorious and powerful truth of God delivered by *Moses*? Yea, they resisted it with such signs and lying wonders, that the heart of *Pharaoh*, and all his people, were hardened against it. And what was the cause of *Babel*'s destruction, but their trusting in the learned? *Thou art wearied in the multitude of thy councils, &c. I destroy the tokens of the soothsayers, and make them that conjecture fools, and turn the wise men backward; and make their knowledge foolishness.* The things of God's dealing none of the learned of *Egypt* or *Babel* could interpret but *Joseph* and *Daniel*.

NEXT come to the learned *Priests* and *Prophets* of the *Jews*, whose lips should have *preserved*

margin: Exod. vii. 12, &c.
—— viii. 7.
Isa. xlvii. 13.
—— xlii. 25.

preserved knowledge, and at whose mouth the people should have sought the Law. But saith the Lord, *They are gone out of the way;* Mal. ii. 7, 8. *they have caused many to fall by the law,* &c. Also, *Stay your selves and wonder; they are* Isa. xxix. *blind and make you blind; they are drunken, but not with wine; they stagger, but not with strong drink: for the Lord hath covered you with a spirit of slumber, and hath shut up your eyes, the prophets and your chief seers,* &c. *Therefore the Lord said, because this people come near to me with their mouth, and honour me with their lips, but have removed their heart far from me; and their fear towards me was taught by the precepts of men. Therefore, behold, I will again do a marvellous work, in this people; a marvellous work, and a wonder; for the wisdom of their wise men shall perish; and the understanding of the prudent shall be hid,* &c. *Their* Isa. lvi. 10, *watchmen are all blind, they have no knowledge,* &c. &c. And *these shepherds cannot understand; for they all look to their own way, every one for his own advantage, and for his own purpose. The* Jer. viii. 9, *wise men are ashamed; they are afraid and ta-* &c. *ken: Lo, they have rejected the word of the Lord, and what wisdom is in them,* &c. *My people*——— xiv. 14, *have been as lost sheep, their shepherds have* &c. *caused them to go astray, and have turned* ——— l. 6. *them away to the mountains,* &c. *Night shall* Micah iii. *be unto them for a vision, and darkness for a divination: The sun shall go down over the prophets, and the day shall be dark over them,* &c. *For they have no answer of God: they build up Zion with blood, and Jerusalem with ini-* Zeph. iii. 4. *quity,* &c. *Her prophets are light and wicked persons; her priests have polluted the sanctuary; they have wrested the law.*

AND

APPENDIX.

AND in the time of our Saviour, *How* Matt. xv. 6. *had they made the commandments of God of no* Acts xiii. 27. *authority by their traditions.* The rulers of *Jerusalem* (the High priest, Scribes and Pharisees) *knew not Christ, nor yet the words of the prophets, which they heard read every sabbath, but fulfilled them in condemning him.* Matt. xi. And our Saviour saith, *I thank thee, Father, Lord of heaven and earth, because thou hast hid these things from the wise, and men of understanding.* John vii. 48. And *none of the Pharisees nor rulers believed on him.* 1 Cor. i. 20, 26. *Where is the wise? Where is the Scribe? Where is the disputer of this world? Hath not God made the wisdom of this world foolishness? Not many wise men after the flesh, not many mighty, not many noble are called.*

AND for the learned, since the time of our Saviour, the council of *Ephesus*, where were 132 bishops. Of *Seleucia*; where were 160 bishops, related by the Protestants. How grievously did they err in decreeing the detestable error of *Arrianism?* Who is ignorant (knowing the histories) that from time to time, both particular Popes and general councils have grosly erred in many things? Only one we will mention, passing by *Trent* and others. The council *Lateran*, we mean (Pope *Innocent*, 1215.) which for universality was behind none; where were present, two patriarchs, 70 archbishops metropolitans, 400 bishops, 12 abbots, 800 conventual priors, the legates of the *Greek* and *Roman* empire; besides the ambassadors and orators of the kings of *Jerusalem, France, Spain, England* and *Cyprus.* In this council it was decreed, That all hereticks,

APPENDIX.

ticks, and fo many as do in any point refift the Catholick faith, fhould be condemned, &c. And alfo that the fecular powers, of what degree foever they be, fhall be compelled openly to fwear for the defence of the faith, that, [they will] to the uttermoft of their power, root out and deftroy in all their kingdoms, all fuch perfons as the Catholick church hath condemned for hereticks: and if they do not, they fhall be excommunicated. And if they do not reform within one whole year, then the *Pope* may denounce all their fubjects abfolved, and utterly delivered from fhewing or owing any fidelity or obedience towards them. Again, That the *Pope* may give that land to be occupied and enjoyed of the Catholicks to poffefs it (all hereticks being rooted out) quietly and without any contradiction. *Tho. Beacon,* in his *Reliques of Rome,* printed 1563, and the Proteftants confefs; that this imperfection hath hung fo faft upon all councils and churches, that *Nazianzen* faith, *He never faw any council have a good end.*

THUS are here fufficient teftimonies proved from fcriptures and experience; that the learned may, and have ufually erred; and therefore the holy fcriptures often warneth us, *To beware of falfe prophets, for many are gone out into the world.*   Matt. xxiv.
1 John. iv.

AND will not your majefty, your highnefs, your honours, your worfhips, be pleafed to confider of thefe *things*? But will your felves fubmit the guidance of your fouls to the learned fpirituality (as they are called) without due examination by the fcriptures? which, if you will ftill do, we can but bewail

wail with the sorrows of our hearts. And not so only, *but will you with your power which God hath given you to use well, compel and constrain your subjects and underlings to believe as the learned believe, not suffering us to read or search the scriptures?* Which if you abhor, as being the *Romish* practice; *will you do that which is worse, letting us read the scriptures, whereby we may know the will of our heavenly Master, and have our consciences enlightened and convinced; but not suffer us to practise that we learn and know? Whereby our sin and condemnation is made greater than* Luke xii. 47. *the blind Papists,* as is proved. And not only so, but will you constrain us to captivate our consciences, and practise in that which in our souls we know to be evil, and contrary to the manifest law of the Lord, and that *only because the learned have so decreed* (whom you acknowledge are subject to err as well as others) or else lie in perpetual imprisonment, and be otherwise greivously persecuted?

May it please you to observe, that the church of *Rome* seeth, and acknowledgeth in words, That *Jesus Christ is come in the flesh,* and hath abolished the priesthood of *Aaron,* and the legal sacrifices; but the *Jews* see it not to this day; nay, the *High Priest, Scribes* and *Pharisees* saw it not; but for the publishing thereof, persecuted *Christ* the Lord, and his *Apostles,* unto the death, calling their doctrine *heresy,* and them *seditious* enemies to *Cæsar,* &c. For the which we all justly condemn them for their wickedness, so often as we read the holy history.

AND the church of *England* seeth and acknowledgeth divers damnable doctrines of the church

church of *Rome*; this among many; That *the scriptures are not the only rule of faith; but that men ought to be conftrained to believe as the church believes.* The *Proteftants* fee the iniquity of this, becaufe they fee and acknowledge all churches *are fubject to err.* But the learned *Papifts* fee it not, but have decreed, That whofoever refifteth in any point, fhall be judged as an Heretick, and fuffer fire and faggot. And every temporal magiftrate that doth not root fuch Hereticks out of their dominions, fhall be excommunicated: And if he do not reform, he fhall be expelled his earthly poffeffions, and his fubjects freed from owing any fidelity or obedience towards him, *&c.* For the which height of iniquity the *Proteftants* and we juftly cry out againft them, for all the innocent blood that they have fhed.

AND we fee moft manifeftly, That *whatfoever is not of faith is fin. And without faith it is impoffible to pleafe God.* And therefore that *no mortal man may make a law to the confcience, and force unto it by perfecutions, and confequently may not compel unto any religion where faith is wanting,* as hereafter more largely we prove. But the learned of this land fee it not (or rather will not practife it) but for our not fubmitting herein procure your temporal fword to perfecute us, by cafting us in prifons, where many of us have remained divers years in lingring imprifonment, deprived of all earthly comforts; as wives, children, callings, *&c.* without hope of releafe, till our God (for the practice of whofe commandments we are thus perfecuted) perfuade the hearts, of your majefty,

Rom. xiv. 23.
Heb. xi. 6.

your

your highness, your honours, your worships, to take pity upon us, our poor wives and children; or his heavenly Majesty release us by death. Will not succeeding ages cry out against the cruelty of the learned *Protestants* herein, as well as they cry out against the cruelty of the learned *Jews* and *Papists?* Yes, we are assured they will, as many millions do in other nations at this day.

THE scriptures declare, the cause of the *Jews* blindness was, not the obscurity of the scriptures, but that they winked with their eyes, lest they should see that which would deprive them of their honours and profits: John xi. 48. And because their fear towards God was taught by mens precepts, and because they looked to their own way, and to their own advantage, and had rejected the word of the Lord; and because they builded their *Sion* with blood, and *Jerusalem* with iniquity, and sought their own honour, and not God's, as before is proved: so the cause of the blindness of the learned *Papists*, in denying the scriptures, the only rule of faith, is not the obscurity of the scriptures, but their winking with their eyes, lest they should see that that would bring them from their honours and profits, and all the forenamed in the *Jews*. And also, as the *Protestants* well observe, White, p. 18. *First, That they might make themselves judges in their own cause: For who seeth not, that if the church be the rule of faith, and theirs be the church, which way the verdict will go?* Next; *For that the greatest points of their religion have no foundation on the scriptures*, &c. So that, take away the scriprures, and establish their religion; but establish the scrip-

APPENDIX.

scriptures, and their religion vanisheth; and that mother of whoredoms, that glorified her self *as a queen*, shall be consumed; and her merchants, that were waxed rich through her pleasures and profits, shall wail and weep, the which they now seeing, shut their eyes, lest they should see that which would bring them from these honours, profits and pleasures. In like manner, it may easily be judged by every indifferent man, that the cause why the learned of this land will not see, or at least practise (that seeing *there is but one Lord,* and *one Lawgiver over the conscience;* therefore no man ought to be compelled to a worship wherein he hath not faith by persecution) is not the obscurity of the scriptures, but their winking with their eyes, lest they should see that, that would take away their honours and profits? For, if *bribes blind the eyes of the wise,* then honours and profits much more. For who seeth not, if none should be compelled by persecution to worship, till the power of God's word had begotten faith in them to worship God in spirit and in truth (*such only worship him,* and none but such *are required to worship him*) that these learned would lose their honours and profits in being lords and law-makers over the conscience and souls of men; although your majesty might lawfully give them what temporal honours and profits your highness liked of. These are the true causes of the blindness of the learned; for so Christ saith; *How can ye believe, when ye seek honour one of another, and seek not the honour that cometh from God alone.* And how can men but be blind in God's mysteries, when they look *to their*

Rev. xviii.

Eph. iv. 5.
James iv. 12.

Deut. xvi. 19.

John iv. 23.

— v. 44.

their own way for their *own advantage,* and for their *own purpose;* for *having rejected the word of the Lord, What wisdom is in them?* They have no *answer of God,* that *build up their* Sion (for so they account their churches and professions) *with blood, and* Jerusalem *with iniquity,* as before is proved.

If these learned could free us from the Lord's wrath, or, if they might answer for us, and we be free; it were safe for us to submit our selves, and captivate our judgments and practice to them; but seeing they cannot so much as deliver their own souls; and that *if the blind lead the blind, both must fall into the ditch.* And *every one must give account of himself to God,* and *be judged by his own works done in the flesh,* and *that the soul that sinneth shall die.* We dare not follow any mortal man in matters of salvation further than we know him to agree with the meaning of God in the scriptures.

Mark xv. 14.

Paul the holy Apostle of *Jesus Christ,* taught, *That we should follow him no otherwise than he followed Christ;* yea, *Christ* himself sent men to the scriptures to try his doctrine. The Apostles suffered their doctrine to be tryed, and commend them that try it. And the Protestants confess, *This doctrine was never misliked, till a church rose up, whose silver being dross, and whose milk poison, could not endure the trial;* which being true, that we may try. Why may not we also judge and practise according as God's Spirit shall direct us in our trial? If a man should drink poison, and know it to be poison, were he not in a worse estate than he that should drink it ignorantly, not knowing thereof?

2 Cor. xi. 1.

White, p. 127.

of? even a murderer of himself in the highest degree: So he that drinketh spiritual poison, knowing it (for according to mens faith it is unto them) he is in a worse estate, and a murderer of his own soul in the highest degree. And therefore that church, or those learned, that will suffer their doctrine to be tried, and yet constrain men to receive and practise it, when upon examination, their consciences are convinced of the falsehood thereof, are worse, and do more highly sin than they that constrain a blind conscience, though both be evil.

WE despise not learning, nor learned men, but do reverence it and them, according to their worthiness; only when it is advanced into the seat of God, and that given to it which appertaineth unto the Holy Ghost, which is to lead into all truth; then ought all, as *Ezekiah* did unto the brazen serpent, detest it and contemn it.

CHAP. VI.

Persecution for cause of conscience, is against the doctrine of Jesus Christ, *King of kings.*

1. CHRIST commandeth, *That the tares and wheat* (which are those that walk in the truth, and those that walk in falshood) *should be let alone in the world, and not plucked up until the harvest, which is the end of the world.* Matt. xiii. 28. —— xv. 14.

2. The same commandeth, *That they that are blindly led on in false Religion, and are offended with him for teaching true religion,* should

be let alone, *referring their punishment unto their falling into the ditch.*

<small>Luke ix. 54, 55.</small> 3. AGAIN, he reproved his disciples (*who would have had fire come down from heaven, and devoured those Samaritans that would not receive him*) in these words; *Ye know not of what spirit ye are: The son of man is not come to destroy mens lives, but to save them.*

<small>2 Tim. ii. 24.</small> 4. PAUL the Apostle of our Lord teacheth, *That the servant of the Lord must not strive, but must be gentle towards all men, suffering the evil men, instructing them with meekness that are contrary minded;* proving, *if God at any time will give them repentance, that they may acknowledge the truth, and come to amendment out of that snare of the Devil,* &c.

5. ACCORDING to these aforesaid commandments, the holy prophets foretold, That when the law of *Moses,* concerning worship, should cease, and Christ's kingdom be established, then all carnal weapons should cease. <small>Isa. ii. 4. Mic. iv. 3, 4. Isa. xi. 9.</small> *They shall break their swords into mattocks, and their spears into sithes,* &c. *Then shall none hurt nor destroy in all the mountain of my holiness,* &c. And when he came, the same he taught and practised as before; so did his Apostles after him: For the <small>2 Cor. x. 4.</small> *weapons of his warfare are not carnal,* &c. But he charged streightly that his disciples should be so far from persecuting those that would not be of their religion, that when they were persecuted <small>Mat. v.</small> *they should pray.* When they were cursed, *they should bless:* The reason is, because they that are now *tares* may hereafter become *wheat;* they who are now *blind* may hereafter *see;* they that now *resist him* may hereafter *receive him;*

APPENDIX.

him; they that are now in the *Devil's snare*, in adverseness to the truth, may hereafter come *to repentance*; they that are now *blasphemers, persecutors* and *oppressors*, as *Paul* was, may in time, become *faithful* as he; they that are now *idolaters*, as the *Corinths* once were, may hereafter become *true worshippers* as they; they that are now *no people of God*, nor under mercy, as the saints sometimes were, may hereafter become *the people of God*, and *obtain mercy* as they. Some come not till the *eleventh hour*. If those that come not till the *last hour* should be destroyed because they came not at *the first*, then should they never come, but be prevented. And why do men call themselves *Christians*, and do not the things *Christ* would?

1 Cor. vi. 9.
1 Pet. ii. 20.
Matt. xx. 6.

CHAP. VII.

Persecution for cause of conscience is against the profession and practice of famous princes.

FIRST, We beseech your majesty we may relate your own worthy sayings, in your majesty's speech at parliament, 1609. Your highness saith, *It is a sure rule in divinity, that God never loves to plant his church by violence and bloodshed*, &c. And in your highness, *Apol.* p. 4. speaking of such Papists as took the oath, thus: *I gave a good proof that I intended no persecution against them for conscience cause, but only desired to be secured for civil obedience, which for conscience cause they were bound to perform*. And, *p*. 60. speaking of *Blackwell*, the arch-priest, your ma-

APPENDIX.

majesty saith, *It was never my Intention to lay any thing to the said arch-priest's charge, as I have never done to any for cause of conscience,* &c. And in your highness's *Expos.* on *Rev.* xx. printed in 1588, and after 1603. your majesty truly writeth thus. Sixthly, *The compassing of the saints, and besieging of the beloved city, declareth unto us a certain note of a false church to be* persecution ; *for they come to seek the faithful ; the faithful are those that are sought ; the wicked are the* besiegers ; *the faithful the* besieged.

Secondly, THE saying of *Stephen,* king of *Poland : I am king of men, not of consciences ;* a commander of bodies, not of souls, &c.

Thirdly, THE king of *Bohemia* hath thus written. *And notwithstanding the success of the latter time, wherein sundry opinions have been hatch'd about the subject of* religion, *may make one clearly discern with his eye, and as it were touch with his finger ; that according to the verity of holy scripture, and a maxim heretofore held and maintained by the ancient doctors of the church ; that mens consciences ought in no sort to be violated, urged, or constrained ; and whensoever men have attempted any thing by this violent course, whether openly or by secret means, the issue hath been pernicious, and the cause of great and wonderful innovations in the principallest and mightiest kingdoms and countries of all Christendom,* &c. And further, his majesty saith ; *So that once more we do protest, before God and the whole world, that from this time forward we are firmly resolved, not to persecute or molest, or suffer to be persecuted or molested, any person whosoever, for mat-*

matter of religion, no, not they that profess themselves to be of the Roman church; neither to trouble or disturb them in the exercise of their religion, so they live conformably to the laws of the states, &c.

AND for the practice of this, Where is persecution for the cause of conscience, except in *England*, and where popery reigns? and not there neither in all places, as appeareth by *France, Poland*, and other places; nay, it is not practised among the Heathen, that acknowledge not the true God, as the *Turk, Persian*, and others.

CHAP. VIII.

Persecution for cause of conscience, is condemned by the ancient and later writers; yea, by Puritans and Papists.

HILLARY against *Auxentius*, saith thus: *The Christian church doth not persecute, but is persecuted: and lamentable it is to see the great folly of these times, and to sigh at the foolish opinion of this world, in that men think, by human aid, to help God, and with worldly pomp and power to undertake to defend the Christian church. I ask of you bishops, what help used the Apostles, in the publishing of the gospel? With the aid of what power did they preach* Christ, *and converted the Heathen from their idolatry to God? When they were imprisoned, and lay in chains, did they praise and give thanks to God for any dignities, graces and favours received from the court? Or, do you think that* Paul *went about with regal mandates,* or kingly authority, to gather and establish the church of Christ? Sought he protection from Nero, Vespatian? &c.

The *Apostles* wrought with their hands for their own maintenance; travelling by land and water, from town to city, to preach Christ; yea, the more they were forbidden, the more they taught and preached Christ. But now, alas! human help must assist and protect the faith, and give the same countenance to, and, by vain and worldly honours do men seek to defend the church of Christ; as if he by his power were unable to perform it.

The same against the *Arrians*. The church now, which formerly, by enduring misery and imprisonment, was known to be a true church, doth now terrify others, by imprisonment, banishment, and misery; and boasteth that she is highly esteemed of the world: whereas the true church cannot but be hated of the same.

Tertul. ad Scapul. *It agreeth both with human equity, and natural reason, That every man worship God uncompelled, and believe what he will; for, another man's religion or belief neither hurteth nor profiteth any man; neither beseemeth it any religion to compel another to be of their religion; which willingly and freely should be embraced, and not by constraint: Forasmuch as the offerings were required of those that freely, and with a good will offered, and not from the contrary.*

Jerom *in* Proem. lib. 4. *in* Jeremiam. *Heresy must be cut off with the sword of the Spirit. Let us strike through with the arrows of the Spirit, all sons and disciples of misled Hereticks; that is, with testimonies of holy scrip-*

APPENDIX.

scriptures. The slaughter of Hereticks is by the word of God.

BRENTIUS *on* 1 Cor. iii. *No man hath power to make or give laws to Christians, whereby to bind their consciences; for willingly, freely, and uncompelled with a ready desire and chearful mind, must those that come, run unto Christ.*

LUTHER, in his book of the civil magistrate. *The laws of the civil government extends no further than over the body or goods, and to that which is external; for, over the soul God will not suffer any man to rule, only he himself will rule there. Therefore, wheresoever the civil magistrate doth undertake to give laws unto the soul and consciences of men, he usurpeth that government to himself, which appertaineth to God,* &c.

THE same upon 1 Kings vi. *In the building of the temple there was no sound of iron heard, to signify that Christ will have in his church a free and willing people, not compelled and constrained by laws and statutes.*

AGAIN he saith upon *Luke* xxii. *It is not the true Catholick Church, which is defended by the secular arm or human power, but the false and feigned church; which although it carries the name of a church, yet it denieth the power thereof.* And upon *Psal.* xvii. he saith; *For the true church of Christ knoweth not* Brachium seculare, *which the bishops now a-days chiefly use.*

AGAIN, in *Postil. Dom.* 1. post. *Epiph.* he saith, *Let not Christians be commanded, but exhorted; for he that will not willingly do that whereunto he is friendly exhorted, he is no Christian. Therefore those that do compel them,*

that

that are not willing, shew thereby that they are not Christian preachers, but worldly beadles.

AGAIN, upon 1 *Pet.* iii. he saith, *If the civil magistrate would command me to believe thus or thus, I should answer him after this manner; Lord, or Sir, look you to your civil or worldly government, your power extends not so far to command any thing in God's kingdom, therefore herein I may not hear you; for if you cannot suffer that any man should usurp authority where you have to command, How do you think that God should suffer you to thrust him from his seat, and to seat your self therein?*

THE *Puritans*, as appeareth in their answer to *Admonit.* to *Parl.* pag. 109. *That Papists nor others, neither constrainedly nor customally communicate in the mysteries of salvation.* Also in their supplication, printed 1609. *p.* 21, &c. much they write for toleration.

Lastly, THE *Papists*, the inventors of persecution, in a wicked book lately set forth; thus they write: *Moreover, the means which almighty God appointed his officers to use in the conversion of kingdoms and people, was humility, patience, charity,* &c. saying, *Behold, I send you as sheep in the midst of wolves.* He did not say, *I send you as wolves among sheep, to kill, imprison, spoil and devour those unto whom they were sent.*

Matt. x. 16.

— ver. 7. AGAIN he said, *They to whom I send you, will deliver you up in councils, and in their synagogues they will scourge you; and to presidents and to kings shall you be led for my sake.* He doth not say, *You whom I send shall deliver the*

the people (whom you ought to convert) into councils, and put them in prisons, and lead them to presidents and tribunal seats, and make their religion felony and treason.

AGAIN he saith; *When ye enter into the house, salute it, saying, Peace be to this house.* Matt. x. 12. He doth not say, *You shall send pursevants to ransack and spoil the house.*

AGAIN he saith; *The good pastor giveth* John x. *his life for his sheep; the thief cometh not but to steal, kill and destroy.* He doth not say, *The thief giveth his life for his sheep, and the good pastor cometh not but to steal, kill, and destroy,* &c.

So that we holding our peace, our adversaries themselves, speak for us, or rather for the truth.

CHAP. IX.

It is no prejudice to the commonwealth, if freedom of religion were suffered, but would make it flourish.

BE pleased not to hearken to mens leasings, but to what God and experience teacheth in this thing. *Abraham* abode among the *Canaanites* a long time, yet contrary to them in religion. Again, *he sojourned in Gerar, and king* Ahimelech *gave him leave to abide in his land.* *Isaac* also dwelt in the same land, yet contrary in religion. *Jacob* lived twenty years in one house with his uncle *Laban,* yet differ'd in religion. The people

Gen. xiii. 7,
16, 3.
— xx, & xxi,
33, 34.
— xxvi. 31.

of *Israel* were four hundred and thirty years in that famous land of *Egypt*, and afterwards seventy years in *Babylon*; all which time they differ'd in religion from the states. Come to the time of Christ, where *Israel* was under the *Romans*, where lived divers sects of religions, as *Herodians, Scribes* and *Pharisees, Sadducees, Libertines, Tkudæans, Samaritans*; besides the common religion of the *Jews, Christ* and his *Apostles*, all which differed from the common religion of the state, which (is like) was the *worship of Diana*, which almost *the whole world then worshipped*. All these lived under the government of *Cæsar*, being nothing hurtful to the state and commonwealth; for they gave unto *Cæsar* that which was his; and for religion to God, he left them to themselves, as having no domination therein. And when the enemies of the truth raised up any tumults, the wisdom of the magistrates most wisely appeased them.

Exod. xii.
2 Chr. xxxvi.

Acts xix. 20.

—— xviii. 14.
—— xix. 35,
&c.

AGAIN, be pleased to look into the neighbour nations, who tolerate *religion*, how their wealths and states are governed, many sorts of religions are in their dominions; yet no trouble of state, no treason, no hindrance at all of any good, but much prosperity brought unto their countries, they having all one harmony in matters of state, giving unto *Cæsar* his due; and for religion they suffer one another.

IF any object the troubles of *France, Germany*, &c. we answer; They are such as have been procured by the learned, but most *bloody Jesuits*, who seek to establish their religion by blood, for the subversion of whom,

your

APPENDIX.

your wisdoms are wise to deal in. Yet be pleased not to let faithful subjects be punished for their wickedness; but let most severe laws be made for the maintenance of civil and human peace and welfare, as to your majesty and others shall seem expedient. And if it be well observed, it is the learned that raiseth up all the bloody wars among the princes of the earth.

CHAP. X.

Kings are not deprived of any power given them of God, when they maintain freedom for cause of conscience.

WE know the learned do persuade, that kings have power from God to maintain the worship and service of God, as they have power to maintain right and justice between man and man. For Christian kings, say they, have the same power that the kings of *Israel* had under the law. For answer to which,

First, LET it be observed, The kings of *Israel* had never power from God to make new laws, or set up new worships, which God's word required not, nor to set high priests, or spiritual lords for the performance of the services, other than such as God, by *Moses*, had expresly commanded; and therefore the power of the kings of *Israel* will warrant no kings to make or confirm *Canons*, set up new worships, and appoint spiritual lords and lawgivers to the conscience, and persecute all that submit not unto them.

Secondly,

Secondly, LET it be well obferv'd, only the kings of *Ifrael* had this power, but no other kings, whofe commonwealths did flourifh to them and their feeds after them, to many generations: and it muft be granted, that he that is king of *Ifrael* now, which is Jefus Chrift (the truth of thofe typical kings of *Ifrael*) he hath the power according to the proportion; the temporal kings had temporal power to compel all to the obfervation of thofe carnal or temporal commandments.

Heb. vii. 16. So Chrift, the fpiritual King, hath fpiritual
— ix. 10. power to compel all to the obfervation of his fpiritual commandments. For when he came,

John iv. 23. himfelf faid; *The hour cometh, and now is, when the true worfhippers fhall worfhip the Father in fpirit and in truth: for the Father requireth even fuch to worfhip him.* If Chrift be only King of *Ifrael*, that fits upon *David*'s throne for ever, as he is; far be it from

Acts ii. 30. any king to take Chrift's feat from him. The wifdom of God forefaw, that feeing the myfteries of the gofpel are fuch fpiritual things, as no natural men (though they be princes of this world) can know them; he left not kings and princes to be lords and judges thereof, feeing they are fubject to err; but he left that power to his beloved Son, who could not err; and the Son left his only deputy the Holy Ghoft, and no mortal man whatfoever, as your highnefs worthily acknowledgeth, in *Apol.* p. 46. *I utterly deny that there is any earthly monarch over the church, whofe word muft be a law, and who cannot err by an infallibility of fpirit. Becaufe earthly kingdoms muft have earthly monarchs, it doth not follow the church muft have*

APPENDIX.

a visible monarch too. Christ is the church's monarch, and the Holy Ghost his deputy. The kings of the nations reign over them; but you shall not be so, &c. *Christ when he ascended* Luke xxii. *left not* Peter *with them to direct them into all truth; but promised to send the Holy Ghost unto them for that end,* &c.

Further, THESE learned alledge the com- Exod. xxiii. mandments, where *Israel* are commanded *to* 33. *destroy all the inhabitants of the land, lest* Deut. vii, & *they intice them to serve their gods, and to* xiii. *slay all false prophets,* &c. These they collect from the time of the *law*; for in the time of the *gospel* they have nothing to alledge; for *Rom.* xiii. maketh nothing for their purpose, *Cæsar* being an heathen king. For answer unto the places of *Moses.*

First, THE *sins of this people, the* Canaanites *were full, and the Lord would destroy them, and give their possessions unto the* Israelites; but the sins of the refusers of Christ are not full until the end, or last hour, as before is proved.

Secondly, THE *children of* Israel *had a special commandment from the Lord to destroy them*; but the kings of the nations have no command at all to destroy the bodies of the contrary minded; nay, they are expresly forbidden it.

Thirdly, THE Canaanites *would have re-* Matt. xiii. 29. *belled against* Israel, *and have destroyed them*; but the contrary minded will not rebel against their kings, but give unto them the things that belong unto them; not so much for fear, as of conscience; and of this the GOD of Gods is witness; if any do, or teach otherwise, let them be destroy'd.

Fourthly,

Fourthly, THE *heads and rulers of* Israel *could command and compel the people to observe those carnal rites and ordinances of the law; even as* CHRIST, *the head and ruler of* Israel *can compel to the observation of his spiritual ordinances of the gospel;* but the heads of the nations cannot compel their subjects to believe the gospel; for *faith is the gift of God;* which *faith,* if they want, all they do in God's worship *is sin.* Therefore they cannot compel any to worship, because they cannot give them *faith;* for which cause the Lord in wisdom saw it not meet to charge kings with a duty which they cannot perform; God will never require it at their hands; the blood of the faithless and unbelieving shall be on their own heads. *He that will not believe shall be damn'd.*

Rom. xiv. 23.
Heb. xi. 6.

Mark xvi. 16.

AGAIN, seeing it is true, as your majesty well observeth in your highness's speech at Parl. 1609. *That the judicials of* Moses, *were only fit for that time, and those persons.*

AND also it is confessed, the law for adultery, theft, and the like, is not now to be executed, according to the judicials of *Moses,* nor directions for the magistrates of the earth to walk by; Why should these be any directions for them, seeing also our Saviour and his Apostles have taught the contrary, as before hath been proved? If all false prophets should be now executed, according to *Deut.* xiii. The kings of the earth would not only be deprived of many of their subjects; but the *cities of their habitation, with all the inhabitants of the cities, must be destroyed with the edge of the sword; the cattle thereof, and all the spoil thereof must be brought into the midst*

APPENDIX. 49

midst of the city, and the city and all therein be burnt with fire, be made a heap of stones for ever, and never be built again; which God forbid such execration should ever be seen. And if these judicials of *Moses* be not now directions for the kings of nations; we read not in all the book of God, any directions given to kings to rule in matters of conscience and spiritual worship to God. But often we read, that the kings of the nations shall give their power to the beast, and fight against the lamb, as lamentable experience hath plainly taught it.

Rev. xvi. 14
—— xvii. 2, .
&c.
—— xviii. 3, 9.
—— xix. 19.

Thus all men may see, there is only deceit in these learned mens comparisons of the kings of *Israel* in the law, with the kings of nations in time of the gospel, in matters of *religion*. Much might be written to prove that kings are not deprived of their power by permitting of freedom of religion; but are rather deprived thereof by using compulsion to the contrary minded; and do sin grievously in causing them to sin for want of faith; but this may suffice, the Almighty blessing it with his blessing, which we humbly beseech him for his *Christ*'s sake, for his own *glory* sake, for the prosperity and welfare of these *kingdoms*, and for the comfort of your faithful and true hearted subjects that are now distressed by long and lingring imprisonments, and otherwise; who of conscience give unto *Cæsar* the things which are his; which is, to be *lord* and *lawgiver* to the bodies of his *subjects*, and all belonging to their outward man, for the preservation of himself and his good subjects, and for the punishment of the evil: In which preserva-

tion

tion the church of Christ hath a special part, when their outward peace is thereby preserved from the fury of all adversaries; in which respect princes are called *nursing-fathers*, as many are at this day, *blessed be the Lord*.

OH be pleased to consider, why you should persecute us for humbly beseeching you, in the words of the King of kings, *To give unto God the things which are God's*; which is, to be *Lord* and *Lawgiver* to the soul in that spiritual worship and service which he requireth. If you will take away this from God, what is it that is God's? Far be it from you to desire to sit in the consciences of men, to be *lawgiver and judge therein*. This is *antichrist's* practice, persuading the kings of the earth to give him their power to compel all hereunto. But whosoever submitteth, *shall drink of God's fierce wrath*. You may make and mend your own laws, and be judge and punisher of the transgressors thereof; but *you cannot make or mend God's laws, they are perfect already. You may not add nor diminish, nor be judge nor monarch of his church*, that is CHRIST's right; he left neither you, nor any mortal man his deputy, but *only the Holy Ghost*, as your highness acknowledgeth. And whosoever erreth from the truth, his judgment is set down, and the time thereof.

Matt. xxii. 21.

Rev. xiv. 9, 10.

Psal. xix. 7.
Deut. iv. 2.
Rev. xxii. 18, 19.

2 Thess. i. 8, &c.
Rom. ii. 8, &c.
Matt. xiii. 40.
—— xxv. 31, &c.
Rom. ii. 16.

THIS is the sum of our *humble petition*; That your majesty would be pleased not to persecute your faithful subjects (who are obedient to you in all civil worship and service) for walking in the practice of what God's word requireth of us, for his spiritual worship,

APPENDIX.

ship, as we have faith, knowing (as your majesty truly writeth in your *Medit.* on *Matt.* xxvii. *p.* 69. in these words) *We can use no spiritual worship or prayer that can be available to us without faith.*

THIS *is the sum of our* most humble petition, *thus manifoldly proved to be just.*

O LORD GOD of glory, raise up in this high assembly the heart of some *Nehemiah*, of some *Ebedmelech*, that may open their mouths (for the dumb, that cannot speak for themselves) in a truth so apparent as this is, lest it be said, as *Isa.* lix. 16. *And when he saw that there was no man, he wondered that none would offer himself; therefore his arm did save it, and his righteousness it self did sustain it.*

AND now we cease not to pray for the king, and his son, and his seed, and this whole, high and honourable assembly, now and always.

Calling the all-seeing God to witness, That we are your majesty's loyal subjects, not for fear only but for conscience sake. *Unjustly* called,

ANA-BAPTISTS.

NUMB. III.

To the Right Reverend THOMAS *Lord Bishop of* LINCOLN.

' *My Lord,*

'HE ground of my humble ten-
' dering these ensuing pages to
' your lordship, is your decla-
' red condescension to peruse
' any brief treatise that should
' be presented to you concerning the proper
' subject and administration of baptism.'

THEN follows a short preface, giving an account of the *English* baptists; at the conclusion of which, the captain says, ' That
' their particular persuasion may be no bar in
' the way of your lordship's charity towards
' them, I shall now proceed briefly to state
' their opinion, with the proofs in general
' upon which they establish the truth of it.'

THE substance, says he, of what is asserted by them, is, *That those who do profess repentance towards God, faith in, and obedience to our Lord Jesus, are the proper subjects of baptism.*

THAT *the due administration of this ordinance is by immersion, or dipping the person in water ; and that they find no rule or example in scripture for baptizing any person in any other manner, or without an actual declaration of faith.*

' For proof hereof they alledge,
' 1. The doctrine and practice of *John the*
' *Baptist,* and of the disciples of our Lord,
' whilst

APPENDIX.

'whilst he was present with them before his
'crucifixion.' *And saying, Repent ye; for the* Matt. iii. 2, 6,
kingdom of heaven is at hand. And were bap- 11, 13, 16.
tized of him in Jordan, *confessing their sins.*
*I indeed baptize you with water unto repentance; but he that cometh after me is mightier
than I, whose shoes I am not worthy to bear,
he shall baptize you with the Holy Ghost and
with fire. Then cometh Jesus from* Galilee
to Jordan *unto* John, *to be baptized of him.
And Jesus, when he was baptized, went up
straightway out of the water; and lo, the heavens were opened unto him; and he saw the
Spirit of God descending like a dove, and lighting upon him.* John *did baptize in the wil-* Mark i. 4, 5,
derness, and preach the baptism of repentance 9.
*for the remission of sins. And there went out
unto him all the land of* Judea, *and they of* Jerusalem, *and were all baptized of him in the
river of* Jordan, *confessing their sins. And it
came to pass in those days that Jesus came
from* Nazareth *of* Galilee, *and was baptized of*
John *in* Jordan. *And he came into all the* Luke iii. 3,
country about Jordan, *preaching the baptism of* 16, 21,
repentance for the remission of sins. John *answered, saying unto them all, I indeed baptize
you with water; but one mightier than I cometh,
the latchet of whose shoes I am not worthy to
unloose, he shall baptize you with the Holy
Ghost, and with fire. Now when all the people were baptized, it came to pass that Jesus
also being baptized, and praying, the heaven was
opened. Then said* Paul, John *verily baptized* Acts xix. 4, 5.
*with the baptism of repentance, saying unto the
people, That they should believe on him which
should come after him; that is, on Christ Jesus. When they heard this, they were baptized*

APPENDIX.

John iii. 22, 23. *in the name of the Lord Jesus. After these things came Jesus and his disciples into the land of* Judea, *and there he tarried with them and baptized. And* John *also was baptizing in* Enon, *near to* Salim, *because there was much*

John iv. 1. *water there; and they came and were baptized. Jesus made and baptized more disciples than* John.

'2. The words of positive and sovereign
Matt. xxviii. 'institution, after the resurrection of our Lord.'
19, 20. *Go ye therefore and teach all nations, baptizing them in the name of the Father, and of the Son, and of the Holy Ghost. Teaching them to observe all things whatsoever I have commanded you, and lo, I am with you always, even unto the end*

Mark xvi. 16. *of the world. Amen. He that believeth and is baptized, shall be saved; but he that believeth not shall be damned.*

'3. The Apostles and Evangelists instru-
'ctions, resolutions of questions on this sub-
'ject and practice, correspondent with the
'command, next and immediately after it
'was given.'

Acts ii. 38. Then Peter *said unto them, Repent and be baptized every one of you, in the name of Jesus Christ, for the remission of sins; and ye*

—— viii. 12, *shall receive the gift of the Holy Ghost. But*
36, 39. *when they believed* Philip, *preaching the things concerning the kingdom of God, and the name of Jesus Christ, they were baptized, both men and women. And as they went on their way, they came unto a certain water; and the eunuch said, See here is water; What doth hinder me to be baptized? And* Philip *said, If thou believest with all thine heart, thou mayest. And he answered and said, I believe that Jesus Christ is the Son of God. And he commanded*
the

APPENDIX. 55

the chariot to stand still; and they went down both into the water, both Philip *and the eunuch, and he baptized him. And when they were come up out of the water, the Spirit of the Lord caught away* Philip, *that the eunuch saw him no more, and he went on his way rejoicing. And he departed thence, and enter'd into a certain mans house, named* Justus, *one that worshipped God, whose house joined hard to the synagogue. And* Crispus, *the chief ruler of the synagogue, believed on the Lord, with all his house; and many of the* Corinthians *hearing, believed, and were baptized.* —— Acts xviii. 7, 8.

' 4. THE manifold use and improvement,
' which after many Christian churches were
' settled, the Apostles made in their epistles
' to them, taken from the due qualifications
' required in persons to be baptized, and built
' upon the due administration of that ordi-
' nance, wherein is shewed the mystical signi-
' ficancy thereof.'

' (1.) As it is by the prayer, stipulation,
' or interrogation of the baptized's good con-
' science therein Godward, the figure of sal-
' vation through the resurrection of Jesus
' Christ; which otherwise, by the waters
' washing away of the filth of the flesh in
' baptism it would not be.' *And now why tarriest thou? Arise and be baptized, and wash away thy sins, calling on the name of the Lord.* —— xxii. 16. *And the Lord said unto him, Arise, and go into the street which is called* Straight, *and enquire in the house of* Judas, *for one called* Saul *of* Tarsus; *for behold he prayeth. The like figure whereunto even baptism doth also now save us, not the putting away the filth of the flesh, but the answer of a good conscience to-* —— ix. 11. 1 Pet iii. 21.

D 4 *wards*

wards God by the resurrection of Jesus Christ.

'2. As it is to the understanding of the baptized person ordained to be a sign of fellowship with Christ in his death and resurrection.' *Know ye not that so many of us as were baptized into Jesus Christ, were baptized into his death? Therefore we are buried with him by baptism into death, that like as Christ was raised up from the dead by the glory of the Father, even so we also should walk in newness of life. For if we have been planted together in the likeness of his death, we shall be also in the likeness of his resurrection.* ^{Rom. vi. 3,4, 5.}

^{Col. ii. 12.} *Buried with him in baptism, wherein also ye are risen with him through the faith of the operation of God, who hath raised him from the dead.*

'And of engrafting into that mystical body the church, whereof Christ is the head.' *For as many of you as have been baptized into Christ, have put on Christ. There is neither* Jew *nor* Greek, *there is neither bond nor free; there is neither male nor female; for ye are all one in Christ Jesus. For by one spirit we are all baptized into one body, whether we be* Jews *or* Gentiles, *whether we be bond or free; and have been all made to drink into one spirit.* ^{Gal. iii. 27, 28.}

^{1 Cor. xii. 13.}

'AND consequently a reproof and conviction, in the baptized's own conscience, of the crime, in case he be guilty of making a schism in the church.' *Is Christ divided? Was* Paul *crucified for you? or were ye baptized in the name of* Paul? ^{1 Cor. i. 13.}

'OR separating from the church,' as, ^{Jude ver. 19.} THESE *be they who separate themselves, sensual, having not the spirit. Not forsaking the assem-* ^{Heb. x. 25.}

APPENDIX.

assembling of our selves together, as the manner of some is; but exhorting one another; and so much the more, as ye see the day approaching.

'3. As the baptized is presumed to know
' himself to be thereby obliged in general to
' a perseverance in holiness, a growth in
' grace, and knowledge of the mysteries of
' God, even of the Father and of Christ, and
' to the yielding a ready obedience of faith
' to all other doctrines and precepts of our
' Lord.' *Know ye not, that so many of us* Rom. vi. 3. *as were baptized into Jesus Christ, were baptized into his death? Buried with him in* Col. ii. 12. *baptism, wherein also ye are risen with him through the faith of the operation of God, who hath raised him from the the dead. There-* Heb. vi. 1, *fore leaving the principles of the doctrine of* 2, 3. *Christ, let us go on unto perfection; not laying again the foundation of repentance from dead works, and of faith towards God; of the doctrine of baptisms, and of laying on of hands, and of the resurrection of the dead, and of eternal judgment. And this will we do if God permit.*

' My Lord, says the captain, if these
' scriptures be rightly interpreted and applied
' by these called *Anabaptists*; and if it be also
' true, as they have often asserted, that there
' is not in the whole scriptures any rule given
' to baptize, or any plain instance of any
' person's being baptized in any other man-
' ner, or without being first further instru-
' cted in the doctrine, and making confession
' of faith; I cannot conceive why this should
' not be accepted without any other additio-
' nal testimonies or arguments, as a sufficient
' de-

'defence for such, as with a due observance
'of all other rules of Christianity, general
'and special, do in this point thus behave
'and do: nor why they should be therefore
'censured, either as varying from the first
'institution, or as being deficient in any
'proof necessary to maintain this their opini-
'on and practice.

'I TAKE it to be agreed, says he, among
'the generality of reformed Christians, that
'in the holy scriptures are contained dire-
'ctions, as well concerning all essential parts
'of worship, as doctrines necessary to be be-
'lieved. And it may be thence safely con-
'cluded, that without the help of any un-
'written traditions, or any other writings,
'the holy scriptures divinely inspired and
'written for our learning, always, since they
'were first written, have been, are, and will
'be, through faith in Christ Jesus, equally
'powerful to render any other person, as well
'as *Timothy*, *wise to salvation:* and to com-
'pleat any other minister of Christ for his
'work, whether it be for doctrine or instru-
'ction in righteousness, reproof of errors, or
'setting to right and restoring the true wor-
'ship of God, if any of his institutions,
'through negligence, omission, incogitan-
'cy, human traditions, frequent and long
'continual examples in the church, or any
'other means have not been rightly observed.
'And if it be admitted, that no power or
'authority was ever committed to any do-
'ctors, assemblies, or general councils, pur-
'posely, or knowingly, in any transcript of
'the scriptures, to vary one letter from the
'original record, or in any translation to vary

APPENDIX. 59

'ry from the true and genuine sense of the
' original text; and that not every individual
' letter, syllable, or word, in a transcript or
' translation; but the sense of scripture is
' of divine authority, and may be render'd
' and preach'd now as well as in the Apo-
' stles time, to every nation under heaven, Acts ii. 5, 11.
' in their respective proper languages. And
' that notwithstanding all accidents of vari-
' ous lections, or different interpretations,
' through the oscitancy of transcribers, or
' various sentiments of translators, through
' human frailty; yet, through the admira-
' ble providence and grace of God, watching
' over and assisting his faithful bishops and
' teachers in the church, we have, in all necef-
' sary points relating to doctrine, worship and
' conversation, the genuine sense and mean-
' ing of the holy scriptures continued to us,
' as they were at first revealed, and divinely
' inspired into, and delivered over by the ho-
' ly penmen thereof, as I am abundantly sa-
' tisfied; I thank God for it, that we have.
' And if it be also admitted that the church
' hath no more power to change the rites and
' forms of sacraments instituted by our Lord,
' than they have to change his word and law;
' for that as the one contains the audible, so
' the other the visible sign of the divine will:
' Then, I humbly conceive, in the decision
' of this controversy, between the *Anabap-*
' *tists* and *Pædobaptists*, we may safely cast
' out of our thoughts all intercurrent centu-
' ries between the primitive and the present
' state of the church; and without having re-
' gard to any intervening canon, tradition,
' or nice school distinction, follow that ve-
          ' nerable

'nerable scripture example of the chief of
'the fathers and the priests, in a case which,
'in many respects, may be said to be of the
'like nature, upon their return out of the
'*Babylonish* captivity; who, when they and
'the people were assembled to read and un-
'derstand the words of the law, which God
'had commanded by *Moses*, and found writ-
'ten therein in what manner the rites of the
'feast of tabernacles were to be observed by
'the *Israelites*, they regulated and kept the
'ceremonies thereof, not by former examples,
'but by the prescript form, which had not
'been so done for about a thousand years be-
Neh. viii. 14, 'fore.' *And they found written in the law*
15, 16, 17. *which the Lord had commanded by* Moses,
that the children of Israel *should dwell in*
booths in the feast of the seventh month:
and that they should publish and proclaim in
all their cities, and in Jerusalem, *saying, Go*
forth unto the mount, and fetch olive branches,
and pine branches, and myrtle branches, and
palm branches, and branches of thick trees, to
make booths, as it is written. So the people went
forth and brought them, and made themselves
booths, every one upon the roof of his house, and
in their courts, and in the courts of the house of
God, and in the street of the water-gate, and in
the street of the gate of Ephraim. *And all the*
congregation of them that were come again out
of the captivity made booths, and sat under the
booths: for since the days of Joshua *the son of*
Nun, *unto that day, had not the children of* Israel *done so: and there was very great gladness.*

'I TAKE baptism, says the captain, to
'have been generally reputed the initiating
'ordinance, or admission of such into the vi-
'sible

APPENDIX.

'fible church, who having been before in-
' ftructed in, and converted to the Chriftian
' faith, have, from that internal perfuafion,
' made an external profeffion of faith in, and
' fubjection to the perfon, doctrine and com-
' mands of the Lord Jefus. Not that I rec-
' kon it in order of nature, or time, the firft
' act of worfhip which any fuch perform to-
' wards him ; for if any thing may in that
' refpect be faid to be firft, I fhould rather
' attribute the priority to the reception in the
' heart, of that *incorruptible feed, the word*
' *of God*, by which a perfon is born again;
' and the demonftration of that fpiritual life to
' be the firft breathing after God, thro' Chrift,
' in holy defires and prayer. Nor do I think
' inftruction in all the fundamentals of Chri-
' ftianity, or in the utmoft extent or fignifi-
' cancy of baptifm it felf, of any more abfo-
' lute neceffity than in the beginning of Chri-
' ftian religion; for in many, if not in each
' individual perfon, Chriftianity may in fome
' refpects have as much its beginning now, as
' when Chrift was firft preached among the
' *Gentiles*. *Apollos* was *mighty in the ſcrip-*
' *tures*, and an accurate teacher of the things
' of the Lord; knowing only the baptifm of
' *John*, until *Aquila* and *Priſcilla* expounded Acts xviii. 24,
' to him the way of the Lord more exquifitely. 26.
' A deficiency is alfo mentioned among the — xix. 1, 7.
' difciples at *Ephefus*. A competent know-
' ledge of the grounds of that obedience, which
' in each individual act of worfhip is yielded
' to God, is requifite in him that fo worfhips,
' to render it acceptable; for God is a *ſpirit*,
' and feeketh and reputeth fuch for true wor-
' fhippers of him, who do worfhip him *in*
' *ſpirit*

APPENDIX.

'*spirit and in truth*. But there may be errors
'on the right hand, as well as on the left.
'God is jealous of his inftituted worſhip, and
'no man is exempt, by the dignity of his
'perſon, or eminency of his gifts, from yield-
'ing obedience thereunto, in due order and
'manner required. It is very remarkable,
'that *Moſes*, the reputed ſon of king *Pha-*
'*raoh*'s daughter, educated in all the learning
'of the *Egyptians*, although God had emi-
'nently appeared to him, ſhewed him divers
'miracles, made him ſignal promiſes of his
'preſence and aſſiſtance, appointed him to be
'the leader of his people; yet, after all this,
'the Lord met him in his journey, and ſought
'to ſlay him. And by the context it is evi-
Exod. iv. 24, 'dent, that this anger againſt him was for that
25, 26. 'he had neglected to circumciſe his ſon. Two
'inſtances alſo we have in the New Teſtament,
'though not of ſuch ſeverity, yet ſuch as ſerve
'to evidence that it may be ſometimes necef-
'ſary to admoniſh thoſe that are moſt emi-
'nently favoured of God, and endued with
'the ſpecial gifts of the Holy Spirit, that
'they defer not that obedience which they
'ought to yield to his inſtituted worſhip, par-
'ticularly this ordinance of baptiſm. Ordina-
'narily, at the firſt preaching of this goſpel,
'baptiſm in water did precede the baptiſm of
Matt. iii. 11. 'the Spirit, and conferring of ſpecial gifts;
'although the latter of theſe was always pre-
'ferred before the other, as moſt eminent.
'But *Ananias* was ſent to *Saul* of the Lord
'Jeſus, who had before appeared to him, that
Acts ix. 17. 'by putting on of his hands, as appears by
'the text, he might receive his ſight, and be
'filled with the Holy Spirit. And this was
'done,

APPENDIX. 63

' done, not only before his baptifm in water;
' but by comparifon of this place with *Acts*
' xxii. 16. there feems to have been, by *Ana-*
' *nias*'s queftion, *Why tarrieft thou?* at leaft
' a neceffary ftirring of him up to an imme-
' diate difcharge of his duty therein. And the
' like we may obferve in *Cornelius* and his
' kinfmen, and near friends; on whom, whilft
' the Apoftle *Peter* was preaching to them,
' the gift of the Holy Spirit was poured out,
' fo that they fpake with tongues, and mag- Acts ix. 47,
' nified God; which as it did fufficiently evi- 48.
' dence they were qualified for it, fo alfo that
' by this anticipation of the baptifm of the
' Spirit, baptifm in water might not be de-
' ferred by them. The Apoftle, not by way
' of teftimony and exhortation only, as in
' *Acts* ii. 40. and in other common cafes;
' but as better fuiting with their before de-
' clared difpofition, and the prefent occafion,
' exprefly commanded them to be baptized. —— ver. 33,

' Touching things relating to the common 34.
' faith, and common falvation of Chriftians,
' it has always been allowed, by the moft emi-
' nently learned and orthodox bifhops and
' doctors, that the fcriptures are eafy to be
' underftood; and were fo plainly in thefe
' points penn'd by the Prophets, Apoftles and
' Evangelifts, that every perfon who will read,
' and diligently fearch and ponder them, might
' thereby of himfelf learn what are therein fpo-
' ken of thefe things.

' Touching the proper fubject and man-
' ner of baptifm, it feems not to me (I fpeak
' with fubmiffion, fays the captain) very ma-
' terial to enquire concerning the different opi-
' nions of men, or how their controverfies here-

I ' about

'about have been decided, by any general
'council since the Apostles days; because each
'person's faith, and practice herein, in every
'succeeding generation to the end of the world,
'is alike to be founded upon, and regulated
'by the scripture, as was theirs who did suc-
'ceed immediately, and were next to the Apo-
'stles. The scriptures in these points are least
'of all liable to be mistaken, when they are
'taken by such as read them, as if sent to
'them immediately by the hands of the Apo-
'stles and evangelists, and by such as hear
'them read openly in the church, as if that
'service was performed by such as had so re-
'ceived them, in obedience to the Apostles
'strict charge to that purpose.' *I charge you
by the Lord, that this epistle be read unto all
the holy brethren.*

1 Thess. v. 27.

'I do not write this, says the captain, to
'derogate from, or diminish any part of that
'honour that is due, and ought to be given
'to those who are pious and learned *overseers*
'in the Lord's vineyard. The wisdom of
'God did foresee it necessary to establish ru-
'lers, pastors and teachers, in his church,
'and to qualify them with suitable authority
'and gifts, as well for the good government,
'ordering and edifying of the body of Christ,
'as on their behalf to watch against and dis-
'cover false doctrines, and false teachers;
'who by transforming themselves into angels of
'light, seek all occasions to destroy the flock,
'remove the ancient foundations of the house
'of God, and to introduce damnable heresies,
'and doctrines of devils; the detection where-
'of is not within the compass of an ordinary
'capacity; therefore in this respect, especi-
'ally

APPENDIX.

'ally even now, when the ravening wolves
'stood watching for the moment wherein they
'might seize their prey, is your lordship de-
'servedly rank'd with the foremost of those,
'whose words are the more excellent and ac- Prov. xxv.11.
'ceptable, because upright, and words of truth,
'spoken in season by a master of collections. Ecclef. xii.10,
'And the grace and good providence of God, 11.
'that qualified and stirred up your lordship,
'upon such a special occasion, to detect and
'expose to open view, the opinions and prin-
'ciples of such false teachers, in their native
'deformity, which renders them so abomina-
'ble, that the disciples of those who are the
'fathers of them, are ashamed to own them,
'is the more remarkable, and calls for an
'humble, hearty and thankful acknowledg-
'ment from all those on whose behalf this
'was done.

'THESE, and all such labours as have a
'tendency either to detect erronious doctrines,
'or reduce the doctrines of Christianity to
'their prime and genuine purity, that inter-
'pret and help others to understand aright the
'holy scriptures of truth, have been, and
'will be always of singular use and advan-
'tage to the church of God, approved, blef-
'sed, and the authors of them highly esteem-
'ed of all sincere Christians for their work-
'sake.

'BUT, my Lord, these and all faithful guides,
'who teach their hearers and disciples pure
'doctrine and worship, speak to them in, and
'guide them to the words of the Prophets
'and Apostles; so that, by common consent,
'all are to be tried, judged and determined
'by the rule of scripture. And in this re-

E   'spect

APPENDIX.

'spect it is, that this sect of *Anabaptists* a-
'mongst us do say,' *That if the doctrine of
baptism, as they teach it, and the form of
baptism as they practise it, be according to
the scriptures, and primitive use of the
Christian church; this alone is a sufficient
defence for them herein, although there should
be no concurrent testimony of any other tradition, custom, decree of council, or opinion
whatsoever.* ' Yet, my lord, with this due
' *salvo* to the sovereign and sole authority of
' scripture, I see no cause they have, if mat-
' ters be duly weighed, to decline, or that
' they do indeed appeal from the judgment of
' the ancient fathers herein.

' To evidence this on their behalf, I shall,
' says the captain, instance in a few of those
' many ancient testimonies which they al-
' ledge as unquestionable, and of such argu-
' ments deduced from thence, as to me seem
' very cogent and natural.

' 1. THAT the general and very ancient
' usage of sponsors or susceptors at the bap-
' tism of infants, to personate and answer to
' articles of the Christian faith ; as if the ve-
' ry person to be baptised is, beyond contra-
' diction, an evidence in it self of a general
' received opinion among all that use this
' custom with understanding, that a confes-
' sion of the principal doctrines of the Chri-
' stian faith, made by the person to be bap-
' tized, did, according to the first institution,
' precede baptism. But then the reason al-
' ledged by this sect, why they do not ob-
' serve this ancient custom, is, because, they
' say, there are no footsteps of this practice
' to be found in the scriptures; neither can
' they

APPENDIX. 67

'they trace the original of it any higher than
'the time mentioned in the *Roman* breviary,
'in their service, the 11th day of *January*,
'celebrated in memory of *Hyginus* bishop of
'*Rome, Anno Christi* 153. who is therein ac-
'knowledged to be the first institutor of suf-
'ceptors in baptism; and is so also by the
'concurrent testimony of other historians.

'AND it is further alledged by them, as
'very probable, that *Tertullian*'s admonition   Tert. *lib. de*
'concerning the deferring of infants baptism   *Bapt. cap.* 11.
'till they could answer for themselves, rather
'than to admit them to it by such underta-
'kers, was occasioned by this novel inven-
'tion of *Hyginus*; the one of them living till
'toward the latter end of the second century,
'and the other at the same time, or about the
'beginning of the third.

'2. THAT practice*, which at first was
'generally admitted by all sorts of converts
'to the faith, *Jews* and *Gentiles*, in all places
'at the same time, and in a continued succes-
'sion from the beginning, without any dis-
'pute or disagreement, *Scil.* to baptize such
'as manifested a joyful reception of the word
'of grace, and made a confession of their
'faith, is to be preferred, as agreeing with
'the first institution and primitive state of the
'Christian church; before that other pra-

---

* It is related by father *Vansleb*. in his *French* history of the church of *Alexandria*, ch. xxxiii. That *Amba Macaire*, bishop of *Memphis*, secretary to *Cosmus*, the third of that name, patriarch to the *Cophti*, or Christians of *Egypt*, who liv'd in the eighth *century*, says, *That in the primitive times, baptism was not administer'd in the church of* Alexandria, *but once a year, and that upon* Good-friday; *and only to those of thirty years of age.*

'ctice,

APPENDIX.

'ctice, *Scil.* admitting infants to baptism by
'sponsors; which obtained but by degrees,
'and in some places before others; and
'which from the first mention of that use,
'successively for several ages, if not to this
'very age, hath been questioned, disputed,
'and sometimes omitted by Christian parents,
'of some who afterwards were of great emi-
'nency in the church, who were not baptized
'until they were adult, although infant bap-
'tism was then admitted by others; as ap-
'pears in the history of their lives, *viz.*
'*Gregory Nazianzen, Chrysostom, Constan-
'tine, Ambrose* and *Augustine.*

Hieron. *in* Matt. xxviii.
'FIRST teach all nations, then dip the
'taught in water; for it cannot be that the
'body should receive the sacrament of baptism,
'unless the soul first receive the truth of faith.

Basil, *mag. de spiritu sancto, cap.* 12.
'THE confession of salvation goes before;
'then follows baptism, sealing our covenant.

Concilium Laodiceum, Anno 364.
'THOSE who are to be baptized ought to
'learn and repeat the creed to the bishop or
'presbyter.

'THIS canon was confirmed in *Constan-
'tine*'s time, at the sixth general synod at
'*Trullo.* Canon 46.

Apolog. Justin Martyr *to the emp.* Antonio.
'As many as believe the things preached
'by the Christians to be true, and promise to
'live accordingly, are taught to fast and
'pray, for the remission of their sins, the
'church also praying and fasting with them;
'and then they are brought to a place
'where water is, and are baptized; then
'they are brought and added to the church
'and receive the Lord's-supper.

Lud. Vives *in* Aug. *lib.* 1. *de Civ. Dei, c.* 27.
'NONE but the adult of antient time were
'used to be baptized.

'THE

APPENDIX.

' The words of *Tertullian* and *Nazianzen*, ' shew it was long before all were agreed ' the time or necessity of baptizing infants ' before the use of reason, in case they were ' like to live to maturity. [Baxter. *more proofs, p.* 279.]

3. That form of baptizing which is ' according to the common acceptation of the ' word and usage of the Christian church in ' its primitive state, and represents all the ma-' terial points of Christian doctrine, whereof ' it is a type, *Scil.* dipping the person bap-' tized in water, to signify his death unto sin, ' purification and resurrection unto newness ' of life, is to be observed rather than any ' other form; which agrees only with one ' thing thereby signified, *Scil.* purification, ' which is mentioned (*Let us draw near with ' a true heart, in full assurance of faith, ha-' ving our hearts sprinkled from an evil con-' science, and our bodies washed with pure wa-' ter*) ' rather as the effect than form of bap-' tism. There appearing no reason why this ' word, by which this ordinance was institu-' ted, should be therein taken in any other ' than a literal sense; and if it be well ob-' served, it may appear, where-ever this word ' is used in the scriptures in a metaphorical ' sense, thereby is represented an overwhelm-' ing, plunging, or large pouring on, whe-' ther it be of sufferings, conferring spiritual ' gifts, or the *Israelites* passing through the ' bottom of the sea, and no where to signify ' sprinkling. It is affirmed by this sect, that ' herein they have the concurrent testimony ' of many learned and approved expositors, ' of those passages of scripture where this ' word is to be taken in a figurative sense. [Sir Norton Knatchbull, *at large in his notes on* 1 Pet. iii. 21. Ambros. *de initiand. c.* 3. Bern. *ser.* 46. Heb. x. 22.]

' Cle-

APPENDIX.

'CLEMENT the 5th is cited for the first, who at the second synod at *Ravenna*, *Anno* 1305, approved, that baptism might be given, no necessity compelling, by sprinkling.

Bugenhagius Pomeranius, *circa finem libelli* Germanician 1542. *editi.*

'JOHANNES *Bugenhagius Pomeranus*, when he saw at *Hamburgh*, an infant brought to baptism, wrapped up in swadling clothes, and water sprinkled upon its head, was amazed; for that except in the case of necessity, for persons sick in their beds, he had neither seen nor heard, nor in any history read of any such thing. Whereupon there being a convocation of all the ministers, it was asked of Mr. *John Fritz*, who had been formerly minister at *Lubeck*, how baptism was there administer'd? who answer'd, infants were there, as in all *Germany*, baptized naked; but he was ignorant how that peculiar manner of baptizing had crept in at *Hamburgh*. At length it was agreed amongst them, that they should send to know the opinion of *Luther*, and the divines at *Wirtenberg* in this matter. Which being done, *Luther* writ back to *Hamburgh*, that this sprinkling was an abuse which ought to be removed, that thereupon immersion was restored at *Hamburgh*.

Monsieur de la Roque, *minister of the reformed church at* Roan.

'A learned *French Protestant*, in answer to the treatise of bishop *Bossuet*, *De communione sub utrâque specie*, answers to an objection concerning the *Protestants* baptizing by sprinkling. That it is true they do so, but that it is certainly an abuse; and that this practice which they have retained from the church of *Rome*, without well examining it, renders their baptism very defective.

'THERE-

'THEREIN is corrupted the inftitution,
'and the ancient cuftom, and the refemblance
'which it ought to have with faith, repen-
'tance, and regeneration. Monfieur *Boffuet*'s
'remark, that plunging had been ufed for
'thirteen hundred years, deferves a ferious re-
'flection.

'IT was very ill done to abolifh the firft
'ufage authorized by fo much ftrength of
'reafon, and for fo many ages. We are
'obliged to return to the ancient practice of
'the church, and the inftitution of Jefus
'Chrift.

4. THEY further alledge, fays the cap-
'tain, that it appears by feveral paffages in
'ancient hiftory, that the variations which
'were made from the firft eftablifhed form
'of baptifm, did not arife from any doubt-
'ful fignification of the words, whereby this
'ordinance was inftituted; but from other
'collateral confiderations, *viz.* The danger
'of perfons, young or old, dying unbapti-
'zed; and thereupon the pouring or fprink-
'ling water upon them in their beds, whence,
'by reafon of ficknefs they could not rife,
'nor without hazard of a real, inftead of a
'reprefentative dying, be baptized in any
'other manner.

'OF this there needs no other evidence *Magn. apud*
'than the many queftions which were moved. Cyprian, *epift.*
'Whether their baptifm might be efteemed Corn. *ad* Fa-
'lawful or compleat, who were baptized only Niceph. *lib.* 6.
'by fprinkling or pouring on of water? which *cap.* 3.
'received no other anfwer, but that neceffity
'urging, it might be fo efteemed.

'My lord, fays the captain, I am mind-
'ful of your direction, not to be prolix;
'and

APPENDIX.

'and have therefore omitted many material
' quotations; which if you will please to read
' a few pages, you will find, in Dr. *Duveil*'s
' treatise on Chap. ii, viii, and xviii. of the
' *Acts*, exactly referred to, and much to the
' purpose. It is not my intent to handle this
' point by way of controversy, but only to
' give some brief hints, that as the form
' of baptism has been varied upon other con-
' siderations than what appears in the insti-
' tution, so may it have been also with re-
' spect to the proper subject of baptism.

Mr. Claude's *Hist. defence*, Eng. transf. Part IV. p. 100.

' THE reverend Mr. *Claude*, in his histo-
' rical defence of the reformation, answering
' to the objections of the author of prejudi-
' ces, about the validity of his baptism, cites
' this passage:' *The promise is made to us and
to our children; and to all that are afar
off, even as many as the Lord shall call*;
' and says, That by a necessary consequence,
' the seal of that promise, which is baptism,
' and all the other rights of the covenant of
' Jesus Christ, belongs to us, and to our
' children; that is to say, to the truly faith-
' ful. I will not undertake, says he, to ex-
' plain Mr. *Claude*'s meaning in these expres-
' sions, nor to set forth the extent of the cove-
' nant which he mentions.

Nehem. Cox on the cove-nants; printed at London, 1683. cited by Duveil, on Acts ii. 41.

' THERE is a short treatise, published by
' Mr. *Nehemiah Cox*, concerning the cove-
' nants before the law, on this subject, which
' may give some light into this matter.

' THERE may be a great difference be-
' tween a direct, immediate, and a remote
' right to what is comprehended in, or be-
' longs to a covenant, not to insist any thing
' on the impropriety or congruity of a seal,

' as

APPENDIX.

‘ as applied to the covenant of grace under
‘ its various miniſtrations. *David*'s ſon by
‘ *Bathſheba*, in the time of the law, dying
‘ at ſeven days old, had no right to circum-
‘ ciſion. *Shem* and *Lot* were contemporary
‘ with *Abraham*; *Job* and his friends, as is
‘ ſuppoſed, with *Moſes*, all true worſhippers
‘ of God, and within the covenant of grace;
‘ yet nothing is ſpoken of circumciſion be-
‘ longing to them, or any of their poſterity.

‘ In the reſolution of the caſe by the Apo- 1 Cor. vii.
‘ ſtle ſaint *Paul*, concerning the cohabitation
‘ of a believer with an unbeliever, in a mar-
‘ ried ſtate, it is determined by the Apoſtle,
‘ that the unbeliever is ſanctified by the be-
‘ liever; and thence he draws this inference,
‘ that their *children* were *holy*: Whence it
‘ ſeems plain, that to the procreation of an
‘ holy ſeed, in the Apoſtle's ſenſe, it was ne-
‘ ceſſary that both parents, as well the belie-
‘ ver as the unbeliever, in that conjunct ſtate
‘ of marriage, ſhould be alſo reputed holy.
‘ And therefore I do not diſcern how the iſſue
‘ of both theſe ſhould have any more im-
‘ mediate right from thence to baptiſm, than
‘ the unbelieving parent. And if *Chriſtiani*
‘ *fideles*, and *baptizati*, were anciently terms
‘ promiſcuonſly uſed one for the other; then
‘ it may ſeem by that character, amongſt
‘ others given by *Paul* to *Titus*, of a perſon Tit. i. 6.
‘ to be choſen an elder, having believing Τέκια ἔχων
‘ children, that it was not a common caſe for πιςα.
‘ all Chriſtian parents to have all their chil-
‘ dren accounted faithful, and conſequently
‘ baptized. But whenſoever it proved ſo, it
‘ was a great evidence of a right and ſucceſs-
‘ ful education in the fear of God, as was
‘ that

2 Tim. i. 4, 5.
2 John v. 4.
'that of *Timothy*, and ground of rejoicing
'to the servants of God; as were those *chil-*
'*dren of the elect lady*, that walked in the
'truth.

'BUT, my lord, my province, says the
'captain, is only to repeat briefly what oc-
'curs to mind in defence of their opinion and
'practice, who are stiled *Anabaptists*; and
'otherwise than what may be presumed of
'necessary consequence, if the terms and
'forms of this ordinance be strictly limited;
'not to intermeddle with the opinion of any
'that teach otherwise, but leave them therein,
'as I ought to do, to stand or fall to their
'own master.

Greg. magn.
lib. 1. ep. 37.
'THE *Anabaptists*, in their own case, do
'say, It is an opinion that the ancients held,
'that what cannot be shewed by certain signs
'to be rightly performed, cannot be said to
'be repeated.

Scotus, in
4 sent. dist. 3.
q. 2 N°. 10.
'IN all doubtful cases, as to matter and
'form, there are three special things to be
'observed,

'1. IF possible to chuse the most safe way.
'2. IF it be not possible to keep that which
'is next to the safest.
'3. THE impossibility ceasing, to sup-
'ply warily what that did for the season pro-
'hibit.

Forbesius
Scoto. Britan.
instruct. hist.
lib. 10. can. 4.
Num. xxx.
'THERE is no doubt but they are again
'to be baptized, who were not dip'd in the
'true sacrament of baptism.

Ordo Roma-
nus de ritibus
ecclesiast.
'To conclude, Whoever undertakes to
'write against the ancient manner of instru-
'cting or confession preceding baptism,
'or form used in baptizing, hath this task
'incum-

'incumbent upon him; To give some other *Sittridus O-*
'proper interpretation of the words of insti- *thonis presby-*
'tution, ancient manner of *catechumens*, use *ter assistens*
'of large *baptisteria* and *Lavacres*, and of *lib. 2. c. 15.*
'the methods and care described for the de- Salmasius *in*
'cent administration of this ordinance, than *epist. ad* Andr.
'is hitherto extant in the frequent mention Calvin. *scrip.*
'of these things in antiquity. *cal. Jul.* 1644.

'IF I have, says the captain, through in-
'advertency, erred in any quotations, or in
'any thing not answered your lordship's ex-
'pectation: I humbly beg your lordship's
'pardon. And if it may be without trouble
'to your lordship, that I may, by the mean-
'est of your servants, receive your lordship's
'further commands herein; they shall readi-
'ly be obeyed by

Your Lordship's

obliged and obedient servant,

RICH. DEANE.

NUMB.

APPENDIX.

NUMB. IV.

A Brief CONFESSION *or* DECLARATION *of* FAITH, *lately presented to king Charles the second; set forth by many of us, who are falsly called* Anabaptists, *to inform all men, in these days of scandal and reproach, of our innocent Belief and Practice; for which we are not only resolved to suffer persecution to the loss of our goods, but also life it self, rather than to decline the same. Subscribed by certain* Elders, Deacons, *and* Brethren, *met at* London *in the behalf of themselves, and many others unto whom they belong, in* London, *and in several Counties of this Nation, who are of the same* Faith *with us.*

I. E believe, and are very confident, That there is but one God the Father, of whom are all things, from everlasting to everlasting, glorious and unwordable in all his attributes. 1 *Cor.* viii. 6. *Isa.* xl. 28.

II. THAT God in the beginning made man *upright*, and put him into a state and condition of glory, without the least mixture of misery; from which he, by *transgression*, fell, and so came into a miserable and mortal estate, subject unto the first death. *Gen.* i. 31.

APPENDIX. 77

i. 31. *Eccles.* vii. 29. *Gen.* ii. 17. and iii. 17, 18, 19.

III. THAT there is one Lord Jesus Christ, by whom are all things, who is the only begotten Son of God, born of the virgin *Mary*; yèt as truly *David*'s lord, and *David*'s root, as *David*'s son and *David*'s off-spring; whom God freely *sent into the world*, because of his great love unto the world; who as freely *gave himself a ransom for all; tasting death for every man; a propitiation for our sins; and not for ours only, but also for the sins of the whole world.* Luke xx. 24. Rev. xxii. 16. 1 Tim. ii. 5, 6. 1 John ii. 2. Heb. ii. 9.

IV. THAT *God is not willing that any should perish, but that all should come to repentance,* 2 Pet. iii. 9. *and the knowledge of the truth that they might be saved,* 1 Tim. ii. 4. For which end Christ hath commanded that the gospel (to wit, the glad tidings of remission of sins) should be preached to every creature, *Mark* xvi. 15. So that no man shall eternally suffer in hell (that is, the second death) for want of a Christ that died for them; but, as the scripture saith, *for denying the Lord that bought them,* 2 Pet. ii. 1. or because they *believe not in the name of the only begotten Son of God,* John iii. 18. Unbelief therefore being the cause why the just and righteous God, will condemn the children of men; it follows, against all contradiction, that all men, at one time or other, are put into such a capacity, as that (through the grace of God) they may be eternally saved. *John* i. 7. *Acts* xvii. 30. *Mark* vi. 6. *Heb.* iii. 10, 18, 19. 1 *John.* v. 10. *John* iii. 17.

V.

APPENDIX.

V. THAT such who first orderly comes into, and are brought up in the school of Christ's church, and waiting there, comes to degrees of Christianity, rightly qualified, and considerably gifted by God's Spirit, ought to exercise their gifts, not only in the church, but also (as occasion serves) to preach to the world (they being approved of by the church so to do) *Acts* xi. 22, 23, 24. *ch.* xi. 19, 20. and that among such some are to be chosen by the church, and ordained by fasting, prayer, and laying on of hands, for the work of the ministry. *Acts* xiii. 2, 3. and i. 23. Such so ordained (and abiding faithful in their works) we own as ministers of the gospel; but all such who come not first to repent of their sins, believe on the Lord Jesus, and so *baptized* in his name for the remission of sins, but are only brought up in the schools of human learning, to the attaining human arts, and variety of languages, with many vain curiosities of speech, 1 *Cor.* i. 19, 21. 2 *Cor.* ii. 1, 4, 5. seeking rather the gain of large revenues, than the gain of souls to God: Such (we say) we utterly deny, being such as have need rather to be taught themselves, than fit to teach others. *Rom.* ii. 21.

VI. THAT the way set forth by God for men to be justified in, is by faith in Christ, *Rom.* v. 1. That is to say, When men shall assent to the truth of the gospel, believing, with all their hearts, that there is remission of sins, and eternal life to be had in Christ. And that Christ therefore is most worthy their constant affections, and subjection to all his commandments; and therefore resolve, with purpose

APPENDIX. 79

pofe of heart, fo to fubject unto him in all things, and no longer unto themfelves. 2 *Cor.* v. 15. And fo fhall (with all godly forrow for the fins paft) commit themfelves to his grace, confidently depending upon him, for that which they believe is to be had in him: Such fo believing are juftified from all their fins, their faith fhall be accounted unto them for righteoufnefs. *Rom.* iv. 22, 23, 24. and iii. 25, 26.

VII. THAT there is one holy Spirit, the precious gift of God, freely given to fuch as *obey him,* Eph. iv. 4. Acts v. 32. that thereby they may be thoroughly fanctified, and made able (without which they are altogether unable) to abide ftedfaft in the faith, and to honour the Father, and his Son Chrift, the author and finifher of their faith. 1 *Cor.* vi. 11. There are three that bear record in heaven; the Father, the Word, the Holy Spirit, and thefe three are one, 1 *John* v. 7. which fpirit of promife fuch have not yet received (though they fpeak much of him) that are fo far out of *love, peace, long-fuffering, gentlenefs, goodnefs, meeknefs, and temperance (the fruits of the Spirit,* Gal. v. 22, 23.) as that they breath out much cruelty, and great envy againft the liberties, and peaceable living of fuch as are not of their judgment, though holy as to their converfations.

VIII. THAT God hath, even before *the foundation of the world, chofen* (or elected) *to eternal life, fuch as believe,* and fo are in Chrift, *John* iii. 16. *Eph.* i. 4. 2 *Theff.* ii. 13. yet confident we are, that the purpofe of God, according to election, was not in the leaft arifing from forefeen faith in, or works
of

of righteousness done by the creature, but only from the mercy, goodness, and compassion dwelling in God, and so *it is of him that calleth*, Rom. ix. 11. whose purity and unwordable holiness cannot admit of any unclean person (or thing) to be in his presence; therefore his decree of mercy reaches only the godly man, whom (saith *David*) God *hath set apart for himself*, Psal. iv. 3.

IX. THAT men not consider'd simply as men, but ungodly men, *were of old ordained to condemnation*, consider'd as such, who turn the grace of God into wantonness, and deny the only Lord God, and our Lord Jesus Christ, *Jude* 4. God indeed sends a strong delusion to men, that they might be damned, but we observe that they are such (as saith the Apostle) that *received not the love of the truth, that they might be saved*, 2 Thess. ii. 10, 11, 12. and so the indignation and wrath of God, is upon *every soul* of man, that doth *evil*, living and dying therein, *for there is no respect of persons with God*, Rom. ii. 9, 10, 11.

X. THAT all children dying in infancy, having not actually transgressed against the law of God in their own persons, are only subject to the first death, which comes upon them by the sin of the first *Adam*, from whence they shall be all raised by the second *Adam*; and not that any one of them (dying in that estate) shall suffer for *Adam*'s sin, eternal punishment in hell (which is the second death) *for to such belongs the kingdom of heaven*, 1 Cor. xv. 22. Matt. xix. 14. not daring to conclude with that uncharitable opinion of others, who though they plead much for

APPENDIX.

for the bringing of children into the visible church here on earth by *baptism*; yet nevertheless, by their doctrine, that Christ died but for some, shut a great part of them out of the kingdom of heaven for ever.

XI. THAT the right and only way of gathering churches (according to Christ's appointment, *Matt.* xxviii. 19, 20.) is first to teach, or preach the gospel, *Mark* xvi. 16. to the sons and daughters of men; and then to *baptize* (that is, in *English*, to *dip*) in the name of the Father, Son, and Holy Spirit, or in the name of the Lord Jesus Christ, such only of them as profess *repentance towards God, and faith towards our Lord Jesus Christ.* Acts ii. 38. ch. viii. 12. ch. xviii. 8. And as for all such who preach not this doctrine, but instead thereof, that scriptureless thing of sprinkling of infants (*falsly called baptism*) whereby the *pure word of God is made of no effect*, and the New Testament way of bringing in members into the church by regeneration, cast out; when as the bond woman and her son, that is to say, the Old Testament way of bringing in children into the church by generation is cast out, as faith the scripture, *Gal.* iv. 22, 23, 24, 30. *Matt.* iii. 8, 9. All such we utterly deny; forasmuch as we are commanded to *have no fellowship with the unfruitful works of darkness, but rather to reprove them*, Eph. v. 11.

XII. THAT it is the duty of all such who are believers baptized, to draw nigh unto God in submission to that principle of Christ's doctrine, to wit, prayer, and laying on of hands, that they may receive the promise of the holy Spirit. *Heb.* vi. 1, 2. *Acts* viii. 12, 15, 17. *ch.* xix. 6. 2 *Tim.* i. 6. Whereby they may *mortify the deeds of the body*, Rom. viii. 13. and live in all things answerable to their professed intentions and desires, even to the honour of him, *who hath called them out of darkness into his marvellous light.*

XIII. THAT it is the duty of such, who are constituted as aforesaid, to continue stedfastly in Christ's and the Apostle's doctrine, and assembling together, in fellowship, in breaking of bread and prayers, *Acts* ii. 42.

XIV. THAT although we thus declare for the primitive way and order of constituting churches; yet we verily believe, and also declare, that unless men so professing and practising the form and order of Christ's doctrine, shall also beautify the same with a holy and wise conversation, in all godliness and honesty; the profession of the visible form will be render'd to them of no effect; *for without holiness no man shall see the Lord*, Heb. xii. 14. *Isa.* i. 11, 12, 15, 16.

XV. THAT the elders or pastors which God hath appointed to oversee, and feed his church (constituted as aforesaid) are such, who first being of the number of disciples, shall in time appear to be *vigilant, sober, of good behaviour, given to hospitality, apt to teach,* &c. *not greedy of filthy lucre* (as too many national ministers are) *but patient; not a brawler, not covetous*, &c. and as such chose, and ordained to office (according to the order of scripture, *Acts* xiv. 23.) who are to feed the flock with meat in due season, and in much love to rule over them with all care,

seek-

seeking after such as go astray: but as for all such who labour to feed themselves with the fat, more than to feed the flock, *Ezek.* xxxiv. 2, 3. seeking more after theirs than them, expresly contrary to the practice of the ministers of old, who said, *we seek not yours but you*, 2 Cor. xii. 14. All such we utterly deny, and hereby bear our continued testimony against them, as such whom the prophets of old bore testimony against. *Ezek.* xxxiv.

XVI. THAT the ministers of Christ tha have freely received from God, ought freely to minister to others, 1 *Cor.* ix. 17. and that such who have spiritual things freely minister'd to them, ought freely to communicate necessary things to the ministers (upon the account of their charge) 1 *Cor.* ix. 11. *Gal.* vi. 6. and as for tithes, or any forced maintenance, we utterly deny to be the maintenance of gospel ministers.

XVII. THAT the true church of Christ ought, after the first and second admonition, to reject all hereticks, *Tit.* iii. 10, 11. and in the name of the Lord to withdraw from all such as profess the way of the Lord, but walks disorderly in their conversations, 2 *Thess.* iii. 6. or any ways causes divisions or offences, contrary to the doctrine (of Christ) which they have learned, *Rom.* xvi. 17.

XVIII. THAT such who are true believers, even branches in Christ the Vine (and that in his account, whom he exhorts to abide in him, *John* xv. 1, 2, 3, 4, 5.) or such who have charity out of a pure heart, and of a good conscience, and of faith unfeigned, 1 *Tim.* i. 5. may nevertheless, for want of watchfulness, swerve and turn aside from the same, *ver.* 6, 7. and became as withered branches, cast into the fire and burned, *John* xv. 6. But such *who add unto their faith virtue, and unto virtue knowledge, and unto knowledge temperance,* &c. 2 *Pet.* i. 5, 6, 7. such *shall never fall,* ver. 8, 9, 10. 'tis impossible for all the false chrifts and false prophets that are, and are to come, to deceive such; for they are *kept by the power of God, through faith unto salvation,* 1 Pet. i. 5.

XIX. That the poor saints belonging to the church of Christ, are to be sufficiently provided for by the churches, that they neither want food or raiment; and this by a free and voluntary contribution, and not of necessity, or by the constraint or power of the magistrate, 2 *Cor.* ix. 7. 1 *Cor.* viii. 11, 12. and this through the free and voluntary help of the deacons (called overseers of the poor) being faithful men; chosen by the church, and ordained by prayer and laying on of hands to that work, *Acts* vi. 1, 2, 3, 4, 5, 6. So that there is no need in the church of Christ of a magisterial compulsion in this case, as there is among others, who being constituted in a fleshly and generational way, are necessitated to make use of a carnal sword, to compel even a small, mean, and short maintenance for their poor; when as many other members of their churches can and do part with great and large sums of money to maintain their vain fashions, gold, pearls, and costly array; which is expresly contrary to the word of God, 1 *Tim.* ii. 9, 10. 1 *Pet.* iii. 3. Alas, *What will such do when God riseth up? and when he visiteth, what will they answer him?* Job xxxi. 14.

XX.

APPENDIX.

XX. THAT there shall be (through Christ, who was dead, but is alive again from the dead) a resurrection of all men from the graves of the earth, *Isa.* xxvi. 19. both the just and the unjust, *Acts* xxiv. 15. that is, the fleshly bodies of men, sown into the graves of the earth, corruptible, dishonourable, weak, natural (which so considered, cannot inherit the kingdom of God) shall be raised again, incorruptible, in glory, in power, spiritual; and so considered, the bodies of the saints (united again to their spirits) which here suffer for Christ, shall inherit the kingdom, *reigning* together with Christ. 1 *Cor.* xv. 21, 22, 42, 43, 44, 49.

XXI. THAT there shall be after the resurrection from the graves of the earth, *an eternal judgment*, at the appearing of Christ and his kingdom, 2 *Tim.* iv. 1. *Heb.* ix. 27. at which time of judgment, which is unalterable, and irrevocable, every man shall receive according to the things done in his body, 2 *Cor.* v. 10.

XXII. THAT the same Lord Jesus who shewed himself alive after his passion, by many infallible proofs, *Acts* i. 3. which was taken up from the disciples, and carried up into heaven, *Luke* xxiv. 51. *shall so come in like manner as he was seen go into heaven*, Acts i. 9, 10, 11 *And when Christ, who is our life, shall appear, we shall also appear with him in glory*, Col. iii. 4. *For then shall he be King of kings, and Lord of lords*, Rev. xix. 16. *For the kingdom is his, and he is the Governor among the nations*, Psal. xxii. 28. *and king over all the earth*, Zech. xiv. 9.

and we shall reign with him on the earth, Rev. v. 10. The kingdoms of this world (which men so mightily strive after here to enjoy) shall become the kingdoms of our Lord, and his Christ, *Rev.* xi. 15. *For all is yours* (O ye that overcome this world) *for ye are Christ's, and Christ is God's,* 1 Cor. iii. 22, 23. *For unto the saints shall be given the kingdom, and the greatness of the kingdom, under* (mark that) *the whole heaven,* Dan. vii. 27. Though (alas) now many men be scarce content that the saints should have so much as a being among them; but when Christ shall appear, then shall be their day, then shall be given unto them power over the nations, to rule them with a rod of iron, *Rev.* ii. 26, 27. Then shall they receive a crown of life, which no man shall take from them, nor they by any means turned, or overturned from it; for the oppressor shall be broken in pieces, *Psal.* lxxii. 4. and their now vain rejoicings turned into mourning and bitter lamentations; as it is written, *Job* xx. 5, 6, 7. *The triumphing of the wicked is short, and the joy of the hypocrite but for a moment: though his excellency mount up to the heavens, and his head reach unto the clouds, yet shall he perish for ever, like his own dung; they which have seen him, shall say, Where is he?*

XXIII. THAT the holy scripture is the rule whereby saints, both in matters of faith and conversation, are to be regulated; they being *able to make men wise unto salvation, through faith in Christ Jesus; profitable for doctrine, for reproof, for instruction in righteousness,*

APPENDIX.

teoufnefs, that the men of God may be perfect, throughly furnished unto all good works, 2 Tim. iii. 15, 16, 17. John xx. 31. Ifa. viii. 20.

XXIV. THAT it is the will and mind of God (in thefe gofpel times) that all men fhould have the free liberty of their own *confciences* in matters of religion or worfhip, without the leaft oppreffion or perfecution, as fimply upon that account; and that for any in authority otherwife to act, we confidently believe is exprefly contrary to the mind of Chrift; who requires, that *whatfoever men would that others fhould do unto them, they fhould even fo do unto others*, Matt. vii. 12. and that the tares and the wheat fhould grow together in the field (which is the world) until the harveft (which is the end of the world) *Matt.* xiii. 29, 30, 38, 39.

XXV. WE believe, That there ought to be civil magiftrates in all nations, *for the punifhment of evil doers, and for the praife of them that do well,* 1 Pet. ii. 14. and that all wicked lewdnefs and flefhly filthinefs, contrary to juft and wholfome (civil) laws, ought to be punifhed according to the nature of the offences; and this without refpect of any perfons, religion, or profeffion whatfoever; and that we, and all men are obliged by gofpel rules, *to be fubject to the higher powers, to obey magiftrates*, Tit. iii. 1. *and to fubmit to every ordinance of man for the Lord's fake,* as faith *Pet.* ii. 13. But in cafe the civil power do, or fhall at any time impofe things about matters of religion, which we, through confcience to God, cannot actually obey; then

APPENDIX.

we, with *Peter* also, do say, That we ought in such cases *to obey God rather than men,* Acts v. 29. and accordingly do hereby declare our whole and holy intent and purpose, That through the help of grace we will not yield, nor in such cases in the least actually obey them; yet humbly purposing, in the Lord's strength, patiently to suffer whatsoever shall be inflicted upon us for our conscionable forbearance.

These things, O ye sons and daughters of men, we verily believe to be the Lord's will and mind, and therefore cannot but speak! And if herein we differ from many, yea, from multitudes, from the learned, the wise and prudent of this world, we, with *Peter* and *John,* do herein make our solemn and serious appeal; namely, *Whether it be right in the sight of God to hearken unto men* (of a contrary persuasion) *more than unto God.* O let the judicious judge righteous judgment, *Acts* iv. 19, 20. And in the belief and practice of these things, it being the good old apostolical way, our souls have found that rest and soul peace which the world knows not, and which they cannot take from us. Of whom then shall we be afraid? *God is become our strength, our light, our salvation*; therefore are we resolved, through grace, to seal the truth of these things, in a way of suffering persecution; not only to the loss of our goods, freedoms, or liberties, but with our lives also, if called thereunto.

Moreover we do utterly, and from our very hearts, in the Lord's fear, declare against
all

all those wicked and devilish reports, and reproaches, falsly cast upon us, as though some of us (in and about the city of *London*) had lately *gotten knives, hooked knives*, and the like, and great store of arms besides what was given forth by order of parliament, intending to cut the throats of such as were contrary minded to us in matters of religion; and that many such *knives* and arms, for the carrying on some secret design, hath been found in some of our houses by search: We say, from truth of heart, in the Lord's fear, that we do utterly abhor, and abominate the thoughts thereof, and much more the actions; and do hereby challenge both city and country (in our innocency herein) as being not able to prove the things whereof they accuse us; and do for evermore declare the inventors of such reports, to be lyars, and wicked devisers of mischief, and corrupt designs. God that is above all will justify our innocency herein, who well knows our integrity in what we here declare, the Lord lay it not to their charge. In the time of building the decay'd house of God, *Sanballat* and *Tobiah (wicked counsellors) hired* Shemaiah, *to make good* Nehemiah *afraid*; and laboured against him, that they might have *matter for an evil report*; that they might reproach him, and hinder the building of the house of God, *Neh.* vi. 12. *For I have heard*, saith the prophet, *the defaming of many*; *Report, say they, and we will report it,* Jer. xx. 10.

SUBSCRIBED by certain Elders, Deacons and Brethren, met at *London*, in the first month called *March*, 1660. in the behalf of

APPENDIX.

of themselves, and many others unto whom they belong in *London*, and in several counties of this nation who are of the same faith with us,

Joseph Wright,	*William Russell*,
William Jeffery,	*Joseph Keech*,
Thomas Monk,	*Nicholas Newbery*,
John Hartnol,	*Samuel Lover*,
Benjamin Morley,	*George Wright*,
Francis Stanley,	*John Parsons*, jun.
George Hammon,	*Thomas Grantham*,
William Smart,	*John Claton*,
John Reeve,	*Thomas Seele*,
Thomas Parrot,	*Michael Whitticar*,
John Wood,	*Giles Brown*,
Francis Smith,	*John Wells*,
Edward Jones,	*Stephen Torie*,
Humphry Jones,	*Thomas Lathwel*,
Matthew Caffen,	*William Chadwel*,
Samuel Loveday,	*William Raph*,
John Parsons, sen.	*Henry Browne*,
Thomas Stacey,	*William Paine*,
Edward Stanly,	*Richard Bowin*,
Jonathan Jennings,	*Thomas Smith*.
John Hammersly,	

Owned and approved by more than twenty thousand.

London, printed for FRANCIS SMITH, at the *Elephant* and *Castle*, near *Temple Bar*. M.DC.LX.

APPENDIX.

NUMB. V.

A DECLARATION *of a small society of baptized Believers, undergoing the name of* Free-willers, *about the city of* London.

E well knowing that we are and have been misrepresented to the people of this and other nations, as well by particular letters from friend to friend, as by publick intelligence in pamphlets and news books, by which means we have been render'd odious in the eyes of almost all, and as it were made a by word, and a hissing to all. Were notwithstanding willing, according to the requirement of our Saviour, *In our patience to* Luke xxi. 19. *possess our souls,* and silently to wait upon our God, for a clearing of our innocency, and the cleanness of our hands in his eye-sight; but lately having had a view of a declaration, dated the 12th of *December* last, made by some persons of the particular judgment; in which some others of another persuasion have joined, to the which, in several particulars, we cannot in the least assent to; we therefore thought it our bounden duty, for the vindication of that truth which we are in present profession and practice of; as also fearing, lest they having declared to publick view, we by our silence should be looked upon either to be of the same judgment with them in what they have declared, or else guilty of all or some of those five particulars they in that declaration say the Baptists in general are

charged

charged withal, have therefore set pen to paper, and shall first give a particular of the said five charges; and then, as in the presence of God, lay down our real judgments and persuasions grounded upon scripture record, to those charges; by which it will be apparent that we are not guilty of them at all, and that we differ from the said declarers in point of judgment: and if we shall in any thing therein derogate from the mind of God, we shall desire, in the spirit of love, to be rectified by better judgments from the word of truth; and shall think our selves happy gainers in such a Christian reproof. Say they, we being misrepresented to the nation,

1. As *such as are opposite to magistracy.*
2. THAT *we would destroy the publick ministry of the nation, who differ from us in some things about religion.*
3. THAT *we do countenance the people called* Quakers *in their irregular practice.*
4. THAT *we do endeavour a toleration of all miscarriages in things ecclesiastical and civil, under pretence of liberty of conscience.*
5. THAT *we desire to murder and destroy those that differ from us in matters of religion.*

To the *first*, we positively say, That we are so far from opposing magistracy, as that it would be to us matter of great rejoicing to know who were our magistrates; but far greater to see such set up who are men fearing God, and hating covetousness, that so justice might be duly executed without respect

APPENDIX.

spect of persons, and judgment run down like water, and righteousness like a mighty stream, that so there might be no more leading into captivity, and that complaining in our streets might have an end. But for our parts, to take a carnal weapon in our hands, or use the least violence, either to support or pull down the worst, or to set up or maintain the best of men, we look not upon it to be our duty in the least; much less to have a thought of endeavouring to set up our selves, either directly or indirectly; for were we abilitated and furnished with such endowments as might render us capable of being rulers, yet could we not allow our selves to act as magistrates, because we are a people *chosen out of the world*, and look upon our selves *as pilgrims and strangers in the earth*. But this we know to be the mind of God, that we are to be *subject to, and not to resist the powers*, because they be *ordained of God*; and as God sets them up, so he requires his sons and daughters to render unto them *tribute, custom, fear and honour*. And we further declare, That it is our bounden duty in obedience to our God, to *pray for kings, and all that are in authority*. So that we are so far from opposing them, as that we say it is our duty to obey them in all civil things that are agreeable to the mind of God; and if they shall require any thing from us that is contrary to his mind and will revealed in his holy scriptures of truth, we say, we are not to resist them; but if in conscience we cannot obey them, then we are patiently to suffer under them, whatever they shall inflict upon us for our non-obedience to their requirements; and

John xv. 19.
Heb. xi. 17.
1 Pet. ii. 11.
Rom. xiii. *beg.*
1 Pet. ii. 13.
Tit. iii. 2.
Rom. xiii. 7.
1 Tim. ii. 2.

to this we yet further declare, That it is our real judgment as to things fpiritual, not to own them as our lawgivers in the leaft; *for there is one Lawgiver which is able to fave and to deftroy*, which is the Lord; and therefore if they fhall at any time impofe upon us laws in point of worfhip; that is, either to worfhip a falfe god, or the true God after a falfe manner; we, by God's affiftance, fhall tell them, with *Shadrach, Meshech* and *Abednego*, That we are not careful to anfwer them in that matter, yet fhall not violently refift, but with them patiently fuffer under them as aforefaid.

James iv. 12.
Ifa. xxxiii. 22.

Dan. iii. 16

To the *fecond, That we would deftroy the publick miniftry of the nation, that differ from us about fome things in religion*. We do declare, That if there be a deftruction intended between us, we muft leave it at their doors, and defire them to judge between the all-feeing God, the fearcher of all hearts, and their own confciences, what they have intended by their fo often prefling *parliament* men from time to time, for a fuppreffion of all, that are not of their judgment in matters of religion; and upon fearch made, if they find themfelves guilty of a defire of any fuch deftruction unto us, we fhall beg them in God's fear, to break off that evil by timely repentance, and make their peace with God: as for our parts, we are fo far from defiring any revenge againft them, or any other that fhall defire or endeavour our ruin; as that in the prefence of God we fhall rather pity than envy them, and, according to the requirement of our Lawgiver, *pray for them*, and their converfion, not at all in the leaft defiring or endeavouring their confufion. That there are

Matt. v. 44.

are many things wherein the publick miniſtry of the nation and we differ in matters of
religion, both in doctrine and diſcipline, is
very clear, and that we deſign or ſo much as
deſire the deſtruction of them, or any other
perſon whatſoever; for ſuch differences, or
any other matters concerning our ſelves, we
hope in our further anſwer to this, and to the
fourth and fifth particulars, we ſhall manifeſt
to be as clear, and alſo therein diſcover our
ſelves to be the *peaceable lambs of Chriſt, the* John xxi. 15.
great Shepherd and Biſhop of our ſouls, who 1 Pet. ii. 25.
doth require us to *learn of him, for he is lowly* —— v. 4.
and meek; yet notwithſtanding we do declare, Heb. x. 20.
Matt. xi.
when or whereſoever ſome of us ſhall conve-
niently meet with any of them, either in private or in publick, we ſhall reſolve (God
aſſiſting us) *to contend earneſtly with them for
the faith once delivered to the ſaints*, according to that exhortation of the Spirit of God
by his Apoſtle *Jude*, and againſt them, and Jude *ver.* 3.
all oppoſitions, and oppoſers whatſoever, as
good *ſoldiers of Jeſus Chriſt, fight the good* 2 Tim. ii. 3.
fight of faith; in which combat we are confi- 1 Tim. vi.12.
dent, we neither ſhall hazard life, nor draw
blood; for through mercy we can ſay with
our Apoſtle, That *though we live in the fleſh*, 2 Cor. x. 3,4.
*yet we war not after the fleſh; for the wea-
pons of our warfare are not carnal.*

To the *third*, That we countenance the people called Quakers *in their irregular practice*.
To this we anſwer, and God is our witneſs,
we lye not, that we are ſo far from counte-
nancing the *Quakers* our ſelves in any irregular practice, as that if we our ſelves be
found in any ſuch actings, we ſhall not violently oppoſe, but patiently ſubject to ſuch
penal-

penalties as the breach of such laws call for; it would have been well if the assertors had declared wherein this irregular practice doth consist, that so we might have given a more particular answer; yet we hope, by what hath and shall be declared, it will easily be judged, that we, for our parts, are no such people as the Baptists generally are reported, and some shew themselves to be.

To the *fourth, That we endeavour a toleration of all miscarriages in things ecclesiastical and civil, under pretence of liberty of conscience.* If by endeavouring a toleration of all miscarriages in things ecclesiastical, the assertors intend amongst our selves in our own assemblies, we shall answer them as in the presence of God, the Searcher of all hearts, that we are so far from any such toleration, as that we, at this very day, go under a reproach by that people we formerly walked withal; because in the reality of our souls, and the integrity of our hearts, we cannot allow of some things that we judge to be of that nature amongst them, we well knowing that the Lord Christ requires a perfect observation of, and a universal obedience to all things whatsoever he commanded; and that as well to what hath been laid down by his Apostles, given in by the incomes of that spirit that was to lead them into all truth, and to shew them things to come; which are also the commands of Christ, as to those that were laid down by himself: So that we positively say, That if we shall allow of any miscarriages either in doctrine or discipline amongst our selves, to thwart the mind of Christ, revealed in his scriptures of truth, we can expect no better

Matt. xxviii. 20.

John xvi. 13.
1 Cor. xiv. 37.
John xviii. 12, 15.

better anſwer for him, than a proclamation of our worſhip, to our vain worſhip, as once he declared againſt the *Jews*: And therefore, if miſcarriages ariſe amongſt us, we are to bring ſuch miſcarriages to the touchſtone of God's word, and ſo weigh them in the ballance of the ſanctuary, and finding them either too heavy or too light, that is, either adding or diminiſhing from or to the mind of Chriſt, we are then to repair to thoſe wholeſome laws left us in ſcripture record, for the regulating of ſuch miſcarriages according to the nature of them, as they are private or publick, or more or leſs in their ſeveral aggravations, and as they are committed by perſons ſtanding in ſuch or ſuch relations. We ſay the more of this, becauſe moſt perſons think, and many do not ſtick to ſay, that we live and act, in things eccleſiaſtical, as libertines, and without church government, becauſe we withdraw our ſelves from the publick aſſemblies. But did ſuch perſons rightly conſider what the diſcipline of the miniſtry of the nation is in their parochial aſſemblies, who profeſs themſelves to be the true ſpouſe and church of Chriſt, and compare it with the mind of Chriſt revealed in the ſcriptures of truth, who gives laws to his church, which is that body of which he himſelf is the head; they would then find themſelves to be the libertines, and not we: and therefore we ſhall earneſtly deſire all that are unacquainted with the true diſcipline of the church of Chriſt, well to weigh, and ſeriouſly to conſider the ſtatute laws of Chriſt, in that caſe provided; the which, as we will anſwer the contrary at the great day of account, we dare not in the leaſt willfully violate or neglect.

Matt. xv. 9.

Eph. iv. 15, 21, 22.
Col. i. 18.
—— ii. 19.

2 Tim. iii. 16.
—— iv. 1, 2.
Eph. v. 11.
Matt. xviii. 15.
1 Tim. v. 12, 19, 20.
—— vi. 5.
—— i. 20.

But

APPENDIX.

Tit. iii. 10.
2 Theff. ii. 15.
2 Theff. iii. 16.
1 Cor. v. 4, 9, 11.
—— v. 13.

But if by miscarriages in things ecclesiastical, they mean that we endeavour a toleration of all miscarriages amongst them in their assemblies, we shall, in the presence of God, clear our selves, and say, We have nothing at all to do with them in such matters; for we say, They are *without*, as to us, and so we look upon our selves to be as to them. And if any one shall seem to be troubled at this term *without*, and object and say, That we are all the creation of God, and what need those expressions of, *Stand at a distance, I am more holy than you*; to such we shall answer in the spirit of love and meekness, and God is our witness, without ostentation, that it is true, all the sons and daughters of *Adam*, are the sons and daughters of God by creation, but

Matt. xx. 16.

few by regeneration and adoption; for *many are called, but few chosen*; for not the

Rom. ii. 13.
Matt. vii. 21.

hearers of the law, but the doers shall be justified, and not every one that saith, *Lord, Lord, shall enter into the kingdom of heaven, but he that doth the will of the Father*; we well know, that many will say, These are hard sayings, and cannot well bear them: but to such we shall give a direction in our postscript, where from one of us they may expect, and we hope also find good satisfaction as to the term *without*.

THAT we own liberty of conscience, we confess, but under that or any other pretence, to endeavour a toleration of any miscarriages, either in things ecclesiastical or civil, we have given (we hope) full satisfaction; for seeing it is the will of our master, to have the tares

—— xiii. 30.

and the wheat grow together till the harvest; and that our heavenly Father doth exercise his

lnog-

APPENDIX.

long-suffering to the whole bulk of mankind, 2 Pet. iii. 9. *not willing that any should perish, but that all should come to repentance;* we look upon it to be our duty to follow God as *dear children,* Eph. v. 1, 2. and thus to *walk in love;* and therefore are *like* Phil. ii. 2. *minded, having the same love;* and therefore do further declare, That we are as free, that all others should enjoy their liberties as we our selves, of what judgment soever they be, we well knowing that some are called at the eleventh hour, as well as at the first and third. And had the Apostle *Paul* been Matt. xx. 1, 6. plucked up whilst he was a tare, a persecutor, a blasphemer, and the chief of sinners, 1 Tim. i. 13, he had never been such choice wheat, to sa- 15. tisfy, refresh, enable, enliven, enlighten, encourage, build up and instruct, correct and reprove, the building of God, the house of 1 Cor. iii. 9. God, the houshold of God, the sons and Heb. iii. 6. daughters of God, nor that body of which Eph. ii. 19. Christ is the head; and therefore we cannot Col. i. 18. but say again, that we are as free, that all others should enjoy their liberties in the things of God, as we our selves, we well knowing that every one must give an account of him- Rom. xiv. 12. self to God; *for every one shall receive the things done in the body according to what they* 1 Cor. v. 10. *have done, whether it be good or bad.* But Matt. xxv. 34, either to procure or maintain our own or 41. others liberties by force of arms, or the least violence, we can find no warrant from the scriptures of truth, in the least, which is that only and alone rule that we walk by; for all the remedy that we find there recorded is, that if they *persecute us in one city, we may flee into another;* and this we see acted by our John vii. 1. Saviour himself, and by his parents, and the Matt. ii. 14.

G 2 Apo-

Acts xii. 17. Apostle *Peter* and saint *Paul*. And to fol-
— ix. 25, low our Master, and to tread in the footsteps
26.
1 Cor. xi. 33. of the flock of God gone before us, we judge
is very safe; but to resist by force of arms, or
use the least violence, we judge unwarrantable.

To the *fifth* and *last* particular; *That we would murder and destroy those that differ from us in matters of religion.* To this we cannot but answer, That so to do, we judge were not so much as common humanity, much less religion or christianity; but our religion is *pure, and undefiled before God and our Father*, which is to *visit the fatherless and widows*; not to make fatherless and widows; and to visit them in their afflictions; not to murder and destroy their relations, to bring them under afflictions: But to this we further answer, That this and the fourth particular we judge seem to contradict one another; for murdering and destroying for difference in matters of religion and liberty of conscience, cannot stand together, nor in the eye of reason can they be charged against one and the same persons; for murdering and destroying for difference in matters of religion, destroys liberty of conscience, and liberty of conscience swallows up and drowns murdering and destroying for difference in matters of religion: so that it argues, that the assertors of these things are yet in *Babylon* and confusion, with those our Apo-
1 Tim. i. 7. stle writ of, not *knowing well what they say, nor whereof they do affirm*; yet, notwithstanding, seeing we are therewith charged, in order to the discharging our selves of this confused burden, we shall, in the singleness of our souls, yet further discover our real judgments, as to the main intent of the charge,

which

APPENDIX.

which is murdering and deftroying; and add this further, that we read of a threefold fword in fcripture.

(1.) THE fword of the fpirit, which is the word of God. *Eph. vi. 17.*

(2.) THE fword of juftice, which is the magiftrates fword. *Rom. xiii. 4.*

(3.) THE fword of fteel, ufually fo called, which is the fword of flaughter. *Ifa. i. 20. Ez. ix. 1, 2.*

THE *firft* of thefe we are required to take to us, and *put on,* and *thus to be ftrong in the Lord, and in the power of his might,* whofe might was evidenced once again and again, by ufing this fword fkilfully; *for it is mighty through God to the pulling down of ftrong holds, cafting down imaginations, and every high thing that exalteth it felf againft the knowledge of God, and bringing into captivity,* &c. and having in a readinefs *to revenge all difobedience,* and *is profitable for doctrine, for reproof, for correction, for inftruction in righteoufnefs, that the man of God may be perfect, throughly furnifhed unto all good works; for we wreftle not with flefh and blood, but againft principalities, powers, the rulers of the darknefs of this world;* not for nor againft the magiftrates, parliament, nor armies of the world, the beft of whofe ftrength is flefh and not fpirit, who fhall be deftroy'd together. *Eph. vi. 11, 13, 17. Matt. iv. 4, 7, 9. 2 Cor. x. 4, 5, 6. 2 Tim. iii. 16, 17. Eph. vi. 12. Ifa. xxxi. 1, 2, 3. Matt. xxvi. 58.*
As for the fword of juftice, or the magiftrates fword we are to be fubject to it, as we have fully declared, and not to refift it; which fword takes revenge on no man before he be apprehended, charged, heard, and by good evidence convicted, and fentence, according to the fact prov'd, given; and then an immediate commiffion given to an executioner,

according to the fact and sentence, for the putting this sword in execution.

But the sword of slaughter, without examination or due consideration, is, many times, put in execution to the slaying and destroying of friends as well as enemies, witness those slaughters and woundings in this city in the late insurrection.

And for our acting in this sword, we can find no warrant from scripture in the least; for that sword being once procured by *Peter*, and another of the disciples, and that by an immediate commission from Christ, the work being finished for which it was intended, we find an immediate and peremptory command for the sheathing it again; and this reason render'd from the lip of truth it self; *for all they that take the sword, shall perish with the sword: for whosoever will save his life, shall lose it*. And we find no toleration in holy writ to the people of God for the drawing it again in the least, neither by precept nor example.

Matt. xxvi. 52.
Mark xvi. 15.

But lest this countermand should not be looked upon to be a sufficient warrant for its continuance in its place, by the people of God, for the time to come; the Lord Christ, among several other weighty things, sent to the seven churches in *Asia*, and in them to us, by *John* the revelator, is not backward to remind them, and us in them of it again, as a matter of no small concernment; and, as we judge, lest it should not be taken so much notice of by us in this our day as he would have it, he bringeth it in, in the midst of a discourse, not long before the rise of the man of sin, when one of the heads of the beast

APPENDIX.

beast is wounded as it were to death, and that deadly wound was healed; intimating thus much, as we apprehend, That as kingly power hath had a wound in thefe nations, even as it were unto death, fo we know that the defign of God fhall be brought about, and the fcriptures muſt be fulfilled; for the deadly wound fhall be healed. And we Rev. xiii. 3. finding the fpirits of the generality of the people of the three nations very high in this juncture of time in the behalf of kingly government, like *Ifrael* of old; fo that by the 1 Sam. viii. face of things, as they appear to us in this laſt change, we do difcern as through a glafs darkly, that the deadly wound is now going to be healed, although we do really judge, that feveral that are in prefent eminent power, intend no fuch thing, no more than the *Jews* in the crucifying of Chriſt, intended the bringing the great defign and fore-appoint- Acts ii. 23. ment of God about; by all which we judge, that caution was intended chiefly to us, *upon whom the ends of the world is come*: and left we fhould not be fo mindful of our duties as he would have us, he makes, as it were, a proclamation, to befpeak our better attention to what he intendeth, and faith, *He that* Rev. xiii. 9, *hath an ear to hear, let him hear: he that* 10. *leadeth into captivity, fhall go into captivity: he that killeth with the fword, fhall be killed with the fword.* Here is the faith and patience of the faints; that whilft others are leading into captivity, and killing with the fword, to pull down, or fet up this or that power, man, or government, to give a deadly wound to kingly power, or to heal that deadly wound again; that then the people of God fhould,

APPENDIX.

Heb. iii. 17. in their *patience possess their souls*, and in the midst of these revolutions exercise their faith, as once that prophet did, and faithfully to depend upon God for his preservation and protection, keeping themselves pure and undefiled, from leading into captivity, or killing with the sword, lest they themselves be led into captivity, and be killed by the sword;
John xv. 19. thereby evidencing themselves to be the *peaceable flock of Christ, chosen out of the world,*
Isa. ix. 6. and following their *master, the Lord and*
2 Thess. iii. 16. *prince of peace*, being regulated by his re-
Rom. x. 15. quirements in the *gospel of peace*, having re-
Eph. vi. 15. ceived from the *God of peace*, that *spirit*,
Rom. xv. 33. whose *fruits is love, joy, peace, long-suffer-*
―― xvi. 20. *ing, gentleness, goodness, faith, meekness and*
2 Cor. xiii. 11. *temperance, against which there is no law*;
Gal. v. 22, 23, 24. that as they are Christ's, so they should evidence that they have *crucified the flesh with the affections and lusts*; but lust being not crucified, it breaks forth into wars and fightings;
James iv. 1, 2. for when *men lust, and have not*, then they *kill and desire to have*: and when the people of God shall act thus, the spirit of God brands them with those ignominious names of adulterers and adultresses; informing them, that what they are fighting for is enmity against God; and that if they obtain it, they
―― iv. 4. are enemies to God: And we well knowing that whilst we are friends to the world we are enemies to God, dare not, in the least, have to do in the world, so as to set up ourselves, or to side with any either in setting up or pulling down; and how can a man's love to the world be evidenced more, than in venturing his life for it, according to that
John xv. 13. saying of our Saviour.

AND

APPENDIX.

AND we further declare, That as we are to be a peaceable people upon the account of action, so we look upon it to be our duty to keep our selves from oaths, engagements and covenants, either for or against this or that person, government, or persons whatsoever: *For because of swearing the land mourneth.* Jer. xxiii. 10. *For the Lord hath a controversy with the inhabitants of the land; because there is no truth, nor mercy, nor knowledge of God in the land; for by swearing, and lying, and killing, and stealing, and committing adultery, they break forth, and blood toucheth blood, saith the prophet.* And saith the same prophet; Hof. iv. 1, 2. *They have spoken words swearing falsly in making a covenant.* 3. *Thus judgment springeth up* — x. 3, 4. *as hemlock in the furrows of the field;* and we not knowing what the cabinet counsel of God is in this our day, upon the account of government, dare not in the least have so much as a thought to engage in any such thing, *lest we be found fighters against God,* Acts v. 39. according to the saying of *Gamaliel*, though in another case.

AND therefore do declare our resolution herein, That we shall not (God assisting us) enter into any engagement whatsoever upon any such account; yet shall this say again, That we shall not violently resist the imposers of any such engagements; but shall patiently suffer the penalty of our non-obedience as aforesaid.

AND we further declare, as in the presence of God, who is the searcher of all hearts, That as it hath been some of our great trouble for a long time, to see some of those that are in the same faith and order with us, so acting;

ing; so it is now become even an overwhelming burden upon our souls, to see them generally running such a precipitant course, by which actings of theirs, the mouths almost of all men are opened against them, and that truth they profess, most ignominiously branded and reproached. And therefore we further declare, That in the sight of God, Angels and men, that we bear our testimony against them in their present actings, and cannot stand by them, nor have communion with them therein, nor with those that strengthen their hands in standing by them; and must tell them, in the words of our Saviour, *That they know not what spirit they are of*; for *the son of man, their master, came not to destroy mens lives, but to save them.*

Luke ix. 55.

THE premises consider'd, we shall appeal to the judgments of all rational men, whether we are guilty of what we are charged withal or not; yet if they shall still go on notwithstanding, to use us reproachfully for the name of Christ, we shall be so far from endeavouring or desiring a revenge, as that, in the words of Christ, we shall, in our requests at the throne of grace, cry out and say, *Father forgive them, they know not what they do.*

APPENDIX.

POSTSCRIPT.

FOrasmuch as the said declarers, in their answer to the first particular in their declaration, do call the *Independants and Presbyterians* their Christian friends, the which however it is they so complement with them, yet in reality (we judge) they cannot own them as such upon a scripture account; as also because one Mr. *William Alleyn*, in a book lately by him publish'd, intitled, *A retractation to separation.* In which book, in the whole current of it, all the scriptures that he brings, which were written by the immediate direction and incomes of the holy Spirit of God, to the churches, as they were in the faith and order of the gospel, he applieth to, and also for, and in the behalf of *Episcopals, Independants* and *Presbyterians*, who are opposite both to the doctrine and discipline of those churches, he intending thereby to persuade us, if possible, to a belief that they are the true and visible members of that body, of which Christ is the head; the which book, by God's assistance, is intended suddenly to be answer'd by one of our society, who resolveth to intitle it, *The retractators work scan'd, or the conceptions and supposals of Mr.* William Alleyn, *regulated by scripture record*; in which, with other things, a gospel believer, or a true church of Christ, upon a gospel account, is intended to be stated; the which is hoped will be so plain, that it may prove instrumental to the undeceiving of some that are under a deceit, by means of that and such deceitful discourses as that is. In which answer it is further hoped, that those that are unsatisfied with our term *without*, in our answer in our declaration to the fourth particular, may receive also good satisfaction; and in the mean time, we desire all to take notice, that though we thus speak, yet we have good thoughts of those friends that go under those denominations, and do own them, and all others, of all other opinions whatsoever, in union, so far as they own God, Christ and their truths: but to own the best of men to be members of that body of which Christ is the head, and so to have communion with them, either to make them our mouth in prayer to God for us, or God's mouth in speaking forth his truths to us, or in breaking of bread at the table of the Lord, we cannot own them in the least, our reasons, we hope, will be fully laid down in the answer to the said book.

Henry Adis, Richard Pilgrim, William Cox, in behalf of themselves, and those that walk with them.

AND if any man shall question the reason why there are no more subscribers to this long declaration; we must answer them in the sorrow of our hearts, in the language of the prophet; *Wo is us, for we are as when they have gathered the summer fruits, as the grape gatherings in the vintage, there is no clusters to eat. The good man is perished out of the earth, and there is none upright amongst men;*

Mic. vii. 1, 2, 3, 4.

they

APPENDIX.

they all lie in wait for blood; they hunt every man his brother with a net. That they may do evil with both hands earnestly, the prince asketh, and the judge asketh for a reward, and the great man he uttereth his mischeivous desire; so they wrap it up. The best of them is as a briar, the most upright is sharper than a thorn hedge: the day of thy watchmen, and thy visitation cometh, now shall be their perplexity.

For thus saith the Lord by his prophet; *Your iniquities have separated between you and your God, and your sins have hid his face from you, that he will not hear: for your hands are defiled with blood, and your fingers with iniquity, your lips have spoken lies, your tongues have mutter'd perverseness. None calleth for justice, nor any pleadeth for truth; they trust in vanity, and speak lies; they conceive mischief, and bring forth iniquity. They hatch cockatrice eggs, and weave the spider's web; he that eateth of their eggs dieth, and that which is crushed breaketh out into a viper. Their webs shall not become garments, neither shall they cover themselves with their works: their works are works of iniquity, and the act of violence is in their hands. Their feet run to evil, and they make haste to shed innocent blood: their thoughts are thoughts of iniquity, wasting and destruction is in their paths. The way of peace they know not, and there is no judgment in their goings: they have made them crooked paths: whosoever goeth therein, shall not know peace. Therefore is judgment far from us; we wait for light, but behold obscurity; for brightness, but we walk in dark-* Isa. lix. 2.

darkness; and so read on to the 18th verse. *According to their deeds, accordingly he will pay, fury to his adversaries, recompence to his enemies, to the islands he will repay recompence.*

BUT lest any man should think us to be what we are not, by what hath been inserted in our paper, after our subscriptions, we shall in fine declare, That, in the presence of God, that what we have said, is against sinful actions, and not persons.

THERE are *three* or *four* lines following so torn in some parts of them, that I chose rather to omit them than supply, for fear of mistake.

FINIS.

Index
to all 4 Volumes
is in the back of
Volume 4.

THE BAPTIST STANDARD BEARER, INC.
A non-profit, tax-exempt corporation
committed to the Publication & Preservation
of The Baptist Heritage.

SAMPLE TITLES FOR PUBLICATIONS AVAILABLE IN OUR VARIOUS SERIES:

THE BAPTIST *COMMENTARY* SERIES
Sample of authors/works in or near republication:
John Gill - *Exposition of the Old & New Testaments (9 & 18 Vol. Sets)*
(*Volumes from the 18 vol. set can be purchased individually*)

THE BAPTIST *FAITH* SERIES:
Sample of authors/works in or near republication:
Abraham Booth - *The Reign of Grace*
John Fawcett - *Christ Precious to Those That Believe*
John Gill - *A Complete Body of Doctrinal & Practical Divinity (2 Vols.)*

THE BAPTIST *HISTORY* SERIES:
Sample of authors/works in or near republication:
Thomas Armitage - *A History of the Baptists (2 Vols.)*
Isaac Backus - *History of the New England Baptists (2 Vols.)*
William Cathcart - *The Baptist Encyclopaedia (3 Vols.)*
J. M. Cramp - *Baptist History*

THE BAPTIST *DISTINCTIVES* SERIES:
Sample of authors/works in or near republication:
Abraham Booth - *Paedobaptism Examined (3 Vols.)*
Alexander Carson - *Ecclesiastical Polity of the New Testament Churches*
E. C. Dargan - *Ecclesiology: A Study of the Churches*
J. M. Frost - *Pedobaptism: Is It From Heaven?*
R. B. C. Howell - *The Evils of Infant Baptism*

THE *DISSENT & NONCONFORMITY* SERIES:
Sample of authors/works in or near republication:
Champlin Burrage - *The Early English Dissenters (2 Vols.)*
Albert H. Newman - *History of Anti-Pedobaptism*
Walter Wilson - *The History & Antiquities of the Dissenting Churches (4 Vols.)*

For a complete list of current authors/titles, visit our internet site at
www.standardbearer.com or write us at:

he Baptist Standard Bearer, Inc.
No. 1 Iron Oaks Drive • Paris, Arkansas 72855

Telephone: (501) 963-3831   Fax: (501) 963-8083
E-mail: baptist@arkansas.net
Internet: http://www.standardbearer.com

Specialists in Baptist Reprints and Rare Books

Thou hast given a *standard* to them that fear thee; that it may be displayed because of the truth. -- Psalm 60:4

www.ingramcontent.com/pod-product-compliance
Lightning Source LLC
Chambersburg PA
CBHW020911020526
44114CB00039B/135

Memoir of the Life and Religious Labors of Lloyd Lee Wilson, a Minister of the Gospel of the Religious Society of Friends, Particularly of North Carolina Yearly Meeting (Conservative),

to describe the workings of the Lord in the various stages of my life, showing how God is at work in all things for good, whether we perceive it so or not, and how our surrender to divine providence allows God's work to be done in and through us for the advancement of the Realm of God

Lloyd Lee Wilson

Inner Light Books
San Francisco, California
2021

Memoir of the Life and Religious Labors
of
Lloyd Lee Wilson
© 2021 Lloyd Lee Wilson
All Rights Reserved

Except for brief quotations, no part of this publication may be reproduced, stored in a retrieval system, or transmitted in any form or by any means, electronic, mechanical, photocopying, recording, or otherwise, without prior written permission.

Editor: Charles Martin
Copy editor: Kathy McKay
Layout and design: Matt Kelsey

Published by Inner Light Books
San Francisco, California
www.innerlightbooks.com
editor@innerlightbooks.com

Library of Congress Control Number: 2021948189
ISBN 978-1-7370112-3-1 (hardcover)
ISBN 978-1-7370112-4-8 (paperback)
ISBN 978-1-7370112-5-5 (eBook)

Scripture quotations marked KJV are from The Authorized (King James) Version. Rights in the Authorized Version in the United Kingdom are vested in the Crown. Reproduced by permission of the Crown's patentee, Cambridge University Press.

Scripture quotations marked NASB are taken from the (NASB®) New American Standard Bible®, copyright © 1960, 1971, 1977, by The Lockman Foundation. Used by permission. All rights reserved. www.lockman.org.

Scripture quotations marked NRSV are from New Revised Standard Version Bible, copyright © 1989 National Council of the Churches of Christ in the United States of America. Used by permission. All rights reserved worldwide.

Scripture quotations marked RSV are from Revised Standard Version of the Bible, copyright © 1946, 1952, and 1971 National Council of the Churches of Christ in the United States of America. Used by permission. All rights reserved worldwide.

Scripture quotations marked BSB are from The Holy Bible, Berean Study Bible, copyright © 2016, 2020 by Bible Hub. Used by Permission. All rights reserved worldwide.

A modified version of an essay in this memoir was published as Lloyd Lee Wilson, "Confidentiality and Community," *Friends Journal* 46 (October 2000): 24–25.

An essay in this memoir was published in two places: "A Statement of Christian Pacifism," *Friends Journal* 49 (December 2003): 18–19; Lloyd Lee Wilson, "Christian Pacifist," *Quaker Life* (April 2003): 15.

An essay in this memoir was published as Lloyd Lee Wilson, "A Deeper Unity," *Quaker Life* (March 1988): 21–22.

Contents

Editor's Note iii

Introduction v

Chapter 1. Laying the Foundation: Maryland, 1947–1965 1

Chapter 2. A Severe Left Turn: Cambridge/Boston,
  1965–1970 22

Chapter 3. Beginning Again: Cambridge and Virginia,
  1971–1979 60

Chapter 4. Vocation and Competency: Virginia,
  1980–1988 94

Chapter 5. Among Conservative Friends: North Carolina
  and Virginia, 1989–1993 215

Chapter 6. Faith, Witness, and Community: Virginia,
  1993–1998 289

Chapter 7. Exercises in the Gospel Ministry: Woodland,
  North Carolina, 1998–2013 340

Chapter 8. New Fields of Service and New Challenges:
  North Carolina, 2013–2019 477

Epilogue: 2021 552

Appendix 1. A Deeper Unity 554

Appendix 2. Who Have Been the Most Important
  Spiritual Friends in My Life? 557

Appendix 3. How Do You Define Ministry? 558

Appendix 4. On a Group Lectio Divina—Luke 5:1–11 560

Appendix 5. How Do I Wait for God in My Life, in Prayer
  and Devotion? 563

Appendix 6. Aspects of Prayer 565

Appendix 7. Reflecting on John Woolman 567

Appendix 8. On a Personal Rule for Daily Life 570

Appendix 9. What the Sabbath Means to Me 572
Publications by Lloyd Lee Wilson 573
Glossary 576
Notes 589

Editor's Note

This book tells the story of a man's life, particularly his spiritual journey as a minister in the Religious Society of Friends. When Lloyd Lee Wilson and I first discussed his intentions to write a memoir, I learned that he had begun keeping a journal when he was eight years old and that he kept journaling his entire life. The content of the journals changed over the years, transitioning from mainly recording life events to a greater exploration of his spiritual state. The journals, along with notes for talks and workshops he has led, various articles that he wrote for publication, written assignments from his seminary studies, as well as letters written and received, are the material used in compiling this book. To create the text, Lloyd Lee transcribed the materials into a digital form making up nearly 1,300 pages when converted to the 6x9 book format. This material was edited down to create the current text.

This book contains descriptions of events taken from the journals, including recountings of vocal ministry and prayers; other writings by Lloyd Lee (and the writings of others); and Lloyd Lee's reflections on events and his inward journey as well as his inward state today as he looks back on his life. The book is essentially a chronological narrative, although there are at times digressions and discussion of the future when he is investigating certain themes.

This book is written in Lloyd Lee's voice and can be read as his being in conversation with the reader. Other voices that appear are noted in quotations to help the reader distinguish whose voice is being read. To help understand whose voice is being presented, the following format is used: long quotes from Scripture are indented in both the right and left margins and are in italics; long quotes from other sources are indented in both the left and right margins but are not italicized; and long quotes from Lloyd Lee's journals and his other writings are indented in the left margin only and are in plain text. All quotes from the Scriptures appear in italics without quotation marks if they are taken from a published translation, and book, chapter, verse, and translation are cited. If the quote is from memory such as in vocal prayer, it appears in quotation marks in plain text; this also occurs when it is a paraphrase of the Scriptures.

In such instances, book chapter, and verse are usually cited. If there is a need for clarification or explanation of some part of the text, endnotes are used. The endnotes are grouped by chapter in the back of the book. Some of Lloyd Lee's longer writings that were published or circulated in one form or another are in appendices at the back of the book.

At times, Lloyd Lee uses archaic wording, such as the term auditory for audience. This is not just a quirk of the writer or editor but is an aid in portraying the language of the traditional faith and practice of Friends. This is also true for the use of numbering instead of names for the days of the week and months. A glossary in the back of the book conveys Lloyd Lee's understanding of certain terms, both secular and theological; his understanding may vary from conventional norms.

Capitalization of words is another area where editorial choices in this memoir sometimes do not follow conventional norms. When denoting God, Christ, or the Spirit of Truth in any of the multitude of names used for all three, the word or phrase is capitalized, such as Teacher, Counsel, Divine Presence. The Realm of God and Kingdom of God are capitalized to emphasize the Lamb's War conflict between the Kingdom of God and all parts of the domination system.

Abbreviations or acronyms are used for certain words that are used often in the text. These are:

CO	conscientious objector
FGC	Friends General Conference
FUM	Friends United Meeting
MIT	Massachusetts Institute of Technology
MEO	Meeting of Ministers, Elders, and Overseers
NCYM(C)	North Carolina Yearly Meeting (Conservative)

In each case, the name is spelled out in full the first time it appears in a chapter and then usually is given as an abbreviation when it appears later in the text.

It is the intent of the publisher to bring this book into print for the benefit of the reader so they might use it in reflecting on their lives and discerning choices and possible calls laid before them. The spiritual journey that leads to putting God at the center of one's life is the beginning point for doing good works in the world.

Introduction

A wise Friend once said that since Friends have no creeds to define us, we have to tell our stories in order to remember who we are as a particular people of faith. These stories from my own life are shared as insights into who Friends have been in the places and times I have occupied, to help us remember. They are an account of my trying to be faithful to a call into public ministry among Friends and others and of my consequent struggles to find the support and accountability among my faith community to answer that call faithfully.

Jacob wrestled with the angel for a night; I have wrestled with God's call into the public ministry for my lifetime. That wrestling has taught me three lessons: God's call to individuals is persistent and perceptible; the call is to a life of surrender, not to a particular mission; and one's vocation in ministry is meant to be lived out in the threefold relationship of individual, God, and the faith community. Sometimes that call has been more perceptible to others than to me; sometimes I have resisted it openly. Acknowledging and surrendering to God's persistent call has been life-giving to me. I have not been called to a specific ministry or equipped with a specific set of "gifts." The call I have heard is a call to a relationship, to total surrender to the will of God, to a complete reorientation of my life to do God's will.

I share this testimony of my life in the same Spirit as public Friend and minister Barbara Blaudone, who wrote in 1691:

> I speak my Experience of the Dealings of the Lord with me, in my Travels and passings through my Spiritual Journey, for the benefit of those that Travel rightly after. And I can speak it to the glory of God, he never moved me to any thing, but that he gave me Power to perform it, and made it effectual, although I [passed] through much Exercise in the performance of it. And the Power of God wrought in me long before I knew what it was; and when Friends came, that my understanding was opened, I soon took up the Cross and came into the Obedience, and the Lord cleansed me by his Power, and made me a fit Vessel for his Use.

Chapter 1
Laying the Foundation: Maryland, 1947–1965

I was almost born on board a sailboat becalmed on the headwaters of the Chesapeake Bay. My soon-to-be parents, Clifton and Betty Wilson, were enjoying themselves on a weekend afternoon in their little sailboat when the wind died. This did not present an immediate problem as they had no schedule to meet and enjoyed each other's company. Then my mother said quietly, "Clif, do you want to deliver a baby?" "No!" my father declared. "Then you'd better start paddling," Betty calmly advised.

Some time later, the young couple made it to shore and on to the hospital in the county seat of Elkton, Maryland. Betty presented herself to the receptionist and explained that she was about to have her baby. "Is this your first child?" asked the woman at the desk. "Yes," replied Betty. "Then don't worry, nothing is going to happen for quite a while. You can even go home." Looking down at the liquid pooling at her feet, Betty responded, "No, I think I'm going to have the baby now—my water just broke."

This persuaded the hospital staff to get a gurney for Betty to lie on, but there was no doctor at the hospital to supervise the delivery. Now convinced that Betty was indeed about to deliver any minute, the head nurse wrapped a sheet around her legs to hold them tightly together and delay delivery until the doctor arrived. This did nothing to slow the natural progression of her labor, of course, and by the time a doctor did arrive to oversee the birth, my head was grossly deformed. The doctor simply stood at the bedside and massaged my newborn skull back into a roughly normal shape.[1]

This story is archetypal of life as my parents perceived it. They often faced challenges with few resources other than their own effort and determination and no one around to help them; when they did encounter persons of authority, those people were as likely to be obstacles as to provide needed help. They depended on each other and their own hard work and perseverance and were distrustful of other people, even those who appeared to be friendly and helpful.

My parents' worldview was to have both benefits and drawbacks for me as I grew up. The values they believed would lead to success were integrity, loyalty to self and family, maintaining a constant vigilance against the suspect motives of anyone outside the family, high moral standards, constant hard work, and personal standards for performance in all areas of life that they themselves set and that exceeded those of anybody else. They felt that their own lack of education had raised real barriers in their lives and were determined that their children would get a college education. Church was an important part of their lives, and they were constantly engaged in service to the church.

My parents' stories are the raw material for the beginnings of my own story, as are the rural setting and isolated culture of the area I grew up in and the culture of the people who were to be my mentors, classmates, and friends. Eventually, each of us must mold our own story, becoming more or less the person God has yearned for us to become, through personal effort and God's continual assistance. The stories into which we are born are the initial foundation on which our own stories are built—but not the ultimate determiners of the lives we lead.

Born to tenant farmers on an orchard in northern Delaware, Clifton Wilson, along with his mother and siblings moved to nearby Elkton, Maryland, when his father was killed in a train wreck (Clifton was three). His mother (who was functionally illiterate) opened a boarding house there and raised her four children. For reasons now unknown, the girls were raised in the Episcopal church but the boys were raised Methodists.

Betty Raye Bare was born to subsistence farmers in the Blue Ridge mountains of Ashe County, North Carolina. Her mother died of complications of childbirth soon after Betty was born. Her father resisted the pressure to place his six children with other families and raised five of them to adulthood. Their Primitive Baptist faith was a strong support for the struggling family.

The Depression hit both families hard, but by the time World War II started, Clif had found steady employment as a telephone

Laying the Foundation

installer/repairman and Betty had come north to Elkton to work in an ammunition plant. Over the course of the war, Clif tried three times to enlist in the Army, but each time the telephone company found out and intervened; his job was considered essential to the war effort by the government, and he was not allowed to leave it. The couple began married life with 2"x4" boards resting on two sawhorses as a table, two empty nail kegs as chairs, and a steady determination that their children were going to have all the opportunities they had missed themselves.

When I was three years old, in 1950, my parents began taking me to Sunday school at St. John's Methodist Church in nearby Charlestown, Maryland. Charlestown was a village of about 350 persons, reputed locally to be the only incorporated town in the nation that had no taxes. Like the town it served, St. John's was small and working class. Average attendance on Sunday morning was about twenty-five persons. In order to support a pastor at all, St. John's had been grouped with three other small churches into a four-church "charge," in keeping with the Methodist circuit rider tradition. In this case, though, the pastor was expected to preach at all four churches each Sunday and to play a full role in the life of each congregation. Even together, the churches in our charge could not support a regular pastor, so the parsonage was filled with a succession of seminary students and their families, interrupted occasionally by the retired pastor called back into service by the prospect of a supplement to what surely was a minuscule pension.

My father had been sent to Methodist Sunday school as a child, but my sense was that it was only after his marriage that he became serious about his faith. The Methodist way of life suited him well in adulthood. The "methodical" approach to faith and worship, with its organized, somewhat repetitive structure for life both in and outside of the church, made religion logical and understandable. There was a procedure for everything. Follow the procedure in all things every day, and everything would be all right. An organized approach to worship, personal prayer, and personal behavior would protect one from the primary dangers to salvation: alcohol, sex outside marriage, dishonesty, and foul language.

Mom had left behind her Primitive Baptist roots in her early teens after she left the family farm to work in nearby West Jefferson, North

Carolina. The boarding house where she worked and lived was across the street from the Methodist church there, and she was attracted by the beautiful singing on Wednesday nights when the choir practiced. (Her childhood Primitive Baptist church had no instrumental music in their worship services.)

Primitive Baptists in the United States share many of the historic values of the Religious Society of Friends: a sense of being "Primitive Christianity Revived" (or preserved), a sense that seminaries are poor preparation for the ministry, a congregational polity, and a sense of not really being Protestants. However, the differences are also striking: a deep sense of original sin, a reliance on Scripture as the only rule of faith and practice, and the importance given to such ordinances or practices as immersion baptism (and only in living water), the Lord's Supper, and foot washing. Senter Primitive Baptist Church, where my mother's family had belonged for generations, met for worship only about once per month in her childhood because of a lack of elders available to bring a message. Foot washing and Communion were observed once per year; my grandfather Lee Bare made the wine the church used for Communion. Full immersion in living water was and still is the standard for baptism. When it came time for my grandfather to be baptized, church members chopped a path in the ice so he and the elder involved could wade out into the New River to a place deep enough for him to slip easily below the water.

A major theme of the preaching at Senter over the years was absolute predestination—the belief that individuals are slated for heaven or condemned to hell before they are born. For this reason, church leaders felt there was little point in putting up a sign or otherwise advertising the church—those who were destined to find it would do so without a sign, and those who were not so destined would not find it even if they were offered a ride to the church door. I shared responsibility for my step-grandmother's funeral and graveside services with an elder from Senter several years ago, and I noted then that in his remarks he offered no assurance that Cordie Bare was or would ever be in heaven—though he did say he was sure we all hoped that was the case. In Primitive Baptist theology, there is just no way to know; one can assume unbelievers will not make it to heaven, but not all believers will be admitted.

My parents steadily moved into leadership positions in the Methodist church in Charlestown. My father served as lay leader of the congregation, and Mom was active in church suppers and other fundraising activities and served on the local "Official Board." They didn't have a lot of money, but they gave of what they had regularly and faithfully to support St. John's.

My brother Damon was born in the fall of 1952. The five-year difference in age was enough to keep us in separate schools and separate youth activities for most of the time we were growing up but not enough for Damon to escape being called Lloyd too many times by teachers and other adults. It was hard for him to escape the expectations others placed on him because they had known me.

I began journaling my experiences quite early; the first journal I still have in my possession begins on June 1, 1956, when I was eight years old. Our family took a trip cross-country that year to visit cousins in Idaho, and I recorded the events of each day in succinct fashion. There is little of an overtly spiritual nature in these early journal entries. I noted one foreshadowing event the following summer (June 15, 1957), when our vacation to visit my mother's family in North Carolina was delayed because my father had burned his eye with cigarette ash and needed to go to a doctor to get it treated; my father's smoking was a factor in his death in 1976 of lung cancer. I continued to journal, and as my spiritual life deepened the nature of my journal entries changed as well, recording my faith experiences and reflections as well as the outward events of my life. Going through those journals decades later, I can identify several themes that have been influential throughout my life: church, schooling, and my relationship with my father.

Church

I attended Sunday school regularly and began acquiring what became a large set of perfect attendance pins. As I got older, the imagined events of adult worship on Sunday mornings became more and more interesting to me, and when I was about eight years old I began pressing my parents to allow me to attend. Once I showed during a trial period that I could be quiet and relatively still for the hour of worship, I was allowed to attend every week. Some of the hymns quickly became my favorites, such as "Holy, Holy, Holy" and "I Love to Tell the Story." The weekly responsive readings, when the congregation spoke our beliefs in unison, impressed me. Sermons, on the other hand, were very much a mixed experience. From time to time, a sermon made a deep impact on me, but more often the sermon was for me a period of learning to sit patiently until it was over.

After I had been attending worship for a while, I was sometimes allowed to help collect the offering, passing the collection plates from pew to pew. One never-to-be-forgotten morning, when the ushers carried the plates up to the front of the church, our pastor looked at their contents and announced to the congregation that the collection was so small that he was going to send the plates back around again—and he wanted to see some folding money in them that time.

In 1959 my parents allowed me to become an adult member of our Methodist church. They felt (and, looking back, I agree) that I should wait until that year, when I turned twelve, before becoming a member. I took the membership class with several adults, was baptized, and then was accepted into membership. The membership class was held in the furnace room on the first floor of the church building. The teacher presented a lot of new material about Methodist doctrines and teachings but nothing that contradicted the basic beliefs that Mom and Dad had taught me.

In the Religious Society of Friends, the meaning of membership changes for both the individual and the meeting as the individual moves from infancy and youth through young adulthood and on into the fullness of life. I have been favorably impressed by the Advices of my yearly meeting (North Carolina Conservative) on this topic, which say (paraphrased) that while our children are clearly a part of our meeting fellowship, they can become members only through an intentional personal commitment to our shared Quaker faith tradition along with the changes in life that such a commitment implies.[2] One can accomplish this, it seems to me, by a three-stage progression. Very young children

Laying the Foundation

are members of our meeting community by virtue of the desire of their parents. Older children (say, below twenty-one or some other arbitrary age) become associate (or junior) members, on their request, through some clearness process that seems appropriate to the community. Sometime before an associate member reaches another limit (twenty-five years old, for example), they must request to become an adult member of the monthly meeting. Again, some clearness process that seems appropriate to the monthly meeting community should be followed. If an associate member does not make this request, their membership would cease at the stated time.

When I was very young, being a part of my family in the church community was all I needed. Later, I began to feel a desire to make a commitment on my own, but in their discernment my parents delayed action on that desire until they felt I had some understanding of the mutual commitments that membership entailed. As I grew into adulthood, those initial commitments proved to be inadequate. What I needed was a deeper understanding of the membership relationship between individual and faith community and a new commitment to that relationship. This didn't happen for me for another ten years, when I encountered Quakerism.

One of the greatest shortcomings of the non-pastoral branches of Quakerism (Liberal and Conservative) is the lack of an effective intentional adult religious education program. This lack has many roots, but its effect is that many Friends have not been exposed to or explored for themselves the deep foundations of our faith and practice. Without teachers to help us understand, many of us make up reasons for why Friends do this or don't do that, and those reasons are often inadequate or misleading explanations of Quaker faith and practice.

The Methodists in our little church started with the assumption that there was a body of knowledge that explained what we believed and why we behaved together as we did, that this body of knowledge was important for each member to learn, and that it was important to teach this to prospective new members before they made the commitment to membership. They made the intentional effort to organize a program to teach that body of knowledge to all who wanted to learn, and especially people who expressed a desire for membership. Their teaching styles and skills may have been open to criticism, but they made this conscious effort, year after year.

Friends in the nonpastoral branches generally don't do this, for several reasons. One common reason is that we are too diverse a community to encompass all the varieties of faith and practice, even within our local monthly meeting. A less healthy expression of this is the feeling that one can't teach any single person's understanding of Quakerism without offending several other members. Another is the surprising resistance of many Quakers and prospective Quakers to admitting that they need to be taught anything; yet another is the overreliance on the Holy Spirit as the only reliable teacher.

Whatever the identified reason is, the result is an increasingly fractured Religious Society of Friends. We do not understand one another's faith because we don't talk about what we believe and why, and every distinctive aspect of Quaker practice seems like an arbitrary invention to be discarded at a whim. Adult religious education as an ongoing, intentional practice makes it clear to newcomers that Quakerism did not begin the first time they attended meeting for worship and that there is a reason why Quakers do each of the unusual things they do. Change is at times good, but we need to know why we've been doing things a particular way before we can tell whether a suggested innovation is a good idea or a bad one.

Baptism was an unexpectedly disappointing experience for me. I remember kneeling at the Communion rail, listening to the pastor go through the ritual words, feeling the drops of water sprinkled on my forehead—and wondering why I felt no different at that moment or afterward than I had felt all my life. Had the baptism not "taken"? Did something go wrong?

In contrast, becoming a member of the church felt important. Unlike baptism, something had changed in me or my relationship to the church when I went through that ceremony. One practical change came from my realization that because I was a member, our local church now owed a sum of money each year on my behalf to the Methodist conference to which our local church belonged, and my current level of weekly giving did not match that amount. So, for the first time, I asked my parents for an increase in my weekly allowance—an additional 10 cents per week—which they granted. I added all of the increase to the weekly donation I was already making to the church. With that increase, I was meeting my minimum financial responsibility as a member.

By now I was beginning to notice that the person who was leading the worship service had a perceptible influence on how well the worship was perceived and received by the congregation. My journal for that summer includes numerous entries comparing the current minister, Rev. Abbott, with his predecessor, Rev. Simpers, as well as critiquing Rev. Abbott's sermons ("preaches too much of a 'dead Amen' sermon"). I was meeting with Rev. Abbott one weekday afternoon each week as part of the Boy Scouts' God and Country program, and over time I began to like him more and more.

I also began teaching Sunday school about this time to what would today be called middle schoolers. Unlike those who had been my Sunday school teachers, I did not have the students read our denominational Sunday school pamphlets aloud paragraph by paragraph. Instead, I summarized the topic for the week and tried to engage the students in a discussion of what it meant and how we could incorporate that principle into our daily lives. Three of my students were my younger brother Damon and his two best friends. I soon learned that they were watching me closely all the time. If my behavior the rest of the week did not seem to them to be consistent with a churchgoer, our Sunday school discussion would be about that behavior, not about the planned lesson.

Christian faith seemed to me, and as far as I could tell to my fellow churchgoers, an intellectual assent to the death and resurrection of Jesus and a personal commitment to certain standards of behavior. For boys becoming men, that meant going to church on Sunday morning, no smoking or drinking, no messing around with girls, no cursing, and no telling lies. An unquestioning national patriotism was expected, both in the church and in the world outside the church. Separation of the races and subordinate roles for women were so much a part of the accepted way of things that they weren't even talked about. Each day in public school started with a Bible reading followed by the recital of the Lord's

Memoir of the Life and Religious Labors of Lloyd Lee Wilson

Prayer and the pledge of allegiance, all led by a student over the school's loudspeaker system. In our classrooms, we learned to "duck and cover" in case the godless Communists launched a sneak attack.

My exposure to different patterns of faith was limited. One of our schoolteachers asked for a show of hands one day on our religious affiliation. Most students in my class were Methodists, as we already knew, and we had a small number of Episcopalians. There was one Nazarene, and one girl described herself as half-Jewish, half-Baptist, but not practicing either. In high school, a lone Catholic boy transferred into our school. At this time, although I was not consciously aware of it, there were only white students in my classes.

As I grew older, more of the content of the adults' conversations around me began to penetrate my consciousness. It became clear that my parents were not simply the sort of people that were in church any time the doors were open; they were often the people who made sure the doors could and would open. When the church was broke and the oil tank was empty, it was my parents who arranged to pay for an oil delivery to keep the parsonage and the church warm. When the pastor's wife called to say they had run out of money and she had nothing except some boxes of macaroni and cheese to feed her family until their next check, it was my mother who assembled a care package and took it to the parsonage.

Pastors and their families regularly came for Sunday dinner at our house, and I soon realized this was a multipurpose event. It was good for the pastor to get to know members of the congregation more closely, for sure, but a bountiful meal for all the pastor's family was also very important for practical reasons. Conversation with my parents away from the church was also a chance for the pastor to let down his hair and vent about the stresses and strains of his position and circumstances.

At age twelve, in response to my growing realization of how difficult life was for these pastors who served St. John's and possibly in recognition of something calling me toward that life, I came downstairs from my bedroom one day to the kitchen where Mom was working, slapped my hand on the table, and said with emotion, "I'm *never* going to be a minister!" and walked out. She never forgot that moment and has often reminded me of the irony of my remark, given the way my life has turned out since.

I certainly never did become a minister in the model that I had seen up to that point in my life: a paid pastor serving as the "one-stop shop" for all the needs of one or several small congregations, balancing the financial needs of his family against the expectations of his parishioners. I disliked the financial neediness our pastors experienced, the long hours of work, and the church politics (the feuds were so intense because the stakes were so small). As I grew older, I realized I did not have the gifts in pastoral care that are so important in that role. I also became aware of the lure and dangers of what I've come to call the "golden shackles" of paid ministry. Desiring to devote one's entire life to service to God, one accepts employment in or for a church. Once there, one realizes that there are things one can't do or say without threatening that very employment that had seemed so liberating. Many times, I've heard a pastor (Friend or non-Friend) say, "That won't preach in my church."

Over the course of my life, I have tried deliberately to minister, to organize myself and my activities to serve God, in both religious and secular settings. As I predicted, I have avoided the paid pastorate. Except for a few years with Friends General Conference, none of my employers were specifically religious organizations; but even there I found the golden shackles to be all too real.

As a Boy Scout, I had the opportunity to speak during worship services on several occasions and filled in once or twice for our pastor when he had to be absent on a Sunday and no supply minister was available. In my fourteenth year, these experiences led St. John's to recommend to the DelMarVa Conference that I be recognized as a certified lay speaker. No one did a search of the records, but fourteen was the youngest anyone present could remember anyone being certified as a lay speaker. Nowadays, such certification includes formal training provided by the Methodist Church, but at that time people like me were on their own.

And on my own I was. I soon learned to prepare several sermons ahead of time and keep them in a loose-leaf notebook as the call to fill in for a pastor somewhere in the area could come unexpectedly and at the last minute. The prime example of this was the Saturday night our own pastor called up and explained, in a voice barely intelligible, that he had had all his wisdom teeth removed that afternoon and would be unable to preach the next morning. Luckily, I had a sermon prepared and was able to fill in for him the next day in all four of the churches on our charge. Of course, I was too young to drive, so Mom or Dad had to take me from church to church so I could preach the sermon.

In high school I became aware of a phrase we used from time to time in worship services that said Jesus Christ was the "propitiation" for our sins. Not knowing what this might mean, I asked our pastor about it one day when we were alone in the sanctuary. He was doing some cleaning; I don't remember why I happened to be there. "What does it mean to be the propitiation for our sins?" I asked. He was silent for several seconds, paying attention to his cleaning. Finally, he said, "I don't know." This disappointed me on two levels. First, I thought that our pastors were supposed to know everything about religious stuff. Second, I thought it upsetting that our whole congregation was saying it believed something when in fact no one knew what it meant (clearly if the pastor didn't know, no one did.) I didn't say anything to anyone else at the time. Like my disappointment with baptism, though, it lingered in the background and played a role later on when I broke my ties to Methodism.

School

I spent the first grade in a two-room, six-grade elementary school in Charlestown, across the street from St. John's Methodist Church and next to the volunteer fire department. My classroom held the first three grades, with the teacher rotating from one group to another to teach us reading, writing, and the rudiments of arithmetic. Mom had already taught me to read and to add and subtract, so I was a bit ahead of the other first graders and wanted very much to be able to read in the second- and third-grade books. This, however, was not allowed.

My parents recognized that the school in Charlestown was not going to meet their expectations and made arrangements for me to attend the second grade in the nearby town of North East, Maryland. The new elementary school there had six classrooms—one for each grade. This

Laying the Foundation

school too soon became seriously overcrowded, but it was much better staffed and equipped than the one in Charlestown.

As the overcrowding grew worse year by year, my parents seriously considered putting me in a private school, which would have been quite a challenge considering their limited financial resources. After investigating a couple of schools that would have been within commuting distance, Dad decided that it was more important that I learn to live with all sorts of people as schoolmates than that I get more advanced academic preparation. This put some challenges in my path in my college years, but I believe he made the right decision.

When I was about twelve years old, I qualified to be on a local quiz show aired on a Baltimore TV station. The show aired live, and during the introductions the emcee asked what I wanted to do in life. "Go to MIT and become an engineer in nuclear physics!" was my enthusiastic reply—much to the surprise of my parents sitting off-camera nearby. They never questioned my choice, however. My college selection was based on my asking many adults which was the best college in the world. More people said MIT than any other institution, so I decided I wanted to go there.

Entering seventh grade meant attending the junior-senior high school in North East. The school library had few new books, but I was allowed to check out any book I wanted, whether it was grade-appropriate or not. I found several old books about the Greek orators, and I read each one carefully. Like Demosthenes, I practiced speaking with small stones in my mouth. but I did not continue that exercise very long as the stones felt very uncomfortable against my teeth. During this time, the school held an oratory contest in which participants delivered a short speech before a panel of judges. I won the contest, which seemed like a good return on my investment of time and effort in that skill.

In the fall of 1963, my junior year of high school, all the county's schools were integrated. This occurred peacefully and largely without incident. We children had been playing baseball in an integrated Little League for several years, and the white children looked forward to having some very athletic black kids added to the school basketball and baseball teams. This is not to say that integration was an entirely smooth process. The next year, when our class put on the traditional senior class play, the white community learned both that there was a local NAACP chapter in town and that there was something offensive about white folks putting on blackface for a stage performance.

Looking back at our community during this period, I see that our rural community was so racist it was ignorant on a conscious level of its racism. The black and white populations were so completely separated from one another that we whites were literally unconscious of the existence of the black population. Racism was pervasive all around us, both formally in our institutions and in the very structure of the culture, yet nobody I knew thought very much about it, one way or another. When racial barriers began to fall, most white people in my community seemed to accept the changes without very much fuss. More than angry or threatened, my remembrance is that they were genuinely surprised and confused when their racism was exposed. Change came about in my town with less pain and suffering, emotional and physical, than in many other communities around the nation. The changes were not universal or complete, as I experienced several years later when dealing with my county's Selective Service board about getting classified as a conscientious objector (CO).

Two or three of us around this time became aware of Mensa, an organization whose only qualification for membership was to score in the 98th percentile or higher on an IQ test. Dad drove me the fifty miles to Baltimore to take the test, which was scored on the spot when the test was completed. As I got in the car for the drive home, Dad asked how I had done. "I scored in the 99th percentile," I replied proudly. Dad's immediate response—"Why aren't you in the 100th percentile?"—took away my sense of achievement. I explained the concept of percentiles to him, pointing out that to be in the 100th percentile would mean that I had scored higher than anyone else who took the test. When I finished the explanation, I had the sense that he still wanted to ask the same question. No matter what I achieved, he wanted and expected more, so I felt I was a constant disappointment to him.

I was in Mrs. Morris's geometry class when the news came over the high school public address system that President Kennedy had been shot in Dallas. My immediate reaction, expressed out loud, was that now there

Laying the Foundation

was no way he could lose the upcoming election. The possibility that he might have been killed was totally outside my realm of imagination.

Two days later, I was with a group of people at the church, gathered in the first-floor furnace room/meeting room for a reason I cannot now recall, when our neighbor Claude Grace came in and announced that Lee Harvey Oswald had been shot. I could see that all the adults were becoming a little frightened, wondering what was happening and when the killing would end. I myself became a little frightened and confused; apparently the world was not as stable and well arranged as I had believed up to that point

My senior year in high school was a time of constant tension between myself and my teachers. I had taken the SAT exam the previous spring, the morning after the junior prom. When the scores arrived at our school, the administration sent mine back, announcing publicly to my classmates and to me that they must have been misprinted. There was no misprint; they simply did not believe I could have achieved the scores reported.

My teachers generally discouraged me from even applying to MIT, saying that the disappointment of rejection would be too big a shock for me to handle. (The previous year's valedictorian had not been able to gain admission to the University of Delaware and had enrolled instead at the University of Maryland, which automatically admitted anyone with a Maryland high school diploma.) My music teacher in particular discouraged me, saying MIT accepted only the "cream of the cream." The guidance counselor refused to cooperate with the MIT application unless I applied to his alma mater, Carnegie University, and one other school. I chose Lehigh University as I had attended a two-week "junior engineering and science institute" there one summer and knew where it was.

I filled out the applications to Carnegie and Lehigh in a rote sort of way, not even bothering to look up where Carnegie was located other than somewhere in New York. Eventually, the admissions offices began to reply, and first Lehigh, then Carnegie offered me admission. When the MIT offer of admission came in, I felt like running up and down the school hallways, waving the letter and shouting, "See! See! I did it after all!"

I did not know this at the time, but the general opinion among both faculty and classmates, after they learned I had been admitted to MIT, was that I would attend for one semester, realize I was out of my league, and return to the University of Maryland to continue my schooling.

Boy Scouts

My father was of the opinion that the Boy Scouts had saved him from a life of delinquency, though he never rose above second class rank. Consequently, he was intent on seeing that I had the full Scouting experience as soon as I was old enough to join. There was no Cub Scout troop in Charlestown, so he and Mom started one. He was cubmaster and my mother was den mother for my group of Scouts. They made sure that I did everything required to attain all the ranks: Wolf, Bear, Lion, and Webelos. When it came time for me to move into Boy Scouts, Dad started a troop in Charlestown; we met in a room of the school building where I had attended first grade that was now being used as the town hall.

All of us in the Charlestown troop enjoyed Scouting activities: camping out, tying knots, building campfires, and the like. What was different for me about Scouting was my father's consistent pressure on me to advance up the ranks. Every activity was a time for me to meet the requirements for some new merit badge or other requirement for the next rank. When my father decided my progress toward Eagle rank was slowing down, he transferred me from the Charlestown troop he had established to an older, more active troop in North East. Several of my classmates were in this troop, and they were making steady progress toward the Eagle. When they finally earned it, they would be the first Scouts in memory in that part of the county in memory to do so. Changing troops did speed my progress up the ranks, but because of the minimum "time in grade" requirements at each rank, I could never catch up to my classmates. They received their Eagle awards a few months before I became eligible. My father was quite displeased that the families of the other boys would not delay receiving their Eagle badges for several months until I became eligible. As I look back, it seems perfectly understandable and reasonable that those parents would not want to delay the moment when their children received recognition for all their hard work.

In addition to the Eagle rank, I had earned my God and Country award and been initiated into the Order of the Arrow, the Boy Scout national honor society. My father saw that I was entered into consideration for Boy Scout of the Year. When I came to him to say that I had been selected Scout of the Year for Cecil County, he asked why I wasn't Scout of the Year for the entire Del-Mar-Va Council (which included all of Delaware and the Eastern Shore areas of Maryland and Virginia).

Earning My Way

My parents had bought some land across the dirt road that ran past our house, and each year they planted a garden there, about one acre in size. This provided most of our vegetables and other produce for the year, either eaten fresh or put up by canning or freezing. I helped with planting and harvesting, but what I did most (as did Damon, as he grew older) was weeding and hoeing. When someone says, "That's a long old row to hoe," I know experientially just what they mean. We sold door to door any produce we could not use ourselves. In the summer months, numerous families from urban areas moved into nearby summer houses for all or part of the season. When I was very small, Mom drove me from house to house and stood behind me as I made my sales pitch. Later on, I rode my bicycle from customer to customer.

Mowing lawns (and the money I earned by doing so), church, and Boy Scouts are the most frequent journal entries of my twelfth summer. At that age, six lawns were the maximum I could handle, as that meant a different lawn each afternoon, with the gasoline push mower. Dad provided the mower and the gasoline. Finishing a lawn meant another one or two dollars in my savings, which I carefully watched grow till I could buy the AM/FM/shortwave transistor radio of my dreams. Daily, I would record in my journal whether I spent the day cutting grass or waiting out the rain, and in the back of the journal I kept a careful account of income and expenses. Two breaks in the lawn-mowing routine came when our family took a trip to New England and eastern Canada and the week I spent at Boy Scout camp.

Memoir of the Life and Religious Labors of Lloyd Lee Wilson

Our New England trip was typical of our family vacations. We packed up the car, drove to the first paved road, and stopped. My father asked my mother, "Which way should we go?" She said, "North," and north we went. In Canada, we stopped at a roadside picnic table and made friends with a local resident who happened to walk by, and he took us to visit a French Canadian farm family a short way down the road. They spoke no English and we spoke no French other than what little Mom remembered from one year in high school, but they had a large album of photographs from their daughter's recent wedding, and the adults spent the afternoon looking at them. There were several other children roughly my age, and I remember we found games to play that required little in the way of language skills.

One of my lawn-mowing jobs was in Charlestown itself, about two miles from home. I was riding my bicycle through town when I noticed an old lady sitting on her front porch. Without thinking about it, I tipped my straw hat to her as I passed by. She took the trouble to find out who I was (not hard in such a rural area) and called my parents to offer me a job cutting her lawn. This added about $2 per week to my income, which was welcome. On the downside, two miles was considered close enough for me to push my lawn mower and gasoline can when neither parent was around to drive me, so I feel I can say I earned every cent I was paid.

I had a full-time summer job after my freshman year in high school helping paint the county schools, earning good wages at $1.00 per hour. When we came to a school that I had never heard of before, I realized for the first time that the school system was segregated. Of course, I'd never seen black children in my classrooms, but I had never before thought about what that meant—that they must have been going to school someplace else.

The income and expense record I kept in the summer of 1963 shows I cut eight lawns on a weekly schedule, earning about $2 per lawn. My weekly allowance was now 85 cents, of which 40 cents went to the church collection. I duly noted additions to my modest coin collection as expenses, along with purchases of Pepsi (10 cents), a slide rule ($5), and a contribution to the Best Teacher contest at school (25 cents). On a regular basis, I purchased a $25 savings bond to go toward my college education, recording the $12.50 expense each time.

Local Culture

Rifles, shotguns, and pistols were part of Eastern Shore culture when I was growing up. My father had several of each at home. We grew up understanding that they were to be respected and that they had good and proper uses. I can remember bringing in my great-grandfather's converted flintlock long rifle, unannounced, to an elementary school "show and tell" event. The rifle was of great interest because it was so big and so old, but there was no comment at all about my just walking into school carrying it.

My own experience with firearms was ambivalent. When I was ten years old, I discovered an old, broken BB rifle at my Aunt Nellie's. When my father found me playing with it, he fixed it and took me to a store where I could buy some BBs. I walked all the way around Aunt Nellie's pond, shooting every tadpole and young frog I could find. I felt joy and a sense of accomplishment with each one I hit, watching it sink to the bottom of the pond. When I went back to the house, I proudly announced my accomplishment. Aunt Nellie, in her quiet way, said she would miss the bullfrogs croaking their songs later in the summer since I had killed them all. I was struck hard by the unforeseen consequences of my actions and have never been able to forget that day. I cannot hear frogs around a pond without thinking of that incident. I realized that killing even a tadpole had consequences and was not to be undertaken lightly and without real need or adequate reflection.

Hunting was an important part of Eastern Shore culture, and the first year a boy went hunting was a rite of passage into young manhood. When the time came, my father introduced me to hunting, buying my first county resident hunting license and taking me to hunt ducks, squirrels, and rabbits. He bought me an over-under combination .22 rifle/.410 shotgun, which was a good multi-use weapon for a young boy unlikely to hit very much anyway. What I remember most about duck hunting is sitting very still out on the water for long periods of time, very cold and miserable. I had to borrow someone else's bigger shotgun, and I don't remember ever getting the opportunity to fire it. Squirrel hunting was much more comfortable since it was possible to move around and get warm, but again I never succeeded in hitting one. Rabbits were the most interesting game to hunt since they ran away in order to escape, but they often ran in a big circle so that if the hunter stayed in one place they came back. I got one unsuspecting rabbit before he began to run, and together Dad and I skinned and butchered it for eating. I had had no qualms about pulling the trigger before the fact, but as we skinned the animal I was struck by the finality of the death I had caused. My experience around Aunt Nellie's farm pond kept nagging at me, and I never went rabbit hunting again after that first time.

My father decided to raise rabbits in order to provide some meat for our table. He brought two home, of which one was pregnant. Before very long he was ready to start killing some to eat, but I protested so strongly he held off. This continued until we were feeding 114 rabbits, at which time he relented and sold them to someone whose children presumably had fewer scruples about killing rabbits. Interestingly, although we also kept chickens at this time, I had no problems with killing and eating chickens. I went fishing for bass, netted herring when they were running, and went crabbing whenever I could without feeling any reservations about eating my catch.

Each of these activities of my childhood had qualities that set me apart from other children my age. Being a preacher at church, my academic achievements in school, the pressure to rise ever higher in rank in the Boy Scouts, working six days a week from a very young age—each of these made me feel and be treated differently from other boys. My parents made these differences feel even more stark as they drilled into me that, as a Wilson, I was different from everyone else, held to higher standards of behavior and performance. No one liked me for myself, according to my parents—only for what they could get from me. My father forbade me to open the hood of any car or be around an exposed automobile engine for fear it would tempt me away from attending college. My mother lectured me that boys were out to make themselves feel better by derailing my plans for college and girls were only interested in getting pregnant by me so they could keep me in Cecil County as their husband. All this talk had its effect on me.

Laying the Foundation

I spent the summer after graduation (1965) as a counselor at Caesar Rodney Boy Scout Camp near home. Some of the other counselors were college students, and one day I came into their cabin and heard them talking about an aerial dogfight that had taken place somewhere called Vietnam. The United States had apparently shot down more planes than it lost, which was reported with cheers and laughter, much like a home team victory on the athletic field. This was the first time I was conscious of the existence of Vietnam or that American soldiers were fighting a war there; I wondered where it was on the world map.

Chapter 2
A Severe Left Turn: Cambridge/Boston, 1965–1970

Arriving in Cambridge to begin my college career seemed to me like one more accomplishment in what had been, to that point, an unbroken series of accomplishments throughout my life—a journey of ascents. My sense of self was robust and confident; I expected that my life would continue to be a series of steady accomplishments.

As a brand-new freshman, I felt the arc of my life for the immediate future was clear and secure. I had always been academically successful; I would continue to be a good student and would enter graduate school immediately after finishing my MIT engineering undergraduate degree. Being a college man would allow me to serve my country as a military officer, which neither my father nor my several Confederate Army or Revolutionary Army ancestors had been able to do. I was respected in the Methodist Church community and was comfortable with the duties and responsibilities of a serious church member as they had been modeled for me by my parents. Life after graduate school and a hitch in the Air Force were pretty fuzzy but would certainly involve more accomplishments and more respect given me by my colleagues and peers.

The next five years would disassemble that vision of the future entirely. Like Horatio, I learned there are more things in heaven and earth than I had ever dreamt of. The world was larger, stranger, and more unpredictable than I could imagine. Most importantly, the world was not under my control. I could not make my fortune or control my destiny or be in any meaningful sense a self-made man.

One of the fundamental lessons we must learn in the spiritual life is that we ourselves are not at the center of our story, despite all the work invested in putting ourselves at the center when we are growing up. That early work, the journey of ascent or the hero's journey, is essential to becoming a healthy adult. Nevertheless, to become spiritually mature we must eventually exchange the hero's journey for the journey of descent. Usually, that requires some dramatic event or events to drive home the reality that the universe does not revolve around us. Then, we can reorganize our world with a more authentic center. Often, we must learn this lesson over and over and each time reorganize until finally God is truly at the center of our story. That first break and reorganization is usually the most dramatic and traumatic. For me, it took five years to accomplish, and it impacted three major areas of my life: education, the military, and religion.

Education

I was more than ready to make a fresh and independent start to my life when my family drove to Cambridge, Massachusetts, to take me to MIT. We were directed to a room in the East Campus dormitories and quickly moved my belongings from the family station wagon to my assigned room. When the job was done, I looked at my parents and said, "Thanks. I'm set now." Mom started to explain that she was ready to stay and help me get settled, but I emphasized that would not be necessary, and my parents and Damon left for the trip back to Maryland.

Like most of my freshman classmates, I had arrived on campus a full week before registration for fall classes because of fraternity rush week. MIT was so short of housing for undergraduates that the fraternities had to house a significant number of entering freshmen, who pledged for fraternities before attending their first classes. As evening drew near, I wandered over to Kresge Auditorium, where a kickoff event was being held. I did not realize that the fraternities carefully researched entering freshmen and had issued special invitations to their desired potential pledges long before. Walking up to some likely-looking fellows under the Phi Delta Theta banner, I introduced myself and struck up a conversation. The senior I spoke with decided that this self-confident, well-spoken young man was worth offering an ad hoc invitation to go back to the Phi Delta fraternity house, even though I was not on their list of prospects. Later, I went back to East Campus to pick up my things; I never did spend a night in a dorm room. Little did I know it then, but this chance encounter very likely saved my MIT career.

Arriving in the Boston area for college at the age of seventeen was for me like setting foot in a foreign land. My haircut and clothes were wrong, my accent was funny, and my cultural assumptions were the stuff of jokes by my classmates. I soon acquired the nickname of "Emperor Bumpkin, the haughty hayseed."

The cultural disorientation I felt would not have been much greater had I been deposited on a different continent. Most of the language I understood, though the accents and pronunciations were strange to my ears and the vocabulary simply weird. If I ordered a milkshake back home at the local drive-in, it was served upside down, and it was free if any of the mixture spilled out. In New England, a milkshake was simply flavored milk. If I wanted ice cream included, I had to order a frappe. Likewise, a tonic was medicine in North East, but in Boston it was a Coke or Pepsi.

Part of my unease was a matter of scale. I had grown up not far from a town of 350 persons, my high school graduating class had 100 students, and Elkton, the county seat, had a population of approximately 4,000 people. Greater Boston had a population of a million people, and the MIT undergraduate student body was larger than Elkton, Maryland. The freshman class alone was the size of North East, the nearest town to my home with a traffic light.

I changed immediately from a big frog in a small pond to a rather insignificant tadpole in a sizable lake. Back home, the guidance counselor had sent my SAT scores back to the College Board because they must have been misprinted—they were too high. At MIT, I learned that my scores were somewhat below average for the entering class. The math teacher back at North East High would spend an entire hour with our class of twenty-five students working through one new concept on the classroom chalkboard and would often mark her work with "Do Not Erase" so we could take the topic up again the next day. In my Differential Calculus lecture hall, there was stadium seating for two hundred students. The professor filled three large whiteboards with one formula after another, writing and talking at a rapid pace. When all three were filled, to my amazement he pressed a button and each was lifted up higher on the wall, revealing three more blank whiteboards awaiting his inscriptions. My mathematics preparation was woefully inadequate; I could barely follow the concepts being presented at MIT, much less take coherent notes. Meanwhile, a group of Japanese students in the first row were writing everything down in detail and taking Polaroid photographs of each whiteboard for later review in their study group. I'd never been in a study group and didn't really understand what they were.

My state of mind was not improved by reading passages like the following I copied from my first-semester chemistry textbook: "Some of the simplified derivations are not difficult to follow, but impossible. These derivations leave mysteries in their wake and give the student the feeling that some sixth sense is necessary, as indeed it is, to decide what to do next." That necessary sixth sense consistently eluded me.

Phi Delta Theta really did rescue me from being lost in this strange place. A pledge class of twelve freshmen and a house of about thirty students overall provided a small group of friends. The pledges were assigned in groups of three to sophomore "room kings" for daily study; during my freshman year each one of the four room kings had earned at least one 5.0 GPA (straight As) as a freshman. As a group, we were tutored by Patrick Henry Winston III, who had earned seven straight 5.0s before falling in love with a Wellesley student the spring of his senior year and earning a single B. I participated in required study hours every weekday night and Sunday afternoon, pretest review sessions, and coaching on how to take an MIT exam. As pledges, we were also required to memorize the Massachusetts Bay Transportation Authority public transit train routes, the numbering system for MIT's academic departments, and other valuable orientation information.

In the midst of all that was different and even shocking about my new life as a university student in a liberal urban environment, intercollegiate soccer offered me a thread of continuity. I went out for the freshman team (freshmen could not play on the varsity teams) and played my way into the starting lineup. Even there I met with the new and exotic in the form of new rules, different formations, and international teammates who demonstrated ball-handling skills and concepts of the flow of the game that alternated between being frustrating to me and breathtakingly beautiful.

Having enjoyed intercollegiate soccer so much, I went out for the freshman indoor track team in the winter season, running the middle distances on MIT's indoor track. I played on the freshman lacrosse team in the spring. In many ways, the exercise and the discipline were good for me, but the time spent away from my studies only contributed to my growing lack of focus on academics. Going to classes seemed more and more like an optional activity. Strictly speaking, that was true; no record of attendance was ever taken at MIT. However, only the best students could keep up with the material without attending classes regularly, and I was nowhere near to being in that group.

With the help of the Phi Delts, I made it through the academic challenges of that first semester. The study time every night after supper was strictly enforced, our room kings were available to answer any questions we had, and weekly quiz reviews oriented us to how MIT organized tests and exams and how to get the most partial credit on each question. The important point, which came as a shock to me, was to demonstrate that one knew how to get to the answer to a problem, not to come up with the answer itself. One's grade almost always depended on those questions on which one didn't get the right answer but showed that one knew the right method to use, thus earning partial credit. I ended the semester with a 3.1 GPA on a 5.0 scale: a C average. Dad had told me he would be happy if I made all Cs. The pressure was off (or so I thought)—I could survive at MIT.

I could not have named it then, but what I was beginning to learn through my college experience was the enabling and equipping power of community. Together, my fraternity brothers and I were able to meet the challenges we faced, both in the classroom and outside, more effectively and more successfully than any of us could have done alone. We were accountable to one another to uphold the character and reputation of Phi Delta Theta (including academic success at MIT) and committed to help one another accomplish that. Our little community had two purposes: to help one another succeed in obtaining a lasting education and to help one another in the transition into adulthood. In both of these, we largely succeeded.

Since then, my thinking about the local Quaker meeting has developed along similar lines. The meeting helps the individual face various challenges successfully because each member brings a different set of skills, knowledge, and abilities to the table. It seems to me that God brings a unique purpose to each Quaker meeting and that together the members of that community have the skills, knowledge, and gifts to carry out that purpose. That purpose may change over time, but God always ensures that the meeting has the spiritual and physical resources to carry out its purpose faithfully.

Near the beginning of the spring semester, our pledge class, along with all the other fraternity pledge classes on campus, went through "Hell Week." We were then initiated into Phi Delta Theta. Hell Week involved a lot of hard work and meaningless exercise, verbal harassment and insults, very little sleep, and almost no time for studies or other outside activities. An incident that stood out for me centered on whether or not to drink a Coca-Cola.

At the beginning of Hell Week, we pledges were required to swear that we would not drink any sodas or partake of any other luxuries for the duration of the week. Near the end of the week, after a long period of hard work, one of the brothers told me to take a break and have a Coke. I refused, citing the oath I had taken not to do so. He insisted, and we were at an impasse for a long, uncomfortable time; he shouted angrily that I had to do what I was now being ordered to do, and I objected that I was prevented from doing so by a prior promise on my honor. After what seemed like a very long time, another brother intervened, and I was persuaded to drink the Coke. It tasted like I had betrayed myself and my word.

Whether or not to have a soda is a small thing, but I would face the same issues with much larger stakes just a few years later. I gave my word that I would serve in the US Air Force as an officer, just as I gave my word that I would not drink a soda during Hell Week. I felt I received instructions from a higher authority later to break that oath and refuse to serve in the military, as I had received instructions from the fraternity brother to break my word and have a Coke. Before Hell Week, I had regarded my word as an inviolable commitment; afterward, I knew that it could be broken, for better or for worse.

One day, we gathered around the radio at the fraternity house and listened to the NCAA basketball championship game in which Texas Western, unranked at the beginning of the season, beat long-time powerhouse Kentucky in a huge upset. What we couldn't see over the radio but had heard about in other ways was that Texas Western was an all-black team and Kentucky was all-white. Once again, athletics seemed to be leading the way toward integration of the races.

My spring semester grades were awful, including a D in physics and an F in integral calculus. The room king system failed me in this instance as my room king had his own issues and went from a 5.0 average his freshman year to a 0.0 that spring. I was not adequately committed to academics and was not using the available resources (such as going to class, which had become an optional activity for me). I'd taken a light load of coursework my first year anyway, and now I was seriously behind the pace needed to graduate in four years.

The cracks in the foundation of my world were already visible, had I had the eyes to see them. Academically and intellectually, I had met my match and more. For the first time in my life, I had failed not just an exam but a semester-long course. I had seen a whole classroom outpace me in calculus and had been unable to stop it from happening. Other strains were slower to develop but present all the same. Spiritually, I was coasting, as a sailboat will continue to move forward for a while after the wind has stopped. Religion was still primarily a matter of personal morality; I had as yet put down no deeper spiritual roots than those I had developed as a child. The war in Vietnam had yet to impinge much on my awareness. I had no qualms about the morality of war in general, and I still felt that a tour in the Air Force as an officer was the best way to fulfill my obligations to my country.

I returned to MIT for the 1966 fall semester determined to bring my grades up above the C level to a 3.0 on MIT's grade scale. This would be possible, I felt, by attending all classes and studying more regularly. I would still participate in sports but would try to limit my time.

I did do better, but not well enough. My fall semester grade average was only 2.9. Some additional change would be necessary. So, I moved across the street to a small apartment with Bill Kampe, an MIT graduate student. Bill had been selected the outstanding Phil Delt in the nation in his senior year and had an outstanding academic record. I knew he would be a good influence on me, and there would be fewer distractions from my studies in that small apartment.

In the spring, I decided to give up lacrosse in order to spend more time on my studies. My spring grades were significantly better, but a second problem now loomed large—the number of academic credits I'd earned was well below the pace necessary to graduate in four years. After four semesters, I was roughly a full semester behind. It would be necessary for me to take significant overloads each semester from then on in order to graduate on time. Family finances, with my younger brother Damon getting ready to enter college the year after I was supposed to graduate, would not stand up to the extra burden if I did not graduate on time.

By happenstance, I attended an evening gathering that fall to hear a Sloan School of Management professor discuss the study of management at MIT, particularly the study of organizational psychology—how people work together in groups. Professor Thomas Allen made a great impression on me, and I took my first management course in the spring. It was a wonderful experience, and I decided to major in management, not nuclear engineering or mechanical engineering.

For my junior year, I shared an apartment with three fraternity brothers. Just before the first soccer game of the season, I injured my foot and could not play. As I healed, I made the decision not to rejoin the team when I was able to practice again but to devote the time to my academics instead.

My grades for fall semester 1967 were my best thus far. I got an A in Managerial Psychology—my first A in an academic subject at MIT. I now hoped to break 4.0 (a B average) in the spring semester and continue to improve in my senior year. My faculty advisor told me that if I continued as I had, and if I did well on my graduate school admission tests, I should not have too much trouble getting into a good graduate school.

Despite my improved grades, an incident that fall illustrated once again the limitations of my background. I signed up for Introduction to Music as one of my required humanities courses. Early in the semester, the professor gave the class the assignment to listen to Stravinsky's *Rite of Spring*. He warned us that it was quite different from most classical music and that it had been quite controversial in its day. This warning had one meaning when heard by someone who actually had some exposure to "conventional" classical music, such as Beethoven or Mozart, but a different meaning when heard by someone like me who did not.

The music library at MIT had recordings on large reel-to-reel tapes that students took to listening booths in the library. I checked out *Rite of Spring,* threaded it through the tape player, and spent an agonizing hour or so listening to the most discordant, upsetting cacophony of noise I could imagine. It was not until many months later that I realized that the last user had not rewound the tape and I had listened to the composition backwards. If this was high-class music, I wanted no part of it, so I stopped attending class or doing homework. Only by some highly focused and strategic cramming during Reading Week was I able to salvage a C in the course.

I took the Admission Test for Graduate Study in Business (now the Graduate Management Admission Test, or GMAT) that fall and scored in the 99th percentile at 719 (the average for the entering Harvard Business School class at that time was 680). My sights were set on staying at MIT's Sloan School, though, not switching to Harvard, but my score on the test gave me more confidence that I would be admitted to Sloan's PhD program.

The spring semester of my senior year at Sloan kicked off with a multi-day T-group experience. Sometimes referred to as "sensitivity training groups," these experiences were designed to teach skills in interacting with other persons through extended personal interactions among participants. The interactions were often quite intense, and the lessons learned were sometimes difficult to accept.

These particular sessions ran for two full days—morning, afternoon, and evening. Over the course of the two days, each of us received explicit feedback about how our interactions in the group were perceived and understood by the others present. The feedback I received was generally consistent with feedback I'd gotten elsewhere:

1. I seemed like an observer too much of the time and a full participant too little of the time.
2. I was perceptive about what was going on in the group.
3. My comments were articulate and meaningful, if sometimes bookish—academic rather than personal.
4. I could be emotionless.
5. I had a tendency to lose touch with the real world by wandering off in my mind.
6. My comments had integrity. They were real to me—they were what *I* wanted to say.
7. I was more of an independent thinker than a follower in the group.

I applied to several Big Ten graduate schools over the winter. I finished the required essay for the University of Wisconsin just in time to hear on the midnight news that National Guardsmen were moving onto the main Wisconsin campus. I wondered whether my application would be opened by the administration, the student militants, or the National Guard.

Finally, the end of the semester arrived, and I received my bachelor's degree from MIT—a major life goal. I graduated from MIT in spite of the doubts of so many people, and I did it in the standard four years.

The Military

Before I registered for any classes as a freshman at MIT, I joined the Air Force ROTC. I had absorbed the culture of the Eastern Shore of Maryland and felt that military service was one of the responsibilities of every able-bodied young man. In spite of growing up on and around the waters of the Chesapeake Bay, I was anxious about drowning at sea, so the Navy was out. The Army and Marine Corps seemed unnecessarily dangerous, so I settled on the Air Force. There, I might become a pilot and serve my country at some distance from the gunfire and torpedoes. The Air Force also promised access to computers and other technology. Being an officer was better than being enlisted, so I chose the Air Force ROTC.

Memoir of the Life and Religious Labors of Lloyd Lee Wilson

As part of my early Air Force ROTC activities, I began reading the official Air Force doctrine, including deterrence through mutual assured destruction (MAD). The idea was that the United States would deter war by being willing to escalate any conflict to a higher level, one at which the opponent could not hope to win. The highest conceivable level of conflict would be one in which both sides were assured of their own and each other's destruction: MAD. If the United States were known to be both able and willing to escalate a conflict up to and including the level of MAD, potential opponents would be deterred from waging war on the United States. I noted in my journal my approval of the doctrine.

MIT had absorbed an old state armory building and converted into a gymnasium. The main floor, now a series of basketball courts, was an exam room for very large classes during midterms and finals. In an echo of its former life, the armory was used by the various ROTC corps on campus once a week for marching drills and other formations. While drilling one afternoon in 1965 with the AFROTC cadet corps, I heard muffled shouts and the sound of people banging on the doors, trying to get in. When marching in formation, there is no opportunity to ask what is going on, and one can look in a given direction only when the marching orders for the group happen to turn one's head that way. Only afterward did I learn that there had been a demonstration against the war in Vietnam outside the armory. The demonstrators wanted to confront the ROTC participants on the issue, but someone had quickly locked the doors, shutting them out. It was not clear to me why there would be such a demonstration; I was still not aware of what was going on in the war.

Developments in my junior year (1967–1968) forced me to pay attention to the moral issues of the war in Vietnam. In the fall semester I became an enlisted member of the Air Force Reserve, assigned to the MIT Air Force ROTC unit, and the Air Force in return began to pay me a small stipend each month. I was now officially part of the Air Force and was committed to following the orders of superior officers, right up to the president. I could not be drafted out of college, but if for any reason I did not become an officer, I would owe the Air Force a four-year stint as an enlisted airman. Meanwhile opposition to the war was growing to unprecedented levels in Greater Boston, especially on university campuses—including MIT. I was caught with one foot in each of two

A Severe Left Turn

opposing camps: the military folks who were obligated to fight as ordered and to win if at all possible and the civilians opposed to the war who felt it was so immoral that drastic acts of resistance were justified. As the tension increased, more and more of my attention outside the classroom was focused on trying to sort out my own feelings about the morality of the war, which was a largely unsuccessful effort.

Entries in my journal from that fall touch on three topics that would become increasingly important to my life and decisions over the next three years. The first was that the commitment to a particular religion or faith tradition can only be assessed from the inside, from the perspective of one who has accepted the premises of the faith and now seeks to fulfill the obligations of those premises. It is only from that perspective that the religion can be truly understood or critiqued. The second topic was that a necessary part of my becoming a man would be to make a decision contrary to a valued opinion of my family or other reference group and defend that decision successfully.

The third topic in my journal entries was the war itself, which had begun to impress itself on my consciousness as it escalated and public debate mounted. I deliberately avoided the questions surrounding whether or not we should have been fighting in Vietnam to begin with but centered on what was the best policy to follow now that the United States was in the middle of a hot war in Southeast Asia. I took refuge in something I had often heard my parents say: our leaders in government know a lot more than we do, and we have to trust them to do the right thing.

Half a century later, I don't find much solace in that attitude. At the time, however, putting responsibility for moral and strategic decisions about the war on the government's shoulders allowed me to avoid facing those issues personally for months. Eventually, a combination of public events and personal experiences forced me to confront the issues of Vietnam and my own military commitment directly.

I was aware of having entered a moratorium on personal decision making, putting off even major decisions as long as possible until outside conditions forced a choice. I was in general aiming at graduate school somewhere, in some field; I was in general trying to broaden my experience and discard narrow prejudices and biases; I was in general trying to explore the craft of being a leader; but in detail I was unable to say where I wanted to go or what sort of life I wanted to live.

Outside conditions soon forced a series of choices in my life, in spite of my reluctance. The controversies surrounding the war in Vietnam were gaining more and more of my attention. Newspapers were full of reports of the Battle of Khe Sanh, comparing it to Thermopylae, stopping the Turks at the gates of Vienna, and the Battle of Britain—all turning points in history. If we didn't stop aggression in Vietnam, we would soon be fighting from bunkers on the California coast.

Orders are orders. Military service was an obligation of citizenship, and that obligation extended to college men in particular. These commitments from my upbringing were still strong in my mind and heart. My beliefs that military action was a legitimate tool of national policy and that military service was an obligation of citizenship were unshaken but were being challenged daily. I could reconcile my support of the US presence in Vietnam, and my membership in ROTC, with my admitted disapproval of certain aspects of the conduct of the war and my aversion to the taking of human life only through accepting the paradox that some things are wrong but have to be done anyway.

In the clear-edged, black-and-white moral universe in which I was raised, paradox was unacceptable. If something was wrong, there was no circumstance in which it was acceptable. Either the war in Vietnam was the right thing to do or I should not participate in any way. My problem was that choices in the real world were not as clear-edged and stark as my moral training had anticipated, and I had no tools to help me work through this different, fuzzier moral territory.

I understand now that a rule-based ethics, whether religious morals or secular laws, is always inadequate to guide our behavior in an ever-changing world. Rules can only reflect what we've already encountered and cannot anticipate what choices we will face in the future. My morals and ethics must be based on a changed heart and a changed perspective from which I attempt to understand situations and choices as the loving God I encounter in worship perceives and understands them. This does not avoid paradox—in fact, it may increase my ability to see paradox. It

A Severe Left Turn

does result in opportunities for love of all persons and all of creation and for giving priority to the restoration of relationships over retribution for "bad" behavior.

When I was an MIT student, however, I had not yet reached that understanding. I wanted an end to the war, but only if it did not compromise US. foreign policy; I wanted an "honorable" end. Till such an end was negotiated, I felt, we had to continue the bloody business of waging war to preserve peace, in defense of the concept of individual liberty. I didn't want to go to war, not even to fight for peace and/or democracy, but if not me, who? If not now, when? I had no answers to these questions.

About this time, the MIT Air Force ROTC held its annual war game.[1] In 1968, as might be expected, the selected battleground was Vietnam. Participants were divided into four groups comprised of the political leadership and military command for both sides: the Chinese Communists (presumed to be the real leadership behind the North Vietnamese forces) and the United States. I was chosen to be the military commander for the Communist forces. Each group did careful advance research to prepare itself for the day of the game.

As the war game began, the Communist forces made a series of surprise attacks with great success, crippling several air bases. Troops and supplies were moving down the Ho Chi Minh Trail without fear of US airpower. Suddenly, it was announced that the United States had bombarded the Ho Chi Minh Trail with multiple nuclear weapons, making it impassable and also causing massive amounts of death and destruction. The referees stopped the game and declared victory for the US side.

I was shocked. What had happened in the game was standard US doctrine, but the implications of that doctrine had never before hit me as it did then. The willingness of my fellow cadets, soon to be up-and-coming leaders in the US military, to use nuclear weapons for a tactical objective was a very unwelcome surprise. Now I saw the escalation inherent in mutual assured destruction in a new light. The death and destruction the United States was willing to inflict seemed completely out of proportion to the political and military objectives to be gained. There was something grossly wrong with the willingness to destroy so much life and land in order to assert political superiority. I continued to think about the reality of war and the real destruction, pain, and suffering it brought from that moment on.

Reflection on doctrine did not extend to questioning my place in the military. I still felt the military role was a necessary and honorable one and that good citizens should serve. As the day to leave for ROTC summer camp—a sort of basic training for future officers—drew closer, I was more and more reluctant to go, but the issue was that I was afraid I wouldn't perform well, not that I didn't belong there.

I reported to Otis Air Force Base on Cape Cod for four weeks of intensive physical and classroom training under the supervision of Major Theophilos (the English translation of his name, "lover of God," was not lost on me). Beyond the physical exercise and various team-building activities, I remember getting to ride in a T-33 jet trainer at 425 mph only ten feet above sea level and watching the ocean spray accumulate on the wings (the pilot was reprimanded for that once we landed). Despite that stunt and the pilot's other acrobatics, I did not lose my lunch—though some others did. I returned from camp less desirous of a career in the Air Force than before but more confident that I could fit in during a stint of four years of active duty.

In many ways, my senior year of college started with that ROTC summer camp and ended with my commission as a second lieutenant in the Air Force twelve months later. I got my SB (bachelor of science) degree the day after I was commissioned, which was a great joy, but by that time my academic sights were already set on a PhD. The military activities of that year that were the most emotionally powerful for me, sidetracking my academic plans and setting the stage for the spiritual and religious breakthroughs I had in the following months.

I received an Air Force financial assistance grant for my senior year, which covered tuition, books, travel to and from home to MIT, and a monthly stipend. The accompanying letter read: "You have successfully competed against top caliber cadets at your institution and throughout the entire Air Force ROTC program. . . . [Y]our interest, academic achievement and officer potential have been singularly recognized." I was

A Severe Left Turn

also promoted to cadet major and appointed deputy commander of the Air Force ROTC.

In the spring of my senior year, the questions and doubts I had about serving in the Air Force grew, though not yet to the point of making me consider finding a way to avoid my commitment. That semester our Air Force ROTC senior class was given a one-page creative writing assignment on a topic of our own choosing. Tom Imrich, the star of our group of seniors, turned in a well-written piece about the adrenaline thrill of flying a jet fighter. Other cadets wrote similar pieces, full of action and all related to the Air Force. Hearing them read gave me a strong sense of being in the wrong place as I had turned in an otherworldly reflection on the second movement (largo) of Dvořák's *New World Symphony* in which I described a vision of an ancient procession through a virgin forest.

A week later, I requested to be relieved from my duties as deputy cadet commander of the MIT Air Force ROTC. I did not have the time or the motivation to do a decent job, and both I and the squadron were hurting as a result. I talked to the major in charge of our unit that same day about what I'd done, and he seemed to understand. I also shared my fears concerning active duty with the Air Force; we talked quite frankly for an extended time. He did not quiet my fears about the morality of being in the military, or about my losing my identity and emerging at the end of four years boxed and packaged like an automaton, but he did help. He led me to think that this latter fear was in large part groundless, or at least not worth spending an overly large amount of time on. Right then, I thought that I could take the Air Force and not crack up if everything he said was true, and I had every reason to believe him.

He also pointed out the other factors contributing to my mental condition, such as the strain of being at MIT and of being about to graduate, and he said that a certain amount of doubt was only normal. In addition, he commented that doubting did not mean that one's present course was wrong per se. All in all, I was helped very much by our conversation, and I admired the man more as a result.

As graduation grew closer, our Air Force ROTC unit announced its annual awards. I received an American Legion award for military excellence, which seemed ironic given my doubts and reservations about military service. I was unreservedly happy, though, to receive a letter from the MIT admissions office saying I had been admitted to the PhD program in the Sloan School of Management. My next year seemed settled. Of course, that was all to change dramatically.

I was commissioned a second lieutenant in the US Air Force on June 12, 1969. Our staff sergeant was waiting outside to give us our first salute as officers, and we each gave him the ritual dollar in return. Several weeks later, I got a letter from the Air Force saying they did not approve of my PhD plans, and if I did not make changes that were acceptable to them, they would call me to active duty immediately. The Air Force wanted me to study something that they felt would make me a more valuable officer (a reasonable enough expectation under the circumstances); I wanted to study something I loved. Once the shock wore off a bit, I became somewhat resigned to being called up immediately instead of after graduate school. As long as I was not in a combat situation, I felt I could serve my active-duty time while spending my off-duty hours preparing to return to graduate school.

Religion

My attendance at church became increasingly sporadic after I arrived in Greater Boston. There were no Methodist churches in sight, and the Congregational church I tried was attended by gray-haired elderly folks who took no notice of me. I visited a number of churches and university chapels over several months, but nothing clicked, and I drifted out of the habit of weekly church attendance. There were about half a dozen Phi Delts who attended services somewhere from time to time, and two or three of us would go together to Harvard Chapel, Boston University, or a nearby church a couple of times a month. In my spiritual life, as in my academic life, I was coasting, not putting much effort into it and not getting very much of solid benefit out of it. In between worship services, I did very little in the way of prayer, Bible study, or private devotions.[2]

Early in that first semester, though, I did recognize an opportunity to act in a spiritual way, and I did my best to be faithful. A fellow pledge came to me around 1 a.m. in a depressed state of mind; he had been reading some of Edgar Allan Poe's poems, and they had struck a dark chord in him. After some conversation, I read the Twenty-Third Psalm aloud, on impulse. When I finished reading, I had the clear sense that I had accomplished a task and made ready to leave the room, but my pledge brother asked me to stay. We talked for a long time, he asking questions and I answering them the best I could and reading from the Gospels, mostly Luke—whatever page the Bible opened to. I was very much affected and felt the Presence of God with us. My pledge brother was also deeply touched and said he felt himself "suddenly very nearly believing in Christianity."

Up to this point, my religious service, whether preaching sermons, teaching Sunday school classes, or something else, had been what I would call methodical in nature. I knew the situation I was entering into, I prepared for certain kinds of interactions in that context, and there was, to use a contemporary term, an "exit strategy" for ending the moment of service. This was the first time when the opportunity was entirely unexpected, I had done no formal preparation, and I had no choice except to continue in the encounter, from moment to moment, until we were given to understand it was over. At the time, I walked away wondering, "What was that?" Many years later, I can answer, "That was my first exposure to what Quaker ministry feels like."

I still wore my Sunday school attendance pins on the lapel of my only sport coat. The required dress for dinner every night at the fraternity house was a coat and tie, so my Sunday school connections were on regular display. The Phi Delts kidded me about this and called me "God-man" because of my open faith; in the spring semester, though, they named me chaplain of the chapter. Whether this was a sign of respect or continued gentle mockery I was not sure, just as I was not sure exactly what it was that the chaplain was supposed to do. Still, I accepted readily and looked forward to whatever might come my way as a result. (Not much, it turned out.)

I went home for the summer, where my father had arranged for me to work for the local electric utility company. I was called upon several times over the summer to preach at St. John's and other Methodist churches in the area, and I was paid a modest fee by the other churches. I was now old enough to drive myself to these churches, which was satisfying.

My spiritual life continued to erode, in part because I wasn't paying attention to it. I was in a faith community that worshipped and worked together, and I had not yet faced a moral crisis that would force me to make an assessment of my faith commitments. The war in Vietnam would make me do that, but that came later.

During the summer of 1967, I came home to spend what was to be my last summer with my family. My father again arranged for me to work with the electric utility company. The last two entries in my sermon notebook are sermons given that summer to my home church, St. John's, and to Bethel Methodist in the northern part of the county. My notation indicates that each sermon was given to one church only, not to the entire charge. At St. John's I preached about the phrase "God is dead" and at Bethel about prayer. Looking back on these notes some five decades later, I am struck by how wholly intellectual they are. I talked about "traveling light" concerning images of God and growing into a close communion with God, but these were ideas in my head rather than lived experience.

By this time, I was no longer attending worship services at any church when in Massachusetts. I attended with my parents when I visited them in Maryland, but organized religion no longer played an active role in my life. It was not that I had rejected the church but that it was no longer relevant to me. The two biggest realities of my life were my college studies and the war, and the church was not helping me with either one. I read the transcendentalists (Emerson, Thoreau) and others but not specifically Christian writings.

These issues spilled over into my correspondence with friends at other colleges and elsewhere. In one letter from this period, I wrote,

> Bible scholars tell us the Commandment should read 'Thou shalt not murder.' Yet better that I should be plagued by guilt, another man die, and you live free than that I should die, and another man live to enslave you. That is how I resolve the conflict.

Looking at that passage now, I see I was mistaken on two counts. Our choices are rarely clear-cut, binary options—there is almost always a third way—and the "resolution" I proposed was not a true solution at all.

Another exchange of letters explored the seeming conflict between a loving God and eternal damnation from the perspective of the eternal willingness of God to let humans choose their own fate. Perhaps hell was the state of existence of the souls of those who refused to accept the love of God and who therefore passed through eternity separate from God. Heaven was life with God—knowing divine love.

That fit my experience of God as a mover of my spirit and a director of my thoughts rather than as a maker of miracles. "Trust God but prepare to do it yourself." God is a spirit and moves like a spirit in order to achieve divine ends. If by knowing God I try to order my life as the Son directed, then my soul should attain inner peace no matter how hard I struggle in the attempt. If I reject God and God's teachings, then in no way can my spirit be at rest, and I am damned to hell as surely as if God had sent me there. But if at some future time I repent and seek God and God's favor, I will get it.

The idea of eternal damnation, that God would punish a human being for doing wrongly rather than help that human restore the right order of things that their wrong action disrupted, was no longer part of my belief. I believed God allowed human beings their free will, even when their choices were contrary to their best interests or the interests of creation, and that our human choices often led us to a state of painful alienation from God. That pain was not punishment inflicted by God but part of the essential nature of those particular choices. God remained ready at any time, before physical death or after, to have the natural shalom restored. All we had to do was decide that restoration was what we wanted.

Fusion of the Educational, Military, and Religious Areas of My Life

The national news in 1968 was disturbing. Eugene McCarthy surged in the primaries; President Lyndon B. Johnson decided not to run for re-election. The major Republican candidate, Richard Nixon, seemed to have no new ideas about Vietnam except massive escalation, which I did not believe would help. My journal reflections at the time, however, concerned racism:

> I am increasingly worried about race relations here in the States. If we cannot make a major effort toward reconciliation between black and white before the end of the summer, it seems the dream of America as we have idealized it will come to an end. There will be two Americas, one black and one white, separate and at war with one another. Dedicating the nation's time and resources to prevent that split seems even more important than victory in South East Asia.
>
> Today Rev. Martin Luther King Jr., Nobel Peace Prize recipient, staunch advocate of the brotherhood of man, and leader of the nonviolent civil rights movement, was shot down in cold blood in Memphis, Tennessee. A great force for peace is gone; the occupants of that white Mustang cannot know—surely do not comprehend—what they have done. God bless Martin Luther King. Like his namesake, he stood his ground. Let us mourn his death now. But not for long; let us gird up our loins and set out again on the long road we traveled with him—the road toward an end of the need for a civil rights movement.
>
> There are times when I am overawed by the greatness and huge deeds of certain people—the ones who seem to have changed history or who have set records that will never be equaled. There are other times when the utter unimportance of any given man or men overwhelms me. The death of JFK affected me in the first way; not that he was a great man in terms of his deeds but that he was an attitude, the personification of the American self-image. The death of MLK affected me in the other way. Reverend King was a great man, working to change the attitudes of Americans about race and race relations. It seems clear that the killer thought that by killing King he was killing the civil rights movement (if the killer were white) or at least the nonviolent part of the movement (if the killer were black). But the onward progress of the civil rights movement will not be stopped or permanently slowed that easily. As long as there

exists racial injustice, there will be a Negro civil rights movement; as long as there remain persons of reason and common sense among the Negro population, there will be a nonviolent Negro civil rights movement.

In my thoughts and feelings, I supported the civil rights movement of the 1960s. I was only very peripherally involved in civil rights activities, but the little action I did take was in support of increasing civil rights. In my personal life, I tried to be open to an expanded circle of friendships and working partnerships of various sorts with black neighbors, fellow students, and others. However, I continued to be blind in two very important ways. First, I assumed that correcting laws that institutionalized racial discrimination and enacting laws that prohibited other racially biased behaviors would be an adequate solution. After this era, I spent decades assuming the larger problem was solved and that reports I heard to the contrary were anecdotal and isolated incidents.

The second area of blindness that afflicted me was that I did not see the close relationship between racism, poverty, and the war economy. Martin Luther King was articulating this near the end of his life, particularly in his Poor People's Campaign, but I didn't catch on (together with many other white people in the United States).

What I did see, based on events in the United States, was that Chairman Mao was wrong—political power did not grow out of the barrel of a gun. Every use of violence in the effort to end racism or to end the war in Vietnam was counterproductive. I couldn't explain and didn't really understand why I felt this way, and I couldn't expand this observation to apply to the use of violence generally, but the violence I saw was universally negative in its effects.

In the summer of 1969, these three areas of my life began to affect each other so strongly that I can only tell their stories together, not separately. In preparation for graduate school, I moved into a two-bedroom apartment midway between MIT and Harvard Square, rooming with a fellow Sloan student. I purchased a used 250cc motorcycle and enjoyed the increased freedom of movement it brought. I thought about riding it to the big music concert in Woodstock, New York, in August but decided at the last minute that there would be too many people there. Missed opportunity . . .

I didn't take my motorcycle to Woodstock, but I did begin riding it each Sunday morning to Walden Pond in Concord, Massachusetts. I would find a comfortable seat near the reconstruction of Thoreau's cabin and spend an hour or so reading some part of Thoreau's writings, usually from *Walden*. In these times of reflection, the need for an answer to my questions about military service grew steadily until it became impossible to ignore.

As I read Thoreau and pondered his writings, the essential 'sameness' of human beings became increasingly clear and important to me. I realized that, despite all the ways we are unique and different from one another, we are identical in many more ways. We search for a unique, individual identity, but it may be even more important, in a time of industrialized wholesale death and destruction, to become more aware of our commonalities. If we could begin to understand the many ways we were similar to one another, perhaps we could begin to learn how to live together in peace.

A quote from William Faulkner's 1950 Nobel Prize acceptance speech also made a deep impression on me: "I believe man will not merely endure, he will triumph; not because he is the only creature with a soul, but because he is the only creature capable of sacrifice and compassion and endurance."[3] And so the practice of compassion became a conscious discipline for me in the summer of 1969. I tried on a regular basis to put myself in the place of another specific person—to walk in their shoes, to feel their hates and fears as well as their ambitions and hopes. In doing so, I found that even those who seemed most different from me were so close to me at the center that we were almost indistinguishable. Our circumstances and life histories were different, and the other person might have chosen different means to achieve their hopes and dreams than I did, but at the core we were very alike. I found that I loved my fellow humans, if for no other reason than that not to love someone so like me would be akin to despising my own self.

And thus I returned to another of the childhood admonitions I thought I had outgrown: love your enemies. But now the reasoning was different. Love not to one up your foes or to please God or the Joneses (my parents' explanations seemed to reduce to these three), but love because to love your enemy is to recognize in them a basic humanness and to love that human nature is to love one's self. Not to love, ergo, is to reject one's own inner nature; it is not healthy.

As my first semester as a grad student commenced, I became less and less able to reconcile these reflections and my underlying beliefs with my commitment to serve in the military. As this disconnect became clearer, it seemed that everywhere I turned I saw another reminder that the Air Force would claim me sooner or later and that I must acquiesce or face jail. I felt there must be some way out, some third path, but though I searched, it remained invisible.

Breaking my promise not to drink a soda during Hell Week as an undergraduate had an effect on me now. I had broken my word then, and the sky had not fallen. In the fall of 1969, I no longer felt that the contract I had signed with the Air Force in my junior year was binding on me. I felt that I had changed so much since then that it was essentially a contract made by someone else, not the person I had become.

I no longer believed that it could ever be right to take a human life. It was never right to kill another person. One can generate very difficult moral scenarios in which particular exceptions to that rule might be justified. But a military is *organized* with the *purpose* of taking life. The argument that the military is necessary to defend the country does not hold; my brother's wrongdoing does not justify my wrongdoing.

I did not feel that I could accept combat duty in the Air Force or duty in support of combat, including duty in logistics or the development of weapons systems. In my mind, the argument that the nation was at war already, and my responsibility as a citizen was to join in, was no longer valid. The choice was not between bad and worse situations, as the major in charge of my Air Force ROTC unit had argued, but between right and wrong—it is right to live in harmony with our fellow man; it is wrong to kill each other. It was as simple as that.

My journal entry for September 7, 1969, notes: "I made the decision not to enter the military service this weekend." I didn't want to spend four years of my youth in involuntary servitude to anybody—military or not. I didn't want to kill, I didn't want to train to kill, and I didn't want to be any part of an organization whose purpose was to kill human beings.

The next day I found a psychologist who was sympathetic and agreed to write a letter supporting my application for discharge (conscientious objector applicants were required to document that they were not mentally unstable). Also, I learned the Air Force had granted me an educational delay of the beginning of my active duty until June 1970. I had time to prepare to carry out my decision.

For the next several weeks, I was in a state of liminality, though I did not learn that term until many years later. It felt as if I were standing at a threshold, facing a door that offered entrance into an entirely different life from my current life. For the moment, everything was quite still, and I was waiting for some sign that I should step through the doorway.

Meanwhile, life on this side of the threshold was exhilarating, as I recorded in my journal. I was in high gear from the moment I arrived at the Sloan School each morning till late at night. Multiple new roles opened up for me. I was twenty-two years old. I was also a teacher, a researcher with a real-world problem to investigate (the effects and effectiveness of system dynamics as a classroom focus), and a PhD student with all the benefits of that status. My reflection on all this in my journal read: "It's wonderful!"

The war would not let me rest in this comfortable space. A banner headline in the *Record American* announced that the war in Vietnam had taken only sixty-four American lives that week—the lowest total in 136 weeks. Standing in Kendal Station that evening, waiting for the subway home, I began thinking of just how large sixty-four was. Name sixty-four male friends. Think of them all dead. Now think of three years of this happening every week. Sixty-four is not such a small number when it is counted in human lives.

I continued to read extensively in Lao-Tzu and Mahatma Gandhi in a search for clarity and a spur to action. They encouraged me to stand firm in my convictions concerning war and the institutions of war (i.e., the military services). It was not just the 'others' we had to reach, it was

A Severe Left Turn

everybody, from the toddler to the totterer. If every person resolved to spend a part of each day working for his brothers around him, the threat of war would be over.

I could see the true nature of the life choices that lay before me, but I had no ability to choose a path and act on it. Looking back, I see that it was God's Light showing me the truth of my spiritual condition, but I would not, could not have named that at the time. At this point, when all choices seemed bad, God began to offer me a way to put my life back together.

A teenaged Quaker, Faith Timberlake, invited her non-Quaker friend Ricki Smith to go to a Quaker meeting with her. I had worked with Ricki's mother in the MIT Hayden Library for several years and had become a friend of her family. Ricki invited me to go to a meeting for worship with her and Faith, and my life was changed as a result.

We decided to go on October 12, 1969, and our first surprise was that there were no empty seats.[4] I'd been going to church since I was three years old, and I had never before encountered a completely full church. We sat on the grass near an open window and tried to hear what was going on, which seemed like not much at all. Still, there was an energy about the place that was strongly attractive. I went back the following First Day, alone this time, and again ended up sitting on the grass outside an open window, trying to hear what was going on.

The third week, I arrived early enough to get a seat on the steps of the balcony at the back of the meeting house. The meeting again began in silence (I still had no idea why), and in that absence of sound I felt that I heard things that were normally lost in the noise of everyday life. It was strange and not entirely comfortable. At some point after I had settled down a bit, I had a spiritual experience parallel to John Wesley's at Aldersgate when his heart was "strangely warmed." Shortly after that, I felt a message—as clear as a voice—that said my spiritual search was over. These people, the Quakers, would be my spiritual home, starting at once.

I was not accustomed to hearing divine personal instruction, but for some reason it never occurred to me to doubt the experience or the message. I began attending worship regularly and reading up on Quakers in the MIT libraries as well as the meeting's library. When David McClelland of Harvard, author of one of our core texts at the Sloan School, stood and gave approving ministry about Woodstock, I discovered he was a Quaker too.

My enthusiasm for the faith tradition I was discovering shows in my journal entries from this period:

> This [Quaker meeting] seems to be the church I've been dissatisfied at not finding. The religion lies not in the [Methodist] *Discipline*, or the Vatican, but in the people. It is not interpreted by the rabbi or priest, but by the faithful; the symbol is not the cross upon the altar but the love in the man. Every aspect of meeting declares its uniqueness. That there should be no professional minister declares a faith of the people, devoid of incomprehensible doctrines, uninterpretable save via a life's training in sophistry. . . .
>
> The faith lives in the people, who live in the real world: the Church is the living church, for there are no trappings to leave behind at meeting's end. How can a Friend help living his faith 7 days a week when he himself is the symbol of his faith? How can he not take the Church to the world when he is the Church? . . .
>
> One last point: I went to meeting on Sunday in bell-bottoms, a worn-out sports shirt, and a peace symbol. God didn't seem to mind at all; nor did anyone else.

By Thanksgiving, I saw a clear path forward. I would become a member of Cambridge Friends, declare myself a religious pacifist, and seek a conscientious objector (CO) discharge from the US Air Force as a Quaker. The discharge still seemed unlikely to be successful, but I felt sure now that one way or another I would never wear the military uniform again. I went home for the holiday concerned about how my family would receive the news.

I broke the news over dinner the night before Thanksgiving. Mom appeared to be hit pretty hard; she was primarily concerned that I had joined or had been seduced into a cult.[5] Dad was angry and felt I was making a series of bad decisions, but we managed to get through the meal without either one of us shouting at the other. Things would get worse between Dad and me for several years before we were, after a manner, reconciled. He had a particular concern, one that I had not realized. He needed to be able to get into Fort Meade, Camp David, and similar places on telephone company business, which required (he told me then) top secret clearance. He was worried that his security clearance would somehow be compromised by my actions.[6] Without that clearance, he would lose his job. Damon was quiet but took this all in to be pondered and considered.

On First Day, after I returned to Massachusetts, I spoke in meeting for worship for the first time. It felt right.

My association with Friends Meeting at Cambridge was rapidly deconstructing my spiritual understandings and beginning to rebuild them on a new foundation, but events in the secular world were having their effect on me as well. Tenth Month[7] 15, 1969, was National Moratorium Day—a day of nationwide protests against the war. I took part in a public protest march, though not without wondering which of the many photographers crowding the sidewalks were taking photos for the government and what would happen if they connected my image with an Air Force Reserve officer.

I began my Moratorium Day activity by attending services at St. Peter's Episcopal Church in Cambridge. The last time I had attended services there, in the fall of my junior year, an antiwar sermon had been preached. The preacher went so far as to say that anyone who wore a military uniform was supporting an immoral and sinful war and was therefore immoral and sinful himself. I was so angry that day that I nearly walked out before the sermon ended, and I think I actually did leave before the service ended. I recall trying, later, to explain my anger by saying that I thought war was wrong but that, as a military officer, I was to obey orders and not to pass judgment on my orders.

As I entered St. Peter's this time, I remembered that other Sunday and realized that I now believed much the same as that minister I had heard preach two years earlier. Though sin had little meaning for me, I agreed that wearing a military uniform meant supporting an immoral and unjust war because *all war was wrong*. Even serving in a noncombatant position supported war because it freed someone else to serve as a combatant. If America were at peace, it would still be wrong for me to enter the military service. No good could come from the sword, in the long run.

I remained of the opinion that the issue was not whether or not the NLF (the National Liberation Front created by the Viet Cong) should win but whether violence could breed anything but violence. Violence can only lead to more violence unless one party elects to absorb that force without striking back. And only that person who has the "perfect right" to be violent can effectively advocate pacifism.[8]

The second pillar of my belief was that God resides in each of us; each man's body is a temple of God, if you will. Believing this, I couldn't kill another person or do intentional violence to anyone, for in doing so I would be attacking God.[9]

I drew the third aspect of my pacifism from the teachings of Gandhi. Because I can never be sure that I am absolutely correct on any issue, it is never correct for me to force another to acquiesce to my opinions. To do so is to risk forcing that person to do wrong. Also, if the opponent bows to my superior force and not to my superior reasoning, I have not cured the ill but merely suppressed it, so it will erupt again at a later time. But if I can win another to my cause through the weight of my arguments (and not by the power of my fist), then we are both reassured of the rightness of our cause, and there are now not one but two persons who believe in it.

As I did more research on CO discharges, I discovered that I had not served enough active-duty days in the Air Force (essentially, I had been on active duty in ROTC summer camp) to discharge my military obligation. If I was successful in getting an Air Force discharge, I would be returned to the tender care of the Selective Service System and could be drafted back into military service.

Criticism of the existing Selective Service System led to the implementation of a draft lottery system late in 1969. The first draft lottery was held on December 1, 1969, and was nationally televised. Those persons with numbers below 100 were very likely to be drafted, in numerical order; those with numbers over 300 would almost certainly never be drafted. I missed the first few minutes of the telecast but watched the rest with interest. As the numbers reached 300 and I had not heard my birthdate called out, I began to relax. Then, a replay of the beginning of the program for men born between 1944 and 1950 made my worst fears come true: September 14, my date of birth, was the first date called, meaning I had 'won' the lottery.

Now it was certain that if I succeeded in getting a conscientious objector discharge, I would be drafted immediately unless I convinced my county Selective Service board that I qualified as a CO by their definition as well as the Air Force's.

When my parents realized that my concerns about the war and my own military service were serious and were about to spill over from opinions into actions, the tension at home began to rise. Dad in particular grew increasingly concerned that what I might do personally could affect not only me but also Damon and his own career with the telephone company. He pressured me to hold off as long as possible on any action about military service so that his career would not be needlessly jeopardized. I could see his point, and I certainly didn't want to mess up his life because I had made a mistake two years ago.

I was in a catch-22 dilemma. To satisfy the requirements of the military for discharge as a conscientious objector, I needed to be acting consistently with my professed pacifist beliefs in ways that could be verified by third parties; to uphold my agreement with Dad, I needed to avoid doing anything that a third party might observe and make the connection between son and father.

During this period, I began describing what I was feeling in letters to Damon. My admitted goal was to make a pacifist of him, but at the very least I wanted to help him avoid being stuck in the dilemma I was in as a pacifist in uniform. If Damon decided to serve in the military, I wanted him to have thought it out in advance and to be sure of his decision, not repeating my mistakes. My letters must have had some visible effect because Dad soon forbade me to write or speak to Damon about anything related to the war or to military service.

Over the Christmas holidays, home became a bitterly divided environment. Damon and I grew closer than ever before as both Mom and Dad seemed to be rejecting principles and values important to the two of us. (Quote of the week at the dinner table: "I know it is going to hurt to learn this, Damon, since your brother has been your ideal for so long, but Lloyd is a hippie.") Damon and I talked late into the night and found excuses to get out of the house together during the day. It was wonderful to learn that he supported my pacifism—it gave me strength to know that one person in my family believed me.

On the other hand, my father told me he would "rather have you come home in a box" than be imprisoned as a conscientious objector. He forbade me from talking to Damon about my religious beliefs and announced that Damon would not be allowed to go to college anywhere north of the Mason-Dixon line as "the Northerners" had clearly corrupted me.

So, my parents denounced anything either of us did that they didn't agree with. They refused to let Damon go to college very far from home and did not let him think about changing his religious denomination or wear the clothes he wanted to or think for himself. He held up quite well, however, despite all the pressure. I wrote in my journal that I was proud of him.

As 1970 began, I was more and more committed to doing specific things in the near future and more distressed at my own choices that had put me in this position vis-à-vis the US Air Force. War became less and less comprehensible. How could I ever have contemplated taking part in such an inhuman act? How could I use the mind and body I was just learning to be creative with to kill other human beings who were just as worthy of living as I was? How could I have ever joined the ROTC? Had I gone to a Quaker meeting three years earlier, had I seen people living their faith—speaking to that of God in every person—then I might not have been in this fix. As it was, I could only hope that the Air Force would believe I was sincere and release me from my obligation. I was more than willing to pay back any money they had given me, with interest; I didn't want to go to prison. They had to believe me; otherwise, I *would* go to prison because I was no longer able to be a part of the military.

A Severe Left Turn

I began preparing my formal application for a conscientious objector discharge. My starting point for the application rested on two beliefs: first, that killing was wrong and that I could not in conscience serve in the armed services, and second, that this belief overrode my pre-existing voluntary enlistment in the US Air Force.

My personal experience with the will of God convinced me that human life is so precious that killing another person is never justifiable. This was inchoate in me until I encountered Quakers, but then I knew and had a name for it. There is "God in every man," as George Fox stated three hundred years ago and as lived and spoken by Quakers and other persons of conscience from his time until the present day.[10] This is what I learned in prayer and meditation with God: each person has something of God in him and that this bit of God is the most important thing about anyone. In some this Light shines forth brightly and in others it is almost hidden, but it is always there. Our approach to all persons should be grounded in love and understanding, not fear and violence.

Weekly worship at Cambridge Friends continued to be a mind-stretching, revelatory experience. Standing outside the meeting house one sunny First Day after the rise of worship, I commented to Tim Nicholson, a member of the meeting, that this was the most radical church group I had ever encountered. "Actually, we see ourselves as conservative," Tim replied. "We are trying to preserve primitive Christianity." Even my perception of how different the Quaker way was from other churches was itself subject to radical reinterpretation.

Another First Day morning that spring, Elmer Brown (executive secretary of Friends Meeting at Cambridge) said that the Revolutionary War had been absolutely unnecessary. I was at first taken aback but saw quickly the truth in his statement. I could think of no ill whose redress demanded war or the spilling of human blood. Case in point: How could any person say that any cause—'communist' or 'democratic'—was worth all the killing, maiming, and destruction that had been going on in Vietnam for the last decade?

Attending the Easter service at my parents' Methodist church in 1970 solidified my decision to join the Religious Society of Friends, and I submitted a letter of application as soon as I got back to Boston. Friends took membership applications seriously. I had only been attending meeting for a few months, and it would have been easy to say it was too soon for me to become a member. My clearness committee, seasoned Friends all, asked good questions and listened carefully to my self-disclosures.

One relevant disclosure was that formal membership would have a positive impact on my CO application. Becoming a member of a historic peace church, after I had been commissioned as an officer, threaded an important needle in the application's very tight logical requirements. Yes, I felt certain that the Religious Society of Friends would be my permanent spiritual home, but it was also true that becoming a formal member *right then* would have a tremendous impact on my immediate future.

The other disclosure was my broken relationship to the Christian church and to Christianity in general. As I had come to new understandings about the nature of humankind and our responsibilities to each other, I had become increasingly angry with the Methodist Church for not teaching me pacifism. I felt they had failed me, and every other young man in the church, by not putting this front and center in their religious education. This spilled over into an anger at Christianity itself. If the institutional church is the interpreter and articulator of Christianity, then Christianity had also failed by not understanding and proclaiming the value of each human life and the consequent necessity of avoiding war at all costs. As I now understood things, it was never right to go to war, and if the institutional church didn't understand that, it was fatally flawed.

Friends found me clear for membership. There was a place for me among Quakers even though I was not Christian—even though I was estranged from and angry at all things Christian. For that, as I've said many times since, I am eternally grateful. At the same time, Elmer Brown gave me the most important, most nurturing bit of eldering I have ever received when he said, "Lloyd Lee, you can believe anything you want and be a member, but you must wrestle with the fact that everything you like about Quakerism stems from its Christian roots." That counsel, over the more than fifty years since he said those words, has reshaped my life.

A Severe Left Turn

In the next several months, I continued to attend meeting for worship regularly, read a great deal about the Religious Society of Friends and their history, and examined my own life from the Quaker perspective. This exposure to Quakers in deed and word convinced me of two truths: an ethic of love for *all* human beings is possible and practical, and such an ethic is meaningless unless it is *lived actively*. I adopted these truth claims as my own faith commitment. How should they be applied to the question of military service and the proper way to treat one's neighbors? This question resolved itself into two subquestions:

> 1) Could I, believing that God exists in every living person, serve in the combat forces of the US Air Force, where I might be called upon to destroy a human life?
>
> 2) Could I accept duty in a noncombatant position within the Air Force, such as in a medical unit or as a chaplain's aide, where I might actually be working to alleviate the suffering of others?

I had spent many hours in prayer and meditation, in reading what other persons had said about the correctness of deciding either to fight or not to fight, and in talking to my peers and elders. I believed that there was no cause, no purpose, no ideal that would justify my killing another human being, anywhere—in Vietnam, in Baltimore, or in my own apartment. I could not be right in killing a robber who was about to kill me because God was part of each of us, and I had no way of knowing God's will; I could not know the ultimate effects of my death vs. the death of the burglar. Because I could not know, and because I believed that there was God in the burglar also, I could not kill him but would meet him with as much love as I could muster, hoping to dissuade him but accepting death, if that were the outcome, as God's will. My conclusion was that I could not be a combatant in any form, as part of either a fighting unit or a support unit.

In meeting for worship late that winter, I was shown that I could not serve in the military as a noncombatant. To serve in noncombatant status is to say that war is a necessary evil and that one should do whatever possible to mitigate the evil(s) associated with war. To refuse to serve at all in the armed forces, I was saying by example that war is always evil and unjustifiable and that the Christian calling is not one of mitigating the evil already done (or in the process of being done) but to live and lead others to live so that the causes of war no longer exist and so that humankind comes at last to live in harmony with men and women of all nations and creeds.

I also questioned the existence of any truly noncombatant position in the US Air Force. During my ROTC summer camp experience, I was repeatedly told by officers and non-commissioned officers in what might be considered noncombatant posts, "Our mission is to keep the planes in the air." They were saying that every unit in the Air Force was dedicated to the same overall mission: defense of the nation by military means. I could not support that mission, not even indirectly.

The first step in becoming a CO was to resign my commission because the Air Force did not want to admit that any of its officers might have such a change of heart. I could then apply for a CO discharge as an enlisted airman. If I did not get the discharge, I'd end up serving my four-year enlistment as an airman, not an officer.

On Fourth Month 15, 1971, I was one of an estimated seventy thousand demonstrators on Boston Common, and I came home with the realization that the peace movement had become an antiwar movement. The call for change had shifted toward a call for revolution, for governmental change and not just foreign policy change. Later, well over three thousand demonstrators in Harvard Square gathered in what was quickly labeled a riot. There were more cops than I'd ever seen in one place before and lots of tear gas—enough to make my eyes sting all along Memorial Drive as I drove my motorcycle back from the Common. The radio reported two police cars burned and about thirty-five policemen injured. I went outside to watch for a while, to observe some mob psychology firsthand. I got gassed and was harassed by a policeman, and it took over an hour to find a safe way to get back to my apartment on Massachusetts Avenue.

On Fifth Month 4, 1970, I and eight other PhD students in the Sloan School circulated this statement titled "A Response to Cambodia":

> We, the undersigned majority of the first year Ph.D. students in Management, ask you to temporarily close the Institute to

A Severe Left Turn

implement anti-war activities as a protest against Nixon's aggression in Southeast Asia. We shall independently strike Tuesday, May 5th, whatever the result of the mass meetings of May 4th. We ask for the support of the MIT Faculty and students for our activities.

The Sloan School did shut down, but much of MIT and other colleges and universities in the Boston area did as well. Also on that day, four unarmed students were killed and nine more injured by units of the Ohio National Guard at Kent State University. Eleven days later, two more students were killed and twelve injured by state and local police officers at Jackson State College in Mississippi. Total chaos seemed imminent.

As events unfolded, I became disillusioned about the effectiveness of rallies and leery of the violence to which they seemed to be gravitating. I spent some time thinking about how to implement a form of Gandhi's soul-force against the war. In an unexpected way, the college strike proved to be that force for me. It was not the rallies nor "teach-ins" but the on-the-street activities such as door-to-door canvassing, leafleting at factories and schools, and organizing telegraph-your-congressman booths all over greater Boston that mirrored Gandhi's approach. By the second morning of the college strike, 140 universities were on strike, with more to come. Over two million college students were freed to mobilize public opinion against the war. And they were working hard!

At the end of the semester, I decided to withdraw from the Sloan School. The dean offered me an indefinite leave of absence, but I felt the need for a complete break. The prospect of spending four years in an Air Force prison seemed all too real, and I couldn't predict how I would feel about graduate studies after such an experience. Even setting that aside, having a PhD felt to me like living in an ivory tower when what the world needed was people working with their hands and hearts to pull us back from the edge of catastrophe. I wanted to be in direct service somewhere.

I cannot pretend that a dramatic turnabout such as the one I had made from military officer to pacifist is made all at once or even over a short period of time. In my case, even a year is too short a time. I cannot say that I had no pacifist leanings prior to June 12, 1969 (my commissioning date), but I can say that at that time my overall balance of sentiment favored the military. What I had then was a heightened sense of the horror of war, of the awful destruction it caused, and an understanding that the only reliable way to avert such a catastrophe was for America to remain so strong militarily that no nation would dare to attack us.

Now, I see the flaws in that argument. Continually building up American military power does nothing to avert wars in which we are not involved, does not predict what will happen if some nation approaches parity with us militarily, and does not consider the price of maintaining such strength—a cost that has included the arms race and the Cold War. This narrow, costly, piecemeal approach to avoiding war was no longer adequate for me. I needed a way to live that would foster peace everywhere.

Quakers speak a lot about love. It seems to me that love means to be in harmony with all that is in or around one's life-space: human beings, other living creatures, and inanimate objects as well. Any notion of love that excludes any part of that whole is incomplete. I believe that to reach that harmony in its wholeness would be to feel a peace that is, for me, impossible to put into words. To feel that peace is to put an end to war. I want to feel that peace.

Even among Quakers, there were few people who faced personally the decisions and consequences that confronted me; role models and exemplars were very important. On Eighth Month 11, 1970, I wrote in my journal,

> Father Berrigan was arrested today. He faces three years in federal prison for protesting the war by pouring blood on draft records in Catonsville, Maryland. I am myself prepared to be arrested in a week or 10 days. I feel a little bit like a condemned man; I find myself taking special notice of little things, like ice cream sodas or the feel of a rocking chair, as if to fix them in my memory.
>
> For the first time, I feel completely in God's hands. I am at the mercy of powers far greater than me, and I can only trust in God to give me the strength to meet whatever is in store for me.

A Severe Left Turn

As 1970 unfolded, I was afloat but dead in the water, as the sailors say. I had no direction, no momentum of any sort. I was alive but was not living into any of the futures I had envisioned for myself. It was time to start over, making a fresh start into a new, as yet unimagined life.

Chapter 3
Beginning Again: Cambridge and Virginia, 1971–1979

So much had changed over such a short time that the next several years felt like a new beginning to my life. Three of the most important themes of my life had come to an end. I had dropped out of an MIT PhD program at the Sloan School of Management; I had left the Methodist Church, angry at what I perceived as its failure to teach me the truth about war; and I had made the decision to break my oath to serve my country as an officer in the US Air Force. I was deeply estranged from my parents back in Maryland. I had few friends and no serious job prospects in Boston. Over everything, the shadow of the looming confrontation with the Air Force and the very real prospect of imprisonment affected everything around me. I felt adrift, out of control, and powerless to have any meaningful impact on my life's direction.

For several years, I had attended the annual summer workshops of the Maryland Association of Student Councils, as a student and later as a staff member. In midsummer I rode my motorcycle to the Maryland student council workshop at St. Mary's College in southern Maryland, only to get a bad sore throat on the way and spend several days in the college infirmary in "isolation" till it cleared up. Medically and emotionally, I felt estranged from my old friends there as well.

Looking back, I realize now that my old life had in a very real sense come to an end. What I needed, though I did not realize it, was to start life over with a new set of goals and aspirations. I was aware in general terms of how much God was protecting me and making my choices easy during this time. I am amazed at just how simply and clearly my path was being marked out and how little conscious attention I paid to this divine guidance. God had provided the faith community I needed for spiritual formation in the Religious Society of Friends and arranged that I discover it, and now God set my "competency" in motion by arranging for me to be employed in a newly created job I hadn't known about and certainly never applied for: business manager of the Medical Clinics at

Massachusetts General Hospital. My understanding of ministry was also shaped as my personal witness against participating in war expanded to helping others with similar concerns.

In my journal for this period, I made numerous entries about the problems of air, water, and noise pollution associated with modern industrial life as well as the importance of protecting as much natural land from "development" by humankind as possible. I did not realize just how important these issues would become, and my approach to them was still rather simplistic: put as much land as possible under protection by means of greatly expanded national parks and forests and conservation efforts. I did not realize until years later that pollution does not recognize legal boundaries and that ecosystems cannot be protected simply by making them legally protected wilderness. Some of these issues and challenges would become more prominent as I worked with the Friends Community Project—but that is skipping ahead in the story.

Spiritual Formation

Soon after I joined Cambridge Meeting, several of us in our twenties began to gather for long lunches after meeting for worship every week in one local restaurant or another. Eight to twelve of us would spend the extended mealtime in conversation about whatever topic captured our shared attention.

These gatherings were fun and were opportunities for learning, but four of us decided that we also wanted a deeper commitment and religious experience on a regular basis. A weekly meeting for worship and discussion seemed attractive, but we didn't feel we knew just what to do or how to do it. We approached two older Friends for advice on what to do, and they took our inquiry as an invitation to participate themselves. Another young adult also joined us, and the first covenant fellowship of my experience was formed. We met weekly for a common meal, worship, and worshipful conversation for a period of several years. The commitment and mutual openness and vulnerability that we soon discovered led us to close fellowship. Two couples from this fellowship eventually married.

Seeing what we were experiencing, other Friends asked to join our group, but we declined. The openness and sensitivity to one another that had been built up over time would be put at risk, we felt, if we added new members. Also, it seemed clear that a larger group would probably not feel as close a bond to one another or share the care we had for one another's welfare. We offered repeatedly to share what we were doing and how so that others could form their own fellowship(s), but this was not satisfactory to a number of Friends, who continued to feel we were being elitist, secretive, and "not Quakerly."

Despite the criticism from some, I have come to believe that long-term participation in a close-knit group of Friends with the expressed intent of fostering spiritual growth has the potential to be a great aid to spiritual formation and maturation. Over time, a committed group of five to eight Friends can develop a community of trust, openness and intimacy that makes it safe to share their personal spiritual challenges and wrestlings and hear those of others without defensiveness or judgment. Two other occasions where this experience has had a definite positive influence on my life were the Covenant Fellowship, which began when I first became general secretary of Friends General Conference, and the fellowship of the various Meetings of Ministers, Elders, and Overseers to which I have belonged as part of North Carolina Yearly Meeting (Conservative) (NCYM[C]).

In spring 1973, I was appointed to the Ministry and Counsel Committee of Friends Meeting at Cambridge. The meeting at this time had over seven hundred members, many of whom were very seasoned Friends. Appointing someone so new to Quakerism to Ministry and Counsel when there were so many other more experienced Friends who could have been asked to serve seemed premature, to say the least. I don't know why Friends made this appointment, but it was a very instructive time for me. Sitting with these solid Friends each month while they discussed the spiritual state of the meeting was an illuminating experience. I began to learn how to discern the spiritual state of the meeting and what could be done to improve it. Importantly, I also learned by example that sometimes it was best to do nothing.

Beginning Again

Soon after I was appointed, a youngish woman began coming to meetings for worship on a regular basis, and she spoke in worship every time she was present. Her ministry was long and rambling, focused more on her own internal condition than on what was "going on" in worship itself. After several weeks, I felt she was being disruptive to the worship and brought the matter to Ministry and Counsel. I wanted someone to speak to this woman directly and explain that she shouldn't be speaking this frequently or this long each time, but Ministry and Counsel did not think this was needed.

The woman continued to speak in worship each week, and the next month I brought the matter up again, and again there was no unity to take any action. After the third month, the woman was absent from worship for several weeks in a row. She came back to meeting only one time after that. She stood up during the worship and described the personal crisis she had been experiencing earlier. The opportunity to talk through her situation in meeting for worship had been of great help to her in resolving this crisis, and she thanked Friends for being patient and providing her this opportunity for healing.

This experience made a deep impression on me. I began to see that the point of meeting for worship was not to have an excellent worship experience but to open ourselves to the work God was ready to do in each of us and in all of us together. Years later, among Conservative Friends, I was to experience this same hesitation to intervene in the face of apparently disruptive behavior. Those Friends spoke of their understanding that there was an Inward Teacher for each person who could guide the individual better than any human teacher could hope to do.

The responsibility of "care for meeting for worship" was shared among the members of Ministry and Counsel, and on Seventh Month 15, 1973, I had that responsibility for the first time. I was sitting in a group of college-age Friends, along with several visitors. I was led to offer vocal prayer during worship in the form of reciting the Lord's Prayer in a slow cadence. The sound of a woman crying began nearby. A glance revealed that a young visitor was holding her head in her hands and sobbing. This was very disconcerting, but I pressed on to the end of the prayer. Later, I learned that her tears were the result of hearing the prayer in a new way that paid more attention to each phrase than she had ever heard done before. This experience made me very aware of the effect that vocal ministry could have on the gathered body and how important it was for the speaker to be a clear channel for that message, not distorting it, adding anything, or leaving anything out. It is a lesson I remember to this day.

I now felt self-confident enough to take a long motorcycle trip on my own, and I made plans to go cross-country to visit my fraternity brother and close friend Norman Hawkins in San Francisco. While I was talking on the phone with him about my plans, he described reading the books of Carlos Castaneda about Castaneda's experiences with a Yaqui Indian elder in Mexico. Norm thought the books were quite good and recommended that I read them when I had the opportunity.

On Seventh Month 28, 1973, I set out cross-country on my BMW touring bike, which was loaded with camping gear and a notebook to journal my experiences. My first stop was Lake Winnipesaukee, New Hampshire, where New England Yearly Meeting's annual sessions were about to begin.

This was my first-ever yearly meeting experience, though I had been part of Friends Meeting at Cambridge for almost four years. Although I stayed only a couple of days, three things happened that changed my life. The first was that the yearly meeting experience itself was so powerfully attractive that I have been a regular participant in yearly meeting sessions ever since. I believe that since 1973 I have missed yearly meeting sessions only twice—when I moved from Boston to Charlottesville, I missed both the meetings completely, and in 2015 I was speaking at Pacific Yearly Meeting sessions when NCYM(C) was meeting. I've also been a visitor at the sessions of many other yearly meetings. The depth of the corporate worship and the fellowship of deeply committed Friends make yearly meeting sessions the high point of my liturgical year.

The second thing that happened was that I sat in on some meetings of people interested in building an affordable retirement community for Quakers in New England. This would, in a few months, result in my leaving my current job to work on the Friends Community Project related to this effort.

The third thing was that I met Louise Brown Wilson, a recorded minister of NCYM(C), while walking along the lake shore one afternoon. She and her husband Robert were visitors at New England Yearly Meeting sessions that year. We only talked for about fifteen minutes, but she made a deep impression on me. I was curious about a yearly meeting that could produce someone of Louise's obvious depth and commitment. Our paths were to cross many times in future years at other Quaker gatherings. When my faith journey and commitments were at a crisis point in 1988, her counsel was instrumental in my decision to transfer my membership to Virginia Beach Friends Meeting and become a Conservative Friend.

All that lay in the future as I set out again on my journey after two days at yearly meeting sessions. The path west took me over the sort of curving small roads across the New England mountains that touring motorcyclists love. I passed over from Buffalo into Canada, and when evening came, I turned off the main road into an apple orchard and made camp for the night. While taking a break from driving the next day, I saw a Carlos Castaneda book for sale and bought it.

I quickly settled into a daily routine that began just before dawn, when I would get dressed and clean up my campsite. If there was no place nearby to see the sunrise, I would ride a mile or so until I found a good spot. One memorable morning, a rooster crowed just as the sun broke over the horizon, and immediately the birds began to sing and the woods and fields came to life. It is difficult to imagine a better start to one's day.

The rider on a motorcycle is much more intimately connected to the surroundings than a person riding in a car. The cyclist is engaged in a direct, embodied relationship with the world, unmediated by roof, soft suspension, climate control, or other "protection." The smells, quality of light, wind, humidity, and sights of the countryside are experienced viscerally. This embodied, intimate mode of experience helped change my understanding of my place in the universe on my way west.

Memoir of the Life and Religious Labors of Lloyd Lee Wilson

Riding across the Canadian plains on a motorcycle, there is nothing in any direction to block one's view—car roof, doors, floor—and everywhere one looks the country is overpowering in its size and magnificence. And the plains are silent. Any time I stopped the motorcycle's engine, I heard only the wind. I could well believe the stories of homesteaders who went crazy with the wind.

I woke up one morning in the rain somewhere east of Moose Jaw, Saskatchewan. Breaking camp in rain always means getting at least a little wet, and riding any considerable distance in the rain will reliably finish the job. Before long I was soaked, cold, and generally depressed. Around Moose Jaw the sky cleared, the sun came out, and I pulled into a roadside rest area to spread my riding clothes on a picnic table to dry out while I warmed myself in the sun. When both my body and my clothes were warm and dry, I set out again, heading west. For two hundred miles there were clear skies and sunshine, making for a glorious ride.

That afternoon, I began to see clouds on the horizon ahead. As I continued to ride, they grew to be a tremendous lineal front stretching from horizon to horizon. I'd never seen anything like it before. The horizon in Saskatchewan is not limited by trees, buildings, hills, or other impediments but reaches from dead horizontal on one side to dead horizontal on the other: 180 degrees of clear vision that seems to stretch out to infinity in either direction. Now I was driving right into that immense storm front. There was no way to drive around it or sidestep its progress. The storm would not be raging outside my car but would be attacking my body directly. I realized at that moment that all the talk about "man against the elements" and the other fables about humans conquering mountains or rivers or overcoming blizzards and hurricanes were just that: fables. Humans and nature do not struggle with each other because individual humans are totally insignificant at the scale on which nature operates.

There was no way for me to escape or conquer this approaching storm; it would have its way with me. The storm was not engaged in a contest of wills or test of strength. It was totally indifferent to my very existence. I was not at the center of the universe or even at the center of

Beginning Again

the story of this particular day on the Canadian plains; I hardly merited a footnote.

As I passed into the storm front, a hard rain began to fall and the wind picked up force. I had never encountered steady wind of such force and duration—hours and many miles without letup, so strong that it was actually difficult to stay in my lane on the highway. For much of the time, I rode way over on the shoulder of the pavement to keep from being blown into oncoming traffic.

This continued without letup all the way to the foothills of the western mountains. Exhausted, chilled, and soaked to the bone, I stopped for the night at a motel that was dry and warm and offered a hot shower and lots of towels to dry off with afterward. This was not a victory over the elements but merely an escape. The day's riding destabilized the foundation of my thinking about the universe, namely, that humans were at the center of everything and that I, as the human of most interest to me, was at the center of humanity. Unmoored from this anthropocentric and egocentric anchor, I was opened to other modes of thinking that have slowly grown in importance to me over the years. In particular, I was opened to the wisdom of putting God at the center of the story and of valuing humanity no differently than the rest of God's creation.

Each evening, after my tent and sleeping bag were set up and I was ready to settle in, I would take out whichever Castaneda book I was working on and read until it was too dark to see the print. Castaneda wrote of twilight as the "crack between the worlds"—a time when otherworldly spirits are able to enter this world and cause mischief. This was a bit unsettling for someone camping alone each night in an isolated patch of woods with no visible evidence of other humans. I had shared no itinerary with anyone other than that I wanted to go to Alaska and San Francisco and the date I expected to return to work. In this time before cell phones and GPS devices, no one would have had any idea where in North America to look for me if anything untoward had happened.

To this day, I don't know how much of what Carlos Castaneda wrote was real and how much was made up. I do know that some of what he wrote struck a chord in me that has continued to resonate through my life. He described a world of dimensions beyond what physical science can measure or describe, a world in which there were spirits who were clearly not human and who were inherently dangerous to those human beings who were unprepared for them. I see this in my present understanding that there is a spiritual world overlapping our physical one and that not all spirits mean us well. Scripture advises us to test every spirit, and for good reason.

Another image that has remained with me from Castaneda is that of the warrior who, having vanquished every previous enemy, engages death—the one enemy who can never be defeated. The measure of the warrior, Castaneda wrote, is shown in the period of time in which the warrior holds back death to continue his work in the world. This image brings humility, reminding us that no one wins every encounter. It also focuses attention on the character of the individual rather than results of their actions.

Heading west out of Calgary brought me into the Rocky Mountains, and I turned north, heading toward Prince George and the Alaskan Highway. I got to asking myself, during this part of the trip, why it was that I would choose to go on this kind of a trip for my vacation rather than any of the myriad other things I might have chosen to do with this much paid free time. First, I decided, I did it to find my rhythm. With no watches, no schedule, no other people who expected me to do this or be there at a given time, however benignly, I was free to find and follow that rhythm that was uniquely mine, in which I was most completely in harmony with the currents of the Way around me (around me in a metaphysical sense, not physically).

Once this harmony had been achieved, this rhythm established, I experienced a minimum of pressure and was free to do some deep introspection. Thus, the initial question, why do I do this, was its own answer: I do this in order to be able to ask that question, not out of quiet desperation but out of contemplative self-examination. Whatever it is I do now—eating, sleeping, looking, etc.—is uniquely mine since I have no other pressures except nature's demands.

A broken front brake cable led me to think that taking the ferry to Alaska might be wiser than riding the Alaska Highway, so I headed west to Prince Rupert on the coast rather than north toward Dawson Creek. I spent several days in Ketchikan, Alaska, and was impressed by the positive attitude and friendliness of everyone I met. I sensed a frontier spirit that pervaded everything and everyone.

On my way south to visit my friend Norman "Hawk" Hawkins in San Francisco, direct engagements with two natural wonders helped strengthen my sense of awe at the scale and power of nature. The first was walking through a grove of mature redwoods in Mendocino County, California. Anyone who thinks a mere human being can make a cathedral should walk through a redwood grove. What majestic trees—what awe-inspiring expressions of God!

The second encounter was seeing the San Andreas fault at the place where it intersects the California coastline. My journal entry at the time read: "It looks serious as a heart attack and tends to make one feel a little tentative about the ground under one's feet." I experienced natural beauty and power over and over again on this trip, on a scale that defies description. Somehow, I'd gotten disconnected from that part of the universe over the years, and that seemed wrong.

Hawk and I spent several days together, catching up on one another's news and renewing our friendship. One surprise came when Hawk said he had never heard of Carlos Castaneda or any of his books. I was sure that I had first heard of Castaneda from Hawk, during a telephone call. I'd been buying books in that series all over the continent on this trip, reading them at the end of each day and trying to absorb the new ideas presented. I decided to leave them all with Hawk—maybe I was supposed to gather them for him.

When it came time for me to begin the journey east, Hawk said he'd come with me for a couple of days. We first went to Yosemite and camped, and the next day we cruised toward Death Valley. There, we had the most dramatic and dangerous encounter with the impersonal power of nature of my entire journey.

On a motorcycle, the constant wind cools everything. In the winter, one is much colder than simply standing out of doors. In the summer heat, even a full set of leathers feels comfortable at 50–60 mph. One's sweat evaporates before there is time to notice it. As we made our way to

Death Valley on a beautiful morning with bright sunshine and no clouds in sight, the temperature seemed just right.

When we stopped at Panamint Springs along the way, a thermometer in the shade read 104 degrees. Continuing down to the valley floor, we could feel the temperature increase even while we were riding. A high crosswind ripped my sunglasses off my face five times. The fifth time I just let them go; by this time, I was simply looking for some shade.

By the time we got to Stovepipe Wells, we had dropped over 1,900 feet in altitude and were just 10 feet above sea level. It was 120 degrees in the shade, and yes, the thermometer was accurate. At the general store, we got something to eat and drink, took a nap, drank some more water, and chatted with the two people who comprised the town's entire summer population.

There were numerous signs of just how hot it was in Death Valley, but their full significance didn't hit me (or Hawk) because the heat was so far out of the range of our experience. There was a hitching post in front of the general store where we spent the afternoon, and the sun cast a parallelogram-shaped shadow from that hitching post. I spent a long time watching small birds land in that shadow and walk along it from one end to the other looking for something to eat. They would not ever leave the narrow shadow of the post as they made their way searching for food; they never landed or walked in the sunlight. There were no hot-water taps in the bathrooms at the general store. The water coming out of the cold-water taps was hot enough to pass for hot water back in Boston.

Finally, the temperature dropped to 112 degrees in the shade, and we decided to make the twenty-five-mile trip to the park headquarters at Furnace Creek. Only after getting back on our motorcycles and into the sunlight did we realize how much energy the heat had taken from us. We arrived after it had closed, so we couldn't get inside to enjoy the air conditioning, but there was plenty of drinking water available and even a few trees for shade. A sign at the headquarters indicated the number of consecutive days the temperature had reached 100 degrees (over 100 days), 110 degrees, and 120 degrees. Hawk and I were not experiencing anything special in the way of weather; Death Valley was inhospitable to humans all the time.

We wanted to delay driving again until the temperature dropped some more, and we also wanted to get out of Death Valley before making camp for the night. We waited until after sunset, but the thermometer still read 111 degrees. We decided on a route toward a pass at about 3,000 feet, which we thought would be significantly cooler than where we were.

We got as far as Badwater Basin, 279 feet below sea level. By that time, I was lightheaded from heat prostration and felt too dizzy to keep my motorcycle upright. Driving any farther that night was out of the question. Hawk was only a little better off than I was. We decided to spend the night where we were and made camp by that truly bad water. It is the lowest point of land in North America; water drains into the basin but has nowhere to drain out. As the water evaporates, it leaves behind whatever minerals and salts it has carried into the basin.

Hawk soaked our clothing in that bitter water; we wrapped our heads in wet towels and tried to stay as quiet as possible. Luckily, we had three quarts of drinking water, which we consumed over the course of the night. We had been trying to take it easy, and maybe in 100-degree weather we would have been OK. But 120 degrees is a whole lot different from 100 degrees (I now know experientially), and we were hurting. Hawk kept us both wet and somewhat cool all night as the water evaporating from the towel and our clothes provided some cooling. I was too ill to get up, so Hawk had to make many trips from our improvised camp to the edge of Badwater to get more water for both of us.

At first light, I managed to stand up and walk across the road and back. There was a small cloud near the horizon just where the sun was beginning to come up. This seemed like a providential protection from direct sunlight for an hour or so, and it seemed important to take advantage of it. I woke Hawk, who had dozed off, and we set out. That cloud stayed in place, shielding us, until we had made it up off the valley floor and out of the worst of the heat. Hawk and I thus became two of the very few people who have camped at 279 feet below sea level. I wish we had been healthy enough to enjoy it.

Memoir of the Life and Religious Labors of Lloyd Lee Wilson

From the moment things began to get bad on the way to Furnace Creek, I was sure we were in a serious situation. When I got really sick at Badwater, I prayed for help and guidance. From then on, I began to gain back a little of the ground I had lost. In the morning, when we expected the temperature to shoot back up again, as the old-timers had told us to expect, there was that cloud blocking the sun until we made it over the pass and out of Death Valley. Thank you, God.

In Shoshone, we stopped at the post office to mail some cards. A passing woman took one look at Hawk as he walked out the post office door and immediately offered us the use of her spring-fed swimming pool to recover. The mineral-rich Badwater water had stained our clothes, faces, and beards with white so that we appeared more than a little ghostly and certainly in need of a place of recovery. We spent most of the day at the side of the pool, occasionally dipping in to wash one more layer of lime and minerals off of our bodies and clothes. Thanks again, God.

Even now, more than forty-five years later, I have no words that adequately express the nature of that experience in Death Valley and the lessons that I learned. The power, majesty, and grandeur of God's creation were certainly part of it. Discarding the last shreds of any illusion I still held that human beings and nature, or a part of nature, could engage in some sort of contest was also a lesson I learned. Hawk and I didn't overcome Death Valley in summer; we simply escaped the consequences of our own inexperience and ignorance. The valley was not doing anything differently than any other summer day, any other year. One can't contest or overcome an opponent that is completely unaware of one's existence. Tasting the quality of nature in such powerful and personal ways on this trip left me with a profound sense of how wrong it is for humans as individuals or as a group to behave in the ways we have been doing: polluting the air, water, and soil; driving uncounted species of plants and animals to extinction; and changing the very climate of the planet.

Hawk and I finally parted company in Lathrop Wells, Nevada, with Hawk heading back to San Francisco and me going east. The temperature was a mere 100 degrees in the shade and felt refreshingly cool. I

Beginning Again

continued to take it easy all day. I cruised to Lake Mead, did the tour of Hoover Dam, and camped at a beach on the Nevada side. Hoover Dam is *really* big and *really* impressive, for a man-made object.

Later, on my journey east, I stopped for a while at Shiloh Battlefield in Tennessee, where more than 23,000 people died in 1862 in a two-day battle. There were only 100,000 combatants in all, and not all of them were on the battlefield the first day. How can a human think that anything justifies the horror of war? My father was right; the old men who declare war should be in the first line of battle. They should have to hit the beaches first. Every beachhead, every time; they should have to be point man on all the patrols all through any war. If that were the case, there would be a lot fewer wars waged.

On my first day back at the medical clinics, I sought out a staffer who had predicted that I wouldn't return after such a long trip. I announced myself and told her that I had indeed come back, to which she replied, "No, you didn't." Physically I had returned, to be sure; but I think it was also true that I was not the same person who had left almost two months previously. I had changed, in ways that I didn't completely perceive or understand yet.

One immediate change in me upon my return was that I received a leading not to wear ties anymore. This was a sharp departure from the explicit dress code for male administrative staff at Massachusetts General Hospital, and it caused some tension with my immediate supervisor. He didn't force an immediate showdown over the ties, but when a couple of months later my leading expanded to prohibit me from wearing suits or sport jackets, he was forced to call me on the carpet.

When it was clear I was not going to reverse my new personal standards of dress, my supervisor offered a compromise. It would be acceptable if I wore a white medical coat while at work. I had to turn down that compromise on grounds of integrity because those white coats were worn by all the clinic doctors, and I was not a doctor. I didn't know what other conversations were going on, but the tension between the two of us was palpable. If I would not cooperate, there was not much he could actually do except fire me, and I knew in my own heart I would give up the job rather than betray this new experience of being led. Eventually, the hospital allowed me to work wearing an open shirt and slacks as long as I wore a name tag.

This was not a leading to adopt traditional "plain dress" or a leading to simplify my life, although I see now that I had been paying way too much attention to the way I dressed and how I looked. It was not a change that I wanted; I can still remember my sense of loss and sorrow when I gave up all my suits and ties. The leading was a lesson in obedience to God's guidance, whatever that guidance might be. The test of whether or not to follow a particular guidance was to ask whether, in my heart, it felt like God speaking. It was a call to obey God's leading, whatever that leading might be.

Looking back after more than forty years, I see a long series of leadings about my personal appearance. Over a period of decades, I have been led to give up collars on my shirts, to wear suspenders rather than belts, to wear hats made for plain people (whether Quaker, Brethren, or Mennonite), and to grow a "believer's beard" (a full beard without mustache). The cumulative effect has been that I am often described as wearing traditional "plain dress," but that was never my intention. I have simply been obedient to God's individual leadings.

At this time, my spiritual life was rather eclectic. I was becoming increasingly active in the Religious Society of Friends, mostly with the monthly meeting in Cambridge. The underlying faith commitments of my activity were ambiguous. I continued to harbor resentment at the institutional Christian church for failing to teach me (and others) that war was wrong, but some parts of my Christian upbringing and the Christian faith of some members of Cambridge meeting still spoke to me helpfully. Those individual faith commitments were highlighted and placed in ongoing tension by the lengthy discussion sparked by a letter from California Yearly Meeting asking Friends to consider "the centrality of Christ" in their faith and their meetings. The members of Cambridge meeting were as varied as one might expect in a large meeting in a university setting; the discussions were long, intense, and at times quite emotional. I remember watching a Christian Friend in tears during one such discussion and feeling myself to be definitely on the "non-Christian" side of the discussion. Concurrently, I felt something deeply and strangely attractive about a faith that would be as dear as that Friend's Christian faith was to her.

I was spending more and more time reading a variety of Zen and Taoist writings and feeling a strong attraction to them. Taoism in particular seemed to speak to my condition and provided a vocabulary with which I could describe my spiritual life to myself and to others. That there is a coherent flow to the universe and that one ought to live in harmony with that flow had the ring of truth to me; that there might be a God with whom I might have a personal relationship did not. I could fit together my understanding of the Tao and the practices of Quakers in worship and meeting for business, so there was no problem for me in that regard.

The other piece of my spirituality was Transcendental Meditation (TM). Two of the Friends in our covenant group practiced TM, and I thought I could see tangible signs of its good effects. Initiation into the practice was personally difficult because it involved bowing one's head to the guru who had started the Western TM movement, but I got past that and began meditating for twenty minutes twice a day.

At this time, I shared a big old house with two other persons in Watertown, Massachusetts. Everyone did their fair share of household chores with a minimum of shirking or complaining. One weekend it fell to me to clean the large eat-in kitchen/dining room. I decided to begin in one corner and work my way around the room in a clockwise direction in order to do an excellent job of cleaning all sorts of nooks and crannies that might get overlooked or neglected by a less-thorough cleaner. I was in high spirits as I began, cleaning out the pantry and washing down the sink with enthusiasm. I continued around the room, methodically cleaning, dusting, and picking up.

By the time I reached the stove, the first flush of enthusiasm was long gone, and everything was less fun than it had been a couple of hours previously. By the time I got to the refrigerator, the fun was gone completely; I was simply working and was not particularly enjoying it. The temptation to cut the task short, to retire to the back of my cave and rest because it hardly mattered anyway, was strong. I was by now almost angry at the work.

Memoir of the Life and Religious Labors of Lloyd Lee Wilson

Nonetheless I saw dust and a paper behind the refrigerator and determined to get back there and clean up. I wrestled the large refrigerator away from the wall enough to reach behind and retrieve a piece of construction paper on which someone had written:

You can do it like it's a big weight on you,
or you can do it like it's part of the dance.

Imagine my chagrin as I realized how this cleaning job had become an ever-greater weight on me all morning. With a changed attitude, I was able to complete the work as part of the great dance of creation and enjoy myself in the process. Over the years since, the memory of this experience has kept me "in the dance" many times when I might have yielded to sloth or burnout. If I am mindful of the great dance, then to work is to pray, and indeed all activity is prayer. Prayer is being in relationship with God, who created and loves us, and all activity is our outward manifestation of that relationship.

In the spring of 1974, I was appointed to the Permanent Board of New England Yearly Meeting—the decision-making body of the yearly meeting when it is not in actual session. I was both chronologically young and inexperienced as a Friend for such an appointment. There was not a lot that I contributed to the quality of decisions made by the Permanent Board, but I gained a great deal by observing these seasoned and weighty Friends as they engaged important challenges facing New England Friends.

In Eighth Month 1975, I married Nano Griffin Rush, under the care of Friends Meeting of Cambridge, Massachusetts. The wedding was conducted after the manner of Friends at the meeting house, and the reception was held after the manner of Nano's South Boston Irish-Catholic community. Here, I was introduced to yet another form of community: four generations of friends and relatives dancing the Hokey-Pokey together with a wide smile on their faces.

My father had undergone lung surgery a few months earlier for reasons that weren't shared with Damon or me. We were told that he was now in great health, and he and Mom drove up from Maryland for the wedding. Six months later, when his declining health could no longer be hidden, Mom finally broke the silence and admitted that Dad was terminally ill. His cancer had been metastatic when it was first discovered, but Dad had been insistent that Damon and I not be told.

Within a couple of weeks of Mom's disclosure, Dad was admitted to Graduate Hospital in Philadelphia; he would not be coming home. He lingered for almost three weeks. Mom moved into his hospital room, sleeping on a cot the staff brought in for her.

I got to come down to Philadelphia to see Dad one last time because the American Friends Service Committee's regional office in New England needed someone to make a presentation to the national finance and executive committees. I said goodbye to Dad just before leaving for the airport for the flight back to Boston. I had just gotten home and settled into bed when Mom called to say that Dad had died. I journaled this prayer:

> Almighty God, who holds us in the palm of one hand, help us feel the comfort of the Spirit that surrounds us; help us surrender ourselves to Thy will; guide us to accept willingly our place in the unfolding of the universe. Grant us the serenity that enables us to perceive Thy hand all around us: in birth as well as death, gain as well as loss, joy as well as sorrow. This we ask that we might be more fully united with Thee, now and forever, amen.

Peace Witness

My immediate concern as 1970 came to an end was the impending hearing for my conscientious object (CO) discharge application. That was scheduled at Hanscom Air Force Base northwest of Boston early in the morning the day after my first day of work at Massachusetts General Hospital. I was nervous to begin with, and the fact that I had a hard time getting my motorcycle started and arrived a few minutes late did not help my emotional state. I'd given my Air Force uniform back to the MIT ROTC when I first turned in my discharge application, so I arrived in civilian clothes: sport coat and tie. My hair had not been cut since I had received my commission, and I'd grown a Fu Manchu moustache as well. When I stepped into the courtroom to face the waiting full colonel, the many ways in which I looked out of place hit me all at once.

Memoir of the Life and Religious Labors of Lloyd Lee Wilson

There must have been an enlisted stenographer there, and perhaps a member of the military police serving as bailiff, but the only person I remember is that colonel. After a moment spent assessing my late arrival and nonregulation appearance, he started to swear me in: "Raise your right hand and repeat after me." "No," I replied. His face clouded even more than before, and my hopes sank. "I will tell you the truth to the best of my ability," I added quickly, "but as a Quaker I will not swear." He obviously did not approve of this development either but decided not to press the issue.

The colonel then embarked on a lengthy interrogation of my beliefs and their chronology. It was essential to my discharge that I convince the Air Force that not only did I fit the description of a legally recognized CO but that I had come to my CO beliefs only after being commissioned as an officer. If I had had reservations at the time I took the commissioning oath, they would simply prosecute me for committing perjury when I was commissioned. The fine line I had to walk was to convince this officer that the following four things were all true:

> 1) I now had sincere beliefs that would qualify me as a CO eligible to be discharged from the Air Force;
> 2) I had not had these beliefs prior to my commissioning in June 1969;
> 3) I had demonstrated these beliefs consistently, beginning at some date after June 1969; and
> 4) by doing so I had done nothing that would warrant my being court-martialed rather than discharged.

My failure to persuade the hearing officer of any of these four points would result in my discharge application being denied. Failure to persuade him of the truth of points 2 or 4 could lead to a trial and punishment under the Universal Code of Military Justice.

The questioning went on for what seemed like a very long time. Finally, the colonel paused. He disclosed that he had never approved an application for CO discharge. I prepared for the worst. He then asked me what I would do if he turned me down, as he had all the other applicants who had come before him. After a moment's pause, I said, "Go to prison, I suppose. I know that I will never wear an Air Force uniform again."

Beginning Again

After a few more exchanges, the colonel said that he would in fact recommend me for discharge and called the hearing to a close. I was so relieved that I could barely walk out of the courtroom under my own power.

The following month (January 1971), I got a letter from the Air Force saying that I had not cooperated with the discharge process and that consequently I was being called to active duty as an enlisted man. The Air Force had no record that I had appeared for my official hearing. An anxious phone call to Hanscom Field revealed that the report of my hearing, including the colonel's recommendation, was at the bottom of a tall pile of paper waiting to be typed up by an airman clerk typist. My sense was that the personnel at Hanscom Field were in no mood to help my discharge move forward. I insisted that they promise to put my report at the top of their pile of work, and they said they would. I didn't hear anything more from the Air Force, neither confirming they had gotten the report nor following through on the threat to call me to active duty. It was an anxious time for me.

Without any other notice, I received my discharge papers in the mail saying I had been discharged from the Air Force as of March 1, 1971, "at the convenience of the government." One half of my journey to becoming a CO was complete. From another perspective, I had managed to leap from the frying pan to the fire and now had to get out of the fire to avoid getting burned. I had not served enough active-duty days in the Air Force Reserve to qualify as exempt from the Selective Service. In addition, I had won that first Selective Service lottery by getting lottery number 1. As soon as the Selective Service System learned I was no longer in the Air Force Reserve, I was sure to be drafted. I was now in the hands of the local draft board in Cecil County, Maryland.

I immediately filled out the Selective Service forms for conscientious objection, added my Air Force discharge package as documentation, and sent it off to Cecil County. I fervently hoped that the fact that the Air Force had already determined I was a CO would be convincing. The best-case scenario would be that the draft board classified me as a CO and sent me someplace other than Boston or Maryland for two years of alternative service—"emptying bedpans," according to the stock image.

There was little chance they would see my current job at Massachusetts General Hospital as suitable service. Alternative service was supposed to be geographically disruptive (like military service) and humbling as well.

In the normal course of events, a county Selective Service board receiving a CO application would schedule a hearing for the applicant before making a decision on the application. As my lottery number was 1, I was in line to be drafted immediately when the draft board was notified of my eligibility. It made sense that I would be scheduled for a hearing almost at once after they received my application, but I heard nothing at all for several months.

When the county board did contact me, it was not to set a hearing date but to send me a new draft card. The new card classified me once more as a member of the Air Force Reserve. As long as this classification remained in effect, not only would I not be drafted, I would not be called into alternative service. This couldn't be correct, and the draft board had to know it wasn't correct as I had sent them my discharge papers myself. I had been preparing to leave my job as a hospital administrator to serve two years emptying bedpans or planting trees or some such assignment. Now it seemed that might not be necessary. Should I point out this error to my draft board?

It took a while for me to sort out what I should do. I had been completely open and honest in my communications with the draft board, so I felt clear in that area. I was then twenty-four years old. If the error was not discovered until after my twenty-sixth birthday, I would be too old to be drafted anyway. If it was discovered before then, presumably my CO application would be processed at that time. If it were approved, I would then be assigned to alternative service. If I pressed the matter now and was assigned to alternative service, my work toward a single standard of care at Mass General would be interrupted for at least two years. It seemed to me that I was doing more good in my current job than I could as a hospital orderly someplace else.

I decided to accept what had happened and to be thankful that things had worked out the way they did. Years later, my mother bumped into the draft board's secretary in the supermarket. In the course of their conversation, my case came up, and the secretary said that the board had wanted to make sure I was not drafted. So, their "error" had been intentional after all.

Issues of racism, class distinctions, and the war economy that were invisible to me at that time or for years afterward now stand out for me all through this incident. My education, formal and informal, had enabled me to make the best use of the resources that were available to draft-age young men to help them navigate the military recruitment/conscription system, eventually bringing my case to the attention of the draft board through my CO application. Clearly, I received special treatment by the county Selective Service board because I was known to them. I was a white man who had garnered the approving attention of the religious and educational communities of the white segment of Cecil County during my high school years. And finally, the implacable demands of the war economy for fresh recruits made it inevitable that some other young man, less articulate and not personally known to the men on the county draft board, would be drafted in my place and in all likelihood sent to the battlefront in Vietnam. I was spared participation in war, but war itself was unchanged.

Over half a century later, I feel that my commitment to personal pacifism is as strong now as it was then and that my commitment to nonviolence in general has grown. The basis or root of my pacifism has definitely changed, however. When I applied for discharge and CO status, I based my claims on the familiar Quaker phrase, "that of God in every one." If God was in every human being, I argued, then an attack on any human was an attack on God, which I was prohibited from doing by my religious beliefs.

I now see weaknesses in that initial claim, and the nature of my fundamental faith commitment to God has changed also. The weakness I see is that if one's claim to pacifism is based on the Presence of God in every person, the rebuttal is a simple "Not in *that* one!" One is reduced to defending the Presence of God even in the persons who appear most godless. The dialogue becomes, "I believe there is God in every one, no matter what they've done" vs. "I don't believe that God is in everyone."

The change in my fundamental faith commitment to pacifism stems from my return to Christianity, which lay several years in the future at the time of my Air Force and Selective Service confrontations. When I began to self-identify as a Christian Quaker, I embraced the moral influence theory of atonement rather than penal or substitutionary atonement. I believed that the purpose and work of Jesus the Christ was directed at humanity, not toward God or the devil. Jesus did not live and die to pay a ransom to the devil or to convince God to accept sinful humans. Christ became human to demonstrate to humans by precept and example God's unbreakable love for all humanity and the proper (moral) way to live in response to that divine love. Christian faith demands of me that I live my life in accord with the precepts and examples of Christ in the historical incarnation and in the guidance of the Holy Spirit in each present moment. Jesus did not come into the world to die for my sins but to *live* and to show us all how to live.

I am a pacifist now because that is the person God calls me to be (virtue ethics). God became human and experienced all the drama and suffering of human life and death in order to redeem every human being, even the most godless-appearing ones. The core question is not whether that "evil" person does or does not have that of God in them but whether I love that person as God certainly loves that person. This, it seems to me, is a much more solidly grounded position and is less vulnerable to attack.

In late 1973, I began resisting war taxes. I felt it was inconsistent for me to help finance military activities in which I was not willing to participate personally. Paying someone else to fight a war and supplying them with weapons and ammunition did not seem very different from pulling the trigger myself. The easiest first step appeared to be to refuse to pay the federal telephone excise tax. This was an easily identified tax with a clear direct connection to financing US wars, the process for resisting was straightforward, and the penalties for resisting the tax were minimal. The tax was first imposed to help finance the Spanish-American War in 1898. It had been repealed but was reinstated in the run-up to World War I and then repealed again after that war. It was imposed once again just before the United States entered into World War II and was made permanent in 1947.

For the novice tax resister, the telephone excise tax offered a clear means of resistance that was easy to implement and risked minimal punishment. One simply reduced one's payment to the telephone company by the amount of the tax, which was clearly marked on the bill. A letter to the phone company included with the payment explained that you were paying all of the telephone company's bill except for the tax. Telephone company policy was that telephone service would not be cut off or disrupted in any way for customers who did not pay the tax. Like many war tax resisters, I loaned the small amount of my resisted taxes to a local charity and stated I had done so in my monthly letter. Symbolically, any forcible collection of the resisted tax amount would mean taking money from a charity and using it for war.

Limiting my witness to resisting the telephone excise tax proved inadequate to clear my conscience. In 1974, I began income tax resistance. I reduced my payment of the federal tax I owed to reflect the proportion of income taxes that went to pay for war, preparations for war, and the interest owed on debt incurred for past wars. I then loaned this amount to an appropriate charity, interest-free. With each year's return I included a letter explaining what I had done and why. The IRS did get the money eventually, along with some penalties and interest, but it was important to me that I was not paying the war taxes willingly. American Friends Service Committee had recently won a court ruling saying they didn't have to withhold payroll taxes for their employees who were conscientious tax resisters, and that seemed to offer hope that there would be a way to do this legally in the not-too-distant future.[1]

My income tax resistance sparked visits by agents from the local IRS office. The agents were without exception polite and good listeners, and they gave every impression of not having encountered a religious war tax resister before. Several promised to take my case back to their supervisor to see what might be done. Always, of course, this was to seize the back taxes, interest, and any penalties from my bank account. As long as the interest and penalties were not excessive, the process seemed satisfactory to me. I had not paid the tax willingly, and the extra expense incurred by the IRS in collection activities reduced the net tax amount somewhat, so I felt I had reduced the total money available for war by some small amount.

Over time, the government ratcheted up the penalties for income tax resistance. Claims of high numbers of dependents (to reduce the amount withheld for taxes from the paycheck) had to be reported to the IRS at the time they were filed with an employer, tax resistance tax returns were labeled "frivolous" and were subject to increasing monetary fines, and the interest rate and penalty amounts charged by the IRS rose significantly. Eventually, I began to feel that by resisting I was now actually increasing the money collected by the IRS so that there was more net money available for war than if I had not resisted. Reluctantly, I gave up that particular witness.

Two other avenues of tax resistance witness were available to me: limiting my overall income and maximizing the amount of approved tax deductions I made each year. My commitment to work only for nonprofit organizations (and small ones, as it turned out over the years) already put a fairly low ceiling on my annual taxable income. I made it my practice to invest as much of my income as I could afford in tax-deferred retirement plans and to give generously to my meeting and other charitable activities. Reducing my net income to below the federal tax threshold remained a goal throughout my working career, and getting to that point in retirement was a great comfort.

During all this time, I was motivated by a desire to be "clear" of war and the seeds of war in my life—to be separate from and uninvolved in those activities. I wanted to be clear of the taint of war. As I've reflected on the degree to which warlike activity pervades every aspect of our culture and society in the United States, I've come to the conclusion that the best one can hope for is to continue to struggle against war as part of the 'implicated resistance'—not as someone completely clear of war who shouts directions from a distance, as it were, but someone in the midst of the community, aware of and implicated by the pervasiveness of war and insisting that *we* need to find a better way to live rather than that *you* need to change.

Career and Competency

Early on in my undergraduate studies at MIT's Sloan School of Management, I realized that the profit motive didn't motivate me. I didn't see anything particularly wrong with it; I simply didn't care about maximizing profits. I was very attracted to the challenge of assembling scarce resources to achieve a shared goal and decided I would focus on the management of nonprofit organizations from then on. At the time, this was simply an intellectual commitment; I did not see my work as calling, or ministry, or even very much "doing good." All those changes in understanding would come about slowly, over many years, as my experience in the workplace and my spiritual insights grew and grew together.

After leaving MIT's Sloan School of Management, I had no clear idea of what I wanted to do in the way of work and little energy to devote to a job search, and the local job market seemed listless at best. One afternoon in November 1970, the phone rang in my apartment and a man at the other end of the line asked for me by name. "Hi," he said, "I'm Dr. Jerry Grossman. I have a job for you at the medical clinics at Massachusetts General Hospital. Come to my office Friday and we'll talk about it."

I met with Dr. Grossman and his colleagues, was excited by their vision, and early in December 1970 I started work at Mass General. A handful of doctors wanted to construct a new model for outpatient medical care. They intended to see all their patients, private and clinic, in the same place, with the same staff, at the same price. Their vision was of a single standard of quality for all the medical care they delivered. They recruited me as their business manager.

A single standard of care would be a big change for these doctors and for the medical clinics system. Mass General is a teaching hospital for Harvard Medical School. One of the requirements for a physician who accepts a teaching position in the hospital is providing free care to clinic patients once a week at the hospital. The physicians saw their private patients (the source of the bulk of their income) in offices elsewhere, with their own staff, laboratory arrangements, and so on, for significantly higher fees. It was an overt two-tier system.

When I arrived, the hospital had four general medical clinics in addition to several specialty clinics (pulmonary, arthritis, etc.). Doctors saw patients in a clinic in three-hour sessions, and every patient scheduled to see a doctor was given an appointment for the beginning of the clinic. Thus, if twenty doctors were scheduled to see ten patients each on a given morning, all two hundred patients were given nine o'clock appointments. The waiting area was overcrowded and shabby, the support staff were overworked, and most doctors looked upon their clinic time as an unrewarding duty, required as a condition of their admitting privileges at Mass General. The clinics were home to some forty thousand office visits a year under this system. Many of these patients were uninsured or inadequately covered. Meanwhile, the physicians were seeing private patients at their upscale offices.

Over the next couple of years, we increased staffing, upgraded the waiting area, implemented an actual appointment system, and demonstrated the feasibility of seeing patients of greatly differing economic status in a single facility with a single standard of care. In the process, the medical clinics went from a money-losing activity for Mass General to a program that stood on its own financially. We also added an Ambulatory Screening Clinic that operated days, evenings, and weekends to serve those folks who came to the emergency ward but had nonemergency medical problems. This freed up valuable ER resources and provided needed care at a greatly reduced cost.

In 1972, I experienced the first significant health challenge I can remember when an old sports injury grew more severe. Since the summer of 1969, I had known there was something wrong in my left hip. I suffered chronic low-grade hip pain that never went away, and the pain gradually intensified as time went on. Finally, the pain began to keep me from going to work, and the Mass General surgeons recommended surgery to remove inflamed tissue around the hip joint.

The operation was less than a success. The surgery did not alleviate the hip pain I was experiencing. Then, as my body began to heal from the operation, it laid down additional bone along the surgical wound—all around and right into my hip joint. The effect was similar to pushing slivers of wood into the hinge of a door. I could not straighten my left hip completely or bend it very far at all.

My surgeons said they could operate again and remove the extra bone, but the prospects were discouraging. The same extra bone growth could very well take place again. There was a 30 percent chance I would emerge from the second surgery with more range of motion than I had at present, 40 percent that things would be essentially unchanged, and 30 percent that I would actually have even less range of motion. I decided against a second operation.

Most of the physical activities and team sports I had enjoyed were now closed to me. I could walk pretty normally, although I kept a cane close at hand for those days when the pain was severe. I could still sit comfortably on my motorcycle, which was a great relief.

Any ethical dilemma about my Selective Service status was now moot. I would be considered medically unfit for military service or alternative service even if my draft board changed its mind or realized its error. Had I had the surgery, with the same results, at the time of the original injury, I would have been discharged from the Air Force as physically unfit without having had to apply for a CO discharge.

The clinical social workers at Mass General were an important part of the care we were providing, and watching them stirred my interest in continuing my own education in the area. I applied to and was admitted to Ohio State's PhD program in clinical psychology. The deadline for confirming my place in the entering cohort came while I was still hospitalized following my surgery. Several doctors from the medical clinics visited me in the surgical wing to try to convince me to stay at Mass General. They offered a very large pay raise, a double promotion on the hospital's organization chart, and other inducements. I eventually agreed and told Ohio State I was not coming. Only after that did it become clear that the doctors did not have the power to deliver on their promises and that the hospital administration, which did have the power, would not agree to what the doctors had promised.

I was frustrated by this development but not so upset that I left the clinics to look for other work. It did teach me to look behind the speakers in any organizational negotiations to see who really held the power to carry out whatever was being proposed or promised. After I recovered enough to get around the clinics in a wheelchair, I went back to work, and the incident did not have any apparent effect on my working relationship with the doctors or hospital administration.

In retrospect, this seems like a significant "road not taken" in my life. An Ohio State clinical psychology doctorate would have meant a sharp break in many different parts of my life well beyond my working career. Living in Columbus, Ohio, for the four or five years needed to earn my doctorate would have introduced me to an entirely different set of friends and colleagues, including a different Quaker "connection."

Though the opportunity at Ohio State was closed, I was still interested in graduate school, and I decided to take some graduate courses at MIT's Sloan School. Sloan and Mass General sit at opposite ends of the Longfellow Bridge across the Charles River, so it was convenient for me to slip away for an hour or two to attend class. I started with accounting since it had direct application to my work at the medical clinics. After that I chose courses that were interesting to me and were also part of the requirements for a master's degree.

Near the end of 1973, I resigned from my job at the medical clinics of Mass General Hospital to accept a one-year appointment as part-time coordinator for the Ad Hoc Committee on Retirement and Friends Community. This was a leap from the security of working for a large institution that had been around for a long time and would likely continue to grow over time to a brand-new group that frankly didn't know where its next dollar was coming from. It seemed right to make the move, and exciting to be in a job that promised even greater unity between my faith commitments and community and making a living.

At the medical clinics, we had a set of fairly well-defined goals: a single standard of care, financial sustainability, and attractiveness to physicians. In this new job, even the goals were undefined. What size of community did we envision? Should it be a retirement home or an entire town or something else? How many Quakers could we attract to whatever we established? We had no answers to any of these questions—not even any criteria for identifying correct answers.

Eventually, the renamed Friends Community Project developed some definition. Friends came to unity that it should be an all-ages intentional community organized around Friendly principles, with the specific goal of providing New England Friends an option for retirement living. We found a site in North Easton, Massachusetts, about halfway

Beginning Again

between Boston and Providence, that seemed promising. We decided to make as much use of solar heating as possible, and I wrote a grant application to Housing and Urban Development to install solar collectors and heat storage equipment in each unit. The grant was approved, and the project took a large step forward. In a meeting with our chosen architect, older Friend Lois Harris radically changed the firm's single-family site plan to cluster housing. This reduced construction costs significantly and preserved as much open space as possible.

The clustered-housing community we envisioned would require a zoning change as the current zoning required single-family houses on separate lots. North Easton, like many New England towns, was run on a town meeting basis; every adult citizen had a vote. Pat Jackson, our Quaker public relations consultant, helpfully announced to the residents of North Easton that Quakers made decisions unanimously and that therefore we would only move forward with our plans if the vote to amend the zoning were unanimous. Friends selected me to make a solo presentation to the town meeting in support of our request. No pressure at all.

The high school auditorium was packed on the spring night of the town meeting. Business dragged on, as it tends to do, and by the time I was called upon the novelty of the meeting had worn off and the residents in attendance were beginning to get a little restless. My presentation seemed to go well, and I answered the questions that were put to me easily, but the improbability of a unanimous decision weighed heavily on my heart after I sat down. Sure enough, when the town moderator asked for the yeas and nays, there were a few negative voices raised even though the large majority was in favor of the change. I was disheartened—we were about to lose because we were holding other people to a Quaker standard for decision making.

The town moderator then announced that it would be necessary to record a roll call vote count on the zoning decision, which would take a long time. In the interest of saving time, he would ask for the yeas and nays again to see if the decision would be unanimous so that a roll call could be avoided. He did so, and the new vote was unanimous in our favor. I was literally weak with relief.

I had continued to take individual courses at the Sloan School of Management at MIT for several years and had accumulated enough credits in the right courses to be close to earning my master's degree. Sloan had a rule that one couldn't earn a degree as a part-time student, so in the fall of 1976 I paid the tuition to be a full-time student and began work on my thesis: "Quaker Decision Making: Applying the Friends' Method to Non-Quaker Organizations." I received my master's degree at the end of the 1977 spring semester.

The thesis was spurred by my observation that the practices of meetings for business were very similar to those of highly functioning small work groups we studied in class. It seemed plausible from a management standpoint, therefore, that one could teach key concepts of the Quaker decision-making process (in secularized form) to groups in the workplace and observe improvements in efficiency, effectiveness, morale, work satisfaction, and so on. From a Quaker standpoint, it would be good to know that the principles we espoused for ourselves were effective when employed outside a specifically Quaker setting.

The setting I chose for a case study was my former workplace: the medical clinics at Massachusetts General Hospital. Medical care settings are highly hierarchical, with medical doctors at the top of the pyramid; decision-making power is very centralized. I chose this setting to introduce a very flat organizational model, with dispersed decision making, to see whether it could survive and flourish.

The organizational goal in the medical clinics was still driven by innovation: to develop new ways of delivering outpatient medical care that would implement a single standard of care for all patients, whatever the method of payment for that care. The new model's encouragement of ideas and suggestions from a broader proportion of the group, giving more people a say in deciding to implement new proposals, was well suited to the organizational goal, and overall the innovation was a success.

Four decades later, I am not so confident that the Quaker way of reaching decisions can be stripped of its spiritual underpinnings successfully. Decision by consensus is not the same as the corporate discernment of God's will for a particular group of people at a particular time. There are many facets of the way we Friends go about making decisions that do translate into a secular setting, but I am no longer clear to say that those facets alone, absent the faith commitments that underlie them, constitute Quaker decision making.

By this time, Nano and I had moved to a large apartment in Jamaica Plain. A sudden large rent increase in the summer of 1977 spurred Nano to conclude that this was the time to make the move we had planned to Charlottesville, Virginia, and we very quickly organized ourselves to do just that.[2]

The move itself seemed easy and without problems; we found rental housing and jobs quickly. House prices were affordable, and in a few months we bought an old farmhouse and a few acres of land in Greene County, about twenty miles north of Charlottesville. However, the culture shock of rural Southern living proved to be very great for Nano. She had never lived outside an urbanized area and had never needed to get a driver's license. The absence of public transportation or even sidewalks in most places was dismaying to her, and the shock of other differences between the South and Greater Boston were as stark and disorienting to her has they had been to me twelve years earlier. These stresses brought to light other issues, particularly in our relationship with each other; a marriage counselor told us that we were "not ships passing in the night, but ships on different oceans." We separated, then divorced. Nano returned to New England quickly and, by all reports, thrived there.

While this was developing, I found work as the community relations director at a local neuropsychiatric hospital in Charlottesville. One of the significant programs of the hospital was a twenty-eight-day residential rehabilitation program for alcoholics. This was my first extended exposure to the problems of alcoholism, and I learned a great deal from being there. Only after beginning work at the hospital did I realize that it was owned and operated by the affiliated doctors as a for-profit enterprise—the only time in my adult work career that I was not working either for myself or for a nonprofit organization. I began to look for a nonprofit I could work for and was soon appointed executive director of Jefferson Area United Transportation (JAUNT), a rural low-income transportation network serving five counties and the city of Charlottesville.

Providing low-income rural people affordable transportation to and from work and medical appointments was very satisfying. The isolation of people in rural poverty makes them invisible, and their problems and challenges are magnified because they can't get to the resources that do exist. This is, however, an ephemeral service: once a trip is completed, there is little to show what happened or what was accomplished. This lack of tangible results began to stand out as the wear of overcoming the numerous challenges of running a publicly funded transportation network began to accumulate on me and in me.

In the fall of 1979, I began to scan the help-wanted ads in the local Charlottesville newspaper. I hadn't said out loud that I was looking to change jobs, but something in me wanted to see what else might be available. One week there was an ad seeking an executive director for a nonprofit organization that aimed to provide affordable housing for low-income families. The brief ad caught my attention, but the name of the organization was a turn-off: Project Home Repair, Inc. It did not seem to be a name that would lead people to take the organization seriously, and I paid the ad no more attention.

Two weeks later, another help-wanted ad appeared. This was identical word for word with the previous one I had noticed except that the name of the organization had been changed to Virginia Mountain Housing, Inc. This was a name that would be taken seriously, and I sent in an application even though the job was located in Blacksburg, Virginia, more than two hours southwest of Charlottesville.

After an interview, I was offered the position of executive director with a satisfactory salary and benefits. Driving home from Blacksburg that night, I tried to weigh the pros and cons of accepting the offer. The organization was doing good work with a permanent effect; a rehabilitated or renovated house lasts a long time. The people were good folks with good motivations, the salary was fine, and the organization had potential for solid growth in years to come. On the other hand, it would require leaving the Charlottesville area I had come to enjoy as well as my

Beginning Again

farmhouse and land in Greene County and making a whole new set of friends.

On impulse, I pulled off the interstate onto a scenic overlook on Afton Mountain. Without quite thinking about what I was doing, I got out of my pickup truck, knelt down at the edge of the overlook, and began to pray for guidance. What should I do? After a little while, I heard words in my mind, as clearly as I might hear any human voice, that said, "If you can't take this job, how are you going to be ready for the next job I have for you?"

The implications of this experience were profound. When I attended my first meeting for worship at Friends Meeting at Cambridge, I had felt a clear meaning without specific words. This time I heard explicit English words, though I did not hear a voice speaking them. This experience said volumes about the nature of God, the potential for personal relationships between God and individual human beings, and the possibility that God might have yearnings or desires for our lives, even to the point of offering choices that would help guide us in the direction God would like to see us develop.

Somewhat shaken by the experience, I got up off my knees, climbed into my truck, and drove the rest of the way home. I called the next morning to accept the job at Virginia Mountain Housing, Inc., effective at the beginning of the new year.

Chapter 4
Vocation and Competency: Virginia, 1980–1988

When the 1980s began, I was thirty-two years old. The next years would be marked by transforming disruptions in my spiritual life that affected my choices in employment and residence as well as my faith commitments. I began this period as a non-Christian committed Quaker. I was unfamiliar with large portions of Scripture and the nuances of the history of our faith, spiritually undisciplined, and unappreciative of the importance of authentic community in the spiritual journey. Wrestling with God over these years led me to a new commitment to the peculiar Quaker understanding of Christianity and with that to the Truth and vast implications of George Fox's epiphany that there is one who can speak to our condition, even Christ Jesus!

These changes led me into (and then, sometimes, away from) three kinds of ministry. I began the decade earning my living doing the corporal works of mercy. Later, I was given opportunities to experience the Quaker "invitational ministry,"[1] and in the end I committed to a "free gospel ministry" in which my vocation as a minister was separated from the competencies by which I earned a living. By the end of the decade, I was again employed doing works of mercy but no longer considered this my vocation. I participated in the invitational ministry but would no longer accept any compensation, and I considered the gospel ministry the focus of my life against which everything else had to be measured.

Following the dramatic guidance I had received on Afton Mountain, I began work at Virginia Mountain Housing after New Year's Day 1980 to help ease the serious housing problems of the rural poor in southwest Virginia. The board of directors were predominantly church-going individuals who saw this work as direct ministry—as faith in action. One of the corporal works of mercy is sheltering the homeless—and we felt that unless a person lived in permanent housing that was safe, decent, and affordable, they were homeless. I also began to consider the prospect of marrying Merrill Varn, whom I had met at Charlottesville Friends

Vocation and Competency

Meeting. This discernment continued for over a year, and we were married under the care of the Blacksburg-Roanoke monthly meeting in Fifth Month 1981.

1980 felt like a hard time to be a pacifist, and things promised to get harder. A rising militarism gripped the nation. New president Jimmy Carter was calling for a renewal of registration for the draft. There were renewed military tensions in Iran, Iraq, and Afghanistan and rumors the Summer Olympics might be canceled.

I could see no role in the national political process for the religious pacifist. There were no pacifist candidates to support. However I voted, the IRS would still seize my money to pay for war. If I left the country, World War III would kill me (and millions of others) as surely as if I stayed home. I concluded that "How can the pacifist remain 'pure?'" must be the wrong question. A better query would be, "To what action is the religious pacifist called in this day in America?"

In this context, I started reading the Scripture straight through, from Genesis to Revelation, using the old family Bible (King James Version). The Bible seemed to me right then to be a treasury of great wisdom, much of which I had been blind to. I was also reading Robert Barclay's *Apology*,[2] with the New Testament close at hand. Barclay opened Paul's epistles to me in a joyous fashion, pointing out meanings that had been obscure. The *Apology* increased my eagerness to read the Bible and to read each book in full rather than in snippets. It began to feel as if Jesus' teachings were especially apt to the present situation. I did not trust any translation as being 100 percent historically accurate or culturally understandable—but I did feel some portion of the same Spirit that moved its authors to write what later became Scripture and was joyful.

I began to understand a new answer to my question about what to do. I should love God with all my heart, all my soul, and all my mind and love my neighbor as myself. No government could prevent me from carrying out those Great Commandments—only my own lack of faith. My proper objective was not success but faithfulness.

When my Bible reading project was about a year old, I had reached Ezekiel. I had also finished Barclay's *Apology for the True Christian Divinity*, Richard K. MacMaster's *Conscience in Crisis* on peace churches in Pennsylvania 1739–1789 and Gandhi's *Non-Violent Resistance*. A reading list this varied could have been fragmenting, but for me it was unifying. Each reading in each book was related to the others. Themes built, climaxed, and fell away as if I were reading rewrites of the same play. Friends speak of seeing God through a Christ-shaped window; this is a window—and only one of many windows—but it is not the Light itself. I was reading several views of God through that window as well as through others. It seemed that this extended study had been opened to me for the purpose of giving me the grounding I needed to carry out a task. I didn't know yet what that task was or even if the time for it had arrived. For the present, there was simply more study, more meditation, more daily work.

Early in First Month 1982, I finished reading the King James family Bible from Genesis to Revelation. Almost simultaneously, an event occurred that spurred my Bible reading immensely but ended my serious study of the King James translation. While at an American Friends Service Committee board of directors meeting in Philadelphia, I happened across a New English Bible, a translation I had not encountered (I really was not aware of any translations other than the King James). I bought a copy and began to read it on the train ride home, starting with Genesis 1:1.

I kept reading during the entire trip back to Virginia. My state of mind was like that of Keats's in "On First Looking into Chapman's Homer," and for much the same reason: a new translation had opened my eyes to vistas not before guessed at. After I returned home, I continued to read through this new translation, book by book.

I was amazed and overjoyed by this contemporary translation. The messages of Scripture were much more accessible without having to fight through archaic vocabulary and syntax to get at the meaning of each phrase. I began to engage Scripture in a way I had not done ever before, to wrestle with the faith claims of Christianity freshly based on my own reading. I discovered a description of the relationship between God and all creation very different from what I had ever heard before. This description matched my personal experiences closely—better than any other I had encountered. I found that if I wanted to describe my inner condition clearly, my best option was to use the vocabulary and metaphors of the Scripture story. I cannot say, as some can, that I became a Christian on a certain date, but the process began in earnest with the purchase of that Bible.

Friends General Conference

Early in 1982, I saw an advertisement for the position of general secretary of Friends General Conference (FGC). Although I had no FGC experience other than attending the 1981 annual Gathering in Berea, Kentucky,[3] I was intrigued. It seemed like an opportunity to use my management training and skills on behalf of the Religious Society of Friends, which had been so valuable to me. After spending time in discernment and discussing the implications with Merrill, I was led to apply. When I was invited to interview, I felt led to take that step, also.

I described to the Search Committee being led to take each individual step in the process one at a time rather than feeling led to become general secretary. When the interview ended, I realized that the "penny had dropped," to use John Punshon's phrase, and I now wanted the job itself, not just to explore the next step. I took a walk outside, settling into prayer.

This was a time for me of great openness to God. I admitted my desire for the job and also my inability to judge whether I ought to take it. It felt faithful to have made my best effort to be the one chosen while also being open with the Search Committee about my uncertainties and apprehensions. Now it was God's turn, and I felt I could accept whatever happened. If God offered the position, I should take it. When I was told that I would be the recommended candidate, I felt a sense of light and joy. Brian Drayton has said one feels more gathered after following a true leading rather than more scattered. I felt more gathered; I had the sense that I had done the right thing in seeking and accepting this job.

Accepting the position meant making numerous adjustments in our lives. Merrill had begun a PhD program in entomology at Virginia Tech in Blacksburg and chose to continue that rather than follow me to Philadelphia. We saw the time of her graduate study and my service at FGC as a time to get an apple orchard started in Greene County so that it would be that much closer to producing income after my expected three- to five-year term as general secretary. The orchard would be home base for both of us. Merrill would travel south regularly for her classwork and research in working apple orchards, and I would travel north to Philadelphia for weekday office work. We returned to Charlottesville Friends Meeting as our spiritual home.

As my starting date drew closer, the clerk of the FGC Central Committee and I began to draft my work plan for the first year. Our intentions were to visit member meetings extensively and to modernize operations in the FGC office. One innovation we planned was to buy one of the new desktop computers and a printer.

I became general secretary of FGC on Seventh Month 1, 1982, less than six months after I began reading the New English Bible intensively. Two days later, I started my actual work at the FGC Gathering at Slippery Rock State College. I was briefly introduced to Friends during an evening plenary session. Leaving the hall afterward, I was accosted by a Friend who was agitated about a particular FGC leaflet. I tried to put him off, being new to the job and tired from the events of the day, but he followed me to my dorm and then inside. I made my apologies and ducked into a men's room, thinking to end the encounter, but he followed me inside to continue his vehement protest. His genuine concern was that the leaflet included on the back page a sentence saying that FGC was an organization with Christian roots; he felt that FGC was "way past that" now and should not be mentioning any Christian history or other connections to Christianity in any of its literature.

I was taken aback by the agitation of this Friend. I was just re-embracing my Christian faith after a long, self-imposed exile, and on my first day at FGC I was confronted by this denial of Christianity's place with my new employer. If there were many other Friends like this in FGC, what had I gotten myself into? Looking back now on my tenure at FGC, I feel this encounter was indeed an indication of FGC's condition and an omen of one persistent characteristic of my employment there.

Vocation and Competency

After the Gathering, I was sent out on the road to visit numerous yearly meeting annual sessions, partly to introduce myself as the new general secretary and partly as part of the regular FGC visitation program. This was the beginning of my introduction to the invitational ministry. I had been invited to work for a Quaker organization, in return for an adequate salary, for the express purpose of promoting that organization to its members and meeting specified needs. The scope and duration of the invitation was under the control of the inviting party, not the minister. My time at FGC began under one set of mutual understandings of the organization's needs and of the content of the invitation. That soon changed dramatically. My understanding of what God was calling me to do was changing as I was drawn toward a new Christian faith. FGC's understanding of its own needs were also about to change urgently.

It took a couple of months, given my crowded travel schedule, to find time to explore FGC finances. The FGC bookkeeping had been very simple up to this time (cash basis, single-entry), making financial analysis quite difficult. What I discovered was that FGC had been running a deficit for six consecutive years and had finally used up all of its reserves. There would not be enough cash to pay the October payroll.

My first FGC Central Committee meeting was held in Tenth Month 1982, and I started off with a bang. "Hi, I'm Lloyd Lee Wilson, your new General Secretary. If you decided to shut down FGC as of Monday morning you wouldn't have enough money to pay the staff, landlord, and other creditors what they would be owed." I spoke for minutes, talking about FGC work seemed vital to me, just how serious a financial bind FGC was in, and how to get out of the hole we were in. The Central Committee members were shocked but not disbelieving of the news, confident that the money needed could be raised in time. My optimism was tempered by the knowledge that the previous year these same Friends had launched a "Leap of Faith" campaign that started the year with $18,000 of pledges in hand to help meet the $45,000 budget—and had finished the year having collected $18,700. This year's fundraising must succeed.

I was particularly grateful during this time for the recurring presence of Patty Levering, who held my feet to the fire on important matters. Patty and I shared on a very deep spiritual level, although we did not have the gift of easy understanding about other things—that was markedly absent. But when we began to speak of spiritual matters, wide gates opened and much was exchanged with just a few words. Patty pointed out that I had spiritual gifts. I began to see the importance of using all those gifts actively. It was not enough to use one gift—management skills—and leave another—gospel ministry—buried like an unused talent in the parable.

My reading of *Salvation by Christ* by Job Scott had opened anew the concept of the Indwelling Christ. If, as Patty said, people wanted simply to be "in my presence," they must sense that Indwelling Christ. My obligation, then, was to live and serve people in a way that directed them to God. What I had thought of as a call to the verbal ministry I now saw as a call to share the Indwelling Christ by word and deed, a calling different from but complementary to other ministries. This was a costly calling; it demanded everything. Christ must come before family, fame, success, even life itself. Christ came first.

This new understanding of my calling affected everything. Instead of giving presentations to large groups of people, my attention was drawn to ways to be fully present to small groups and individuals in settings that encouraged informality and spontaneous reactions to dialogue. I saw the necessity of living in such a way that my presence would be more transparent to the Light of Christ Within. I felt unburdened, though I was aware of having a larger calling than I had realized, one with a harder and more costly discipline. If this was God's wish for me, I would accept.

For well over a year, FGC's financial woes continued as we took two steps forward followed by a giant step backward. Financial woes notwithstanding, work on rearticulating the spiritual purpose and mission of FGC continued. In Fifth Month 1984, the Executive Committee gathered to consider the latest attempt at this statement along with a set of priorities for FGC activities and outlines of specific programs. Friends were keenly aware that there were not enough resources to go around and that some important tasks had to be left

Vocation and Competency

undone. Our hope was to be able to say we were doing the most important tasks with the available resources.

The statement of purpose could have sidetracked this whole train because work on earlier drafts had highlighted our spiritual disunity. If we could not agree on our purpose, how could we find agreement on what we should do? The hope in earlier meetings had been in Friends' refusal to give up—their gentle tenacity, softly pressing toward an understanding of one another that could lead to honest language to which all could give assent.

Carolyn Holden of Canadian Yearly Meeting was asked to take the various drafts and suggestions and draft a new statement for this meeting. She was unable to set pen to paper for several weeks, but one morning it was given to her all at once. It was an excellent piece of work; Carolyn had been touched by grace when she wrote it.

As the executive committee began to consider the statement, I could feel the spirit of disunity begin to rise up and manifest itself. I gave up following the speaking and concentrated on praying for God's blessing on our group and its deliberations. I prayed quietly but vocally for Christ to be present in our midst and to drive out the spirit of disunity and unfaithfulness. It really seemed as if God's blessing were being poured out like honey flowing down, over, and around us all. The tone of the vocal sharing changed, and Friends agreed to accept the statement as Carolyn had written it with one change, to *add* a phrase about the importance of the Judeo-Christian tradition! With God's help, we were over the first hurdle.

Holding the 1984 Gathering in upstate New York seemed like a risky experiment; would Friends travel so far from Philadelphia for an FGC event? My attention was occupied by a more personal set of questions. I had seriously injured my back in the Virginia orchard just before leaving for the Gathering and was able to make the drive to Canton, New York, only with the help of powerful pain relievers. For the first couple of days, I struggled to keep up with my usual responsibilities while holding the pain at bay. On the third evening, several dear friends who were also Friends staged an intervention to get my attention. Tom Ewell, Thom Jeavons, Patty Levering, and Rachel Ruth took me aside after supper and gently and lovingly disciplined me for the pace I'd been trying to maintain recently, especially at the Gathering, and stated their concern about my planned trips to California and Alaska.

It was disturbing to hear that they had been concerned about my work, but I could see the truth in their words. I asked their forgiveness for outrunning my Guide, which Tom Ewell quickly and graciously tendered, and agreed to cut back on the number of meetings I attended and people I interacted with at the Gathering and to spend as much time as possible either in my room or on my back, or both, in an attempt to get some physical relief and rest.

This and similar encounters sparked ongoing discussions with the Personnel Committee and others about how much work I could be expected to do and about the content of that work. One concern was my growing call into the gospel ministry, which was different from the call of the typical FGC general secretary. This had become a public image problem for some FGC supporters as well as one more demand on my time and energy. Central Committee members made it clear that I was employed for my administrative skills only, not for any activity in the public ministry. To prevent Friends and Friends meetings from concluding that because I was Christian FGC was a Christian organization, a clear separation was needed between my public ministry and the theological commitments of FGC as an organization. In other words, I should not accept or undertake any new ministry on FGC time. Over the next twelve months, that concern expanded into whether I should be allowed to undertake public ministry at all, even on my own time, as long as I was an FGC employee.

I was not a "released Friend" but a "constrained Friend." The salary and benefits I accepted constrained me to do the tasks assigned by my employer and to restrain from activities my employer deemed detrimental to the organization. This was fine as long as I felt led to do the tasks my employer wanted to pay for, but if God led me to some other activity, my "faith-based" employment became a form of golden shackles. Over the years, I've come to recognize this danger in all sorts of invitational ministry, from Protestant pastors to religious institutions to gigs like workshops or retreats. Any time money is exchanged, the risk of distortion of the gospel is present, hindering faithfulness rather than enabling it.

In a time of private retirement in early 1985, I was released by the Holy Spirit from continuing as FGC general secretary. This change would take several months, but probably not more than a year. The Holy Spirit had not said that I should leave immediately and offered no instruction about how to prepare for the transition.

I sought guidance from my Charlottesville oversight committee. They affirmed that I had fulfilled my obligations to FGC and was clear to leave when way opened. They said that the sign of way opening would be the appearance of the right job, and they went on to suggest that a new job might be created that I would be suitable for and interested in. During the 1985 FGC Gathering, Janaka Casper of tracked me down and called me. He had created a new job at Virginia Mountain Housing and wanted me to fill it at the same salary I was earning at FGC. This was the sign I needed that the time had come for me to leave FGC. I accepted the job and resigned my position at FGC that same day.

The Free Gospel Ministry

Now I was working at Virginia Mountain Housing again, providing shelter for those without a safe, decent, and affordable home. Rather than coming full circle, my life was describing a spiral, moving in a third dimension. I was experiencing the difference early Friends described between "competency" and "vocation." Working in the field of low-income housing (I now realized) was my competency—what I did to earn a living. It was good work. It helped establish the Kingdom of God, but I no longer understood it to be my calling. I still participated in the invitational ministry, although not as anyone's employee or paid resource. Now I saw those invitations as the excuse God had used to get me to a particular place at a particular time in order to catalyze something completely unknown to me. In later years, the last words in my ears as I left home for a speaking engagement or to lead a retreat were often those of Susan (my future wife): "Remember—thee has no idea why thee is going there!"

Memoir of the Life and Religious Labors of Lloyd Lee Wilson

I was about to be introduced to something new in my experience: the free gospel ministry, for lack of a better name. A journey through New England would immerse me in this service, and I understood it to be my vocation. Chronologically, the transition from FGC employment to this new form of ministry was short and abrupt, but of course God had been preparing me for this shift long before it happened. Looking back long after, I can see this preparation going on in "the background" years ahead of time.

My daily Bible reading and study had continued while I was at FGC, and I set aside time each day for personal worship. I had thought of nurturing the Spirit like nurturing an acorn—giving it the right amount of light, moisture, and nutrients to sprout and grow. Now I was learning that the growing tree needs even more of all these things than the acorn. It has deeper, more numerous roots and more leaf area to enable the tree to meet its greater needs. In my own journey, I found an ever-greater need for specific spiritual practices such as prayer, contemplation, study, and worship. My ability to pray increased, but it was more important than ever to me to be regular in my practice of prayer. I don't know whether the oak has joy in its broader span of limbs, but I did have greater joy in the Lord.

A topic I frequently reflected on was the proper relationship between my newly reestablished Christian faith and other spiritual paths. I had never been very eclectic. I liked to learn about other spiritual paths, but the salad bar approach to enlightenment seemed to me like a cop-out because people needed to commit to a single spiritual path in order to make long-lasting progress. Still, it became clear that the great paths can and do illuminate one another. As Jesus taught not to lay up treasures on earth, where rust corrupts and thieves break in and steal, Lao Tzu taught that to hold on to material wealth makes us poor and that struggling against acquiring material goods distracts us as much as the goods themselves. The Taoist master is in effect giving a commentary on Jesus. John (1:1–5) and Barclay would say this is the Light illuminating itself. I am comfortable with that.

My embrace of Quaker Christianity led me to deal with possessions through a *spirituality of subtraction*: eliminating anything in my life that

Vocation and Competency

distracted me from God. Jesus teaches that material things can be a major distraction; Lao Tzu adds a warning that making a fetish of not having material things can be equally distracting. Both teachers are speaking about the same Living Water.

Around this time, several Friends in various parts of the country started praying "together," wherever we were physically, at 8:30 a.m. Eastern time on Monday mornings. Numerous other Friends joined us over time. This came to be a very important time in each week for me. When the Covid-19 pandemic hit in 2020 and social distancing measures kept Friends from worshipping with one another physically, the memory of this group praying "apart together" helped me adjust to the new reality and to trust in the authenticity of online meetings for worship.

In 1982 the American Friends Service Committee board of directors was wrestling over whether or not to include homosexuals in their affirmative action policy. I was invited to make a presentation to the board "from the Christian perspective." I called my remarks *Homosexuals and the Christian Sexual Ethic*. The goodness of *all* of God's creation led me to conclude that homosexuality is a good part of God's creation, just as heterosexuality is. Each is to be honored and devoted to God and considered a gift from God. My conclusion was that homosexual persons share a viable Christian ethic for life and are "full members of the body of Christ: not fallen brothers, not weaker sisters, but equals entitled to our full acceptance and love."

New Year's Day 1983 brought this reflection:

> I have recently been made much more aware of how blessed I am and have been, in so many ways. Little encounters or passing observations gently but firmly push home the point till it penetrates my waking mind. All of this is a direct and free gift of God, which I have done nothing to deserve and much to indicate I do not deserve. What complaint would I have if God were to take it all away? Is it not all God's from the beginning? Have I not already been blessed far more than I deserve? If the trials of Job were to befall me this evening, I would do better to praise God for what God had lent me and whatever God had been

pleased to let me enjoy for a little while than to complain about my loss or protest my undeservingness.

Why should I not devote "my" life to working in God's vineyards—it is more God's than mine anyway, and all I could do in a lifetime would not begin to repay all the blessings I have received. Praise God, who does not keep strict books of account but blesses us beyond our desserts and beyond all measure, even offering Christ, the gift of new Life! The continuation of each blessing each second is another free blessing. How can I mourn the loss of one blessing for even a second when an infinity of blessings remains?

While at FGC, I spent a great amount of time visiting monthly meetings. These visits were occasions of great learning for me. Some were "covered gatherings," no matter how many or how few people were physically present. It was not obvious on these journeys that anything I did or didn't do made any difference—God does as God sees fit. There were times when something I did triggered an already existing condition, such as the time when I was moved to vocal prayer during worship and was eldered immediately afterward with the harshly spoken words, "We don't do that here."

A steady stream of letters from strangers gave me the opportunity for conversations on numerous spiritual topics. Some correspondents were seeking information, and others posed specific challenges to Quaker faith and practice. One of the latter evoked the following journal notes as I prepared a response:

- Meeting for worship is not sitting down to tell God "Here I am—speak!" It is entering into that calm that enables us to hear what God is saying all the time. God has a message for each of us always; we often aren't listening. The mystic and monastic have recognized this and devote much of their lives to structured listening. We need to practice the Presence of God as they do; to hear God among the pots and pans.

- The basic process of this part of worship, learning to listen, is one in which we can participate all week long. In fact, we cannot do it adequately for just one hour per week.

Vocation and Competency

- We gather with others to worship because there is a mutual reinforcement, like bringing many candles into a single dark room, that occurs when several people worship together. It helps to have others around who are embarked on the same journey, caught up in the same endeavor. Our attention to God is not changed by the presence of other worshippers—only our clarity of vision and hearing.

- Vocal ministry, in the sense of prophecy, is only one aspect of worship. Equally important are the aspects of contemplation, adoration, repentance, intercession, and praise. These may or may not involve outward speech.

- We should not store up experiences or observations during the week for possible use during worship but should offer them up to God at the moment when they occur. The object is to become constantly aware of God's Presence and direction in our lives, not to become centered on one hour of the week during which we will get direction for all the others. Friends once called these experiences "opportunities" and were not shy about settling into a period of worship in the midst of a walk, or conversation, or other activity. We should strive to regain that spirit.

- To carry a thought into meeting with the intention of sharing it vocally is wrong on two counts. First, it implies that we have not shared that thought with God when we first had it but have stored it away in some fashion. Secondly, it means that during worship we will be thinking about our idea, how and when best to share it, rather than listening for God's idea.

- To enter into meeting for worship with an intent not to speak is equally dangerous, for it risks disobedience to God's will. To carry out our intent to be silent, we may have to shut out a message we are intended to speak or to hear the message and still refuse to give it voice. Our fellow worshippers are thereby deprived of the message, and we have defied God's will.

- Yes, every spoken message—prophecy—*should* be by divine revelation, for several reasons. (1) Messages that are not divinely inspired are in fact interruptions of the attempts of other worshippers to hear the Divine Voice. (2) The purpose of meeting is not to be edified in the worldly sense but to be drawn close to God. Only God can do that. (3) To give a message that is not inspired may actually confuse other worshippers who expect divine inspiration and seek it in what you say. (4) There is no need for the spoken word; a meeting for worship can be powerful, beautiful, and influential in the lives of those who attend without a word being spoken.

• Must prayer be by divine inspiration? Here, we do indeed talk to God and are (perhaps) not directly inspired. Vocal prayer may be by inspiration—we may feel led to a particular vocal prayer that unites a worshipping group into a single organism—or it may be on our own hook—a spoken prayer of confession or repentance that becomes a covenant with the community to recognize, accept, and support our changed condition. Vocalized prayers of adoration will most likely be inspired as we can adore silently.

• We can never be sure of our own motives when we stand to speak in worship without a sense of divine impetus. The Adversary is real, and temptations are strong. We may be succumbing to a desire to set our neighbors straight, or demonstrate our erudition or oratorical style, or any of a number of harmful impulses if we speak without inspiration.

• How then can we tell that we are inspired? (1) We are surprised by the impulse and the message—at least when it first presents itself. (2) Both impulse and message persist in us until relieved by speaking. (3) Physiological signs are present, such as a heavy pulse, a sense of having one's heart in the throat, or a sense of being almost pulled to one's feet. (4) After we have spoken, a sense of calm pervades, of being more gathered and of having discharged our obligation. (5) The full message is not quite clear when we first stand, and usually we are surprised by at least one or two phrases of the message that seem quite unusual, not like us at all. (6) Succeeding messages are complementary—not on the surface, but on a deeper level they draw the worshippers together.

Vocation and Competency

Merrill's advanced pregnancy in early 1983 brought these reflections about intercessory prayer:

> It is easy to pray for a healthy baby and for Merrill to come out of the experience in good health. Intercessory prayer in general is a better experience for me now than ever before. It's not just 'holding people in the Light,' which seems a little off-balance to me—sort of like the spiritual equivalent of holding a dirty dish under the hot water tap. Since I have come to experience the reality of our brokenness and of the Adversary, I feel the need for God's active intervention on my behalf and am buoyed up by the prayers of others to God on my behalf, asking for the intervention I need—a fresh hit of grace, if you will. I feel the reality, in turn, of my own prayers on behalf of others, asking God's blessing on them.

Praying for myself is more problematic. Is it legitimate to pray for my own healing—for example, for reduced blood pressure? Or for strength to resist temptation, for the necessities of life, for deliverance from the snares of the Adversary? Perhaps the answer is in Christ's model prayer: "Give us this day our daily bread." What is a more basic daily need than the health to sustain a normal life? Is it to be believed that the God who tells us not to be anxious about our food and clothing (Matthew 6:25–33) truly intends not to offer the same assurance for our very bodies and minds? Jesus said in Matthew that if we ask, it will be given to us, and later that if we seek the Kingdom of God first, then everything else we might need will be ours as well.

It cannot be wrong to ask, in humble obedience, to be preserved in our physical bodies. We do not know God's will and must accept what God gives, but we can certainly ask for what we believe, in our limited way, to be the good. I feel at liberty to pray for physical health, for the health of those near to me, and for my own release into the ministry, sensing all are legitimate requests and all will be granted if God so wills it.

My blood pressure had returned to unhealthy high levels, which gave me impetus to resume regular practice of Transcendental Meditation. I had started meditating about ten years earlier but let it lapse when my blood pressure dropped back down toward normal levels. Not only had my blood pressure gone up again, but Merrill told me that she could tell by my personality that I had stopped meditating.

A colleague at Massachusetts General Hospital had made a similar observation after announcing she had signed up for Transcendental Meditation training. I asked what had influenced her to do so, and she said I had. I would take a break when the pressure or stress peaked to go off privately and meditate. The change in my mood and personality before and after meditation had convinced her that it was real and worthwhile. Odd how others can see us more clearly than we can see ourselves. How important it is to live in community!

The 23rd and 24th of Third Month 1983 were twin days of beginning. On the 23rd, Merrill and I with the help of friends and family planted over 730 apple trees on the land we'd been preparing for so long. It was a thrill to walk along the rows after the planting was over in that quiet time before dusk when even the air seems soft. The orchard seemed a thousand times more real to me than it had even the day before. Then, on the 24th, Asa Cadbury Varn Wilson was born. When the moment arrived, I was in tears—overcome by the miracle of birth, by the sight of my/our son, and by relief that Merrill's pain was over. Washing him after his birth was a holy sacrament. Praise God, the circle was unbroken.

I was able to stay on with Merrill and Asa for two weeks before FGC called me back to Philadelphia. Parting after that time was the hardest of the many partings we'd had since I had become general secretary. In the ensuing days, my thoughts strayed often to Virginia. Soon Asa had been without me as long as he and I had been together; when you've only been alive a few days, each hour seems like a long time!

In midsummer 1983, I took Asa with me to Philadelphia while Merrill was out of the country. On the drive, we stopped in Rising Sun, Maryland, and visited Penny Haines. I hadn't planned to stop at Penny's house; it happened to us. Asa and I were heading up the interstate, and I took the North East/Rising Sun exit, thinking even as I did so that I was making a mistake because traveling by US Route 1 would take longer than staying on I-95. Even so, I continued to Rising Sun. When I got into town, I turned aside, again without intending to, and stopped at Penny's

Vocation and Competency

house. It turned out that she was feeling sad and had been praying for someone to visit her whom she could talk to. We had a good long visit, talking of spiritual consolation and desolation and about the difficulty of waiting for the Lord to give us a sign. It was a stimulating conversation for its content but even more so for the sense of having been an instrument of God for Penny's support. It was a pastoral visit planned by God, not human beings.

That summer, my travels brought me back to New England Yearly Meeting sessions after six years. While I was there, Jan Hoffman shared advice from Gordon Browne, who had told her that as yearly meeting clerk many people would ascribe to her power, insight, and wisdom that she might not in fact possess. If she allowed her ego to get caught up in believing she was who people acted as if she was, her spiritual life would suffer. I felt I should take this to heart. There was an increasing number of people who approached me for personal counsel, from the adulterous clerk of a monthly meeting to the rising Earlham School of Religion student concerned about the state of his monthly meeting to family members who were struggling with unemployment, marital troubles, personal integrity, and esteem. If I started believing I had the wisdom and discernment to help all these people myself, I'd be in big trouble.

In Eleventh Month 1983, I traveled to Homewood Meeting in Baltimore. During worship I felt a leading to speak, but the ministry was so frequent that I felt no opening to do so. Before I would finish reflecting on the previous message, a new speaker would rise. Shortly before noon, I felt an opening and was led to speak on Micah 6:8, *What doth the Lord require of thee . . . ?* (KJV). This seemingly discharged my obligation. This was a time of struggle for me with respect to my vocal ministry. I had been unfaithful at times by cutting short a message that I really should have developed at greater length. This time I had had the additional worry of knowing that noon was approaching and the Friend with care of the meeting would want to end shortly. I did finally rise, and though there were points I did not make and illustrations I did not use, I sensed I had been faithful.

In Twelfth Month 1983, a group of us organized a Scattered Fellowship Retreat at Powell House. The weekend gathering was deliberately unplanned, dependent on the immediate guidance of the Holy Spirit to direct our actions throughout. It was a very powerful experience. One Friend came to accept Christ into her life, and others reported deeply moving insights and openings. For me, it was another time of wrestling with God. I struggled with the choice between visitation on the West Coast in the summer and giving a lecture at New York Yearly Meeting but had no sense of the Lord's guidance. I realized on the drive back that I needed only to ask specifically for that wisdom/discernment and God would give it to me. I made that prayer explicit there and then, and I offer it here:

> Dear God—Abba—grant me the wisdom and spiritual insight to choose wisely, with the help of my faith community, my places and types of intentional ministry, from now on. Grant that wherever I go, that your Presence and blessing will inform, direct, and transform my every word and deed so that those I encounter praise You and are brought to Christ. You can make me a powerful instrument of your will; grant that blessing.
>
> Protect me from the Evil One and his attacks. Prevent me from being a stumbling block to any other person and grant instead that I may be a window through which others see God. All this I ask in Jesus' name, knowing and believing in faith that all I ask will be granted, or something better; also, that we are promised to do greater things even than the deeds of Jesus before his crucifixion.
>
> Grant that souls may come to Christ a week after I leave a place so that I not be made proud.
>
> Pour thy blessings on Merrill and Asa and on our parents and relatives, especially Aunt Nellie. Guard thy laborers wherever they are and grant them thy peace. Forgive us all, and me especially. Amen.

Seven months later, my faith community gave me the specific guidance to lay down the western journey.

On Second Month 22, 1984, I noted in my journal:

Vocation and Competency

I finished reading the Bible cover to cover for the second time in Second Month 1984 and recorded the event in the old Wilson family Bible, near a note written by my great-grandfather W. C. Alexander: "Finished reading the Bible through the fourth time Monday, Nov 14, 1870—W.C.A." He had not stopped in 1870. Below that are his notations for his fifth through twelfth readings, the last completed on Sunday, August 4, 1878. About that time, according to the inscription on the flyleaf, this Bible must have passed into the possession of his descendants.

A century later, when I made my commitment to read the Bible front to back at least once, I was not a Christian and certainly not a fan of the Bible. There were parts of the Gospels I could read and feel benefit from, but the rest of the New Testament seemed questionable to me, and the Old Testament was definitely out of date. I was in considerable spiritual travail and was looking for some spiritual guidance that would help me make sense of what was happening to and around me and would point out a direction for my spiritual renewal and eventual growth. The Bible provided all that and more.

I read in that old Bible daily, with its archaic seventeenth-century English, hard-to-read typeface, and brittle pages. I had no commentary or concordance to help me understand what I was reading.[4] As I read a chapter or two each day, some themes took shape in my mind that deeply and truly spoke to my condition.

Out of the tumult and violence of the Old Testament I saw God's persistent loyalty to whatever remnant of the covenant people was faithful. God is active in human events, the Old Testament chroniclers were saying. Even when, like Job, we cannot understand why God is doing (or allowing) the terrible things around us, God desires to be in a covenant relationship with us. Over and over, humans try to live up to God's expectations, fail, and reap the consequences of their failure. Yet God never tires of starting over, of trying yet again. I could truly understand this theme because it was the theme of my life: my failure to live up to the standards that I thought God prescribed for me and living through the consequences of those failures. Picking up the pieces, I would try again—and fail again.

Reading the New Testament Gospel message in its own words was like cutting the rope that had held a helium balloon tethered to the ground. My heart soared. Here was the Way out of the endless cycle; Christ had come to demonstrate irrefutably that nothing we could do would drive God away, that God's grace released us from the cycle of brokenness and failure if we only had faith in the Truth of the gospel. Not immediately or quickly, but inexorably, I became a Christian.

It took two years to finish the Bible for the first time. After several times through, I began reading it differently, spending more time with a selected book, reading about the culture and historical setting of that book, and meditating on what I'd read, often discussing it with spiritual friends. As I became familiar with the biblical characters, I began to look to specific persons for guidance for specific situations I was facing: Job, Timothy, the church at Ephesus, Jacob. I also became part of Bible study groups that followed the weekly readings in the Common Lectionary, giving us a sense of fellowship with other Christians around the world.

The Bible has layer upon layer of meaning, and as we progress in our faith more and more meaning becomes accessible. All of the hurdles we face and issues that we must resolve in our personal spiritual journeys have been faced before by persons whose stories are recorded in Scripture. Sometimes they made good decisions and sometimes bad ones; either way, we gain by studying their experiences.

The Bible is not for me the final authority on spiritual issues; I believe strongly in continuing revelation. I also believe that the words of the 1661 declaration by George Fox and others are still true: "The Spirit of Christ is not changeable, so as now to lead us from a thing as evil and then unto it." Our present revelation is an outgrowth and unfolding of past understandings

Vocation and Competency

recorded in Scripture and so should demonstrate some clear harmony with Scripture. If I were to sense a leading or insight that seemed to run against the grain of the Scripture message (in overall intent, not just in some detail), that contradiction would be a clear sign to me that prayer, study, discussion, and contemplation were needed to clarify both my leading and my understanding of Scripture. To understand Scripture, one must be guided by the same Spirit that inspired Scripture, and that is a state we attain only infrequently and briefly.

Writing this journal entry in 1984 highlighted for me how much I'd changed. When the 1970s began, I wanted no part of the Bible or Christianity; in 1984, I had at least one Bible with me wherever I went and enthusiastically encouraged others to read and study Scripture. As I wrote the above entry, I had several translations of the New Testament as well as multiple commentaries and study guides on my shelf. The Bible and the Holy Spirit affected this change. There were no weighty Friends or others convincing me of the importance of the Scripture record—the Bible spoke for itself. I was able to hear because I laid aside my prior opinions of what was wrong with Paul, the Old Testament vision of God, the divinity of Jesus, and the violence of the Israelites at God's command and simply read. Instead of my previous attitude of "prove yourself," I adopted an attitude of "Help me—speak to my condition." Scripture did.

One day that spring, Sam Caldwell, general secretary of Philadelphia Yearly Meeting, told me he'd been given a message for me. The message was, "Tell Lloyd Lee to remember we are all soldiers of Christ." Now, *that* is food for much meditation! I'd been thinking about issues of discipline, obedience, conflict, and mutuality. A continuing theme had been the difference between being an individual seeking enlightenment (progress along the path, to use a common Quaker metaphor) and being a soldier of Christ. While the individual determines right action on the basis of what will help them along the spiritual journey, the soldier follows orders—orders whose overall purpose or plan may be obscure but that are certainly aimed at some goal larger than the individual's enlightenment. Our aim as soldiers is to be constantly preparing ourselves to be used by the Head of the church and putting ourselves at

God's disposal—literally, if need be—for bringing about the Kingdom of God on earth.

I gave the 1984 Rufus Jones Lecture (in Pittsburgh, Fourth Month), and this was an intense spiritual experience. I had doubts about what I had planned to say right up to the time we settled into opening worship. During worship, I had the sense of being lifted up, prayed for, and steadied by those close to me. My ego was lifted out of the way, and in its place came a strong sense of being God's instrument, that I was not to worry for God was answering my prayers to preach the Word as God would have it preached and for the audience to hear the Word as God would have them hear it. This was the strongest experience I had yet had of being God's instrument. I surrendered to that present Spirit and "let 'er rip" without self-consciousness or concern for how I was being received.

When the lecture was complete, we settled back into worship. Friends were rooted in their seats for about two hours from the beginning of the opening worship until the closing worship broke yet were unwilling to rise, even then, until prodded repeatedly by the organizer. Friends approached me, some with tears in their eyes, to say the lecture had "plowed deep," named for them what was trying to happen in their own life, or otherwise touched them at a place of spiritual struggle. I knew that I had said nothing but merely made myself available to be used.

I'd resolved in the Rufus Jones Lecture to witness to the power of Jesus Christ in my life and stop there. The preparation period and delivery were both profound experiences for me. The delivery was the best preaching I'd ever done—or that had ever been done through me. It did seem that some people were brought closer to Christ. Tapes and transcripts were circulated for study group use.

Following the 1984 FGC Gathering, I entered into a two-week period of complete bed rest in Virginia in an effort to recover from the back injury I had suffered in the orchard. This proved to be a fruitful time for reflection. One fruit was to see the need to make different arrangements for support and oversight of my ministry. I approached Charlottesville Friends and shared my growing, continuing call into the public ministry

Vocation and Competency

and the strong sense that this call should be lived out in the context of my "home" faith community. I hoped for their support in the form of acknowledging the call, admonishing and encouraging me to be faithful, aiding my discernment, and helping me through the dry times. The monthly meeting clerk responded very positively, exploring how to set up and sustain such a relationship through Ministry and Worship.

In leading me to establish new relationships of accountability, I can see now, God was preparing the foundation for my service in a new form of ministry—the free gospel ministry. The first leading into that new form was about to appear.

I began to reflect on the specific aspects of the spiritual life that are of central importance to a Friend active in the public ministry and are affected by the relationship between a monthly meeting and a member who is a "public Friend."

Exemplary obedience is certainly one such aspect. We each have the responsibility to live so as not to discourage or lead astray the brother or sister weaker in the faith, but it seems to me this burden falls with added weight on the public minister. Woe to the one who causes the least of these to stumble—it would have been better for them never to have been born (Matthew 18:6)! Particularly in these times, the public minister's life and behavior, as well as their words, will be under special scrutiny, both by those who seek an example of a life led under the Spirit and by those who are skeptics. Obedience to the guidance of one's faith community will help ensure that one "give[s] no offense in anything, that the ministry be not blamed."[5]

Discernment applies equally to discerning how to exercise one's gifts rightly as it does to discerning errors in one's behavior elsewhere. In particular, the community can see more clearly how a Friend's gifts are developing and what sorts of opportunities they should seek out to exercise those gifts. Is the public minister's life balanced among their responsibilities to family, competency, and other areas? Along with exercising their gifts, is the public Friend nurturing and developing them adequately?

Identification was an issue for earlier generations of Friends. How could one tell whether a visiting Friend should be given an opportunity, at a called meeting or otherwise, to be heard? This was not an issue when I'd traveled only where invited and not on my own initiative (in the invitational ministry). If that changed, as it might, it would be important to have some outward confirmation that Friends should take me seriously. It seemed as if a traveling minute from my monthly meeting would serve that purpose.

Admonishment is important. I already knew from experience that things I did for one reason were at times understood to signify something quite different. The frank admonishment of sincere Friends could minimize this and also prevent other errors that would diminish my effectiveness as a carrier of the gospel message.

Encouragement is the other side of admonishment and is equally necessary. Perhaps all times are difficult ones in which to preach the gospel, but these present times seem more difficult than most, and they are the times in which I live. There would be times I need encouragement to keep going, to trust that what I was doing was having a good effect even if I couldn't see it.

Worship is a critical aspect of the relationship. The monthly meeting relationship that I was seeking grows out of regular worship with a group of Friends well known to one another who seek to know God's will for all of us as a body. The corporate experience of the Presence of God in worship is by far the best means we have of determining God's will and obtaining the strength to be obedient to that will.

These aspects of my desired relationship with Charlottesville Friends occupied my thoughts and reflections over the following weeks, but the issue of exemplary obedience was prominent. I would be under increased scrutiny as a result of asking for this help in my faith walk. What I sought was a recognition by my faith community of my calling into the public ministry, a sharing of the burdens and responsibilities of that calling, and a mutual commitment to minister and to be ministered to.

Vocation and Competency

In Ninth Month, the new Charlottesville oversight committee met for the first time and was clear to continue as a committee under the care of Ministry and Worship. One Friend thought that I ought to be able to do all this discernment myself, to know and carry out God's will without help from her or others; another said that if I were looking "to spread my influence" in the committee, he wanted it known that he had no intention of becoming a born-again Christian (my term for myself). I assured him that I was seeking to be influenced, not to influence, and told the other Friend she was welcome to be a part of the group as long as she felt it right to do so. I was not made uncomfortable by her model of the ministry, though it was a different model from mine; I might learn from her in the future.

We planned to meet monthly for worship to share what felt real and alive in my public ministry, discuss areas where I lacked clear discernment, and explore ways to develop my spiritual gifts more fully. I would share tapes of my talks, copies of my essays and published articles, and so on. The group would go to meeting for business with requests for travel certificates on a case-by-case basis. I was ecstatic to be heard so completely and sympathetically; to be supported as these Friends had agreed to do was a marvelous development.

On Ninth Month 14, 1984, I marked my thirty-seventh birthday by taking a trip in a VW van to Hartford, Connecticut, on FGC business. I spent the trip lying down across the bench seat in the back, trying to minimize the pain in my back so I would be able to participate in the discussion when we arrived. I felt like a young man with an injury, not a middle-aged man beginning to deteriorate and grow older. Still, nearly all the baseball major leaguers were younger than I was that year. So was my chiropractor, my insurance agent, and my lawyer. Somebody had slipped a few extra years into my portfolio when I wasn't looking, and suddenly my threescore years and ten were more than half gone.

Something spiritual in me had changed that summer, not unlike growing older or gaining maturity but more profound and, I hoped, more of an unmixed blessing. It was as if God had reached inside me and turned down my rheostat, a divine intervention to grant me the patience, gentleness, and lovingkindness I'd been lacking. These qualities still struggle for preeminence within me, but the odds are more even than before, perhaps even tilted in their favor; God be praised.

Traveling in the Gospel Ministry

As noted earlier, I began to participate in the invitational ministry in 1982 when I became FGC general secretary. In 1984, about twelve months before leaving FGC, I had the first of a series of leadings into a different ministry format, what Friends have called traveling in the gospel. In this form of public ministry, the initiative stems from the individual's discernment of a leading from God, not a group's discernment of their need or desire. The standard of faithfulness is whether the individual does all that God requires—and nothing more—not whether the expectations of the inviting group are met. The content of the ministry itself is not known until it unfolds in the moment and is often not understood by the minister or auditory until much later, if ever. The invitational ministry is authentic, well suited to aspects of Friends' contemporary spiritual condition and the society we live in (North American society in particular), and of great benefit to Friends wherever it happens. Travel in the gospel ministry changed my life.

My first leading to gospel ministry appeared during a secretaries and superintendents conference in Ninth Month.[6] Kara Cole and I started talking at breakfast on the first morning about traveling in the ministry "in the old style" and kept going right through meeting for worship. It was a genuine "opportunity," and I felt the Presence of the Holy Spirit strongly enough to feel easy about missing corporate worship—which was extraordinary for me.[7]

What began to open to Kara and me during that weekend was very different from the ministry with which we were familiar. We were being drawn to visit Friends in a distant place not because we knew them or because they invited us to make a presentation but because God was leading us to do so. We would visit simply because that was what we were led to do, without a prearranged topic, trusting that if we were faithful something divinely good would happen. We would bring to this travel our differences in age, sex, Quaker affiliation, and spiritual journeys, all surmounted by our unity in Christ. We would meet with individuals or with groups of Friends in various places who felt led to the opportunity to

Vocation and Competency

meet with us. I envisioned gathering in homes or meeting houses, speaking out of the worship as moved by the Holy Spirit, and proceeding as way opened.

I hoped to witness to the love of Christ that is over all and in all, uniting everyone in a bond that transcends earthly differences. We would share the good news and witness to the difference that the gospel had made in our lives. Meeting with small groups of Friends, witnessing to the love of Christ among us, sharing what we had found in the course of our spiritual journeys, encouraging others to press on and leaving them some road maps—these things felt very right, and I was eager to be about them.

Being firmly grounded and supported by my home meeting would be essential. The oversight committee in Charlottesville meeting would have to be deeply involved and strongly supportive. To travel under my own initiative to other yearly meetings in this way (as contrasted with a speaking engagement by invitation) called for a certificate from Charlottesville meeting stating their unity with me (and Kara) and with this service. The old Quaker journals I had read spoke of certificates being considered and then issued by a yearly meeting for ministry outside that yearly meeting's boundaries, though I had never seen one myself. How could that be accomplished?

Our planning horizon gave us a full year to consider all this, and we would need that time. Kara and I researched the established procedure for the long-dormant practice of considering travel certificates and followed that procedure. The first step was to bring the leading to my oversight committee. They were in unity and were very positive about the witness such a journey would make about unity among Friends. They recommended that monthly meeting issue a certificate for travel for Kara and me, which the meeting did in First Month 1985.

Kara and I sent out letters announcing our intended presence in New England and asking meetings willing to receive us to contact us. Brian Drayton agreed to help with arrangements in New England. I felt clear that this was right action. The trip would be a time to witness joyfully and gently to the Lord and to the unity that the Lord had brought to Kara and me, different as we were. I felt was no anxiety about not having anything to say but rather a deep curiosity about what the Lord would say through us. I prayed:

> Lord Jesus Christ, grant me a heightened sense of Thy Presence during my travels in New England, and let that Presence be manifest to others. Let my words and deeds be such as will draw others to Thee. Keep us all safe until we each reach home again. In Your Name we pray.

Charlottesville Meeting forwarded its certificate for my travel to Baltimore Yearly Meeting, and that summer the yearly meeting endorsed the certificate with essentially no discussion. It troubles me when important meeting decisions are reached without discussion or extended silence. I wonder whether Friends see the precedent they are setting or whether they think they are deciding one way and really deciding another. What did it mean for a meeting uneasy over issues about Christ to approve a minute endorsing travel "in the gospel ministry" and commending the travelers to "the Christian care" of the Friends visited? Had Friends understood what they were doing?

The Charlottesville oversight committee had recognized the validity of my leading and trusted in their experience of me as one bound up in the love of that faith community, regardless of theological differences. I didn't feel that same sense of community of faith in the yearly meeting. The reluctance to thresh out decisions involving issues where we differed significantly troubled me. I was rarely if ever free to engage this problem directly because if I agreed with the decision the yearly meeting was making I felt I should keep quiet, and if I disagreed I felt obliged to constrain myself to speaking to the issue at hand and not to the process being followed.

Paradoxically, I'd have felt more support had there been some doubts or even opposition expressed before unity was reached. Where there is not an underlying unity in a faith community, we must generate it anew with each decision or else do without. We must start by expressing our initial disunity and work from there.

I realized that God had purposes for this trip that remained unknown. I had been saying for some time that invitations were only "the excuse" by which I had been brought to a particular place and time in order to interact with some person(s) in unexpected and unrecognized ways. This seemed to be also true of the trip to New England. My leading to go had been confirmed at the personal, monthly meeting, and yearly meeting levels. What I realized in a fresh way was that in this, too, God probably had purposes I didn't discern and couldn't comprehend even if I did discern them. That meant it was important to "sit lightly" on any concept of why we were making this trip. We could be modeling a form of ministry for some infant minister who would not speak to either of us directly; our words might bring one person to Christ though no one else was affected; this might be a dry run for a second journey as yet unimagined.

Preparing for a journey when one does not know the trip's true purposes is surprisingly difficult. I felt I was prepared to the extent that I had taken time in prayer to ask for God's Presence and guidance that I might be a faithful and obedient servant—nothing more specific. In prayer, I asked Christ's blessings on the journey, that we might complete it in safety, that we might speak the Word as God wished it spoken, and that our audiences might hear that Word God intended for them. Let our every word and action point to God; let nothing happen that would cause anyone to stumble in their faith. What I did not feel clear to do was to plan what I would say on that first evening (or any subsequent evening) when we gathered with a group of Friends.

> Jesus, you are my Lord and have by your intervention in my life redeemed me from a hopeless life apart from you. I am forever grateful and indebted to you for your gift and sacrifices for me and wish only to become who and what you desire of me. Help me do Your will.
>
> Lord, I pray particularly for your blessing on our journey to New England. Grant us the purity of heart and intent that will keep us from being offensive to anyone who desires to hear the good news. Give us your tongue to speak the Word as you wish it spoken in each place and to each person we encounter. Give us your eyes that we may see the person you wish us to encounter,

not the person which the world sees. Give us Your Love that we might give it to everyone we meet.

Protect us, Lord, from accidents, ill health, and other dangers that might prevent us from accomplishing your intention. Strengthen us to do Your will as it should be done. Guard our loved ones while we are away and grant that we might return to find all healthy and happy and our bonds to them stronger and more Christ-like than before.

We seek to do Thy will. Purify our intent and grant that we might help in some small way to carry out Your plan for bringing about your Kingdom.

In Your name—amen.

Traveling in the Ministry in New England: Journal Excerpts

Ninth Month 10, 1985. Tomorrow I leave for New England to undertake with Kara Cole this gospel ministry which we've been planning for a year. As the date has approached, I've given up any preconception of what this trip is for and what it will 'accomplish' and am now simply waiting, like Habakkuk, to see what I will say.

Some New England Friends bought a plane ticket for me so I could meet with Friends "traveling under concern" on our last day and avoid beginning a 12-hour drive home late in the day. When a Friend called with this offer, I was *very* surprised and uncertain about whether to accept, so told her I would call back. I settled into prayer and reflection, and almost at once the words of one of our Advices came to mind (Friends should be careful that the ministry is not hindered for lack of funds). I called back to accept the offer.

I found this plane ticket humbling. Who was I to deserve such treatment, that people were willing to spend money to ensure that I attend an informal gathering? Nobody, to be sure; yet Friends are willing to spend money to ensure that the Christ in me attends. There is a part of me that wants to be worth their

Vocation and Competency

'investment'; the rest of me knows that any effort on my part will only ensure that I am not. All I can do is what I've been trying to do anyway: get and stay centered in the Lord so that everything I do and say is God's work, not mine.

Ninth Month 11, 1985. All the preparation has come to an end. There remains only driving to the airport. Either I've been receptive to the work of the Holy Spirit to prepare me for this journey or not. In either case, there is nothing to do about it now. There is time only for unceasing prayer, underlying and undergirding every moment:

Lord, no matter what my spiritual state, grant that I speak the Word you wish spoken in New England. Tender the hearts of those who hear me so that they can hear in my words the Word you intend for them personally. Have compassion for me, and grant that this ministry prospers not as I deserve but as will suit your perfect will for the bringing about of your Kingdom on earth.

I have no vision of success—no measure of what size audiences will indicate we've done well, no desire that any persons should profess a profound spiritual experience as a result of our ministry. I do hope that some Friends will endorse my traveling certificate, I must admit. To have been open to the leading as Kara expressed it first, to have been faithful to good process about pursuing the leading, and finally to have gone to New England and spoken in those places that were interested in hearing us (and where, once there, the Spirit gave us something to say) – this will be success. Whether New England Yearly Meeting is outwardly affected (or inwardly affected) by this trip is not our concern and not a measure of our faithfulness. Whether our trip becomes, in Bill Taber's words, a model for new forms of Quaker ministry is equally not our concern. Only the doing of the trip itself, staying close to our Guide throughout, is of importance to us. It may well be that the visible impact of this journey may be in Indiana Yearly Meeting or Baltimore Yearly Meeting, at Friends United Meeting or even Charlottesville

Monthly Meeting. Some infant minister in some other yearly meeting may read of our exploits years from now and be changed for the better. Or, as is often the case, this exercise may be simply preparation for the next. "You know, O Lord!" Certainly, I do not.

The thought that I might die on this journey has been strong in my mind. That's not a premonition but a reminder that we ought to comport ourselves at all times in such a way that we are prepared for the transition from life to Life. If I am called home before I return to Virginia, God will receive a poor sinner who was at least trying to do right. I have an Advocate who is capable of uniting me with God in eternity and who has promised to do just that—so I do not worry.

Asa, in the next room, has just awakened and is singing "Itsy Bitsy Spider." I am reminded of the journals of Samuel Janney and Elias Hicks that describe receiving mail from home that sometimes bore bad news, or of returning home and discovering to their joy that everyone was still alive and healthy.

Ninth Month 12, 1985. The covenant fellowship spent the day in retreat at the home of Sylvia and Finley Perry in Dover, Massachusetts, reflecting on the ministry that Kara and I will begin tomorrow.[8] I feel a continuing sense of calm, that it is the Lord's will for us to be about this work, confirmed both by Friends who say clearly, "This is the Lord's will," and indirectly in the way that the schedule has fallen into place, a car has become available to us, and Friends have volunteered to underwrite our airplane tickets.

When asked what I thought that the audience in Wellesley meeting tomorrow would be expecting, I replied that I didn't know what they expected—it wasn't really my concern to meet their expectations but to be able to discern their conditions and as way opened to speak to those conditions. I asked for prayer for speedy and accurate discernment for us and also for what I always pray before public ministry, that our words might be the Word as the Lord would have it preached to this audience and that the hearts of the auditory might be softened and their ears

Vocation and Competency

so tuned that in the words we are able to speak they can hear the Word as the Lord would have them hear it.

We are here to be obedient to the Lord, free of preconception about what that will mean. We have no measure by which to know we've been successful other than coming to the end of our journey with a sense that we have done our best to follow the path set before us by our Inner Guide.

We may be setting forth a model for years from now, when Kara and I are both dead and buried; we may be in fact only in training this time around for ministry that one or the other of us will do ourselves five or ten years from now; we may be involved in some other work not even imagined, which the Lord knows but which it is not important for us to know. I am curious to see what happens. I am curious to hear what I will say, if anything, tomorrow night. It may be my part to set an example by starving them of words entirely. (I would say that was unlikely; but the Lord has chosen stranger instruments to do stranger things.)

I am reminded of the Rule of Saint Benedict, which admonishes us before we begin any good work to pray for its perfection; I certainly pray tonight that this work of ministry in New England might in fact be made perfect in the Lord. A large number of people throughout the East Coast are holding this journey in their prayers very consciously and intentionally and will continue doing so through the entire trip. I feel the effect of those prayers, and I am grateful for them.

Kara has had at least one person call, write, or stop by her office about this trip almost every day for the past five or six weeks. These inquiries fall into two groups. One group is those people who are "professional Friends" and find it surprising that she would spend her vacation time traveling among Friends in the ministry, and the other includes Friends who are generally supportive of this venture and who wonder if she would be able to undertake a similar kind of journey in their own yearly meeting. I have been essentially on retreat from Quakers over the same period of time and have had very few inquiries except from close friends.

Kara has gathered excitement and enthusiasm from the people who have been in touch with her, and that's a very good thing; I have gathered a certain amount of calm, and I think that's very good for me. I could not have gained or maintained a centeredness about this trip had I been in contact with as many people asking about it as Kara had been. So, once again the Lord acts to give us what we need.

Ninth Month 13, 1985. I started the day with a walk through the MIT campus, sparking many memories. I got to Cambridge meeting house about 11 o'clock and spent over an hour in silent worship and prayer in the meeting house, hoping to center myself in such a way that I could be a useful instrument for the Lord at the evening's meeting at Wellesley. I had the sense coming out of this worship that things would work out as the Lord intends.

There were 16 Friends at Wellesley Meeting this evening. We shared dessert and then gathered in the meeting house living room for worship. We soon felt the Presence of the Lord, and Kara was favored to offer a message about fear, the way that perfect love casts out fear, and how her experience of God's love and her understanding of how to live a life of love is mediated by the life and Presence of Jesus Christ.

I was aware, soon after we settled into the silence, that there was a decision in the room that had been put off but needed to be made and to be faced confidently and firmly. I had never had this kind of leading before and was quite uncertain about how to deal with it. I spoke aloud that I perceived that the decision was there, waiting to be made, and went on to offer some testimony about the Lord being present in my life to help these decisions turn out correctly, ending with a reference to Corinthians 10:13 which promises that God "with the temptation provides the way of escape, in order that we might endure." I was not pleased with this ministry, feeling that I had perhaps spoken too soon and that

Vocation and Competency

I had not had a clear enough understanding about what to do or insight about the decision. However, I did not feel that I had done harm, simply that I had not done as much good as I might have.

The ministry then spread to several others in the meeting and was useful to all. After we closed the meeting, an informal discussion continued for some time. We returned to our hosts for the night and discovered that one frustration that Kara and I would have as we traveled was that we did not have an immediate time to debrief in private, although we had a wonderful conversation with our hosts about other matters.

Kara and I gave our certificates to the clerk of the meeting, and she endorsed them. It seemed that the first meeting of our journey had gone well; our nonspecific preparation had been just right. Kara had carried most of the burden of the spoken ministry. I might well have either spoken much later in the meeting or kept silent entirely, holding discernment of the pending decision in silent prayer.

Ninth Month 14, 1985. A set of handwritten directions and a loaned car brought us to Dartmouth Meeting in southeastern Massachusetts. On the way, Kara and I shared what had gone on the previous evening, what conclusions we drew from that, and what changed intentions we might have had about today's work or the rest of the trip. We arrived about 11 a.m. and were greeted by the pastor and the clerk of the meeting. There were ten people besides ourselves present for a potluck lunch; seven were able to stay for the worship following. The wonderful weather and the extraordinarily beautiful views that we had enjoyed on the drive highlighted the many unmerited blessings that we receive from the Lord, and I was opened to expand on this topic. It seemed acceptable service, and I was more at ease than I had been the previous night. Kara later offered ministry on the topic of hospitality, making several points in a direct and simple yet eloquent way, which clearly spoke to the conditions of several persons in the room. Vocal ministry continued, all developing some theme on the topic of hospitality raised by Kara. All three of the pastors present offered vocal ministry.

After worship we discussed why we were traveling in the ministry, what we hoped might be accomplished by our travels, and what the process had been to get us here. This discussion was an opportunity to share some thoughts close to my heart about the calling into ministry, the risks one takes in claiming that leading and the gift of ministry in one's faith community, and the effects that I hope it might have for us to model that process and to take those risks—to show that they can be braved and to provide the opportunity for some private encouragement given to some new minister.

After visiting Apponegansett Meeting House, built in 1790, we returned to the parsonage for dinner—a time of Christian fellowship and of personal support and sharing. Then we returned to the home where we had hospitality and spent a long time in fellowship with our host family. This was an important part of our visit.

I saw during worship that day that my vocal ministry must start close to my heart and be personal, closely related to my lived experience, if it is to be faithful and acceptable service. This requires that I take the risk of opening up to strangers about my wrestling with inward promptings and urgings into the public ministry, the work of sharing that with my community, and carrying out authentic leadings in the trust that the community's discernment has been genuine.

Ninth Month 15, 1985. This morning we drove to Providence Meeting for First Day worship. There were roughly fifty persons present, about half a dozen of whom were first-time attenders at any meeting for worship. Worship was good, the Spirit ran deep, and we were both moved to offer vocal ministry. Kara began with thoughts about physical hunger in Ethiopia and elsewhere and reflected from that on the spiritual hunger that we feel in North America. Later, I was opened to a fuller understanding of Romans 8:28 and was freed to share that, emphasizing our need

Vocation and Competency

to respond to the call God gives each of us according to God's purposes—to take the risk of living into the new life that will come into us as we respond to that call. I felt particularly favored in this communication, and a number of the auditory came to me after meeting to confirm this.

About 40 people stayed for a potluck lunch, and many stayed for more worship and discussion after that. Afternoon worship included considerable vocal ministry, spread widely throughout the meeting. Kara and I were opened to speak about the risks of coming and why we did come, sharing again our inability to plan and the requirement that we lean on the Lord. This seemed to speak to a number of the people present. After some time, we ended the formal meeting and continued a question-and-answer session in which the spirit of worship continued to be felt. We were given openings to share many things close to our hearts about the ministry and about Christian ministry among Friends, and good connections were made.

Today I felt fully in harmony with the rhythm of this trip. It was clear what we should be doing at each part of the day in order to be prepared for the rest, and we were able to do it all without any sense of forcing the schedule or being hurried. If we were to do this again next year, it would probably still take us a couple of days to find this rhythm, but we had been hoping for it, and it came today. I am beginning to understand what it is to be traveling in the ministry, and where my focus and attention needs to be, and how I need to open myself up to other people in order to be fully faithful to this calling.

One Friend reflected on our presence in Providence, drawing on a quotation from Henri Nouwen to say Kara and I had reached the point where vocal ministry was not necessary; our simply being and being present with them was a powerful statement and a powerful ministry. He shared how strong a witness it was that we did not have a prepared program or a statement that we felt we needed to make but were willing just to be, to settle into worship, and to see what happened—confident that the Lord's will would be done.

Kara and I are 'participant observers'; the ministry is being shared by everyone who has responded to hearing of this call and this leading by doing something to advance it: arranging our itinerary, putting us up for the night, giving us a meal, coming to hear us, worshipping with us, or bringing something to the potluck. All of those people have had a role in the ministry as important as Kara's and mine. We have had little conscious role for which we can claim any responsibility—we've just been letting ourselves be used. We get to travel and see more of it than anyone else, but that doesn't mean we have a larger responsibility than anyone else; it is just our role to be the traveling observers watching it happen. I think also Charlottesville Meeting, Baltimore Yearly Meeting, and West Richmond Meeting [Kara's monthly meeting] have a role in this ministry and have themselves received some fruits from it. We've been to meetings that are quite different in membership, geography, and history, and something very good has happened in each one.

Something good and precious will happen every place we are, and with every person we encounter, if Kara and I can simply stay centered and open to that potential and hold ourselves in prayerful readiness for that to happen. That, it seems to me, is where we need to be as travelers in the ministry. We are right not to have prepared any further, and we are right not to carry any particular message but to have the simple faith that something special will happen and that we are participant observers in the process of making that happening.

Ninth Month 16, 1985. We spent this morning at Moses Brown School in Providence. Kara went to a Bible study class, and I went to a class on ethics. Our experiences were very good. In the Bible class, Kara was invited to share her personal history with the Bible and how it has changed over the years, and the students met someone much more orthodox than anyone in their

Vocation and Competency

previous experience who was at the same time clearly a kind and caring and loving soul. My experience in the ethics class was also excellent as the class explored truth-telling—what to do when faced with Immanuel Kant's problem of being at a crossroad when a pursuer comes up and says "Where did X go? If I catch him, I'm going to kill him." I was impressed by how a teacher must establish an atmosphere where the students can really share their own feelings without having them be stepped on or ridiculed in any way and how necessary these first steps are before students can begin to examine their own beliefs for consistency and fairness.

After lunch we set out for Manchester, Connecticut. One teacher asked if he could share the ride, so Kara rode with him as far as Abingdon, where he lives, and I followed behind. This seemed to be a reactivation of the old practice of one Friend feeling a desire to travel for a time with the traveling Friends in order to have the opportunity for a private conversation or simply to share with their spirit. I was very pleased that this opportunity had become clear to this Friend and that he had suggested it.

We managed to get lost coming into Manchester. On a whim, we picked an exit arbitrarily to get off the interstate and ask directions, only to find we had chosen the exit absolutely closest to our destination and were now only a few blocks away. We were able to drive directly to our hosts from that spot.

After dinner we went to the meeting house in Hartford, where 18 other Friends were gathered. This meeting opened with extended silence. Eventually, Kara was moved to speak, and considerably later I was also. It seemed to me that a lid was over the rest of the meeting, representing their desire not to take the initiative but to be spoken to.

Then one Friend was moved to vocal prayer, and it seemed to me the entire condition of the meeting was changed. Slowly, questions began to come to the surface, and the other Friends in the meeting began to answer in ways that were spiritually perceptive and deep. By the end, every person in the room had spoken at least once, and there was a clear sense that the meeting was ministering to itself. There was clear personal authenticity and validity in what was said.

The subject was the way that we reach out to other people, especially two points. One was a reflection on the Greek tense "to have already been doing" something; Friends wanted to so live that when someone began a period of trouble we would have already been doing those things that made us present and available and helpful and supportive so that we were not a new face appearing in a time of trouble. The other was that Friends wanted to have the courage to do things that we thought we might do badly but thought we were called to do nonetheless, to take the risk of attempting something we didn't yet know whether we could do or whether we would have the ability to do well, and to have the faith in the Lord that is necessary to undertake those ministries.

It was a covered meeting, both in our silence and in our vocal sharing. Meeting closed with another prayer that seemed to speak for each one of us from the heart. Once again, this was a very different meeting from any others we've attended and yet very wonderful also. Kara and I shared afterward how much more precious and more wonderful and more powerful each meeting seems than the one before it. I want more and more, but I also want God to strengthen me so that I can absorb the powerful spiritual energies that are beginning to flow around us without burning myself up.

The rhythm of our travels carries us through the day without any sense of extra exertion or exhaustion. Several people commented tonight that we must feel tired, or "isn't this a tiring journey," but I really had to say no. The worship and opportunities with people each day are tremendously refreshing; I have a sense of what Bill Taber meant when he talked about the personal refreshment that he felt as he began to offer new opportunities for worship around Pendle Hill.

Vocation and Competency

It feels that this knowledge that the Lord is always with us, that God is always going to make things work, to make wonderful things work, could be a constant part of my life. I have the sense that if I did this it would change my spiritual and my worldly activities and impact. It seems similar to Roger Bannister's first four-minute mile; it took decades for someone to run the mile under four minutes for the first time, but within a few years of Roger Bannister's doing it, half a dozen other people had done it and had run significantly faster than he did. The difference was simply that they now knew it was possible. I now know it is possible to live this way, so if I break my stride or lose my focus, it should be possible to regain it.

It seems in right order that we are not traveling with any constant companion. The time driving from one place to another is the only private opportunity we have to debrief about what has happened, to share our current spiritual condition, and to give each other insight or assistance on our patterns of ministry. All this would be inhibited if we had any other companion, and even if it were another seasoned minister the dynamic would be changed.

If there is anything I miss, it is that there are so few times during the day for focused prayer. It is very important to me to rise early each day and spend the time until our host family is stirring in prayer, journaling, and devotional reading. This devotional time is very refreshing—I hunger for more. It is also important to take a good walk each day. The times I haven't exercised I've felt some mental and spiritual staleness as well.

Ninth Month 17, 1985. From Hartford we worked our way northward, stopping to meet with a Friend who had asked for an opportunity. From the moment we arrived, I was struck by a sense of spiritual unrightness that had physical manifestations in me. Kara later commented that my speech—sentence patterns, choice of words, and pronunciation—was affected so that she was immediately aware of my condition. The entire time of our visit was spiritually draining to both of us. Unsettled by the experience, we were ready quite early to move on toward our evening meeting with Friends.

After arriving in New Hampshire, we took a walk along a beautiful wooded stream and later had tea with our host. During our walk and during our conversation on the porch, we felt opportunities for deep worship and ministry to one another, and we sought to settle each time into a time of waiting for the word that the Lord might give us. Each time, we were pulled away from that communion of the Spirit. We felt we might be unable to be as centered as we ought that evening.

We called Thom Jeavons and Tom Ewell, asking for their special prayer support for that night. Thom immediately mentioned that he had been in prayer for us each day on our journey and that he has had each day a vision of Kara and me walking down the roads of New England with Christ between us, an arm around each one of us. This had been a powerful experience for him and had a powerful impact on me.

The meeting was covered, and our prayers were answered; neither Kara nor I felt adversely affected by whatever had affected us that afternoon. Discussion had a slow beginning but grew steadily. We talked about how to know when a leading is true, about obedience and the role it plays in our spiritual lives. The endorsements on our certificates for travel commented that we had brought Light into their dark places; I wondered greatly at what this might mean.

I shared the model of my relationship to Charlottesville Meeting and what its structure and its effect on me and the meeting has been. This focused attention on me for a long period of time. It felt in good order, but I was made aware that soon a question would appear which would be the time to let Kara take the lead in the discussion. I could feel Kara preparing herself to take a more active role in the discussion and could feel the approach of the question that would effect the transfer. The right question arrived shortly after; I sat back in my chair, Kara leaned forward, and the transition had been made. I don't believe that we could have been this sensitive to one another's condition or to the flow of the discussion or to our readiness to work in tandem a week ago. It was another example of the way the Lord is making us sensitive to one another in order to advance His work.

Ninth Month 18, 1985. Marian Baker of Contention Pond, New Hampshire, gave us hospitality for the night. After excellent conversation over breakfast, Kara and I set off for Maine. This leg of the journey was one of several for which we had no directions and no human guide. However, we found our way not only to the right town (which was not actually marked on our map) but also to our hostess's house, making a number of choices as unmarked dirt roads forked on the way from the paved road to the house we sought. Kara was driving and made the right choice every time without faltering. This was certainly a case of following one's Inward Guide!

Over dinner we conversed with Friends from five monthly meetings about the Spirit and how it was moving among us and among Friends generally. After dinner we went to Portland Meeting. We had both deep worship and a smooth transition to sharing about times in which the Lord has been tangibly present in our lives.

Afterward, two Friends approached us individually about what a landmark meeting this seemed to have been for another of the Friends present, who had been a strident universalist—almost argumentative, even during meeting for worship—in her desire to make sure that "Christ" was always understood as more universalist than specifically Christian. Tonight, this Friend had been open to explicitly Christian ministry, able to speak about a time when the Lord had been perceptibly present to her and to confess that this was the life into which she would like to live. It seemed very tender and authentic to me and was striking and heartwarming to others.

Later that evening, we and our hosts spent a long time talking about our faith journeys. This turned out to be a deep and precious time of sharing. It became clear that it would be important for our hostess to have an opportunity to share a particular spiritual issue, but I was not free to bring the topic up. I felt sure, however, that it would be brought up the next morning.

This was the third in a series of insights or discernments that occurred to me that day that were very unusual in my experience. The first was during an afternoon prayer time, when it became clear to me that tonight's meeting would be focused on Christian witness to a much larger extent than previous meetings—which it was. The second happened during the meeting itself when the imagery of my worship was laced with compasses, magnets, and setting one's heart toward the Lord as a compass needle is set toward the pole of a magnetic field. I learned later that one Friend present was still carrying a vision that she had had twice during yearly meeting sessions involving the Holy Spirit generating a field of magnetism.

Ninth Month 19, 1985. We lingered with our hostess until noon. This was especially a time for her and Kara to establish a place of friendship in the Lord and share experiences of spiritual growth—the sharing I had felt the previous night had to happen. Kara said later she had had the same discernment the previous night and knew also that the discussion would occur the next morning.

We then drove to Beacon Hill Friends House in Boston, where Anne Buttenheim was the new director. I felt my role in this meeting for worship was to pray the Holy Spirit into the room and was exercised in this task throughout much of the meeting. However, Anne spoke out of the silence to make a specific request that Kara and I share our experiences of the Christ Spirit. Kara did so quickly, and eventually I was led to share also. I believe that without that specific request it would have been my place to remain silent.

Later, Anne and I spent a long time talking about her spiritual condition and regular spiritual practice. The bond between us has been increased immeasurably by the time spent

Vocation and Competency

together with Donna Moore and Patty Levering in Richmond, Indiana, the previous Sixth Month, when those three women spent such a long time with me, helping me understand where I had been unfaithful in my faith walk and where my relation to God could be improved. This example of Christian care on their part and accountability on my part has been important to them and to me, serves to bond us more closely together, and makes me more intentional about being present to them in time of need.

The next afternoon, our worship in the Friends House formal garden was interrupted by a bomb scare as a female voice on the telephone warned that a bomb had been placed in Friends House and was set to go off in ten minutes. We evacuated and waited on the side of Chestnut Street until the bomb squad finally came, about 20 or 25 minutes later. They found nothing and left us to our own devices. I lay down in my room for about 20 minutes, using the Jesus Prayer and the simple repetition of "Jesus" to evoke the relaxation response and recover both physiological and emotional peace.

The late afternoon was occupied by a formal opportunity at Friends House, and it was a time of extremely close work. I was impressed but no longer surprised by the way in which Kara and I worked together, that we knew without looking at each other, talking to each other, or planning ahead how the lead in conversation would pass from one to the other and had some instinctive idea of where our own strengths were and where the other's were stronger.

When we were clear of that work, Kara and I set off for Lynn, Massachusetts. Friends from Lynn, North Shore, and Amesbury meetings were waiting for us with a potluck meal. A strong sense of excitement and joy met us immediately when we entered their fellowship hall, and I found this to be the most striking part of the entire evening. The worship room was set up in the standard Protestant fashion, capable of holding one hundred and fifty people. We worshiped in one corner of this space, arranging pews to make three sides of a square.

Once again, Kara was given a ministry of the word, in this case "require" in the passage from Micah asking what the Lord requires of us. Each night, she has been given one word around which her vocal ministry is gathered, a most unusual experience for her—and for me since I am the only person who has heard her every night. It has been marvelous to see this gift bestowed and to see Kara's faithfulness to it. While Kara said she had not thought about that passage from Micah for several years, it had been present to me in a real way in each of the previous two nights. It was brought to mind so that I contemplated it, but it was made clear that I was not being given it to speak. Once again, this is an example of the mysterious and marvelous way in which Kara and I were being knit together on this journey. Brian Drayton also appeared in the vocal ministry; his vocabulary, terminology, and style reflect the old journals that, as is commonly known, he reads in so much.

During worship, a middle-aged man wandered in off the street and eventually wandered out again. This was a point of discussion after worship when we returned to the fellowship hall. A woman Friend shared that it was frightening to her to think about trying to reach out to the local community, to share their pain, and to find the words to make the experience of Christ real to them. I suggested that if she or other Friends could do that for just one or two of the people who already seemed to be wandering into the meeting house, they would become more effective proclaimers of the gospel to the community than she or anyone else could be conventionally.

In response to a question about how to make the church grow, I gave what Kara later described as a "pep talk" with an energy and enthusiasm that surprised both of us. I called upon both the passage from Ezekiel where God brings dead bones back to life (Ezekiel 37) and the experiences of Sand Creek meeting in North Carolina and Doylestown meeting in Pennsylvania as meetings that had almost faded out and were regathered to a new vitality. Checking with Kara about this later, it seemed as if it was rightly ordered and the energy was well received by Friends. The

Vocation and Competency

later part of the evening included a quieter conversation about First Day schools and other matters, including ways to keep a sense of community in a growing meeting.

Although it was a long and vigorous day, at least in terms of spiritual work, I did not feel overly tired at the end but rather that by waiting for the Lord's leading throughout the day and then being obedient to that leading we had lived into the promise that those who wait upon the Lord shall run and not be weary, walk and not faint.

Ninth Month 21, 1985. This was a day of rest: no travel, no public meetings. Kara and I went to Darcy and Brian Drayton's for a hearty and tasty supper. Afterward, we gathered in their living room and soon realized we had an opportunity for worship, which at a word from Darcy we seized. It was a refreshing time, in which we were grateful for the way in which the Lord is working in each other's lives. It seemed to me that the work that Brian and Darcy are doing in Lynn Meeting is the Lord's witness in that place, and while we do not know the outcome, they are faithful to be present there and to try to bring new life.

This home opportunity felt very good to me—a premonition of future experiences in my own monthly meeting. I know that future home opportunities will be less extensive and possibly less deep since Brian, Darcy, and I have known each other for so long. They may not look and feel exactly like this one, and yet I am happy to know that they can feel like this one and will hold that as my heart's desire.

Ninth Month 22 (First Day), 1985. Kara and I were up and away early on the last morning to get to Worcester, Massachusetts, in time for worship. We were each exercised in vocal ministry. After worship, we shared in one last wonderful potluck meal. It was coming to an end all too soon; I had the sense of having been faithful and of not being ready to return to "normal" life. About 15 Friends gathered to hear Kara and me speak of our journey and our leading. Afterward, the group of

Friends traveling under a concern gathered, and we settled into worship for the third time.

Afterward, Kara and I drove to Logan Airport, and there we took leave of one another. What a rare and precious experience this has been! Kara and I had come to know one another so well that little speech was necessary. We shall never be the same to one another; probably we shall never be the same to ourselves again.

We were traveling in this ministry for 12 days, counting the Covenant Fellowship retreat on Ninth Month 11 and 12. We held or attended 16 meetings for worship, including the covenant group, one at Moses Brown School, two First Day meetings, and a home opportunity at the Draytons'. I traveled approximately 1,000 miles by air to get to and from New England; Kara and I drove together an additional 1,300+ miles on the journey itself.

Friends attending our meetings came from twenty-three monthly meetings and five yearly meetings: Wellesley, Cambridge, Smith's Neck, Mattapoisett, North Dartmouth, Providence, Westerly, Hartford, Mount Toby, Hanover, Burlington, Haverford (Philadelphia Yearly Meeting), Dover, Portland, Beacon Hill, Washington (D.C.), Lynn, Amesbury, North Shore, Worcester, West Branch (Iowa), Vienna (Austria), and Bethesda (Baltimore Yearly Meeting). We had numerous individual opportunities in addition to the general meetings.

I journaled at the outset of this journey that we would be unable to tell which were the right things that needed to happen in this ministry and that our only measure of success would be to come to the end of our labor knowing that we had done our best to follow the promptings of the Spirit. We have done so and have been blessed beyond our expectations; I believe others have felt that blessing also.

Traveling Further on the Spiritual Path

As I read my journal entries for the next several months, thirty-five years after writing them, the importance of the spiritual experiences I went through is made clearer by the passage of time. However, I also have a clearer understanding of the power of specific words to facilitate or obstruct our ability to express our experience well. My vocabulary at this time was drawn from the "heaven or hell" branch of Christianity that had been my schoolroom, but the experience I was describing was an ongoing encounter with a God of reconciling love who offered Life to every human being, not a God of judgment and punishment. I have not changed the language I used at the time. I invite the reader to read "compassion" for mercy; acknowledgment of our true self, imperfect and error-prone, for confession of sin or brokenness; and (as always) to listen for the Truth behind imperfect words.

By early 1985, the Jesus Prayer[9] had replaced Transcendental Meditation as the focal point of my daily meditation periods and was the most common short prayer in all my daily activities. It was my first prayer when I awoke in the morning and usually the last before I fell asleep. My days were punctuated by fresh convictions of my brokenness. When these realizations poured over me, my cry was, "Lord Jesus Christ, Son of God, have mercy on me!" The mercy of God, God's forgiveness and love, seemed to fall down on me with great gentleness, warming me to the core, so that my experience was not the despair of Puritan depravity but grateful joy due to unmerited grace. Each conviction of sinfulness brought a fresh outpouring of God's love—unexpected and unearned happiness filled my days.

How many would pursue God's judgment, rather than flee it, if they realized that the end of that judgment was the joy of being harmoniously in God's Presence? Their flight is futile for God will make all things new in God's own time, even those who flee from God; all they accomplish is to delay knowing the joy of God's blessing.

On Second Month 10, 1985, I wrote the following in my journal:

> As Asa and I drove to meeting, I was looking forward to a time of deep worship, when I could withdraw from the world to be nourished by God. On the way, I was struck by how important a sense of our sinfulness is to our ability to be joyful for God's grace and mercy. Only because I had known the sorrow of being sinful can I begin to realize how precious God's mercy is—how

invaluable Jesus' work is as redeemer and reconciler. This bore down on me with such force that I was unable to get out of the car for several minutes after arriving at the meeting house.

Asa was particularly quiet during worship, leaning back against me while looking at a book. I was filled with the warmth of the love I have for him yet also aware of my earlier insight. Would I be required to share it this morning? The time came for Asa to go to First Day school, and I still had no clarity. My thoughts developed along the lines of a vocal message, but I did not feel free to speak. An awareness of God's grace accompanied this, yet I did not feel at peace. I resolved that I would not speak in worship today—without relief.

After some time, others began to share vocal messages. As they progressed, they seemed to stray further and further from knowledge of the Indwelling Christ. I was filled with grief at the brokenness of our meeting as a faith community, trying so hard to be faithful yet falling so short. I cried a heart prayer to God to forgive us, to heal and reconcile us with the Divine. At last, I knew there was no choice, and I rose to speak. The message was very emotional and personal; my voice broke when I talked of how my continued sinfulness breaks my heart, and I was nearly at a loss for words to describe the joy Jesus brings. When I sat down, a wave of release swept over me so strongly that I dove deep into a prayer of thanksgiving. Rarely have I felt so clearly that I had done the right thing by speaking and that God approved.

Friends have a rich and precious heritage from generations of careful Friends who sought lovingly to express their insights and advices to one another through minutes, formal epistles, journals, and personal correspondence, and yet it seems we often neglect this treasure for trinkets of more recent manufacture. While rereading Samuel Janney's memoirs, I glanced here and there through the book at sections I'd highlighted during earlier readings. The impact of such pure and tender Truth moved me greatly; his observations on the public ministry convicted me all over again of my personal unworthiness for it—yet it is not I, but Christ in me, who is the true minister. I wish that all that is ego in me could sink down so low that nothing could or would obstruct God's will for me, that this body and mind might become an unresisting tool for God. God forgive my foolish struggling in the divine hand!

> O God, thank you that you do not discard this untrustworthy tool but patiently set about to redeem it, healing it by your love and bending it to your Will. God grant that I might become ever more peacefully and joyfully resigned to God's purposes for me, surrendering my flawed will to God's perfect control. I love you God—help me love you still more!!!

The Pendle Hill gathering on Quaker ministry in Third Month 1985 was as powerful a spiritual experience as I'd had in a long time. There were about three dozen people there, ranging from Bill Taber (as seasoned and powerful a minister as I've ever encountered among Friends) to a Friend who had been a member for just a year and had only recently begun to appear in the ministry. It was my part to appear in the gospel ministry several times, both preaching and praying. That service seemed acceptable; Bill Taber sought me out Saturday afternoon to say how much he had appreciated my presence and vocal contributions thus far. It seemed almost inevitable that I immediately went dry for the rest of the day.

In the First Day worship, I spoke of the one Master of us all, His commandment that we love one another, the broken state of the Religious Society of Friends, and the need for a ministry of reconciliation among us. I claimed it as "a personal concern," which is unusual terminology for me. I felt that I had been faithful to a true leading to speak, yet in place of a sense of peace came tears and a broken heart lasting the entire remaining period of worship. I cried tears of joy for the visible fellowship of those gathered in that meeting for worship and tears of pain that such fellowship is so rare while distrust and disrespect are so prevalent among the various groups of Friends. "Slain in the Spirit" is the only phrase I can call up that expresses the totality of my surrender to that experience.

At the rise of meeting, Bill Taber announced that he would be praying in the porch room with anyone who felt led to join him, so I rose quickly and followed him. The experience there was quite similar to that known as "afterglow" in evangelical circles and helped me "come back to earth" after the great intensity of meeting for worship.

Shortly afterward, I was accosted by a Friend who wanted to let me know that she felt excluded by the Christian language I had used in vocal ministry. I was so depleted by the intensity of worship, prayer, and healing that I could not respond to her concern very well, and we found no unity at that time. (Later, I did feel we were reconciled.)

By day's end, I was spiritually exhausted. The feeling was similar to that at the end of a day of hard physical labor, when one knows one has done good work—and a good amount of it—but is glad nevertheless to see the sun go down. I felt it in the pit of my stomach and saw it in my inability to engage the Friend upset by Christian language at the deep level at which her trouble should have been addressed. As good as the weekend had been, I needed alone time to ponder all these things in my heart.

Over the following week, I began to feel more at ease about the events at Pendle Hill. When we think we know God's work and style as well as God knows it, God often sets us straight. My comfortable preconceptions of how and when God might be at work are in reality my attempt to keep God in a box, to set finite limits on the infinite Lord of Creation, and part of the meaning of the past weekend was a reminder that I shouldn't be doing that. As for the experience in First Day worship, I now felt released to share the message of God's reconciling love more widely.

Travel is often liminal space for our spiritual life. I read the account of Abraham's servant (Genesis 24) while in the airport in Third Month. Two aspects of this familiar story stood out with fresh impact: first, that we never learn the name of the servant who plays such a pivotal role in the story; and second, that the story offers an unequivocal example of specific prayers being answered specifically. Who else in the Bible has so many speaking lines, is a central actor and not just an interlocutor for Jesus or another teacher, and yet remains nameless? God must have known his name, for God heard his prayer, knew who was praying and why, and answered clearly—yet we are never told it. Why is that so?

Vocation and Competency

Perhaps if we knew his name, we might honor the person rather than the moral of the story. We might be tempted to say, "God answered Bebop's prayer, so Bebop must have been righteous," rather than saying, "God answers the prayer made in faith." If God can provide such specific help in response to the prayer of a person so unimportant that their name is not even recorded, helping them be so faithful and successful that their story is told thousands of years later, then God can help me, today, with the challenges and tasks I face.

What a prayer that servant prayed! "Lord, help me by letting me say thus-and-such, and by letting the woman respond by saying and doing thus-and-such, so that I can know she is the right one." Not "Send me a sign," but "Send me this specific sign!" Is God offended by this? Apparently not, for God responds in just the way Abraham's servant has requested—immediately—before the prayer is completed. God has not been influenced to do this by the stature or reputation of the one making the prayer—the servant is nameless. It is the prayer itself that is important. We need to recover that prayer of faith today.

> O Lord of Creation, take the lessons of Thy Scripture and write them in my heart. Even more, dwell in me and be my Teacher always, pointing out for me the way in which I should walk. Bring me into such harmony with Thy will that my prayer *is* Thy will and my desire is Thy desire.
>
> Help me to be not a disciple of great renown but a servant of great faithfulness. Let my life direct those who encounter me in this world to Thee. Wherever I go, let me be a midwife to the birth of Thy Kingdom into this world. Surely, the prayer of your servant will be granted out of Thy infinite mercy and love.
>
> In Christ's Name I Pray. Amen.

On Third Month 11, 1985, I wrote the following in my journal:

> "There is a faith which overcomes the world, and there is a faith which is overcome by the world."[10] Our faith can be overwhelmed by worldly events: the burnout among peace activists who lose hope after years of struggle or the despair of the disciples on Saturday night after the crucifixion.

These present days can feel very much like that Saturday night: the world had apparently overcome the vision of God's shalom and all hopes had been shattered. Simon the Zealot was thinking of turning again to armed revolution as change's only hope. Matthew the collaborator felt he had gambled everything and lost; neither Roman nor Jew would have anything to do with him now. Peter was thinking about going back to the boats and fishing for a living.

Think of the next morning—the first excited, confusing report of the women, the doubts of the men, and finally the dawning realization that the resurrection was real at this moment! This change came about not because the women (and later the men) failed to locate the dead body of Jesus but because they did encounter the living Presence of Christ. The faith of that tiny band of men and women, which had been momentarily overcome by the world, was transformed into a faith that overcame the world—a light shining in the darkness that the darkness has never been able to put out, never been able to comprehend. The conflict between God and our Adversary was settled that weekend, and though skirmishes remain to be fought, God's victory was conclusive. Our faith in that victory, and in the Lord of Creation, is a faith that overcomes the world.

In Third Month 1985, I made a presentation to Charlottesville Friends about my understandings of ministry and of my particular role as a minister. I said that a minister of the gospel of Jesus Christ is one who acts under the orders of Christ in all they do. Ministry is any action undertaken in that role, not just speaking. Finally, a minister is a spiritual midwife, facilitating new life in other people.

I claimed my role as a minister of Christ. Ministry was my vocation; my entire life was under the leadership of Christ, and I dedicated each day to ministry. I tried to live like Christ, following the commandments to love God and to love my neighbor. This meant obeying the rules of the spiritual world, not the physical world—being a fool for Christ's sake. To do ministry was to serve the Inward Guide, risking everything on the relationship with God. I was learning to sit lightly on everything: money and security and images of what success is, where home is, what my gifts are, and what my ministry is. I was learning by experience the divine approbation that is the reward of faithful ministry: a simple "Well done,

Vocation and Competency

good and faithful servant" (Matthew 25:21). Faithfulness leads to a clearer sense of our Shepherd's Voice and Presence. Faithfulness also brings joy at bringing God and one's fellow humans closer together.

In this presentation, I shared that I didn't have all the spiritual gifts—no one did. I did have the gift of administration. Using the gift of administration faithfully meant taking numerous risks, but my experience was that God preserves and protects. The gift of administration is part of a larger gift, which is partly a gift of healing. More and more, people were seeking me out when they were spiritually troubled. I'd been able to help by letting the Inward Christ work through me.

This presentation ushered in the brief "golden era" of my participation in Charlottesville Meeting. It was well received, with no protest or pushback as far as I was aware. I felt known and accepted in my identity of a devout Christian devoted to public service, to the ministry. This feeling persisted for perhaps two years but then was replaced by a profound sense of the opposite—that many Friends in Charlottesville Meeting rejected who I was, a devout Christian, and could accept me only if I remained silent about my faith.

I was invited to give the J. Bernard Walton Lecture at Southeastern Yearly Meeting sessions in Florida over Easter weekend 1985. My time there was a time of Presence—of Christ working through me to gather God's flock in gospel order. My only task was to make myself available to the Inward Teacher and otherwise stay out of the way. The outward signs of approval were not scarce. Each time I spoke, a Friend or Friends commented on my eloquence, asked if I could write up my comments for their *Faith and Practice*, etc. There was outward and deliberate opposition, but the power of the Lord was over all.

Two events stood out above all: a faith conversion and a running confrontation with one Friend that came to a climax in the middle of the Walton Lecture that I was giving. A woman approached me Friday evening after attending a workshop titled Challenges Facing Unprogrammed Friends. Participants in that workshop had made it clear that they felt one problem facing Friends was that they weren't Christian enough. As a non-Christian, she was concerned that these attitudes would exclude her. (I was impressed by her lack of defensiveness; she perceived a difference in spiritual approaches and was seeking more information.) We talked for at least two hours that evening. I shared my spiritual journey as a Quaker and later as a Christian Quaker and my experience of the personal attributes of God; she shared her experience of God as a glorious Light. We closed with a period of worship and prayer. When I began to pray about her gift of the vision of the glory of God, the chapel seemed to me to get lighter all around us—which she saw too.

The next morning, she told me she had lain awake thinking about our conversation, and around 3 a.m. she had realized that there was one, even Christ Jesus, who could speak to her condition. We had one or two chances to talk after that, and the opening stayed with her, seeming to strengthen over time.

Just before I gave the Walton Lecture, I saw her and asked for her prayers, if she felt able to pray (she had never experienced God as capable of being prayed to before). Later, this woman told me her prayer had been that my lecture would be such a powerful spiritual experience that even non-Christians would find it spoke to them. I was able to share with this woman that another Friend had already approached me to say that although Christian terminology was a source of difficulty to her, my message had spoken to her and that I'd been a channel to God for her for that evening. Praise God to demonstrate so specifically that prayers are answered!

Then there was the lecture itself. As a prelude, it is necessary to know that Southeastern Yearly Meeting on Friday afternoon had established Bonifay Monthly Meeting in Florida, with a membership of two Friends and three additional seekers. It seemed to me unfair and unrealistic to lay on just two Friends the responsibility for establishing and nurturing a meeting, educating seekers, centering the worship, witnessing to Truth in the region, and all the other activities of a monthly meeting, but it was not my place to say anything in a meeting I was not a member of. I did speak privately with the immediate past clerk of the yearly meeting and the current clerk. They felt that there had been no other loving alternative for the yearly meeting given the history of this

Vocation and Competency

group, and they expressed the hope that the new meeting would grow into health and stability.

Ben, one of the members of the new Bonifay meeting, subsequently spoke several items during meeting for business. Much of what he said seemed like word salad to me, but Friends told me he was actually improved over a year ago.

During worship sharing on Saturday morning, I was moved to share my sense of being surrounded by a cloud of witnesses—living and dead, near and far—and concluded with a word of thanks to God for making Her Presence manifest.[11] Ben responded shortly afterward with a monologue about how beards and moustaches, bushy eyebrows, and long hair are evidence of an aggressive personality—witness a psychology professor he once had, or our ape and chimpanzee ancestors and cousins who have very fuzzy faces and are *quite* aggressive. (I wore a long Fu Manchu moustache and longish hair at this time and have always had very bushy eyebrows.) Ben then denounced all those who would take away God's maleness, including an extensive and detailed list of the genitalia of God that would be amputated or mutilated by these despicable persons.

Ben spoke again to say that something another worshipper said had disturbed him, and he wanted a committee established to look into the matter—naming me and two other persons to that task. After worship, he asked me if I would "participate." I explained my understanding of worship sharing and said that I heard judgment in his voice and would not take part. He then criticized me for my poor judgment.

Had he known my thoughts, Ben would have been even more upset, for I'd spent the latter part of worship sharing trying to decide whether I should walk over and cast out the evil spirit in him. I came to feel eventually that I was not called to do so. This was extraordinary; I was not dubious that he needed exorcism, not doubtful that I could do the job in the name of Jesus Christ, but satisfied that God had other plans and I should not interfere. This seemed to be an extension of the feeling I had all week that I was simply to stand in the power of Jesus Christ *as a witness*.

Memoir of the Life and Religious Labors of Lloyd Lee Wilson

As I stood in the chapel, beginning my last preparations for the lecture just ahead, Ben showed up again, asking what I thought of Scripture passages about men sleeping with boys and spilling their seed on the ground. I declined to discuss Scripture with him until together we looked up the specific passages he had in mind and assured ourselves of the correct quotation and the context for each passage. Ben was quite upset and promised to challenge me in open meeting. I allowed that he had that right, and he left the chapel.

I left the chapel a moment later, found two seasoned Friends, explained the situation to them briefly, and asked for their prayers. I was then filled with a sense that everything was in Christ's hands, happening just as God would have it. I had nothing to fear or worry about. Ben would discover he'd taken on not a liberal churchman but Christ, who happened to be occupying my body at the time.

When Friends gathered to hear the lecture, I rose out of the silence to speak, walked to the podium, and discovered I'd left my notes in disarray after Ben's appearance in the chapel. Rather than shuffle through the pages to put them in order, I decided to trust in God's guidance. The first half of the lecture went well. Ben walked into the room at about the halfway point, however, and soon began shouting out questions about Jesus' and my own homosexuality. The rest of the audience began to shout back "No!" each time he would ask if he could get some answers to his questions.

I stood mute. It felt as if Christ had interceded between me and the rest of the world—especially between me and Ben—and that I was perfectly protected from any possible harm. Calmly, I watched Ben shouting his questions until three or four seasoned Friends rose to escort him out of the chapel; he went reluctantly. I then returned to normal and picked up where I'd left off.

The next morning, at meeting for business, a Friend reported that Ben now realized that Bonifay's request for monthly meeting status should be withdrawn. Southeastern Yearly Meeting approved and laid down Bonifay Monthly Meeting some forty hours after it had been established.

Vocation and Competency

In Fifth Month 1985, I participated in the Friends Ministers Conference in Chicago as a way of understanding more about pastoral Friends. Soon after arriving, I found myself in an opportunity with a pastor for Evangelical Friends Church—Eastern Region, who sought me out for advice and counsel as to whether he should stay at his present church in Rhode Island or accept a call to a church in Ohio. We waited on the Lord's will in silence for some time, after which it seemed clear to me what I should say, and I did so, which brought tears to the pastor's eyes. The stillness and calm of waiting broke in upon him with the force of fresh insight, and he was much tendered. I was learning to cease clinging to my own conceptions of why I was anyplace or what I should be doing and to do simply, but with all my might, whatever the Lord gave my hand to do.

The ministers' conference became a conference of contrasts for me. I heard affirmations of basic Quaker testimonies by leaders of pastoral Friends groups, followed closely by statements from others that showed no comprehension of those same testimonies. There was hustle and bustle everywhere, no planned silent worship, and the workshops had little audience participation. Yet after the keynote address a pastor did stand and ask for silent worship, and the group did sit silently for a short time. There were eloquent prayers at every opportunity, and every transition of any sort was an opportunity for vocal prayer from the designated leader. Eloquent phrases slid easily from these lips but at times seemed to lack authenticity. I found myself hungering for some inarticulate spiritual groanings.

I went to a workshop on the devotional classics, hoping to find something useful for a spiritual formation program. The young pastor who led the group was so intent on telling us of his change in teaching from an emphasis on commitment to an emphasis on transformation that he treated audience comments as interruptions—even though his audience knew more than he about his chosen topic. Yet, it was in this workshop, in response to comments I made about the journals and memoirs of Samuel Bownas, Job Scott, Samuel Janney, and Elias Hicks, that I had encountered the pastor who had occupied the rest of my afternoon.

Memoir of the Life and Religious Labors of Lloyd Lee Wilson

I looked forward to the 1985 North Carolina Yearly Meeting (Conservative) (NCYM[C]) sessions as an opportunity to be with Louise Wilson and to renew some other friendships and Friendships. I arrived at Belk Hall at Chowan College in Murfreesboro just in time to turn a corner and hear Louise Wilson say, "I can't bear to wait another minute for Lloyd Lee to arrive." Yearly meeting was a grand reunion, with Louise and Bob Wilson, Pam Snyder, and Hannah Gosling all there. The sessions were a wonderfully healing place to be. How much deeper into God's Love we could go together when we did not first have to discuss whether we all believed in God! What wonderful things God was doing among these Friends, and how they loved one another! I recorded this prayer in my journal later that night:

> Thank you, Lord, for making me aware of this gathering of your disciples and for making it possible for me to have fellowship with them for these few days. Help me to bring you into my life as fully and personally as these Friends have done and enable me to be a blessing to others as they have been a blessing to me. Heal my heart of its hurts and my flaws by your Presence and Love and make of me who you would have me be. I pray in the name of Jesus the Christ, who suffered and died for me. Amen.

After the evening session one night, seven of us retired to a quiet room for prayer. I felt the Presence of the Lord very strongly among us from the start and soon felt as if the top of my head had been opened and the Spirit was pouring in a torrent into my body. It did not stay there but flowed just as strongly out of my arms and legs and torso into the room, permeating and enveloping everyone present. Later, this image changed to one of breathing in the Holy Spirit and breathing the Spirit out to everyone else with every exhalation. As God's Presence worked its healing on me, I found myself able for the first time to pray for the people at FGC who had been the most difficult for me. My prayers before this had been the prayers I felt obligated as a Christian to pray for anyone; now I wanted to pray for them as human beings who were going to face difficult work in the months ahead and would need God's Presence and guidance in their lives. Now I prayed for them because I loved them. It was wonderful!

Vocation and Competency

At a later gathering of the same group, Hannah Gosling was given a vision of and for each of the others. Hannah saw me approach Jesus from the front, lift his arms into the cross position, and embrace him strongly; Jesus simply melted or was absorbed into my body. The scene shifted, and I was alone, walking down a rural path—wearing a crown and a purple cape and holding a staff. Suddenly, I was brought to a halt by an invisible barrier. No matter how I tried to get around the edge or over the top of this barrier, it always blocked my way; I could find no door or other way through. As I continued to search for an opening, my expression grew increasingly distraught.

Jesus approached me from behind while I was still searching, took off my crown and cape, and took my staff away. I turned my head to see who it was, and when I recognized Jesus I fell to my knees. At that moment, my hand reached out and found a way through the barrier; on my hands and knees, naked, I moved forward into a space beyond the invisible barrier. This vision was similar to comments Bill Taber had made the previous month about my taking off the clothes of office and beginning a "naked ministry" in my meeting.

This may be a good place to share a bit about my personal experience of visions. My own visions are "second sight" in the sense of "seeing" the future (precognition), but visual images are not a large part of my experience. I often see visions with my eyes open because for me visual images are secondary to other senses and feelings. The experience is mostly a sense of the future—of knowing what the future is going to feel like at some particular moment. The sensation comes on me unbidden and often makes no sense except that, by force of experience, I know that the sensation will make sense eventually. Often, I feel I will be bonded with a person, place, thing, or office or institution in the future, though there is no connection now.

I felt that bond with the office of general secretary the first time I saw Dwight Spann Wilson, before I ever got involved with FGC, and I felt the same bond again when I stopped in at the offices to visit a friend who was working there temporarily. I felt that bond with a pickup truck owned by Virginia Mountain Housing when I left there for FGC. Without my ever saying anything, the same truck was assigned to me when I returned to Virginia Mountain Housing three years later.

More conventional visions—visual and auditory—have been common in my mother's family. I remember her recounting a vision in which she saw Pueblo Indians going about their daily life during a visit to an ancient Pueblo village one summer. Occasionally, my involvement with a vision was more direct. After a long illness, my Aunt Nellie died on Twelfth Month 23, 1983, and was buried on the 27th. Merrill and I decided to follow through with a commitment to visit Merrill's family over the holiday, so I didn't get to the funeral. Mom approved of our decision because Nellie had told her on the day she died that Asa and I had visited her that day. It happened this way.

Nellie had been an increasing part of my prayers since she first fell ill. That day, I had an extended prayer session in the morning at home. I finished my prayers at 9:15 a.m. and then made several telephone calls. I am sure of the time because I had to make arrangements to call one person back in half an hour. At the same time, Mom was in the hospital room in Winston-Salem with Nellie. Nellie saw me in the room with her, holding Asa in my arms. She commented on how quiet and well-behaved Asa was. (He really was that way, but Nellie had never seen him before.) Her vision ended at 9:15 a.m., according to Mom (who made a point of checking the time), just when my prayers ended.

That night I dreamed of Nellie looking about herself anxiously and at another nearby figure. In the dream, I spoke to her, saying, "It's all right Nellie, it's the risen Christ—accept him!" She looked very relieved and turned to the other figure, now recognizable as the Christ. At that moment, the dream ended.

On the last day of the yearly meeting, we all caravanned to Woodland, North Carolina, for closing worship at Cedar Grove Meeting House and a picnic lunch afterward. I was occupied through much of meeting for worship with a leading to speak that I greatly desired would go away but would not. I realized that the real issue was not the message but whether I was going to be obedient to God's will—to speak when God said to speak and to be silent when God said be silent, not when I felt it was fitting for me to speak or be silent. Whether the message I finally

Vocation and Competency

delivered had any impact on anyone there is God's business, not mine, but I felt immeasurable consolation in submitting to the Divine Will and standing to speak when the creaturely in me desired to be silent. It seemed to me later that a crucial fork in the road had been passed successfully and that if I had not been faithful then, I would have begun to wander farther from God's will for me until all my gifts, including the gift of God's Presence, were withdrawn.

Throughout that summer, I gained insight about acknowledging and accepting the reality of my spiritual calling. A Friend wrote a wonderful letter pointing out the inconsistency of my wanting to be a faithful witness to my Lord and also wanting not to upset anyone—wanting all people to approve of me and what I do. There was much truth in her observation that I needed to give up this desire to be liked and approved of, to rest more confidently in the approval of God, not humans, and to live more fully into the reality of what the Lord was doing in my life.

When Bill Taber visited me for an opportunity that summer, his simple statement that he had come in part to see whether I had any word for *him* turned me upside down. It became clear that he was depending on others for nurture, support, and direction in his own spiritual life, even as he was depended upon by so many. Before that moment, I had been lazing along, letting Bill carry us both through the currents of the Spirit, thinking I had no responsibilities. I was wrong—my friendship was important to him and his work. I had become part of the tapestry of this invisible meeting of ministers and elders, and there were burdens and responsibilities that fell to me because of that. I was needed; others depended on me to do my share. They were hurt if I was not diligent about my work and ministry.

After I returned to Virginia, I continued to rise at 6 a.m., giving me over an hour for morning devotions before the workday began. I prayed and read at the desk in my office until I heard Asa awaken and begin to talk. This made for a very good start to each day. My devotions began with my prayer list, which was over 150 names long. I offered specific prayers for the top five or six persons on the (rotating) list and for any others that were in my heart that morning, as well as a general prayer for everyone else. Often, I sent a postcard to one of those I'd prayed for.

Then I read the day's reflection from Oswald Chambers's *My Utmost for His Highest* and a chapter or two from the Bible and meditated on what I'd read. The rest of the devotional time varied greatly—sometimes more Bible reading, sometimes a letter to a spiritual friend who was also a Friend, sometimes an entry in my journal—depending on how I was led.

I had so much to do in prayer; there was a far greater need for intercessory prayer than I could meet. God did not need my prayer in order to accomplish the Divine Will, but I couldn't see how to decide to pray for this one and not that one. What of other prayers—of adoration, thanksgiving, and so on; where was the time/energy/perseverance to do all I needed to do? My prayer became:

> Lord, I cannot accomplish what I intend or desire in prayer. Accept my flawed efforts not on their merits, Lord, but as a response to thy gift of grace. Let it not be that any of these thy children stumble or suffer because I have been inconstant in prayer on their behalf.
>
> Sweet Jesus, even this is not enough, for I do not even know for what I should be praying! You, God, see and know your loved ones truly and completely, while I have only glimpses seen through a dark glass. How can I bear to hurt You by confessing that at times I do not want to pray for what is best for them truly, but rather only for what I want for them—but You know that already, have felt that pain already, and my confession is only the first step in my lifting that wound from your heart. Have compassion on me, thy creation!
>
> Christ, You are my Advocate, pressing my cause with Your Father as only that Advocate can who has already suffered for His clients. You love me that much, Lord—and I do so little to deserve that love, and so much that deserves Your detestation—and you love me still, Lord. You have called me to Your side, called me by name in spite of my broken nature; even though I continue to wound you, You have given me Your heart. Surely You love these Your saints more than me, Lord; surely You love the greatest sinner as much as me, the worst of all, for You know better than I what I do. If you love me as I am, surely you will

Vocation and Competency

answer our imperfect prayers of intercession for these of your flock.

Save them all—call them each by name—Jesus, we pray this by thy Holy Name itself—answer our prayer!

And You answer, patiently: "It has been answered already, My son."

I attended Baltimore Yearly Meeting sessions in Eighth Month 1985 in the midst of an extended dry spell verging on a drought. We awoke one morning to a gentle rain that persisted through breakfast and as we gathered for our business meeting. In the worship before business began, I offered a vocal prayer:

> Spirit of Christ, descend on us with thy blessings
> as softly as this morning's rain
> falls on this dry soil.
> Open us to thy blessings and Presence
> so that we may receive them
> as readily as the soil receives the rain.
> Grant that we might bring forth a bountiful crop
> and be joyful to bear Thy harvest
> knowing that we are Thine
> that You endure from age to age
> and that we shall surely be gathered to Thee one day.

Both before and after yearly meeting sessions, for most of 1985 I had felt a persistent nudge toward undertaking a home visitation ministry in Charlottesville Meeting. After yearly meeting sessions, I realized this nudge had become an infant leading, and so I brought it to my oversight committee for their discernment. The committee and I discussed it over the summer months. In Tenth Month 1985, when I returned the certificate for the New England travel to Charlottesville Meeting, Ministry and Counsel presented my leading to do family visits. Meeting for business approved, and Ministry and Counsel agreed to arrange the visits.

One hopes that a leading comes from immediate and perceptible guidance. It is also true that the Holy Spirit prepares us; in retrospect, we can see ways in which the possibility of a particular service and/or the skills needed to serve in a particular way are laid before us in advance. In the case of home visits, a contemporary example was Bill Taber's work with individual opportunities. Another glimpse of the possible came from the numerous Quaker journals that I had begun reading almost as soon as I became a Quaker. Among my favorites, which I copied out for my own use, was the following entry in Hugh Judge's *Journal* for Tenth Month 9, 1786, almost exactly two centuries before I embarked on this work myself:

> In fifteen days we visited about one hundred families and parts of families of our members. John Perry being then quite unwell, we postponed the remaining visits. In this service, we witnessed seasons of renewed favor, in which the baptizing power of Truth was felt to the tendering of many minds. In some places, it seemed like a time of searching out the hidden things of Esau.
>
> Surely no service in the church is so deeply humbling as this: to be truly honest, and place things where they properly belong, giving everyone their due, is a work that requires close attention to the Divine Guide. Although some few seemed shut up in their shells, yet in general, Friends hearts and houses were open to receive us, to my humble admiration. May the praise be given Him who was not wanting in furnishing with fresh supplies from place to place, to minister to the states of the people.

Ministry and Counsel was concerned that some Friends might be uncomfortable with my making a religious visit to their home, so they arranged to schedule the visits themselves. At meeting on First Day, I'd get a note with an individual's or family's name and the time of the visit, and I'd make that visit according to schedule. The next week I'd get another note with another appointment. Eventually, the clerk of Ministry and Counsel simply told me I was done. I made no attempt to figure out who might be missing from my list of homes visited. Everyone on the meeting's mailing list had been offered a home visit, and I had made visits to all those who accepted.

The first home visit was in Tenth Month 1985, and visits continued weekly until First Month 1987. In an adults-only household, we would begin with fifteen to thirty minutes of waiting worship, followed by a time

Vocation and Competency

of quiet conversation. The entire visit lasted no more than about seventy-five minutes. It was clear from the very first visit that the deep sharing reached in Friends' homes could not have taken place in our normal meeting activities and that our worship time was especially deep and moving. Sometimes no words were spoken for an extended period, and other times we moved easily into a centered discussion after only a few minutes. On one visit, I spent a full hour in silent worship with a single-parent Friend, aware of the ebb and flow of a strong Presence in the room with us. I felt very much that I had been ministered to in that encounter and could understand with new clarity Bill Taber's early fears that he was becoming a "spiritual vampire" via these opportunities. The silences were profoundly moving, and the conversations were full of God's grace and glory. Again and again, I was drawn to Hugh Judge's *Journal* and prayed with him that "praise be given Him who [is] not wanting in furnishing with fresh supplies from place to place, to minister to the states of the people.

Throughout that year, the home visitations and meetings for worship clarified and shaped my self-understanding; the testimony of the faith community was that others were helped and changed as well. I meditated often on 1 Corinthians 14:1–5: it is unfaithful to shrink from spiritual gifts that the faith community needs.

I could make no specific report about the families I had visited, but I did share general observations with the monthly meeting. One was that I was convinced that Charlottesville Meeting had about the same proportion of members involved in 12-step programs as the population at large. The other was that there were parents in young families in the monthly meeting who wanted to participate in activities in addition to First Day worship but could not because they could not arrange or afford child care for other times.

Two changes in meeting practice occurred as a result. The meeting began opening the meeting house for 12-step meetings. This was a change in heart as well as a change in practice—the meeting began to feel that this was a service for "people like us," not simply a charity that might be offered to "those people." The second change was that the meeting made a commitment to provide childcare at any meeting function for anyone who needed it. This did indeed increase the number of young parents who were active in the meeting at various times during the week.

During all this time, I continued reflecting about gifts, both spiritual and worldly. Worldly gifts include all those physical and mental talents and abilities that we see in people all around us: athletic prowess, mental acuity, and articulate speech or writing. These gifts are distributed evenly over the population, whether the recipients are spiritually mature or even spiritually awake. As a mother loves all her children equally, whether they behave or not, and gives tokens of her love equally, so also God gives us our share of these worldly gifts. Moreover, there is no requirement that they be used in gospel order—physical prowess may be used to amass a fortune for one's own use or to give money to orphans, or it may be squandered; God gives the gift anyway. If we nurture a physical gift, it may grow, but that is a question of how the gift is developed and nurtured.

Spiritual gifts are harder to discern. I believe one must be open to and responsive to the grace by which the gift is given in order to receive it at all. Many of us are asleep to our spiritual selves and never perceive the spiritual gifts we are being offered by God. The ways in which we use spiritual gifts also affects their development. There are many stories of Quaker ministers who have felt that unless they were obedient *that moment* to the workings of the Holy Spirit, their gift (of vocal ministry or of something else) would be withdrawn forever. A spiritual gift improperly used—that is, out of harmony with God's will—will shrink and eventually disappear.

Spiritual gifts are fruits of the life of the Spirit in us and prosper as the Holy Spirit prospers in us and we use the gifts offered in harmony with God's Spirit. To claim for ourselves a gift we've not been given or to fail to use a gift that has been entrusted to us are equally damaging errors. How is one to avoid them?

Just as the eye cannot see itself, we cannot discern our own gifts nearly as well as our brothers and sisters can see us. We must be committed to call each other out into accurate recognition of our true spiritual gifts, into proper exercise and development of those gifts, and

Vocation and Competency

into that life that is permeated by the Spirit of Christ, source and sustenance for all our gifts.

As 1985 came to an end, I did an examen of current issues in my life and identified four. Reviewing the list reminded me of how the Lord's blessings were abounding all around me. There were many things that could be troubling me that didn't, and that was the Lord's doing.

- Maintaining the proper balance of time spent with Merrill and/or Asa with the demands of work, the orchard, daily chores, and personal time for devotions, correspondence, etc.
- Reflecting on and praying about my faith life. Do I have a right relationship with Christ that will allow me to live free from sin? What does it mean to be "free from sin?"
- Being active in and nurtured by Charlottesville Friends. This feels so good I am tempted to look over my shoulder and ask how long God will let me go on this way before sending me back out "on the road."
- Trying to stay in reasonable physical condition while respecting the limits imposed by my back.

The next month, as 1986 began, I had a series of nightly dreams about my death. Sometimes I drowned, sometimes I was killed in a car accident. Sometimes I had no choice, and sometimes I could (and did) choose to die at that time and place—not suicide, but accepting what was happening to me as part of God's will.

Dying did not frighten me anymore, and these dreams didn't either. I would be happy enough to shuffle off this mortal coil when God called, and I looked forward to being remade in the divine image (whatever that entails). Then all this would probably seem unimportant except for those I have left behind, for whom it seems to me I would yearn deeply, as God yearns for us. Still, as I dreamed at night and reflected on dreams by day, I realized that sooner or later Asa would have to get along without me and that I would have to let him go.

Perhaps my dreams were of the death of the old Lloyd Lee, who had to die before Christ could bring the new person to life. If my physical body happened to die in that process, so be it, I concluded. God would do what was best for me, I knew. This I knew as "experimental knowledge," for God's Presence was as tangible and joyful and precious to me at the start of 1986 as ever I'd felt it. I could feel myself unwinding and relaxing in God's Presence, slowly letting down my guard and soaking up the warmth of Divine Love. I was more vulnerable than ever before, but I had less to "lose," having given it all to Christ already.

I have continued to reflect on my inevitable death in the decades since these dreams. They continue to give rise in me not a morbid mood but a sense of celebration. Each time I am reminded, in the words of the Easter morning greeting, HE IS RISEN! Because Christ is risen, nothing can happen to me that is not within God's permissive will; angels really are watching over me. If I die, I will go straight to God; if I live, I live for God. I am no longer what I was before but not yet what I will be when I come fully into Christ's fellowship.

Daily life had three other aspects at this time, not new but fresh and vital: family, orchard, and faith community. The home visitations, life among Charlottesville Friends, and my personal spiritual life were full of grace. They reminded me that my family life was also full of grace. The orchard continued to thrive, and the setbacks that we experienced from time to time were insignificant.

These aspects of my life took up all of my time and would easily take up much more time than I had to give. By God's grace, I was able to do what was most important in each area, and those things left undone were not allowed to cause serious trouble. What was not integral to those four activities, however, had to be set aside for the time being.

In Third Month 1986, Bill Taber and Brian Drayton led another powerful retreat at Pendle Hill, this one titled A Surrendered and Accountable Ministry, different from the previous year but just as impactful. I was led on Seventh Day evening to share about the relationship of my encounter with the risen Christ to my earnest desire to be surrendered, entirely obedient, and accountable. (The discussion had been drifting toward talk of how distasteful it is to surrender—on the basketball court or anyplace else.) The room was then silent for some minutes, after which Bill Taber rose, explained that he felt he had to rise to speak about authority, and declared that we had just heard the voice of

Vocation and Competency

authority speaking. He clarified that the Source of that authority is not the individual Friend, no matter how beloved or disliked, etc. I had never before had the ministry that sometimes flows through me affirmed more clearly. I had very little sense of what was happening; I had to ask others later to describe what I had said. I wasn't even sure at first that Bill was referring to what I had said (of course, in a very real way he was not; he was referring to words that had been channeled through me).

In my encounters with individual Friends between scheduled happenings, I felt a still center within me, unmovable and still, the source of a new love. I could anchor in that center and was capable of a new level of love for other people with far less defensiveness or self-consciousness than ever before. I had died to the world a little bit more, and "not I, but Christ in me" was alive a little bit more. It was another spiritual rebirth—and an extremely joyful time.

The meeting room in the Pendle Hill barn was spiritually oppressive to me when I sat there on Sixth Day, and I didn't go back. Later, I learned that Richard Hall, an Ohio Conservative minister who had been visiting Quaker families in the Philadelphia area, had also been unable to sit there.

A journal entry I wrote in early 1986 counseled patience without ever using the word:

> After 16 years as an active Friend, I'm beginning to understand what it means to *be* a Friend. After a thousand meetings for worship (First Day and midweek, at yearly meeting sessions, committee meetings and retreats), I am beginning to see what worship can be and how one might get to that spiritual condition. How much energy I've expended in the attempt to live and worship after the manner of Friends, and how much of that was misdirected.
>
> These small pieces of grace appear precious to me now as they break into my life little by little. How foolish I have been, acting and talking as if I knew what in actuality I did not know—did not, as I now realize, have even a clue! What great encouragement these memories give me to keep low always.

There is an encounter in worship which I never suspected before I became a Christian and which was not real to me for several years after I did give my life to Christ. Now that encounter, that realization of God's Presence, comes softly into meeting after meeting, changing the very nature of my worship. I come into awareness of the Presence of the Living God; that changes everything!

That is what being a Friend is coming to mean for me: a life centered in and surrendered to the Presence of the Living Christ. As that encounter permeates my life, everything else falls away into meaninglessness. In the refiner's fire of God's gaze, my imperfections are made perfect, my weaknesses are made strengths. Lifetime ambitions are discarded—I want only to know God's Presence and to do God's will forever. Instead of plowing forward to make my mark on the world, I seek to do God's will without distorting it by my own.

Meeting for worship is not a place to be affirmed but to be transformed and changed. The blessing of the faith community is not that it supports and strengthens us where we are but that it is the potter's wheel on which we are shaped by One whose Hand never trembles and whose Vision never blurs. Here, if we allow it, we are made more nearly whom He would have us be.

"Lord, make us clay in Thy Hands. Amen."

Reading *The Interpreter's Bible (Revised Standard Version)* with its extensive commentary also helped me during this period of my life. I was getting more out of the Old Testament than either of my first two times through Scripture (the King James Version and the New English Bible). Though I was eager to get back into the New Testament, I felt I'd be better prepared for that by learning as much as I could about and from the Old Testament.

God's Presence was real to me throughout each day during this time. Evil persisted, and I gave in to temptation at times, but overall I felt like the person who has bathed whom Jesus described in John 13:10.[12] My feet got dusty and needed regular cleaning, but overall I'd been washed clean by Christ's compassion. Christ had been *so* patient with me; how

Vocation and Competency

could I help but love Him? I declared my allegiance to Christ and proclaimed this small corner of creation to be part of the restoration, God's Kingdom. Praise God!

I arrived at the 1986 NCYM(C) sessions in time to join the evening intercessory prayer group in Louise Wilson's room. I felt the Presence very strongly, as if the Holy Spirit were being poured out among us as we offered various prayers. I prayed for the newborn Nathan Gorgen, who had heart defects, and for his parents. I was led to offer my life for Nathan if that were within the perfect will of God. It was the first experience in my life of a spirit of self-sacrifice of the type I read of repeatedly in Julian of Norwich and Teresa of Avila. I had not thought such a spirit could or would come through me; I pondered the experience in my heart.

Our intercessory prayer the next night brought spiritual danger. Louise asked for specific prayer for Jonathan and told a story of spiritual attacks over a span of several years experienced by Jonathan's father. Since Jonathan had been born, his father had had no more attacks. Jonathan had been born with severe medical problems; that he had survived at all was a medical miracle.

We settled into prayer to see what might be done for father and son. Two Friends had stark black and white visions, evil and disconcerting. A third also had the sense of blackness, relieved only by a prayer of thankfulness for the gifts of grace God gave each of us daily. One Friend prayed for protection from the evil spirit and cast it over water. I felt danger and prayed for God's protection for us all, then immediately felt the drowsiness and inability to focus my thoughts that I have associated in the past with demonic attacks.[13] I fought that off, and the group took some time to decide what to do.

We decided to pray for the boy's healing and moved into a close circle, sitting on the floor of the dorm lounge where we had gathered. I felt at once the need to claim that space, the boy, and all those present for Jesus Christ against all attack and all harm. Three times I felt a rushing sensation as of fire being pressed against my skin from the inside out, from the base of my neck to the top of my head. Then I became normal again and continued my prayer for protection.

There were more vocal prayers for healing. At this point, the door to the room opened and Arthur Berk entered, in some apparent distress. I felt certain he had been drawn by the strength of the spiritual vibrations around us. Louise pulled him gently to the floor beside her, and we began to pray for him. I was led to walk behind him and place my hands on his shoulders (I was on my knees, and he was sitting with his legs extended in front of him). We continued in prayer until Arthur volunteered that he was feeling some relief from his condition. On my way out, I described my experience to Louise and asked for her blessing. She told me to claim Christ as Lord and to cast out any entity I felt in my room tonight, saying that some very subtle spirits were around right then.

After breakfast the next morning, most of the prayer group of the previous night gathered in a side room and formed a circle around Jonathan and his parents. Shortly after we settled into worship, there was a powerful sense of Presence evident to all, and I knew that however powerful and dangerous our Adversary might be, our Advocate was greater and Lord of all. Soon Louise rose, and standing behind Jonathan with one hand on him and one on his father, prayed for cleansing and the break of any harmful link, genetic or otherwise, between generations. When she sat down, a Friend came forward to kneel in front of Jonathan, who was in his father's arms. The bond between man and infant as they gazed into one another's eyes was palpable to all; love was pouring into Jonathan.

A few moments later, I was moved to stand before Jonathan (one hand on his head, my Bible in my other hand) and say words to this effect: "I seal this soul and mark it for Jesus Christ, Lord of all creation. I set the sword of Truth at the gate of this soul—let nothing harmful or unholy enter in. You will grow in wisdom and stature and in favor with God and man. God bless you and keep you forever."

When I returned to my seat, Louise asked Jonathan's mother to sing "Balm in Gilead." We all stood and had a benediction, and then Jonathan left with his parents. The rest of us reflected on how each one of us had been given a task to do and how the tasks fit together well and formed a cohesive whole: casting out while some stood guard, cleansing that morning, filling the cleansed soul with love, and sealing and guarding the

Vocation and Competency

newly filled soul through the prayer God had given me. It seemed more a prophecy or forthtelling than a prayer of petition, more a statement of Truth about to happen than an intercession.

The question "Who do you want to be?" occupied my thoughts and prayers for several weeks afterward, though after much prayer I began to ask instead, "Who does God want me to be?" I saw differences between the two questions and their answers that had escaped me. I felt the experience of Jonathan's healing was a watershed, a qualitative change in my willingness to claim the ministry being offered. It was a time of learning not to presume on the Lord's gifts while also learning not to limit, in my thoughts or prayers, what the Lord could do with this raw material. As it says in the First Epistle of John, we don't yet know what God intends us to be. The Holy Spirit was moving powerfully, and I needed to stay still and centered, inertia-less, so it might have perfect freedom.

How I should share with other people what God was changing in me inwardly was a constant question. In Eighth Month 1986, I struggled with the sense that I must speak publicly in witness to a new understanding of the wrongfulness of abortion—that it was not enough to change without testifying to the change in me.[14] This could be necessary in both the monthly and yearly meetings, but I had been hoping that I would be released from the witness in my monthly meeting.

When I settled into worship one First Day, the leading to testify came again. I clung to my seat while two other frequent ministers spoke of children and Jesus' love for them and of the special qualities children have that adults would do well to emulate. Still I resisted, thinking of how out of step I would appear to the majority of Friends there and throughout the yearly meeting. At about a quarter to the hour, a visitor spoke on the Scripture verse from Romans 12 about not being conformed to the world, and I had no more excuses. I rose, gave my testimony, and sat down with considerable peace of heart.

That summer was a time of increasing stress and distress in my marriage. It was important for me to remember that the body of Christ was with me in this time of difficulty. I took advantage of my solitary time in the orchard to be intentional about that. I realized that over the past several years I had come to the body of Christ like a refugee from my marriage. What a joy it would be for my home to be part of that body!

The members of the body of Christ were both known and unknown to me. Those persons who were unknown to me could have little impact on my decision (regarding divorce) or its fruits. They were a source of general support, but the body becomes real as it is manifest in specific individuals whom I encounter day by day. That week, as I wrote a letter to a different friend who was also a Friend each day and often called another, the body seemed almost physically tangible. I knew that the known body of Christ would be loving and supportive no matter what decision I made. Jesus Himself would love me whatever I did, even though some of the things I might do would cause Him pain. These thoughts were a source of considerable comfort to me as I continued to seek to know what to do.

In Ninth Month I stayed overnight with Benigno and Karen Sánchez-Eppler at the Friends Burial Ground in Baltimore, sleeping in a small room inside the perimeter wall. It was a night of spiritual warfare, in two stages. Soon after I arrived, I was moved to walk around the perimeter stone walls of the burial ground and identify myself to the dead. At the midpoint of my circuit I stopped, prayed for the souls of all who were buried there, and cast out any and all entities present in the burial ground who were not of God. I then prayed to seal the perimeter against the return of any entities I had cast out and completed my walk around the walls. It seemed important to go all the way around.

I went to bed and was awakened just before 1:00 a.m., no longer sleepy at all. Turning on the light, I found the passage I was seeking: 2 Corinthians 4:8–10. It came to me that I was supposed to be in intercessory prayer for someone, so I got on my knees and started praying. I prayed the Jesus Prayer mostly but also offered my life and body in place of the unknown person(s) for whom I was praying. It came to me that Jesus could take my life and lend it back to me to be used according to His will. I waited for the first sensations of dying, but they did not appear—only a violent tingling in my legs when I stopped praying and lay down again, I suppose a result of kneeling for so long. When I felt the prayer was done and looked at my travel alarm, it was exactly 2:00

a.m. I fell asleep as soon as the sensation in my legs subsided. Truly, Jesus was calling me into new kinds of service that were less and less understandable to my mind. I prayed that I would be a worthy tool for His purposes.

In the fall of 1986, I began a daily spiritual practice of speaking with Jesus as if He were my human therapist or counselor. That daily practice led me to read through my journal for the previous several years. I was struck both by the depth of the Presence of God in my life over that time and by my continuing struggles with the same set of issues: trust in God vs. being overly sensitive to the criticisms of others, my inability to receive the love that humans and Jesus each offered to me, and the long-continuing brokenness of my marriage to Merrill. God had been faithful through all this.

In Twelfth Month I visited Bill Taber while in Philadelphia. I felt a need to give an accounting of myself. I felt he might be disappointed in me, but that proved not to be the case. We had a solid time together. It was particularly reassuring to me that he did not act as if my marital struggles directly affected or interfered with my work in the ministry.

I shared my leading to travel in the gospel ministry in North Carolina, and we settled into silence, holding this leading in the Light of Christ. Bill suggested that traveling with an 'ordinary Friend,' one not known as a public minister, would be best for me at this time. After some more silence, he was given the name of Frank Massey as a companion— an ordinary Friend valued for his faith, commitment, and obedience. I wrote Frank the next day, describing my leading and Bill Taber's sense that he would be the right companion.

As 1986 drew to a close, my personal examen focused on my felt need for financial security. One reason I had become an apple grower was to escape the risks of being financially dependent on government funding and other "soft" money, such as contributions. Until then, that had always seemed like wisdom, but it had begun to feel more like blasphemy. It is so simple, straight out of the Sermon on the Mount: if I am doing what God would have me do, God will take care of me. If I'm working in winterization for the poor and the federal government eliminates the program so I become unemployed, God will take care of me. How insulting I had been to God to demonstrate with my actions that I didn't believe God would take care of me and that therefore I would have to change my career, do something else, in order to take care of myself. God forgive me.

I was not led to stop saving money for retirement; nor did I believe that changing from changing career paths from nonprofit employment to being an independent farmer was necessarily unfaithful. I did see that I would be OK in retirement (should I live that long), not because I had saved enough but because God would take care of me if I trusted God—if I had faith in God. Changing from a nonprofit manager to an apple grower would not make me more secure, but coming to lean more fully on God's care would make me more secure whether I was managing housing rehabs or apple orchards. My commitment to becoming an apple grower had to be evaluated in the context of my reliance on God, not total control of the means of generating my income. The judgment would come to rest on other qualities, then: degree of service to others, quality of workday life, freedom to follow religious leadings, and so on.

For many months, I had one revelation after another along these lines, changing and deepening my understanding in many areas; it seemed that my entire faith had been undergoing renovation and renewal. I had thought of myself as a Christian before but now saw that my faith and understanding were still shallow. I was moving from the intellectual to the heart; I had had the factual knowledge of history, theology, and Quaker practice, but their life in me was almost mechanical. Now, I was living more in my heart. I began to feel like the nun who, when asked how long she'd been a Christian, said, "Just since this morning—I have to start over every day!"[15]

It became easier to accept that God loved me, and in Christ lived out that love for me, while at the same time accepting that I had been unable to stay married. Much of my previous experience and understanding of love had been conditional; I could be loved only if I were already perfect and always behaved properly. How backwards I had been! God loved me not because I'd earned it but because I was God's creation.

We humans can be certain of God's love because God lived with us as a human in Jesus of Nazareth—what greater sign could there be? My fears that if I strayed from the righteous path one more time God would desert me, or withdraw all spiritual gifts from me, had been foolishness. There is nothing that can separate me from the love of God except my own refusal to be loved. This affects my human relationships as well. Knowing that God truly loves me removes my anxiety over whether person X thinks I am worthy of their love.

As Christmas approached, I was reading two apparently unrelated books: a history of Santa Claus legends and Job Scott's *Salvation by Christ*. One First Day morning, these were catalyzed into a single vocal offering. I contrasted Kris Kringle/Santa Claus, who makes a list of who's naughty and nice so as to be able to leave good gifts with good people and lumps of coal with bad people, with the Krist Kind/Christ Child, who makes no such lists and gives of Himself unconditionally because of His great love for us. Just as Mary said in the first chapter of the Gospel according to Luke, we must also be the handmaid of God, willing to do as God wills and cooperating with God's desire that Christ be born in us.

There was considerable silence after I sat down. Eventually, a Friend was moved to respond that one of his yearnings had been answered—that the meeting for worship would begin to show an unbroken continuity from week to week. This had happened because "Lloyd Lee has spoken to the question of suffering, which we wrestled with last week." He said that I had spoken to the fruits of suffering since my insights would not have come had I been healthy and occupied with the normal routines of daily life.

I had not been present the week before, and such a role for my ministry had never occurred to me. Once again, I saw that I don't really know what I am saying when I stand to speak in worship. I may have some idea of the words I will use, but their meaning is often starkly different from what I may think. The importance of the prayer I use before speaking in worship is abundantly clear: "Lord, grant that I may speak the words you would have me speak; that your Word is expressed in my words. Grant that the auditory hears Your Word as You would have them hear it in the words I speak."

On Christmas Eve 1986, I went to the meeting house for midweek meeting, not really knowing whether I should expect more Friends than usual because of the date or fewer because of the bad weather. As it turned out, there was no one at the meeting except me. I settled into worship with a sense of having begun my Christmas Day retreat already. After a few moments, I was led to open my Bible and read the Christmas story aloud, as recorded in Matthew and Luke. The literal sound of the words had a strong effect on me; it was an essentially liturgical time. This smallest of all possible meetings for worship was indeed covered.

The next morning, after chores were completed, I drove up to Swift Run Gap on the Skyline Drive. I parked the truck on the shoulder where the Appalachian Trail crosses the drive, shouldered my day pack, and set off toward an unfamiliar peak.

The day was not unrewarding. Although there were no views to compare with those at Bearfence Mountain, or bold deer like the whitetail I met at Byrd's Nest #4, there were hawks and woodpeckers, places to sit with views through bare-limbed trees of the play of sun and clouds throwing shadows across the mountains, plenty of homemade bread and tasty cheese for lunch, and pecans to shell for dessert. The world all around me vibrated with the news that God has come to be in the creation. The Creator has become united with the created. Bethlehem and Calvary are the endpoints of a single event: God with us, Immanuel. Calvary is the inevitable denouement of the incarnation that began at Bethlehem, and Calvary is of little importance unless the One who hung there was Christ Incarnate.

Bethlehem and Calvary were not frozen in time twenty centuries ago. The seed of Bethlehem is planted in each human heart, and we have the calling to nurture that seed as Mary nurtured the boy Jesus, in harmony with the will of God. If we do, then Christ is crucified in us as our old self dies and we rise with Him to a new life with the Father. That day, I prayed:

> Dear Lord, thank You for the gift of Yourself at Christmas. Grant that I may always keep the reality of your Presence in my heart and in my mind and allow myself to be guided and corrected and comforted and protected by that reality. I ask in Jesus' Name, amen.

Vocation and Competency

Once I was released into this new (to me) gospel ministry, the leadings and formal commitments continued one after another, with no perceptible break in between. After New Year's Day 1987, I returned the certificate for home visits in Charlottesville Meeting, and Friends then approved a certificate for my travel in the gospel ministry in North Carolina. This travel certificate meant a great deal to me, possibly even more than the one for New England in 1985. One reason why was that I now knew experientially the quality and intensity of experience that was opening up, while two years ago I was only guessing what travel in the ministry might be like. Another reason was the affirmation I felt by the meeting being clear to approve this certificate in light of my marital struggles.

In these events, including the core group/base community sense I wrote of earlier, I felt drawn to and bound up with Charlottesville Meeting in fresh and strong ways. One of the strong points I brought away from my Christmas Day retreat was Thomas Merton's emphasis on the vow of stability; a monk vows not to change monasteries simply because his first does not seem ideal but to move only when instructed to do so by his abbot.

After Bible study one evening, several Friends continued discussing spiritual matters. Three of us agreed to help one another discern, name and claim, and exercise our respective spiritual gifts. This seemed like the final step in the transition away from the Covenant Fellowship (Kara, Thom, Sam, and Tom) as my primary accountability group. That covenant group was no longer capable of serving in that way, and I saw the beginnings of a group that could do so better than my oversight committee.

I say this because these Friends shared a common Christian faith experience and therefore were closer to understanding my experiences and my motivations for desiring to develop and exercise those spiritual talents that had been entrusted to me. I hesitate to say "gifts," for ownership transfers in the act of giving, and I don't feel that is what has happened to me. In our culture, giving is understood to be permanent, whereas I feel that spiritual gifts are reclaimed by the Giver if not properly used.

Memoir of the Life and Religious Labors of Lloyd Lee Wilson

There had been a progression in my thinking from a period of assuming I made a great difference in any group of people with which I might be associated (this phase lasted many years) to a time of denying that I had much of any impact at all (this lasted a shorter time). Being willing and able to accept the clerkship of Ministry and Worship, which I had been asked recently to do, seemed linked to a third, more recent phase of recognizing that I had an impact and of taking responsibility for that impact in a wise manner.

Late in First Month 1987, I made a trip in the ministry to Friends Meeting of Washington (D.C.). Lisa Liske, Marshall Sutton, and I were the only vocal ministers in worship that morning. Marshall and Lisa gave Penington-like messages of real beauty and grace. I felt again that longing, a near envy of their state of grace that would bring out such beautiful ministry. It was finally given to me that different persons are given different kinds of grace—flavors as it were—for God's purposes and that we are not all able to sound like Marshall and Lisa because we are not all meant to by our Creator. This gave me considerable comfort. I hoped then to be able to give over this sense of being flawed and simply appreciate these other gifts in other people as they were shared and exercised. Thanks, God.

Back in Charlottesville, my vocal offering one First Day was a story by Lao Tzu about an old man and his son who had many adventures. After relating each adventure, the old man asks the village elders, "How can you tell whether this is good fortune or bad fortune?" I related this to my own condition of often being unable to tell whether what was happening to me was "good" or "bad." Luckily, we do not have to be able to discern end results directly. We have only to have faith that there is a Pole Star that gives direction, orientation, and structure to all of creation; after each disorienting experience, we have only to seek that Star that is seeking us, and somehow by that very double search the whole of creation is redeemed.

After the rise of meeting one First Day, an occasional attender took my hand and said, "You are the reason I come to meeting: to hear you speak." When I demurred politely, he insisted, "No, really! I come to hear what you have to say!" I disengaged myself as quickly as I could politely

Vocation and Competency

do so and moved on to other Friends. Only in retrospect could I absorb what he'd said. Powerful testimony! I prayed that neither he (nor anyone else) was ever led astray or misguided in any way by listening to my ministry or observing my life and witness.

I continued to reflect on my evolving relationship to Charlottesville Meeting. Friends were helping me accept, name, and claim my gifts and role in the meeting and were holding me accountable for doing my part responsibly. My concerns about speaking too often had been relieved. Many different Friends had volunteered affirmations of my vocal ministry and in many different settings; I could no longer deny that something special was at work through me (e.g., "When we first met, I did not like you, Lloyd Lee, but every time you spoke, in worship or in meeting for business, you spoke to my condition").

At the same time, a few trusted friends who were also Friends were helping me become aware of ways that my patterns of vocal ministry got in the way of communicating the gospel ("When you quote others so much . . ." or "Your ministry recently has not been closely connected to your own experiences"). I felt that something that had been good was now beginning to become better, a process made possible because I was now aware and accepting of its reality.

It was a joy to spend another weekend at a Pendle Hill retreat with Bill Taber in Second Month. The first evening I was content—even glad—that Bill closed our opening worship before I rose to offer a message (moments before, as I was already praying for faithfulness in delivering that message when he acted). Bill then read a passage by Tilden Edwards about orientation toward the spiritual life in which much of the imagery and metaphor were the same as the message I had been about to deliver. The message had been given without my need to speak, and I was at peace.

On the second day of the retreat, Bill asked if there were any last comments arising out of worship before he read some brief announcements and we adjourned. Kim Hollingsworth sang a song she'd been thinking of, but Bill said he felt there was another message and he was not clear to move on to the announcements. At this time, a young man from Sandwich Preparative Meeting shared some insights he'd gained from reading Emanuel Swedenborg. After that, Bill announced that he was still not clear to close, and in a moment Kim's father Ned shared an anecdote that had helped him decide about his own conscientious objector commitment in 1949.

By this time, I was beginning to think Bill had me in mind. "Surely," I thought, "he won't hesitate now to close meeting. But if he does, I must speak." Bill then announced that he was still waiting for a message, and I felt compelled to speak. I rose, and quaking interiorly if not exteriorly, spoke about gospel order as our response to God's initiative (the catechism's definition of covenant)—the good news. There can be no gospel order without the gospel—the good news that Christ came, arose, and has come again. The gospel must be personal, not merely that Christ is a Savior but that Christ is a Savior for me. When we open to that reality, we are indeed reoriented, and as a pile of iron filings under the influence of a magnet orient themselves toward its pole, every aspect of our life is oriented toward the Source of the gospel. The mark of the life lived in gospel order is not that it achieves certain things or even looks a certain way but that it points in every particular toward the good news— the gospel.

The body had been full of laughter during Ned Hollingsworth's story but was now covered with solemnity as I took my seat and we all settled back into worship. After a few minutes, Bill said quietly, "Now we can close." As Friends began to move around the room and begin conversations, I sought out Bill and asked him directly, "What just happened?" He looked at me with his gentle smile and said only, "Some things we should not talk about very much."

Frank Massey agreed to be my companion in the North Carolina ministry, and we went on retreat at Quaker Lake to begin preparing. We had put off the trip itself until the fall, which allowed my travel certificate to be considered at yearly meeting sessions in the summer. The leading seemed part and parcel of the healing process going on in me. The Lord continued to be able and desirous to use me for His work. Even as I came to face and accept my own brokenness, I was learning that God loves me anyway, as I am. At the same time, it seemed that the ministry that came through me was changing as I was changing, and all for the better. What happened in the fall would be significantly different than what might have happened had we taken the same trip and met the same people the previous winter.

Frank and I shared a desire to remind Friends of various flavors that they are more alike than they are different and that the similarities are more important than the differences. It seemed important to visit meetings and churches from all branches of Friends, if that could be arranged, and to encourage the meetings and churches we did visit to invite Friends of other flavors to join them in worshipping with us.

We also shared not knowing what we would say on the trip, or what purpose would be advanced, or how that would be accomplished. This was a familiar feeling for me, having gained seasoning from the New England journey and from my home visits, and I welcomed that uncertainty with a sense of expectation. For Frank it was largely a new experience, but he recognized this position as the correct one for us.

It seemed important to begin preparing early for this gospel labor. Preparing seemed so simple as to be a cliché: to become as centered, Spirit-led, and Spirit-fed as possible. Yet it is precisely the profoundly simple things that do not come about without attention to detail. Daily devotions, individual and group prayer, and time with Frank were all part of my preparation.

I needed to declutter my life and mind so that I would be sensitive to the gentle proddings of discernment and so that I didn't rush past opportunities in order to be present to and helpful to other people. I needed to build my confidence in God's loving guidance in my life so that I would dare to do and say the things God would have me do and say, neither adding to nor subtracting from the divine message. I needed to clarify God's witness in my life so that the Nouwen quote a Friend had given Kara and me would come true and words would be unnecessary.

As Easter 1987 approached, my reflections took note of much sadness, endings, and even symbolic death in my life. The overriding sensation was one of leaving the chrysalis: dying to the life of a caterpillar in order to be born into the life of a butterfly. Much of the life I had been leading was well suited to my previous condition, and some of it had been good in absolute terms. My condition had changed, and those things and people unable or unwilling to change with me had necessarily to be left behind.

> *As for the man who is weak in faith, welcome him, but not for disputes over opinions. One believes he may eat anything, while the weak man eats only vegetables. Let not him who eats despise him who abstains, and let not him who abstains pass judgment on him who eats, for God has welcomed him. Who are you to pass judgment on the servant of another? It is before his own master that he stands or falls.* (Romans 14:1–4a RSV)

This passage offers strong counsel not to disparage our brothers and sisters in Christ, no matter how different from us they may appear.

I changed my seat in meeting for worship one First Day in Fourth Month. I'd been a "back bencher" for a long time, sitting on the very back bench at one end of the meeting room. My overt reasons for sitting there had been to have adequate support for my back (those benches have higher backs than the ones away from the wall), a sounding board for my voice when I was exercised in the ministry, and the ability to see all the worshippers during meeting. I think an unspoken reason had been a certain (false?) humility and a reluctance to be seen as thinking of myself as central to the meeting.

This morning I sat in a new spot, on one of the benches nearest the middle of the room. I stayed there for worship and business meetings. Seated facing the clerk across an open space, I was now in a position to be seen easily. Those two front benches are not "facing benches" in any normal Quaker configuration or as other Charlottesville Friends would think of them. For me and God, however, they were the facing benches, and sitting there was acceptance of my responsibility toward God and the meeting. My responsibility to this meeting included being a leader in it, not only in my formal role as clerk of Ministry and Worship or in my words but also nonverbally, in the way I worshipped or attended to the business of the meeting. To sit in this new spot was a conscious choice, an acceptance of responsibility for the potential and reality of my presence in the meeting. I felt my actions were saying, "This is my

Vocation and Competency

practice; this is my faith. I accept responsibility for my witness in this faith community."

This sense of commitment seemed confirmed when a Friend called afterward to say that she had been too brief after the rise of worship when thanking me for my ministry. She added that she was grateful for my nonverbal ministry as well; the example she used was my continuing effort to be open to the leading of the Spirit in whatever we were doing as a group and in whatever was said. She had found my example helpful that day as she had been dealing with her own anger at something that had been said. She was seated in business meeting in a place where she could not have seen me had I been in my regular seat.

In a number of informal ways, individual Friends in Charlottesville were able to recognize my gifts and I could acknowledge that recognition. Sitting on the "facing bench" and hearing affirmation afterward were examples of that. The existence of my oversight committee and the way that new members of that committee had been provided as needed over the years was another. The monthly meeting was too fragmented spiritually to be able to recognize my ministry corporately. What I was already receiving in support was what the meeting could do. I realized that what I should be striving and praying for was that the meeting would be brought closer to God's will for it as a faith community—whatever that might mean for me.

Fourth Month 12 was Palm Sunday in the liturgical calendar. Near the close of worship, I was led to ministry starting with a recollection of Jesus on the hill overlooking Jerusalem and weeping. I recounted His activity during the days after Palm Sunday when he taught during the day in Jerusalem, to the great approval of the people, but left each night to sleep in Bethany. The people of Jerusalem were willing to shout "Hallelujah!" and to call him a great teacher but were unwilling to find a place for him in their homes. We were like the people of Jerusalem, I said; we were unwilling to let Jesus into our hearts to dwell and abide with us. When we did, God would change us completely. Then what we did would be holy, and what was holy was what we would do.

I continued to pray for Christ's Presence in my life and His continued teaching in my heart. I felt that my prayer was acceptable to

God and that my stiff-necked past was forgiven. Conviction and convincement may be nearly instantaneous, but conversion may take years. I felt that the work being done in me was conversion of my old life into a new life. I was eager for the process to move along but was beginning to understand it enough that I was not dismayed that it was moving slowly. God's will, according to God's plan, in God's time.

One First Day in Fifth Month, I was engaged in vocal prayer and felt constrained to pray on my knees. Having recently spent devotional time reading Samuel Bownas, I was keenly aware of his admonitions against unneeded gestures. However, the prayer given to me was not one I could pray while standing. Once I gave myself up to it, there was no nervousness or hesitation, and peace flowed like a river when I resumed my seat. Only one Friend said anything afterward, simply commenting that the meeting must have been powerful for me, as it had been for her. She had spent most of the meeting in a deep mystical experience of being bonded to the meeting community and of having those persons bonded to her. Love flowed through her so strongly, she said later, that her only possible response was to cry. This was a powerful experience for both of us.

At the 1987 Friends United Meeting (FUM) Triennial sessions, Jan Hoffman shared a story of the recent New England Yearly Meeting Committee Day in Hartford, Connecticut. A faith and witness group made up of Friends wanting to encourage travel in the ministry or under a concern met that day, and Friends began to share their personal stories and motivations for attending that gathering. One couple described themselves as new to Quakerism, having started attending meeting only two years earlier. Shortly after they first came to worship, they heard two out-of-town visitors would meet with Friends in the Hartford meeting house one weekday evening. This couple decided to attend that gathering, and they were impressed that the visitors had no agenda or planned program; they had come to town with the simple expectation that something good would happen if they were faithful.

The events of that evening had so impressed this couple that they decided to become Quakers. They were at the faith and witness group's meeting to help this kind of visitation occur more generally. When Jan

Vocation and Competency

told them that the visitors were Kara Cole and Lloyd Lee Wilson, the couple replied, "Perhaps those were their names, but that wasn't important. Their witness was important." In such a manner, years later and hundreds of miles distant, God affirmed the faithfulness of that journey. I felt that God allowing me to hear this at that time was also the affirmation I yearned to have of the intention to travel in the gospel ministry in North Carolina.

I had a dream one night at the triennial that lingered in the background of my mind. In the dream, I had gone to Louise Wilson and asked her permission to transfer my membership from Charlottesville Monthly Meeting to Virginia Beach Friends Meeting. That transfer would mean moving from Baltimore Yearly Meeting to NCYM(C), thus leaving FUM and FGC for Conservative Friends. The dream raised questions of my true commitment to Charlottesville Friends Meeting and of my true unity with either the Hicksite or the Gurneyite faith traditions. Was I forcing myself to feel committed to Charlottesville, and was this dream my deeper self, warning the rest of me that my true commitment was elsewhere? I certainly felt estranged from the center-less faith of many non-Christian Friends and uncomfortable with the way in which many Gurneyite pastoral Friends had become acculturated to Protestant forms and beliefs.

The Richmond Declaration of Faith of 1887 was a focus of dissension all week, despite the efforts of many people over the previous eighteen months to keep that from happening. Southwest Yearly Meeting representatives pressed for a reaffirmation of the Richmond Declaration by the triennial, and Friends from East Coast yearly meetings spoke strongly against it. No unity seemed possible, even though one evening we stayed in session until after midnight, adjourning only when the Guilford College security guard showed up to lock the building.

As Friends made their way to the exits, numerous persons could be heard questioning why FUM should continue to exist if we could not agree on a statement of faith. How could we unite on mission or any other work if we could not agree on what we believed? Some of these Friends came over to where Kate Newman and I were sitting to labor with us or to say that a schism was now inevitable.

Kate and I ended up in a long conversation with Chuck Fager, Ann Thomas and her daughter Helen, Johan Maurer, Mark Minear, and Tom Klaus. We labored with one another until 2:00 a.m., frankly and forcefully but in love, looking for a way to preserve an organization that seemed to each of us worth saving. We found unity on a single sentence we had written that described the reality of FUM and those Friends who gathered to do its work. This seemed to us much more useful than wrangling over longer descriptions of what Friends in FUM yearly meetings ought to believe.

Tom Klaus and I presented the "Two O'Clock Minute" at the next day's business session. It was approved, everyone seemed satisfied, and the triennial avoided making history. I was grateful to have been a part of bringing that minute to the light of day and grateful that it seemed to have helped FUM through a difficult time. Nevertheless, I was disheartened by both parties to this dispute. Those demanding a specific profession of Christian beliefs had forgotten that Truth can never be adequately be expressed in words, and those who took umbrage with the Richmond Declaration or any similar statement were for the most part simply upset with Christian language, not with the attempt to confine Truth to any finite set of finite words. Perhaps, I thought, I really was supposed to become a Conservative Friend, in spite of the distance between the closest monthly meeting and my home. I felt I would have to sit with this very attentively.

Back in Charlottesville, Friends began to express similar tensions between Christians and non-Christians. I became aware of this when a frequent attender shared during worship that he was concerned that "the humanist faction in meeting" would "dilute" the message of Christ so that His divinity would be missed. He had considerably more to say, to much the same effect. It was very troubling to me that such name-calling was beginning in our meeting, particularly in meeting for worship. Up till then, Charlottesville Friends had been remarkably free of Christian-humanist tensions (under any label), and I had been thankful that our high mutual regard had given us tolerance and respect for one another and one another's theologies. It seemed that time of mutual respect might be coming to an end.

Vocation and Competency

Soon afterward, my oversight committee told me some Friends might ask the meeting to withdraw the certificate it had approved for my ministry in North Carolina. Apparently, Charlottesville Friends were not as supportive of my faith and work in the ministry as I had thought them to be. I was not sure of the basis for the discontent—perhaps it was as straightforward and fundamental as my outspoken Christianity. As it turned out, the topic was not mentioned in meeting for business, so nothing happened immediately. This was, however, a harbinger of things to come.

Over the rest of the summer, I wrestled with the tension between the Spirit I felt among Conservatives and the expressions of the Spirit among Charlottesville Friends. Charlottesville was affiliated with both FGC and FUM —and I was finding I had not just less and less unity but active disharmony with these two branches of Friends. As I said to a Friend, where FUM or FGC Friends and I differed, I often wished they were more like me. Where I differed from Conservatives, I often wished I were more like them.

Is it better to be a member of a nearby faith community with which I had little unity or of a more distant community with which I was in more harmony and from which I felt more nurture? In which setting did God want to work through me? Where was my witness most faithful and most visible? In which locus was I being obedient?

I was reminded of the words of Miguel de Unamuno: "May God deny you peace but grant you glory." Christ leads us out of safe harbors to the seas where storm winds blow. If I transferred to Virginia Beach in hopes of a safe harbor where I would be nurtured, it was certain that He would lead me out to some other labor. Whether I went or stayed, however, as I reminded myself, *My grace is sufficient for thee* (2 Corinthians 12:9 KJV). The places God wished to send me were the places I should be content to go. For the time being, it seemed I should be content to be placed among Charlottesville Friends.

During the 1987 NCYM(C) sessions, Fran Taber spoke on the rhythms of Quaker life, comparing them with the Rule of Saint Benedict. Her comments on stability in particular hit home and bore in on me a fresh sense of the value of staying where I was. Deborah Shaw of

Friendship Meeting read a Howard Thurman quote in one of her reports that said each spirit has in its immediate surroundings exactly the sustenance it needs for its right growth. I prayed that the Lord would grant this for me in the Charlottesville meeting.

There were four points of teaching during the NCYM(C) sessions that I found personally applicable, even though I was not a member:

1. *Stability*—Until I received clear guidance to change, Charlottesville Friends Meeting should be my faith community.
2. *Commission*—I was charged to witness publicly to the gospel, in my home meeting and especially while traveling.
3. *Inward workings of Christ*—The troubled times I often felt, when I was most uncertain that I was doing anything worthwhile spiritually, were signs of the inward working of Christ, who was calling me forth and making me whole.
4. *Generations*—In the past year I'd passed sufficiently through the age forty transition to identify more fully than ever with Louise Wilson and David and Mae Brown and to see without longing or regret the generational distance between myself and the generation of the twenty-somethings. It all felt rightly ordered.

Meanwhile, my Charlottesville oversight committee was true to their stated intention of taking a stronger role, asking difficult questions, and refusing to acquiesce to just any response I might make. It felt very good. It was difficult for me to communicate clearly to the committee my sense that, however difficult the next weeks might be, with Baltimore's yearly meeting sessions, Asa's departure for Florida to live with his mother, and my fortieth birthday all coming within a month of each other, I had full confidence in a promise of wholeness afterward. The committee seemed to feel that if I were not centered on the coming pain of these three difficult transitions, I was denying their strength and reality in an unhealthy way. All of this was hard work. I am grateful for the new attitude of the committee and their willingness to put this effort into my care and nurture. I felt that as they learned, in the months to come, how

Vocation and Competency

to hold my feet to the fire, they would be increasingly important to my spiritual growth and faithfulness.

During Baltimore Yearly Meeting's sessions, the appointed clearness committee met with Frank Massey and me about our leading to gospel ministry in North Carolina. I had hoped for a searching clearness process—not inquisitorial but deep in the Spirit—but this was not to be. There were questions about the mechanics of the journey and about our reasons for choosing North Carolina but none of the bright searchlight I felt when sitting with, for example, Bill Taber. It was evidence of growth that they attempted a clearness process at all rather than just receiving my request and forwarding it to the yearly meeting for approval. The yearly meeting approved endorsing Charlottesville's certificate. As in 1985, there was no discussion. I wondered how many Friends understood what they were doing and how many were simply following a policy of "live and let live."

I was lifted to my feet during the closing worship of Baltimore Yearly Meeting sessions to speak on 2 Corinthians 12:9. Another Friend spoke later in the meeting, objecting to the use of "Lord" to refer to Christ—finding it unsupported exegetically and unacceptable personally. These words seemed to drain power from the meeting. This Friend approached me after worship and within a few moments was yelling at me about my starting a new separation among Friends. It was quite painful and highlighted our broken state as a religious society, unable to hear one another's vocabulary with generosity and inclusiveness.

I had been aware for some time of the need for vocal ministry during the first part of worship when our children were with us but had not been released into that ministry myself—and *very* few others had spoken during that time, either. Soon after we settled into worship one First Day in Ninth Month, I was brought to my feet with words to this effect:

> It is difficult to understand why there should be a drought, or why it should end with four straight days of rain that bring more precipitation than the previous four months. We can only have faith that God's plan is being worked out.
>
> It is like walking through a dark forest holding our mother's or father's hand. The path is rough and difficult, with many

roots, stones, and low branches. To the side we see a meadow with bright sunshine and lush grass, or a hill that seems to beg to be climbed. Our parent keeps us on this cloudy, narrow path, and we can't see why. Mother (or Father), keep us moving toward the destination—thy destination—that we can't see or even properly imagine.

The opening retreat for the Baltimore Yearly Meeting's Spiritual Formation Program was held in Ninth Month 1987. In the retreat's opening worship-sharing, I shared around the transition from being a minister to being an elder, which had been in my thoughts for the previous month or so. A minister stands in direct relationship to God; an elder stands in direct relationship to a faith community. I was becoming an elder not because my relationship to God was less important or less strong but because that relationship was becoming much clearer. Because I was (literally) more confident in and of my vertical relationship to God, I was freer to build up my horizontal relationships with God's people. My own spiritual well-being was more and more intimately tied up in the well-being of my faith community.

If I were to choose a book in the Bible as my personal theme over the previous year, it would be Galatians, for I had come to know the freedom of the gospel—the good news that God loved me unconditionally. I was much freer to be exactly myself because I recognized that that was exactly the person God loved. In the presence of that love, I was much freer to love other people as they were without insisting that they change to meet my needs or expectations. I love because I am loved. We say that God forgives us because we first forgive other people, but can it be with forgiveness as with love—that we are able to forgive because we recognize that God has first forgiven us?

On the second day of this retreat, we were asked to write a personal 'credo' and examine it for inconsistencies—the areas of inconsistency were probably areas of needed or current growth. I'd been attracted to the Apostles' Creed for the previous eight or ten months, and so I began there and made modifications and additions. I've added some comments reflecting my current thinking; these are inside square brackets in the text that follows.

Vocation and Competency

I believe in God the Father/Mother Almighty, Maker of heaven and earth: God is One, infinite and without limit, Creator of all the universes, omnipotent, omniscient, and ubiquitous (this does not mean God imposes predestination of any sort on any part of creation). God is Person yet is far beyond conceptions of personhood as gender-linked. Humans are made in the image of God, and all the best in humanity is a reflection of the totality that is God.

and in Jesus Christ God's only Son our Lord: For me, Jesus of Nazareth is/was/will be the Christ, God's own Self given to this creation to reconcile it to the Creator. This cosmos-changing event is unique in this creation, though universal in its effect and infinite in its manifestations. Wherever the Christ is recognized [in Christian settings or elsewhere], S/He is proclaimed as very God of very God and Lord of Creation.

who was conceived by the Holy Spirit: Jesus of Nazareth was the Christ, very God of very God. He was not merely an extraordinary human being, but also divine. [Scripture proposes several different timelines about when this divinity was accomplished or activated, which remains a personal choice for the believer.]

born of the Virgin Mary, Jesus of Nazareth was fully human, born of a flesh-and-blood mother. Whether or not Mary was a virgin is not important to my faith. [Years after this exercise, I became aware of the tremendous irony of the comma after "Mary," which passes over Jesus' human life as if it did not matter.]

suffered under Pontius Pilate, was crucified, dead, and buried: As a fully human being, Jesus shared fully in the human condition. He shared all human emotions, including true suffering during the Passion and crucifixion. Jesus actually died on the cross and was buried as a dead man would be buried. His suffering was total, His sacrifice was complete, His faithfulness total. [Jesus was crucified as an enemy of the empire (the domination system), not sacrificed as an atonement for human sin.]

on the third day He arose from the dead, ascended into heaven and sitteth on the right hand of God Almighty: The resurrection was real, total, and complete. He has come back from the dead and is not visible among us today only because He continued to heaven—which by implication is a real place (though not necessarily in this universe). [The resurrection was real, total, and complete. We know this not because we couldn't find a body but because we have encountered the living Christ.]

from whence He ~~shall~~ [has] come [to teach His people Himself and] to judge the quick and the dead: Christ has already returned from heaven and is among us today, teaching all who acknowledge and will accept divine guidance. Christ is the final arbiter of good and evil; it is God's standard, and not our own, to which we are all held accountable. God is Lord of life and death and everything else in creation, and all persons throughout eternity are accountable to God.

I believe in the Holy Spirit: The Holy Spirit is the spirit of God, even Christ, who can speak to our condition and who has come to teach willing people directly and inwardly.

The holy catholic church: There is one *church universal*, made up of all who acknowledge and accept Christ, and that church has the special blessing of Christ's Presence.

the communion of saints: There is a special fellowship among believers. [This is the spiritual gathering that one feels at certain times of souls living and dead, present and distant, gathered in worship—what Bill Taber sometimes called the Gathering of Ministers and Elders that is always in session.]

the forgiveness of sins: God does not hold grudges eternally but forgives us immediately. We feel this release as soon as we acknowledge our errors and our need for metanoia—a complete change of heart.

the resurrection of the body: This old body, made new in ways that I cannot know ahead of time and which I would not now understand if I were told, will be the seat and center of my awareness when I am resurrected. [On this point, my understanding has since changed dramatically. There is resurrection, there is life everlasting—but I no longer believe that it will involve this present body of mine.]

and the life everlasting: We will all be raised up into eternal life. Before God every knee will bow, and Divine Harmony will prevail universally. We will be lifted out of time to be eternally with our Creator. [I now place this event not "out of time" but in the present time. We know a new Life, which is Eternal because it is in harmony with the eternal Creator, when we turn our hearts toward that harmony as our only goal.]

The time had come for Frank Massey and me to set out on our gospel ministry in North Carolina. My journal for that trip follows.

Traveling in the Ministry in North Carolina: Journal Excerpts

Tenth Month 8, 1987. This trip in the gospel ministry, over twelve months in the preparation, is finally about to begin. I have nurtured the leading, held myself accountable to my faith community in determining how to follow this leading, and done my best to prepare myself mentally, physically, and spiritually. Now it is in the hands of God; there is nothing more for Frank and me to do except to carry out our itinerary—unless the Lord leads us in some other direction—and to be faithful to the promptings of the Holy Spirit at each moment.

I made it to Frank and Beth's in time to break bread with them at their evening meal; afterward, Frank and I had an opportunity together before retiring for the night. It took us a good six hours to get to Virginia Beach the next day. The journey gave us time to get more familiar with one another's rhythms and our spiritual condition—a time of tuning ourselves to one another that advanced this ministry significantly. When we got to Virginia Beach, Frank and I took a long walk and then went over to the meeting house ahead of time. Frank had a chance to see the room where we would gather, and I got to reacquaint myself with it.

Charlie Ansell directed early arrivals downstairs and shut the doors to the meeting room so Frank and I could have a period of prayer and preparation. This was covered time; we were both exercised in vocal prayer and felt the Presence and blessing of the Holy Spirit on this room, on this group of people about to be gathered, and on this labor which we had begun. About a dozen people from Virginia Beach Friends Meeting came. Frank and I had said from the beginning that it was our belief that the people who needed to come or who were supposed to come would, so we were freed from disappointment that it wasn't a larger crowd.

As covered as our time of preparation had been, when the meeting began we had a significant amount of work to do. For myself, the work was first centering down, then giving up the idea of having a profound message to give, and finally giving up the fear of not having anything to say at all. I was helped by remembering that Job Scott once went to fifteen meetings in a row while traveling in the ministry before he felt released to speak in any. I eventually gave up to the will of God and received some peace of mind from this. After a little while, Frank stood, and my heart was filled with spontaneous prayer for him and in support of his ministry. Frank later had vocal prayer to offer, and it was deep and accessible.

I was given the story of Naaman, and, with the sense of an elder brother giving advice, I rose to share that story—to remind Friends of the danger of taking the long journey we were all on and then being unwilling to do the things that the Lord called us to do because they seemed to be different from what we wanted to do, too trivial, or didn't suit what we knew to be our gifts or station in life. I alluded to Philip, who had been chosen by the apostles in the early church to be a deacon—a waiter of tables—and yet did not hesitate at the prompting of the Lord to go up to the Ethiopian's chariot and be an evangelist. This felt like acceptable service, although the strange feeling of giving counsel continued.

Vocation and Competency

After meeting for worship ended, Frank and I spontaneously went to each of the people there to shake their hands and speak a word of greeting. I was drawn to a Friend who had seemed afflicted when I first saw him come into the meeting house and who now sat with his arms and legs crossed, hunched over as if he were extremely cold even though he had on a bulky pullover sweater and the meeting house was comfortably warm. When I asked him if he were all right, he said, "Yes, I'm fine," which was so at odds with every physical and spiritual indication he was giving out that I took it to mean that he did not want to talk to me about it, and so I went on.

After everyone else had gone, Frank and I spent a few moments sharing our experience in meeting for worship, and Charlie Ansell joined us. Frank had felt a sense of disease in the meeting and asked Charlie if there were any indication of that. Charlie spoke first of the Friend who had appeared so cold, whose condition was such that Charlie and Jan wanted to speak with Frank and me about it in an opportunity (to which we readily agreed), and then of a couple who had made public two nights previously that they had separated and then had each resigned from Ministry and Oversight.

Tenth Month 10, 1987. We spent Seventh Day morning in a long opportunity with a married couple who was wrestling with the mental and emotional condition of another member of the meeting who was involving them in his troubles. The four of us began with prayer directly after breakfast; when we rose, it was time for lunch. Frank and I were able to affirm that these Friends had done the right thing and had involved the meeting in an appropriate way all along the line. We were all heartened to realize this trial had in fact drawn their family closer together and pointed out the importance of attending to the condition of their family and family affairs. It was close work and not pleasant, but it was joyful in the sense of bearing one another's burdens, of feeling that we were useful, that here was good solid work that could not have been done unless Frank and I had been faithful in carrying out the call to travel in the ministry in this place at this time.

After lunch Frank and I drove to Woodland, where we met with Bob and Barbara Gosney. After an hour or so of quiet conversation, we walked the block to Cedar Grove Meeting House, where Rich Square Monthly Meeting is held.

About twenty-two Friends, from eight to eighty years old, shared a wonderful potluck dinner in "the lunch room," a separate building. We then moved to the library in the meeting house since the heating system in the meeting room was not functioning, and Frank and I settled immediately into worship. Here in Rich Square, it felt like we were in the traces alone: Friends were waiting for us to perform ministry for them. This was in contrast to Virginia Beach, where I had had the sense that we were all doing ministry together. This feeling of being alone really did, in Elias Hicks's words, "make hard work for the poor minister[s]." I was brought to my knees in vocal prayer about midway through the meeting, which I felt was acceptable service, and was grateful to be prayed through.

Sometime later, Frank rose in ministry, which also ended in a prayer. There was some hesitation in his delivery partway through. I learned later that he had a hesitation in his leading at that point, not that he had outrun his Guide but that he was left without knowing how he was supposed to finish. Later, I was called to my feet to speak of the old definition of a Christian, attributed to G. K. Chesterton, as one who is completely fearless, absurdly happy, and in constant trouble—the first two relating directly to how we are as little children but the last referring to a life lived constantly at the edge of our faith, not necessarily in constant trouble with the civil authorities (although that can be true also). It was a new insight to me, and I was happy to have been given this understanding.

In both meetings, I spoke in a style that was somewhat unfamiliar, closer to a preaching style than I ordinarily approach. I didn't have any feeling positive or negative about this change

Vocation and Competency

other than to notice it. I felt led both times, and I felt both times that I'd been faithful to a sincere leading.

After worship, we walked back to the Gosneys' house and talked about various topics. Gwendy Gosney stayed up with us, and it was a pleasure to get to know her a little better. We have similar tastes in music, and I was able to empathize with her sense of being a little isolated in a small town without used bookstores and with only a country music radio station. As we retired, Frank and I talked briefly about the sense we'd had of tonight's meeting. Even though it would not have changed the response very much at Rich Square, we thought we ought to do a short introduction before meeting for worship on the rest of this journey.

Tenth Month 11, 1987. On First Day, we once again gathered in the library because the heating system in the main meeting room was still not working. Sabbath Day school was first, based on the International Sunday School lesson for the day. George Parker offered Frank and me an opportunity to speak, but neither of us felt led to do so. When we gathered for worship, I experienced a renewed time of "the Inward work of Christ," to use Bill Taber's term. It was clear to me from the very beginning that I was not going to be exercised in public ministry that morning but had considerable interior work to do.

After worship, eleven of us went back to the Gosneys' for lunch, which lasted until four o'clock. The five men spent most of that time sitting in the dining room after all the dishes had been cleared away, talking about the various journeys that had led them to live where they are now, their reaction to Woodland and Rich Square Friends, and why that experience spoke to them so strongly. It was a time when we could be open and honest, without pretense or facade. I was very grateful for that time and for the sense of covering—of the timelessness of our afternoon together. It seemed afterward that this conversation with men Friends was one of the main reasons we had been led to come to Woodland. For me, another was the contact with Gwendy

Gosney; I hoped to follow up our conversations that weekend with a letter of encouragement.

We spent that evening with Frank's father, Lloyd Massey. Lloyd Massey told us a story about Thomas and Ann Fisher, who were visiting his home when Lloyd's father died. The elder Massey had had a heart attack several days before and was obviously failing in one bedroom, and the Fishers were in another. They came into the living room, and Ann said to Thomas, "Thomas, perhaps we should go and come back another time, when we would not be such a burden on the family." Thomas Fisher laid his hand on his wife's knee and said, "No, let us wait a little while." Shortly after that, Lloyd Massey's father died, and the Fishers were able to be a real comfort to the new widow and her family during the next hours and days. Lloyd was pointing out to us the importance of being open to the promptings of the Holy Spirit about what to do in unusual situations.

Tenth Month 12, 1987. We traveled to the home of the clerk of Wilmington Monthly Meeting, only to find that despite our initial conversations, a follow-up letter later on, and a telephone conversation with him last week, he had not made arrangements for us to meet any Wilmington Friends that evening; he and his wife had plans to go to the ballet. Frank and I took a walk to sort through this information, seeking guidance about right action. We were easy eventually to leave Wilmington without meeting with Friends there, explaining to the clerk that we did not seek to impose ourselves on them or to cause them to change their plans. We drove on to Ralph and Patty Levering's house in Davidson, arriving about 10:30 p.m. After these events, I thought a lot about Lloyd Massey's story.

Tenth Month 13, 1987. Our breakfast conversation with Patty Levering centered on the call of Friends to be indifferent to their material well-being while putting high priority on their spiritual condition. The state of being indifferent does not require tremendous attention to being as poor as possible and

Vocation and Competency

does allow one to achieve that level of material well-being that seems most effortless—that distracts one least from the promptings of the Holy Spirit. We are not to try to cling to the mountaintop experience but to use it as a guide and inspiration for everyday life down in the valleys, which is where we are expected to lead the life of Christian devotion and Christian service. We had extended periods of prayer with Patty before and after lunch, punctuated by some quiet discussion about the basis of decision making in the Spirit and possible new areas of service for each of us.

We had dinner with members of the Charlotte meeting and their daughters. It was a happy occasion for all, with lots of laughter and good-natured joking back and forth. We then went on to the meeting house, where fifteen Friends gathered in addition to Frank and myself. We settled into worship after a short introduction about what we were about and what we expected to happen this evening. Early in the worship there was vocal prayer, which moved the meeting to a much deeper and more centered spot in the Spirit. I was very aware of the spiritual presence of those Friends who had said they would be praying for us, and I felt companioned, supported, and lifted up.

I was exercised in the ministry about the love of the faith community and the importance of being open to one another—loving and being loved as we are in our actuality and totality. Partway through, I found the force of the message pulled right out from me, as if there were a drain in the soles of my feet and someone had taken the plug out of the drain. So, I stopped and sat down. Frank said later that he had been, in his words "right with me" through the message and was surprised that I quit when I did and that my body language changed the rest of the meeting. I did go through a time of searching to figure out whether I had been unfaithful. I don't think so—I just had the message taken away for some reason.

After the rise of meeting, we continued in our places to answer questions about our leading and how we had decided to come to North Carolina, which seemed helpful, and then rose for general socializing. Frank remarked after we got home that it seemed to him that a lot of things were happening to me on this journey. They seem to be good for me; I do hope they are not interfering with the ministry, but there is not anything I can do about that except to be faithful and face these changes, walk through them as obediently as I can, and trust that that is what the Lord wants me to do right now.

Tenth Month 14, 1987. Our next stop was Greensboro. We arrived to find that the New Garden Meeting House was without heat (an apparent theme for the journey). We took a walk around the Guilford campus and then settled under the trees near the New Garden Meeting for a time of worship and prayer. We had discerned that we weren't taking enough time to worship by ourselves each day, and this was an opportunity to do that. It was quiet, covered, precious worship, after which I felt much more at ease about how this evening's activities would prosper.

The heat was fixed in time, and we went inside. Friends from about four different monthly meetings, pastoral and Conservative, attended; we had twenty-one Friends plus Frank and me gathered in the Brotherhood Room of the meeting house. Frank and I gave a longer introduction this time, describing a little about what the intent of the journey was in terms of expectancy, obedience, and sensitivity to leadings and adding that we hoped Friends would share in the worship and in the ministry and reflect afterward on how the Spirit was at work in their lives. Worship lasted about forty-five minutes, in which time one Friend offered a song and I was moved to vocal ministry on George Fox's phrase "Christ has come to teach His people Himself," emphasizing the roles of Christ as Teacher and ourselves as students willing to learn and all of creation being His people. Frank was moved to petitionary prayer for God's blessing on each of us in our desire to learn and to become more of what God dreams for us. A period of reflection followed worship, in which several Friends recounted taking the risk to share about Friends and to invite individuals to their meeting for

Vocation and Competency

worship. A couple of Friends expressed their gratefulness for the faithfulness of Frank and me for taking the risk of coming on this journey of ministry. Several Friends spoke to Frank later about how good it was for four meetings in the area to get together like this; they had not done it in the past and felt like they ought to do it in the future.

A Friendship member offered a reflection on Acts 5:15, which describes early Christians carrying their sick to places where Peter's shadow might fall on them so that they might be healed. He had heard from an old preacher that at the time of day when Peter would be doing this, the sun would be in his eyes and his shadow would be falling behind him, so that Peter would not know where his shadow was falling and in fact might be unaware of which people were being healed, or even that people were being healed, unless someone brought him a report later. The point was that when we are faithful in ministry we do not know where our shadow falls. I felt that we've been faithful, that our time of worship outside the meeting house was a time of reconsecration and rededication, and that this journey continues to be a journey of faithfulness and obedience in which the will of the Lord is being carried out.

Tenth Month 15, 1987. We got to Jamestown Meeting a little before 10 o'clock and had some good discussion with the pastor. Friends here see themselves as different from a major thread running through North Carolina Yearly Meeting (FUM). They viewed with disapproval the report that one pastor in Deep River Quarter within the past month has "sprinkled a baby"— performed an infant baptism—in order to get the parents into the meeting as members. There was also discomfort at the type of prayer that went on at a recent ministers' association meeting because it was interspersed with ejaculations and assurances from all over the room: "Yes, Lord!" "Amen!" etc.

We didn't dwell on negative topics for long, though. We spent most of our time talking about methods of church outreach, what kind of role seemed right for Jamestown Friends, and how Friends might liberate one another to do the kind of ministry that is released from other career demands and compatible with their sense of an enabling and equipping ministry. I am very much in harmony with these Friends and their attempts to be released for the work for which they are called while working within the pastoral system where they also feel called. I feel very clear of working within the pastoral system; it is not a place where I am called, but I understand what it feels like to be called to a particular situation and to want to be as faithful as possible in that situation, and I think that's what they are feeling.

Frank and I set off for White Plains in the afternoon. White Plains Meeting has about 350 members on the mailing list, and about 90 persons attend a typical meeting for worship. We had five adults, not counting the day care person, who had about five children in tow. We met in a small room in the back of the building and were blessed by a real sense of the Presence. I sat on Frank's right in response to his request—he did not know why I should sit there other than that the Spirit seemed to flow better when I did—and it seemed to me to be good and deep worship. Frank was again moved to vocal prayer about transforming power. I spoke in a more informal way than I had been doing, starting with the old hymn "I Love to Tell the Story" and talking about my inability to speak the story without first surrendering and being transformed in such a way that my life is the story or points directly at the story. Other Friends later spoke in the meeting both about transforming power and the willingness to surrender to it. After worship, we retired to the kitchen and had tea and coffee and cookies. The children had a good time, and the adults talked for another hour.

Tenth Month 16, 1987. This morning, Frank and I drove to the home of Jeff and Trish Seben in Carroll County, Virginia. Jeff was working two small orchards (which he bought from Sam Levering) and Trish teaches school, and together they raise their children. This was Jeff's first year as an apple grower; he had about seven acres of full-sized trees. We helped pick a couple of

Vocation and Competency

trees and afterward walked through the orchard talking about apples, the American Friends Service Committee, and Friends in general. Picking apples, Frank said, brought the fifteenth chapter of John to mind; pruning does not always bring forth a bigger crop but a better crop.

Jeff and Frank and I discussed the deep rift that currently exists between American Friends Service Committee and North Carolina Friends; we could not see any way that rift could be healed. We felt there was still a need and desire for service opportunities for Friends in the North Carolina area and that it might be a wise thing to begin a regional service organization close to the grassroots, which would provide direct service opportunities for young Friends, old Friends, and like-minded persons. In the event of national service, or mandatory national service, such an organization might be a real asset for Friends.[16]

Frank and I went on to the Parkway Cooperative, where we found Sam Levering helping grade apples. I was surprised that he knew my name and where I lived and had some nice things to say about my ministry. He was impressed that Frank and I were traveling in the ministry and encouraged us in that endeavor; he was discouraging about starting out in the apple business right now because the profit margin was very small.

Tenth Month 17, 1987. We drove to Seth Hinshaw's house near Asheboro and spent the morning in conversation and worship with Seth. He has recently published a book on the spoken ministry among Friends, and some points he raised in that book about the traveling ministry, preparation, and vocal prayer provided the springboard for our discussion. I was again impressed by that sense of being at home with one's self and of being unrushed that has characterized the deepest and most tender Friends I have met on this journey. Seth was as interested in hearing our views as he was in giving us his, in a self-effacing manner that encouraged us to a similar humility.

We drove on to Chatham in the late afternoon, where we stayed with Jim Hood and Sara Beth Terrell. After supper, we went over to the meeting house fully expecting that we might have a total attendance of five: Frank and me and Sara Beth and Jim and their daughter Julie. To our joy, there were 21 people in addition to Frank and me in attendance, including Alfred Newlin, who came in after we had settled. Frank and I sat on a front pew while everyone else sat on the pews behind us, so we couldn't see who came in and I had no idea Alfred was there until later in the meeting when he spoke.

Frank offered ministry on the fifteenth chapter of John. He began by reading the chapter in its entirety, then described the process of pruning as bringing us to be producers of better fruit, not necessarily of more fruit. I was very happy to hear this message come to fruition and to feel this different style of ministry from Frank, much more declarative than usual. It seemed very deeply led.

When Alfred Newlin spoke, I recognized his voice immediately. His message was tender and graceful. Two other Friends spoke, one about Jesus as the lighthouse who we very much need and one about Jesus and God speaking to us all the time, not just in the thunderstorm or other dramatic moments of our life. Alfred rose a second time, later in the meeting, to speak about prayer and Scripture and the value of spending time in retirement, prayer, and Scripture at the beginning of the day and at the end of the day.

Near the end of the meeting, I was brought to my knees in vocal prayer, which must have been an unusual sight for other Friends since in effect I disappeared from view in front of them, but it felt like acceptable service. Frank and I turned to one another to close meeting at exactly the same moment, which was an indication of how much closer we've been drawn over the course of this journey.

The discussion after worship was brief and fairly quiet; it seemed that Friends were still in a centered state. Frank described a little bit about our travels, and Alfred Newlin made a comment or two. All in all, it was the most talkative I've ever seen

Vocation and Competency

Alfred. We then adjourned to refreshments, and the conversation was immediately intense and loud and joyful and happy. I talked with several Friends but spent most of my time talking and playing word games with a young girl named Amber. Always when I am engaged like this now, I wonder whether this is someone who in future years may either take up the ministry or support the ministry, in part out of remembrance of a childhood experience. I pray that each of these children might be touched by the Holy Spirit.

Tenth Month 18, 1987. We arose this morning for a leisurely breakfast before First Day activities began. Frank seemed troubled in spirit, and when I talked with him about it, he said he felt he should stay in Chatham rather than go to Chapel Hill this morning. We held this possibility in silence for a short time without much clarity and decided to reconsider after I got back from a prayer meeting with Sara Beth.

Sara Beth and I and two other Friends gathered for an hour of open worship, centered sharing, and prayer. Afterward, Frank and I considered further whether or not he should go to Chapel Hill. Frank concluded, since he had made a commitment and was not clearly led to stay away, that he should go.

Meeting for worship at Chapel Hill was well attended; there were perhaps 50 persons present. Reading briefly in the Epistle to the Hebrews brought me great comfort, and I centered down easily and quickly to a place of consolation and real joy at the way the Lord has led us through this week and taught us things that we needed to know while bringing blessings to the people among whom we traveled.

I was given vocal ministry on invitation as a prime characteristic of our spiritual life: the invitation of Christ to us, "Come unto Me"; our invitation to Christ in answering His knock on the door of our hearts; and the invitation that our lives should be to others to enter into the more abundant life that has come to us as a result of accepting and giving those invitations to God. After I finished, there was deep and centered testimony on the words "In the beginning God," on the parable of the good Samaritan, and on the ambivalence with which we receive invitations because they are times of growth for us and growth is not always comfortable. It felt to me afterward that the ministry had fallen on prepared ground.

After meeting, Frank was clear that he was not supposed to stay in Chapel Hill but was not exactly sure what he was supposed to do. We parted at that time with an embrace and with feelings that went far beyond any words that we might have been able to use.

I went back into the library for a simple lunch, and we settled into a circle of over 20 people. I described the process by which I found clarity for the leading to this travel and where Frank and I had gone these past ten days. We settled into a discussion of spiritual matters: the ways in which we nurture the spiritual in us, the pulls between service and inward spiritual life, the paradoxes that are at the heart of our spiritual experience. We broke this portion of the meeting after an hour or so, and I stayed around for another 15 minutes talking to individuals.

There was one question about whether I felt free to use Christian language when I traveled in the ministry, given the condition of Friends. It felt as if this were the question I had been preparing for over the past ten days, and I was able to answer it with some degree of giftedness and grace, speaking about the importance of being authentic in our spiritual life, the link between being authentic and being able to use the language that speaks to our hearts and to our condition, and the exact equivalence between my freedom to be authentic and the freedom that I give others to be authentic and to use the language that speaks to their heart and their condition. This answer seemed to be understood and well accepted by all. There was none of the defensive response that often occurs when this topic is introduced.

Near the end of our time together, a Friend remarked that I had taught Chapel Hill Friends something about being faithful in

Vocation and Competency

a task because it is the task we are given. He said that they didn't have a language with words to understand and describe and conceptualize a journey in the ministry that is not goal-directed or results-oriented but that I had given them an example of that and that he thought the meeting had learned from it, and he hoped that the meeting would continue to learn from it. The meeting clerk alluded to this same thing in her endorsement to my certificate.

Then I headed home, the journey in the ministry very nearly over. I felt that the whole trip had been faithful, joyful, obedient ministry and acceptable to the Lord. I was very grateful that the Lord led me into this service and that I was given the grace to hear the call and respond to it and be faithful to it and that Friends in Charlottesville Monthly Meeting and Baltimore Yearly Meeting were given the discernment to feel the validity of the leading and to find unity with it. In Paul's words, "Thank God for His indescribable gift!"

Growing Deeper into the Spiritual Life

During the opening worship of the FUM Communications Commission meeting later in 1987, I offered vocal ministry, and the editor of *Quaker Life* asked me later to write it down for him to the best of my ability. I did, and it was published in their March 1988 issue as "A Deeper Unity" (see appendix 1).

This was quite unusual for me. More often than not, I can't remember what I said as soon as I sit down after speaking. When I do remember it seems the words were meant to fit a particular audience at a particular place and time so that they don't have meaning for a wider audience. In this case, the words stayed with me, and they seemed to have an effect for good when circulated broadly.

I spent twenty-three days on the road in Tenth Month 1987. This included the North Carolina journey in the ministry described above, FUM Board and Commissions, Baltimore Yearly Meeting committee meeting day, a weekend in Jacksonville, Florida, to visit Asa, and a "normal" amount of work-related travel. I was very road-weary by month's end and thankful for a week at the farm, being nurtured by home. Catching up on farm work prevented me from doing much reflecting or writing about the trip with Frank other than one letter to a distant Friend beginning to travel in the ministry in her region:

> Dear Friend—
>
> It is good to hear from you. The prayer support of many Friends was tangibly present to me during my travels; I was exercised in ministry on that subject while at Charlotte.
>
> Our gospel labors in North Carolina were blessed by a sense that there was in each place we visited at least one person or couple for whom our visit was an important event. It is vital to remember, of course, that God's perspective is different from ours, and that what seems important to us may, from the divine viewpoint, seem rather beside the point. Beyond that, things take time; the knowable effects of our New England journey are still unfolding, two years after the fact.
>
> To respond directly to your question, I do not "justify . . . the briefness of [my] contact with Friends in North Carolina" to myself or to others. It is simply not my place to pretend to understand what God intends that my faithfulness should accomplish; my place is to be tender to the promptings of the Spirit, and to be faithful in doing what those promptings direct me to do—no more, no less.
>
> As to the opportunity for faithfulness in a called meeting for worship or in receiving hospitality from Friends while on the journey, my answer is similar: faithfulness lies in doing what one has been led to do. I have been led to travel without a specific concern or message, to meet with Friends in the trust that something good will happen; that trust has been well placed and abundantly rewarded. The repeated affirmations of the Friends among whom I have traveled is that my willingness to travel in this way is itself a strong encouragement to faithfulness in others—an encouragement that (I feel) might be diluted if I were to change to a format that, as you put it, "made more sense."

Vocation and Competency

Aside from old friendships that were strengthened or renewed, there are one or two Friends whom I met in New England in 1985 who stay in my mind, and one with whom I continue in a sporadic correspondence. Those who give evidence of being most profoundly influenced, however, are people with whom I am not in continual contact; I know of their experiences only from the reports of other Friends.

Beyond the direct impact of the journey, I have come to realize that there is an indirect effect that may in the long run be of far greater import. There are a growing number of ministers who are traveling at some distance from home, or visiting Friends in their home meetings, for whom my own travels and visits have been a model (though perhaps not the only model). I had a strong connection with one or two children in each meeting Frank Massey and I visited on this journey and continue to feel that some of these young Friends may themselves be "public ministers" one day. We simply don't know where our shadow falls.

You don't mention whether you have a companion in the visitation you are now doing; I greatly hope you do. Your readings in Woolman's *Journal* will affirm the valued position of companions in our history, and my own experience witnesses to the importance in so many ways of having a tender companion. That and a group of 'elders' to which you can be accountable for your gospel labors are to my mind the most important parts of any public ministry.

I look forward to hearing more about your work, and to sharing with you our common experiences in the ministry.

In Peace,

LLW

When I had more time for reflection on the North Carolina travels in the ministry, several things seemed notable. The trip was a time of considerable learning for Frank and me around our role and behavior as ministers and how to be faithful to that calling. I also had much more contact with children than Kara and I had had in New England, and I had the sense that one or more of those young Friends might be called into ministry themselves in years to come—especially Gwen Gosney in Rich Square Monthly Meeting in Woodland.

During the journey, I moved a considerable distance away from the Quietist position that all human thoughts and emotions are bad, that one must wait for one's humanness to be overwhelmed by a powerful leading that forces one to speak in meeting, toward a sense that our human natures (as God's creation and made in God's image) are capable of a harmony with the Divine Will that enables us to recognize and be faithful to more subtle promptings. It felt as if my old way of being in meeting was like a rock (Here I am, Lord, but You are going to have to blow me away before I speak today), and the new way was like a fruit tree (My Master has planted me in good soil, pruned me, and sent the sun and rain in order that I might bear fruit—and here it is.)

The change left me able to speak out of my own experience, in my own terms and words, with greater confidence that the Word would be spoken and heard in the words I spoke and that the auditory heard. It also raised up in me the need to live in that Harmony that enables such Divine Cooperation to continue. I was as likely to remain silent through a full meeting as before and more likely to speak "prophetically" in conversation outside of worship.

In Eleventh Month, I found a prayer scribbled on a yellow legal pad in my office. It was undated, but I seemed to remember stopping by the side of an interstate sometime in the previous year and writing down what had been rumbling through my head:

> Jesus and the Father are One. Jesus Christ is Lord. We thank you, God, for the joy and beauty of thy creation and for the manifold ways You make Yourself manifest in creation.
>
> We ask to become even more aware of Your Presence all around us in the places, people, and events of everyday life.
>
> We seek to become more and more like Jesus, who emptied Himself of heavenly glory in order to bring about God's Kingdom in creation.

Vocation and Competency

Help us to be Jesus' hands and feet and tongue in this day and place, helping the Spirit come into this creation wherever we go.

Give us the gift of community that we may know the present blessing of Your Kingdom among the people who are the Body of Christ, living in the Holy Now at the same time we work toward a new creation beyond time and space. Help us to be built up ourselves and to build up others in the community of faith.

Help us to love ourselves as others love us so that we might love others as we are loved. Open our eyes to the ways in which You are present in everyone so that we might love everyone. AMEN.

On the last day of 1987, I wrote the following in my journal:

Asa crawled into bed with me this morning. It was both a wonderful way to start the day and an immediate reminder that this was the last time he'd be here with me for a while. It has been a truly blessed time. He has so much personality now that we can be really good friends, and we are "real pals," as he says so often. I love him so much and miss him so much when he's not here. If he were sad in Florida, I don't think I could bear it; thank God he is enjoying life there with Merrill—enjoying life and thriving as well.

Dear Father of humankind and Creator of all that has been and is and will be, pour down your love and blessings on my son Asa. You know my love for him and my desire that he not suffer from my mistakes and shortcomings. Protect him from arbitrary pain and suffering; help him learn from whatever sorrow You see fit, in Your omniscience, to let him experience. Spark and nurture in his heart a love and yearning for You and Your Son and grant that Asa may reflect Jesus' life and light each day of his life.

Father, help me be the best father to Asa that I can be. Pour the fire of Your love into my heart, burning out everything there that is not of You and making me more nearly the person You created me to become. Help me commit my ways to You, that my plans might become established.

Righteous Judge of all creation, forgive me for my many sins this past year. Remember the loving sacrifice of Your Son who is my Advocate, who gave His life for me and for all human beings. I confess my sinfulness and repent of my evil deeds and thoughts; I accept with eternal gratitude the gift of forgiveness and renewal offered through the life, death, and resurrection of Jesus Christ.

Christ, my Counselor, Guide, and Daystar, hold my heart each day of the year to come. Help me listen always for your gentle voice and help me to be obedient to Your will. Give me Your eyes, that I see all that happens from Your perspective. Give me Your tongue, that I might be your herald wherever I go. Give my Your hands, that I might do Your work here on earth. Give me Your patience, that I might always be in harmony with Your intentions.

Amen.

On First Month 3, 1988, I wrote in my journal:

During First Day worship, way opened for me to speak about the young boy who shared his lunch with Jesus (who then fed 5,000 other hungry people). I said a few words of thanks for that young boy's mother also, who packed an extra fish and some extra bread with her son's lunch just in case he came upon someone who didn't have anything to eat. That loving woman put the idea in her son's heart that sharing is right so that when the opportunity came, he knew what to do. Ultimately, all we can do in this brutally broken world is to put ourselves in a position for miracles to happen, to share our lunch, however inadequate it may seem. If we share our loaves and fishes, God will take care of the rest.

Later in First Month, I was moved to "throw in my mite" concerning the weeks and months and years following the first Christmas. The magi made the long trip home having seen the prophecy fulfilled, yet the world did not seem to have changed. When the heavenly choir went back to

Vocation and Competency

wherever it came from and the shepherds returned to their flocks, it was just as cold as the night before. The Messiah had come—and the shepherds were still watching over their sheep. Most of all I spoke of Joseph, the man of three dreams, who was obedient to the leadings given him and who most probably never knew the shape of Jesus' ministry, much less the true nature of His role in creation. All Joseph had was the faith to do what he was given to do. The church calendar stretches from Christmas to Easter through the long cold nights of winter; we know that Easter is coming, but these faithful ones did not. Are we not called to be at least as faithful, trusting, and obedient as Joseph?

A discussion with several Friends produced an interesting insight. Some Friends saw my reluctance to explain my personal feelings on topics under consideration at meetings for business as an indication that I had some hidden agenda. I was trying to avoid having an undue influence on the meeting but was giving Friends who don't know me very well an excuse to mistrust my motives. Friends pointed out that the meeting could probably defend itself against my personal feelings and that it would be helpful for me to trust the meeting that much. I promised I would try to change, beginning that week.

Over the next several months, a number of incidents occurred that indicated my relationship with Charlottesville Friends was not nearly as harmonious as I had thought. One was the clerk's request to meet with me in the meeting house for a talk. Her first words of substance were that whenever I rose to speak in ministry, some Friends were thinking to themselves, "Here comes Christ." This did not seem like a problem to me, but it was definitely a problem to the clerk. She asked if I would change my ministry so that I did not speak so much or so often about Jesus or Christ, which stunned me—all the more because she was one of the Friends to whom I had felt close spiritually.

Several other similar but less dramatic incidents followed. The climax came when I posted an old FUM poster on the meeting house bulletin board. It displayed some of the more than two hundred words George Fox used to refer to Christ: Great Physician, Teacher, Inward Guide, and many more. I put the poster up because it was an indication of the many ways Friends encounter God and Christ. After about a week, the poster disappeared, but no one admitted they knew what had happened to it. After a considerable time had passed, one of the older Friends in meeting, very active and well respected, told me she had taken down the poster and hidden it "because we don't believe those things here." I felt that I was being told, by a weighty Friend, that I did not belong in Charlottesville Friends Meeting. I began to pray over this situation, trying to figure out what I should do.

Eventually, I drove to Virginia Beach to ask guidance from Louise Wilson, thereby fulfilling the prophecy of my dream during the FUM Triennial a year earlier. After hearing my description of my time of membership with Charlottesville Friends and recent events, Louise sat in silence for a time and then said simply, "I believe thee has discharged thy obligation to Charlottesville Friends." Thinking of the spiritual hospitality I had experienced among Conservative Friends, I asked Louise if it would be acceptable for me to apply to transfer my membership to Virginia Beach Friends Meeting. She said she thought that it would, and I made the long drive back home feeling released from a painful situation and that I had a welcoming place to go. I composed a letter to Charlottesville Friends Meeting in Fourth Month 1988 requesting transfer of my membership to Virginia Beach Friends Meeting, NCYM(C).

One First Day morning in Fifth Month, I worshipped with Virginia Beach Friends before driving back to Charlottesville for an evening meeting for business because it had been announced that a question concerning my membership would be discussed. To my genuine surprise, the Charlottesville meeting was not clear to approve my (and Asa's) transfer but instead appointed a committee to meet with me and consider the issues I'd raised. If after meeting with them I renewed my request for transfer, Friends said they would approve it.

It took a while to sort through all that was said, to figure out what Friends meant by their comments and what all that might mean for me. I was not being nurtured or enabled to grow and mature spiritually by current conditions in Charlottesville; I felt that I needed to be a part of a community that shared a greater devotion to Christ. The meeting that night made some Friends feel that certain incidents were distressing to

Vocation and Competency

me as a Christian in ways not immediately obvious to them as non-Christians. It was not clear that very many people saw those incidents as evidence of a larger pattern. Part of my uncertainty about the meeting's ability to change its attitude stemmed from the particular Friends who were absent from the meeting that night, including four active Friends who had helped set the recent tone of nonacceptance of the Christian message.

I was committed to work with this new committee, to help them understand more clearly why I felt that Virginia Beach was the community to which I should belong. I did not feel led to delay renewing my request for transfer beyond the next meeting for business. It might emphasize to Charlottesville Friends that an important part of my concern was the acceptance and nurture that all Christians needed, not just me, if I were to offer to continue to work with them after my transfer.

I began worshipping with Virginia Beach Friends most First Days while my transfer request was pending. During this time, I heard personal testimony about the effect of Christ on an individual's heart, quotations from Scripture, and vocal prayer in Jesus' name—all signs of a community welcoming to Christians and gathered to worship after the manner of Friends. I felt like a weary, thirsty traveler who had walked into a lush oasis after a long journey through a dry land. With the exception of brief conversations with a few attenders, I heard little reaction from Charlottesville Friends about my transfer. The silence from Charlottesville and enthusiasm from Virginia Beach Friends spoke strongly to me about the rightness of my decision.

The strongest sign that I'd made the right decision was the sense of lightness and rightness that I felt every time I thought about the change, about being a Conservative Friend, part of Virginia Beach Friends Meeting, part of NCYM(C), part of a faith community that had already welcomed me into their fellowship and was feeding me what I needed: the risen Christ. It was a peace beyond understanding, an indescribable gift.

I received the following letter, dated Sixth Month 14, 1988, from the clerk of Virginia Beach Friends Meeting, after the approval of my transfer:

Memoir of the Life and Religious Labors of Lloyd Lee Wilson

Dear Lloyd Lee and Asa,

    Meeting forwarded the enclosed letter to Charlottesville Friends Meeting reporting your transfer to Virginia Beach Friends Meeting. Future Friends will know the formal act of your transfer by reading musty minutes, but matters of heart will not be as clearly perceived. The matter of heart is wrapped up in the joy and care we hold for you, your physical and spiritual presence in the meeting and the continuing brotherhood/sisterhood we share in the Body of Christ. The Lord gives us a gift, unqualified love, with the start of each new day. This is the matter of heart we share with you that a minute cannot report. Welcome, Friends.

    In Christ's Love,
    Charles Ansell, Clerk

Chapter 5
Among Conservative Friends: North Carolina and Virginia, 1989–1993

Road trip songs were the soundtrack of much of my life in the mid- to late 1980s. Sometimes the song was as enjoyable as "On the Road Again" (made popular by Willie Nelson) and other times as bleak as Jackson Brown's "Running on Empty," but I seemed to always be on my way to someplace else. I had traveled to more individual places while employed by Friends General Conference, but now I was covering many more miles working with Virginia Mountain Housing. Being accepted into membership by Virginia Beach Friends Meeting only accentuated this pattern. I lived along the sides of a great triangle, with my home at Daybreak orchard north of Charlottesville as the northern apex. Each First Day I would drive down the eastern side of that triangle to Virginia Beach for meeting for worship. This was just over 181 miles each way—over six hours of driving for the round trip. The next morning, I would drive down the western side from Daybreak to the Virginia Mountain Housing offices in Christiansburg, Virginia. This was just over 160 miles, or slightly under three hours if the traffic was good. As needs and opportunities arose, I made other trips during the course of the week to potential or actual project sites across the state or to attend a Quaker workshop, retreat, or other gathering. Near the end of each week, I'd head back to Daybreak to do my laundry, cut the grass, or cut wood for heating and prepare for the drive to Virginia Beach early First Day morning. The one place I did not spend much time was home.

Mentally and spiritually, this was a very fruitful time for me. I was learning a great deal about how to operate a growing nonprofit organization efficiently and effectively without losing its original vision, and we continued to make real, positive changes in people's daily lives. Being among Conservative Friends opened me to a new understanding of the Quaker faith tradition I had only guessed at before. It was also a costly time for me, physically and emotionally. It soon became clear that

I had to find a way of life with more roots. That would take time, wisdom, and patience to accomplish.

I was driving once a month from Virginia to Jacksonville, Florida, to visit Asa at his mother's new home. If I set out immediately after work on Friday afternoon, twelve hours of driving would get me to their house just before he woke up on Saturday morning, and I'd have time for a short nap before we started our day. I'd take him to a worship service on First Day, then leave immediately afterward to drive back to Daybreak, wash my clothes, and collect whatever mail had accumulated in the mailbox since I'd last been home. The next morning, I was off to Virginia Mountain Housing again. Asa was not aware of what I was undertaking to be with him, but I trusted it would have a beneficial impact one day. The important thing was not that he appreciated my effort but that my monthly presence made a difference in how he grew up.

I was also helping out in Baltimore Yearly Meeting's Spiritual Formation Program. Driving home from a Bible study meeting in Harrisonburg, Virginia, one evening, I began once again to mull over whether I had been too forceful, too definitive that evening in my Christian interpretation of Scripture. I felt the discussion had been lively and a number of important pieces of the Truth were raised up for people to see, which is the important work of such a session. My primary worry was how non-Christians had received what I had to say.

Three decades later, I find the same concern is a lively issue all across Quakerism. Wherever I travel in the ministry, I feel the need to preface my words with an explanation of ways we can talk to one another and hear one another more clearly. In North Carolina Yearly Meeting (Conservative) (NCYM[C]), we call this practice "listening in tongues." Our goal is to create a safe place to be brave in our meetings so that individuals feel they can express themselves in the language and vocabulary that feels most authentic to them, that most clearly expresses their personal spiritual experience. Everyone in the meeting is committed to listening behind the words in order to hear and understand the reality that the words point toward. Each hearer does the work of translating whatever language the speaker uses into the language they personally prefer—listening in tongues. Today, I know that I have to help build this safe place to be brave and to encourage others to speak their truth using their own words. I must be consistent in hearing their words as pointers toward a spiritual reality that is in fact beyond the power of any words to capture fully. We all speak in metaphors. I also have to model how to speak in that place by sharing the words of metaphor that are most precious to me in describing my spiritual experience and by being brave in my own expression.

Service

So much time spent traveling made it important for me to set aside time daily for private devotions. One morning I was given an image from a meeting for worship at Cambridge, Massachusetts, in 1973 when I had been moved to offer the Lord's Prayer without preface or other additions. Toward the end, a nearby worshipper began crying. After meeting, she told me she had been overwhelmed by the beauty of the prayer.

As I asked God what I should see in this image from a decade earlier, I felt God had given me a gift—speaking the Word, telling the story—that I had yet to appreciate fully, develop properly, or use consistently. In God's patience and kindness, God had not taken the gift from me, even though I had not used it as God wished me to use it. I'd been too easily distracted by "real work," too sensitive to the criticisms of others, and unable to connect with a base community that would hold me accountable, under Christ, for using this gift properly.

This interior dialogue evoked in me a desire to be more intentional in my vocal ministry—to have more confidence, to be encouraged by and accountable to those brothers and sisters in Christ whom God sent to me for this work, and not to be discouraged by criticism. I did not want to outrun my Guide in anything, but I had allowed insecurity, fear, and distractions to interfere with being faithful in this gift. I was lagging behind my Guide, which was equally wrong.

That afternoon I spent time in a guided meditation on the parable of the merchant and the pearl and felt a strong connection between that story and the morning's image. I felt that I was the merchant in the parable and that I had not sold all that I had for the pearl—for the gospel. This needed to be balanced with Friends' advice to be patient and not to make great changes hastily, but it was clear that I was not yet making God the first priority in my life.

At that time, I was spending much time thinking about being a minister of the gospel and the resistance that the word 'minister' evoked in many Friends. Without surrendering my sense of the rightness of the word, I began to feel that perhaps going back to root meanings would be helpful. I began trying out the phrases 'servant of my Lord Jesus Christ' and 'herald of the gospel of Jesus Christ' in my mind, feeling the rightness of the words and trying to figure out how to say them without appearing arrogant or self-righteous. These phrases still do feel right, and I feel there are ways to say them that would be helpful to listeners.

While visiting the meeting in Lexington, Kentucky, I was led to ministry:

> Those ancient Friends who made it possible for us to gather in worship this morning often spoke and wrote of being enrolled in the school of Christ. We stand in the same relationship to the world and to Christ as those Friends; it would be good to ask ourselves regularly whether we are being teachable in the school of Christ. Do we make time each day to listen to our Teacher? Do we do the daily readings that help explain our Teacher's plans and intents? Do we do our 'homework?' Is our home a place where the life and Spirit of Christ is made manifest? It is important to ask these questions and answer them honestly, not only for the joy it brings us to do the Lord's will in this world but because that day is coming when we will join those ancient Friends and, like them, pass from works to rewards.

I sat down again with a sense of having discharged my obligation and spent the balance of the meeting for worship with a sense of the Divine Presence nearby.

When the Lexington Friends gathered after worship for meeting for business, I was mostly silent, conscious of being a guest rather than a member of the faith community. I did feel led to comment when Friends began to discuss the importance of having children walk into the meeting room and sit down immediately, even when they come to the door (at the end of First Day school) while vocal ministry is being offered. (This had happened that morning as I was speaking. I had stopped and waited for them to find seats, then continued.) I pointed out, as gently as I could, that if it were to be their practice to teach their children to do this, it would be wise for them to tell visitors that this was their intention, for nowhere else are Friends of any age taught to walk into worship during ministry, and without explanation visitors might draw a mistaken conclusion about the meeting for worship.

Inwardly, my ongoing work centered on letting go of the orchard in order to get on with my life—to free myself to follow the leadings of the Holy Spirit as they became perceptible to me. I had told my clearness committee that my family was going to be the hardest hurdle for me in selling the orchard and moving, and this turned out to be the case. Mom and my brother Damon had personal and emotional investments in Daybreak that were not closely linked to my own wants, needs, or investment in the place—emotional or financial. It was important to remember that I was not responsible for protecting those emotional investments and that I needed to do what the Lord was leading me to do, the best I could discern that, even if it led me on paths contrary to the wishes and desires of my family. Explaining my leading to move in terms that made sense to Mom and Damon proved very difficult, and I worked to remember that the leading could be valid even if they misunderstood it or disapproved.

A letter from my brother expressed his surprise and disappointment that I was "abandoning" Daybreak, and he predicted that I would be very unhappy in Virginia Beach. He called Daybreak "the family homestead," although I had owned the property only a decade. In a telephone conversation, my mother urged me to buy as much land as possible around Daybreak so that I could leave it to Asa when he was grown. To dedicate my life to acquiring a few acres of land for my son to inherit—that seemed a divinely uninspired life. It was hard to keep to my leading in the face of this unanimous family disapproval. Taking some consolation from Matthew 19:29, I sold Daybreak on Sixth Month 3, 1989.

I also found some consolation from contemporary Friends. I read Brian Drayton's monograph on the practice of recording Friends in the ministry once again and was struck as before by his observations near the end of the piece. He writes that the abiding characteristic of the minister is that nothing can be more important than obedience to the leading: "the essential fact which defined a minister was a sense of calling to the work, which was an abiding concern, shaping all decisions in life." As Bill Taber says, ministers are expected to do *everything* and *nothing*: everything the Spirit requires and nothing that is not required. The effect of these words and the spirit behind them was to reinforce my intent to move to Virginia Beach, where I felt my service was to be centered.

During this time, I had a conversation with a Charlottesville Friend in which she said that I had been so important to her spiritually that she felt permanently indebted to me. For most of my life, this sort of conversation would have played directly to my ego or I would have erected such defenses as to be unable to hear it at all. This time, I was better able to hear her without distortion, to recognize that God had been at work through me to reach out to her and that I had been nothing other than an earthen vessel, and to accept her thanks for being that vessel. It felt as if I was finally beginning to learn a little bit about how to be the person God intended me to be.

I had begun leading Bible study during adult First Day school in Virginia Beach. It was well received, and I felt a special joy in our time together, which I attributed to my increased acceptance of the role of teacher. It felt very "right" for me to lead a group in Bible study or other spiritual exploration. I came to accept this giftedness with thanks to the Giver and to seek opportunities to use it for God's purposes.

In Eleventh Month 1988, I went to see the Cascades in southwest Virginia for the first time in six or seven years. On the way, I inadvertently pulled out in front of another car while I was passing a slower vehicle. This led me to think about the protection the Lord had given me those past years and over all those miles I had driven. If I ever thought that it was my own driving skill that had kept me safe, I would be greatly mistaken. God had protected me, not because I deserved it but because God loved me.

These thoughts led me to reflect on the 'miraculous medals' of Jesus, Mary, Christopher, and other saints that many of the faithful carry in their automobiles. These images are the object of considerable scorn from unbelievers, and, in fact, the images do not protect the automobiles in which they ride from all accidents or unfortunate happenings, as the skeptics seem to think the faithful believe. Nor do the images enable the drivers of those vehicles to abdicate their own responsibility for safe driving.

What those images could do, I realized, looking at the small cross that hung from my sun visor, was remind the driver of how much they owed each day to the merciful protection of God. Even my best efforts to drive safely, and the best efforts of those with whom I share the roads, are not enough to keep us from harm. God's merciful hand is at work every day, every hour, every trip; the crucifix or other image is a reminder of how much we owe to God's loving interventions. I would not have purchased the small cross on my own, but it came as a gift from a Charlottesville Friend, and I accepted it as a gift and as a spur to mindfulness.

With God's grace, I arrived at the trailhead to the Cascades shortly after noon, made a cheese sandwich on homemade bread, tucked my travel Bible into my vest, and set off on the trail. Early morning rain had dampened the leaves and undergrowth, muting the noise of the wind blowing along the gorge. The tangible presence of the grace of God along the walk did much to calm my mind.

The first sight of the falls, framed by an enormous boulder and an overhanging pine tree, was as spectacular as ever. Only as one moves past that point and approaches more closely does the scale of the waterfall become clear; it is much bigger than one can at first conceive. That the far wall of the gorge rises 1,000 feet above the valley floor where the trail follows the stream should have prepared me for this, but though I read the sign carefully and stopped to gaze awhile at that high cliff face, the height of the waterfall did not penetrate to my heart until I sat by the pool at the foot of the Cascades and looked up.

Scripture and prayer seemed to be the only authentic response. Taking out my pocket Bible, I read Revelation 19:5–7:

And a voice came from the throne, saying,

"Give praise to our God, all you His bond-servants, you who fear Him, the small and the great."

And I heard, as it were, the voice of a great multitude and as the sound of many waters and **as** the sound of mighty peals of thunder, saying,

"Hallelujah! For the Lord our God, the Almighty, reigns. Let us rejoice and be glad and give the glory to Him, for the marriage of the Lamb has come and His bride has **made herself ready**." (NASB 1977, emphasis mine)

After a time of contemplation and prayer, it seemed right to stand and read that passage again, aloud, so I did so, there being plenty of rocks near at hand suitable for the purpose. Having done that, I turned and made the hike back to my car, full of the glory of the Creator and feeling God's Presence and grace in and all around me. Joy, Joy, Joy!

In Twelfth Month, a controversy developed at Virginia Beach Friends Meeting over a portrait of Jesus on the library wall in the meeting house. The portrait had been made by a faithful attender of the meeting in its earliest days and later given to the meeting. It was then hung in the library without further thought. Recently, some people had begun to question its placement and the details of the painting itself. Objections were raised to the portrayal of Jesus as a blue-eyed Caucasian with light brown, gently wavy hair, to the placement of an image in the meeting house, and to the placement of an image of Christ there in particular. The meeting of MEO was unable to reach clarity on what (if anything) to do about the painting, and the regular meeting for business was also unable to find unity. A special meeting was called. I was touched when, while seeking a satisfactory date for the called meeting, Friends specifically expressed the desire that I be able to attend and asked when I could make the drive down from my home in Greene County.

The meeting itself was remarkable in that Friends quickly moved past the ostensible reason for the meeting—whether or not the portrait of Jesus should hang in the meeting house permanently—to the underlying issue of our personal relationship to Christ. I felt hearts were tendered and Friends were enabled to speak openly and clearly about their faith and their relationship with Christ, whether that was personal, primary, ambivalent, or distant. By evening's end, whether or not the painting continued to hang in the library did not seem to be very important to most Friends present.

I made a number of comments that pressed out of me, some of which seemed helpful enough and some of which left me distinctly uncomfortable—particularly trying to explain the importance of maintaining single-pointed devotion to our own (Conservative Quaker) path to God, honoring other people on other paths but not trying to mix paths. I made a profession of my Christian faith. I added that if the painting had never been hung on the library wall, I would never have missed it nor felt that my spiritual experience was incomplete in any way. However, now that the painting was there—blue eyes and all—taking it down would feel to me like a statement about Christ and our relationship with Christ that would be contrary to my own faith commitments, and I did not want to make that statement.

These comments were as personal as any I had ever made about Christ in public, and they left me quite vulnerable. What I had to say seemed likely to be very uncomfortable for certain Friends present to hear, which made me uncomfortable saying them, yet I felt led to do so and felt that I should follow my leading. The affirming comments of more than one Friend after the meeting helped but did not entirely ease my discomfort. After what had happened at Charlottesville Friends Meeting, this seemed to me like highly risky behavior.

The Ansells offered me overnight hospitality, which I gladly accepted, and sleep came quickly. I try in the first moment of wakefulness each morning to review the coming day and lay it before God for divine blessings and guidance. That morning, lying half-awake in bed, I had a clear vision of myself on my knees in the dust at Jesus' feet, tying the laces on his sandals, which extended to just below His knees. Then I kissed His feet tenderly. Rising up again on my knees, I hugged His legs, content to stay right there indefinitely. Jesus, however, grasped my shoulders and lifted me to my feet, embracing me warmly and firmly. This vision seemed to be a clear message telling me that my devotion, witness, and service to Him was accepted and approved by Him with love; specifically, that my words and silences the previous night were acceptable service.[1]

I didn't say anything to the Ansells at the time, but I pondered the experience all day. Over the years and decades since this event, this vision has remained an anchor point in my life. To take the risks I felt I was taking by making the Christian witness I did in that meeting, and to have Christ affirm my actions so unequivocally, has cemented in my inmost being my identity as an acceptable servant of God through Christ. Events have rocked that sense of identity and calling from time to time, but nothing has been able to displace them for long.

Early in 1989, after a particularly blessed First Day worship at Virginia Beach, I had lunch with Curt and Ann Shaw. We had a long conversation about spiritual gifts. Curt volunteered that just by my presence I often ministered to him. I'd been thinking mostly about verbal gifts in ministry, spoken and written; it was good to be reminded that there is a silent ministry as well and that this silent ministry was an important part of my own service.

Curt said that my spiritual gift was that of being an apostle—one under spiritual authority and caring for several faith communities. Ann confirmed this, adding that her own spiritual gifts included discernment, meaning that she was right about what she said she had discerned. Being an apostle was not a gift I had ever heard mentioned among Friends, and it sparked a lot of reflection.

I am a conservative in religious matters, skeptical of innovation in our faith and practice. If change does come, I want to be certain that it grows out of and is consonant with our historic understanding of Truth. Of course, revelation continues, and our understanding grows; our faith and practice *will* change over time, becoming more nearly molded to the divine image. Yet not all change is helpful, and we must be willing to prune some strong shoots that appear in the wrong place or grow in the wrong direction.

The closest connection I was able to make between "apostles" and Friends' thought was Bill Taber's description of "mothers in Israel." A "mother in Israel" carries the meeting (at whatever level) or Friends at large in her or his belly, caring for and nurturing its spirit as a physical mother does her unborn child. The case of a mother in Israel seems to me to parallel the "care of several meetings" Curt sees as part of the role of an apostle, and thus I could name and claim being a mother in Israel— one who cared for the corporate body of the faithful.

Another aspect of the apostolic role, according to Curt, was "speaking under authority." Friends know that authority does not come from outward credentials but inward grace; the self-giving, other-directed love of the mother in Israel is conducive to being empowered to speak with authority for the good of the meeting although not sufficient by itself. A Virginia Beach Friend observed that whatever I said in response to the query in meeting for business ended up in the final minute. It had been given to me, with some frequency, to speak with authority on spiritual as well as worldly matters, and I could name and claim this gift (or gifts plural, I suppose) as well: discerning and articulating right vision or right action for a group. Thinking of the responses of several individual Friends and meetings to my articles in *Quaker Life* and elsewhere, I named and claimed the gift of written ministry, of articulating the gospel in written words that inspired and stimulated readers to delve deeper into the Holy Spirit.

Does my inward acknowledgment and consciousness of these gifts carry implications for my ministry among Friends? Yes and no. No in the sense that way will open for me to do the right thing, in God's time and place, while my settled intention to do this or that can interfere with God's will. Yes in the sense that God gifts us for a purpose, which is that God's will might be perfectly realized in God's Kingdom on earth. God does not waste gifts or call His servants to tasks they are unequal to. These gifts are meant to be used in God's service, and I should be ready to use them that way. Using them fully involves recognizing them and being willing to exercise them as God directs.

Shortly after my conversation with Curt and Ann Shaw, they transferred their membership from Xenia Meeting to Virginia Beach. Their recording as ministers was accepted as part of the transfer. No one else in living memory had transferred a recording in ministry into this yearly meeting,[2] so George Parker of Rich Square Monthly Meeting was consulted to see whether it could be done and, if so, how. His response was that a generation or two ago this might have been more difficult, but these days Friends were on better terms with one another. On his advice, we recorded in our minutes that the Shaws were recorded ministers and that we received them as such. There was no question raised about doing this.

One night while Asa was visiting me in First Month 1989, we went out for pizza. As we always do at home, we held hands for silent grace before beginning our meal. Soon afterward, a man eating dinner with his family nearby came over and thanked us for saying grace; he said it meant a lot to his family to see us pray. Asa and I had been entirely unself-conscious about silent grace; it was just who we were. Yet the Lord made it an opportunity to witness to God. I am grateful that we were made witnesses to the gospel, all unknowingly.

Sam Caldwell came to visit in First Month, and we went to Charlottesville meeting together. We received a warm welcome from numerous Friends at the rise of worship. I was struck by the difference between the apparent warmth of this reception and my struggles a year ago, when my reception had been very different. One Friend observed that the entire meeting seemed to "sit up" when I appeared at the door, which she attributed to Friends knowing how I led my life.

These comments came to mind some fifteen years later, when Friends had just settled into worship at Cedar Grove Meeting House in Woodland, North Carolina. I looked up and saw Bill and Frances Taber through the window, making their way down the side porch toward the front door of the meeting house. The effect of the Tabers' unexpected arrival was electric.

One First Day in meeting for worship at Virginia Beach, I offered vocal ministry along the same lines as I had the previous week in Charlottesville. I had read in the old journals that Friends expounded on the same themes again and again in their public ministry, but this was a very out-of-the-ordinary experience for me. It is difficult to balance the sense of being led in the moment with my intellectual opinions about what I should be doing or saying in ministry; the leading to offer a particular message often seems to be in conflict with what my head says my behavior and speech should or should not look like, or sound like, or resemble. Still, I let God have the reins this time and sat down with a sense that I had been faithful.

One of the elders approached me at the rise of meeting to express appreciation for my ministry, and we then talked for several minutes about how important specific feedback is to me and how difficult it is for me to rise to speak during worship. She was surprised, as most Friends seem to be, to learn that speaking in meeting is not the easiest thing in the world for me to do. This Friend was blind and intentionally paid closer attention to sounds, including speech, than anyone else I had encountered. One came away from a conversation with her feeling more deeply listened to and heard than when speaking with nearly any sighted person. It was a gift that was very helpful to her in carrying out the activities of an elder.

In Fourth Month 1989, I led a retreat at the Pine Mountain Settlement School in Bledsoe, Kentucky, for Friends in that part of the state. The first evening's session opened with a period of worship, during which I was moved to vocal prayer on behalf of all of us gathered for the weekend that we would be receptive to the gentle nudging and prodding of the Holy Spirit. After worship, I gave everyone a task to think about until our session the next morning.

I played the weekend by ear, other than the barest of outlines that I formulated before I got to the retreat site. This was the first time that I felt confident about trusting so much to discernment in the moment, and the success was gratifying. Louise Wilson worked this way all the time, and it gave her great flexibility and the ability to respond to the condition of those present; I was learning that I could operate that way also.

After the morning sessions, a Friend took me aside to question my vocal prayers during the periods of worship with which we'd begun each general session. He told me he questioned anyone's right to pray for or on behalf of any other person, in a meeting for worship or otherwise, and was himself praying for clarity about whether or not he should elder me for the practice. I told him I'd be glad to talk with him about this when he reached clarity in his discernment.

I gave a lot of thought to that Friend's concern throughout the day, though he did not approach me a second time. This was an opportunity to stand as a clear witness to the Truth that I knew and to claim my right to religious expression that was true to my own religious experience. Too often, it seems to me, Christian Quakers give ground to non-Christian Quakers on these matters, ceding to non-Christians both the right to express themselves in their own terms and to prevent Christians from doing the same.

The meeting to which most of these Friends belonged was not Christ-centered and did not give much sign that it was God-centered. Friends expressed the purposes of the meeting as mutual self-help and healing, with little outreach and almost no mentions of yearnings after the Divine. I began to wonder, as the day progressed, what good it was for me, a devout Christian, to try to work with these people. What help could I be to them since our spiritual paths were so different?

As I centered down in the evening worship that closed the day, I raised these questions to God in silent prayer and looked up at the beams holding up the roof of our meeting room. They crossed at an angle that wasn't 90 degrees, as if to say that the cross of Christ was distorted by the condition of these Friends. As I continued in prayer, I was led to look directly over my head, where I saw a wooden chandelier made of crossed beams at right angles with a light at the end of each beam. It was the True Cross with a lamp at the head, foot, and each arm, and it was suspended directly overhead, shining its Light down on one and all, believer and skeptic alike. This was an ecstatic experience for me, making me feel that I was in just the right place (bathed in the Light of the cross) and that all was right in the world (as it was being flooded by the Light of the cross). A smile played across my face as all anxiety and doubt faded from my heart.

I felt extremely close to Bill Taber and Louise Wilson all weekend. We were all together in that spot where the meeting of ministers and elders is always in session, true brothers and sisters of one another. I was present with them as a full brother (if a younger one) in ministry, not by sufferance or tolerance. I was stepping on ground they had trod and prepared before me, stepping into my inheritance and the role prepared for me—the role I was created to fill. One attender said later that I "just glowed" all morning long.

I was exercised in the ministry during our closing worship, speaking on Gideon and God's desire that we undertake tasks that would be utterly impossible without divine intervention so that the glory would be unmistakably God's, not ours. It seemed acceptable service.

In the spring of 1989, George Stabler, a recorded minister, visited me on behalf of the Virginia Beach Friends Meeting of Ministers, Elders, and Overseers (MEO)[3] to see whether I would accept being recorded as a minister myself. I had not expected this visit or its purpose, but I had, however, spent considerable time over several years reflecting on the right relationship between the meeting community and its individual members. I explained to George that I did not feel that I had any say in the matter; it was a matter of corporate discernment on the part of the meeting. If the meeting discerned that I had been entrusted with spiritual gifts that should be developed and exercised for the good of the meeting, then my part was to say yes to that discernment and serve the meeting accordingly.

This was apparently satisfactory to the members of MEO. In due course, they recommended to the general monthly meeting that I be recorded in the minutes as a minister of the gospel. This was placed on the agenda for the Fifth Month 1989 meeting for business. I was then serving as recording clerk, and I requested to be excused from taking minutes that month—if not for the entire meeting, at least while the committee gave its report on that topic. The clerk turned me down, expressing the desire to have me formulate that very personal minute.

So, I sat at the clerks' table trying to remain outwardly calm and composed while feeling very exposed and vulnerable in front of all these Friends, listening to a recommendation for action that I had thought would never happen. When a Friend asked whether we had "resolved the issue" of recording ministers, I thought I would sink right through the floor; my worst of all fears about recording had always been to be recommended for recording and then turned down by a monthly meeting for business.

Memoir of the Life and Religious Labors of Lloyd Lee Wilson

The clerk pointed out that a discussion of recording gifts had been held as requested, and another Friend reminded those gathered that we were part of a yearly meeting that provided for the recording of elders and ministers in its *Discipline* so that there was no larger issue about recording per se but only decisions to be made as to whether certain Friends should be recorded. That seemed to settle Friends' minds. The clerk asked if the meeting was in unity, and Friends approved without further comment.

By this time, my hand was shaking so that I could hardly read my writing when I stood to read the minute aloud, and I thought my voice would crack. Friends told me I appeared calm and sounded normal, which only goes to show that the ear as well as the eye can be easily deceived! During that same meeting, it gave me a certain degree of satisfaction—or at least company in my misery—to watch Charles Ansell, reporting for MEO, have to recommend himself for appointment as an elder. This was clearly a right discernment, and Friends quickly approved. Both minutes were reconsidered the following month, as was standard procedure, and given second approval.

In Sixth Month 1989, I met with local Friends to negotiate the sale of Friendship Village Apartments by Virginia Beach Friends Meeting to Virginia Mountain Housing. Friendship Village was a 110-unit HUD-subsidized apartment complex sponsored by Virginia Beach Friends Meeting but largely ignored in the years since. It needed major renovation and better property management overall to regain and sustain an acceptable quality of life for its residents. This was part of a long process of seeking to find the proper way to find competent owners for Friendship Village. I was very happy to be so close to the end of the negotiation process and to the beginning of the financing process.

I continued to have difficulty "doing business" with Quakers and continued to be a bit puzzled about the root of the difficulty. Friends are very diverse and my difficulties were so universal that it was hard to attribute the stresses I felt to Quakers per se. I do feel, though, that our religious society has attracted in recent decades a group of people who are not decision makers—social workers, college professors, schoolteachers, and the like—and an overlapping group who are deeply suspicious of any transaction involving larger sums of money than they keep in their personal checkbook. This is a shift from the business owners, large and small, who were once prominent among Friends. I feel decision making is 5 percent about making the right decision and 95 percent about making the chosen decision right. I am also at ease with large sums of money; by training, by experience, and by nature, it doesn't have very much hold on me. While I may never have a very great deal of it (it sticks to me much like eggs stick to Teflon), it doesn't fascinate me, either.

Perhaps the matter was simply that I was different from the large majority of present-day Friends and that some of these differences came to light when our common activity lay within the bounds of my chosen profession. If I had felt more understood and affirmed as a manager in my past Quaker experience, it might not have been so important at this time to be understood and affirmed as a manager.

Part of the gift that Virginia Beach Friends Meeting was for me during this period was the presence of devout, competent businessmen like Bob Wilson and Charlie Ansell. For as long as I'd been a Friend, I had felt the lack of strong male role models in my "competency"; at times, it had seemed that Friends felt that being a businessperson was an open compromise of one's principles. Bob and Charlie's presence in the Virginia Beach Friends Meeting not only helped me directly, but their lives had already witnessed to others in the meeting so that the prejudice against businessmen I'd felt elsewhere was not as strong there.

This acceptance of business people was part of a generally nurturing atmosphere in the meeting that had helped me accept who I was. I was a businessman—a manager—and a good one, at that. What is more, my business was a vital part of the gospel: housing those who might otherwise have no decent place to live. Charlie Ansell had been right a few months earlier when he said that I was a full-time minister. I was just beginning to understand and accept that I had several flocks to care for.

The key to my effectiveness in doing business with Quakers has been to stay aware that God knows to the last decimal point just how competent a manager I am; God's discernment and affirmation are infinitely more important than the opinion of human beings. What is important is that Truth be served and right action followed, whether Friends understand my role in that process or not.

In Sixth Month, Charlie Ansell and I made the first of our planned visits in the gospel ministry together. At Greenville Meeting, both Charlie and I offered vocal ministry during meeting for worship. It seemed to me that his offering was the more important of the two and spoke most directly to the condition of Friends present, though I know that such seemings and appearances are often deceptions and not to be trusted. I offered my affirmations afterward and told Charlie that it felt today as if I were the one carrying the bags for the two of us (Charlie had said earlier that he was not sure what his role was to be in this labor except perhaps to carry the bags).

After table fellowship, the adults gathered again to talk about the state of the meeting and what they and we could do to strengthen it. I was heartened to hear a Friend say that although the meeting had been larger in the past, it has been small before also and would be larger once again in the future. There is not much specifically that we as traveling ministers could do in such a situation except to be present in the Spirit with these Friends, remember them in our prayers, and encourage others to make the journey to Greenville as way opened.

As a newly recorded minister, I began attending the Virginia Beach Monthly Meeting of MEO. Louise Rothrock was clerk, and I began taking the minutes. Louise, though blind, was a very good clerk; she had an excellent memory, was well organized in her thoughts and plans, and knew how to "put the question" before the group in such a way that it could be answered. She and I had a quick rapport about the minutes, finding unobtrusive ways from the start for me to let her know when I was finished writing and ready to read back a minute for approval.

It was strange to sit down with a group of Friends and feel that I might be meeting with them, God willing, for the rest of our lives. This added to my sense of commitment to the group to do and be the best I could with them, and to be patient because we had a long time to work things out, to come to an understanding of the demands of Truth in our lives. I journaled at the time: "I think, by and large, that a lifetime spent as a minister or elder may be just barely long enough to do the work necessary. (Check back in 20 years or so.)" Looking back now, over thirty years later, this is true. A lifetime apprenticeship is just barely enough as there is always more to learn.

The importance of making a long-term commitment still looms large in my heart, but I understand much more clearly now the dangers of considering being recorded as a minister as a lifelong condition. Clearly, one's gift should be recognized only for as long as the gift is manifest and properly used. God's task for a meeting community changes over the years, and as time passes different gifts are distributed to different people to equip the community to carry out that changing task.

The importance of the right balance between long-term commitment and moment-to-moment surrender to the perceptible guidance of the Holy Spirit was also highlighted around this time in two other contexts. I'd spoken in worship several First Days in a row and was feeling the familiar tension about whether I should speak so much or not. What was different this time was that I knew right down to the core of my being that the decision was not mine to make and that the One whose decision it was knew far better than I what was best. What I say and when I say it have meanings and impacts I cannot imagine—so the best thing I can do is to be listening and obedient.

Also about this time, I served on a committee for clearness for membership. In our preparation, we talked about the consequences of not being faithful to our Guide when we seek clearness about a membership application. One committee member confessed that she had not spoken out when she felt uneasy about an application a few months previously. The individual involved had since had a hard time acclimating to the meeting and accepting our norms and values; recently, her attendance had dropped off dramatically. It really is better for all involved in a clearness committee to defer any action, especially a recommendation for membership, if there is a stop or hesitation in any Friend's heart. We share a long-term commitment to the health of the meeting community, but that must not blind us to correct decisions about individual membership matters.

The committee for clearness for membership is one of the two most important types of committees in any monthly meeting; the other is the nominating committee. The decision as to who we accept into membership affects not only the individual making the application and their family but also changes the composition of the entire meeting community. No monthly meeting can afford to give this clearness process less than its absolute best effort at discernment, and no relaxation of our expectations concerning prospective members can be accepted without an impact on the meeting as a living faith community.

At NCYM(C) sessions in Seventh Month, I joined Louise Wilson, David Eley, and some others for a time of evening prayer in Louise's room. I surprised myself by sharing my feelings of loneliness and pain early in the silence, and we spent until after midnight working together to search out and heal the causes of my dis-ease. A fundamental issue seemed to be that I had not yet fully forgiven myself for two failed marriages, even though I believed that Christ had forgiven me. I later prayed:

> I name [claim] the forgiveness of Jesus Christ for all my wrongdoings in relationships, especially my two marriages, and claim the reality and power of that forgiveness to enable me to forgive myself. I do forgive myself for past mistakes, and resolve to take the lessons they teach me into my future with joy. Thanks be to God for what He has given me, for what He has taken away, and for what He has left me.

Later in those sessions, I was moved to vocal prayer during worship and found myself once more kneeling to speak; that practice was apparently not over for me. (Like other distinctives in my appearance or behavior, I did not myself choose to kneel; it was presented to me as part of my obedience.) I felt uncomfortable about having knelt until later in the meeting when Alfred Newlin also knelt in vocal prayer. He had a harder time of it than I had, as I was in a front row seat and had plenty of room, while Alfred had to turn around sideways to have enough space to get even one knee to the carpet. His faithfulness gave me assurance.

At the First Day meeting for worship when many Virginia Beach Friends were attending yearly meeting sessions, another Friend delivered an extended diatribe against Christians. More than one seasoned Friend apparently considered eldering her. I had not been present and could not take part in such an action, but I spent considerable time in prayer about it anyway.

Can the meeting elder a Friend for the content of their message? It seemed to me that the answer was yes, but with some context. The eldering this Friend seemed to need was not a slap on the hand for outrunning her Guide but a loving inquiry as to whether she felt as alienated from the meeting community as her ministry indicated. If yes, one set of responses was needed; if no, another.

I have come to understand the process of eldering as discernment of the spiritual condition of each of the members of the faith community as revealed by their vocal ministry and other signs. An elder's goal is not the correction of a person's behavior but an improvement in their spiritual direction and health. What sincere seeker would not welcome such assistance?

Hearing the query responses at yearly meeting sessions convicted me that the time I spent watching television was largely wasted and in some measure glorified exactly those values and attitudes that were most in conflict with the Kingdom of God. When I got home, I turned the television set to the wall. Two weeks later, I gave away my indoor antenna. It was remarkably easy to live without television. There was no time when I felt I had nothing of value to do, which highlighted just how much watching TV had kept me from the truly useful. It was mildly surprising to see how little Asa protested the lack of TV viewing. He had until then been a heavy watcher at every opportunity, but aside from a few half-hearted complaints in the first few days, he hardly mentioned TV. I eventually gave the TV set to the Things Unlimited store, where it was sold to support our Friends School.

I received a lovely letter from Brian Drayton in which he wrote (concerning our both having been acknowledged as ministers), "Every year, I discover how this covenant has changed me, and it has led me further into integrity, though I was (am!) often unwilling to follow the Guide." I feel my leadings about my television viewing habits are an example of how this covenant—my sense of responsibility to the meeting that has acknowledged my giftedness—affects my own behavior. It is not that television itself is bad (which it may or may not be), nor that I am taking on some penance above and beyond the general membership, but that I have found watching television to be inconsistent with my own need to nurture and develop the gift with which I have been entrusted. Watching television is just one more way that I avoid becoming the person God knows I can be and yearns for me to become. I am now much more aware of the importance of being constantly vigilant so as to be always the most transparent channel, the clearest witness to God and the gospel, that I can possibly be.

I started working on an essay about abortion in the summer of 1989, exploring what seemed to me valid arguments on both sides of the issue, searching for a position consistent with Quaker beliefs and testimonies that I could endorse personally. I hoped by writing formally I could clarify my own thoughts. This marked the beginning of the extended writing project that eventually became my book *Essays on the Quaker Vision of Gospel Order*. This first essay on abortion was the only one that was *not* included in the collection when it was published.

Charlie Ansell and I continued our travels in the ministry that summer, visiting Wilmington meeting in Eighth Month. We arrived at our hosts' home in time for supper, which was tasty and simple. There is a wonderful quality of "table fellowship" when Friends offer their hospitality of home and table without any affectation or apprehension, accepting the traveler completely and trusting without even thinking about it that the traveler accepts them as they are. This quality of hospitality abounded that evening. After dinner, we talked at length about things Quaker and non-Quaker in the life of faith.

I had the sense that these Friends were strong in their faith and were also in search of some encouragement as they strove to be faithful witnesses in their daily lives—especially in their employment. I think the most important encouragement we could give them was what we did: to simply come to their meeting in response to a leading, to stay in their home and share with them, without pretense or facade, who we are and Whose we are. In that regard, I believe we were faithful.

The one lack of faithfulness, which I perceived too late, came at the very end of the evening when the conversation broke up and we all went to bed. We had an opportunity then for a few minutes of worship, but

Among Conservative Friends

both Charlie and I let it pass unthinkingly. It was only a missed opportunity, but it points out how important it is to be always aware, always sensitive to the opportunities being presented to us.

While driving to Christiansburg several days later, I was passed by an earnest young man who flashed his headlights and waved his arm as he overtook my vehicle. We both pulled over to the shoulder. It turned out he had a burning idea about the relationship between America and Israel connected to the relationship of Judah and Israel in the Old Testament. Since my license plate was *A Quaker*, he thought I ought to know what he had discovered so that I could help spread the word. I listened for several minutes as he patiently explained his reasoning. As he finished, he confided that the authorities in Fluvanna County, Virginia, thought he was insane and that he was at that moment on his way to Charlottesville for a psychiatric evaluation. I assured him that I would share what he had told us with other people, and we parted company on good terms.

Shortly after Labor Day, I was up before dawn to drive to Gunpowder Meeting in Sparks, Maryland, for a gathering of Christian Quakers in Baltimore Yearly Meeting. We had a meeting for worship and a meeting for eating, as well as a time of general sharing about the way Truth prospers in our lives and meetings. I was saddened to hear Friends speak of how threatened others in their monthly meetings feel that Christian Quakers were gathering to worship together from time to time. The gathering broke up in the early afternoon. I returned home glad that I had surrendered to the leading to attend.

I clerked a meeting for business for the first time that fall when the clerk was unavoidably out of town. At the suggestion of the monthly meeting of MEO, I recorded the minutes as well. Overall, I thought it went well. There were a few elements that I hoped to improve over time, but no major faux pas. We got all the business completed with what seemed to be a genuine sense of unity on each item and used our time effectively.

I had not been eagerly awaiting the chance to clerk a meeting, but I was not reluctant to take on that responsibility when asked. I had participated in, thought about, and studied our decision-making process for nearly twenty years and felt confident that I would be competent. One always does feel just a bit excited at the prospect of finding out whether one really does have the skill one thinks one has, and I felt that. This did not, I believe, adversely affect my performance.

The clerking task that day was not particularly difficult because there was no business about which I held a deep personal conviction. The hardest part of clerking, for me, is separating oneself from personal opinions and becoming fully the servant of the meeting. Most of the hard part of any ministry, it seems, is exactly that—the giving up of one's self and dedicating all of one's efforts to serving others. One must truly die to self in order to serve God and God's creation (including humans); otherwise, one gets inextricably involved in satisfying one's own needs and wants, to the detriment of the service.

In Tenth Month 1989, I began an informal home visitation program among the one hundred or so members of Virginia Beach Friends by visiting the home of one of the recorded ministers in the company of an overseer of the meeting. I was uncertain about how the visit would proceed but turned it over to God and resolved to assume that God would arrange events to suit divine purposes. The visit went well, with a period of covered worship at the beginning followed by tea and some quiet conversation.

Global warming was much in the news that fall, as was the piecemeal progress being made toward "safe" fusion power. Whether the promises being made about the safety of fusion power would turn out to be true or not, this much seemed certain: unless we did something fairly radical about the carbon dioxide we were discharging into the atmosphere, and did it soon, our children and their children would live in a radically different world, one different in climate, in food production, in shorelines. The differences would not be pleasant.

My personal examens that fall included my financial stewardship, especially in relation to Virginia Beach Friends Meeting. I reviewed these things regularly, but the decisions I reached never stayed "made," which seems right. This time I discerned that my practice of giving 4 percent of my salary to the meeting, 1 percent to Right Sharing of World Resources, and 5 percent elsewhere should continue.

Among Conservative Friends

There were many opportunities to be of service to Virginia Beach Friends Meeting now that I was a member, and I had to remember that my no to one opening sanctified my yes to another at a later time. I did say yes to becoming the recording clerk, on the condition that the meeting go back to the older tradition of reading draft minutes back immediately for approval. I found the personal discipline of listening carefully in order to draft an acceptable minute a very helpful experience and did not miss being able to speak to the issues myself.

As recording clerk, I didn't miss the opportunity to speak to an issue brought before meeting for business; it felt even more spiritually appropriate now for me to be silent than it had felt before for me to speak up (which I had done frequently). Unexpectedly, not only was I more at ease with the decisions of the meeting, but the decisions themselves seem to be reached more harmoniously. One could say that I had embarked on a silent ministry (à la Nouwen) or a *poustinia* (desert) retreat in the meeting house or that I had gone into retreat for my own benefit; all of these were true in their own way.

As recording clerk, I could speak in an indirect fashion since I did draft the minute for approval by the meeting, but this is so subtle a feat and so easily misused or abused that I hesitate even to mention the possibility. A recording clerk who attempts to color minutes to reflect a personal perspective will find them rejected and will be out of a job very quickly. Still, there is a witness in the very style and vocabulary of the minutes, if properly worded, that reminds Friends always of the One with whom we seek to be in unity and Whose perspective we seek.

Later in 1989, Virginia Beach MEO held a special meeting to discuss Wilmer Cooper's *The Gospel according to Friends*. We discussed Cooper's five points about Quaker distinctive perspectives on the gospel and felt all were important, though some more than others. The emphasis on a personal experience of Jesus Christ, for example, was felt to be still essential to the Quaker gospel but no longer a Quaker distinctive. Too many other Christian groups were emphasizing the need for a personal relationship with Christ for our experience to do very much in the way of distinguishing us from the world's people (at least to an outsider—I suspect that the Quaker experience is substantially different from the fundamentalists' personal relationship.)

The universality of Christ and of Christ's redemption, on the other hand, was generally felt to be both essential and distinctive. Here, Friends seemed to be reacting to those who claimed to see nothing of Christ or of goodness in anyone or any spiritual path outside of Christianity—sometimes nothing outside their own small portion of Christianity. It seemed to be that George Fox and Robert Barclay were clear that everything that was good in other spiritual paths was due to the Presence and intervention of Christ in those paths and that persons who had never heard of Christ but were faithful to the measure of Light entrusted to them (in the path that they followed) would nevertheless be saved.

There are a couple of ways to understand this. One is that Christianity is the perfect and complete expression of the divine Creator-creation relationship and that people who think they are following a different spiritual tradition are unknowing Christians because it is the hidden Christ that redeems their faith and practice.

My own understanding is that Christianity and all the other great spiritual traditions are incomplete understandings and incomplete expressions of the great Truth and Reality that cannot be fully comprehended by any mortal being. Any of these traditions will lead a devout follower closer and closer to that Truth over time. The tradition I follow is a "happy accident" of time and circumstance. What is important is that I make an authentic choice and follow that chosen tradition with full devotion. The great traditions are not "all the same"—they are profoundly different, with profound implications for their followers. They each lead their followers toward the Truth that is beyond all faith traditions.

I also believe everyone will come to be with God in eternity—eventually. I believe everyone has the ability—the "right," so to speak—to reject God in the context of any of the faith traditions. This state of turning away from God, however perceived, is personal hell. This can last all of one's life and into death, but even in death each soul continues to have the ability to accept God and God's love. As soon as the soul does that, the personal hell of alienation from the Divine ends and the heaven of Divine Union begins. Every knee shall bow, every tongue confess that Jesus Christ is Lord, however manifested; every soul shall eventually acknowledge its Creator, however named or understood. There is no need for punishments in hell; simply being apart from God is punishment enough.

In late 1989, I offered a program on Quaker history in the Virginia Beach meeting house, using an approach I'd never tried before of reading extensively from the journals of Friends in each period of Quakerism rather than talking about them in the abstract. I gave context for each reading to set the stage and spoke a bit afterward to point out some important aspect of what had just been read. I included readings from George Fox's *Journal* and one of his epistles, Elias Hicks's *Journal*, Thomas Kelly's *Testament of Devotion*, Robert Barclay's account of his own convincement, Marmaduke Stephenson's account of his call to be a prophet to the nations, and part of the 1873 Epistle from NCYM(C) to Dublin Yearly Meeting, as printed in the 1950 *Discipline* of NCYM(C). Louise Rothrock, who of course could not see me, said that I sounded as if I were glowing with the joy of sharing these dear ancient Friends who were also friends of mine with these gathered present-day Friends. Bob Wilson approached me after most others had left, shook my hand, and said simply, "Thee has a gift, Friend. See that thee uses it."

I felt happily drained afterward, as if I had given away all the energy that I was supposed to give away, had been faithful, had discharged my obligation, and had done good work—expressions that somehow don't quite reach the reality, only point toward it in a way that others who have themselves felt that same reality can recognize. Telling the story, sharing the good news, spreading the message, is very near what it is that I am supposed to be doing. God grant that I become ever more clear and more faithful in my service.

I have long believed that the heart of the Quaker understanding of the gospel is in Fox's statement that "Christ has come to teach His people Himself." By 'Christ' I understand the Truth and Reality that stand behind any attempt to express the divinity in words—our metaphor for the Creator and Sustainer of all that is. The Creator, to whom our word

'Christ' points, *has come*—God has not ignored us until some future event or until our physical death but has come in the present moment to the place where we are. In the midst of our messy, imperfect, confused lives, God has come to us.

God has come to *teach* us—not to snatch us away from our difficulties, not to erect some impermeable barrier between us and the world or our troubles, not to fight our battles for us like a spiritual Clark Kent, but to teach us. In the midst of our troubled, messy lives, Christ has come to teach us how to have true Life and how to have it abundantly. God has come to teach us so that all things will work for good; God has come to teach us how to have a peace that passes all understanding.

If the Divine is here to teach us, then we are capable of learning—we can change our habits, our deeds, our thoughts, and even our hearts. We can change; we can cast aside those parts of our old selves that are unhealthy for ourselves and others and become profoundly different people. And finally, we are all God's people. I think often of the bedtime prayer that Asa and I prayed each evening when he was a child. First, we prayed for ourselves, then for our relatives, then for people we knew and people we didn't know, and finally for "all the aliens on all the other planets, if there are any." This was as large as we knew how to cast the net. Not only are all human beings everywhere God's own children, but all sentient beings throughout creation are as well—the Divine has come to enlighten everyone who has come into creation. When we say that Christ has come to teach His people Himself, we are saying that God has come to teach you and me so that we can learn and improve, for we are all inalienably God's people. Let us now, therefore, enroll in the school of Christ the Teacher.

In Twelfth Month 1989, I attended the Consultation on Worship—Earlham School of Religion's tenth in its annual series of consultations—with Louise Wilson and Charlie Ansell of Virginia Beach Friends Meeting. I was eager to see many Friends I'd been separated from for several years, eager to be going to a gathering of Friends who valued worship so highly, and eager to attend my first Quaker ecumenical gathering as a representative of Conservative Friends. High expectations can lead to disappointment, but there were more old friends who were also Friends present than I could possibly speak deeply with, the worship was deep, and I was a Conservative Friend by definition if nothing else.

Some of those conversations raised familiar and painful questions. Why do we make it so hard for God-led, God-fed individuals to lead lives of acknowledged ministry among us? Is it even harder for women—is there unconscious sexism among Friends? It is hard to a greater or lesser extent for everyone, but it seems even harder for women.

I offered vocal prayer during worship the first morning at Earlham. The core of my prayer was this: "Lord, thank You for what You have given me; thank You for what You have taken from me; thank You for what you have kept from me; thank You for what You have left me." I added to each portion of the prayer as I was led, but I don't remember what I said. The Friend sitting next to me reached out and touched me on the shoulder for as long as I was kneeling. Afterward, Louise Wilson simply said, "I *do* love thee!"

Louise's plenary talk was well presented and well received. Her style is very much her own, and if the listener is willing to uncover that tender spot we all have near our heart, Louise's words and presence can't help but have a powerful effect. It is possible to be unmoved by her testimony, but only by choosing to be hard. Yet, when one looks at her offerings intellectually, there is no immortal prose or poetic imagery in her words; it is instead the obvious testimony of her whole being that lends power to what she says. Louise has let God have God's way with her, and it shows. Her spoken words are simply the carrier waves by which God's message is transmitted.

One afternoon, Wil Cooper announced that there would be worship "after the manner of Conservative Friends" at the rise of lunch. About forty Friends were in attendance, and Richard Hall spoke "in the heavenly tones." Charlie Ansell and I ended up alone on the facing bench, without any of the other Conservative Friends present. I felt able to sense the state of the meeting pretty generally but was faced with a dilemma as the meeting began to come to an end because I could tell Charlie was still wrestling with a message. I held off closing the meeting for several minutes, though I could feel the mood of the meeting ripening quickly and did not want to prolong worship beyond its time. At last, I could delay no longer and extended my hand to Charlie, and the meeting was ended. With a word or two we confirmed what had been happening to each of us and that each had been faithful. Charlie's message had not been for this meeting after all, and I had been right to close meeting when I did.

That Charlie and I were on the facing bench and came to have care of the meeting was symbolically very important to me. Certainly, several other Conservative Friends could have been there with or even instead of us, but they chose to sit in the body of the meeting. I was the first of the Conservatives to arrive, and I sat on the facing bench by choice as one likely to offer vocal ministry. This enables one to be more easily seen and heard. Louise Wilson was the next to arrive, and I expected her to come forward—I even made eye contact with her, which I often avoid once I'm seated, but she deliberately turned aside partway up the center aisle and sat down. Charlie then came into the meeting and walked to my side as if he had read a script directing him to do so.

What this symbolized to me is that the active ministry had passed to a new generation, from others to Charlie and myself and our contemporaries. To use Louise's metaphor of a symphony, new instruments had begun to carry the melody. This seemed God-incidence and not coincidence; I was moved to tears as I tried to relate this metaphor and its power to another Friend.

I realized that the call into public ministry that I was seeing acted out in this worship required a personal acknowledgment, acceptance, and surrender that I had begun but not yet fully embraced. The work is never done. This led me into prayer:

> I embrace the ministry God has sent me and give wholehearted assent to God's call for me, without reservation.
>
> I confess my past unfaithfulness to this call through allowing fears and doubts to silence my voice or cloud my message of God's story; I repent and ask forgiveness; I accept Christ's forgiveness with thanksgiving and celebrate God's continuing love for me and acceptance of my service.

> I commit myself to sustained, intentional preparation for ministry through direct prayer, Scripture, and other devotional readings, a rightly ordered life, and other practices as way opens.
>
> I commit myself to unreserved exercise of my gifts of ministry through my physical presence at places and times where way may open for ministry and to a readiness to be God's instrument, casting out in Christ's name all fears, doubts, and other hindrances to faithfulness.
>
> I know that Christ can empower and enable me to overcome all obstacles to the ministry to which God calls me, and I call upon God's power to make me whole and wholly God's, the minister God calls me to be and knows I will be if I am faithful.

Plenary worship on First Day closed the consultation. A Philadelphia Friend rose to call on Friends to repent, naming specific individuals present in the meeting who should repent of action or word. After some time had passed in silence, I was moved to offer my pence, roughly as follows:

> When we consider our spiritual state, and how we have failed to live up to our own standards or the will of God, then our condition seems black indeed—as it did on that Friday night when our Lord died. But let us not linger there but pass on to First Day morning, that first Easter, and gaze upon an empty tomb; the stone is rolled away, Christ has risen, and all the world is changed. Our accounts are settled, and we are made new creatures in a new creation.

After worship, Thom Jeavons, who had been sitting next to me, said that he had never heard me as clear in my ministry as I had been then. Louise Wilson commented that I had never let myself be this transparent before.

After returning from the Consultation on Worship, I was curious to see whether I would be moved to ministry in my home meeting—and if I was, if any change would be noticeable, inwardly or outwardly. I did speak in worship that First Day, beginning with the passage from Luke in which the angel first speaks with Mary (who is troubled by the experience) and closing with John 3:16. Our encounter with the Divine must always be troubling to us in our own strength, which cannot stand divine intervention, but we can embrace the promise that God has sent His Son to give us everlasting life.

I did feel an inward change toward more freedom of action, more confidence that I was an instrument of the Lord's plan, more freedom to state my experience of Christ without veil or hedge. It was as if a rusty hinge, which formerly operated only with resistance and as a result of considerable pressure, had been cleaned and lubricated. Now the hinge moved freely and easily, doing what it was designed for with a minimum of outside force. Joy!

On New Year's Day 1990, I took a homemade New Year's cheesecake with strawberry and blueberry toppings to the Ansells, keeping a smaller cheesecake for myself with no toppings. I added some fatback to the black-eyed peas and hominy this year and must confess that it adds considerably to the taste. It is important to remember that we as a family have been poor, and this simple New Year's Day meal does that. It is equally important to remember that to be poor does not mean to be entirely without pleasure. Black-eyed peas and hominy taste *good* and are also inexpensive. When I am tempted to adopt a jaded perspective and think that only those things that are expensive can be of high quality, it is good to be reminded of hominy and peas with a bit of fatback thrown in, which makes a substantial meal and tastes very good in the bargain.

In First Month 1990, Charlie Ansell and I made a visit to Durham Monthly Meeting. We arrived at our hosts' house the evening before to discover a potluck supper and about eight Friends awaiting us. There was lively discussion during the meal and afterward because Quaker Oats Corporation had acquired the rights to Popeye the Sailor and launched an advertising campaign in which Popeye ate Quaker cereals to get the energy to beat up other people. Several Durham Friends had written letters of protest, but to no apparent effect. The Durham children were getting involved in the effort to stop this connection of Quakers to personal violence.[4]

Both Charlie and I were active in the vocal ministry on First Day. I continued to be moved by the increasing depth and power of Charlie's vocal ministry, which rang clear as a bell once again.

Among Conservative Friends

Durham Friends were used to a formal presentation during their "forum" after meeting for worship, but Charlie and I treated it as a called meeting for worship from which, as we explained before settling down, Friends might feel led to share in a worshipful way about issues important to their spiritual life and condition. There was a good response to this as Friends and attenders shared about spiritual pride and arrogance, the difference between appearing humble and really being humble, and the importance of others in one's own spiritual life. I felt the meeting was covered and that Charlie and I had given acceptable service in both meetings that day.

I was still driving many miles a week for work, family, and Quaker service. In Third Month 1990, a vehicle breakdown put me on an unplanned three-day retreat in North Charleston, South Carolina, prompting this journal entry:

> The Hand of God at work in my life is at brief moments unveiled, and I glimpse a bit of divine mercy and grace—all unheralded and unmerited and but a small part of the infinite gifts I receive every day. It is as if a fish discovered just one or two drops of the ocean that surrounds it every moment and marveled that God had provided these specific bits of wetness just where and when they were most needed; that is exactly my experience. I find myself thanking God for my Saab's blown head gasket and warped head that have already kept me here in unexpected isolation for two days and at least one more to come. I've been surrounded by clouds of angels bringing undeserved gifts and protections I didn't realize I needed, shielding me from evil I'd never seen, taking burdens from me I could never have borne, and leaving me with just what I need: not a jot more, not a tittle less.
>
> In the sparseness of a retreat, all the facades and illusions by which we hide from ourselves are removed. Into the emptiness and silence they leave behind, if we will allow it, come the issues with which we should be wrestling before God. Retreat has come to have the meaning of a safe haven for rest and recuperation—physical, emotional, and spiritual; it would be better thought of as a clearing away of all the clutter that

impedes our spiritual battles. In retreat, naked before God, there is no more hiding, no more excuses. Either we face the adversary with God at our side or we run away. The choice is ours, to fight or to run, but there are no other alternatives.

In normal life, we might put this choice off for weeks or months or even years under the illusion that other matters were important just now or that we were not even under attack in just that way. But in retreat, we cannot avoid seeing the choice that is ours. We are promised that if we choose to face the adversary we cannot lose, for God is with us. It is at times more than we can bear to bring this truth into our hearts, and we choose to run away. No one can run farther than God's love can reach, and whenever we choose to stop running, God's love is there, and the retreat is prepared, and the choice is offered again.

So, unexpectedly, I am in retreat, here in the Cricket Inn in North Charleston, with a few days of absence from normal existence providentially provided for me since I would not see for myself how much I needed them. Here, I've been isolated from working and moving and meeting. In the silence and emptiness of my isolation, some issues have been bubbling up to consciousness, and I have been doing some wrestling.

In my prayers and listening silences, a number of Scripture passages have been lifted up to my attention, including Luke's admonition not to look back after putting one's hand to the plow and passages in Matthew about letting the dead bury the dead, loving Jesus even when it means conflict within the family, and the father who asked his two sons to work in the vineyard.

These verses seem to describe a God at great odds with creation—a stark conflict. But this morning I took a long walk, as I have done each day of this unexpected retreat. I discovered the Sunset Gardens Perpetual Care Cemetery, and near the middle of the cemetery I encountered a white marble statue of Jesus at Gethsemane.

Gethsemane conjures images of Jesus on His knees, sweating blood in His struggle to remain faithful and obedient in the face of the painful death that will be one fruit of obedience: winning an individual victory by individual effort. This Jesus, however, was sitting on the rock with his hands folded on one thigh, looking gently to heaven as if listening to His Father's voice. "Son," I imagine Jesus hearing, "continue to love these people; give yourself to them unstintingly even though they misunderstand both You and Your love and will choose not to love You in return. They will disappoint You and hurt You far more than the cross or the sword, and they will desert You when You most need them. Love them anyway. Be infinitely vulnerable to them because only then will their smallest flicker of love in return be sufficient to bring them home to Me."

As I sat in prayer and contemplation of this vulnerable Savior, I realized that it is just this vulnerability to which Christ calls each of us, to which Christ is calling me now. Only by being as vulnerable as Jesus can I become the person God yearns for me to become, and only as that person can I be the channel and instrument of God's love in our lives and the world around us that God calls me to be.

A few weeks later, as Friends left the Virginia Beach meeting house following midweek worship, Louise Wilson asked me if I would consider becoming clerk of the yearly meeting. At first, I thought she was talking about the monthly meeting. When she said "yearly meeting" I literally stopped in midstride. Louise didn't know whether I would be asked or not but wanted me to have some advance time for spiritual preparation just in case. She said it had taken her a long time to decide to accept the appointment as clerk and that she was at first inclined to decline but eventually accepted the burden. I had thought the yearly meeting clerkship was twenty years or more away for me so had not given the slightest thought about the matter and was glad for the extra time for prayer and discernment.

My first reaction was that the yearly meeting clerkship would involve a great deal of travel. I'd prefer to stay at home and be present to my own monthly meeting. The important thing, of course, was to do what God wanted me to do, not what seemed more attractive or appealing to my creaturely self—or what seemed less appealing to my creaturely self, which would be an equally wrong basis for choosing among alternatives.

Memoir of the Life and Religious Labors of Lloyd Lee Wilson

With God's help, I hoped to be faithful and discerning of right action no matter what combination of choices had to be faced.

My private devotions one First Day in Fourth Month 1990 were particularly deep and profoundly moving. I spent a timeless period in prayer for healing and forgiveness in all aspects of my relationships with my parents and brother, ending in the sense that both had been granted to me if I would accept them. After such a profound early morning, I was not particularly expecting anything profound during the meeting for worship, but on entering the meeting I was reminded of a Virginia Mountain Housing phrase: "That house should be rehabilitated with a torch." Thinking of the hopeless structures that drew such a phrase from our mouths, I was given the image that our lives have been rehabilitated, made livable again, through Christ.

After the meeting had reached a pretty settled state, I was moved to rise and speak at some length on these images and related matters. I said that as the various 12-step programs begin with the acknowledgment that one has a problem one cannot resolve, we gather in worship because we acknowledge we cannot manage our lives in our own power, though there is One who can. Ancient Friends reminded themselves that they were not in control of their lives with such phrases as "intending to meet again [on such and such a date] if consistent with Divine Will" and "if way opens." We feel the ordering influence of the One who redeems and rehabilitates our lives by faithfulness, even to the call of the cross, and offer ourselves in holy obedience to the one who tears down our flawed construction and builds a new life on a solid rock foundation, a new home in Christ.

I could not see him and did not hear anything, but soon after I began to speak, a young man sitting behind me on the other side of the meeting house began to cry openly. (Louise Wilson could see him clearly and told me afterward.) After I regained my seat, this young man stood up, apologized for anything he might be doing wrong since he had never been in a Quaker meeting before, and said he felt he must speak since "the gentleman who just spoke" seemed to have been speaking directly to him. He confessed to living a life he did not like but could not control; he was seeking a way to live better but did not know how. He said he didn't know Christ but was seeking help.

Among Conservative Friends

At the rise of meeting, several Friends spoke with him at length. He and I had a brief opportunity a little later to speak about his spiritual condition, and I gave him a ride down the road to the place he was staying. He said he intended to come back next First Day "if consistent ... ," and I prayed that he would.

Over the summer, I met with Phyllis Sullivan, head of Friends School, to discuss my being the Quakerism teacher at the school in the coming year. She said she very much wanted me to be present in the school in some fashion because my "presence is potent." A year earlier, I would have fussed over that in some way to deny or minimize it; this time I let it pass, knowing in the first place that it is not my presence that is potent but Another's and in the second place that God is indeed present and I should not deny that or God.

This seemed to be a step toward devoting more of my time to direct and intentional ministry and therefore toward clearer discernment of my leading and ways it might be carried out. I accepted the responsibility and spent one morning per week over the next school year meeting with middle and upper school students to discuss Quaker history, public witness, and current affairs as seen from a Quaker perspective. It was personally rewarding and seemed to be faithful service.

Meeting for business in Eighth Month 1990 was my first as presiding clerk. Susan Sieg, the new recording clerk, and I had agreed previously that we would sit in the body of the meeting during the opening worship and that she would read the opening minute as soon as we assumed our seats at the head of the meeting for the regular agenda. Opening worship was deep; then, out of the silence Louise Wilson spoke of perceiving Christ at the head of the meeting and of being moved to that perception by the fact that the clerks were not yet in their usual seats.

A major part of MEO in Ninth Month was taken up with a discussion of discontinuance of ministers and elders who were no longer exercising their gifts. According to the minutes of the monthly meeting for business, one Friend had never been discontinued from his station as an elder although he had been inactive, even as a member, for a number of years. Friends were reminded that the recognition of ministers and appointment of elders was not for a lifetime but for the duration of the presence and exercise of the gift being recognized. Friends were chosen to meet with the inactive elder to learn about his current spiritual condition and to begin to feel out what might be done.

An attender rose in prayer during First Day worship one morning in Ninth Month asking God that Saddam Hussein be deposed. This was the second time in three weeks that she had spoken in some way about the situation in Iraq and Kuwait, and both times I felt her ministry was not in keeping with the faith and testimony of Friends. Her ministry implied she had taken sides in the conflict, which is contrary to Friends' witness, and that she advocated retribution, not restoration of right relationships. Toward the end of the meeting, I was released to speak of Jesus' response to those who committed injustice or other sins—He forgave them. On one level, this was in response to the woman's prayer, which I felt to be out of gospel order, and so I was very tender about what I said and how I said it. I was careful not to refer directly to her or to her prayer in any way; George Fox's admonition not to criticize other ministers in public meetings was on my heart. Yet, it also seemed important to me that ministry that is not in keeping with Friends' faith and practice not be allowed to stand unquestioned lest we lead astray some visitor or attender who might believe that what has been said is what Friends believe to be the Truth.

On reflection, it seemed that I found the right balance between making a clear witness and being tender toward the earlier speaker. Her vocal ministry continued without noticeable change over the next several weeks, though, and I began to feel led to call on this Friend at her home. I shared this leading with one of the elders, who united with my concern and agreed to join me. We made a home visit to labor with this person about her vocal ministry and were very frank about the specific things she had said that seemed to us to be out of keeping with the peace testimony. We also spoke about ways in which she could try to be more centered and Spirit-led in her ministry.

She was not very open to what we had to say and not at all ready to be accountable to our faith community. She told us she was not interested in learning more about Quakers because she got no spiritual nourishment from meeting for worship. She was stimulated by the four television evangelists she watched each First Day morning before meeting, and she came to worship with Friends only to share that televangelical fire with us. Our suggestions that she cut back to only two or three TV shows before meeting or sit longer with a message before standing to share it were not well received. The elder and I left feeling that we had been faithful but probably had not been heard. We had spoken honestly and openly, with the desire of helping her become more fully a part of the meeting, but that was not her desire.

I was at this time responsible for property management at Friendship Village Apartments, the 110-unit Section 8 complex built by Virginia Beach Friends. I came home late one night in Tenth Month 1990 to find a death threat on my answering machine. It called me out by name and (profanely) called me dead. I was stunned. I reported the death threat to the Virginia Beach police; the investigating officer thought the threat was well within the range of behavior of the family of a well-known local activist who had taken issue with my involvement with the apartments.

I called Charlie Ansell to request a clearness/support committee, including at least the three persons who served on both the Virginia Beach Friends Housing Corporation board and the monthly meeting of MEO. This clearness committee met quickly and was quite helpful. They allowed me to express my unease and also think about how to protect Asa, and I came away considerably calmer. I was in God's hands, and I accepted that God would protect Asa from the consequences of my death just as God would not let me die before my time. Nothing more happened other than this one threat.

In Tenth Month 1991, there was a called meeting to consider various hurts in the Virginia Beach Friends Meeting community. I attended that evening and brought Asa, but very soon after I settled into worship I had the sense that this was not my meeting to attend and that I would be better off not attending it. This feeling persisted for some time, and I eventually gave in to it, retrieving Asa and going home. No sooner had I gotten Asa into bed and finished our prayers than the telephone rang. It was a woman I knew asking if I would be willing to explore giving her husband some work so he could get an early release from prison to a halfway house in Norfolk. This call seemed to me to be the reason I was not easy to stay in the meeting earlier, and the validation of that leading made me feel easy to agree to explore those possibilities.

In Second Month 1992, I led a retreat at Quaker Hill Conference Center in Richmond, Indiana, titled A Serious Call to a Devout and Holy Life (an homage to William Law). The theme was to introduce participants to some of the basics and distinctives of Conservative Friends. While there, I met with Steve Main of FUM to explore the possibility that Friends United Press might publish my manuscript of essays. He was generally optimistic, but his primary agenda was discussing his plan for "realigning" Quakerism and enlisting Conservative support on his side of the realignment. Steve wanted to purge FUM of those Friends who did not accept the Richmond Declaration of 1887 and the authority of the Scriptures (i.e., the unprogrammed Friends who belonged to Friends General Conference as well as to FUM) and thereby draw Evangelical Friends Alliance back into FUM. This would take several years, he said, but in the end would produce a single organization representing about 3/4 of all Quakers and would remove what Steve called "a thorn in FUM's side" that took up energy and reduced financial support.

Steve said it would be at least two years before my manuscript would get to the top of the waiting list for publication. I doubted that my essays titled "Waiting Worship" and "Reading the Scriptures" would prove theologically acceptable to the realigned organization since the former disapproved of the paid ministry and the latter placed the authority of the Holy Spirit above that of the Scriptures. I concluded it would be wise for me to look for another publisher.

It seemed to me that Conservative Friends would have no role in the realignment discussions or process but that we should have a care and concern for Friends who were left without a spiritual home as a result. There are many Christian Friends in unprogrammed meetings who look to FUM for spiritual nurture as they are in a minority theologically in their own meetings. The realignment process, if it succeeded, would cut them off from FUM support and nurture. Whether or not it succeeded, it would be likely to alienate these Friends even more deeply from their non-Christian brothers and sisters, who would view the realignment as a negative judgment on themselves—as it indeed was. It might be that I would have a role in the public ministry to provide some of the spiritual nurture these isolated Friends would need. Way would open if it was the right thing to do.

Outside these conversations, the retreat went well. There were about a dozen of us, which I think is a good number for this sort of work. It seemed that Friends found the spiritual food for which they had been hungering. I had several opportunities. Each seemed covered and was a time of spiritual refreshment for me. I had the sense of being worked hard and at the same time being fed and otherwise being given the care I needed to carry out the work set before me. Retreats seemed to be an appropriate setting for my ministry, or at least a portion of it.

Each of the retreat participants had something meaningful to say in appreciation during our closing session, commenting on the time I had put into preparation and the helpfulness of the queries I had given the small groups. One Friend said she had heard all her Quaker life about shared leadership but had never seen it in practice until this weekend. I had a sense of having given acceptable service and having received the Lord's approbation.

About the same time, I became aware of a change in my vocal ministry. I felt the need to speak with greater clarity for Christ growing in me and felt that I was ready to be bold for Him. I preached the everlasting gospel, declaring unequivocally our need for reconciliation and Christ's redemptive love and the necessity to make Christ Lord in our lives. This was couched in terms of God's everlasting invitation to each of us to a closer communion with the Divine, not as condemnation or "fire escape theology."

In the course of supper one night, Asa asked if we could have intercessory prayer at bedtime. "Of course," I replied. "Who do you want to pray for?" Asa said we could make a list, which we did. When I asked why he would like to have intercessory prayer, he said because his First Day school class did every First Day. I asked him if he liked that class, and he said, "Very much." The only problem, he confided, was that the next time he came to live with me he would be too old to be in that class again. I called his First Day school teacher that night to tell her all about this and to thank her for doing such a good job. She was very touched; I think we were both close to tears. To see a young soul in one's care begin to learn to love the Lord is a very precious thing, indeed.

In Third Month, I led a spiritual gifts workshop for the Virginia Beach Friends Meeting. Mostly, I wanted to get across some fundamental concepts about spiritual gifts, and that seemed successful, with a few exceptions. One Friend pushed back against the idea that God might give us something that we did not have beforehand or that a divine gift might improve us or add to us in some way. Her spirituality seemed to be expressed as upholding herself and honoring herself just as she was at that moment, without admission that she might need to improve or be improved in any way.

Another Friend said that she had difficulty understanding what I was saying because she did not know enough of my personal story or spiritual history. At the end of our time together, when I gave Friends the assignment of forming quintets who would get to know one another closely over the next three months to help one another name and claim their spiritual gifts, she said she did not have the time to be involved.

Two of our elders were present and expressed appreciation for the evening. Another Friend came up to me to say she had dreamed of me recently and that in her dream I was skating gracefully on thin ice. Now it seemed to her that the dream referred to this workshop and symbolized my interactions with these two difficult Friends. I'd done well, in her eyes; she felt I had gone just where I needed to go without falling through the thin ice. So, all in all, the feedback was positive, and I had the internal confirmation of having been poured out in giving what I knew without reservation and having spoken clearly about the Truth without condemning or judging those two Friends for being where they were.

That same month, I also spoke at a gathering of Friends held at Durham Meeting. There were twenty-eight adults in attendance, in addition to several children and the adults who were looking after them. I felt equipped and empowered in the teaching ministry, which was affirmed by a number of Friends afterward. I found myself speaking with some authority on several topics, simply stating what I believed to be the truth, for example, about the way that nominating committees should go about their work. This was accepted as helpful, not as threatening. The lesson this taught me was that when I am more secure about my own identity and worth (and thereby less vulnerable to what others may think about me), I am more able to share what I know in ways that are less emotionally charged and therefore less threatening. (It turns out also that what I have to share is valued by those who hear it and that my own worth is affirmed more often than not.)

We are indeed wonderfully and fearfully made, that our psychological nature and our spiritual condition should be so closely linked that healing in one sphere should release the other into greater growth and service. I felt that I had stepped into another level of ministry, due in large part to the liberating of my gifts made possible through the gains I had made in the course of psychotherapy the past year.

Controversy

I received a call in Fourth Month 1991 from the yearly meeting nominating committee saying I was under consideration to be yearly meeting clerk. I replied that I felt clear to accept the nomination if it were offered. I did feel clear to accept the responsibility; the timing was right in that it would begin just as Asa returned to his mother and my duties as a single father slackened. The year of being clerk at Virginia Beach had given me excellent preparation for the yearly meeting clerkship. It felt like a doorway for service to the yearly meeting, to put to further use God's gifts and equipping to further the Kingdom.

I did get one cautionary phone call, from a Friend in the western part of the state who advised me to pray solidly about whether or not to accept the clerkship. He knew of no obstacles but said he feared that the clerkship might be a distraction to me, diverting my attention and energies from my "seedling ministry" of speaking, writing, and traveling in the Truth. This seemed more an affirmation of my public ministry than an admonition about not becoming clerk, but I agreed to sit with it and see what guidance I might receive.

Memoir of the Life and Religious Labors of Lloyd Lee Wilson

A Friend in Virginia Beach resigned from the station of elder in Fifth Month, leading me to reflect on elders generally. She did not feel capable of counseling Friends who came to her for help when her own life was under stress. It seemed out of order to her to continue in the station for even a little while if she could not serve outwardly as she felt elders should, and so she resigned. My sense was not that she had lost her service in the station of elder but that the nature of that service had changed for a time—that elders serve in their station even in those circumstances in which they are so broken that they are unable to give much outward advice or counsel. How they comport themselves in times of difficulty is in fact a powerful witness to the rest of the faith community.

I shared this understanding at the next MEO meeting. Friends have spoken of following Jesus' precept *and example,* of how the witness of Jesus' life teaches us as deeply as His words. Friends today learn from the example of elders (and other seasoned Friends) as much as from their words of wisdom. In the past, I would have kept silent, masking my inner turmoil at the failure of Friends to understand things as I saw them; now I saw that it was unrealistic to expect Friends to share my views unless they heard what my views were and why I held them. On one level, it is a sort of teaching ministry; on another, it is a fruit of my increased spiritual and emotional health.

Friends seem to forget that ministers and elders are not appointed for life but for the duration of their gifts, which may or may not be lifelong. It seems to me those Friends most uneasy about acknowledging these spiritual gifts are the ones most likely to state that the acknowledgments are for life and then to complain about that. Of the seven Friends appointed to the station of elder by Virginia Beach Friends Meeting, none have died in that station and four have been discontinued while still in membership with the meeting.

At meeting for worship later that spring, I spoke about Christ as our Shepherd and the shepherd as the one who leaves his home to live with and care for his sheep, as Christ did. He knows us each and cares for us individually, and we come to know and trust His voice. When we wander, He seeks us out; He protects us from dangers we never see as well as those that startle us. The witness of those who have gone before us testifies to the possibility of a life spent listening to that voice and following its guidance. In closing, I said, "Let us not be stubborn."

In a few moments, a Friend rose to share that he had trouble with the image of humans as Christ's sheep as his experience with sheep as a boy led him to think of sheep as very dumb and likely to do irrational things. I could not help but think that was often a good description of human beings.

By this time, the time for ending meeting had arrived, but I did not feel that hearts were yet clear. In a little while another Friend rose to say that pride goeth before a fall. Now I did feel easy, and in a few minutes I turned to the elder on the facing bench with me and shook her hand. This last speaker and I had a short opportunity after the rise of meeting, in the course of which he said my message was the most powerful he had ever heard in nearly twenty-five years of attending Quaker meetings for worship.

David Martin and I attended the Gathering of Conservative Friends at Olney School in Barnesville, Ohio, in Sixth Month 1991 and had "early morning communion" at 6 a.m., as had become our regular practice whenever we were together. In addition to coffee, we always shared worship and good spiritual conversation on a topic of individual concern. One morning we talked about my collection of essays, and David recommended that I publish a selection of four essays in paperback, similar to the latest New Foundation Fellowship publications. He suggested asking the yearly meeting of MEO for a minute of encouragement in support of my work in the written word and volunteered to take the lead in raising the $3,000 or so he thought it would take to cover the publishing costs. When the final text was prepared, he suggested that we get a minute from the yearly meeting in session or the Representative Body to be printed in the front of the book certifying (in David's words) that I was not "a loose cannon on deck." This was all very encouraging and motivating for me.

Next month at yearly meeting sessions, events began to unfold much as David Martin had suggested. In its business meeting, the North Carolina (Conservative) Yearly Meeting of Ministers, Elders, and

Overseers minuted its encouragement of my writing and appointed a committee to prepare a suitable portion of it for publication. It was understood that in time this committee would probably ask the Representative Body for a minute of endorsement to be inserted in the front of the book.

During the next day's general business sessions, I was nominated to become yearly meeting clerk, although two Friends voiced their reservations that this new responsibility would interfere with my other ministry. When George Parker said, "I believe the young man can do it," the matter was settled and my nomination was approved.

I met with these Friends later to hear more of their concerns, together with David Brown, a former yearly meeting clerk. One spoke of a "great ministry" that he perceived I had, saying that none of us knew what I might be doing ten years in the future and that he didn't want me to do anything that would interfere with that ministry. It troubles me greatly when people express this sort of expectation about me because it seems to ignore who I am in favor of who they wish I were; it also seems to set me up for failure. David Brown was helpful in this discussion, saying that it was to the yearly meeting's benefit to have a clerk who was deeply spiritual and that he felt no conflict between the clerkship and my ministry. The next day, the representatives made their report to the body, and the yearly meeting approved me as their new clerk.

During "collection" at the end of the day, a Friend offered a devotional reading. To my complete surprise, she chose to read a portion of my unpublished essay on gospel order. It had quite an impact on me to hear my words read in a public setting like that and to realize that someone had considered them appropriate for such an occasion. I was made more thankful for God's grace in making me its steward for a time, and I prayed God would help me be a good steward.

Two nights later, after the evening session ended, I was approached by one of the visitors from Ohio Yearly Meeting. He was concerned that several West Grove Meeting members had reported to him that they might "take West Grove out of the yearly meeting" because I had been appointed clerk. He said another visitor from Ohio Yearly Meeting had left yearly meeting sessions early so as to avoid giving the impression that she supported this separation. Just why I was persona non grata was unexpressed. Perhaps it had something to do with my previous experience as Friends General Conference general secretary, or perhaps it was something else. I already knew that some older Friends were concerned that I not wear short pants anymore now that I was clerk.

I didn't think wearing long pants would be any great hardship, but I decided to visit West Grove at the earliest opportunity and let Friends there have more firsthand data with which to work. If they were going to reject me, let them do it with facts, not their conjectures about who I might be.

During closing worship of yearly meeting sessions, I offered vocal ministry about the way in which the gospel story we tell is the story of this current moment and noting that we are writing it ourselves each day. It is important that we write it as well as those who have gone before wrote and lived out their portion, worthy of the Kingdom days yet to come. Afterward, a Friend came over to express her appreciation for my ministry, which she said solved a problem with which she had been wrestling for some time. She did not say what the problem had been.

After yearly meeting sessions ended, I shaved off my moustache while preserving the rest of my beard. It was very interesting to see my upper lip again for the first time since my junior year in college. I did not realize until later the pacifist symbolism of a full beard with no mustache (the believer's beard), but when I did I embraced it completely.

About the same time, I took several shirts to a tailor shop to have the collars taken off. After spending time with plain Friends at the Gathering of Conservative Friends and at our recent yearly meeting sessions, my leading to adopt this statement in my clothing was greatly strengthened. I did not feel led to adopt the old plain dress, which seemed no longer "plain" since it took so much effort to dress that way. I did feel rightly led to remove the collars from all my shirts and to continue to wear only simple, plain pants.

In Eighth Month 1991, Susan Sieg and her estranged husband signed legal separation documents, agreeing to live as if they were not married. In my mind and hers, she was now free to see other men socially, and we began spending time together at meeting functions and at other times. This point of view was not universally shared among Conservative Friends. For some, divorce was barely acceptable, and remarriage after divorce was definitely beyond the pale.

It was common knowledge that I was divorced from Asa's mother, but the matter had never been raised in my hearing. The first hint that there might be trouble with seeing Susan came when I shared with the local MEO that David Martin and I were feeling led to travel in the ministry. After the meeting ended, a recorded minister asked for an opportunity. She asked if I thought I was walking in right order as a public Friend. Her concern was that I had spent too much time in public with Susan at the last yearly meeting sessions, which she felt was wrong because I was now a public Friend. If I felt no stop or hesitation about this, however, she was easy to allow the request to go forward.

This was the first hint of what became a long-lasting and painful controversy involving Friends across several yearly meetings. The only recent change in my role among Friends was that I was now the yearly meeting clerk. Did that make me a public Friend? Were the standards of behavior different for some Friends than for others? Why did my role as yearly meeting clerk make my behavior wrong but my role as a recorded minister or monthly meeting clerk did not? Why did certain Friends find it so difficult to let this issue rest, in spite of their repeated assurances that they would do so? Eventually, Susan and I accepted that we were an anvil on which Friends were hammering out their own problems. It was a painful process.

In Eighth Month 1991, I made a visit to West Grove meeting—the lion's den. If West Grove Friends did have anything to say about my being clerk, I wanted them to say it to me directly. No one did, but the day was memorable nonetheless. Of the nine Friends at worship, six were Newlins (one of the founding families), two were visiting from Ohio Yearly Meeting (Conservative), and the ninth was me.

The meeting house sits on rock pilings in a grove of old oak trees. There was almost no traffic passing by on the road; other than a distant airplane, the only noise was natural. The building had no indoor plumbing, but there was a sink with running cold water outside one of

Among Conservative Friends

the privies. The meeting house had two entrances and was partitioned inside. The inner partition was a nearly solid wall, with shuttered windows and one doorway cut through. Though Friends now use only one half of the meeting house for worship, they sit separately, with women on the left side of the aisle and men on the right. Luckily, I noticed this and was about to sit on the right (and correct) side when Alfred Newlin brought me up to the gallery.

I was comforted by the perceptible Presence of the Holy Spirit among these few Friends gathered in the shade of these old oaks in unobserved faithfulness. In the quiet, I came to a fresh appreciation of their spiritual depth and how different their lives and worship were from those of us who lived and worshipped in a city. They might be stubborn, ancestor worshipping, and overly distrustful of all other Quakers, but there was something valid and powerful about what happened in their meeting for worship that had be respected. After some time, Alfred Newlin stood in vocal ministry. About midway through the worship, I knelt in prayer, after which Alfred stood in ministry once again.

Afterward, we went to David and Dixie Newlin's dairy farm for dinner: two kinds of chicken, fresh biscuits, and three desserts. While the women were putting this together, David Newlin told me about his grandfather, who was clerk of Chatham Monthly Meeting at the time of the separation of the original North Carolina Yearly Meeting into two separate yearly meetings, one affiliated with Five Years Meeting and one not. The traditionalists met in the Chatham meeting house on First Day afternoons for a number of years until one day they arrived to find the meeting house had been locked against them. At this point, the decision was reached to build West Grove meeting house just down the road from Chatham meeting. (A similar sequence of events at Holly Springs meeting had led to the establishment of Friendsville Monthly Meeting.)

David Newlin was then clerk of West Grove. His father had been clerk of NCYM(C). Alfred Newlin, a recorded minister, had uncles who were at one time simultaneously clerks of the two North Carolina Yearly Meetings—FUM and Conservative. Quakerism and service to Quakers is deep in the blood of these Friends.

Memoir of the Life and Religious Labors of Lloyd Lee Wilson

The Newlins told the story West Grove and many other rural Quaker meetings in the last century whose children married out of meeting or moved away in search of better employment. A sense of inevitable decline and demise pervaded the conversation. There was no sense of convincement as a means of continuing the meeting; the universe of possible younger members of West Grove and these other meetings was limited to the children of present members. When those young people moved away or married out of meeting, there was no way to replace them. Alfred Newlin told me that his father had been very enthusiastic about the establishment of Virginia Beach Friends Meeting as a possible beginning of an upswing in the membership of the yearly meeting. No one seemed to have thought that something similar might happen at West Grove.

In Ninth Month, the same Virginia Beach minister who had raised the question about my relationship with Susan asked for a meeting with both of us together with an elder of the meeting. Contrary to what she had said before, she had continued to be distraught about the relationship. The four of us had a frank discussion in which Susan and I tried to communicate the depth of our prayer and the search for discernment that we had undertaken before beginning our relationship and the degree to which we felt God's blessing on our being together. At the end of our time together, the minister said that although she wished we had waited longer before beginning our relationship, what was done was done and what was right now was to get on with our lives. I was glad that her previously hidden discomfort had apparently been laid to rest. If only that had been the case.

In Ninth Month, I attended a retreat for yearly meeting clerks from across North America. I was impressed by how different NCYM(C) was from the other meetings: smaller, less social action oriented, more unified spiritually. The issues that gripped and separated other yearly meetings, such as the proposed realignment of yearly meetings, Christian-universalist tensions, inclusion of gay persons, were much less fraught with tension in our yearly meeting. I loved NCYM(C), and hearing these other clerks describe their yearly meetings brought my affection into sharper focus. We need to change as we grow in Christ, but I truly love the faith people we are now.

Among Conservative Friends

In Tenth Month 1991, two Conservative Friends from Ohio, Richard Hall (a recorded minister) and Katherine Roberts, visited Virginia Beach Friends Meeting in the ministry. It seemed that Richard's message in worship was aimed at me directly, and events that afternoon proved it to be true. Almost forty Friends came to my house to have lunch with Richard and Katherine, which was a very festive time. After other Friends had gone, Richard had an opportunity with me in which he urged me to stay away from Susan in order to avoid the eternal flames of hell. He said Christ could forgive me for having been previously married and then divorced, but if I were to marry again that would be adultery, for which Christ would not forgive me. He said he would certainly never remarry himself after being divorced. I replied that I had been married twice and divorced twice already, so if he was correct then I was condemned to hell already, no matter what I did. He then implored me to break off the engagement for Susan's sake, to save her from hell. I responded that Susan was an adult who could make those decisions for herself and that he should speak to her directly. (He did have an opportunity with her after he finished with me.)

Richard ended by stating that he thought it was imperative that I not see Susan again socially until a year after her final divorce decree was issued—a somewhat incongruous statement, given what he had said earlier about going to hell. I thanked Richard for his loving concern and for being faithful enough to speak to me in person.

I really did appreciate Richard's faithfulness in coming to see me, although I wondered who had been stirring things up in Ohio; Richard and I had known about each other but had not been friends or even acquaintances before this. A Virginia Beach minister had said that week that she had been in correspondence with Richard Hall, so I suspected that it was her and that she continued to be pretty upset, no matter what she said to me personally.

As for Richard's advice, it seemed like fire insurance theology to me—and still does. I do not believe that a loving God will condemn anyone to eternal flames and punishment, so I am not likely to change my behavior merely in order to avoid hell. God works by invitation, not by coercion or intimidation, and God's messengers do the same.

One of the ironies of this visit was that the various critics who agreed that I was violating Quaker standards of behavior disagreed with each other about what those standards were. Earlier that year, Susan and Louise Rothrock had planned to go to a Quaker gathering in Barnesville, Ohio. When Louise had to cancel at the last minute, she encouraged Susan to ride with me to Barnesville and back. David Martin criticized me for doing this, saying Louise was wrong. As an illustration, he shared that he had refused to give Katherine Roberts an automobile ride from Barnesville to Earlham College because she was not his wife. Richard Hall, however, apparently had not seen anything wrong with traveling the much longer distance between Ohio and Virginia Beach by automobile on an overnight trip accompanied by the same woman, also not his wife. This pattern of our critics disagreeing with each other about what the standards were became commonplace.

Later in Tenth Month, while in Greensboro for several Quaker activities, I met David Martin at a local ice cream parlor to speak with him about my relationship with Susan. He heard me out and said that he had only one question to ask: "Have Susan and you taken this before the Lord?" I assured him that we had done so and that we continued to pray for God's guidance and protection in our relationship. "Then," said David," I have nothing more to say." I was glad to think that David was no longer upset about us. (I was wrong about this, but I did not know that at the time.)

Travel in the Ministry to Virginia, Maryland, and Pennsylvania

In Tenth Month 1991, I made a short trip in the ministry among meetings belonging to Baltimore Yearly Meeting. For this trip, it seemed most feasible to ask a local Friend to serve as a companion in the ministry, and for the first days of the trip Chuck Hughes did this. I spent the early part of the day of my departure reading the Bible and some other devotional material, praying, and resting. It felt good to have a little time to practice on my mountain dulcimer, which had been too much neglected for several weeks.

The trip began on Tenth Month 13 with a visit to Midlothian Preparative Meeting outside Richmond, Virginia. There were considerably more people there this time than the last time I was there, and most of the growth had been among families with elementary school-aged children. I was exercised in the vocal ministry, speaking on the great unconditional love that God has and the many opportunities that we present for God to exercise the gifts of unmerited grace, mercy, and unconditional love. About the most that can be said of us is that we are a people learning to love God—but that seems to be enough.

After worship, about fourteen adults gathered for what the meeting called Meeting for Nurture. A large box stood in the center of the room into which each person was invited to place a symbol of their spiritual life, which they later drew out again and used it to disclose some aspect of their spirituality to the group. The majority of persons gathered were using some form of A Course in Miracles as the centerpiece of their spiritual life, one (European) woman was interested in native American religion, and two were universalists of one sort or another. I and two other persons were the only self-described Christians. After most of the others had spoken, I was led to a testimony about the One who teaches us directly, without textbooks, and enables us to live in the community and harmony with one another and with nature that others in the room yearned for.

This meeting lasted until 3:30 as Friends began to acknowledge the great disparities in their spiritual paths and to express their desire to find ways to be mutually nurturing in spite of their diversity. There was an acceptance by the non-Christians present that Quakerism gained its historical vigor and vitality from Christ, which seemed to me to go further than many other meetings.

This meeting ran later than expected, which made it hard to get to Adelphi Meeting on the outskirts of Washington, D.C., for evening worship, but Chuck Hughes was waiting patiently at the appointed rendezvous with a box of fried chicken, and we set out together immediately for the meeting house, arriving only a few minutes after the appointed time. There was a spirit of fatigue and lassitude over this group; Chuck felt this well and seemed to think it accounted for the absence of several Friends who had been expected to attend that night.

The next day I called at the Baltimore Yearly Meeting offices to visit Frank Massey. Frank appeared to be healthy and happy, though he said he was tired to the very core. My affection for him was renewed during our time together, and I was moved to pray fervently for his protection and blessing.

That afternoon I asked Chuck Hughes to describe things five years from now if all his best hopes came true. His response was "a Conservative meeting, in a Conservative context." That context, he explained, would be affiliation with other Conservative Friends, which was important to the long-run stability and nurture of a Conservative monthly meeting. Chuck believed that Ohio Yearly Meeting would offer affiliation to such a group, as they did with Glenside Preparative Meeting near Philadelphia.

We went next to Langley Hill, where we met with Friends from Langley Hill and Alexandria meetings in Virginia. I explained what it meant for me to be traveling in the ministry and described the process involved in testing my leading and receiving the liberty of my monthly meeting to make the journey. One of the points I emphasized was the sense of not knowing what would happen but having faith that if I was faithful in rendezvousing with God and distant Friends, something divinely good would happen. We settled into a time of waiting worship, and after a while I spoke a few words about allowing God to be at work in ways unknown to us by being faithful to the Divine Call.

The worship slowly made that familiar transition into a discussion proceeding from a deep place among us. We talked about taking responsibility only for being faithful and not for the apparent outcomes of our actions and about the ways an apparently irritating personality in a meeting or spiritual formation accountability group could be a pathway to spiritual growth for all concerned, teaching us patience, lovingkindness, gentleness, and intercessory prayer. One Friend spoke of his reluctance to "dump his baggage" on others, which became an opening for discussing how much a willingness to do just that could be a blessing to all concerned, giving others an opportunity to exercise their gifts. The Friend concerned could receive some healing and would become in turn better able to help those who had first helped him. This exploration seemed to give this particular Friend considerable comfort.

A Friend asked for an explanation of an "opportunity," so I gave some concrete examples of what had gone on in opportunities in my own experience. It seemed right to close with another period of waiting worship, during which time I was brought to my knees in a prayer of thanksgiving for all those things that God had given us, or taken from us, or kept from us, or allowed to remain with us. Chuck Hughes said later that this was the first time that "knees had hit the floor" in Langley Hill Meeting and that he had had the impulse to stand in unity, being stopped only by the realization that of those present only I would know what he was doing and why.[5]

I spent the next day sightseeing in Washington, starting at the Vietnam Veterans Memorial and then working my way up one side of the National Mall and down the other. It was drizzling rain when I started, but a steady stream of people was walking down to the memorial anyway, and fresh flowers were in evidence along the base of the wall. I came away with a fresh sense of how much useless waste that particular war (and all wars) had caused. How could one conceive of anything being so important that one could send so many young people to their deaths, with instructions, training, and equipment to kill and ravage as much as possible before they were killed themselves?

The rest of the day was much less bitter and sad. I enjoyed the National Museum of Industrial History and the Smithsonian National Museum of Natural History. At the geology exhibit in the latter museum, a young man, seeing my plain dress (Chuck had lent me a black cardigan sweater to go along with my black broad-brimmed hat, collarless white shirt, and believer's beard), felt led to explain to me, in *very* basic terms, the principles and uses of the seismograph on exhibit. I could not resist; in a near whisper, I explained that I had two degrees from MIT, understood the physics, and was comparing the design to a similar instrument I had built in mechanical engineering class as an undergraduate.

That evening, Chuck Hughes and I attended the midweek meeting for worship at Friends Meeting of Washington. I had the sense throughout the worship that there was a person present who was close to making a decision about Jesus Christ. During the first half hour or so of worship, I was brought to my knees in a prayer of thanksgiving for God's creation and our place in it and for God's mercy and generosity in sending Jesus Christ to live with us, share in our pain and death, and rise to live again among us. I was later exercised in the vocal ministry, recalling some of the many names for Jesus that George Fox had used such as Healer, Counselor, Great Physician, Comforter, and Advocate. These draw such a distinctive picture of Christ that it is not remarkable that Quakers are considered a third form of Christianity. Set aside any other experiences of Christian thought or faith when you come to Quakers and experience Christ directly and immediately. We are in need of Christ in each of the roles Fox described, and Christ is searching us out more strongly and clearly than we are searching for Him. Let us put our Hands in the Hand that stilled the waters. This seemed like acceptable service.

On the evening of the seventeenth, about fourteen Friends and attenders gathered at Sandy Spring meeting in Maryland for midweek worship. It seemed for some time that this was, at long last, going to be the meeting in which I was given nothing to say, despite being on a journey in the gospel ministry. I gave myself up to that prospect in good spirit, trusting that my silence would itself be a message. However, it seemed right a little while later to go to my knees in vocal prayer, and I did so, thanking God for mercy and consistent guidance in all we think and do. After a little while, another worshipper offered some vocal ministry on the Thirteenth Psalm, and some time after that I was brought to my feet in vocal ministry on the theme of letting our lives speak. If that is our response to the Great Commission, I said, then it is imperative that our lives be characterized by holy obedience and the greatest consistency.

The next day dawned clear and mild, and the entire day was beautiful. The fall colors were much further advanced than at home, making the forest as colorful as Joseph's coat. I arrived at the Broadmead retirement community in Cockeysville, Maryland, early enough for a brief walk around the grounds before heading for my home visit with Marshall and Virginia Sutton. After a period of solid worship, we began reflecting on the spiritual condition of the yearly meeting. They were concerned about anything that appeared separatist, including both the "call for realignment" and local attempts to form a new covenant group in the Washington area. Marshall felt that Baltimore Yearly Meeting could not accept a new monthly meeting that said it accepted everything in the yearly meeting's *Discipline* and *Manual of Procedure* yet restricted membership to those who professed a belief in Jesus Christ. He also thought that the geographic obstacles to affiliation with a Conservative yearly meeting could not be overcome. They were both concerned that non-Christian persons might be scared off from Quakerism by explicit Christianity but had never thought, until I posed the possibility to them, that there might be Christians who left Quakerism because it did not support them in their Christianity.

From Broadmead, I drove to Blue Mountain Nurseries in Harford County, Maryland, operated by Dick and Janet Simon. Dick was clerk of Gunpowder Meeting in Sparks, Maryland. He had to work all afternoon, so I had a mixture of time to myself and an extended talk with Janet. It was a pretty open and tender time, and I believe I was able to offer some consolation and resources to Janet for matters on her heart.

After an early supper, I left for York Meeting in Pennsylvania. Only one Friend was there when I arrived. He told me of the meeting's "bad experience" with another traveling minister from Ohio who had arrived unannounced and was moved to give "a twenty-minute sermonette on sin and righteousness." Apparently, some Friends had been concerned that this traveling minister intended to come to their meeting every week. All in all, I did not feel welcomed to York by hearing this story. When no one else showed up, we went inside to begin worship. I asked to use the facilities, which in this case was a brick outhouse, but it was locked with a padlock and my host could not find the key. I was not in urgent need, which was fortunate, but this was beginning to feel like the kind of night about which stories are told in later years.

We settled into worship, sitting on the facing bench, and after a while other people began drifting into the meeting house by ones and twos until at last there were eight of us altogether. After some time, I was moved to my knees in a prayer of thanksgiving that we lived in a time and place that allowed and enabled us to gather for worship without threat or hindrance and that for 225 years Friends in this meeting had been faithfully preserving the meeting and the meeting house in which we were worshipping. Later, another Friend offered ministry to the effect that God offered us a relationship rather than perfection in solitude. Otherwise, the meeting was silent.

After the rise of worship, we talked about a number of things, including the process of traveling in the ministry, how spiritual gifts could or should be recognized, and how people's various gifts relate to and support one another. This seemed to be a helpful discussion to several of the persons in attendance, and it seemed to me that what I had to say was coming from a centered place. Five of us then went on to a local restaurant for dessert and more discussion, which centered on a couple who had not been attending meeting recently, supposedly because another member had made an offensive remark to the husband of the couple about his apparent sexism. The offending Friend had sincerely apologized, but there had been no reconciliation. I felt led to share the story of the foot washing at Marlborough and that "more is required of some than others."[6] The offending Friend, present at this discussion, accepted this as a bit of good counsel, saying that she might have to do more to attempt reconciliation.

My hosts for that night lived in Carlisle, Pennsylvania. We lingered over breakfast for an extended time, talking about Quaker practices and procedures and how to nurture Christians in a deeper spiritual life in the context of Baltimore Yearly Meeting. The conversation continued until it was time to walk down to Carlisle Meeting House and have lunch. In worship afterward, I was moved to my knees in prayer and later stood in ministry about the invitation of Christ, who stands at the door and knocks and will sup and abide with us if we will only invite Him in. There was one other spoken message; otherwise, the meeting was silent.

The monthly and quarterly committees of ministry and counsel then gathered around a large table to meet with me. We talked for about two hours in a question-and-answer format. Their questions included the progress of my spiritual journey, how God had been active in my choice of career and work life, how ministers of the gospel were acknowledged, and what I did to keep from feeling selfish about my time and the demands on it. Finally, it seemed that hearts and minds were clear, and we parted in love. I set out in the late afternoon and early evening through the wooded countryside toward and into Amish country, arriving at the home of my hosts for that night shortly after dark.

I was back at Nottingham Meeting in Oxford, Pennsylvania, for First Day worship after several years' absence. I spoke during worship, but the words I spoke have since escaped me, as is often the case. I have a sense that the general feeling was joy and optimism springing from God's intimate love and care. After worship, we all joined for lunch downstairs. There was much good fellowship and conversation, demonstrating a real feeling of friendship and community among the members of the meeting community. Finally, it was time to take my leave and head homeward. It was difficult to leave such sweet spirits.

Once home, I felt that the trip had been acceptable service. There was new growth aplenty among the Friends I had visited; although some of the directions this growth was taking troubled me, it was not my concern. I had been the instrument by which they had received some nurture from their (and my) Master, which is all that I could ask. It seemed to me that during this trip my ministry and prayers had been more than usually gentle and inviting, expressing the unconditional, patient, long-suffering, redeeming love of God and Jesus Christ for each of us. This was not a radical change but a difference in emphasis, which I trusted God put into my words for a reason. Thank God for giving me this opportunity and for enabling me to accept it and Virginia Beach Friends to release me into it.

More Service and Controversy

Representative Body met at West Grove meeting late in Tenth Month, and I had my first opportunity to clerk at the yearly meeting level. All in all, it went well for both me and Jeanne Rose, who was serving as yearly meeting recording clerk for the first time as well. Several Friends came up afterward to say that our service had been more than acceptable. I felt at my ease, even though the meeting house at West Grove requires that the clerks sit high in the gallery. I expected Friends to give respect to the meeting for business, not the clerks, and had some success. As one Friend observed, by the end of the meeting even Alfred Newlin was standing and waiting to be called on before speaking.

During the meeting, the Young Friends of Durham Monthly Meeting proposed a new query to replace the yearly meeting's tenth query on living in harmony with nature. The proposal was well done, and most of those present felt it would be an improvement over the current query. Unfortunately, there was no mechanism that would enable the yearly meeting to revise just one query without opening the entire *Discipline* to review and revision. That project was something the yearly meeting was not prepared to undertake at that time.

I kept this incident in mind for many years. While serving on the yearly meeting's Discipline Revision Committee some twenty-five years later, I proposed language that would make it clear that the yearly meeting could revise any part of the new *Discipline* without necessarily opening up the entire document to change, and I cited the Durham Young Friends' proposed query as the prime example of why this would be a good idea. That language was approved.

At the next meeting of MEO at Virginia Beach, a recorded minister began to criticize me for being away from meeting too much, depriving Friends of my leadership and ministry. Others pointed out the meeting had appointed that Friend as assistant clerk that year specifically to enable me to travel in the ministry and that they thought the arrangement was working out well. The Lord lifts up ministry from those who are gathered, Friends said, and if we depend too much on any one person we are being unfaithful to our own tradition and experience as Friends.

This minister persisted in her statements of unease in spite of this lack of support from others until at last I volunteered to cancel my scheduled retreat at Powell House that weekend if any Friend present felt I should not go. This went not only to her stated issue with my frequent travel in the ministry but also to her unstated issue with my relationship with Susan. Deliberately, I polled each Friend present, asking them whether they were easy with my going to Powell House as planned. No one voiced any objection. Finally, I asked the concerned Friend herself if she was easy with my going, and she agreed that I should go.

Among Conservative Friends

I then reiterated my long-standing desire to be under the care of the local MEO in my ministry, especially for travel outside the monthly meeting, and reminded Friends that they had been unwilling to provide that. The minister who had just objected to my travel stated her unwillingness for that meeting to provide oversight for me because she was "unwilling to be accountable to anyone else" for her own ministry. She said she had experienced too much pain in this manner to be willing to make herself vulnerable. However, an elder and an overseer said they were willing to meet with me to help me discern whether to undertake new activities in the ministry.

The Powell House retreat, titled A Serious Call to a Devout and Holy Life, was held as scheduled in Old Chatham, New York, in Eleventh Month 1991. This was the second time I had given a retreat inspired by William Law's book by the same name. The underlying premise was that if our encounter with Christ is real, then we ought to be about the business of re-ordering our entire lives around that encounter. No halfway measures made sense. What did it mean to answer God's serious call to a devout and holy life in the context of the Quaker Christian tradition?

I learned from a staffer that sixty Friends were registered. Powell House itself was full to capacity, and they had lodged sixteen participants in nearby B&Bs. It was momentarily daunting to think there would be literally ten times as many participants as I had expected, but I turned it over to God and trusted that my format was flexible enough to serve a large number as well as a smaller. Seeing a wall plaque in my room about the Flushing Remonstrance, I spent some time in silent prayer and thanksgiving for those brave souls who had made it possible for these sixty folks to gather.

Opening worship settled quickly and deeply, and the gathered Friends seemed hungry for the gospel message in my presentation. I felt enabled and empowered, truly released into service. There was great spiritual enthusiasm in the group, perhaps because they felt restrained from celebrating the gospel in their home meetings. It was a great joy just to be gathered together, whatever I might have to offer.

Scripture tells us that Jesus was unable to work any miracles in his hometown because of their lack of faith. What I felt was the other end of that phenomenon: the strength that comes when one's auditory is full of faith and enthusiasm for the gospel. Even the Bible passages I read seemed to be filled with an extra power to touch the hearts of Friends there, as individual after individual came to me and thanked me for opening the Scriptures to them in new, fresh ways. Between plenary sessions, I would revise the material for the next session in light of our experience in the session just finished.

I had felt for a long time that if I ever seriously strayed from the Lord's favor or from doing the Lord's will, one consequence would be that God would remove my gifts in the ministry. The experience of that weekend was powerful confirmation that I had not fallen under condemnation, and I was thankful.

The retreat finished as strongly on First Day morning as it had been all weekend. Friends were already talking about scheduling another retreat in a few months and asking me about possible resource persons. The drive home gave me several hours to reflect on the weekend. God had been very generous and merciful to us all.

In Virginia Beach Friends Meeting, the controversy continued as the months passed. Susan and I continued to meet with Louise Wilson and others in the hope of coming to some reconciliation. Often, we would be joined by one or more elders or other seasoned Friends willing to try to serve as mediators. Sometimes there seemed to be some progress toward healing, but at other times I left these meetings feeling we were more at odds than we had been before.

Our accusers agreed with one another that there was something seriously "wrong" about my relationship with Susan, but they did not agree on just what that "wrong" was. Sometimes our relationship took a back seat to some other perceived flaw. In that case, an evening might be spent on that subject without mentioning our relationship. Often, I felt it was futile to try to respond and simply listened until the other person(s) ran out of steam.

Among Conservative Friends

During this period, an elder, two other recorded ministers, and I met to explore the monthly meeting's role in clearness for proposed marriages under the care of the meeting. After the rest of our business was completed, I shared with these Friends an update on my relationship with Susan and offered to answer any questions or hear any comments they might have. All three were quite positive, decrying the attitude that Quaker leaders must be perfect as well as the "leader-bashing" that one Friend in particular saw going on in our meeting. After this meeting, I was reassured that what I felt to be so right was in fact not opposed to Quaker thought and practice. I wanted to make myself available to talk directly with the rest of the members of MEO, as way opened.

In Twelfth Month, all the old issues arose once again at the MEO meeting, ranging from my car (an old Mercedes sedan) to my broad-brimmed hat to my relationship with Susan. One Friend lingered for some time on the subject of my car until Lucy Stone remarked that when she was living in England, the clerk of London Yearly Meeting had driven a Rolls Royce. After that, the critical Friend changed the subject.

When the same Friend then started in about Susan and me again, I told her that I had talked with every member of MEO about my relationship with Susan save two and had an appointment to talk to one of those scheduled that coming week. Her response to this was, "Well, that doesn't make me very happy, Lloyd Lee." I replied, "I didn't do it to make you happy." The comments of Friends during these conversations, I added, was that my personal life was my personal life and that criticism should not be allowed to interfere with my duties as clerk. The Friend was still unwilling to give up her opposition to the relationship. I told her once again that if she thought I should be removed as clerk of monthly meeting, she needed to bring it before meeting for business. She said, also once again, that she would take it up in prayer.

Susan and I felt a continuing divine affirmation of our relationship in our prayers and worship together that I wished other Friends could share. Of course, some did; perhaps others would one day.

Just before Christmas 1991, the Friend who had been most critical of our relationship wanted to talk to me about it once more, and I agreed to meet her in the meeting house. She said that after a long period of prayer and fasting she had come to see how much the clash between us had been her own doing and not mine. She had been obsessed with seeing the monthly meeting develop just so and in seeing me develop just so. In her words, she had treated the monthly meeting as her child and had put me on a pedestal of her own making. She now saw that those actions were wrong, and she asked my forgiveness. I told her I was glad to hear that she had come to that realization and that I believed her sincerity.

I was so taken aback by this unexpected reversal that I could not be sure that I could truly forgive her for her actions. Could it be that all this turmoil was over at last? I truly hoped and prayed so. I believed she was more correct than she realized and that all this had been primarily about her own issues. Could she really be finally ready to own up to that and let go of her concerns about me? For my part, over the next few days I prayed to be given the spirit of forgiveness for her.

After New Year's, I took this Friend aside privately and told her that I forgave her for what she had done over the previous six months. She expressed appreciation that I had not just said I forgave her when she first confessed because she knew that could not have been true, fully and deeply, so quickly. She asked whether I thought she should say something at MEO next week. I said that I thought she should say something but that it did not have to be in any great detail—just enough to let other Friends know that we were no longer in conflict and that she did not oppose my relationship with Susan any longer. She in fact did do this at the next meeting.

In First Month 1992, I had a vision during worship in which I was trying to get out of a room but could not. My surroundings had Salvador Dali-like characteristics, with distorted perspectives, no roof to the room, and solid footing only on large stepping-stones distributed at some distance from each other throughout the room. At first, I was trying to open a closed door, but it resisted all my efforts to force it open. When I turned around, there was an already-opened door across the room. Trusting that the stepping-stones would prove trustworthy, I crossed the room and attempted to pass through that door, only to become stuck partway through. At this point, I became aware of several large burdens distributed around my body: a backpack, several suitcases, and a number of growths on my body in several places that looked like large tumors. With all these extra items to carry, I was simply too large to pass through the door. Only when I put aside all my burdens/baggage and stood naked before the door was I able to pass through.

It seemed to me that the meaning of the vision was the difference between being willing and being willful. As long as I was trying to force open closed doors and carry my own baggage through open doors, I was being willful, standing in the same relationship to God that a two-year-old often stands in relation to their own parents. What God is calling us to be is willing—to turn around and pass through the door God is opening for us, leaving behind everything, for everything except God is a burden to us and a hindrance to our passing through. It seemed to me also that this was a vision for the entire meeting. Shortly after the children joined us for the second half of worship, I stood and recounted my vision. It seemed to be acceptable service.

Later in First Month, I attended a Housing and Urban Development conference in Philadelphia near Arch Street meeting house. Over a dinner break, I set out on a walk to reacquaint myself with Center City. I stopped to buy a hot pretzel at a shop that catered to tourists by dressing its staff in "old-time plain Quaker apparel." The surprised look on the young woman who served me when she looked up and realized she had the real thing as a customer was worth the price of the pretzel! In my black broad-brimmed hat, black sweater, and believer's beard, I looked the part.

As I began walking back toward my hotel, a man of about my age walked past me and began to window shop. Then he turned and began to walk back in the way he had come, lagging behind me. It soon became clear that he was following me. Before too long, he quickened his pace, caught up with me, and started a conversation. He was a plainclothes policeman, as it turned out, on his way home after work. He asked if I were Amish, and when I said no, just a plain Quaker, he remarked that not many were seen these days. Then he told me a story about hitchhiking home one night in the rural area where he grew up. He was offered a ride by a man with a believer's beard, which frightened him so much he took off running cross-country to get away. He now figures it was the safest ride he would ever be offered.

About this time, a young black man came up to us and asked for 50 cents to make up the rest of the fare he needed to get home. I stopped walking, counted out the amount he needed, and gave it to him. My policeman acquaintance continued to walk on, but slowly so I could catch up easily when I was done. He then began to talk about how he never gave money to beggars because he could never be sure how it would be used. I wanted to talk to him about how the gospel says to give to anyone who asks, not just to people who deserve money or who will use it well, but for some reason I was reluctant to do so. In the end, all I said was that we can never know another person's story and so can never judge. He seemed to be chewing on this as we parted company; I hoped it would bear fruit at some future time.

The controversy over my relationship to Susan continued unabated in the months that followed. After I returned home, two well-respected Friendship Meeting Friends sent me a letter in Third Month advising me to resign as yearly meeting clerk immediately so that they could recommend a replacement to be appointed at the spring Representative Body meeting. They claimed not to be judging my relationship with Susan but acting in the best interests of the yearly meeting, whose members must respect and have confidence in the yearly meeting clerk. I also learned that a third Friendship member had been telling Friends of his deep concern about the relationship between Susan and me and his concern that I was a womanizer.

This was an especially painful development because it revealed that at least two Friends I respected had said one thing to me and quite another behind my back. I had approached the Friend who was concerned that I was a womanizer several months previously to discuss my relationship with Susan, and he had raised no objection to our relationship. He had not raised that issue to me since, in person or via telephone or letter, though we talked by phone periodically.

The other Friendship members advising me to resign had been approached by the Virginia Beach Friend who had apologized to me in Twelfth Month for her criticism of Susan's and my relationship. It came to light that, about a month after apologizing to me, she had assembled a group of Friends in Greensboro to talk about Susan and me and what should be done. All this felt like a body blow; I was both sick and angry.

Susan and I met with these three Friends when we could. They felt that yearly meeting clerks are and should be held to a higher standard of behavior than other Friends and that I had not lived up to that standard. This higher standard was unwritten and undiscussed.

I said I believed most Friends in Virginia Beach were now reconciled, explaining that I had approached each member of Virginia Beach MEO save one to give each an opportunity to share their concerns with me directly. Their most common response was that my personal life was my personal life and not a concern of the meeting at large. One Friend immediately asked if he could write each member of the Virginia Beach MEO directly to confirm this. I consented, though it seemed to me that his purpose was not to find out the truth but to catch me in a lie.

None of these Friends wanted to speak with Susan; they each claimed they had no quarrel with her. Yet, if it was my relationship with Susan that disturbed them, was not she as involved in that relationship as I was? I found this treatment of Susan as a nonperson both fascinating and highly objectionable.

I concluded our time together by reminding these Friends that I was appointed clerk of the yearly meeting by the yearly meeting and that I did not feel that any two or three Friends, no matter how weighty, should be able to undo the will of the yearly meeting. If they persisted in their concern, I said, they should speak at the Representative Body meeting next month and see what the will of the yearly meeting was. None of the three seemed particularly eager to do this, but I expected that they would find the wherewithal when the time came.

About a week later, an overseer of Virginia Beach Friends Meeting asked to meet with me, saying that she had received a letter from a Friendship Meeting member and wanted to talk about it. From her description of the letter, its primary objective was to try to catch me in an untruth. She said that she would reply that she was supportive of Susan's decision to leave her previous marriage and happy that Susan and I had found each other and had felt blessed by God in our growing relationship.

I continued visiting each of the meetings in the yearly meeting, joining Fayetteville meeting in Third Month to attend First Day worship. Attendance was small by Virginia Beach standards—five adults and three children—but very good by Fayetteville standards. Bruce Pulliam told me later that this was the first time a sitting yearly meeting clerk had ever visited Fayetteville Friends.

I am convinced that traveling to worship with distant Friends in gospel love bears fruit every time, whether we can see it or not. When we are obedient, God gives our every word and action meaning far beyond our understanding to accomplish the Divine Will in ways we can never comprehend in anything approaching its true fullness.

The morning worship when Representative Body gathered for its Fourth Month meeting gave no indication of the storm that was to break on us that afternoon. Immediately after we settled into the afternoon meeting for business, a Friendship member stood to share his concern that I should no longer be clerk of the yearly meeting. His concern was seconded by another of the Friendship Friends Susan and I had met with the previous month. She argued that behavior that was in fact acceptable in other Friends should disqualify me from being clerk.

Several Friends then spoke either of their own concerns or of their sense that I was doing a good job as yearly meeting clerk. I asked whether the meeting was in unity with the recommendation that I step aside. There was no unity on this question. I asked Ray Treadway to serve as clerk pro tem and took my seat with the body while discussion continued.

A Friend asked why I did not resign immediately to save the yearly meeting from painful dissension. I explained that having been appointed by the yearly meeting as a united body, I was not free to resign at the urging of two or three individual Friends. After some more discussion, I stood again to ask whether the Representative Body was easy to allow me to resign, and there were Friends not easy with that—George Parker, in particular. So, there we were: no unity to remove me from office, no unity to allow me to resign on my own. Friends were going to have to deal with

Among Conservative Friends

this potentially messy situation directly. A committee was appointed to look into all this with Carole Treadway as convenor.

The yearly meeting committee asked Susan and me to meet with them at Rich Square Monthly Meeting on a First Day afternoon about a month later. Their first question was whether Susan and I had been traveling to other yearly meetings together and living at those sessions as man and wife, as rumored. This was a brand-new question to Susan and to me, and we could deny it absolutely and unequivocally. We spent two more hours with the committee, answering questions and trying to explain the process we'd undertaken of seeking divine guidance through prayer and worship—a process that had been central to our relationship (and still is).

I felt the central question and answer came when a Rich Square elder asked what I thought George Fox would have said about our relationship. I speculated about the amount of gossip there must have been when George Fox married the widow at whose home he'd spent so much time when her husband was still alive. My main response, though, was that George Fox set all else aside and clung to the guidance of the Holy Spirit. Susan and I might not be adhering to some Friends' ideas of right behavior, but we were following, to the very best of our ability, the guidance of the Holy Spirit.

The committee then sent us out and continued their deliberations in private. After two more hours, they asked me, without Susan, back into their meeting. Carole Treadway said the committee had found no unity on any reason why I should resign, that the actions of the Friends who had brought up the charges against me had raised serious questions in the committee members' minds about right order and procedure, and that I had the full support of the committee. Carole went on to say that the committee felt I should not continue as yearly meeting clerk beyond the current year, which was fine with me. Finally, Carole said that the Friends who had ridden down with us from Virginia Beach would have some other matters to discuss with me in the near future. After Carole read the committee's findings to me, I repeated them back to her for confirmation, which she gave. She asked if I wanted a written copy of the

283

minute at that time. "No," I said, "I trust the committee." At that, we adjourned.

As we drove home, I felt finally vindicated, both on the basis of what Carole Treadway had reported as clerk of the committee and on how that report had been interpreted and expanded on by the conversation with Virginia Beach Friends on the ride home. It had been a long struggle, but it was over.

But it wasn't over yet. The following week, the written report of the special committee's work was circulated, with several changes from the verbal report I had heard, repeated back, and had confirmed at the meeting at Rich Square. The changes were so great that I felt I had no choice but to resign. The sentence expressing the full support of the committee now read only that I might come to any member of the committee for advice and counsel. Carole admitted these changes were made after the committee had adjourned, following private communications from individual members. I wished I had asked for a written report at the time of the committee meeting, but it was too late now.

I sent a letter of resignation to the clerk of yearly meeting's Nominating Committee without delay and announced the vacancy to Virginia Beach Friends at the rise of First Day worship, saying the Nominating Committee of yearly meeting would be proposing an interim clerk to yearly meeting for approval. I said that Friends who had suggestions should make them to the Virginia Beach representative on the Nominating Committee: Susan Sieg.

Discerning between Competency and Vocation

Sixth Month 1992 was a time of transitions for Susan and me, with the turmoil of the yearly meeting clerkship behind us and the end of our respective monthly meeting clerkships near. I spent hours contemplating what it might be that the Lord was leading Susan and me toward as a ministry. I was also wrestling with the difference between a competency and a vocation. Both my experience at FGC and at Virginia Mountain Housing had revealed some of the benefits and costs of thinking of my employment as both competency and vocation, but I was not yet clear that, for me, they should be separate.

Two thoughts that persisted in this time were (1) that I had not yet learned to rely completely on the Lord and (2) that it would be good for me to be in a ministry where I had a greater impact, doing things that would otherwise not happen at all. Nothing specific felt like a divine call, but I had the sense of doing the necessary prior work of truly opening myself to whatever the divine call might be.

None of the examples I thought about carried much in the way of a dependable salary or job security; I felt I would have to give up some of the financial security that I'd garnered so far in order to do them or anything similar. As I contemplated this, I began to realize how limited my trust in God was. If I really trusted God, it should not feel so scary to risk my financial security. My next move, whatever else it might be, would also be a vehicle by which I learned to trust the divine more completely.

The last meeting for business where Susan and I were the monthly meeting clerks went smoothly enough. As we expected, no one suggested a minute of appreciation for the work we had done over the previous two years as recording clerk and clerk. We were prepared for this but were saddened at this reminder of how broken the meeting had become over this issue.

The 1992 NCYM(C) sessions were held at Chowan College. Asa and I packed up and headed south on the second Fourth Day of Seventh Month (the traditional date of the start of the annual sessions). It was good to see these Friends again and wonderful that so many of them seemed unaffected by or were overtly supportive of Susan and myself, in spite of all the furor that had surrounded us over the past year. I felt that a goodly number of my relationships with individual Friends in the yearly meeting had not been damaged beyond repair, after all.

In the business meeting of the North Carolina (Conservative) Yearly Meeting of MEO, I was appointed (to my surprise and probably to the surprise of several other Friends as well) to plan the group's midyear retreat. Apparently, it was the opinion of the body of recognized ministers, elders, and overseers that I was not evil or flawed beyond useful service. In the general sessions, when Woodland Monthly Meeting in Goldsboro, North Carolina, asked to join our yearly meeting, I was appointed to convene the clearness committee.

Reflecting on these developments later, I realized they made sense if in fact there actually was a different, stricter standard of behavior for the yearly meeting clerk than for other Friends. By this higher standard, I was unfit in the minds of some to be yearly meeting clerk, but by the lower criteria that applied to everyone else I was suitable to help discern whether to recommend a meeting affiliate with our yearly meeting, to plan a spiritual retreat for Friends, and even (as it turned out) to publish a book of essays purporting to describe Conservative Quakerism.

George Stabler was appointed clerk of the yearly meeting. George asked for an opportunity to address the yearly meeting in session and began by making it clear that he had accepted the nomination only if it were clear to all that he was in no way a part of any "coup" to overthrow "Lloyd Lee and Susan" and put himself in our place. He said he was concerned that historians might read the minutes decades hence and see that he was part of the special committee appointed by Representative Body, after which I resigned and he became yearly meeting clerk himself. I resolved at that time to put a note in my journal about this to further protect his reputation.

The matter of publishing my essays came before the body later in the sessions. There was a general sense that the yearly meeting should allow me to publish the essays at my own expense if a preface could be drafted that indicated yearly meeting permission without implying yearly meeting endorsement of everything I had written. Such a preface was composed and read at the afternoon session, and the decision to allow the essays to be published was minuted. I whispered to Susan, "I'm going to be a daddy—I'm having a book!"

Over the summer of 1992, Susan and I consulted several ministers, elders, and overseers of Virginia Beach Friends Meeting, seeking to be married in right order and if at all possible under the care of the monthly meeting. The consistent message of those we consulted was that getting married was all right but that obtaining approval for the wedding to be under the care of the meeting would be disruptive to the unity of the meeting and probably nearly impossible to achieve. As a result, we decided not to ask for the care of the meeting and to be married in a civil process by a "marriage commissioner" (in the vocabulary of the Commonwealth of Virginia). This was accomplished on Ninth Month 9, 1992. The marriage commissioner drew strongly from his own heritage as a Native American. We prayed together for God's blessing on our marriage and acknowledged the importance of what we were undertaking in God's sight. All in all, it felt as "religious" as any wedding I had seen.

Susan and I rented the meeting house for a second wedding celebration, unofficial but conducted after the manner of Friends, attended by a few of our closest friends. We had a covered meeting for worship, said our vows, and signed the calligraphed wedding certificate that a friend of Susan's had made for us. I felt very married, having had two weddings in less than a week, and very happy.

Unfortunately, the turbulent times for me among Friends were not over. For a time after the wedding, some of the Friends who had previously been critical of me continued to express their disapproval in ways both thinly veiled and very direct. Any matter under discussion might be recast as a moral issue. Given the behaviors that "some Friends recorded as ministers" were getting away with, some said, why shouldn't we do or approve this other thing as well? This was painful, but it seemed best to bear it in silence rather than attempt a defense.

In Twelfth Month 1993, Ben Hebner and I attended the Earlham School of Religion Friends Consultation on Personal Service in Richmond, Indiana. In one evening session, unexpectedly, John Punshon called on Ben and me to share about our affordable housing work in Tidewater Virginia. We gave a thumbnail sketch of the conditions in the area and how we worked to improve them in a small way. It was good work, needed work, but it was my competency—I no longer considered it my vocation.

At the end of that evening, I opened a time of worship by reading a passage from the beginning of my essay titled "Waiting Worship." It did seem that we reached a deeper state afterward than we had achieved up till then at this consultation, and Ben said that the reading "worked."

When worship ended, Ben and I spent about ninety minutes talking about Conservative Friends with a couple of the other attenders of the consultation.

One afternoon, John Punshon took several of us on a tour of Richmond. Along the way, he and I began talking about Conservative Friends. He sensed a widespread growing interest in Conservative faith and practice and felt that nationwide as many as one person per monthly meeting was "desperately hungry" for the Conservative message but that there was no prophet, no writer, to articulate the vision. "Perhaps I'll find that in your book," he said. He thought that a neo-Conservative message was needed, relatively orthodox doctrinally but willing to apply doctrine to current issues, such as homosexuality, and come up with new answers.

I was much more confident of the value of the book now than before we had come to Richmond but was waiting for the published reviews. Then again, I realized there was no reason to put much weight on the reviews as the periodicals who would review it were not Conservative and were therefore not likely to be favorably predisposed to its content. The real value would be indicated by whether or not, after its existence became known, the book was bought and read by those hungry for the message I was attempting to convey.

Chapter 6
Faith, Witness, and Community: Virginia, 1993–1998

Susan's and my life over the next half-dozen years was characterized by the interplay of faith, witness, and community. Each of these engaged the others continually, acting either to build up or break down the strength and integrity of all three through the choices and commitments we made in our lives day by day.

We both continued to be deeply invested in the worshipping community in spite of painful relationships in past years. In worship on the morning following Christmas in 1993, Susan offered vocal ministry (which was rare for her) with a strength of emotion that was remarkable. Her voice broke several times during her brief message, and by the time she sat down she was in tears, which continued for several minutes afterward. She spoke in the person of Jesus, inviting each of us to rest our broken bodies in His arms, to be transformed into the beings He had in mind for us to become next. This ministry seemed specially applicable to a family in the meeting grieving over the sudden loss of their husband and father on Christmas Eve, but I soon realized that it was universal.

I was silent, but my own meditations centered around the word *Emmanuel*, "God with us." Until Jesus was born, the wise and religious people of the world knew of "God at a distance," the Lord God Jehovah on Mount Sinai or in the pillar of fire or of smoke. The pagans knew of God at a distance also, on Mount Olympus or in the stars. With the birth of Jesus, the world began to experience Emmanuel, God with us—in diaper changes, games in the town square, trips to Jerusalem, and discussions in the desert. As we, the created, began to experience the Creator among us, we realized that God experienced life among us as well; God could be trusted to understand and empathize with us because God was with us. Christ promised his disciples that he would be with them everywhere and forever (Matthew 28:20). God at a distance had become Emmanuel forever.

Memoir of the Life and Religious Labors of Lloyd Lee Wilson

In spite of moments when we felt great spiritual unity with the other members of the Quaker community, there were also times it was difficult to feel that unity. About two weeks after the meeting described above, a Friend who had been mentioned for possible recording in the ministry spoke in First Day worship. She opened by mentioning previous ministry about John the Baptist, misquoted the relevant Scripture passage(s), and went on to misquote the parable in Luke 18:1–8. It troubled me that a Friend who was looked to by members of the meeting for spiritual inspiration should misquote Scripture in this way. If our Bible literacy were higher, this would not trouble me because Friends would be able to sort things out on their own and those who spoke in worship would be more concerned about getting their Scripture references correct. As it is, Friends know so little of the Bible that it is incumbent upon those who quote it to do so correctly.

In Fourth Month 1994, John Punshon stayed in our home while visiting Virginia Beach and Rich Square Monthly Meetings. At Virginia Beach, John spoke about the way in which many Friends look to Conservatives as closer examples of early Quakerism than has otherwise survived, and he briefly described why that might happen. He pointed out dangers in "celebrating diversity" in the way that Friends General Conference Friends do, but he was clear that Evangelical Friends have also deviated from the historic Quaker vision.

John discussed the idea of a "normative" Quakerism: a set of beliefs and practices that should be accepted as standard by the faith community but at the same time not completely binding on every individual Friend. For example, pacifism is a normative Quaker belief, but it would be possible and acceptable for an individual who is not a complete pacifist to be accepted into membership. As long as there is general agreement about what the normative Quaker beliefs and practices are, individual diversity can be tolerated. However, as the consensus about what constitutes normative Quakerism breaks down, our health as a faith community breaks down as well.

John observed that the Quaker periodicals have been dominated by questions "at the margin" of Quakerism posed primarily by those who want to move or expand the bounds of normative Quakerism, either to

Faith, Witness, and Community

include their own perspective or to exclude some contrary perspective. As a consequence, the Quaker periodicals are not expounding the central themes and doctrines of Quakerism and cannot be expected to do so. These questions at the margins need to be addressed, and perhaps the periodicals are the best place to do that. The point John made was that Friends who wished to see the principles of normative Quakerism preached, understood, and applied could not depend on these media to do that. We would have to be active in the ministry ourselves (in various ways) to find opportunities for direct personal exposition and effective means for delivering our message.

Meeting for business is a good place to observe the health of a Quaker meeting. If we truly believe that there is one Truth that all can perceive, then we will enter meeting for business expecting to reach unity. If we believe that each person has their own truth, then we will not expect unity and meeting for business will reflect that.

John made his way downstairs the next morning at the appointed hour, confessed his need for more sleep, and went back to bed. He appeared again just before time to leave for Rich Square Monthly Meeting; Susan inserted him into the car with a mug of coffee in one hand and fresh muffins in the other.

He spoke at Rich Square about loving God with all our heart, mind, soul, and strength and loving our neighbor as ourself. Again, one theme was the importance of a core of beliefs that everyone understands to be normative for the community. It is all right for a croquet player to join a tennis club, John said, as long as everyone understands that this does not change the tennis club into a croquet club.

The annual North Carolina (Conservative) Yearly Meeting (NCYM[C]) sessions in Seventh Month revealed a healthy faith community putting forth new growth—although not all our visitors saw it that way. The state of the meeting reports indicated a thriving yearly meeting with real growth in membership, financial strength appropriate to our needs, and spiritual depth. I was deeply impressed, as were other Friends, by the report from Durham meeting, which had concluded a two-year search for clarity by adopting a minute expressing their intent to accept and process applications for marriage from homosexual couples in the same manner as those from heterosexual couples. They had taken their time, not outrun their Guide, and by so doing had moved together as a community rather than fracturing.

Several of the Ohio Yearly Meeting (Conservative) visitors to our sessions were quite upset by this report and spoke against it with some feeling. One of them read an extended Scripture passage to demonstrate that homosexuality is a sin, and two others spoke against Durham's decision as unwise and disappointing. They pressed the argument that Durham Friends had moved contrary to the yearly meeting's *Discipline* and therefore threatened the authority of the yearly meeting over the monthly meetings. This was not true; a careful reading of the marriage portion of our *Discipline* reveals a remarkably gender-free document that, to most NCYM(C) Friends, in no way prohibited Durham's discernment. I reminded Friends that the first "discipline" by the Elders at Balby included the statement that they were not setting up rules because "the letter killeth, but the Spirit giveth life."[1] Durham Friends had followed the Spirit in their deliberations, and their outcome demonstrated it. An Ohio Friend rose a second time to protest that the *Discipline* had already been violated, which Friends thought was directed at me personally, but his comment was given the Philadelphia treatment—resounding silence.

Our clerk proposed that a discussion of the Durham report be added to the next Representative Body agenda. I expressed my general reluctance to have business initiated by the clerk. There was no action needed on the part of the yearly meeting concerning these reports from monthly meetings, and if some member of our yearly meeting had a concern, it would work its way to Representative Body through our monthly meetings, according to good procedure. Friends were satisfied with this, and the clerk withdrew his proposal.

In the concluding meeting for worship of the yearly meeting sessions, I rose and spoke of the nature of God—to hear the cry of God's people, to care, to take sides, to get involved, and finally to get other people involved—as in Exodus and elsewhere throughout the Bible. God's heart must be breaking, I said, to hear the cries of five billion souls; can we believe God does not hear or care? Can we pretend God is not involved, not breaking into the world right at this moment? Can we deny that God calls on us to be equally involved on behalf of the poor and oppressed?

This message seemed risky enough as it contained themes of liberation theology. To my dismay, when I regained my seat it was immediately clear that I had not yet discharged my obligations for the morning. A few minutes later, I moved into the aisle and went to my knees in prayer. This was the unusual part of the ministry, for I prayed with greater emotion than ever before in vocal prayer, asking God's forgiveness for ignoring opportunities to clothe the naked, feed the hungry, house the homeless, and visit those sick and in prison. I thanked God for the forbearance and patience to keep giving us new opportunities to be faithful, not because we deserved them but for the sake of God's Son, Jesus Christ. This time, when I regained my seat I knew I was clear and felt the assurance that I had been faithful.

There was no direct response other than a silent squeeze of the hand from Susan. George Parker did rise later in the meeting, reflecting on the ministry he had heard in meeting that morning and concluding that, based on what he had heard this morning, the yearly meeting was in good hands. There was nothing to indicate that he had my words in mind any more or less than those of other Friends who had also spoken. However, Susan commented later that I did not appear to be desiring any approval other than our Lord's.

I felt that if liberation theology was the direction in which God is leading me, and if God was helping me get out of my head and into my heart and gut, then experiences like these—deep emotion on my part and silence from the auditory—were likely to be my lot in the days and months to come. If I continued to be faithful to the Inner Guide and listened to Susan's counsel, I would be able to do what God asked without need for encouraging words from others.

Susan and I continued to work on discerning our calls and vocations, both individually and jointly, in the following months. It seemed clear that I was to use my gifts as a writer in the ministry, and that meant I must structure my life to provide opportunities for that giftedness to be exercised and developed. For the past year, I had used the 6 a.m. hour to do consulting work at home, but Susan reminded me that I had once reserved this time slot to write *Essays on the Quaker Vision of Gospel Order*. We agreed that I should begin using this time to write once again, before our daily devotions. Susan's only condition was that I bring her a cup of coffee as soon as it was ready each morning, which I was more than willing to do. I intended to spend this time journaling and writing new material for public consumption.

Late in Seventh Month, Susan and I drove to Langley Hill Meeting in McLean, Virginia, to meet with a yearly meeting spiritual formation group. This was the third year I had done this and the second time Susan accompanied me. My chronic back pain was flaring up, so Susan did all the driving and I spent the time with my head immobilized with pillows against the motion of the pickup truck, which made the trip bearable.

After a potluck dinner, we gathered for a period of waiting worship and whatever else the Spirit might bring. Prepared messages continued to be less comfortable for me than the give and take of question-and-answer sessions because the latter format assured me that I was dealing with matters of importance to people in the group. So, after the worship ended, I spoke a little about gospel order and the restored harmony of creation, about the mystery of "Christ died, Christ arose, Christ has come again," and about George Fox's message to seventeenth-century England. Then we moved to questions and answers. Questions came fairly quickly, and the energy level immediately rose. In this case, some of the questions were, "Who was Jesus?" "How do we deal with the contradiction between 'Be thou holy' in the Old Testament and 'Be thou compassionate' in the New Testament?" "Could a non-Christian be accepted into membership in a Conservative meeting?" "What about plain speech and plain dress?" and "What or who is a Christian?" We had entered into worship at 7 p.m. and did not close until after 10 p.m. Several Friends were taking notes during the question-and-answer period, and all seemed to be paying close attention—it seemed to be meaningful for all.

One First Day in Eighth Month, I shared a message in worship recounting the plights of several women (without giving names) who had been tenants at the small apartment building in Norfolk that Ben and I owned through New Dominion Housing and had sought housing there or had sought shelter from domestic violence at Samaritan House (where I did the financial record-keeping). The gist of the message was to ask where the gospel was for these women if their circumstances were not changed for the better. I concluded by offering a query: "How are we, as individuals and as a meeting, the body of Christ for these women today?" I did not want to give this message, but it seemed to be the message I was given to share, so I did. I had a sense of having been faithful when I regained my seat. Meeting had been entirely silent before I spoke and was pretty much silent afterward except for a message about the importance of praying for people one couldn't help physically.

Around this time, we began discussions with other Friends and peace activists that led to the formation of Norfolk Quaker House, a military counseling center on religious and moral issues for servicemembers and those considering enlistment. As we did, the need for such a service became clearer and closer. A young Friend shared with Susan and me that he would be eighteen years old in a week, but he felt constrained by his religious beliefs not to register for the draft. Our announcements at meeting had prompted him to come to us requesting guidance.

We talked about the possible and probable consequences of nonregistration and the importance of building a portfolio of documents that would demonstrate his consistent commitment to this position and to pacifism overall. I promised that I would record our encounter in my journal so that I could point to the date it had happened and to this young man's strong convictions at that time, if the need ever came, and told him he should do the same. This was the second young man to seek out counseling since our first meeting, and it seemed like additional confirmation that we were pointing in the right direction.

A key participant in these discussions was Steve Baggarly from Norfolk Catholic Worker. One evening, after a wide-ranging discussion about mission, specific activities, organizational structure, and a name for the project, I asked Steve how the Norfolk Catholic Worker House was funded. His answer was simple and without hesitation: "We beg." This made a deep impression on me as an example of trusting in the Lord.

Memoir of the Life and Religious Labors of Lloyd Lee Wilson

Part of our discernment process was attending the twenty-fifth anniversary celebration of Fayetteville (North Carolina) Quaker House in Tenth Month. After listening to the first set of speakers, Susan said that this was the type of ministry that the Lord was calling her to do and for which she had been prepared over the last year. This seemed to me like the final confirmation that we were supposed to go forward with Norfolk Quaker House, and there now seemed little reason to delay.

The celebration included a bus tour of Fort Bragg guided by a pair of lieutenant colonels from the Delta Force—which at the time did not officially exist. Our primary guide was a friendly, knowledgeable officer who spoke very articulately about life on the base and the military in general. I had to keep reminding myself of the actual content of the things he was describing. For example, he pointed out the marked trees in one area we passed that was used for training exercises. Those trees, he explained, were nesting sites for the red-cockaded woodpecker, which is protected under the Endangered Species Act. When on maneuvers, troops were prohibited from coming too close to those trees to avoid disturbing nesting woodpeckers. That sounds like a caring, sensitive military—until one remembers that the purpose of maneuvers is to prepare the participants to kill other human beings efficiently and effectively.

At the end of the tour, our guide remarked that he had enjoyed being with us but felt a little like Harrison Ford in the movie *Witness* in which Ford takes refuge in an Amish community and experiences profound culture shock. We all laughed together at that, but there was culture shock on all sides. We went into one chapel and saw a large stained-glass window depicting a church surrounded by modern soldiers with automatic weapons and cigarettes dangling from their lips. The wall behind the altar had two large silhouettes of soldiers kneeling in prayer, their rifle butts resting on the ground and helmets on their heads. I was impressed by how well the military had co-opted religion to support its mission and how seamless the integration of all aspects of the military life was. We cannot afford to be Pollyannas and think that we're going to walk up to the military and convince them all to lay down their weapons. The dominant culture is too strong, and we'll be lucky if we are able to

Faith, Witness, and Community

maintain a consistent witness ourselves. If we are present to help one person through their conversion, that will be success.

Later, the Quakers present held an afternoon meeting for worship on the base. Bruce Pulliam announced we were the largest group of Friends in Fayetteville since 1770.

In Twelfth Month 1994, I was given another hard message in ministry. The Christmas story—thinking of Christ's family as homeless refugees, as the rural poor—struck me with fresh power, and I began to compare their circumstances with the responses we in the United States make today to the homeless, the refugees, and the rural poor. (President Clinton had just proposed that federal funding for emergency shelters be terminated, California had voted to exclude illegal aliens from all social benefits programs, and the US Department of Defense had announced that it intended to build another nuclear attack submarine.) After some time, I was moved to rise and speak, and I was obedient, though it was not a message I was happy to be called upon to share.

After I regained my seat, there was a deep silence in the room. After some time, a Friend rose in response to the ministry I had offered. I was protected from almost all of what she had to say—I did not hear it then and could not remember it afterward. Other Friends later told me that she took my message personally and defended herself. After the rise of meeting, a seasoned Friend came to me with a fervent look on his face and said, "Thee was favored, Friend. Any time thee afflicts an entire meeting like that, thee was favored!"

For several months, Susan and I had been looking forward to the 1994 year-end retreat at the Center for Action and Contemplation in Albuquerque, New Mexico, led by the Franciscan Richard Rohr.[2] I'd discovered his cassette tapes sometime in the 1980s, and Susan had spent a six-week internship at the center shortly after we were married. His teaching had had a profound impact on us both. I called him a couple weeks before the retreat and described my desire to have an "opportunity" with him while Susan and I were there. I needed some reassurance that my discernment and understanding of liberation theology were correct and, if possible, some guidance about the right use of my gifts.

When the time came, I laid out my concern to Richard. Then, in response to his questions, I outlined my introduction to and my study of liberation theology. The conversation went on for over an hour. Richard asked about the books I had read and suggested others, walking over to the liberation theology bookshelf and pulling out *Binding the Strong Man* by Ched Myers and *When Theology Listens to the Poor* by Leonardo Boff. We talked about themes of liberation theology and how they might match up with or conflict with Friends thinking and beliefs and about my own spiritual condition.

About two-thirds of the way through our conversation, Richard began affirming my foundation in liberation theology, my gifts as a writer and speaker, and my balanced place from which to speak to Quakers about liberation theology. "God is preparing you for something," said Richard, "and it may well be this." He had several more things to say that added up to affirmation that I had the balance and spiritual maturity to speak the message without being inflexible or judgmental. "Don't push the river," said Richard, "but I know you won't. You're standing right in the middle of it."

I expressed my joy at this affirmation and how much it meant to me to hear it. "Yes, the *vox externa*," said Richard, "the external voice. We all need to hear from somebody outside the system to tell us we are not crazy. Well, you are doing fine." I came away feeling anchored at one end of the stream I was attempting to navigate.

Richard Rohr's presentations at the retreat seemed far removed from the specific liberation issues of suffering, poverty, and praxis with which I'd been wrestling and the nitty-gritty of battered women's shelters, unpaid rents, and state bureaucracies that engaged me much of my workdays. What he offered was a way to engage in a liberating praxis: a deep identification of myself and all of creation with God. Then, I would have no need to create or protect my ego or self-interests, to control others, or to make them serve my interests. I would be "in the river" with no need to push it in any direction.

Social action, then, springs out of love for those who suffer along with compassion for their pain—not outrage at the injustice being done by other people. The call is to act so that all suffering ends, not so that evil people are punished. As Jesus' healing took concrete action through a mixing of mud and spittle, so must ours, whether with hammer and nail or general ledgers and databases. When we cease to act from that place in the river of Love, when we want more to punish the wrongdoer than to love our neighbors, then it is time to stop all doing and return to the silence. Unless we do, all our efforts will serve to entrench the evils we oppose and disguise them in new forms.

New Year's Day 1995 in Albuquerque was glorious, with clear blue skies and high, scattered clouds. We began the day in contemplation, facing the sunrise over the mountains, which was spectacular. During breakfast, half a dozen hot air balloons launched to our north, one of which eventually passed right over us at a very low altitude and landed just the other side of where we were meeting.

My day started in the dark and as a writer—in what I was increasingly coming to know to be my time and role. Susan and I arose at 5 a.m., and I went downstairs to get our coffees while she dressed. The first draft of the afterword for my manuscript on liberation theology and Quaker praxis came pouring out, almost faster than I could write it down. There is a wonderful, almost ecstatic feeling one gets when the words flow like that and one realizes the strength of the current and that the words are good, the structure is good, and a creation is underway that is very nearly born complete. Some fine-tuning might be needed, but nothing very extensive. This doesn't happen every day, or even every week, but it is a true joy when it does. The Holy Spirit was active through me that day, for which I gave thanks, and I took heart that I was doing the right thing.

Reflecting on my current life, I felt easy that I had the right ingredients present. I had good work, family, spiritual life, Norfolk Quaker House, time to write, and a commitment to be available for the spoken ministry as way and opportunity and leading opened. There seemed to be the proper mix between action and reflection. I hoped that I could, over time, reduce the amount of other work in favor of Norfolk Quaker House activities and writing and speaking, but that remained to be seen. Richard's admonition not to push the river seemed applicable here—just do my practice, and everything else would take care of itself.

Memoir of the Life and Religious Labors of Lloyd Lee Wilson

After breakfast, Richard spoke to everyone about prophets. I took careful notes because I wanted to understand this important role in the faith community better and because it had become uncomfortable for me to think about being in that role. Richard's presentation was helpful but did not give me much comfort. He made six points:

1. Prophets are rooted in their own faith (e.g., "good Jews"); they start conservatively, from a love of the tradition as it has been transmitted to them.
2. Prophets are not eclectic. There is no "salad bar prophecy."
3. Prophets are accountable to someone, somewhere, somehow.
4. Prophets have one great thing they believe absolutely, and that relativizes everything else.
5. Prophets can recognize in themselves the sin that they hate in the world.
6. Prophets are able to wait, not pushing the river, for kairos—when the time and place is right for their action.[3] In the meantime, they expect and are willing to receive the grace to love those who disagree with them.

Applying these points to myself, I certainly felt rooted; this was what Richard was referring to when he described my loyalty to Quakerism as it had been passed to me. I had been aware of and spoken against the dangers of eclecticism for years. I felt the need for accountability, and I had worked to establish it for myself when it was not available.

What one great thing did I believe? I believed that Jesus Christ has come to teach his people himself—and that included every human being. That communion between God and human beings relativized everything else. Susan understood Richard to be referring to a place of personal groundedness—the personal faith on which everything else depends. That was it for me. I could see in myself a repeated failure to act in accordance with this great Truth—a failure to behave as if God's guidance were directly and constantly available—even as I lamented the same failure in others.

Would I be able to wait for kairos? Could I avoid the temptation to push the river? That remained to be seen, but I prayed for that gift.

Faith, Witness, and Community

The early months of 1995 brought a steady stream of young enlisted men and women to Norfolk Quaker House for help, many of them already in trouble with the military legal system. About half had left their duty station without permission, which meant our first job was to arrange their safe return to base to surrender. One such client wanted to be a SEAL, so he had signed up for that training when he enlisted at the cost of another two years of service. After he began active duty, his superiors did not approve his application to the SEALs but still held him to the extra two years of active-duty service. Every few months, he felt like he couldn't take the Navy anymore, so he would take a break. When he spoke to us, he was facing forty-five days in the brig for his third unauthorized absence in a year. He was very pleasant and soft-spoken and seemed in every way a fine young man—he just didn't fit in the Navy.

Visiting the United States Navy Brig was a powerful experience. I had not been inside a prison or jail of any sort since visiting a one-cell town jail when I was in elementary school. Getting inside the brig the first time was an adventure—proving who I was, emptying my pockets, and then being repeatedly rejected by the metal detector. Finally, they took me aside to use an electronic wand. They discovered that every part of my body was tripping the alarms. When I pushed my sleeves up to my shoulders, my bare arms tripped the metal detectors. The guards recorded this as an equipment failure, though they could not duplicate the effect with anyone else; I took it as a sign that I was doing God's work.

I had the experience of Sarah Barney and Comfort Hoag much on my heart throughout meeting for worship one First Day but was not given a leading to say anything. The topic did not linger in my consciousness after meeting, but soon after settling into worship the next First Day they were back in my awareness with such power that I knew that I would be led to speak. Still, I gave the leading time to season and mature until it seemed certain that the Spirit was the true source and not my own ego.

While this was going on, Susan was acutely aware that I was being called to speak. Her own heart was pounding in her chest, and she could see angels all around me with beating wings and arms outstretched to help me stand up. It seemed to her that God was opening hearts to hear the words I was being called to speak. At length, she was herself silently urging me to stand and speak.

After praying my usual request that the words I was about to speak be the gospel God wanted expressed in that meeting and that the words heard be that gospel, whether I was faithful or not, I rose to speak. As always, what I said was different from what I had been thinking, although the starting point—Sarah and Comfort's journey—was the same. What I said in essence was that in spite of having gone through an expansive clearness process before being released for their journey to England, Comfort Hoag was free enough to hear a fresh word from the Lord in the middle of the ocean and to attend to that word without a striving for foolish consistency or the fear of appearing foolish. Comfort had recognized that the Lord had released her from her previous commitment to the ministry in England and would enable her and Sarah to return home immediately. We too needed to listen to what the Lord had to say to us that morning rather than rehashing what God had said to us yesterday or last week.

It seemed like acceptable service, and I was content when I took my seat. After the rise of meeting, a number of Friends came to me with a complimentary word, including Friends with whom I was not on close terms. I am suspicious when a ministry seems too popular, concerned that the comfortable may have been comforted rather than afflicted. In this case, it may well have been that Susan's vision was more accurate than my suspicion and that hearts were indeed opened for the message that it was my lot to articulate.

Charlie Ansell, our newest elder, came to me in the library after work and thanked me for my ministry. He then asked me a question: "Is there a difference between ministering and preaching?" My first reaction to his question was the same as Susan's when I repeated the conversation to her after we got home: "Yes, they are different, and a Friends meeting needs both!"

It seems to me that ministering, which of course comes from the Latin for "to serve," includes a wide range of service to one's faith community and to humankind (and the rest of creation!) in general, of which vocal ministry is only one example. It is for my gifts in the vocal ministry that I have been acknowledged as a gospel minister. Vocal ministry occurs primarily within meetings for worship and includes several different activities, including prayer, confession, praise, teaching, exhortation, and preaching. D. T. Niles (in *The Preacher's Calling to Be a Servant*), says that preaching and evangelism are the same thing and that one evangelizes because it is the great work to which all Christians are called. Webster's unabridged dictionary says that to preach is to expound or proclaim, to advocate, to urge with earnestness, to advise or teach. So, ministering and preaching overlap but are not identical. Probably, there is more ministering that is not preaching than there is authentic preaching that is not ministry.

I began sharing drafts of my book manuscript exploring the relationship of liberation theology to normative Quakerism in Fourth Month 1995. The responses were not encouraging. One reader said that she did not think it was up to the standards of my earlier book; it just didn't hang together in her mind, and she didn't think I should be in a hurry to publish it. She admitted her inability to be more specific than that. Another reader gave a similar "go slow" response. Neither reader pointed to specific issues with the manuscript; they did not say whether the problem was in the content or the writing style or give any examples of passages that illustrated their concern. After a period of personal discernment, I put the draft aside and did not work on it any more.

Worship on Palm Sunday 1995 started out well but ended painfully for me. At first it seemed well centered, with solid ministry from three Friends, all around the idea of seeking and doing God's will rather than our own. After the children joined us in the latter part of meeting, I was moved to prayer, in petition that the God in me would be increased and the "me" in me would be decreased. I also recalled Jesus' pain and Passion during the week leading up to the first Easter. By the time my prayer was done, I was in tears, and a broader than usual chorus of "Amen" echoed my own as I got up off my knees and back into my chair. My tears were unexpected, but I was deeply moved, and I continued to weep for a minute or two afterward.

Very soon, though, the silence was broken by a Friend who announced that Jesus had laughed and joked on the way to the crucifixion.[4] She then proceeded to tell a series of jokes that her meditation had revealed as the sort of thing Jesus said while carrying the cross. This included a joke about Veronica collecting divine sweat on her towel (like rock music fans collect towels with their favorite stars' sweat today), Simon of Cyrene's bodybuilding class, and their good fortune at missing rush hour traffic with the cross. Jesus, she said, died with a twinkle in his eye. She ended by encouraging Friends to think of other jokes about the last day of Jesus' life.

I was shocked, pierced, incredulous—folded up in my chair—because Jesus was being mocked once again, just as He had been mocked during his Passion. I did not see the parallel to the first Easter at that moment but felt only that my faith had been mocked as well as the faith of all Christians who esteem the Passion, atonement, and resurrection and view them as central to their faith. After the rise of meeting, I went to this Friend to express how shocked I had been by her ministry, but her only response was to say, "You are wrong to feel that way." It would have been simple (and enough) for her to say that she had meant no offense and had not realized anyone would be hurt by her words, but she stood her ground. Later, she followed me into the meeting library, where I had gone to get some coffee and recover my composure, and told me I had no right to come to her as I had—essentially saying that I had no right to my emotions or my faith.

It is a reality that those who attend our meetings for worship embrace a wide variety of beliefs that differ in some very important ways from each other. We must be always working to keep our meeting communities safe for the expression of that wide variety of beliefs and at the same time to sustain them as places where spiritual formation and development can thrive. This requires tact and forbearance on the part of all of us—a lesson it seems we all find difficult to remember.

On another First Day that spring, I was not active in the vocal ministry, though the seed of a message was growing in my awareness when the clerk shook hands to close the meeting. It is difficult to discern, when this happens, whether one has been considering a message God has

Faith, Witness, and Community

not inspired, whether the message was intended personally and not corporately, or whether those responsible for closing meeting have misjudged the spiritual condition of Friends. I know that when I was responsible for closing meeting, I found it difficult to discern the proper time to do so. It was made harder for me personally because being open to inspiration that might lead to vocal ministry interfered with my giving attention to the condition of the meeting for worship overall. There is a good reason that historically it was elders who had the responsibility of closing meeting, not ministers.

I had spent the last portion of this meeting holding two passages of Scripture in my awareness, unsure what, if anything, I was meant to do or say. The first passage was from the Old Testament, where God takes Ezekiel to the valley of dry bones and asks whether these bones can live (Ezekiel 37). The other passage was the assurance that God is at work to bring some good in all things, even tragedy (Romans 8). What message might have issued from these seeds, if any, I don't know. Just as it seemed that things might be building toward getting me on my feet, the clerk shook hands and the meeting for worship ended.

At the meeting for business in Sixth Month, a nomination to the station of elder was brought up for its second consideration, having been approved for the first time in Fourth Month. There was again general approval of the nomination, but this time one Friend said she was not in unity with the nomination. She said she knew something about the individual that in her mind disqualified her from the station of elder, but she did not feel free to disclose what that was to the meeting for business. No one else having spoken against the appointment at either meeting for business at which it was considered, I rose and asked the objecting Friend if she would bear the burden of not allowing the meeting to move forward on this matter—would she be willing to bear the burden of having kept the meeting from making the right decision if it turned out that she was wrong. She responded that she would indeed be willing to bear that burden, and the matter was laid aside.

In Eighth Month, Susan and I spent all of one day painting a Samaritan House shelter residence, getting it ready for new residents— women and their children fleeing domestic violence. Soon after we got home, the Samaritan House executive director called, saying that she had been given a message for me and a vision for Susan while praying for us just then.

The message for me was in two parts. The first was, "The truth has been revealed to you already. You are to be a witness to that truth," and the second was, "Take comfort in the truth and wisdom that has been revealed to you." When she took up her Bible for confirmation, she opened it to Matthew 16:17–18, which in her Living Bible translation read, "*God has blessed you, Simon, son of Jonah,*" *Jesus said, "for my Father in Heaven has personally revealed this to you—this is not from any human source. You are Peter, a stone; and upon this rock I will build my church; and all the powers of hell shall not prevail against it.*"

The vision for Susan was of a colorful blanket or quilt that was in her lap when she was sitting and around her shoulders when she was standing or walking. The words that went with this vision were that Susan was to be a comfort to many people, but for that to happen she must be unafraid; the blanket would be her protection and would always be with her. The blanket or quilt was the equivalent of a shield, and Susan's putting it on was a deliberate act of the will, not automatic.

One First Day in the summer of 1995, I spoke in worship about the change that happens when one puts God at the center of one's story. Susan had been out of town that weekend, but as soon as she got home she asked whether I had spoken in meeting, and when, and how I had stood when speaking. She had had a vision of me speaking at about fifteen minutes before the hour, which was approximately when I did speak, and she saw me wearing gray (I was) and resting my hands on the bench in front of me (which I did). This close spiritual connection between us is a precious blessing to us both.

In Ninth Month, Susan and I spent a First Day in Greensboro, North Carolina, making a presentation about Norfolk Quaker House after morning worship at Friendship Meeting and leading a workshop titled Elders and Community at the Glenagape Retreat Center in the afternoon. I gave a few opening remarks at the workshop and then, as usual, moved quickly into question-and-answer mode. The discussion was good, although I soon realized that the clash going on within North Carolina

Faith, Witness, and Community

Yearly Meeting (Friends United Meeting) colored the way these Friends could see particular matters. One pastor was "disappointed" to hear that I would participate in the Eucharist with other Christians in an event if led by the immediate guidance of the Holy Spirit. He said there were pastors in that yearly meeting who wanted to install baptismal fonts in their worship rooms "in case" they were moved by the Spirit to perform a baptism during worship.

Our faith tradition affirms that the spiritual baptism needs no outward sign, but I also believe that we must be willing to be obedient to the immediate leading of the Holy Spirit, not to forms or lack of forms. The wisdom of the faith community is a counterbalance to the leadings of individual Friends; this is upset by the unequal balance of power in the pastoral system. The congregation would in fact be hard-pressed to stop a pastor from performing a water baptism.

Another individual kept probing me for universal minimal outward behavioral requirements for Friends. Surely Friends had to at least be involved in the ecological awareness movement or the peace movement or whatever. This Friend was unsatisfied with my response that no specific outward behavior was required, although change in many areas could be expected as one came into closer and closer communion with the Holy Spirit. Most Friends present did not have such strong and specific personal issues to address and seemed fully engaged in the exploration of what it would mean for them to be completely dependent on the leading of the Holy Spirit.

Relying on God's guidance in all things is frightening for many human beings, including many Friends. We look for a safe haven, outward reassurance that we are "OK"—and this desire for an outward behavioral requirement is a search for a safe haven. What Quakerism has to offer is a witness that God's guidance is both available to all and fully reliable. Those who depend on that guidance and follow it are OK. The witness of Friends who have endeavored to do this over the centuries declares that following divine guidance leads an individual to change one's life in predictable ways. But Friends have drawn the circle of membership broadly, to include all those who have started on the path, rather than narrowly, to exclude those who have not finished the journey.

We aspire to the normative witness of Quakerism, but we move unevenly and at varying speeds, being careful not to profess in any place that which we do not possess.

In Ninth Month, I spent a memorable time with a Norfolk Quaker House client, meeting with the Navy recruiter who had signed him up for the Delayed Entry Program. We arrived on schedule at the recruiting office but discovered that the petty officer who had set up the meeting was running late. Without introducing herself, she walked up to us, announced the meeting had been moved to the district recruiting headquarters about a mile down the road, and turned to walk away. I had to speak up quickly just to be sure she was the petty officer we were supposed to meet.

Once at the new meeting site, we were told to sit in a hallway while she searched for the chief recruiter. When he arrived, he spoke to our client while the petty officer asked me a question. Before I realized what was happening, our client had been whisked away into a separate office. When I heard the door close and latch, I wished—too late—that I had impressed on him more thoroughly the importance of our not being separated. Now there was nothing to do but wait in the hallway, praying for our client and the meeting now going on in the chief recruiter's office.

From the hallway, I could hear a loud conversation taking place in the recruiter's office, with the repeated high-volume refrain, "Bottom line is, you are in the Navy and have to report!" This was followed unfailingly by our client's equally loud response, "Bottom line is, I'm not going!" Eventually, the door opened and I was invited inside.

I sat beside my client on a couch, with a petty officer on each side of us, facing the chief recruiter behind his desk. He asked me what I was doing there, and I said I was a Quaker minister in the role of a spiritual advisor. He asked what I had counseled our client, and I said that was privileged information I could not divulge. The chief recruiter then turned to his fellow petty officers and said, "Let me explain about Quakers. They go around forcing other people to accept their way of thinking." I replied that this was not the case, that Quakers believed strongly that no one should be forced to behave contrary to their conscience. The recruiter then said we persuaded weak-willed people to believe what we believed. Our client replied he had spent a year in seminary and was quite capable of making his own moral decisions.

After a little more verbal sparring, the chief recruiter said that we were right: the client did not belong in the Navy—he did not deserve to be in the Navy. Neither one of us deserved to be on federal property, and we should both get off immediately. Our client would get his discharge papers in the mail in a couple of weeks. As we rose to leave, I offered my hand in friendship to the recruiter, who pushed himself back in his chair to get as far away from me as possible and refused to shake my hand. "Get out!" was all he could say. As we walked out, I put my hand on our client's shoulder and encouraged him not to laugh until we were out the door. Truth be told, that advice was for me as much as for him.

One afternoon that fall, I scanned some of the latest Quaker-P discussion group postings. I started reading a conversation thread that I picked more or less at random and discovered it was a discussion about whether entire world governments could be converted to gospel order or whether a complete conversion was even necessary to provide real benefits. I was amazed to encounter this use of the concept of gospel order in a setting so removed from that of the essays that I had written. When I described this to Susan, she was nonchalant, saying that she already assumed that I had changed the course of Quaker debate by writing about gospel order. I felt like someone who had dropped a single crystal into a pool of supersaturated liquid and was now watching the spread of the crystalline structure out to the horizon. God had used and prepared me and had prepared many other parts of creation for this tiny slice of the Truth.

Opportunities for a greater commitment of both time and energy were opening up in both my competency (consulting for nonprofit housing groups like Samaritan House) and my vocation (symbolized by my ministry through Norfolk Quaker House). Samaritan House was interested in establishing a division for housing acquisition that would acquire new housing units as well as generate revenues for other Samaritan House programs. Meanwhile, the Norfolk Quaker House board approved the work-for-hire agreement that made me the coordinator for $1 a year—a symbolic payment reflecting a deeper, more formal commitment to that work. I needed to discern the basic issue of what the Lord wanted me to do. Both opportunities were good work; which was right for me?

One of the resources for discernment that I could bring to the process was my new understanding of myself in terms of the Enneagram.[5] I had discovered that I was a Five on the circle of Enneagram types and thus moved toward integration as an Eight—I was a gatherer of information who used that information on behalf of other people, especially the powerless and marginal. When I sat in the silence and listened, Norfolk Quaker House (and Quaker Ministries, Inc.) appeared to be the better fit with my basic nature.[6]

As my commitment grew, the number of calls we fielded for the GI Rights Hotline continued to grow in 1996. At the time, Susan and I were the only volunteers regularly answering the hot line 24/7. It was part of our ministry at Norfolk Quaker House. Those we counseled faced one challenge after another. One sailor called to say that the Navy had "lost" his letter requesting conscientious objector status and discharge. He turned the letter in again, only to be told that now he had forty-eight hours to turn in his completed application or be ordered immediately to a ship on the West Coast. He had done a considerable amount of work on the application already, but helping him finish it took an all-night effort by both Susan and me.

Just a few days later, Susan and I met with a new client. As I drove him back to his duty station, he began talking about his former life in Texas, where he'd had a good job at an oil refinery, his own apartment and car, and a girlfriend. He had joined the Navy because they promised to train him for a higher-paying job. Now the Navy was training him to help land jet fighters on an aircraft carrier. "How many civilian jobs are there," he asked, "for people trained to land jet fighters on a carrier?" His only post-discharge option, he felt, would be to go home and ask for his old job back. If he did that, he would be four years behind everyone else in terms of seniority and pay grade. He would be working *for* the people he had once worked *with*, and he would never catch up because of those four years in the Navy.

Faith, Witness, and Community

One client reached out to us from the carrier *USS George Washington*. This young man was a devout Christian but not at all a pacifist when he enlisted, but sleeping beneath the steam catapults that launched the fighter planes and bombers led him to a conversion of heart. He began to read his Bible more carefully and was persuaded that a true Christian life was a pacifist one. He told us of the deep despair he felt reading the Bible in his "rack," listening to the catapults launching plane after plane, and thinking that he was the only Christian pacifist in the entire world. We assured him that he was not alone. At the evening's end, I took him back to the *George Washington* so he could board before it sailed for Bosnia the next day.

Asa, Susan, and I made a spring trip to Cambridge Massachusetts, in 1996 to help Asa begin his search for a college. This was an opportunity for me to visit my old stomping grounds again and introduce Asa to places that were significant in my own youth.

Once in Boston proper, we decided to walk the Freedom Trail, following the guiding red line in the sidewalk up the hill to the State House. We finally found Mary Dyer's statue hidden off to the side behind General Joseph Hooker's. I told Asa a little of the story of early Friends Mary Dyer, William Robinson, William Ledra, and Marmaduke Stevenson. These four Friends were hanged in colonial Boston for being Quakers, which was a capital crime at that time.

The temperature was in the 30s and the wind was very brisk, so the walk itself was not pleasant, but the history was grand. We took our time in spite of the cold, reading tombstones at the Old Granary Burying Ground and plaques at Old North Church and even stepping inside St. Stephen's, the Kennedy family's church. After visiting Paul Revere's house, we walked down Causeway Street to the subway. Asa and Susan got to ride on the Green Line for the first time, which was mostly unchanged since thirty years ago: noisy, slow, and uncomfortable. Asa began to get a feel for the possibility of living in the city without an automobile, and all of us were thankful for the ride.

The next day, we made the trip on the Red Line to Harvard Square and Friends Meeting at Cambridge. It was an eye-opener for me to see that the annual budgeted revenue for the monthly meeting that year was slightly more than $172,000. Later, I learned the meeting had spent almost $1,000,000 expanding and renovating its office space and library, including adding a tunnel to the American Friends Service Committee room for used clothing.

There had been no apparent renovations in the meeting room, however. The bench cushions looked twenty years older and the cork floor was more heavily worn than in my memory, but they otherwise were the same as when I had left for Virginia in the late seventies. During worship, there was some heady vocal ministry and a relatively large number of speakers, though perhaps not so many when one considers there were well over one hundred people at worship. Late in the meeting, I was moved to my knees in a prayer of the heart, giving thanks for God's Presence and grace and mercy in our lives. It seemed like acceptable service.

Just as meeting was rising, a young man immediately to our left rose and spoke, quoting Julian of Norwich and her vision of the acorn in God's hand. He introduced himself later as Max Hansen, a California Friend who had been corresponding with me via email about *Essays on the Quaker Vision of Gospel Order*. What a God-incidence that he should come into this meeting for worship on this First Day and sit next to us.

After learning that I was coming to Cambridge, a Friend had asked for an opportunity to talk with me. At the rise of worship, we got some coffee and found a corner of the new dining room in which to talk. She had no specific concern but had felt helped by me at several points in the years immediately following our last conversation and felt led to make contact again. I shared with her that for several years after that conversation she had been on one of my prayer cards. I had been explicitly praying for her and her welfare once a week.

About this time, Max approached and asked to join us for the afternoon. We readily agreed, believing that there are no coincidences and that some important connection was being made. We took the subway to Kendall Square and began walking the length of the MIT campus ("two miles long, two blocks wide"). We spent a little time in the economics library and in the Sloan building where I had spent most of my MIT student days, then walked through the main campus.

Faith, Witness, and Community

The Great Court was as impressive to me that day as it had been thirty-three years earlier when I'd seen it for the first time. The honor given those scientists and thinkers whose names are on the buildings around the Great Court still gives me shivers. We walked down part of the Great Gray Womb—now called the Infinite Corridor—and got a taste of some of the classroom and lecture spaces. The next day, we did more sightseeing on the MIT campus, then drove past Fenway Park and began the trip home.

Susan and I worshipped at Providence Meeting near Pendle Hill Retreat Center in Pennsylvania on Easter morning 1996. As I settled, the words of an old Easter hymn slowly came to mind—at first only part of one verse, and then a few more lines, and then finally the whole song and melody. I savored the message as being for myself, chided myself for being so prideful as to consider singing in a meeting for worship, and attempted to move on. I could not move away from "Down Came an Angel," however, and was eventually caught up in the strongest inner quaking that I had felt in a long time. My heart was pounding faster and faster, my head was spinning, and I realized that I was being called to stand and sing.

My attempts to find release by reciting the verses or singing just the last verse or two were earnest but futile. I prayed for release and then for the ability to stand and be faithful, and finally I was able to get to my feet and sing. When I was finished and regained my seat, I felt an unusual flush and tingle all over and an inner certainty that I had done my assigned task acceptably. A deep peace came over me that lasted for the rest of meeting for worship.

Two other people spoke. One woman spoke of the sacrifice and suffering we celebrate at Easter and the joy and peace that she had as a result, which the world did not give her and could not take away. She concluded by saying that we must, "as my brother has said," go and tell our brethren that Christ is risen today. Toward the end of meeting, an elderly man spoke of convalescing at Massachusetts Eye and Ear Clinic some forty years prior and being read to by an elderly retired nun. She took him to Catholic Mass on Good Friday—the day he was discharged from the hospital—and then to the train station for his trip home. When he tried to send her a thank-you letter, he discovered she had died that very night.

After the rise of worship, this Friend, who was named John, greeted us and told us the rest of the story. When he was feeling pretty down about his impaired vision, the nun told him a story that "her friend Paul" had told her about being shipwrecked. "When the ship goes down," Paul said, "hold on to a broken piece. Everyone who does will be saved." That was exactly what happened. Paul had told this nun the story, and she then told John the story. He felt assured then that he would be all right.

The next morning, Susan and I took the train into Central Philadelphia for a visit to the "Quaker Kremlin." At 1501 Cherry Street, we got to visit with Asia Bennett at Friends World Committee for Consultation and spent a few minutes with Kara Newell at American Friends Service Committee before an appointment whisked her away.

On our return to Pendle Hill, I went over my notes for the evening's lecture and joined Susan in an afternoon nap. After that, it was time for dinner. As we sat over a cup of coffee in the dining room, a man came up to the table looking for Lloyd Lee Wilson. His name was William Geary. He wanted to start a Conservative Friends meeting in Cape May, New Jersey, to be affiliated with NCYM(C). We talked for about fifteen minutes about the options and the challenges of his hopes; Susan and I invited him to Representative Body later that month and to yearly meeting sessions that summer. This was the beginning of a relationship between our yearly meeting and Southern State Worship Group, in New Jersey's Southern State prison, that extended over more than twenty-five years. Friends in the two groups write to each other, pray for one another, and build relationships that at times continue well after release from prison.

Turnout for the lecture was good, probably 130–140 people. The questions afterward were good and sometimes quite difficult, which is always exciting, so overall I felt the lecture was a success. Anne Buttenheim took a copy of the text to post on the Pendle Hill website and suggested that I submit the text to Rebecca Mays for consideration as a Pendle Hill pamphlet. Dan Seeger and other Friends had several good things to say about the lecture afterward.

Faith, Witness, and Community

I began thinking about writing another book, fueled in part by the comments of Friends wherever I traveled who told me how valuable *Essays on the Quaker Vision of Gospel Order* had been in their lives. Susan pointed out the difference between having the desire to write and having something to say and suggested that it was simply not yet the right time because the spiritual changes in both of us due to our exposure to and acceptance of liberation theology had not yet had time to season. I realized that she was right but still struggled with my discernment. I didn't want to waste time by not writing when I should be, just as much as I didn't want to be writing when it was not the correct time for me to write. There is no benefit to trying to push the river; when the time came, I would know it. My only task was to be awake and prepared.

I reached my forty-ninth birthday in 1996 in harmony with my aging process and grateful for the gifts of life I enjoyed. I missed the competitive athletics of my youth, appreciated the joys my current age offered, and was not terribly interested in appearing younger than I was. God had blessed me bountifully, and I was deeply grateful. My relationship with Susan grew deeper and more precious each day; my love continually grew stronger and more profound as I learned and gained so much from her presence. I was truly a happily married man.

I had been idly speculating for a while about a hypothetical future in which Susan and I attended Somerton Friends Meeting in Suffolk, Virginia, as sojourning members while retaining our primary membership at Virginia Beach. We had talked some about the possibility of moving to Suffolk for a few years. Suffolk offered more rural space and a lower cost of living, which was attractive. What it didn't have was the pull we associated with a true leading. This led us to consider whether we might move to some other place, perhaps near the Center for Action and Contemplation in Albuquerque or to the Shenandoah Valley of Virginia.

In Tenth Month 1996, I was invited to preach at Somerton Friends Meeting and to lead two or possibly three sessions of a faith and practice study group Somerton Friends were organizing, including a session on clerking. After thinking privately about Somerton meeting, I had been offered two opportunities to be more involved with Friends there. Such God-incidences carry meaning, and it was important that I discern what lessons God was offering me there. It could be the beginning of a relationship with Somerton Friends or perhaps a nudge to look more widely than Virginia Beach Friends Meeting for both nurture and ministry.

When the day came, I preached from the first chapter of the Gospel according to Mark as that had been lively in my heart since before the invitation came. I spoke without written text or notes, using only the Scripture itself for a guide. The thrust of my comments was that our "reading position" was taking the edge off the gospel message and had impaired our ability to understand what Mark was trying to say. To understand the gospel as Mark understood it, we needed to make the effort to hear his story as his first audience heard it.

I was more comfortable in the pulpit than I had expected—after all, it was the first time I had given a sermon since I was a teenager. Afterward, Susan said my delivery had been good and she thought my main message of the need to read the gospel with fresh eyes had been communicated, though she thought some of my references to more radical ideas and liberation theology were not understood by the congregation. I felt settled and at ease; it seemed like acceptable service.

Susan and I welcomed 1997 with a weekend of retreat and discernment in a log cabin just off the Blue Ridge Parkway. To our joy, there were about two inches of snow on the ground when we arrived, and after we settled in it started to snow again. For folks who are starved for the sight of snow, the ability to stand outside in falling snow is a joy. We spent the weekend in worship, reading, and reflective conversation, along with hiking nearby trails. Over the years, we have continued the practice of a New Year's retreat, and since retirement we've dedicated all of each First Month to a Sabbath rest, putting as much of our life as possible "on hold" while we spend the month in rest, reflection, and discernment. It is a precious time each year.

On this 1997 retreat, I reflected on the change I felt in my identity as I shifted away from identifying as a manager toward being a writer, teacher, and minister. The change in focus seemed like the right thing, and it felt like the right time to do it. There seemed to be few opportunities to earn a living in this new role without transgressing the

Faith, Witness, and Community

Quaker testimony against the hireling ministry, but I trusted that way would open.

Later that month, I got a call at Norfolk Quaker House from a sailor at Naval Air Station Oceana. She had just made a statement to the JAG officer there (a member of the Judge Advocate General's Corps) that she was homosexual and was worried that she would be in physical danger if she was not immediately removed from her unit and allowed to go home. She had been given the GI Rights Hotline number somewhere, remembered it, and called us. She was in need of immediate accompaniment, which preempted any other plans Susan and I'd had for the next couple of days. We met her at the base gate that evening (she was not allowed to leave the base), and we went to the base bowling alley to talk. She was thirty-three years old and had decided to fulfill a lifelong desire to be in the Navy. She thought she would get money to finish her schooling and had been promised that she would be eligible for the full $30,000 Montgomery GI Bill plus admission to the service school of her choice. When she reported for duty two pounds overweight, she was told she would have to go home, lose the weight, and report again later. The delay meant she lost her $30,000 eligibility and her choice of service school but was still bound to her enlistment. She had been in the Navy for four months and said it was the worst experience of her life.

The whole Navy experience had been an unhappy one for her, even though she had been at the top of her class throughout her training. She did not like the crudity of Navy life and language, and she wanted to go home. She was lesbian, but that was not the focus of her problems with the Navy—just a convenient way out, one provided by the Navy itself. She was very aware of the way Navy personnel talked about gays and lesbians and did not want to be the subject of that kind of verbal abuse herself, much less face the physical harassment that some homosexual men and women experienced in the military.

We agreed that I would meet her again the next day to accompany her as she made her formal declaration and began the process of getting a discharge. Late-night phone calls confirmed that I would be allowed to do this as her minister.

I met her at the main gate at noon the next day to accompany her as she made her formal declaration and began the process of getting a discharge (I was allowed to do this because I was now her minister). First, we met with the lieutenant who was preparing her request for administrative leave. His title was in fact defense counsel, and he was clearly on her side. Unfortunately, this was the first homosexuality case in which he had been involved, so all he could do was read the military manual carefully and follow the regulations.

We then met with the base legal service representative. She was a civilian who had been in that office for ten years, and she was competent, compassionate, and very helpful. She confided that her babysitter was lesbian, so our client's declaration did not upset her at all. She was very attentive to our client's emotional condition, reassuring her that she did not have anything to worry about and patiently explaining the process that would be followed.

This base had had only one other case since the regulations about homosexuality had changed. That case had begun just two days previously and was still in process. The legal services rep made sure that the chain of command was fully informed but went out of her way to ensure that our client's confidentiality would be protected. When it appeared that our client might have to wait over a week to get a separation medical exam performed, the rep arranged for one at a different base the next day.

Our client's concerns about personal safety were met by transferring her immediately to the base's "holding company" barracks to be processed and discharged from there. Everyone in that barracks was there only until their orders for transfer or discharge were processed. There would be no reason for anyone to learn about her sexuality. Our client would sign blank discharge papers before leaving for home, and her discharge papers would be mailed to her.

I was at the base gate at 6 a.m. the next morning to meet our client and walk her through her separation medical exam, staying with her until it was complete and the paperwork signed. Afterward, she was moved directly to the holding company. Her sexual orientation remained secret until her discharge was complete. I did not have any need to intervene in

Faith, Witness, and Community

the process, although I suppose the presence of an "outside" observer may have helped the Navy personnel stay on their best behavior. I know our client was reassured by having a friendly presence close by throughout those days.

My own spiritual formation continued during this time of service to others, sometimes dramatically. A short course at Pendle Hill in Sixth Month led by Ched Myers accelerated my inner work around the teachings of liberation theology. Most of the course explored Jesus' testing in the desert, reported in Luke chapter 4. I am often reminded that there was no witness to report these events—only Jesus could have told the disciples what happened. Jesus knew these were not simply tests that the Son of God had to face but tests that every Christian must face and survive in the course of discipleship.

Ched set the stage by pointing out how crossing the Jordan River and spending forty days in the desert evoked memories of the Israelite people crossing the Jordan to enter the promised land and how the river was parted by the ark to let them cross (Joshua 4). Those forty days sparked thoughts of the forty-year Exodus journey and the manna that fed the Israelites' hunger.

The first temptation Jesus faced was turning stones into bread to satisfy his own hunger. Palestine is so stony that had Jesus begun turning stones into bread he would have been rich indeed. Instead, he quoted Deuteronomy 8:3—a direct reference to the manna experience. Each family got just enough manna to meet its needs, but hoarding caused the manna to spoil. Jesus was saying, "God will provide your needs. Trust God, not your own efforts." In Ched's words, the first principle of the Kingdom of God is "No silos."

The second temptation was toward worldly power, and Jesus here quoted Deuteronomy 6:13. This quotation would have evoked memories among the Jewish people of their early prosperity (while they were decentralized; remember the twelve stones in Joshua 4) and their rapid fall later, once they had installed the human (centralized) monarchy. In Ched's words, the second principle of the Kingdom of God was "No kings."

Memoir of the Life and Religious Labors of Lloyd Lee Wilson

The third temptation was harder for Ched to characterize. Jesus quoted Deuteronomy 6:16, which in turn refers to Exodus 17:1–7 and Numbers 20:1–13. Both of the latter recount an incident when the people doubted Yahweh, who then demonstrated His power by bringing forth water from a rock. In Exodus, the people were wrong and Moses struck the rock, as he was instructed to do. In Numbers, Moses was told to speak to the rock but instead struck it, and in punishment he was prohibited from entering the promised land.

The Israelites tested whether God could provide for their needs and whether YHWH was deserving of their loyalty—they must have been considering other gods. Moses felt obliged to embellish on YHWH's instructions as if God were not all-knowing. The sin seems to be idolatry (the Deuteronomy quote comes right after a warning against following other gods). The test seems to be whether Jesus will attempt to force God's hand by jumping and thereby make God save him. When we try to force or control God's actions, we are placing ourselves above God, and that is idolatry. So, for me, the third principle of the Kingdom is "No idolatry"—no god but YHWH.

No silos, no kings, no idolatry. These three form the basis for an economy of grace rather than an economy of debt, which we explored during the retreat. The economy of grace rests on the understanding that God has given us the Kingdom to live in as a free gift, so there is no need for worry or fear (Luke 12:32). We ourselves have not built this economy of grace; we have not climbed the pyramid to earn or achieve it, and no god other than Yahweh has provided it—God has given it to us. Ched illustrated this point with two other passages from Luke 12, one about the rich man who tears down his barns to build bigger ones and the other about the lilies of the field. The first parable illustrates the futility of trying to store up wealth for oneself and would have evoked memories of Egypt in Jesus' audience because the Israelites built the storage cities of Pithom and Rameses for Pharaoh by forced labor (Exodus 1). Yahweh disrupted that system and instituted the system of manna in its place.

The Genesis account is very clear on the imperial economy of debt and Joseph's role in implementing it. The imperial power extracts value from throughout its empire and stores it in the capital. It controls the

Faith, Witness, and Community

economy so as to create debt relationships and uses that debt to enslave the populace even further. To receive the basic necessities of life, one has to go into debt to the provider—a debt to be paid in money, obedience, reverence, and respect. Jesus pointed out that even being at the top of that system is futile.

In Luke 12, the lily of the field is compared to Solomon—the apex of Israel's experiment with earthly kings. Even Solomon, the best of the best in that system of hierarchy, domination, and power, could not match what God gave freely and unstintingly to multitudes of mere flowers. The birds and flowers participated in an economy of grace; God provided enough for them each day. They did not need to store up wealth nor to organize as a domination system to gather food.

The lesson is that if we share what we have as a grace to all who are in need, there will be enough for everyone. If some hoard, others must go hungry. There is no reason for the pyramid of power except to enable some persons to hoard. As long as we feel the need to hoard and organize ourselves to do so, we are in a state of idolatry.

A Catholic Worker house is an economy of grace. A home is an economy of grace. Norfolk Quaker House is an economy of grace. The debt economy is constantly trying to overwrite these and similar examples as "charity." Statements about the worthy poor and expectations of obedience, reverence, or other strings that are attached to gifts identify charity. The practice of a grace economy deconstructs the structure of the debt economy, which in turn reacts to protect itself. If there is no opposition, the project is probably charity. If the system protests or opposes, the project may be grace.

Ched also spoke during the retreat about Luke 11:24–26, where the unclean spirit is driven out but returns with seven other even more wicked spirits who set up housekeeping. This is a sign of how hard it will be to move into the economy of grace—the more we clean our lens and clean up our practice, the more stuff we will dredge up from within that must be dealt with and the more outward practices we must clean up. Seen this way, the parable seems to be a companion to Luke 19, which describes the external world's reaction to our efforts. From either perspective, the effort to live in the Kingdom of God looks to be lifelong, painful, and full of discouragement.

So, we have on the one hand the doctrine of perfection—be perfect as your father in Heaven is perfect—being affirmed by Friends and Scripture. On the other, we have Jesus apparently teaching that the forces of opposition are so strong and so stubborn that we will never wholly reside in the Kingdom. We live in that tension, never allowed by the doctrine of perfection to rest short of the Kingdom yet never arriving in that promised land—wandering painfully and with great effort in the desert. Yet we follow the pillar of fire and column of smoke, and there is a pattern to our lives of effort that we can only briefly, rarely, and incompletely glimpse. And also, always, there is Emmanuel, God with us, infusing and redeeming the present moment with infinite, unmerited grace.

We are caught between the now and the not yet, as Paul wrote in 2 Corinthians 6:4–10. We are in pain and yet always full of joy, poor and yet making many people rich, having nothing and yet owning everything. We have the assurance of things not seen, setting out by faith from this Kingdom to the next, living ever after as strangers in our own land that has become strange to us, living in the promise of the new heaven and the new earth foreseen in John's vision. O come, Emmanuel!

Later that summer, I gave a plenary address at Lake Erie Yearly Meeting sessions. Just before leaving home, I read the text to Susan and asked her whether it was worth traveling that far to deliver; I was not sure. She said the material was so familiar to her she could not tell how valuable it would be, either—so I came to the podium at the appointed time without a clear sense that what I was about to say would be anything but mediocre. Before speaking I got down on my knees and prayed aloud what I normally pray silently—that God would guide my speech so that I spoke God's gospel and that God would open hearts so that God's gospel would be received in each one, no matter whether I was faithful or not.

When the meeting broke, Friends began to approach me, speaking their thanks for a prophetic message. One Friend had tears in her eyes. Others spoke of how afflicted they were by the call to put God at the center of their lives. But no one questioned whether or not the message was true—they only confessed that it was hard and sought to explore various aspects of it. There was an electric sense that something good and exciting had just happened.

In the worship-sharing time that followed, it became clear that Friends had been spoken to. That afternoon, I offered a workshop devoted to following up on the plenary in which about twenty Friends and I explored the Kingdom of God and our need to be located with the poor, and we did some Bible exegesis on passages ranging from "Turn the other cheek" to Jesus' testing in the desert after his baptism. Free times and meal times were occasions of continued conversation with various Friends about a wide range of topics related to the lecture.

My sense of having been used powerfully by my Master continued the next day and throughout the sessions. While we waited for the breakfast line to open, several Friends and I continued a discussion about the economy of grace and community discernment. Breakfast included a discussion with four or five other Friends about the nature of evil and Walter Wink's book *The Powers That Be*. At the morning session, the Friends Committee on National Legislation representative opened her report by quoting and expositing the closing part of my lecture concerning the vision of new Jerusalem—the Reign of God.

When we gathered for the final meeting for business, the teen program report included a drawing of the high schoolers' most vivid images of the yearly meeting sessions: a burning bush and a slow-moving cow covered by a quilt (the latter was a reference to my description of my mom as a child hanging quilts on fences, hedgerows, and anything else that was available to clean them of the winter's dust and musty odor). The general epistle opened with a lengthy summary of my remarks.

In the closing worship, from the first ministry to the last, Friends rose and cited some part or another of the plenary or the workshop discussion to begin their ministry. Meeting for worship was deeply covered, building to a final message from a woman from Toledo Meeting about community, the preferred location among the poor, and what we should learn from their perspective. She ended by committing her life to living into this kind of community. By the end, my eyes were filled with tears and I was holding Marty Grundy's hand. She offered me a handkerchief, but I wiped away the tears without it. "I am glad," I told her, "to have been present at this meeting where the Spirit has been so active." Marty added, "And to have been a catalyst." No, thought I, for a catalyst is unchanged by the reaction it instigates—and I was not unchanged.

The plenary address immediately worked its way into the vocabulary of the yearly meeting sessions. When Friends thanked the clerk for faithful service, he replied that it had been an "encounter with the taproot" (referring to the title of my lecture). When the meeting approved a minute on a social concern, a Friend cried out, "We're going upstream to save the babies!" The economy of grace was the buzzword of the day as Friends excitedly looked for present examples and future opportunities. Over thirty copies of the plenary audiotape had been ordered the last time I saw the list, and multiple Friends spoke of organizing study groups back home to explore the topics of the plenary in more depth.

It certainly seemed that I had touched a match to a tinderbox. God had clearly and carefully prepared the fireplace before I arrived, and the spark was God's, not mine, but how wonderful to have carried it to Lake Erie Yearly Meeting and watched it take hold! "Encounter with the Taproot" is included in *Wrestling with Our Faith Tradition* and was reprinted by Friends World Committee for Consultation.[7]

I ended the yearly meeting sessions totally exhausted—physically tired, full of minor aches and pains, emotionally wrung out, mentally depleted—in other words, wonderfully used up! I looked forward to the journey home, being reunited with Susan and Asa, and finishing Father's Day at home and at rest with my family. Thank God.

A First Day experience in Tenth Month 1997 illustrated the adage "Life is what happens while you are making other plans." Susan and I began the day by making biscuits and gravy for breakfast. I made the biscuits, and she made the sausage gravy. Just as we sat down to eat, a Samaritan House client called to say that her estranged husband had just told her he was going to put all her belongings out on the sidewalk in the rain at noon. So, instead of First Day School and worship, we spent the morning and early afternoon helping this woman through the next step in unraveling her relationship with her husband. Susan and I accompanied her to her house. Her husband's car was in the driveway, but he did not answer the door, and he had changed all the locks. After knocking repeatedly with no response, we decided to get a cup of coffee and wait until noon.

When we came back to the house, a few boxes were on the front porch, and a handwritten "no trespassing" sign had been taped to the screen door—with half a dozen spelling errors. We took a couple of photographs with the disposable camera Susan kept in her pickup. The husband was in his car, and at the first sign of our arrival, he backed out of the driveway and parked across the street, one house down. He sat there, motor running, the whole time we were loading things into a borrowed van and our truck. Susan and the client got about half a dozen plants from the back of the house in addition to the things from the porch, while I sat in the pickup as a sort of watchman. As we drove off, the husband pulled into his driveway again. After all this was over, the woman observed, "The Samaritan House people were right—they said this would happen, and I did not believe them. I surely can tell anybody else who comes to Samaritan House that they know what they're doing."

I was glad to have been able to refer this woman to Samaritan House for help and to have been able to intervene with Samaritan House when she did not get the specific help she needed when she first called. I was glad the Samaritan House staff had shown themselves so "on the money" in their predictions of how the situation would develop and what the client should do, even though she did not always take their advice. I was glad to have been able to be a male presence twice that weekend to help defuse the situation and make sure the husband did not make a scene—or worse. Finally, I was thankful for the wonderful relationship that Susan and I had and for God's graciousness and generosity and bringing us together.

Later that year, at another retreat Ched Myers led, he and I got to talking, and I asked how he'd made the leap of faith into the itinerant ministry he was now following. He said he had been doing retreats and workshops for about ten years, at first on weekends when he was not busy with American Friends Service Committee work, then on vacations and holidays as well. Eventually, he cut back his work hours to three-fifths time so he could devote more time to leading retreats and workshops.

About sixteen months earlier, he'd left American Friends Service Committee entirely to test the waters fully, trying to discover the answers to three questions:

1) Was there a desire and hunger for this kind of ministry?

2) Did he have the gifts to carry it out?

3) Could he make it financially on the income this work generated?

Sixteen months later, he was able to say yes to numbers one and two but the jury was still out on question number three. He was on the road 75 to 80 percent of the time, which was too much to be sustainable, yet he was barely making ends meet financially. Emotionally and spiritually, he needed to cut back on his schedule, but financially he couldn't afford to do so.

This was unexpectedly disturbing to me. I realized afterward that I was asking him questions to see whether there was something in his experience that could help me with my own discernment. I sensed that my gifts could be most fully utilized in a life dedicated to old-style ministry, but I knew that the Religious Society of Friends was not equipped to support me in that life. Ched was telling me that he himself could not do it, not even with his decade of experience, vast contacts, and high visibility among many different faith traditions. If he couldn't make it work, who could? If there was no way to devote myself full-time to the ministry to which I was called, what was I to do? Could God really be calling me into a place of such unease and compromise?

Another conversation with Ched explored the joys and problems of the ministry to which he was committed and to which I felt increasingly called. He affirmed that the need for "rabbis" was great and that the desire to learn more of what the Scriptures had to teach us was widespread. The road was a difficult place for him—he hated it—yet the itinerant ministry brought him into contact with people who would not ever come to him if he were based in a retreat house. Still, he said he

Faith, Witness, and Community

would take a position in a retreat center in a minute if it were offered because the burdens of travel would be taken away.

Ched found what Scripture said about the hireling ministry to be ambivalent. On the one hand, Paul insisted that the laborer was worthy of his hire. On the other, he bragged that he himself had been financially independent—although it seems clear that he had accepted some financial support from other believers. Ched felt that Paul's concern was the patronage system, in which a wealthy individual would become the patron of a priest or scholar, providing for his financial needs in return for some influence or control over the content of the message and activities of his protégé. Ched felt okay in principle about accepting the support of individuals to release a gifted person into the ministry by having a group of people each pledge a certain amount of financial support per month for the released minister's living expenses. The rub was that he was not at all comfortable asking for that support for himself. I knew how he felt.

One evening, Ched led us through an exploration of Jesus' dinner at the Pharisee's house when "the woman with a bad name" came and washed his feet with her tears, drying them with her hair (Luke 7:36–50). We all got down and reclined on the floor, which helped us get the proper perspective on the story. Then Ched talked about inappropriate touching and the scandal and shame that this touching would have caused at the dinner. Finally, he asked for someone with long hair to demonstrate what the woman had done. There were only two of us who qualified, and the other one (a woman) did not respond, so I let down my hair and used it to rub the foot of one of the other retreatants. It was a powerful moment for all of us, which Ched used to point out how charged a moment it must have been then as an increasing number of guests saw and became upset at the presence and behavior of the woman. (I enjoyed myself thoroughly.)

On the drive home from Pendle Hill, I realized that I had been waiting for God to tell me what was going to happen for Susan and me in the next several years before I committed myself to a plan. I wanted assurance that I was committing to a long-term successful project before I started. Yet it is God who starts and sustains ministry, not me and not

Susan and me together; God will fill in for us if it is the Divine Will that whatever we become involved in should continue once we leave. I wanted God to give me a guarantee that we would be in for the long run when in fact God never gives that sort of promise. Jesus' parable of the silos is a teaching that we should not expect that sort of sign from God or act as if we know what will happen tomorrow.

This seemed to liberate me to act on a leading even in the midst of my uncertainty. God never gives guarantees, and I felt I should not wait for a guarantee of success before starting a new project. So, late in 1997 Susan and I began intentional discernment to see where God was offering us a way to serve. This would not bear fruit for about a year, and then it did so in an entirely unexpected way.

One possibility that came to mind was starting a new Friends meeting. If Friends are really "in the world but not of it," like extraterrestrials, then perhaps one can think about Conservative Friends using the Drake equation and the Fermi paradox the way some people think about extraterrestrial civilizations. If one-quarter of the North American population would be attracted to a religion with Christian roots, and one-fifth of those were apophatic in spirituality rather than kataphatic, and if one-sixth of the apophatic folks were pacifists, there were potentially over 11,600 unprogrammed Quakers in Tidewater Virginia alone.[8] If 10 percent of those people would be interested in the Conservative Quaker branch, that would amount to 1,600 Conservative Friends in southeastern Virginia—roughly three times the current membership of NCYM(C). That's the Drake equation side of this thought experiment. The Fermi paradox side is simply the question, Where are they? There is a market here, as my management school vocabulary would express it. There is room for another meeting and more—there are yet many people to be gathered.

Establishing a new meeting was not the only possible course of action. We could make an equal commitment to grow Virginia Beach Friends Meeting (perhaps to divide at some future date when it became too large). There was much I loved and respected at Virginia Beach Friends Meeting, and I would be forever grateful to that meeting and those Friends for accepting me into the Conservative tradition and

Faith, Witness, and Community

helping me along a significant part of my spiritual maturation. But the "angel" of Virginia Beach Friends Meeting, to borrow the metaphor Walter Wink used in his trilogy *Naming the Powers*, *Unmasking the Powers*, and *Engaging the Powers* was one of individual spiritual healing—a task it did reasonably well. It was not a community of radical faith; there was no commitment to a radical Christianity located among the poor and powerless. There was certainly a place in the divine plan for a community like Virginia Beach Friends Meeting, but that did not appear to be the ministry for which Susan and I were being prepared.

In all the possibilities we considered during this long discernment, one constant was having a base in a faith community, probably small and probably Friends, who gathered to worship God and live as disciples of Christ after the manner of Friends. "Christ has died, Christ has risen, Christ has come again to teach his people himself" would be at the core of this community, and the cycle of action and reflection would be its modus operandi. Part of the life of such a community would be proclamation—sharing what it discovered with others.

This led me to more reflection on aspects of membership in a faith community, and I realized my understanding had changed. I had thought membership was a choice by the individual that a particular faith community could best support the individual's spiritual growth. Now I began to think of individual membership as a commitment to the mission and work of the community. To paraphrase what John F. Kennedy said in 1961, "Ask not what your meeting can do for you—ask what you can do for your meeting."

Even setting that issue aside, I would not want any meeting to grow very fast. Those who were attracted to such a meeting should stay because of their commitment to our worship and witness, not because they had been enrolled on a roster. If after an extended period of time they made a personal commitment to the welfare and faithfulness of the community, then perhaps a membership decision would have meaning for them and for the community.

In Eleventh Month 1997, another difficult meeting for business illuminated just how difficult it is to have authentic community. The query that month asked whether love and unity were maintained among us, and the meeting spent a goodly time considering its efforts—not insignificant—to overcome the pain and hurt engendered in a previous meeting for business and to restore a sense of unity and community in the meeting. A Friend rose to encourage us to send letters to the president supporting the United Nations Convention on the Rights of the Child, which the United States had not ratified. A young mother then rose to say with emotion that she could not support that convention because the US Constitution said international treaties overrode federal and state law and thus she would not be able to exercise proper parental control over her children (i.e., corporal punishment).

In an attempt to keep this Friend in the discourse, I recalled that the Prince of Peace Plowshares activists had not been allowed to cite international law in court earlier that year and that I was unclear about the extent to which international treaties in practice abrogated federal law. Perhaps the Peace and Social Concerns Committee could research the matter and report back to the meeting for the general edification of Friends. The clerk of that committee then rose to say she considered what we had heard to have come straight from the Christian Coalition—at which point the distraught mother began crying out that this was not so and that the meeting never listened to what she had to say, and then she stormed out of the meeting house.

One of the elders went out to speak to her, and after a short time I did also. She was extremely upset, at or near tears all the time we talked. I told her I was sorry for the pain she had experienced in the meeting, and we embraced. We talked for awhile, during which time she remarked that I was no longer present in the meeting enough "to be the salt you could be."

Between the meetings for business and worship, another Friend also remarked to me that I had been absent a lot and asked what I had been doing. I told him I'd been traveling in the ministry to Charlottesville, Pendle Hill, and other places. He shared that several Friends had commented to him on my absences recently and that they interpreted them as my disengagement from the meeting.

These and similar experiences over the years have convinced me that authentic spiritual community is not a stable state but is inherently unstable and needs constant attention. All of us need to be nurturing the faith community all the time, helping repair its breaches and strengthen its weak areas. The work of community is constant work, and it is hard work—but without it we have no hope of being models of the Kingdom of God, which is our calling.

While our discernment about our future was underway, Susan and I continued our work in the public ministry. In First Month 1998, we met with Friends at Wicomico River Friends Meeting in Salisbury, Maryland, as the culmination of their study of *Essays on the Quaker Vision of Gospel Order* over several months. About fifteen people were present for the discussion and perhaps twenty for the meeting for worship that followed. We talked about diversity, the need for a core vision for a meeting, and the importance of corporate action and reflection to the spiritual growth of a community. Friends were fully engaged, and their questions and comments had substance. Susan and I felt that the group was poised on the edge of exciting spiritual growth while at the same time facing challenges such as the geographic dispersion of their membership.

I was active in the ministry during worship, speaking to the effect that God seems always to have worked with imperfect people and that they often could not agree with each other, like Paul, John, and Mark and their discussions about whether or not to be vegetarian. God seems to have sought out people like this to be the vessels of the gospel, and Scripture seems to go out of its way to remind us of this.

Discussion continued during and after the potluck meal following worship until the last of us finally rose to leave about 2:20 p.m. Friends seemed able to hear what I had to say, and more than one admitted they had been challenged or had had long-standing excuses shattered by the discussion. Susan and I felt that the gospel had been well served by the day's activities.

I talk now of corporate vision and corporate action as the sine qua non of growth and of the cycle of praxis, action, and reflection as the path. Right membership seems to me no longer a recognition that the Quaker setting is the best for my personal spiritual journey but a commitment to the vision and the praxis of the faith community. It is time to get out of our heads and into our guts—to put feet on our gospel order and see how it walks around on the ground. For example, Friends have asked me how to conduct outreach to a university community. I tell them to "talk their talk" unabashedly when asked why they walk the way they do.

These things seem vitally important to me, and not only for the Religious Society of Friends. The old order, the old ways of being religious, are falling apart because the center cannot hold. Sectarian piety and focusing on personal salvation are both inadequate to the times. If the gospel is to be indeed good news, it has to be involved in the daily struggle of the poor and marginalized, and it has to be good news here and now—not another brand of spaceship theology or an escape to the hereafter.

Friends at business meeting in Virginia Beach began discussing whether an ex officio member of a meeting committee could vote. Those present were reminded that no votes were taken among Friends and that the settled policy was that all present had a voice in deliberations. A Friend then rose to say, with some feeling, that in meetings for business one individual's objection blocked the entire group from action or decision and that her understanding was that this committee was not honoring that veto power.

At that point, I rose to say our practice is to seek out the sense of the meeting, which we recognize when the clerk has articulated it acceptably to Friends present. We do not have a one-person veto system (the so-called
tyranny of one), and complete unanimity is not required. We should understand our own practices before reflecting them onto another group. There were several head nods at this, a few smiles, and one sotto voce "Thank you." A seasoned Friend rose to affirm what I had said, adding that this was why it was so important to give the clerk time to discern what the sense of the meeting might be. Discussion of ex officio committee members then came to a halt.

Virginia Beach Friends began their meeting for business in 1998 by hearing a report on clearness for membership for a man who had been a Methodist pastor for many years. They reported him clear for

Faith, Witness, and Community

membership but had neglected to discuss with him his membership in the Methodist Church. When I asked about this, the meeting began a discussion of dual membership, and it quickly became clear that the meeting was of two opinions. Some Friends felt dual membership was not in good order, and others saw no problem in belonging to two faith communities, even if they held conflicting beliefs and faith commitments. When I was in this same position in New England many years ago, I was instructed that I must resign from the Methodist Church in order to become a member of the Religious Society of Friends. In Virginia Beach, there was precedent in the refusal of the meeting to approve the membership application of a Friend who had wished to belong to our monthly meeting and another meeting at the same time. If membership is "a commitment to the welfare and faithfulness of the community" and reciprocally a commitment to the welfare and faithfulness of the individual by that community, it is difficult to see how one can be a member of two communities at once, no matter how much their abstract faith commitments are in harmony.

In early 1998, I led a Pendle Hill short course on gospel order. We spent the opening session introducing ourselves and sharing our expectations. Two of the participants proved to be true gems: Takashi Mizuno, a Japanese immigrant with a concern for peace and justice on Okinawa, and Pak Sung-Joon, a Korean liberation theologian. I had met them both at a retreat weekend with Ched Myers the previous fall and was very pleased that they came to this course.

Pendle Hill arranged for Pak Sung-Joon to talk to the on-campus community. He shared some of his life story, including his thirteen and a half years of imprisonment, and his concern that transnational corporations were working tremendous injustices on the people of Korea and other Pacific Rim nations.

At the suggestion of Deborah Fink, I also offered Pak Sung-Joon one of our class sessions. He led us in an exercise listing all the things in our personal storehouses, old and new, that we should bring out and offer to Jesus (Matthew 13:51–52). Then he explored the Good Samaritan Parable in Luke. Korean *minjung* theologians[9] consider that Jesus told the story to draw attention to the beaten man and that Jesus himself played the role of the beaten man to teach us that we should pay heed to the cries of the poor and suffering. The class was very powerful.

Takashi Mizuno had asked me to meet with him to discuss his call to ministry and help him in his discernment. When we met, he said most of his discernment questions had been answered in the worship-seeing exercise I had led earlier that day. Our time together was therefore spent mostly on the details of his plans for an Okinawan shalom ministry to promote grassroots organizing for peace and justice in Okinawa and a parallel organization in the United States to assist Okinawan immigrants to this country. We planned some reciprocal visitation later in the year, he and his wife to Norfolk to visit Susan and me and Norfolk Quaker House, and Susan and I to Riverton, New Jersey, to see his organic farm (which he hoped would finance other ministries).

The short course seemed to go well, and I got indirect feedback that participants felt it was a good experience for them. After each session, I reflected on what had gone on so far and then determined the content to offer in the next session. The hopes and expectations shared by the students included learning about the role of Scripture in gospel order, which led me to share some examples, including the economy of grace and the visions of peace and justice contained in Jesus' report of his temptations by the devil. As at New York Yearly Meeting, the section on "no kings" met with some resistance. Friends seem to be able to hear the "no silos" proposition as a challenge with which they should wrestle, but they often hear the "no kings" proposition as offensive, especially when I confess that it has led me to an increasing withdrawal from participation in national government. We Friends are such good citizens, and we work so hard to increase the good works that we perceive our government does, that we live in a state of constant denial about the largest activity of the national government—national "defense"—and the fact that Scripture seems to say pretty clearly that centralized governments are a form of idolatry in that they represent our depending on human institutions to do the work of *Ha-Shem*.

I shared with a Pendle Hill staffer the proposition that Linda Chidsey and I lead a weekend retreat for ministers and elders among Friends, and she ran with it in a big way. She planned a three-day or four-day event with an attendance of about fifty persons, to be held no earlier than Ninth Month 1999, and she promised to help in the advance work, including mailings, publicity, and planning. I was excited by her enthusiasm and told her I would be able to devote time to the project after I gave the Philadelphia Yearly Meeting opening address in Third Month.

A lunchtime conversation with Doug Gwyn was another real treat. He had just finished a book about seventeenth-century Seekers and now was turning his attention to Truth—once again writing for an audience that extended beyond Friends. Doug had discovered four kinds of truth—or, at least, four ways in which we accept new truth into the corpus of belief. The first is *direct affirmation by personal experience*, the classic "This I know experientially" of Quakers. The second is *coherence*, by which a new truth is accepted because it fits into the scheme of already accepted truth. There is also an *operational* truth, accepted because a particular methodology of testing it has been developed and applied with positive results, and, fourth, a *pragmatic* truth that is accepted because using it gives good results. Doug felt a healthy religious body uses all four types of truth and that part of what had happened in the schisms among Quakers was that the various branches of Friends had come to overemphasize one or another type of truth. I see conflicts between the first two types of truth as a strong factor in much of the conflict over doctrine among Friends at the monthly and yearly meeting levels.

We talked for a time about various writing projects, and I described my efforts to be accountable to the yearly meeting regarding my writing of the essays on gospel order and the decision of the reading committee members that the second manuscript should not be published. Doug reminded me of George Fox's comment when the Second Day Morning Meeting rejected one of his manuscripts: "I did not set this body up to reject my work!"

One evening, our group was joined by about half a dozen members of the Pendle Hill community who were curious about the short course. I gave a short introduction to gospel order and then the members of the class each shared what had been important to them about the experience. It seemed to have been important for everyone. One Friend broke into a spontaneous, emotional prayer of thanks to Jesus for the week and all who had helped bring it about. Another Friend said that I had redefined for him what it meant to be a minister and that he realized he had not met one before. I take that sort of thing with a grain of salt, but it was nice to know that my efforts at least had not prevented the gospel from being heard.

On Third Month 26 1998, I spoke to the opening session of Philadelphia Yearly Meeting on John 3:30 in Arch Street Meeting House. I felt energized by giving the talk and felt a good response from the auditory. In the period of worship afterward, an older Friend rose to say he had been reminded of Tom Kelly giving his "Holy Obedience" lecture in the same room many years ago—that the same truths were to be found all through both lectures. No one else spoke.

On Nissan 14, 5758, in the Hebrew calendar, which happened to be Good Friday 1998 in the Christian liturgical calendar, Susan and I observed Passover with a Seder of our own. We didn't have a ritually correct meal, but it felt authentic internally. We had unleavened pitas and red wine and read aloud the passages from Exodus instituting the Passover and an essay that did an excellent job of expressing the importance of Passover in today's terms, stressing the centrality of justice. We ate this simple meal slowly, reading and eating and discussing what that first night must have been like. The room was lit by a single candle; we sat in a small circle of light surrounded by the darkness, much as the Israelites did on that first Passover.

I had always thought of Jesus as the Passover lamb, and that was part of it; the tenth of Nissan would have been what we call Palm Sunday. The crowd's selection of Jesus as their chosen one as he rode into the city became the equivalent of the selection of a lamb without blemish on the tenth of each Nissan. Now I thought about Jesus celebrating the Passover with his friends to remind them that what was about to happen, however frightening and terrible it might be, was in fact part of the one Big Story of God at work in the universe. God was in charge on that first Passover, God was in charge on Maundy Thursday and Good Friday, and God is in charge today.

Faith, Witness, and Community

In Fifth Month 1998, I attended a gathering of Friends in West Chester, Pennsylvania, staying with Michael Wajda and Alison Levie. Alison and I had a good conversation about the kinds of personal relationships ministers needed in order to develop and exercise their gifts properly. We agreed that ministers of the word were unlikely to find these relationships in their own monthly meetings as meetings were unlikely to have more than one or two persons with this vocation; we saw the quarterly meeting as a more likely place to find these needed relationships.

There were about twenty people present. We began and ended in solid worship, with time in between for table fellowship and small group discussions about various subjects. One Friend and I shared on a very personal level about the challenges we had faced in accepting our callings. In particular, it was an opportunity for him to share how he was wrestling with a sense that he had not yet fully shared his spiritual journey with his wife. That generated a sense of incompleteness in him, which he now seemed ready to address. The conversation renewed in me a sense of thankfulness for the deep communion Susan and I had on spiritual matters. We were not identical, but we were each deeply devoted to the Lord and respectful of the way God had been at work in each other's life.

I thought the group was headed in the right direction and was already accomplishing a crucial thing: establishing a place of deep worship where the headship of the Lord Jesus Christ over all matters pertaining to the church was acknowledged without dispute. Beyond this leaping-off point, I saw territory the group had not yet explored— covenant accountability. Friends had a growing sense that something like this was needed, though most didn't have a clear sense of what that something might be. To move from discussions about how to grow and season ministers and elders to actually growing and seasoning ministers and elders, I felt that we needed to establish stable groups of folks called to ministry and eldership, with infants to adults in their service, who would establish ongoing relationships that would endure over time and give them a stable point from which to observe each other's growth in grace and to give good and loving counsel. Secondly, members of these groups needed to see each other in their ministry in order to give the guidance that would be truly helpful. This would mean making a commitment to visit each other's meetings and to be present for one another in other times and places of public ministry.

I had been rereading Samuel Bownas and was chewing on his initial qualification for the ministry, which was more or less a sanctification experience. The response to this experience may well be the kind of reorientation of one's life that I had been writing about. This, too, needs to be discussed openly and frankly; there are some prerequisite qualifications to the ministry that cannot be skipped or finessed.

In Seventh Month, Susan, Asa, Susan's son Dan, and I made the trip to Chowan University in Murfreesboro, North Carolina, for the 1998 sessions of NCYM(C). When we got to Chowan, there were immediately opportunities for conversation that I found very rewarding. Barbara Gosney and I talked about realizing that the "transition of generations" was over and that we were now the ones who had to do the "heavy lifting" of keeping the tradition healthy for the next generation. The first night's dinner table consisted of Bob and Barbara Gosney of Rich Square Monthly Meeting, Linda and Peter Chidsey from New York Yearly Meeting, Sid Kitchens and Deborah Shaw of Friendship Friends, Marty Grundy of Lake Erie Yearly Meeting, and myself. It was excellent fellowship, and I was refreshed in body and soul. Takashi Mizuno arrived near the end of our meal, bringing his Okinawa photo exhibit.

The yearly meeting of MEO gathered for worship and business after supper, clerked by Bob Gosney. His summary of the previous winter's gathering was received with approbation, and Friends agreed to hold another Twelfth Month gathering and also to look for monthly meeting events to co-sponsor in order to provide opportunities for Friends from several monthly meetings to gather in the fall and spring. I agreed to convene a planning group for the new retreat.

After the other business of the meeting was completed, Bob Gosney reminded Friends that he had asked the previous year to be replaced as clerk of the yearly meeting of MEO at this meeting, and he asked for recommendations or a volunteer to serve as clerk. There was a period of silence, and after a while Sid Kitchen passed me a note saying, "I think thee would make a good clerk." I leaned over and said to him, "Then speak up." He did, and shortly thereafter Carole Treadway said that the same name had occurred to her. Bob looked at me, and I said that I was willing to serve if Friends were easy with the appointment. He put the question to the meeting, and there was general approval.

So, after seven years, I was once again a clerk at the yearly meeting level. Susan says this was a symbolic olive branch; the yearly meeting was offering something it could offer and I was accepting something I could accept in an effort to bring closure to that whole episode. She was right, but there was more. It was also affirmation that the concerns about ministry and eldering that I carried were right for me to carry and that I should continue that work. It was affirmation from the yearly meeting that intentional efforts to nurture the health of our faith tradition were in order. I was happy to have this acceptance and affirmation from the yearly meeting and believed it did bring a sort of closure. At the same time, it was not an accomplishment or the end of anything but simply something that happened to me (and to the yearly meeting) while we were on our way to do other work.

Closing worship of Rich Square Monthly Meeting on First Day, held in Cedar Grove Meeting House in Woodland, was rich and deep, and the fellowship over lunch afterward was hearty and uplifting. This was a special place, made holy by the generations of faithful Friends who had lived here. The town itself, only about eight hundred souls, seemed to have an aura about it from more than two hundred years of Quaker presence.

As we left the meeting house for the drive home, Susan turned to me and said, "We're supposed to live here and nurture Rich Square meeting." Something in her voice let me know this was not just idle conversation. My heart was so full of positive feelings about the meeting, its importance in the history of the yearly meeting, and the sense I'd had all through the sessions that we were supposed to be at work nurturing the faith tradition of our yearly meeting that I immediately accepted Susan's statement as prophecy—a forthtelling—that this was indeed what we were supposed to be doing. "OK," I said, "let's be looking for the path opening for us to do that."

Chapter 7
Exercises in the Gospel Ministry: Woodland, North Carolina, 1998–2013

While Susan and I discerned how to carry out our leading to move to Rich Square Monthly Meeting in northeastern North Carolina, our outward life in Virginia Beach continued without immediate change. In Ninth Month 1998, I had lunch with a Friend about his recent appointment to the station of elder. I wanted to encourage him to be proactive and assertive in his new role, more than he otherwise might think to be. He had been a listener all his professional life, and he had commented when the Monthly Meeting of Ministers, Elders, and Overseers (MEO) were discussing his possible appointment that listening was the most important part of being an elder. This is true, but it is not the *only* important part of being an elder. The faith community needs both those who can hear without condemnation and those who can offer words of insight. I hoped this Friend would work to balance the actions and activities of the elders in our meeting.

I also wanted to take up the accountability of ministers to elders. Our meeting's elders had been very reluctant to exercise this responsibility, though some had tried. I yearned for a rigorous accountability that constructively questioned my efforts to develop my gifts, to steward them properly, and to exercise them rightly.

Ministers need to be accountable to elders because the elders can see aspects of the minister and the ministry that are not visible to the minister directly. The elders have been identified by the community as both having a passion for the welfare of the community and "knowing" when things are in gospel order. The faith community is blessed when the elder combines this passion and knowing with a willingness to be articulate about what they see to be true about the community's circumstances. An elder should be able to say to the community, "This is what I see happening here, and this is the effect it will have on the community," and the community should be able to hear this without defensiveness, relying on the elder's perception—just as the minister can rely on the elder's advice and counsel.

Susan and I traveled to Wilmington, North Carolina, in Ninth Month 1998, the first of several planned visits to monthly meetings that year in my service as clerk of the yearly meeting MEO. Wilmington Friends were considering whether or not to reinstate their MEO, and if so in what form. There had been two problems with maintaining this meeting in Wilmington: the meeting's reluctance to recognize spiritual gifts, and the last meeting's appearance of meeting and acting outside the knowledge of the monthly meeting. I did what I could to encourage Wilmington Friends to reinstate their MEO. It is an important asset of the monthly meeting, with its chief responsibility being, as our *Discipline* states plainly, to foster the spiritual life of the monthly meeting.

For many with some familiarity with the Religious Society of Friends, and others who share our discomfort with the hireling ministry, the first issue to address in considering whether to establish a meeting of ministers, elders, and overseers (or a ministry and oversight committee or other similar body) is the question of singling out specific individuals as ministers in a religious society that attempts to live as a priesthood of all believers. A deeper understanding of our faith and our practice leads to the realization that the question of elders, the "nursing mothers in Israel" who "feel an exceptional concern for the deeper spiritual life of the meeting"—a passion for the welfare of the faith community—must come first.

God raises up in each meeting those spiritual gifts necessary to the nurture of that group and its faithfulness to the Divine Will. Central to those gifts, and to the raising-up process, is the gift of eldership. In every meeting, there are one or more individuals who care deeply for the well-being of the meeting, who seem to know in their bones what is the right order and right action for the group, and who articulate that understanding for the meeting community in word and deed. These people are the elders of the meeting and are the first Friends who should be appointed to the monthly meeting of MEO.

There is also a set of material responsibilities assigned to MEO, including the responsibility "to foster peace, alleviate want, discourage tale-bearing." These are sometimes lumped together as pastoral care matters, and persons gifted in these areas serve in the meeting as "overseers." These are folks who are sensitive regarding when a Friend needs a visit or how and when to arrange for financial support or physical assistance during an illness. In larger meeting communities, the group is often set apart as a separate committee of overseers, and I approve of that division being made even more widely than it is currently practiced. The North Carolina Yearly Meeting (Conservative) *Discipline*, however, says that overseers will commonly serve together with ministers and elders in a single meeting of MEO, and it works well enough that way.

When these gifts have been identified, and when both elders and overseers have had ample time to exercise their gifts in the meeting of MEO, it will often happen that ministers are raised up in the meeting community. The direction of causation points so strongly in this direction that one Conservative *Discipline* (that of New England Yearly Meeting) advised that if there were no ministers apparent, the meeting should appoint elders! When the true gift of vocal ministry is lifted up in an individual, that Friend will want nothing more than the company of elders and more seasoned ministers to guide them in the proper development and exercise of that gift. It is the joyous responsibility of the meeting community to assist that development as well as to receive the gift as it is exercised. The naming of the gift does not convey authority or privileges to the individual but acknowledges (this is the word used in our *Discipline*) that a gift has been granted and that both individual and community are obliged to see that the gift is developed, exercised, and received faithfully.

The need for a special committee to carry out these tasks is sometimes questioned. A separate committee enables those persons with gifts and experience appropriate to the special specific responsibilities of MEO to address these responsibilities without the distraction of other tasks and responsibilities. In the case of very small meetings, it may be impractical to divide the entire community into smaller groups. I was a member of a small meeting (Charlottesville) that for some years had no committees at all but met as a committee of the whole to consider the tasks that in a larger meeting would be assigned to a committee. One week we would meet as the Peace Committee, another as Ministry and

Oversight, and so on. This worked well while the meeting was very small but was abandoned in favor of separate committees when the meeting began to grow.

The Virginia Beach Monthly Meeting of MEO modeled some of these tasks in a recent meeting. A discussion about the condition of adult First Day school ended with a commitment on the part of all members of MEO to attend First Day school regularly and to make it clear that our approach to Bible study was formational rather than intellectual or scholarly. Later in the meeting, there was some discussion of a perceived lack of unity in the monthly meeting and among members of MEO. We agreed that much of our trouble had come from "cutting corners" rather than taking the time to discern and be faithful to the leadings of the Holy Spirit and from keeping silent when we should have spoken up, especially when that meant speaking difficult truth in a given situation. We agreed to pray for reconciliation and healing among us and to strive to speak the truth clearly and fully in all our dealings.

Susan and I led a workshop on liberation theology at Guilford College in Greensboro in Eleventh Month. We had brought some hard candy with us, and I started distributing it right away, one piece for everyone, with the explanation, "The Kingdom of God is a party!" I used a candle to symbolize a campfire and sang the spiritual "Mary Don't You Weep." Then we talked about the meaning of the song and went on to explore the story of the healing of Jairus's daughter. We acted the story out, and it was as powerful as always. Finally, I talked about Jubilee, and we looked at what had happened with the candy. Sure enough, accumulation had happened! We talked about accumulation and redistribution for a while, and then our time was up. I had a sense that the time was well spent and that Friends brought something away with them—including, as Deborah Shaw said later, a new way of looking at the Bible. I came away feeling that I had given everything I could during those two days.

One year during yearly meeting sessions, a sensitive incident transpired in which members of the yearly meeting of MEO intervened to ensure that two individuals did not encounter each other during our time together. This was handled quietly and with confidentiality. When it became known in later months that something unusual had happened, some Friends pressed for details, but those who had been most directly involved felt providing detailed information about the incident would violate the privacy of one of the individuals involved and possibly damage the reputation of the other. This led to several conversations in different settings about the proper balance between confidentiality and community. I wrote a reflection on this topic to help guide the discussion in our yearly meeting:

> There is an inherent tension between the desire for confidentiality in a Friends meeting and the desire for community. The assurance of complete confidentiality between two individuals, which may lead to a strong bond and great trust between them, can work in just the opposite direction in a faith community. Confidentiality is important—even vital—to maintain if we want and expect Friends to disclose their problems and areas of struggle to the overseers, elders, and others who have pastoral care gifts and responsibilities in the meeting community. Communication (which seems to share the same root as community) is called for if we hope to achieve true community, where we know one another in the context of the Eternal who is our life and breath and being.
>
> If the meeting errs too far in the direction of confidentiality, true community is never achieved because we never really get to know one another. Efforts at community can also be damaged by selective "leaks" of information on the part of one or more parties to confidential information. The meeting becomes a hive of secrets, where one's status and position in the group depends on what one knows about whom.
>
> If the meeting errs too far in the direction of sharing all communication, true community is never achieved because we never trust one another enough to divulge our true selves. A sort of "false community can be achieved, where the façade is maintained but the reality is always masked.
>
> How can the meeting determine how much information to share, when to share it, and how? What can we do to create the

sort of context and relationships that encourage proper sharing of information and proper use of information once shared? I suspect there is no *a priori* rule, but only the hard and painful path of praxis: the cycle of action and reflection.

There is at times a reluctance on the part of attenders to apply for membership because they feel that they have not "achieved" enough in their spiritual work or traveled far enough on their spiritual journey. I believe this feeling does not spring spontaneously in the hearts of the attenders, but results from their picking up on a pretense that is perhaps more common among Friends than we want to admit: that we have indeed achieved a great deal in the way of expunging from our lives those things we would be loathe to divulge to our Friends. Sure, we may talk about embracing our dark side, or draw back from the historic Friends doctrine of perfection; but there is precious little true confession among us. It is rare that we admit to one another just what our struggles are, where we have stumbled or fallen—what it is that demonstrates that we are indeed still sinners in need of redemption.

I have witnessed faith communities that practiced public confession: where a man might stand before the worshipping community, confess that his continued unemployment had driven him to drink and drugs over the previous week, and ask for forgiveness and restoration. In this instance, the community publicly forgave him for his failings. Sitting him down in their midst, the community gathered to put hands on the confessing man and pray for his healing and restoration. It is my strong sense that those sins lost their hold over that man in that experience of being confessed and forgiven.

In contrast, Friends communities have largely lost this practice (once exemplified in the confession leading to restoration after disownment). In a Friends meeting, this same man would very likely never publicly confess. If he did share his experience with an elder, the elder would certainly feel bound to protect his confidentiality. As a consequence, the man would forever carry a secret unknown to the rest of the community: he could never be fully known by his faith community. As his name came up in consideration for various positions in the meeting, those Friends "in the know" would squirm uncomfortably with their knowledge, unable to disclose why they felt this Friend might be unsuitable for the position being suggested. Suspicions of hidden agendas or prejudices would be natural, and true community would be hindered. The specific incidents would have power to impact the entire community negatively for many years to come. The individual is chained by the power of that sin for much longer than necessary because the "secret" remains for years and years.

Two principles suggest themselves. First, I think there is general agreement that when an individual approaches an elder or overseer—or any Friend, for that matter—for help with a specific problem, the confidentiality of that conversation should be protected. Without this assurance, the willingness of individuals to come to members of the meeting for help would be greatly diminished. As a corollary, it seems to me that when the individual requesting confidentiality begins to divulge part of that conversation or the situation that led up to it, the other Friends should be released from that request for confidentiality to some extent. Otherwise, undue power is given to the original Friend to control the general perception of the situation, to the harm of the Gospel Order, that is, that state of wholeness for the faith community and the relationships among its members that God intends and yearns for us to enjoy.

Second, I think that as a community we should encourage the practice of public confession. We are gathered together not because we deserve or have earned community, but because God has mercifully forgiven us and called us together. Public confession reminds us of this fundamental truth and establishes a context in which other Friends can also face up to their failings, be forgiven, and get on with their lives. When this practice is established, then we as a community can encourage those Friends who come to us in confidence to speak of their situation openly. The broader forgiveness, love, and base of prayers found

Exercises in the Gospel Ministry

in the faith community can only help the individual break the power of sin more quickly and completely.[1]

As the date approached for a discussion of these issues at yearly meeting sessions, I was plagued by a steadily worsening, literal "pain in the neck" for which I could find no physical cause. Susan finally named what was happening: I was approaching a time of public ministry and was once again expressing my anxiety through bodily pain. This pattern has persisted throughout the years of my public ministry, both before and after Susan named what was happening. Rather than try to "solve" this pain or make it go away, it seems best simply to recognize it as a cost of ministry. Like Paul, I am afflicted but not crushed, struck down but not destroyed.

When the time for the discussion of confidentiality at yearly meeting arrived, it was much less lively than expected. Some Friends thought the topic itself was difficult for Friends to talk about—we couldn't even talk easily about what we should or should not talk about. The yearly meeting of MEO decided to circulate my short paper on the topic to monthly meetings and to local MEOs, and a visiting couple from Philadelphia Yearly Meeting asked for a copy to take back to their yearly meeting's Ministry and Counsel.

During these sessions, I continued David Martin's practice of "early morning communion" since he was unable to be present. It was not on the official schedule, but Friends were invited to gather early each morning for "God talk" and hot beverages. This unstructured time with no agenda might involve discussion of a Scripture passage, the spiritual foundations underlying a difficult topic that had come up in meeting for business, or some other issue with which a Friend was struggling.

I also led Bible study at yearly meeting that year using a series of props as teaching aids. One morning I used a tea bag, telling the story of the tax protestors in Boston during my college days who used tea bags as a symbol to evoke the story of the Boston Tea Party and claim their role in continuing and extending that story—just as Jesus' account of his own temptations claimed his role in continuing and extending the exodus story. Another morning I used the clerk's table to represent the ark of the covenant, with a chair on top of the table to represent the (empty) mercy seat.

During morning worship one day, a visiting Kenyan Friend traveling in the ministry was moved to speak about the importance of reading the Bible, prayer, and repentance. I felt her ministry was sweet and acceptable, but it stirred up a spirit of defensiveness and divisiveness in the worshipping group that greatly saddened me. One of our older members felt compelled to speak about not needing to read the Bible, repent of her sins, or pray, and others stood to speak similarly, although more gently. Another visiting Friend spoke twice in his usual fashion—very Christ-centered and very much centered in what he perceived to have been the belief and practice of early Friends. Both Deborah Shaw and a visitor from Philadelphia felt led to sing, but their songs did not seem to gather the meeting as much as one would have hoped. At length, I felt led to go to my knees in prayer, petitioning the Lord to send the Holy Spirit down upon us as the rain, for we were parched and thirsty. I asked that we be kept from the sin of believing that there was any part of creation in which God could not be found or Truth revealed and that we be united in unity of spirit in the bond of peace.

Reading and hearing the responses to the queries from our monthly meetings is one of the ways in which we come to know one another in that which is eternal—one of the primary tasks of our yearly meeting sessions. In the response to the twelfth query, Friendship Meeting made reference to difficulties surrounding a particular American Friends Service Committee project that had been laid down and noted that the process of doing so had been painful to some members of the meeting. In the silence that followed the responses, I asked whether love and unity had been restored at Friendship. After a few minutes, another Friend rose and renewed the inquiry. A Friendship member soon stood and explained that the decision had eventually been agreed to by both the organization's regional office and Friendship Meeting. Coming to this decision had been difficult, but true unity had been reached and the meeting was in harmony once again.

In Ninth Month 1999, the long-planned Gathering of Ministers and Elders took place at Pendle Hill. That provided an opportunity for me to make a long-desired visit to the Friends worship group at Southern State Prison in New Jersey. My day began with teaching Quaker studies at Friends School in Virginia Beach, followed by the drive to Pendle Hill. After dropping some things off there, I continued to Mullica Hill Meeting in New Jersey. There, a potluck dinner preceded a discussion of Friends' call in the present day and how to be faithful to it. (I used *Essays on the Quaker Vision of Gospel Order* as a jumping-off point, which led a Friend to tell me afterward that her favorite essay in the whole book was the first one—which I have always considered difficult reading and generally unpopular. Everything is there for some purpose, for some reader.)

After a couple of hours, Bill Geary and I drove on to Southern State Prison and had an evening meeting for worship with seven prisoners. When Bill and I had last talked, the approval for me to enter the prison had not yet arrived, and it was doubtful that I would be able to visit. On the drive up that afternoon, I had felt a strong sense that I would be allowed inside after all. Discussing this after the fact, Rashon Dinshah (the other Friend who visited there regularly) told me he found out the approval had been issued at just about the same time that I had the sensation in the Saab. So, all in all, I drove 435 miles and met with three different Friends groups that day.

The prison gave me a sense of foreboding, with its double fences of concertina wire, floodlights, and the like. We emptied our pockets of everything except car keys and driver's licenses, then went inside to the first "sally port" door, where we surrendered these items and our names were compared to the approved visitors list. We had to go through a metal detector to get to the sally port, and our car keys set it off each time, but no one seemed to care. We stayed in the middle room until the first door was closed and securely locked again. Then the second door was opened. Once we had passed through that door and it was again locked, we signed a logbook, received visitor's passes, and were stamped on the back of one hand with fluorescent ink. After passing through one more set of double locked doors, we were finally inside the prison itself.

There were two prisons at this site, mirror images of each other, and they shared a single perimeter for security purposes. Each was divided into three sections, with hundreds of men in each section. The size of our nation's prison population passed from abstract numbers to physical reality for me as we walked through the open yard to the building where worship would be held. The yard was several acres in size, and although no trees were allowed to grow there, flower beds were everywhere and the grass was luxuriant. (Trees and bushes were forbidden because a prisoner might hide behind one.)

At worship, there were seven prisoners and three visitors: Bill Geary, Rashon Dinshah, and myself. From the moment I walked in the door, everyone was on their feet and shaking my hand, welcoming me to their group. I felt deeply and genuinely welcomed. I don't know what I had expected, but I was surprised that no one in the room looked like someone who had gotten in trouble with the law; they looked more like folks I might run into in a meeting for worship or at the church down the street from our house. Most of the attention was focused on a man named Linwood, who was to be released the next day. The other prisoners gave him spiritual advice and recalled all that had happened during the time he had been part of the group. A Hispanic man quoted most of the tenth chapter of Matthew from memory. Another recited a poem he had written about the differences between the man who is convicted, the man who is a prisoner, and the man who will be released. I could feel another meaning, that of the spiritual progress of one who gives their life to God.

After the meeting, several of us stayed to talk until it was time for the evening lockdown. Bill, Rashon, and I then went back through the succession of gates and talked some more in the lobby about the slow but steady reduction of spiritual and counseling resources available to prisoners. The others returned to their cells.

The next morning, I was back at Pendle Hill for the Gathering of Ministers and Elders. Marty Grundy, Linda Chidsey, and I gathered in the Brinton House dining room to center our spirits for the upcoming gathering. Brian Drayton arrived late in the afternoon, and our team was complete. He had been at the last moment uncertain about whether he should come, but after consulting with some seasoned Friends he felt clear. Now that he was at Pendle Hill, he felt that it was indeed right for

Exercises in the Gospel Ministry

him to be there. Our hearts were very much in unity; we shared a great anticipation and expectation for what might transpire over the next few days. Forty-five participants had signed up, which was exactly the number we had hoped for.

At the first session that evening, we gathered in the Barn, the leaders spoke briefly about hopes and expectations for the four days, and we settled into waiting worship. There were moments when the worship seemed quite deep, followed fairly quickly by ministry that seemed to pull us back nearer the surface. Afterward, the four of us decided this was simply the normal state of affairs when a group of Friends gathers for the first time. It takes a while to find its rhythms.

It quickly became clear the next day that numerous Friends were feeling led into the ministry who had neither role models nor mentors and no adequate oversight from their monthly meetings. They spoke about their pain and frustration in ways that were very unsettling. There seemed to be little that could be done for them in this gathering, but their expectations had been different—they had come hoping for immediate relief. Those who were most outspoken seemed to be those whose pain was deepest. This was an unexpected development, and we weren't sure how to respond to it.

One helpful response to the situation was that some participants whose personal gifts were in eldering organized to exercise that role here. Several of them sat behind the gathering leaders at each session and were proactive in their role of offering nurture as well as guidance. Their work seemed most effective among Friends who were familiar with named elders and made less of a difference among those Friends whose experience did not include the corporate recognition of gifts of eldership or ministry.

I went to sleep one night thinking about how to express my calling and commitment to this gathering and woke up still engaged in that process. Individual Friends in our yearly meeting came to mind, each bringing forth in me a smile, or a tear, or some memory of our life together. I realized that those individual Friends also had an identity as a faith community, as a people of God engaged in the work of bringing about the Kingdom of God. They sometimes bumbled around in this work, and they wrangled with one another, but they were my people, my community, and the calling I felt was to live with them and to help them in their labors.

After morning worship with the Pendle Hill community was over, we regathered in the Barn. Linda Chidsey introduced a time for individuals to share their commitments for the coming year, beginning with the four leaders; we expected this process would lead us gently into our closing worship. She then shared her own commitment for the year, and in a few moments Marty Grundy followed.

At this point, a seasoned Friend interrupted to give a message that, she informed us, she had felt led to give during meeting for worship but had not. This led to other vocal ministry in rapid succession, lasting for some time. When a sense of quiet listening resumed, Kenneth Sutton, sitting with the elders, observed that our Friend had been unable to deliver her message earlier not because she had been unfaithful, nor because the time spent in worship had been too short, but because other Friends had spoken too much and too quickly, one after another.[2] This seemed to have no perceptible effect on the Friends present, who again rushed to fill the silence with their own words once he resumed his seat.

When the opportunity presented itself, I shared my love for this particular, peculiar people of God, with all the joy, sorrow, and aggravation that they bring into my life. My calling and commitment, I said, was simply to go live among this particular people of God and nurture them. This seemed so different from what I might have been expected to say that I wanted to take it much deeper into the silence, but events soon overtook us all and silence became scarce indeed.

Soon after I sat down, Brian Drayton rose to share his commitment. He talked about his desire to nurture and build up ministers of the gospel wherever they might be scattered. In particular, he offered to stay in correspondence with anyone who wrote him, and he described the benefits of doing so. Brian then offered specific advice to infant ministers about staying close to their gifts and not "rushing"—either rushing to deliver a specific message in a meeting for worship or rushing into a course of ministry before they had done the work to qualify themselves for that service spiritually and had received the fresh putting forth of the

Exercises in the Gospel Ministry

Spirit to equip them for it. No sooner had he sat down than a young man was on his feet to announce that he was one of those infant ministers and he was going to rush anyway. There was more of this type of vocal ministry and individual testimony from several individuals. We got through it and our sessions came to a close, with seasoned Friends giving those in distress whatever support they could.

These events seemed scandalous to some seasoned Friends who did not approve of infant ministers running about without accountability, nurture, or the fellowship of more seasoned colleagues. I did not approve either, but I saw it as evidence of the brokenness of the Religious Society of Friends as a whole, not the irresponsibility of people newly called into the public ministry. There was a great deal of work that needed to be done.

We Friends should be in a constant state of discernment, always asking ourselves, "What is God leading me, leading us, to be doing now?" As a people professing the immediate, perceptible guidance of the Holy Spirit and the authority of the Holy Spirit over all worldly laws or written creeds, it would be hypocritical to do otherwise. After this Pendle Hill gathering, I began to feel God was asking me to serve in a different way than I had been doing. I began questioning whether I was supposed to continue in the public ministry and looking for resources to help me wrestle with that question.

The resources available to me included my spouse and partner, Susan, and the named elders of my meeting. Susan confirmed that there had been a clear change in the nature of my public ministry over a sustained time, and the elders I consulted helped me name and describe what had been happening.

My vocal ministry had become increasingly a teaching ministry—a retelling of our stories as a people; my public prayer had become an expression of Friends' corporate longing for a closer walk with God. I had become more active in working outside the meeting for worship to deepen the spiritual life of the meeting, to remind the body of "right order"—why we do things a certain way and how our practice illuminates and witnesses to our faith and experience.

The call that was growing in my heart was to preserve and strengthen Conservative Friends in their own faith tradition. At the Pendle Hill gathering, when I expressed my "commitment" in the way I did, it seemed to me more the work of an elder than a minister. Was this clear discernment? Were the gifts I had exercised as a public minister being withdrawn, and should the recognition of my gifts (my recording) be withdrawn as well? I needed help to be sure, but the possibility brought a sense of release and relief and not any sense of loss. It felt like I would be able to lay down a burden.

Thankfully, this was not a discernment I was expected to make alone. Named elders have a special responsibility to support and nurture public ministers, holding their feet to the fire when needed. I told the elders with whom I met that I was prepared to turn back, take up the yoke again, and try to be faithful. But if their discernment supported my own, I would need guidance as to what to do next. These elders affirmed the changes in my ministry, though they expressed them differently, and agreed that I had been active in new ways in other parts of the meeting's life. The recommendation was that I lay my condition before the Virginia Beach MEO to see whether they were clear about what should be done.

Almost anything could happen. MEO could agree that my giftedness in ministry had ended and recommend to the monthly meeting that my recording be discontinued, or they could decide in the other direction and tell me to get back to the plow. Or, looking forward to my impending transfer to Rich Square, they could decide to take no action and let Rich Square Friends sort all this out. At that moment, I hoped that Virginia Beach would be clear to discontinue their recognition of my recorded ministry. However, I was determined to be obedient to the discernment of the faith community, whatever that turned out to be.

I looked forward to the next MEO meeting with enthusiasm and arrived at the meeting house early and centering down for about forty-five minutes before the meeting started. I explained my condition in some detail and asked Friends to do some corporate discernment, not about what was best for me but what would be best for the monthly meeting. There was a good discussion after that, but the group was

Exercises in the Gospel Ministry

unable to come to unity about a recommendation for various reasons. In consequence, the matter was laid over for another month.

The process of describing my condition to others further clarified my own understanding and settled my intent, if way opened, to be freed of the station of acknowledged minister—at least for the time being. It seemed important to be among Friends in Rich Square as a private Friend to give me time to find my place of service in that community and for Friends there to encounter me without the preconceptions that labels bring. In the meantime, I continued to be presented with opportunities to learn patience.

The Virginia Beach Monthly Meeting of MEO was unable to reach clarity on whether or not I should continue as an acknowledged minister before the monthly meeting acted on the transfer requests from Susan and myself. I was able to ensure that the minute of transfer reflected that Virginia Beach Friends Meeting did not expect my recording as a minister to transfer. The principle that only the local faith community can discern spiritual gifts and my need for fresh discernment joined hands.

Susan and I attended the 1999 year-end retreat at the Center for Action and Contemplation in Albuquerque. The first leg of our trip was a flight to Dallas. Soon after we took off, a small child sharing the seat just behind me with her mother began crying incessantly. The mother patiently tried one thing after another to quiet her little girl, to no avail. I was not particularly bothered at first, but eventually it began to wear me down. I finally thought to pray for the little girl, that she would be comforted and stop crying. At once, she quieted down and remained silent for the rest of the trip. An occasional gentle kick against the back of my seat seemed no more than God's smile, reminding me that I had underestimated the power of prayer—again.

When we arrived at Dallas/Fort Worth International Airport, we learned that the next leg of our journey had been oversold. We agreed to be bumped until the next morning and were given first-class accommodations at a nearby hotel. When Susan called the motel in Albuquerque to let them know we would not arrive until the next night, she learned that our reservation had been canceled and the motel was completely booked up. Had we not agreed to be bumped, we would have arrived in Albuquerque with no place to stay. As it turned out, we were given a hotel room for free plus a total of $600 in flight credits for use anytime in the next year. God had been looking out for us once again.

Early in the retreat, Richard Rohr shared a lesson he had received when a novice from his spiritual director: "Richard, you will get what you pray for. Richard, you will get what you pray for. Richard, you will get what you pray for. Repeat after me: you will get what you pray for." I thought of the baby on the flight to Dallas and smiled.

On New Year's Eve, those of us on retreat were supposed to write out a list of all the hurts and grievances that we had been holding on to until then so that we could release them by casting the list into a fire that night. I had the sense of having done this work already over the past several years so that what I had to work on—and this was not trivial—were the small annoyances of everyday life. Feeling that one has already done a spiritual task being recommended is always dangerous, and I examined myself closely to see whether I could detect any signs of denial, but I could not. I felt better that evening when Susan and I discussed the day. She'd had the same reaction as I did, both the sense of having done most of this work already and checking herself closely for signs of denial.

One of Richard Rohr's comments that seemed particularly apt was that individualism is a myth (or, as I would put it, an illusion) that does not and cannot work. Human beings can't thrive or even survive in isolation because we need to be in community. We are *holons*—entities that appear to be autonomous, especially when viewed at close quarters, but are actually related cosmically to a much larger universe. Some theologians argue that everything is a holon, that there is no part of creation that exists in isolation from the rest of creation. But the dominant culture teaches us that individualism is true, so we holons go around acting like individuals and can't understand this craving for community or why it is so difficult to find or sustain. If we acknowledged that we were created for relationship and community and acted on *that* knowledge instead, things would be much better for us and for the rest of creation. Another helpful comment from Richard was that the vertical aspect of the cross is transcendence and tradition, which liberals find

Exercises in the Gospel Ministry

very frightening. The horizontal aspect is inclusivity and breadth, which conservatives find equally frightening.

We began the second day of the new millennium with a contemplative sit before breakfast. After that, Richard spoke largely in a question-and-answer mode. This mode made the encounter more focused, which was good. One question was how a Christian who believes all prayer is mediated by Christ can describe that experience to a Buddhist without offending the Buddhist. Richard's response was immediate and clear. He said that he agreed with leaders of the great world religions that "nondenominationalism" was a great fallacy; personal eclecticism and cafeteria religion were not the same as ecumenism. Rather than dig twenty-five shallow wells all over the spiritual landscape and try to take a little sustenance from each one, Richard said, one should dig deeply in one's own chosen tradition. Eventually, one will strike the living water that enables one to be in fellowship with everyone else who has dug deeply in their own tradition.

Richard also shared a story told by Gil Bailie about six Buddhists and six Christians who gathered for an ecumenical conference. The Buddhists stood up after a couple of hours and announced that they were leaving and not coming back. When pressed for an explanation, they said that the Christians did not know who they were—they had no identity. The Buddhists had come to compare the two religions and find common ground, but the Christians had spent the entire time apologizing for Christianity. When the Christians come to know who they are, the Buddhists said, then the conference could begin again.

We had just enough time after the retreat ended to drive to Albuquerque Friends Meeting, joining about forty Friends gathered for First Day worship. After a bit, I engaged in vocal ministry on the George Fox quotation "Christ has come to teach his people himself." It seemed acceptable service, and peace was given when I regained my seat.

Back home, Susan and I were accepted into membership of Rich Square Monthly Meeting in First Month. The clerk said Rich Square ministers and elders would meet next in Second Month and take the matter of my acknowledged ministry under consideration. George Parker said he saw no reason to question Virginia Beach's discernment, so the outcome of that discernment was predictable; I would again be acknowledged as a minister of the gospel.

On the night before Easter 2000, Susan and I celebrated a Passover Seder with Bob and Barbara Gosney. Susan roasted a leg of lamb, Barbara prepared the rest of the food, and we followed a Haggadah Bob had compiled after studying a great many different examples. It was a deeply moving spiritual experience.

One aspect of the Seder that impressed me was the section that reminds the participants to have compassion for the Egyptians, who suffered greatly in the process of liberating the Israelites from their slavery. Another was the list of all the miracles associated with the exodus story, each beginning with "It would have been enough, Lord, . . ." before naming yet another miracle. In the midst of the celebration of their own liberation, and in light of all they have suffered, the Jews remember and have compassion for the suffering of their oppressors, the Egyptians. It is a powerful lesson for us all.

Familiarity with the Exodus story leads us often to gloss over it with a single generalization: God freed the Israelites. The litany of miracle blessings repeated at the Seder reminds us that a whole series of miracles made up this liberation story, each of which was memorable in its own right. I came away with a renewed sense of just how wonderful and magnificent the exodus story is and of how patient God is, working with the Israelites and intervening in human history again and again until they were safe in the promised land.

The move to Woodland, North Carolina, to support Rich Square Monthly Meeting progressed in slow stages. Following Susan's original vision at the 1998 yearly meeting sessions, we began to look for a house to buy, but the market in a town of eight hundred souls did not offer very much. Eventually, we enlisted the help of an older Friend who had grown up in Woodland. He called a childhood friend and asked, "Have you ever considered selling the old family home in Woodland? No? You should." As 2000 began, Susan and I were members of Rich Square Monthly Meeting, but we still had jobs in Virginia Beach, and it was not clear when we were supposed to complete the move. In Ninth Month, an unmistakable sign appeared when I lost my biggest nonprofit housing client with two days' notice. It was time to start looking for work near Woodland to follow through completely on the vision Susan had been given.

Northeastern North Carolina is an agricultural region that has been in economic decline for half a century. My best opportunity for a familiar job in the several neighboring counties was Chowan College, a private Baptist-affiliated liberal arts school that had been a two-year college until four years previously. Their website listed an opening for a first-ever institutional researcher, but when I sent in my résumé they said they had closed applications and were conducting the final interviews. I was left with no viable job possibilities in the area. Two weeks later, Chowan called me, saying they were reopening the position if I wanted to make a formal application. I did, and I was hired as director of institutional research that fall.

Susan was still employed in Tidewater Virginia, and her youngest children were still in high school. We decided that she would stay in Virginia Beach till her children graduated and I would split my time between there and our house in Woodland. The driving times were just short enough to make this doable, though tiring. This entire process seemed divinely ordered and propelled, from the initial leading through each step of the move. Whenever an obstacle arose, the means of overcoming it was also lifted up.

Alfred Newlin, a West Grove dairyman and recorded minister, had been a model Conservative Friend and model minister for me since I had become familiar with this yearly meeting in the mid-1980s. His death in Fifth Month 2001 affected me deeply; I still feel his presence often, especially in times of my own public ministry. Friends often thought of him humorously, with his very soft, often inaudible voice, his archaic manner of speaking, and his deep attention to getting the details of our procedures and practices correct, but to me his sincerity, integrity, and pure faith were much, much more important. He was very devout but always open to perceiving how the Light of Christ was unfolding in the present moment rather than acting from preconceptions of right and wrong.

Alfred was very affirming of my ministry and often took me aside when we met to ask about my condition and about my family. When he showed up at Chatham Meeting when Frank Massey and I were traveling in the ministry, I felt powerfully supported in the rightness of what Frank and I were trying to do—in the shape of our attempt to be faithful. When Alfred came into the body at West Grove and brought me back with him to the facing bench, I was deeply moved.

Alfred's funeral was at a funeral home; the number of people who attended was far greater than could have fit into the West Grove meeting house. David Hobson, a pastor from the other body—North Carolina Yearly Meeting (Friends United Meeting)—had been asked to officiate. He suggested that there be a facing bench set up in front. Eight of us ended up sitting on chairs behind the casket and flowers; perhaps some of those in attendance could see the tops of our heads, but I am not sure. David Martin read very movingly from the "Advices to Meetings of Ministry and Oversight" in the *Discipline*.[3] Deborah Shaw sang, and David Hobson read a poem requested by a family member. I spoke about Alfred's importance to me as a model and as one who had taken a personal interest in my condition.

Life in the Rich Square faith community was not without its challenges. At the Sixth Month meeting for business, it was suggested that George Parker might welcome some help preparing the annual treasurer's report, which was several months overdue. I offered to help with the report if needed and wanted. Friends seemed generally approving of this plan, but after the rise of meeting an elder approached me to say that he would have a conflict of interest if I were nominated for assistant treasurer or treasurer since "some Friends" felt I was financially untrustworthy. He said that he couldn't allow me to become treasurer and go to yearly meeting to meet with other treasurers as the representative of Rich Square Monthly Meeting.

I was shocked. I told him that I had no desire to be treasurer or assistant treasurer and would step away from that possibility immediately. Reflecting on the matter a little later, I realized that what he said cast doubt on my integrity generally in a way that had to affect my

Exercises in the Gospel Ministry

station as an acknowledged minister of the gospel. How long had he felt this way? He never told me.

In the query answers at yearly meeting sessions that summer, Rich Square reported it had minuted its support of a member who had decided not to register for Selective Service. This member was my son, Asa. At that point, I rose in ministry, recalling George Parker's words in support of Asa and his story of facing the same set of questions sixty years earlier. There were Bob Gosney and I from the Vietnam era, with George Parker on one side of us and Asa on the other. The sense of continuity across the generations, of keeping the faith and testimony alive through the years, was very strong and very precious. Bob Gosney later shared with me that he too had felt that sense of intergenerational continuity at the time.

At another point in the reading of answers to the Queries, I was again active in the ministry to the effect that this was holy ground, the root principle of our life as Conservative Friends. I used the term "interrogatory theology" that Ched Myers used and connected it to the understanding Friends have that the same Light that illuminates our sins has power for our salvation. Because this is so, what we need to do is live lives of example and ask the penetrating questions of one another. If we engage the questions faithfully, the Inward Light of Christ will do the rest. There are no right or wrong answers to the Queries. The answers we heard that day indicated that these eight faith communities were faithfully engaging the right questions.

Those times when community is hardest are when we have reached the edge of our growth, both individually and collectively. This is the growing edge where Christ can be at work in us and through us for the redemption of all creation. It is true that authentic community is that place where the person thee least likes lives because that is the place where we can best be in community, best carry out the threefold purpose of community. Even Thomas Merton could not be a hermit until he learned how to live in community.

Community is not our first calling. Christ is our first calling. Community is the inevitable outgrowth of our embrace of Christ. Community is not an end in itself—a goal—though it is a wonderful gift when we experience it. Community is not a warm fuzzy to make us feel good—though the experience of community is almost always expressed as a good feeling. Community is often painful, difficult, costly work. It is precisely then that community is most real, its witness most clear, its efforts most effective.

Jesus' message extended the prophetic tradition, not spiritualized it. He added the individual aspect without eliminating the community. He continued the vision of leadership and community based on service to others, even unto his death.

God's salvation is for all of creation—not just humans, and certainly not just for some humans. No part of creation is disposable. No part is beyond God's saving and transforming power.

As Christians, we are called not only to be radically changed people—to be born again—but together to constitute the body of Christ here on earth—to be a prophetic witness and critic of the dominant culture(s), to be a model of gospel order for all of creation, and to be an agency for bringing about the transformation of society. Our faith tradition, Christian and Quaker, begins with a prophetic understanding of being called to transform the world. As with our Latin American brothers and sisters, as has been true across the generations everywhere, this inevitably leads to sacrifice, suffering, and martyrdom. Community is not only the means by which we do this, but it is the context and support that makes it bearable.

I spoke at Illinois Yearly Meeting in the summer of 2001 and was favored in the ministry. Meeting for worship on the last day was very deep, and the Holy Presence was perceptible. Eventually, I rose in outward ministry, calling upon the vast fields of corn surrounding us to evoke the image of fields white with the harvest calling for workers to bring it in. As in Joel, we have God's assurance that the day of the Lord is coming when God's Spirit is poured out on all who will accept it. A younger Friend approached me afterward to say that this message was why I had been called to the yearly meeting and why I had come. I was able to say honestly that this was quite possible because I did not know why I was there. I never know; that is God's business—mine is to be faithful to the leadings I am given.

Exercises in the Gospel Ministry

Later that summer, I spoke at Ohio Valley Yearly Meeting sessions held at Earlham College. When I joined the early worship the first morning, six or eight other Friends were present. When I closed my eyes, the meeting room seemed to be filled with seasoned Friends and the quality of worship was quite deep, but when I opened them again, there were only those few Friends who had been present before. This experience repeated itself whenever I closed my eyes. It was as if the cloud of witnesses had become especially tangible.

The clerk asked if I would like some Friends to worship with me in advance of my lecture, and I accepted. We gathered in a small upper room about half an hour before the scheduled start of the lecture. Soon, one woman began to pray aloud. In the prayer, she alluded to the fact that I had already had a great impact on many Friends unknown to me, including herself—she had returned to God and Christ as a result of my spoken ministry years earlier. I was deeply humbled and my eyes were wet with tears, though I kept my head bowed so others did not notice. The event she spoke of was the Rufus Jones Lecture I had given in Pittsburgh years before. She had returned home that evening, she said, and "sat down in a chair and told my husband that I was a changed woman." Evidently, she was. (I had always considered that lecture a bit of a failure because before I gave it the Friends General Conference Religious Education Committee wanted to publish it, but after hearing it they never mentioned publication again. I figured nobody had liked it. Little did I know!)

After that prelude, anything that might happen in that night's lecture would be all gravy. As it turned out, it went well, and the question-and-answer time afterward was engaged and thoughtful. Friends continued individual conversations with me for two hours afterward.

I was led to leave an afternoon workshop a few minutes early the next day. Heading to the yearly meeting bookstore, I began looking at the selections very carefully, although I had already decided that I didn't have enough cash to buy anything. After a few minutes, a young woman approached me to ask whether I could give her a few moments of my time, and we found a place nearby to sit down and talk. Although she had been a Friend for less than a year, she was feeling strong leadings toward the vocal ministry and was looking for guidance. My sense from our discussion was that she probably did recognize a true leading to speak and that she was properly concerned not to outrun her Guide. We talked about ways she could get some guidance, including reading the journals of earlier Friends ministers and Samuel Bownas's writings and communicating with Fran Taber.

The next day, I was drinking my morning coffee on the deck outside the coffee shop when I saw the same young woman pass by. I called out to her, but she showed no sign of hearing. Her eyes were set on some distant point, and her face was set as one going toward Jerusalem. A little later during early worship, the same woman rose in ministry and reported, in a way that gave evidence of how strongly she had been moved, that the Lord had called her into service and she had said yes to the call. I felt that she had taken up the cross of the vocal ministry and that she had entered the second covenant—beyond simple membership to the covenant between God and the spiritually called and equipped. A short time afterward, I was moved to my knees in a prayer to seal her decision for the Lord. I went to her at the rise of meeting, and we sat in silence for a few moments. I let her know I would be available later on, when she was ready, if she wanted to process what had happened with a listener. She thanked me for the offer, and we all made our way to breakfast.

We ran into each other a few minutes before suppertime and decided to eat together, then found a quiet place and talked. She had had a purification experience a few weeks earlier that seemed to me to have been preparation for the call and response she had experienced that morning. Unfortunately, no one in her monthly meeting seemed able to understand what was happening to her. She seemed to be well grounded and mature spiritually and was handling this experience very well. Part of me wanted to point her in a given direction, part wanted to protect her from influences that might have a negative impact, and part just wanted not to interfere with a powerful work of the Holy Spirit. I decided it was best to let the last prevail.

Exercises in the Gospel Ministry

I returned from these yearly meeting sessions to the familiar rhythms of family life and my work, unaware of the disaster that was about to overtake us all. Just before I left my office to go teach my morning class at Chowan College on Ninth Month 11, 2001, Dean Lowe crossed the hall from his office to say two airplanes had crashed into the World Trade Center in New York City. My immediate speculation was that they had collided in midair somehow and then struck the World Trade Center on their way down to the ground. Class had just begun when the vice president for student life came into the room, pulled me aside, and whispered, "This is not George Orwell. We are under terrorist attack. We need to tell the students and let them know what resources we have available for them."

I told the students that the World Trade Center and the Pentagon had been attacked and took them to the student center, where they could watch the developing news on a big-screen TV and where those who were most upset would have someone close at hand who could talk with them. As I watched the second tower collapse, all I could think of was the newsreel of the Hindenburg disaster, where the newsman just repeated over and over, "Oh, the humanity! The humanity!" How could one even begin to grasp the number of deaths and the amount of suffering in those two buildings alone?

By evening, we knew that four different airplanes had been hijacked in a well-organized plan. One had hit the Pentagon, where the fires were still burning and the death toll was near one hundred. Hundreds of rescue workers were feared dead at the World Trade Center, killed by the collapse of the second tower as they tried to reach folks trapped by the collapse of the first. Radio news had broadcast an interview of an eyewitness who saw people leaping from the upper floors of the two towers to certain death below. No one had ventured a guess about the total number of deaths, the dollar value of the damages, or how long it would take to recover. Numbers came in bits and snippets—266 dead on the four airplanes, 200 firefighters dead—any one of which would have been a major disaster in itself. It seemed to me the worst peacetime disaster in US history.

What would this country do in response? I feared that we would identify a convenient scapegoat (Osama Bin Laden was the early favorite), pick a spot where we said he was located, and obliterate it—"Bomb it into the Stone Age," as General Curtis LeMay would say. Suppose President George W. Bush decided that the only proportionate response was a tactical nuclear weapon? I would not have put it past him or his military advisors. I prayed he would not come to that decision. A poorly thought-out response, conventional or nuclear, would succeed only in uniting the Islamic world against us, with bloody consequences.

The Gosneys and I opened the Rich Square meeting house that evening and held meeting for worship with the doors open to the night air. It seemed far from the violence and death of the day, but the suffering and death was not distant from our hearts and prayers.

A week later, some of the shock of the 9/11 attacks had worn off. The frantic search for survivors had given way to the grim search for body parts. The officials in charge of such things reported they expected as many as one million tissue "samples" that needed to be identified. Decomposition and the effects of the still-burning fire at the World Trade Center were degrading the tissue to the point that normal DNA testing would be ineffective, so plans were made to test mitochondrial DNA instead—the largest single use of this type of testing in history.

Reports began to circulate that some of the terrorists had lived in and prepared for their mission in the United States for years, and no one seemed very surprised. Anything seemed possible. If they could hijack four planes at once and kill thousands of people, why shouldn't they be able to live among us indefinitely beforehand, enrolling in our own flight schools to learn how to turn our airliners into instruments of mass destruction?[4]

Meanwhile, the US president spoke of a "crusade" against the terrorists—a word that affects Muslims much as "holocaust" affects Jews. The secretary of defense refused to rule out the use of tactical nuclear weapons, and the government warned that those who supported terrorists or gave them shelter (such as the Afghan Taliban) would be treated the same as if they were themselves terrorists. The Taliban in turn swore jihad to protect their country, and I wondered if anybody

Exercises in the Gospel Ministry

remembered that Afghanistan was known as the land where empires go to die.

It seemed to me that the strongest "statement" people in the United States could make in response to the attacks would be to go about our daily business, with increased security and watchfulness, to be sure, and to mount a concerted effort to catch the criminals who had done this awful thing but essentially to continue our lives as before, refusing to be intimidated by these evil acts. The one change truly needed was a close examination of our personal and collective lives to eliminate those activities that led to injustice or suffering anywhere. The image of the watchful father in the parable comes to mind. The father would not let the actions of either son, however hurtful or insulting, change the way he had decided to live his life—i.e., with great love for each of them. What a powerful witness it would be for our country to emulate that example!

Meanwhile, the nation careened toward a war that proved to be disastrous in so many ways for so many people—people in the United States included. Warplanes moved to advanced positions closer to Afghanistan, and the Bush administration pressed for greatly expanded powers to eavesdrop on a wide range of people and to detain even legal immigrants and resident aliens indefinitely on no grounds stronger than suspicion. Reports of violence—some of it lethal—against American citizens and others who were in this country legally came in every day and from every part of the country. If your name sounded Middle Eastern or your appearance seemed Arabic or related to any part of the Indian subcontinent, the United States was not a safe country to be in. I feared this would become a religious war, Christians against Muslims, and that the United States would find itself trapped in the same sort of violent circle that had held Israel for so long, including the loss of significant civil liberties as casualties of that war.

If this continued, how long until Hampton Roads would become a target of terrorist attention? At the time, this area held the largest group of naval installations in the world, with military bases and civilian areas (including Virginia Beach) mixed in together; it was both an attractive target and easy to penetrate. I feared that a biological or chemical attack might harm Susan or her family. Benjamin Netanyahu said that the terrorists were sophisticated enough to deliver and explode a nuclear weapon on American soil—they just hadn't gotten hold of one yet. If it got too bad, I believed that Susan and I would close down the household in Virginia Beach and consolidate ourselves in Woodland.

In other ways, life went on normally. On Tenth Month 12, 2001, I wrote the following to a distant Friend newly called into the gospel ministry:

Greetings—

I am glad to read thy account of Iowa (Conservative)'s business sessions. I have never visited that yearly meeting, and recent reports from others have been mixed. Thine is the most detailed information I have received, and from the best-known and therefore most reliable source so far (i.e., the others have been mostly hearsay).

Though our details vary, the sense of groundedness in worship thee describes is similar to my experience of NCYM(C). It takes a little over a day for our yearly meeting to find its rhythm each year. My simile has been an 8-oared crew with coxswain, which rocks a bit when the crew is first assembled but after some practice time together becomes steady as a rock, even when someone is getting in or out of the shell.

The observation thee shares is the perspective from which I intend to present a workshop at next year's FGC Gathering: that what so many Friends seem to find attractive and/or powerful about Conservative practices are in fact our common heritage, available for all Friends if they so desire.

Here in Woodland, the monthly meeting of ministers, elders, and overseers has forwarded my leading to travel in the gospel ministry among Friends in the Carolinas to the monthly meeting, which is scheduled for this coming First Day. Since my leading includes travel among Friends of other yearly meetings and unaffiliated Friends, if the monthly meeting issues a certificate it will be forwarded to the Representative Body at the end of this month for yearly meeting endorsement. If they are in unity about the matter, I could be free to travel by the beginning

Exercises in the Gospel Ministry

of Eleventh Month. My companion, if in keeping with divine providence, will be Mike Arnold—a younger (than me, anyway) Friend from West Grove meeting. West Grove has already issued a certificate for him to accompany me to visit Charlotte Friends and will consider a broader certificate this First Day.

These are difficult times for everyone, particularly for those who hold all human life as sacred to God. There has not been the rush to make public statements or hold public witnesses among Friends here that one reads of elsewhere. There seems to be rather a sense that if we attend to truly living in that life and power that takes away the occasion of all wars and outward fighting, our witness will take care of itself.

Five days later, I wrote the following in a letter to a Friend in the public ministry:

Well! There seem to be a few minutes to attend to thy message, so I will seize the time to do so. It sounds as if Truth prospers and Love abounds in thy life; may it be continually and deeply so. Wonderful things happen when we let go and let God. The plan thee has received seems to be a great gift, and certainly a reassuring one. The only bit of cautious advice I might offer is to remember not to "freeze" this gift into exactly the shape it was when thee first received it. Like Peter at the Transfiguration, we often want to grab hold of our spiritual experiences and insights and put them in familiar, static structures, but the Spirit is living and growing and the world is changing all the time, and how this gift becomes reality in kairos may not be what thee first perceived. Don't force it—but thee knows that already.

Thee asks about feeling intolerant of another Friend's use of "Dear Father and Mother," saying, "It just felt so wrong and still does." My immediate response is to ask whether it feels wrong for thee to use that phrase to address God or wrong for other Friends to do so. I would say the former is not intolerant, but the latter may be.

Truly, God is beyond gender, but certainly our archetypes of father and mother originate in the Divine, as thee knows. To call

God by any descriptive name in some way neglects an infinite number of other descriptions that could be used. Scripture uses primarily (but not exclusively) male imagery in references to God because that was the best available language available to communicate important aspects of God's nature and relationship to human beings. In a different culture twenty centuries later, we don't have to be limited by that vocabulary if we don't want to be.

Many people in our contemporary culture are sensitive to gender issues; manhood and fatherhood have gotten a bad press in recent decades here in the West. If addressing God as "Dear Father and Mother" helps an individual approach God in prayer, bless 'em! If a simple "Our Father" resonates with Scripture and childhood memories of church services and family prayer, do it! If any name at all seems sacrilegious and all we can manage is *Ha-Shem* ("the Name"), fine. I've used all three at various times over the years. God seems to hear me just fine no matter what names or titles I use (or leave out). God is already at work in the heart of one who prays. Praise God, who hears us always!

David Eley (from Texas) and I are attempting to write a joint article on the use of the Queries in NCYM(C) to appear in an upcoming issue of our journal. This seems more difficult than it might be because David doesn't do email, so there is a long pause between thought and reply. I won't know until it is all over whether that pacing helps or hinders the process. I expect all is as it should be.

I enjoy hearing from thee and wish abundant blessings on thy unfolding life.

Later, while on the road for the fall Representative Body meeting, I was up early and read extensively in Hugh Judge's *Journal* before my hosts awoke. Judge was an articulate writer on spiritual matters and a great advocate of the value of home visits among Friends. One of those God-incidences happened during the adult discussion that day that preceded meeting for worship. The group read and discussed a passage from John Main on silence. I had read Hugh Judge's passage about three kinds of silence earlier that morning and was able to share that with Friends present.[5]

Mike Arnold and I began our gospel travels in Eleventh Month with a visit to Sumter-Black River Allowed Meeting in South Carolina. Meeting for worship was held in the "sessions house" of Salem-Black River Presbyterian Church, the oldest Scottish Presbyterian congregation in South Carolina. The building was constructed by slaves who afterward were allowed only in the balcony, which they entered by means of two doors in the back of the building. The stairways up to the balcony were enclosed, with no connection to the first floor of the sanctuary itself. How it must have felt to those folks, to have worked so hard to build that handsome building and then be limited to entering it from the back door and sitting out of sight of the white worshippers below!

In First Month 2002, Rich Square Friends again began to discuss possible outreach activities that the meeting might undertake to make itself more visible in the local community. I was struck by the apparent fear in some Friends of any change or project that might involve increased work or responsibility for members of the meeting. I understood we were a small group and had limits. Nevertheless, we had a choice and a responsibility as a meeting community. If we were going to do nothing other than make ourselves spiritually comfortable, I believe we would lose our mandate as a Christian community. To be true to the gospel, some significant portion of our energy had to be directed toward other humans and the rest of creation.

In meeting for worship, I was moved to rise up in ministry on this choice that we had before us: either to reach out toward our neighbors in some meaningful way(s) or to wither away. Afterward, I thought that if other Friends had not already invited themselves into the Rich Square community, the meeting would have been laid down by now. Present at worship that morning were three old-timers and six newcomers. All six newcomers were convinced Friends, but none had been convinced at Rich Square. All had been Friends before they came to Woodland. Susan and I were in Woodland specifically because we were called to nurture and sustain the monthly meeting.

Our traveling ministry led Mike Arnold and me to the Beaufort Worship Group on the North Carolina coastline in Second Month. It felt very important to us to be traveling in the ministry, and it felt in right order as well. That is to say, traveling in the ministry seemed to be a very important task for some Friends in our various yearly meetings to be undertaking in the present day, and it seemed in right order for the two of us to be taking a share of that responsibility.

About fifteen people attended meeting for worship. Afterward, we stayed in our places and talked for about another hour. Mike and I soon perceived that the real issue was that these Friends felt isolated and unsupported in their beliefs. We talked about the importance of staying within one's guidance and not taking on the whole world as an adversary, and we used the imagery of leaven in bread. We also emphasized the opportunities for fellowship and association with Wilmington meeting, which was only about ninety minutes away, and with NCYM(C). Yearly meeting sessions that year would be at Chowan College, which was much closer to this worship group than Guilford.

In Third Month 2002, I co-officiated the funeral for my stepgrandmother Cordie Bare in West Jefferson, North Carolina. I got to West Jefferson in time to walk around a bit —Ashe County was as beautiful as ever. Unlike other trips to "Bare country," I did not feel an immediate desire to move to Ashe County this time. What I did feel was an acceptance that to make one commitment is to forgo making other equally valuable or desirable commitments. I'd made the commitment to live in Woodland and to build up the Friends meeting there to the best of my ability and with divine assistance; that commitment eliminated living in Ashe County as a possibility. So be it.

Uncle Dallas was just inside the funeral home door, and we embraced immediately. Cousin Anne Marie was sitting in the family space farther inside, and Aunt Ethel was standing by the open casket. Cordie's body was well presented, and she seemed at rest at last after years of illness.

The same couple that had sung at Aunt Ella Mae's and Uncle Bertie's funerals sang that morning, and the harmonies were as beautiful as ever. The man who sang also offered a prayer—getting down on his knees beside the pulpit to do so—and a sermon/eulogy. After a little while, he settled into a sing-song cadence that combined the phrasing I associated with black preaching and what almost seemed to be a tune, reminding me of the sing-song chanting of old Quaker preaching. This message was delivered with a lot more emotion than I expect those old Quakers were allowed to show, however.

The preacher made it a point to say during his eulogy that "we just don't know whether Cordie is in heaven or not," which is good Primitive Baptist theology but offered no comfort to the grieving family, as I could see. In my own remarks from the pulpit, I emphasized my experience of a loving God who always desires to be reconciled with each and every one of us. Multiple family members thanked me afterward for my offering.

The funeral procession took us to a cemetery just outside of town. All along the way, every car and truck stopped as we went along, whether we were on a four-lane highway or two-lane byway. Even tractor-trailers stopped for us.

On the way out of town, I stopped by the farm; it was my first chance to see the ruins of the old farmhouse since it had burned.[6] The chimney still stood, as did the cinder block root cellar—but there was nothing in between. The other buildings and signs of farming seemed out of place without a house to tie them all together. More connections had been broken between me and this land. I cut diagonally northeast to Galax, then took Route 58 east to Virginia Beach. It was a long trip home, but I wanted to be with Susan that night.

In Third Month, Mike and I visited the meeting of the Friends General Conference (FGC) Traveling Ministries Program near Nashville, Tennessee. I had not flown since the terrorist attacks on 9/11. Some of the increased security measures now in effect were comforting, but some were frightening. We were asked by three different people for a government-issued photo ID, which was new but not onerous. However, at key traffic nodes throughout the terminal there were soldiers on guard with assault rifles held at the ready, trigger fingers extended but not yet inside the trigger guard. Their camo uniforms, black berets, and combat boots certainly stood out from the crowd. Who were they supposed to shoot? Giving loaded automatic weapons to a group of nervous nineteen-year-olds and distributing them throughout a crowded public place did not, I thought, make me safer. I certainly didn't feel safer.

What would have made me feel safer? I would be safer if my country did not sell weapons of war all over the world; if we did not constantly support oppressive regimes and dictatorships in the name of stability; if we increased our foreign aid to needy countries and devoted it to projects that would truly help people rather than simply "open up markets and resources" to our own businesses; if we renounced the use of nuclear weapons for any reason or under any provocation . . . the list goes on. No foreseeable US government was going to do these things (although we may pray and work for change along the margins.)

So, I am not safe. What should be my response to the threat of terrorism? First, as Thomas Chalkley reports in his journal about being threatened by privateers at sea, I should be prepared to "go to heaven."[7] If we tend to our relationships with God (and creation), we will be prepared to die whenever that happens. Second, when faced with an actual incident (not just the threat of one), we should pray, as Chalkley did, for a bloodless solution. Third, we need to work constantly to root out the causes of war in our own hearts and lives—thoughts and behaviors that are the seeds of conflict. Finally, we must work to make our community (however we define that group) void of offense toward God or human kind. If we have done these things, we are as safe as we can be in an uncertain world.

We met Marty Grundy at the Nashville airport, and a Friend gave us all a ride to the camp together. It is a joy to meet any of the servants of Christ after a long separation, but some are more dear than others. Marty is one of those for me. I was very glad to see her again.

After dinner, we gathered for worship, which was settled and sweet and mostly silent. We then divided into small groups to discuss "how the Spirit has been challenging us this past year." Here again, I was aware of what Elaine Emily has called "the great need for and lack of eldership." The gift of eldering is mostly not understood or even recognized, and there is a significant unmet need for this sort of discernment and guidance.

Exercises in the Gospel Ministry

The next morning, I arose a couple of hours before breakfast, then walked down to the dining hall to journal and to read in Thomas Chalkley's *Journal*. It was a good time, with quiet woods all around and an unlimited supply of fresh hot tea to be made and enjoyed.

The extended meeting for worship that morning (two and a half hours) was owned and blessed by the Master. There was an appropriate amount of ministry for a meeting that long—not the overabundance that sometimes is heard when a group of Friends gather who think of themselves as ministers. Some of the ministry seemed to call us to reflect on the type of service we were being called to offer among Friends to help lead them to a deeper, more authentic spiritual life.

At length, Mike Arnold rose and walked into a kitchenette adjoining the meeting room. We could hear water running. After a short while, he emerged wearing his broad-brimmed hat with a pan full of warm water in his hands and a pile of towels over one arm. Walking into the center of our circle, he knelt before a Friend and washed her feet. Leaving his hat on the floor in the center of the circle, he then washed the feet of three more Friends around the room.

I felt this ministry to be powerful and articulate. During our extended closing worship the next day, Jack Davis of Ohio Valley Yearly Meeting rose to testify the powerful effect this foot washing had had on him and the lessons that he now had to apply to his own life. It was moving ministry and brought tears to my eyes.

There were persons present who opposed and tried to undermine the foot washing example. One woman rose to share what she called her own midrash on the false prophet Hananiah (Jeremiah 28). She went on at length, speaking for about half of the entire time Mike was on his knees washing Friends' feet.

Near the close of this meeting, I was brought to my knees in prayer. I gave thanks for the unconditional love of God and asked that we be made content with our humble station as God's servants, knowing that the universe is God's creation and that the Divine Will prevails. It seemed acceptable service.

That afternoon, Mike and I attended an interest group on recording ministers. This was a good discussion, without some of the "allergic reaction" that short-circuits many such opportunities. All agreed on the importance of bringing a group to a clear understanding of spiritual gifts before attempting to recognize gifts of ministry. I suggested that it would be wise to consider appointing elders before considering ministers; this was favorably received.

Over dinner, Elaine Emily told a group of us about some powerful spiritual experiences in her life in recent months. She was seeking a vocabulary that would express the power of these events without scaring those who heard her accounts. Mary Grundy suggested that she look at some of the metaphors used by early Friends to describe their experiences—that would be vivid and would remind others that this sort of thing was within our own faith tradition.

Our evening session was spent in open consideration of the ways Friends had been changing over the past ten years, those in FGC in particular. Phrases such as "becoming the body of Christ," constant prayer, reading the Bible, extended worship, and terms such as Jesus, Christ, elders, and God prevailed. As Mike Arnold commented, "West Grove Friends would not believe FGC Friends said these things." This was clearly not a representative sample, but what they reported that evening and the fact that FGC would sponsor such a group as this did say a lot about the spiritual state of Liberal Friends.

We met in extended worship again on the last morning. Just before meeting, I exchanged Chalkley's *Journal* (which I had been reading before breakfast) for my Bible. On impulse, I picked up our *Discipline* also and brought it with me. Soon after settling down in one corner of the meeting room, I was impressed by a sense of the strong presence of "that meeting of ministers and elders which is always in session" all around and among us and of the approbation of that group for the labors, faithfulness, and integrity of Friends gathered there that day. My heart was broken open by the love and encouragement being poured out on us and for us, and tears literally ran down my face despite my wiping them away repeatedly. I was brought to a near sense of those meetings Alfred

Exercises in the Gospel Ministry

Newlin described where the Holy Spirit was so strongly present that there was not a dry eye to be found and the floor was wet with tears.

This went on for some time, in successively stronger waves. At length, I opened the *Discipline* and read the "Advices to Meetings of Ministry and Oversight" to myself. After more time had passed, with my heart still broken open and tears still flowing, I was led to stand in vocal ministry and explain my sense of the presence of this "cloud of witnesses" and their approval. I was then led to read these Advices aloud, saying that while the words came from the *Discipline*, I felt the message was from a larger and older body (that other Meeting of Ministers, Elders, and Overseers that is always in session). When I regained my seat, I had a great sense of relief and comfort, though my heart was still tender and tears came to my eyes from time to time throughout the rest of worship and even two hours later. I felt the ministry had been owned and approved by the Master.

Some time later, Mike Arnold rose in ministry to give a message on the unconditional love, exampled and directed by the gospel, toward our enemy and those who meant us ill as well as those for whom we humanly felt a near affection. His message was clear and strong, giving evidence of being Spirit-led and Spirit-fed.

Later that spring, I spoke about Christian pacifism to a Christian Ethics class at Chowan College of about twenty students. This could have been a difficult audience; the professor said that in their recent discussions about Christians and war they had focused on just wars and the "end times" and had not even touched on the Sermon on the Mount or any of Jesus' other teachings about peace and justice.

Quakerism is a woven fabric, not easily teased apart into individual strands, so I also talked about other aspects of the tradition, including waiting worship, simplicity, and some social justice issues. The class seemed interested and asked some good questions in the discussion period, so I felt they had heard and were processing what I had to offer. A man who asked some pointed questions about whether any Quakers would be "allowed" to serve in the military was himself, I learned later, a veteran who had served in Bosnia.

One never knows what seeds one plants in a session like this or how they may or may not come to bear fruit at some unknown time in the future. Had I not pressed for the opportunity, nothing would have happened, and the potential maximum effect would have been zero. At least this way I did what I could to make the gospel of peace known. One turns the ground, another waters the garden, but the increase is the Lord's.

Father's Day 2002—a First Day—was a day of travel in the ministry for Mike Arnold and me. After a special breakfast, Susan and I met with Charlie Ansell and Louise Rothrock at Virginia Beach Friends Meeting for a short period of worship, after which I took my leave and headed on to Mike Arnold's place in Snow Camp. Mike and I then continued on to Fayetteville meeting. There were about ten people gathered at the meeting house when we arrived, and we shared a common meal before gathering for some discussion and worship.

During the discussion, I felt it necessary to share my sense that these Friends could go deeper in their consideration of the Queries by attempting to come to a sense of the meeting in their answer rather than simply cataloguing the responses of individuals. The incoming clerk seemed to take this suggestion seriously, and I had some hope they would make the attempt. I was convinced that the process would strengthen their meeting community and assist their corporate spiritual growth. This was difficult for me to broach because it arose from my listening to their responses at yearly meeting sessions over a period of years and did not come from a leading that arose that evening. However, it seemed rightly led, and afterward I had a sense of having discharged my obligation.

Meeting for worship did not appear to be very deep or fully covered. It was silent until near the end, when I was drawn to speak a few words on the parable of the sower and the seed, pointing out the generosity of God in supplying enough seed not only for the good soil but also for the stony soil, the beaten path, etc. Likewise, the sower was not judgmental but instead sowed the seed in all places so each patch of earth had the opportunity to be fruitful. I drew no other conclusions, feeling that I had come to the end of my leading. After worship ended, a Friend remarked

Exercises in the Gospel Ministry

to me privately that he considered me a prophet because I always seemed to speak directly to the condition of the Friends present. Two other Friends also confided that I had spoken to their condition—but I did not know then, nor do I know now, what their condition (or conditions) might be.

In Sixth Month, Susan and I went to a talk by Garchen Triptrul Rinpoche[8] at a Unitarian church in Norfolk. Some of the things he had to share, many stemming from his imprisonment by the Chinese government, were quite powerful. He told us, "I immediately decided this is what I owed. Then it was a pleasure, in that it was an opportunity to purify myself. Now I appreciate a normal life all the more." I took the following notes on his teaching:

- All sentient beings are my parents.
- The more technologically advanced we become, the more pain and suffering we experience.
- Throughout his talk, Rinpoche was spinning a small prayer wheel. Inside the prayer wheel were 40 million mantras on microfiche. Each rotation of the wheel 40 million prayers.
- Turning the prayer wheel reminded him to be mindful of generating lovingkindness.
- Once action is taken, karma is inevitable.
- The only antidotes to negative emotions are lovingkindness and compassion. The method he was taught was to regard all sentient beings as our parents. That is reason enough to be loving and kind to them.
- In the subjugation of your coarse mind lies the entirety of Buddha's teaching.
- There is so much suffering in the world—it makes people justifiably angry. But we must ask whether anger does us any good. It does not. If we give in to anger, not only does the suffering remain, but we are consumed by negative emotions.
- The six perfections are simply lovingkindness.

Shortly after the end of the 2002 spring semester, the Chowan dean let me know that the next day he and the college president would offer me the position of registrar, which would be added to my portfolio as director of institutional research. At the time, this seemed like a very positive affirmation, a significant promotion, and a significant pay increase since I would be doing two people's full-time work at the same time. The reality, as I learned the next day, was that the college was near bankruptcy and would be laying off staff and tenured faculty while cutting the salaries of those who remained employed. I could accept a doubled workload with a cut in pay and remain employed or I could be out of a job completely. I proposed to the dean that I receive an extra two weeks of paid leave each year to undertake gospel ministry. He agreed to this side deal, and I told the president I would accept the newly merged position and the cut in pay.

Having breakfast with Susan one morning in Sixth Month, our conversation turned to the general religious mood in the country. She felt many might be ready to come to a new relationship with God as they realized the identification of triumphal Christianity with American imperialism was not satisfactory. I hoped that this was so, for the nation-church wars that were building or already upon us promised suffering almost beyond comprehension: Hindu India vs. Muslim Pakistan, Jewish Israel vs. Muslim Palestine, Christian United States vs. Muslim terrorists. I couldn't help but place this in the context of apophatic and kataphatic spiritualities. Could the number of adherents to apophatic paths increase to a level that would counterbalance kataphatic triumphalism? God grant that it would be so. As William Penn wrote in 1670:

> I would have thee and all men know that I scorn that religion which is not worth suffering for, and able to sustain those that are afflicted for it. Mine is; and whatever may be my lot for my constant profession of it, I am no ways careful, but resigned to answer the will of God by the loss of goods, liberty, and life itself.[9]

> We took our solemn leave of them, recommending to them holy silence from all will-worship, and the workings, strivings, and images of their own mind and spirit; that Jesus might be felt by them in their own hearts.[10]

The Kingdom of God is upon us—it is here. It is not delayed until a future coming of Christ; it is not deferred until all humans have entered in. It is here now. The table is set, the banquet is prepared, the Master has issued invitations to everyone in every state and condition. The only needful thing is to accept the invitation. The Mistress of Hospitality says, "Come, eat"—but will you? The Master's invitation is for all and forever—but for how long will you make excuses and stay away? All that is needed is to accept the decision to eat in the house of the Lord. After that, it may be hard for us in the world's eyes, but we will have all joy in the Lord. This is our purpose in creation.

I offered a workshop on Conservative spirituality and practice at the 2002 FGC Gathering. Over thirty people signed up, which is more than I had imagined would want to participate. Friends at the workshop had a wide range of hopes and expectations focused around a deeper faith that was shared closely with the rest of their meeting community. The workshop was a very intense experience for me; our discussions were deep and substantial in content. We covered topics such as the Queries and meetings for business but also spent the last day covering topics and answering questions posed by the participants. At the close of our time, I read the final paragraph of the Advices from our *Discipline*, and after a time of silence I went around the room, shaking each person's hand and speaking a short word of encouragement or blessing to them. I felt that I had lived up to the Light I had been given as to this workshop and generally in this Gathering, for which I was most grateful to God.

I spent part of each day in opportunities with Friends, whether or not they were enrolled in the workshop. One day culminated with a group opportunity with the group of young adult Friends Elaine Emily called the "California cabal." These were intense folks—committed, talented, and gifted. Gordon Bishop in particular—son of Adrian and grandson of Muriel—had as strong a gift of discerning states and conditions as I'd felt in any Friend of any age for a long time.

Some of the speakers at the Gathering were just delightful, and I got great pleasure from their teachings. John Punshon's talk one evening was classic pungent Punshon. If I had to pick one point to highlight, it would be his observation that "the natural Quakers in the community around us don't need us. It is the rotters we should be going after. Fox called for a personal transformation." A second to remember was his observation that Faith communities are growing that

    1) know who they are;

    2) know why they are [have a purpose];

    3) have boundaries [this is us—that is not]; and

    4) require a commitment.

I had agreed to join what I thought was a private discussion about dressing plainly one afternoon and was surprised when it turned out to be a public, advertised event sponsored by the Friends Committee on Unity with Nature and that I had been advertised as a co-facilitator. Afterward, I was able to have a private word with the woman who had requested a discussion with me on this topic to explain why the changes in nature and sponsorship obligated that I be consulted to see if a public discussion was agreeable. She indicated her intent to be more careful in the future.

As it turned out, at least thirty-six people attended. Each of the four named co-facilitators gave a short testimony of our leadings into one form or another of dressing more plainly, including the religious principles that we felt had been advanced in our own lives by the practice.[11] There was not enough time for all of those in attendance to ask even one question, and no time for true dialogue, but the questions we did hear showed Friends had been feelingly engaged on the subject. Most seemed to be focused on the right use of the world's resources and similar environmental concerns. All in all, I felt it was a good meeting even though not what I had expected.

In Eighth Month, Rich Square Meeting for Business heard the endorsements of my certificate for travel in the ministry over the past year and united in issuing another. The new certificate was open-ended as to time and expanded the geography covered to "Friends in the Carolinas and elsewhere." Mike Arnold and I felt that there might be openings for us to travel to more distant locations.

There was a called meeting of the Yearly Meeting of Ministry and Oversight of NCYM(C) at Rich Square in Ninth Month, and twenty-two Friends gathered for the morning worship. As clerk, I asked Friends to

Exercises in the Gospel Ministry

begin the after-lunch session more as a discussion than a meeting for business in order to facilitate a free sharing of ideas and experiences. This seemed to have the desired effect, and we eventually heard from every Friend present except one (I spoke to her during a break, and she was at ease with being silent). Friends spoke of their sense of vocal ministry in their own meetings and of their understanding of when they were rightly moved to rise in ministry. One Friend spoke of the increasing unease some Friends in his meeting felt with Christian theology, an unease that frequently led him to attend worship at a Disciples of Christ church before attending Quaker meeting.

After about two hours, I asked Friends to consider actions we might take or recommend to monthly meetings to address the concerns that had been shared. About half a dozen suggestions were made, but at the end the depth and power of the shared spiritual experience of the day were greater than our suggestions and we decided to make no recommendations other than to plan to meet again in Tenth Month and to invite other Friends to join us. We would gather at the rise of Representative Body in Virginia Beach, God willing, and see what our Guide had in store for us then.

Carole and Ray Treadway, Bob Cooper, and Sam and Jeanne Rose elected to stay overnight, and we had a hearty if simple dinner together in the lunchroom together with the Gosneys and Edward Pearce. We lingered over the dinner table for a long time, talking about the state of the yearly meeting and how to nurture our Christian roots without falling into dogmatism or creedalism. Carole spoke of the need for a description of Quaker Christianity in terms that were accessible to our attenders and that would differentiate us from the various versions of Christianity that had led many of them to take refuge with Friends.

The Tenth Month Representative Body ran long, so we had only about an hour for the called meeting of MEO. The Representative Body had asked the yearly meeting MEO to consider how to strengthen the ties between Durham and the rest of yearly meeting, so after an extended period of worship I raised that issue for consideration. Friends had been expressing how important our own worship together had become, so I suggested that we meet in Durham for their regular meeting for worship in First Month and then gather that afternoon for another called meeting of MEO. This was met with approval, and we decided to meet in Durham First Month 26, 2003, if consistent with Divine Will.

I was on the road early on the appointed First Day to arrive in Durham in time for worship. The meeting house was packed; there were adults sitting on the floor and every seat was filled, even after the children left for First Day school. There were about half a dozen messages in worship, about half from Durham Friends and half from the MEO visitors. At the rise of worship, Durham Friends produced an excellent potluck lunch—lots of food and all of it tasty. It seemed to me, looking over the crowd, that there were lots of conversations going on between Durham Friends and visitors. Just what we had hoped!

The afternoon MEO meeting started with worship. After a time, I read the first and fourth Queries for ministers, elders, and overseers from the *Discipline*. Worship continued for another ninety minutes or so, guided somewhat by the themes of previous meetings (concerns for the vocal ministry, the nurture of ministers, etc.) but also touching on our call as a people of faith to share the gospel with the world. We closed with an intent to meet again on First Day following the next Representative Body meeting, planned for Wilmington. My sense continued to be that something special was happening in these meetings. If they were nurturing those who attended, perhaps they were in that way nurturing each of our monthly meetings.

I was invited to speak at a Chowan College colloquium on the impending war with Iraq in Second Month 2003 as the faculty antiwar speaker. My remarks were as follows.

> Hi. My name is Lloyd Lee and I am a Christian pacifist. For 300 years following the resurrection of Jesus, that would have been a redundant statement; it was understood that all Christians were pacifists. We know that some Christians even allowed themselves to be killed rather than to join the Roman army. But that sort of belief is very rare today, so allow me to explain.
>
> Becoming a Christian is not an intellectual declaration but a transformational experience. In that transformation Christ breaks the shell and the bonds of our old life and gives us each a

Exercises in the Gospel Ministry

new life with a new spirit and a new heart, a new desire to do God's will and a new strength to do it.

It is the shared experience of my faith tradition—the Religious Society of Friends, or Quakers—that as that transformation progresses, one discovers the guidance and companionship of Christ within. Christ's "Behold, I am with you always" has become literally true. When we examine ourselves in this new life, we discover that among many other blessings, we are now living in that life and power that takes away the occasion of war—all the reasons and excuses for fighting other human beings have fallen away.

As a Christian, there are at least four reasons why I "utterly deny" all wars and preparation for war and fighting with outward weapons.

1. The first reason involves lust. We usually think of lust as involving intense sexual cravings, but when the Epistle of James tells us that wars come from the lusts (James 4:1), a broader meaning is intended. Lust is the intense desire for those things that I do not have and that it would be wrong for me to possess. As a Christian, I've been redeemed from my bondage to the lusts in all their multiple forms. The freedom Christ gives me from the covetousness of my old life frees me from the urge to fight to fulfill those desires. There is no longer an occasion, or reason, for me to make war.

2. The second reason is an explicit command—Christ my King has by command (Matthew 26) and example disarmed me. Peter attempted to defend Christ by violence, cutting off the ear of the servant of the high priest. What better justification could there be for fighting than the defense of the perfectly innocent and defenseless against a violent enemy with evil intent? But Christ said to Peter, "Put your sword back in its place, for all who draw the sword will die by the sword." When Christ disarmed Peter he disarmed all Christians.

3. The third reason is that war is counterproductive—as a Christian, I yearn for and work for the coming of the Kingdom

of God; but the Kingdom will come not by might or the power of the outward sword but by the spirit of God (Zechariah 4:6). I can't hurry the Kingdom by waging war. It is impossible to "fight for peace." The cessation of outward fighting at the end of any war already always contains the seeds for the next war.

4. The fourth reason is transformation—as a Christian, it is no longer my aim to replace one earthly government with another but to speed the day when all the kingdoms of this world become the Kingdoms of God (Revelation 11:15). My task as a Christian in this regard is to continually examine my life and remove the seeds of war and injustice wherever I find them. The most and best I can do to bring about the Kingdom of God is to live myself as if it were already here. I may be called to witness to others but never to force them to change. "Regime change" is an unchristian concept.

A key vision for God's Kingdom is the biblical Jubilee—where everybody has enough and nobody has too much; where debts are forgiven and people are restored to their ancestral lands. Jubilee was a periodic redistribution of wealth to prevent some people from becoming wealthy at the expense of others.

When we accumulate an unfair portion of the world's wealth, when so many others are poor, ill, and hungry without resources or opportunity to improve themselves, we deny the vision of Jubilee and refuse to live into the Kingdom of God that is now coming into being on earth. We become gluttons.

When we go to war to protect our wealth, our standard of living, or our physical belongings, we deny Christ. We deny the redeeming and renewing power of Christ to give us a new spirit and a new life where outward wealth is irrelevant.

When we take up arms against our enemies, we disobey the clear command of Christ and become lawbreakers ourselves.

When we rely on our national military force to protect us rather than placing our faith in God, we become idolaters.

The first Great Commandment is to love God totally. Therefore, my first loyalty is to God, not to my country. Christ

Exercises in the Gospel Ministry

calls us to love our enemy, to pray for them, and to do good to them. I cannot do these things and also take up arms against them. The second Great Commandment is to love our neighbor. Therefore, my second loyalty is to my neighbor, helping those who need help as the Good Samaritan did.

My third loyalty, then, can be to my country—but no higher than third. We are told to render unto Caesar what is Caesar's and unto God what is God's. But, like Dorothy Day, I find that after I render unto God what is God's, there is nothing left for Caesar.

Is this a risky position to take in life—to place all my trust in an unseen God rather than in military defenses I can see and touch? Of course it is; it places me and people like me in a very vulnerable position. But that is the nature of faith: to put ourselves at risk on behalf of what we believe to be true. Discipleship is costly.

Even if my pacifist position results in apparent failure in the eyes of the world, I believe it is more Christ-like to suffer wrong than to oppose it by methods that are themselves wrong in Christ's sight. The standard for Christians is always faithfulness, not success.

So. I am a Christian, and therefore I am a pacifist. I oppose and denounce the impending war on Iraq. It is an unjust war, as others will readily point out, but it is not merely this particular war that I oppose. The basic issue for me is that war itself—any war—is never an acceptable means toward any end for a Christian. In God we really do trust.[12]

These remarks proved to interest a wider audience than just Chowan faculty and students and were later published in slightly modified form by *Friends Journal* and *Quaker Life*.

A worldwide peace vigil was held on Third Month 16, 2003, starting in New Zealand and moving across the globe as the local time reached 7 p.m. in each zone. Susan and I attended a local vigil at the meeting house in Virginia Beach. Rain caused the vigil to be moved indoors. The meeting house was packed. Electric lights were turned off, and the only illumination was provided by the small candles each vigil-keeper held. The meeting clerk gave a short introduction to Quaker proceedings, and we settled into what was, for both Susan and me, very deep worship.

After forty-five minutes or so, I was moved to vocal worship, reminding those gathered of the promises made in the Sermon on the Mount and of the necessity for each of us to be the "salt of the earth" and not to lose our savor. Someone had alerted Channel 13 news of the vigil, and they had a camera in the meeting room. They were able to get some remarkable shots in the semi-darkness, including shots of both Susan and me in worship and a sound bite from my ministry. It was a wonderful time, refreshing our spirits and renewing my felt desire to live a peaceful life, but I doubted it would have the desired effect on the Bush administration. He seemed set on waging war in spite of the opinions of so many people in America and the rest of the world.

The next day I stopped by the Baptist church in Woodland and spoke to Heath Lloyd, the pastor. Partly I wanted to give him positive feedback about the radio broadcast of his sermons that the church had recently begun, and partly I wanted to open to him a concern I had that if/when war began, the churches should have some sort of ecumenical prayer opportunity to give individuals an opening to share their concerns and desires about the suffering of war with the Lord in the company of their neighbors. Heath was fairly open to the idea, though he did not embrace it immediately. I asked him to hold the idea in prayer and went on my way.

President Bush went on national TV that evening to talk about the impending war with Iraq. He'd given Saddam Hussein and his two sons forty-eight hours to leave Iraq, saying that war could begin at any time after that period was over. It seemed evident that he could not have gotten a majority vote to support the war in the United Nations Security Council, much less avoided a veto from France or Russia. Now he was leading the country into a preventative war—not even a preemptive war—that fell short even of the most liberal "just war" test. We were going to war not because of anything Iraq had done and not because of anything that Iraq was about to do but because of things that Bush thought that Iraq might do sometime in the future.

Exercises in the Gospel Ministry

The previous month, Senator Robert Byrd had given an excellent speech in the US Senate that echoed in my thoughts often. He asked, How could it be consistent with the highest moral principles of the United States to wage war on a country in which over 50 percent of the population was under the age of fifteen? I believed that historians would look back on this time one hundred years later and call it a watershed, the moment when the United States unambiguously assumed the persona of empire.

Mike Arnold and I attended another FGC Traveling Ministries Program retreat later in Third Month. I had a chance for some conversation with Marty Grundy at dinner and shared my distrust about attempting a "new Barclay"—a systematic exploration of Quaker theology. Her response was useful: "Good. The problems he was addressing aren't relevant any more." This, I thought, could be the basis for a book—What are the relevant questions today for the Religious Society of Friends?

Time after dinner was occupied by a short worship-sharing time in small groups and a plenary meeting for worship. After the end of worship, a Friend I knew by name only approached me, and we fell to talking about his current dual membership in one monthly meeting belonging to a Liberal yearly meeting and another belonging to a Conservative yearly meeting. I asked him a couple of gentle questions about who had care of him and where his spiritual home was, and in both cases he named the Conservative meeting. I suggested that his true membership might be with the Conservative meeting. I then made a little hop on one foot and then on the other, but he did not get the allusion. I suggested that he read Elijah, and we parted company.

Later, this Friend approached me again. After thanking me for recommending Elijah, he began to protest that I knew nothing about his spiritual condition, his prayer life, his oversight and support, etc., including his anguish and suffering. I agreed that I knew nothing of those things and had been told nothing by others. He did not seem to understand that my disapproval of dual membership had everything to do with my sense of the nature of membership and nothing to do with any sense I might have of his individual circumstances or condition. He did not seem open to hearing this, so I abandoned the effort to explain.

The next day was one intense encounter after another. At breakfast, a retreatant began telling me of a crisis in an Ohio Valley Yearly Meeting group that had already been the cause of a court injunction. Other Friends joined us and ended up asking me to write up my recommendations about how to handle the situation. The rest of the morning was taken up with an extended meeting for worship in which it was my part to be silent. I felt the worship was deep and that the Counselor was present.

Back home again, I spent some time reflecting on interfaith relations. Ecumenism is a difficult subject, and my understanding of appropriate ecumenical activity has changed frequently as I have matured spiritually. It seems to me that both endpoints of the discussion, total exclusivity and the assertion that all religious traditions are the same, are equally wrong and to be avoided. To believe that the Creator is only satisfied with my perceptions and my mode of worship to the exclusion of all others seems to me the height of hubris. To assert that all faith traditions are the same, in spite of mutual claims to distinctives, is to claim that no person understands their own faith commitments except me—an equal hubris.

I believe true ecumenism acknowledges and honors the distinctives of different faiths, understanding that each strives to achieve the shared goal of a more authentic life. This applies when thinking of Christians and Muslims and Hindus; it is equally true among Christians whose worship is intricately woven of complex liturgy and those whose worship is rooted in silent listening for the Divine Voice. Paul had something like this in mind when he wrote:

> *One man regards a certain day above the others, while someone else considers every day alike. Each one should be fully convinced in his own mind. He who observes a special day does so to the Lord; he who eats does so to the Lord, for he gives thanks to God; and he who abstains does so to the Lord and gives thanks to God.* (Romans 14:5–6 BSB)

Exercises in the Gospel Ministry

Isaac Penington articulated this truth from the Quaker perspective when he wrote:

> It is not the different practice from one another that breaks the peace and unity, but the judging one another because of differing practices. He who keeps not a day may unite in the same Spirit, in the same life, in the same love, with him who keeps a day; and he who keeps a day may unite in heart and soul with the same Spirit and life in him who keeps not a day; but he that judgeth the other because of either of these errs from the Spirit, from the love, from the life, and so breaks the bond of unity.[13]

As I have matured spiritually, I have become more involved in ecumenical activities, not to minimize our differences but to celebrate the mystery of that Presence that is beyond any human ability to comprehend fully or to contain in any description. Whether to carry out the acts of mercy, to remember the mighty acts of God at Passover and Easter, or to witness to our shared belief in the dignity and worth of every human being wherever born or however labeled, authentic ecumenical activities bring joy to God.

Mike Arnold was my companion again in Sixth Month when I spoke to the annual sessions of Southern Appalachian Yearly Meeting and Association at Warren Wilson College in Swannanoa, North Carolina. Carole Treadway and Deborah Shaw came down from Greensboro to meet with Mike and me and to hear the first of my two lectures, the first focused mostly on faith and the second on the implications that faith has for our common practice. We also discussed what the proper vetting procedure should be for printed versions of lectures such as those I was about to give. Carole gave the opinion that although I was a Friend traveling with a certificate from my monthly and yearly meetings, there was an assumption that I would speak in good order but that the text of what I said should be vetted in some fashion by the yearly meeting before it appeared in print. This was agreeable to all, and we resolved to tell inquirers that there would have to be a yearly meeting review before they could be printed. What eventually happened was that these lectures became the core of my second book, *Wrestling with Our Faith Tradition*.[14]

My ability to deliver either of these lectures had been in doubt. I had continued to have chest congestion and a persistent cough left over from two weeks of illness and was often unable to speak more than one or two sentences without having to stop for a coughing spell. I had been asking for prayer support all week, and I asked again in the hours leading up to the lecture. In what Susan later called "the hand of God," I was enabled to deliver the entire first lecture without coughing, stopping only once for a sip of water.

The lecture was very well received. There was a long time of worship immediately after the lecture, and when it broke there were at least three other events scheduled to begin, but about sixteen Friends stayed for a question-and-answer period that lasted for another hour. The questions were good, indicating both serious listening and the questioners' desire to understand the implications of some of the points I had made.

I felt a little better the next day but was still concerned about my ability to give the second lecture. Again, God was with me, and I had only one cough the entire time—and that barely more than clearing my throat. The lecture was well received, and again I had to turn people away after over an hour of questions and answers. God was blessing this ministry bountifully.

At the same time, my visit was not without criticism. One morning at breakfast, a Friend began to labor with me about how people who believed in a single faith were the cause of all wars and suffering in the world—especially fundamentalist Christians like myself. When I protested that I did not qualify as a fundamentalist, she insisted that I certainly did—by her terms. She was quite taken with a pamphlet by Dan Seeger about universalism and was disappointed to discern that I probably was not going to be converted away from Christianity by reading that pamphlet.

Earlham School of Religion

In Eighth Month 2003, I began pursuing graduate studies at the Earlham School of Religion through their Access program—a mix of online studies and on-campus intensive two-week courses. My motivation for undertaking this formal religious study was straightforward. People were listening to what I said and reading what I wrote—paying attention. I needed to learn what I didn't know to fill in the gaps, and I needed to unlearn what I thought I knew that wasn't true so as not to lead people astray. One of the learning tools at Earlham was the reflection paper, where the student was asked to reflect on the concepts explored in class and how they were applicable (or not) to the student's own life. Excerpts from some of these reflection papers, on topics such as "What is Ministry?", lectio divina, and John Woolman, are included in an appendix to this memoir. Taken together, they constitute a written examen that both highlighted and clarified my spiritual self-understanding in important ways.

The seminary experience frequently turned my understanding of a Scripture passage upside down. An early example of this was a group class exploration of Henri Nouwen's book on Rembrandt's painting *The Return of the Prodigal Son*.[15] Since that time, my name for this story has been the parable of the watchful father. Some of the insights that made the most impact on me were these, from my journal:

- When the father says to the elder son, "Everything I have is yours," this is literally true. The estate has already been divided. On top of being unfair (the prodigal is being accepted back without penance or other punishment), this party is being held at the elder son's expense!
- This reminds me of Ched Myers describing Jesus talking to Nicodemus. "Hey, Nick! Come down from that tree! I'm throwing a party at your house tonight, and I'm bringing fifty of my weirdest friends!"
- It is all a "distant country"—everything that is lived without God at the center is a distant country. Every time I place anyone or anything other than God at the center of the story (including myself), I am in a distant country. To come home is at last to turn toward God with all my being.
- "My favored one." I hear this when I have put aside my own will and allowed God to speak and act through me.
- My soul coming home and receiving forgiveness—one by one, little by little, no blanket dispensation, but serial review and release. Not so much a second innocence but a new start, scars

and all, broken open to allow the mercies of God to enter in. Broken to remind me that I am not the center. "He must increase, and I must decrease." Blessed balm of being returned to right relationship with my God.

- Elder son—been there, done that, have the T-shirt but it is worn out. For a long time I was jealous of others' spiritual gifts, and especially of attention given to newcomers. I've given up the pretense that I've done things right (i.e., the hard way) while others have not. I think I am over being the elder son of this parable.
- I do trust that God feels I'm worth finding—not perfect, but worth finding. I have gratitude for all God has done and is doing for me—more than I ever deserve.

At Earlham, learning to be open with others about what was happening in my spiritual life was a struggle for me. This was not a skill much practiced or valued in my family growing up, and in my experience it had been risky, even among Friends. It was apparent to me from this very first class how important authentic sharing was to the spiritual formation process, but if others knew what I was thinking and feeling, it would be fuel for their fire – and I'd be in the middle of it! If I was going to live up to my responsibilities as a student, then, I had to be self-revealing. Three old tapes from my teen years were especially troubling now:

"If I tried to explain, you wouldn't understand."

"If you really knew me, you wouldn't like me."

"You're a Wilson—you aren't like other people. There are different rules for you."

How long those old tapes persist, and how long their power continues to have its influence.

I was helped at this time by Callie Marsh, a seasoned Friend from Iowa Yearly Meeting (Conservative), who let me know that she also wanted to pursue an M.A. through the Access program, as I did. Callie understood the nuances of the Conservative faith tradition, she had a similar goal at Earlham School of Religion, and she helped me learn to share about my inward experience. This was a great encouragement.

Exercises in the Gospel Ministry

The full Access program included an on-campus course in First Month and online courses in the spring and fall semesters. I took the online courses regularly but could not leave my duties as registrar at the beginning of Chowan College's spring semester. As I look back over this time, the online courses were quite valuable, but the on-campus intensives had the greatest impact on me.

I had more difficulty during my on-campus class in the summer of 2004 as I was suffering from asthma (probably due to mold in my office at Chowan) in addition to my usual aches and pains. This time, I did not feel obligated to walk to and from campus each day, and the medicines I carried for my asthma were not always effective. By practicing more meditation and deep breathing exercises and not allowing myself to get overly upset, I persevered through the class.

One day, Doug Gwyn and I met for lunch. We talked a great deal about his book *Seekers Found: Atonement in Early Quaker Experience* and its underlying premise that the cultural context of the early decades of the Quaker movement and the decades of the '60s and '70s we had both lived through had much in common. We each enjoyed conversing with someone of a similar age who remembered those decades from much the same perspective.

While on campus in the summer of 2005, I was troubled one night by what I'd come to recognize, over the years that this had been happening to me, as an attack of the Adversary—a series of embarrassing incidents brought to my mind in quick succession that made me feel that my efforts in the ministry were foolish at best and embarrassing or actually harmful to the gospel at worst. This particular type of attack is a twisting of the true need for humility. It is important to remain humble so that I do not outrun my Guide, but the Adversary twists this to try to convince me that I am worthless and should do nothing at all.

This was familiar enough territory that, although I was troubled, I did get to sleep, but when I awoke, the trouble was still with me. When time came for early worship, I headed for Earlham's worship room and once there walked straight to the seat where I had been led to worship that week. Callie Marsh was the only person in the room, but we did not make eye contact or acknowledge each other.

Over the course of the worship, I brought the attack before the Lord and gradually felt relief so that by the time we rose and met in the middle of the room to shake hands, I understood the attack was over. Callie's first words to me were to the effect that she had sensed that I was troubled in spirit when I walked into the room, and she had spent a goodly portion of the worship time in prayer for me.

At the beginning of class that morning, I shared the above as a testimony to the power of prayer for one another. Later in the class, during our discussion of the spirituality of dreams among Quakers, I shared the story of my dream/vision of my tying Christ's sandals the night after the Virginia Beach called threshing meeting about the portrait of the blue-eyed Jesus. This is not a story I tell often, and when I do it affects me strongly. Looking back, I see that remembering and telling of Christ's acceptance of my ministry was another bit of healing and recovery from the earlier spiritual attack.

Another Access student crossed my path after class, and she stopped to remark, "You look great! You are smiling, and it becomes you! The Spirit is just radiating out of you!" Christ is our Healer and Physician; intercessory prayer is powerful.

During class, Steve Angell passed out an excellent paper written by Carol Holmes of New York Yearly Meeting on her experience of intervisitation in that yearly meeting. In the paper, she shared some of her personal emotional and psychological struggles over several years as well as described yearly meeting efforts at building the larger community through visitation. She quoted from my essay in *Walk Worthy of Your Calling* to describe the motion of love that begins a person's movement toward visitation. In her conclusion, she quoted me again and then paraphrased my words to summarize the whole purpose of the yearly meeting's visitation program. This was so direct a refutation of the attack I had experienced the previous night and early that morning that it brought tears to my eyes, and I sat in silence at my table long after my meal was complete. When it seemed that I really ought to get up and go, I went back to Earlham School of Religion and returned to the worship room to give thanks for God's grace and generosity in accepting my ministry and in helping me stave off the Adversary.

Exercises in the Gospel Ministry

At the end of several years of part-time study at Earlham School of Religion, I asked myself what I had learned about theology. One simple realization was that, without labeling it as such, I'd been doing a good bit of theological reflection for a number of years. I also could see more clearly now the breadth and depth of the field. I had kept aspects of theological work at a distance by intention or through simple oversight (e.g., I had been by intention and public declaration a non-Trinitarian via my simple refusal to consider the topic—an interpretation of an early Quaker witness that got me out of more than one theological tight spot).

I was even more committed to the Christian metaphor for ultimate Truth and meaning than I had been when I started at Earlham School of Religion. As for pluralism, my sense was that there is one Truth behind it all but that none of us has a perfect or even very comprehensive understanding of that Truth; the answer Job got to his questions rings very true to me (Job 38–41). All of us, on whatever path, have only an incomplete sense of that Reality. Christ is the Way, the Truth, and the Life for me, but I did not believe that to be the case for every person. I chose to spend my life digging one well deeply into Christianity rather than digging a great number of shallow wells. There are other paths to the Truth—other wells also yield Living Water—and they are just as authentic and have just as much internal integrity as Christianity. Those who dig deep wells will find the same Living Water no matter what tradition they dig in.

The various methodologies for doing theology strike me as tools that should be used for specific tasks rather than adopted as one's sole approach to the work. Having wrestled for some years with the task of writing a systematic theology for conservative/classic Quakerism, I sense that this is not particularly well suited to the postmodern congregation. It may be an excellent thought experiment for the theologian—sort of a test circuit to ensure that we are not, after all, "believing six impossible things before breakfast," as the White Queen told Alice—but it is not a methodology to win contemporary hearts and souls for Christ.

Dogmatic theology is attractive to me as I am naturally conservative. It is not that I don't want any change at all from the doctrines and principles of early Friends; it is that I want to examine each and every change to ensure that we understand what we're changing and why and what the likely effect of the change might be. Brian Drayton's woven cloth of Quakerism is a good metaphor here; we can remove a thread or two from warp or woof, but if we remove too many the cloth will no longer hold together. But dogmatic theology by itself is too conservative, too inert to meet my needs.

Narrative theology has an interesting name, but the lack of a coherent definition or even a single meaning limits its usefulness as a general method. Quakers as a people should have a natural affinity for narrative theology as we use narrative so often to ourselves and to inquirers of all sorts. Wil Cooper remarked at a NCYM(C) session that we Quakers talk about ourselves so much because we have no creed or dogma that defines who we are. Narrative is more useful as an example of theological principle than as a tool for uncovering that principle—a tool of communication, not investigation.

Where I feel most at home, and where I've done the most reading and studying, is liberation theology, which Gustavo Gutiérrez calls "critical reflection on praxis." I'm realizing that our praxis—on the personal, community, national, and global scales—does not meet the standards of the gospel. I've read Gutiérrez, the Boff brothers, and the rest and have studied with folks in this country such as Ched Myers and others who espouse Jubilee economics and other liberation-type approaches to the Word and the world. Through them, I'm beginning to see the interlocking systems of injustice we've constructed everywhere that oppress human beings, especially the poor and powerless. My sense is that Scripture has been read from the top (of society) down for millennia and that Christians need to learn to read it from the bottom up. Our understanding of and relationship to God will inevitably change as we do this. I feel that my own engagement in the world has changed as a result of my engagement with liberation theology. I understand the "problem of violence" presented by this theology, but it is a problem with which I am willing to wrestle; the gains of the approach outweigh the costs of the problem.

I am strongly committed to liberation theology's understanding of theology as "the second step—reflection on practice." A priori logic just

Exercises in the Gospel Ministry

leads to too many dead ends and injurious doctrinal conclusions. At the same time, I see that one needs to make an attempt at a comprehensive (constructive) theology, at least for oneself if not for one's faith tradition, in order to live an integrated, harmonious life.

It seemed to me (and still does) that one's theology has to be integrated into one's actions—that what one believes and how one believes it has to be reflected in the way one moves in the world. Be doers of the word and not hearers only (James 1:22), as Paul advises in that "epistle of straw."[16] It is not true that "anything goes" because we Friends don't put our faith in written creeds. I had a sense that my formal theological study at the school of religion would shape my actions and my writings for years to come—which they did.

I presented and defended my master's thesis research while on campus for an intensive course.[17] There were about a dozen faculty and students present, the atmosphere was quite friendly, and it did not seem to me that I was asked any difficult questions at all. At the end of the defense, Earlham School of Religion's dean asked me what was the most important thing I had learned from my research. My immediate answer, echoed from the audience by Callie Marsh, was that "We are not Wilburites!" Both Iowa and North Carolina Yearly Meetings (Conservative) developed along their own lines, under different circumstances and at different times from Ohio Yearly Meeting. Places where we differ from Ohio in doctrine or practice are not instances of our falling away from the Wilburite vision but are expressions of the result of our own spiritual discernment and development. This was for me a very liberating realization.

Susan and I returned to the Earlham campus in Fifth Month 2009 for commencement. The baccalaureate dinner beforehand was wonderful. Various faculty speakers gave testimonials to the graduating students; it was heartfelt, very affirming, and deeply touching. Later, we gathered in Stout Meeting House for programmed worship with a period of open worship included. I had been asked to speak a few words of explanation about waiting worship, and I did. (The irony of having to explain waiting worship at a graduation service at a Quaker seminary was not lost on me.)

A Time of Reflection

Throughout this time, I was reading old minutes of North Carolina Yearly Meeting and its member monthly meetings from before and after the separation. Reading in the Civil War era, I encountered this minute of advice from the 1861 sessions of the yearly meeting:

> We do not believe that religion consists in a garb of peculiar shape; but we do believe that the man of solid principles will not adopt that dress of the fop. He will dress in a plain and simple manner. But in addition to this, the style of Friends points them out as members of a body, believing as very few other Religious Societies do, in the peaceable nature of Christ's Kingdom, and its incompatibility with every species of injustice and oppression; and thus the plain coat and plain speech become real though silent testimonies against oppression and war.[18]

Friends from 150 years ago were expressing what I had experienced over the years about dressing simply and distinctively. It felt like a warm embrace and affirmation from the faith tradition itself.

Another discovery brought home how disruptive the Civil War was in every part of life. In 1862 the yearly meeting minutes noted that they were "cut off by the lines of the contending armies" from all other Friends and had received no epistles from other yearly meetings. They wrote an outgoing epistle anyway in the conviction that they would not be cut off forever. "This too shall pass."

I also spent considerable time reflecting on the idea of salvation and what I believed about it. The common idea one hears from contemporary Christians is that the religious life consists of believing or acting in a particular way so that one is "saved" rather than "damned." This often seems associated with attempts to control how God will act. If a person behaves this way, the logic goes, God will be forced to save them, and if a person acts in this other way, God will be forced to damn them. The purpose of religion is to be saved rather than damned, and in many accounts being saved results in material benefit (prosperity theology), rescue from hell (fire insurance theology), or escape from worldly tribulations (spaceship theology).

Exercises in the Gospel Ministry

Friends have understood the purpose of religious life differently—as obtaining true knowledge of God, which is the source of true happiness. This knowledge comes from an unmediated relationship with Christ, not from secret knowledge imparted by Christ (which would be Gnosticism) but from the relationship itself.

Coming to know God directly and intimately is such a life-changing experience that it can truly be called being born again; one becomes a new person as Christ comes to abide in oneself and as one abides in Christ. One's outward behavior is a reflection of this new relationship and of the love that exists between oneself and God. One acts not to avoid damnation or to ensure salvation; one simply manifests one's life in God in the world. This is not a withdrawal from the world because we know experimentally that God is lovingly involved in all of creation constantly and continually. As we come to know and share in God's love, our love for all of creation will necessarily increase and become more manifest.

Our "witness" to God's love cannot fail because it is not evaluated by its effects but by its source. The peace witness of Christians in the months leading up to the most recent war against Iraq did not fail because the witness did not prevent the war. It succeeded to the extent that it was a faithful manifestation of our transforming experience of being in relationship with God and a manifestation of God's love for all of creation. If we manifest the loving relationship we have found with God, the manifestation will be an invitation to others to come to the same source and experience a similar relationship. As that happens, the world will be changed.

While I was at Earlham for the first intensive course, Susan and Mike had been talking about the Old-Time Farmers' Day near his farm later that month. The Baptists regularly held an old-time worship service there, and Mike once held a Quaker meeting. That meeting was too quiet and not accessible enough to newcomers as no one had a way to figure out what was going on. Mike and Susan had decided to hold another Quaker meeting for worship at this year's Old-Time Farmers' Day, only this one would be a "public meeting" in the old style and they would invite a visiting Quaker minister in the old style—me—to bring the message. Like the old public meetings, Susan, Penny, and Mike would be available to "work the crowd," answer messages afterward, and direct interested folks to a regular meeting for worship. What could I do but say yes? If I was going to be accountable, I needed to be accountable in all things, so I agreed to take this on. It would be a valuable field test of an old style of outreach to see if it could still yield a harvest in the twenty-first century—and to see whether I could make it work (with divine and human help). So, I got clearness from my meeting, and we held worship in a large barn on site. Folks sat on benches and hay bales, I preached, and some other folks offered ministry as well. I don't know if any hearts were touched, but it seemed to be acceptable service.

The local membership of Rich Square meeting was small, but occasionally we were joined in worship by visitors who outnumbered us by three or four to one. One First Day about that time, there were a surprising twenty-one persons at meeting for worship at Rich Square. Lib Parker and four generations of her Parker descendants and Tom and Betty Feamster from Durham meeting. Tom, a former professional football lineman, was wearing a black felt broad-brimmed hat, white collarless shirt, black braces, and black trousers—he looked like a (much) bigger version of me at a "special occasion" meeting for worship!

Tom and Betty Feamster are strongly committed to their new path as Quakers and want to be more than First Day Quakers, just as they had been more than Sunday Episcopalians. However, they lived more than an hour's drive from Durham Meeting and had reached the age when they no longer drove at night. They had come to the conclusion that they needed either to begin a new meeting in Louisburg, North Carolina, where they lived, or to move closer to an established meeting—preferably one not located in a metropolitan area. We spent considerable time discussing the obligations and responsibilities of starting a new meeting, and they seemed to have a clear idea of what it would take. We also talked about the advantages of coming to Woodland and joining Rich Square Monthly Meeting and the importance of nurturing and sustaining this "mother meeting" of NCYM(C).[19] We told them that the meeting could certainly use two new members of their gifts and commitment, that real estate prices and cost of living were low in Woodland, and that there were lots of social ministry opportunities.

The conversation over the lunch table (and long into the afternoon) was especially centered and nurturing. Bob Cooper of Fayetteville, North Carolina, reported that he hoped after next week to have visited every monthly meeting in the yearly meeting in a span of twelve months. He had a clearness/support committee from his monthly meeting, but since his call was visitation and not ministry, he did not feel it necessary to obtain a certificate from the meeting for business.

We talked a lot about community and membership. A community needs a memory of its own history, and each member needs to address that history and be shaped by it even as they shape and form the present into a new, extended history. A group needs to be willing to discuss personal beliefs in the context of that community history in order to pass beyond faux community into true community.

Friends experience God in the individual and God manifest in the community. The tendency is to ignore God manifest in the community, but the opposite error is to believe one must completely subvert one's identity to the community. As Christians, we believe that individual identity is fulfilled and completed in the faith community.

We reminded the Feamsters that dual membership doesn't work. One cannot give allegiance to two faith traditions at once or to two faith communities at once. They each—a faith tradition or a faith community—require our full commitment, our presence, and our presents—and to give less is to cheat both ourselves and the communities involved.

Travel in the Ministry: California

Ben Lomond Quaker Center in California offered to sponsor Susan and me in a two-week tour of Pacific Yearly Meeting faith communities in Eleventh Month 2003. After the necessary discernment and approval of certificates, we accepted and began the journey with a flight to San Jose, California. Walter Sullivan of Ben Lomond was waiting for us when we emerged from the airport.

Our hosts for the first night were Joe Magruder and Laura Magnani (Carl Magruder's father and Zac Moon's mother). Laura gave me to understand that Zac's recent practice of plain dress was at least in part due to my influence. I was glad that the first part of our journey was safely over and prayed for divine blessings on our gospel labors.

Our first visit was to Redwood Forest Meeting in Santa Rosa, California. We met at Friends House, a retirement facility where a number of meeting members lived. There were about thirty-five people at the potluck before the meeting, and about fifty gathered for the meeting itself. I began by speaking in a general way about deepening our Quaker faith, knowing and engaging our faith tradition in its own vocabulary and on its own terms. To my joy, the auditory soon began to pose its own questions, and we shifted to addressing the circumstances of Redwood Forest Meeting more directly. I felt the Spirit grow in perceptible Presence as we proceeded. After the meeting ended, about two-thirds of the group stayed to ask questions about Christian vocabulary, the nature of eldering, and vocal ministry. We closed a second time a little after 9 p.m. Susan and I retired to our quarters for the night and were asleep after a short debriefing session with one another.

The next morning, thirty-five to forty people gathered in the Redwood Forest meeting house. The focus of discussion became suffering, especially within the meeting regarding some unreconciled hurts Friends had done to each other, their shared lack of forgiveness, and issues around having two centers of worship (one at Friends House, where we had met the previous night, and one at the meeting house, where we were meeting that day).

Just before embarking on this journey, I had read the bestseller *When Bad Things Happen to Good People* by Harold Kushner. I had bought it on a whim at a used book store, and it sat unread for months before I picked it up on what I thought was another whim and read it carefully. What seemed whimsical was in reality divine providence. The book prepared me for dealing with the questions of suffering, pain, and evil that I encountered in California beginning that afternoon in Santa Rosa.

I announced early on that I would be available for opportunities on Seventh Day afternoon and that interested Friends should make arrangements through Susan. The first person I met with was an East Asian woman who had recently lost her husband and had spoken that morning of her sleepless nights and general sustained misery over the loss.

After just a few moments of silence together, this woman began to share her grief and guilt over a small spat she and her husband had had just before he died. She had rebuffed his attempts at reconciliation, and it was heavy on her heart. I recognized what was happening from similar descriptions in *When Bad Things Happen to Good People* and was able to say some things to relieve her of that guilt and help her focus on the years of happiness she'd had with her husband. We closed with some silent prayer, and she left after saying a few words of thanks. I went on to my next opportunity.

The next day, as the retreat participants gathered for lunch, this woman sought me out and sat down at our picnic table. She said she had gotten the best night's sleep she had had since her husband had died and that she felt as if the world had colors again. After thanking me once again, she sang "Jesus Loves Me" in her native language.

I have never lost a spouse to death and cannot possibly know or imagine what that feels like. But I believe that God arranged my circumstances, including reading that book at just the right time, so as to work a healing on that woman in that moment. This was a result of my willingness to get out of the way entirely and let God be at work in me and through me. Whatever one calls it, praise God.

Eight other people also requested opportunities, and I was busy for both the "free hour" between lunch and our afternoon session and for two more hours between the end of our session and the supper hour. I was asked for help with grieving the death of a spouse, reconciling a mother to her adult daughter, discerning right order in seeking a new job, and more. Three people specifically asked for vocal prayer—a sign that the whole meeting was probably thirsty for that.

There were numerous hard questions asked of me, but I felt guided and equipped to give an answer in each case that was kind but firm. Hearts were tendered and some broken open to the love of the True Shepherd. Tears flowed freely in some, both outwardly and inwardly. At the end of the day, I felt I had given acceptable service but knew that there was more work I would be called to perform and that it might or might not be contained in the next day's formal program.

The previous day, I had mentioned extended "worship before worship," a practice at Friendship Friends Meeting in Greensboro, North Carolina, and Susan mentioned the power of a lighted candle in the center of the room during some discussions and group events. We arrived at Redwood Forest meeting house on First Day to discover that Friends had rearranged the chairs to make room for a lighted candle in the middle of the room and that three Friends had already begun worship an hour early.

The meeting room was soon packed, and worship quickly reached a solid place. About forty minutes into the worship, I was moved to my knees in vocal prayer. I started and ended with a time of silent submission, on my knees but not speaking. Susan said later that she was physically shaking in the time leading up to my prayer, knowing that I was being given significant ministry. When I regained my seat, I received confirmation both that my ministry had been acceptable and that this had been the unfinished business that I had sensed.

The final program of the weekend was a ninety-minute session on membership. This proved to be a "hot-button" topic, and I was called on more than once to divide the Word of Truth so as to be clear without being needlessly hurtful. It was necessary to say to one Friend that I had little of comfort to say in response to her description of her situation. After the program ended, this Friend and her husband asked for an opportunity, which I granted. It quickly became clear that they wished mostly to describe how other Friends had behaved poorly toward them. This did not seem productive, so I closed the opportunity as soon as that could be managed.

Several people approached me to say how helpful the weekend and/or their opportunity with me had been to them spiritually. I had an extended conversation with one young woman who said that as a result of the last group discussion she had decided to apply for membership in the meeting after being an attender for many years.

Exercises in the Gospel Ministry

I felt tired in the best way after all was over. While waiting for Susan and Walter Sullivan to say their goodbyes, I wandered behind the meeting house and discovered an apple tree with ripe apples still on the branches. I thought of Jesus and the food the disciples didn't know about (John 4:32) and of birds bringing food to the prophets. Truly, God provides me sustenance, physical and spiritual, for my labors.

Susan and I stayed with Elaine Emily that night. After a relaxing morning, we went to the San Francisco meeting house. After dinner with several Friends at a neighborhood Indian restaurant, we gathered for the evening meeting. John Helding arranged for the gathering to be videotaped—a first for me. The woman who did the videotaping, I later discovered, was transgender and the married father of two children. Now she was living as a woman and was still part of the same, intact nuclear family. God is good.

I talked again about nurturing our faith. The audience there—about twenty-five persons—was more heavily Christian than in Santa Rosa, and the predominant condition was thirst. When asked for an example of a corporate experiment with Truth, I described our yearly meeting's consideration, over decades, of issues of inclusivity regarding homosexuals, up to and including the approval of same-sex unions. This both illustrated the point and implicitly uncovered an important difference between NCYM(C) and Ohio Yearly Meeting, which I've discovered to be wrongly conflated among many Liberal Friends

On my arrival, I had given the meeting clerk my travel certificate, which she said she would sign right away. When I suggested that she might want to see what happened first, she said she only intended to say I had been there on that date. During the meeting, she asked me to say more about being a recorded minister as she and others were of a divided mind, being against "hireling priests." I used the occasion to make clear that I was not a hireling because I accepted no honorarium or other pay for any of my gospel labors other than travel expenses and my bed and board while traveling—which I understood to be consistent with the beliefs and practices of early Friends. This provided an opportunity to discuss the recording process and open the importance of recognizing spiritual gifts of all types in the faith community. I described the ways recorded ministers are the servants of and accountable to the rest of the community, no longer able to make their own decisions about many things.

After closing worship, most Friends stayed on, engaging Walter, Susan, or myself on one or more of the subjects that had been touched on. Many seemed energized; some were thoughtful; few if any appeared to be skeptical. Susan said she was well pleased with the night's work. I also felt it had been owned and accepted by the Master.

We spent Armistice Day in Berkeley. As usual, reflections on the tragedy of war and the futility of believing any war (other than the Lamb's War) could "end all wars" occupied much of my thoughts, both as 11 a.m. approached and afterward. I spent the morning journaling in a neighborhood park. I got lunch at the neighborhood deli, then found a table and chair at a sidewalk cafe that was closed for "Veterans Day." I spent the afternoon at that sidewalk table, eating, journaling, reading Thomas Story's *Journal*, and people-watching in the afternoon sun.

In the evening, we went to Berkeley Friends Church for a gathering jointly sponsored by that church, Berkeley Friends Meeting, and Strawberry Creek Meeting. My friend Max Hansen was the new pastor of Berkeley Friends Church and seemed energized by that role. After an excellent meal, about twenty Friends gathered in the worship area to talk. The discussion started slowly, perhaps because for many the church-type setting was foreign. Participation increased steadily, and I believe that by the time we closed Truth was over all. This was lively spiritual exercise, and I again felt the sense of spending and being spent for the Lord. Each night's sleep brought refreshment so that I felt no accumulated tiredness in body or spirit.

The next day, Eleventh Month 12, we drove to Davis, arriving early enough to enjoy the bountiful farmer's market there—buying food for the road as well as a loaf of bread for the evening potluck. The unfamiliarity with which Friends here faced the challenges of setting up for the meal seemed to indicate a meeting that did not spend much time in table fellowship, and the meeting for worship afterward was marked by ministry that seemed clearly not Spirit-led or Spirit-fed. I felt I was faithful throughout the evening and kept close to my Guide, but the response was mixed. There were repeated smiles and head-nodding throughout by some Friends, but others seemed resistant, even offering pushback in various ways.

We had a long drive the next day to San Luis Obispo, through beautiful scenery and lots of farmland. We paralleled the great aqueduct for a long time, and I marveled at this civilization of ours that goes to such great lengths (literally, in this case) to move water from its natural locations to places more convenient for human activity.

That evening, I was led to speak on the shift in meaning and usage of the phrase "that of God in every man" from Fox's time to our own. This was a hard message for some to hear, though once again I was also given to feel that some hearts were reached and some consoled. I also acted out Walter Wink's explanations of the three "hard" parables about turning the other cheek, walking the extra mile, and giving up one's cloak.

On the fourteenth, we arrived at Ben Lomond Quaker Center, located in a beautiful setting in the midst of eighty acres of redwood forest. Susan and I were in a separate little cabin downhill from the rest of the weekend's activities, offering an important private space for us to debrief, relax, and be "off stage."

At our first gathering that evening, I was surprised by the relative youth of this group—many of the Friends were in their thirties. The next morning, I held "early morning communion" in the dining hall. There was solid conversation that carried over into breakfast. We then spent the morning discussing the principles of classic Quakerism in the Casa de Luz meeting space at the top of the hill.

Susan had requests for more than ten opportunities with me that afternoon, and I was powerfully used in that work. The range and intensity of the spiritual issues brought to me in these meetings was nearly overwhelming. I did the best I could, with divine assistance. When it was over, I went down to our little cabin to shower away the karma and to change shirts before starting the next session. I did not want the spiritual energies from the opportunities to spill over into the plenary sessions.

Certain ways the discussion developed in that session made me feel stopped up so that I could not speak for most of the session. Finally, Gordon Bishop asked me to tell my spiritual journey, and I felt released to speak and to witness. Two issues that came up were a Friend who shared he had a leading to ministry he did not want to share with his meeting because it would be too much hard work and another who described a dual membership situation in her meeting. I felt constrained to speak to both issues, and I hope it was helpful. One Friend thanked me afterward for disagreeing with her.

After dinner, we gathered around the wood stove in the dining hall. After some discussion, it seemed as if worship was called for, and we centered down. In due course, we closed and retired for the night.

First Day morning brought another good "early morning communion" session over coffee. These less formal times are an excellent way to explore topics that the larger group, for reasons of time, must pass over too quickly to meet the needs of some. I was more direct in the large group that morning, guiding the discussion into several areas I thought it was important to touch upon before we ended. We had a time of extended worship after lunch; it was deep and the ministry was generally helpful. I felt some hearts were broken open and fresh springs of Living Water put forth.

After the larger retreat ended, Susan and I met with the "New Year's group"—some Friends who had shared a powerful corporate spiritual awakening while on retreat at Ben Lomond the previous New Year. These Friends spoke of being increasingly drawn to Conservative Friends and proposed that the group constitute itself as a new preparative meeting that would have dual affiliation with Pacific Yearly Meeting and NCYM(C). I spoke up at this point, saying that it seemed to me that doing so would fatally compromise their prophetic stance inside Pacific Yearly Meeting. If they were seen as an outpost of Conservative Friends, their message would be much more easily dismissed than if their sole affiliation were with Pacific Yearly Meeting. They determined to follow this latter course, though it would mean much work for them.

I had one last opportunity the next morning before we headed for the airport for the flight home. We had a wonderful flight—completely

Exercises in the Gospel Ministry

uneventful—and arrived in Raleigh in the middle of the night. We were tired, as anyone might be after such a long day and long flight, but without any "back-home blues" or "spiritual hangover." We had been given a job, and by God's help we had been able to do it faithfully; now it was time to move on to the next job.

Early in Second Month 2004, Mike Arnold, Susan, and I visited Virginia Beach Friends Meeting "in the ministry." Very early in the worship, a Friend stood and reported that she had been asked to represent Quakers at a public event recently and had chosen to read James Nayler's last words. She described Nayler as being persecuted for his universalist Christian theology of the Christ Child within each of us and then made a transition to naming individual Friends in the meeting who were active in social concerns issues, briefly describing their activity and then concluding with, "I'm proud of [the person's name]."

I was shocked at both parts of her message—the historical inaccuracy of the first part and the unsoundness of the second. I was silent for about half an hour, but the inner trembling I felt increased minute by minute, and finally I rose to my feet. "Pride is a slippery thing," I said, "Just when you think you've got a grip on it, pride shifts in your hands and takes on a meaning you didn't intend." I went on to say that Nayler was arrested because he rode a donkey into Bristol, surrounded by a crowd of his followers who threw their coats and tree branches down in front of him and shouted "Hosanna." Nayler may have thought he was giving a sign to Bristol residents, but to his fellow Englishmen it seemed clear he was claiming to be Jesus Christ, a blasphemy. As Friends, we are committed to a spiritual path of subtraction, which results in our doing only what the Holy Spirit directs, in the power given to us by the Holy Spirit, and persevering through the courage given us by the Holy Spirit. What then is there for us to be proud about? As Scripture says, when we have done all these things, we will have done only what is expected of us. About all we can claim for our own is the will to pray, and we should be in prayer constantly, breathing in God with each breath and breathing out our petitions, our thanksgivings, and our praises.

Near the end of the meeting, I was brought to my knees briefly in vocal prayer for the gift of constant prayer for all gathered there this morning. All in all, this was some of the most difficult ministry I had ever given, and I could not have delivered it had I not been completely clear that this was God's doing, not my own. By the time I rose to speak, I had been trembling inwardly, and outwardly as well, for several minutes.

Later that month, Mike Arnold and I traveled to First Friends Church in Knoxville, Tennessee, for a weekend workshop on peace issues. My Seventh Day presentation went well, but afterward, back at our hosts' house, Mike and I began to feel unsettled. At first, I thought it was the predicted snowstorm in the mountains and our concern over whether the roads would be clear for us to return home the next day, but as the early evening progressed it became clear that something else was going on. Improvements in the forecast did not lead us to feel better about staying on as planned. Finally, I called Susan to get her input. After talking briefly with me and with Mike, Susan said, "You two are supposed to be in West Grove tomorrow." This had the ring of truth, and we immediately began preparations to leave that night. We packed, ate a simple dinner, and set out for Snow Camp about 8 p.m.

As soon as we left our host's driveway, Mike said that he felt as if a great load had been lifted from him. I felt the same. Although the trip was somewhat more exciting than usual, with snow falling all through our trip across the mountains toward Asheville, it seemed to us both that we had made the right decision. About 1:45 a.m., we pulled into Snow Camp and I gratefully fell into bed.

The next morning I approached Eric Ginsberg, the clerk of West Grove meeting, and explained that Mike and I were present "by surprise" that morning—but that here was my certificate, just in case. As it turns out, I was active in the vocal ministry during worship, and Eric did endorse my certificate.

My final journey in the ministry in that Second Month was to attend a Prophetic Ministry Retreat sponsored by the School of the Spirit at the Sisters of St. Francis retreat center near Philadelphia. There were almost fifty participants, including several faces there I was especially glad to see. The highlight of the evening was the opportunity to eat dinner with

Exercises in the Gospel Ministry

Bill and Fran Taber. They seemed to be in as good shape and good humor as ever, though Bill had had some recent medical problems.

In the opening session, we were asked to introduce ourselves with a short statement of the ministry to which we were each called. There were a lot of "ministry of prayer" and "ministry of manifesting the love of Christ" sorts of statements, but when it came round to me I said I was called to nurture, sustain, and articulate a particular strand of the Quaker tapestry, that of classic Quakerism. From somewhere behind me I heard a sotto voce "Amen!" from Bill Taber.

Bill gave a talk the next morning on the motions of prophetic ministry. His leaping-off point was a quotation from Howard Brinton that all Quaker ministry is prophetic because it all stems from the immediate guidance of the Holy Spirit. Bill made it clear that being in constant touch with the Living Stream is required for prophetic ministry. He named ten specific motions of prophetic ministry:

1. Being in touch with and radiating from the Living Stream
2. Being moved to change lifestyle and/or occupation
3. Being moved to pray for or to speak to specific persons
4. Being moved to seek opportunities
5. Being moved to speak in meeting for worship
6. Speaking prophetically in meetings for business or committee meetings
7. Being moved to set up workshops, retreats, or give public talks
8. Offering prophetic witness and testimony—individual and corporate
9. Being drawn to witness to someone in authority
10. Being called to a specific project of research or writing

One afternoon, Marty Grundy and I had a good conversation about whether my own ministry was prophetic. I started out saying no, but Marty had some excellent insights I hadn't recognized. My point was that I did not actually critique what existed—my message was not to say "That's not it" or the equivalent. Marty's point was that when I described classic Quakerism as the "city on the hill," the implication that contemporary Quakerism was not that was clearly and broadly understood.

Later that afternoon, I had an opportunity with Bill Taber. After some time to center down, Bill said that his immediate impression was of great firmness, the sort of thing that would enable one to perform intricate work—threading a needle—in the midst of a windstorm. I shared with him the feedback from the California trip. Friends there saw me as able to hear where my questioners were spiritually and answer their questions sensitively while being firm about my own beliefs and my sense of where Truth lies.

Bill went on to say that he greatly appreciated my expression of my call (to nurture, sustain, and articulate classic Quakerism) the previous night. This was very meaningful to me. If Bill Taber approved of my work, I felt, then I was on solid ground. After the opportunity ended, I went outside to walk the labyrinth on the retreat grounds. I walked the entire way looking straight down at the toes of my shoes, trusting that if I stayed in the path each moment I would arrive at the destination safely.

Memorial Day 2004 seemed especially poignant given that soldiers, resistance forces, and civilians were dying daily in Afghanistan and Iraq. It was increasingly clear that events had not proceeded as forecast by the administration and that US soldiers would be in Iraq—and in mortal danger—for an indefinite period of time. Some news reports were speculating on a tenure as long as five years.

NCYM(C) sessions met in Seventh Month as usual. There were almost fifty Friends present for the Ministry and Oversight business meeting—the highest I could ever remember. I stepped down as clerk, and the body was "enthusiastic" (the word used in the minutes) in its approval of Charlie Ansell as the new clerk. My sense was that I had done good work in my time as clerk. The group had a revived sense of purpose and was meeting more frequently than in previous years. We had engaged important issues facing the yearly meeting and had been proactive in developing activities to address them.

Later in Seventh Month, I attended Iowa Yearly Meeting (Conservative) sessions at Scattergood School in West Branch to deliver a plenary address. The first morning, Callie Marsh and I decided to spend the time before breakfast in worship in the meeting house. Soon after we settled, I felt the presence of many spirits questioning and to some extent challenging my presence there. It seemed to me that these were the spirits of Friends who had nurtured and sustained this faith community over many decades and that they were concerned that I might be a troublemaker of some sort. I reassured them that this was not so—I came as a friend, to share the gospel message that they also loved. Getting down on my knees, I bowed my head and let them search out my heart. After a short time, I felt that they were reassured and accepted my presence. Our worship continued without further interruption until the bell for breakfast rang.

After breakfast, we returned to the meeting house for Bible study led by Marshall Massey. We explored the passage in Acts 16:11–40 and at one point began discussing the spirit that possessed the slave girl. One Friend asked if we believed in spirits in the present day, and I volunteered that I had felt spirits in the meeting house that very morning, without giving any further details. "Oh, yes!" said Callie, "They made the building creak!"

I attended the Ministry and Counsel meeting one afternoon. When Friends had gathered, I explained I was following an old custom of traveling ministers when their journey took them near a select meeting, and Friends were easy with my presence. I could not help noticing that of the fifteen persons present (other than myself), fourteen were women and only one was a man, my old friend Wilmer Tjossem. They read the State of the Meeting reports from each monthly meeting; I got the impression of a younger body, chronologically, given the number of reports of Young Friends concerns, weddings, and births, than was the case in North Carolina (Conservative).

One afternoon I had an extended "sit" in the courtyard area outside of Central Hall in open worship and contemplation. I did try to be listening for any guidance related to my presence there at Iowa Yearly Meeting (Conservative), but otherwise my thoughts were undirected. It felt like time well spent, and I felt that Susan would approve. She feels that I do not spend enough time in contemplation, and in truth I do not devote as much time to that as she does. I do try, however, to be listening at other times. On that day, however, I felt that she would be content.

At dinner, I took a place at an empty table, as was my custom. I was soon joined by five very pleasant and agreeable Friends. As we finished our meal, one Friend asked me to discuss the concept of gospel order as she had been reading my essays and did not want to lose the opportunity to discuss them with the author. This seemed agreeable to the others, so I briefly outlined the primary concepts of gospel order, showing how all our testimonies spring from this fundamental understanding of the relationship between Creator and creation. This led to an extended discussion of topics such as being born again and our understanding of Christ. Several of the topics I planned to touch on in my First Day talk were discussed with great interest. This led me to be less worried about my First Day intentions.

Bible study the following morning considered the eighth chapter of Romans and was very rich. This chapter includes the statement about nothing being able to separate us from the love of God, and thus yet another idea for my draft text for First Day had come up ahead of time in the regular course of events.

I took a little while to peruse Scattergood's William Penn Room, which houses the older and rarer books in the local collection. I ended up spending considerable time reading in John Wilbur's *Narrative and Exposition*, which details, from the Wilburite perspective, the events leading up to the charges against the author, his exoneration by South Kingston Meeting, and the action by the quarterly meeting of laying down South Kingston Meeting and transferring all members to Greenwich Monthly Meeting. Even allowing for some bias in the recounting of the events, the yearly meeting's various actions did seem outrageous, but both sides seemed to be acting more like canon lawyers than like Friends seeking a deeper understanding of Truth.

One morning I was certain that Marshall Massey was going to pick a passage out of the Old Testament for Bible study, so certain that I left my complete Bible behind and brought only the Tanakh. I was correct in my feeling. Marshall was a good leader for the Bible studies; he chose passages with deep meaning and allowed us to wrestle with them in our

Exercises in the Gospel Ministry

own way, not imposing his own reading on the rest of us. I am not sure I could have done as well or chosen as appropriately.

I was active in the ministry during one morning meeting for worship, taking as my starting point the statement "This may be my last time to attend this yearly meeting," which I'd been hearing in NCYM(C) from numerous older Friends over the years. The thrust of my remarks was to remind Friends that we don't have any promises about next year, next month, or next week—all we are given is this moment, and all we can do is strive to be faithful in this moment.

In meeting for business, we heard an extract from the annual report by Deborah Fisch, the yearly meeting clerk, to her oversight committee ("anchor committee," as it is called there) that drove the gathered body into the deepest worship of these sessions. The extract included an account of her prophetic ministry at the Traveling Ministries Program retreat that spring in which she had recounted the parable about the unfruitful tree given one more year to produce. The true evidence of the baptizing power of the Holy Spirit was plainly and powerfully present. I was brought to my knees in thanksgiving and supplication on behalf of the gathered body.

Iowa Friends offered some of the duplicates in their collection to the Rich Square Monthly Meeting library, so I began working through three boxes of duplicates to compare titles with the Rich Square collection. I ended up selecting nine or ten hardcover editions and about half a dozen pamphlets. The most important addition was an 1806 edition of Clarkson's two-volume *Portraiture of Quakerism*. I suggested that Rich Square Monthly Meeting might be moved to make a donation to the Archives Committee of Iowa Yearly Meeting (Conservative) for the repair and preservation of their collection, which was immediately acceptable.

At their request, I had dinner one night with the Friends of Yahara Preparative Meeting along with Larry and Callie Marsh, who were on the care committee for Yahara from West Branch Monthly Meeting, and Deborah Fisch, yearly meeting clerk. Yahara Friends wanted to discuss right order in their relationship with West Branch and with the yearly meeting. I recommended that they should probably not be communicating with the yearly meeting or yearly meeting committees directly but should route their communications and concerns through the West Branch Monthly Meeting. This they were glad to promise to do. Larry and Callie stated their intention to labor with the monthly meeting clerk to see that the overall relationships between the three levels of meetings were given more attention and handled both speedily and properly.

The other matter on which we spent much time and attention was the recognition of spiritual gifts. Yahara Friends, or at least those who were present, apparently felt that one of their number had a calling and a gift for prison ministry, and they were looking for the right way to recognize that gift and to call out its development and exercise. The last recorded minister in Iowa Yearly Meeting (Conservative) had died about a decade earlier; although the mechanism for recording spiritual gifts was still in the *Discipline*, there appeared to be a tacit agreement among the generation of Friends now in their seventies and eighties that no minister was to be recorded or elder appointed. I talked to Yahara Friends about the meaning of and reasons behind recognizing spiritual gifts and laid out the procedure that would be followed in my own yearly meeting. Deborah said that procedure would be appropriate in their yearly meeting, and the West Branch Friends present agreed that their monthly meeting would also follow that procedure.

I was interested to see that the recorder reported a total of 565 members in the yearly meeting, including active and inactive, resident and nonresident, etc. The approved yearly meeting budget included $49,000 raised by apportionment from the monthly meetings, which worked out to just under $87 per member. I didn't know the exact figures for NCYM(C), but I knew we were paying much less per member to the yearly meeting. From about the same number of individual members, our total amount raised from monthly meetings was only about $19,000. The largest item in the Iowa budget was a donation of $31,500 to Scattergood School. We had no item of comparable size in our budget; we supported four Friends schools but only for about $4,000 total.

When it came time for me to speak on First Day, Callie Marsh introduced me as her friend rather than repeating my résumé, which suited me exactly. I felt my presentation was faithful; I used my printed text for reference to make sure I didn't leave anything out and to help me express nuanced ideas precisely but spent a fair amount of time looking away from the text toward the audience. After I finished, audience questions filled up the rest of the time available. I felt the questions were very good, addressing important issues and not at all defensive. Callie gave away the dozen copies of the NCYM(C) *Discipline* I had given her and said she could have given away ten more.

After a short break, we settled into meeting for worship. Although they made a specific effort to set up a facing bench, Friends then failed to sit in it! I thought the empty facing bench was a stark symbol of Iowa Yearly Meeting (Conservative), which has tacitly refused to record the gifts of vocal ministry or eldering for many, many years.

In Ninth Month 2004, I attended a Methodist church service while visiting my mother in Maryland. The worship service that morning included "the sacrament of baptism" for two young children, a girl and her younger brother. If they weren't poster children for adult baptism, I don't know what would be. The young boy—maybe six or seven—acted as if he had absolutely no idea what was going on. He was not disobedient or protesting, but his attention and body wandered from place to place, and it was clear he did not understand the meaning or importance of the event at all. His older sister was actively resistant to the whole affair, refusing to approach either the communion rail or the baptismal font just behind it. Her father finally had to pick her up and carry her forward as she clung to him desperately with her hands, feet, and head turned away from events and voicing her desire not to participate. I was frankly embarrassed for the parents.

Surely, if Christian baptism means anything other than a magical "cleansing" of some sort, it involves the willing commitment of the individual being baptized to God through Christ. How can these parents believe their children, one of whom didn't know what was transpiring and the other of whom was actively resisting it, would be spiritually better off than they were before? It seemed to me that nothing of spiritual significance happened during the ceremony that morning. I understand that for some Christians outward baptism with water carries a deep significance, and although I don't share that view I will not say it is not true for them. It is harder, though, for me to feel that significance applies when the individuals being baptized are not themselves able or willing to open themselves to that spiritual significance and the commitment it implies.

In Eleventh Month 2004, I began to have a serious headache every day, and my primary care doctor prescribed an MRI to try to discover the cause. One outcome was the discovery of a brain tumor. It turned out to be benign and quite old, the calcified fossil of an unknown illness cured perhaps thirty years previously. This potentially fatal illness had been turned away when I was not even aware that it was threatening me. God truly cares for us and protects us more than we can possibly know.

Reading and reflecting on Doug Gwyn's *Seekers Found: Atonement in Early Quaker Experience* spurred my own wrestling with atonement and how atonement in the early Quakers' experience compared with my own personal experience. I could affirm much of what he described, but one passage seemed particularly powerful:

> This stance implied a Copernican revolution regarding the usual understanding of atonement in Christ. No human reading of Scripture or reflection upon Jesus' death on the cross could communicate its saving power to the soul. It must be known within, through the individual's own death to self and the raising of Christ the seed within. . . . Early Friends thus argued that there could be no **justification** by Christ's death on the cross without **sanctification**, the mystery of the individual's own death to self-interest and new life for others. . . . But the apocalyptic horizon of the early Quaker understanding of atonement made it a drama of reconstruction not only between the individual and God but throughout the entire social and natural order of creation.[20]

The Quaker experience of atonement is a Copernican shift—a change in the location of the central work of atonement itself. Most Christian understandings of atonement make God the central actor and describe humankind as unable to leave its sinful state. God does the heavy lifting and the individual needs only to give intellectual assent. Even Abelard's moral influence approach involves God doing the hard work of incarnation, suffering, and death while we observe and learn from the example. The Quaker experience (and mine) has been that the work of atonement happens inside the individual as God enables and equips each person to live a new, sanctified life and model that life in our relations with all of creation, especially within our own meeting communities.

Bill Taber died on Fourth Month 15, 2005. He had been fighting cancer and I knew it had metastasized, so his death was not a total surprise to me, but death is a shock even when expected. He and George Parker had been my role models as Conservative Quaker men; they seemed to me, more than anyone else, to embody what it meant to be a man deeply steeped in our peculiar faith tradition. Not only what they said but their every behavior demonstrated how our faith is lived. Now Bill was gone from this life; George, now ninety-two, would remain for a little while.

Over the years, I have felt the spirit of Bill Taber very much with me and on my heart at particular times. I have much gratitude for the deep guidance he gave me, often with few words, and for his clear example of an impeccable life—the embodiment of a Quaker man in the classic tradition. He taught me to feel into that spiritual space that is all around us yet not in the physical dimensions known to science and to feel the presence of those who have gone before. My mother had some of this gift, and I feel she passed it to me, but Bill affirmed this and showed me how it applies to the Quaker life.

Bill had been present to me most strongly and movingly in person, but his impact through his written work had also been important to me and to many other Friends. His reintroduction of Samuel Bownas to contemporary Friends through his editing of a new edition of *A Description of the Qualifications Necessary to a Gospel Minister* had had a widespread and deep impression on Friends in the unprogrammed branches of Quakerism.

My first exposure to Samuel Bownas's *Journal* was a loose-leaf photocopy of an 1847 edition gifted to me by Rachel Ruth of New York Yearly Meeting in the early 1980s. She had found a copy in the yearly meeting archives and made copies for herself, me, and one or two others.

It was hard to read due to the old font and poor-quality images, but I was fascinated by Bownas's insights. To have Bill Taber's new edition, which had more contemporary language and was easier to read, was a gift in itself. I recall Louise Wilson telling me at yearly meeting sessions in 2004 that she was rereading the book. She had been a recorded minister for over fifty years at that point.

Bownas said that he was writing out of his own experience. Reading him, I have felt continuously that he was speaking directly to and about my own experience. It seemed to me that the call into ministry is the same call now as it has ever been and that the necessary qualifications and the pitfalls are also still the same. Two changes are that there seem to be fewer Friends called into the ministry per capita now than in earlier generations and there are fewer extended journeys in the ministry. The fewer extended journeys may reflect that we live different personal lives now and have very different occupations. I also wonder whether there are really fewer people called nowadays or just fewer people saying yes to the call. The book was of personal value to me in confirming the authenticity of my call into the gospel ministry (as there has often been little guidance to be found among contemporary Friends); giving personal guidance about a minister's deportment and behavior; serving as a benchmark against which to evaluate my own progress (or lack of it) in the ministry, beginning as an infant minister; and offering a resource to be shared with others who were also experiencing a call into the public ministry.

The very next month, George Parker and his sister, Esther Wethington, died. We spent most of a day cleaning up the meeting house and lunchroom in preparation for two memorial services in two days. We powerwashed the siding, cleaned the interior, scrubbed the bathrooms, and more. I felt that our work was really a gesture of respect for George and Esther rather than trying to look good for our visitors; other Friends agreed.

The day of George Parker's burial and memorial meeting was very full. There were nearly sixty Parkers present, and several of them spoke, including John Parker, who shared his father's love for the passage from Micah 6:8. Bob Gosney was eloquent in his opening prayer and closing comments. Near the end of the worship, I mentioned that an early Friend had been described as being "stiff as a tree and clear as a bell." George Parker had been as firm, strong, and stable as a great oak tree, and his ministry, his witness, and his many activities on behalf of others had been as clear as a bell regarding their source and inspiration.

We went from the family cemetery to the meeting house and lunchroom, making sure the caterer had everything she needed for the lunch and enlisting several of the Parker grandchildren to help move two benches back into the meeting room from the library, where they had been located in recent years. We added some folding chairs at the end of some benches, and the funeral home added another row along the back of the meeting house. All in all, we had seating for 206 persons, and they were all occupied except a very few.

Once again, Bob Gosney was eloquent in his welcome and explanation of Quaker worship. Shortly after he finished, I rose and read Psalm 46, which had been George Parker's special request for this occasion. All of George's children spoke fondly and lovingly of their father, as did his wife, Lib Parker. Louise Wilson rose in a centering prayer, and Bob closed the meeting shortly after she finished.

When the memorial service was over, Susan made coffee and heated water for tea, and we invited Friends who had come from a distance to the lunchroom for light refreshments and fellowship. This was a blessed time. I was tired at the end of the day but felt I had been useful in the Lord's service.

I attended yearly meeting sessions in Seventh Month 2005. The powerful experience of the opening worship elicited these reflections:

> This is holy ground—not by force of ritual or institutional authority but by the power of hearts turned inwardly and corporately toward God. Here is the eternal Presence of God made manifest. This is the sanctuary of the Most High—where we are prepared, guided, and strengthened for the service God desires of us as God's people. Let our demeanor and behavior be consonant with this holy space we now inhabit. Set aside all preconceptions and expectations about what could or might happen—this is the eternal moment, when God's Will is the only rule.

Memoir of the Life and Religious Labors of Lloyd Lee Wilson

Some time after yearly meeting, Jan Hoffman of New England Yearly Meeting told me she had accidentally knocked a copy of Howard Brinton's 1931 Swarthmore Lecture, *Creative Worship*, off its shelf in a Quaker library.[21] When she bent to pick it up, it was open to a sentence that looked familiar. It turned out to be almost identical to a sentence in our NCYM(C) *Discipline*. Jan was inquiring why this might be so. When I found a copy of Brinton's lecture in a library at Earlham sometime later, it seemed like a good opportunity to photocopy the sentence in question, if I could find it, for comparison to our *Discipline*'s "Group Worship" section.

I did find it and noticed another sentence that also looked familiar. I reviewed the lecture systematically, comparing it to our 1983 *Discipline*. It became apparent that everything in that section of our *Discipline* after the first paragraph had been lifted from Brinton's lecture. Words or phrases were occasionally changed, but at other times entire sentences or groups of sentences were lifted from the lecture and placed in the *Discipline*. There was no attribution to Brinton.

The sentence Jan alerted me to had first appeared in a 1969 draft revision of the *Discipline*. Brinton died in 1973, so conceivably he could have given permission to use his words, but there was no indication of this in the *Discipline* itself. The wording had been changed enough so that the section was not an exact quotation. Would Brinton have given permission for an unattributed paraphrase? I doubted he would have. To my academically sensitive mind, this appeared to be intentional plagiarism.

It was hard to describe my emotions. I didn't disagree with the meaning of the words—and, as Richard Rohr says, the question is "Is this truth?" not "Who said this?" The problem was in the plagiarism itself, which in its extent and the revisions made almost persuaded me it was deliberate. What else in the *Discipline* had been plagiarized from some as yet undiscovered source? Where was our integrity?

This incident led me to search our yearly meeting minutes for information about the process for revising the *Discipline*. I started with the decision in 1966 to start the process of revising the then current *Discipline* (published in 1950). To my surprise, the process seemed to

Exercises in the Gospel Ministry

extend unbroken from Eighth Month 1966 to Fourth Month 1984. There seemed to be no time in that nearly eighteen-year period when there was not a revision committee actively at work. Proposed new disciplines in 1969 and 1970 never received full approval, and I couldn't find a minute of approval for the full 1983 *Discipline* either—only for the Queries.

This highlighted the large and extended expenditure of time and energy that would be required to revise any yearly meeting's discipline. This was true not just for our yearly meeting; the recent process in New York Yearly Meeting had taken fourteen years to complete. It seemed to me that such an effort would take vital energy and attention away from matters that might be more important for the yearly meeting. The process itself could be divisive, as during the last NCYM(C) revision when different monthly meetings were answering different sets of queries and reporting their answers to the yearly meeting.

The current *Discipline* was deeply flawed. There was the matter of the extensive borrowings from Howard Brinton and the various places quarterly meetings were mentioned even when there were no longer any quarterly meetings, to name just two areas of concern. However, I feared that an effort to "improve" the *Discipline* at that time would create more problems than it resolved and would distract us from the work God would have us be about. For the time being, I did nothing.

Other encounters with the writings of Friends were more nurturing. One of the benefits of reading the journals of earlier generations of Friends is realizing that they shared the same spiritual insights that we experience in the present day. An example is this passage from eighteenth-century Friend Sarah Grubb:

> 'Blessed is that servant that watcheth, and keepeth his garment, and who, when his Lord cometh, is found ready.' It appeared to my mind that all those who have enlisted under the spiritual, unconquered Captain, have received a mark thereof, a change of heart, an awful covering of spirit, a loving one another, and means whereby such might stand in readiness for the word of command; and that therefore the peculiar blessing of the divine hand rests upon these faithful servants, who when not actually in service, so remember their office, as to be fit, when called

thereto, to step into it, and move only in that raiment, and with that armour, which the Master gives them.[22]

Grubb seems to capture the sense of having received the second call into the ministry and of responding faithfully not by always doing but by so living that one is always prepared when the leading comes. There is a spiritual mark and there is a change of heart, and thank God there is a means by which we may stand in readiness for the word of command.

Work as a college registrar was ordinarily routine, but one semester a matter of integrity arose that nearly cost me my job. One of my tasks was to report to a nationwide database how many students were enrolled at the end of the last day students were allowed to add classes for the semester. This semester's report showed 797 students enrolled on that day. The president directed me to change the report to show 800 students enrolled because it made a better news story to have 800 students rather than almost 800. I tried to make it clear to the college provost how this request conflicted with the ethical principles I taught students in my accounting class. The president insisted I change the report.

The crisis was resolved when I prepared a report that showed 800 students but took my name off the report and removed any source; it became unattributed data. I used the correct census figures in all my reports and other work, both internally and to national agencies and databases. The provost later confided how close the president had come to firing me over this issue; I confided to him I preferred losing my job to losing my integrity.

One evening, I started reading *Memoirs of Martha Routh*.[23] Routh was an eighteenth-century British Friend. Within a few pages, two incidents in her life reminded me that divine instruction is to be found everywhere if the mind and heart are open to receive it.

The house that Martha Routh's family occupied while she was a child abutted an inn of good reputation that was frequented by Friends and others. One night a military officer began to argue with other customers and decided to "take it outside," where the argument might be settled by force of arms. The proprietor of the inn was not present, and his wife fainted dead away. A crowd gathered to watch the fight. Martha's mother became aware of what was going on in back of her house and made her way to the center of the crowd. As the officer drew his sword and raised it to the sky, the brave woman simply took it out of his hand and returned to her house; apparently everyone was too stunned to take any action to restrain her. She returned to report that the sword was now safely locked away until the next morning, when the officer was invited to come to retrieve it—which he did, with some appreciation of the ill that had been prevented by the fearless action of Martha's mother.

The second incident concerned Martha's reaction to her call into the ministry. She understood that one step in this process was to change certain habits of clothing, even though she was considered proper by Friends and no one had criticized her current practice. After some inner struggle, she complied with this guidance and found considerable comfort (and even joy) in doing so. This has been my own experience with dress; each successive change has been a matter of specific guidance and not a negative judgment on either what I had been wearing previously or on what other Friends wear. The dominant Christian culture has so ingrained the idea of a judgmental God—judgment in the sense of condemnation—that the idea of a guiding God, who leads each of us in the paths most beneficial to our spiritual growth, is almost entirely foreign to us all.

After dinner one Christmas Eve, I retired to the front hall to meditate on the Christmas season and our tree. I thought about the vast changes between the daily lives of my grandparents, parents, myself, and Asa. After a while, I shared these reflections with Asa, who had joined me in my "tree meditation." I also took the opportunity to share with Asa how much I valued and honored the start he had made in life and his prospects for the future.

Another part of my meditations was the extent that the Christmas story of Jesus, Mary, Joseph, and the others could be excised without significantly affecting my Christian faith. Not only was the question of the virgin birth/immaculate conception/perpetual virginity immaterial to me; the entire story was secondary. It seemed to me that Jesus took on the divine project at the time of his baptism, when the dove descended and words were heard claiming him as God's own. I am thus an adoptionist, a view that has officially been considered heretical for the past seventeen centuries.

My biblical studies through Earlham School of Religion have made me aware of many different threads of belief that made up the early church and of many different beliefs that were held as orthodox by serious Christians in those first few centuries. My awareness was only deepened by doing some New Testament exegesis and seeing how varied the witnesses were that made up the "received canon" of the Bible. These experiences have made me more comfortable in accepting and admitting (confessing?) heterodox beliefs of my own—including an adoptionist Christology.

This is not equivalent to saying that any belief is acceptable. There are some strands of thought and belief that seem to me acceptable and some that are not. At present, I do not have a good rubric for identifying and separating the one from the other. Perhaps there is none—perhaps there is only a gestalt in which some beliefs can participate and some cannot. I have more work to do.

As I was working at home one morning in 2006, I looked out the window and saw an older couple walking toward the front door. They introduced themselves as fellow Woodland residents who wanted to talk to me (or whoever opened the door) about a verse of Scripture. I invited them inside, and we had a friendly discussion in the front parlor.

My visitors' text was Romans 16:20, which is about God putting Satan under the feet of those to whom Paul was writing. That served as a springboard to many other topics, and we had a lively discussion of the immediate and perceptible guidance of the Holy Spirit, whether the world and all its governments were under the control of Satan, the role and authority of Scripture in the lives of Christians, and more. I was able to witness to the Truth as understood by Friends and invited the couple to attend worship and/or discussion times at the meeting house. They may have been Seventh-day Adventists, though they never said so; in any event, they pronounced themselves satisfied and we parted on good terms.

Exercises in the Gospel Ministry

During a discussion of membership at Virginia Beach recently, Louise Wilson spoke movingly, using some very mystical terminology. I reflected that the Conservative spiritual path, if followed with integrity, often brings devout Friends to such a place—Bill Taber comes to mind—but that the vocabulary used is apt to be misunderstood by those who haven't done similar work. What is happening, it seems to me, is that while the vocabulary of these seasoned Conservatives appears to have come full circle; their spiritual growth has moved them vertically so that they actually describe an ascending spiral, as one might move up a spiral ramp or staircase. Louise's speaking of Christ everywhere was not the starting point but the fruit of her many decades of faithfulness.

I had been thinking about the possibility of starting a blog since the previous yearly meeting sessions. It seemed like a way to utilize new technology to reach new inquirers with information about Quakerism and to provide regular content to Friends and attenders who felt an affinity for Conservative Friends. Way has never felt entirely clear, so I haven't taken action, but the idea has never really gone away.

Now the balance tipped away from starting a blog to the point that I could lay the idea down. Part of the attraction of blogging is its immediacy: it allows authors to record their thoughts on a subject very quickly, responding to personal insights or external events while they are fresh. One blogger described her blog as a "rough draft" of her thoughts and ideas. Those immediate reactions and rough-draft comments have an indefinite half-life in cyberspace, and that half-life was getting longer with the advent of web archiving technology.

I was not easy with thinking of a blog as a rough draft and did not feel that I could generate final-draft material frequently enough to justify the blog format. It bothered me that an item of lesser quality, one that I might later wish had never been made public in that form, might through the medium of a blog be launched beyond my ability to correct or explain. A large part of my motivation for studying at Earlham School of Religion had been to prevent misleading people through my writing or vocal ministry; I didn't want to undo that effort by releasing into cyberspace material that had not been properly seasoned.

It also seemed to me that, because of its potentially wide readership, blogging is a form of publishing, so that by blogging I would in effect be sidestepping the practice of accountability that I had tried to build up around my publications. Both for my personal spiritual well-being and because I am a public Friend closely identified with my yearly meeting, I don't want to lose this accountability or to give the impression to others, by my example, that it is not important.

Later in 2006, Susan and I made a gospel ministry visit to Gwinnett Preparative Meeting in Norcross, Georgia. They were a small group, separated by choice from the much larger Atlanta monthly meeting nearby on theological grounds; they wanted a clearer Christian witness in their worship. Susan and I were able to be witnesses to a Conservative Quaker faith that is neither the same as FGC nor too closely related to the more common, but more judgmental, orthodox Christianity. While holding close to Christ, I also spoke of the need to be loving toward the non-Christians in our meetings and used myself as a case in point. Had Friends not been willing to accept me as a non-Christian when I first came to Quakerism, I would not be among them now as a devout Christian.

We met for several hours on Seventh Day afternoon, breaking for a potluck dinner and lingering over our meal for more discussion. We gathered for worship near 10 a.m. on First Day, and remained for well over an hour at the rise of meeting for more discussion. Some Friends had read one or both of my books and put questions to me that showed they had been thinking about what they had read. Others were still struggling with their previous church affiliations, especially with Roman Catholicism. Susan was able to be particularly helpful to these persons, speaking of her own experience of what Catholicism has to offer and where it falls short of Quaker sensibilities.

About four of the Gwinnett Friends expressed a definite interest in attending our yearly meeting sessions, which we encouraged. The clerk was thinking about affiliation with our yearly meeting, but all agreed that was premature. There was a dual-affiliation question that would have to be resolved as Gwinnett was already affiliated with Southern Appalachian Yearly Meeting and Association through Atlanta Monthly

Exercises in the Gospel Ministry

Meeting. I wasn't sure that Gwinnett Friends were yet ready to sever their ties with Atlanta, although some of the comments offered that weekend led me to conclude that was not inconceivable. All in all, it seemed right for us to have visited them.

On a whim, Susan and I bought tickets for a Durham concert by George Thorogood and the Destroyers, our long-time favorite roadhouse blues/rock band. It was a great concert. The band was on top of its game, and we even had seats (unlike the last time we'd heard them live, when we'd had to stand for the whole time). This was an unusual activity for me, and in the time between getting the tickets and the concert itself, I did some reflecting on my growing reluctance to be social even though I usually had a good time when I did get out and mingle. I called it my "hermit nature" and on one level took it lightly, but on another I took it very seriously and wondered if my desire to be reclusive was a harbinger of some deeper psychological imbalance. Would it continue to grow as the years went by? I would much rather, even now, be at home and go through my mundane routines than get out and mingle with other than a very few friends.

The one exception to this is my work/ministry/service with Friends. Susan has said for years that I appear to be a different person when I'm in a Quaker setting, whether our own yearly meeting sessions or with some other Quaker group. This continues to be the case, and I don't feel the slightest hesitation about breaking up my routines to go way out of my way to be with Quakers (provided, of course, the discernment committee gives its approval). While with Friends, I am often open, vulnerable, social, and sharing. I come away from these times feeling emotionally wrung out and physically worn out, but it always feels great at the time and worthwhile afterward.

Perhaps related to this is my sense that there is an emotional analogue to my travels away from Woodland. It feels as if I am climbing out of a deep place whenever I leave Woodland on a journey, and the farther the trip the higher the elevation to which I must climb. The return trip is a welcome descent from these heights to my familiar badger hole.

One trip I found easy to make was to watch Asa's team compete in the 2006 Ultimate Frisbee National Championships in Columbus, Ohio. I took the opportunity to attend the entire tournament and enjoyed myself thoroughly, both as a proud papa and as a fan of the athleticism and spontaneous movement of the game. It closely resembles the flow of soccer, the "beautiful game" I enjoyed playing so much in my younger days.

On the trip, I read in Mary Capper's *Memoir*[24] and reflected on the sentiment that "unchurched" people who live "moral lives" are just as good, beloved by God, and bound for heaven as devout Christians (or any other religious group). This raised three issues in my mind:

- How do "unchurched" people determine what is "good"? By what standard? If not by divine revelation, mediated or unmediated, are they not constantly at risk of being misled?
- The great purpose of human life is not to be moral but to be in relationship to God. Nor do we act morally in order to be justified to God—being in love with God is our inspiration, guidance, and empowerment to live the moral life.
- Heaven is not some later reward for good behavior in this life; it is a state of being in right relationship with our Creator, who loves us. That relationship can begin this very moment and last forever!

In another place, Mary Capper reflects on the importance of resignation to the divine will, even in intercessory prayer. I had a similar reluctance to petition in prayer, though it was somewhat easier to intercede on behalf of others than to pray "for myself." "Resignation is our lesson"—but are we to be resigned to injustice and oppression? To all the evil this world holds? Ought we fight against that evil and injustice or be resigned that evil will continue even as we strive to embody the Kingdom of God in this time and place? To be resigned is not to be inured to the pain and suffering of those around us but to keep our eyes on the prize.

During this time, I also finished my work for the yearly meeting of reviewing the historical Quaker use of "overseer" terminology and forwarded it to the clerks of the yearly meeting and the yearly meeting of MEO for their use. My search of the Digital Quaker Collection pretty much confirmed my previous sense that Friends have used this term from their earliest days, based apparently on Acts 20:28: *Take heed therefore unto yourselves, and to all the flock, over the which the Holy Ghost hath made you overseers, to feed the church of God* (KJV). When the term began to be applied to the plantation supervisors of chattel slaves, Friends used the same word for both applications, depending on the context to make the meaning clear. I see no reason why Friends cannot continue the same practice.

Feeling out the topic that became my address on holy surrender to the 2006 New England Yearly Meeting sessions led to reflections on our unwillingness to be vulnerable to God. That sensibility that balks at holy surrender is the one that still believes that I can do it myself—that I have the innate ability to live successfully on my own terms. There is a certain outward success that is attainable in this way, but it is hollow, like the great beech tree that stood on the campus green at Chowan University. One day it appeared tall and magnificent, the very picture of strength and permanence. That night there came a strong wind, and by noon the next day, when I made my usual post-lunch walk around the green, the workmen were sawing up the branches and hauling them away. For all its apparent strength, a ring less than three inches thick all around the circumference of the tree was sound wood. Inside that, the tree was completely hollow—not just rotted wood but wood that was completely gone. I could have sat in my favorite easy chair inside that stump without touching wood in any direction.

Preparing to speak at New England Yearly Meeting sessions proved to be a time of self-examination, of reflecting on how I might stand up to the counsel that was growing in me to be given to others. As was typical, I found much room for improvement. The way forward was to describe what we all aspire to and share the obstacles we find along the way.

Charlie Ansell and I visited New England Yearly Meeting sessions at Bryant University, Rhode Island, in Eighth Month 2006. On the first day, we attended the meetings of the yearly meeting's Ministry and Counsel Committee, which were burdened by deep and painful divisions among Friends. Thus far, all efforts to aid reconciliation had been fruitless, but prayer and outward efforts both continued.

We left the afternoon plenary worship after about an hour and sought out the hall where I would speak. The Friend who would be operating the sound system and recording equipment was present, so we did a sound check, I familiarized myself with the microphone, and we chose seats for Charlie and for Brian and Darcy Drayton to help me counter my natural stage-left shift when I speak. There was time to go over my text one last time; I made some minor changes.

After dinner, the four of us found an empty classroom and centered down. We decided on some logistical details, and I opened my spiritual condition to them pretty freely. After worship and vocal prayer, we walked over to the evening venue. I felt much supported by these Friends, and my anxieties about how my words would be received were relegated to their proper place; my words' reception was much less important than my being faithful. When it came time, I was able to "trust my stuff" and give myself fully to the delivery. It was a comfort to look over to Charlie and see his smiling face. His body seemed to take in what I had to say and literally inflate as I spoke. I finished strong and regained my seat with a solid feeling that I had discharged my obligation—that my labors were owned and accepted by my Master.

Only one message broke the silence afterward. An older Friend spoke of crossing the Pacific years ago on an empty oil tanker and feeling the different, strong ocean swells that said the ship was finally approaching the shore. He said he felt those swells in this room tonight and hoped they signified we were approaching a new land or the rediscovery of an old land that had been lost. Later feedback from others was very positive, from many simple thank-yous to a woman who asked a follow-up question and, to my simple "yes" in response, fell into my arms in tears.

New England Yearly Meeting had planned to offer a simultaneous Spanish translation of my talk. My old friend Betsy Cazden was the designated translator, and when we met beforehand I offered her a printout of my planned remarks. She said that she was confident that she could keep up by listening as I spoke, so I kept the printout myself. In the actual event, Betsy found that I spoke from the podium a good bit more

Exercises in the Gospel Ministry

quickly than she was used to hearing me in conversation, and not far into the lecture she simply gave up the effort to keep up. Oh, well . . .

I attended a gathering of all the recorded ministers in the yearly meeting who were present, which was seven people other than myself. The talk was mostly about how to nurture one another, including a number of recorded but inactive ministers. The desire was expressed that more Friends be recorded for their gifts, and several clear-cut possibilities were named. No clear way was seen for those already recorded to advocate for these Friends with potential.

At the yearly meeting sessions, I had a couple of remarkable conversations with friend and Friend John Kellam of Rhode Island. John recounted going to the local prison, before his World War II trial as a conscientious objector (CO), to inquire about the way prisoners were assigned to work details. He learned that prisoners were considered perfectly interchangeable—anyone could be assigned to any job. This played an important role in his experience later, after he was convicted on charges related to his pacifism and sentenced to that very prison. He refused to work in the prison shop on tasks to advance the war effort. That much was expected, but John went further and refused to do *any* work since he knew that doing anything would free another inmate to work in the shop supporting the war. This total refusal to work was new to the warden's experience.

John served twenty-two and a half months of his five-year prison term and then was released because the war had been over for fifteen months and the prisons were crowded. He had refused to apply for parole because that would have required him to say that he had been rehabilitated in prison and would do better now than he had done before being jailed. John felt he had not been rehabilitated and had no need of being rehabilitated; he felt certain he would continue to hold those beliefs dear that had gotten him imprisoned to begin with, though they might get stronger after his release.

When a guard told John he was to be released, John said that he would believe that when he saw the outside of the prison walls. A few days later, a couple of guards came to take John out of the hospital bed where he had been kept for the previous year to support the (prison's) illusion that he had not been working because he was sick. The guards put him in a wheelchair and took him to another room, where they took off his hospital gown and dressed him in a suit and overcoat. Then it was back into the wheelchair and to the prison gates. They didn't stop for paperwork or to process his release in any way.

Once outside, the guard told John he was free to leave. John replied that since he could now see the outside of the prison walls, he believed that was so. It was Eleventh Month. The guard said there was a train station in Lewisburg, Pennsylvania, the next town over, and that he had a train ticket in the suit pocket. John was free to get to Lewisburg any way he could and then to take the train home. The guard then said he was going to Lewisburg and would give John a ride if he wished. John accepted since he was offered the ride as a free man and not as a prisoner.

On the way, John and the guard began to talk about their families, and the guard revealed that his son was also a CO and was helping transport medical supplies along the Burma Road. John recalled an incident when this same guard had dragged a CO in the prison along the floor by his hair. This guard had also tried to move John by pulling at his arm, which had resulted only in pulling John to the floor since he refused to allow his feet to cooperate with any prison order or direction. John wondered aloud about how the guard, who had a CO son himself, could treat other COs that way.

The guard replied with his own story. He had been an orderly at Byberry Mental Hospital in Philadelphia for several years but had not been given a raise during that time. A job at the prison opened up, offering considerably more pay, so he took it. Almost from the first day, he realized he had made a mistake—but by that time the federal government had declared certain jobs essential to the war effort and employment in those jobs was frozen; no one in those jobs could quit, including prison guards.

After being told he couldn't quit, this prison guard went AWOL; he just left the prison and went back to Byberry, where he was hired back at his old job of hospital orderly. However, the prison officials found him and made him return to work at the prison.[25] He then tried to get fired,

Exercises in the Gospel Ministry

which was the cause of the incident John had reminded him about. The guard hoped that if he treated the prisoners poorly he would get fired. He discovered that no matter how poorly he behaved, he could not get fired because his supervisors realized what he was trying to do. He eventually relented and started treating the prisoners as well as he could, given the circumstances.

All this time, the guard had been as much a prisoner as John—but while John was a prisoner for conscience, the guard was a prisoner against his conscience. This was an example of the liberation theology insight that the oppressors are also themselves oppressed by an unjust system.[26]

One day that fall, I was walking back from my Chowan Bible class when a student from another class approached and asked to talk. He was both attracted and intimidated by my outward appearance but overcame his reluctance to ask some very good questions. We found a bench nearby on which to sit and spent over an hour together, him firing questions and me responding—though it seemed each response triggered another question even before I finished talking. What fun!

He raised several faith-related topics—doubt, inclusivity, rational proof—directly related to what he could observe of my Quaker life. A self-described atheist, he nevertheless expressed appreciation of the honesty and "fairness," as he put it, of the Quaker way. He did advise me strongly not to let the word get around that I would not use violence to defend myself against a robber. All this reminded me that we live our theology every day; it is not an abstract intellectual exercise. Those abstract exercises do exist, but theology gains real meaning in the way it is incarnated in our lives—the way it grows legs and walks around in our neighborhood.

Attending a Quaker funeral in Tenth Month sparked in me a period of internal reflection about death and the possible shape of eternal life, if there is such a thing. I'm not immortal. I've seen enough death, human and otherwise, to know that we die, that our bodily ego identity ceases to exist. We may be eternal, at least in part—I believe so—but we are not immortal. That's probably for the best. My eschatology, my vision of last things, doesn't have too much to do with there being an identifiable

Memoir of the Life and Religious Labors of Lloyd Lee Wilson

Lloyd Lee Wilson after death. It centers on the reign of God throughout creation. I don't believe in an endlessly turning wheel of life but in a more or less linear history proceeding from an unknown point of creation to an equally hazy but definitive end. Somewhere or sometime before the end, everything in creation will be returned to that harmony with God in which it was made and is intended to remain. My role as a believer is to live so that this great project is advanced, to act and speak so that my influence is toward a greater harmony with God everywhere. If I do, with the help and grace of God, then I am part of God's eternal Truth, and that is enough. If there is something that survives death and that remembers being Lloyd Lee Wilson (I think that may be the case), that's icing on the cake. Eternity is not something after death; it is a state of being that is available to us in this chronological life—a touch of kairos, perhaps. Anyway, death no longer scares me so much, and the idea of a heavenly life after death doesn't motivate me so much. Reaching a greater harmony with God in this present life, knowing and feeling the Life that infuses us as we move into that harmony—that is what I hunger and thirst for.

My theological studies at Earlham School of Religion encouraged sustained reflection on my personal faith. My interactions with students and faculty of the Chowan Department of Religion put me in daily contact with Christians who could clearly and concisely articulate the basis of their faith. What did I believe? Was there some religious or spiritual Truth on whose universal, ultimate validity my faith was constructed? Or did I believe that all such truths were relative and that my understanding of God was a happenstance of perspective and point of view—where and when I grew up, so to speak? Was I willing to say, "Yes, war is *never* the answer, and there *is* a loving God with whom one can have an I-Thou relationship"? In the vocabulary of epistemology, what did I know and how did I know it?

George Fox seemed to say that our deepest knowledge is experimental; we see Truth revealed and confirmed in our personal experience. My experience in life—spiritual, emotional, physical, intellectual—reveals the Truth of a divine Creator and Sustainer that is best expressed in the metaphor of the God of the Judeo-Christian tradition. I write this with some humility because there is much I do not understand, much that is paradoxical, much that remains mysterious, much that is claimed for that tradition that I cannot claim or endorse. But I know that this faith tradition, and especially the little Quaker corner over by the edge, is home.

At the same time, I recognize that there is Truth in the other great religious traditions—in all paths with heart. When we dig our own wells deeply, mine in Christianity and other folks in their own traditions, we find the same Living Water. How can we start with such differing assumptions and contradictory claims and yet strike the same Stream? This is paradoxical to the intellect, but I no longer see paradox as a problem.

When we study wisdom literature in my Bible classes at Chowan University, I get to share my favorite Jack Nicholson moment with my students, the one where God says to Job, "You want the truth [about why this is happening to you]? You can't handle the truth!" I love that moment in the movie![27] As finite humans, we can't grasp the entirety of the Truth of God or of God's ways. And yet, like Job, we can't give up the attempt. And although, like Job, we can't grasp the entirety, we can understand enough so that God shows up to talk with us.

I (with others) operate in a Christian gestalt that is deeply integrated and has great explanatory power. It is not the only possible gestalt, and the set of "true" gestalts is not limited to those that overlap heavily with the Christian one. We're too limited in our ability to understand the Divine. As I like to say, when we get to heaven *everyone* is going to be surprised—both those who expected a heaven and those who didn't. I claim Truth for the Christian gestalt, but it is not an exclusive Truth. There are other ways of approaching the Divine, other paths from which the view is much different.

Is this a gnostic, hidden, God-behind-God belief? I don't think so. The problem is not that God is hidden or hiding but that human beings are too limited to absorb all the ways that God is self-revealing (including those ways in which there appears to be no God at all). We're not alone. Each of the great faith traditions has utilized metaphor to express an understanding of the infinite reality in which we live and move and have our being.

I believe that behind the metaphors there is Truth, and that Truth is absolute for me. One piece of that Truth, for me, is that war is never the answer. I'm not willing to kill for that Truth, but I am willing to suffer for it and perhaps to die for it. Believing in an absolute Truth is not the same as saying that my faith is the only one that expresses the Truth. My understanding of that Truth binds me but not anyone else.

Christ is the metaphor by which I approach and try to understand the Truth, and I have much work to do. I am clear that Jesus Christ is the only path to God for me, and I am equally clear that the other great spiritual traditions are also authentic—that individuals committed to those paths are no more spiritually disadvantaged by their path than I am by mine.

My explorations of gospel order some fifteen years ago had some important implications related to our human attitudes and relationships to the rest of God's creation that slowly grew in my awareness as time passed. By 2006, these implications had risen to a place of importance in my mind. I journaled that "earthcare" issues were more important than almost anyone realized and that we all needed to be much more engaged in improving our behavior. At the same time, I didn't see anyone articulating a good Quaker *theological* position about this (which I realized might say more about my isolation than about the actual work being done), and I wondered how that would work out. An "earthcare witness" not founded on an articulated Truth would be a house built on sand.

Susan and I reflected on our own practices and tried to make changes that would reduce our ecological footprint and be fairer to our neighbors, but I wondered if it would be enough. What was clear was that it would be a lot easier to live simply if we had more money! Being rich means one has options; being poor means one has to do what one can.

Late in 2006, I was recruited to apply for the position of executive director of Pendle Hill. The process of discerning whether that would be a good fit for Pendle Hill and for Susan and me occupied much of what would have been "free time" over the next several months. One key question I asked myself was, Why would I want to be the executive director of Pendle Hill? I believed (as I had said often) that the teaching

Exercises in the Gospel Ministry

ministry was (and still is) the greatest challenge facing unprogrammed Friends. How do we teach the essentials, the root, of our faith tradition to newcomers in a way that is authentic, accessible, and relevant to the circumstances that shape our daily lives? Pendle Hill could be a large real-world laboratory for developing and implementing those teaching and learning techniques.

Susan and I spent a long time sitting in the silence with this development. It felt like liminal space, much like when I was recorded by Virginia Beach Friends. A door into new service was opening that I might or might not cross through, but I recognized the ways in which I had been prepared and equipped to begin that service.

Susan and I continued our exploration and discernment about the possible Pendle Hill position over the winter break and into Second Month. My interactions with Pendle Hill board members and staff seemed to go very well, both via conference calls and in person. I felt confident that the position would soon be offered to me and that I should accept it. However, after a couple of conflicting telephone calls from Pendle Hill board members, it became clear that another Friend had been chosen.

This left us with the question of why we had been put through this process and why we had felt so strongly that God was leading us to Pendle Hill when nothing came of it. Susan and I had done everything we could think of to be spiritually certain about this possibility, and the responses we had heard from other friends and Friends we consulted, as well as our own prayer life, seemed to point clearly and favorably in Pendle Hill's direction. Were we so mistaken in our perception of God's guidance? Had God really been trying to tell us not to go through the application process?

Once again, the only clarity we reached was that the details of our part in God's intentions for creation are unknowable. God does not promise us success, and God does not promise to explain everything eventually; God promises that our faithfulness will lead to fulfilment and divine accompaniment. God had led us to engage carefully and fully in the discernment and selection process for the Pendle Hill executive director position; we had done so to the best of our ability and understanding.

At Chowan, the lows and highs of teaching a Bible course to twenty-first-century freshmen were extreme. Early in the 2007 spring semester, I assigned Genesis chapters 1–11 to my Religion 101 class for weekend reading and gave a pop quiz when we next met. All the questions were straightforward, such as "According to Genesis, who was the first murder victim?" or "According to Genesis, why do people speak different languages?" I should have been forewarned by the phone call I got from a student one day after class asking where to find Genesis: "Is it in the big red book?" (Our only textbook was a Bible: large, red, and prominently titled *The New Annotated Bible*). The quiz was worth fifteen points, and after I graded generously and gave everyone a one-point bonus, twenty of the twenty-seven students who took the quiz failed.

On the other hand, one of my students from a previous semester came to see me about the same time. Her excuse was to talk about her final grade, but the real reason was to talk about whether or not her infant son's illnesses could be due to some sin that she or the infant's father or grandparents had committed in the past. The baby had been sick a lot of the time in the fall and became seriously ill again over the Christmas break. The student's mother-in-law had told her this could be punishment for some sin the baby's parents or grandparents had committed and that the Bible teaches this is so.

I talked with her about the different things the Tanakh says about these things and how—contrary to the rules—people don't seem to be punished for what their parents or grandparents may have done. For example, Ruth's descendants should not have been Israelites for ten generations, but in three to four generations David was king of Israel. I also talked about Jesus' offer to forgive all our sins if we repent and sincerely ask forgiveness. If she or the baby's grandmother really thought some sin of theirs was afflicting the baby, relief was as close as a prayer of repentance and a desire for forgiveness. The mother seemed to gather considerable comfort from our discussion and said when she left that she would talk with the baby's grandmother and suggest that the grandmother pray for forgiveness for any unwitting sin or error that might be contributing to the baby's illnesses.

This brought to mind the conversation I had with another student about whether or not her friend who had recently committed suicide was condemned to hell. I had reassured her the Bible does not condemn those who commit suicide. On the final exam, when I asked students to write down the most important thing they had learned in the course, this student wrote that for her it was learning her friend was not going to hell for committing suicide.

It seems that, for some students, the contact with a religion professor is an important opportunity to discuss important spiritual problems with someone who can bring a knowledge of the Bible and evident Christian belief to their personal circumstances. If Religion 101 were not a required course, they might never find their way to these resources. It is a responsibility I didn't know I was sharing with all other professors of religion in the world.

In Third Month 2007, Charlie Ansell and I were invited to a portion of the School of the Spirit residency being held near Raleigh, North Carolina. We'd been asked to come as models for the traveling ministry and to share what we knew about the spiritual gifts of vocal ministry and being an elder. We were several miles down the road when I realized that I had left my certificate for travel in the ministry behind, and we had to reverse course back to Woodland so I could retrieve it. It would be poor modeling not to have a certificate!

Avila Retreat Center, where the residency was being held, was as pretty and restful as I remembered it from a previous visit. One of the sisters remembered me from that visit, which was remarkable. Immediately after supper, we entered into the grand silence, spending about an hour together in "active silence" before going our separate ways and intentionally "doing nothing" until the next morning.

It was good we began our sojourn in the grand silence because we certainly got a workout when the silence ended! We rose, ate breakfast, and entered worship still in the grand silence. Worship was held in the retreat center's chapel, complete with an altar and a large wooden crucifix; the Presence was palpably among us, and worship was quite deep. There were a few offerings in vocal ministry, but not too many, and they were well grounded. Near the end of the time, I rose to speak a few words and felt I had been faithful. Later, both Susan and Charlie told me that they knew and felt physically that I was supposed to speak. Susan said it was like having two hearts inside her, both pounding furiously; her mind kept hearing Christ say, "You are crucifying me by not speaking!" (meaning me, not her). Charlie said it was the first time he had had the physical sensation of knowing someone *else* was supposed to offer a message.

The rest of the morning was spent in plenary session. I spoke at length about travel in the ministry, without notes or even a clear outline in my head. This had been a spiritual exercise for me over the last several weeks, to sit with my heart open to the topic, feeling out what might be said without writing anything down. It seemed to work as the school's staff members came to me afterward to say that many things I had said had been especially pertinent to this group and the spiritual work they had been engaged in during the first days of the residency.

After lunch, the group had some free time, which I spent offering opportunities to individual students. Charlie was faithful as doorkeeper, and I spent time with seven people in two hours. I would bring one opportunity to a close, and within a few seconds of the last person leaving, the next would arrive. There were deep emotions revealed, and tears were shed more than once. It felt like good work. Charlie said six of the seven persons had looks of obvious relief on their faces as they left.

In 2007 I discovered a restatement of the peace testimony that had been approved by the 1943 North Carolina (Conservative) Yearly Meeting in session. I'd never heard this statement referred to, and a quick email to Gwen Erickson at Guilford revealed that there was no printed copy of the statement in the historical collection there. My immediate thought was that this statement should be distributed widely in the yearly meeting.

I felt a certain personal affirmation in that the theology of the statement I had found was close to the theology of the peace testimony as I had articulated it ("I am a pacifist because God has wrought a change in me") rather than "I am a pacifist because there is that of God in the other person" that I once believed, abandoned, and have since critiqued as structurally weak and easily confuted. The 1943 statement speaks of living in the life and power that takes away the occasion of war, and it also speaks of the qualities brought out by the Spirit.

Fourth Month brought the horrible mass shooting on the Virginia Tech campus in Blacksburg, Virginia, where Virginia Mountain Housing was located. All the news media, and lots else besides, was filled with aspects of the massacre. There was the shock and grief that always surrounded an event this tragic, but there were also persons attempting to gain from it in some way—politicians pressing onto the scene, news organizations descending on Blacksburg in groups of up to one hundred staffers per network, folks using the event to promote their opinion ("Guns don't kill people," "We need stiffer gun controls," "Our company offers automated notification services that would have avoided the second round of shootings"), and so on. So pervasive was the rush to publicity that a company offering automated emergency notification services to campuses made news by suspending sales calls in the immediate aftermath of the tragedy as a matter of (unusual) good taste.

At least one major league baseball team wore Virginia Tech hats for a game, and vigils and other memorial services took place all over the region, if not the country. Chowan University scheduled a candlelight vigil for one week after the shootings. I was not moved to take part, not drawn (as many seemed to be) to see how closely I could connect myself to the tragedy, though Merrill and I had lived there for a time, my brother Damon got his undergraduate degree there, and I used to play basketball in the Virginia Tech gym daily. Yes, over 30 people died there, but 187 persons died in bombings in Baghdad the following day, and the death and suffering in Darfur for years is beyond measure. Perhaps we North Americans mourn excessively for suffering close to home because we keep ourselves in denial about the greater suffering that continues beyond our borders day after day, month after month, year after year.

My detachment could also have been a defense. If I made myself vulnerable to this small suffering, I might be overwhelmed by the larger suffering. There was nothing I can do about any of it directly; the dead were already dead, and from a distance I could have had no influence on events at Virginia Tech. In spite of the suffering, of the great cloud of darkness, we must press on, trusting that if we are faithful, if enough of us are faithful (and God only knows how many are enough), something divinely Good will happen.

The trick is to be alive to the reality of suffering without being overcome by the sheer magnitude of pain in the world, to be sensitive to what one is being personally led to do without being discouraged by the enormity of what still needs to be done, to keep to one's task throughout the day and into the evening without exaggerated optimism that will fade away, to ward off despondence that will rob our efforts of their vitality. God bless us in the effort.

In the midst of this inner work, Woodland seemed like a protected sanctuary. Meanwhile, small-town life in Woodland was just right for me. When it came time to leave my office for home at the end of work one day that spring, I could not find my car keys. I decided that I must have left them in my car that morning, so I walked down the hill to find out. There they were, still in the door lock, in plain view of all passersby. This seemed like one more sign that this was a blessed place to live; in many areas, my car would have been long gone by the time I got back to it.

The informal ways of local government, the ability to know and be known by government officials, shopkeepers, and neighbors, and the ability to leave my house (and car!) unlocked—these and many more aspects of country life made me feel deeply at home. I realized that there were other places Susan and I could live that would be as nice as Woodland, but none that would be better. About the only thing I would change would be to move about a block back from the traffic on Main Street—and half the time I wouldn't even want to change that.

Sitting in the back yard and watching birds late one afternoon, Susan and I talked about how much this period in our life seemed like a honeymoon, with time to give uninterrupted attention to one another. It was a very good time; we were both very happy and very grateful for this time of divine blessing.

Exercises in the Gospel Ministry

We were now beginning to look more intently at retiring when Susan reached sixty-two in a little over three years. We wouldn't have a lot of money, but we would have each other, and we craved the free time to do things that seem more important than the work we were doing then. Susan was concerned about our ability to keep our old house in good repair and pay the utility costs in our retirement years. This was an important question, but if we had to move, I didn't want to change our lifestyle very much at all. I wanted to live in a small town where we could listen to stained glass bluegrass on Seventh Day mornings and the host of the show would encourage us to make plans to go to church the next morning and where I could walk most places I needed to go.

There would always be special trips on Quaker matters, but if I were retired, most of my days could be spent between the town hall at one end of the town and the meeting house at the other, with the post office and local "supermarket" in between. The Internet offers so much material I can access from home, and what it doesn't offer directly I can order online for delivery.

In the summer of 2007, I was reminded how important and how hard it is to listen openly and carefully to vocal ministry. Susan and I were visiting Virginia Beach Friends Meeting, and I offered some ministry on the ways that the creation stories in Genesis point out humankind's position as part of God's creation with responsibility to care for our brother and sister creatures. I also said that much of our human conflict has environmental underpinnings and causes and that our classic peace efforts can only be partial and incomplete until we are as committed to the gospel order in creation as we are to harmony among humans.

Soon, a Friend rose to claim a special affinity to dirt, as the grandchild of a farmer, and on that basis to say we had to stop thinking of creation as something we manage and more to that effect. My immediate sense was that she had not heard anything I had said other than that I referred to the Bible, and she assumed I was preaching the "dominion over creation" doctrine when in fact I was advocating the opposite. Soon afterward, another Friend rose and reported on a book that she had read recently advocating vegetarianism and abstinence from the use of any animal products due to the extreme violence done to animals. She was quite explicit about the dire consequences of eating meat or wearing leather; there seemed very little love for anyone in anything she said—not even for the animals. Every time we gather to worship, we need to be listening in tongues, asking ourselves what God has to say to us through the ministry we hear without letting the human speaker or our own humanness get in the way.

That summer, Bloomington Friends Meeting in Indiana invited me to lead a retreat/workshop for their meeting on corporate discernment. After listening to my discernment group, I accepted the invitation and obtained a certificate for travel in the ministry. In the time between their invitation and the projected date of the retreat, Bloomington Friends changed the schedule and structure of the retreat little by little until what had started as a full weekend retreat was a single presentation after meeting for worship on Seventh Day morning, which would be attended by not only Bloomington Friends but Friends from other meetings in their quarterly meeting and members of a meeting from Western Yearly Meeting who would be holding a gathering of their own at the same facility at that time.

This was so markedly different from what I had agreed to do that it called the entire discernment process into question. On reflection, I felt that I did not feel led to travel so far, taking Charlie Ansell with me, in order to make a relatively short presentation (for which I was not prepared) about corporate discernment. What I had agreed to do was to lead a retreat over a full weekend for members of Bloomington Friends Meeting, which would allow time to create a safe space where individuals would feel free to express themselves fully and deeply. I took the question back to my discernment group, who agreed that I was released from my previous commitment and should contact Bloomington Friends to let them know I no longer planned to come.

Throughout the following day, I felt lighter in spirit for having taken this action; I had been released from what would not have been in good order. I would have to explain what happened to our monthly and yearly meetings, of course, since they had issued and endorsed a certificate for me to make this trip, but I was ready to do so with a clear conscience and a calm heart.

God is often at work in individuals being called into public ministry long before that call becomes visible to others. Two incidents involving Jan Ansell from 2007 and 2008 seem, in hindsight, to be examples of this, though we did not recognize it at the time.

We were attending Representative Body, and I was active in the vocal ministry in the latter half of worship. A short time after I regained my seat, Jan rose and also offered ministry. This was unusual for Jan, who at that time spoke in meeting quite infrequently. After the rise of meeting, she shared that she had been given a message quite early in the meeting but had wrestled with the leading. She was told that not only was she to offer this message at this meeting but that she had to be brave enough to speak after Lloyd Lee Wilson spoke. Of course, when she was receiving this instruction I had no idea myself that I would be led to speak. In fact, if someone had asked me about the prospect, I would have said something like, "Not likely today." Jan said she thought the leading meant that she had to be brave enough to speak after a seasoned Friend had spoken and her ministry risked being compared to that Friend's ministry. As it turned out, I did speak, and she was faithful afterward, and I have the sense that all was owned and accepted by the Master.

Jan had similar leading during MEO at yearly meeting sessions in 2008. Charlie Ansell shared his sense that it was time for him to step down as clerk, and Friends centered down to consider who might be right to take up the clerkship. As the silence continued, I felt led to rise and ask whether Janis Ansell would feel free to serve as clerk. She said that she would take this under consideration, and we agreed to postpone a decision until Seventh Day. Jan told me later that when Charlie made his announcement she heard internally that if God wanted her to take the clerkship, some other Friend in the body would name her in the face of the meeting. Her first question to me after we rose, therefore, was whether Charlie had put me up to it! I assured her that he had not.

In these and other unreported incidents, I believe God was teaching Jan to trust leadings even when they seemed risky, to be confident enough to allow herself to move with the Divine Stream without "pushing the river." About five years later, Jan was recognized as an elder in West Grove meeting, and about five years after that she was recorded as a gospel minister. God had been preparing her long before anyone knew that was what was going on.

Brian Drayton quoted the following passage from James Nayler's *Saul's Errand to Damascus* during a retreat I attended, and I encountered it again reading a draft of his pamphlet on Nayler:

> If I cannot witness Christ nearer than Jerusalem, I shall have no benefit by him; but I own no other Christ but that who "witnessed a good confession before Pontius Pilate"; which Christ I witness suffering in me now.[28]

A historically distant Christ leaves me rudderless, whatever His atoning efficacy, for I cannot see sufficient contemporary guidance in the written word alone. The perceptible guidance of the risen and present Christ is sufficient, having both shown the path to reconciliation with God and showing me each moment how to follow that path and live into that reconciliation.

In the spring of 2008, I went through a time of spiritual dryness. At the same time, I had several opportunities for public ministry, and in each case it seemed that the Holy Spirit was palpably present and Truth was served. The lesson I took away from this was that faithful service to God does not depend on our feeling particularly holy or Spirit-filled but on our being obedient, following the leadings we are given no matter how we are feeling internally.

Carl Magruder was the plenary speaker at our 2008 yearly meeting sessions. I was happily impressed to learn that he had not prepared a text for the presentation; he had prepared the messenger but not the message. Few Friends follow this old pattern today—Deborah Fisch and Carl are the two who immediately come to mind among public Friends. My reluctance to do the same in most situations has been part of my growing awareness that I am a writer, not a speaker. It is so important to me to get the exact words right that I feel obliged to write them ahead of time, rework them and refine them until they say what I want them to say, and then follow that text closely in my speaking. Carl and Deborah show by example that the Holy Spirit can reach through and around the

Exercises in the Gospel Ministry

words with Truth and real power. Perhaps there is room for both of us—writers and speakers—in Truth's service.

Later that summer, I drove to New Garden Friends Meeting in Greensboro, North Carolina, for Elmer Brown's memorial service. My car radio wasn't working, which was a surprise, but I didn't really mind the quiet and used the driving time to reflect on my time with Elmer and the quiet role he had played in shaping my Quaker experience. He had been a spiritual director to me, although I did not realize it at the time, and he had framed my understanding of Quakerism in a way that had persisted over five decades.

From time to time, I would poke at the radio controls or wiggle the control face, which sometimes got semidisconnected from the body of the radio, to no avail. When I arrived in Greensboro, I even checked the fuse box to make sure the radio had not blown its fuse. Everything was in order, and nothing prompted the least response from the radio. Not very upset about this for the moment, I entered the meeting house and settled on a bench to center down.

There was a decent number of Friends at the memorial, though not as many as someone who knew Elmer's service and life might have expected. He had come to Greensboro in the last decade or so of his life and had outlived many of his contemporaries, so the absence of a large crowd was understandable.

I spoke at some length in the service because I had come to realize that Elmer had been very important to me. His admonition that I could believe what I wanted but could not ignore the fact that everything I liked about Quakerism came from its Christian roots not only had provided the frame and space for my return to Christianity but had been my watchword for issues of membership and belief ever since. His witness and example over the years had more impact on me than I knew, and his manner of working with diverse Friends (including me) demonstrated more patience, tact, wisdom, and humility than I had recognized for many years.

After staying briefly at the reception after the memorial meeting, I returned to my car to head home. To my surprise, the radio worked as soon as I started the car, and it worked flawlessly all the way home. I believe its earlier silence had been a spiritual intervention to ensure that I spent the drive to Greensboro in a properly reflective frame of mind—and it had worked. Since this date, it has become my intentional practice not to play the radio on my way to a meeting for worship of any kind.

I experienced a mix of highs and lows at Representative Body in Tenth Month. The meeting for business heard a report on the School of the Spirit experiences of four yearly meeting Friends who were finishing up their two-year course. It was a good report, but a visiting Friend stood immediately to say that the School of the Spirit was unnecessary since we had an Inward Teacher. I was disappointed that this visitor once again rose to speak to the business of the yearly meeting, as he had done on other occasions in the past. He was a fine Friend, but he and his monthly meeting were not in membership with our yearly meeting. Until that happened, I wished he would speak less often about what the yearly meeting ought to do or how our minutes and epistles should be worded.

After the business ended, I gave a talk titled "Friends—A Different Kind of Church." There were a number of very good questions at the end, and several Friends expressed their appreciation. The only disappointment was that the digital recorder once again failed to operate, so I have no recording of the presentation. That recorder had worked every time I used it outside of Cedar Grove Meeting House and has never worked in the four times I have tried to use it in the meeting house. I was led to wonder what that meant!

Like early Friends, I often say to other people, "I'm a Christian, but not *that* kind of Christian." A Pendle Hill lecture[29] in 2009 gave me the opportunity to expand on this sentence, and I spent many months thinking about what I wanted to say about the differences.

My understanding of atonement is an important difference from other Christians. Rather than believing that Jesus' death produced an atonement between God and humans that overcame an otherwise unbridgeable chasm between the two, I believe that Jesus' death and resurrection demonstrated the already-existing fact that nothing humans can do—even torturing and executing the Christ—will break the bond of love God feels with all of creation. Jesus' death and resurrection are the visible signs of God's always-existing covenant of love with creation.

About the divinity of Jesus, I'm an adoptionist; I look to the *bath qol* at Jesus' baptism (Mark 1:11) as the moment. The doctrines of the virgin birth, immaculate conception, and perpetual virginity are unimportant to my Christian faith. I believe that the actions of Adam and Eve represent a pattern common to human beings, not an archetypal mold in which all human souls are formed. I don't believe in original sin and therefore don't need the birth narratives to free the infant Jesus from original sin.

Like early Friends, I'm not Trinitarian. The word is not in Scripture, and the doctrine seems to me part of a series of attempts (as with the birth narratives) to resolve problems concerning the effectiveness of Jesus' death as a sacrifice to produce salvation.

Regarding evangelizing and proselytizing, I occupy a middle ground. Jesus is the way, for me, to God. I have discovered a wonderful treasure; naturally, I want to share what I have found with others, to be always ready to give an account of the hope and joy I have. At the same time, I remember always an incident in John's Gospel (21:20–23); it is not my concern to know how others stand with God, only to pay attention to my own spiritual condition.

Jesus models a life that is fully human yet fully in harmony with our Creator in every way. Jesus is a precept and example for the life lived in God—the life that is the true goal of every Christian. But, as James Nayler wrote, "If I cannot witness Christ *nearer than Jerusalem*, I shall have no *benefit* by him" (emphasis added). It is not ideas or even beliefs about the historical Jesus who lived near Jerusalem so many centuries ago that are of benefit to us as Quaker Christians. It is the inward experience of the Living Christ, the Holy Spirit of God that brings grace, mercy, illumination, healing, teaching, and guidance (not an exhaustive list) that matters, that makes a difference in my life.

My sense is that the emphasis that both Catholics and Protestants have placed on substitutional (penal) atonement theory, and the subsequent need for additional doctrines to explain and support that, has seeped into Friends, both pastoral and nonpastoral. I believe the effect is to add an obstacle to persons who would otherwise be ready to "repent, be (spiritually) baptized, and receive the Holy Spirit" but cannot accept a violent God or the intrafamily violence seemingly inherent in the mainline atonement teaching. We also weaken the foundation of our peace testimony when we try to base it on a violent God or do not base it on the nature and intent of God at all.

In Ninth Month 2009, Susan and I facilitated a two-day retreat for Virginia Beach Friends titled "Building Spiritual Community." It felt very good to be working with Susan in this service. Happily, we work very well together, with each pulling hard in some spots and letting the other lead when that seems rightly led. There was no vying for top spot, no competition for the spotlight. Personally, I pushed my envelope in some good directions. Susan said I was favored throughout but especially when I was called forth in vocal prayer.

I had been trying to depend on the immediate guidance of the Holy Spirit more and more and on my own preparations less and less. I tried very hard not to prepare for this retreat, but I made sure not to neglect my spiritual practices so that I could arrive as centered as possible. This worked out well; God is good and on time, every time. The retreat unfolded in specific ways appropriate to the conditions and circumstances of Virginia Beach Friends, which I could never have anticipated in specific plans formulated ahead of the event. It seemed to me that I was more aware than usual of the spiritual flow of conversations and better able to hold back on my comments or observations until the appropriate moment.

My sixty-second birthday later that month sparked thoughts of retirement. As I aged, my vocation as a minister of the gospel was becoming more and more important to me (and it had always been quite important), while my competency became less important. However long the remaining time before my death would be, it was getting shorter daily, and I wanted to be of service in the gospel to the fullest extent possible. If I had access to health insurance, I would have retired then, but retiring without health insurance, given my physical condition, seemed like willfully cutting short my remaining time of ministry.

Exercises in the Gospel Ministry

On the other hand, my competency as registrar, director of institutional research, and assistant professor of religion and accounting at Chowan was becoming less and less manageable. It was no longer possible for me to do all the things I was assigned to do, and I survived by figuring out what could be neglected with the least negative effect.

It was my hope that the provost would allow me to make the shift over to full-time faculty that academic year, but he told me he couldn't move me because he'd have to hire two people to take my place, which he couldn't afford to do. So, there I was, in the same positions but with an even greater workload because Chowan's enrollment was at a record high that fall.

I wrote the following description of a trip to School of the Spirit in my journal on Ninth Month 20, 2009.

> First Day—Charlie Ansell and I traveled to the School of the Spirit as we did for the previous cohort two years ago. We arrived last night as the group was entering the grand silence, which ended this morning in worship. I spoke with the group afterward, first about my experiences as a traveling minister of the gospel and moving to an extended Q&A session that included dressing plainly, my understanding of Christ, individual and corporate discernment, and much more.
>
> Charlie did some very good work himself, describing his experience as an elder and also as a companion during many of my travels in the ministry. The contemporary conflation of those roles—particularly calling a traveling companion an elder—makes it very helpful when someone like Charlie, who has been in both roles, can explain the difference. Ears perked up also when Charlie described the time in Greensboro when he and I were traveling together and he realized that our leading was ended even though we had additional visits planned. The equality, or balance, between (identified) minister and (identified) companion in that type of discernment was new to several people in the room, I am sure.
>
> I again worked this visit entirely without notes or specific preparation other than trying to be as spiritually centered as I

could manage. This is hard work for me as I always want to be very exact and complete, and a completely written-out manuscript always seems best. This weekend was a visitation, not an address, and I felt "safer" to work without anything written down. All I had to do was prime the pump with some initial comments and then sit back and wait for the questions to come at me. It worked very well, of course, since we spent our time together paying attention to the issues and questions most important to these Friends rather than on some preplanned message of my own. We covered a very wide variety of subjects, including several I never expected, and it all felt like covered work.

Offering personal opportunities continues to be a powerful personal experience. This time I spent 2½ hours in a series of opportunities with students. Every time I make myself available, the complete time fills up almost immediately, and often (like this weekend) people squeeze themselves in before and after the announced time. This time I allowed 15 minutes each. Even in that short time, individuals go very deep spiritually and share profoundly about their conditions.

I have worried occasionally that offering opportunities might be a conceit on my part—a spiritual fraud I perpetuate simply to get a feeling of self-importance. It helped to remember Bill Taber's reflection on his own experience with opportunities. He said that at first he felt that he was involved in something like spiritual vampirism because the experience was so powerful for him. Over time, he came to feel that the opportunities were authentic experiences for everyone involved; he was not taking spiritual energy from the other person in the encounter, but they were both being energized in helpful ways. I believe that is the case for me, as well.

That fall, Susan and I were invited to attend the FGC Traveling Ministries Program retreat in Asheville, North Carolina. After the opening worship, the retreat leader asked us to go around the room introducing ourselves, our meetings, and our ministries. When my turn came, I said that I had been a Friend for forty years, active in the public ministry for thirty years, and a recorded minister of the gospel for twenty years—ten years each in two monthly meetings. I did not feel I "had" a ministry; in fact, it felt dangerous for me to talk about or think about "my" ministry. What I had was a commitment to following God's leadings in whatever direction they led so that it seemed I moved one time in a given direction and afterward in some quite different direction. God hadn't given me a ministry as much as God had given me a series of opportunities to follow divine leadings.

In worship the next morning, I was called to my feet in vocal ministry to express the Twenty-Third Psalm in my own words, line by line. It felt quite different from the tone of the meeting to that point, but it felt like authentic service, and when I regained my seat I was reassured that the ministry had been owned and accepted. After meeting, the Friend next to me asked whether I was reciting something I had read before or whether the words had just risen up during the meeting. When I said that the words had been given at the moment, it seemed to me that we were both disappointed—she that there was no written source she could consult and I that she would think there might be.

Around lunchtime, one of the women from Southern Appalachian Yearly Meeting and Association approached me to say that when I had spoken at that yearly meeting several years previously, I had told her after a meeting for worship that I thought she had been faithful in her vocal ministry. She had continued to hold that in mind over the ensuing years, and it had been helpful and encouraging to her as she worked to remain faithful to her leadings. I do not remember the original incident, but it underlines the importance of following one's Guide in even the smallest thing as one never knows what importance it may have to another person.

During a break in the group activities, Susan and I met by chance on the meeting house porch and realized that we each had the feeling that we were done at this gathering. After checking with each other about the seriousness of this shared feeling, we went immediately to the retreat leader, shared our sense of being complete, and made our goodbyes. Once we got on the road, Susan expressed a great sense of relief, confirming our decision to leave. I immediately thought of the trip Mike

Arnold and I had made to Tennessee and our decision on that trip to leave the evening before we had planned. Susan and I had no outward confirmation of our decision, as Mike and I did not, but I was clear that we were being faithful to the Divine Will.

In early 2010, I spent some time thinking about the meaning of membership among Friends, spurred by my reading of John Howard Yoder's *The War of the Lamb*.[30] The meeting is a covenant community, individuals drawn together by God into a shared corporate life, to be sure. But what is the nature of the covenant? How has God called us to be with one another and with God? Reading Yoder highlighted the covenant commitment, to God and to one's community, to work out one's salvation in the context of the faith tradition (in our case, the Quaker tradition—or perhaps the particular tradition of one branch of Quakers). Inseparable from this is the commitment to give and receive specific nurture and accountability to one another as one manifestation of that work.

A key distinctive of our tradition is that it emphasizes the importance of forming and sustaining an outpost of the Kingdom of God as the shared workspace where this happens. This is a difference that has become more important and more difficult to maintain in the last century as North American Christianity has doubled down on individual piety and become less concerned with social justice.

The membership covenant is a commitment that one accepts that this particular faith tradition is the proper context for one's long-term spiritual work. To keep me honest in my wrestling with that tradition, and to provide necessary perspective on my condition and circumstances, my relation to fellow members must be one of honest, loving mutual accountability. Avoidance of the hard issues and difficult conversations makes it impossible to help one another and undermines our goal of making our meetings witnesses to the possibilities of life together and invitations to others to "come and see."

Brian Owen wore his Boy Scout uniform to worship one First Day when I was visiting West Grove meeting. He was about to become an Eagle Scout, and his Eagle project was to build a utility shed on the meeting house grounds. Many memories and emotions washed over me, and I tried to let them have their way without thinking deliberately about them. Eventually, I was drawn to remember a repeated experience from my Boy Scout days of encountering a challenge that seemed way beyond my abilities or even aspirations, deciding to attempt the one small part of that challenge that I felt was possible for me and discovering eventually that I had done everything required. This seems transferable to the world of faith, where God's invitations and calls seem impossible, yet if I am faithful to attempt what little I can, it is always the case that God has prepared a place for my feet and yet another step for me to take.

This seemed throughout most of the meeting for worship to be unusual ministry and applicable primarily to one person, Brian, so much so that I was reluctant to stand and speak. However, I was given a clear sense that another Friend would also want to hear what I had to say, so I gave in to the leading and spoke. After meeting rose, that Friend engaged me in conversation and privately acknowledged that the ministry had been helpful to him.

In Ninth Month 2010, I was invited to write a chapter for the forthcoming *Oxford Handbook of Quaker Studies* on the history of Conservative Quakers from 1845 to 2010.[31] The first thing I did was to tell Susan of the invitation—and the next thing I did was accept. The invitation itself was so affirming on so many levels I couldn't put it all into words. From their description of the project, Oxford University Press wanted this to be an important book—the successor to the Rowntree series of the early twentieth century. They could literally have asked anyone to write about Conservative Friends, but they selected me. This seemed like another facet of the experience I had had at the School of the Spirit retreat in Second Month 2004 when I'd said I felt a call to nurture and articulate a particular strand of Quakerism and heard Bill Taber issue an emphatic sotto voce "Yes!" This is an affirmation from the academic side that I am seen to be one who truly understands and can articulate that strand that is Conservative Quakerism.

I retired from Chowan University on the first day of 2011, ending ten years of service, and the university named me registrar emeritus. I taught one introductory Bible class at Chowan that spring but soon realized that even two days a week of teaching as an adjunct professor was more stressful than I wanted. I let Chowan know I would not be continuing as an adjunct, and I felt more settled in my mind immediately.

There were numerous other opportunities for service. For several years I had been the only Woodland resident who attended every town board meeting whether I was interested in a particular agenda item or not; it seemed part of my responsibilities as a citizen of such a small town. Early in 2011, the Woodland Town Board of Commissioners appointed me to fill a vacancy in their membership. I recognized that in important ways the town commissioners were in an impossible position as most of the problems facing the town were beyond the ability of the town government to influence in any way. I agreed to join them because I thought there were things that could be done to make the town a better place to live and that someone needed to do them. I was "affirmed in" just before their next meeting and put my shoulder to the wheel.

I'd wrestled with the obvious "Quaker issues" of voting rather than seeking unity and of supporting a budget that funds a town police force armed with deadly weapons, and I felt that, in this circumstance, being involved outweighed being "pure." My answer to the voting question came out unexpectedly in my Michener lecture at Southeastern Yearly Meeting just before I was appointed when I said that voting was acceptable when the underlying assumption was that the source of wisdom was secular rather than divine. I sought for divine assistance in determining how I should vote but was willing to cast that vote in a secular process. Because I knew the town police officer and his predecessor and had heard them describe their work in dozens of town board meetings over the years, I knew that their work was overwhelmingly nonviolent and that they would only use deadly force to save their own lives or the lives of innocent civilians. I hoped that I would not make the choice to use deadly force even in that situation, but I could not deny them the right to protect themselves and at the same time send them out to do work necessary to enhance the safety of everyone in Woodland.

My time in office began just as the board started to build its budget for the next fiscal year, which was some of the hardest and least-appreciated work that the board did each year. I'd seen Woodland residents complain in the same meeting that taxes were too high and that the police weren't doing enough to keep the town safe—when I knew the work that was being done to keep taxes was as low as possible and how thin the police were stretched to give the rest of us the quality of service that we received. It would be even harder in the coming year because tax revenues had dropped again in the "jobless recovery" from the recession. My work on the board did fit the "think globally, work locally" mantra and felt appropriate because it was working for the Kingdom in my own neighborhood.

Susan and I went to the spring Representative Body meeting at West Grove. One incident during the business meeting was upsetting. While Patty Levering was speaking, another Friend got up and sat down in his seat repeatedly and went out the door to the parking lot and back, up the aisle again, in front of Patty, and into the other room—only to come back, walk in front of Patty again, and sit down where he had started. Patty was reading a description of a young Friend's encounter with Christ while visiting West Grove meeting, and my reaction was that the other Friend's interruptions were the work of a spirit of confusion trying to distract us from listening to what Patty was reading.

I don't go around interpreting events as the work of spirits as a general rule, and to perceive this incident this way was surprising to me. Susan and I discussed it during the drive home, and we acknowledged that this Friend certainly had psychological and emotional issues. It seemed to me that this spirit (if that's what it was) took advantage of that vulnerability to distract the rest of us. Susan suggested that someone—perhaps I—should make a point of sitting next to him at the next meeting for business to try to help anchor him. I would certainly feel this out to see if it seemed the right thing for me to do.

Early one First Day in Seventh Month 2011, I headed north to visit the Old Town Friends Fellowship at the Aisquith Street Meeting House in Baltimore. These Friends had sent a visitor to our last yearly meeting sessions, and I'd had a growing desire to travel to Baltimore and worship with them ever since. This was my first visit under a general travel certificate that Rich Square had approved earlier that year.

Memoir of the Life and Religious Labors of Lloyd Lee Wilson

Since Old Town Friends didn't meet until 5 p.m. on First Days, I timed the journey to be able to worship with Alexandria Friends in Virginia in the morning. I had never worshipped there before. The meeting house dated to the early 1850s, and there were carved graffiti from Union soldiers visible on the outside walls. The meeting house and grounds were completely surrounded by Fort Belvoir, which made for an interesting feeling as one approached from any direction.

I had time after I arrived to walk through the graveyard and look at the burial mound, which included remains and headstones removed from another Quaker cemetery elsewhere in Alexandria. Seeing the graves of Janneys, Stablers, and Gillinghams reminded me of the long history here. The shutters had been preserved; during worship they sparked in me vocal ministry related to how there is spiritual work we need to do ourselves with shutters closed, some we do in the company of the faith community with shutters open, and some we do outside in witness and testimony—and each depends on having done the others in the proper proportions. It seemed when I took my seat again that I had faithfully discharged my obligation.

The Aisquith Street Meeting House was just off Fayette Street in a pretty poor neighborhood. There were fairly wide streets on two sides, a burial ground behind, and outdoor basketball courts on the fourth side. Its exterior architecture reminded me more of St. John's Methodist Church back in Charlestown, Maryland, than a traditional Quaker meeting house. Of course, wood frame construction for Quakers is more familiar to me than brick, but brick is more suitable for urban environments. The meeting house, which dated from 1781, was the oldest house of worship still standing in Baltimore.

Friends began to gather a few minutes before 5 p.m. There were four members of Old Town plus myself and Betsy Myers, the clerk of Baltimore Yearly Meeting, who had a certificate for visiting meetings in that yearly meeting and had decided to visit the Old Town meeting that afternoon because she had seen on their website that they expected me to be present.

We had a good time of sharing in the hour before worship. Old Town Friends described their desire to be an inclusive Christian fellowship in downtown Baltimore affiliated with a larger Quaker body and how those commitments affected their search for the affiliation that would be right for them and the larger body. They were drawn to the faith witness of Conservative Friends but did not want to be "pioneers" on gender issues, which seemed to rule out Ohio Conservative and direct affiliation with Friends United Meeting at that time. They felt their Christian commitment was an uneasy spot in their discussions with various Baltimore Yearly Meeting monthly meetings and were concerned that the yearly meeting had officially ruled out recognition of specific spiritual gifts. They felt gifts of ministry and eldership rising up in individuals in the group and were seeking affiliation with a body that had an understanding of those gifts and a structure for guidance and nurture. They were drawn to North Carolina (Conservative) but were worried that the challenges of distance would be hard to overcome.

    I shared with them copies of our *Discipline* and minutes of last year's business sessions and talked about the yearly meeting in relation to several of the issues they had raised. In the modern world, distance is not the handicap that it once was, provided there is a solid commitment on both sides to be physically present with one another on a regular basis. Physical travel is less demanding than was in previous generations, and electronics can fill in the gaps in important ways. Betsy Myers was generally supportive of the group's searching in Baltimore Yearly Meeting and elsewhere, indicating that the right fit was more important than whether that fit was inside her yearly meeting or elsewhere. I pointed out that once a monthly meeting or other group was affiliated with some other yearly meeting, NCYM(C) would no longer engage in affiliation discussions with the group because dual affiliation was not generally permitted in our yearly meeting and we did not want to be perceived as "poaching" from other yearly meetings. We did not recognize a geographic franchise for yearly meetings, and individuals were always welcome to pursue membership in any of our monthly meetings.

    I stayed overnight with Kevin-Douglas Olive and his partner, who had a nicely renovated townhouse not far from the meeting house. Kevin-Douglas and I had some excellent conversation deep into the night and again the next morning. It seemed to me that NCYM(C) was the best fit for this group, but sustaining the relationships that would make that affiliation effective would be a long-term challenge.

Later in the year, Bob Gosney was my companion at a School of the Spirit retreat at the Franciscan retreat center near Philadelphia. There were thirty-five participants, including alumni of each of the school's On Being a Spiritual Nurturer program cohorts. On the first night, I shared the concepts of the covenant triangle and the prophet as "covenant advocate"—concepts that were new to many present and that resonated strongly with several. My usual fear when preparing for or leading a retreat like this one is that I will not "prime the pump" enough for the participants to start flowing on their own. There were no problems along those lines this time as Friends quickly engaged with the presentation and advanced the discussion on their own. I felt the topic and presentation were well matched to the audience.

I had two opportunities the next day, and Bob Gosney had one. Mine were solid times, though not as dramatic or draining as some I've experienced. This was a grounded group of individuals who had paid attention to their spiritual work.

In the evening session, Friends began to ask questions about the nature of the covenant between their faith community and God on the one hand and themselves on the other. It seemed clear that many feel these relationships were broken or impaired. It felt necessary to abandon my plans for the next day in order to address this directly. Making this sort of change on the fly felt quite risky as I prefer to be thoroughly grounded in my subject and presentation, even when I don't have precise words written out in advance. However, the tradition in which I claim to walk teaches that God will guide us in these circumstances, so I discarded my advance preparation and trusted that God would lead me in the way we should go.

The next morning was given over to the School of the Spirit staff collecting feedback about their various activities, so I had time to sit with Bob and feel out what to do that afternoon and evening and then to be alone to follow up on those insights. Bob is a wonderful companion in the ministry as he understands my role and has an excellent sense of where a group is spiritually and intellectually. He is able with a few words to share an insight that triggers all sorts of stuff in me in response, making my work much easier for me and much more on target for gathered Friends.

I had three opportunities that afternoon, completely filling up the time between lunch and our first session, so I had little time to be nervous about the changed plans and how they would play out. There was little to worry or be nervous about, however. We talked about covenant relationships in general, explored what the expectations might be of and from the faith community, and then asked each person to write out their personal desired covenant with their faith community. By then, it was time to break for dinner.

In the evening, we shared some of the expectations that participants identified and explored how we might begin the process of making them a reality—remembering that we may plow for another's planting and for yet someone else to harvest, all for the Lord. Friends were obviously tired at the end of the evening, but the session went well.

Morning worship on First Day was deep—as all the worship had been during this retreat. Afterward, we had about an hour to wrap up unfinished topics, which I used to sum up Jeremiah's "love letters"—his message to the exiles describing the new covenant. It felt like good service. Finally, I asked all to stand in a circle holding hands and facing inward. I told them they were the blessed community, called to encourage and nurture and hold each other accountable in covenant relationship to each other. Then I asked them to face outward, still holding hands. What they saw now was their mission field: serving God by serving (ministering to) the world outside the blessed community. You can't see one another, I continued, but you are still just as close, still connected, and still able to give and receive each other's support and gifts. My last words were, "Preach the gospel always; if absolutely necessary, use words." That quote, which is attributed to St. Francis, seemed appropriate and even obvious given that we had been meeting in a Franciscan convent, but several Friends came up to me afterward to ask whether those were my words or a quotation from someone else.

Bob drove most of the way home, which allowed me to sleep; I was very tired. I came out "even" at this retreat, expending the last of my energy at the close of that morning's session. Bob had been an excellent companion and had had service of his own as well. I felt we could say, with Alfred Newlin, "It was right for us to be here."

In Bible study at Rich Square one First Day morning, we read in Isaiah 64. As I often do, I looked before and after the chosen verses, looking for context in which to understand what had been selected. The verses describing the Holy Land as a wilderness, with Jerusalem destroyed and the Temple burned down, sparked in me a near sympathy with the plight of the Jewish exiles. How could one be in covenant relationship with God without the promised land, or the holy city set on a hill, or even the Temple itself, God's dwelling place?

Later, in worship I felt led to offer ministry comparing the seeker, the finder, and the pilgrim. *Seekers* were in search of what they had not yet experienced and knew only by the reports of others. *Finders* knew of their own experience but often became like the disciples at the Transfiguration, wanting to build monuments to what they had experienced and settle down there, shutting themselves off from continuing revelation. The Jews in exile, it seems to me, were coping with the reality that they had experienced covenant with God, but they misidentified that experience with the monuments of the promised land, the city of David, and the Temple.

In the context of contemporary Quakerism, I had called myself a finder rather than a seeker, but I feel that more truly I have been a *pilgrim*. I seek what I have already tasted, but I must always be "on the way" because I know the reality of the living covenant relationship cannot be sustained if I try to freeze or preserve it in a permanent configuration. Living relationships mature as they are nurtured and sustained over time, and this must be true of one's faith commitments and relationship with God as well. My relationship with God grows from the historic roots of Quakerism, and I do not expect that it will ever take a shape that denies those roots—but roots are not branches, not leaves or fruit, and to be alive that relationship must be growing in ways that God only reveals from moment to moment, not in advance. So, I am a pilgrim; I know where I've been and I know to Whom I am going. Where I am now is not my destination.

Exercises in the Gospel Ministry

In 2012, I journaled some reflections on the many Friends who say they want nothing to do with "theology." A common definition of theology, of course, is "faith seeking understanding," which puts these Friends in the awkward position of stating that they don't want to understand their faith. That implies that they are professing a faith they don't really possess, a situation condemned by early Friends.

What these Friends probably mean is that they don't want to have anything to do with *deliberative theology*—second-order reflection on the embedded theology that shapes our actions and speech.[32] Embedded theology is the set of assumptions and understandings of the ground of our ultimate concern and our relationship to that concern that shape our daily life. In other words, we all have a personal theology that expresses itself in everything we do or say. We attend Quaker worship rather than Orthodox mass or Islamic prayers because Quaker meeting is a better fit for our embedded theology. Likewise, we are pacifists, vegans, or advocates for renewable energy because of our theological understanding of the ground of our ultimate concern—in my case, of God.

Embedded theology is taught by the *praxis* of the church community, our parents, and other role models. As Conservative Friends have learned to their sorrow, these "osmotic" methods of learning can often produce a faith that is rather brittle, unable to stand up to challenges presented by life crises or a changing world. To strengthen the faith embedded in our daily lives, we need a process of reflection on this embedded understanding of God and our relationship to God that both honors the stream of tradition and looks for new understandings that accommodate new learnings and present crises. Deliberative theology is that reflective process.

We call ourselves Seekers and describe ourselves as being on a spiritual journey, yet many Friends neglect the deliberative theology process as a tool for gaining greater understanding of spiritual Truth, of moving from our starting condition toward a deeper and more authentic faith. In particular, we neglect the practice of deliberative theology in our meeting communities. Friends are not alone in this corporate neglect, but we share in the lack of fruit. Since we don't practice corporate theology and don't nurture the mutual respect and freedom to articulate our theology that the corporate practice requires, we fall short of the understanding we might otherwise have. We also fall short of that supportive, nurturing faith community we might be a part of.

I also spent time in 2012 deliberating on and journaling my understanding of atonement. My spiritual friend Professor J Brabban, chair of Chowan's Department of Religion, had been warning me that in order to develop a satisfactory understanding of the atonement I would have to develop a systematic Christian theology and that the atonement reaches into almost every part of Christian faith. On the first point, we disagreed (I prefer a constructive theology approach to a systematic one), but the more reading and study I did, the more I realized J was correct on the second.

One of the first questions is why we need atonement at all. Why are we alienated from God to begin with, and why can't we restore that right relationship on our own? Isn't God wishing for and inviting us into a harmonious relationship, already and all the time? Original sin is the best-known concept that aims to explain this need. The details vary, but basically this doctrine holds that humans all inherit from Adam a propensity to sin, ensuring that every human sins personally to a greater or lesser extent. Since humans all share in Adam's sin, we are each guilty of sin even before we commit a sin ourselves. Our divinely intended relationship with God is implemented by God's actions alone—there is nothing humans can do other than to believe after the fact.

I do not find these arguments persuasive on several grounds. We do not understand ourselves today as the literal descendants of historical Adam and Eve; they are not our genetic ancestors but mythical figures that embody the relationship of human beings to our Creator. The Jewish interpretation of the creation and the Garden of Eden stories understands Adam and Eve to be archetypes, representing the essential nature of human beings, and not prototypes, representing a fixed pattern to which all subsequent human beings must adhere. To understand Adam and Eve as imposing an inescapable sinful nature on us as their descendants and making us guilty of sin before we have done anything requires both that we read back into the Genesis stories a meaning different from that understood by the faith community that originated them and that we have a literal understanding of the biological link between Adam and Eve and the rest of humanity that is no longer credible.

In his Proposition IV, seventeenth-century Quaker Robert Barclay agrees that humankind is "fallen" and incapable of responding to the seed of God within, but he also dismisses the concept of original sin as simply unbiblical. He rejects those who advocate a "natural light" or inherent goodness that would allow an individual to choose and act on the good without the necessary help of God and at the same time dismisses the idea that Adam's sin is imputed to infants at birth. We each become sinners, in Barclay's mind, when we actually transgress on our own. This is inevitable, Barclay writes, quoting from Genesis and Jeremiah, because our hearts are deceitful and our imaginations are wicked. There is the seed of God in us, but that seed is not our nature.[33]

It seems to me that a satisfactory contemporary response to the question of why we humans need to be reconciled to God—why atonement is necessary—might look something like this. God desires to be in an entirely good and harmonious relationship with us and for us to be in an entirely good and harmonious relationship with the rest of creation, but we individually and corporately fail to live up to our end of those relationships. We fail because God has given us free will, the freedom to choose either to do the will of God or to do differently. Given finite understanding and finite abilities, we are unable on our own to choose to do the will of God consistently. Inevitably, each one of us becomes more and more estranged from God, wandering farther and farther from being the individual God created us to be and yearns for us to become.

We are unable to correct this state of affairs on our own, through our own willpower or repeated efforts. God must intervene by offering a means of overcoming our estrangement—a path of reconciliation, or atonement. Jesus of Nazareth, the Christ, is that path of atonement. Atonement is necessary not to appease God's offended honor, nor to satisfy God's unyielding justice, but to enable human beings to hold up their end of the love relationships with God and with the rest of creation.

Atonement is not effective because Christ suffered and died on the cross as punishment for our sins. Atonement works because of the moral influence of Jesus Christ, the Human One, who modeled Divine Love. We have the opportunity to be at one with God because God loves us enough to become human, to share our joys and pain; Jesus' life and teachings are a guide to how we should live in order to please God.

But even the historical account of Jesus' life and death and resurrection is not enough to reconcile us fully to God. As James Nayler said (paraphrased), "If I can experience Christ no closer than Jerusalem, I can have no benefit from him." It is the Presence of Christ in the present moment, our loving relationship with the Divine and our attention to the immediate guidance of the Inward Guide, that holds the atoning power. God enables us to be in right relationship with the Divine and equips us to nurture and sustain that relationship, but we must also do our part, committing to and working to live up to the Light we have been given.

George Fox's account of his childhood and youth leading up to his life-changing encounter with the Inward Christ fits well into this schema. Fox says of his childhood that he "knew pureness and righteousness" and of his teenage years that he "never wronged man or woman in all that time." Nevertheless, he was subjected to great temptations and mighty troubles that brought him to the edge of despair. Neither his own efforts nor those of others recognized for their spiritual maturity and profession of faith were able to give him comfort or release from his condition. Although he had great openings to the meaning of Scripture during this time, they were not enough to release him from his troubles. Then he heard the voice that said that there was one, even Christ Jesus, who could speak to his condition. In his relationship with the Inward Christ, Fox found reconciliation with God and creation that healed him of his temptations and troubles and restored his unity with creation.

As in Fox, so in us. My estrangement from God and my need for atonement is not inherited from Adam and Eve but stems from my own free will. When we are too young to understand right from wrong and make informed choices, we are capable of being pure and righteous, but as we grow in understanding and know the consequences of our choices, we inevitably become estranged from God because we do not have the wisdom or insight to choose rightly without the intervention of the Holy Spirit, Christ present inwardly. We all need atonement because none of us can always make the right choices, or carry out the right choices when made, on our own.

If all people need atonement and atonement comes from the faithful life, death, and resurrection of Jesus the Messiah, is atonement then universal? Are all souls saved, whether or not they explicitly repent, are baptized, and receive the Holy Spirit in this life? It seems to me that our free will requires that the answer to this question must be no. If free will is real, then God must allow some persons to refuse to be reconciled, to continue in a state of estrangement from their Creator.

Is the moment of death the last opportunity for a person to repent? In the Roman Catholic catechism and elsewhere, provision is made for those who died without making a profession of Christian faith because they died before Christ's time—that is, without freely accepting the offer of atonement—to receive atonement and salvation anyway. If we commit to the principle of free will, then those souls must also have had the free choice to say yes or no to this opportunity after death. The Roman Catholic teaching of *baptism by desire* also addresses the issue of persons who die without making a full profession of faith, whether they are catechumens or non-Christians who try to do God's will in whatever form they perceive it. The issue for catechumens is the lack of water baptism itself, which does not concern Quakers. For non-Christians, it is the absence of a decision to accept the offer of atonement that presents a problem. I believe we have the opportunity after physical death to make that decision if we have not already said yes to God.

Heaven, it seems to me, is not a place but a state of living in atonement with God, wherever and whenever we are—whether or not we have left this physical life for whatever comes next. Hell is not a place of condemnation but a state of being estranged from God, also wherever and whenever we are. All it takes to move from one to the other is our own decision.

Transfer to West Grove Meeting

Charlie and Jan Ansell had continued to look for suitable land on which to carry out Charlie's vision of "Feed my sheep." Unable to find suitable land near Rich Square Monthly Meeting, they purchased a farm in the center of the state and renamed it Wings of Dawn (from Psalm 139). After a long discernment, Susan and I decided to join them in an intentional Quaker community practicing sustainable agriculture and embodying Quaker witness in other ways. We agreed that when Charlie and Jan broke ground on their net zero-energy house at Wings of Dawn, we would "go public" about our plans to move into the old farmhouse Charlie and Jan would be vacating. That time came in Fifth Month 2012.

I felt (and still do) that if possible one should be a member of the closest Quaker meeting to one's home, so our plans for moving implied plans to change our meeting memberships. Susan and I were in somewhat different places concerning transfer to West Grove Meeting, the closest meeting to Wings of Dawn.

I was ready to transfer my membership immediately. I was also clear that my recording as a gospel minister should not transfer automatically. West Grove Friends should go through a discernment process and decide for themselves whether I still held a gift in the ministry. Either of two outcomes could result, and either would satisfy me. West Grove Friends could discern that I still held the gift, in which case I would continue working to develop and exercise that gift faithfully. Or, West Grove Friends could discern that I no longer held that gift, in which case I would be a "formerly recorded minister" and would do my best to do and speak according to the Guide in concert with the monthly meeting. The latter outcome would be a witness to Friends that recording is not for life and is not a personal status but recognition of a spiritual gift that may move away at any time.

West Grove Friends approved my transfer of membership at meeting for business in Eleventh Month, and Ministry and Oversight was asked to take up the matter of discernment of my gift in the vocal ministry at its earliest convenience. I asked the meeting to consider issuing me a travel certificate for the upcoming trip Charlie and I were planning to make to Palm Beach Monthly Meeting and to help with discernment around a pending invitation to travel to Indiana to lead a workshop there.

Historically, recording as a minister (but not as an elder) has transferred with membership, but it seemed to me that a person may be gifted differently in a new meeting than in a previous meeting as the new meeting may have need of different gifts. It seems unfair for a meeting to inherit a recording from a previous meeting; it provides no opportunity for Friends in the new meeting to develop a shared sense of the minister's gifts—even in a situation like mine, where I was well known to everyone.

Susan's concern was more basic. She wondered whether, at that time in her spiritual formation, it was right for her to be attached to any specific faith community at all. She was considering letting her membership rest in Rich Square for the present or, if she did apply for transfer, asking West Grove Friends to appoint a clearness committee to ensure that she and the meeting understood each other's expectations and intentions. I could see the integrity of her position and assured her that whatever arrangement suited her was fine by me; I laid no expectations on her one way or the other. It seemed to me that we were exploring or expressing two sides of the same truth. She was pointing out that no single spiritual path had a monopoly on opportunities for growth for the committed student, and I was pointing out that any student could benefit by being committed to a specific spiritual path.

Membership is too often treated as a status of the individual rather than as a relationship between the individual and the faith community. Thus, nominal members are able to go for years or even decades without ever attending meeting for worship at the meeting of which they are members yet when queried claim membership status because they have such fond memories of the old meeting, or they will always be Quakers in their hearts, or they wish to be buried in the old Quaker cemetery, or whatever. As a thought experiment, I have wondered about abolishing formal membership and simply watching to see who carries the water and chops the wood for the meeting on a regular basis. Those who invest in the meeting (in a wide variety of ways) should have a say in meeting decisions, and those who do not invest should not have a say. Everybody is "going to heaven"—formal membership doesn't matter in that way—

but one should earn the right and responsibility to participate in community decisions in meetings for business.

I read in a blog posting about that time that Britain Yearly Meeting's *Faith and Practice* lists the word "discipline" twice in its index, once pointing to the sentence "Membership is a spiritual discipline" and once to the sentence "Membership is a commitment to the discipline of Friends." I thought it might be an improvement to add the word "corporate" to each sentence: "Membership is a corporate spiritual discipline" and "Membership is a commitment to the corporate discipline of Friends." This seems to capture the relational nature of membership. Membership among Friends is or should be a commitment to the corporate spiritual disciplines of the Religious Society of Friends, including corporate worship, meeting for business, and mutual accountability. These are disciplines we practice under the headship of the Holy Spirit of God, who provides immediate guidance in all things to those willing to hear.

When Representative Body met in Tenth Month 2012, Friends were ready to explore the process that might be used to revise our *Discipline* section by section rather than as a whole. This would allow some needed changes in procedure (such as revisions to reflect that the yearly meeting no longer had quarterly meetings) without miring the meeting interminably in conflicts over wording of the Advices or whether the 1671 letter to the governor of Barbados ought to be deleted. Previously, I had resisted a *Discipline* revision for both personal and corporate reasons. Personally, I was concerned that a revision would be less Christian and would include less of the traditional wording and terminology that I valued highly. Corporately, my understanding of the revision process that had stretched from 1967–1983 led me to believe that a new revision could divert the yearly meeting's attention and energies from more important work that should engage it fully.

Now my sense was that it was time to attempt a revision and that my role should be to do what I could to ensure that it was done rightly. The work the yearly meeting had done over the previous five or six years had gotten us to the point that we could discuss and embrace a diversity of beliefs in the context of a Christian core and tradition. By breaking the revision process up into manageable parts undertaken serially, we should be able to keep the time and energy devoted to the revision process to a manageable level. Representative Body appointed me to a committee charged to recommend a specific process for the revision. As the first named member, I would convene the first meeting of the committee.

Before the committee addressed its charge directly, I hoped we would consider just what the *Discipline* was, what role the *Discipline* played in the lives of individual Friends and Friends meetings, and what attributes would characterize a good *Discipline* for our yearly meeting. I think of a good *Discipline* primarily as a resource for individual members and monthly meetings, as providing guidance as we navigate some of the most common and/or most difficult issues we face in the course of daily life. It is not comprehensive and does not try to address every issue that any person or meeting will encounter, and it is not a rule that prescribes how each part of the day and each situation must be addressed. It is not creedal, but it is principled.

An ideal *Discipline* provides guidance for individuals and meetings and points the way to other resources as well. It should address common activities in more detail than less frequent matters as well as activities that have more serious consequences if undertaken wrongly more directly than those with less serious consequences. One would expect the procedure for marriages to be covered in detail since there are consequences for the couple and legal fines for the meeting if marriages are not done according to the law. Sojourning membership would be covered in less detail since the consequences of mistakes are less severe.

In the tradition of NCYM(C), the Queries and Advices are an important resource for both individuals and meetings as well as a means of strengthening identity and community, so I felt they should be given careful attention in our *Discipline*. Respect for the tradition is important, but at the same time modern vocabulary and wording are important to keep this resource accessible and usable in the present day.

The national elections in 2012 drew great attention. I went to bed before the West Coast returns were in. Obama and Romney were neck and neck, but a solid Democratic showing on the West Coast would give Obama the victory. Once again, I did not vote in the national election.

Although I had a clear preference for Obama and the Democratic platform over Romney and the Republican platform, both candidates and their parties were committed to the use of lethal force in foreign policy and domestic situations. If there had been a pacifist candidate that otherwise espoused the Democratic platform, I would have had no problem voting for that candidate. Sadly, there was again no such candidate that year.

So many people buy into the hope that if we just elect different people the whole government will change and if the government changes our society will change (for the better). It seems to me that real change will have to come from below, from a changed populace. If at the local level the Kingdom of God breaks out, the elections, our government, and our society will inevitably change for the better. Until that grassroots change happens, there is little hope for more than incremental shifts in policy at the top. One can argue that I've not done enough to work toward that grassroots change; that is a criticism that should be part of every Christian's self-examen. It does seem to me, however, that what is needed is not limited to grassroots social justice activism but must include changed lives in situ. There is a place for everyone in the revolution, as the old saying goes—if there isn't, then it's not the revolution.

The most profoundly effective lives are those lived in one's normal place, as if the Kingdom were here already in all its fullness. When one lives one's daily life as part of the Kingdom, at home, in the workplace, in the neighborhood, then lives are truly changed, beginning with our own, and that change will find its way into every part of the society.

Chapter 8
New Fields of Service and New Challenges: North Carolina, 2013–2019

The next few years brought many changes in where Susan and I lived, how we spent our days, and the monthly meetings we were part of, as expected. What was unexpected was the number and type of changes in my public ministry that also happened.

We closed on the sale of our Woodland house on Valentine's Day 2013 and moved to Wings of Dawn Farm in the central part of North Carolina. There were many adjustments to be made, such as remembering how to heat with wood and how to keep a fire going all night, but the process was smooth and enjoyable. The Ansells had moved into their new zero-energy home just a couple of days before Susan and I moved into the old farmhouse, so there was lots of unpacking for everyone to do in addition to the regular farm chores. There were hundreds of chickens to feed and move from pasture to pasture in mobile coops we called "hennabagos" as well as ground to prepare for a large truck garden selling to the local farmers' market (or, later, to a newly formed CSA). Time was short; soon the spring planting season would be upon us without mercy.

Just eight days later, Charlie and I drove through predawn near freezing temperatures and sporadic rain to catch a flight to Palm Beach, Florida, to lead a weekend retreat. There were about twenty-five people for the first night; some had made a four-hour drive to get there.

Charlie is an excellent companion in the ministry. He makes the travel itself smooth without being intrusive about it, and he finds a place for himself when I speak that is easy for me to see and for him to give unobtrusive visual feedback about volume, pace, and so forth. He stays centered when others might get flustered, and that makes it easier for me to stay centered myself, no matter what might transpire.

As we gathered the next day, Friends were well prepared; the discussion was insightful and well centered. The afternoon session included an enactment of the incident involving Jairus's daughter and the woman with a flow of blood, which seemed to grab people's imagination. The individual performances were enthusiastic and very appropriate to the context of the story. Acting out the story made it alive to their thoughts and emotions.

We gathered before worship on First Day to review our work and to address any last questions. The discussion took the form of informal worship-sharing, with individuals speaking out of the silence as led. It seemed clear that the weekend had been meaningful to Friends personally and in the life of the meeting community. As I was standing to bring the session to a close, John Bucholz interrupted to give me his walking stick. He was just two weeks past open-heart surgery (at age eighty-five), so this gesture was more than unexpected. He went through an elaborate demonstration of the ways the walking stick could be used, ending with getting down on his knees to pray for God's help for me. I was more touched than words could say.

Our first weeks and months at Wings of Dawn Farm were blessed by a strong sense of community being established together with a warning not to cling too tightly to our vision of what the future held. The community aspect brought to mind words of Francis Howgill:

> The Kingdom of Heaven did gather us and catch us all, as in a net. . . . We came to know a place to stand in and what to wait in; and the Lord appeared daily to us, to our astonishment, amazement and great admiration, insomuch that we often said one unto another with great joy of heart: 'What, is the Kingdom of God come to be with men? And will he take up his tabernacle among the sons of men, as he did of old?' . . . And from that day forward, our hearts were knit unto the Lord and one unto another in true and fervent love, in the covenant of Life with God; and that was a strong obligation or bond upon all our spirits, which united us one unto another.[1]

At the same time, while thinking about what the future might hold for us at Wings of Dawn, Susan heard a voice say to her, "You're not going to be here in three years." She had come to know and trust the Voice of her Shepherd and recognized it now. We discussed this new experience for some time. Clearly, it could mean any number of things other than her immediate reaction that she would die sometime in the next three years. Any number of other events could contribute to her not living at Wings of Dawn. This could even be good news in the sense that God might have something even more wonderful to offer us between now and then than Wings of Dawn – though it was hard to imagine in the present moment what that might be. It seemed important not to get too attached to our own expectations.

Throughout that spring, the four of us at Wings of Dawn lived in the tension between an invitation to a Spirit-led, Spirit-fed community and the unrelenting call to accomplish more on the farm. It was difficult to set aside enough time to devote to spiritual work and the work of the ministry because there was so clearly much more to be done than there was time and energy to do. Each of us was constantly making decisions about which items had priority – what was screaming most loudly, as Charlie put it. At a weekly farm meeting, Jan shared her sense of losing her spiritual centeredness as a consequence of being so busy on the farm. We affirmed that staying spiritually centered was very important to us all, and if farm activities were getting in the way we needed to look for ways to correct that.

Soon afterward, West Grove ministers and elders met to hear the Advices and consider the Queries for our meeting. When we got to the part about not letting the business of everyday life interfere with our service to the meeting, Jan spoke again to great effect, and Charlie observed that in order to improve in this area the first thing he would have to do would be to begin getting eight hours of sleep each night. Later, he told me that he and Jan had committed to having a half hour of worship after breakfast every day, so he would not be starting farm work until that was completed. I wanted to call out "Amen!" Our spiritual commitments were making real changes in our outward lives—and I thought that all the work we were really supposed to do on the farm would still get done because we would see more clearly what was our calling and what was attractive distraction.

The yearly meeting committed to revising its *Discipline* at its 2013 sessions, and I was appointed to the revision committee along with

Deborah Shaw, Andrew Wright, and Patty Levering. I asked the clerk for some time on Seventh Day to speak to the yearly meeting about the *Discipline* revision process. Before addressing the specifics, I spoke about two groups I saw forming in the yearly meeting: those who feared something precious would be lost in the revision process and those who were licking their chops (metaphorically) to change uncomfortable or awkward wording or eliminate parts of the *Discipline* altogether. Each group needed the other, and I spoke to the need of the traditionalists to find words that would reappropriate and rearticulate timeless truths in the context of the present world. The innovators also needed the traditionalists because change without context would be meaningless, like a swimmer trying to change direction while floating in midair. This had been on my heart for a couple of days, and I found relief in finally being able to express it. Bob Gosney later said it had been needed and that I had "nailed it."

By high summer, the high excitement of starting our little intentional community had given way to some troublesome truths. Shared decision making had not developed in the way I had hoped and anticipated. Susan and I weren't helping make decisions but were doing what we were asked and able to do in return for the ability to live on the farm.

Where before I was looking for a sense that I had contributed toward the long-term vision for the farm, I now focused on whether I'd done a good day's work in and of itself. This shift in perspective was a good exercise in humility for me—practice in littleness of mind. It kept me mindful of the work I was doing right then, staying in the present moment. That allowed me to release all the other stuff without attachment, emotional or otherwise—just the right thing for my spiritual health.

We processed thirty-seven chickens one day that fall, setting up in the driveway between the farmhouse and the brooder house. I spent much of the time meditating on the death of these chickens. The ideas that sacrificial death is an integral part of the universe and that death is necessary to allow new life both felt important and true to me. I found myself thanking each bird for its contribution to our well-being and the

New Fields of Service and New Challenges

well-being of those who had eaten its eggs, somewhat in the manner of Native Americans. There seemed to me to be no moral "wrong" being done in our harvesting these chickens at the end of their productive lives and eating their bodies to sustain our own lives. Taking any life should never be done thoughtlessly, but I did not feel an absolute prohibition against taking any life under any circumstances.

Early in Ninth Month, I had an injection in my left hip to try to reduce the increasing pain I'd been experiencing. This was supplemented by taking extra NSAIDS, heating pads applied to the hip area, and to the extent possible a lessening of my physical activity. The results were underwhelming, and in less than a week I was experiencing the same level of daily pain I had been prior to the injection. When my physician called, I was ready to listen. X-rays showed "severe arthritic degeneration" in my left hip. My increased pain was not due to a strained muscle or tendon after all and would not heal over time.

The message was very straightforward: I would be a candidate for immediate total hip replacement except that the extra bone around the joint laid down after my previous hip surgery made it probable that the same thing would happen again, quite possibly leaving me with even less range of motion than I currently had. I chose to continue attempting to manage the pain nonsurgically in order to avoid just the sort of outcome she was describing.

Those attempts were unsuccessful, and a round of MRI scans doubled down on the reasons. I had severe degenerative changes in my lumbar spine as well as severe arthritic degeneration of my left hip. I tried to stay optimistic, but my options going forward seemed to fall short of happy endings: hip replacement, which one surgeon had already declined to do for fear it would leave me even worse off; long-term narcotics to reduce the pain, which might leave me dependent on drugs; or spinal fusion, which would relieve some of the lower back pain at least but would make moving about even more difficult.

Susan was a solid support throughout, and I thanked God constantly for her presence in my life. She never complained about my increasing inability to help with chores or made me feel inadequate or a slacker in any way and was always encouraging about the possibilities of finding a way to reduce the pain and possibly regain a good portion of my mobility so that I could contribute to the farm physically as well as mentally. Frank Massey's earlier advice to "be a presence" at Wings of Dawn was beginning to appear prophetic as there was little I could do physically.

I had a talk with God one afternoon, giving thanks for all the blessings I'd received throughout my life and was still receiving moment by moment. I shared my frustration at being so limited in movement and at feeling my condition worsen week by week. There was no way I deserved divine assistance—as I often said, I was already better off than I deserved—but it would surely be nice to regain some ability to move about and be helpful as well as to be rid of most of the pain. Susan and I were just beginning to find our rhythms around the farm and to begin to live into what seemed like a wonderful new phase of our lives together. It was still wonderful, and we were still thankful for every day, but I felt curtailed by this degenerative illness.

While she was at a spiritual renewal retreat, Susan called me to say that she'd described my illness during the opening session, saying that she felt as if she'd lost a companion. That hit me hard. I knew she did not mean it as completely and permanently as it might sound, but it brought home to me just how much she had been affected by my disability. It was not fair that she should suffer in any way from my problems, yet that does seem to be the way this world works.

A new surgeon described a presurgical radiation therapy that promised to prevent extra bone from being laid down during the healing process. On that hope, I made the choice to have my hip replaced, and the surgery was performed early in First Month 2014. I awoke afterward to early indications that it had been successful; I had survived, all my toes still wriggled, and I felt very little pain. Of course, my bloodstream was saturated with narcotics, so if I could have felt any pain it would have been a bad sign indeed. My thanks went to God for allowing me to pass through this danger safely. The medical staff sent me home with clear instructions about what not to do until the home health care people started making regular visits for my rehabilitation. The new hip had nothing impeding its full range of motion. The radiation treatment before surgery was successful in preventing more excess bone being formed during this surgery, and the surgeon spent time removing a considerable amount of bone fragments from the muscles and other tissues surrounding the joint so that post-surgery I had increased range of motion in my left hip, for which I was grateful. My level of chronic pain was not reduced as much as I had hoped, due to issues related to my spine, not my hip.

Achieving and maintaining the right balance between the farm and public ministry was unexpectedly difficult. Susan and I were interested in Friends General Conference's New Meetings Project, which matched two-person teams of seasoned Friends with new Friends meetings and worship groups over an eighteen- to twenty-four-month period. It seemed like an excellent way to help new meetings succeed in growing and becoming stable, and we felt we'd like to be involved together. When we first mentioned it to elders at West Grove Meeting, they were positively inclined toward it, saying it seemed to be a good match for our gifts and abilities.

When we brought up the subject a little later, they replied with some pretty discouraging remarks about our use of the discernment process and their unwillingness to be involved. One stated her unwillingness to be involved in any discernment for us as she was too busy with other responsibilities. Another said he chose not to participate in the discernment process outlined by the New Meetings Project but would say publicly that he supported our involvement in the project anyway. So, one elder in my meeting had refused a direct request for help in discernment from a minister for whom she had oversight responsibility, and another elder had short-circuited the discernment process, saying he was willing to support the proposal without going through any discernment.

Susan and I talked a lot about the discernment process for public ministry I had been using, which was asking a small group to help me with discernment prior to bringing a leading to the monthly meeting for discernment. It seemed best to us to move back toward the older pattern, which would be to present my leadings and opportunities directly to the monthly meeting for business rather than to a formal or informal discernment group ahead of time. We also laid the New Meetings Project aside for the present.

Late in 2013, I made a visit to the worship group in Southern State Prison in New Jersey and to other places where way opened. The ride north on the Carolinian was my first train trip in several years and was more pleasant than many of my earlier train journeys. This train was clean, spacious, staffed by friendly conductors, and close to on time all along the way.

Wi-Fi had not been possible on those earlier trips, of course, but I made good use of the service on this trip, doing some writing as well as reading several online articles about the recent schism in Indiana Yearly Meeting. The disparate understandings of the authority relationship between that yearly meeting and its constituent monthly meetings seems to be the real driving force behind the separation. If the "identified problem" had not been gender relations, it would have been something else with very similar results. The center of gravity of the range of understandings of that relationship between North Carolina Yearly Meeting (Conservative) (NCYM[C]) and its monthly meetings was much different from the one that prevailed in Indiana, but the example did emphasize the importance of articulating the relationship clearly and usefully in our own revised *Discipline*.

The morning after I arrived in Philadelphia, Bill Geary and I went to the Quaker Center at 15th and Cherry, where we met with Robin Mohr of Friends World Committee for Consultation. I'd never met Robin before, although we had been aware of each other for years. We had an excellent conversation about the Friends World Committee for Consultation and its perspective on various aspects of Quakers in the Western hemisphere before heading over to the meeting house for a meeting for worship with the Friends Select School student body.

The meeting house was pretty well filled with students. I was given some vocal ministry to share, which I did, and two students also spoke during the worship. Afterward, I was able to greet one of those students and give a word of encouragement, but the press of young people wanting to get outside was too great for me to locate the other. Three Japanese

New Fields of Service and New Challenges

students each stopped and bowed to me on their way by, which touched me; I bowed with the gesture of namaste in return.

After worship, Chris Mohr joined us and we returned to Robin's office for a religious opportunity. This was a blessed time; I was glad to have asked for this time together.

After the meeting with Robin, Bill offered to take me anyplace I wanted to go in Philadelphia. I told him that what I craved was an authentic Philly cheesesteak. So, we walked down to the Reading Terminal Market, and my craving was satisfied as I got the real deal and savored every bite. That evening, we had dinner with Jack and Peggy Warner before driving down to Southern State Prison. Their hospitality was warm and genuine. Afterward, Bill and I set our hearts toward the prison. The prison itself was as stark and desolate as I remembered it, with perhaps even more concertina wire than before gleaming brightly in the glare of the sodium floodlights. We set up the assigned room for worship and waited for the inmates to arrive. They were not allowed to leave their cells until the announcement was made at the stroke of eight p.m. that the worship would happen.

The first inmates to enter (after signing in outside and being patted down by a guard) greeted me with, "You look just like your photo." It turns out Jeff Ginsberg had sent them an 8" x 10" photo she had taken of Friends attending Representative Body at West Grove in 2011, and with Bill's help they had identified all the Friends who had been writing them or otherwise supporting them over the years. Six prisoners in all came to the meeting, which was filled with deep conversation and testimony. At one point Jimmy, their clerk, read the passage in Matthew about visiting the prisoner being visiting Christ (Mark 25:36), which nearly brought tears to my eyes.

I described the process of obtaining a travel certificate and shared with them that the unity required in that process meant that West Grove Friends were with me in spirit on my visit to them, which seemed to reach several deeply. It turned out that one of the group had hopes of being paroled that year, and if that happened he hoped to return to the Siler City-Pittsboro area of North Carolina. I shared how close that would be to Wings of Dawn and expressed the hope that way would open for us to meet again in North Carolina.

I spent the next day in contemplation and reading before a potluck supper gathering at Mullica Hill Meeting in New Jersey. There were about ten Friends in attendance. The food was good and was largely vegetarian or vegan. To my ears, the absence of any discussion of organic or non-GMO food was curious. On the trip, I'd heard several persons discuss the importance of eating rightly in terms of dietary supplements or certain food groups but almost none in terms of avoiding antibiotics, hormones, or other nonsustainable agricultural practices. I realized that there might be more of a disconnect between producers and consumers of food than I had previously thought.

The discussion after dinner was warm and genuine. Bill Geary primed the pump, as he called it, by undertaking a "Bill Moyer-type" interview of me for fifteen minutes or so, after which he opened it up to everyone, and we moved fairly quickly from folks asking me questions to a general sharing of insights and challenges in the spiritual life. It was authentic and deep, and I was given the opportunity to testify to the perceptible guidance of the Inward Christ in my life. I believe the evening was owned and accepted by the Holy Spirit.

The train ride home on the following day offered ample opportunity to read, rest, and reflect on the journey. I felt that it was clearly right for me to have made this trip, including all the stops. I felt blessed by an exceptional Divine Presence in my several opportunities for ministry over the previous several months, in travel, writing, and presence. It felt important to remain mindful of this and to nurture the Divine Presence by my practices and my behaviors so that I would not bring it to an end prematurely. If I were faithful and diligent, it would remain just as long as suited the Divine Will.

As I got off the train in Burlington, North Carolina, and walked toward the station, I met the stationmaster walking in the other direction. He greeted me with "Good evening, Mr. Wilson, good to have you back." I greeted him in return and indicated that I was headed inside to look for my wife. To this he replied, "I haven't seen her yet." This exchange, with a man Susan and I had only met once for a brief conversation several days earlier, epitomized one of the characteristics of small-town life that is hugely appealing to me: the degree to which people are able to and desirous of treating each other as individuals rather than anonymous mannequins. In the small-town setting, everyone knows everyone else, at least by sight—and if by chance you don't know each other, you act as if you do. That's just not possible in the city.

One of the attractions of Greensboro for someone like me is the numerous Quaker-themed events. In 2014, David Johns, my constructive theology professor at Earlham School of Religion, was at New Garden meeting in Greensboro one evening to give a talk titled "Can Quakers Quake Again?" One of his points was that Quakers do theology all the time, in spite of protests to the contrary, and that we need to be doing more of it communally rather than in individual isolation.

As David talked about the importance of Friends doing theology together, my mind was drawn to reflect on why the corporate aspects of Quakerism are so important. I had long felt so, but I also felt that my attempts to articulate the reasons had been inadequate. Now I saw that the corporate aspects of Quakerism are the work that God has given us to do—to learn how to be the Kingdom of God together and to live into that new reality as colonies of leaven intent on transforming the world. Our meetings are supposed to be examples of the Kingdom, showing the world how we can live together and inviting all to join us. To opt out of that exciting, difficult, and exhausting process is to opt out of God's project for creation; it is like sharpening a tool or tuning an engine but never putting the tool or engine to its intended use.

To be open to and to follow the Inward Guide personally is hard enough, even with divine assistance. To learn how to love and trust and live in gospel harmony with the very human people in our meetings is even more difficult. As the saying goes, it is easy to be holy on the mountain but hard to be holy in the marketplace. Yet that is the purpose for which we have been gathered as a people and the content of what Christ has come to teach us individually and corporately.

On Third Month 2, 2014, I recorded the following in my journal:

> First Day—At meeting for business this morning we considered the Third Query, concerning love and unity. I spent the time reflecting on the great stresses the Wilsons and the Ansells have experienced from time to time over the past year, times in which there was little unity to be found. Yet we were all continually desiring unity and trying to restore it. That process is not instantaneous; it requires effort and humility and persistence over extended periods of time. We are not restored fully even now, but we are closer than we were a little while ago, and I trust in a little while longer we will be closer still.

I spent one morning rewriting the section of the *Discipline* titled "Special Occasions" (weddings and funerals). Soon I had reworked the old language into a new format that included same-sex couples as well as heterosexuals and had worked in language that opened the door for a meeting to have care of a wedding that was only a religious, not a legal, union. Reflecting on this work made me realize how far I had come personally in this area.

My attitude about homosexuality coming out of high school was essentially ignorance. I'd heard a couple of derogatory words about homosexuals but had had no real sense of what they meant or that they might refer to real people. They were just reference-free insults that boys could hurl at one another. Early in my freshman year of college, I was accosted while riding the subway by a young man who hugged me fiercely and went on and on about how good I looked, etc. I pretty much froze, making no response at all, and he ran off at the next subway stop. Even afterward, I had no real understanding of what had happened.

Living in greater Boston in the late '60s and '70s, I was exposed to the reality that some men were homosexual; I don't recall that the existence of lesbians had penetrated my consciousness at that point. Homosexuality seemed strange and not understandable to me, but I didn't have the fundamentalist extreme reaction of labeling it as mortal sin and perdition. I can clearly remember saying that homosexuals could do or be whatever they wanted—but behind closed doors. I did not want to be exposed to homosexuals being affectionate toward one another in public. I was confused when the homosexuals to whom I expressed this opinion did not welcome it. They said they wanted to be free to act as heterosexuals acted in public—a point I did not understand and did not approve of until much later.

By 1983, when I was part of a panel on homosexuality and affirmative action in a national board meeting of American Friends Service Committee, my thinking had progressed considerably. At that time, I said that the sexual ethical standard for heterosexual and homosexual people was the same: no fornication (i.e., promiscuity), no adultery, and monogamy. Bisexual people, I recall saying, were also called to the same standard; no matter how many people (or groups of people) might be attractive to a person, the standard was to choose one person and be faithful to them in a committed relationship. This drew the strong approval of most of the board and also an anonymous handwritten letter of protest. I shared the note with Asia Bennett, then head of American Friends Service Committee, who issued a memo to all staff condemning anonymous communications of that sort.

Now, in 2014, here I was, working to ensure the full integration of LGBTQ+ folks into all aspects of our religious and community life. I'd come a long way; God had been patient and persevering. If I can change so much, other people can too, on a wide range of subjects.

One spring First Day morning, I worshipped at the pastoral Friends meeting down the road from the farm in Liberty, North Carolina. The meeting had been established around 1943 and had thrived for several decades before shrinking in membership in recent years. They had a meeting house and fellowship hall along with two former parsonages that the meeting was renting out. There were about eight members in attendance and seven visitors besides myself who were middle schoolers from a neighboring Friends meeting who were there as part of a membership preparation program.

The back page of the church bulletin offered a full list of officers and committee members, but closer examination revealed that there were only a few different names—each showed up multiple times in different roles. The worship room itself gave evidence of declining numbers. It was laid out much like a Baptist or Methodist sanctuary, with rows of pews facing a raised conventional pulpit front and center and a choir section on the left front on permanent risers. Behind the pulpit, there was a large portrait of Jesus hanging on the back wall. A low railing separated the pulpit and choir section from the other worshippers. There were microphones hanging from the ceiling to catch the sound of the choir, but no one stood near them. The interim minister spoke from a small podium at floor level in front of the pews on the right side of the room, where we were all invited to sit.

The worship was informal, personal, and sincere. There were a couple of hymns (a cappella since there was no one to play the piano), a pastoral prayer, a children's message, a sermon, and a collection of "tithes and offerings." One part of the collection was dedicated to an outreach project that helped local persons in poverty. I could appreciate the value and intent of each part of the service while feeling nevertheless that it was not worship of the sort that had become most meaningful to me. There was no time to settle down into silence and simply be present to the Living God. I don't worship as well as I ought because I am often distracted, but I feel most like I have truly worshipped when I have done nothing more than open myself to God's Presence.

Susan had been worshipping regularly at Friendship Friends Meeting, even though it was a little farther away from the farm than West Grove. One First Day, feeling a strong desire to worship with her, I attended Friendship as well. Attendance was good and the worship was deep. The first vocal ministry came from Ted Benfey, who was by then an old man, physically bent but sweet in spirit. Some time afterward, I was led to offer my penny's worth reflecting on the tremendous change wrought on the world by the mystery of the resurrection. A young woman later added her words on the grief she was feeling around the loss of her relationship with her mother.

Friendship seemed to be in a very good place both spiritually and in terms of community. They had made the commitment to build a new meeting house to accommodate increased numbers at meetings for worship and other meeting activities but were approaching that large project carefully and spiritually, not rushing ahead of their discernment and their level of unity. There were a variety of activities to attract new

New Fields of Service and New Challenges

attenders: extended worship, discussion forums, weekday bag lunches for conversation, and social concerns such as feeding the poor.

In light of the postmodern world's unbelief, I reflected somewhat on my own faith during worship. It was clear to me that Jesus of Nazareth was a historical human being whose life is roughly outlined in the Gospels (they are not strictly biographical accounts so should not be judged by modern standards) and that he taught an ethic and a relationship with God that is described in the New Testament. Something happened soon after he died that radically transformed those who had been his followers in life and that spread contagiously all over the world, and it has sustained those followers for some two thousand years. It is a mystery to me, and I have no better description of that mystery than resurrection. In short, Easter happened. I can't explain it or even describe it in much detail, but that it was and is a real event is not in doubt in my heart and mind.

The Discipline Review Committee met in Fourth Month to review the responses to our discussion draft for section I of the revision. We spent well over an hour in worship before embarking on the business portion of our meeting. During that time, each of us spoke of our concerns and our hopes for the *Discipline* revision process and for a developing situation regarding Piedmont Friends Fellowship. When the worship was completed, I could feel a marked decrease in the general level of anxiety and a corresponding increase in our trust that Christ was indeed head of all things regarding the church and that our part was to continue our specific tasks in obedience and faith.

As we gathered around the table, signed on to the network, and began reviewing the responses from each meeting in turn, we were able to truly hear and respond to each comment in an open and nondefensive way, better, I thought, than any of us had been able to do earlier when looking at them in isolation from each other. Soon, we had a marked-up text that reflected numerous comments from meetings. Some suggestions we did not adopt, after careful consideration, but there were a great many that had real merit.

Each of us was aware that Piedmont Friends Fellowship had made the decision (after years in discernment) to form a new yearly meeting

(Piedmont Friends Yearly Meeting and Association).[2] This move seemed threatening to us, even though the plan seemed intended to be as minimally disruptive to existing yearly meetings as feasible. There were four NCYM(C) monthly meetings in the Fellowship then—Davidson, Durham, Fayetteville, and Friendship—and we recognized the risk that some or all of them might join the new Piedmont yearly meeting. Dual affiliation across yearly meetings had never seemed feasible to me as it entailed commitment to mutually exclusive doctrines and values. How could a monthly meeting maintain the NCYM(C) doctrine of waiting worship and inspirational ministry, to give an obvious example, when it also belonged to a yearly meeting that included meetings that hired pastors who read prepared sermons? So, the formation of the Piedmont yearly meeting seemed to threaten the loss of some or all of those four monthly meetings that were currently in NCYM(C). If one or more of those meetings were to leave us, I feared that Virginia Beach might also leave our yearly meeting in order to affiliate with Baltimore Yearly Meeting because their ties to and participation in our yearly meeting had been diminishing in recent years.

In Fifth Month, Susan and I traveled in the ministry to the Farmington-Scipio Regional Gathering in New York State. Several generations ago, there had been a strong Conservative presence in Scipio (they had even exchanged epistles with our yearly meeting), and we were looking forward to the opportunity to renew relationships. I was to give two lectures, and we were scheduled to lead a workshop together on our personal spiritual journeys.

Due to travel difficulties, we arrived at the gathering a full four hours behind schedule. The evening lecture I was to give, titled "Radical Hospitality," had been canceled, and there seemed to be no appropriate time to reschedule it.

The next morning, I gave my lecture titled "Leaven of the Kingdom of God: Our Corporate Purpose as a People Gathered and Taught," and it seemed to go quite well. Callid Keefe-Perry, sitting in the first row, had a troubled look on his face and troubled body language all through the talk, which I wondered about at the time, but I pressed on anyway. Later, I spoke to him and learned that he was feeling discouraged about whether any of what I was saying could or would be heard by Friends in Farmington-Scipio. My sense was that some heard and some did not; I got several questions afterward that indicated individuals had been paying attention. It is the prophet's responsibility to speak the Truth as clearly as possible and as closely as possible to the leading. What the people do with that Truth is their own responsibility. This may be part of the difference between a prophet and a pastor—a pastor spends time working within the faith community to put the prophetic word into daily practice.

That afternoon, Susan and I led a workshop together on the topic of our individual and mutual spiritual journeys. Each of us told our story, and the other asked questions or made comments as we went along. It was very informal, and Friends responded enthusiastically. Susan and I learned a little bit about each other that we hadn't realized before, and the audience seemed to be able to identify with each of us in a personal way. Susan was the big hit, and I was both proud and happy for her to allow herself to be on the public stage and to be received so positively. Several Friends suggested that we put on the same workshop for other audiences.

I sat down at the dinner table that evening and stayed there until time to retire for the night as various Friends joined us, shared in the conversation for a while, and then departed, only to be replaced by new faces. It felt like good ministry as I was able to speak to specific conditions and to answer personal questions that needed this more intimate setting rather than the lectern or the workshop.

After meeting for worship on the last day, the group gathered to share some of the attributes they had experienced in Susan and myself. Each one was written down on newsprint, and the sheets for each of us were then given to us to take home. Several Friends I had spoken with that morning encouraged me to publish my memoirs so that more Friends could hear my story. I expressed my sense that after publishing memoirs one was then obliged not to do anything else significant, to which the response was that I should publish volume 1 now and subsequent volumes later on. I had gotten this same encouragement from several independent sources recently, and I began to feel that I should listen carefully.

On Sixth Month 8, 2014, I reflected in my journal on West Grove meeting:

> First Day—I continue to sense that there is little of the Life in West Grove meeting at the present time. We seem to go through the motions rather listlessly. I have tried to give voice to my concerns through the responses to the queries, but that does not seem to have any effect. We do nothing to attract or welcome new people, and several of those who have attended do so no longer. I hold the meeting in prayer regularly and ask God for clarity about what we should do or what I should do, but so far I perceive no guidance—so I keep the watch, and pray, and wait.

At one of our periodic farm meetings that summer, the Ansells and Wilsons ended up discussing our understandings of discernment, which was illuminating to me. It came up in the context of differences between the Ansells' commitment to the farm and Susan's and my commitment. The Ansells were fully committed to Charlie's original vision of being told to "feed my sheep" and to the farm as the embodiment of that vision, no matter what. Jan contrasted that with my commitment to work on the farm, as she described it, "until the Lord leads you to go someplace else." This startled me. It was a true description of my own commitment to continuing discernment, but I hadn't realized the variety of ways my commitment to discernment could play out in our Quaker faith tradition. On deeper reflection, I concluded that the right path for me was to commit until the Lord led me elsewhere.

These and other experiences left Susan and me with the sense that our earlier sense of what Wings of Dawn would become and our roles there were not achievable. We spent an increasing amount of time seeking clearer discernment about what our proper roles might be, but guidance came slowly.

Friends gathered at Guilford College for the 2014 sessions of NCYM(C). Susan led that year's Bible study, talking about transformation and about ways of knowing other than the intellectual, and she followed that up with lectio divina on Bible passages that illustrated her content.

New Fields of Service and New Challenges

She was articulate, engaging, and informative, and she exuded the confidence of a skilled and experienced public speaker. Everything she did, from the way she opened up her topic to the style of her speaking, made her material accessible and attractive to the audience. It was a great start to the week, and several Friends approached her afterward to tell her so. I certainly did.

My own special services were as yearly meeting treasurer and member of the Discipline Revision Committee. One evening, I took part in a panel discussion of the distinctive spiritual and historical characteristics of our yearly meeting. I spoke about our history, Carole Treadway told some stories about yearly meeting members over the decades, and Rachel Miller spoke of her experiences growing up in the yearly meeting. Carole was good, as she always is, and Rachel really exceeded my expectations. She gave a good presentation and delivered it well.

In Tenth Month 2014, Susan and I left Wings of Dawn Farm and moved into a small house about ten minutes away. It felt very right for us to leave. At the same time, it still felt that it had been right for us to move to Wings of Dawn when we did. Some purpose had been served, and it was not our place to demand that God explain everything to our satisfaction. Job attempted to get that same satisfaction and learned that he could not understand God's ways and reasons; I felt that was also true of me. God led, Susan and I were faithful to what we were able to discern and were obedient, and we both felt God's assurance that we had done the right things at the right time. That is all we need to know; it is all we are entitled or enabled to know.

It seemed best to make a clean break from the Wings of Dawn experience. At meeting for business the next month, Friendship Friends heard the letter from West Grove meeting and approved my becoming a sojourning member at Friendship. Now Susan and I were officially in the same meeting again, which made me glad. There was much to appreciate and to be thankful for during my two years at West Grove, but listening at Friendship to the sounds of fellowship before meeting, to the vocal ministry of others during meeting, and to the nature of items brought to meetings for business illuminated for me the abundance, diversity, and energetic life of the faith community there. It was right for me to transfer my membership to West Grove when I did earlier, and also right that I now be at Friendship. I would listen to see if, after some period of sojourning, I was led to transfer my membership outright.

Nothing was said, either in West Grove's letter or in Friendship's meeting for business, about my being recorded as a minister of the gospel. I was content not to push the matter in any way; when it became a concern to some Friend, it would come to the attention of Friends generally. It was conceivable that West Grove Friends might discern that as I was no longer worshipping with them regularly the necessary relationship of mutual accountability could not be sustained. That could lead them to discontinue me from my station as a minister. I saw no objection that could be raised to that argument. Or, some Friends at Friendship might object to my being a recorded minister and on their rolls as a member, sojourning or regular. They had recorded Deborah Shaw only after much painful work (although I believed one of the most vocal opponents to the recording process was no longer active in the meeting). Ted Benfey was listed in the directory of ministers and elders as a member of Friendship but had been recorded by Philadelphia Yearly Meeting, and I supposed something like that could be possible for me.

As I saw it then, if/when I asked for a final transfer of membership from West Grove to Friendship, my recording would end; this had been the process followed, at my request, when I transferred to Rich Square and to West Grove. It would then be up to Friendship to decide whether to consider recording me themselves. It seemed to offer a teaching moment either way. If they undertook the process, it would teach us all a little more about what it means to have a gift of ministry recorded in the meeting minutes. If they didn't, it would offer me an opportunity to describe to others that being recorded is not a lifetime office but is always subject to the discernment of the faith community. I would attempt to sustain the same relationships of mutual discernment and accountability in either case.

That winter, I was invited to deliver the keynote address at the 2015 Pacific Yearly Meeting sessions that summer. My immediate reaction was joy at the opportunity to visit Friends in California in the ministry as I

New Fields of Service and New Challenges

hadn't done that since Susan and I had traveled there in 2003. I felt a connection with Friends there, known and unknown. One disappointment was that their sessions overlapped our own that year since NCYM(C) was taking place a week later than its usual schedule. If I were to accept, it would be necessary to ensure that other Friends were willing and able to assume my responsibilities during our annual sessions.

When the Discipline Revision Committee met again, I shared the invitation to Pacific Yearly Meeting and asked the group if they were willing and able to release me from my committee obligations during yearly meeting sessions next summer so that I might accept the Pacific Yearly Meeting invitation. They were ready to do so and saw some advantages in that. If I were absent from our sessions, some otherwise skeptical Friends might be more accepting of the revision process as something that was widely shared and not just a one-Friend project.

The Worship and Ministry Committee at Friendship meeting had a full agenda for its next meeting. I shared the invitation I'd received from Pacific Yearly Meeting, Susan introduced her leading to offer an opportunity for regular contemplative practice at the meeting house, and Deborah Shaw opened a prospect for her to lead a workshop/retreat during the next year. The committee found unity in forwarding both prospects for travel to the monthly meeting. Susan's description of a weekly day (or afternoon) of contemplative practice was also well received. She and the committee mutually agreed to season the possibility for a month or so to see more clearly what the format of such a day might be.

Travel minutes for myself and Deborah Shaw were approved without hesitation at the next meeting for business. I let Friends in Pacific Yearly Meeting know I was free to accept their invitation and began the spiritual preparation needed to prepare a keynote lecture.

The Discipline Revision Committee had drafted a new section on membership and distributed it to the monthly meetings for discussion and feedback. Friendship's discussion was very good – both insightful and positive. The proposed end of birthright membership was the most controversial part of the revision. Two birthright members spoke movingly of how important knowing they had a place in the meeting had been to them as they were growing up. Other Friends reminded us that as "convinced Friends" they felt were somehow second-class members of their meetings. Friends were open and frank without being defensive. As we sat tenderly with one another, it was opened to the birthright members that if the *Discipline* kept the terminology of birthright membership but added a requirement that such members must make a positive declaration that they want to continue to be members sometime before their twenty-fifth birthday, their needs and concerns would be met. As this requirement for a positive declaration of desire was at the heart of my desire to see the membership policy revised, this seemed to me to be an important breakthrough in the discussion.

When the Discipline Revision Committee met to review the responses received on the proposed revisions to membership, our opening worship reminded us that we did not gather to do our own work but to do God's work as it was shown to us. Each one of us felt deeply about the words we drafted on every subject, but each one of us was ready to put personal preferences aside when it became clear that the yearly meeting as a body was not in unity with the words we'd used or the practices we'd recommended. We realized that birthright membership was not a practice that Friends were in unity to give up or to modify in any great manner. The committee withdrew the bulk of what we'd written and in its place strengthened the section that emphasized that monthly meetings made membership decisions as they were led.

There was a worshipful discussion of spiritual gifts one morning before meeting for worship at Friendship touching on many of the usual topics. What claimed most of my attention was an internal, heart-warming affirmation that I felt as the discussion continued—an inward assurance that I had received a spiritual gift and that this would continue to be true whether or not my local faith community recognized it consciously, whether or not they provided nurture and accountability for the development and exercise of that gift, and whether or not they consciously made space to receive the fruits of the gift. I felt the joy of being able to offer the gift in both seen and unseen ways and was released from the angst of any tensions within the local meeting about the gift.

New Fields of Service and New Challenges

I was shown the prospect of my exercising my giftedness in the service of the Lord for the rest of my life, and it gave me deep contentment and joy to contemplate. This seemed to be both numinous and liminal space. It seemed to indicate a new phase to my ministry (perhaps one I had been moving into without yet realizing) in which I was freed from both the angst of "Am I gifted?" "Does anyone else recognize my gifts?" "Dare I say or do anything in this place and moment of time?" and the dangers of ego. The gift is simply there, as I am simply left-handed; it is time to simply use the gift in the service of God.

A short time later, I was active in the vocal ministry on First Day. Before speaking, I had to deal with some doubts about how often I had been speaking in worship recently and whether my too-frequent speaking would lead some to discount the messages I had been given. As I held both the leading to speak and my doubts before God in a search for clarity, the experience of this earlier discussion returned, and I felt joy at being able to share the joy of God's immediate Presence. Doubt melted away, and I was able to share what I had been given in a faithful manner, without reservation but also without undue or artificial enthusiasm.

I felt a great spiritual energy in the worship at Friendship that I did not feel at West Grove or for that matter at Rich Square. I spent part of each meeting just feeling the Holy Spirit moving about the meeting room, rejoicing in its Presence and energy. At the same time, I was feeling more frequent and more powerful leadings to speak in meeting. I had no sense outside of meeting of anything that I should say in meeting, but once in worship with other Friends there was hardly a First Day when I did not feel some promptings to speak. Over the past couple of months, I had actually gotten to my feet a little bit less than half the time, which is much more frequently than I had ever felt the urge at West Grove or Rich Square. It was a joyful experience in every way—like surfing on the waves of the Holy Spirit—but I wanted to be careful to do no harm and to always stay close to my Guide.

Carole Treadway led another discussion in the Deepening the Spiritual Life of the Meeting series on First Day. She began by passing around a postcard-sized photo of a grid of panels, similar to quilt panels, of responses to the sentence "Jesus is _____." Each panel expressed one possibility, such as "denial of reason" or "a mythical figure." We were invited to offer our own responses to the incomplete sentence. Friends were deliberate, open, and quite nonjudgmental of each other's offerings. I had no sense that anyone felt offended by anyone else's statement or that any speaker felt their statement had been judged in any way. It was an example of Carole's ability to create a safe space for such sharing to take place and of the nature of the Friendship faith community.

There was a large range of responses, though everyone was apparently engaging with Jesus in some way. I heard no one who outright rejected Christianity due to a past injury, for example. In all, the discussion portrayed Friendship Friends as people serious about their faith journey who were engaging Jesus in ways relevant to the twists and turns of their particular journey. In my response, I described Jesus as the pivot point around which the entirety of cosmic history turned and the point at which God and humanity most strongly connected. I also said that Christianity was a large tent and that we didn't have to all find the same answers—we were only required to continue to engage the question.

I entered worship afterward feeling strong movements of the Spirit but uncertain of what they meant or how I should respond to them. Susan told me afterward that it was first uncomfortable and later actually painful for her to sit beside me. Her neck and shoulder on the side nearest me began to ache; she had to spend time doing some mental pain-reduction exercises in that area of her body. Meanwhile, I was neither calm nor distracted. Something spiritual was going on in me, and I was doing the work needed to let it develop and discern what it meant.

Eventually, the vision of Jesus that I had experienced at the Ansells' house in Virginia Beach came to mind, and I reflected on that experience internally for a while. The leading came to share this experience in worship, and though I resisted for several minutes, the intensity of the leading was too great to resist. There were physical indicators, such as an elevated and intensified heartbeat, that I hadn't felt in a long time and that could not be ignored. Some part of me was reluctant to engage in yet another bit of what was becoming quite frequent vocal ministry, and I felt reluctant to make myself vulnerable to other people in the way I knew such an account would make me vulnerable. It was difficult to stand but impossible to remain seated.

So, I rose, put on my glasses, shut my eyes, and gave my testimony of an encounter with Jesus in a vision. At the end, I confessed that I still did not know everything that the vision meant but said that knowing was not as important as continuing to engage the question, continuing to seek the meaning.

When I went to the Worship and Ministry meeting to present my request that they recommend that monthly meeting issue travel minutes for me to go to Community Friends Meeting in Cincinnati in Eighth Month and to Broadmead Monthly Meeting in Ohio in Tenth Month, they were willing and in unity and had some affirming comments about the way this ministry would fit into the desire expressed by the yearly meeting to share more widely the source and foundation of our particular faith tradition as North Carolina Conservative Friends. Darlene Stanley, Worship and Ministry clerk, told me she had received a message as she reviewed the invitations from the two Ohio meetings in preparation for that meeting. She perceived the Divine Presence and was told that the trip to Cincinnati in particular was important in the unfolding of the next step in my service in the ministry.

I spoke with Darlene privately, saying that it would be good for me to talk with her in the near future and asking her to be sensitive to an opening for a conversation. I felt it would be good to have someone who was part of Worship and Ministry be privy to the sorts of interior conversations I had been having. Darlene could be both a reflective observer helping me stay close to my Guide in terms of vocal ministry at Friendship and a ready help in the event that some Friend(s) approached Worship and Ministry with a concern about my vocal ministry.

Darlene and I met at the meeting house early one morning and spoke for over an hour. Simply put, I wanted help in making sure I didn't outrun my Guide. It became clear to us that what I was desirous of was eldering and that Friendship didn't do much in the way of explicit eldering for vocal ministers. She agreed to do what she could to help me personally and suggested that Ministry and Worship might explore what it should be doing for the meeting in this area.

After the rise of meeting that week, George White approached me on his walker and said, "When in doubt, speak." He went on to add, "To most people I say the opposite, but to you I say, when in doubt, speak. What you say is important to me and helps me live a better life, so speak!" It is so like God to give us unexpected signs in unexpected ways. I still yearned for a solid eldering relationship in meeting, but I was reassured that at that time I was being faithful, neither outrunning nor lagging behind my Guide.

One of the members of the Southern State Worship Group had been transferred to a facility in central North Carolina, and I wanted to continue to visit him. My initial attempt to visit "Tom" after his transfer from Southern State Prison was derailed by his unexpected transfer from Johnston Correctional Institution in Smithfield to Southern Correctional in Troy, North Carolina. I renewed my efforts once he got settled, and we spent two hours together without a break in our first conversation. I came away feeling blessed to have had the opportunity.

Tom was open about the mistakes he had made in the past that had brought him to the place he was now in, and he did not put the blame for that on anyone but himself for the bad decisions he had made. He'd done what he could do in terms of NA and AA programs and other opportunities offered by the prison system. Southern Correctional was a minimum-security facility, and Tom was able there to work under prison supervision on an off-campus rehab project not far away. This gave him the opportunity to get outside the prison and outdoors on a regular basis and to pass the time more quickly than just sitting idly inside.

We talked about his limited experience of Quakers and how the Quakers he had met had had an influence on him. Bob Cooper had given him copies of *Who Do You Say I Am?* and *Wrestling with Our Faith Tradition*. He had some good questions to ask about the latter, indicating he was reading closely and thinking about what he was reading. I tried to bring him a copy of *Radical Hospitality* but couldn't get it past the guard at the gate because he had to request a specific title before I could give it to him. He said he'd like to read more about George Fox, so he and I planned to do the dance to get him some books and pamphlets to read. Once he had been at Southern long enough, he'd be able to get a four-

New Fields of Service and New Challenges

hour pass to attend worship services. It was about an hour's drive from Southern to Friendship Meeting. I thought it would be possible to pick him up, drive to Greensboro, attend worship, and get him back to Southern within that time frame.

Also that spring, Frank Massey invited me to speak over dinner to some Guilford College students about my spiritual journey and ministry over the years. This is part of an ongoing practice he had of inviting different Friends to share their stories; all students were invited but not required to sit in and listen. Max Carter and Deborah Shaw were there the night I came, along with Frank and a few students, and we had a good time. Afterward, Frank said he would like to have me speak to his third-year students on the same topic because my story was not a "straight line" and he thought some of those students would benefit from hearing and realizing that.

As I spoke, I was very aware of how much reviewing my journals recently had brought back to mind both larger patterns and specific incidents in my life. I was able to give a much fuller and better organized presentation because I'd been immersed in my journals. God organizes opportunities in our lives to a much greater extent than we usually are aware. This is not predestination but an invitation into a more perfect harmony with God's yearnings and desires.

Friendship did not address recognizing me as a recorded minister when the meeting accepted my transfer of membership. At a later meeting for business, Worship and Ministry recommended that I be recorded. There was no unity at that meeting; several actions to familiarize Friends with the meaning of that practice were recommended, and the decision was deferred. Though these actions were carried out, the subject was not brought back to business meeting, as had been agreed. This meant to me that I was no longer a recorded minister.

As I reflected on traveling to California for Pacific Yearly Meeting and related events, what felt different now was a certain internal confidence in the reality of my gift and the rightness of exercising it that stemmed from its formal recognition by the faith community. My relationships as a minister with the three monthly meetings that had recorded gifts they saw in me were not ideal in any fashion. However, the act of recording—however incompletely followed through on afterward—was to me an important affirmation that there was something going on in me that is important to the health of the faith community and that should be developed and exercised carefully.

After feeling that corroboration for roughly twenty-five years, I now felt its absence. Even when my meeting had done very little corporately to be involved in the development or exercise of my gifts, that initial affirmation had said to me that I wasn't crazy, that it was right for me to be concerned with deepening my spiritual life in order to act as a public Friend more nearly in the gospel order and more nearly to what God had in mind for me. Being known outwardly as a recorded minister did not matter very much other than as a witness to others that particular spiritual gifts are still being entrusted to individuals in our faith tradition, as they have been from the beginning, and that it is important to recognize when that has happened and to do what we can to see that those gifts are developed and exercised as God would have them be.

This led to some interesting conversations with Sid Kitchens, clerk of Friendship Meeting, about whether or not I was still a recorded minister. Sid was inclined to feel that I was—that the gift did not disappear simply because I transferred my membership from one meeting to another down the road. At the same time, he felt it would be highly unlikely for Friendship Meeting to record me as there were some Friends in the meeting who felt "sensitive to issues regarding titling" (as the monthly meeting's website puts it). Sid suggested that I continue to be on the roll of recorded ministers under Friendship but with a note saying I was recorded by West Grove Meeting.

There were two Friends on the yearly meeting roster of recorded ministers who had been recorded while members of other yearly meetings, one from Iowa (Friends United Meeting) and one from Philadelphia (Orthodox). After sitting with this possibility for some time, I found it unacceptable for me because it would refer to a past relationship between West Grove and myself and not a present relationship or spiritual condition.

With these thoughts in mind, I set off in Seventh Month 2015 to speak at Pacific Yearly Meeting sessions and to visit other California

New Fields of Service and New Challenges

Friends groups along the way. My companion in this ministry was Elaine Emily of Berkeley.

Before the yearly meeting began, I spent a day on retreat with the Young Adult Friends—roughly defined as Friends under forty—at the Berkeley meeting house. We had some excellent conversations and a group discussion during the day. After dinner we gathered again, together with some other folks from Berkeley Friends Meeting. A couple of people had asked questions of me that afternoon that there had not been time to answer, so I primed the pump by responding to those, and we were on our way. This question-and-answer format I enjoy very much, and the audience seemed well engaged. We talked for more than two hours about recording spiritual gifts, the testimonies, whether Quakers were still relevant, how NCYM(C) came into being, the immediate and perceptible guidance of the Holy Spirit, and more.

These folks were asking good questions of their faith, of the Quaker faith tradition as they saw it, and of the world. They didn't know very much of the story of the tradition beyond what they saw acted out in their monthly and yearly meetings, and these meetings were both relatively new in the history of Quakerism.

A significant part of the opportunity that presented itself to me here, as elsewhere at other times, was opening the fullness of the faith tradition, and of Christianity itself, to their view. They'd seen such a small slice of each that they often didn't realize the possibilities for them in the broader tradition or the big tent of Christianity. These young adults would rather hear a committed person with whom they disagreed be honest with them than listen to a wishy-washy non-answer from someone who didn't want to be offensive to anyone else. "Friends believe all sorts of things" didn't cut it with them. "I believe this and this because of that and that" was what they wanted to hear—and they would then argue Torah in an informed, engaged, noncombative way.

Going in, I had no real sense that I as a writer was in any way relevant to this age group of Friends on the West Coast. The book of essays was more than twenty years old, and I had no indication that anyone in Pacific Yearly Meeting had read or paid attention to what I'd written since then. Much to my surprise, many of them had read and wrestled with what I've written over the years and felt strongly that this wrestling had been a real help to them in the development of their own spirituality. Carl Magruder was a formal and informal mentor for several of these Friends. I discovered later that he had been telling them that the Friend who was going to "show up" in Quakerism was the one who would read the *Gospel Order* essays through to the end. They had been doing just that. Sometimes they felt like underlining an entire page, sometimes they just wanted to throw the book across the room—but they kept going back and wrestling with what's there. What they've been getting out of that process has changed their spiritual journey.

At almost every moment of the retreat that wasn't taken up by a scheduled activity, I was engaged with one or more Young Adult Friend in a spiritual discussion. These were deep discussions because they were serious about their faith commitments—whether those commitments were Christian in nature, Buddhist, or something else. At several points, Friends in private conversations became quite emotional as they described how important something or other that I had written had been to them.

After the retreat, Elaine and I drove to Walker Creek Ranch in Petaluma, California, for the yearly meeting sessions. From the moment of our arrival, I encountered numerous persons who told me they had been present at this meeting or that meeting when I had visited them back in 2003 and how much they were looking forward to my presence at the yearly meeting sessions. Others approached to say how much they appreciated my various writings. Far from being a stranger, I felt very much included in the community

I had the sense that the lecture I had prepared touched on a number of points of interest and concern to Pacific Yearly Meeting Friends. (In my experience things almost always work out that way, but it is a surprise and joy to me every time.) The audience was engaged throughout, and I felt my delivery was guided and supported by the Master. When I finished and stepped down to my seat among the audience, Friends sang a couple choruses of "Amen." I had mixed feelings about that, but it seemed sincere and spontaneous. If one stays on the road long enough, one gathers a string of unusual personal experiences.

New Fields of Service and New Challenges

That same afternoon, I did a follow-up session in the same tent where the lecture had taken place. In format, it was an "ask me anything" time, and Friends had lots of questions to ask. The crowd was big enough that I was told to wear the same headphone mike that I had worn to give the lecture, and Friends were asked to wait until a portable microphone could be brought to them before voicing their question. Again, the questions were deep and serious. I found myself being more open and more vulnerable than I had been in a long time, if ever. The session felt owned and accepted by the Master.

Throughout our time together, Elaine was engaging me in some spiritual direction. Overall, she seemed to be urging me to fully recognize and accept the impact I had had and was still having among Friends and to consider whether I ought to change my manner of being engaged in the ministry as a result. She encouraged me to find ways to be more proactive in reaching out for opportunities to be in the public ministry, seeking out—or having my support committee seek out—chances to offer workshops, lectures, and so on at Quaker centers such as Powell House, Ben Lomond, and Pendle Hill.

Elaine had scheduled numerous opportunities during the sessions for me with individuals and one couple. Given the number of people who were approaching Elaine, it seemed as if I could have spent all the free time in the rest of the yearly meeting sessions doing opportunities. I was able to do only half a dozen before news of Mom's ill health intervened.

Mom had had some sort of "event" at the assisted living facility where she lived, possibly a heart attack. Her pulse was erratic, and she had been admitted to the local hospital. The family had been called to her bedside. I left the yearly meeting sessions immediately. All her children and grandchildren and their spouses were able to be with her as she died.

In the meantime, late summer and fall of 2015 were taken up with a trip to Cincinnati with Sydney Lee Kitchens to participate in an exploration of the diverse forms of ministry among Friends and a weekend retreat sponsored by Broadmead Monthly Meeting focused on my Pendle Hill pamphlet *Radical Hospitality*. Susan was once again my companion in the ministry for that work.

Memoir of the Life and Religious Labors of Lloyd Lee Wilson

Late in 2015, Susan suggested that Deborah Fisch and I undertake a joint teaching ministry for individuals interested in the Conservative tradition. This brand-new (to me) possibility resonated with me immediately, and I sent an email to Deborah exploring the possibility. What I said was, "Basically, I would like to work with thee to teach/share the fundamentals of the Conservative faith and way of being in the world with interested Friends." Deborah responded favorably, and Friendship Meeting united in issuing a travel minute in the spring.

This project fell somewhere in between the long-term commitment of School of the Spirit students who go through a two-year program as a cohort and a collection of one-off weekend gatherings of folks who don't necessarily know each other or the leaders. We proposed two or possibly three long weekends per year (Fifth Day through First Day), with preference given to folks who had attended a previous event in the series. My target audience was Friends who wanted to understand and embrace the tradition, not folks who wanted to argue against it and/or change it to better suit them as unique individuals. I think, in Wess Daniels's terminology, we were hoping to attract people who were interested in becoming "apprentices of the tradition."

I had begun to experience voice fatigue as I prepared the plenary address to Pacific Yearly Meeting. As I rehearsed sections of the lecture, my voice would tire, and I wondered if I had written too long a talk even though the total length was less than forty-five minutes. The fatigue continued after the yearly meeting sessions, and near Thanksgiving I went to see an ear, nose, and throat specialist. His exam revealed that my right vocal cord was paralyzed and the left cord was having to do all the movement required for speech. The cause of this type of paralysis was not immediately clear but was often related to damage to the vagus nerve.

Because the damage was by this time several months old, it was probably already permanent. I learned that there are treatments and speech therapies to help ameliorate the effects and slow future degradation, but it was unlikely that the frozen vocal cord would recover very much of its motion any time in the future. Given how important speaking was to me, I felt a little like someone who had lost one eye and now wanted to take extra care to protect and nurture the remaining eye.

During a First Day worship about this time, my mind was drawn away from other thoughts to a query for monthly meetings and similar Quaker groups. Eventually, I was led to share something like the following:

> A query for meetings and other Quaker organizations: Does our meeting community possess the values that we profess as ideal for the world? Do we as a meeting work to incorporate our faith commitments into our life together as a community of faith? Does our life together demonstrate that the ideals we profess are both desirable and achievable? Do we strive to maintain the right balance between the needs and aspirations of the individual, the meeting, and the wider creation?

After meeting, Jim Fernandes shared with me that his wife Jane (then president of Guilford College) had written a message to the Guilford community and shared it with him earlier that morning. His reaction was that what she had written needed a query added, a query that addressed whether or not the Guilford community was living up to its ideals. Imagine his surprise when, in the middle of meeting for worship, someone stood up and offered exactly that sort of query, with no commentary, and sat back down!

I continued to reflect on corporate discernment for some time. The type of corporate discernment involved in testing a leading to public ministry is of the same sort as the discernment in testing a leading to marry under the care of the meeting or a leading for the meeting community to undertake a particular social justice service ministry. In the case of a leading to marry, the initial leading comes to the couple themselves. After appropriate testing, they bring their leading to the meeting for business, which discerns whether Friends can unite with that leading. Are these particular individuals (the couple) "clear" to carry out this particular leading (to be married) at this particular time (the proposed wedding date)?

If the answer to these questions is yes, the meeting minutes its unity with the leading and helps accomplish the wedding. Individual Friends are involved in this to a greater or lesser extent as they feel led and comfortable. As Friendship Friends recognized, the meeting had some continuing responsibility for care and oversight of the couple after the wedding, if only to check in from time to time to ensure that they were thriving.

In the case of a leading to public ministry, the initial leading also comes to one or two individuals. After appropriate private testing, the Friend or Friends bring their leading to the meeting for business, which then discerns whether Friends can unite with that leading. Is this Friend "clear" to carry out this particular leading at this particular time?

If the answer to these questions is yes, the meeting minutes its unity with the leading and helps initiate the ministry. Individual Friends are involved in this to a greater or lesser extent as they feel led and comfortable. The most common involvement is a private commitment to hold the Friend in prayer for strength and guidance about how to proceed. Some Friends will probably want to check in with the concerned Friend over the ensuing months, if only to give a word of encouragement and ensure that the ministry is thriving.

It is not necessary that every Friend agree personally with the content of the concerned Friend's ministry—only that it seems right for that Friend at that time. By way of illustration, neither John Woolman's monthly meeting nor his quarterly meeting ever approved a minute against slavery while he was alive, but they regularly approved travel certificates for him to make religious visits under his concern that slavery was evil.

Support for a leading does not mean total agreement or even being comfortable with the content of the leading. It means sensing that the concerned individual(s) should carry out the activities described in the time period discussed. The most desired and needed support is often intercessory prayer.

Travel in the ministry in New England in 2016

Brian Drayton and I had been exchanging emails discussing a manuscript he was working on. In Eighth Month, he raised again the prospect that we might travel together in the ministry in New England

New Fields of Service and New Challenges

sometime soon. This was something we'd both expressed a desire to do, but it had not previously risen to the level of a leading. Now it did seem to have life in it, and we agreed to begin sitting with the possibility to see if it continued to grow. It did, and Friendship approved a travel minute for my service in New England that spring.

Susan and I set off on Fourth Month 20, 2016, to begin our travel in the ministry in New England with Brian. Unlike our Quaker predecessors, for whom it would have been an arduous journey lasting weeks, we arrived in Cambridge in time for lunch in Harvard Square and a walk to Longfellow Park in beautiful weather.

Sharon Frame offered hospitality at the meeting house there, and we spent a long evening sharing experiences and perspectives on various spiritual matters. Susan and I went to bed refreshed rather than tired from our travels.

Our work began in earnest the next day, beginning with a home visit to Marty and Ken Grundy in Wellesley. Afterward, we returned to Cambridge, where Brian joined us in the early afternoon. He and I talked nonstop until it was time for supper; it felt as if we were taking up the conversation as if the intervening decades since I had left New England had never happened.

One topic was how best to respond to the current situation of the brokenness of the Religious Society of Friends in terms of its understanding of how to nurture and guide public ministry. Should we spend our energy trying to repair what seemed almost irreparably broken or work to build new systems of support and guidance, such as informal meetings of those who seemed to be gifted and active in the roles of ministers and elders gathering regularly to support and nurture one another? This would be a throwback to the early days of Quakerism when there were no structures and ministers coached one another. There are risks and opportunities associated with either path.

That evening, Salem Quarterly Meeting Friends with a concern for ministry gathered at the Cambridge meeting house. There were twenty-one folks at the potluck dinner and more than thirty at the gathering afterward. We had a spiritually grounded discussion. I quickly felt Brian and myself moving forward and back on our chairs as Kara and I had done in New England years ago as we responded to spiritual shifts in the room. It felt like very solid sitting. I was surprised at the number of people who intended to be present multiple times during this visit, saying that they planned to come again that weekend at Cambridge or later on in Putney, Vermont. Marty Grundy was there even though we had met together earlier in the day.

On Sixth Day, Susan and I spent the morning in devotional reading and quiet retirement before Brian joined us for an afternoon meeting with local Quaker Voluntary Service volunteers. They were bright, energetic, and quite young. I sometimes felt a chasm between us that was hard to bridge, but it did seem that some of what we had to share was reaching them. Brian and I pointed out that they were now public Friends, whether they realized it or not, and were witnesses and examples to other persons of what it meant to be a Quaker. Positively, that meant understanding that their lives did preach, both in words and in deeds; negatively, that meant (per the "Advices to Meetings of Ministry and Oversight" of NCYM[C]) to be careful to do nothing that would give offense so that the ministry would not be blamed.

That evening, the three of us had dinner with Callid and Kristina Keefe-Perry and their housemate Honor Woodrow. It was a blessed time, with spiritual communion during the common meal and a deep exploration of various spiritual matters.

Seventh Day began by sharing morning coffee again with Sharon Frame. When I mentioned that the time we'd spent with the Grundys and with Callid, Kristina, and Honor seemed to me to be home visits in a slightly different format, Sharon said she considered these morning coffee gatherings to be a home visit to her as well.

An afternoon workshop titled Spiritual Gifts, Traveling Ministry, and Unity amidst Our Diversity attracted twenty-five persons. Discussion was good right from the start and got deeper as the afternoon progressed. I was active in ministry about the significance of unity near the end. Brian was faithful and greatly favored throughout. I felt my loss at not sitting under his ministry more often over the years and told him so in a private "afterglow" time when the forum ended.

New Fields of Service and New Challenges

After some private time over dinner in Harvard Square, the four of us (Brian and Darcy and Susan and myself) celebrated with wonderful ice cream cones that we finished in Radcliffe Yard on our way back to Longfellow Park for the appointed meeting for worship. There were about twenty Friends present; Brian and I were silent throughout. A couple of gathered Friends gave vocal ministry, all of which seemed to me to be helpful.

First Day began with a forum at Friends Meeting at Cambridge titled Language for the Inward Landscape, attended by about forty-five persons. Friends filled the front parlor and spilled into the library, where they could hear but not see what was going on. Brian spoke about "baptism," and I spoke about inward states and spiritual experiences in the Quaker tradition. Friends were engaged, the Spirit seemed to be tangibly present, and the end of our time came all too soon.

Both Brian and I had service in the vocal ministry during the regular meeting for worship. I began by recounting my experience in the balcony of the Cambridge meeting house the very first time I came inside during meeting for worship and the extensive changes that my life underwent after hearing the Divine Voice telling me this would be my spiritual home. I described that encounter and commitment as being grafted onto a living community as a new branch and said how thankful I was for all the Friends who had made that grafting possible for me by their faithful lives. Each person who affected me had also been affected by someone earlier in the procession, and that person by someone else, back to and through George Fox and to all those souls who kept the Christian faith alive and those who kept the faith of Judaism, which was the fertile soil of Christianity, and so on.

After the rise of worship, several memorable things happened. Two different women came to me, separately, to praise my vocal ministry. One said that if she thought she could get that kind of preaching by making the change, she would become a pastoral Friend. The other came a little later and said she had never heard ministry in a meeting so eloquent, so poetic, so Spirit-led, so articulate and organized (and on and on) ever before. My unspoken reaction to this was, "I'm sorry"; I felt I had been faithful to the measure given me, but I'd had no sense of having done anything more than that.

A third woman was the mother of a transgender child now at the age of looking at colleges. The mother wanted to know about the anti-transgender law recently passed by the North Carolina legislature and the atmosphere around Guilford and our meeting. I was able to answer truthfully that this law did not represent the beliefs or behavior of folks at Guilford or our meeting, and I described the work of Guilford to nurture and sustain an inclusive community and to follow Quaker principles in doing that as well as the conversations currently going on at Friendship Meeting to raise our own awareness of the relevant issues and to ensure we were not unconsciously making visitors or members uncomfortable by actions we didn't see as they did. This felt like a covered conversation, and I felt at the end that she had been given some comfort by what I had to share.

This ended the southern New England portion of our gospel journey, and we spent the night with Brian and Darcy at their home in New Hampshire. The next day, we four drove to Putney, Vermont, for an evening gathering of young adult Friends in Vermont concerned with ministry and how to guide and support it faithfully. About a dozen Friends gathered in the home of Noah Baker Merrill for a potluck meal, worship, and conversation.

Before these Friends gathered, Brian and I went to the Putney meeting house, where Jan Hoffman was waiting to have a private opportunity with us. Some aspects of Jan's public service to the yearly meeting over the previous fifteen years had gotten to the point that she was feeling considerable spiritual pain. Jan was able to be open and nondefensive in sharing her condition with us, and I believe Brian and I were able to hear her and empathize with her. We were able to make a suggestion for change and for a symbolic act that would signify her commitment to that change. It was my sense that Jan accepted the wisdom of this advice and left our meeting in better condition than that in which she began it.

The rest of the evening in Putney was solid and encouraging. The Friends gathered were mostly in their thirties and were involved in solid

New Fields of Service and New Challenges

service and ministry in a number of fields, from medicine to environmental action to inclusive education. They felt the religious underpinning to these efforts strongly and wanted to strengthen them so they could be both sustained and guided in their service. We talked about the importance of getting together with folks carrying similar commitments for mutual guidance and support, and we described specific spiritual practices that would be helpful. In particular, Friends asked specifically to hear more from me about doing a daily examen.

On Third Day (Fourth Month 26, 2016), we drove to Gonic, New Hampshire, for an appointed meeting for worship there. The evening began with a potluck meal and solid conversation, followed by waiting worship and a centered time of spiritual discussion. These Friends were isolated from the bustle of urban life and its rich spiritual resources, but they had found their own source of the Living Water and made sure to stay close to the Source. That ended our service in New England at that time, and the next day we flew back home without incident.

In Sixth Month, Susan and I decided to attend the annual Quaker Spring gathering in Barnesville, Ohio, for Friends interested in the Conservative tradition. This was our first return in twenty-five years—the first, before we were married, had been the occasion of considerable pain after we returned home. This trip brought some welcome healing.

I was a little disappointed that the average age at the gathering was so high—probably near my own age. The opening worship was gathered and a balm was felt in Gilead, but not the fresh springs that I had hoped for. The joys and sorrows shared at the end of worship were all about pain, suffering, and injustice. My offering about the joy of the fresh movement of the Spirit Deborah Fisch and I felt in our joint teaching ministry seemed out of place.

At breakfast the next morning, Susan Smith asked me if I and Susan (Wilson) would time the morning meeting for worship. I agreed, and we did. To be asked to sit on the facing bench at Stillwater and to time meeting seemed a great symbol of healing.

Stephanie Crumley-Effinger approached me later for some advice. She had been asked to lead a retreat for a monthly meeting that was in some conflict. What made me relevant was that one of the parties to the conflict had invoked my writing to say that the others were violating gospel order by not hiring him to do some repair work for the meeting: "Lloyd Lee Wilson's teachings" said that the meeting should preferentially hire him because he was a member of meeting, over any others. Apparently, the meeting had chosen not to hire him for this work because in the past the quality of the work he had done for members of the meeting had not been of acceptable quality. I told Stephanie that my writing was applicable only to situations when all else was equal. In this situation, the meeting had no obligation to hire the Friend, but it did have an obligation to talk frankly with him about the quality of his work, and they should have done that the first time his performance was unacceptable.

One of the afternoon discussions was titled "The Role of the Ego in Ministry: The Water Tastes of the Pipes." We stayed on topic for a while, but eventually talk shifted to how to find and sustain a right relationship between the minister (of whatever type of service) and the meeting community. It seemed to me that it was now time for those of us who were based in meetings that still had active procedures for naming and developing spiritual gifts to acknowledge that those procedures were not going to be adopted widely in Liberal yearly meetings and that even in our own yearly meetings the practice was flawed and in places broken. We needed to identify the support and accountability functions that were needed and find new ways to provide them.

In the fall, Susan and I helped with a residency of the School of the Spirit's On Being a Spiritual Nurturer program. I gave a couple of talks on discipleship, forms of ministry, and spiritual gifts as well as offered several individual opportunities, and Susan was my (excellent) companion in that ministry. All the group work felt Spirit-led and Spirit-fed yet somewhat different from the norm. Susan's term for it, which seemed appropriate, was that I gave teaching ministry rather than prophetic ministry.

Friendship meeting still had not returned to the question of whether or not I should be recorded as a minister, though the work it intended to do before addressing that had been completed for some time. In the interim, the monthly meeting clerk added my name to the yearly meeting roster as a minister in Friendship, even though the monthly meeting had not reached unity to do that. The listing noted that I had been recorded by West Grove meeting, though an important principle in our yearly meeting history was that only the local community could discern the presence of a spiritual gift in ministry.

I found both the unapproved listing and the note very uncomfortable. To me, the important thing about having one's gifts recognized by inclusion on the roster of ministers was the relationship between the individual member and the faith community for the purpose of nurturing and exercising those gifts. That relationship had ended when I transferred my membership out of Virginia Beach and out of Rich Square and again when I transferred from West Grove to Friendship. To list my name on the roster when no such relationship existed between myself and Friendship Friends meeting was not a source of happiness but a reminder of pain and loss.

I continued to be in an awkward situation regarding whether or not I was a recognized minister of the gospel. There were some in Friendship Friends meeting who believed that I was still a recorded minister since I had once been recognized as such. I disagreed with them, as my actions on the occasion of my previous transfers of membership demonstrated. There were others in our meeting who clearly and outspokenly felt that no person should be recognized for spiritual gifts, that we were all identical in that regard—"We are all ministers! We are all elders!" When Ted Benfey, who had been recognized in Philadelphia, asked me whether I was a recorded minister, I said, "That's a tough question. I used to be!"

Bill Taber's observation that the minister is supposed to do "everything and nothing" was frequently on my mind. Remembering the 'nothing' part of that construction seemed important to me, especially in the matter of whether or not the meeting would record me. The issue was really about the meeting and its understanding of itself. Did it want only to be a safe place for individuals to work on their own spiritual work, or did it also want to be a community working together to accomplish the task(s) God was offering for the healing of the world? Only the latter option required the corporate discernment of spiritual gifts. The meeting needed to figure that out, I thought, without interference from me. I needed to be very careful to do nothing that was not required of me by the Holy Spirit.

In the absence of formal recognition by the meeting, I worked to establish the structures and processes needed to identify, develop, and exercise spiritual gifts in the ministry responsibly. I asked four Friendship Friends to serve as my anchor committee; some but not all of these Friends were also part of the Worship and Ministry Committee. The anchor committee in turn reported as needed to Worship and Ministry. This anchor committee made the discernment that I was still gifted and should be recognized, and they made their discernment known to Worship and Ministry, which then recommended to the Friendship meeting for business that I be recorded. I made sure never to indicate that I wanted to be or should be recorded—which was easy to do because I thought in principle that doing so was wrong and in the present case that perhaps God was indicating I should withdraw from public ministry.

During this period, opportunities for public ministry and leadings to travel in the ministry presented themselves regularly, and I held fast to the principle that all travel outside the monthly meeting required a travel minute and all travel outside the yearly meeting needed an endorsement from the yearly meeting. After excluding events that conflicted with my schedule or reflected a clear mismatch between the nature of the opportunity and my gifts and background, I brought the remainder to the anchor committee for shared discernment. Those items we reached unity on were forwarded to Worship and Ministry, and items on which they too were in unity were forwarded to the monthly meeting for business.

This resulted in a steady flow of requests for travel minutes coming to the meeting for business, along with a flow of reports and endorsements to those reports returning a few months later as the envisioned ministry was completed. (It is hard to tell from this why I thought God might be telling me to retire from the public ministry.) Eventually, the monthly meeting approved an annual travel minute for me with the understanding that my anchor committee would be accountable for good discernment for the duration of the travel minute.

New Fields of Service and New Challenges

Once a year, each endorsement of the travel minute was read aloud to the meeting for business.

Friendship meeting had a history of conflict avoidance. The stock phrase was used that "an open discussion of [insert topic here] would tear the meeting apart" to indicate that the topic should be avoided at all costs. I saw the clerk's unilateral decision to list me on the yearly meeting roster of ministers and elders as a Friendship minister "from West Grove M.M." as an example of this. The persons recommending recognition of my gifts might be satisfied by that listing without ever bringing it before the meeting for business, and those opposed might never notice that the listing was there since it would not have come before the meeting for business.

Susan's weekly afternoon of contemplative practice "alone together" at the meeting house was thriving. Occasionally, when she was out of town, she asked me to help host the gathering. One afternoon as I did that, I began a thought piece that by the end of the day had become a piece that I titled "Two Models of Quakerism: Community and Collection of Individual Souls."

> I see an important difference between Stephen Grellet's preaching and the preaching of early Friends. In the middle of the seventeenth century, Friends primarily attempted to draw their hearers into a gathered people through which God would act to accomplish his redemptive purposes in history. Grellet's chief aim was to save souls, to convert individuals to the true faith so that they would go to heaven, not hell, after their death.[3]
>
> Grellet was an important evangelical minister—the latter period of Quietism. His aim was the same as that of evangelical Friends generally, past and present: to save souls. I believe that to the extent that this is a true characterization, Evangelical Friends have indeed strayed—but it seems to me that Liberal Friends have made the same underlying mistake of believing that it is the individual's condition that is paramount. Evangelicals may be focusing on a single type of journey (the soul to God through Christ) and Liberals may be considering a wide variety of spiritual journeys, but they both look too much to the

individual journey and miss the centrality of the faith community to the Quaker expression of Christianity.

Early Friends felt they were living in the end times, that Christ's return was being enacted in and all around them. The Lamb's War was already decided, Christ was victorious, and they were engaged in the necessary final cleanup operations. Their task was to discern and carry out their corporate role in bringing the transformation into the Kingdom to its fullness. The transformation that they experienced in stepping into this emerging gospel order was so great that whatever happened at the time of death seemed like a grace note.

Whatever we profess, contemporary Friends act as if we are living in a time of delayed eschatology—that nothing much is changing in the ongoing Lamb's War, that the ocean of darkness seems still to prevail, and that our task is to look to our own spiritual journeys.

These same perspectives and understandings of the Quaker path are active in Friendship Meeting today; they are still very much in tension, and the differences over whether or not recognizing spiritual gifts is a Quaker or a good thing to do are a reflection of this tension. For those who see Quakerism as concerned primarily with one's individual spiritual path, community recognition of individual spiritual gifts makes little sense and could be detrimental to both the individual recognized and to others in the community.

The concept of outward ministry propelled by spiritual giftedness is foreign to this model of Quakerism. One's concern is rightly directed toward one's own journey, not primarily toward service to others. In this model of Quakerism, the sense of being called into a vocation of outward service, and of being divinely gifted for that vocation, can be a serious threat of inflated ego for the individual and a potentially harmful distraction of other Friends from their own journeys.

For a people who believe both that God speaks directly to individuals and that the content of God's communication is the

New Fields of Service and New Challenges

spiritual journey of each individual, the prospect of one person being gifted to work on behalf of others seems like an intrusion of the model of intermediation that Friends have supposedly rejected. To recognize an elder or the gift of vocal ministry does seem to be a violation of some understanding of Quaker equality, a conferring of distinctive status on certain Friends to the detriment of others. Arguments about the servanthood to the community of those whose gifts have been recognized are unpersuasive because it is the individual, not the community, that is of primary importance. Discussions around the metaphor of the different parts of the body of Christ working together toward a goal are also unsuccessful because the operative metaphor for these Friends is the multitude of autonomous individual creatures, each with its own purpose(s).

The standard of adequacy for the meeting–individual relationship in this model is, "Does this meeting give me the thing(s) I need for my own spiritual growth and journey?" The meeting must meet the demands placed on it by each of its members. As many Friends can attest, this is not a standard that meetings can meet consistently.

For those who see Quakerism as concerned to marshal the resources of communities of Friends to usher in the Kingdom of God (by whatever name or metaphor), the appearance of a spiritual gift in the community is a welcome additional resource for carrying out that task. It becomes the responsibility of the community to use that resource wisely and to see that it is developed well, exercised properly, and protected from harm due to untoward behavior on the part of the person stewarding that gift or any other danger. Because the focus of these Friends is how to discern and carry out their work in redeeming the world, the appearance of distinctive spiritual gifts meshes easily with the metaphor of the various parts of the body of Christ, each offering a different contribution toward a shared goal.

The standard of adequacy for the meeting–individual relationship in this model is the question "Am I giving the meeting what it needs from me to carry out its work in redeeming the world?" The meeting must address the work God has given it to help heal the world, and individual members are responsible for seeing that they have each provided the meeting with what they can to make that work possible. This is a standard to which each of us can reasonably aspire.

To some extent, this change in focus from community to individual is an influence of the Enlightenment, which began to make its impact on general society at just about the time Friends were getting established in England. Since that time, the individual has gained steadily in importance in the dominant culture that surrounds Friends at every time and in every place. It would be more than remarkable if the culture of the Religious Society of Friends, over time, did not reflect these changes in the much larger dominant culture.

Rampant individualism, in religion, politics, and economics, came to have unparalleled power and influence in North American society in the late twentieth and early twenty-first centuries. Individualism in the guise of religion that cares more about one's own spiritual welfare than the plight of one's neighbor, politics that values obstructionist policies far more than collaboration toward a shared goal, and winner-take-all capitalism appear to be in uncontested ascendance. I feel they have actually run their course, though, as demonstrated by their inability to address the challenges that now face the global village, and they must be replaced.

Einstein said we cannot solve the problems we know we face with the same technologies that created them. Our current dominant models of religion, politics, and economics cannot get us out of the problems of global economic injustice, climate change, sectarian conflict, and political inequity we all face together.

It is my sense that taking another look at the community model preached and lived out by early Friends can be valuable. It is certainly true that simply replicating their views and understandings, or trying to do so, will be unsuccessful. Asking the question "How can the idea of a redemptive community, seeking to embody the work of God in healing the world of its hurts and reconciling us to one another, the great creation, and to our Creator and sustainer?" may guide us into unexpected Truth.

Soon after I wrote this, my thoughts about the nature of Friends crystallized around a new pattern. It seemed that the primary "objective" of a monthly meeting is to help the community learn how to live together in God's shalom as the blessed community or as inhabitants of God's holy mountain (Isaiah). This state of shalom is both God's desire for our own community and the foundation of our witness to the rest of the world. Our shalom is desirable for its own sake, but it also informs our work to heal the rest of the world. Without shalom among ourselves, we have no standing to tell others how they should behave, and the power of anything we do or say will be undermined by the fact that we don't behave that way ourselves.

The work of the meeting is to use our life together to learn how to live more fully and more authentically in gospel order. If a committee is not accomplishing its assignment(s) effectively, it is more important to use the occasion as an opportunity for learning than to intervene in order to achieve a particular desired outcome. The meeting that cannot unite on a particular minute but uses the opportunity to build its skills in communications, mutual understanding, and basic faith commitments builds its capacity to find unity in a multitude of difficult situations in the future.

Susan's and my blended family had been blessed in many ways over the years. Now it would be challenged as well. A phone call on First Month 19, 2017, ushered in a year full of health crises, natural disasters, and personal disappointments that deeply affected every part of our blended family. Daughter-in law Randi called that afternoon to let us know that Asa's work colleagues in Raleigh (where he'd been at corporate headquarters) had taken him to the ER with what seemed to be the flu or meningitis. A later call said he'd probably had a stroke and had been admitted to the neurological ICU. Susan and I packed our bags and headed for the hospital.

Scans at the hospital indicated an arteriovascular malformation in Asa's brain, a congenital condition in which an artery connects directly to a vein without the normal capillaries in between that safely reduce the blood pressure and protect the veins from leaking. Asa had had a stroke at this spot, and the lost blood had left a fairly large clot in his left frontal lobe.

While the gathered family waited for the ICU team to determine the best course of treatment, night turned into day and Donald Trump became president of the United States. It seemed to me much less important than what was going on in the neuro ICU at the same time.

The decision was to attempt to repair the leak and remove the clotted blood. It would take a couple of days to gather the right surgical team for the operation. Meantime, more and more of Asa's family and friends from all over the country gathered at the hospital. Asa was slightly more alert and less disoriented than he was when admitted, which improved our spirits—but we all knew that without the surgery the improvement would be only temporary.

Asa's surgery was carried out on First Month 23 and was largely successful, though not without its own problems. The procedure triggered a stroke in an area of the brain that coordinates leg movements. That was repaired within five minutes, but the surgeon couldn't say whether there would be any detectable effects.

The next few days were a blur of IV tubes, monitors, and heavy medications to reduce the swelling in Asa's brain. His ability to move his feet and legs had indeed been compromised, in addition to the original damage to the area of his brain that managed impulse control and decision making. My prayers included an offer to God to substitute my life for his, even though I'm pretty sure God doesn't make that sort of deal. In a few days, Asa was moved from the ICU to a step-down unit that cared for recovering patients.

On First Day, I stopped for worship at Durham meeting on my way to the hospital. It was a covered time for me, but a text message immediately following the rise of worship disturbed my calm. Asa had become seriously ill that morning and was now back in the neuro ICU.

New Fields of Service and New Challenges

Over the next few days, Asa reached what would be the bottom point of his illness, although we had no way of knowing that there was any future improvement to expect or hope for.

He had wide swings between being fairly alert and having little idea of what was going on. In one of his more alert periods, we had a good cry together, confessed how painful and frustrating his condition was, and expressed how much we cared for one another.

We learned that there had been more damage than we'd been told or suspected previously; much of the left anterior lobe was damaged. This includes areas that provide impulse control; his overt annoyance at being questioned and at attempts to remove IVs, leads, etc., were examples of a deficiency there. About this time, I overheard the physical therapist talking with one of the ICU nurses about scheduling future therapy visits. "Have you seen his scan? It is awful—he'll be here a while."

Asa continued to struggle with the aftereffects of the stroke and the surgery. There were times when he could be helped to get out of bed and sit in a chair and other times when he couldn't—or wouldn't—say his name, say what year it was, squeeze a hand, or wriggle his toes. We couldn't tell at this point how much of his cognitive abilities might return when the swelling went down or what it would take to bring the swelling to an end.

Groundhog Day was an apt metaphor for Asa's experience over the next several weeks of waking up every morning to the same windowless room with the same rat's nest of electronic leads and tubes and with the same lack of comprehension about what had happened to him and what was going to happen next.

Eventually, Asa improved enough to be transferred to a rehabilitation center in Atlanta (where he and Randi lived). A second brain surgery was performed there to repair the remaining damage from the arteriovascular malformation, and he received inpatient and outpatient physical and cognitive therapy. He was still severely compromised mentally and physically, but he was well enough to live at home.

In Fifth Month, Asa and Randi celebrated their wedding anniversary with an added sense of gratitude for having survived a great deal in the past few months and for a recovery process that seemed to promise continued gains in the months to come.

Two days later, we learned that Susan's five-year-old grandson Alex had been hospitalized with the dengue virus, and she went off to Puerto Rico to be with the family. Luckily, the infection did not develop into full-blown fever and Alex recovered completely. The infection did leave him more vulnerable to developing the full-blown dengue fever the next time he was bitten by an infected mosquito—which are endemic in Puerto Rico. The practice of intercessory prayer continued to be a regular part of our daily life.

In Eighth Month, Alex suddenly became unresponsive one evening. His father took him to an emergency ward, and soon ADEM—acute disseminated encephalomyelitis—became an unwelcome addition to our family's medical vocabulary. Alex was suffering from an inflammation affecting his brain, damaging the coating that protects nerve fibers. He was admitted to a local hospital once again, and our intercessory prayers took on new vigor.

On Ninth Month 6, shortly after Alex was released from the hospital after his ADEM episode, Hurricane Irma's winds and rain passed over northern Puerto Rico. Although not a direct hit, the storm helped saturate soils and weaken tree limbs, utility lines, and other structures that would be severely damaged and often completely destroyed just a couple of weeks later.

Two weeks later, Hurricane Maria struck Puerto Rico hard, where Susan's son Ryan and his wife Melissa were living. This time, their house was directly in the path of the eye of the storm. They survived without injury by sheltering in a windowless room in the lower level of their house, and the concrete house itself suffered only minor damage, but the damage to the island and its inhabitants overall was devastating.

As federal government dependents, Melissa and the two children were evacuated to Miami as soon as the storm had passed. They stayed there for six months and then were sent back to Puerto Rico, whether or

New Fields of Service and New Challenges

not their previous home was habitable. As a federal law enforcement officer, Ryan stayed in Puerto Rico and spent several weeks providing security for the National Guard soldiers who were delivering food and water to residents across the island, often by helicopter as that was the only way to reach many remote areas.

For both Asa and Alex, being discharged from the hospital was only the beginning of a long period of rehabilitation and recovery. For Alex's family and the rest of Puerto Rico, the end of the rain and high winds was only the starting point for a slow recovery that would take years.

While these family dramas played out, events outside our family proceeded unabated. Deborah Fisch and I gave our joint ministry a name (Broken Vessels Quaker Ministries) and a website and developed an initial program with residencies to offer to interested Friends (Deeper Roots). As the date for that first gathering approached, I experimented with a blog post on the website that I titled "Anticipation":

> It is almost time for the participants in the Deeper Roots program to gather near Nashville for our first weekend together, and my anticipation is building in a combination of excitement, wonder, and anxiety. All sorts of wonderful things are possible when a group of intentional souls like these Friends come together; the possibilities fill one's imagination.
>
> At the same time, I find myself increasingly anxious about outcomes and results. What if the whole project is a flop? What if no one feels they've gained anything worth the time and money they are investing in participation? I want to store up silos of stuff to talk about, bushels of insights to share with the other participants; I want to ensure that all our available time is filled with appropriate and useful material for spiritual enlightenment. I want to be able to be certain that everyone carries away a sense that the outcome of the program has been worth their investment.
>
> But the School of Christ is a garden, not a guaranteed certificate of deposit, and as gardeners our responsibility is in our inputs, not in outcomes. Here in North Carolina, we have been busy in our own garden for more than a month now,

trucking in organic compost, building new and improved fencing, assembling new raised beds, starting seeds, and transplanting perennials. As the season progresses, we will be watering plants as needed, adding support for tomatoes and other climbing vines, pruning them as needed, and watching for harmful pests. All these things can be very helpful inputs toward a successful garden, and they are all things we can control and accomplish on our own.

What makes the garden worthwhile, however, is the miracle of life that is beyond our control. Life in the sprouting seed, the growing plant and the maturing fruit for harvest is an unmerited gift of God. We do what we can to prepare the garden for God's gift and to nurture the gift as God develops it day by day, but it is God's gift and God's miracle that gives the garden meaning.

This is as true of our life as spiritual beings as it is of our work as gardeners. The Seed is the unmerited gift of God to each one of us; we cannot create it or bring it to life through our own efforts. We can only prepare ourselves to receive God's gift and order our lives to nurture and sustain that growing Life as it comes to maturity and we can share in the ongoing fruits of the Spirit. Nothing I can do will guarantee that anything at all will grow in our garden. We prepare the soil and plant every year in the confidence that God is faithful and God's promise is true; we seek to be ready to receive Life at God's hands. Nothing I can do will guarantee that anything good at all will happen in Deeper Roots. In our individual lives scattered across the continent, we prepare the soil of our souls to receive the seeds of God's new planting in confidence that God is faithful and God's promise is true, that wherever we gather in God's name, God will be present with us. We seek to be ready to receive Life at God's hands.[4]

The gathering itself lived up to my anticipations. Alfred Newlin, dairyman and recorded minister of West Grove Meeting, would pause when leaving a place where he had had religious service and, if fitting, conclude aloud, "It was right [for us] to be here." That was an "A" grade in Alfred's book. It seemed to me that the seventeen folks who gathered for the long weekend gathering could each say, "It was right for us to be

New Fields of Service and New Challenges

here." Though we were each demonstrably human and imperfect, we each had religious service over the course of the long weekend that were owned and accepted by the Master.

Friends seemed especially hungry for the Scripture. I spoke a little about the various collections of texts that make up the Judeo-Christian Scripture in various faith traditions and about the possibility of using literary and other criticism to help us understand what a passage was saying to us personally. I then gave three examples: John's story of Lazarus to illustrate how looking at a manuscript as narrative helps us identify and appreciate how the biblical author constructed a story to emphasize certain points or to maintain narrative tension; Walter Wink's commentary on "Resist not evil" and the three examples Jesus gave to illustrate how knowledge of the historical and cultural setting of the text opens up unexpected meanings; and liberation theology's "reading from the underside" of the parable of the talents to show how the reader's historical and social position can give new perspectives on Scripture—in this case, perspectives then confirmed by other analyses of the text.

A short time later, I wrote the following reflection to describe an unexpected (but not unfamiliar) encounter:

> I saw him out of the corner of my eye as I stepped up to the coffee urn to refill my cup before heading home: he was backing through the door, soda cup and bag of food in his hands. He hesitated mid-step as he saw me, and then my attention was turned to not over-filling my cup. This happens to me a lot: between the "believer's beard," the hat, and the suspenders, I elicit a lot of covert looks, open second takes, and wide-eyed stares from adults as well as young children. Often there is nothing more to the encounter (except perhaps a smile and a wink to a child).
>
> This time, when I looked up a moment later, there he was right next to me, looming. He seemed about a foot taller than I am and a foot wider: a rock of a man who, if set on a solid foundation, would never be moved. He was wearing the sort of telephone that clips to one's ear; it looked incongruously small attached to such a large man.

He hesitated for a moment and then asked the title of the book I held in my other hand. *"Engaging Scripture: Reading the Bible with Early Friends.* It is about how early Quakers read the Bible and how we can learn to do that again." This lowered the barriers, and he began to share with me how he's seen that many of us read the Scriptures with blinders on (he covered his eyes with both hands) and don't see what the Bible has to offer us.

He knew his Bible and led me quickly and easily along a trail from the woman at the well to Mt. Gerizim to Sinai to the Law to the person of Jesus. Our religious and spiritual vocabularies were quite different, but I felt we were speaking, underneath the words, the same message: that without the person of Christ, I cannot truly understand what Scripture has to say for me, in my condition, in the present moment. Time became irrelevant, the world fell away, and we shared the joy we each feel when the Scriptures are opened to our understanding.

Suddenly he blinked and said, "I have to be going." We shook hands earnestly and exchanged heart-felt blessings. He turned back to the door he had been about to pass through earlier, and I walked in the opposite direction to the door leading to my pickup. As I passed into the sunlight, I saw my new friend at the wheel of a large semi tractor-trailer—his size and the truck's size seemed properly matched. He was a long-haul truck driver; it would be many hours before he had his next chance for a face-to-face conversation with anyone. I found myself waving to every truck driver I saw on the drive back home.

It happened again yesterday. Somebody took the risk of initiating a conversation with somebody else who had taken the risk of inviting one. It has happened to me repeatedly since God started interfering with my wardrobe all those years ago, but each time is as fresh and as precious as the first. "If you build it, they will come," says the line from the movie; if you risk being invitational, they will take the risk of accepting the invitation, says Radical Hospitality. In this terribly fractured, partisan, splintered time we live in, it is important to do both: to inspect our lives to see that they are invitational to all sorts of people and to take the risk of accepting the invitation others may extend, knowingly or unknowingly, to interact in a way that builds community rather than breaking it down. Unexpected joy awaits.

At about the same time, I joined a weekly half-hour online meeting for worship with special attention to ministry Zac Moon might be led to during the annual sessions and to the shalom of Pacific Yearly Meeting's 2017 annual sessions. This was a positive experience in spite of my initial reservations about the medium. That many participants were already known to me helped make me more open to this new mode of worshipping. Praying for the ministry of a Friend was familiar territory, but praying for yearly meeting sessions felt right only if I jettisoned all possibility of judgment and lived entirely in that space where I can pray for anyone, at any time, that they might experience a fresh encounter with the Living God.

Spurred perhaps by the life-threatening challenges faced by Asa and Alex, I wrote a "final examen" for myself that summer, an exercise similar to writing my own obituary but with a more explicitly spiritual focus.

> I am seventy-five years old and dying. For what am I grateful? For what am I least grateful, and what do I wish had done differently with my life?
>
> **Most Grateful**
> Life with Susan.
> Watching Asa and Randi in their life together.
> Sense of God's abiding, guiding Presence in my life.
> Having produced writings that other people find spiritually helpful.
> Gifts of intelligence, education, learning, communication.
> God's protection from evil and tragedy.
> North Carolina Yearly Meeting (Conservative) and my mentors there.
>
> **Least Grateful**
> My lack of self-assurance and excess vulnerability to the real or imagined opinions of others.

My lack of more widespread acceptance in Friendship Meeting.
Flawed relationships with my parents—especially Mom.
How easily I've been distracted from God's guidance.

Wish I had done differently
Learned to play a musical instrument well.
Found a way to last longer working for Friends General Conference.
Found a way to last longer as yearly meeting clerk.
Written more for publication.
Spent more time intentionally teaching Friends.
Had more confidence in God; been more willing to follow God's guidance.

Conclusions
- I have to put all hope and concern for a better past behind me.
- God forgives me for whatever I've done wrong—I should, too.
- God forgives those around me for whatever they've done wrong—I should, too.
- God liberates me from the chains of my past deeds and experiences and heals me of my wounds—I need to accept my freedom and healing.
- I am given a clean start, every day of the rest of my life.
- My joy and God's gifts to me are in the practice of the gospel ministry.
- I feel most alive and most true to myself when I am sharing the gospel.
- God's gifts to me enable and equip me to share the gospel: gifts of communication, gifts of insight—the Lord's favor, gifts of a stable home life and family, and in general the ability to concentrate on the gospel.
- God calls me to be engaged in this work.

New Fields of Service and New Challenges

I wrote the following in my journal on Sixth Month 25, 2017 (First Day):

> I was active in the vocal ministry this morning. The message connected two gospel passages, one about Jesus healing ten lepers (only one of which came back to offer thanks) and the other about the persistent widow. Of the first, I said I was one who "kept running," lost in the moment of healing and forgetting why and how I had been healed. In similar fashion, I am often oblivious to God's many healings, gifts, and blessings in my life, taking them all in without giving thanks or even acknowledgment.
>
> Usually I think of the parable of the persistent widow (Luke 18:1–8) as a commentary on how to work for justice—by being persistent and faithful even when there seems to be little realistic hope that those in power can be persuaded to change. Today I saw myself as the sleeping judge, uninterested in the One knocking on the door, shutting God out from my innermost life. One day I hope that I will come to my senses, give thanks for all that God has and continues to do for me and those I love, open the door, and invite God into my life fully.
>
> Another morning, I settled into worship about fifteen minutes before the appointed time and found the Center. As other Friends and visitors came into the meeting room, I was given the image of the members of a symphony orchestra coming on stage by ones and twos and making their quiet preparations for the music to come. Each musician has a different part to play—a unique contribution to the music of the symphony. If we are physically or spiritually absent, the quality of the music that can be and is produced is impaired.

At yearly meeting sessions that summer, I went to the door of the room where the recorded ministers and elders were meeting and waited for an opportune moment. Stepping into the room, I said that, like a new minister showing up at Second Day Meeting, I was presenting myself for acceptability. (West Grove had reported that I was again a recorded minister of their monthly meeting.) Would it be acceptable for me to join them "at the table" at this meeting? Mary Miller, an elder of Greenville, asked, "Have you sat at this table before?" When I attempted to give a qualified answer, she interrupted, "One word—yes or no?" "Yes." "Then come and sit," she said.

I felt full acceptance from those gathered. The worship was solid. The conversation later on was primarily focused on the work of elders and pastoral care for those in spiritual depression, so I listened but did not contribute.

Shortly after Hurricanes Irma and Maria had landed their one-two punches on Puerto Rico, I traveled to Ben Lomond Quaker Center in California to lead a weekend retreat about the roots of Quakerism called In for the Long Haul. The damage and suffering on the island were close to my heart, and I asked participants to pray for Puerto Rico during the weekend.

At this point in time, Melissa, Alex, and Victoria had been evacuated from Puerto Rico to emergency housing in Miami, where they were separated from their home, school, Melissa's job, and husband and father Ryan. Ryan's reports and cell phone photographs of the damage to homes and roads and the suffering of individuals and families were at times heart-wrenching.

Susan had not felt a leading to be my companion in the ministry for that weekend, but Charles Martin, a San Francisco Friend, had agreed to the role. When I introduced Charles as my companion, I said that if he intervened, his word was a "fatwa." Events soon showed how important the role of companion is and how important it is that the companion be willing to be active in that role when needed.

Early in the weekend, one Friend contended wholeheartedly that the hurricanes "were the best things that could have happened to Puerto Rico" for various reasons. Affected by the personal accounts of the pain, suffering, and loss that thousands of Puerto Ricans were experiencing, including my own family, I allowed myself to lose my center and began reacting to this person's contentions in the general meeting rather than sticking to the topic of the weekend.

As we began to drift more and more into a two-person debate with a room full of spectators, Charles intervened, clearly pointing out what was happening. I took my own advice about what to do if Charles intervened, stopped speaking, and spent some time discerning what had been happening. After a time of silence, I apologized to the contentious Friend and to the rest of the group for allowing myself to be drawn off-center to the detriment of all.

We then went on with the planned subjects of the weekend, and our time seemed owned and blessed. All the evaluations by participants afterward were very positive except for one non-Friend who had happened to be at Ben Lomond on personal retreat over the weekend and had decided to attend our workshop. The next day, this person submitted a second evaluation, explaining that they had misunderstood the purpose of the weekend. On rereading the advance description, they saw it had been exactly what it was promised to be.

After the events of the 2017 yearly meeting sessions, I asked for an opportunity with Charlie Ansell to explore the report West Grove Friends had made at yearly meeting sessions about my still being a recorded minister at that meeting. I felt a sense of detachment regarding the issue, combined with a sense that my life would be considerably less complicated if the report had been a mistake. After a time of worship, I opened the topic to Charlie and asked whether or not West Grove's report had been intentional. Somewhat to my surprise, Charlie said that West Grove still thought of me as their recorded minister. He went on to say that West Grove Ministry and Oversight had recently laid itself down, and he asked whether I was now a member of Friendship or was still sojourning there.

I shared with Charlie briefly the deliberations at Friendship over my recording, the counsel of folks such as Darlene and Carole Treadway, and my sense that I was not to be personally involved in those deliberations. I described what Darlene had told me about Ohio Yearly Meeting and recorded ministers.

Charlie asked me whether I thought he should bring the matter up again with West Grove Friends. After thinking it over, I replied that I did not think he should do anything as a result of my instigation because it would risk muddying the waters over a false issue of whether I was actively seeking to be recorded. I did not want to do anything that would appear as if I were trying to bring about a particular outcome.

Finally, Charlie said to me that whether or not I was a recorded minister, he was certain that I had had a gift in the gospel ministry and still had such a gift and that I should be faithful in using that gift. Looking at the social and political scene around us, Charlie said, he felt there were folks out there who said they had the gospel but really didn't understand the gospel. "You," he said with a smile, "understand the gospel."

At another Contemplative Tuesday afternoon at Friendship meeting house, I journaled these events and my understanding of their meaning. These were the things I brought away from my time with Charlie:

- West Grove's report was intentional, not a mistake. They still feel I have a gift and a connection with their meeting.
- West Grove as a meeting is becoming less institutionally precise. Committee structures are deteriorating. At present, there is no one who is "clear about the details" and also committed to the long-term growth and welfare of the monthly meeting.
- I feel no need to explore the mutual responsibilities West Grove and I have toward each other regarding the gospel ministry. I don't sense, based on my conversation with Charlie, that there is any person at West Grove who would find this exploration helpful.
- The clerk of Friendship's Worship and Ministry Committee should consider the West Grove report as real and intentional, not a clerical error.

Over the course of the spring months, I began to feel drawn to travel in the gospel ministry in the Pacific Northwest, particularly with Wess Daniels as my companion. However, it seemed to me that before I could do or say anything about this growing leading, Wess would have to suggest the same thing himself. One summer First Day as he and I were talking after the rise of meeting with several other Friends, Wess proposed a joint trip in the Pacific Northwest. I immediately said, "Yes,

New Fields of Service and New Challenges

and I'll tell thee later why I'm so clear to say so." In Ninth Month, we began to meet for discernment around this journey in the ministry.

I was called to jury duty in Third Month 2018. This had happened once before, while we were living in Northampton County, North Carolina. That trial was avoided by a last-minute plea bargain. There was no opportunity to speak directly with anyone in the justice system about my doubts about being a juror, and my hesitations were not so clear then as they were now.

I'd been rereading Walter Wink and his discussion of the domination system as a result of the interest of one of the Deeper Roots students. I had also become newly aware of the issues of privilege, class, and race embedded in the criminal justice system through recent white privilege and Black Lives Matter discussions. I was reminded of the depth and force of meaning when one says "Jesus is Lord" rather than "Caesar is Lord." Now, I wondered what the proper response was to being called to participate in (and thereby legitimize) a power in the domination system—the legal system with its emphasis on redemptive violence.

I'd been to court enough times to have worked through the issues of taking off my hat, rising when the judge walks in, affirming rather than swearing, and so forth. My hypothetical attitude toward jury duty had been that I would refuse to take part in a trial involving the death penalty but would serve otherwise. But was that enough? I knew enough of prisons through my visits to understand they were not about rehabilitation or penitence but were about punishment—the myth that by punishing the perpetrator one can achieve justice for the ills that had been done. A prison sentence continues to punish long after the sentence has been completed through parole supervision, voter disenfranchisement, limited employment opportunities, the stigma placed on the ex-convict by society, and much more.

There are inequities at the front end of the system as well. Black men are more likely to be stopped and/or arrested than white men, more likely to be charged with a crime, and more likely to be convicted when charged. Once "in the system," individuals are much more likely to be charged and convicted again and again.

The situation is similar to the one many folks faced during the active draft years. The Selective Service System itself was unfair. Should a person like myself, who had the legal ability to obtain and keep a deferment, use that ability or refuse to participate in the system at all by refusing to register with Selective Service to begin with?

I continued to be concerned about what was right for me to do about my upcoming date for jury duty. It would be easy if I were asked something like, "Is there any reason you might be unable to provide the defendant a fair trial?" Then I could explain my reservations in straightforward terms, and certainly any prosecutor would then excuse me during voir dire. But, by doing that, was I actually helping or hurting the defendant? By excluding myself, would I make it less likely that the defendant would receive a just sentence—if a just sentence was indeed possible, which was something I believed was not likely? Could I find a defendant innocent when the evidence indicated legal guilt without violating my promise(s) as a jurist and my integrity as an individual?

When the day finally came, I reported as directed and was informed that the time to express my reservations would come when I was called and questioned individually by the opposing attorneys. As it happened, I entered the courtroom with about twenty-five other potential jurors and watched the selection process. The jury was selected before I was called; I believe I was the last remaining potential juror out of my group of potentials.

In Third Month, the Nominating Committee asked if I would be willing to serve as clerk of the monthly meeting. I said that my initial stance was twofold: (1) I have a high regard for the work of nominating committees as people who match the spiritual gifts of individuals with the spiritual needs of the meeting, and (2) I look upon myself as the servant of the meeting who should serve where and as the meeting calls. Therefore, the request from the Nominating Committee carried weight with me, and I did not feel that there were some places I "ought" to be serving and others where I did not want to serve.

Nonetheless, the clerkship is a spiritually demanding position and a time-consuming one as well, so saying yes would require that I make adjustments in the other things I did and ministries that I undertook.

New Fields of Service and New Challenges

There would be an expectation of a minimum two-year commitment, with a third year being desirable if it still seemed rightly led by Friends. I said I'd need to spend some time in discernment to ensure that other commitments I had already made would not interfere with the needs of the clerkship.

I did a careful examen of all my existing commitments and those potential commitments I could identify, noting which ones would be ending and which continuing over the next two years and how much time each required to be carried out faithfully. I identified places where I would need to say no in order to say yes to the clerkship. My conclusion was that given the other commitments that were ending and the ones I could bow out of or say no to, I would have the time and energy needed to clerk the monthly meeting well.

During my discernment, the monthly meeting decided to spend up to $15,000 to begin the pre-design phase for the new meeting room. There could be stakes in the ground to indicate the dimensions of the new construction as early as Tenth Month 2018, with construction taking place over the following six months or so. The actual pace of events would in all likelihood not be that fast, but the reality was clear; the next clerk would have the big job of shepherding the meeting through the many difficult tasks associated with this project. Given how many difficult choices would have to be resolved, and the meeting's reluctance to have the difficult conversations needed to reach deep unity, the challenges facing the clerk would be great. Even after construction was complete, there would be another difficult period while the meeting adjusted to living in the new, larger space. Meanwhile, all the other activities of a healthy monthly meeting/faith community needed to continue with as little disruption as possible.

It would be my responsibility to keep the rest of my life in order so that I had the time, energy, and spiritual groundedness to clerk well. My anchor committee would be a definite help in that work. A particular need that pressed home on me was for a personal practice of constant intercessory prayer on behalf of the meeting, prayer that it would grow steadily in its depth and maturity as a community of faith and that I would not fail to be a spark for that growth as clerk.

I also needed to be always listening closely to all the members and attenders of the meeting. Being a good clerk would require me to do as much as possible to ensure that every person felt heard. Part of this would involve being present for as many meeting activities as possible, which I'd been conscious of wanting to do for some time.

Shortly after saying yes to the Nominating Committee, I received an invitation from Trinity Episcopal Church in Bloomington, Indiana, for a proposed ten-day sojourn with them during Holy Week 2019 during which I would preach four times, lead a contemplative retreat, host a family event, and provide spiritual direction to individuals and couples throughout. My first reaction was "Wow! What an opportunity!" My second reaction was "Wow! What a lot of work!"

I'd been thinking about this possible ministry since I'd received the initial inquiry, but to get the actual formal invitation brought a sense of near glee. I was well aware of how much work this task would involve and how great the opportunity would be to fall flat on my face, but it also felt like something God would enjoy seeing me do and that God would hold me up and guide my heart as I prepared for and carried it out. My anchor committee would not meet for a couple of days, but until then I had no perceptible stop in me from saying yes.

Susan was happy when I told her about the invitation and then fell immediately into a consideration of who might be best as my traveling companion. It was premature to spend too much time on this (at least until the anchor committee had its say), but the image of Mark Wutka came to mind. It was a discernment that could be put off for a little while.

One First Day morning, Carole Treadway's monthly Deepening the Spiritual Life of the Meeting included a reading from the third servant song:

> The Lord GOD has given me
> the tongue of a teacher,
> that I may know how to sustain
> the weary with a word.
> Morning by morning he wakens—
> wakens my ear

to listen as those who are taught.
The Lord GOD has opened my ear,
 and I was not rebellious,
I did not turn backward. (Isaiah 50:4–5 NRSV)

As I read and then sat in silence with these verses, I had a deep sense that I could say them for and about myself using the first person. The Lord has indeed given me the tongue of a teacher that I might sustain the weary with a word. Each day God awakens in me the ability and desire to listen and be taught. This is a fierce gift, and like all gifts from God it carries with it responsibility. I have not been rebellious and have not turned away but have done my best to live up to that responsibility. My efforts have been imperfect, but I have faced in the right direction.

The leading to travel in the ministry with Wess Daniels in the Pacific Northwest had matured, passing through all the tests of corporate discernment, and in Sixth Month 2018 we set out.

Traveling in the Ministry in the Pacific Northwest: Journal Excerpts

Sixth Month 5, 2018. Wess and I met up at the Seattle airport this afternoon—Wess from San Francisco, myself from Greensboro—and found our way to Ann Stever's house on the edge of Lake Washington. Ann and her spouse Dorsey Green had prepared a wonderful salmon dinner for us. Promise Welkin joined us for dinner and some excellent conversation.

Afterward, the four of us headed to Seattle Friends Church for the evening event. About 35 Friends were there from North Pacific Yearly Meeting, Sierra-Cascades Yearly Meeting, and I believe others as well. The opening worship was sweet and deep. I had difficulty discerning whether or not I should speak but was given a few words to say near the end of worship that seemed at least to do no harm.

We moved into a time of Spirit-based sharing during which Friends shared various matters of concern, to which Wess and I responded as led. This seemed well-grounded and helpful to several folks. We closed a little before nine o'clock, but Friends stayed for informal conversations for almost another half hour. By that time (being still on EST internally), I was quite worn out.

Tom Ewell was there, to my surprise and joy. He is looking well and very happy. He said my teaching style was just right and that I had obviously worked on it over the years.

Several people came up to me afterward and shared how my books or writings—even the audio of my "Holy Surrender" lecture at New England Yearly Meeting—had been important to them in some way.[5] One younger Friend said that the first time she read the gospel order essays she couldn't figure out what I was talking about, but when she reread the book years later it made sense and was now quite valuable to her.

Sixth Month 6, 2018. The next evening, Wess and I met with Friends at Camas Friends Church and then were hosted by Ruth Ann Hadley Tippin and her husband Jon. There were 22 Friends who gathered to worship with us at Camas (according to the elder who endorsed my travel minute); their hospitality was evident from the time we walked in the door.

This was Wess's church before he came to Guilford College, and they clearly held a deep affection for him. There were lots of hugs and backslaps, expressions of joy, and the gentle teasing of men who care for one another as each person or family arrived, so that although we arrived early we didn't settle into worship until well after our appointed time. This didn't seem to me like a delay but instead as the first part of our sacred time together—a celebration of the return of a son and brother who had been away.

I felt less anxious and more centered as we settled into worship and more connected to Wess spiritually than I had been the night before. It was my part to be silent tonight, but Wess was favored in a message he offered about the difference between looking and seeing, asking what might it take to see what we are looking at more clearly and truly.

New Fields of Service and New Challenges

After our worship ended, Friends shared on a number of topics, including how remarkable it was for two Friends to travel so far to gather with distant Friends and simply listen—as Ruth Ann put it later, simply to make ourselves available to the Holy Spirit. We talked for a little bit about how and why Quakers tell stories about Quakers so much and the importance of knowing one another's stories and our faith community's stories. Another Friend spoke about the need to see our likeness to "the other" rather than to focus on our differences, and yet another opened the topic of what gave us hope. Thinking about this question, I found that my present answer was the Poor People's campaign and shared a little about why.

Sixth Month 7, 2018. This was a day of retreat for me. Wess went back to Camas to meet with his spiritual director and spend time later visiting with friends and Friends from his time there. I enjoyed my solitude in the little one-room house next to our hosts, surrounded by Ruth Ann Tippin's extensive library. The "little house" is a one-room structure set a little apart from the (decidedly) big house where our host and hostess live, set high on a hillside overlooking the Columbia River. Outside the window, I could see a beautifully landscaped area of large rocks and small bushes and beyond that a profusion of untamed trees and undergrowth that could possibly be the edge of the world. Behind me was the Columbia River far below and a range of low hills on the other side of the river. I could hear nothing other than the occasional plane flying overhead. This was once a wood shop, converted into a wonderful living space by a widow who thought she might rent the big house to tourists and live herself in the little one.

Each day on this journey I have been reading in the *Memoirs and Journal of Hugh Judge*, a recognized minister who traveled a great deal in gospel love in America in the late eighteenth century. At one point he describes receiving a packet of letters from home that were "the first since leaving my family, and they were truly acceptable." This reminded me of the profound separation of traveling ministers of the past from everything dear and familiar to them while they were on such a journey as Wess and I are now. In one journal I read the account of a trans-Atlantic traveler receiving a series of letters from home, one at a time, describing the illness, decline, and eventual death of one of his children. Each letter had been 6 weeks or more in transit; by the time he received each letter, he had no way to know whether the child had already recovered, the illness had continued, or death had overtaken the young one. There was nothing to do but continue to be faithful to his calling and pray for his child and entire family.

In a parallel situation, by means of email I was able to learn of my mother's last illness in time to cut short my time at Pacific Yearly Meeting in 2015 and, by the further blessing of transcontinental air travel, could make it back to North Carolina in time to be with her when she died. May we all have due regard for the risks and sacrifices undergone by our spiritual ancestors in order to preserve and pass on our faith tradition in the past, and may we be willing to undergo the like in our own time to share the gospel. With all this in mind, I called home early this morning and talked to Susan. What a joy to hear her voice and to know she is well and had a wonderful time yesterday working on the meeting house lawn with Judy Williams and later sharing supper and conversation with Judy.

This afternoon I picked up a workshop outline by one of our Deeper Roots participants that I had put aside to study at an appropriate time. It began with some readings from the Gospel of John, so I took down the *New Interpreter's Bible* volume on John to read and reflect on the opening lines from his gospel, comparing the NIV and NRSV translations and reflecting on the possible variants ("The true light, which enlightens everyone, was coming into the world" *or* "He was the true light that enlightens everyone coming into the world").

From there, the workshop offered half a dozen or so Quaker quotations, including some of my favorite Quaker writers, especially Isaac Penington and Francis Howgill. This led to more

New Fields of Service and New Challenges

reflection, this time on the familiar curves and smooth surfaces of well-worn words that only gain in beauty and worth from frequent use over a long time.

My morning reading in Hugh Judge's *Memoirs* had included the following, dated Ninth Month 5, 1786:

> Low in mind, but sensible of Divine Good. This is a favour, supernatural to human conception, to know that God is in us and we in him. Oh! that mankind universally were sensible of this great mercy, that he condescends to dwell in us, and walk in us. Surely a due sense of his Divine presence, ever with us, would produce fruits of love, meekness, gentleness, patience, brotherly kindness, charity. Was this the case with all professing christianity, envy with all its evil offspring would be rooted out—tale bearing and evil speaking one of another, would cease—the rending devouring nature of the wolf being subdued, it would dwell with the lamb—the spotted leopard would lie down with the harmless kid, and the calf and the young lion, and the fatling together—and the innocence and gentleness of the little child would lead them. What a blessed state to individuals! and what a happy condition of the human family, when this glorious gospel day is more and more risen.[6]

Like a good jazz musician, surely Hugh Judge had been "sitting in" on my reading of this workshop today, helping me prepare for a meditation on the Presence that we indeed often experience all too fleetingly.

Sixth Month 8, 2018. I had a covered time with Ruth Ann Tippin in the morning, talking about various things over coffee while Wess slept in and Jon worked from his office upstairs. Retired from the pastorate herself, she feels a concern for the nurture and development of other pastors, especially in the Quaker distinctives, those aspects of theology, spirituality, and practice that are distinctive to Quakers within the wider

Christian church. (Both Ruth Ann and Wess have spoken about their sense that the practice of hiring pastors who are not well versed in Quakerism has weakened our witness and our tradition itself.)

That afternoon, Wess and I met with Mike Huber, a former pastor and current QuEST staffer, for some coffee (of course) and God talk. He's a very impressive figure—tall, well built, with a handsome Marlboro Man type of face. West Hills meeting in Portland, Oregon, was a participant in the events that led to the formation of Sierra-Cascades Yearly Meeting, so Mike as pastor has been through a lot; I think he's glad to be out of the line of fire now. He exudes a spiritual groundedness and practicality that is charismatic. As I encounter more of the people who were most directly involved/affected by the events leading up to the split, I see more clearly that these are not crusaders for some principle but simply people who believe that Jesus taught that we should love everybody, no exceptions—and who have set out to live that teaching out in their own lives and congregations.

This evening we made a home visit to Peggy Senger Morrison and her wife Alivia. Peggy seems to have aged noticeably since I met her at Guilford last year, and Alivia is wrestling with a couple of serious medical conditions. The discussion went quite deep as Alivia and Peggy described their physical and spiritual conditions, especially the stress and anguish Peggy feels over the broken lives of the children she teaches and tries to help navigate the institutions and settings of "normal" life. The stories she shared of her student's lives (and deaths) were quite moving in their tragedy. We had a prayer time that went quite deep very quickly; Peggy and Wess each offered a powerful, moving vocal prayer.

Sixth Month 9, 2018. We returned to Peggy and Alivia's for breakfast this morning. I stayed in the kitchen and talked with Peggy while she cooked, while Wess and Alivia conversed in the living room. Peggy looked and acted as if the weight of the world had been lifted off her shoulders overnight. She said that she had gotten a good night's sleep for the first time in months. Prayer really does change things in perceptible and wonderful ways.

In the evening we met with a small group of Friends in Newberg, Oregon, at the home of Cherice and Joel Bock. There were about eight or nine folks altogether—pretty much all in their thirties, several with children at home. A common theme among them was a combination of pain felt in their relationship with Northwest Yearly Meeting before the split, pain of a different sort felt during the breaking apart itself, and bright hope of healing and other good things that they expect in the emerging Sierra-Cascades Yearly Meeting.

Cherice was the first presiding clerk of the new Sierra-Cascades Yearly Meeting, so I delivered to her oral greetings from the Interim Body[7] of North Carolina Yearly Meeting (Conservative) and our welcome to them as a yearly meeting into the wider family of Friends.

One question we shared and each person answered was, "Why am I still a Quaker?" It was amusing but not quite surprising to me that Wess and I answered in the same vein. Essentially, we are still Quakers because the choice to become Quaker was not entirely our own and God has not yet given us release from that decision. Wess went on to say he felt Quakers was the only place there was someone waiting for him; I said, "Where else would I go?"

Sixth Month 10, 2018. I'd been hearing about Reedwood Friends Church in Portland, Oregon, ever since Kara Cole and I became friends in my Friends General Conference years, but I'd never been there until this First Day morning. The physical plant was huge, well designed, well maintained, and beautifully landscaped, but the membership was greatly diminished from earlier decades. Wess was asked to bring the message in worship, and he preached to about 25 worshippers in a stadium-seating room that could have held at least 200. Carole Spencer (formerly on the faculty of Earlham School of Religion) is a member here, and her husband operates the sound system from a wraparound station up in the back of the room that reminds one of an airplane cockpit. Hymns and the Scripture reading were in English and Spanish, and everyone was quite welcoming. After worship Wess and I led separate discussion groups, which were well attended and quite lively.

In the evening we went to the Multnomah Friends Meeting for an appointed meeting for worship. Worship was deep, and the Presence of God was palpable.

Sixth Month 11, 2018. This was perhaps our busiest single day of the journey. We began with the morning Bible study at Multnomah, then had lunch with Vail Palmer and his wife Izzy. We ate an early supper with Clyde Parker, then went on to Eugene Friends for a Spirit-led, Spirit-fed discussion there.

Over the course of our trip, we had six called meetings for worship plus the regular worship at Reedwood at which Wess preached, made seven home visits, and met in more informal ways with several groups of Friends and individuals. As I made my way homeward on the twelfth, I felt clear to say in my heart, "It was right to be here."

Clerk of Friendship Meeting

The Friendship Nominating Committee did recommend me for the clerkship of the monthly meeting, and meeting for business approved the appointment. As the Eighth Month meeting for business that would start my term grew closer, I perceived five practices, spiritual disciplines, that would help me be as useful to the meeting as I could:

- Kenosis (self-emptying): to focus always on "What can I do for the meeting?" rather than "What do I want the meeting to do/be for me?"

- Constant prayer: to be in the constant practice of intercessory prayer for the meeting and for individuals.

- Inclusiveness: to spend time with monthly meeting members, more than my personal desire for solitude would lead me to do.

- Invitation: to always be vulnerable and not be offendable; to create a safe place for meeting members to be brave.

New Fields of Service and New Challenges

- Commitment: to be committed to the meeting community that is, not to the meeting community I wish for.

I expected that my hardest job would be shepherding the meeting through the rest of the planning and building process for the new meeting room, and that challenge showed up at my very first meeting for business as clerk. During the Planning Committee's report, a member of the committee stood up to say he would stand in the way of any site plan that would result in the loss of a particular large tree near the meeting house and would never stand aside in his opposition. As this tree was possibly threatened by one of the two parking plans being presented for consideration by the committee, this came as a surprise to many in the room. The way he made his statement, and the emotion with which he expressed it, led me to surmise that he has in fact closed his mind and heart to any continuing guidance from the Holy Spirit that might lead him to a different understanding of what the meeting should do.

Two Friends came to me after the rise of meeting for business, concerned about these comments. My response to each of them was that the "tyranny of one" is in fact not part of the good order of meeting for business and that I felt clear that in the case of a meeting in unity about a particular decision with the exception of one Friend, the clerk in good order can express that the sense of the meeting was to proceed with that decision in spite of the lone exception. Later, yet another Friend asked to speak with me privately and expressed similar concerns about the objecting Friend. Here I was, only a few hours into my clerkship, and I was already practicing all five of the spiritual disciplines I had set for myself as fervently as I knew how.

After a period of individual devotion, I wrote this journal entry in Tenth Month 2018:

> God does not love us because we have changed in some way pleasing to God. God loves us so that we can be free to change in ways that bring us nearer to actualizing our full potential, more nearly becoming the person that God has always known was truly our individual self and has yearned for us to achieve.
>
> In the process of becoming a whole and fully realized individual, we also come to realize that we are fully incorporated

in the totality of creation that is the manifestation of God. We do not realize our true self, our whole developed personhood, in isolation but in divine community—a marvelously unique and beloved part of the community of the universe, in God and of God as part of God's divinely good creation.

Late in Tenth Month, Susan and I attended an interfaith rally against hate and violence at Temple Emanuel in Greensboro. The synagogue was packed; Susan and I had seats only because we made sure to arrive very early. The immediate cause of the rally was a need to respond to the recent shootings in Pittsburgh. Religious leaders from just about every faith tradition represented in Greensboro were present that night, and most if not all had an opportunity to speak or pray or sing as part of the worship service/rally.

Those of us most deeply yoked to a particular faith tradition need to do more public witness to the truth that being deeply committed to our tradition does not mean or imply that we are opposed to any other faith tradition, whether that opposition is expressed in violent or nonviolent terms. We are all, as Richard Rohr says, seekers after that same Living Water. Many individuals do not listen to our words, so we must see to it that our actions express the same message clearly and loudly.

At the rise of morning worship at the 2019 North Carolina (Conservative) Yearly Meeting sessions, a woman Friend whom I did not know approached me with a postcard created by Quaker Earthcare Witness and a story. She recalled that in the closing worship of the annual sessions last year, I had offered vocal ministry about the darkness and how we should deal with it that had moved her to tears. She could not leave her seat when everyone else left for lunch, and by the time she regained her composure she was late for the meal. Shortly afterward, she attended a meeting of the Quaker Earthcare Witness leadership and shared her experience with them. Affected by what she had to say, the organization had produced the postcard, which included a quotation from James Nayler.

I had no memory of having offered any ministry as the last yearly meeting sessions came to a close, and James Nayler is not a Friend I commonly quote or reference in ministry. Nonetheless, this was her story, and the postcard was the tangible result. God is good.

On Ninth Month 8, 2019 (First Day), I wrote the following in my journal:

> It was my lot to keep silent in worship this morning. It was a very sweet, covered meeting, in which several Friends took the risk of making themselves vulnerable in quite personal ministry. The cumulative effect was quite powerful, and I felt it knit those in attendance in a closer community, a greater awareness of how similar we are, even in those aspects of life that we often keep to ourselves.

During the meeting for business after worship, the Worship and Ministry Committee made a recommendation that I be recognized as a minister and that my recording be "transferred" from West Grove to Friendship Friends. This was approved with very little spoken comment. One Friend, a transfer to NCYM(C) from Brooklyn Monthly Meeting, stepped aside from the decision but at the same time said she did not want or intend to stand in the way of the meeting's discernment.

Deborah Shaw had replaced me at the clerk's table for this item of business. She was very quickly able to propose a minute of unity with which Friends were agreeable, and the whole affair was over in a very few minutes. I had worried that the discussion would be long and challenging, taking up most of the time available that day and quite possibly more before unity could be reached (in either direction), but this proved not to be the case.

After several years of being unwilling to return to this task of discernment, Friendship Meeting had taken the risk and had found unity where previously there had been none. I hoped that the meeting had found some new confidence in its ability to tackle difficult conversations in the process.

Epilogue: 2021

> While at this place I had often to look back on the many trials I have had to pass through in the course of my life; and more especially since I joined the Society of Friends, and have been called to the work of the ministry; and on taking a retrospective view, I am ready to say, how little has been my progress! What need to double my diligence in advancing life! I have read much, and travelled more than most others, yet have advanced nothing to what I apprehend many others have, that have been called long after me. A sense of my own infirmities has of late much impressed my mind; but I hope that a greater improvement will be made, so that when the time of my dissolution cometh, I may be found ready.
>
> —David Sands (1745–1818)[1]

Reading David Sands's journal entry from a similar point in my own life, I feel a near sympathy with his condition and a similar hope that "a greater improvement will be made" in days to come.

In this most recent phase of my spiritual journey, the work of the ministry continues, though it has changed in certain aspects. "To do everything God asks of me and nothing else" is still a watchword for me, and what God is asking of me is still changing. It seems God's guidance these days is to "do less, better." Both my abilities and God's expectations for outward service are diminished, but there has been no reduction of the standard for each piece of work, which is to do the absolute best I can by staying as close to my Guide from moment to moment as I am able.

The kinds of ministry to which I've been called have also changed. Helped by the restrictions on travel and group gatherings brought on by the Covid-19 pandemic, I've done fewer in-person events such as leading workshops or retreats or speaking engagements. The time and energy I spend in pastoral care and intentional spiritual direction or formation has noticeably increased. The one-on-one time I spend with Friends newly called into the public ministry is also much greater. These changes

Epilogue

seem to reflect new growth in my own spiritual condition as well as a reaction to the pandemic.

After a lifetime of wrestling with God, I am still doing so. Now we wrestle together, like dance partners in an intricate movement, as I try to gain an understanding of what God is saying rather than to gain an advantage that will help me to avoid the difficult parts of the Divine Word. I continue my long apprenticeship to the Quaker faith tradition and hope to finish my journey as a faithful apprentice.

Appendix 1
A Deeper Unity

Lloyd Lee Wilson, "A Deeper Unity," *Quaker Life* (March 1988): 21–22.

For many years I was a person for whom the concept of sin did not have much meaning. I believed in God and strove to do what was right, but did not feel that "sin" was very relevant. As I continued my spiritual journey it became clear that no matter how fiercely I resolved to do God's Will and no matter how hard I tried to carry out my resolve, there was something at work which inevitably defeated me and separated me from God. Disturbingly, it soon became clear that this alienating force was within me—a blackness that I could never defeat, never drive out no matter how hard I tried to live a virtuous life. It would always be present and would always get between me and the God I have come to love. I would never be able to overcome this blackness using my own resources. Thus, I came to understand that sin is real, that it is an important part of my life, and one with which I must grapple in order to live an authentic life, the kind of life I desire to live.

At the same time, I began to realize another force active in my life, working to free me from the alienating effects of this personal blackness and to reconcile me again and again with my Creator. Patiently, tirelessly, this other Presence—someone other than me active in me—worked to call me into a new, fuller life in closer harmony with God. As I began to recognize, turn inward, and put my life in harmony with this Inward Presence, I felt the blackness in me made powerless and the good in me lifted up. And thus I came to recognize the work of the Inward Christ, who is my only hope of escaping the power of that blackness in me and coming to live always in the Light of God.

I strive now to assist Christ in His work in every moment of my life, to set my heart and mind on those things which He would have me think and do. He is my most faithful and most trustworthy Friend, who has said, *You are my Friends [sic] if you do what I command* (John 15:14 NIV). In that same paragraph of John's Gospel, Christ is quite specific about His meaning: *This is my command: Love each other* (John 15:17 NIV).

Christ expands this in what is sometimes called the High Priestly Prayer: *I pray also for those who will believe in me . . . that all of them*

Appendix 1: A Deeper Unity

may be one. . . . So that the world may come to believe that you have sent me. . . . May they be brought to complete unity to let the world know that you sent me and have loved them even as you have loved me (John 17:20, 21, 23).

As I grow in faith it becomes increasingly important to me to be worthy of being called His friend—and it breaks my heart to see how greatly we who call ourselves the Religious Society of Friends have fallen short of His desire for us. We seem to revel in emphasizing the ways in which we differ, rather than taking joy in those things which we have in common. It seems to me that our own spirits and our message to the world will continue to be seriously flawed until we learn to live in the unity for which Christ prayed.

The unity which Christ desires for us is not a unity of institutional structure nor of doctrine nor testimonies. The unity He desires is deeper, based on our common recognition that there is One who can and does speak to our condition. There is one God, one Logos who is present in our worship, who reaches out to us in our broken condition and calls us by name, healing us and reconciling us to Himself. Whatever our finite experience of God, whatever nouns or pronouns or other words we use to name and describe that experience, there is one Author and Perfector of our faith.

We are a people who claim that it is the inward experience of God that is important, not the outward form—yet we distrust and show little respect for others in our own faith tradition whose outward form of worship differs from our own. We honor our ancestors in the faith who could minister across language barriers where no translator was present with such power and authenticity that their audience would exclaim, "I love to hear where the words come from"—yet we ourselves are unable to overcome our different choices of words in the same language to be able to acknowledge our own unity in that place "where the words come from."

This, Friends, is sin—that blackness in us which draws us away from God's will for us and works to delay the coming about of the Kingdom. It is a difficult adversary to defeat, for it is persistent and has twisted a basic truth to form an underpinning of its work. It is true that each of the subgroupings of Friends has preserved and emphasized a portion of our common faith tradition that it feels is most important. Where sin comes in is to deny that any other portions of the tradition are important or worth emphasizing, or that persons who don't emphasize the same portion of the tradition as we do are Friends at all. We want to say, in our pride, that we have it right, and that therefore no one else does.

We have a difficult adversary to overcome, but our task is not impossible. We have as our Ally and Guide the infinite tenderness and mercy, patience and power of the Inward Christ, the Friend who can lead us into the humility of realizing that no one or group has all the Truth, no one form of worship can be sufficient for the Lord of Creation, no one understanding of this work in our lives can be comprehensive. Let us recommit ourselves today to building in our lives, with the help of the Inward Guide, that foundation of Love that will bring us to the unity of the fellowship of all believers, the family of the Children of God. Let us seek that diversity that will let the world know the validity of the message we bring and the relationship we have with the Christ within.[1]

Appendix 2
Who Have Been the Most Important Spiritual Friends in My Life?

Lloyd Lee Wilson, Earlham School of Religion reflection paper, 2003.

I have been fortunate in having experienced two long-term group spiritual friendships in my life. One was in the 1970s in Cambridge, Massachusetts, and one was in the early 1980s, when I was general secretary of Friends General Conference.

I have a deepening spiritual friendship with Mike Arnold, my traveling companion in the ministry. Though we live several hours apart in North Carolina and belong to different monthly meetings, we are committed to one another in the various ways enumerated by Howard Macy in his article titled "The Joy of Spiritual Friendship." We encourage one another as well as hold each other's feet to the fire; I especially appreciate Mike's ability to tell me "No, thee shouldn't attempt that (or take on that task or responsibility)." I depend implicitly and explicitly on his discernment and my wife's to guide my public ministry. If they agree I should, I do; if they don't agree, I won't.

All these Friends were different from me theologically and in many other ways, although I think we grew closer together over time as we all matured spiritually (at least in part because of our spiritual relationship). In each case, they have indeed been a gift that I could not have imagined, much less brought about, in my own will and by my own efforts. Our long-term commitment (monastic "stability") has been important to our being present to one another, as has the practice of a common meal. As my wife says, there is a reason so many meals are mentioned in the Gospels and Acts!

The overall impression that remains with me is of the generosity and "courtesy" of God, who has offered these blessings when I haven't even been aware of needing them or being able to benefit from them. It gives me courage to take risks in the ministry and in my spiritual life generally, trusting that God is there to work all things for good in new and unexpected ways.

Appendix 3
How Do You Define Ministry?

Lloyd Lee Wilson, Earlham School of Religion reflection paper, 2003.

I am uncomfortable with attempts to define ministry because it seems to me such definitions inevitably lead to tests of whether this action or that (on the part of someone else) is true ministry or not. In a general sense, ministry is "service to God," but let me immediately put an apophatic spin on that by saying "that's not quite it." No definition of ministry can quite capture the fullness of the reality.

It seems clear that whatever ministry is (and we know it when we experience it even if we can't adequately define it), some Friends are called to re-order their lives around being ministers to God and doing ministry. This second calling was well known among Friends of earlier generations but is much less so now. Our sense of equality in the eyes of God has given way to a declaration of uniformity among Friends. This is contrary to the evidence of our eyes and ears and acts to prevent numerous persons who have received this second call from the proper development and exercise of their gifts.

My experience of "offering ministry" includes a wide range of activities: standing to offer vocal ministry or kneeling to pray in Quaker meeting for worship; preaching sermons in Methodist worship services; serving breakfast to homeless men with the Catholic Worker folks; public speaking to Friends or non-Friends groups; reading to shut-ins at the local nursing home; leading workshops and retreats; working for twenty years to provide safe, adequate, and affordable housing; writing for publication; leading Bible study or other study groups; teaching Quaker studies at a Friends School; serving as registrar at Chowan College (a Baptist school); serving on yearly meeting or monthly meeting committees; being general secretary of Friends General Conference; counseling young men and women about military service as part of Norfolk Quaker House; clerking various business meetings or serving as recording clerk for meetings and committees. I have traveled extensively in the public ministry among Friends and have described those experiences in an essay ("Faithful to the Promptings of Love") in the

Appendix 3: How Do You Define Ministry?

book *Walk Worthy of Your Calling: Quakers and the Traveling Ministry*.[1]

What is the common thread linking all these activities? It seems to me these are all the fruit of a positive response to that second call mentioned above. Because I responded to that call—in various ways at various times, in keeping with my spiritual maturity and understanding—there was room in my life to undertake these tasks, and I was listening when the specific leading was presented. I see many times that faithfulness in an earlier task prepared me for faithfulness in a later task. Sometimes that experience also prepared my faith community to help me develop and exercise my spiritual gifts more nearly as the Lord wished them to be exercised.

Implicit in this is the understanding that ministry involves the exercise of spiritual gifts—that God enables and equips us to carry out the ministries to which we are divinely led. These spiritual gifts are not often as dramatic as the ability to speak in many languages that was given at Pentecost, but the principle is the same; we serve God with the tools God has given us—not with abilities we have given ourselves. It is furthermore my experience and belief that God entrusts those gifts to the faith community, not the individual, but that is another matter for another forum.

All of this work in the ministry is the most serious endeavor on which one might embark, and at the same time it is in my experience the source of the greatest happiness and peace one could experience. Hannah Whitall Smith points to the same double reality when she recounts this conversation between her uncle John and her brother James about their work in the ministry:

He was speaking with my brother about a "religious visit" he had lately paid to some neighboring Meetings, and as they separated, he said in a very solemn and mournful tone, "So thou wilt see, dear James, what a heavy cross has been put upon me." . . . In a moment or two my uncle walked hastily back, and touching my brother on the arm said, "I am afraid, brother James, that I conveyed a false impression in what I said about my ministry being a cross. Truth compels me to confess to thee that it is not a cross at all, but a very blessed and delightful privilege. Amen![2]

Appendix 4
On a Group Lectio Divina—Luke 5:1–11

Lloyd Lee Wilson, Earlham School of Religion reflection paper, ca. 2006.

Peter's character is easy for me to assume as he seems to be the archetypal older brother—responsible, dependable, sensible, and hard working. This has been my role throughout life. As Peter, I *want* these folks to see me cleaning my nets after working all night (although I would rather have a pile of fish on the dock as well). Where do they get the time and money to wander around the countryside, following one more itinerant preacher? Do they think food just magically appears on the plate? Fish don't just grow on fig trees—it takes hard work by folks like me to keep folks like them fed!

Sounds like this one's name is Jesus—haven't heard any bad reports about him, at least. Whoa! What a crowd! Looks like they're going to push him right into the water if they don't let up soon. Now what—he's on my boat! Argh!

Well, OK, I'll carry him out a little ways from shore. The nets are done, and the combination of sun and breeze will dry me off. Besides, sitting a little while as he preaches will be a welcome rest and a good reason not to be working at something else. Let's hope he does more than just spout the usual drivel.

He was talking a little sense there for a while, but now he wants to tell me about my own trade? I've fished these waters all my life—there's nothing he can teach me about when and where to catch fish around here! In the heat of the sun, with an east wind, there aren't any fish to be caught today. OK, just to show him his place, I'm going to do as "the master" asks—we'll see how his tune changes when we don't catch anything.

By the hair on Abraham's beard—look at those fish! Andrew! John! Get out here, now! Forget your nets—it will be hard enough to lift mine! If I try to pull this catch in over the gunnels the boat will founder—we'll have to tow the net between us, still in the water, until we reach shore.

Appendix 4: On a Group Lectio Divina

Who is this guy, anyway? He's got to be a holy man to do stuff like this. Must be able to see right through me, to know all about me. No, look—stay away! I'm a sinner myself—can't keep the law and catch enough fish to feed my family at the same time—go back to your fans and leave me alone!

It's all right, you say? That's not what you're interested in? You want *me* to travel with you? But I've got responsibilities, people who depend on me . . .

Wait—don't go yet! Caleb! Joash! Get over here! Look, I'm going to be gone for a while. The boat's yours to use—my share of the catch goes to my wife till I get back—no, I don't know how long I'll be gone. Jesus! Wait up!

While I can readily imagine myself as Peter, with his carefully assumed and managed burden of responsibility, it is much more difficult to imagine myself in Jesus' place, as His responsibility seems infinitely greater. Once He's called the disciples, He is responsible for their lives and for the disruption He's caused all around them. He is responsible for "messing everything up" in the lives of all those who hear and try to follow Him. Once He's started, he has to follow through to the end. He can no longer lead His own life—He is the servant of His own followers and hearers.

Long ago, at MIT, we used to talk about the Jonah complex—the drive of some talented folks to avoid being successful because they were afraid of what success might bring—ever-increasing expectations, etc. I know I've had some of that in my life—had it then, at MIT, and have had it since. Could this be part of the same behavior? Am I unconsciously muting my voice in order to avoid the burdens/responsibilities of being a leader among Friends?

I am an intellectual hermit. I can bear to be with people some of the time, but I need long periods of alone time in order to stay happy. The treasure I am reluctant to give up to follow Him completely is my privacy, my solitude, my old books. What we did in secret as children is often a sign of who we really are. I read books and wandered alone in the woods. Already I have had to give much of that up whenever I am among Friends. (An acquaintance sitting nearby during our yearly meeting sessions last month while I received and scheduled requests for opportunities and other demands on my time finally exclaimed, in a moment of quiet, "My God, Lloyd Lee—is it always like this for you?" I had to say, "Yes—but sometimes worse.")

If we are to do what Mike and Susan and I and a few others are seeing is our leading and our task—to write the new primer, to fuel the revival, to knit new Friends and new meetings into the cloth of classic Quakerism—it seems clear I will have to give up a lot of privacy and solitude. Not all, of course, and I will depend heavily on Mike and Susan for discernment. But I will have to be with people much more of the time than I would presently prefer.

Sometimes I feel like repeating the old American Friends Service Committee joke from the time when Clarence Pickett was the head of the organization: "Here am I Lord! Send Clarence!" God grant that as the vision becomes clearer and the demands of the ministry increase, I am willing to give, cheerfully, whatever it takes to be obedient.

Appendix 5
How Do I Wait for God in My Life, in Prayer and Devotion?

Lloyd Lee Wilson, Earlham School of Religion reflection paper, ca. 2006.

I can't write about my personal waiting without writing about the Conservative faith tradition, which teaches me how to wait and provides important models of corporate waiting in which I can participate. It seems my life is a continuous practice, in both senses of the word, of "waiting for and moving under divine inspiration" in all things, trying neither to outrun nor to lag behind my Guide.

The first formational doctrine of North Carolina Yearly Meeting (Conservative) [in 1904] lifted up "the immediate and perceptible guidance of the Holy Spirit." (The second, and only other, stated "the headship of Christ over all things to his church.") If the guidance of the Holy Spirit comes in a perceptible way, without any intermediary, then the onus is on me to prepare for that guidance by removing anything that might be in the way, might come between that guidance and me. The spirituality of subtraction—central to Conservative faith—is a continual removal of anything that might get in the way of waiting.

Corporately, that happens in waiting worship in a powerful way as one joins with the whole community in waiting upon the Lord, listening for and attending to that still small voice that may break in upon us at any time, through any person, or through us all in the silent miracle of a gathered meeting. Together we create a space in which there is only the Lord and waiting upon the Lord. Both First Day and midweek meetings for worship are important times of waiting for me, in the midst of my faith community.

Beyond these large expressions of waiting, my personal practice is an attempt to orient my whole person toward listening for guidance in all things. I try to make it that no decisions, even minor ones, are made without "sitting with" them or "seasoning" the matter. My plans become divinely tentative. The corporate practice supports and reminds us of this principle in various ways. For example, the concluding minute of each of our monthly business meetings says: ". . . meeting closed, purposing to meet again on the ___ day of ____ month, if consistent with the Divine Will." We live "as way opens," knowing and embracing the possibility that God may indeed lead us to change our plans at any time.

Practice at listening and waiting for guidance on the small matters of daily life has caused several things to happen. One, I recognize the Voice when I hear it. Two, I am better able to hear that guidance on larger matters because I have practice on how to listen. Three, I have faith, based on experience, that if I follow that Voice I will be all right. And four, I trust that when I have followed that Voice to the best of my ability, whatever happens is within God's plan. "Unplanned" events or changes that would once have caused me frustration or anxiety can now be accepted with equanimity as it is God's plan unfolding, not mine, and God works all things for good.

Another word for this orientation toward listening for guidance in all things is simplicity. I prepare myself for listening and receiving guidance by removing competition for my attention. I want not to clutter my mind with concerns about what I will wear, how my car or house compares with my neighbor's, etc. Developing this single-pointed awareness oriented toward God is an important part of my waiting for God's guidance.

In this attitude of body and soul, knowing the outcome or end result of one's life is not so important as knowing one is being faithful to the guidance one is receiving right now, in this moment. In the slough of despond, the important thing is not to know how things will eventually turn out but to accept the guidance of where to put one's feet, one step at a time, to find those "certain good and substantial steps" that God is always offering. If I do that, then "all will be well, and all will be well, and all manner of things will be well."

Appendix 6
Aspects of Prayer

Lloyd Lee Wilson, Earlham School of Religion reflection paper, ca. 2006.

    I kneel when praying vocally in worship, with bowed head and eyes closed. I know this is archaic among unprogrammed Friends, and I don't expect others to stand and face the rear of the meeting house as was once the practice. Still, to pray for/on behalf of the gathered body seems to me a holy undertaking, one that invokes the Presence of God in a special way. It is similar to, but different from, offering vocal ministry to the meeting. I stand in ministry, but it seems right to kneel in prayer. I remember the first time I did this. It was during a weekend retreat on vocal ministry at Pendle Hill with Bill Taber. We had been talking about the schisms and divisions among Friends, and when we settled into worship, I was overcome by the brokenness of the Society of Friends. I fell to my knees in prayer and was (nearly) in tears. . . .

    In private prayer, I am not aware that I have any consistent physical postures or actions. My eyes may be open or shut; I may be silent or speak out loud, etc. I often begin with the Jesus Prayer or a personal equivalent that goes, "I'm such a jerk! God forgive me!" This is often followed by words or yearnings to God about some specific thing or person or circumstance. Prayer can happen at any time, from getting out of bed to moving through my morning routines to a sentence or two thrown out in the midst of my workday. My early morning prayers tend to be of thanksgiving, especially for the "trinity": waking up, being able to get out of bed, and going to work/having a (very good) job. Often, my daytime prayers are for other people who face some difficulty. I still follow my father's advice and try to review the day each evening, holding it up to God as I drop off to sleep.

    It has been my lot to do a great deal of driving these past three years, and my musings on the road often bring to mind incidents in my past when I have behaved poorly—these are also times when I pray the Jesus Prayer, either in the classic formulation or my shorter, blunter personal version. This is a continuing theme of my prayer life as I try to get out from under the burden of the many mistakes and outright sins that I have committed. There is a Jackson Browne song with the line, "Don't confront me with my failures, I had not forgotten them." Amen! There is grace and mercy and forgiveness in abundance, this I know experientially—but it seems I must repent for each sin individually. This I'm willing to do, but it takes so long. . . .

I find it very difficult to pray for some good thing for myself as this seems to be a misuse of the relationship with God. I may lift a situation up to God and ask that God's will be done in that situation, and that I be an instrument, not an obstacle, in making that happen, but it is extremely rare for me to pray that event A happen rather than event B. For example, I was able to ask my classmates to pray that I put on paper a fair and accurate representation of my knowledge of the Old Testament but unable to ask them to pray (or to pray myself) that I pass the proficiency exam. I just don't know enough about God's plan to know that the best thing is for me to pass.

The faith tradition—classic Quakerism articulated in the present day—is always a participant in my thoughts and ruminations these days. When I read about the work of elders, I see not the usual concern about the individual's spiritual formation but an overriding concern for the right nurture and sustaining of the tradition. My concern for Quaker content is not for myself but for the tradition. This care for the tradition is, I think, the ground on which I stand. I have much to learn and much spiritual formation to undergo—but even here, I am not at the center of the story.

Perhaps this begins to get at what Paul was writing about, which has always mystified me, when he said, "Not I, but Christ in me." One lives not so much for oneself but for the sake of the gospel to serve others. This is part of the reordering of life that accompanies accepting the call into ministry. How bold to claim that Christ lives in me—yet this is clearly the claim of primitive Christianity. And I am so flawed. Yet, as Paul found treasure in earthenware vessels, perhaps that can be the case for me, too.

Appendix 7
Reflecting on John Woolman

Lloyd Lee Wilson, Earlham School of Religion reflection paper, ca. 2006.

I haven't dipped into John Woolman's *Journal* for several years, and I found last night's reading a delight. As a Southerner, I find the (to my mind) "bias" of northern readings of Woolman a bit hard to take sometimes, especially as it is not politically correct to question that bias in any way, but Woolman's life itself is a model of humility, accountability, and "holy obedience" that just stops me in my tracks. This is how a life should be lived in gospel order.

Some readers observe that we have in his journal only Woolman's account of how he was received. This is true, but there was another report made at the time by the people he visited, and although we don't have access to those reports in his journal (they may still exist in a meeting or college archive), we can draw some conclusions based on what Woolman does tell us. His certificate for travel in the ministry was regularly endorsed by the Friends he visited, and those endorsements were reviewed by his monthly and yearly meetings upon his return. Had those endorsements given the consistent message that he was abrasive, arrogant, and/or condemning of the Friends he visited, it is very unlikely that he would have been granted another certificate. So, the fact he made multiple journeys in the ministry is evidence that he was as well received as he himself reports.

Beyond the formal accountability of endorsements of his certificate, other Friends in the yearly meeting undoubtedly had observed Woolman in his travels at some time or other or had received a letter from visited Friends about him. When Mike and I brought our certificates back to our yearly meeting sessions for review last month, four Friends present stood and gave their testimony about our ministry. Two were from our yearly meeting who had seen us elsewhere, one was from another meeting we visited who decided to attend our sessions, and one had belonged to a yearly meeting I visited and had since moved to North Carolina to be part of our yearly meeting, "not entirely due to Lloyd Lee's ministry" is the way I remember her expressing it. I expect these same sorts of testimonies were going on with Woolman, also.

I can't say that I identify with Woolman, but I do feel there are many points of contact between us. The content of our ministry is different, but the desire to be faithful to that call and at the same time to be accountable to our faith community is, I believe, very similar. Our desire to live outward lives consistent with our spiritual profession of faith is similar, though I've come to somewhat different conclusions about providing for my children, at least in terms of educating them. By conscious decision, both of us earned far less than we had the opportunity to earn in our competencies. I have had the additional opportunity, because of the times I live in, to choose that the content of my work would be a direct ministry as well. Working for teaching hospitals, nonprofit housing organizations, and shelters for battered women were not career options for John Woolman.

Woolman wore an undyed hat as a testimony of simplicity and against the fashions of the vain world. When for a time undyed hats came into fashion, he had to decide whether to change his hat style in order to continue a testimony against fashion or continue to wear the same hat and wait for the style to change again. He chose to wait. I wear shirts without collars for the same reason. When for a time collarless shirts came into fashion, I had the same decision to make. Like Woolman, I chose to wait out the fad, and soon enough fashion changed and I got my testimony back.

There is a matching event in my life to Woolman's experience at London Yearly Meeting of Ministers and Elders. *Essays on the Quaker Vision of Gospel Order* contains the Quaker equivalent of a nihil obstat [declaration of no objection] from North Carolina Yearly Meeting (Conservative), and I have tried to explain openly how seriously I took the approval process. I would not have gone ahead with publication without the approval of my faith community. Nonetheless, this often doesn't really seem to sink in. Consequently, when folks ask me when I'm going to write another book (as they often do), I typically brush off the question by saying something noncommittal. What they don't know is that I wrote a second book a couple of years after *Essays* came out. I felt it was good work on an important topic. When I showed the manuscript to a few seasoned Friends in the yearly meeting, however, they were not clear that it should be published. The manuscript still sits on my

Appendix 7: Reflecting on John Woolman

bookshelf in a three-ring binder—but I have never looked at it again and no one else has ever seen it. John Woolman, I believe, would have understood this immediately. The majority of contemporary Friends, it seems to me, value their individualism too much to understand.

I often compare Woolman to his contemporary Benjamin Lay, a hunchbacked dwarf who carried pigs' bladders full of blood into meetings for worship so he could spray the blood of slavery on the assembled worshipers. We remember Woolman with respect bordering on awe; Lay is a forgotten man. Somehow through all the years, through all the difficulties and all the resistance to his ministry, John Woolman remained tender to the immediate promptings of the Holy Spirit and tenderly loving of his auditory, while never wavering from the prophetic message he had been called to deliver to that auditory. God grant me a measure of Woolman's tenderness, and his faithful perseverance!

Appendix 8
On a Personal Rule for Daily Life

Lloyd Lee Wilson, Earlham School of Religion reflection paper, ca. 2006.

1. Morning devotions (with my wife, whenever possible)

2. A page or an hour of writing each morning, whichever comes first

3. Some moderate physical exercise each day

4. Evening devotions (with my wife, whenever possible)

5. An hour of Quaker study or preparation for public ministry each evening

6. Regular journaling (unscheduled)

7. Personal examen before going to sleep

Although this looks like a rigorous rule, these seven practices are not that different from what I am doing already or have done in the past. I feel most comfortable when there is routine in my life, and I feel that routines help me make sure to give the right amount of attention to the various activities that vie for my attention.

My wife and I have practiced morning devotions in previous years, and I look forward to re-establishing that the week after I return to North Carolina and when we are fully moved to Woodland. She suggested that we add evening devotions, and I am in unity with the prospect. These devotions consist primarily of contemplative prayer. I also already practice a form of examen each night before retiring, and I propose to continue this.

I wrote *Essays* by arising early each morning and writing a page or for an hour before anyone else got up. Whether this is before or after morning devotions, the same commitment seems right to me for working on other projects.

I try to get some exercise each day when I can; it will be beneficial to make this a more intentional practice. I have been journaling, in one style or another, since I was twelve. This is a practice I will continue.

Appendix 8: On a Personal Rule for Daily Life

This leaves the evening hour of study and preparation for ministry as the only completely new practice. I have been irregular in this area, and I need to be more intentional. The preparation for ministry on one level can happen only as I am given inspiration, but making space for that cannot be a bad thing. I have a high stack of Quaker-related materials that I want to read, and my intent is to be reading this material when I am not ready to work directly on whatever my next public ministry commitment might be and to give up the reading for preparation as led.

Appendix 9
What the Sabbath Means to Me

Lloyd Lee Wilson, Earlham School of Religion reflection paper, ca. 2006.

Be careful to make a profitable and religious use of those portions of time on the first day of the week which are not occupied by our meetings for worship.

—"Advices," in North Carolina Yearly Meeting (Conservative) *Discipline* (1983)

For me, keeping the Sabbath has meant no gainful employment or labor related to gainful employment and no unnecessary purchases or other commerce. Chowan College knows that I do not work on First Day, even during orientation weekends or other times when previous registrars did work. I arrange to buy food and other items on Seventh Day or Second Day; I don't shop or "go to the mall" on First Day. Susan and I walk to the meeting house for worship and often from there to the Grapevine Café if there is a sufficient group able to break bread together (I see the café as providing an important ministry of hospitality). The afternoon and evening may be spent in reading or writing, baking bread, playing with our dogs, or caring for our garden—mostly just being together.

Keeping the Sabbath is for me a matter of obedience (after all, they aren't called the Ten Suggestions!), but other issues are more important. It is a matter of faith in God, having faith that God is indeed taking care of me and that maximizing my work production is not essential to the proper functioning of the universe; it is a matter of receiving God's grace for rest and renewal; it is one way to respond to my yearly meeting's query: "To what extent is the performance of my worldly duties promoting or hindering my growth in grace and my service for God?" It helps me remember that everything I have is a gift from God and not the earned and deserved reward for my own effort. It helps me remember about Jubilee—that the purpose of work is not to maximize my own possessions but to see that everyone has enough.

Publications by Lloyd Lee Wilson

Books

Essays on the Quaker Vision of Gospel Order. Burnsville, TN: Celo Valley Books, 1993; repr. Philadelphia: Quaker Press of Friends General Conference, 2007.

Wrestling with Our Faith Tradition. Philadelphia: Quaker Press of Friends General Conference, 2005.

Contributions to Edited Books

"Conservative Friends 1845–2011." In *The Oxford Handbook of Quaker Studies*, edited by Stephen W. Angell and Pink Dandelion, 126–37. Oxford: Oxford University Press, 2013.

"Faithful to the Promptings of Love." In *Walk Worthy of Your Calling*, edited by Margery Post Abbott and Peggy Senger Parsons, 95–111. Richmond, IN: Friends United Press, 2004.

"Gospel order." In *The A to Z of the Friends (Quakers)*, edited by Margery Post Abbott, Mary Ellen Chijioke, Pink Dandelion, and John William Oliver Jr., 120. Lanham, MD: Scarecrow Press, 2006.

Pamphlets

The Exercise of Spiritual Authority within the Meeting. The School of the Spirit Ministry, 2014.

Radical Hospitality. Pendle Hill Pamphlet #427. Wallingford, PA: Pendle Hill Publications, 2014.

Change and Preservation in the Same Current. 41st Michener Quaker Lecture in Florida. Orlando, FL: Southeastern Yearly Meeting Publications, 2011.

Who Do You Say I Am? Pamphlet #409. Wallingford, PA: Pendle Hill Publications, 2010.

Encounter with the Taproot. Philadelphia: Friends World Committee for Consultation, 2007.

Holy Surrender. Worcester, MA: New England Yearly Meeting of Friends, 2006.

Why Do You Still Read That Old Thing? Philadelphia: Friends World Committee for Consultation, 1996.

Articles

"Historical Background and Spiritual Characteristics of North Carolina Conservative Friends." *Journal of the North Carolina Yearly Meeting (Conservative)*, no. 7 (2016): 11–22.

"Discernment: Coming under the Guidance of the Holy Spirit." *Journal of the North Carolina Yearly Meeting (Conservative)*, no. 6 (2012): 1–9.

"Earth Care and the Great Commandments." *Journal of the North Carolina Yearly Meeting (Conservative)*, no. 5 (2008): 3–12.

"The Baptisms of John and Jesus: An Exegesis of John 1:19–34." *Quaker Theology* 7, no. 2 (2007): 136–72.

"A Conservative Yearly Meeting Is Born." *Quaker Theology* 6, no. 2 (2005): 78–91.

"On the Advices." *Journal of the North Carolina Yearly Meeting (Conservative)*, no. 4 (2005): 7–19.

"Concerning Birthright Members: A Response." *Newsletter*, North Carolina Friends Historical Society 19 (2005).

"A Statement of Christian Pacifism." *Friends Journal* 49 (December 2003): 18–19.

"Christian Pacifist." *Quaker Life* (2003): 15.

"Reading the Query Answers: A Conversation" [with David Eley]. *Journal of the North Carolina Yearly Meeting (Conservative)*, no. 2 (2003): 26–32.

"Wrestling with Our Faith Tradition." *Journal of the North Carolina Yearly Meeting (Conservative)*, no. 3 (2003): 3–38.

"Confidentiality and Community." *Quaker Monthly* (Nottingham, UK) (2001).

"Accountability and Vocal Ministry." *Journal of the North Carolina Yearly Meeting (Conservative)*, no. 1 (2001): 8–10.

"Confidentiality and Community." *Friends Journal* 46, no. 10 (2000): 24–25.

"A Deeper Unity." *Quaker Life* 29, no. 2 (March 1988): 21–22.

"Spiritual Profession and Our Daily Activity." *Quaker Life* 29 (June 1988): 37.

"Unprogrammed Friends & Growth." *Quaker Life* 29, no. 10 (December 1988): 13–14, 15.

"Prayer." *Fellowship in Prayer* 36, no. 1 (1985): 14–19 (reprinted in *The Evangelical Friend*, June 1985).

"It Speaks to My Condition." *Quaker Life* 25, no. 4 (May 1984): 10–12.

Publications by Lloyd Lee Wilson

"Reliquary of the True Cross." *Friends Journal* 29, no. 14 (October 1, 1983): 3.
"Looking Ahead." *Friends General Conference Quarterly* 16, no. 1 (1983): 1.
"I Have Stopped Paying for War," *Quaker Life* 22, no. 4 (1981): 22–23.
"A Fellowship of Friends Is Gathered in the Appalachian Mountains of Virginia." *Quaker Life* 21, no. 4 (1980): 12–13.
"Building a Conscious Community." *PeaceWork* 50 (1977).
"New England Friends Community." *The New England Friend* (1974): 3.

Book Reviews

Where the Wind Blows: Vitality among Friends by Jay Marshall. *Friends Journal* 52 (December 2006): 26.
Pilgrims in Their Own Land by Martin Marty. *Friends Journal* 31 (April 1, 1985): 22.
Nuclear Holocaust and Christian Hope by Ronald Sider and Richard Taylor. *Friends Journal* 30 (Feb. 15, 1984): 27–28.
Christians and Nonviolence in the Nuclear Age by Gerard Vanderhaar. *Friends Journal* 29 (Feb. 15, 1983): 24.
God and Government: The Separation of Church and State by Ann E. Weiss. *Friends Journal* 29 (February 1, 1983): 24–25.
Getting the Books Off the Shelves: Making the Most of Your Congregation's Library by Ruth S. Smith. *Quaker Life* 16, no. 12 (1975).

Videos

Lloyd Lee Wilson Interview with Hilary Burgin and Marcelle Martin, November 2019. January 24, 2020. https://www.youtube.com/watch?v=fkhJIXiYgsI
Are Quakers Christian? QuakerSpeak, October 31, 2019. https://quakerspeak.com/video/are-quakers-christian/
Why Do Quakers Worship in Silence? QuakerSpeak, October 18, 2018. https://www.youtube.com/watch?v=BcF948A_Mqo
Committing to the Quaker Spiritual Path. QuakerSpeak, July 5, 2018. https://quakerspeak.com/video/committing-to-the-quaker-spiritual-path/

Glossary

accountability. Our need to be answerable to one another in our Quaker meetings. Two major areas of accountability are the balance of freedom and discipline inside the meeting and whether our lives reflect the core vision of early Friends.

adoptionist Christology. A "low Christology" that holds Jesus was the adopted son of God, not a preexistent divine being. Often combined with a disbelief in doctrines of immaculate conception, virgin birth, perpetual virginity, or the Trinity.

Adversary. In some Christian thought, a term referring to the collection of forces, systemic injustices, and temptations that together form obstacles for the Christian pilgrim. Not a person, like Satan or the Devil, but a recognition that there is opposition that the believer must face.

Advices (Quaker). A formal document summarizing specific advice given by a yearly meeting to its individual members over a period of years, often published in conjunction with the Queries.

Aldersgate. During a time of great personal and spiritual disappointment in 1738, John Wesley reluctantly attended a group meeting in a Moravian chapel on Aldersgate Street in London. While someone was reading from Martin Luther's Preface to the Epistle to the Romans, he felt that his heart was "strangely warmed," and he became a Moravian.

apophatic spirituality. A way of theological thinking and practice that attempts to approach the Divine by negation, speaking and thinking only what may not be said about God—the set of sentences that begin "God is not . . ." Also called the *via negativa*.

atonement. The means by which God and God's creation are reconciled. Christians have never agreed on a single understanding of atonement, though individual denominations may do so. See moral influence theory, penal atonement.

auditory. Synonym for audience in the seventeenth century, favored by Quakers and their religious contemporaries but implies that the individual listening is actively engaged in the message and not a passive consumer.

Glossary

authority. The power to influence thought, opinion, or behavior. Among Friends, authority is not vested in persons but in the Light itself and is manifested in various ways through Scripture, institutions, or individuals.

care of meeting for worship. The responsibility to hold the spiritual and physical state of the meeting for worship in discernment and prayer, to sense when the time has come to close the meeting; often includes overseeing introductions and announcements at the rise of meeting.

centrality of Christ. Phrase used to highlight the differences among Friends between those whose faith commitments are closer to orthodox mainline Protestantism and those who express a more mystical faith, less explicitly Christian

circuit rider. Methodist clergy assigned to serve a number of small, isolated churches (a "charge"), which they visited on a specific "circuit" and a set schedule.

competency. What an individual does to earn a living. See vocation.

concern. An assignment from God, to an individual or a group of individuals, requiring a specific response in deed, word, or prayer.

constructive theology. A method of doing theology that draws on our experiences to infer tentative descriptions of God, which are then subject to experiential testing; an *a posteriori* approach. See systematic theology.

contemplative. In religious life, a contemplative is one who practices a spirituality of contemplation, the practice of intentionally setting aside the intellect in order to be fully open to the experience of the Presence of God beyond words or rational constructs. In Western Christianity, closely related to mysticism.

convicted. Among Friends, the sense that one's behavior has been wrong and a better way must be found. Can apply to some specific act or to one's spiritual life generally. Followed by convincement (or a better way), and conversion of manners (the full adoption of that better way).

corporal works of mercy. Acts focused on relieving the physical needs of other creatures, based on Matthew 25, Isaiah, and the Book of Tobit. They include feeding the hungry, giving water to the thirsty, clothing the naked, sheltering the homeless, visiting the sick, visiting the imprisoned or ransoming the captive, and burying the dead.

covenant community. An understanding of a group of individuals (such as a monthly meeting) as being called together by God to carry out an agreed-upon purpose; distinct from a collection of individuals who like each other or gather because they share other common interests.

covenant fellowship. A small group of individuals who commit to meet with each other regularly for worship, discernment, spiritual nurture, and accountability.

covered meeting. A meeting for worship in which the presence of God is so strongly felt that those present are united in a profound silence of "waiting upon the Lord." Vocal ministry that is offered is often united in unexpected ways. See also gathered meeting.

cycle of action and reflection. In religious contexts, a concept of spiritual growth that involves three steps in any action, whether personal or corporate: planning, acting, and reflecting on the outcome contemplatively.

deliberative theology. An understanding of faith through carefully reflecting upon embedded theological convictions and asking "Why?" See embedded theology.

discernment. The work of recognizing the will of God for an individual or a group, coming to understand it more clearly, and deciding to accept it.

docetism. The belief that Jesus' body was not fully human and therefore that he did not suffer during his Passion and death on the cross.

doctrine of perfection. Quaker doctrine that the scriptural admonition "Be ye perfect" should be taken literally as a promise Christ can enable us to fulfill. Friends have long discussed what it means to be perfect.

dogmatic theology. A method of doing theology that starts with the essential dogma of the church and builds logically on that foundation to articulate all the truths about God. A characteristic of dogmatic theology is that to deny the truth developed in this way is considered heresy.

Eagle (Boy Scouts). Highest rank in the Boy Scouts. In the 1950s and '60s, this was achieved by very few Scouts.

Glossary

economy of debt. An economy built on a scarcity of resources, unevenly distributed. Ultimate concern rests in the size of one's silo and the available worldly force to protect it, which is idolatry.

economy of grace. An economy built on God's infinite grace, available to all without limitation. Ultimate concern rests in living a life pleasing to God and one another.

elders. Formal leadership role in many Christian denominations. In churches without a paid or ordained ministry, elders take on a more central role in the life of the congregation.

embedded theology. Our first understanding of the faith and the subsequent actions and practices that it entails—those things that have been learned and reinforced by our environments. Embedded theology is similar to cultural heritage or the presuppositions and assumed beliefs that one holds. See deliberative theology.

fatwa. In Islam, a formal ruling or interpretation on a point of Islamic law.

fire escape theology. A stream of popular theology that represents escaping from the trials and tribulations of this life as the primary motivation for Christian faith and practice.

fire insurance theology. A stream of popular theology that represents ensuring one does not spend eternity suffering in hell as the primary motivation for Christian faith and practice. See spaceship theology.

foot washing. Ritual washing of feet practiced by numerous Christian denominations in response to John 13:14–17. Often observed on Maundy Thursday of Holy Week. Sometimes clergy wash the feet of lay members; in other denominations, members wash one another's feet.

free will. The ability to act on one's own, without constraints of divine will, fate, or necessity. Theologically, the opposite of predestination.

gathered meeting. Meeting characterized by an unusually strong sense of the Divine presence. See Thomas R. Kelly, "The Gathered Meeting," in *A Testament of Devotion*. See also covered meeting.

Gnosticism. A Christian heresy dating to the second century CE, teaching that the world was created and ruled by a lesser divinity, the demiurge; that Christ was an emissary of the remote gods; and that secret knowledge (gnosis) of these things was required for redemption of the human spirit.

gospel order. The harmonious relationship among all the myriad parts of creation; God has always yearned for it to prevail everywhere.

God and Country Award (Boy Scouts). Boy Scouts medal awarded in conjunction with a Scout's chosen religious denomination after the Scout satisfied a number of requirements specified by the denomination.

Great Commission. Jesus' instruction to the disciples in Matthew 28:19–20a, considered by many to be binding on all Christians.

Holy Spirit. God's continuing presence in this world; the experience of God as spiritually active in the world. Among early Friends, a close synonym of Christ.

immaculate conception. Dogma of the Catholic church that Mary, mother of Jesus, was free of original sin from the moment of her conception.

immediate and perceptible guidance of the Holy Spirit. One of two primary doctrines of North Carolina Yearly Meeting (Conservative). Divine guidance is available to anyone. It is immediate in the sense that it is available in the moment it is needed and that it is available without intermediary; no clergy, holy writing, or church teaching is required. It is perceptible in that the guidance can be felt and understood directly by the individual. The other primary doctrine is "the headship of Christ over all things to His church."

immersion baptism. The practice of baptizing by submerging the individual completely, in contrast to baptism by pouring water over the head or sprinkling some water on the top of the head. Immersion "in living water" can take place only in a natural body of water such as a river and not in a large baptismal font inside a church.

implicated resistance. The understanding that in a modern society no individual can be completely free of any involvement in systemic injustice. One may resist injustice and act to minimize or reduce it, but one is always still implicated in the injustice one is working against.

infant leading. The first indications, often vague and uncertain, that the Inward Guide is preparing specific guidance about a task one will be expected to carry out in the future.

Glossary

intercessory prayer. A form of petitionary prayer directed toward the welfare of people and creation other than oneself.

interrogatory theology. A theological practice based on asking probing questions about how various faith commitments are reflected in the praxis of individuals and the faith community as a whole. Asking and answering queries by monthly meetings is an example.

Inward Christ. Reference to the Christ Spirit, or Holy Spirit, who gives us direct and perceptible help and nurture inwardly, i.e., without the need to consult outward books or authoritative people. See Inward Guide.

Inward Guide. One way that the Inward Christ is experienced—as a guide to our behavior and moral choices.

Inward Light. Among early Friends, the inward illumination provided by Christ that shows our spiritual condition clearly and points out where we need to change. In the present day, often used to denote the Inward Presence of Christ.

Jubilee. The Torah divides time into cycles of seven years. Each seventh year is a year of release, when debts are forgiven, farmland lies fallow, and stores of food are distributed freely to all. After seven cycles of seven years, the fiftieth year is the Jubilee. That year, prisoners are released, slaves are given their freedom, and all property is returned to its original owners or their heirs. Jubilee has not been observed (for various reasons) since about 600 BCE.

lay leader (Methodist). An elected leadership position in the local Methodist church; often also the chair of the Official Board. Works with the pastor to plan, carry out, and evaluate all the programs of the congregation.

lay speaker (Methodist). A member of a local church certified by the Quarterly Conference to conduct services of worship and hold meetings for prayer and exhortation and to serve as needed in other kinds of church or church-related activities.

leading. Immediate, perceptible guidance from the Holy Spirit to do (or not do) some specific thing.

lectio divina. The ancient spiritual practice of reading Scripture contemplatively as a form of prayer, as an individual or in a group.

liberation theology. A theological movement emphasizing liberation from social, economic, and political oppression as a necessary part of general salvation. Began among Roman Catholics in Latin America and has since spread around the world.

Light. Another name for Christ, referring to John 1:1–9.

liminal space. Spiritually, a threshold—a time of transition between what was and what could be. Often a time of profound change.

listening in tongues. A practice dealing with spiritual diversity by asking everyone to use the religious vocabulary that seems best to them and asking listeners to take responsibility for translating the language of the speaker into their own preferred vocabulary.

liturgical calendar. The annual cycle of seasons and days observed by the Christian church in commemoration of the life, death, and teachings of Christ and of his followers.

Lord's Supper. Holy Communion, an ordinance of most Christian churches. It can be "open," meaning that anyone can participate, or "closed," meaning that only baptized members in good standing with the church can participate.

meetings of ministers, elders, and overseers. In previous centuries, those Friends recognized as ministers and elders were sometimes organized into a system of monthly, quarterly, and yearly meetings parallel to but separate from the meeting system to which all Friends belonged. Sometimes named overseers were also included. In North Carolina Yearly Meeting (Conservative), this organization still exists nominally but is weakening in practice.

monthly meeting. In North American Quakerism, a local congregation, so called because members meet monthly to conduct business. In Great Britain, often a regional meeting encompassing several local congregations.

moral influence theory. The understanding of atonement in which Christ became incarnate to be a moral influence on human beings, demonstrating and teaching how to live in a way pleasing to God.

narrative theology. A way of doing theology that takes the narratives in Scripture as the model for theological thinking and action; the narrative story of people "bumping into God" is the material from which our understanding of and relationship to God is built.

normative Quakerism. The idea that there can be an agreed upon set of faith commitments and practices that are the "normative" story of

Glossary

Quakerism, without expecting that any individual Quaker will necessarily agree with all those commitments and practices.

nonpastoral (Quaker). Two of the four branches of Quakerism are often called nonpastoral Quakers: Conservatives and Liberals.

North Carolina Yearly Meeting of Friends (Conservative). One of two groups, both called North Carolina Yearly Meeting of Friends, that emerged from the separation of the original North Carolina Yearly Meeting in the early years of the twentieth century. Called Conservative because it was slower to embrace innovation than its counterpart.

Official Board (Methodist). Governing body in local Methodist churches.

opportunity. The recognition by two or more persons that an opportunity for communion with the Holy Spirit is being offered and their response to set aside whatever they have been doing to listen and worship. Can be planned or spontaneous.

Order of the Arrow (Boy Scouts). Honor Society in the Boy Scouts of America. Members are elected by their fellow Scouts, approved by their adult leaders, and must meet a set of other specific criteria. Membership is limited.

original sin. Christian doctrine that, because of the sin of Adam and Eve, all human beings are born into a state of sinfulness.

oversight. The exercise of pastoral care functions in a Quaker meeting; the specific responsibility of those appointed as "overseers." Sometimes used as a synonym for under the care of. See under the care of.

Passion, the. Events surrounding the arrest, trials, and eventual crucifixion of Jesus Christ.

penal atonement. The understanding of atonement in which wrongdoers must be punished before God can forgive them. Since humans cannot bear the punishment they deserve, Jesus substituted for all humankind and suffered the necessary penalty. A subgrouping of substitutionary atonement.

Permanent Board (New England Yearly Meeting). The decision-making body of New England Yearly Meeting at times when the yearly meeting is not in session.

perpetual virginity. Catholic dogma that Mary, mother of Jesus, was a virgin before, during, and after giving birth.

petitionary prayer. A general category of prayer characterized by requests for good outcomes for oneself, others, or specific parts of creation.

plain dress. Mode of clothing adopted by Quakers in the seventeenth century and continuing until the early twentieth, characterized by lack of ornamentation, bright colors, or fashionable style. Think broad-brim hats, suspenders, and collarless shirts. Still worn by a few Friends today.

poustinia. A Slavic term made popular by Catherine Doherty in *Poustinia: Encountering God in Silence, Solitude and Prayer*. A *poustinia*—as this word is used in the Eastern Christian tradition—is a simple cabin or room to which one goes to pray and fast in silence and solitude, typically for a day.

praxis. Spiritually, the customary conduct of an individual or group that reflects faith commitments or doctrines.

precept and example. The combined witness of the teachings and the life of Jesus Christ as a guide for Christian decisions and acts.

predestination. The Christian doctrine that everything that happens has been predetermined by God; humans have no real free will. In particular, God had already determined before the moment of creation who would be saved and admitted to heaven and who would not. Particularly in versions of this doctrine where the total number of saved souls is a fixed number, one can never know who has been predestined for heaven: obvious sinners can be eliminated, but there is no way to know whether a good person has been good enough to qualify. See free will.

Primitive Baptist church. A small sect of "Particular Baptist churches of the Old School" distinguished by their articles of faith, which are:

1. We believe in one true and living God, Father, Son and the Holy Ghost and these three are One.
2. We believe that scriptures of the Old and New Testament as translated in the 1611 King James Version of the Holy Bible is the written word of God and the only rule of faith and practice.
3. We believe in the doctrine of election by grace.
4. We believe in the doctrine of original sin and in Man's impotency to recover himself from the fallen state he is in nature by his own free will or ability.

Glossary

5. We believe that sinners are called, converted, regenerated and sanctified by the Holy Spirit, and that all who are thus regenerated and born again by the Spirit of God shall never fall finally away.

6. We believe that sinners are justified in the site [*sic*] of God only by the imputed righteousness of Jesus Christ.

7. We believe that baptism and the Lord's Supper are ordinances of Jesus Christ and that true believers are the only subjects of those ordinances and we believe the only true mode of baptism is by immersion.

8. We believe in the resurrection of the dead and a general judgement and the joys of the righteous and that the punishment of the wicked will be eternal.

9. We believe that no minister has the right to administer the ordinances of the gospel except such as are regularly called, and come under the imposition of hands by the presbytery.

primitive Christianity. Christianity as it existed during the lives of the apostles—the original faith. Early generations of Quakers considered themselves "Primitive Christianity Revived."

propitiation. Theologically, an atoning sacrifice that appeases an angry God.

prosperity theology. A theological understanding based on the premise that financial wealth and physical health are always God's will for believers and that these blessings can be secured through faith, positive speech, and donations to specific religious organizations.

quarterly meeting. A regional gathering of monthly meetings. Historically, quarterly meetings met once every three months to conduct business.

Queries (Quaker). A set of formal questions addressed to individuals or groups (e.g., meetings of Ministers, Elders, and Overseers) to stimulate examination of particular parts of their lives that may present particular challenges. See also Advices.

recorded minister. A Friend who has shown a continuing gift for nurturing the faith community in various ways and whose meeting has recorded the existence of this gift in its minutes. Sometimes this is done by the yearly meeting, but in North Carolina Yearly Meeting

(Conservative) it is the responsibility of the monthly meeting. This is an open-ended recognition but can be rescinded if the individual shows signs of having "lost the gift" or behaving in ways detrimental to the good name of Friends.

released Friend. A Friend whose leading to carry out a particular course of action has been met with approval by a meeting; the meeting then promises to provide enough support to enable the Friend to follow that leading.

Representative Body. The deliberative body that has decision-making responsibility for North Carolina Yearly Meeting (Conservative) when that body is not in session. Now known as the Interim Body.

Richmond Declaration of Faith of 1887. A world conference of Orthodox Friends meeting in Richmond, Indiana, in 1887 issued this declaration in an attempt to set a standard of beliefs and practices for all Orthodox Friends. Yearly meetings that adopted this declaration as their own became members of the new Five Years Meeting (now Friends United Meeting), one of the four branches of Quakerism.

rule of life (personal). A daily schedule and set of practices designed, if followed closely, to help individuals and communities live closer to the heart and mind of Jesus by spending appropriate amounts of time in prayer, work, worship, and service to others.

Rule of St. Benedict. A collection of directions (rules) about how monks should order their lives while living in community under an abbot. Has been used by the Benedictine order, among others, for over 1,500 years.

rule-based ethics. Also called deontological ethics; one of three schools of ethics (the others are virtue ethics and consequential ethics). Ethical decisions should be based on preestablished rules applied universally.

school of Christ. Quaker term for the individual and corporate experience of being life-long students with Christ as our Teacher. Similar to the concept of being apprentices to the faith tradition.

separation. Quaker term for schism. The Great Separation(s) refers to the nineteenth-century schisms that divided North American Quakers into Hicksites, Wilburites, and Orthodox Friends.

shalom. Hebrew word meaning peace, harmony, wholeness, completeness, prosperity, welfare, and tranquility.

Glossary

slain in the Spirit. Sociologist Margaret Poloma has defined slaying in the Spirit as "the power of the Holy Spirit so filling a person with a heightened inner awareness that the body's energy fades away and the person collapses to the floor" (*The Assemblies of God at the Crossroads: Charisma and Institutional Dilemmas*, 1989).

spaceship theology. A stream of popular theology that represents escape from the suffering and tribulations of this life through the Rapture and Second Coming as the primary motivation for Christian faith and practice. See fire insurance theology.

spirituality of subtraction. A spiritual discipline, closely linked to apophatic spirituality, in which the practitioner intentionally subtracts everything in life that is not God or that hinders them from the direct experience of God. See apophatic spirituality.

substitutionary atonement. See penal substitution.

swear (an oath). Quakers have historically understood Matthew 5:34 literally as prohibiting Christians from all formal oaths, including swearing to tell the truth in a court of law.

systematic theology. An ancient method of doing theology in which everything is deduced logically from one or a small number of foundational principles—an *a priori* approach. See constructive theology.

Teacher, the (Quaker). A name for Christ; related to Fox's epiphany, "Christ has come to teach His people Himself."

testimony. The witness of a life lived under the immediate, perceptible guidance of the Holy Spirit

that of God in everyone. A phrase used by contemporary Friends that posits a part or seed of God resides in every human being; never used in this way by George Fox.

theodicy. Study and reflection on the question of why an all-knowing, all-powerful, and perfectly good God would allow evil to exist in the world.

traveling under a concern. Travel to other Quaker meetings or non-Quaker groups in response to a divine leading to articulate a particular concern or to share the joy of the gospel with other believers.

Trinitarianism. Belief in the Christian dogma of the Trinity: the unity of Father, Son, and Holy Spirit as three persons in one Godhead. This term is not found in Scripture.

under the care of. For events, the phrase means that the event's sponsor is responsible for preparations and for seeing that all aspects of the event are carried out in right order. For individuals, the phrase indicates a group of Friends who guide and nurture the individual in the exercise of a gift or carrying out a leading. See oversight.

virgin birth. The Christian doctrine that Jesus was conceived and born to Mary without sexual intercourse with a man, through the power of the Holy Spirit.

Virgin Mary. A name for Mary, mother of Jesus of Nazareth, reflecting the doctrine that she became pregnant with Jesus without losing her virginity. Catholics and Orthodox Christians believe that she was a virgin her entire life.

virtue ethics. A school of ethical thinking that understands decisions in terms of the virtue, or moral character, of the person making the decision.

vocation. The work to which God calls an individual; a field of ministry. See Competency.

Wilburites. Followers of John Wilbur, one of the key figures in the Great Separations of the nineteenth century.

yearly meeting. An organization of Friends or monthly meetings covering a larger area than a single quarterly meeting; in session once each year to conduct business. Once yearly meetings covered distinct separate areas, but since the separations of the nineteenth century it is common for yearly meetings representing different branches of Quakerism to overlap each other geographically.

Notes

Introduction

¹ Barbara Blaugdone, *An Account of the Travels, Sufferings and Persecutions of Barbara Blaugdone* (1691), 9–10, available from Early English Books Online Text Creation Partnership, https://quod.lib.umich.edu/e/eebo/A26118.0001.001?view=toc.

Chapter 1

¹ My mother felt this reshaping process was incomplete and spent several weeks hiding my skull under a concealing cap, continuing to massage my skull herself in private moments until she was satisfied with the results.

² North Carolina Yearly Meeting of the Religious Society of Friends (Conservative), *Faith and Practice: Book of Discipline of the North Carolina Yearly Meeting (Conservative) of the Religious Society of Friends* (1983), https://www.ncymc.org/home/faith-and-practice.

Chapter 2

¹ A war game is a simulated military conflict carried out as a game, leisure activity, or exercise in personal development. These games are roleplaying exercises intended to develop the players' skills in strategic planning. In our case, we had two groups representing each side in the conflict. The four groups were put in separate rooms, had limited communications with the other group on their team, and were expected to out-strategize their opponents over a finite set of simultaneous "moves."

² Looking back, my spiritual condition was not much different from that of Samuel Bownas as a young man when Anne Wilson declared that "thou comest to meeting as thou went from it (the last time), and goest from it as thou came to it but art no better for thy coming; what wilt thou do in the end?" Joseph Besse, *The Journals of the lives and travels of Samuel Bownas, and John Richardson* (Philadelphia: repr. 1759), 3–4. http://name.umdl.umich.edu/N06545.0001.001.

³ William Faulkner, "Banquet Speech," 1949, The Nobel Prize, accessed April 18, 2021, https://www.nobelprize.org/prizes/literature/1949/faulkner/speech/.

⁴ The meeting room of Friends Meeting at Cambridge holds 175 persons; there were at that time two meetings for worship each First Day morning, one at 9:30 and one at 11:00.

5 A little later, I gave my mother a copy of Daisy Newman's *A Procession of Friends* to help her get a feel for the sort of people Quakers are. After reading it, she said to me "Quakers are just like Methodists!"

6 Only many years later did I learn just how big a promotion and increase in pay Dad's recent transfer from Charlestown to the Laurel, Maryland, area represented. Certainly, his angst over the possibility of losing the financial security he had only just obtained must have been great.

7 Early Friends developed a distinctive vocabulary as a result of the importance they attached to strict truthfulness in all things. A striking example of this "plain speech" was their renaming of the months and days of the week. It was clearly not true that October was the eighth month of the year or December the tenth (as the Latin numbers embedded in those names would indicate). Also, Friends could not honor the pagan god Janus (January) or Juno (June). Friends called all months by their true order in the year: First Month, Second Month, and so on. In addition, to avoid honoring the Sun or Moon god, Thor or Woden, Friends called the days of the week First Day, Second Day, and so on. As I immersed myself ever more deeply in this new faith, I began adopting plain speech as well. In this memoir, I have used the common names for the months and days of the week when I used them at that time. As I came to adopt plain speech, I have switched to plain speech in the memoir.

8 After I returned to Christianity, this point became even more important to me. I am pacifist because Jesus Christ, who had the perfect right to defend himself (as an innocent) and to punish the wrongdoer, chose to be pacifist, absorbing violence without striking back.

9 This argument is now unpersuasive to me. My pacifism does not depend on my perception of the spiritual condition of other people—on whether or not they have "that of God" in them. I am pacifist because God has modeled a new way to live and has enabled me to live that way myself.

10 I now know that George Fox never used the declarative sentence "There is that of God in every man" or "in every one"—but this was my understanding at the time. See Lewis Benson, "'That of God in Every Man'—What Did George Fox Mean by It?" *Quaker Religious Thought* 12, no. 2 (spring 1970): 2–40.

Chapter 3

1 American Friends Service Committee v. United States, 368 F. Supp. 1176 (E.D. Pa. 1973), https://law.justia.com/cases/federal/district-courts/FSupp/368/1176/1802936/

2 It had become clear to Nano and me that we were priced out of home ownership in Greater Boston, given our jobs as nonmedical health care staff. I was tired of

Notes

shoveling snow after frequent winter blizzards in New England. On our motorcycle honeymoon, we visited Charlottesville, Virginia—a small city that met our criteria of being at least two degrees south of Boston with a business school and a teaching hospital. Other than an early morning visit to our small tent by a foraging brown bear, we had a very enjoyable visit and decided that we would eventually move there, as way opened.

Chapter 4

[1] The invitational ministry is the predominant form of ministry among contemporary North American Quakers. In this format, a group of Friends decides that they want to learn about certain aspects of a spiritually related topic and that a certain Friend would be a good choice to do this teaching or inspiring. They issue an invitation to that Friend to address them at a particular place on a specific date, the Friend accepts, and a presentation on the topic takes place as planned. This individual is often compensated for their time and effort. The invitational ministry may describe anything from the call of a congregation to a pastor to an invitation to lead an afternoon workshop at a yearly meeting session.

[2] Robert Barclay, *Apology for the True Christian Divinity* (1676).

[3] I had been curious about the FGC Gathering for some time and took advantage of being relatively near the 1981 Gathering site to see what it was like. What made the greatest impression on me was the constant friction between Gathering attenders and local residents throughout the week. When we went through the cafeteria line on the last morning of the Gathering, all the staff had on identical T-shirts with *ISTQ* written across the front in bold letters. It stood for "I Survived the Quakers."

[4] See Acts 8:30–31.

[5] "Advices to Meetings of Ministry and Oversight," in *Faith and Practice: Book of Discipline of the North Carolina Yearly Meeting (Conservative) of the Religious Society of Friends*, rev. ed. (1983).

[6] Secretaries and superintendents were the terms at that time for the chief administrative officers of the yearly meetings and the various umbrella organizations in the United States and Canada.

[7] At this time, Kara Cole was administrative secretary of Friends United Meeting and I was general secretary of Friends General Conference. We were the chief administrative officers of the two largest branches of Friends in North America.

[8] The covenant fellowship consisted of Kara Cole, Thom Jeavons, Sam Caldwell, Tom Ewell, and myself.

[9] Dating to the early Desert Fathers and Mothers of the third century, the ancient form of this prayer is "Lord Jesus Christ, Son of God, have mercy on me."

10 Thomas Loe, speaking in Cork, Ireland, in 1666, as reported by William Penn, who was in attendance. "The Life of William Penn," Providence Forum, accessed July 24, 2021, https://providenceforum.org/story/life-legacy-william-penn/.

11 God is truly beyond gender but manifests qualities that we humans perceive as gender-related. There are times when it is good to use feminine pronouns for the divine simply as a reminder that solely masculine pronouns are misleading and inadequate, even when we would ordinarily use gender-free wording.

12 Jesus said to him, *"One who has bathed does not need to wash, except for the feet, but is entirely clean. And you are clean, though not all of you"* (NRSV).

13 Talking about demonic possession is not common among Conservative Friends, though I have known some who use that language on occasion. I have been pressed on numerous occasions, public and private, to expound on the Adversary and our encounters with it but have declined to do so on the grounds that this only gives more power to that which we do not want to have any power at all.

14 This is a story about spiritual resistance and obedience, not about the morality of abortion. The need to consider abortion arises from the most tragic of circumstances. Weighing those circumstances and discerning right action in them can only be undertaken, it seems to me, by the prospective mother. I have given thanks to God that I have never faced such a choice, even indirectly, and know I could not make it for another person.

15 Richard Rohr shared this story with me; the nun was celebrating the fiftieth anniversary of taking her final vows.

16 The North Carolina Friends Disaster Service was formed five years later, in 1992.

Chapter 5

1 Although much of the surface controversy leading up to the called meeting had to do with whether the portrait accurately portrayed Jesus' face, and I had just had an intimate encounter with Jesus, I didn't look Him in the face in my vision, so I still can't say who was 'right' in the controversy! That seems appropriate since His facial appearance wasn't the real, underlying issue at stake.

2 Since this date, I have learned that Cyrus W. Harvey, an eminent Kansas Friend, was a recorded minister when he transferred to Rich Square Monthly Meeting on Third Month 15, 1913. George Parker was only one year old at the time and can be forgiven for not remembering. The process followed in Harvey's case was parallel to the one George recommended for Virginia Beach.

3 North Carolina Year Meeting (Conservative) has a parallel meeting structure—sometimes called a "select" structure—of ministers, elders, and overseers in addition to the more familiar monthly, quarterly, and yearly meetings for all

Notes

members. So, there are two monthly meetings, one of which is made up of only ministers, elders, and overseers.

4 They were successful in the effort; Quaker Oats abandoned the campaign.

5 It was a common practice among Friends until the mid-nineteenth century that whenever a Friend knelt in prayer during meeting for worship, everyone else present stood and faced the rear of the room while the prayer continued. Aspects of this practice were continued among some Conservative Friends groups well into the twentieth century.

6 See "The Marlborough Footwashing," Marlborough Meeting, www.marlboroughmeeting.org/V2/FootwashingV2.html.

Chapter 6

1 *The Epistle from the Elders at Balby*, 1656, Quaker Heritage Press, qhpress.org/texts/balby.html. For more on this epistle, see Martin Kelley, "Dusting off the Elders of Balby," *Quaker Ranter*, January 28, 2010, https://www.quakerranter.org/dusting_off_the_elders_of_balb/.

2 Father Richard Rohr (b. 1943) is an American Franciscan priest now living in New Mexico who has become a widely followed ecumenical spiritual teacher and writer. At this time, he was best known as the founder of the New Jerusalem Community in Cincinnati, Ohio, in 1971 and of the Center for Action and Contemplation in Albuquerque, New Mexico, in 1986. I had been introduced to his teachings by Louise Wilson about a decade earlier than this retreat. Susan spent a six-week internship at the Center for Action and Contemplation shortly after we were married.

3 Kairos is "the appointed time in the purpose of God," the time when God acts (e.g., in Mark 1:15, the time [kairos] is fulfilled and the Kingdom of God is at hand).

4 The idea that Jesus did not suffer during his Passion and death on the cross is a form of docetism, declared a heresy in 325 CE and considered so by much of the Christian church ever since.

5 The Enneagram is a modern synthesis of a number of ancient wisdom traditions. The synthesis was developed by Oscar Ichazo, born in Bolivia and raised there and in Peru. He began teaching the system in Chile in the late 1960s before moving to the United States, where he still resides. As taught in the United States, the Enneagram divides human personalities into nine interrelated types, each with its gifts and brokenness. Study of the Enneagram can lead to greater self-awareness of areas where personal growth is needed, as well as to understanding of why we interact with certain individuals in particular ways.

6 Around this stage of my life, I was forming a new 501(c)3 corporation every year or two, getting federal tax-exempt, tax-deductible status, and using it for some relevant purpose. Quaker Ministries, Inc., served as a container for a variety of activities, including providing a tax-deductible way for people to support Ched Myers while he was deciding to make the full plunge into ministry, before he got his own nonprofit, Bartimaeus Cooperative Ministries, up and running.

7 "Encounter with the Taproot," in Lloyd Lee Wilson, *Wrestling with Our Faith Tradition: Collected Public Witness, 1995–2004* (Philadelphia: Quaker Press of Friends General Conference, 2005). Reprinted 2007 by the Wider Quaker Fellowship, La Asociación de amigos de los Amigos, Friends World Committee for Consultation Section of the Americas.

8 Apophatic theology approaches God, the Divine, by negation, by speaking only in terms of what may not be said about the Divine ("God is not . . ." It contrasts with kataphatic theology, which approaches God or the Divine by affirmations or positive statements about what God *is*. The apophatic tradition is often linked with mysticism, with the experience of God, the perception of the divine reality, beyond ordinary thought or perception. Silent worship can be seen as an example of apophatic spirituality, while "programmed" worship is an expression of kataphatic spirituality.

9 *Minjung* theology is a Korean variation on liberation theology.

Chapter 7

1 A modified version of this essay was published as Lloyd Lee Wilson, "Confidentiality and Community," *Friends Journal* 46 (October 2000): 24–25.

2 As William Bacon Evans is rumored to have commented at the end of a meeting for worship, "If some Friends practiced more moderation in speaking, others would not have to practice abstinence!"

3 "Advices to Meetings of Ministry and Oversight," in *Faith and Practice: Book of Discipline of the North Carolina Yearly Meeting (Conservative) of the Religious Society of Friends*, rev. ed. (1983), 36.

4 We soon realized that Khalid Sheikh Mohammed, thought to be the "architect" of 9/11, had been a student at Chowan College some years earlier. A few of our professors remembered having him in their classes. Later, as college registrar, I had several extended conversations with journalists about exactly what information I could share with them about this former student and what had to remain private, following federal privacy law regarding students.

5 Judge wrote:

> There are three kinds of silence; the first, from action; the second, from speaking; and the third, from thinking. The last is the most difficult to

attain; so that perhaps few of those, esteemed as spiritually-minded christians [sic], have fully arrived at this degree of perfection. The apostle speaks of 'every thought being brought into subjection to the obedience of Christ.' To attain this state, requires close watchfulness and humble dependence on the aid of Divine grace.

Hugh Judge, *Memoirs and Journal of Hugh Judge* . . . (Philadelphia: John and Isaac Comly, 1841), 90.

⁶ For an account of this event and its impact on me, see my plenary address to Lake Erie Yearly Meeting, included in *Wrestling with Our Faith Tradition: Collected Public Witness, 1995–2004* in 2005 and published separately by Friends World Committee for Consultation as "Encounter with the Taproot" in 2007.

⁷ Thomas Chalkley, *The Journal of Thomas Chalkley: A Minister of the Gospel in the Society of Friends* (Philadelphia, 1866), 187.

⁸ Garchen Triptrul Rinpoche (b. 1936), a Tibetan Buddhist teacher in the Drikung Kagyu lineage and the eighth in the Garchen Rinpoche line, is believed to be an incarnation of Siddha Gar Chodingpa, a heart-disciple of the founder of the Drikung Kagyu lineage in the thirteenth century CE. He is also believed to have incarnated as Mahasiddha Aryadeva in ancient India—the lotus-born disciple of Nagarjuna himself.

⁹ William Penn wrote this when he was on trial for preaching before he was sentenced to six months in Newgate Prison. Thomas Pym Cope, ed., *Passages from the Life and Writings of William Penn, Collected* (1882), 104.

¹⁰ Cope, *Passages from the Life and Writings of William Penn*, 150.

¹¹ North Carolina Yearly Meeting approved the following minute of advice at their 1861 annual sessions (North Carolina Yearly Meeting Minutes, November 7, 1861, pp. 5–6). It speaks my mind:

> We do not believe that religion consists in a garb of peculiar shape; but we do believe that the man of solid principles will not adopt the dress of the fop. He will dress in a plain and simple manner. But in addition to this, the style of Friends points them out as members of a body, believing as very few other Religious Societies do, in the peaceable nature of Christ's Kingdom, and its incompatibility with every species of injustice and oppression; and thus the plain coat and plain speech become real though silent testimonies against oppression and war.

¹² These remarks proved to interest a wider audience than just Chowan faculty and students and were later published in slightly modified form by *Friends Journal* and *Quaker Life* : Lloyd Lee Wilson, "A Statement of Christian Pacifism," *Friends Journal* 49 (December 2003): 18–19; Lloyd Lee Wilson, "Christian Pacifist," *Quaker Life* (April 2003): 15.

[13] Isaac Penington, *The Works of Isaac Penington*, vol. 4, 4th ed. (Sherwoods, NY: David Heston, 1863), 360.

[14] Lloyd Lee Wilson, *Wrestling with Our Faith Tradition: Collected Public Witness, 1995–2004* (Philadelphia: Quaker Press of Friends General Conference, 2005).

[15] Henri Nouwen, *The Return of the Prodigal Son: A Story of Homecoming* (New York: Image Books, Doubleday, 1992). Henri Jozef Machiel Nouwen (1932–1996) was a Dutch Catholic priest, professor, writer, and theologian. He taught at the University of Notre Dame, Yale Divinity School and Harvard Divinity School. Later in life, Nouwen lived and worked with individuals with intellectual and developmental disabilities at the L'Arche Daybreak community in Richmond Hill, Ontario.

[16] This was Martin Luther's epithet for the Epistle of James.

[17] Lloyd Lee Wilson, "'The Remnant of Like Faith': The First Fifty Years of North Carolina Yearly Meeting (Conservative)" (master's thesis, Earlham School of Religion, 2009).

[18] North Carolina Yearly Meeting, *Minutes* (1861), pp. 5–6.

[19] In 1768, Rich Square Monthly Meeting was established in Rich Square, North Carolina. The monthly meeting had its own meeting house. In the mid-nineteenth century, Cedar Grove Preparative Meeting was established in the nearby town of Woodland; Friends there built their own meeting house. In 1904, the yearly meeting separated. Inside Rich Square Monthly Meeting, those Friends who accepted the recent innovations, including membership in Five Years Meeting, met in the Rich Square Meeting House and continued to call themselves Rich Square Monthly Meeting. Those Friends who were not in unity with the innovations met in the Cedar Grove Meeting House and called themselves Rich Square Monthly Meeting as well. Cedar Grove Preparative Meeting has never been laid down but does not meet as a separate body from Rich Square Monthly Meeting (Conservative). Rich Square Monthly Meeting (Friends United Meeting) ceased to meet around the 1930s, and that meeting house no longer exists. For many years, the name of our yearly meeting was North Carolina Yearly Meeting at Cedar Grove as the other body was North Carolina Yearly Meeting at High Point. Woodland Monthly Meeting is in Goldsboro, North Carolina, and belongs to North Carolina Yearly Meeting (Friends United Meeting).

[20] Douglas Gwyn, *Seekers Found: Atonement in Early Quaker Experience* (Wallingford, PA: Pendle Hill Publications, 2001), 301.

[21] Howard H. Brinton, *Creative Worship*, Swarthmore Lecture (London: George Allen & Unwin, 1931).

[22] Sarah Grubb, *Life* of Sarah Grubb, in The Friend's Library, vol. 12, ed. William Evans (Philadelphia: Joseph Rakestraw, 1848), 282.

23 Martha Routh, *Memoirs of Martha Routh*, in The Friend's Library, vol. 12, ed. William Evans (Philadelphia: Joseph Rakestraw, 1848).

24 Mary Capper, *A Memoir of Mary Capper*, in The Friend's Library, vol. 12, ed. William Evans (Philadelphia: Joseph Rakestraw, 1848).

25 My own father made three attempts to enlist during World War II, but each time he was turned down when his "essential job" as a telephone installer/repairman was discovered by the recruiting office.

26 The parallels between John's life and my own were more extensive than I realized. He had been in ROTC while an undergraduate at the University of Minnesota (1933–1938) and was commissioned as an Army officer upon graduation. He went to graduate school at MIT and resigned his commission in the winter of 1940–41. John also had the experience of finding his paperwork down near the bottom of someone's piled high inbox and had to intervene personally to get it processed. He also was immediately draft eligible upon being released from his service commitment, but his interactions with various draft boards and the legal system resulted in a prison sentence.

27 Rob Reiner, dir., *A Few Good Men*, Beverly Hills, CA: Castle Rock Entertainment, 1992.

28 Brian Drayton, *James Nayler Speaking*, Pendle Hill Pamphlet #413 (Wallingford, PA: Pendle Hill Publications, 2011).

29 Lloyd Lee Wilson, *Who Do You Say I Am?*, Pendle Hill pamphlet #409 (Wallingford, PA: Pendle Hill Publications, 2010).

30 John Howard Yoder, *The War of the Lamb: The Ethics of Nonviolence and Peacemaking* (Grand Rapids, MI: Brazos Press, 2009).

31 Lloyd Lee Wilson, "Conservative Friends, 1845–2010," in *The Oxford Handbook of Quaker Studies*, ed. Stephen W. Angell and Pink Dandelion (Oxford: Oxford University Press, 2013), 126–37.

32 See Howard W. Stone and James O. Duke, *How to Think Theologically*, 2nd ed. (Minneapolis: Augsburg Fortress, 2006).

33 Robert Barclay, *An Apology for the True Christian Divinity*, 8th ed. (Birmingham: printed by John Baskerville, 1765), 77.

Chapter 8

1 Francis Howgil, "Francis Howgil's Testimony Concerning the Life, Death, Tryals, Travels and Labours of Edward Burrough, That Worthy Prophet of the Lord," in Edward Burroughs, *The Memorable Works of a Son of Thunder and Consolation* [. . .] (1662) ([E. Hookes], 1672), 39.

² Piedmont Friends Fellowship was an association of meetings, independent as well as those belonging to several different yearly meetings, which worked together to produce some shared programs, especially activities designed for younger Friends. The situation which attracted our attention was a proposal that the fellowship become a yearly meeting in its own right (discussed later in the chapter). Later on, it did establish the Piedmont Friends Yearly Meeting, while maintaining the old fellowship. Several NCYM(C) meetings are still part of the old fellowship, but none changed their affiliation to the new yearly meeting.

³ T. Vail Palmer Jr., *Face to Face: Early Quaker Encounters with the Bible* (Newberg, OR: Barclay Press, 2016), 232.

⁴ I did not post this draft blog.

⁵ Lloyd Lee Wilson, *Holy Surrender: 2006 New England Yearly Meeting Keynote Address* (Worcester, MA: New England Yearly Meeting of the Religious Society of Friends, 2006).

⁶ Hugh Judge, *Memoirs and Journal of Hugh Judge* . . . (Philadelphia: John and Isaac Comly, 1841), 80.

⁷ Interim Body is the new name for the former Representative Body of NCYM(C).

Epilogue

¹ David Sands, *The Journal of David Sands* (The Friends Library, 2016), 92.

Appendix 3

¹ Lloyd Lee Wilson, "Faithful to the Promptings of Love," in *Walk Worthy of Your Calling: Quakers and the Traveling Ministry*, ed. Margery Post Abbott and Peggy Senger Parsons (Richmond, IN: Friends United Press, 2004), 95–111.

² Mrs. Pearsall Smith (Hannah Whitall Smith), *The Unselfishness of God and How I Discovered It: A Spiritual Autobiography* (New York: Fleming H. Revell Co., 1903), 61.

Also available from Inner Light Books

Messages to Meetings
by Brian Drayton
    ISBN 978-1-7370112-0-0 (hardcover)
    ISBN 978-1-7370112-1-7 (paperback)
    ISBN 978-1-7370112-2-4 (eBook)

Movings of Divine Love: The Love of God in the Letters of John Woolman
by Drew Lawson
    ISBN 978-1-7346300-3-9 (hardcover)
    ISBN 978-1-7346300-4-6 (paperback)
    ISBN 978-1-7346300-5-3 (eBook)

A Call to Friends: Faithful Living in Desperate Times
by Marty Grundy
    ISBN 978–1-7346300–6-0 (hardcover)
    ISBN 978–1-7346300–7-7 (paperback)
    ISBN 978–1-7346300–8-4 (eBook)

Surrendering into Silence: Quaker Prayer Cycles
by David Johnson
    ISBN 978–1-7346300–0-8 (hardcover)
    ISBN 978–1-7346300–1-5 (paperback)
    ISBN 978–1-7346300–2-2 (eBook)

A Guide to Faithfulness Groups
by Marcelle Martin
    ISBN 978-1-7328239-4-5 (hardcover)
    ISBN 978-1-7328239-5-2 (paperback)
    ISBN 978-1-7328239-6-9 (eBook)

A Word from the Lost: Remarks on James Nayler's Love to the Lost
by David Lewis
    ISBN 978-1-7328239-7-6 (hardcover)
    ISBN 978-1-7328239-8-3 (paperback)
    ISBN 978-1-7328239-9-0 (eBook)

William Penn's 'Holy Experiment'
by James Proud
    ISBN 978-0-9998332-9-2 (hardcover)
    ISBN 978-1-7328239-3-8 (paperback)

In the Stillness: Poems, prayers, reflections
by Elizabeth Mills
    ISBN 978-1-7328239-0-7 (hardcover)
    ISBN 978-1-7328239-1-4 (paperback)
    ISBN 978-1-7328239-2-1 (eBook)

Walk Humbly, Serve Boldly: Modern Quakers as Everyday Prophets
by Margery Post Abbott
    ISBN 978-0-9998332-6-1 (hardcover)
    ISBN 978-0-9998332-7-8 (paperback)
    ISBN 978-0-9998332-8-5 (eBook)

Primitive Quakerism Revived
by Paul Buckley
    ISBN 978-0-9998332-2-3 (hardcover)
    ISBN 978-0-9998332-3-0 (paperback)
    ISBN 978-0-9998332-5-4 (eBook)

Primitive Christianity Revived
by William Penn
Translated into Modern English by Paul Buckley
    ISBN 978-0-9998332-0-9 (hardcover)
    ISBN 978-0-9998332-1-6 (paperback)
    ISBN 978-0-9998332-4-7 (eBook)

Jesus, Christ and Servant of God
Meditations on the Gospel According to John
by David Johnson
    ISBN 978-0-9970604-6-1 (hardcover)
    ISBN 978-0-9970604-7-8 (paperback)
    ISBN 978-0-9970604-8-5 (eBook)

The Anti-War
by Douglas Gwyn
    ISBN 978-0-9970604-3-0 (hardcover)
    ISBN 978-0-9970604-4-7 (paperback)
    ISBN 978-0-9970604-5-4 (eBook)

Our Life Is Love, the Quaker Spiritual Journey
by Marcelle Martin
    ISBN 978-0-9970604-0-9 (hardcover)
    ISBN 978-0-9970604-1-6 (paperback)
    ISBN 978-0-9970604-2-3 (eBook)

A Quaker Prayer Life
by David Johnson
    ISBN 978-0-9834980-5-6 (hardcover)
    ISBN 978-0-9834980-6-3 (paperback)
    ISBN 978-0-9834980-7-0 (eBook)

The Essential Elias Hicks
by Paul Buckley
    ISBN 978-0-9834980-8-7 (hardcover)
    ISBN 978-0-9834980-9-4 (paperback)
    ISBN 978-0-9970604-9-2 (eBook)

The Journal of Elias Hicks
edited by Paul Buckley
    ISBN 978-0-9797110-4-6 (hardcover)
    ISBN 978-0-9797110-5-3 (paperback)

Dear Friend: The Letters and Essays of Elias Hicks
edited by Paul Buckley
    ISBN 978-0-9834980-0-1 (hardcover)
    ISBN 978-0-9834980-1-8 (paperback)

The Early Quakers and 'the Kingdom of God'
by Gerard Guiton
    ISBN 978-0-9834980-2-5 (hardcover)
    ISBN 978-0-9834980-3-2 (paperback)
    ISBN 978-0-9834980-4-9 (eBook)

John Woolman and the Affairs of Truth
edited by James Proud
    ISBN 978-0-9797110-6-0 (hardcover)
    ISBN 978-0-9797110-7-7 (paperback)

Cousin Ann's Stories for Children by Ann Preston
edited by Richard Beards
illustrated by Stevie French
    ISBN 978-0-9797110-8-4 (hardcover),
    ISBN 978-0-9797110-9-1 (paperback)

Counsel to the Christian-Traveller: also Meditations and Experiences
by William Shewen
    ISBN 978-0-9797110-0-8 (hardcover)
    ISBN 978-0-9797110-1-5 (paperback)

www.ingramcontent.com/pod-product-compliance
Lightning Source LLC
Chambersburg PA
CBHW021413300426
44114CB00010B/474